ENCYCLOPEDIA OF
AMERICAN IMMIGRATION

ENCYCLOPEDIA OF AMERICAN IMMIGRATION

Volume 1
Abolitionist movement—French immigrants

Edited by
Carl L. Bankston III
Tulane University

SALEM PRESS
Pasadena, California   Hackensack, New Jersey

Editor in Chief: Dawn P. Dawson

Editorial Director: Christina J. Moose   *Research Supervisor:* Jeffry Jensen

Project and Development Editor: R. Kent Rasmussen   *Photo Editor:* Cynthia Breslin Beres

Manuscript Editor: Tim Tiernan   *Production Editor:* Andrea E. Miller

Indexer: R. Kent Rasmussen   *Design and Graphics:* James Hutson

Acquisitions Editor: Mark Rehn   *Layout:* William Zimmerman

Editorial Assistant: Brett S. Weisberg

Frontispiece: New citizens celebrating after a ceremony in Florida in which more than one thousand immigrants were naturalized in July, 2009. (AP/Wide World Photos)

Cover photo: (The Granger Collection, New York)

Library of Congress Cataloging-in-Publication Data

Encyclopedia of American immigration / edited by Carl L. Bankston III.
    p. cm.
   Includes bibliographical references and index.
   ISBN 978-1-58765-599-9 (set : alk. paper) — ISBN 978-1-58765-600-2 (vol. 1 : alk. paper) —
ISBN 978-1-58765-601-9 (vol. 2 : alk. paper) — ISBN 978-1-58765-602-6 (vol. 3 : alk. paper) —
  1. United States—Emigration and immigration—History. I. Bankston, Carl L. (Carl Leon), 1952-
   JV6450.E66 2010
   304.8′73003—dc22

                                            2009054334

First Printing

PRINTED IN THE UNITED STATES OF AMERICA

CONTENTS

CONTENTS

Publisher's Note

Encyclopedia of American Immigration is a three-volume encyclopedic reference set that covers the full depth and breadth of American immigration history—from the arrival of the early ancestors of Native Americans more than ten millennia ago to a broad range of twenty-first century immigration issues. In addressing all the diverse demographic, economic, legal, political, and social aspects of immigration, the set provides both a comprehensive picture of the role of immigration in American history and up-to-date perspectives on modern immigration.

Immigration in History

A commonplace of American history is the notion that the United States is a "nation of immigrants." That notion is accurate, as every person in the country is either an immigrant or is descended from immigrants. There are no exceptions. When Europeans first arrived in North America during the sixteenth and seventeenth centuries, they found well-established communities of Native Americans, whom newcomers regarded as "indigenous." However, even the Native Americans were descended from immigrants from the distant past. It was not long until the Native Americans were outnumbered by modern immigrants from Europe and Africa. As these new arrivals spread throughout what would become the United States, their own descendants would come to think of themselves as "native" Americans and would typically look upon later arrivals as unwelcome newcomers. As articles in *Encyclopedia of American Immigration* richly document, this process has continued into the twenty-first century, with each new wave of immigrants looked upon by many of their predecessors with resentment and distrust.

The flow of immigrants into North America since colonial times has been continuous but has gone through many shifts—both in the numbers and in the composition of immigrant groups. The first real large waves of immigration began during the mid-nineteenth century and continued into the early twentieth century, bringing millions of Europeans into the United States. These waves were followed by several decades of relatively slow immigration, but during the late twentieth century, the flow of immigrants again accelerated. This new wave of immigration, which has continued into the twenty-first century, has brought very different types of immigrants—people mostly from Asia and Latin America. It has also brought new issues and controversies, particularly as many of these immigrants have entered the country illegally.

Coverage

The goal of *Encyclopedia of American Immigration* is to answer all the questions about immigration in American history that students are likely to ask. Among the issues that the set's articles address are these:

- The regions from which immigrants have come
- Why immigrants leave their homelands
- Why they choose to come to the United States
- How immigration patterns have changed over time
- How government immigration policies have changed
- What the role of public opinion in immigration policy has been
- When "illegal" immigration became an issue
- How immigrants become American citizens
- How immigrants adapt to their new homeland
- How the experiences of different immigrant groups have varied
- What special forms of discrimination and opposition immigrants have faced
- How immigrants have fought and organized to assert their rights
- How immigration patterns have differed across the United States
- What immigrants have contributed to American culture and society
- How American immigration history fits into worldwide migration patterns

To answer these and other questions, *Encyclopedia of American Immigration* offers 533 alphabetically arranged articles covering almost every imaginable facet of American immigration history. About one-third of its essays—which account for nearly half its total pages—are overviews of issues ranging from AIDS, affirmative action, and Amerasians through women immigrants, world migration patterns, and xenophobia. Among the overview topics of special interest are essays on art, music, foodways, films, and literature.

The next large category of essays might be considered the set's core: 65 articles on specific ethnic and national immigrant groups, ranging from Africans, Arabs, and Argentines to Vietnamese, West Indians, and people from the former Yugoslavian states. Each of these essays outlines its group's immigration history, emphasizing what has made the group unique. All these articles include tables summarizing demographic data, and most include line graphs showing the groups' immigration histories.

The next largest category of topics encompasses 54 essays on historical events and eras. In addition to three long essays covering the full history of American immigration, these topics range from the abolitionist movement of the early nineteenth century, anti-immigrant movements targeting specific groups, and the Bellingham incident of 1907 to Westward expansion, both world wars of the twentieth century, and the "yellow peril" campaign of the late nineteenth and early twentieth centuries. Other event topics include the slave trade, the Great Irish Famine, the California gold rush, the bracero program, the Elián González case, and the building of the border fence.

Encyclopedia of American Immigration addresses regional differences within the United States through essays on all 50 states and Washington, D.C. Averaging nearly 1,000 words in length, these essays survey the unique immigration histories of each state and provide tables summarizing demographic data. Another 10 essays cover cities that have particularly significant immigrant populations. The set also has overview articles on ethnic enclaves.

U.S. immigration policy, a large and fascinating subject in itself, is addressed from several perspectives. In addition to overview essays on such topics as alien land laws, the U.S. Congress, the U.S. Supreme Court, and quota systems, the set has 45 essays on specific laws and international treaties, 45 essays on individual Supreme Court rulings, and 17 essays on government agencies and commissions. Information on additional laws, court cases, and government agencies can be found in appendixes at the back of volume 3.

The life stories of individual immigrants add another dimension to the study of immigration. *Encyclopedia of American Immigration* has articles on 45 individual persons, most of whom were post-independence-era immigrants who have made marks on American history. These range from the Czech-born U.S. secretary of state Madeline Albright and the Russian-born writer Mary Antin to Arnold Schwarzenegger, the Austrian bodybuilder and actor who became governor of California, and Anzia Yezierska, the Polish-born author who wrote extensively about immigrants in New York City. Briefer sketches of an additional 53 immigrants can be found in the biographical directory of volume 3. All these biographical essays and appendix entries focus on the experiences of their subjects as immigrants.

ORGANIZATION

Like other Salem encyclopedic works, *Encyclopedia of American Immigration* is organized and formatted to be student friendly. Essays are arranged alphabetically under the headwords students are most likely to seek. More help can be found in volume 3's indexes, which contain cross-references to variant names and terms. Additional finding aids include extensive lists of "See also" cross-references at the end of each essay, a category list in volume 3, and a complete list of contents in every volume.

Individual essays use the same types of ready-reference top matter for which Salem reference works are noted. The specific types of top-matter information vary among essay types, but all essays have "Significance" statements that summarize the relevance of the subject to American immigration history. Special care has been taken to illustrate articles. In addition to more than 200 tables, graphs, charts, and maps, the set contains more than 240 photographs.

All articles provide extra bibliographical help. Every essay, regardless of length, has a "Further Reading" list. The lists in essays of 1,000 or more words are annotated. The appendix section in volume 3 also contains an annotated bibliography of general works on immigration. Other appendixes include a glossary of immigration terms, an annotated filmography, and a lengthy time line. Finally, volume 3 also contains five indexes:

- Categorized List of Articles
- Court Case Index
- Law and Treaty Index
- Personage Index
- Subject Index

ACKNOWLEDGMENTS

Salem Press would like to thank the more than 210 scholars who contributed original articles to *Encyclopedia of American Immigration.* Their names and affiliations are listed in the pages that follow here. This publication is especially indebted to its editor, sociology professor Carl L. Bankston III of Tulane University, an expert on Southeast Asian immigrants whose contributions to this project have been many and substantial.

CONTRIBUTORS

Richard Adler
University of Michigan, Dearborn

Stephanie M. Alvarez
University of Texas, Pan American

Emily Alward
Henderson, Nevada,
District Libraries

Nicole Anae
Charles Sturt University

Carolyn Anderson
University of Massachusetts

Terry A. Anderson
Grant Management Solutions
Project

Jacob M. Appel
New York University

Jahaira Arias
Rutgers University

Charles F. Bahmueller
Center for Civic Education

Amanda J. Bahr-Evola
Southern Illinois University,
Edwardsville

Jane L. Ball
Yellow Springs, Ohio

Carl L. Bankston III
Tulane University

David Barratt
Montreat College

Cordelia E. Barrera
University of Texas, San Antonio

Melissa A. Barton
Westminster, Colorado

Keith J. Bell
The Citadel

Alvin K. Benson
Utah Valley University

Milton Berman
University of Rochester

R. Matthew Beverlin
Rockhurst University

Cynthia A. Bily
Adrian, Michigan

Pegge Bochynski
Salem State College

John Boyd
Appalachian State University

Kevin L. Brennan
Ouachita Baptist University

Sarah Bridger
Columbia University

Howard Bromberg
University of Michigan

Christine M. Brown
Bridgewater State College

Thomas W. Buchanan
Ancilla Domini College

David R. Buck
Thiel College

Michael H. Burchett
Limestone College

Hugh Burkhart
University of San Diego

Susan Butterworth
Salem State College

Joseph P. Byrne
Belmont University

William Carney
Cameron University

Jack Carter
University of New Orleans

Dennis W. Cheek
Ewing Marion Kauffman
Foundation

Michael W. Cheek
Kennett Square, Pennsylvania

Douglas Clouatre
North Platte, Nebraska

Kathryn A. Cochran
Longview Community College

Elizabeth Ellen Cramer
Appalachian State University

Rochelle L. Dalla
University of Nebraska

Richard V. Damms
Mississippi State University

Dolores A. D'Angelo
American University

Eddith A. Dashiell
Ohio University

Antonio Rafael de la Cova
*University of North Carolina,
Greensboro*

Dianne Dentice
Stephen F. Austin State University

James I. Deutsch
Smithsonian Institution

Joseph Dewey
University of Pittsburgh, Johnstown

Marcia B. Dinneen
Bridgewater State College

Thomas Du Bose
*Louisiana State University,
Shreveport*

Darius V. Echeverría
Rutgers University

Howard C. Ellis
*Millersville University of
Pennsylvania*

Robert P. Ellis
Northborough, Massachusetts

Victoria Erhart
Strayer University

Thomas L. Erskine
Salisbury University

Mauricio Espinoza-Quesada
Ohio State University

Thomas R. Feller
Nashville, Tennessee

Gregory C. Ference
Salisbury State University

Jacqueline H. Fewkes
Florida Atlantic University

Dale L. Flesher
University of Mississippi

Charles H. Ford
Norfolk State University

Lydia Forssander-Song
Trinity Western University

John K. Franklin
Graceland University

Timothy C. Frazer
Western Illinois University

Joy M. Gambill
Wake Forest University

Richard A. Glenn
Millersville University

Raymond J. Gonzales
*California State University,
Monterey Bay*

Nancy M. Gordon
Amherst, Massachusetts

Hans G. Graetzer
South Dakota State University

Scot M. Guenter
San Jose State University

Michael Haas
*California Polytechnic University,
Pomona*

Randall Hannum
*New York City College of
Technology, CUNY*

Dennis A. Harp
Texas Tech University

A. W. R. Hawkins III
West Texas A&M University

Sandra C. Hayes
Jackson State University

Bernadette Zbicki Heiney
*Lock Haven University of
Pennsylvania*

Torrie Hester
Roanoke College

Joan Hope
Palm Beach Gardens, Florida

Aaron D. Horton
University of Arkansas, Little Rock

Mary G. Hurd
East Tennessee State University

Raymond Pierre Hylton
Virginia Union University

Earl G. Ingersoll
*State University of New York
College, Brockport*

Ron Jacobs
Asheville, North Carolina

Ramses Jalalpour
University of Wisconsin, Madison

Bruce E. Johansen
University of Nebraska, Omaha

Barbara E. Johnson
University of South Carolina, Aiken

Sheila Golburgh Johnson
Santa Barbara, California

David M. Jones
University of Wisconsin, Oshkosh

Mark S. Joy
Jamestown College

Jonathan Keljik
George Washington University

Steven G. Kellman
University of Texas, San Antonio

Leigh Husband Kimmel
Indianapolis, Indiana

Matjaž Klemenčič
University of Maribor

Paul M. Klenowski
*Clarion University of
Pennsylvania*

Gayla Koerting
Nebraska State Historical Society

Grove Koger
Boise State University

Margaret A. Koger
Boise, Idaho

James C. Koshan
Thiel College

Elitza Kotzeva
Appalachian State University

Beth Kraig
Pacific Lutheran University

M. Bahati Kuumba
Spelman College

P. Huston Ladner
University of Mississippi

Laurie Lahey
George Washington University

Wendy Alison Lamb
South Pasadena, California

Philip E. Lampe
University of the Incarnate Word

J. Wesley Leckrone
Widener University

Jennie MacDonald Lewis
University of Denver

Thomas Tandy Lewis
St. Cloud State University

Roy Liebman
*California State University,
Los Angeles*

Huping Ling
Truman State University

Heather R. Love
*Slippery Rock University of
Pennsylvania*

M. Philip Lucas
Cornell College

R. C. Lutz
CII Group

Andrew F. Macdonald
Loyola University, New Orleans

Gina Macdonald
Nicholls State University

Robert R. McKay
Clarion University of Pennsylvania

David W. Madden
*California State University,
Sacramento*

Daniel Melero Malpica
Sonoma State University

Philip L. Martin
University of California, Davis

Laurence W. Mazzeno
Alvernia College

Scott A. Merriman
*Troy University, Montgomery
Campus*

Eric Yitzchak Metchik
Salem State College

Julia M. Meyers
Duquesne University

Michael R. Meyers
Pfeiffer University

Randall L. Milstein
Oregon State University

Robert D. Mitchell
Ohio State University

William V. Moore
College of Charleston

Lincoln Austin Mullen
Brandeis University

Debra A. Mulligan
Roger Williams University

Alexandria J. Murnan
University of Kansas

B. Keith Murphy
Fort Valley State University

Alice Myers
Bard College at Simon's Rock

John E. Myers
Bard College at Simon's Rock

Jerome L. Neapolitan
*Tennessee Technological
University*

Leslie Neilan
*Virginia Polytechnic Institute and
State University*

Caryn E. Neumann
Miami University of Ohio

Norma Corigliano Noonan
Augsburg College

John O'Keefe
George Washington University

James F. O'Neil
Florida Gulf Coast University

Amy J. Orr
Linfield College

Shannon Oxley
University of Leeds

William A. Paquette
Tidewater Community College

Robert J. Paradowski
Rochester Institute of Technology

Diana Pardo
University of Central Oklahoma

David Peck
Laguna Beach, California

William A. Pelz
Institute of Working Class History

Noelle K. Penna
Bronx High School of Science

Barbara Bennett Peterson
*University of Hawaii and Oregon
State University*

Allene Phy-Olsen
Austin Peay State University

Bethany E. Pierce
Bridgewater State College

Julio César Pino
Kent State University

David L. Porter
William Penn University

Kimberly K. Porter
University of North Dakota

Laurence M. Porter
Michigan State University

Jessie Bishop Powell
*American Public University
System*

Tessa Li Powell
University of Denver

Luke A. Powers
Tennessee State University

Victoria Price
Lamar University

Maureen J. Puffer-Rothenberg
Valdosta State University

Aaron D. Purcell
Virginia Tech

John Radzilowski
University of Alaska Southeast

Sara A. Ramírez
University of California, Berkeley

John David Rausch, Jr.
West Texas A&M University

Rosemary M. Canfield Reisman
Charleston Southern University

H. William Rice
Kennesaw State University

Mark Rich
Cashton, Wisconsin

Betty Richardson
*Southern Illinois University,
Edwardsville*

Robert B. Ridinger
Northern Illinois University

Edward A. Riedinger
Ohio State University

Rudy Rodríguez
University of North Texas

Stephen F. Rohde
Rohde & Victoroff

Francine Sanders Romero
University of Texas, San Antonio

Barbara Roos
Grand Valley State University

Joseph R. Rudolph, Jr.
Towson University

Virginia L. Salmon
*Northeast State Technical
Community College*

Richard Sax
Lake Erie College

Martha A. Sherwood
Kent Anderson Law Associates

Ji-Hye Shin
*Rutgers State University of
New Jersey*

Wayne Shirey
University of Alabama, Huntsville

R. Baird Shuman
University of Illinois

Karen Manners Smith
Emporia State University

Sarah B. Snyder
Yale University

Alvin Y. So
*Hong Kong University of Science
and Technology*

Karel S. Sovak
University of Mary

David R. Stefancic
Saint Mary's College

Arthur K. Steinberg
Salisbury, North Carolina

COMPLETE LIST OF CONTENTS

VOLUME 1

VOLUME 2

VOLUME 3

Contents

ENCYCLOPEDIA OF
AMERICAN
IMMIGRATION

A

ABOLITIONIST MOVEMENT

THE EVENT: Widespread and diverse movement that sought to end slavery in the United States
DATE: Early nineteenth century to 1865

> **SIGNIFICANCE:** Debates over slavery touched every aspect of American life during the decades leading up to the U.S. Civil War (1861-1865). As was the case with Americans in general, immigrants could be found on all sides of the issue. Some immigrants became active abolitionists, but ethnic, political, and economic issues often kept recent immigrants from playing a major role in the efforts to end slavery. Abolitionism was strongest in the Whig Party, and later in the Republican Party. However, because immigrants did not find these parties congenial, only a small number of recent immigrants played a significant role in the antislavery movement.

Between 1800 and 1860, nearly five million immigrants came to the United States, mostly from Ireland, Germany, and Scandinavia. Most of these immigrants settled in northern states, and those who went to the South tended to settle in cities, where they became laborers, artisans, or small businessmen. Few recent immigrants had the money to become slave owners, but some immigrants did own slaves. There were also others who defended slavery although they were not directly involved with it, and still others who were active in the antislavery movement.

Abolitionism was strongest in the Whig Party, and later in the new Republican Party that emerged during the mid-1850's. Before the Civil War, most immigrants joined the Democratic Party, because the Whig and the Republican parties had many evangelical Protestant members, and their reformist platforms were perceived as anti-immigrant. This connection of ethnicity and religion with party affiliation meant that recent immigrants generally did not become part of the political parties in which abolitionism flourished. Therefore, rela-

tively few immigrants were prominent abolitionists.

IMMIGRANT OPPOSITION TO ABOLITIONISM

Often on the lowest rungs of the economic ladder, immigrant laborers—like their native-born counterparts—were generally not supportive of the abolitionist movement. Many feared that freed slaves would compete with them for employment. However, just as relatively few immigrants were actively involved in the abolitionist movement, few were active defenders of slavery or outspoken critics of the abolitionist movement. Nevertheless, there were exceptions. For example, John Mitchel, who had been banished from Ireland for his revolutionary activities, eventually became a slave-owning farmer in Tennessee and a vocal defender of the slave system. When Tennessee was being occupied by Union forces during the Civil War, Mitchel spent four months in prison for his outspoken support of the Confederacy.

The German immigrant Francis Lieber is a good example of the ambiguous position on slavery that many immigrants held. Lieber was a liberal activist in Germany before migrating to the United States in 1827. Although he had often spoken out against slavery, when he moved to Columbia, South Carolina, he bought two slaves to serve as family servants. He justified this by saying he would treat them better than others might, and that they would be educated and uplifted by contact with his family. Nevertheless, he continued publicly to maintain that American slavery was "a great evil and misery."

IMMIGRANT SUPPORT OF ABOLITIONISM

Economic concerns led some immigrants to fear competition for jobs from freed slaves, but other immigrants came to believe that they shared common class interests with the slaves. Immigrants who had risen above the lowest levels of the working-class poor did not feel they were in competition with free blacks for employment and were often more sympathetic toward the condition of the slaves. Many German immigrants, who tended to be artisans, skilled workers, or small businessmen, were more actively antislavery. The black abolitionist Frederick Douglass saw poor Irish immigrants as "a great obstacle" to the efforts to end slavery, but he considered German immigrants to be "our active allies" in the struggle.

After the failure of the revolutions of 1848 in Europe, many politically radical Germans came to America, where many of them become outspoken critics of slavery. Immigrants who had been active in the effort to end slavery in the British Empire also became abolitionists in America. For example, the Reverend George Bourne was a British Presbyterian minister who became a pastor in a Virginia church around 1815. However, he was fired by this church soon after he published *The Book and Slavery Irreconcilable* (1816), which argued that slavery violated biblical principles. Bourne then moved to the North and became an active abolitionist. He on the board of the American Anti-Slavery Society when it was founded in 1833.

In general, immigrants were not unlike native-born Americans in the antebellum era in their attitudes toward the abolition of slavery. They were found on every side of the debate, and they based their positions on economic interests, philosophical or theological principles, or general humanitarian ideals.

Mark S. Joy

CONGRESSIONAL ACT PROHIBITING THE SLAVE TRADE TO THE UNITED STATES

The following passage is excerpted from the 1807 act of Congress that banned the importation of African slaves to the United States and its territories.

An act to prohibit the importation of slaves into any port or place within the jurisdiction of the United States. . . .

Be it enacted, That from and after the first day of January, one thousand eighteen hundred and eight, it shall not be lawful to import or bring into the United States or the territories thereof, from any foreign kingdom, place, or country, any negro, mulatto, or person of color, with intent to hold, sell, or dispose of such negro, mulatto, or person of color, as a slave, or to be held to service or labor.

SECTION 2: *And be it further enacted,* That no citizen or citizens of the United States, or any other person, shall . . . for himself, or themselves, or any other person whatsoever, either as master, factor, or owner, build, fit, equip, load, or otherwise prepare any ship or vessel, in any port or place within the jurisdiction of the United States, nor shall cause any ship or vessel to sail from any port or place within the same, for the purpose of procuring any negro, mulatto, or person of color, from any foreign kingdom, place, or country, to be transported to any port . . . within the United States, to be held, sold, or disposed of as slaves, or to be held to service or labor. . . .

Approved, March 2, 1807

FURTHER READING

Berlin, Ira, and Herbert G. Gutman. "Natives and Immigrants, Free Men and Slaves: Urban Workingmen in the Antebellum American South." *American Historical Review* 88, no. 5 (December, 1985): 1175-1200. Excellent study by a major scholar of American slavery and a leading labor historian.

Foner, Eric. *Free Soil, Free Labor, Free Men: The Ideology of the Republican Party Before the Civil War.* New York: Oxford University Press, 1970. Classic work on the rise of the Republican Party and its connection to antecedents such as the Free Soilers and the Know-Nothing Party. Especially helpful in showing why immigrants did not feel at home in this new party during the 1850's.

Morrison, Michael A., and James Brewer Stewart, eds. *Race and the Early Republic: Racial Consciousness and Nation-Building in the Early Republic.* Lanham, Md.: Rowman & Littlefield, 2002. Collection of essays that are helpful for understanding attitudes toward race among abolitionists, the general American public, and European immigrants.

Osofsky, Gilbert. "Abolitionists, Irish Immigrants, and the Dilemmas of Romantic Nationalism." *American Historical Review* 80, no. 4 (October, 1975): 889-912. Excellent study that shows how the abolitionist movement hoped to attract the support of Irish immigrants and why this attempt was largely a failure.

Roediger, David R. *The Wages of Whiteness: Race and the Making of the American Working Class.* London: Verso, 1991. Excellent study of the attitudes of working-class Americans toward race.

Wittke, Carl. *The Irish in America.* Baton Rouge:

Louisiana State University Press, 1956. Standard study on Irish immigration; gives some examples of prominent Irish immigrants on both sides of the slavery and sectional debates.

SEE ALSO: African Americans and immigrants; American Colonization Society; History of immigration, 1783-1891; Irish immigrants; Know-Nothing Party; Liberia; Nativism; Political parties; Slave trade.

ACQUIRED IMMUNODEFICIENCY SYNDROME

DEFINITION: Disease state caused by infection with human immunodeficiency virus (HIV) that leads to slow destruction of victims' immune systems, making victims highly susceptible to potentially life-threatening infections and cancers

ALSO KNOWN AS: AIDS

SIGNIFICANCE: The emergence of acquired immunodeficiency syndrome (AIDS) during the early 1980's fostered a national hysteria in which fears of contracting the disease were directed against categories of people who were believed to be its main carriers, most notably homosexual men and intravenous drug users. In an effort to prevent the diseases' spread, federal laws were modified to restrict travel and immigration into the United States.

The first official mention of what would become known as acquired immunodeficiency syndrome, or AIDS, by the U.S. Centers for Disease Control and Prevention was issued on June 5, 1981. That report chronicled the cases of five white gay residents of Los Angeles, California. Soon, public hysteria over the apparently high mobility of the disease's high-risk groups—homosexual men, intravenous drug users, hemophiliacs, and Haitian immigrants—erupted. Medical experts added to this frenzy by recommending quarantine measures on the basis of limited facts. They apparently assumed that prosperous gay American and European men—who were the first visible faces of AIDS—were more prone to travel internationally

than their heterosexual counterparts and that they might therefore spread the disease rapidly during their travels. Equally compelling to the public health establishment at that time was the fact that the market for medical blood supplies was no longer local but international. Because intravenous drug use had increased tremendously around the world during the permissive 1970's, the danger of HIV-tainted blood reaching uninfected patients was growing.

IMMIGRATION ISSUES

Public fear of the spread of AIDS and HIV was growing at the same time the public was becoming more concerned about the immigration of undesirables. Some of this fear had a racist element. Scenes of black Haitian boat people trying to reach the United States were frequently in the news. Whereas lighter-skinned refugees from communist-ruled Cuba had been welcomed into the United States, the black-skinned refugees from Haiti's right-wing government were looked upon with suspicion. The U.S. government officially classified them as economic, not political, refugees who could be turned away at will. Moreover, the fact that many Haitian would-be immigrants had been found to be carrying tuberculosis during the 1970's's and AIDS during the 1980's made them even less welcome. Meanwhile, growing fears of AIDS and HIV in the United States raised new calls for restricting the immigration of possible carriers.

During the summer of 1987, President Ronald Reagan faced mounting pressure to do something dramatic about the spread of HIV/AIDS. This pressure led to his embrace of North Carolina senator Jesse Helms's proposal to add HIV to the U.S. Public Health Service's list of "dangerous and contagious diseases" so it could be used as grounds for barring possible carriers from immigrating into or even visiting the United States. Only one month earlier, Reagan had ordered the Public Health Service to add HIV to its contagious disease list through an executive order, even though it was becoming generally known that the infection was not spread through casual human contact—which was the conventional legal and medical interpretation of "contagious." Under this ruling, travelers carrying HIV could be banned from entering the United States. Congressional ratification of the ban made it much more politically appealing in the short term. It also made the ban bureaucratically stronger over the long haul. Enacted during the height of the culture wars over both morality and immigration, restrictions on the immigration of AID/HIV carriers would remain on the books until the year 2008.

EFFECTS OF THE BAN

The codified American ban on the entry of HIV carriers into the United States had the ironic effect of interfering with the exchange of academic and scientific information designed to stem the disease's spread. A typical example of this obstruction was the harassment of Dutch AIDS-prevention specialist Hans Paul Verhoef in April, 1989, by the Immigration and Naturalization Service (INS). The INS apparently detained Verhoef after specimens of the only known medication for HIV/AIDS were found in his luggage. His detention was temporary, but it caused Verhoef to miss an important professional conference on AIDS in San Francisco.

International conferences on AIDS held in the United States during the early and mid-1990's secured waivers for foreign participants infected with HIV/AIDS to enter the country. However, the granting of these waivers was slow, arbitrary, and begrudging. Consequently, the growing militancy of AIDS advocacy groups such as ACT UP during the administration of George H. W. Bush connected the travel and immigration ban to what they perceived as bureaucratic indifference and contempt that had made a bad situation worse. Even the merciful inclusion of persons infected with HIV/AIDS as a protected group under the Americans with Disabilities Act in 1990 did little to mitigate the effects of the travel and immigration ban.

DEVELOPMENTS DURING THE 1990'S

Bill Clinton's presidency brought new hope to end the travel ban. However, as was often the case in gay-related and AIDS issues at that time, these hopes were dashed. Indeed, Clinton and the U.S. Congress renewed the ban, apparently to appease advocates of traditional family values. Shifting demographic trends in the incidence of the disease, which was afflicting increasing numbers of heterosexual Americans, had little effect in galvanizing support for repeal of the ban. The adoption of safer-sex practices during the 1980's had leveled off the disease's mortality rate and spread among

gay white men by 1995, but the incidence of the disease was continuing to rise among both male and female African Americans of all sexual orientations.

The introduction of retroviral cocktail drugs after 1996 transformed HIV/AIDS from a deadly to a chronic disease, at least among victims who could afford the taxing regimen of medications that were becoming available. Meanwhile, the worldwide and increasingly heterosexual scope of HIV/AIDS was becoming publicly evident, and the disease's ravages were a growing concern for American national interests and security, particularly in sub-Saharan Africa.

The trend toward an African—or foreign—face for HIV/AIDS may have ironically given the travel ban within the United States a second wind at the turn of the twenty-first century. That attitude was further strengthened by a fresh set of fears about immigrants in general after the September 11, 2001, terrorist attacks on the United States that prompted unprecedented new security measures to protect national borders.

In the meantime, routine obstruction and harassment of AIDS victims by federal government agencies continued. For example, Andrew Sullivan, the noted English pundit and editor, could not apply for American citizenship because of his HIV-positive status. Christopher Arnesen, an immigrant from New Zealand, had to fight a protracted legal battle to get the Social Security benefits he had earned from working for twenty-eight years in the United States. Eventually, however, the federal government relented. In what may be regarded as one of the most positive legacies of his administration, President George W. Bush committed the United States to help stop the spread of HIV/AIDS and assist its victims in Africa. At his prompting, the Democratic-controlled Congress quietly repealed the ban in 2008, ending nearly a full generation of discrimination against AIDS sufferers.

Charles H. Ford

FURTHER READING

Andriote, John-Manuel. *Victory Deferred: How AIDS Changed Gay Life in America.* Chicago: University of Chicago Press, 1999. Excellent analysis of the devastating impact of the disease in the United States during the 1980's and 1990's.

Chalmers, James. *Legal Responses to HIV and AIDS.*

London: Hart, 2008. Comprehensive look at interconnections between immigration and HIV/AIDS issues.

Gordenker, Leon, Roger Coate, Christer Jonsson, and Peter Soderholm. *International Cooperation in Response to AIDS.* London: Pinter, 1995. Excellent account of the conference controversies of the late 1980's and early 1990's.

Lalou, Richard, and Victor Piché. "Migrants and AIDS: Risk Management Versus Social Control—An Example from the Senegal River Valley." *Population, English Edition* 59, no. 2 (March-April, 2004): 195-228. Study of the interrelationships among migration, immigration, and HIV/AIDS fears in sub-Saharan Africa.

Nelson, Leonard J. "International Travel Restrictions and the AIDS Epidemic." *American Journal of International Law* 81, no. 1 (January, 1987): 230-236. Early survey of global exclusions put in place before the Helms amendment.

SEE ALSO: Gay and lesbian immigrants; Haitian immigrants; Health care; History of immigration after 1891; Immigration law; Infectious diseases; "Undesirable aliens."

AFFIRMATIVE ACTION

DEFINITION: Policies used by government agencies, private businesses, and other organizations for the purpose of increasing the representation of members of specified minority groups

SIGNIFICANCE: The convergence of affirmative action policy and mass immigration into the United States from Latin America and Asia has had some unintended consequences. Immigrants have often benefited from affirmative action programs, although they do not share the long histories of slavery and discrimination suffered by African Americans and members of other American minority groups.

Before the 1960's, private American educational institutions and most employers could legally discriminate on the basis of race or other classifications. In 1964, the U.S. government took the lead in ending racial discrimination in education and employment by enacting the Civil Rights Act of 1964. Title VII of that law prohibited entities receiving federal funding from discriminating on the basis of race, color, religion, sex, or national origin. The language of the law itself and the content of the floor debates leading up to passage of the law make clear that nothing in the act required or even permitted preferential treatment for any group.

Shortly after the Civil Rights Act was passed, President Lyndon B. Johnson, in Executive Order 11246, promoted "affirmative action" programs to increase educational and employment opportunities for African Americans, women, and members of other disadvantaged minorities. Johnson justified affirmative action as necessary for achieving equality of opportunity and as a means of overcoming the effects of past discrimination. This "soft" approach to affirmative action called for nondiscrimination enhanced by aggressive recruiting of, and remedial training and internships for, members of minorities.

Following the urban riots that swept the nation during the late 1960's, affirmative action programs shifted from the principle of nondiscrimination to the principle of preference. "Hard" affirmative action sets goals and time lines, in some cases set-asides and quotas, specifying numbers or percentages of minority group members who were to be hired to jobs or admitted into programs. Regardless of the law's intentions, the Civil Rights Act of 1964 led to preferences for minorities. One of the most controversial programs that followed in its wake was the Public Works Employment Act of 1977, which required at least 10 percent of public work contracts go to minority-owned business enterprises. Since that time, the affirmative action landscape has been littered with statutory and constitutional legal challenges. Judicially created limits on affirmative action have diminished its value to all minorities.

CONVERGENCE OF AFFIRMATIVE ACTION AND IMMIGRATION

During the 1960's, the U.S. Congress also reformed national immigration policy. The Immigration and Naturalization Act of 1965 eliminated ethnic distinctions among prospective immigrants. This change resulted in a wave of new immigrants from Latin America and Asia. While estimates of their actual numbers vary, the immigrant population living in the United States grew enormously—from about 5 percent of the total national population in 1965 to more than 12 percent, or about thirty-eight million immigrants, in 2009.

The Civil Rights Act of 1964 and the Immigration and Naturalization Act of 1965 were developed without reference to each other. The convergence of legislated nondiscrimination and racial preferences with mass immigration from Latin America and Asia resulted in some unintended consequences. Because the post-1965 immigrants were mostly Hispanic and Asian—both protected classifications under federal affirmative action policy—approximately 75 percent of all post-1965 immigrants qualified for affirmative action benefits immediately upon their arrival in the United States. In contrast, members of such immigrant groups as Hasidic Jews, Iranians, and Afghans did not qualify. The majority of new immigrants did, however, benefit from affirmative action remedies that had been developed to compensate African Americans for the disadvantages imposed by their heritage of slavery and discrimination. This fact has lead to intraminority tension and white native opposition.

Economic studies have established that poor African Americans have suffered as a result of employers hiring immigrants in order to obtain cheap labor while satisfying minority hiring requirements. Some studies have demonstrated that the chief beneficiaries of affirmative action have been women, Hispanics, and Asians—not African Americans, who were the primary target group of affirmative action programs. Also, by extending favored treatment to members of immigrant groups who have not suffered from the American legacy of slavery and discrimination, affirmative action itself has lost some of its philosophical coherence. This has led many to conclude that the original intent of affirmative action—compensation for the consequences of slavery and discrimination—has been undermined by mass immigration. Early twenty-first century recommendations have included excluding immigrants from the benefits of affirmative action under the logic that those who have only recently entered the United States have no claim to preferential treatment to make up for past wrongs. Critics of such recommendations respond that the purpose of affirmative action was not merely to compensate for past wrongs but also to give equal opportunities to those who still suffer discrimination, which would include many immigrants because of their race or ethnicity.

IMMIGRANT VIEWS ON AFFIRMATIVE ACTION

"Hard" affirmative action has never had strong public support, but "soft" affirmative action has. The vast majority of Americans, immigrants included, have supported equality of opportunity but have been opposed to preferential treatment for members of racial and ethnic groups. For example, polls have shown that more than 70 percent of Hispanics dislike racial preferences. Throughout the United States, anti-affirmative action ballot measures have been passed in individual states. Studies have shown that opposition to affirmative action is grounded largely in its inconsistency with the twin national values of individualism and merit. Members of numerous immigrant groups have pointed out that immigrants come to the United States looking for economic opportunity, not preferential treatment. As such, immigrants and immigrant families are largely ambivalent about affirmative action.

Richard A. Glenn

FURTHER READING

Graham, Hugh Davis. *Collision Course: The Strange Convergence of Affirmative Action and Immigration Policy in America.* New York: Oxford University Press, 2003. Explores how affirmative action and immigration policy came into conflict when employers, acting under affirmative action plans, hired new immigrants while leaving high unemployment among inner-city African Americans. Details how affirmative action for immigrants has stirred wide resentment.

Kellough, J. Edward. *Understanding Affirmative Action: Politics, Discrimination, and the Search for Justice.* Washington, D.C.: Georgetown University Press, 2006. Surveys the historical developments and impacts of affirmative action policy and procedures.

Robb, James S. "Affirmative Action for Immigrants: The Entitlement Nobody Wanted." *The Social Contract* 6, no. 2 (Winter, 1995). Argues that immigrants are taking advantage of affirmative action programs that were originally created to benefit disadvantaged native-born minorities and supports ending all preferences for immigrants.

Skrentny, John D. *The Minority Rights Revolution.* Cambridge, Mass.: Belknap Press, 2004. Shows how Hispanics, Asians, and other groups of immigrants changed the face of American politics.

_____, ed. *Color Lines: Affirmative Action, Immigration, and Civil Rights Options for America.* Chicago: University of Chicago Press, 2001. Examines the role of affirmative action and civil rights in the light of shifts in America's minority populations.

SEE ALSO: African Americans and immigrants; Civil Rights movement; Congress, U.S.; Constitution, U.S.; Employment; Immigrant advantage; Immigration and Nationality Act of 1965.

AFRICAN AMERICANS AND IMMIGRANTS

SIGNIFICANCE: The unique circumstances arising from the manner in which the vast majority of African Americans came to the Western Hemisphere and the question of whether African Americans should be considered an immigrant group in the strict sense of the term have contributed substantially to the overarching debate over the role of race in American society. Adding to whatever racial tensions might have arisen among African Americans and certain immigrant groups, resentment has been manifested in some quarters over perceived preferment of newcomers over the long-established African American population.

Over the general, long-term perspective on history, the relationship between African Americans and other immigrant groups to the United States has revolved around mutual suspicion and competition. This aura of suspicion and competition has been heavily overlain and exacerbated by the racial issues that had already been set in place during the early colonial era. During the early seventeenth century, the few Africans who were transported to colonial Virginia, Maryland, and New England colonies held the status of indentured servants. Chat-tel slavery similar to that already in place in Spanish and Portuguese America had yet to secure legal status in the North American colonies. However, events moved rapidly. Spurred by concerns about the long-term stability of the system of indentured servitude and questions of interracial marriage and sexual unions, the various English colonial governments put into place legalized systems of permanent, racially based chattel slavery.

Massachusetts was the first North American colony to institute slavery on the Latin American model. However, it was in Virginia in 1661 that the southern slavery model, which would persist to 1865, was set in place. By the end of the seventeenth century a legal and social code of separating the "black" and "white" races was firmly fixed. This system of racial separation endured, in its various permutations, into the late 1960's. As it would prove, this was to be the general rule whether or not these "whites" were long-established, and mainly of English stock; or part of subsequent waves of immigration from Ireland, Scandinavia, or central, southern, or eastern Europe. When society was defined in racial terms, all white persons, regardless of their condition in society, could look upon themselves as "preferred" over all African Americans.

GREAT DRAFT RIOT OF 1863

Communities of free African Americans existed from early colonial times. However, because of the growing incompatibility of the chattel slavery system outside the South, they flourished to a far greater degree in the northern colonies and states, particularly in the more vibrant economic climate of northern urban centers. As a distinctly identifiable and socially denigrated minority, African Americans invariably competed with newly arrived white immigrants for the lowest-paying jobs. With substantial white immigrant communities in nearly every major center by the 1860's and increasing numbers of African American slaves escaping into the North on the Underground Railroad, relations between black and white communities grew more tense.

The U.S. Civil War (1861-1865) was resented by many white northerners as being waged to eliminate slavery. These people feared the prospect of a tidal wave of freed black slaves coming north from southern plantations to threaten the livelihood of

Harper's Weekly *illustration of the burning of New York City's African American orphan asylum during the 1863 draft riots.* (The Granger Collection, New York)

poor whites. In 1863, the first military conscription in the United States brought this resentment to fever pitch, as lower-class whites saw themselves as being compelled to participate in a struggle to free black slaves that would work against their own interests.

In New York City, this resentment sparked a series of events that culminated in a bloody draft riot. In July, 1863, a motley group white of protestors, among whom German and Irish immigrant laborers were prominent, rapidly degenerated into a mob and began a rampage of vandalism, arson, assault, and murder. Over a four-day period, they burned down an orphanage for black children and relentlessly brutalized African Americans, as many as two thousand of whom may have fled the city seeking safety.

TWENTIETH CENTURY DEVELOPMENTS

The great New York City draft riot, notorious and horrific in its scope as it was, set the tune for subsequent northern and midwestern riots against African Americans. This ongoing violence was partially fueled by the anxieties and feelings of insecurity on the part of white immigrant groups. Anti-African American sentiment among white immigrants grew after the Civil War and during the early twentieth century. Meanwhile, during the first three decades of the new century, a movement that became known as the Great Migration saw the movement of many thousands of African Americans from the South to the North, where they sought employment in urban centers. The same years also saw a massive influx of European immigrants into the United States.

As Jim Crow segregation systems became more rigid throughout the South and economic conditions there generally worsened, African Americans sought comparative freedom and better employment opportunities in northern cities, in which they formed ethnic enclaves. New York City's Harlem and Boston's Roxbury became two of the largest and best known of such communities. As black southerners were moving north, large numbers of eastern and southern Europeans were entering the United States, enlarging or creating their own ethnic enclaves. They were also coming into competition—at times violently—with African Americans for jobs. Interactions between Jews and African Americans were more ambiguous because of the existence of small but vocal groups within both communities harboring attitudes of racial exclusivity and religious anti-Semitism.

The decade of the 1960's witnessed both the ebbing of the old immigration patterns and the crest of the Civil Rights movement. Although African Americans made major political and economic strides as a result of the successes of the Civil Rights movement, their very success engendered a new consciousness among members of other minority groups, particularly Asian Americans. Through the ensuing decades, the numbers of Asian Americans were considerably augmented by refugees from military conflicts in Vietnam, Cambodia, and Laos. However, the great rise in Latin American immigration would prove to have the greatest impact on African Americans.

"NEW IMMIGRATION" AND AFRICAN AMERICANS

By the last decades of the twentieth century, American Latinos and Latin American immigrants—who are often collectively known as Hispanics—combined to overtake African Americans as the largest ethnic minority category in the United States. However, Latinos comprise people from many highly disparate nationalities, including Puerto Ricans, Cuban Americans, Mexican Americans, and other groups with roots in Central America, South American, and the Caribbean. To complicate their relationship with African Americans even further, many Latin groups contain strong black elements. Consequently, there has been measurable outreach between African Americans and Latinos. Some African American community and legislative leaders have joined with Hispanic leaders to support liberalized immigration policies. Many educational institutions, especially historically black colleges, have actively recruited students from Hispanic communities.

Despite increasing African American cooperation with Hispanics, the major American political parties have tended to treat Hispanics and African Americans as separate and distinct voting blocs. For example, the Republican Party heavily courted Hispanic voters during the 2000 and 2004 national elections, and a modest outreach initiative by the George W. Bush administration to enlist greater African American support was stymied by the handling of the Hurricane Katrina disaster in New Orleans. What was perceived as a belated and inadequate response by the Bush administration was roundly criticized.

A question generating great differences of opinion has been what the impact of increasing Hispanic immigration—both legal and illegal—might have on already high unemployment rates within the African American community. Moreover, as African Americans have seen many Hispanics reach higher levels than most African Americans, black resentment has grown over the possibility that favoritism has been shown to the newer arrivals. However, there is no evidence that disparities between black and Hispanic incomes are any more than a perception.

Raymond Pierre Hylton

FURTHER READING

Chang, Iris. *The Chinese in America: A Narrative History.* New York: Viking Penguin, 2003. Though this book is mainly about Chinese Americans, it often offers comments on African Americans that present interesting juxtapositions of the historical interplay of African Americans with a large nonwhite immigrant group.

Katz, Loren William, ed. *Anti-Negro Riots in the North, 1863.* New York: Arno Press, 1969. Compilation of historical documents that illuminate the reasons why immigrants rioted.

Learner, Michael, and Cornel West. *Jews and Blacks: A Dialogue on Race, Religion, and Culture in America.* New York: Penguin Books, 1996. Two intellectuals, one Jewish, the other African American, discuss the long and paradoxical interplay between their marginalized communities.

Morgan, Edmund. *American Slavery, American Freedom: The Ordeal of Colonial Virginia.* New York: W. W. Norton, 1975. Useful for providing background information for and chronicling the advent of slavery and racism into the American social and legal fabric.

Morrison, Toni. *What Moves at the Margin: Selected Nonfiction.* Edited by Carolyn C. Denard. Jackson: University Press of Mississippi, 2008. Contains the Nobel Prize-winning author's 1993 essay "On the Backs of Blacks," which presents a stark analysis of the dilemma of race as relating to nonblack immigrants and their attitudes toward and interactions with African Americans.

Swain, Carol Miller, ed. *Debating Immigration.* New York: Cambridge University Press, 2007. Collection of essays on immigration, the most significant of which concerning racial issues are those by Swain and Jonathan Tilove.

SEE ALSO: Abolitionist movement; Affirmative action; African immigrants; American Colonization Society; Civil Rights movement; Ethiopian immigrants; Garvey, Marcus; Liberia; Slave trade; Stereotyping; Universal Negro Improvement Association; West Indian immigrants.

AFRICAN IMMIGRANTS

SIGNIFICANCE: Many early African immigrants came to the United States as students during the early 1920's. By the 1990's, many were coming as refugees seeking a better life. Their physical resemblance to African Americans sometimes caused confusion, so they distinguished themselves from the descendants of slaves by retaining their native speech accents and many of their native customs and costumes. They typically have assimilated quickly into American lifestyles, establishing themselves in careers and professions that have provided comfortable livings, stability, and social respectability.

During the seventeenth, eighteenth, and nineteenth centuries, many thousands of Africans were forcibly brought to what is now the United States. Since the early twentieth century, it appears that more Africans have immigrated voluntarily than all those who had been brought earlier as slaves. Many have come as students to attend American schools. Others have been refugees fleeing repressive regimes, persecution, natural disasters, and harsh economic conditions in their home countries.

African immigration intensified after World War II, and an even more significant flow began during the 1970's, after the American Civil Rights movement improved conditions in America for people of color. Substantial numbers of refugees came from Ethiopia and Somalia, northeast African nations that were embroiled in civil wars and beset by drought and famine. Some 80,000 Africans entered the United States legally during the 1970's. During the 1980's, that number grew to about 176,000. It is probable that these numbers do not fully reflect the many illegal immigrants who also entered the country in those years.

During the 1990's, the number of sub-Saharan immigrants tripled. Africans constituted only about 2 percent of all documented immigrants in 1991, but by 2000 their numbers had increased to about 5 percent. At the start of the twenty-first century, the U.S. Census Bureau reported that nearly 1 million African immigrants were living in the country, 50 percent of whom arrived and settled between 1990 and 2000. Only about 18 percent came before 1980; 26 percent came between 1980 and 1989. In 2001, 31 percent of African immigrants came from the Sudan, which was engulfed in a devastating civil war. Food, housing, and health care shortages plus drastic curtailment of civilian rights caused a debilitating struggle between that nation's dominant north and its rebellious south.

By 2004, of approximately 1 million African immigrants living in the United States, 35 percent

PROFILE OF AFRICAN IMMIGRANTS

Countries of origin	All African nations
Primary languages	English, French, Portuguese, Arabic, and others
Primary regions of U.S. settlement	East Coast cities
Earliest significant arrivals	Early twentieth century
Peak immigration period	1990's-
Twenty-first century legal residents*	632,042 (79,005 per year)

*Immigrants who obtained legal permanent resident status in the United States.

Source: Department of Homeland Security, *Yearbook of Immigration Statistics,* 2008.

were from West African countries such as Ghana, Nigeria, Senegal, Sierra Leone, Liberia, and Mali. Twenty-six percent came from such eastern and northeastern African countries as Ethiopia, Kenya, Malawi, Rwanda, and Somalia. Fewer than 3 percent were from such equatorial African countries as Cameroon, Chad, Congo, and Gabon.

LOCALES FAVORED FOR SETTLEMENT

A high proportion of Africans who have immigrated to the United States have come from urban backgrounds and have already been accustomed to Western ways. Many speak English well when they arrive and are, for the most part, from families headed by married parents. These attributes have made it easier for immigrants to adapt to life in the United States, and a high proportion of them, about 95 percent, have settled in large cities. About half reside in New York City, Washington, D.C., Los Angeles, Atlanta, and Minneapolis. Nigerians and Ghanaians in particular have favored New York City. Immigrants from Somalia and the Sudan have differed by tending to settle in the Midwest.

African immigrant enclaves have churches and mosques that reflect their traditional religious rituals and customs. Their businesses are African-themed, especially in such cities as New York, Chicago, Houston, Washington, D.C., and other cities with large numbers of immigrants. Immigrants who have attained measures of stability and economic success have generally shared their prosperity with their families in Africa. During the early twenty-first century, African immigrants remitted to their relatives more one billion dollars annually. In some countries, most notably the Sudan, these remittances have made important contributions to the balance of trade.

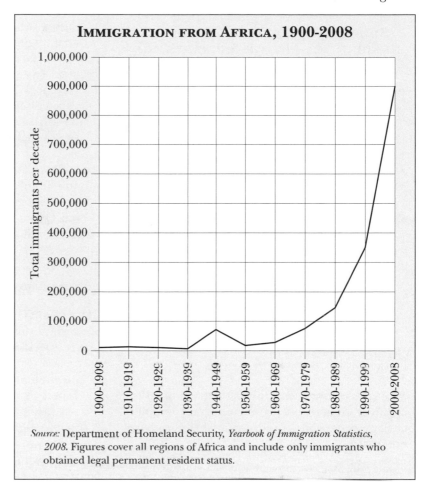

IMMIGRATION FROM AFRICA, 1900-2008

Source: Department of Homeland Security, *Yearbook of Immigration Statistics, 2008.* Figures cover all regions of Africa and include only immigrants who obtained legal permanent resident status.

EDUCATION

U.S. Census data from 2000 indicate that black African immigrants have the most education of any population group in the United States. Indeed, they even have higher levels of academic achievement than Asian Americans. They are more likely to be college educated than any other immigrant group. They are also more highly educated than any native-born ethnic group, including white Americans. About 48.9 percent of Africans who have immigrated since the late twentieth century have college degrees.

During the first decade of the twenty-first century, Africans who came to the United States as students made up only 13 percent of the total black population of the United States. However, that group accounted for 27 percent of all black students in twenty-eight top American universities. These figures are even more impressive in the elite

SUB-SAHARAN AFRICAN NATIONS SENDING THE MOST IMMIGRANTS TO THE UNITED STATES, 2001-2008

Rank	Nation	Immigrants
1	Nigeria	82,583
2	Ethiopia	80,004
3	Ghana	49,681
4	Somalia	46,202
5	Kenya	42,398
6	Liberia	32,727
7	South Africa	26,979
8	Sudan	26,928
9	Sierra Leone	18,309
10	Cameroon	15,551
11	Togo	11,119
12	Cape Verde	10,468

Source: Department of Homeland Security, *Yearbook of Immigration Statistics, 2008.* Figures for other sub-Saharan nations ranged from 55 immigrants from Mali to 6,937 from Senegal.

Ivy League universities. Only 6.7 percent of all Ivy League students were from immigrant families, but 40 percent of all the universities' black students were Africans.

Jane L. Ball

FURTHER READING

Arthur, John A. *The African Diaspora in the United States and Europe: The Ghanaian Experience.* Burlington, Vt.: Ashgate, 2008. Examines Ghanaian communities in the United States, especially permanent residents since 1980 and the relationship between new African immigrants and native-born African Americans.

D'Alisera, JoAnn. *An Imagined Geography: Sierra Leonean Muslims in America.* Philadelphia: University of Pennsylvania Press, 2004. Discusses attempts by Sierra Leonean Muslims to retain their religion, customs, and ethnic identity.

Koser, Khalid, ed. *New African Diasporas.* New York: Routledge, 2003. Describes the waves of immigration of the late twentieth century from Africa to the United States and to northern Europe and the United Kingdom.

Ndubuike, Darlington. *The Struggles, Challenges, and Triumphs of the African Immigrants in America.* Lewiston, N.Y.: Edwin Mellen Press, 2002. Discusses the struggles of African immigrants in adapting to American society.

Olupona, Jacob K., and Regina Gemignani, eds. *African Immigrant Religions in America.* New York: New York University Press, 2007. Collection of essays discussing African immigrants' widely diverse African religious and moral traditions and their role in shaping Christianity in America.

SEE ALSO: African Americans and immigrants; "Brain drain"; Civil Rights movement; *Clotilde* slave ship; Ethiopian immigrants; Higher education; Liberia; Quota systems; Settlement patterns; Slave trade; South African immigrants.

AFROYIM V. RUSK

THE CASE: U.S. Supreme Court ruling on revocation of citizenship
DATE: Decided on May 29, 1967

SIGNIFICANCE: The *Afroyim* decision established that U.S. citizenship may not be revoked involuntarily for actions such as voting in a foreign country.

Beys Afroyim, a naturalized citizen from Poland, moved to Israel and voted in an Israeli election in 1951. When he attempted to renew his U.S. passport in 1960, the U.S. State Department refused his request, based on the Nationality Act of 1940, which stipulated that voting in a foreign election would result in a loss of citizenship. In an earlier decision, *Perez v. Brownell* (1958), the Supreme Court had upheld the law by a 5-4 vote. In a civil action against the secretary of state, nevertheless, Afroyim argued that the revocation of his citizenship was unconstitutional.

By a 5-4 margin, the Supreme Court agreed with Afroyim's contention. Writing for the majority, Justice Hugo L. Black emphasized that the first clause of the Fourteenth Amendment was written in order to ensure that U.S. citizenship would be "permanent and secure." The decision had the result of encouraging the right of U.S. citizens to hold dual citizenship. In *Vance v. Terrazas* (1980), the Court held that the intent to give up one's citizenship must be proved by clear and convincing evidence, not simply inferred from acts such as voting in a foreign country. According to the State Department, citizenship may be revoked for treason. In a few other cases, particularly *Fedorenko v. United States* (1981), the Court would uphold the government's power to revoke citizenship if deception had been used in the naturalization process.

Thomas Tandy Lewis

FURTHER READING

Starkey, Lauren. *Becoming a U.S. Citizen: Understanding the Naturalization Process.* New York: Kaplan, 2006.

Wernick, Allan. *U.S. Immigration and Citizenship: Your Complete Guide.* Roseville, Calif.: Prima, 2002.

SEE ALSO: Citizenship; Dual citizenship; *Fedorenko v. United States*; Immigration law; Supreme Court, U.S.

ALABAMA

SIGNIFICANCE: Patterns of immigration in Alabama have varied markedly among different areas of the state, making the state as a whole ethnically diverse; however, arrivals of large groups of new immigrants sometimes prompted eruptions of nativism. Late in the twentieth century, an influx of Mexicans provoked protests from taxpayers and from workers who felt their jobs were threatened.

During the sixteenth century, Spanish explorers found Alabama populated by Iroquoian and Muskogean Indians, large numbers of whom were killed by Europeans. Most of those who survived were forced off their land and sent to what became the state of Oklahoma. Many died on the infamous Trail of Tears during the 1830's.

After several unsuccessful efforts at colonization by the Spanish, the French established a colony at Mobile, which was still a part of French Louisiana, in 1711. In 1780, that

settlement was taken over by the Spanish. In 1813 it was claimed by the United States. Nevertheless, the French and the Spanish had left their imprint on Mobile, and as a port city, it would continue to have a more cosmopolitan atmosphere than any other place in Alabama. Baldwin County, which lies on the eastern shore of Mobile Bay, also attracted a diverse population.

After the U.S. Civil War ended in 1865, immigrants from Italy, Scandinavia, Greece, Germany, central Europe, and French Canada settled in the county, cleared the land and farmed the fertile soil, and fished in the coastal waters. The ethnic origins of the communities they founded are still evident. For example, Fairhope, a town in Baldwin County, was the site of two unusual ventures, both organized by midwesterners. It was originally founded as a semisocialistic single-tax colony, and it was also the home of an early educational experiment, the School of Organic Education.

Alabama's central and northern parts were settled largely by people from other states. Planters from South Carolina and Georgia, who could no longer grow cotton on their depleted soil, moved to the Black Belt in the central part of Alabama, and Scotch-Irish from the eastern Appalachians traveled westward into northern Alabama. From time to time, new European arrivals attempted to carve out places for themselves. For example, in 1817, two years after the final fall of France's Emperor Napoleon, some of his officers and office-

PROFILE OF ALABAMA

Region	Southeast
Entered union	1819
Largest cities	Birmingham, Montgomery (capital), Mobile, Huntsville
Modern immigrant communities	Mexicans, Asian Indians

Population	Total	Percent of state	Percent of U.S.	U.S. rank
All state residents	4,599,000	100.0	0.0154	23
All foreign-born residents	130,000	0.028	0.35	33

Source: U.S. Census Bureau, *Statistical Abstract for 2006.*
Notes: The U.S. population in 2006 was 299,399,000, of whom 37,548,000 (12.5%) were foreign born. Rankings in last column reflect total numbers, not percentages.

holders went to western Alabama to establish vineyards and grow olive trees. Their enterprise was a failure, and they left, but the town they named Demopolis remains. During the 1890's, immigrants from Sweden, Denmark, and Norway were persuaded to move to Fruithurst, a model town in eastern Alabama, but their winemaking project, too, was a failure. German immigrants who founded Cullman in 1848 had no better luck with viniculture, but they remained and succeeded at other enterprises.

During the 1880's, Birmingham became the center of a new industry, the making of coke pig iron. To the local labor force the manufacturers added immigrants from England, Scotland, Ireland, Italy, and Holland. Because these immigrants made up less than one-fifth of the local workforce, there was no concerted protest to their presence. After World War I, however, when immigrants flooded in from southern and eastern Europe, local workers saw their jobs threatened. Moreover, longtime residents, who were mostly of Protestant Scotch-Irish stock, looked with suspicion on the languages, customs, and religions of the new arrivals, many of whom were Roman Catholics or Jews. The result was a storm of protest and the resurgence of the Ku Klux Klan.

Native Alabamians welcomed well-educated immigrants who could fill obvious needs, such as the German scientists who transformed Huntsville into a technological center, and Indian physicians who came to Alabama to work in understaffed hospitals. However, they resented the presence of uneducated immigrants who began flooding into the state from Latin America, and especially from Mexico, during the 1990's. They believed these people took jobs away from native Alabamians and burdened taxpayers with their demands for schooling, health care, and social services. The fact that as many as half these immigrants had probably entered the United States illegally and that some were involved in drug trafficking also concerned Alabamians. Some Alabamians supported taking legal steps to expel undocument immigrants. However, others made efforts to teach English to Spanish-speaking immigrants and help them in other ways to become integral members of the community.

Rosemary M. Canfield Reisman

FURTHER READING

Cobb, James C., and William Stueck, eds. *Globalization and the American South.* Athens: University of Georgia Press, 2005.

Hamilton, Virginia. *Alabama: A Bicentennial History.* New York: W. W. Norton, 1984.

Mohl, Raymond A. "Globalization, Latinization, and the *Nuevo* New South." In *Other Souths: Diversity and Difference in the U.S. South, Reconstruction to Present,* edited by Pippa Holloway. Athens: University of Georgia Press, 2008.

Rogers, William Warren, Robert David Ward, Leah Rawls Atkins, and Wayne Flynt. *Alabama: The History of a Deep South State.* Tuscaloosa: University of Alabama Press, 1994.

Waters, Mary C., and Reed Ueda, eds. *The New Americans: A Guide to Immigration Since 1965.* Cambridge, Mass.: Harvard University Press, 2007.

SEE ALSO: *Clotilde* slave ship; Florida; French immigrants; Iron and steel industry; Ku Klux Klan; Labor unions; Mexican immigrants; Mississippi; South Carolina.

ALASKA

SIGNIFICANCE: Alaska saw considerable Russian immigration during the late nineteenth and early twentieth centuries, but by the early twentieth century, Russians constituted one of the state's smaller immigrant populations. Filipinos have also entered Alaska since the early twentieth century to become the state's the largest immigrant population. Filipinos have long provided an important source of labor to the Alaskan fishing industry, particularly in the state's canneries. Although immigration to many other states slowed during the early twenty-first century, Alaska's immigrant population has continued to grow, and immigrants from Mexico have become one of the state's fastest-growing immigrant populations.

Many of Alaska's immigrant communities were established long before Alaska achieved statehood in 1959. Notable among these were Russians, who began settling the region during the eighteenth and nineteenth centuries. The first Russians came to Alaska for the fur trade, but the Russian colony was never very successful. The United States bought the territory from Russia in 1867. During the late 1890's, the Klondike gold rush drew thousands of miners to Alaska. These new arrivals included many Germans and Irish, who would become two of the state's largest immigrant ancestry groups.

Filipinos have also played an important role in Alaskan history since the eighteenth century, when they were involved in the fur trade. Known as "Alaskeros," they began to settle permanently in Alaska during the early twentieth century, when many of them worked in fishing canneries. Seafood would eventually become Alaska's main export, but its economy is based primarily on petroleum. However, during the early twentieth century, oil had not yet been found in Alaska. Filipinos and other immigrants, including Koreans, provided crucial labor to the fishing industry, particularly in canneries.

Most Filipinos who arrived in Alaska during the early twentieth century were men, who quickly established ties with members of such Native communities as the Tlingit, Haida, Eskimo, Aleut, and Tsimshian. Intermarriage between Filipinos and Native Americans was common, and these unions produced many future community leaders.

A major wave of new immigration developed after oil was discovered in 1968. Many immigrants came to work on the Trans-Alaska Pipeline. Many of them stayed after the pipeline was completed in 1977. Immigrants from Central and South America and Asia played an important role in the Alaskan fishing industry as both permanent and seasonal workers. Many brought the experience of working in fishing industries in their native countries.

Korean immigration to Alaska increased during the late twentieth century. Koreans typically entered Alaska through Canada or other U.S. states. Many of them owned restaurants, hotels, and other businesses. During the 1980's, Korean American business leaders planned and developed Korean

PROFILE OF ALASKA				
Region	Northwest of Canada			
Entered union	1959			
Largest cities	Anchorage, Juneau (capital), Fairbanks			
Modern immigrant communities	Filipinos, Koreans, Mexicans			
Population	Total	Percent of state	Percent of U.S.	U.S. rank
All state residents	670,000	100.0	0.002	47
All foreign-born residents	47,000	7.0	0.13	43

Source: U.S. Census Bureau, *Statistical Abstract for 2006.*
Notes: The U.S. population in 2006 was 299,399,000, of whom 37,548,000 (12.5%) were foreign born. Rankings in last column reflect total numbers, not percentages.

neighborhoods in Anchorage along Fireweed Lane, Northern Lights Boulevard, and Benson Boulevard. Anchorage's Korean Chamber of Commerce helps Korean immigrants build community and establish and expand their own businesses.

Immigrant businesses generally have become more numerous and economically important since the late decades of the twentieth century. Most immigrants—from both abroad and the lower forty-eight states—come to Alaska seeking work. Many begin as blue-collar workers and save enough money to establish their own businesses and to send remittances to their families.

Compared to the experience of other U.S. states, Mexican immigration is a relatively recently development in Alaska. Many of these immigrants enter Alaska from other states. Some have come for dangerous but highly paid fishing jobs. Others have established businesses, particularly restaurants. Mexican workers also work in canneries, tourism, and construction. By 2008, the Mexican presence in Alaska had become important enough for the Mexican government to open a consulate in Anchorage.

Melissa A. Barton

FURTHER READING

Berton, Pierre. *The Klondike Fever: The Life and Death of the Last Great Gold Rush.* New York: Basic Books, 2003.

Buchholdt, Thelma. *Filipinos in Alaska, 1788-1958.* Anchorage, Alaska: Aboriginal Press, 1996.

Cole, Dermot. *Amazing Pipeline Stories: How Building the Trans-Alaska Pipeline Transformed Life in America's Last Frontier.* Kenmore, Wash.: Epicenter Press, 1997.

Haycox, Stephen W. *Frigid Embrace: Politics, Economics, and Environment in Alaska.* Corvallis: Oregon State University Press, 2002.

SEE ALSO: Asian immigrants; Canada vs. United States as immigrant destinations; Canadian immigrants; Filipino immigrants; Korean immigrants; Latin American immigrants; Mexican immigrants; Russian and Soviet immigrants; Washington State.

ALBRIGHT, MADELEINE

IDENTIFICATION: Czechoslovakian-born American who became U.S. secretary of state

BORN: May 15, 1937; Prague, Czechoslovakia

SIGNIFICANCE: A scholar who became the first woman to serve as a U.S. secretary of state, Albright drew on her life experience and extensive knowledge of world affairs to champion human rights and gender equality around the world.

Madeleine Albright was born Marie Jana Körbel, a member of an established Jewish family in Prague, Czechoslovakia, in 1937. Had German expansionism and the events of World War II not intervened, she might have known a comfortable, urbane existence in her native land. However, Nazi-ruled Germany advanced into Czechoslovakia the year after she was born, and her native country was forever transformed. Because the Körbels were Jewish, three of Albright's grandparents would later die in Nazi concentration camps during the Holocaust. However, she herself would not learn her full family history until many years later, after she became U.S. secretary of state. When she was five, she and her immediate family members were baptized into the Roman Catholic Church. The family also dropped the umlaut from the name "Körbel"; the resulting "Korbel" had a less Jewish and more Czech sound. From that time, Marie Jana became known as Madeleine and was the only member of the family who attended Catholic mass regularly.

During the war years, as German armies advanced across eastern Europe, Albright's family fled to England. After the war ended in 1945, they returned briefly to Czechoslovakia, where her father, a noted scholar in international relations, entered the Czech diplomatic service as ambassador to Yugoslavia and Albania. However, after it became evident that her father was not in harmony with the communist regime that assumed rule in Czechoslovakia during the late 1940's, her family became refugees a second time. In 1949, they immigrated to the United States and settled in Denver, Colorado. Madeleine's father accepted a professorship at the University of Colorado in nearby Boulder. There he developed a distinguished international relations program and mentored two future U.S. secretaries of state—his own daughter and, later, Condoleezza Rice, who would served as President George W. Bush's secretary of state.

LIFE IN THE UNITED STATES

As a teenager, Madeleine adapted easily to American life, pleasing her father with her academic accomplishments. In the private girls school she attended in Denver, she was described as neither the brightest nor the prettiest but always the most highly motivated. It was thus not surprising when she matriculated on scholarship to Wellesley College in 1955. Active in campus organizations, she made lasting friends from different backgrounds. She also acquired the ultimate mark of acceptance for an immigrant woman of modest means when, a few days after her graduation from Wellesley. she married into one of America's most prominent and wealthy families. Her journalist husband, Joseph Patterson Albright, was heir to a newspaper empire that included the *Chicago Tribune.* Demonstrating again the Korbel family flexibility in religious affiliation, Madeleine complied with her new mother-in-law's request that she become an Episcopalian. However, she explained to the Episcopal bishop who instructed her that she could not renounce her Catholic devotion to the Blessed Virgin Mary.

Throughout her marriage years, Albright suppressed her own ambitions while promoting the career of her husband. Meanwhile, she earned master's and doctoral degrees from Columbia University, specializing, like her father, in international relations. She also acquired a second mentor, Zbigniew Brzezinski, another eastern European immi-

Madeleine Albright in 1997. (U.S. Department of State)

in European languages and her wide acquaintance with eastern European diplomats gave her an advantage over most American officials. At the United Nations she dealt with problems in Iraq, Haiti, Somalia, and Rwanda and closely monitored events in the Middle East. The plight of women, particularly in underdeveloped countries was a concern she shared with the president's wife, Hillary Clinton, a fellow Wellesley graduate who became her close friend.

In 1997, President Clinton named Albright to the highest government office ever held by an American woman: U.S. secretary of state. The drama of her personal story, her charm, and even the jewelry she wore attracted wide press attention. More than most diplomatic officials, she was able to interest the general public in international issues. She traveled tirelessly, addressing a variety of pressing problems: ethnic conflicts in countries recently liberated from communism, the growth of religion-based terrorism, the proliferation of weapons of mass destruction, and the ever-present Middle Eastern tensions. Perhaps because she had herself escaped the prime European tyrants of the twentieth century, Germany's Adolf Hitler and the Soviet Union's Joseph Stalin, she reacted forcefully to "ethnic cleansing" in the Balkans and genocide in Africa.

grant professor, who would later become national security advisor to U.S. president Jimmy Carter.

Diplomatic Career

In 1982, after twenty-two years of marriage, Joseph Albright left Madeleine for another woman. Traumatic as the divorce was for Madeleine, it enabled her for the first time to follow her own career path. Now firmly identified as "Albright," she taught at Georgetown University's School of Foreign Service in the District of Columbia and advised Democrat politicians such as Walter Mondale, Michael Dukakis, and Geraldine Ferraro, the first female vice presidential candidate. Ferraro became a friend with whom Albright attended mass, when she briefly reverted to the Roman Catholicism of her childhood.

The election of Bill Clinton to the presidency in 1992 catapulted Albright into national prominence. After taking office, Clinton appointed Albright ambassador to the United Nations. Albright's facility

Lasting Achievements

Albright was much admired in Europe. As a patriotic American, she rejected Václav Havel's extraordinary suggestion that she might succeed him as president of the Czech Republic. Her legacy was already impressive. She made the highest levels of U.S. government secure for talented women and worked to improve the lot of women everywhere. While acknowledging the dangers of a new world order, she maintained cordial relations with post-Soviet Russia and the People's Republic of China. Even in difficult peace negotiations between Israelis and Palestinians, she could claim modest gains. Because she had become an American citizen by choice rather than through birth, she unceasingly promoted American ideals of justice and freedom. Although she did not employ the phrase "manifest destiny" of an earlier era, she spoke and wrote of her conviction that her adopted country did have the special task of spreading its ideals.

Allene Phy-Olsen

FURTHER READING

Albright, Madeleine. *Madame Secretary: A Memoir.* New York: Miramax, 2003. Revealing memoir in which Albright covers both her personal life and her professional career after she completed her term as U.S. secretary of state.

_____. *The Mighty and the Almighty: Reflections on America, God, and World Affairs.* New York: HarperCollins, 2006. Accessible study of religious movements throughout the world and their political ramifications.

Blackman, Ann. *Seasons of Her Life: A Biography of Madeleine Korbel Albright.* New York: Charles Scribner's Sons, 1998. Straightforward biography of Albright by an admirer.

Dobbs, Michael. *Madeleine Albright: A Twentieth-Century Odyssey.* New York: Henry Holt, 1999. Critical examination of Albright's career by the journalist who uncovered the Korbel family's Jewish past while Albright was secretary of state.

Lippman, Thomas W. *Madeleine Albright: A Twentieth-Century Odyssey.* Boulder, Colo.: Westview Press, 2000. Balanced account of Albright's relations with both world figures and journalists.

SEE ALSO: Anti-Semitism; Czech and Slovakian immigrants; Higher education; Holocaust; Jewish immigrants; Marriage; Refugees; Religions of immigrants.

ALIEN AND SEDITION ACTS OF 1798

THE LAWS: Four federal laws restricting immigration and making certain criticism of the government illegal
DATE: Enacted in June and July, 1798

SIGNIFICANCE: These laws were the first example in the United States of repressive immigration legislation enacted amid fear of foreigners and war hysteria, coupled with a willingness to suppress dissent and punish free expression.

Fearing war with France and fed by nationalist suspicion of foreigners, the Federalist-controlled U.S. Congress passed a series of four laws signed by President John Adams in 1798. The Naturalization Act (officially An Act to Establish a Uniform Rule of Naturalization), enacted on June 18, 1798, extended the duration of residence required for aliens to become U.S. citizens from five to fourteen years. It was repealed in 1802. The Alien Friends Act (officially An Act Concerning Aliens), enacted on June 25, 1798, authorized the president to deport any resident alien considered "dangerous to the peace and safety of the United States." It expired after two years. The Alien Enemies Act (officially An Act Respecting Alien Enemies), enacted on July 6, 1798, authorized the president to apprehend and deport resident aliens if their home countries were at war with the United States. It had no expiration date and remained in effect into the early twenty-first century. The Sedition Act (officially An Act for the Punishment of Certain Crimes Against the United States), enacted on July 14, 1798, prohibited the publication of "false, scandalous, and malicious writing" against the U.S. government and its officials. It expired on March 3, 1801.

By 1798, Adam's Federalist Party and Thomas Jefferson's Republican Party were clashing over U.S. policy toward the new revolutionary government in France. A war was raging in Europe between England and France. Jefferson, who had served as minister to France, was sympathetic to the French, but Adams had signed a treaty with England and, seeing France as a threat to America's interests, put the country on a war footing as part of an undeclared "quasi-war," which bred antagonism toward French immigrants and unleashed widespread xenophobia.

Republicans depended on recent immigrants to enlarge their voting strength, a fact that provided the Federalists with a good reason to postpone immigrants' access to citizenship and the right to vote as long as possible. Federalists, by and large the party of the established propertied class, sought to create a homogeneous American nation and viewed immigrants with suspicion and disdain and as a source of unrest and even revolution. In this anti-immigrant atmosphere, the Federalists pushed through the Alien and Sedition Acts. Under the Alien Enemies Act, with no right to a hearing or to present evidence in their defense, noncitizens could be arrested, detained, and deported. When Republicans objected that this was unconstitutional, the Federalists responded that aliens had no rights under the U.S. Constitution because they were not part of the document's "We the People."

The Sedition Act was intended to quell a flood of orations and pamphlets critical of the policies promoted by the Federalists. In 1799, four Irish immigrants were charged in Philadelphia with violating the law by urging Irish natives to sign petitions against the acts. The prosecutor opened their trial by telling the jury that "the greatest evils this country has ever endured have arisen from the ready admission to foreigners to a participation in the government and internal arrangements of the country." He accused the defendants of being among those "who are stirring up sedition and strife, who plant confusion, tumult and national ruin."

Jefferson called the Alien and Sedition Acts "an experiment on the American mind to see how far it will bear an avowed violation of the Constitution" and objected to Federalist attempts to purge the country of foreigners and their new ideas. Jefferson and James Madison helped draft the Kentucky and Virginia Resolutions, which condemned the acts and called on the states to nullify them.

President Adams never signed any deportation orders under the acts. In the end, the laws backfired on the Federalists and may have cost them the election of 1800, in which Jefferson defeated Adams's bid for reelection. As president, Jefferson pardoned all those convicted under the Alien and Sedition Acts. In 1964, in a landmark First Amendment case, *New York Times v. Sullivan*, the U.S. Supreme Court declared, "Although the Sedition Act was never tested in this Court, the attack upon its validity has carried the day in the court of history."

Stephen F. Rohde

ALIEN AND SEDITION ACTS

Congress passed the Alien and Sedition Acts in the summer of 1798, condemning subversiveness not only among immigrants and noncitizens but also among citizens who dared disagree with the federal government. The acts, excerpted here, were adopted without regard for the civil rights outlined in the U.S. Constitution and the Bill of Rights, and were so unpopular that they were repealed after two years.

AN ACT CONCERNING ALIENS.

Sec. 1: That it shall be lawful for the President of the United States at any time during the continuance of this act, to *order* all such *aliens* as he shall judge dangerous to the peace and safety of the United States, or shall have reasonable grounds to suspect are concerned in any treasonable or secret machinations against the government thereof, to depart [be deported] out of the territory of the United States. . . . (June 25, 1798, p. 571)

AN ACT FOR THE PUNISHMENT OF CERTAIN CRIMES AGAINST THE UNITED STATES.

Sec. 1: That if any persons shall unlawfully combine or conspire together, with intent to oppose any measure or measures of the government of the United States, which are or shall be directed by proper authority, or to impede the operation of any law of the United States, or to intimidate or prevent any person holding a place or office in or under the government of the United States, from undertaking, performing or executing his trust or duty. . . shall be punished. . . .

Sec. 2: That if any person shall write, print, utter or publish . . . any false, scandalous and malicious writing or writing against the government of the United States, . . . or to stir up sedition, or to excite any unlawful combinations therein, for opposing or resisting any law of the United States, or any act of the President of the United States, . . . shall be punished. . . . (July 14, 1798, p. 596)

Source: Statutes at Large, 5th Cong., Sess. II, June 25 and July 14, 1798. Library of Congress, U.S. Documents and Debates, 1774-1875. http://memory.loc.gov/ammem/amlaw/lwsl.html. Accessed August, 2005.

---

tucky and Virginia Resolutions, which condemned the acts and called on the states to nullify them.

FURTHER READING

Miller, John Chester. *Crisis in Freedom: The Alien and Sedition Acts.* Boston: Little, Brown, 1951.

Smith, James Morton. *Freedom's Fetters: The Alien and Sedition Laws and American Civil Liberties.* Ithaca, N.Y.: Cornell University Press, 1967.

Watkins, William J., Jr. *Reclaiming the American Revolution: The Kentucky and Virginia Resolutions.* New York: Palgrave Macmillan, 2004.

SEE ALSO: Deportation; Espionage and Sedition Acts of 1917-1918; French immigrants; History of immigration, 1783-1891; Naturalization Act of 1790; Political parties.

ALIEN CONTRACT LABOR LAW OF 1885

THE LAW: Federal law prohibiting the importation of immigrant laborers under contract
DATE: Enacted on February 26, 1885
ALSO KNOWN AS: Contract Labor Law of 1885

SIGNIFICANCE: This law and later federal labor legislation targeting immigrants prohibited American employers from recruiting and importing foreign laborers by promising them jobs on arrival in America. The law targeted primarily Chinese immigrants on the East and West coasts who worked for lower wages than those demanded by unionized American citizens.

During the mid-nineteenth century, large numbers of laborers were brought into the United States to work mines in the California gold rush, help build the first transcontinental railroad, and work in other expanding industries. A large portion of the imported workers with limited skills were Chinese and Irish immigrants, who worked more cheaply than native-born Americans. California's gold rush was mostly played out by the 1860's, and the transcontinental railroad was completed in 1869.

As the need for cheap labor in the United States diminished, the federal government began enacting laws to discourage the importation of more foreign laborers, particularly from Asia. The Naturalization Act of 1870, for example, limited U.S. citizenship to persons of European and African descent, thereby excluding the thousands of Asian workers already in the United States. The Chinese Exclusion Act of 1882 went further. It placed a tax on each immigrant arriving, blocked entry of convicts and less intelligent individuals, and restricted all Chinese immigration to the United States. These laws launched a new era of restricted immigration into the country.

Enacted by Congress in 1885, the Alien Contract Labor Law had two purposes: to promote the unionization of skilled laborers through groups such as the Order of the Knights of Labor and to prohibit contracting immigrants from being employed upon their arrival in the United States. The law aimed at reducing immigration to the country and supplying the workforce with better skilled trained craftsmen. The act prohibited all companies and individuals from bringing immigrants into the United States under contract or through indentured servitude. A less overt purpose of the law was to raise the quality of new immigrants by excluding people who could not pay their own way to reach the United States. Immigrants who could afford to travel to the United States on their own income were most welcome. Exceptions to this law were people in the arts and higher education, and those with special skills and talents in short supply in the United States.

After the Contract Labor Law was passed, the federal government lacked the resources to enforce it tightly. In 1888 and 1891, it was amended to include provisions for government inspections of ships carrying immigrants and for investigations of illegal employment contracts. The law effectively prevented small and midsize American employers from contracting with immigrants, but the full effect of the law on immigration is not known. Awareness of the limited effectiveness of the law created an impetus for the federal government to create the Bureau of Immigration in 1891.

Keith J. Bell

FURTHER READING

Lee, Erika. *At America's Gates: Chinese Immigration During the Exclusion Era, 1882-1943*. Chapel Hill: University of North Carolina Press, 2007.

LeMay, Michael C., and Elliott Robert Barkan, eds. *U.S. Immigration and Naturalization Laws and Issues: A Documentary History*. Westport, Conn.: Greenwood Press, 1999.

Steinfeld, Robert J. *Coercion, Contract, and Free Labor in the Nineteenth Century*. New York: Cambridge University Press, 2001.

SEE ALSO: Alien land laws; Anti-Chinese movement; Chinese immigrants; Contract labor system; Immigration Act of 1882; Immigration Act of 1891; Immigration and Nationality Act of 1952; Immigration and Nationality Act of 1965; Immigration and Naturalization Service, U.S.; Railroads.

ALIEN LAND LAWS

DEFINITION: Laws of individual states that limited land ownership by noncitizens, particularly Asian immigrants

SIGNIFICANCE: Targeting mainly Asian immigrants, the alien land laws demonstrated an anti-immigrant hysteria in a nation that prided itself on the welcome it extended to immigrants. The discriminatory laws were upheld by the courts into the 1940's.

The United States of America, even before it became independent from Great Britain, has always had a schizophrenic relationship toward immigrants. It has prided itself on being a nation of immigrants, but its citizens have also frequently complained about the types of new immigrants entering the country, arguing that the new immigrants are not as worthy of becoming Americans as those who have already arrived. Part of this xenophobia has been reflected in laws enacted by some states that banned noncitizens—especially those not permitted to become citizens—from owning land.

EARLY LAWS

Some of the earliest alien land laws occurred in California, which began enacting laws during the nineteenth century that banned aliens who could not become citizens from owning land. California directed these laws mostly against Asians, the main racial group banned from naturalization. Many local California jurisdictions passed such ordinances, and eventually the state government did as well. These laws were not the only manifestation of anti-Asian discrimination, as both laws and customs discriminated. One such custom was a law banning laundries from operating in wooden buildings without permits; it discriminated against Chinese laundry owners who generally could not afford brick buildings. The government officials who issued the permits granted them to virtually all white applicants, while denying them to virtually all Chinese applicants. In 1886, the U.S. Supreme Court declared this practice illegal. California's state and local governments continued to enact a variety of discriminatory laws targeting against Asians.

In 1913, the state of California passed its Alien Land Law. This law forbade those who were not American citizens and were not eligible for citizenship from owning agricultural land. This law targeted Asians, who constituted the only important category of immigrants in the state who were not eligible for citizenship under federal law. Because immigrants from Europe and Africa could become citizens, the law did not affect them. It would not be until the 1960's that the U.S. government revamped its naturalization policy to hold that people from all continents could become citizens. California's law did not conflict with a 1911 U.S. treaty with Japan that protected the right of Japanese immigrants to own commercial land in the United States, as it covered only agricultural land.

In 1920, the state of California passed a new Alien Land Law that made the restrictions of the 1913 law even more stringent. Up to that time, many Asian immigrants had circumvented California's land law by purchasing agricultural land in the names of their American-born children and made themselves the managers of the land. Thanks to the unambiguous language of the Fourteenth Amendment to the U.S. Constitution, even the children of Asians born in the United States were full citizens:

> All persons born or naturalized in the United States and subject to the jurisdiction thereof, are citizens of the United States and of the State wherein they reside. No State shall make or enforce any law which shall abridge the privileges or immunities of citizens of the United States . . .

California's 1920 law was designed to make it even harder for Asians to own land. It required all persons purchasing land in someone else's name to prove they were not doing so to circumvent the terms of the 1913 law. The 1920 law also prohibited naming as trustees persons ineligible for citizenship and effectively reversed the traditional burden of proof, requiring people to prove themselves innocent. Two years later, California's supreme court struck down the law's provision on trusteeship. In 1948, the U.S. Supreme Court addressed the law's burden-of-proof provisions in *Oyama v. California*. In that ruling, the Court held that the reversing of proof provision violated the equal protection clause of the Fourteenth Amendment because it treated noncitizens differently. However, the Supreme Court did not strike down California's 1913 law.

California was not the only U.S. state to enact alien land laws. Other states that added or modified such laws and provisions during the 1920's included Arizona, Florida, Idaho, Kansas, Louisiana, Montana, New Mexico, Oregon, and Washington. During World War II, anti-Japanese fervor caused Arkansas, Utah, and Wyoming to enact such laws. Most of these states' laws remained in effect until at least the 1950's.

END OF THE LAWS

California's alien land laws were finally invalidated in 1952, when the state's supreme court struck them down in its *Sei Fujii v. State of California* ruling because they violated the Fourteenth Amendment's equal protection clause. The California court was initially considering a claim by an immigrant named Sei Fujii that California's alien land laws violated the human rights provisions of the United Nations (U.N.) Charter, which, ironically, had been drafted in San Francisco. California's supreme court held that the charter's human rights provisions were not self-executing, and because neither the state of California nor the federal government had acted to implement legislation to bring these provisions into effect, the charter was not in force in California. Instead, the court cited the Fourteenth Amendment of the U.S. Constitution to invalidate the law. However, the state legislature waited another four years before formally voting to remove the invalid statute.

Later court decisions have largely rendered unconstitutional further attempts to enact legislation discriminating against legal immigrants. However, the absence of a direct ruling from the U.S. Supreme Court striking down such laws (*Oyama* struck down only the 1920 strengthening statute, not the original 1913 law) meant that laws had to either be invalidated by each state supreme court or be repealed state by state. Some states took considerable time to do that. For example, as late as 2008, the state of Florida had a ballot initiative that would have removed a constitutional provision on the matter. The provision in question allowed the legislature to forbid alien land holding. Although the provision had never been enforced, Florida voters refused to vote for its removal in 2008. Some opponents of the ballot measure argued that removal of the constitutional provision' would somehow aid terrorists and illegal immigrants.

By the early twenty-first century, only four states still had alien land laws on their books. Other states had already removed their own laws or had had them overturned by courts. Oregon and Montana, for example, had their laws overturned by their state supreme courts during the 1940's and 1950's. Washington State required a ballot proposition to overturn its law. That measure went through three elections before it received a majority vote, even though only one state legislator publicly opposed the measure.

Scott A. Merriman

FURTHER READING

Bender, Steven. *Greasers and Gringos: Latinos, Law, and the American Imagination.* New York: New York University Press, 2005. While examining the roots of negative Hispanic stereotypes and their effect upon laws, Bender shows how many land-use laws were directed against Latino immigrants and members of other groups.

Chappelle, Diane. *Land Law.* New York: Longman, 2008. Examination of all aspects of American land laws, including prohibitions and regulations.

Jordan, Maria Elena Sanchez, and Antonio Gambaro, eds. *Land Law in Comparative Perspective.* Boston: Kluwer Law International, 2002. Collection of essays that examine land law throughout the world. They look at historical and contemporary issues, including land ownership.

Pincetl, Stephanie. *Transforming California: A Political History of Land Use and Development.* Baltimore: Johns Hopkins University Press, 1999. Focuses on land use in California, where some of the strongest alien land laws were enacted. Examines California's past and present, including its environmental history and other land-use issues.

Singer, Joseph William. *Property Law: Rules, Policies, and Practices.* 4th ed. New York: Aspen, 2006. Illuminates a wide variety of different aspects of property law, including such topics as trespass, ownership, adverse possession, and landlord-tenant relations.

SEE ALSO: Americanization programs; Anti-Chinese movement; Anti-Japanese movement; Asiatic

Barred Zone; Burlingame Treaty of 1868; California; Chinese Exclusion Act of 1882; Empresario land grants in Texas; Paper sons; *Sei Fujii v. State of California*; *Yick Wo v. Hopkins*.

ALVAREZ, JULIA

IDENTIFICATION: Dominican American author
BORN: March 27, 1950; New York, New York

SIGNIFICANCE: Alvarez came to prominence as a novelist with the publication of *How the García Girls Lost Their Accents* (1991), the semi-autobiographical story of four immigrant sisters who struggle to find their place in a new home and life in America. Much of her work examines her bicultural heritage.

Julia Alvarez was born in New York City, but her family returned to the Dominican Republic shortly after her birth. Her early years were spent in comfort surrounded by many loving relatives. She attended American schools, ate American food, and dreamed about America. Initially, her parents and grandparents experienced social and political acceptance in the Dominican Republic because of their wealth. Her father, a doctor, was in charge of the local hospital. When the political situation worsened and her father became involved in a plot to overthrow the dictator of the country, Rafael Trujillo, the family was forced to flee. They returned to New York, having lost most of their possessions and material comforts, and moved into a small apartment in Brooklyn. The shock of leaving her former lifestyle and adjusting to America deeply affected Alvarez.

Though Alvarez and her family were familiar with all things American, she herself was treated as a foreigner. Alvarez's experience as an outsider led her to immerse herself in books and writing. Her cultural background emphasized storytelling, and she was encouraged in school to develop her talents. She attended Middlebury College in Vermont, graduating summa cum laude with a bachelor's degree in English in 1971, and she earned a master's degree in creative writing from Syracuse University in 1975. Alvarez received tenure as an English professor at her alma mater in 1991, the year she published her best-known book, *How the García Girls Lost Their Accents*, a coming-of-age novel based on her experience and that of her family in their transition from a life of privilege in the Dominican Republic to the challenges of growing up in a diverse neighborhood in a disadvantaged area of New York City. The sequel *¡Yo!* (1997) focuses on the character of Yolanda García.

Although her first book was a volume of poetry, *Homecoming: Poems* (1984), Alvarez has been recognized primarily for her prose. Her novel about the García sisters was awarded the PEN Oakland/Josephine Miles Literary Award in 1991. *In the Time of the Butterflies* (1994), a fictionalized account of the lives and murders of the Mirabel sisters under Trujillo's regime, was a 1995 National Book Critics Circle Award nominee and was later made into a feature film. Alvarez's other works of fiction include *In the Name of Salomé* (2000), an ambitious historical novel that weaves together the lives of two women and their political causes, and *Saving the World* (2006), which tells parallel stories about humanitarian missions.

Alvarez's historically rooted stories of assimilation provide a voice for immigrants and young Latinas in particular. She is one of the first Dominican American writers to achieve international acclaim.

Dolores A. D'Angelo

FURTHER READING
Heredia, Juanita, and Bridget A. Kevane, eds. *Latina Self-Portraits: Interviews with Contemporary Women Writers*. Albuquerque: University of New Mexico Press, 2000.
Johnson, Kelli Lyon. *Julia Alvarez: Writing a New Place on the Map*. Albuquerque: University of New Mexico Press, 2005.
Sirias, Silvio. *Julia Alvarez: A Critical Companion*. Westport, Conn.: Greenwood Press, 2001.

SEE ALSO: Child immigrants; Dominican immigrants; Education; Families; Literature; Santiago, Esmeralda; West Indian immigrants.

AMERASIAN CHILDREN

DEFINITION: According to definitions in congressional legislation of the 1980's, "Amerasians" are the children of women of specified Asian nations and American men who were born during a certain time period. More generally, however, the term is often used colloquially to describe children of non-Asian U.S. citizens and Asian nationals

SIGNIFICANCE: The vast majority of Amerasian children who immigrated to the United States after the early 1970's were of American and Vietnamese descent. Those of American and Korean ancestry were a distant second. After 1987, Vietnamese Amerasians were permitted to immigrate to the United States and bring along close relatives, thereby adding to Vietnamese immigration to America.

After World War II ended in 1945, American troops remained stationed in East Asian countries such as Japan, the Philippines, and South Korea. After the Korean War ended in 1953, additional troops remained stationed in South Korea. The years that followed saw an increase in the numbers of children born to American soldiers and local Asian women. The vast majority of the American fathers were European Americans and African Americans. Very often, these fathers abandoned their children and the children's mothers when they returned to America.

AMERASIANS AND AMERICA

The plight of fatherless Korean American children moved American writer Pearl S. Buck to call attention to their neglect, and she chose the term "Amerasians" for them. In 1954, Harry and Bertha Holt promoted American adoption of Korean War orphans. Some of these orphans were abandoned Amerasians facing discrimination in Korea as *honhyol*, or "mixed blood" children.

From about 1962 to 1975, as the United States became more deeply involved in the Vietnam War, relationships between American men and Vietnamese women increased. On average, relationships in which children were born lasted about two years. As American military authorities discouraged American-Vietnamese marriages, only the most determined Americans brought their Vietnamese wives and Amerasian children home to the United States, where these immigrants constituted the vast majority of the 20,000 residents of the country who were counted as Vietnamese by early 1975.

After the communist victory in Vietnam in early 1975, the situation in Vietnam for Amerasians deteriorated badly. Even before that time, life had been difficult for them after their fathers left the country. The communists, however, made their lives even harder by showing active hostility toward the children of their American enemies, and they discriminated severely against them and their mothers. Called *con lai*, "half-breeds," or *bui doi*, "children of the dust," the children were bullied and rejected and denied good educations and job opportunities—which were already scarce under communism.

IMMIGRATION RIGHTS FOR AMERASIANS

When the plight of Vietnamese refugees known who tried to leave their homeland by sea caught the free world's attention after 1978, the U.S. government became willing to admit them as refugees. The first Vietnamese Amerasian children arrived together with other Vietnamese refugees through the Orderly Departure Program (ODP) after 1979. However, this program did not address all the special needs of the Amerasian children. For three years, U.S. Senator Jeremiah Denton introduced and fought for what would become the Amerasian Immigration Act of 1982. On October 22, 1982, that act became law.

The first of two important pieces of federal legislation on this issue during the 1980's, the Amerasian Immigration Act defined Amerasians as children whose fathers were U.S. citizens and whose mothers were nationals of Kampuchea (Cambodia), Korea, Laos, Thailand, or Vietnam, and who had been born between January 1, 1950, and October 22, 1982. This definition of Amerasian was a narrow legal term. Critics of the law objected that it did not immediately award citizenship to the Amerasians it defined, and that children of American fathers and women from Japan, Taiwan, and the Philippines were not considered Amerasians under the law.

The first five hundred Amerasian children admitted to the United States under the 1982 law left

Vietnam in 1982 and 1983. As many as 5,500 Vietnamese Amerasians also left under the ODP. Soon, however, the Vietnamese government objected to the U.S. government's calling these people "refugees" and halted their departure. The 1982 law also allowed only the children to immigrate, leaving behind their mothers in favor of American institutional or private sponsors if the children were under eighteen years of age. This provision explains why relatively few Amerasians from Korea and other eligible nations immigrated under this law.

The Amerasian Homecoming Act of 1987, which was enacted on December 22, 1987, corrected some of the deficiencies of the 1982 law. Under this new legislation, all children born to American fathers and Vietnamese mothers between January 1, 1962, and January 1, 1976, and their close relatives could immigrate to America.

The 1987 law quickly turned Amerasians in Vietnam from despised "children of dust" to "children of gold." Some ordinary Vietnamese posed as relatives of Amerasians in order to go to the United States. By 2009, it was estimated that almost all eligible Vietnamese American children who wanted to leave Vietnam had done so. About 25,000 had immigrated under the Homecoming Act and as many as another 10,000 may have entered the country through other means. Additionally, Vietnamese Amerasians facilitated the immigration of some 60,000 to 70,000 of their Vietnamese relatives.

ADJUSTING TO LIFE IN AMERICA

The majority of Amerasians admitted through the immigration laws of 1982 and 1987 generally succeeded in America. However, they did so only after adjusting to the English language and American culture and overcoming their limited formal educations, traumatized lives, and issues of abandonment and discrimination. Moreover, only about 3 percent of

them could locate their American fathers. Those who came with their mothers and already had some command of English were among the most successful. Alcoholism, depression, drugs, and crime troubled some Amerasians, but most eventually adapted well.

Through the 1990's and the early twenty-first century, there were persistent efforts by U.S. lawmakers to widen the definition of Amerasian children eligible for immigration or to bestow automatic citizenship to them. However, none of these efforts had succeeded by the year 2009.

Many Asian Americans have objected to the colloquial use of the term "Amerasian" for all children of non-Asian American fathers and foreign Asian women, arguing that such usage implies that Asian Americans are not real Americans. The 2007 American Community Survey listed 1,707,488 Asian

Barry Huntoon (left), an American Vietnam War veteran, with his wife and infant child in 1987, greet a teenage Amerasian girl whom Huntoon believed to be his daughter, born after he left Vietnam. However, the girl's natural mother later denied Huntoon's claim. Huntoon's well-publicized story, later made into the 1990 television film The Girl Who Came Between Them, *pointed up the difficulties of establishing the paternity of the many Amerasian children left behind by American war veterans. (AP/Wide World Photos)*

Americans living in the United States who were also descended from one or more other racial heritages. Among these people, about 170,000 were foreign born, and 66 percent of them—112,200 people—were born in Asia. Under the broadest, if controversial, definition of the term, they might also be called "Amerasians."

R. C. Lutz

FURTHER READING

Gage, Sue-Je Lee. "The Amerasian Problem: Blood, Duty, and Race." *International Relations* 21, no. 1 (2007): 86-102. Scholarly analysis of the passage of the Amerasian Immigration Act of 1982 that is strong on the U.S. background regarding Amerasians. The author criticizes the law's exclusion of Japanese and Filipino Amerasians.

Lamb, David. "Children of the Dust." *Smithsonian* 40, no. 3 (June, 2009): 28-37. Informed journalistic overview of the fates of Vietnamese Amerasians and the key events facilitating their immigration to America. Praises the immigrants' general resilience and corrects stereotypes. Illustrated.

McKelvey, Robert. *The Dust of Life: America's Children Abandoned in Vietnam*. Seattle: University of Washington Press, 1999. Powerful and sympathetic portrayal of the fate of Vietnamese Amerasians before, during, and after their immigration to the United States.

Nguyen, Kien. *The Unwanted*. Boston: Back Bay Books, 2001. Autobiography of a Vietnamese Amerasian left in Vietnam after 1975, his sufferings, resentments, and eventual immigration to the United States.

Yarborough, Trin. *Surviving Twice: Amerasian Children of the Vietnam War*. Dulles, Va.: Potomac Books, 2005. Portrayal of five Vietnamese Amerasian children and their challenging lives in Vietnam and, after immigration, in America.

SEE ALSO: Amerasian Homecoming Act of 1987; Asian immigrants; Child immigrants; Families; Intermarriage; Korean War; *Nguyen v. Immigration and Naturalization Service*; Orderly Departure Program; Refugees; Vietnam War; Vietnamese immigrants.

AMERASIAN HOMECOMING ACT OF 1987

THE LAW: Federal legislation designed to ease immigration of Vietnamese Amerasian children and their close relatives to the United States

DATE: Enacted on December 22, 1987; effective on March 21, 1988

SIGNIFICANCE: This was the first federal law that substantially eased the immigration of Amerasian children born during the Vietnam War—mostly the offspring of American fathers and Vietnamese mothers. By 2009, about 25,000 Vietnamese Amerasians and 60,000 to 70,000 of their relatives had immigrated to the United States under this law.

During the long conflict in Vietnam in which the United States was involved from the early 1960's until 1975, many American soldiers and civilian personnel working in Vietnam fathered children with Vietnamese women. Because U.S. authorities discouraged marriages between Americans and Vietnamese, only the most determined Americans managed to take their Vietnamese wives and children to the United States before American involvement in the war ended in early 1975.

At the time Vietnam was officially reunified under communist rule on July 2, 1976, it was estimated that tens of thousands of Vietnamese Amerasian children were living in the country with virtually no contact with their American fathers. The communists detested these Amerasians, whom they regarded as contemptible half-breeds, or *bui doi*, "children of the dust." Their most severe contempt was for children who had African American fathers.

In 1982, the U.S. Congress passed the Amerasian Immigration Act, which theoretically allowed for the immigration of Vietnamese Amerasians to America. However, because the Vietnamese government was not cooperative, only about 6,000 Amerasians and 11,000 of their relatives reached the United States under this law, which was part of the Orderly Departure Program that began in 1979. However, in 1987, even this limited avenue for Amerasian immigration appeared to close as

Vietnam objected to the program's classification of Amerasians as refugees. In response, the U.S. Congress passed a bill sponsored by Robert Mrazek and others in the House of Representatives and John McCain in the Senate as the Amerasian Homecoming Act. The law became effective on March 21, 1988. It was set to expire in two years but was extended. In 2009, it was still the basis for processing a shrinking number of applicants, who had to be children of American citizens and had to have been born between January 1, 1962, and January 1, 1976.

Under the law, Amerasians and their relatives could apply for immigration to the United States. They were given full refugee assistance, even though they were not officially classified as refugees. During the peak years of immigration under this law, from 1988 to 1993, about 95 percent of all applicants and their relatives were admitted. By that time, the law had facilitated immigration for about 20,000 Amerasians and about 50,000 of their relatives. In 1993, however, the U.S. government learned that there had been widespread misuse of the law, as ordinary Vietnamese citizens eager to go to America had been paying bribes in order to pose as relatives of Amerasians who were pressured to participate in the scheme. It was estimated that about 17 percent of the immigrants admitted under this law were fake relatives. In response, U.S. government approval of later applications fell to as low as 5 percent after 1994.

By 2009, about 25,000 Amerasians and 60,000 to 70,000 of their relatives had immigrated to America under the Amerasian Homecoming Act. By then, however, the annual numbers had severely declined. In fiscal year 2007, for example, only 129 immigrants were admitted to the United States under the law. In June, 2009, the U.S. consulate in Ho Chi Minh City began processing applications on a special appointment basis only.

In general, the Amerasians who came to the United States with their mothers did the best in assimilating to American society. Many faced great hardships, but most proved resilient and successful. However, only 3 percent of them managed to contact their American fathers after arriving in the United States. By 2009, about 50 percent of all the immigrants who arrived under the law had become U.S. citizens.

R. C. Lutz

FURTHER READING

McKelvey, Robert. *The Dust of Life: America's Children Abandoned in Vietnam.* Seattle: University of Washington Press, 1999.

Nguyen, Kien. *The Unwanted.* Boston: Back Bay Books, 2001.

Yarborough, Trin. *Surviving Twice: Amerasian Children of the Vietnam War.* Dulles, Va.: Potomac Books, 2005.

SEE ALSO: Amerasian children; Asian immigrants; Child immigrants; Families; Indochina Migration and Refugee Assistance Act of 1975; *Nguyen v. Immigration and Naturalization Service*; Orderly Departure Program; Refugees; Vietnam War; Vietnamese immigrants.

AMERICAN COLONIZATION SOCIETY

IDENTIFICATION: Charitable organization to send former slaves to Africa

DATE: Established in 1816; dissolved in 1964

SIGNIFICANCE: The public and private funds raised by the American Colonization Society led to the settlement of approximately thirteen thousand African Americans in West Africa by 1867 and the establishment of the independent nation of Liberia. The organization's guiding philosophy represented a middle ground between abolitionists and proslavery advocates.

Although the American Colonization Society (ACS) was not formed until December, 1816, the desire to remove black slaves from the United States had long existed. The gradual elimination of slavery in the northern states created a concern for the inferior status of free blacks in society. Some slaveholders in the South grew uneasy about their human property, and many more feared free blacks. These motivations led to the creation of the ACS, but their diversity contributed to the organization's modest success.

The organizers of the ACS were varied and well connected. Reverend Robert Finley, a Presbyterian minister from New Jersey, organized the first meet-

Liberia College, which opened in Monrovia only two decades after the American Colonization Society helped establish the first settlement of African American emigrants in Liberia. In 1951, the college became the University of Liberia. (Library of Congress)

ing, while Virginia politician Charles Fenton Mercer, Congressman Henry Clay of Kentucky, Francis Scott Key, and Congressman John Randolph of Virginia were among the early supporters. Supreme Court justice Bushrod Washington, a nephew of George Washington, was the society's first president. After founding the society in Washington, D.C., the officers sought federal funds to carry out their mission. Former presidents Thomas Jefferson and James Madison soon supported the cause, as did their successor, James Monroe, who used his influence to arrange public funding.

The goal of the ACS was to establish an African colony where free blacks and manumitted slaves would be sent. However, persuading northern free blacks to volunteer was difficult. Southerners were often eager to export free blacks but not their own slaves. Nevertheless, the first shipload of eighty-six emigrants sailed from New York on January 31,

1820. No one in Africa welcomed the settlers taking tribal lands, and the unfamiliar climate, disease, and lack of supplies ravaged the first wave of immigrants. In December, 1821, with the armed assistance of the U.S. Navy, the ACS purchased Cape Mesurado, the present site of Monrovia, Liberia. By 1833, more than thirty-one hundred African Americans had arrived. Ironically, the ACS's mission was aided by southerners, who wanted to rid society of free blacks in the wake of Nat Turner's rebellion in 1831. Pennsylvania, New York, Maryland, Mississippi, and Louisiana created their own colonizing missions during the 1830's. All were incorporated into the Liberia colony, and the ACS increasingly became a federation of state societies.

The most notable success was Liberia's declaration of independence in 1847. This action was encouraged by the ACS, whose financial difficulties made it impossible for it to care for the colony properly. In the years between Liberian independence and the U.S. Civil War, almost six thousand African Americans emigrated. In the five years after the war, more than two thousand more went to Liberia, but with contributions down, the ACS was practically bankrupt. In the decades to come, it functioned as a Liberian aid society focusing on education and missionary work.

The ALS evoked a wide variety of reactions before the Civil War. Certainly tinged with a racist belief that blacks would never earn equal rights, many white northerners sincerely thought that colonization was the best solution. Beginning in the 1830's, abolition societies portrayed the ACS as antirepublican and proslavery. White southerners were largely apathetic. Most free blacks identified their future with the United States rather than an uncertain fate in a remote colony. The lack of consensus about the status of African Americans undermined the organization's efforts and reflected the bitter divisions in American society. The ACS was formally dissolved in 1964.

M. Philip Lucas

FURTHER READING

Burin, Eric. *Slavery and the Peculiar Solution: A History of the American Colonization Society.* Gainesville: University Press of Florida, 2005.

Staudenraus, P. J. *The African Colonization Movement, 1816-1865.* New York: Columbia University Press, 1961.

SEE ALSO: Abolitionist movement; African Americans and immigrants; African immigrants; Emigration; Garvey, Marcus; Liberia; Slave trade; Universal Negro Improvement Association.

AMERICAN JEWISH COMMITTEE

IDENTIFICATION: International think tank and Jewish advocacy organization
DATE: Established in 1906

SIGNIFICANCE: Through its fund-raising and the work of its national and international subdivisions, the American Jewish Committee (AJC) has exerted a major influence on the welfare of Jews throughout the world for more than a century. According to its mission statement, the AJC is committed to countering world anti-Semitism and terrorism; promoting human rights, religious pluralism, and interfaith relations; strengthening Jewish life in the United States and abroad; and seeking an enduring peace for Israel.

The American Jewish Committee (AJC)—not to be confused with the American Jewish Congress, another advocacy group—was founded in November, 1906, by wealthy German American Jews in the wake of deadly anti-Jewish pogroms in czarist Russia. The founders included members of such socially prominent American Jewish families as the Strauses, Sulzbergers, Warburgs, and Schiffs. Among its original goals was to "prevent infringement of the civil and religious rights of Jews" and "alleviate the consequences of persecution." One way of accomplishing the latter was to facilitate the emigration of Jews to the United States or other countries of their choice.

During the early years of the organization, one of its stated tasks was to ensure that the U.S. government did not attempt to limit the influx of Jewish immigrants, most of whom were coming from eastern Europe. President Theodore Roosevelt was enlisted to help in this cause and proved to be very cooperative. In fact, he had appointed one of the AJC's founding members, Oscar Straus, to his cabinet. Straus is believed to be the first Jew to serve in such a capacity.

One of the main activist Jewish organizations in the realm of immigration policy, the AJC played a prominent role in aiding Jewish victims of both world wars. Toward the beginning of World War I, the AJC established the American Jewish Joint Distribution Committee and the American Jewish Welfare Board to assist both Jewish and non-Jewish servicemen and war victims. To those displaced coreligionists who looked to America after surviving the horrors of the Holocaust, the AJC offered material assistance in facilitating immigration. After World War II, the AJC supported increased immigration for the purpose of family reunification, opposed the denial of government benefits to noncitizen but legal immigrants, and called for increasing the intake of refugees from countries where continued residency can pose a danger to their lives.

During the 1980's, the AJC launched a campaign to pressure the Soviet Union to allow its Jews to emigrate. To this end, the AJC organized the Washington, D.C., Freedom Sunday Rally in December of 1987, attracting an estimated 250,000 people. Ultimately, Soviet Jews were allowed to leave, and thousands came to the United States, with particularly large contingents settling in New York and Los Angeles.

In the early twenty-first century, as Jewish immigration became less of an issue, the AJC added its powerful voice to combating what it considered anti-immigrant views and vigilantism against Hispanics, urging cable television stations to reveal the backgrounds of "so-called immigration experts" to their viewing public and stating that "issues such as immigration can be explored legitimately . . . without demonizing an entire group of people." The AJC has also been a strong proponent of increased funding for the acculturation of new immigrants as part of a sound immigration policy, including the learning of English and an "American values education."

The AJC's ongoing influence was amply demonstrated at its hundredth anniversary celebration in 2006, which U.S. president George W. Bush, U.N. secretary-general Kofi Annan, and German chancellor Angela Merkel attended. In 2009, the AJC's membership was estimated at more than 100,000, with branches in more than thirty U.S. cities as well as eight overseas offices. It was also the first American Jewish organization to establish a full-time presence in Germany. The organization continued to involve itself in various humanitarian causes, raising significant amounts of money to alleviate the consequences of crises such as the South Asian tsunami in 2004 and Hurricane Katrina in 2005.

Roy Liebman

FURTHER READING

Cohen, Naomi W. *Not Free to Desist: The American Jewish Committee, 1906-1966.* Philadelphia: Jewish Publication Society of America, 1972. Discusses the founding and history of the American Jewish Committee up to the mid-1960's, including the role it played following the world wars and in helping Israel to become an independent state in 1948.

Ivers, Gregg. *To Build a Wall: American Jews and the Separation of Church and State.* Charlottesville: University Press of Virginia, 1995. Examines Jewish advocacy groups such as the AJC, B'nai B'rith, and the American Jewish Congress that are strong advocates of church-state separation.

Robin, Frederick. *The Pursuit of Equality: A Half Century with the American Jewish Committee.* New York: Crown, 1957. Provides an overview of the first fifty years of the AJC's accomplishments.

Sanua, Marianne R. *Let Us Prove Strong: The American Jewish Committee, 1945-2006.* Waltham, Mass.: Brandeis University Press, 2007. In its coverage of the post-World War II activities of the AJC, this book overlaps with Cohen's. Thus, it is most useful in its account of the history of the AJC in the four decades following 1966. As an official publication of the AJC, its tone is generally laudatory.

SEE ALSO: Anti-Defamation League; Anti-Semitism; European immigrants; Holocaust; Jewish immigrants; Religion as a push-pull factor; Russian and Soviet immigrants; World War I; World War II.

AMERICAN PROTECTIVE ASSOCIATION

IDENTIFICATION: Anti-Roman Catholic organization

DATE: Founded on March 13, 1887; dissolved in 1911

LOCATION: Clinton, Iowa

SIGNIFICANCE: The American Protective Association was one of several American organizations created to counter the growing presence and influence of Roman Catholic immigrants in the United States. Its purpose was to protect the United States from the Catholic Church, which it viewed as a foreign organization with international designs.

Between the end of the Civil War (1861-1865) and World War I (1914-1918), approximately 25 million immigrants came to the United States. Many of these immigrants were working-class Roman Catholics who settled in the cities of the North. The presence of these immigrants and their growing economic and political influence resulted in a

Protestant nativism that based its appeal primarily on conservative political values designed to appeal to the common person.

The American Protective Association (APA) was the largest anti-Catholic organization in the United States during the late nineteenth century. It was founded in Clinton, Iowa, on March 13, 1887, by attorney Henry Francis Bowers and seven other men. While its original motivation was linked to local political activity, it began to spread to other locales within a few years. The group was a secret organization with uniforms and elaborate rituals. Its purpose was to defend "true Americanism" and fight the growing power of the Catholic Church in America. The APA advocated immigration restrictions, a free public school system to counter the growth of parochial schools, and a slower naturalization process for immigrants. All members took an oath never to vote for a Catholic, never to employ a Catholic if a Protestant were available, and never to go on strike with a Catholic worker. The organization appealed primarily to conservative working-class Protestants who perceived the growing Catholic population as a threat to their values, economic status, and political influence.

Unlike the Know-Nothing Party movement of the first half of the nineteenth century, the APA did not form a political party. Rather, it focused on working through the Republican Party. The APA's greatest success occurred in school board and municipal elections in the Midwest. It promoted anti-Catholicism by distributing forged documents designed to promote fear of Catholics among local citizens. Before elections, it circulated lists of candidates marked *C* for Catholic, *c* for Catholic sympathizer, and *P* for Protestant.

The American Protective Association's greatest national success occurred in 1893 and 1894 as it capitalized on the fear of Catholic success in national and local elections. It also began to publish newspapers; by 1894, approximately seventy APA weeklies were in circulation. While the organization claimed to have a membership of 2.5 million at its peak, historians estimate that its dues-paying membership was approximately 100,000. Though it was a national movement, its greatest strength was in the Midwest and West. The organization declined rapidly during the last half of the 1890's because of internal dissension. Bowers's death in 1911 effectively marked the end of the organiza-

tion; however, its prominence during the 1890's illustrates the continued strains between native Protestants and Catholic immigrants in the United States during the nineteenth century.

William V. Moore

FURTHER READING

Bennett, David H. *The Party of Fear: From Nativist Movements to the New Right in American History.* Chapel Hill: University of North Carolina Press, 1988.

Kinzer, Donald L. *An Episode in Anti-Catholicism: The American Protective Association.* Seattle: University of Washington Press, 1964.

Lipset, Seymour Martin, and Earl Rabb. *The Politics of Unreason: Right-Wing Extremism in America, 1790-1970.* New York: Harper & Row, 1970.

SEE ALSO: Anti-Catholicism; Employment; European immigrants; History of immigration, 1783-1891; History of immigration after 1891; Know-Nothing Party; Ku Klux Klan; Nativism; Religions of immigrants; Xenophobia.

AMERICANIZATION PROGRAMS

DEFINITION: Amorphous movements that emerged in the second half of the nineteenth and the early twentieth centuries in response to the influx of non-English-speaking immigrants

SIGNIFICANCE: At the turn of the twentieth century, non-English-speaking immigrants flooded American shores, setting off a wave of nativistic fears. In order to combat rising nativism, reformers constructed a number of programs aimed at absorbing immigrants into American civic life.

During the decades following the U.S. Civil War (1861-1865), demands for the creation of a national culture emerged in response to increasing concerns that new non-English-speaking immigrants, if left to their own devices, would erode the moral and economic fabric of the United States. The assassination of President William McKinley in 1901 by Leon Czolgosz, the anarchist son of a Polish immigrant, fueled fears of radicalism on the part of immigrants and galvanized the efforts of many Americans to assimilate immigrants in order to moderate their radicalism. Under the guise of combating neglect and exploitation, Progressives embraced the notion of Americanization and developed programs to promote immigrant acculturation.

SETTLEMENT HOUSE MOVEMENT

Emerging social science programs in universities during the early twentieth century played a key role in fostering immigrant integration into American society. Progressive reformers believed that immigrants could be converted into valued American citizens. Settlement house programs in large cities offered immigrants respites from the crowded, dirty tenements as well as places to learn. This and

other initiatives, such as the Young Men's Christian Association (YMCA), provided health services, vocational training, and civics and English classes.

Other efforts focused on motherhood as a key to assimilation. The domestic science movement published information and research on diet, nutrition, health and cleanliness. Programs sought to limit the sizes of families on the premise that unrestricted population growth ought to be abandoned in modern industrial societies. Many of these programs aimed at giving immigrant women tools to work outside their homes as housemaids, seamstresses, and laundresses.

EMPLOYER PROGRAMS

Many industrialists designed worker education programs to influence the behavior of their immigrant workers and to reduce the growing problem of labor turnover. For example, in 1913, Ford Motor Company instituted what it called its "Five Dollar a Day" program. To receive that level of wages, workers had to be certified by Ford's sociological department that they were thrifty, sober, and diligent. The emerging theories of scientific management assisted industries by creating a structure of strict organization of production combined with pay incentives. Other companies opened libraries and offered classes aimed at fostering acceptance of American ways, as defined by the employers. Management argued that speaking English was fundamental to unifying the workforce and creating industrial prosperity.

Company medical staffs taught oral and physical hygiene in both the workplace and the home. They also offered married women instruction on household finances and child care. One railroad company used a boxcar converted to reflect its image of the model American home to transport Americanization instructors. The state of California created a Commission of Immigration and Housing to investigate work and living conditions and to teach English and good health practices to immigrants. The state commission recruited religious leaders, social workers, and government bureaucrats to design and implement Americanization programs.

MANY PEOPLES ONE NATION
Let us unite to Americanize America

THE FLAG SPEAKS

I am whatever you make me, nothing more. But always, I am all that you hope to be, and have the courage to try for.
I am song and fear, struggle and panic, and ennobling hope.
I am the day's work of the weakest man, and the largest dream of the most daring.
I am the constitution and the courts,
statutes and the statute makers, soldier and dreadnaught, drayman and street sweep, cook, counselor and clerk.
I am no more than what you believe me to be.
My stars and my stripes are your dream and your labors. For you are the makers of the flag and it is well that you glory in the making.

FRANKLIN K. LANE

Patriotic poster issued during World War I to promote the idea of Americanization. (Library of Congress)

EDUCATION PROGRAMS

During the late nineteenth century, many efforts to Americanize adult immigrants did not provide the desired results. Employers and reformers recognized that they might reach immigrant parents more effectively through their children, reasoning that children were potentially easier to shape into responsible citizens. Accordingly, companies established kindergarten programs for the children of its immigrant workers, while progressives shifted their focus to creating a system of compulsory public education. Schools in urban settings became vehicles for maintaining social order and inculcating American values. The schools afforded vocational training and English-language classes, taught the value of good citizenship and respect for authority, and provided programs in health and grooming. By the 1890's, most states with increasing immigrant populations had passed laws mandating compulsory schooling from the ages of eight to fourteen. Historian Richard Hofstadter noted that the intent of public education was to forge a nation, make it literate, and foster civic competence.

PATRIOTIC EDUCATION PROGRAMS

Progressives were convinced of the need to mold immigrants into "100 percent Americans" and to create a national culture to promote loyalty to American civic ideals. Many patriotic expressions that Americans would embrace during the twenty-first century were developed in response to fears that non-English-speaking immigrants would erode the national identity. For example, the schoolhouse flag movement required public schools to fly the American flag and conduct daily flag-salute ceremonies. In 1891, Francis Bellamy wrote the Pledge of Allegiance to promote national unity and civic patriotism by honoring the American flag.

Public education emphasized the importance of civic service and duty to country. Patriotic programs emphasized the sacrifices made by past citizens to preserve the union. Laws were passed requiring public schools to observe President Abraham Lincoln's and President George Washington's birthdays, and to participate in Memorial Day and Flag Day activities. The invention of the idea of Betsy Ross as maker of the first American flag, patriotic pageants, pictures of national heroes, and teaching of citizenship were all part of the public school Americanization programs.

Progressive teachers advanced ideas of civic patriotism, while Theodore Roosevelt and members of the Grand Army of the Republic (GAR) advanced programs of martial patriotism. Martial patriotism was infused with heroic images of soldiers, wars, and the honor of dying for one's country. Stories of military adventures written for schoolchildren abounded. Symbols of soldiers and war cropped up in public parks, newspapers, and literature across the nation.

Linda Upham-Bornstein

FURTHER READING

Bodnar, John. *The Transplanted*. Bloomington: Indiana University Press, 1985. Major work on the experience of immigrants in transitioning to American capitalism.

Fitzpatrick, Ellen. *Endless Crusade: Women Social Scientists and Progressive Reform*. New York: Oxford University Press, 1990. Examination of the lives of four progressive women who played a crucial role in the establishment of settlement houses and social reform.

Higham, John. *Strangers in the Land: Patterns of American Nativism, 1860-1925*. New Brunswick, N.J.: Rutgers University Press, 2002. Significant scholarly study of the history of nativism in America.

O'Leary, Cecilia Elizabeth. *To Die For: The Paradox of American Patriotism*. Princeton, N.J.: Princeton University Press, 1999. Important work on the construction of American patriotic culture and the struggle to solidify a distinctly American identity.

Sánchez, George J. *Becoming Mexican American: Ethnicity, Culture and Identity in Chicano Los Angeles, 1900-1945*. New York: Oxford University Press, 1993. Examination of programs in California designed to assimilate Mexican immigrants.

SEE ALSO: Anglo-conformity; Assimilation theories; Citizenship; Education; English-only and official English movements; History of immigration after 1891; Hull-House; Nativism; Progressivism; Settlement houses.

ANGEL ISLAND IMMIGRATION STATION

IDENTIFICATION: Federal government's main immigrant processing and detention center on the West Coast
DATE: Operated from 1910 until 1940
LOCATION: California's San Francisco Bay

SIGNIFICANCE: Angel Island served as the West Coast port of entry for Pacific Rim immigrants arriving in the United States between 1910 and 1940. The station also functioned as an interrogation and detention center during the height of national hostility toward Chinese and other Asians seeking new lives in the United States.

Sometimes called the Ellis Island of the West, the Angel Island immigration station was not precisely a West Coast counterpart of the East Coast's main immigrant processing center. In fact, owing to the anti-Asian immigration laws in force during the center's years of operation, Angel Island officials often devoted themselves to keeping newcomers out of the United States, rather than welcoming them in.

EARLY HISTORY OF THE ISLAND

The largest island in California's San Francisco Bay, Angel Island is a natural land mass of 1.2 square miles located about one mile from the mainland of Marin County, north of San Francisco. In sharp contrast to the much smaller and mostly flat Ellis Island, Angel Island is dominated by an 800-foot-high peak. After serving for thousands of years as hunting and fishing territory for the coastal Miwok people, the island came under Spanish colonial control during the late eighteenth century and passed to the United States in 1848, after the Mexican War. In 1863, the U.S. Army established a camp on the island and built artillery installations along its shore. The island served as a departure and homecoming port for troops during the Spanish-American War and both world wars. Some prisoners of war were detained on the island, and the Army operated a quarantine station there for many years.

In 1905, the federal government decided to expand beyond military use of the island by building an immigration facility near an inlet called China Cove on the island's northeast coast. Opened for business five years later, the Angel Island Immigration Station became the principal site where U.S. officials detained and interrogated thousands of new arrivals from China, Japan, and other Asian countries. Unlike European immigrants, who were welcomed to the United States after cursory examinations, Asian immigrants passing through Angel Island experienced targeted discrimination in the form of exclusion policies mandated by U.S. laws originally enacted during the 1880's.

CHINESE IMMIGRATION

Large-scale Chinese immigration to the United States had begun in 1848, at the start of the California gold rush. Tens of thousands of Chinese workers dug for gold, built railroads, and worked for rock-bottom wages at many other jobs, often sending remittance money home to families in China.

Angel Island immigration reception center in 1915. (Library of Congress)

Meanwhile, they encountered widespread hostility from Americans of European ancestry, many of whom feared competition from cheap Asian labor. In 1882, the Chinese became targets of federal anti-immigration legislation in the form of the Chinese Exclusion Act, which one U.S. senator denounced as "legalization of racial discrimination." The act barred all Chinese laborers and most other Chinese from entering the United States, and placed numerous restrictions on those already in the country. China at this time was a politically weak nation, unable to protest the discriminatory treatment its sons and daughters received in the United States, so the policy faced no effective international challenges and was later renewed.

After 1910, immigration officials at Angel Island developed elaborate procedures to identify and deport would-be immigrants from China who sought ways around the ban on their immigration. The immigrants knew that the Exclusion Act could not apply to the children of American citizens, so if Chinese Americans born in the United States had offspring in China, those children should have the legal right to enter the United States. After many public records were destroyed by San Francisco's great earthquake and fire of 1906, it became common for young men in China to buy documents that identified them as American citizens by claiming U.S.-born Chinese men as their fathers. Immigration officials at Angel Island had no way to tell "paper sons" from real sons, so they detained many male immigrants for weeks or months and tried to expose them as frauds by quizzing them in minute detail about such topics as family histories and ancestral villages. Typical interrogations included questions about habits or facial characteristics of relatives and odd bits of information about the histories and customs of the home villages. Immigrants prepared for weeks for the dreaded Angel Island interrogations, which were conducted through interpreters and could result in deportation because of misunderstandings or miscommunication. Chinese women immigrating as wives or daughters of American-born Chinese experienced similar detentions and interrogation. Whole families in detention were frequently separated and housed according to sex, a policy that was particularly hard on young children.

A small number of immigrant detainees were held for more than two years and interrogated numerous times. Despair was common among these long-term detainees, several of whom committed suicide during the center's years of operation. Some detainees at Angel Island responded to their imprisonment and interrogation by composing poems that they painted or carved on walls inside the immigration station's detention barracks.

JAPANESE IMMIGRATION

During the early twentieth century, the Japanese population in the United States was less than one quarter that of the country's Chinese population, but the Japanese also endured anti-Asian prejudice. However, because Japan was then a more powerful country than China, the U.S. government tried to avoid formal exclusion of Japanese immigrants. Nevertheless, in 1907, a Gentlemen's Agreement forged between the United States and Japan created severe restrictions on further Japanese immigration. At Angel Island, Japanese men and women met with detention and interrogation techniques similar to those used on the Chinese.

During the early twentieth century, many Japanese arrivals at Angel Island were "picture brides" who had never met the husbands who arranged for their passage to America. It was common for Japanese men living in the United States to find brides in Japan by employing traditional matchmakers and exchanging photographs. After surrogate weddings, the newlywed women could embark for America and present themselves to immigration officials as the wives of U.S. residents. Japanese "picture brides" were detained at Angel Island for medical examinations and other immigration procedures. If a new husband did not collect his bride in a timely fashion, the woman was deported. Some couples had to go through weddings performed by Christian ministers before the brides were formally admitted into the United States.

The federal government stopped processing immigrants through Angel Island in 1940, three years before Congress finally repealed the Chinese Exclusion Act. Angel Island was later transformed into a California state park, and its immigration station was made a National Historic Landmark. A restored barracks building houses a museum in which visitors can view the Chinese inscriptions on the walls.

Karen Manners Smith

FURTHER READING

Lai, Him Mark, Genny Lim, and Judy Yung. *Island: Poetry and History of Chinese Immigrants on Angel Island, 1910-1940.* Seattle: University of Washington Press, 1991. Scholarly treatment of the immigrant experience shaped through oral history and detainee poetry in Chinese and English translation.

Okihiro, Gary Y. *Margins and Mainstreams: Asians in American History.* Seattle: University of Washington Press, 1994. Asians in the broader context of U.S. national and international history.

Soennichsen, John. *Miwoks to Missiles: A History of Angel Island.* San Francisco: Angel Island Association, 2001. Popular history of Angel Island, including military uses of the island as well as the history of the immigration station.

Takaki, Ronald. *Strangers from a Different Shore: A History of Asian Americans.* Boston: Little, Brown, 1998. Highly readable background for the Asian immigrant experience in the United States. Covers local Chinese, Japanese, Korean, Indian, and Filipino immigrant history.

SEE ALSO: Asian immigrants; California; Chinese immigrants; Deportation; Ellis Island; Japanese immigrants; Korean immigrants; Paper sons; Picture brides; San Francisco.

ANGELL TREATY OF 1880

THE LAW: Agreement allowing the United States to regulate, limit, or suspend immigration of Chinese laborers to the United States

DATE: Signed on November 17, 1880

SIGNIFICANCE: By placing restrictions on the number of Chinese workers permitted to immigrate to the United States, the Angell Treaty marked a turning point in the U.S.-

Editorial cartoon by J. A. Wales commenting on the convergence of anti-Chinese policies of the Democratic and Republican Parties in 1880. (Library of Congress)

Chinese relationship on immigration issues that paved the way for the passage of the Chinese Exclusion Act of 1882, which suspended Chinese immigration for ten years.

In 1880, James Burrill Angell, president of the University of Michigan, was nominated as minister to China by U.S. president Rutherford B. Hayes. Angell was confirmed by the Senate on April 9, 1880. Angell's first task was to negotiate changes to the Burlingame Treaty of 1868 that would reduce the number of Chinese immigrants moving into the western United States. Angell and fellow members of the treaty commission to China, John F. Swift and William Henry Trescot, traveled to Peking (now Beijing), China, in June, 1880, to seek an agreement.

Using the argument that Chinese laborers did not readily assimilate into American culture, Angell and his colleagues negotiated a treaty to regulate and limit the immigration of Chinese laborers to the United States but not to prohibit it outright. The resulting Angell Treaty was signed on November 17, 1880, and proclaimed U.S. law on October 5, 1881. This treaty ended free Chinese immigration to the United States and separated U.S. trade interests from the immigration issue. It also provided an avenue for anti-Chinese lobbyists to push for an exclusion law. Most of the protections that the treaty secured for Chinese immigrants were reversed by passage of the Chinese Exclusion Act of 1882.

Alvin K. Benson

FURTHER READING

Lee, Erika. *At America's Gates: Immigration During the Exclusion Era, 1882-1943*. Chapel Hill: University of North Carolina Press, 2007.

McClain, Charles J. *In Search of Equality: The Chinese Struggle Against Discrimination in Nineteenth-Century America*. Berkeley: University of California Press, 1994.

SEE ALSO: Anti-Chinese movement; Burlingame Treaty of 1868; Chinese Exclusion Act of 1882; *Chinese Exclusion Cases*; Chinese immigrants; Page Law of 1875; Taiwanese immigrants.

ANGLO-CONFORMITY

DEFINITION: Tendency of immigrants to lose much of their native cultural heritage and conform substantially to the core Anglo-Protestant culture of the United States

SIGNIFICANCE: Immigration has been an ongoing and important source of growth and development for the United States. Attitudes toward these new arrivals, both legal and illegal, have varied with time and circumstances. One constant concern has been the assimilation of immigrants, who are often required to seek acceptance by means of Anglo-conformity.

The United States is a relatively young nation. In contrast to the makeup of older nations, its population has been, and continues to be, drawn from all over the world. The country's colonial era saw a struggle for cultural dominance among English, French, Spanish, and Dutch settlers. Eventually, the English became both the majority and dominant group in what became the United States. For this reason, English language, English laws, and English customs became central to the national culture. Those who shared, or were willing and able to share, this culture were most easily assimilated. Within the United States, Anglo-conformity is said to form the basis of a single unifying culture that is important for any heterogeneous nation.

During the early formative years of the independent American nation, most new immigrants came from western Europe. Some nationalities were considered questionable in regards to how well they would be able to assimilate into American culture. For example, Germans were regarded as questionable because of their different language and different culture, while English-speaking Irish Protestants were generally acceptable. However, Irish Roman Catholics were regarded as questionable because of their religion and because of the long-standing antagonism between Ireland and England. Eventually, immigrants from both Germany and Ireland constituted a large part of the new anglocentric nation. Assimilation was accomplished through Anglo-conformity.

TYPES OF IMMIGRANTS AND ANGLO-CONFORMITY

Individual immigrants fit into various types or categories that can influence society's reaction to them. The immigrants may be

- legal or illegal
- voluntary or involuntary (such as slaves)
- refugees who have well-founded fears of persecution because of their race, religion, ethnicity, or political affiliation
- migrants who are seeking work
- safe-haven seekers who want temporary safety from disasters
- sojourners who come for a specific short-term reasons, such as tourism or study.

Immigrants who are interested in remaining in the United States are expected to conform to Anglo culture. The most basic requirements are conformity to language and laws. A certain degree of Anglo-conformity is required, not only for general social acceptance but also for citizenship.

Anglo-conformity has been expected of immigrants and is encouraged, but it has generally been regarded as voluntary. However, that has not always

---

BARRIERS TO ASSIMILATION

Over time the United States became identified as a white, Anglo-Saxon, and Protestant ("WASP") nation. Barriers to assimilation were cultural and physical in nature. The former were more common and able to be overcome, while the latter were not. This is reflected in the findings of a longitudinal study conducted by the distinguished California sociologist Emory Bogardus in 1926, 1946, 1956, and 1966 that found that Americans favored white western Europeans over white eastern Europeans, and both over nonwhite non-Europeans.

The acceptability of an immigrant group appears to be influenced by a combination of five variables:

- how long the group has been in the country
- how or why its members came
- visibility or identifiability of its members
- positive and negative stereotypes of the group
- social and economic success of the group's members

All these factors help to explain the findings of Bogardus.

---

been the case. For example, although Native Americans are not considered to be immigrants to the United States, they were subjected to involuntary and forced Anglo-conformity. There was a period when the government took children from Native American parents, placed them in boarding schools, and forcibly replaced their Native American cultures with Anglo-American culture. The children had their hair cut short and were given English names, clothed in uniforms, and forced to speak English and learn Anglocentric culture, including religion and education.

THREE GREAT WAVES OF IMMIGRATION

The United States has experienced what have been called "three great waves" of immigration during its history as a nation. Each succeeding wave was more diverse culturally, ethnically, and racially than its predecessor, thereby making Anglo-conformity more problematic. Political, economic, and social changes occurring in Europe during the late eighteenth and early nineteenth centuries pro-

vided the incentive for the first wave of immigration. Immigrants during that period were mostly from northern and western Europe. Some came as indentured servants. Some were Africans whose status was quickly changed to slaves, making them ineligible for citizenship.

The second wave occurred during the late nineteenth and early twentieth centuries and brought many southern and eastern European immigrants as well as non-Europeans. These groups were usually considered less acceptable and less able to be assimilated than earlier immigrants.

The third wave began in the second half of the twentieth century and was the most religiously, ethnically, and racially diverse of them all. The most numerous immigrants during this wave were Hispanic, with the greatest number coming from Mexico. The second most numerous were Asians, the majority of whom came from the Philippines.

Prior to the passage of the Immigration and Nationality Act of 1965, the U.S. Congress attempted to preserve the racial and cultural characteristics of the nation that had been established by the first wave of immigrants. To that end, it passed laws limiting or excluding Asians and, in the Immigration Act of 1921 (also known as the Emergency Quota Act) and the Immigration Act of 1924, allocated immigration quotas for countries based on the percentages of Americans whose ancestors had come from each country. These legislative acts favored northern and western Europeans, while placing limitations on the immigration of southern and eastern Europeans and non-Europeans. In addition to legislation aimed at preserving the original racial and ethnic makeup of the United States, legislation was also used to preserve the Protestant nature of the WASP society. This was accomplished by restricting immigration from non-western or northern European nations and non-European nations, which were generally not Protestant countries.

Immigration legislation passed after 1965, when the national-origins emphasis on quotas was eliminated, has been less concerned with religion, race, and ethnicity and more concerned with family unity and economic assets, including education and occupations. The result seems to be a trend away from Anglo-conformity and a move toward cultural pluralism.

Philip E. Lampe

FURTHER READING

Deveaux, Monique. *Cultural Pluralism and Dilemmas of Justice.* Ithaca, N.Y.: Cornell University Press, 2000. Thoughtful exploration of the ethical and legal problems arising in a pluralistic society such as that of the United States.

Gabaccia, Donna R. *Immigration and American Diversity: A Social and Cultural History.* Malden, Mass.: Blackwell, 2002. Survey of American immigration history, with attention to ethnic conflicts, nativism, and racialist theories.

Kramer, Eric Mark, ed. *The Emerging Monoculture: Assimilation and the "Model Minority."* Westport, Conn.: Praeger, 2003. Collection of essays on a wide variety of topics relating to cultural assimilation and the notion of "model minorities," with particular attention to immigrant communities in Japan and the United States.

Myers, John. *Dominant-Minority Relations in America: Convergence in the New World.* 2d ed. New York: Allyn & Bacon, 2006. Textbook that examines intergroup relations through both conflict and assimilationist perspectives and encourages readers to see them as part of the process of dominant-minority interaction. The second edition of this work has added a chapter on Arab Americans.

Singh, Jaswinder, and Kalyani Gopal. *Americanization of New Immigrants: People Who Come to America and What They Need to Know.* Lanham, Md.: University Press of America, 2002. Survey of the cultural adjustments through which new immigrants to the United States must go.

Wiley, Terrence G. *Literacy and Language Diversity in the United States.* 2d ed. Washington, D.C.: Center for Applied Linguistics, 2005. Comprehensive study of language and literacy in American education.

SEE ALSO: Americanization programs; Anti-Catholicism; Assimilation theories; Cultural pluralism; English as a second language; English-only and official English movements; Hansen effect; Identificational assimilation; Language issues; Multiculturalism.

ANTI-CATHOLICISM

DEFINITION: Efforts to discriminate against immigrant groups with large numbers of Roman Catholic members

SIGNIFICANCE: Rooted in antipapist feelings brought to the New World by Protestant English colonists, prejudice against Catholics shaped attitudes of those residing in the United States toward Catholic immigrants. Campaigns to deny Catholics basic rights persisted throughout the nineteenth century, leading to discrimination against immigrant populations from predominantly Catholic countries and forcing Catholic newcomers to demonstrate that they were loyal Americans and not tools of the papacy.

Anti-Catholicism was a fixture in the British North American colonies, where Protestants of every denomination were united in their antipathy for the Roman Catholic pope and his followers, and institutionalized discrimination against Catholics was commonplace. After the formation of the republic, the guarantee of freedom of religion in the U.S. Constitution, coupled with the low number of Catholics in the country, led to a reduction in overt discrimination, although individual prejudices among the Protestant majority still existed. Beginning in the 1820's, however, when Catholics from Germany and Ireland began arriving in the United States by the thousands, latent hostility erupted in a series of overt efforts to control what was portrayed as a potential menace to the new American nation.

ANTI-CATHOLICISM PRIOR TO THE CIVIL WAR

By the 1820's, those already settled in America had begun to see new immigrants as a threat to the economic stability of the nation, and the fact that so many entering the country after that time were Catholics provided an easy excuse to target the newcomers as foreigners whose presence threatened the civic values of the new nation. Catholics were seen as being loyal first to their church, and orphanages, refuges, hospitals, and schools established by Catholic religious orders were condemned as incubators of un-American values. Dozens of anti-Catholic pamphlets and books appeared touting the notion that the pope was in league with foreign heads of state to overthrow the American government. Prominent among these was inventor Samuel F. B. Morse's *Foreign Conspiracy Against the Liberties of the United States* (1835), a virulent attack charging that these new immigrants were being used as dupes in a conspiracy to turn America into a vassal state of the papacy.

Numerous evangelical groups sprang up to counter the alleged Catholic threat, often sending missionaries to meet ships containing immigrants to urge them to convert to Protestantism upon arrival in their new homeland. During the 1840's, the Native American Party, later known as the Know-Nothing Party, emerged as a political force, campaigning on a platform to keep Catholics out of public office. Efforts by these groups made it difficult for new immigrants to assimilate quickly and often prompted more radical Protestants to engage in violent acts against churches and Catholic establishments.

LATER ANTI-ROMAN CATHOLIC CAMPAIGNS

Although anti-Catholicism subsided for a time during and after the Civil War, a new wave of hysteria about the influence of Catholic immigrants rose during the 1870's, largely as a result of an influx of Catholics from Italy and eastern Europe. Once again, immigrants were seen as a threat to the economic prosperity of those already residing in the country, and the newcomers' religion became an easy way to stir up antagonism among the Protestant majority. The most prominent group to emerge during this new round of anti-Catholic activity was the American Protective Association, which was highly influential during the 1890's. Strongly linked with the Progressive movement that swept the nation at the turn of the twentieth century, this group sponsored a number of newspapers and journals that called readers' attention to the menace posed by large groups of citizens seen to be intensely loyal to a foreign power.

By this time, Catholics had established political presence in a number of American cities, and most Catholic politicians were Democrats. The overwhelming tendency for Catholics to vote Democratic gave further ammunition to those who argued that Catholics could not be trusted to think independently; eventually, it was claimed, Catholics would be led to support leaders and laws inimi-

cal to traditional American values of individual liberty and freedom of choice. At the same time, leaders of the temperance movement targeted Catholic immigrant populations as being morally inferior, since their cultural values encouraged consumption of alcohol. As had happened before the Civil War, as a result of these attacks new Catholic immigrants found it difficult to become fully accepted in American society and were often forced to remain in geographic and social enclaves for support and protection.

By the end of World War I, anti-Catholic attacks on immigrant populations had begun to wane. While there remained within the country a tendency to distrust Catholics (evidenced by the voting patterns in the 1928 presidential election, when Catholic Al Smith received only a small percentage of Protestant votes), by midcentury the impact of such prejudice on newly arriving Catholics was minimal. While the new wave of Catholic immigrants from Latin America and Asia who began arriving after 1965 were subjected to intense discrimination, there is little evidence that it was based on their religion. Nevertheless, many were encouraged to question whether their loyalty to their church was compatible with the American values of individualism and freedom of religion.

Laurence W. Mazzeno

FURTHER READING

Hurley, Mark J. *The Unholy Ghost: Anti-Catholicism in the American Experience.* Huntington, Ind.: Our Sunday Visitor, 1992. Traces the continual struggle of Catholics in America to fight prejudice and discrimination, especially from proponents of "nativism" who branded Catholics as un-American.

Jenkins, Philip. *The New Anti-Catholicism: The Last Acceptable Prejudice.* New York: Oxford University Press, 2003. Contains a discussion of the historical development of anti-Catholicism in America, including its origins in xenophobic responses to immigrants during the nineteenth and early twentieth century.

Massa, Mark S. *Anti-Catholicism in America.* New York: Crossroad, 2003. Provides a synopsis of the relationship between the rise of anti-Catholic sentiment and the influx of largely Catholic groups of immigrants into the United States during the nineteenth century.

Nordstrom, Justin. *Danger on the Doorstep: Anti-Catholicism and American Print Culture in the Progressive Era.* Notre Dame, Ind.: University of Notre Dame Press, 2006. Concentrates on the outpouring of anti-Catholic writings during the first two decades of the twentieth century. Explores motivations for anti-Catholic feelings in the United States at various times during the history of the nation.

Walch, Timothy. *Catholicism in America: A Social History.* Malabar, Fla.: Krieger, 1989. History of the Roman Catholic Church in America detailing its struggles against persistent prejudices that led to misunderstandings, discrimination, and sometimes violence against Catholics as their numbers grew within the general population.

SEE ALSO: American Protective Association; Anglo-conformity; Catholic Charities USA; German immigrants; Irish immigrants; Italian immigrants; Know-Nothing Party; Nativism; Political parties; Religions of immigrants; Stereotyping.

ANTI-CHINESE MOVEMENT

THE EVENT: Era that saw widespread opposition to Chinese immigration at the local, state, and federal levels
DATE: 1850's-1940's
LOCATION: West Coast of the United States, primarily California

SIGNIFICANCE: The Anti-Chinese movement developed out of anti-Chinese attitudes in the mining fields of California during the 1850's to become a more widespread movement during the 1870's. The movement was successful in helping to get the federal government to pass legislation restricting Chinese immigration that was enforced from the 1880's until the 1940's.

When Chinese immigrants first arrived in the United States, they were accepted because they performed work considered undesirable by European Americans. However, as their numbers increased, strong resentment developed on the West Coast, particularly in California. Chinese immigrants encountered prejudice and discrimination

that were sometimes manifested in violence. Ultimately, the anti-Chinese movement helped foster federal legislation that severely restricted Chinese immigration for several decades.

CALIFORNIA AND THE EARLY MOVEMENT

The discovery of gold in California in 1848 initiated the first significant wave of Chinese immigration to the United States. The state of California attempted to limit the ability of Chinese immigrants to assimilate. Miners of European descent were angered that the Chinese were gaining mining permits and finding gold that, in their minds, was rightfully theirs. The state government of California passed Foreign Miners' License Tax laws in 1850 and 1852 that required all miners who were not U.S. citizens to pay three dollars per month in taxes (later increased to six dollars, and finally lowered to four dollars). Because Chinese workers were ineligible for U.S. citizenship, more of them had to pay this tax than members of any other immigrant group.

In 1851, John Bigler was elected governor of California on an anti-Chinese platform. Four years later, the state's supreme court ruled that Chinese had the same limited rights as African Americans and Native Americans, meaning that they could not testify against white citizens in court. There was such a strong anti-Chinese feeling nationally that when a bill was introduced in Congress that would give Chinese Americans the right to vote, it was rejected. Many Americans who supported the anti-Chinese movement in the West regarded the Chinese as morally and intellectually inferior to all other minority groups in the region. These people consistently blamed the Chinese for the ills of the community.

As time passed, anti-Chinese sentiment gained support among the wider population. As the national economy suffered during the 1870's, labor union leaders led the outcry against the Chinese for keeping wages low and taking potential jobs from white Americans. Labor leaders, along with politicians, used the charge that Chinese would work for lower wages as a way to win votes. Along with the economic issues, the movement focused on the cultural differences and stereotypes of the Chinese immigrants. Those opposed to Chinese immigration pointed to opium smoking, gambling, and prostitution as examples of the negative

Contemporary newspaper illustration of the anti-Chinese rioting in Denver, Colorado, in 1880. (Library of Congress)

influences that Chinese immigrants had on American society. Furthermore, they looked down on the Chinese reluctance to assimilate and adopt the mainstream American way of life.

CHINESE EXCLUSION AND VIOLENCE

The anti-Chinese movement continued to grow during the 1880's. With pressure from California, the federal government became involved as the movement gained national support. The federal government moved to stop Chinese immigration altogether. In the 1868 Burlingame Treaty with China, the U.S. government had encouraged the immigration of Chinese nationals to the United States. Just over a decade later, the Chinese Exclusion Act of 1882 suspended all immigration of Chinese to the United States. This act was amended in 1884 to make it more difficult for Chinese laborers working in the United States who left the country to return.

After new Chinese immigration was mostly eliminated, the anti-Chinese movement turned its at-

tention against Chinese who were already residing in the United States. There had been scattered incidents of violence in California against Chinese during the 1870's, but the movement became more violent throughout the West during the mid-1880's. This tension had been growing in both the mining fields and along the railroads—two sectors of the economy that employed large numbers of Chinese workers. In 1885, large-scale violence erupted in Rock Springs, Wyoming, where white vigilantes stormed through the Chinese community, killing many people and driving away many of the rest. Additional incidents later occurred in other Chinatowns throughout the Far West.

STRICTER ENFORCEMENT

After violence on the West Coast, the United States strengthened its anti-Chinese stance. First, the government approved the expulsion of Chinese laborers who owned property in the United States or had wives living in the country. In 1888, Congress passed the Scott Act, which banned both the immigration and the return of Chinese laborers to the United States. This law had the impact of refusing reentry to tens of thousands of Chinese who had temporarily left the United States. The anti-Chinese movement was successful in renewing the Chinese Exclusion Act in 1892 and establishing a permanent ban in 1902. Because of the anti-Chinese movement, Chinese immigration remained outlawed until 1943.

David R. Buck

FURTHER READING

Gyory, Andrew. *Closing the Gate: Race, Politics, and the Chinese Exclusion Act.* Chapel Hill: University of North Carolina Press, 1998. Good analyis of why the federal government passed the Chinese Exclusion Act of 1882.

McClain, Charles J. *In Search of Equality: The Chinese Struggle Against Discrimination in Nineteenth-Century America.* Berkeley: University of California Press, 1994. Focusing on the San Francisco

Bay Area, McClain examines Chinese efforts to mobilize against discrimination in employment, housing, and education.

Miller, Stuart Creighton. *The Unwelcome Immigrant: The American Image of the Chinese, 1785-1882.* Berkeley: University of California Press, 1969. Documents American anti-Chinese feeling from the arrival of the first Chinese in the late eighteenth century to 1882, the year in which the Chinese Exclusion Act was passed. Bibliographical references and index.

Sandmeyer, Elmer Clarence. *The Anti-Chinese Movement in California.* Champaign: University of Illinois Press, 1991. Considered by some historians to be the best work on the subject of anti-Chinese discrimination in California. Bibliographical references.

SEE ALSO: Angell Treaty of 1880; Burlingame Treaty of 1868; California; Chinese Exclusion Act of 1882; *Chinese Exclusion Cases*; Chinese immigrants; "Mongrelization"; Nativism; San Francisco; Stereotyping.

ANTI-DEFAMATION LEAGUE

IDENTIFICATION: Civil rights organization founded to combat anti-Semitism
DATE: Established in October, 1913

SIGNIFICANCE: Although the Anti-Defamation League was founded to correct injustices toward the Jewish people, it later broadened its mission to seek justice and fair treatment for all social groups.

The Anti-Defamation League (ADL) was founded as an American Jewish defense organization by the Chicago chapter of B'nai B'rith. A decade before World War I, the United States experienced a vast influx of immigrants. More than 10 percent were Jews, who tended to settle in the cities of the East Coast such as New York City. Many of these Jewish immigrants were living among other immigrants who had carried their hatred and fear of Jews from their home countries, and the seemingly endless Jewish immigration from eastern Europe increased anti-Semitism. Wearing unfamiliar clothing, speaking a language most Americans did not

understand, and engaging in religious practices that seemed bizarre, Jews were "othered" by some non-Jewish Americans who experienced discomfort and fear.

At the 1908 meeting of the executive committee of B'nai B'rith, Rabbi Joseph Silverman of New York proposed establishing an agency to promote "the Jewish name" and to combat stereotypes of Jews. Five years later, Chicago lawyer Sigmund Livingston, himself an immigrant from Germany, suggested the formation of a National Caricature Committee, the name reflecting the negative portrayals of Jews in the media. Early film, the vaudeville stage, dime novels, and even daily newspapers introduced the stereotype of the repulsive Jew. On stage, the Jew was a cheater, an arsonist, or a liar; on film, he was a usurer, smuggler, or worse. These stereotypes reinforced anti-Semitism and helped lay the groundwork for mob violence against Jews.

A few months before the founding of the organization that was finally named the Anti-Defamation League, Leo Frank, a Jewish factory manager, had been found guilty of rape and murder in an Atlanta trial where crowds outside the courthouse chanted, "Hang the Jew." After reviewing the evidence, the governor of Georgia commuted the death sentence to life imprisonment. In August, 1915, a mob inflamed by anti-Semitic propaganda took Frank from prison and lynched him. Anti-Semitic words turned to deeds.

Livingston and fifteen leaders of the Jewish community convened the first meeting of the ADL in Chicago. They established a 150-member executive committee representing Jews across the United States. With a budget of two hundred dollars from B'nai B'rith and two desks in Livingston's law office, the organization began its mission: "to stop, by appeals to reason and conscience, and if necessary, by appeals to law, the defamation of the Jewish people." The league was also committed to securing "justice and fair treatment to all citizens alike." One of the first actions of the ADL was to eliminate negative images of Jews in the media. Adolph S. Ochs, a member of the ADL executive committee and publisher of *The New York Times*, wrote a letter to newspaper editors nationwide decrying the use of "objectionable and vulgar" references to Jews in the national press. By 1920, such references had virtually ceased.

Leo Frank, whose lynching helped prompt the creation of the Anti-Defamation League. (Library of Congress)

A CONTINUING MISSION

The work of the ADL was carried forward through aggressive campaigns to educate people about anti-Semitism. Through the publication of pamphlets and short films, the league sought to eradicate negative stereotypes of Jews and to promote awareness of Jewish contributions to American life. However, serious attempts to defame Jews continued. For example, in 1920, industrialist Henry Ford began publishing the widely circulated anti-Jewish tabloid *The Dearborn Independent.* The Ku Klux Klan (KKK), proclaiming its hatred of Jews, experienced a resurgence in the South and several northern states, with four to five million members throughout the United States. KKK activities including boycotting Jewish merchants, smashing shop windows, and burning crosses outside synagogues.

The *Protocols of the Elders of Zion* (first published in English in 1919) was introduced to America and spread throughout the country. This document, later proved to be a forgery, stated that Jews were plotting to overthrow all governments and take over the world. Many Americans, conditioned to negative beliefs about Jews, accepted the document as truth. By September, 1920, anti-Semitism was so widespread that the ADL and other Jewish groups met to consider action. One outcome was a manifesto denouncing anti-Semitism signed by 116 of the nation's leaders, all of whom were Christians, including U.S. president Woodrow Wilson, former president William Howard Taft, and Cardinal William O'Connell.

During the 1930's, as National Socialism (Nazism) gained momentum in Europe, attacks against Jews in America increased. The Nazis spent millions of dollars on propaganda in America; the ADL estimated that by the end of the 1930's there were more than five hundred anti-Semitic organizations in the United States. During the lowest point of the Great Depression, many non-Jewish Americans believed that the Jews were responsible for their economic woes. The anti-Jewish radio propaganda of Father Charles Coughlin, broadcast over 475 stations, fueled this conspiracy theory.

Following World War II, the ADL worked toward ending social discrimination against Jews, focusing on barriers against Jewish memberships in organizations and prohibitions in housing. The ADL also started a "crack the quota" campaign against anti-Jewish discrimination in college and medical school admissions. The league's weapons were the media and the law.

Over the years, the ADL has fought discrimination against Jews and other groups. During the 1960's, for example, the ADL was actively involved with the Civil Rights movement. Headquartered since 1947 in New York City, the ADL works to provide civil liberties for all. It continues its original mission to heighten awareness of anti-Jewish propaganda, such as Holocaust-denying Web sites. The ADL alerts people to white supremacist pronouncements and denounces those who defame Jews.

Marcia B. Dinneen

FURTHER READING

Forster, Arnold. "The Anti-Defamation League." *The Wiener Library Bulletin* 28, no. 33 (1975): 52-58. A detailed look at the background of the ADL and the league's continuing efforts to combat anti-Semitism.

Friedman, Saul A. *No Haven for the Oppressed: United States Policy Toward Jewish Refugees, 1938-1945.* Detroit: Wayne State University Press, 1973. Discusses how the intensification of Judeophobia in the United States led to the founding of the ADL.

Grusd, Edward E. *B'nai B'rith: The Story of a Covenant.* New York: Appleton-Century, 1966. Describes the context that led to the founding of the ADL.

O'Brien, Lee. *American Jewish Organizations and Israel.* Washington, D.C.: Institute for Palestine Studies, 1986. Includes general background on the ADL, including its founding, structure, and projects.

Svonkin, Stuart. *Jews Against Prejudice: American Jews and the Fight for Civil Liberties.* New York: Columbia University Press, 1997. Focuses on the post-World War II activities of the ADL.

SEE ALSO: Affirmative action; American Jewish Committee; Anti-Semitism; Israeli immigrants; Jewish immigrants; Ku Klux Klan; Stereotyping.

ANTI-FILIPINO VIOLENCE

THE EVENTS: Racially motivated riots and assaults directed against Filipino agricultural laborers

DATE: Late 1920's to early 1930's

LOCATION: West Coast of the United States

> **SIGNIFICANCE:** Although Filipinos have been generally less well known in the United States than immigrants from other parts of Asia, they have suffered much of the same kinds of discrimination and mistreatment as other members of other Asian groups.

The Pacific island group that now constitutes the independent republic of the Philippines came under American control after the Spanish-American War in 1898. The archipelago had been a Spanish colony since the sixteenth century, and its people were fighting for independence from Spain at the same time that the United States was fighting Spain in a war that had been triggered by a conflict over Spanish rule in Cuba. However, instead of recognizing the independence of the Philippines after defeating Spain, the United States entered into an agreement with Spain to transfer possession of the islands to its own rule. Afterward, American forces replaced Spanish forces in the bitter fighting with the Filipino insurgents.

ORIGINS OF ANTI-FILIPINO PREJUDICE

As Americans fought the Filipinos, prejudicial attitudes toward them arose among American soldiers, who applied derogatory terms, such as "Goo Goos," to native Filipinos. Even American officials who were favorably disposed toward the Filipinos after the fighting ended often took condescending attitudes toward Filipinos. For example, future U.S. president William Howard Taft, who was the first American governor-general of the Philippines, famously referred to Filipinos as "our little brown brothers." He maintained that these new subjects of the United States would need special guidance if they were to rise toward the level of Anglo-Saxon civilization.

Large-scale Filipino immigration to the United States began during the early twentieth century, after the Filipino insurrection was suppressed, in response to American demand for agricultural workers. By 1920, the West Coast of the United States was home to perhaps 5,600 Filipinos. Within a decade, this number grew to more than 45,000 immigrants. Filipino migrant workers provided much of the seasonal labor for fruit and vegetable farms in California, Oregon, and Washington, where they harvested asparagus, grapes, strawberries, carrots, lettuce, potatoes, and beets. The racial attitudes of white Americans sometimes prompted violence against Filipino farmworkers. Relationships between the sexes were frequently the source of such violence. Most Filipino agricultural laborers were men. In the absence of comparable numbers of Filipino women, these men sometimes took up romantic relations with white women. White American workers not only resented competition from lower-wage Asian workers but also were angered by the thought of brown men with white women.

FIRST VIOLENT INCIDENTS

On October 24, 1929, an anti-Filipino riot erupted in Exeter, a farming community in central California's San Joaquin Valley. A mob attacked the local labor camp in which Filipino workers lived and burned it to the ground. In early 1930, an anti-Filipino riot occurred in Watsonville, another California town nearer the coast, where a mob of about five hundred white youths marched on a Filipino dance hall. Around the same time, about four hundred white vigilantes attacked a Filipino club in nearby Monterey, where they severely beat a large number of Filipinos. When police attempted to stop the beatings, the vigilantes called them "Goo Goo lovers"—the racist term for Filipinos that had originated among American soldiers.

In his 1946 autobiography, *America Is in the Heart,* the celebrated Filipino American writer Carlos Bulosan wrote of the harsh treatment and violence he endured after arriving in the United States as a laborer in 1930. One California mob even tarred and feathered him and chased him out of a town as he was traveling from place to place seeking work.

Anti-Filipino violence never again reached the intensity of the late 1920's and early 1930's. However, Filipinos were still among the victims of an apparent rise in anti-Asian prejudice during the 1980's and early 1990's. In early 1991, for example, fights broke out at a party at the estate of Chicago mayor Richard Daley, Jr., when white guests called two Filipino Americans racist names and attempted to force them out of the estate.

Carl L. Bankston III

FURTHER READING

Bankston, Carl L. "Filipino Americans." In *Asian Americans: Contemporary Trends and Issues,* edited by Pyong Gap Min. 2d ed. Thousand Oaks, Calif.: Pine Forge Press, 2006.

Bulosan, Carlos. *American Is in the Heart: A Personal History.* 1946. Reprint. Seattle: University of Washington Press, 1974.

_____. *On Becoming Filipino: Selected Writings of Carlos Bulosan.* Edited by Epifanio San Juan, Jr. Philadelphia: Temple University Press, 1996.

Karnow, Stanley. *In Our Image: America's Empire in the Philippines.* New York: Random House, 1989.

SEE ALSO: Anti-Chinese movement; Anti-Japanese movement; California; Exeter incident; Filipino immigrants; Filipino Repatriation Act of 1935; Hawaii; Nativism; Oregon; Washington State.

ANTI-JAPANESE MOVEMENT

THE EVENT: Widespread reaction against Japanese immigrants at the local, state, and federal levels

DATE: Early twentieth century

LOCATION: West Coast of the United States

> **SIGNIFICANCE:** Japanese immigrants began arriving in small numbers during the 1890's, but it was not until the twentieth century that organized political groups formed against them, mostly in California. Japanese immigrants began arriving in large numbers in California around 1900, alarming local citizens who feared the "yellow peril" and causing nativist political groups to pressure the government to restrict future immigration and to restrict the Japanese to their own schools and neighborhoods.

Although the Japanese were excellent workers and became one of the most successful immigrant groups in America, many native-born Americans resented their presence in the United States. A wide range of political organizations and activist groups formed coalitions to push for laws restricting the rights of Japanese immigrants and their children at the local, state, and federal levels. Some American workers believed that the Japanse were taking away jobs that belonged to Americans. The movement was successful in influencing the passage of anti-Japanese legislation beginning in the early twentieth century, peaking with the official exclusion of all Japanese immigrants from the United States in 1924. These restrictions were not lifted until passage of the Immigration and Nationality Act of 1965, which abolished restrictions based on national origin.

FORMATION OF ANTI-JAPANESE GROUPS

Racist attitudes and fear of foreign workers caused Americans to band together and form several anti-Japanese groups in the early twentieth century. The first and most significant anti-Japanese group was the Asiatic Exclusion League (AEL), which was organized in 1905 in California. The AEL wanted to stop further Japanese immigration and to prevent the Japanese already living in the United States from integrating into mainstream society. In 1906, the AEL successfully pressured the board of education in San Francisco to force Japanese schoolchildren to attend classes at the segregated Oriental School, which had been established for children of Chinese immigrants. Another anti-Japanese group, named the Immigration Restriction League (IRL), was organized in 1894 by wealthy East Coast businessmen who wanted to allow European immigration but put a halt to the Japanese, Koreans, and Chinese, who they felt were racially inferior and products of repressive governments who would be unable to participate in a free, democratic society.

GENTLEMEN'S AGREEMENT AND PRESSURE FOR ANTI-JAPANESE LAWS

In 1907, President Theodore Roosevelt was pressured by the AEL to ban future Japanese immigration, but he did not want to give in to the group's xenophobia and racism. However, Roosevelt signed the Gentlemen's Agreement that prohibited Japanese workers from immigrating to Hawaii or the continental United States, but parents, wives, and children of workers already living in the United States were allowed to join their families. Therefore, the Japanese immigrants who came after 1907 were almost exclusively women who were either mothers or "picture brides" sent to marry men through arranged marriages. Photography was becoming readily available, and potential husbands and wives could exchange photographs of each other before they were married, even though they had never met each other in person. The Gentlemen's Agreement severely reduced new immigration, but anti-Japanese sentiment continued to increase in California, Oregon, and Washington State.

The AEL and the IRL continued to pressure the federal government to pass new laws restricting Japanese immigration during the 1910's and 1920's. For example, these anti-Japanese groups wanted to pass a law requiring that immigrants be able to read English, which many of the Japanese were unable to do. The AEL argued that Japanese workers sent their earnings back home instead of spending their money in the United States. Moreover, they believed that Japanese workers were willing to accept lower wages and unsafe working conditions. The state of Oregon passed a law in 1907 that made it illegal for Japanese immigrants to be-

come permanent residents. In California, anti-Japanese sentiment reached a fevor pitch in the years leading up to the beginning of World War II in 1939. The state's Webb-Hartley Law of 1913 (also known as the Alien Land Law) made it illegal for foreigners to purchase real estate or lease land for longer than three years. California also passed laws prohibiting Asians from owning businesses, and the state raised the cost of commercial fishing licenses for all people of Asian ancestry.

The anti-Japanese movement resulted in laws that prevented immigrants from becoming legal residents, owning land, or owning a business, but the combined effect did not diminish the success of the Japanese. The Japanese tended to live in segregated communities, and they combined their resources to set up their own savings and loans and banks to offer assistance to businesspeople and farmers. The anti-Japanese laws were aimed at preventing future immigration, but they did not affect the children of Japanese born in the United States, who were legally U.S. citizens. Racist and nativist groups such as the IRL and the AEL mounted a fierce resistance, and the Immigration Act of 1924 prevented all Japanese immigration to the United States. Furthermore, the Great Depression of the 1930's severely reduced job opportunities. During the 1930's, the Japanese government became more authoritarian and militaristic, using the anti-Japanese American laws as evidence that the outside world did not trust them. The ultimate expression of the anti-Japanese movement was the forced internment of about 120,000 Japanese Americans during World War II, about 80,000 of whom were U.S. citizens.

Jonathan L. Thorndike

FURTHER READING

Curran, Thomas J. *Xenophobia and Immigration, 1820-1930.* Boston: Twayne, 1975. A cogent history of immigration and anti-immigrant sentiment.

Daniels, Roger. *Asian America: Chinese and Japanese in the United States Since 1850.* Seattle: University of Washington Press, 1988. A well-researched overview of Chinese and Japanese Americans from 1850 to 1980.

Hatamiya, Leslie T. *Righting a Wrong: Japanese Americans and the Passage of the Civil Liberties Act of 1988.* Stanford, Calif.: Stanford University Press, 1993.

The Civil Liberties Act of 1988 granted reparations to Japanese Americans who had been interned during World War II. The author provides an immense amount of detail on the events leading to its passage.

Takaki, Ronald. *Strangers from a Different Shore: A History of Asian Americans*. Boston: Little, Brown, 1988. A popular history of Asian Americans that draws upon a variety of primary sources, from newspapers to court cases.

SEE ALSO: Alien land laws; Anti-Chinese movement; Asiatic Exclusion League; Gentlemen's Agreement; Japanese American Citizens League; Japanese American internment; Japanese immigrants; "Mongrelization"; Nativism; "Yellow peril" campaign.

ANTIN, MARY

BORN: June 13, 1881; Plotzk, Russia
DIED: May 17, 1949; Suffern, New York
IDENTIFICATION: Russian-born American author and political activist

SIGNIFICANCE: One of the most prominent voices of the early twentieth century wave of immigration to the United States, Mary Antin is best known for her 1912 book *The Promised Land*, describing her experience and that of her family in settling in America and attending American schools.

Born in Russia in 1881, Mary Antin was the daughter of a Jewish merchant who had been trained as a rabbi only to reject Orthodox Judaism and instead go into business. Her birthplace, Plotzk, was in the region known as the "Pale of Settlement," where Russian Jews were allowed to live. After Czar Alexander II was assassinated by political radicals in March, 1881—exactly three months before Antin was born—Jews became scapegoats for political and popular reaction. Antin later described how she and her family had to hide inside their house during Christian holidays for fear that celebrations would turn into pogroms—violent persecutions of the Jews that were often supported by the Russian police. Jews were subject to arbitrary fines, and

their children could be admitted to schools only in limited numbers.

Seeking to escape Jewish persecution in Russia, Antin's father sailed for America in 1891 and settled in Boston, while his wife and six children waited until he established himself in the new country. Three years later, when Mary was thirteen, the family followed her father and took up residence in the Boston slum district called Revere. Later, they moved to Boston's South End. Although Antin's family was poor, in the new country she was free to attend Boston's public schools, including the demanding Boston Girls' Latin School. Antin later wrote about the great opportunity the school offered to her; it gave her both a dedication to learning and an intense sense of patriotism for her adopted nation.

In October, 1901, Antin married Amadeus Grabau, a German-born paleontologist and geologist who was eleven years her senior. A graduate of the Massachusetts Institute of Technology, Grabau was then completing his doctorate in geology at Harvard. He would later become a prominent scholar and author of numerous books. The year they married, Antin and Grabau moved to New York, where Grabau taught at Columbia University. Meanwhile, Antin began studying at Teachers College and Barnard College of Columbia University.

WRITING WORK

Even before undertaking her college studies, Antin had begun her autobiographical writings. Her first book, which she wrote in Yiddish as a set of letters to an uncle still in Plotzk, was later published in English as *From Plotzk to Boston* (1899) with a foreword by Israel Zangwill. Zangwill himself was a prominent immigrant writer of Russian Jewish heritage best known for coining the term "melting pot" in a play of that name. Antin's first book told the story of her own immigration experience, and it brought her name to the attention of the reading public.

A dozen years after *From Plotzk to Boston* appeared, the immigration experience became the subject of Antin's most widely read book, *The Promised Land* (1912). Before its publication, it appeared in serial form in *The Atlantic Monthly*. The magazine serialization and the book brought the lives, experiences, and ambitions of America's new immigrant populations to a wide readership. The writing helped bring public sympathy and understanding to people who had seemed alien to many Americans. Antin's portrait of self-reliant, hard-working immigrant families, eager to become patriotic Americans, soon became required reading in civics courses in schools around the nation.

In 1914, Antin published *They Who Knock at Our Gates: A Complete Gospel of Immigration*. She also lectured widely on the subject of immigration from 1913 to 1918. At a time when the American government was considering adopting more restrictive immigration policies, Antin was an outspoken advocated of openness to new immigrants. She also became a strong supporter of former president Theodore Roosevelt, who sought to recapture the presidency on the ticket of the Progressive (Bull Moose) Party in 1912.

Mary Antin's life became more difficult after the United States entered World War I in 1917. Her husband held widely known pro-German views, and war between the United States and Germany made such views intensely unpopular. When Grabau left the country to do research in China in 1919, Antin remained behind with her family. After the war, Mary Antin wrote relatively little until her death in 1949.

Carl L. Bankston III

FURTHER READING

Antin, Mary. *The Promised Land*. 1912. Whitefish, Mont.: Kessinger, 2004. Reprint edition of Antin's most famous and influential book.

Howe, Irving. *World of Our Fathers: The Journey of the East European Jews to America and the Life They Found and Made*. New York: Galahad Books, 1994. Comprehensive history of the experience of East European Jewish immigrants, including Jewish Germans, such as Antin and Grabau.

Mazur, Allan. *A Romance in Natural History: The Lives and Works of Amadeus Grabau and Mary Antin*. Syracuse, N.Y.: Syracuse University Press, 2004. Sympathetic joint biography with special attention to Antin's and Grabau's writings.

SEE ALSO: Education; Jewish immigrants; Literature; Melting pot theory; Progressivism; Religion as a push-pull factor; Russian and Soviet immigrants; Yezierska, Anzia.

ANTI-SEMITISM

DEFINITION: Dislike of Jews, based solely on their being Jewish, sometimes expressed in public pronouncements and hostile actions

SIGNIFICANCE: Except for isolated instances, most notably the lynching of Leo Frank in Georgia in 1915, anti-Semitism in America never acquired the malevolent levels that it frequently reached in Europe. Discrimination had its greatest effects on U.S. immigration policies during the decades between the late nineteenth century and the era of World War II. The refusal of the United States to admit European Jews trying to flee German Nazism during the 1930's condemned most of these persons to murder at the hands of the Nazis.

The lure of freedom for Jews can be found in the earliest decades following the founding of the first settlements in what became the United States. The first Jews arrived in New Amsterdam, which would later become New York City, in 1654, when twenty-three Dutch colonists fled Recife off the coast of Brazil after the Portuguese occupied the island. Despite the reputation of Jews as productive citizens in Holland, even in the New World they continued to face discrimination, and at times even hatred. New Amsterdam governor Peter Stuyvesant considered them a "deceitful race," "blasphemers of Christ." Jews were permitted to worship only in their private homes—a situation that did not immediately change even after the British replaced the Dutch as rulers of New Amsterdam in 1664.

The period from the mid-seventeenth century to approximately 1830 represented the first, albeit limited, immigration of Jews from Europe to the United States. A second period, of greater immigration levels, occurred between 1830 and 1880. It saw the arrival of mostly of German and other western European Jews. The third and largest influx of Jews took place between 1880 and 1924, when most Jewish immigrants were from eastern Europe, particularly from Russia. The search for religious and political freedoms as well as economic opportunities was a primary driving factor during each of these periods. However, the relative importance displayed by each of these issues varied during the respective eras.

COLONIAL ERA AND EARLY INDEPENDENCE

Most American settlers during the colonial era of North America were British. What little anti-Semitism they displayed was reflected primarily in attitudes or verbal attacks rather than in statutory legal restrictions. At the time of the late eighteenth century American Revolution, approximately two thousand Jews lived in the North American colonies. New York City and Charleston, South Carolina had the largest concentrations. Many of these people had immigrated from Spain and Portugal or those countries' colonies, not from England, which was itself home to only about eight thousand Jews at that time. In the British colonies, Jews had been granted full rights of citizenry by an act of Great Britain's Parliament in 1740—a privilege not then available to Roman Catholics. Nevertheless, while interactions between individual Christians and Jews were generally amicable, British attitudes toward the Jewish "race" often reflected contemporary prejudices about allegedly unscrupulous Jewish business practices.

The United States gained its independence in 1783. The U.S. Constitution that was ratified in 1789 contained no clauses discriminating against Jews or members of any other religious group and specifically guaranteed that "no religious Test shall ever be required as a Qualification to any Office or public Trust under the United States." The First Amendment of the Bill of Rights, which was ratified two years later, specifically guaranteed that the federal government would not interfere in the free exercise of religion. However, while federal laws did not discriminate against Jews, some state laws restricted Jewish officeholders into the nineteenth century. In 1780, as prominent a figure as John Quincy Adams, the son of one of the nation's Founders and a future president himself, said that Jews were willing "to steal the eyes out of your head if they possibly could."

Even during this period, Jews in the public eye could be subject to personal attacks. Benjamin Nones, a Revolutionary War hero from Philadelphia and a member of Thomas Jefferson's Republican Party, was forced to defend himself against Federalist attacks denouncing him not only for being a Jew, but for being poor as well. New York politician Mordecai Noah, whose father and grandfather had fought in the American Revolution, was likewise denounced as an "enemy of Christ." His position as a diplomat in Tunis was revoked because of his Judaism. Despite such obvious examples of antipathy toward Jews, Jew willing to convert to Christianity were generally accepted into what was considered polite society.

NINETEENTH CENTURY IMMIGRANTS

Between 1830 and the 1880's, the number of Jews in the United States rose to approximately 200,000. Most of this increase was the result of immigration of Ashkenazi Jews from central and western Europe, in contrast to the Sephardic immigrants from Iberia of earlier years. Many of these transplanted Europeans settled in the cities along the East Coast, from which they gradually moved inland to the growing cities of Cincinnati, St. Louis, and New Orleans. In this they differed little from the millions of other European immigrants then entering America.

Complex reasons prompted the emigration of Jews from Europe through the mid-nineteenth century. Before the 1870's, most of them left Europe for economic or political reasons, in contrast to later immigrants who fled from lethal pogroms. The decades of the 1830's and 1840's were a period of political turmoil that culminated in a series of mostly unsuccessful revolutions around the year 1848. After these revolutions failed, many young Europeans filled with revolutionary ideals looked elsewhere for their future. During this same period of political change, a population explosion was taking place in Europe while economic changes were limiting opportunities for young people. Jews were particularly affected, as merchant, trading, and skilled artisan occupations at which they had historically worked were disappearing.

Meanwhile, American attitudes toward Jews were undergoing changes as new German, Irish, and other immigrants brought their own prejudices against Jews to America. Attacks on Jews became increasingly common, and acts of discrimination against Jews increased. In Cincinnati, Ohio, for example, Roman Catholic priests told domestic workers not to work for Jewish employers. The speaker of California's state assembly tried, unsuccessfully, to levy a special tax on Jews to induce them to leave the state.

THE "NEW TRANS-ATLANTIC HEBREW LINE"

FOR THE EXCLUSIVE USE OF "THE PERSECUTED."

Puck *magazine cartoon lampooning Jewish immigrants from eastern Europe in 1881.* (Library of Congress)

Some eight thousand Jews fought in the U.S. Civil War. Most fought for the Union army, but the most prominent Jew during the war was arguably Judah Benjamin, a former U.S. senator who became secretary of state for the Confederacy. Early during the war, Union general Ulysses Grant issued what may have been the most blatantly anti-Semitic official statement in American history. In December, 1862, he issued an order in which he accused Jews "as a class" of war profiteering and ordered all Jews to leave certain parts of Kentucky, Tennessee, and Mississippi within twenty-four hours. However,

after the order was brought to the attention of President Abraham Lincoln, it was revoked.

During the decades following the Civil War, Jews increasingly integrated into mainstream American society. Many became prominent merchants. Nevertheless, anti-Semitic discrimination persisted. For example, the prominent businessman Joseph Seligman was refused admittance to an upscale hotel in Saratoga Springs, New York, because he was Jewish. However, Jewish communities were becoming increasingly accepted as part of the American landscape.

TWENTIETH CENTURY WORLD WARS

Wholesale changes in the demographics of American Jews, and the response of the country at large, began with the mass influxes that began during the 1880's and continued into the 1920's. During those years, nearly 2.4 million Jews immigrated to the United States. Most came from eastern Europe, and most of them settled in the cities of New York, Philadelphia, and Chicago. Poverty was among the forces that drove Jews to emigrate from Europe, but increasingly virulent anti-Semitic nationalism in some eastern European countries was rising to the level of lethal pogroms against Jewish communities.

Educated Jewish immigrants from western Europe integrated into American society relatively easily, but more poorly educated immigrants from Russia were considered by many Americans as less intelligent and of poor genetic stock. As these immigrants' names revealed their Slavic ancestry, many immigrants changed their names to appear more American. It was common for these persons to change their names to reflect their "Americanization." For example, the name "Pakerevich" became "Baker," and "Israel Baline" became "Irving Berlin."

While overt hatred, particularly in the South, was generally directed against members of racial minorities, such feelings were also occasionally directed against Jews. The most blatant example was the 1915 lynching of the Jewish Atlanta businessman Leo Frank, who had been unjustly convicted of the rape and murder of an employee. Henry Ford, the founder of Ford Motor Company and a major figure in business during the 1920's, regularly published anti-Semitic editorials in his own newspaper, the *Dearborn Independent*. Father Charles Coughlin preached anti-Semitism to the nation from his pulpit in Royal Oak, Michigan.

The growing anti-Semitic attitude was reflected most clearly in changes in immigration laws that were directed against eastern and southern Europeans in general, but against Jews from those regions in particular. For example, the Immigration Act of 1924 established a quota system that severely restricted Jewish immigration from most of Europe. These new limits on immigration had an immediate impact on Jews attempting to flee Europe following the rise of fascism during the 1930's. The appointment of Adolf Hitler and the Nazi Party to power in Germany in 1933 was rapidly followed by German legalization of discrimination against Jews. The anti-Jewish riots that began during November, 1938, were merely the prelude to the rounding up and eventual murder of Jews throughout Europe.

The resistance of the United States to Jewish immigration during the 1930's was dramatized in the *St. Louis* affair in 1939. When the German ship *St. Louis*, carrying more than 900 Jews attempting to escape from Europe, arrived in Cuba, its passengers were not allowed to disembark, and they were ultimately refused permission to enter the United States. Most had to return to Europe, where they were eventually murdered. In 1939, the Wagner-Rogers Bill designed to admit 20,000 Jewish children from Europe was voted down in Congress. Despite the admittance of prominent individuals. such as Albert Einstein, few Jews were allowed to enter America during the 1930's.

AFTER WORLD WAR II

Although there was strong evidence that Nazi Germany was trying to exterminate European and Russian Jews throughout the war, the full extent of German atrocities became widely known only after the surrender of Germany in May, 1945. Hundreds of thousands of European Jews who survived the Holocaust became stateless; even the idea that they might return to what was left of their prewar homes was unrealistic. Whether public awareness of the extent of the Holocaust changed American attitudes or merely rendered overt anti-Semitism no longer acceptable is unclear. Returning American soldiers regarded the elimination of racial and religious discrimination to be a major priority, and criticism of Jews as a people was significantly reduced. Although Jews within some individual professions continued to endure some discrimination, often in the form of hiring quotas, legal barriers against Jews were gradually eliminated. Even the Hollywood film industry addressed discrimination and hatred against Jews. In the film *Gentleman's Agreement* (1947), for example, actor Gregory Peck played a reporter pretending to be Jewish in order to investigate discrimination, while the plot of *Crossfire* (1947) involved the murder by bigots of a Jewish war hero.

U.S. immigration policies that had historically discriminated against Jews began to change as well.

A bill proposed by Congressman William Stratton of Illinois in 1947 to admit 400,000 displaced persons, including Jews, went nowhere. However, one year later Congress did pass a similar bill to admit more than 200,000 displaced persons, the Displaced Persons Act of 1948. Efforts by members of Congress to establish into law provisions of the 1948 act that continued to create barriers to immigration of displaced Jews were defeated, and by 1960 an estimated 250,000 survivors had arrived. The Civil Rights movement during the 1960's, while primarily addressing discrimination against African Americans and members of other racial minorities, ended most remaining legal barriers directed against Jews as well.

The last major influx of Jewish immigrants to the United States began during the late 1970's and continued through the presidency of Ronald Reagan, as emigration barriers in the Soviet Union slowly beginning to lift. Approximately two million Jews had remained in Russia following World War II. An increasing number of activists, largely but not solely Jewish, began a campaign directed at the Soviet government to allow these Jews to emigrate. Pressure from the United States as well as internal Russian *refuseniks* eventually proved successful. Ultimately, nearly 200,000 Russian Jews immigrated to America between 1979 and 1990.

Richard Adler

FURTHER READING

Diner, Hasia. *The Jews of the United States, 1654-2000.* Berkeley: University of California Press, 2004. In addition to treating Jewish history from a religious viewpoint, Diner addresses economic and cultural changes within the community. A feminist perspective underlies much of the history.

Dinnerstein, Leonard. *Antisemitism in America.* New York: Oxford University Press, 1994. Comprehensive history of anti-Semitism that addresses the earliest European Christian biases toward Jews and the influence of those beliefs during the earliest years of Jewish immigration. Chapters divide American history into specific periods, emphasizing the evolution of anti-Semitism and effects on immigration policy during each period.

Gerber, David, ed. *Anti-Semitism in American History.* Champaign: University of Illinois Press, 1986. Collection of essays analyzing both the roots of anti-Semitism and resultant discrimination against Jews. Subjects such as mythological accusations against Jewish practices, and interactions among Jews and other minorities are covered.

Sheldon, Harvey. *Encyclopedia of the History of Jewish Comedy.* Charleston, S.C.: BookSurge Publishing, 2008. Although not strictly a history of anti-Semitism, this self-published work addresses the development and use of "Jewish comedy" as a means to address perception of Jews by outsiders. The premise of the book is that one cannot hate if one is laughing.

Wenger, Beth. *The Jewish Americans.* New York: Doubleday, 2007. Comprehensive history of 350 years of Jewish history in America. The book contains extensive first-person accounts of the Jewish experience, accompanied by a large number of photographs.

SEE ALSO: American Jewish Committee; Anti Defamation League; Displaced Persons Act of 1948; History of immigration, 1783-1891; History of immigration after 1891; Holocaust; Israeli immigrants; Jewish immigrants; Nativism; Religion as a push-pull factor; Stereotyping.

ARAB IMMIGRANTS

SIGNIFICANCE: Christian and Muslim Arab immigrants from the Middle East and North Africa, initially drawn to the United States by economic opportunities, have both assimilated into and remained distinct from mainstream American culture, creating a distinctive literary and ethnic identity and working to address stereotypes and prejudices arising from the unfamiliarity of Middle Eastern peoples in the United States.

Tracing the historical presence of Arab immigrants during the various periods of their arrival in the United States raises questions of cultural complexity and religious diversity as well as problems of identification. During the early years of the first major period of immigration, which lasted from 1881 to 1914, the U.S. Bureau of Immigration used no standard terminology to identify from what parts of the Ottoman Empire Arab immigrants originated. Instead, the bureau used such labels as Greeks, Turks, Armenians, Ottomans, and Syrians. After 1899, the bureau simply labeled all Arab immigrants as "Syrians."

EARLY IMMIGRANTS

The initial wave of immigration brought roughly 110,000 Arabic speakers to the United States before World War I (1914-1918). A second, much smaller, number entered between 1920 and 1924, when passage of a new federal immigration act set a quota on Arab immigrants. The 1924 law represented a shift in American opinion away from the open immigration policies of the earlier era, limiting the entry of members of designated ethnic or national origin groups to 2 percent of the numbers of those groups who had been counted in the 1890 U.S. census. This had the practical effect of further

limiting the number of immigrants from Arab lands who could qualify for admission, as the bulk of immigrants to the United States before 1890 had come from northern Europe.

The first Arabic speakers to arrive in the United States were Christians from Lebanon. Higher percentages of Muslim immigrants arrived during the next major period of Arab immigration, from the early 1950's to the mid-1960's. Another increase came after the passage of the Immigration and Naturalization Act of 1965, which abolished the quota system. The Arab countries that contributed the greatest numbers of immigrants after 1965 were Egypt, Morocco, Yemen, Jordan, and Iraq.

The first Arab immigrants generally settled in the urban areas of the Northeast and Midwest of the United States, forming their own ethnic neighborhoods. By the beginning of World War II, they had established major presences in New York City, Boston, and Detroit. Their economic profile was both as members of the industrial workforce and independent businesspeople who traveled widely in search of customers for their lines of household goods.

The second wave of Arab immigrants, who came during the 1950's, brought a significant number of professional people seeking better conditions. Their numbers were augmented by university students who chose to remain in the United States and followed employment opportunities to new homes, often creating an Arab presence where none had been before. The third wave, after 1965, contained a mixture of skilled and unskilled workers, many fleeing civil strife or instability in their homelands. However, equal numbers simply sought better lives for themselves and their families. The third stream of Arab immigration contributed most of the visible face of Arab America known to the rest of the United States.

ACCEPTANCE AND EXCLUSION

All three waves of Arab immigrants initially encountered a variety of prejudicial attitudes beyond those associated with belonging to any group of newcomers to America working to establish themselves. The initial group from Syria and Lebanon entered the United States at a time when nativism was widespread and a cultural imperative on making all immigrants assimilate completely into white Protestant society was in vogue. The newcomers

PROFILE OF ARAB IMMIGRANTS

Countries of origin	Algeria, Bahrain, Egypt, Iraq, Jordan, Kuwait, Lebanon, Libya, Morocco, Oman, Qatar, Saudi Arabia, Syria, Tunisia, United Arab Emirates, Yemen
Primary language	Arabic
Primary regions of U.S. settlement	Northeast, Midwest
Earliest significant arrivals	1880's
Peak immigration period	Mid- to late twentieth century
Twenty-first century legal residents*	262,468 (32,809 per year)

*Immigrants who obtained legal permanent resident status in the United States. These figures are only for immigrants from nations whose populations have the highest percentages of ethnic Arabs—those listed above. Other nations with large Arab populations include Chad, Israel, Somalia, and Sudan.

Source: Department of Homeland Security, *Yearbook of Immigration Statistics, 2008.*

were viewed as suspect for multiple reasons. Not only were they foreign born and speaking limited English, they also were dark skinned, often unskilled, and members of either the Roman Catholic or the Eastern Orthodox faiths. Their village backgrounds, family loyalties, and relatively small numbers worked to preclude the establishment of a distinct and visible Arab ethnic segment of the population in a fashion similar to the process undergone by such groups as the Italians, whose own provincial origins took second place to their identification with their native country. The question of Arab eligibility for admission as American citizens proved contentious after 1910, due to federal government restrictions on Arab immigration. However, a series of successful lawsuits filed between 1910 and 1923 by members of what was loosely known as the "Syrian" community eventually established that Arabs were to be considered eligible for American citizenship.

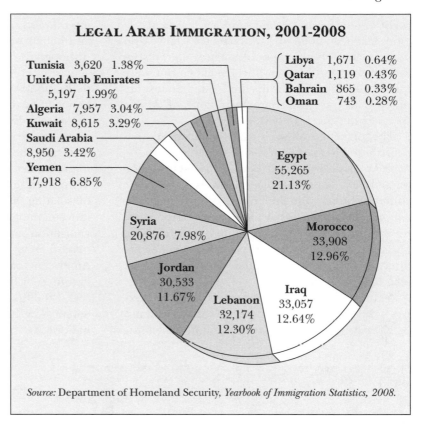

LEGAL ARAB IMMIGRATION, 2001-2008

Tunisia 3,620 1.38%
United Arab Emirates 5,197 1.99%
Algeria 7,957 3.04%
Kuwait 8,615 3.29%
Saudi Arabia 8,950 3.42%
Yemen 17,918 6.85%
Syria 20,876 7.98%
Jordan 30,533 11.67%
Lebanon 32,174 12.30%
Iraq 33,057 12.64%
Morocco 33,908 12.96%
Egypt 55,265 21.13%
Libya 1,671 0.64%
Qatar 1,119 0.43%
Bahrain 865 0.33%
Oman 743 0.28%

Source: Department of Homeland Security, *Yearbook of Immigration Statistics, 2008.*

CIVIL RIGHTS AND STEREOTYPES

The predominantly Muslim Arab immigrants who arrived during the 1950's and early 1960's usually arrived with greater economic resources and higher levels of professional education than the members of the first wave had possessed. They were far less flexible in blending with America society than their Christian Arab predecessors had been. They preferred to retain their allegiance to Islam and remained engaged in Middle Eastern political issues. Mainstream American general opinion toward Arab immigrants altered sharply following the Six-Day War of June, 1967, in which the American ally Israel fought several of its Arab neighbors. After a series of highly publicized airline hijackings by Middle Eastern groups, U.S. President Richard M. Nixon issued an executive order in September, 1972, that was intended to prevent terrorists from gaining entrance to the United States. His order authorized special measures against Arabs, ranging from the imposition of restrictions on their entry and ability to apply for permanent resident status to surveillance of community organizations under the code name Operation Boulder.

The fact that no incidents of terrorist activity connected with the Arab American community had occurred raised questions about the necessity of the president's measure. However, the situation was further complicated by the subsequent oil embargo and the sharp rise in petroleum prices imposed by the Arab-dominated Organization of Petroleum Exporting Countries (OPEC) after the conclusion of another Arab-Israeli War in October, 1973. Before these developments, Arab Americans had drawn little public attention in the United States. However, these events prompted a cultural redefinition of what it meant to belong to this community. No distinction was made in political language or mass media journalism to reflect the actual diversity of the contemporary Arab world, which was publicly cast as made up of vicious terrorists intent on destroying America, fanatical religious leaders—no matter which sect of Islam—and unscrupulous businesspeople. These stereotypes were based partly on political realities but were widely disseminated within the United States, unrelieved by positive characterizations of Arabic speakers in American culture.

The presence of such inaccurate images has contributed to a sense of social marginality among Arab Americans that has been addressed in several ways. While some Arab immigrants have made complete breaks with their home cultures and have adopted American lifestyles and values, others stress their uniqueness to distance themselves from being associated with a particular Arab nation or withdraw into ethnic communities, following the pattern of earlier arrivals.

A third response has been to confront stereotypes directly by stressing points of commonality between Islamic and American culture by calling attention to common emphases on strong families and beliefs held by both Muslims and Christians. Although the history of Arab immigrant civil rights activism can be said to begin with the protest by a delegation representing the Association of Syrian Unity made to the federal government during the citizenship disputes before World War I, most such groups came into being during the 1980's. Perhaps ironically, the success of Arab Americans in adapting to mainstream culture during the earlier part of the twentieth century had the unexpected result of isolating them from the issues of the Civil Rights movement of the 1960's. The largest civil rights organization countering stereotypes and misinformation about the Arab communities has been the American-Arab Anti-Discrimination Committee. Founded by South Dakota politician James Abourezk—the first Arab American to serve in the U.S. Senate—in 1980, it quickly established chapters nationwide. In 1985, the Arab American Institute

Arab immigrant accountant helping a Latino man prepare his income tax forms in Chicago in early 2007. Known as Al-Muhaseb (the accountant) in Arabic, the man's company was affiliated with H&R Block, the giant tax-preparation firm. (AP/Wide World Photos)

was established in Washington, D.C., to encourage and promote greater involvement by Arab Americans in civic life and the political process.

MISTRUST OF THE FEDERAL GOVERNMENT

In 1987, the Reagan administration attempted to prosecute two longtime Palestinian American residents of California and six of their associates who had been distributing literature and working at fund-raising for the Popular Front for the Liberation of Palestine. The government charged that they were promoting communism. Dubbed the "LA 8," the Arab defendants were not deported, as a federal judge ruled the Immigration and Nationality Act of 1952, under which they were being prosecuted, to be unconstitutional. The government continued to attempt to revive the case six times over a period of twenty years, using successive pieces of antiterrorist legislation including the Patriot Act. In 2007, the Board of Immigration Appeals announced that no further action would be taken, following a ruling by a Los Angeles federal immigration judge that the plaintiffs' civil rights had been repeatedly violated. This long, drawn-out case served as the focus for Arab immigrant distrust of the federal government and, despite the eventual vindication of the accused, created a legacy of wariness that was only exacerbated by the terrorist attacks on America of September 11, 2001.

The varied social impacts of the events of September 11, 2001, on the Arab immigrant communities were based upon several pieces of legislation passed by the U.S. Congress in the immediate aftermath of the attacks. There was an intensification of existing negative stereotypes about Arabic speakers and an erosion of certain civil rights and elements of due process in investigations carried out by the Federal Bureau of Investigation (FBI) with the stated aim of identifying possible terrorists and their accomplices, based in large part on racial profiling. Male immigrants from Arab nations regarded as terrorist havens who did not possess green cards were frequently required to be photographed, fingerprinted, and registered by the federal government. More than 140,000 people were registered. Only a handful of the people investigated were actually accused of having terrorist links, but the process resulted in hundreds of Arab immigrants leaving the United States for their home nations, Canada, or Europe to avoid official deportation.

Many of the actions taken by the FBI were sharply criticized by the U.S. Justice Department. These actions also helped energize civil liberties organizations within and outside the Arab community to oppose the selective enforcement of immigration law being utilized to target them. Arab immigrants found themselves having repeatedly to deal with the domestic political consequences of policies and actions they did not condone. They also were repeatedly obliged to emphasize and assert their adoption of American national culture, a process complicated by ignorance among mainstream Americans of the actual core values of Islam.

Despite these problems, the numbers of Arab nationals applying for immigrant status to the United States held firm after 2001—at an average of about 4 percent of total U.S. immigration. However, there was a sharp decline in the numbers of foreign student visas issued to applicants from Middle Eastern countries. The drop in student visas ranged from 31 percent for persons from Lebanon to 65 percent for persons from the Persian Gulf states. At the same time, however, the U.S. government actively sought persons fluent in all dialects of the Arabic language to work in its counterterrorism campaign. Ironically, the scarcity of Arabic-language programs in American institutions of higher education forced the government to accept applicants for these new positions from among recent Arab immigrants, who faced lengthy periods of security evaluation before they were hired.

These cultural and political challenges resulted in a new awareness of the presence of Arab immigrants in the mind of the American public and offered the immigrants an unprecedented opportunity to educate other Americans on the realities of Arab life. A prime example of this new assertiveness was the appearance in public settings across the United States of women wearing head scarves as required by the Qur'ān, a practice widespread within the Muslim world but not well known in the United States before 2001. In May, 2005, the Arab American National Museum opened in Dearborn, Michigan. These and other outreach efforts by Arab political and religious organizations has begun to create a degree of balance in how the American public regards Muslim and Christian Arab Americans.

Robert B. Ridinger

FURTHER READING

Arab American National Museum. *Telling Our Story: The Arab American National Museum.* Dearborn, Mich.: Author, 2007. Profile of the history and exhibits of this unique collection of Arab immigrant history.

Ewing, Katherine Pratte, ed. *Being and Belonging: Muslims in the United States Since 9/11.* New York: Russell Sage Foundation, 2008. Collection of eight ethnographic essays that explore how questions of identity and assimilation have been and are being addressed in contemporary Arab Christian and Muslim communities.

Hooglund, Eric J. W. *Crossing the Waters: Arabic-Speaking Immigrants to the United States Before 1940.* Washington, D.C.: Smithsonian Institution Press, 1987. Collection of original research essays on the first wave of Arab immigration.

Kayyali, Randa A. *The Arab Americans.* Westport, Conn.: Greenwood Press, 2006. Detailed yet readable history of the cultural background of Arabic-speaking immigrants to the United States and their participation in and impact on American society.

Mehdi, Beverlee Turner, ed. *The Arabs in America, 1492-1977: A Chronology and Fact Book.* Dobbs Ferry, N.Y.: Oceana, 1978. The history of Arabic speakers in the Americas is followed from 1789 to 1977 through fifty-five primary documents.

Naff, Alixa. *Becoming American: The Early Arab Immigrant Experience.* Carbondale: Southern Illinois University Press, 1985. History of the first wave of Arab immigrants before World War II and their economic and social networks.

Orfalea, Gregory. *Before the Flames: A Quest for the History of Arab Americans.* Northampton, Mass.: Olive Branch Press, 2006. Collection of oral histories of 125 Arab immigrants of three generations of migration, with background information.

SEE ALSO: Asian immigrants; Asian Indian immigrants; Asiatic Barred Zone; Iranian immigrants; Israeli immigrants; Muslim immigrants; 9/11 and U.S. immigration policy; Patriot Act of 2001; Religions of immigrants; Stereotyping.

ARGENTINE IMMIGRANTS

SIGNIFICANCE: Reflecting significant Italian as well as Spanish influence, Argentines constitute a small immigration population of mostly easily assimilated professionals, scientists, artists, and craftsmen, mainly of European descent (British, French, German, Jewish, Italian, Polish), escaping political and economic trouble in Argentina.

Before the 1970's, the U.S. government had classified Argentine immigrants within the larger category of "Other Hispanics." Consequently, Argentine-focused statistics before that decade are absent. Anglo-Argentines in particular had fled dictator Juan Perón's regime during the 1950's, and during the 1960's Argentine professionals (predominantly medical doctors and scientists) sought improved economic conditions, resulting in a "brain drain" to Australia, Canada, and the United States, with more women than men entering the United States. In 1970, there were 44,803 Argentine immigrants nationwide, with 20 percent living in the New York metropolitan area. These numbers soared during the mid- to late 1970's because of political persecution during Argentina's "dirty war": Jorge Rafael Videla's military junta snatched off the streets college students, protest-

PROFILE OF ARGENTINE IMMIGRANTS	
Country of origin	Argentina
Primary language	Spanish
Primary regions of U.S. settlement	New York, California, South Florida
Earliest significant arrivals	1910 to 1930
Peak immigration period	1975-1990
Twenty-first century legal residents*	40,298 (5,037 per year)

*Immigrants who obtained legal permanent resident status in the United States.

Source: Department of Homeland Security, *Yearbook of Immigration Statistics, 2008.*

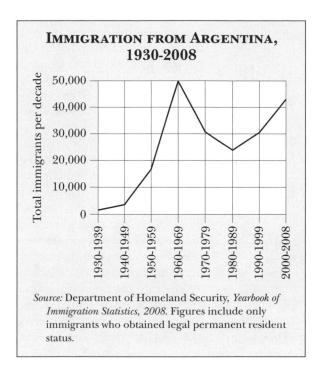

IMMIGRATION FROM ARGENTINA, 1930-2008

Total immigrants per decade

Source: Department of Homeland Security, *Yearbook of Immigration Statistics, 2008.* Figures include only immigrants who obtained legal permanent resident status.

ers, trade unionists, and rights activists, who "disappeared" forever.

The 1970's political refugees were less educated and more diverse than the 1960's immigrants, though more highly educated than the general Argentine population. The Argentine debt crisis of the 1980's brought another wave of immigration. The 1990 U.S. Census shows the 1970 figure more than doubled over the intervening twenty years to 92,563 Argentines nationwide. There were 15,115 Argentine immigrants in Los Angeles. By comparison, there were only 15 in North Dakota and Montana combined. Argentine American business and scientific associations, tango dance clubs, and the Italian community made New York City so attractive that the 1990 U.S. Census reported 17,363 Argentine Americans residing there. These figures may be low because they exclude more than half the population of Argentine immigrants who fall into other categories, such as Anglo-Argentines, Korean Argentines, Japanese Argentines, Arab Argentines, and especially Italian Argentines. Figures may also be skewed because the "Hispanic" or "Latino" category does not accurately apply and because Argentines tend to assimilate quickly.

From 1995 to 1999, 9,086 Argentines entered the United States as permanent residents, and the 2000 U.S. Census recorded 100,000 Argentine Americans overall. In 2002, South Florida claimed more than 21,000 in Miami's Little Buenos Aires alone. San Francisco claimed 6,000. In the first decade of the twenty-first century, poor employment opportunities, especially after the 2001-2002 economic collapse in Argentina; strong foreign-labor demands; and the possibility of entry under family reunification provisions created a new wave of Argentine immigrants. Between 2000 and 2004, 17,306 Argentines entered the United States as permanent residents, leading the U.S. Justice Department to tighten rules for temporary visas to discourage illegal residence.

Andrew F. Macdonald and Gina Macdonald

FURTHER READING

Marshall, Adriana. "Emigration of Argentines to the United States." In *When Borders Don't Divide: Labor Migration and Refugee Movements in the Americas,* edited by Patricia R. Pessar. New York: Center for Migration Studies, 1988.

Viladrich, Anahí. "From 'Shrinks' to 'Urban Shamans': Argentine Immigrants' Therapeutic Eclecticism in New York City." *Culture, Medicine and Psychiatry* 31, no. 3 (September, 2007): 307-328.

_____. "Tango Immigrants in New York City." *Journal of Contemporary Ethnography* 34, no. 5 (October, 2005): 533-559.

SEE ALSO: American Jewish Committee; "Brain drain"; California; Canada vs. United States as immigrant destinations; Economic opportunities; Florida; Green cards; Latin American immigrants; New York City; San Francisco.

ARIZONA

SIGNIFICANCE: Arizona has always been an important destination for Mexican immigrants to the United States. With its large population of American-born Hispanics, the state offers a cultural atmosphere familiar to Latin American immigrants. However, because of the large number of undocumented immigrants in the state, Latin American immigrants often encounter problems of acceptance by the general population.

PROFILE OF ARIZONA

Region	Southwest
Entered union	1912
Largest cities	Phoenix (capital), Tucson, Mesa, Glendale, Scottsdale
Modern immigrant communities	Mexicans

Population	Total	Percent of state	Percent of U.S.	U.S. rank
All state residents	6,166,000	100.0	2.05	16
All foreign-born residents	929,000	15.1	2.47	7

Source: U.S. Census Bureau, *Statistical Abstract for 2006.*
Notes: The U.S. population in 2006 was 299,399,000, of whom 37,548,000
  (12.5%) were foreign born. Rankings in last column reflect total numbers,
  not percentages.

Although Arizona has always attracted more Hispanic immigrants than those from any other group, immigrants from both Europe and Asia have also come to the state seeking work and opportunities to improve their lives since the late nineteenth century. The state's ethnic mix includes immigrants came from China, Japan, Great Britain, Ireland, France, Germany, Poland, Italy, and Russia. Many of these immigrants reached Arizona after having already settled in other states. Many set out for Arizona after Arizona's copper mines opened and the Southern Pacific Railroad started construction. With the completion of the railroad in 1876, copper mining became a commercial enterprise and increased the number of immigrants coming from east of the Mississippi River.

During the 1860's, Arizona's Chinese immigrants tended to remain in isolated communities, as they had in California. Many of them located in the Prescott area. Most had no intention of staying in Arizona, as they hoped to return to China after amassing their fortunes. Other Chinese arrived in Arizona as contract laborers to help build the Central Pacific Railroad. However, the Burlingame Treaty of 1868 between China and the United States changed things by giving Chinese immigrants a legal right to remain permanently in the United States and its territories. Consequently, even more Chinese immigrated to Arizona and other western states during the 1870's. The large increase in the number of Chinese prompted an anti-Chinese sentiment throughout the country that resulted in the passage in 1882 of the Chinese Exclusion Act. The new legislation severely restricted the lives of Chinese immigrants in Arizona as it did throughout the rest of the country, and the restrictions remained in force until 1943. Nevertheless, the Chinese made major contributions to Arizona with their work as miners and railroad laborers, as both the mines and the railroad were of primary importance to the economic development of the state.

Most Japanese who immigrated to Arizona settled in the southern part of the state, where they established farms. In later years, many of them moved to Phoenix. By the early twenty-first century, approximately twenty thousand Japanese Americans were living in Arizona.

The major immigrant population in Arizona, however, is Mexican. Sharing a border with Mexico and offering better opportunities for work than Mexico can provide, Arizona experiences a continuous flow of Mexican immigrants, both documented and undocumented. Many of these immigrants settle in the southern and central areas of Arizona. The counties of Santa Cruz and Yuma have especially large populations of Mexicans and Mexican Americans. In 2006, Arizona was home to the fourth-highest number of Mexican immigrants in the United States.

Shawncey Webb

FURTHER READING

Gutiérrez, David G. *Walls and Mirrors: Mexican Americans, Mexican Immigrants, and the Politics of Ethnicity.* Berkeley: University of California Press, 1995. Good account of the ongoing immigration from Mexico.

Rodríguez, Havidán, Rogelio Sáenz, and Cecilia Menjivar. *Latinas/os in the United States: Changing the Face of America.* New York: Springer, 2008. Emphasizes diversity in Latino communities and assesses its effects.

Sheridan, Thomas E. *Arizona: A History.* Tucson: University of Arizona Press, 1995. Well-researched and comprehensive treatment of Arizona's full history.

Telles, Edward, and Vilma Ortiz. *Generations of Exclusion: Mexican Americans, Assimilation and Race.* New York: Russell Sage Foundation, 2008. Good investigation of four decades of the Mexican American experience.

SEE ALSO: California; Chinese Exclusion Act of 1882; Chinese immigrants; Illegal Immigration Reform and Immigrant Responsibility Act of 1996; Japanese immigrants; Mexican immigrants; New Mexico; Railroads; Texas.

ARKANSAS

SIGNIFICANCE: Arkansas has experienced less foreign immigration than many other states. Nevertheless, by the late nineteenth century, small groups of immigrants were leaving their cultural and economic marks on the state. During the early twenty-first century, a growing presence of undocumented Latino laborers was fueling a lively and sometimes heated public debate about illegal immigration in Arkansas.

Before the U.S. Civil War (1861-1865), Arkansas's population was made up mostly of English, Scotch-Irish, and Scottish stock from Kentucky and Tennessee. People of African descent, mostly slaves, also arrived in significant numbers during this period; they constituted about 25 percent of the state's total population by 1860. Immigration during the antebellum period was slow, however, and Germans—including hundreds of German Jews—constituted one of the largest immigrant groups. In 1833, a planned German colony centered in Perry and White Counties collapsed, but 140 of the Germans remained, providing a support base for postbellum immigrants. German families continued to trickle into Arkansas over the next three decades, and by 1860, 1,143 Germans resided in the state.

As happened in many southern states during the years immediately after the Civil War, many leading Arkansans feared that their state's small population and lagging rates of immigration were hindering economic development. During the 1870's, the state began to circulate promotional literature abroad and dispatched agents to attract western and northern European immigrants to Arkansas. Such efforts were most successful in attracting more Germans, whose population grew to 5,971 by 1900. Although German accounted for only 0.46 percent of the state's population, they left an enduring cultural imprint on the state's landscapes—especially in the scattered agricultural communities they founded in the Ozarks.

Italians were also a small but notable presence inlate nineteenth century Arkansas. Indeed, while several Italian agricultural communities appeared in the South during the late nineteenth and early twentieth centuries, Arkansas's Tontitown, founded during the 1890's, was by far the most successful. Small influxes of French, Irish, Czech, Slovak, Syrian, Greek, and even a few Chinese laborers also arrived during the late nineteenth and early twentieth centuries. Some of these people were agriculturalists, but many more gravitated toward such population centers as Little Rock and Fort Smith.

PROFILE OF ARKANSAS

Region	South
Entered union	1836
Largest cities	Little Rock (capital), Fort Smith, North Little Rock, Fayetteville, Jonesboro
Modern immigrant communities	Mexicans, Salvadorans

Population	Total	Percent of state	Percent of U.S.	U.S. rank
All state residents	2,650,060	100.0	0.09	32
All foreign-born residents	107,000	3.8	0.29	37

Source: U.S. Census Bureau, *Statistical Abstract for 2006.*
Notes: The U.S. population in 2006 was 299,399,000, of whom 37,548,000 (12.5%) were foreign born. Rankings in last column reflect total numbers, not percentages.

On the whole, however, Arkansas remained a state with few immigrants.

This picture began to change during the late twentieth century. During the 1990's, Latin American—mostly Mexican—workers began rapidly replacing African Americans in the state's farm labor sector, as well as in poultry and other agricultural product processing plants, construction trades, and light manufacturing. Indeed, Arkansas's 337 percent rate of increase in Latino population between 1990 and 2000 was one of the nation's highest. This growth—in large part the result of economic pull factors in the United States (demand for cheap, unskilled labor) as well as the potent push factors of poverty and limited labor markets in Mexico and other Latin American countries—has led to significant changes in Arkansas's cultural fabric. It has also led to increasingly heated political discourse over the desirability and future of illegal immigrants in Arkansas society.

Although other immigrant groups—including Vietnamese and other Asians—have begun increasing their presence in Arkansas, their growth rates lag far behind those of other, more rapidly developing southern states, and Asian immigrants are vastly outnumbered in Arkansas by Mexicans and Salvadorans, who together constitute more than 50 percent of the state's immigrant population. The fact that Arkansas's third-largest single immigrant group in 2000 was Germans showed a surprising continuity with the state's immigrant past. However, the number of Germans remained tiny in comparison to that of Latinos and the state's general population.

Jeremiah Taylor

FURTHER READING

Ray, Celeste, ed. *Ethnicity*. Vol. 6 in *The New Encyclopedia of Southern Culture*. Chapel Hill: University of North Carolina Press, 2007.

Trumbauer, L. *German Immigration*. New York: Facts On File, 2004.

Watkins, Beverly. "Efforts to Encourage Immigration to Arkansas, 1865-1874." *Arkansas Historical Quarterly* 38 (1979): 32-62.

SEE ALSO: British immigrants; Czech and Slovakian immigrants; German immigrants; Greek immigrants; Italian immigrants; Jewish immigrants; Mexican immigrants; Mississippi; Mississippi River; Missouri.

ART

SIGNIFICANCE: American art forms, like American music and literature, has been immeasurably enriched by the contributions of artists from every land coming to the United States to add their unique ideas and styles to the artistic tapestry.

Few art forms created in the United States have been completely free of foreign roots. American music, literature, and art have all been shaped from the beginning by artistic trends, figures, and movements from other countries, by artists immigrating to the United States, and by those moving back and forth between the United States and other countries. Scholars consider jazz the unique contribution America has made to the world's music and wonder what American jazz would be without its African, Caribbean, and Latin elements—the heritage of jazz artists who carried their native musical traditions to the United States. American folk music has its tangled roots in Irish, Scottish, and English ballads, and the American musical goes back through George Gershwin and Irving Berlin (himself an immigrant from Russia) to W. S. Gilbert and Arthur S. Sullivan in England to a long tradition of the European music hall. Twentieth century American literature is notable for the modernism of William Faulkner and other native-born writers, but modernism is Anglo-American in origins and was fostered by Americans such as T. S. Eliot, Ezra Pound, and Gertrude Stein, who emigrated to the Europe of James Joyce, Virginia Woolf, and others; by Europeans bringing modernist voices to the United States (such as the German novelist Thomas Mann, who settled there in 1936); and by American writers such as those of the lost generation (Ernest Hemingway, F. Scott Fitzgerald, and others), who lived abroad during the 1920's.

PHOTOGRAPHY, ARCHITECTURE, AND SCULPTURE

The history of the visual arts is a similar story of cross-fertilization and immigrant imagination, coming from every direction of the globe. American photography—to take the simplest example—is hard to imagine without the studies of locomotion by Eadweard Muybridge, who was born and

Danish-born photographer Jacob Riis in 1904. (Library of Congress)

From its beginnings, American architecture had been an eclectic mix of styles, but it emerged during the twentieth century as leader of the International Style thanks in large part to immigrant artists: Louis Kahn (Estonia) came to Philadelphia in 1905, Rudolf Schindler (Austria) to Chicago in 1914, and both Richard Neutra (Austria) and Eero Saarinen (Finland) to the United States in 1923. The biggest boost to American architecture, as to other artistic forms, was the rise of Nazi Germany: With the closure of the influential Bauhaus school for architecture and design in Berlin in 1933, painter and art theoretician Josef Albers was hired at the newly opened Black Mountain College in North Carolina; László Moholy-Nagy took his experimental design, sculpture, and photography to Chicago; and Walter Gropius became a professor of architecture at Harvard, to be followed in that chair by Ludwig Mies van der Rowe (who had headed the Bauhaus after Gropius left), the most influential American architect after 1945. Ulrich Franzen (Germany) studied with Gropius at Harvard and then went to work for another immigrant artist, I. M. Pei, who had immigrated from China in 1935.

Sculpture in America tells a similar story. Possibly the best-known sculptor of the nineteenth century was Augustus Saint-Gaudens (1848-1907), born in Ireland of French descent and brought to the United States as an infant, who created public memorials such as the Diana statue at Madison Square Garden in New York (1891) and the Robert Gould Shaw Memorial in Boston Common (1884-1897). Alexander Milne Calder, the grandfather of the twentieth century American artist Alexander Calder, came from Scotland in 1868 to create public sculptures (such as the statue of William Penn atop Philadelphia's city hall). Other sculptors from Europe included Arthur Lee (who emigrated from Norway to the United States in 1890), Louise Nevelson (Russia, 1905), Louise Bourgeois (France, 1938), Eva Hesse (Germany, 1939), Jacques Lipchitz (Lithuania, 1941), and Naum Gabo (Russia, 1946).

PAINTING

The history of American painting is studded with immigrant names. John James Audubon (1785-1851), America's most famous wildlife painter, was born in Haiti of French parents and

died in England but who did his most important photographic experiments as a resident in the United States; the social documentation of immigrant life by the Danish-born Jacob Riis (*How the Other Half Lives*, 1890); or the studies of San Francisco's Chinatown during the 1890's by the German-born Arnold Genthe. Also notable is the creative work of Luxembourg-born Edward Steichen from the early twentieth century up to *The Family of Man* exhibition at the Museum of Modern Art in New York (which he curated in 1955), the most popular photography exhibition ever mounted; the abstract experiments of László Moholy-Nagy (who came to the United States from Hungary in 1937); and the work of Ben Shahn (Lithuania, 1906), Andreas Feininger (France, 1939), Robert Frank (Switzerland, 1947), and the famed portrait photographer Yousuf Karsh (Armenia, 1928).

came to the United States in 1803. Thomas Cole, the ablest of early American landscape painters, came from England in 1818. Albert Bierstadt's panoramic landscapes have defined the American West ever since he came to the United States from Germany in 1832. William Michael Harnett, the still-life painter, came to the United States from Ireland in 1849. One of the most endearing American images, the painting of *Washington Crossing the Delaware*, was made by the German-born Emanuel Gottlieb Leutze in 1851.

The second major wave of European immigration, from approximately 1880 to 1920, included a number of painters who would gain fame in the United States. The 1913 Armory Show in New York first introduced America to modern European artists such as Paul Cézanne, Marc Chagall, Henri Matisse, and Pablo Picasso. However, it also included a number of immigrant artists, such as the painters Oscar Bluemner (from Germany, 1892), Abraham Walkowitz (Russia, 1893), Joseph Stella (Italy, 1896), and Jules Pascin (Bulgaria, 1914), and the sculptors Gaston Lachaise (France, 1906), Elie Nadelman (Russia, 1914), and Alexander Archipenko (Russia, 1923). The most controversial work at that show was *Nude Descending a Staircase* (1912), a painting by Marcel Duchamp, who worked intermittently in the United States after 1915 and became a U.S. citizen in 1955.

Other noted artist-immigrants from this period include Max Weber (who came from Russia in 1891), Louis Lozowick (Ukraine, 1906), Peter Blume (Russia, 1911), and Raphael Soyer (Russia, 1912). Artists continued to immigrate to America during the twentieth century, and especially after the rise of Nazi Germany. George Grosz came from Germany in 1932, Hans Richter in 1941, and Max Beckmann in 1947. The noted abstract painter Piet Mondrian electrified the American art scene when he arrived from the Netherlands in 1940, but such paths of art influence are often fluid and difficult to define. The famed Mexican muralists of the 1920's and 1930's—Diego Rivera, José Clemente Orozco, and David Alfaro Siqueiros—were all residents of the United States at one time or another and worked on a number of mural projects in New York, Los Angeles, Detroit, and other cities. The legacy of these muralists' powerful social realism has lasted since then, yet one of Siqueiros's students when he taught in New York City

during the 1930's was Jackson Pollock, who would become one of the most famous abstract expressionist painters, dominating American art after World War II.

Many of the postwar painters were immigrants: Mark Rothko came from Russia in 1913, Jack Tworkov from Poland the same year, Arshile Gorky from Turkish Armenia in 1920, Willem de Kooning from Holland in 1926, Hans Hoffman from Bavaria in 1932, and Saul Steinberg from Romania in 1941. American art since the 1950's has continued to see an influx of immigrant artists: The painter David Hockney (born in Bradford, England) settled in Los Angeles in 1976; and the sculptors Claes Oldenburg (who came from Sweden in 1936) and Christo (Bulgaria, 1964) and the architect Paolo Soleri (Italy, 1947) have transformed the American landscape with their work.

LATIN AMERICAN, ASIAN, AND MIDDLE EASTERN INFLUENCES

American art has been enriched not only by Europeans but also increasingly by people from other continents. Waves of immigration after 1980 have come from Asia, Latin America, and the Middle East, and American art has experienced an infusion of styles and images from all these directions. The Mexican tin *retablo* tradition of altar paintings lives on in the early twenty-first century, as do Aztec and Aztlán images and myths that have infused the art of the Southwest for centuries and can be found in the multimedia assemblages of Guillermo Pulido, the prints of Enrique Chagoya, and the quilts of Maria Enriquez de Allen, all three of whom are immigrants to the United States from Mexico. Other Latino artists have come from Cuba (the painters Luis Cruz Azaceta, Juan González, and Cesar Trasobares), from Brazil (Lito Cavalcante, who came to the United States in 1972), from Uruguay (the painter, sculptor, and woodcut artist Naul Ojeda), from Chile (the painter Jorge Tacia has lived in New York since 1981), and from other South and Central American countries.

The influx of Asian art has also been significant: Chinese (painters H. N. Han and Bing Lee), Korean (video artist Nam June Paik), and Japanese (painters Masami Teraoka, Henry Sugimoto, and Yuriko Yamaguchi) artists immigrated to the United States during the twentieth century, as well as artists from Southeast Asia—Vietnam, Cambo-

British-born painter David Hockney, with friend and model Celia Birtwell, standing in front of his painting Mr. and Mrs. Clark and Percy *at a 2006 exhibition.* (AP/Wide World Photos)

dia, and Thailand. Artists from the Middle East include the Iranian-born sculptor Siah Armajani, best known for designing the Olympic torch presiding over the 1996 Atlanta Olympic Games, and the American sculptor and painter Zigi Ben-Haim, who was born in Baghdad, Iraq, and later lived in Israel.

Art in the twenty-first century knows few national borders. Though some artists are unable to emigrate, images from their art as well as its forms and techniques can travel around the globe in nanoseconds through the Internet. The 1913 Armory Show in New York was the first time that most Americans were able to witness the modern European masters; less than a century later, art could be transmitted throughout the world instantly. For example, in 1989 David Hockney sent work for the São Paulo Art Biennial via fax. Art can be viewed online, and "Internet art" has itself become an important artistic form. Technology and immigration are both sources of art inspiration and tradition during the twenty-first century.

David Peck

FURTHER READING

Lippard, Lucy R. *Mixed Blessings: New Art in a Multicultural America.* 1990. New York: New Press, 2000. Survey of late twentieth century multiethnic art, especially its Native American, Latino, Asian American, and African American forms. Lippard does not identify artists as native or immigrant, but she fully illustrates the ways that artistic forms, idioms, and styles from other cultures have become a necessary part of the language of American art.

McCabe, Cynthia Jaffee, ed. *The American Experience: Contemporary Immigrant Artists.* New York: Balch Institute for Ethnic Studies, 1985. This exhibition catalog includes curator McCabe's introduction ("Immigrants and Refugees: The Internalization of American Art") as well as essays by Yi-Fu Tuan ("Immigrant Artists: A Conceptual Framework") and Thomas Kessner ("Immigration and the American Experience"), followed by portraits of the twenty-eight contemporary immigrant artists in the show, including Christo, Patrick Ireland, and John Stockdale.

_____. *The Golden Door: Artist-Immigrants of America, 1876-1976.* Washington, D.C.: Smithsonian Institution Press, 1976. This volume, which emerged from an exhibition at the Hirshhorn Museum and Sculpture Garden as part of the bicentennial celebration of 1976, includes introductions by historian Daniel J. Boorstin ("The Immigrants' Vision") and curator McCabe ("A Century of Artist-Immigrants"), a sixty-page "Chronology, 1876-1976," and a "Catalogue of the Exhibition" with date of arrival, date of U.S. citizenship, and analysis and examples of the work of some sixty-eight artist-immigrants, from Max Weber to Paul Rotterdam.

See also: Berlin, Irving; Literature; Music.

ASAKURA V. CITY OF SEATTLE

The Case: U.S. Supreme Court ruling on priority of treaties over state laws
Date: Decided on May 26, 1924

SIGNIFICANCE: The *Asakura* ruling provided a relatively liberal interpretation of treaties with foreign countries that guarantee the civil rights of their citizens residing in the United States.

R. Asakura, a subject of the Japanese empire, operated a pawnbroker business in Seattle, Washington. In 1921, the city issued an ordinance requiring pawnbrokers to obtain a license and stipulating that only U.S. citizens were eligible to acquire the license. In a civil action against the city, Asakura argued that the ordinance was invalid because it violated the U.S.-Japanese treaty of 1911, which guaranteed that the citizens of each country would have the rights "to travel . . . to own or lease and occupy shops . . . to carry on trade . . . upon the same terms as native citizens or subjects." Washington State's high court upheld the validity of the ordinance.

The Supreme Court, however, reversed the decision and struck down the ordinance. Writing for a unanimous Court, Justice Pierce Butler began by observing that an established treaty was part of the "supreme law of the land" and therefore superior to the laws of a state. Second, the ordinance made it impossible for Asakura to operate his business,

thereby denying him the equal opportunity that was guaranteed in the treaty. Finally, in explaining why the business of pawnbroker was a form of "trade" specified in the treaty, Butler wrote:

> Treaties are to be construed in a broad and liberal spirit, and, when two constructions are possible, one restrictive of rights that may be claimed under it and the other favorable to them, the latter is to be preferred.

Thomas Tandy Lewis

FURTHER READING
Aust, Anthony. *Modern Treaty Law and Practice.* New York: Cambridge University Press, 2007.
Reuter, Paul. *Introduction to the Law of Treaties.* New York: John Wiley & Sons, 1993.

See also: Alien land laws; Asian immigrants; Japanese immigrants; Supreme Court, U.S.; Washington State.

ASIAN AMERICAN LEGAL DEFENSE FUND

IDENTIFICATION: New York-based nongovernmental organization established to foster Asian American civil rights through the provision of legal services
DATE: Established in 1974
LOCATION: New York, New York
ALSO KNOWN AS: Asian American Legal Defense and Education Fund; AALDEF

SIGNIFICANCE: Prior to the establishment of the Asian American Legal Defense and Education Fund (AALDEF), no reliable sources of assistance were available for special legal issues faced by the Asian American community in the eastern United States. Because of language barriers, racial discrimination, and other considerations, Asian Americans were often among the "forgotten" ethnic groups with limited access to those in power.

The first major influx of immigrants into the United States from Asian countries, particularly China, began during the mid-nineteenth century with the discovery of gold and the building of transcontinental railroads. Following the repeal of various nineteenth century exclusionary laws, the influx began to increase anew. By the end of the twentieth century, the Asian American community was growing rapidly, mainly through immigration, and was expected to reach a total of some twenty million people by the year 2020. Despite these developments, Asian immigrants were still to be found working in unsafe sweatshop conditions during the early twenty-first century and often had nowhere to turn for legal help. Human smuggling continued to be a problem, and its unfortunate victims cannot seek redress from the appropriate authorities because they face imprisonment or deportation. These are some of the constituencies served by the Asian American Legal Defense and Education Fund.

AALDEF PRIORITIES AND SERVICES

Among the important issues addressed by AALDEF for the benefit of immigrant and lower-income members of the Asian American community are voting rights, economic justice, employment (including hiring discrimination and labor and workplace rights), education, civil rights, anti-Asian violence, affirmative action, police misconduct, government benefits, and immigration issues, including naturalization assistance and human trafficking. The organization works with a relatively small permanent staff, a few of whose members are lawyers, and a contingent of several hundred volunteers, among them attorneys who serve on a pro bono basis. They work with Asian American communities across the United States, assisting an estimated twenty thousand annually, all without government funding but with support from foundations and corporations.

AALDEF provides its legal services free of charge to those unable to afford them and litigates cases that may have a wide-ranging impact on the Asian American community as a whole. The organization also provides legal training workshops for community organizers, community education that may impact thousands of people at the grass roots, training of students for potential careers in public interest law, and efforts to influence governmental policy to ensure equality for Asian Americans.

The fund also coordinates with other ethnically based interest groups, such as the National Association for the Advancement of Colored People (NAACP) and the Puerto Rican Legal Defense and Education Fund, to maintain hard-won gains in civil rights. It is also a founding member of the Public Interest Law Center in New York City.

One example of the assistance AALDEF provides occurred in connection with the events of September 11, 2001, including the terrorist destruction of New York City's World Trade Center towers. This disaster affected the Asian American community as seriously as members of other ethnic groups. Particularly hard-hit were residents and workers in New York's Chinatown, especially those in the restaurant and garment industries. AALDEF provided legal services to at least five hundred displaced workers and used a $100,000 grant to hire additional case workers for outreach to the community.

TWENTY-FIRST CENTURY ACTIVITIES

In 2008, AALDEF won a settlement of $4.6 million in back wages for thirty-six Chinese immigrant workers at a Manhattan restaurant. During that same year, it organized the first National Asian American Education Summit to bring together youth advocates and students from across the United States to discuss strategies for improving public school education. AALDEF represents clients in school districts across the country and files amicus briefs in education-related court cases, including those pending before the U.S. Supreme Court. Some of these cases concern controversies about English proficiency criteria for non-native English speakers.

Another example of AALDEF activism occurred during the 2008 presidential election. With record turnouts from first-time Asian American voters and those who had recently become American citizens, there were numerous problems with inadequate language assistance, misspelled names on election rolls, lack of appropriate materials in voters' native languages, and even evidence of anti-Asian hostility. AALDEF dispatched more than 1,400 attorneys, volunteers, and law students to numerous polling stations in areas with large Asian American populations to hear complaints and gather exit-polling data.

The 2008 national election also generated hundreds of complaints about voting problems that were registered on the AALDEF hotline. In 2009, the fund presented a policy report and recommendations about Asian American voter participation to a committee of the U.S. Congress. It identified obstacles to voting in eleven states and the District of Columbia. During the same year, AALDEF filed an amicus brief with the Supreme Court in a case relating to the enforcement of voting rights supposedly guaranteed by the Voting Rights Act of 1965. Meanwhile, the fund planned to work during the 2010 census to ensure that Asian American immigrants would be fully counted.

Roy Liebman

FURTHER READING

Asian American Legal Defense and Education Fund. *Asian American Access to Democracy in the 2008 Elections.* New York: Author, 2009. Report presented to the U.S. Congress about problems faced by Asian Americans in several states while voting during the 2008 elections. Available online in PDF format.

Kim, Hyung-chan. *A Legal History of Asian Americans, 1790-1990.* Westport, Conn.: Greenwood Press, 1994. Examination of legal issues relating to Asian immigrants, especially during their early years in the United States. Bibliography, index.

Outlook Newsletter. Biannual Asian American Legal Defense and Education Fund newsletter outlining the accomplishments of AALDEF in the period since the previous publication. Also available as an online PDF file.

Redondo, Brian. *Left in the Margins: Asian American Students and the No Child Left Behind Act.* New York: Asian American Legal Defense and Education Fund, 2008. Passed during the George W. Bush administration, the No Child Left Behind Act has not greatly benefited Asian American children. This AALDEF report enumerates the failings of the law. Available online in a PDF format.

SEE ALSO: Asian immigrants; Bilingual education; Chinese immigrants; Chinese Six Companies; Immigration law; Immigration lawyers; Issei; Japanese American Citizens League; Japanese immigrants; United Farm Workers; Vietnamese immigrants.

ASIAN AMERICAN LITERATURE

DEFINITION: Fiction, poetry, drama, essays, and other works written in English by Asian immigrants and Americans of Asian ancestry

SIGNIFICANCE: Through their writing, Asian American authors have portrayed the Asian immigrant experience as seen by themselves rather than through the eyes of American mainstream press and literature. Their early works focused strongly on the Asian American family and communal adaptations to life in America. As the Asian American community matured, its writers moved beyond the immediate immigrant experience, often featuring Asian American characters of many different ethnic backgrounds and often retaining a focus on Asia.

Toward the end of the nineteenth century, Chinese American immigrants were the first Asian Americans to write about their experience in English. Their primary impulse was to combat negative racist stereotypes held about the Chinese by the popular American press and literature of the day. In his autobiography, *When I Was a Boy in China* (1887), Yan Phou Lee, who converted to Christianity and immigrated to the United States to study from 1872 to 1875, sought to show that education could turn a young Chinese into a person suitable to fully participate in American society. A similar goal inspired Yung Wing's autobiography, *My Life in China and America* (1909).

EARLY ASIAN AMERICAN LITERATURE

The Chinese American author Edith Maude Eaton, who wrote under the pen name of Sui Sin Far, was the first Asian American writer fiercely sympathetic to common Chinese immigrants in Canada and the United States, the two countries where she lived after her birth in England. Her short stories and articles, first published in 1896, painted an accurate picture of the struggles and aspirations of the first Chinese immigrants in America who worked hard, menial jobs, lived in Chinatown enclaves, and endured racist taunts and violence. Her last collection of short stories, *Mrs. Spring Fragrance* (1912), was rediscovered and republished in 1995.

Eaton's younger sister, Winnifred Eaton, chose a different path. Adopting the Japanese-sounding pen name of "Onoto Watanna," she entertained readers with lighthearted and sometimes risqué romance novels and short stories with Japanese American themes, but without focusing on the darker sides of the immigrant experience. From her first novel, *Mrs. Nume of Japan* (1899), and including her greatest bestseller, *Tama* (1910), Onoto Watanna's Asian-themed fiction proved popular. During the 1920's, she turned to writing screenplays in New York City. After returning to Canada in 1932, she worked as a dramatist until her death in 1954.

Etsu Inagaki Sugimoto's autobiography, *A Daughter of the Samurai* (1925), introduced her readers to the Japanese American immigrant experience, albeit from an upper-class point of view. Sugimoto's subsequent fiction chronicled her return to Japan with her two daughters, followed by a return to America for her children's education, a move not uncommon among some Japanese Americans.

Younghill Kang's *The Grass Roof* (1931) was well received, in part because immigration to America was the goal of the novel's Korean protagonist. As the American public came to sympathize with China in its conflict with Japan, Lin Yutang's work *My Country and My People* (1935) became a bestseller. Even H. T. Tsiang's critical novel *And China Has Hands* (1936), about the oppressed life of a Chinese laundryman, saw publication.

Mainstream American taste for Asian American literature turned sour when Younghill Kang's second novel, *East Goes West* (1937), looked critically at European American society from an educated Korean American immigrant's point of view. Decades later, however, the work was considered an early Asian American classic.

WORLD WAR II AND THE 1950'S

Japan's attack on the U.S. Navy base at Pearl Harbor on December 7, 1941, not only brought America into World War II but it also brought decisive changes for the Asian American community that Asian American writers reflected in their literature. Pro-Chinese sentiment led to publication and success of Pardee Lowe's *Father and Glorious Descendant* (1943), a story about a Chinese American father and son published during the same year that U.S. Congress repealed the Chinese Ex-

clusion Act. Jade Snow Wong's *Fifth Chinese Daughter* (1945, revised 1950) depicted the daughter of immigrant parents finding her place within American society.

Lowe and Wong's literary popularity paved the way for the success of Chin Yang Lee's *Flower Drum Song* (1957), an insider's humorous look at San Francisco's Chinatown. The novel was also adapted into a popular Broadway musical in 1958, followed by a 1961 film version that featured an almost exclusively Asian American cast led by Nancy Kwan. Later Asian American critics faulted Chinese American writers of this era for being too accommodating to mainstream tastes, but most critics eventually acknowledged that these early works provided a nonstereotypical view of Asian American life as written by Asian Americans themselves.

Louis Chu's bitter *Eat a Bowl of Tea* (1961) presented a starkly realistic but always sympathetic look at the prewar, urban bachelor Chinese American immigrant community. Chu's novel initially failed to win a large mainstream readership before becoming a classic.

Japanese American literature was deeply affected by the internment in remote relocation camps of Japanese and Japanese Americans living on the West Coast from early 1942 until 1945. This infamous political event, for which the United States formally apologized many years later, became a key subject of Japanese American literature. It also delayed publication of Toshio Mori's short-story collection *Yokohama, California* from 1942 to 1949. Mori's stories perceptively and gently chronicle mostly prewar Japanese American life in rural California.

The internment camp experience also influenced the work of Hisaye Yamamoto, who began to publish in 1948. Her best stories were republished in *Seventeen Syllables and Other Stories* (1988). The impact of the camp experience on young Japanese American women was rendered also in Shelley Ota's *Upon Their Shoulders* (1951) and Monica Sone's *Nisei Daughter* (1953). John Okada's novel *No-No Boy* (1957) compared the equally bitter fate of two Japanese American men who said either "no" or "yes" to camp authorities who asked male internees if they were ready to renounce Japan and were willing to join the U.S. armed forces. Subsequent works of Japanese American authors, such as Jeanne Wakatsuki Houston's autobiography, *Fare-*

well to Manzanar (1972, with James D. Houston), continued to describe the camp experience.

REBELLION, CONTROVERSY, AND SUCCESS

During the early 1970's, a group of young Asian American authors rebelled against style and themes of much classic Asian American literature that they rejected for promoting subservient immigrant assimilation to the point of cultural self-denial. In their anthology *Aiiieeee!* (1974), writer-editors Frank Chin, Jeffrey Paul Chan, Lawson Fusao Inada, and Shawn Hsu Wong presented radical short stories, plays, and poems deeply antagonistic to Asian American conformity with mainstream American values. Chin's play *Chickencoop Chinaman* (1974) offered a cynical view of Asian American masculinity threatened by European American racism.

The 1970's and 1980's saw a substantial rise of successful Asian American writers whose focus on immigrant families and first- and second-generation Asian immigrant protagonists captivated an enthusiastic readership. Maxine Hong Kingston's *The Woman Warrior* (1976) became a critically acclaimed bestseller. Readers loved its thinly disguised autobiographical tale of a Chinese American girl growing up in Stockton, California's Chinatown who overcomes both outside indifference and Chinese misogyny with her belief in a mythic Chinese heroine. The book won Kingston the National Book Critics Circle Award.

On the stage, David Henry Hwang dramatized the Asian American immigrant experience. His first play, *F.O.B.* (pr. 1978, pb. 1983), alluded to the pejorative term "fresh off the boat" for recent immigrants, particularly Asians. His great critical success, however, came with his play *M. Butterfly* (pr., pb. 1988), which moved beyond the immigrant experience to dramatize traditional Western views on Asia and Asian femininity.

Since the 1980's, the growing ethnic diversity of Asian American writers has offered readers views of Asian immigrant experiences from quite different national backgrounds. Under the pen name Ron-

Frank Chin, the author of The Chickencoop Chinaman, *the first play by an Asian American to be produced.* (Corky Lee)

Amy Tan, author of The Joy Luck Club. *(Robert Foothorap)*

ton and Tan for what he called an anti-male bias and pandering to white audiences in their writings. Kingston and Tan rejected his criticisms by pointing out that their works were fiction about individual characters, not anthropological or literary studies of Asian American immigration. Both Kingston and Tan continued to enjoy success even as their fiction turned away from immigrant themes to issues of world peace, in the case of Kingston's writings, and to the inhumanity of the Burmese military dictatorship in Tan's *Saving Fish from Drowning* (2006).

THE IMMIGRANT EXPERIENCE

The 1990's also saw the rise of the poet and critic Shirley Geok-lin Lim, a first-generation immigrant from Malaysia. Her memoir *Among the White Moon Faces* (1996) won the American Book Award. Lim also brought further critical attention to Asian American literature through her work as a college English professor. Another Asian American writer and college professor, Bharati Mukherjee, published her first novel, *The Tiger's Daughter*, in 1971. Her novel focuses on the vaguely autobiographical journey back to India of a Bengali-born Indian girl educated and married in America. Mukherjee later turned to historical fiction, closing a two-volume tale of Indian rebellion against British colonialism in *The Tree Bride* (2004).

young Kim, the Korean American author Gloria Hahn wrote *Clay Walls* (1987), a moving account of a Korean family's coming to California during the 1920's. Le Ly Hayslip's memoir *When Heaven and Earth Changed Places* (1989) presented a Vietnamese woman's view of the Vietnam War and the postwar Vietnamese American immigrant experience. Bapsi Sidhwa's novels told of the Pakistani American experience, from *The Crow Eaters* (Pakistan, 1978; United States, 1982) to *A Pakistani Bride* (2008).

Amy Tan's runaway bestseller *The Joy Luck Club* (1989) told the interwoven tales of four sets of Chinese American mothers and daughters. The book depicts conflicts between first- and second-generation immigrants whose families make the transition from China to America. In 1993, the novel became a successful Hollywood film with an almost entirely Asian cast.

Igniting controversy, Frank Chin criticized Kings-

Many mainstream American readers continued to prefer writings by Asian American authors that focused on Asian American experiences, or at least on Asian topics. Jhumpa Lahiri's writings were successful in meeting this demand. Her first collection of short stories about first-generation Bengali immigrants, *Interpreter of Maladies* (1999), won for her the Pulitzer Prize for Fiction in 2000. In 2008, her novel about second- and third-generation Asian Indian Americans, *Unaccustomed Earth* (2008), topped the bestseller list of *The New York Times* during the week in which it was published.

As Asian American literature has matured, some authors have strived to move beyond immigrant themes and autobiographical works. In general, however, Asian American writers who have tried to do this have had limited success. For example, Cynthia Kadohata and Chang-Rae Lee both moved away from celebrated first works that focused on immigrant Asian Americans. Kadohata's *The Floating World* (1989) and Lee's *Native Speaker* (1995) were both successes. In contrast, Kadohata's science-fiction novel *In the Heart of the Valley of Love* (1992) flopped. However, she regained her audience with *Kira-kira* (2004), the story of two Japanese American sisters that won the Newbery Medal. Lee's novel *Aloft* (2004), with an Italian American protagonist, failed to attract critics and readers. Lisa See, who gained literary fame with her family memoir *On Gold Mountain* (1995), triggered by the rare occurrence of her Chinese great-grandfather marrying an European American, gave her subsequent works Asian—but not necessarily Asian American—themes. Her novel *Shanghai Girls* (2009) followed her heroines from China to America during the 1950's.

By the early twenty-first century, most Asian American literature still focused strongly on the Asian American immigrant experience and featured many Asian American immigrant characters. Those Asian American authors who sought alternative topics generally retained links to Asia. The crime series of Laura Joh Rowland, whose sleuth Sano Ichiro operates in seventeenth century Japan, was a noticeable example.

R. C. Lutz

FURTHER READING

Cheung, King-Kok, ed. *Words Matter: Conversations with Asian American Writers*. Honolulu: University of Hawaii Press, 2000. Interviews of nineteen Asian American authors who talk about the influence of the immigrant experience on their work.

Huang, Guiyou. *The Columbia Guide to Asian American Literature Since 1945*. New York: Columbia University Press, 2006. Comprehensive reference work with narrative overview, six review chapters organized by literary forms and genres, a bibliography of literary criticism, and an overview of periodicals focused on Asian American literature. Readable, accessible, and well researched.

Kim, Elaine H. *Asian American Literature: An Introduction to the Writings and Their Social Context*. Philadelphia: Temple University Press, 1982. One of the first studies of the subject; still widely available and influential. A good starting point for the study of the emergence of Asian American literature.

Leonard, George J., ed. *The Asian Pacific American Heritage: A Companion to Literature and the Arts*. New York: Garland, 1999. Written for high school students, this volume contains a section on literature that is particularly useful, as it discusses major Asian American authors and places their works in their social and historical contexts.

Oh, Seiwoong, ed. *Encyclopedia of Asian American Literature*. New York: Facts On File, 2007. Comprehensive work with author entries, bibliography of secondary sources, and list of major literary works. Especially good for the study of individual writers.

Srikanth, Rajini. *The World Next Door: South Asian American Literature and the Idea of America*. Philadelphia: Temple University Press, 2004. Scholarly analysis of Asian Indian authors that focuses on the interaction of literature and the immigrant experience. The book's last chapter, "Trust and Betrayal in the Idea of America," is especially perceptive.

SEE ALSO: Child immigrants; Chinatowns; Families; Intermarriage; Lahiri, Jhumpa; Lim, Shirley Geok-lin; Marriage; Mukherjee, Bharati; Sidhwa, Bapsi; Stereotyping.

ASIAN IMMIGRANTS

SIGNIFICANCE: Through almost an entire century after the first wave of Chinese immigrants to California laid a strong foundation of Asian immigration during the 1850's, Asian immigrants faced racist legal barriers seeking to exclude them from the United States. After these barriers were lowered during the 1940's and finally fell in 1965, Asian immigration flourished. By 2007, some 14.5 million people of full or partial Asian descent lived in the United States, accounting for almost 5 percent of the U.S. population, with early twenty-first century trends showing promise of continued growth.

Asian immigration to the United States began in earnest during the mid-nineteenth century, when the California gold rush attracted thousands of Chinese miners. By that time, Asian workers were also beginning to immigrate to the kingdom of Hawaii, which the United States would annex as a territory in 1898 and later make into a state. Immigration to Hawaii thus contributed to U.S. immigration. The indigenous peoples of Hawaii and other Pacific Islands that came under the control of the United States were not immigrants, but they are often counted among Asian Americans.

EARLY ASIAN IMMIGRATION DESPITE LEGAL BARRIERS

When the first 4,000 Chinese miners arrived in California in 1849-1850, they found significant legal barriers to Asians already in place. As early

as 1790, the U.S. Congress limited the right of immigrants to become naturalized U.S. citizens to free white people. The state of California tried to prevent further Chinese immigration by passing laws of its own in 1855 and 1858 that would later be ruled unconstitutional. The 1860 U.S. Census listed Asian residents for the first time. Almost all the 34,933 Asians in the country that the census counted were Chinese living in California; 90 percent of them were male. At that time, they accounted for only 0.1 percent of the entire U.S. population.

Passage of the Fourteenth Amendment in 1868 inadvertently aided Asian immigrants. The amendment explicitly granted citizenship to all persons born in the United States, which meant that children born to Asians in the United States were automatically American citizens. During that same year, the United States and China signed the Burlingame Treaty. That document affirmed the mutual right of emigration but granted only residency, not naturalization rights, to immigrants from each country. With the gold rush over, thousands of Chinese immigrants worked on the new transcontinental railroad that would link California to the East in 1869.

In 1869, the first Japanese immigrants arrived in California. Nevertheless, the 1870 U.S. Census showed that the vast majority of 63,199 Asians in America were still Chinese, 49,277 of whom lived in California, with only 55 Japanese adding to the Asian total.

The federal Page Law of 1875 outlawed importing immigrants against their will, transporting them in slave-like conditions, or bringing them into the United States if they were convicts or prostitutes. Hostile white Californians unjustly believed that many Chinese immigrants fell into these categories. The U.S. Census of 1880 counted 105,465 Chinese living in the United States, along with 145 Japanese, almost all in the West, particularly California.

FIGHT AGAINST LEGAL BARRIERS

In 1882, the U.S. Congress passed the infamous Chinese Exclusion Act. It pro-

IMMIGRATION FROM ASIA, 1850-1949

Source: Department of Homeland Security, *Yearbook of Immigration Statistics, 2008.* Figures cover all regions of Asia, including Turkey and other Middle Eastern nations, and include only immigrants who obtained legal permanent resident status.

hibited the further immigration of laborers from China for ten years, forbade Chinese laborers in America to bring in their wives from China, and affirmed Chinese ineligibility for naturalization. Only Chinese merchants and scholars were allowed to come. The act severely halted growth of the Chinese population in America. Consequently, the 1890 U.S. Census revealed an increase of only 2,000 Chinese over the previous decade, with a total of 107,472. There were also 2,039 Japanese U.S. residents. Facing hostility in California and the West, Chinese immigrants began to move to the Northeast, the Midwest, and the South.

While the Chinese Exclusion Act was renewed for another ten years, the 1890's saw a surge in Japanese immigration to America. To ensure a positive, family-based immigrant society, Japan encouraged the emigration of both men and women. In California, many Japanese took to labor-intensive farming, cultivating produce and flowers. The 1900 U.S. Census showed a total of 114,189 Asian residents and a tenfold increase of Japanese residents, to 24,326. The Chinese population increased to 89,863 against considerable legal odds.

In 1907-1908, a series of "Gentlemen's Agreements" between the governments of Japan and the United States established that no more Japanese laborers would immigrate to America. Instead, Japan promoted the emigration of women to help form Japanese families in the United States. The U.S. Census of 1910 showed 72,157 Japanese residents and 71,531 Chinese. For the first time, Japanese outnumbered Chinese in the United States. Indicative of the growing diversity of Asian immigrants, the census also showed, for the first time, 2,545 Hindus, who were mainly Asian Indians, as well as 462 Koreans and 160 Filipinos. Most of the latter were students who came after the Philippines became a U.S. colony in 1898.

The Immigration Act of 1917 established the Asiatic Barred Zone—a vast region of Asia from which no immigration to the United States was to

Chinese and Japanese women waiting within an enclosure to be processed at the Angel Island Reception Center during the 1920's, a period during which very few Asian immigrants were admitted to the United States. (AP/Wide World Photos)

be permitted. The zone included all of Asia with the exception of Japan, a World War I ally of the United States, and the Philippines, then a U.S. dependency. Coinciding with a rise of racist attacks on Asian communities in the United States during the 1920's, the Immigration Act of 1924 barred entry to all Asians other than Filipinos. However, the right of Filipinos to immigrate was terminated by a legal subterfuge in 1934. Despite these barriers, Asian immigrants were able to make their living in America, and their children treasured their U.S. citizenship. Ethnic Asian enclaves such as Chinatowns in major cities provided comfort to many Asians in face of white hostility.

WORLD WAR II AND AFTER

After Japan attacked Pearl Harbor on December 7, 1941, the United States reacted harshly against Japanese Americans. Executive Order 9066, signed by U.S. president Franklin D. Roosevelt on February 19, 1942, directed federal authorities to relocate from their homes on the West Coast all persons of Japanese ancestry, both aliens and U.S. citizens alike. Eventually, more than 110,000 ethnic Japanese were sent to relocation camps dispersed in remote regions of the Far West.

The internment order was the infamous high water mark of anti-Asian U.S. sentiment. The Chinese Exclusion Act was repealed in 1943, as the United States and China were wartime allies. Repeal of the discriminatory law carried much symbolic weight. By 1944, internees were starting to be released from the Japanese relocation centers, which were finally closed in 1945. Meanwhile, Japanese American volunteer soldiers fought bravely in World War II.

After World War II ended in 1945, U.S. immigration policy shifted positively toward Asian immigration. In 1946, Filipinos and Asian Indians were given the right to become naturalized citizens. In 1947, Asian American soldiers were allowed to bring home their Asian spouses. After Mao Zedong's Communist Party created the People's Republic of China in 1949, the United States granted refugee status to 5,000 Chinese studying in America.

The Immigration and Nationality Act of 1952

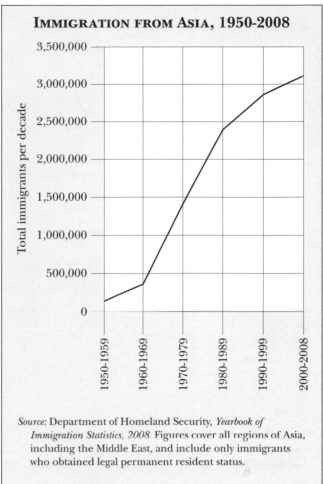

IMMIGRATION FROM ASIA, 1950-2008

Source: Department of Homeland Security, *Yearbook of Immigration Statistics, 2008.* Figures cover all regions of Asia, including the Middle East, and include only immigrants who obtained legal permanent resident status.

gave Asian immigrants the right to become U.S. citizens. The act set national quotas for immigration while establishing nonquota immigration rights for spouses and unmarried children of U.S. citizens. This provision greatly helped male Asian immigrants, particularly Chinese and Filipinos, bring in their wives after they obtained citizenship.

Indicative of the 1952 act's positive effect on Asian immigration, the number of Asian Americans living in the continental United States, which had risen from 254,918 in 1940 to 321,033 in 1950, climbed to 565,443 in the U.S. Census of 1960. As always, the census did not distinguish between citizens and alien residents. Nevertheless, its data offer a valuable tool to measure success of Asian immigration. When Hawaii became a U.S. state in 1959, it added some 315,000 Asian Americans to the U.S. population, as well more than 100,000

PROFILE OF ASIAN IMMIGRANTS	
Countries of origin	East, Southeastern, South, and Southwestern Asian nations
Primary languages	Chinese, Japanese, Filipino, Vietnamese, Hindi, Arabic, and many others
Primary regions of U.S. settlement	West Coast, Hawaii
Earliest significant arrivals	Mid-nineteenth century
Peak immigration period	After 1965
Twenty-first century legal residents*	2,856,706 (357,088 per year)

*Immigrants who obtained legal permanent resident status in the United States.

Source: Department of Homeland Security, Yearbook of Immigration Statistics, 2008.

people of either full or partial Hawaiian descent. In Hawaii, Asian Americans immediately won political power, as Daniel Inouye and Hiram Fong became the first two Hawaiian representatives in the U.S. Congress. In 1962, Inouye became the first Asian American senator.

BENEFITS FROM IMMIGRATION LIBERALIZATION

The Immigration and Nationality Act of 1965 finally did away with national quotas and established race-blind immigration. Instead of quotas for individual nations, as before, each nation could send up to 20,000 immigrants per year to the United States, including people with special skills. The Eastern Hemisphere, including Asia, was allotted an annual total of 170,000 immigrants.

The 1970 U.S. Census showed that 1,538,721 Asian Americans, including 100,179 Hawaiians/Pacific Islanders, lived in the United States. They accounted for 0.8 percent of the population. As only Japanese, Chinese, Filipinos, and Koreans were counted as "Asian Americans," Asian minorities from countries, such as India, fell into the census's "Other" category. Consequently, the total Asian American population was undercounted.

After communist regimes took power in Vietnam, Cambodia, and Laos during the mid-1970's, the composition of Asian immigration to the United States altered significantly. To welcome new Southeast Asian refugees, Congress passed the Indochina Migration and Refugee Assistance Act on May 23, 1975. The 1980 U.S. Census showed that of the 3,500,439 Asian Americans, including Hawaiians and Pacific Islanders, there were 261,729 Vietnamese living in the United States. Six years earlier, only 260 Vietnamese were known to be in the United States; most of them were students.

The 1980 census also revealed that the number of Asian Indians had risen to 387,223. This made them the fourth-largest Asian American community in the United States, after Chinese, Japanese, and Filipino Americans. Each of the latter groups numbered about 700,000 to 800,000 people. In contrast to other Asian immigrants, most Indians arrived in the United States already speaking English. Many of them were attracted by the booming American computer and electronics industries.

During the 1980's, Asian immigration to the United States doubled the population of Asian Americans, who numbered 7,273,662, or 2.9 percent of the total U.S. population, in 1990. The Immigration Act of 1990 sought to diversify immigration to America. This worked against Asian countries with many potential immigrants. However, family members were still given preferences.

The 2000 U.S. Census recognized the increasing national diversity of Asian Americans. For the first time, it listed six different ethnic categories, as well as "Other Asian." Also for the first time, people could be listed as members of more than one racial or ethnic category, reflecting the growing significance of interracial marriages. The census counted 11.9 million Asian Americans, including 1.7 million people with mixed Asian heritage, or 4.2 percent of the U.S. population.

Asian immigration to the United States continued strongly during the early twenty-first century. In 2007, the American Community Survey estimated that almost 13 million Asian Americans and 1 million "Asian/Caucasian" Americans were living in the United States, accounting for 4.7 percent of America's total population. At the same time, Asian Americans gained much greater visibility in all aspects of U.S. society, including politics, economics, and popular culture. The United States continued to attract Asian immigrants, leading to a strong growth of Asian American communities.

R. C. Lutz

FURTHER READING

Chan, Sucheng. *Asian Americans: An Interpretive History.* Boston: Twayne, 1991. Survey of key common dimensions of Asian immigrant experience in America from the 1850's to 1990. Good, college-level overview of the topic. Photos, maps, chronology, and bibliography.

Kim, Hyung-chan. *A Legal History of Asian Americans, 1790-1990.* Westport, Conn.: Greenwood Press, 1994. Look at the legal framework for Asian immigration with strong focus on legal control and exclusion during the late nineteenth and early twentieth centuries; discusses how liberalized immigration policy changed patterns of Asian immigration after 1952 and 1965. Bibliography, index.

Kitano, Harry H. L., and Roger Daniels. *Asian Americans: Emerging Minorities.* 2d ed. Englewood Cliffs, N.J.: Prentice Hall, 1995. Good, readable introduction. Covers key immigration laws, major Asian immigrant groups, and important events in history of Asian immigration. The last two chapters discuss issues affecting Asian Americans and their communities on the eve of the twenty-first century. Tables, bibliography, index.

Lee, Joann Faung Jean, ed. *Asian Americans in the Twenty-first Century.* New York: New Press, 2008. Collection of twenty-seven oral histories covering a wide range of Asian American immigrant experiences on the personal level. Interviewees came from East and Southeast Asia with backgrounds ranging from professionals to activists, politicians, and homemakers. Their stories illuminate past and contemporary immigration issues. Photos.

Novas, Himilce, and Lan Cao. *Everything You Need to Know About Asian American History.* Rev. ed. New York: Plume, 2004. Written in accessible question-and-answer format, very suitable for middle and high school students. Covers key issues and people. Illustrated.

Okihiro, Gary Y. *The Columbia Guide to Asian American History.* Paperback ed. New York: Columbia University Press, 2005. Comprehensive work with special focus on early Asian American immigration to Hawaii, hostility toward Chinese immigrants in America, internment of Japanese Americans during World War II, and contemporary issues of Asian Americans. Illustrated, with detailed bibliography, overview of visual and electronic resources, and index.

Takaki, Ronald. *Strangers from a Different Shore: A History of Asian Americans.* Rev. ed. Boston: Back Bay, 1998. Most widely available, accessible standard work covering major groups and events in the history of Asian immigration to America. Comprehensive survey with an eye for telling individual details, well written. Illustrated, notes, index.

SEE ALSO: Asian Indian immigrants; Cambodian immigrants; Chinese immigrants; Filipino immigrants; Hmong immigrants; Hong Kong immigrants; Indonesian immigrants; Japanese immigrants; Korean immigrants; Laotian immigrants; Malaysian immigrants; Pacific Islander immigrants; Pakistani immigrants; Taiwanese immigrants; Thai immigrants; Vietnamese immigrants.

ASIAN INDIAN IMMIGRANTS

SIGNIFICANCE: The Asian Indian diaspora followed three waves of immigration to the United States: The first wave occurred in the first decade of the twentieth century, the second during the 1970's, and the third during the early twenty-first century, when the highest level of immigration from India occurred. Accounting for more than 2.5 million people in 2007, Asian Indians constituted the third-largest Asian immigrant population in the United States.

Although most immigration from India to the United States occurred during the early twenty-first century, the earliest signs of international migration from India occurred after 1830, when Indian merchants, sailors, and indentured workers traveled on East India Company ships to North America. The 1900 U.S. Census reported that 2,545 "Hindus" whose birthplace was listed as India had settled in the United States.

FIRST WAVE OF IMMIGRATION, 1900's TO 1920's

Between 1907 and 1917, thousands of Sikh landowners and peasants left the Punjab in northern India to search the western shores of North America for employment and higher wages. First immigrating to Vancouver, Canada, Punjabi Sikhs settled in Oregon, Washington, and Northern California to work on the Western Pacific Railroad. Legally prohibited from bringing their wives and families, some young, male Sikhs married Mexican women, creating a "Mexican Hindu" culture. The small Sikh immigrant community remained faithful to its religious and cultural practices, establishing temple settlements for other Asian Indian travelers.

Leaving employment on the railroad and in the lumber mills, by 1910 Asian Indians began contracting for agricultural jobs in California, where there was a dire need for farmworkers. Comfortable and experienced working in the fields, Asian Indians moved from working as day laborers to tenant farmers. Transacting bank loans, Indians purchased acreage. By 1914, as prosperous landowners, the Asian Indian immigrants started moving inland to central California to establish independent ethnic agrarian communities. Hard-working and English-speaking, the Asian Indians posed little threat to the socioeconomic fiber of the region. However, by the 1920's the hostilities toward the growing number of "Asiatics" escalated as the competition between Asian immigrants and white workers increased.

ANTI-ASIAN LEGISLATION

As early as 1905, an association known as the Asiatic Exclusion League (AEL) organized to oppose Asian immigration. It launched an anti-Asian crusade toward not only the Chinese and Japanese immigrant populations but also the three thousand new Asian Indian immigrants who had arrived in California at the end of the decade. After years of fighting for congressional legislation to limit immigration, the exclusionists were successful in adopting a series of laws that led to turning away hundreds of Asian immigrants. The Immigration Act of 1917 (also known as the Asiatic Barred Zone Act) restricted immigration from Asia. Soon afterward, the Supreme Court ruled in *United States v. Bhagat Singh Thind* (1923) that Indians were not included under the "statutory category as white persons"; consequently, Indians were denied the right to naturalization, and previously naturalized Indians were stripped of U.S. citizenship.

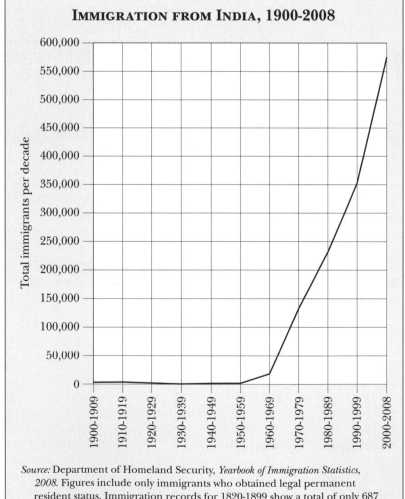

IMMIGRATION FROM INDIA, 1900-2008

Source: Department of Homeland Security, *Yearbook of Immigration Statistics, 2008.* Figures include only immigrants who obtained legal permanent resident status. Immigration records for 1820-1899 show a total of only 687 immigrants.

Sikh immigrants to California posing for a group portrait in 1910. (California State Library)

Seven years later, the Immigration Act of 1924 limited the number of new immigrants to 2 percent of the number of people from their country who were already living in the United States. Over the next twenty years, the number of Indians in the United States dwindled to fewer than 2,500. In 1946, the Luce-Celler Bill reinstated naturalization to Asian Indians and allowed an immigration quota for Indians and Filipinos; 6,000 Indians entered the United States between 1947 and 1965.

SECOND WAVE OF IMMIGRATION, 1965-1990

The tides turned under President Lyndon B. Johnson when he signed into law the Immigration and Nationality Act of 1965 (also known as the Hart-Celler Act), lifting the national-origin quotas system and issuing visas on the basis of preferred skills or family reunification. The initial post-1965 immigrants were professionals and their families; after the mid-1970's, the Asian Indian immigrants moved into small business ownerships and self-employment ventures in restaurants, travel agencies, and motels. Almost 40 percent of all Asian Indians who entered the United States after 1965 arrived on student or exchange visitor visas. By 1990, the Indian population had increased to 786,694.

With the passage of the Immigration Act of 1990, preference was given to immigrants with high technology-based skills, advanced degrees, and exceptional professional talents. Contributing to the "brain drain" in India, colleges throughout the United States hosted a significant number of Indian students, making India one of the top five sending countries. By 2000, Asian Indians constituted the fourth-largest immigrant community in the United States.

PROFILE OF ASIAN INDIAN IMMIGRANTS

Country of origin	India
Primary languages	English, Hindi, Urdu, Bengali, Marathi, Tamil, and others
Primary regions of U.S. settlement	California, New York, New Jersey, Texas, Illinois
Earliest significant arrivals	Early twentieth century
Peak immigration period	Early twenty-first century
Twenty-first century legal residents*	535,988 (66,998 per year)

*Immigrants who obtained legal permanent resident status in the United States.
Source: Department of Homeland Security, Yearbook of Immigration Statistics, 2008.

BEYOND 2000

The Asian Indian immigrant population increased by 38 percent between 2000 and 2005, becoming the third-largest immigrant population in the United States. Asian Indians have attained the highest level of education and the highest median income among all national origin groups in the United States. More than 40 percent are medical professionals, scientists, or engineers concentrated in metropolitan areas across the United States.

Entering the United States English-knowing, highly educated, socially and professionally connected, and geographically mobile has made Asian Indian assimilation fairly smooth. Asian Indian immigrants tend to identify themselves not with the Indian national origin group but with their particular regional, linguistic, religious, or professional subgroups. After arrival, Bengalis, Punjabis, Marathis, and Tamils tend to maintain their languages, religious practices, foods, and dress.

Tamara M. Valentine

FURTHER READING

Bacon, Jean Leslie. *Life Lines: Community, Family, and Assimilation Among Asian Indian Immigrants.* New York: Oxford University Press, 1996. Examination of the Asian Indian experiences in Chicago.
Jensen, Joan M. *Passage from India: Asian Indian Immigrants in North America.* New Haven, Conn.: Yale University Press, 1988. Cultural history of the immigration patterns of Asian Indians to the United States.
Joshi, Khyati Y. *New Roots in America's Sacred Ground: Religion, Race, and Ethnicity in Indian America.* New Brunswick, N.J.: Rutgers University Press, 2006. Analysis of second-generation Indian Americans and their identities.
Leonard, Karen Isaksen. *The South Asian Americans.* Westport, Conn.: Greenwood Press, 1997. Examination of the social, political, and cultural history of South Asian immigrant communities.
Sheth, Manju. "Asian Indian Americans." In *Asian Americans: Contemporary Trends and Issues,* edited by Pyong Gap Min. 2d ed. Thousand Oaks, Calif.: Pine Forge Press, 2006. Sociohistorical look at the diverse Asian Indian communities that developed across the United States.

SEE ALSO: Asian immigrants; Asiatic Barred Zone; Asiatic Exclusion League; Association of Indians in America; Bellingham incident; "Brain drain"; Immigration and Nationality Act of 1965; Lahiri, Jhumpa; Motel industry; Mukherjee, Bharati; Pakistani immigrants; *United States v. Bhagat Singh Thind.*

ASIAN PACIFIC AMERICAN LABOR ALLIANCE

IDENTIFICATION: Labor-activist organization
DATE: Founded on May 1, 1992

SIGNIFICANCE: The Asian Pacific American Labor Alliance was formed to address the workplace and community needs of a growing Asian and Pacific Islander population in the United States.

The Asian Pacific American Labor Alliance (APALA) convened for the first time on May Day, 1992, in Washington, D.C. That gathering drew five hundred Asian American and Pacific Islander labor and union activists from around the United States, including hotel and restaurant workers from Honolulu, longshore laborers from Seattle, garment factory workers from New York City, nurses from San Francisco, and supermarket workers from Los Angeles. The establishment of APALA was the culmination of several decades of Asian American labor activity.

AFFILIATION WITH THE AFL-CIO

After the mid-1970's, Asian American labor organizers in California worked to strengthen unionization efforts by holding organizational meetings in the larger Asian American communities of San Francisco and Los Angeles. Neighborhood-based organizations such as the Alliance of Asian Pacific Labor (AAPL) grew out of these efforts, forging stronger ties between labor and community and uniting Asian union staff members more closely with rank-and-file labor leaders. The creation of the AAPL was a successful local movement, but it soon became clear to AAPL administrators that to organize significant numbers of Asian American workers, a national organizing effort would be needed. Led by Art Takei, the AAPL solicited organizational aid from the American Federation of Labor-Congress of Industrial Organizations (AFL-CIO).

AAPL vice president Kent Wong attended the 1989 national AFL-CIO convention in Washington, D.C., to lobby for the establishment of a national labor organization for Americans of Asian and Pacific Islander descent. AFL-CIO president Lane Kirkland acknowledged Wong's lobbying attempts by noting the local accomplishments of the AAPL in California and recognizing the organizing potential of the burgeoning Asian American workforce.

Two years after that AFL-CIO national convention, Kirkland appointed a national Asian Pacific American labor committee, comprising thirty-seven Asian American labor activists. The committee spent more than a year planning the founding meeting of the Asian Pacific American Labor Alliance, finally releasing an invitation for Asian American and Pacific Islander unionists, labor activists, and workers to bridge the gap between the national labor movement and the Asian Pacific American community.

APALA CONVENTION

More than five hundred delegates attended the May, 1992, APALA convention to adopt a constitution and set up a governmental structure with a national headquarters in Washington, D.C., and local chapters throughout the United States. Organized in this way, APALA could receive recognition and legitimacy from a national administration guided by the AFL-CIO, while still using its powerful techniques of community organizing at the local level.

During the convention, APALA organizers and delegates recognized and honored Asian Pacific American labor pioneers whose achievements they believed had melded national and local unionization efforts successfully or who had made significant contributions toward heightening the recognition of Asian American laborers. Honorees included Philip Villamin Vera Cruz of the United Farm Workers union and Ah Quon McElrath of the International Longshore and Warehouse Union.

APALA conventioneers looked ahead to the organization's role in continuing such activism and achievement. They drafted a commitment document calling for empowerment of all Asian American and Pacific Islander workers through unionization on a national level, as well as the provision of national support for local unionization efforts. APALA also promoted the formation of AFL-CIO legislation that would create jobs, ensure national health insurance, reform labor law, and channel financial resources toward education and job training for Asian and Pacific Islander immigrants. Toward that end, a revision of U.S. governmental policies toward immigration was called for. APALA's commitment document supported immigration legislation that would promote family unification and provide improved access to health, education, and social services for immigrants. Finally, the document promoted national government action to prevent workplace discrimination against immigrant laborers and strongly supported vigorous prosecution for perpetrators of racially motivated crimes. APALA delegates passed several resolutions, which they forwarded to the AFL-CIO leadership. These documents decried the exploitative employment practices and civil rights violations alleged against several U.S. companies.

Convention delegates also participated in workshops that focused on facilitating multicultural harmony and solidarity, enhancing Asian American participation in unions, and advancing a national agenda to support broadly based civil rights legislation and improved immigration policies and procedures. From these APALA workshops, two national campaigns were launched. The first involved working with the AFL-CIO Organizing Institute to recruit a new generation of Asian Pacific American organizers. The second campaign involved building a civil and immigration rights agenda for Asian Pacific American workers that was based on APALA's commitment document and its convention resolutions.

Through the legislative statement of its goals and by lobbying for their societal implementation, the Asian Pacific American Labor Alliance was the first Asian American labor organization to achieve both national and local success. Although by the time of the 1992 APALA convention Asian Americans had been engaged in various forms of unionization activity for more than 150 years, the establishment of APALA within the ranks of the AFL-CIO provided it with more powerful organizational techniques. APALA was able to unite Asian Pacific workers, simultaneously integrating them into the larger American labor movement.

Cynthia Gwynne Yaudes

FURTHER READING

Aguilar-San Juan, Karin, ed. *The State of Asian America: Activism and Resistance in the 1990's.* Boston: South End Press, 1994. Explores the connection between race, identity, and empowerment within the workplace and the community. Covers Euro-American, African American, and Asian American cultures.

Espiritu, Yen Le. *Asian American Women and Men: Labor, Laws, and Love.* Lanham, Md.: Rowman & Littlefield, 2000. Examines the Asian American labor experience from a gendered perspective, asking how the oppression of Asian American workers has structured gender relationships among them.

Friday, Chris. *Organizing Asian American Labor.* Philadelphia: Temple University Press, 1994. Analyzes the positive impact of Asian Pacific immigration upon the formation of West Coast and Pacific Northwest industries between 1870 and 1942.

Rosier, Sharolyn. "Solidarity Starts Cycle for APALA." *AFL-CIO News* 37, no. 10 (May 11, 1992): 11. Summarizes the AFL-CIO conference report on the establishment of the Asian Pacific American Labor Alliance.

Wong, Kent, ed. *Voices for Justice: Asian Pacific American Organizers and the New Labor Movement.* Berkeley: University of California Press, 2001. Collection of interviews with Asian Pacific American labor organizers and workers.

SEE ALSO: Asian American literature; Asian immigrants; Chinese immigrants; Civil Rights movement; Issei; Japanese American Citizens League; Japanese immigrants; Pacific Islander immigrants.

ASIATIC BARRED ZONE

IDENTIFICATION: Region of the world from which new immigration was not allowed by federal law

DATE: 1917-1952

SIGNIFICANCE: Creation of the Asiatic Barred Zone by the U.S. government highlighted the country's negative attitude toward Asian immigrants during the early twentieth century.

The California gold rush during the mid-nineteenth century attracted an influx of Asian immigrants to the Far West. The arrival of the gold began to run out. After, Asians were forcibly removed from mining areas and blamed for the dry-up in profits from gold mining. This led to Congress passing the Chinese Exclusion Act of 1882, the first piece of legislation that restricted who could immigrate into the United States. Among other restrictions, the act denied Chinese immigrants entry into the United States, unless they obtained certification from the Chinese government.

American fear of Asian immigration continued into the twentieth century with the passage of the Immigration Act of 1917. This law created the Asiatic Barred Zone, which designated a region whose native peoples were barred from entering the United States. The act extended the exclusion formerly limited to the Chinese to all Asians and Pacific Islanders from Turkey and Saudi Arabia in the west to the Polynesian Islands in the east. The fact that President Woodrow Wilson's veto of this law was overwhelmingly overridden by Congress demonstrated the nation's nativist attitude at the time. The Immigration and Nationality Act of 1952 eliminated the Asiatic Barred Zone, improving American relations with Asian countries. Nonetheless, quotas and preferences based on occupational skills continued to limit Asian immigration through another decade.

Ramses Jalalpour

FURTHER READING

Lee, Erika. *At America's Gates: Chinese Immigration During the Exclusion Era, 1882-1943.* Chapel Hill: University of North Carolina Press, 2007.

Tichenor, Daniel. *Dividing Lines: The Politics of Immigration Control in America.* Princeton, N.J.: Princeton University Press, 2002.

SEE ALSO: Anti-Chinese movement; Anti-Filipino violence; Anti-Japanese movement; Asian immigrants; Asiatic Exclusion League; California gold rush; Chinese Exclusion Act of 1882; Chinese immigrants; Immigration and Nationality Act of 1952; Japanese immigrants.

ASIATIC EXCLUSION LEAGUE

IDENTIFICATION: Organization whose goal was to stop all Japanese immigration to the United States and disrupt the lives of Japanese already residing in the United States

DATE: Operated from May 14, 1905, until after World War II

LOCATION: San Francisco, California

ALSO KNOWN AS: AEL

SIGNIFICANCE: The Asiatic Exclusion League concentrated on opposing Japanese immigration, but it was against the immigration of all Asians, including Koreans and Hindus from India. It opposed Chinese immigration, too, but Chinese immigrants were already effectively blocked from entering the United States during the early twentieth century. By constantly reinforcing negative stereotypes of Japanese as "coolies" who threatened the American way of life, the league contributed to the passage of anti-Japanese legislation at the entry of the United States into World War II in 1941.

The Asiatic Exclusion League was a white supremacist organization active along the West Coast of the United States and Canada through the early twentieth century. Its supporters were primarily English-speaking labor union members who opposed all forms of Asian immigration because of the downward pressure on wages that Asian immigrants caused. Wage preservation was the reason most often cited for the need to restrict Asian immigration. The vast majority of Asian immigrants were unskilled laborers who did not speak English and could not qualify for labor union membership. They consequently would have had only a minimal impact on union wages.

The AEL was actually a latecomer in a series of anti-Asian immigration bodies and movements. The AEL feared massive Asian immigration, due to real or imaginary problems of social integration, language and cultural barriers, increased crime, and depressed wages. Tacitly understood among the various anti-Asian groups was the idea that America and its opportunities should be reserved for peoples of European descent, preferably English-speaking peoples.

Anti-Asian sentiment had long played a role in American politics, beginning with various pieces of legislation such as the Bayard-Zhang Treaty of 1888, which severely restricted new Chinese immigration, and the Geary Act of 1892, which prohibited all Chinese immigration for a period of ten years and required all Chinese residents in the United States to carry residency permits at all times or face immediate deportation. Anti-Chinese initiatives were on the AEL agenda, but the group's main targets were Japanese and Korean immigration. The AEL later expanded its definition of Asian to include Hindus from India, and it regarded all Asians as "coolies."

Although AEL membership comprised mainly labor union members and leaders, the organization was influential at the state level, particularly in California, whose state attorney general argued in favor of laws to prohibit Asians from owning property and mandated that Asian children should attend segregated public schools. The AEL also lobbied successfully on the national level, finding members of Congress willing to vote against legislation that would ease existing restrictions on Asian immigration. One particularly vehement anti-Asian congressman was E. A. Haynes of California, who denounced Japanese immigration as an evil influence.

After an earthquake devastated San Francisco in 1906, real estate agents and bankers banded together to help residents rebuild. Newspapers carried advertisements with designations as places where only white residents would be allowed to build homes and own property. These advertisements guaranteed that no Asians, no saloons, and no cheap apartments would be allowed in or near white-only residential districts. Around this same time, Asians were blamed for rising crime rates in West Coast cities because of their opium smoking and other drug crimes that were blamed on Asians.

The AEL helped pressure the U.S. Congress to ask President Theodore Roosevelt to restrict all Japanese immigration from Hawaii territory in 1907. The Immigration Act of 1924, signed by President Calvin Coolidge, restricted Japanese immigration to the United States from any location. Japanese immigrants already living in the United States were denied the option of applying for U.S. citizenship—a ban that lasted until after World War II. Meanwhile, the unprovoked Japanese attack on Pearl Harbor on December 7, 1941, galvanized long-standing American animosity against Asian immigrants, particularly Japanese living along the West Coast. President Franklin D. Roosevelt's February, 1942, Executive Order 9066, directing that all Japanese and Japanese Americans living on the West Coast be removed to intern camps, was the logical culmination of decades of AEL campaigns against the presence of the Japanese in the United States.

Federal government discrimination against persons of Japanese descent continued until 1965, when President Lyndon B. Johnson signed an immigration reform bill that granted persons of Asian ethnicity equal standing with those of European descent for immigration purposes.

Victoria Erhart

FURTHER READING
Hyung-chan, Kim. *Asian Americans and Congress: A Documentary History.* Westport, Conn.: Greenwood Press, 1996. Provides an analysis of U.S. policies on Asian immigration from 1790 to the 1990's. Discusses general stereotypes Americans held about Asians, and how those stereotypes in-

fluenced specific pieces of legislation restricting Asian immigration.
Ingram, W. Scott. *Japanese Immigrants.* New York: Facts On File, 2004. Young-adult book that focuses on when and why Japanese immigrants came to the United States. Also covers the history of attempts by Japanese to assimilate into American society and the legal and social discrimination they faced.
Takaki, Ronald. *Strangers from a Different Shore: A History of Asian Americans.* Boston: Little, Brown, 1988. Very readable history of Asian Americans by a leading Japanese American scholar that draws upon a variety of primary sources, from newspapers to court cases.
Teitelbaum, Michael. *Chinese Immigrants.* New York: Facts On File, 2004. Young-adult book that traces the history of Chinese immigration to the United States. Includes a time line of immigration events as well as U.S. legislation relevant to Asian immigration. Also touches on the role Chinese and Chinese Americans play in current U.S. economy and politics.
Tichenor, Daniel. *Dividing Lines: The Politics of Immigration Control in America.* Princeton, N.J.: Princeton University Press, 2002. Comprehensive history of U.S. immigration policy that highlights shifts in restrictionist policies.

SEE ALSO: Alien land laws; Anti-Chinese movement; Anti-Japanese movement; Asian American Legal Defense Fund; Asian immigrants; Asiatic Barred Zone; Chinese Exclusion Act of 1882; Gentlemen's Agreement; Japanese American Citizens League; Japanese immigrants.

ASSIMILATION THEORIES

DEFINITION: Theories derived from assumptions supported by empirical studies to explain the varied processes and paths that immigrants have undertaken to incorporate into the mainstream of the destination country

SIGNIFICANCE: Assimilation theories prevailing at different times are barometers of the political and socioeconomic environments experienced by immigrants. They have profound influence on social policies designed

Chinese American children playing football in California in 1928.
(Time & Life Pictures/Getty Images)

for the incorporation of immigrants and public attitudes that directly affect the perception and reception of immigrants. Different assimilation theories therefore could trigger the emergence of varied coping and adaptive strategies among immigrants as a response.

Several assimilation theories have evolved since the mid-nineteenth century as immigration to the United States gained scale. Anglo-conformity dominated much of the second half of the nineteenth century, when the majority of the immigrant stock were from northwestern Europe. The advent of rapid industrialization of the labor force around the turn of the twentieth century produced fertile ground for the emergence of the process theory and melting pot theory when sources of immigrants expanded to all over Europe and beyond. Ensuing theories of segmented labor market and multiculturalism took shape in the latter half of the twentieth century. As leading theoretical perspectives in contemporary times and in contention with earlier assimilation theories, they dominate the study of immigrants and influence social policies that address immigrant issues. Recognizing immigrants' proactive role, the new theories highlight the different incorporation strategies immigrants have employed in response to the mainstream political and socioeconomic conditions while taking comfort in their transplanted ancestral cultural traditions.

ANGLO-CONFORMITY

Early arrivals of Anglo immigrants from primarily northwestern Europe established the values and norms in the United States. Being the majority among all immigrants and with a head start in political and economic power, the Anglos upheld their cultural traditions as the standards, and Anglo-centrism was widespread during much of the nineteenth century. Immigrants of non-Anglo origins were compelled to discard their ancestral cultures upon arrival and conform to the prescribed Anglo way of life as the only option. Legislation was passed to discriminate against and to curtail the immigration of particular population groups. Immigrant enclaves were therefore consolidated as one of the most important protective strategies in response.

PROCESS THEORY

Studies of immigrants' incorporation in the first half of the twentieth century was heavily influenced by the process theory developed by the Chicago School. In an irreversible streamline, immigrants were to be incorporated into the mainstream through a progressive process of contact, conflict, accommodation, and assimilation. Instead of forcing rapid conformity, proponents of the streamline process acknowledged a stagewise progression of immigrants' incorporation. However, this theory fails to articulate the reciprocal cultural influence from the immigrants and suggests that some immigrant groups are unassimilable.

MELTING POT

Growing diversity of immigrants and rapid industrialization of the labor force during the late nineteenth and early twentieth centuries gave rise to the melting pot theory. Taking reference from a stage play titled *The Melting-Pot* (pr. 1908) by Israel

Zangwill that celebrated interracial marriage, the symbolism of the melting pot caught on socially. Proponents of the theory forecast the future of the United States as a melting pot. Immigrants of different cultural backgrounds with varied skin pigmentations dressed in their colorful ancestral costumes would walk through a symbolic melting pot upon arrival in the United States and reappear on the other end as members of a homogeneous culture. The melting pot theory acknowledges the reciprocal contributions of the immigrants to the mainstream.

SEGMENTED LABOR MARKET

The segmented labor market theory evolved in the second half of the twentieth century, mainly to explain the experiences of immigrants from non-European countries. Social and cultural resources of immigrants upon arrival and covert discrimination suggested or practiced in the mainstream have shaped the labor market into formal and informal sectors. In the formal sector, where greater potential for job security, promotion, and upward mobility is built into the structure, the presence of immigrants tends to be more limited. Immigrants, however, are highly concentrated, voluntarily or involuntarily, in the informal sector (for example, ethnic enclave economies), where there is a lack of structural buildup for security and advancement, by comparison. The segmented labor market theory suggests that there is unequal access to opportunities for immigrants and therefore retardation of immigrants' incorporation into the mainstream. The segmented labor market may also be a voluntary transition that cushions immigrants with necessary ethnic support and facilitates their incorporation into the mainstream at a more comfortable pace.

MULTICULTURALISM

Multiculturalism arose in the wake of the Civil Rights movement and the reform of the immigration policy during the 1960's. Rising presence of cultural diversity and the strengthening voice of immigrants and minorities have propelled social and political transformation. Diversity is perceived with growing appreciation, and multiculturalism highlights cultural diversity as enrichment to the mainstream. Cultural traditions and economic contributions of immigrants are respected, acknowl-

edged, and applauded. Instead of forcing immigrants to be assimilated to any prescribed cultural norm, different cultural groups are encouraged to express themselves in reshaping and redefining what the mainstream culture is. Multiculturalism is in strong contention with earlier assimilation theories in immigrant studies.

Linda Q. Wang

FURTHER READING

Glazer, Nathan. *We Are All Multiculturalists Now.* Cambridge, Mass.: Harvard University Press, 1997. Examines the reality of multiculturalism in American public school curricula and highlights the inadequacies of minority assimilation in the past and present.

Gordon, Milton M. *Assimilation in American Life: The Role of Race, Religion, and National Origins.* New York: Oxford University Press, 1964. Refines the streamline process theory into cultural and structural assimilation.

Kivisto, Peter. "The Transplanted Then and Now: The Reorientation of Immigration Studies from the Chicago School to the New Social History." *Ethnic and Racial Studies* 13, no. 4 (1990): 455-481. Critiques the streamline process theory and the melting pot model and proposes a change of venue in addressing immigrant studies through a pluralist and multicultural perspective.

Miller, John. *The Unmaking of Americans: How Multiculturalism Has Undermined the Assimilation Ethic.* New York: Free Press, 1998. Advocates the assimilation perspective through critiquing the inadequacies of multiculturalism.

Park, Robert E., and Herbert A. Miller. *Old World Traits Transplanted.* New York: Harper & Brothers, 1921. Empirical foundation to the streamline process theory of contact, conflict, accommodation, and assimilation.

Renshon, Stanley A. *The Fifty Percent American: Immigration and National Identity in an Age of Terror.* Washington, D.C.: Georgetown University Press, 2005. Advocates the significance of Americanization in twenty-first century national security.

SEE ALSO: Americanization programs; Anglo-conformity; Cultural pluralism; Ethnic enclaves; Eugenics movement; Hansen effect; Identificational assimilation; Melting pot theory; Social networks.

ASSOCIATION OF INDIANS IN AMERICA

IDENTIFICATION: National association of Asian Indians
DATE: Founded on August 20, 1967

SIGNIFICANCE: The association has provided a unified voice and sense of purpose for the nearly two million people of Asian Indian descent living in the United States, gathering them under the common bonds of Indian heritage and commitment to the United States.

In 1965, Congress passed a new Immigration and Nationality Act, repealing the Immigration Act of 1917 and opening the door to immigrants from India, who soon arrived in large numbers. Founded in 1967 and incorporated in 1971, the Association of Indians in America (AIA) is the oldest association of Asian Indians in the United States. The AIA has three goals: to support the social welfare of Asian Indians living in the United States and to ease their transition into the mainstream; to help members work for development in India; and to provide charitable, cultural, and educational means for Asian Indians to participate in American community life. The AIA is a grassroots organization with chapters throughout the United States. It has worked to gain political recognition of Asian Indians by the federal government, to lobby for the reunification of families, to promote scholarship in areas affecting public policy, to support voter registration, and to assemble resources to aid victims of natural disasters around the world.

Cynthia A. Bily

FURTHER READING

Bacon, Jean Leslie. *Life Lines: Community, Family, and Assimilation Among Asian Indian Immigrants.* New York: Oxford University Press, 1996.

Das Gupta, Monisha. *Unruly Immigrants: Rights, Activism, and Transnational South Asian Politics in the United States.* Durham, N.C.: Duke University Press, 2006.

Ng, Franklin, ed. *The Asian American Encyclopedia.* Tarrytown, N.Y.: Marshall Cavendish, 1995.

SEE ALSO: Asian immigrants; Asian Indian immigrants; Immigration Act of 1917; Immigration and Nationality Act of 1965; Motel industry.

ASTOR, JOHN JACOB

IDENTIFICATION: German-born American businessman
BORN: July 17, 1763; Waldorf, near Heidelberg, Germany
DIED: March 29, 1848; New York, New York

SIGNIFICANCE: John Jacob Astor established the first American monopoly with his American Fur Company (1808-1834) and devoted his business acumen and enterprising energies to controlling the fur trade from the Great Lakes to the Pacific coast and beyond to China, where he traded furs for tea and Chinese porcelains at great profits.

John Jacob Astor. (Library of Congress)

Born to German parents of French Huguenot descent Johann Jacob Astor, a butcher/village bailiff, and his first wife, Maria Magdalena Vorfelder, youngest son John Jacob Astor immigrated to New York City in 1783. He opened a musical instrument/fur store that he expanded into a worldwide fur empire with his American Fur Company and its subunits, the Pacific Fur Company and the Southwest Fur Company. The American Fur Company was organized into departments after 1822, with St. Louis serving as the western headquarters, controlling Missouri, the lower Mississippi River, and Illinois, and the northern department headquartered at Mackinac Island, dominating the Great Lakes and the upper Mississippi River regions. Originally based at Astoria at the mouth of the Columbia River in Oregon (until the War of 1812), Astor engaged trappers and Native Americans to secure the fur pelts that he shipped to Canton, China, and Astor's ships also traded with South America and Hawaii, where they purchased cargoes of sandalwood marketed in China (1816-1828). Astor's biography appeared in *Astoria* (1836) by Washington Irving.

Astor was selected as one of the directors of the Second Bank of the United States. Following the War of 1812, he profited from the elimination of Canadian and British fur trading competition. Astor advised President James Monroe on appointments to the port of New York. Astor carefully selected his ship captains and business agents who sold his goods abroad, and he supported a network of relatives whom he employed in his fur business, banking interests, and Manhattan real estate investments. Astor married Sarah Todd on September 19, 1785, and they had four children. His greatest benefactions were the Astor Library and the German Society of New York (1836), which dispensed information to immigrants.

Barbara Bennett Peterson

FURTHER READING

Madsen, Axel. *John Jacob Astor: America's First Multimillionaire.* New York: John Wiley & Sons, 2001.

Porter, Kenneth Wiggins. *John Jacob Astor: Businessman.* Cambridge, Mass.: Harvard University Press, 1931.

SEE ALSO: German immigrants; Melting pot theory.

ATLAS, CHARLES

IDENTIFICATION: Italian American physical fitness expert
BORN: October 30, 1892; Acri, Italy
DIED: December 24, 1972; Long Beach, New York

SIGNIFICANCE: Arguably the best-known physical fitness advocate of the first half of the twentieth century, the muscular but not muscle-bound Atlas became the physical model of the ideal American man. He epitomized personal transformation, self-reliance, and a quest to impress others.

Charles Atlas was born Angelo Siciliano to farmers in the Calabria region of southern Italy. After his parents separated when he was ten, he joined his mother when she immigrated to Brooklyn, New

Charles Atlas in a characteristic bodybuilding pose on a beach. (Popperfoto/Getty Images)

York, in 1904. As a teenager, Atlas suffered bullying from other young men. The experiences left him with a lifelong fear of weakness. In search of an identity, he found the ideal model of a man while viewing classical statuary at the Brooklyn Museum. Soon he pasted a picture of strongman Eugene Sandow on his mirror and religiously read Bernarr Macfadden's magazine, *Physical Culture.* Atlas undertook an exercise program with the aim of imitating Sandow. A friend likened the results to the mythological figure Atlas, thus giving the bodybuilder his professional name.

Atlas followed other strongmen into vaudeville. In 1921, he won *Physical Culture's* contest as "World's Most Handsome Man." A year later, he began the mail-order bodybuilding course that brought him fame. Advertisements in pulp magazines portrayed Atlas in a breechcloth alongside the slogan, "You, too, can have a body like mine." He became synonymous with health, muscles, and manliness.

Caryn E. Neumann

FURTHER READING

Fair, John D. *Muscletown USA: Bob Hoffman and the Manly Culture of York Barbell.* University Park: Pennsylvania State University Press, 1999.

Gaines, Charles, George Butler, and Charles Roman. *Yours in Perfect Manhood, Charles Atlas: The Most Effective Fitness Program Ever Devised.* New York: Simon & Schuster, 1982.

Grover, Kathryn, ed. *Fitness in American Culture: Images of Health, Sport, and the Body, 1830-1940.* Amherst: University of Massachusetts Press, 1989.

SEE ALSO: History of immigration after 1891; Identificational assimilation; Italian immigrants; Name changing; New York City; Schwarzenegger, Arnold.

AU PAIRS

DEFINITION: Live-in child-care assistants, who are typically young immigrant women, who work in exchange for room and board and opportunities to learn English

SIGNIFICANCE: Au pairs have helped satisfy the need of working parents to find care for their children at a reasonable cost while enabling young foreigners to visit the U.S.

American mothers traditionally worked within their homes. However, after the United States entered World War II in 1941, the growing needs of the national labor force and new economic demands on families led many women to take jobs outside their homes and to seek alternative arrangements for their child care. Parents who lacked available assistance from extended family members sometimes arranged for daycare services. However, a preferred arrangement among families in the middle and upper classes was to provide substitute care within their home. In-home services allowed children more continuity and permitted parents more flexibility in their schedules.

The pool of available live-in child-care providers generally included local college students, young women from midwestern states, and immigrant women. Caregivers from foreign countries, who often did not have proper working papers, afforded reasonably priced choices for child-care services. The initial legal provision for immigrant child-care workers was limited to visitor's visas for those who had bona fide friends or family members with whom they would live for up to one year. Because there were limited options available for hiring domestic child-care services at a time when demand was growing, many parents employed helpers who lacked legal documentation.

In 1985, the U.S. Information Agency (USIA) received a proposal from the American Institute for Foreign Study requesting the addition of a new category, "au pairs" (from French *au par* for "equal to"), to the exchange visitor program. This new classification was added to the list of opportunities available under the Mutual Educational and Cultural Exchange Act of 1961. It provided one-year J-1 visas to foreign students aged eighteen to twenty-six who wished to become au pairs in America. Au pairs were given the opportunity to experience life in America and receive room, board, and cash stipends in exchange for forty-five hours per week of child care. Despite some skepticism about the appropriateness of the new plan under this act, a pilot au pair exchange program was instituted, renewed, and maintained.

Under the official au pair program, which was overseen by a bureau of the U.S. Department of State, authorized agencies evaluated potential au pairs and host families and partnered the two. In contrast to "nannies," who are technically salaried employees, au pairs are legally regarded as members of their hosts' households and not as servants. However, although au pairs are not officially classified as employees, federal guidelines require that their stipends must meet minimum-wage standards.

Federally authorized au pairs are in the United States through an exchange program that is intended not to lead to permanent residence, but to allow one- to two-year stays. Au pair candidates must be young and proficient in English, have proof that they have completed their secondary education, and pass a background check. Many other child-care workers fill similar roles in U.S. homes. Some of these individuals have successfully obtained other work visas. Those people and their hosts who have not obtained legal work authorization can face potentially costly legal consequences if discovered. In 2001, the regulations for the au pair program were revised to include an alternative EduCare program allowing fewer hours for child care and more for studies. Au pairs may originate from any country with U.S. diplomatic relations, but most come from western Europe.

Cynthia J. W. Svoboda

FURTHER READING

Bloodgood, Chandra. *Becoming an Au Pair: Working as a Live-in Nanny.* Port Orchard, Wash.: Windstorm Creative, 2005.

Griffith, Susan. *The Au Pair and Nanny's Guide to Working Abroad.* Guilford, Conn.: Globe Pequot Press, 2006.

Miller, Cindy F., and Wendy J. Slossburg. *Au Pair American Style.* Bethesda, Md.: National Press, 1986.

Wrigley, Julia. *Other People's Children.* New York: Basic Books, 1995.

SEE ALSO: European immigrants; Families; Foreign exchange students; Higher education; Immigration Reform and Control Act of 1986.

AUSTRALIAN AND NEW ZEALANDER IMMIGRANTS

SIGNIFICANCE: The numbers of Australians and New Zealanders who have immigrated into the United States have never been great, but the increasing numbers of highly skilled and educated immigrants who began entering the country during the late twentieth century have brought with them the potential to make significant contributions to their new homeland.

The earliest waves of Australian and New Zealander immigration to the United States coincided with significant cultural developments. During the late 1840's and early 1850's, colonials from Australia and New Zealand arrived along with a flood of immigrants from other parts of the world to California after news of the California gold rush beginning in January, 1848. The discovery of gold represented an important push-pull factor between the United States and Australia and New Zealand during this period. Just as California's gold rush attracted thousands of Australian and New Zealand-

PROFILE OF AUSTRALIAN AND NEW ZEALANDER IMMIGRANTS	
Countries of origin	Australia and New Zealand
Primary language	English
Primary regions of U.S. settlement	West Coast
Earliest significant arrivals	1850's
Peak immigration period	1970's-1990's
Twenty-first century legal residents*	Australians: 21,232 (2,654 per year) New Zealanders: 8,663 (1,083 per year)

*Immigrants who obtained legal permanent resident status in the United States.
Source: Department of Homeland Security, *Yearbook of Immigration Statistics, 2008.*

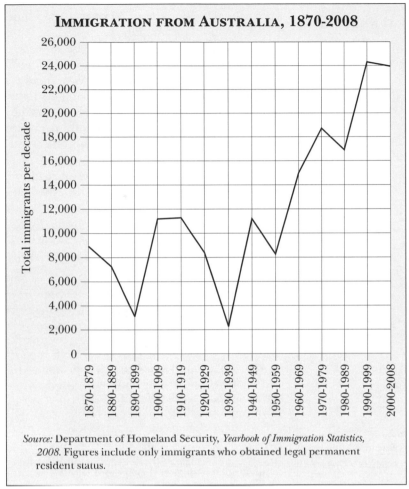

IMMIGRATION FROM AUSTRALIA, 1870-2008

Source: Department of Homeland Security, *Yearbook of Immigration Statistics, 2008.* Figures include only immigrants who obtained legal permanent resident status.

immigration steadily increased with 3,976 Australians entering the United States between 1951 and 1959. A sharp increase occurred during the 1960's, when 19,562 Australians immigrated to the United States. Another sharp increase in both Australian and New Zealander immigration during between 1971 and 1990, when more than 86,400 Australians and New Zealanders arrived in the United States. The numbers of people immigrating from Australia and New Zealand to the United States grew steadily between 1960 and 1990.

By 1990, the U.S. Census reported that slightly more than 52,000 Americans reported having Australian or New Zealander ancestry. This figure represented less than 0.05 percent of the total U.S. population. The 2000 U.S. Census reported the presence of 45,650 Australian-born noncitizens and 15,315 Australian-born U.S. citizens in the United States. A little more than one-half of these people were female.

ers hungry for gold, a gold rush that began in Australia during the early 1850's attracted thousands of American prospectors. Meanwhile, the building of faster steamships made long-distance transoceanic transportation cheaper and more endurable, and the opening in 1869 of both the Suez Canal and the transcontinental railroad in the United States increased the flow of people between the continental United States and Australia and New Zealand.

Between 1861 and 1976, 133,299 Australians and New Zealanders were recorded as entering the United States. This flow peaked during the years following World War II (1941-1945) as the American economy boomed. The war itself played a role in immigration. In 1944, American servicemen married 15,000 Australian women, who came to the United States as war brides. During the 1950's,

"BRAIN DRAIN"

As an immigrant group. Australian immigrants are comparatively highly educated. Among those counted in the United States in 2000, 26 percent held bachelor degrees, and 20.3 percent held graduate or professional degrees. Over the next several years, record numbers of Australians left their homeland. Most of these emigrants were younger and better educated than Australia's general population. Their major destinations have been North America, the United Kingdom, and the European Union. Emigrants have been motivated primarily by the attractions of higher salaries, better working conditions, better educational opportunities, and the possibility of better lifestyles in other countries. Although the numbers of emigrants have been relatively small in comparison to Australia's total pop-

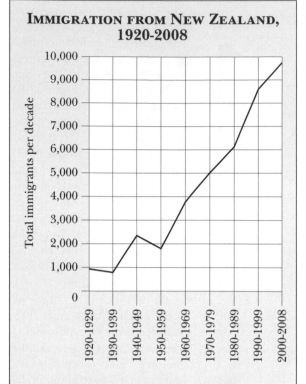

IMMIGRATION FROM NEW ZEALAND, 1920-2008

Source: Department of Homeland Security, *Yearbook of Immigration Statistics, 2008.* Figures include only immigrants who obtained legal permanent resident status. Incomplete earlier records show only 72 immigrants from New Zealand between 1870 and 1920.

ulation, the consequences of their leaving their country has been significant because they represent a much higher proportion of the country's future cultural, intellectual, and economic leaders. The other side of this issue is the significant contributions that these well-educated immigrants make to their new homelands.

Nicole Anae

FURTHER READING

Bedford, Richard, Elsie Ho, and Jacqueline Lidgard. "Immigration Policy and New Zealand's Development into the Twenty-first Century: Review and Speculation." *Asian and Pacific Migration Journal* 10, no. 3-4 (2001): 585-616. Argues that New Zealand's indigenous population constitutes the largest share of the total population and has the most prominent role in debates about the development of social and economic policy, including immigration.

_____. "International Migration in New Zealand: Context, Components and Policy Issues." In *Population of New Zealand and Australia at the Millennium,* edited by Gordon Carmichael and A. Dharmalingam. Canberra, A.C.T.: Australian Population Association, 2002. Useful overview of New Zealand's place in world migration patterns.

Cuddy, Dennis Laurence. "Australian Immigration in the United States: From Under the Southern Cross in the 'Great Experiment.'" In *Contemporary American Immigration: Interpretive Essays.* Vol. 1, edited by Dennis Laurence Cuddy. Boston: Twayne, 1982. Although now old, this study

U.S. VISITOR AND IMMIGRANT STATUS INDICATOR TECHNOLOGY PROGRAM

Australia's contribution to U.S. immigration and security strategies after the terrorist attacks on the United States of September 11, 2001, offers an interesting insight into global networking. The U.S. Visitor and Immigrant Status Indicator Technology program (US-VISIT), established by the new U.S. Department of Homeland Security, implemented an integrated entry and exit data system to record all entries into and exits out of the United States by covered individuals. It was designed to verify identities of travelers and to confirm their compliance with the terms of their admission to the United States. The key step in implementing these legislative requirements was a test conducted between June and September of 2005 in partnership among Australia, New Zealand, and the United States. The key airports involved were the international airports in Los Angeles and Sydney, Australia. The test evaluated the operational impact of the new technology as well as the performance of the e-Passports and the reader solutions being tested.

In 2006, Australian and New Zealander delegates, together with partners from a number of other Asia Pacific countries, worked in conjunction with the U.S. Department of Homeland Security to devise and endorse a multilateral framework for detecting and preventing the use of lost, stolen, and invalid passports for travel and entry.

remains an important source of information concerning Australian immigration to the United States before the 1980's.

Hugo, Graeme, Dianne Rudd, and Kevin Harris. *Emigration from Australia: Economic Implications.* CEDA Information Paper 77. Melbourne, Vic.: Committee for Economic Development of Australia, 2001. Study examining the causes and consequences of rising emigration from Australia.

LeMay, Michael C., ed. *The Gatekeepers: Comparative Immigration Policy.* New York: Praeger, 1989. Compares immigration policy and politics in the United States, Australia, Great Britain, Germany, Israel, and Venezuela. Helpful in understanding overall immigration issues.

Lynch, James P., and Rita J. Simon. *Immigration the World Over: Statutes, Policies, and Practices.* Lanham, Md.: Rowman & Littlefield, 2002. International perspectives on immigration, with particular attention to the immigration policies of the United States, Canada, Australia, Great Britain, France, Germany, and Japan.

SEE ALSO: "Brain drain"; California gold rush; History of immigration, 1783-1891; History of immigration after 1891; Immigrant advantage; Pacific Islander immigrants; Push-pull factors; War brides; War Brides Act of 1945.

AUSTRIAN IMMIGRANTS

SIGNIFICANCE: Although some estimates suggest that the numbers of Austrians in the United States have represented less than one-tenth of 1 percent of the entire U.S. population, Austrian immigrants and Austrian Americans have had a profound impact on the arts, sciences, and popular culture of the United States.

Austrian immigration provides an example of the difficulty of defining certain American immigrant populations because of changing borders and ethnic identifications. An analogue of modern Austria existed in ancient times as a province of the ancient Roman Empire. In later centuries, the region persisted, at various times and in various forms and sizes, as a duchy, as a powerful empire in its own

PROFILE OF AUSTRIAN IMMIGRANTS

Country of origin	Austria
Primary language	German
Primary regions of U.S. settlement	Northeastern states, West Coast states, and Florida
Earliest significant arrivals	1730's
Peak immigration period	Late nineteenth through mid-twentieth centuries
Twenty-first century legal residents*	3,686 (461 per year)

*Immigrants who obtained legal permanent resident status in the United States.
Source: Department of Homeland Security, *Yearbook of Immigration Statistics, 2008.*

right, and as a partner with Hungary in the Austro-Hungarian Empire.

The modern state of Austria was not established until 1918. Therefore, pre-1918 statistics on Austrian immigration cannot be authoritative for several reasons. For example, under the Austrian and Austro-Hungarian empires, members of many ethnic groups were technically Austrian citizens. These included Serbs, Czechs, and Slovenians. However, when these peoples, who were technically Austrian nationals, immigrated to the United States, American immigration officials did not always distinguish between ethnicity and national citizenship. For this reason, Austrian immigrants of Serbian descent might have been recorded as "Serbians," not as "Austrians." Conversely, immigration officials were also not always clear about distinctions between Austria and its fellow German-speaking neighbor Germany. It is likely that more than a few immigrants who should have been recorded as Austrians were listed as Germans.

FOUR WAVES OF IMMIGRATION

Four different periods in U.S and European history have seen the most significant numbers of immigrants from Austria. The first occurred before the American Revolution and was prompted by quests for religious freedom. Much of German-speaking Europe from the seventeenth through the nineteenth centuries consisted of dozens of small duchies and principalities and kingdoms. The religious preferences of their rulers—who could be either Roman Catholics or Protestants—were usually identified as the state religions. Citizens of other religious persuasions were often discriminated against, if not persecuted outright. This religious intolerance often led to emigration.

The first Austrian immigrants on American shores, who arrived in 1734 in what is now the state of Georgia, came from the Salzburg area, where Roman Catholicism was dominant. Several hundred in number, they established a community called Ebenezer not far from Savannah. After the American Revolution (1775-1783), one of their number, Johann Adam Treutlen, became the first governor of the new state of Georgia. When U.S.

president Bill Clinton later proclaimed September 26, 1997, to be Austrian American Day, he recalled the contributions of Georgia's early Salzburger pioneers.

The second major wave of immigrants began in 1848, when a series of small prodemocracy rebellions broke out in what would become modern Austria. The suppression of these mini-revolutions led to the immigration to the United States of many of the intellectuals who had waged them. Called the "Forty-eighters," these Austrians tended to settle in large American cities in the North and Midwest, where a number of them became active in the abolitionist movement.

The third immigration wave was the largest and took place during the first decade of the twentieth century, during which more than two million Aus-

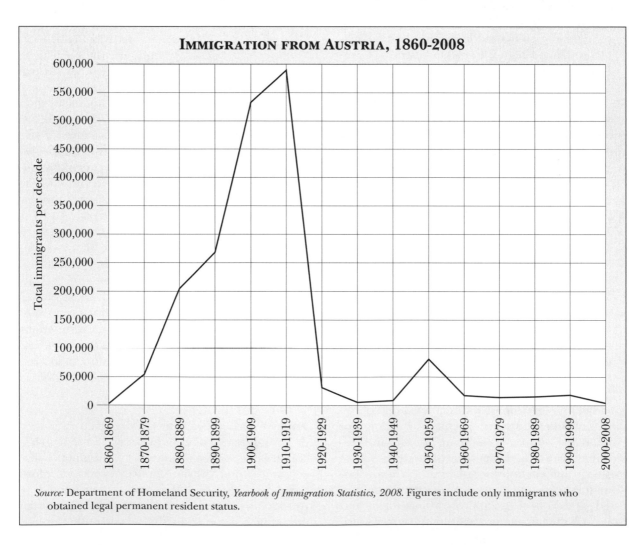

IMMIGRATION FROM AUSTRIA, 1860-2008

Source: Department of Homeland Security, *Yearbook of Immigration Statistics, 2008.* Figures include only immigrants who obtained legal permanent resident status.

Already well known before she arrived in the United States during the 1930's, Hedy Lamarr (right) became one of Hollywood's most glamorous leading ladies. In 1953, she naturalized as an American citizen. This film still is from Comrade X *(1940), in which she plays opposite Clark Gable (center) as a Russian streetcar conductor anxious to spread the communist message.* (Time & Life Pictures/Getty Images)

trians arrived on American shores, in large part because of the political and ethnic conflicts that eventually led to the outbreak of World War I. The fourth and final wave was motivated by World War II. During the years leading up to that conflict, many Austrian Jews fled their homeland to escape the Holocaust. After the war ended in 1945, more Austrians—this time from many backgrounds—immigrated to escape the desolation and disorganization left in its wake. From the mid-1930's through the mid-1950's, approximately 70,000 Austrians arrived in the United States. After Austria emerged as a prosperous, democratic country during the 1960's, Austrian immigration to the United States became negligible.

FROM CINEMA TO SKIING

Austrian immigrants have proven that even a small immigrant population can strongly affect the cultural and intellectual life of America, as Austrian immigrants and Austrian Americans have been prominent in a wide array of fields. From the earliest days of motion pictures, Austrian immigrants and their offspring have been prominent in cinema. Examples include silent-screen star Ricardo Cortez, the celebrated dancer Fred Astaire, actor Peter Lorre, and legendary screen star Hedy Lamarr. During the late twentieth/early twenty-first centuries, three of the best-known actors in America were of Austrian descent: Arnold Schwarzenegger, who was a superstar during the 1980's and

1990's and became governor of California in 2003; Erika Slezak, of *One Life to Live*, who is, after Susan Lucci, perhaps the most respected and recognizable American soap-opera star; and Natalie Portman, who played Princess Amidala in the enormously popular *Star Wars* films. Three of Hollywood's most respected directors of the early and mid-twentieth century were of Austrian descent—Fritz Lang, Otto Preminger, and Billy Wilder. One of the most popular musicals in Broadway and Hollywood film history, *The Sound of Music*, is based on the true story of an Austrian family that eventually immigrated to America.

Other areas of endeavor in which Austrians in America have triumphed have included law (Supreme Court Justice Felix Frankfurter), musical composing (Arnold Schoenberg and Erich Korngold), physics (Wolfgang Pauli), literature (Franz Werfel), and food preparation (Wolfgang Puck). A little-known area in which America has been greatly influenced by Austrian immigrants is that of skiing, as much of the art and practice of alpine skiing in the United States follows Austrian traditions first taught in American ski resorts by such immigrants as Hannes Schneider and Stefan Kruckenhauser.

Thomas Du Bose

FURTHER READING

Boernstein, Henry. *Memoirs of a Nobody*. Edited and translated by Steven Rowan. Detroit: Wayne University Press, 1997. Autobiography of a Forty-eighter that provides insights into a little-known source of American activism during the nineteenth century.

Leamer, Laurence. *Fantastic: The Life of Arnold Schwarzenegger*. New York: St. Martin's Press, 2006. Perhaps the definitive biography of the most famous Austrian American of all time, the bodybuilder and film star who became governor of California in 2003.

Naiditch, Hannah. *Memoirs of a Hitler Refugee*. New York: Xlibris, 2008. Similar to Perloff's book but broader in scope.

Perloff, Marjorie. *The Vienna Paradox*. New York: New Directions, 2004. Autobiography of a major American literary critic who was Jewish and fled Vienna as the Holocaust approached. Records the impact of specifically Viennese culture on Austrian and American thought.

Spalek, John, Adrienne Ash, and Sandra Hawrylchak. *Guide to Archival Materials of German-Speaking Emigrants to the U.S. After 1933*. Charlottesville: University of Virginia Press, 1978. Invaluable for historical or genealogical research into German/Austrian immigration during the mid-twentieth century, especially Holocaust-related immigration.

SEE ALSO: Albright, Madeleine; Citizenship and Immigration Services, U.S.; European immigrants; European revolutions of 1848; Frankfurter, Felix; German American press; German immigrants; Hamburg-Amerika Line; Holocaust; Schwarzenegger, Arnold.

AVIATION AND TRANSPORTATION SECURITY ACT OF 2001

THE LAW: Federal legislation designed to improve the security of transportation systems throughout the United States, with particular emphasis on airport security

ALSO KNOWN AS: Public Law 107-71

DATE: Signed into law on November 19, 2001

SIGNIFICANCE: The Aviation and Transportation Security Act was enacted following the terrorist attacks of September 11, 2001. In addition to instituting new security procedures, the act established the Transportation Security Administration to assess and amend security policies for all types of public transportation. The act made airport security and other modes of transportation the responsibility of the federal government and changed the way that Americans view travel.

Preceding the September 11 attacks, airport security was shared between airport authorities and commercial airlines. Security screening focused on searching for handguns and bombs (following the suitcase bombing of Pan Am Flight 103 over Lockerbie, Scotland, in 1988). The Aviation Security Improvement Act of 1990 and the recommendations of the White House Commission on Aviation Safety and Security (1996) were either ineffective or not implemented. Aviation security was secondary to concerns about economic efficiency, and there was a strong resistance to spending money to improve security. The Federal Aviation Administration (FAA) was focused on congestion and delays in civil aviation, and Congress was attempting to reduce flight delays by requiring the airlines to provide passengers with better information and to improve baggage handling. In 1999, a Fox News survey showed that 78 percent of respondents saw poor maintenance of airplanes as a greater threat to airline safety than terrorism. Although Great Britain and Israel had created strong passenger- and luggage-screening regulations, there were no such protocols in the United States.

On September 11, 2001, America's vulnerability to terrorist attacks was exposed when four commercial airplanes were hijacked and directed toward specific targets. Two of the airplanes were flown into the World Trade Center, destroying the twin towers. The third plane hit the Pentagon, while the fourth crashed into a field near Shanks-

ville, Pennsylvania, after passengers attempted to retake control of the plane. Nearly three thousand people were killed in the attacks. Although nine of the nineteen hijackers were given special security checks at the airports, they were not questioned or personally searched. Only their checked luggage was given an extra look.

On September 21, South Carolina senator Ernest F. Hollings sponsored an aviation security bill that was quickly discussed in both the House and the Senate. President George W. Bush, speaking in the lobby of Terminal A at Ronald Reagan Washington National Airport, signed the Aviation and Transportation Security Act (ATSA) into law on November 19, 2001.

SUMMARY OF THE AVIATION AND TRANSPORTATION SECURITY ACT

The purpose of the ASTA was to set up layers of security that would prevent future terrorist attacks. Once the ATSA became law, security in all types of transportation, including aviation, rail, other sur-

Travelers passing through a security checkpoint at St. Louis's international airport in October, 2009. (AP/Wide World Photos)

face transportation, and maritime transportation and port security, became the direct responsibility of the federal government. The act established the Transportation Security Administration (TSA) within the Department of Transportation, headed by an undersecretary of transportation. In 2003, the TSA became a part of the federal Department of Homeland Security. Important sections of the ATSA outline procedures for hiring and training screening personnel, who must be American citizens. Rather than being hired by private companies, those screening passengers and luggage at the 429 commercial airports are federal employees. All employees and law-enforcement officers who enter a secure area of an airport must have their identities verified. The ATSA mandates that cockpit doors be reinforced and remain locked during flight, and flight crews are trained to handle suspicious travelers. Following the September 11 attacks, the number of air marshals increased from thirty-three to more than a thousand. (The exact number is classified information.)

Even general aviation was mandated to make security changes, and those running flight schools were required to enhance background checks for foreign nationals who wished to learn to fly. Communication between various agencies was improved, and a "no-fly" list—a secret watch list maintained by federal authorities to prevent those suspected of terrorist ties from boarding commercial aircraft—was expanded. Deadlines for implementing certain requirements were also set. By November, 2002, a federal workforce was to be in place to screen all airport passengers and property, and by the end of 2002 all checked luggage was to be screened for explosives.

Although the ASTA covers all modes of transportation, the resources and focus have been on aviation. Subsequent acts have developed more regulations and assigned responsibilities to other agencies to provide additional security for maritime, rail, land, and other types of transportation.

IMPLEMENTATION AND PROBLEMS

New security procedures took effect immediately after the act became law. Parking to drop off passengers was not allowed, and restrictions for carry-on luggage were implemented. Access to departure and arrival gates as well as airport concourses was restricted to ticketed passengers.

Checked luggage was extensively screened, and all passengers—not just those with checked baggage—were prescreened. The Computer Assisted Passenger Prescreening System database (in place since 1997), along with the Advance Passenger Information System, provides information on potential security risks used to create a no-fly list. This list has caused problems and complaints about political and ethnic profiling. Screening of passengers at security checkpoints has also raised a number of issues, from privacy concerns regarding screening devices to complaints of racial profiling.

Despite complaints about invasion of privacy and delays with long security check-ins, most Americans accepted the provisions of the Aviation and Transportation Security Act. Travelers realized that the freedom to travel without layers of federal oversight and restrictions was lost on September 11, 2001.

Marcia B. Dinneen

FURTHER READING

Bradley, Elizabeth. "Safety in the Skies." *Women in Business* 55, no. 2 (March/April, 2003): 18-21. Discusses airline safety in the United States. Statistics from the Transportation Security Administration.

Downey, Mortimer L., and Thomas R. Menzies. "Countering Terrorism in Transportation." *Issues in Science and Technology* 18, no. 4 (Summer, 2002): 58-65. Argues for a well-integrated counterterrorism system to replace piecemeal tactics.

Johnstone, R. William. *9/11 and the Future of Transportation Security.* Westport, Conn.: Praeger, 2006. A former member of the 9/11 Commission, Johnstone investigates the causes of aviation security failure on September 11, 2001.

Levine, Samantha. "Toward Safer Skies." *U.S. News & World Report*, September 27, 2004, 32-37. Details improvements in aviation security since 9/11 and problems that still exist.

Smith, Norris, and Lynn M. Messina, eds. *Homeland Security.* New York: Wilson, 2004. Includes reprints of published articles on aviation security.

SEE ALSO: Citizenship and Immigration Services, U.S.; Homeland Security, Department of; McCarran Internal Security Act of 1950; 9/11 and U.S. immigration policy; Patriot Act of 2001.

B

BAYARD-ZHANG TREATY OF 1888

THE TREATY: Unratified treaty between the United States and China that was designed to resolve certain immigration issues involving the two nations

DATE: Signed in March, 1888

SIGNIFICANCE: The Bayard-Zhang Treaty attempted to prohibit all new Chinese immigration for twenty years and limit the right to return of Chinese workers who had temporarily left the United States for home visits in China. However, despite the severity of the treaty's immigration restrictions, they would prove more moderate than those of some later legislation.

Provisions of the Bayard-Zhang Treaty of 1888 were instituted by the U.S. government despite widespread public protests in rural China and the Qing government's refusal to agree to the treaty's restrictive terms. As early as 1868, the United States and China had agreed upon unrestricted Chinese immigration. However, this agreement, formally termed the Burlingame Treaty, was not ratified in its entirety by representatives of both countries, but portions of the agreement were nonetheless implemented.

Tens of thousands of Chinese laborers, overwhelmingly young adult males, immigrated to the United States during the decades before and after the U.S. Civil War. They worked on massive railroad construction projects in the West and in large-scale mining operations to supply the coal to run the railroads. So many Chinese immigrated and were so poorly integrated into American society that the first restriction on Chinese immigration for both males and females was passed under the Page Law of 1875. The act passed as a direct result of an 1875 decision by the Union Pacific Railroad to use Chinese laborers as strikebreakers in coal mines around Rock Springs, Wyoming Territory, the site of later anti-Chinese violence. Despite the fact that the Page Law violated the spirit and terms of the unratified treaty of 1868, it was only the first of increasingly restrictive treaties sought by the U.S. government, including the Bayard-Zhang Treaty.

Beginning in 1885, rising anti-Chinese sentiment resulted in widespread violence against Chinese laborers throughout parts of the West. The U.S. economy was depressed, and unemployment was high and rising. Despite the fact that many of the railroads paid all workers according to the same pay scale, many English-speaking miners and railroad workers felt that the presence of a large pool of Chinese replacement workers artificially suppressed wages. In Rock Springs, Chinese miners outnumbered English-speaking miners by a margin of two to one.

The local affiliate of the Knights of Labor was vehemently opposed to so many Chinese miners and urged English-speaking miners to demand that the railroad fire the Chinese and have them expelled from the country. Relations reached a flash point on September 2, 1885, when the English-speaking miners demanded that the Chinese miners join them to strike for higher wages. The Chinese miners refused. Later that day, English-speaking miners descended on the Chinese miners' camp and burned it to the ground. Many Chinese miners were attacked. Twenty-eight Chinese miners were murdered, and $150,000 worth of Chinese-owned property was damaged. The U.S. government sent federal troops to restore order as local law enforcement either refrained from taking action or joined the rioting. Eventually, the U.S. government paid the Chinese government some monies as compensation for the deaths and destruction of property, but neither individual Chinese miners nor their families received compensation.

As news of anti-Chinese violence spread to other towns in the West, other Chinese communities were attacked and the Chinese population was threatened with death or expulsion. In March, 1886, mobs attacked the Chinese community in Seattle. All the Chinese who were caught were taken to the port to be forcibly put aboard a ship sailing for San Francisco. Again, federal troops were necessary to restore order, and martial law was declared. Tacoma, Washington, also faced the same threat to public order, necessitating deployment of additional federal troops. Mortified by its inability to protect Chinese persons and property, the U.S. government asked the Chinese government to agree to the terms of the Bayard-Zhang Treaty. These terms included a twenty-year ban on all new Chinese immigration to the United States and severe restrictions on the return to the United States of Chinese immigrants who had temporarily left America.

The year 1888 was an election year in the United States. The race was very tight between Democratic incumbent Grover Cleveland and Republican challenger and eventual winner Benjamin Harrison. The economy was the most important campaign issue. Neither candidate gave any credence to protecting Chinese rights. Congress did not allow time for negotiations to permit the ratification of the Bayard-Zhang Treaty. Instead, it passed the Scott Act of 1888 that banned all further Chinese immigration and excluded any Chinese from returning to the United States. Opponents of the Scott Act argued in court that the act was unconstitutional, as it contradicted previous immigration arrangements. The U.S. Supreme Court ruled that immigration issues were a matter of national defense. Congress was authorized to pass whatever legislation it considered necessary to protect U.S. security interests. The Scott Act restrictions were expanded by the Geary Act of 1892, which prohibited all Chinese immigration for an additional ten years and required all Chinese in the United States to carry residency permits at all times or face immediate deportation.

Victoria Erhart

FURTHER READING

Chang, Iris. *The Chinese in America: A Narrative History.* New York: Viking Press, 2003. Examines U.S.-Chinese immigration relations using many Chinese sources.

Lee, Erika. *At America's Gate: Chinese Immigration During the Exclusion Era, 1882-1943.* Chapel Hill: University of North Carolina Press, 2007. Concentrates on immigration policies and their effects on both Chinese immigrants and American immigration officials charged with enforcing discriminatory laws.

McClain, Charles J. *In Search of Equality: The Chinese Struggle Against Discrimination in Nineteenth-Century America.* Berkeley: University of California Press, 1994. Overview of Chinese immigrant history and experience. Extensive treatment of the legal history of Chinese immigration.

Pfaelzer, Jean. *Driven Out: The Forgotten War Against Chinese Americans.* Berkeley: University of California Press, 2008. Uses many nineteenth century sources, including letters and newspaper accounts.

Sandmeyer, Elmer. *The Anti-Chinese Movement in California.* Champaign: University of Illinois Press, 1991. Covers California labor legislation and its impact on Chinese immigrants.

SEE ALSO: Anti-Chinese movement; Asian immigrants; Asiatic Exclusion League; Burlingame Treaty of 1868; Chinese Exclusion Act of 1882; Chinese immigrants; Coolies; Page Law of 1875; Railroads.

BELGIAN IMMIGRANTS

SIGNIFICANCE: As skilled tradesmen and farmers, early Belgian immigrants contributed significantly to the economic development of the United States. Those who came after World War II made important contributions to the scientific and intellectual development of the country.

PROFILE OF BELGIAN IMMIGRANTS

Country of origin	Belgium
Primary languages	French, Flemish (Dutch)
Primary regions of U.S. settlement	Northeast, Midwest
Earliest significant arrivals	1820's
Peak immigration periods	1881-1930, 1941-1960
Twenty-first century legal residents*	5,531 (691 per year)

*Immigrants who obtained legal permanent resident status in the United States.
Source: Department of Homeland Security, *Yearbook of Immigration Statistics, 2008.*

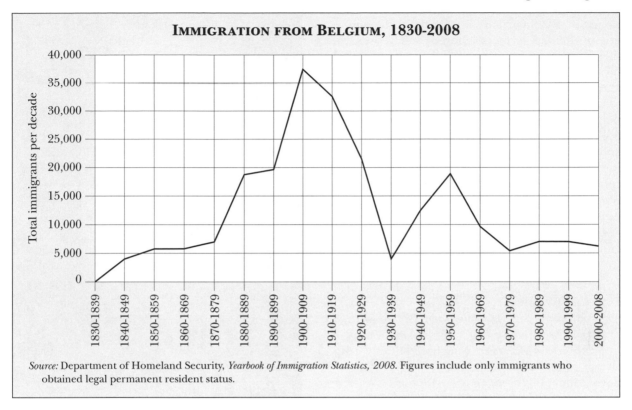

IMMIGRATION FROM BELGIUM, 1830-2008

Source: Department of Homeland Security, *Yearbook of Immigration Statistics, 2008.* Figures include only immigrants who obtained legal permanent resident status.

During the seventeenth century, a small number of Belgian Protestants fleeing religious persecution in Europe immigrated to the Hudson River Valley in what would later become New York State. However, the nineteenth century was the period when significant Belgian immigration to the United States began. Due to land shortages and a potato blight in Belgium in 1840, many farmers and farm laborers came to the United States from 1840 through 1884. The Belgian government actually encouraged emigration and skilled craftsmen including carpenters, brick masons, lacemakers, and glassblowers also left Belgium to find work and improved economic conditions in the United States.

After arriving in the United States, Belgians settled in areas where they could most easily continue to pursue the types of work they had done in Belgium. Farmers settled in the Midwest, especially in the Great Lakes area. Many Belgians settled in Wisconsin, where they found an abundance of fertile farmland. Glassblowers found employment in West Virginia, Pennsylvania, Michigan, and Indiana. Many of those skilled in trades were drawn to urban areas such as Chicago and Detroit. Skilled

Belgian tradesmen made significant contributions to Detroit's becoming a major manufacturing and industrial city.

Belgians quickly established close-knit communities in which their customs and traditions thrived. The Festival of Kermiss, the traditional Belgian harvest celebration, was first observed in the United States in 1858. Since then, it has continued to be celebrated in Belgian American communities throughout rural sections of the United States. These communities also founded self-help associations to assist community members who were ill or impoverished. In addition, the associations offered health and life insurance at a low cost.

Although Belgian immigrants maintained much of the culture of their native country, they did not segregate themselves from the general American population but were willing to assimilate. Learning English and becoming active in both the social and political lives of their new country, they quickly blended into American society and suffered much less discrimination than members of many other immigrant groups.

After World War II, another wave of Belgians

came to the United States. Unlike the earlier immigrants who were farmers, laborers, and tradesmen, these new immigrants were mostly well-educated professionals seeking employment in corporations and universities. From 1950 to 1970, few Belgians came to the United States. However; revisions in Belgian tax laws and a generally depressed Belgian economy prompted an increase in Belgian immigration for a short period during the early 1970's. Individuals born in Belgium make up a small percentage of the late twentieth and early twenty-first century immigrant population. However, many Americans can trace their ancestry to individuals who immigrated to the United States from Belgium before 1950.

Shawncey Webb

FURTHER READING

Amato, Joseph. *Servants of the Land: God, Family and Farm: The Trinity of Belgian Economic Folkways in Southwestern Minnesota.* Marshall, Minn.: Crossings Press, 1990.

Bayer, Henry G. *The Belgians: First Settlers in New York and in the Middle States.* 1925. Reprint. Bowie, Md.: Heritage Books, 1987.

Cook, Bernard A. *Belgians in Michigan.* East Lansing: Michigan State University Press, 2007.

SEE ALSO: Assimilation theories; Claiborne, Liz; Employment; European immigrants; French immigrants; Indiana; Michigan; Pennsylvania; Wisconsin.

BELL, ALEXANDER GRAHAM

IDENTIFICATION: Scottish American inventor and educator
BORN: March 3, 1847; Edinburgh, Scotland
DIED: August 2, 1922; Baddeck, Nova Scotia

> **SIGNIFICANCE:** Entering the United States at the invitation of a Boston institution and speaking excellent English, Bell may not have thought himself an immigrant until his first attempt to patent his telephone was rejected on the grounds that he was an alien. Once naturalized, Bell proudly proclaimed himself an American citizen.

Alexander Graham Bell around 1902. (Library of Congress)

Alexander Graham Bell's grandfather taught correct pronunciation and elocution, as did Bell's father, Alexander Melville Bell. Young Bell became adept at teaching "Visible Speech," the system of symbols his father invented showing the positions of the lips, tongue, and soft palate needed to reproduce all sounds. In May, 1868, Bell used Visible Speech for the first time to teach the deaf to speak English.

After both of Bell's brothers died of tuberculosis, his father moved the family to the more healthful climate of Canada, settling at Brantford, Ontario, in August, 1870. When the Boston School for the Deaf invited Bell's father to teach Visible Speech there, he sent his son instead. There were then no requirements that Bell hold a passport or have a visa to enter the United States, and Bell did not think himself an immigrant in March, 1871, when he traveled forty-five miles east to Buffalo, New York, and casually boarded a through train to Boston.

Bell found the city congenial, teaching at the School for the Deaf, becoming professor of vocal physiology and elocution at Boston University, and privately tutoring deaf students, including Mabel Hubbard, who later became his wife. He experimented at night, seeking a way to transmit speech over an electric wire. Bell was rudely awakened to his alien status when he tried to file a caveat (notice of intention to file a patent) with the United States Patent Office to establish priority as the inventor of the telephone. Told that, although aliens were eligible to apply for patents, only citizens could file caveats, Bell began the process of naturalization. He took out his first papers in 1874, which granted him most rights of citizens, except the right to vote. He did not complete the process and become a full citizen until November 10, 1882, by which time he had patented the telephone (1876) and moved to Washington, D.C., where he still could not vote in presidential elections.

Bell and his wife honeymooned in Great Britain, where his wife became pregnant and gave birth to their first daughter. Her birth there made the daughter technically a dual British American citizen, as was her father; British law counted all born in Britain as subjects of Queen Victoria for life. Because wives assumed the status of husbands under both British and American law, the entire family could have, but did not, consider themselves dual nationals.

Bell was proud of his American citizenship, specifically rejecting in 1915 the notion that he was a hyphenated American and flying the American flag at his summer home in Nova Scotia. At his instructions, the plaque marking his burial place at his Canadian summer home bears the inscription: "Died a Citizen of the United States."

Milton Berman

FURTHER READING

Bruce, Robert V. *Bell: Alexander Graham Bell and the Conquest of Solitude.* Boston: Little, Brown, 1973.

Grosvenor, Edwin S., and Morgan Wesson. *Alexander Graham Bell: The Life and Times of the Man Who Invented the Telephone.* New York: Harry N. Abrams, 1997.

Shulman, Seth. *The Telephone Gambit: Chasing Alexander Graham Bell's Secret.* New York: W. W. Norton, 2008.

SEE ALSO: British immigrants; Canadian immigrants; Canada vs. United States as immigrant destinations; Citizenship; Dual citizenship; Naturalization; Passports; Science.

BELLINGHAM INCIDENT

THE EVENT: Racially and economically motivated riot and expulsion directed against Sikh laborers
DATE: September, 1907
LOCATION: Bellingham, Washington

SIGNIFICANCE: During the first decade of the twentieth century, Asian Indian immigrants, most of whom practiced the Sikh faith, working in the United States met organized discrimination and even violence.

Asian Indians began to leave India around 1900 to earn money for their families in India and for the independence movement of India against Great Britain. Most were men and identified as members of the Sikh faith. Between 1900 and 1905, several hundred immigrated to the United States and British Columbia, Canada. Since Sikhs often understood English and were hard workers, some Canadian employers began to promote Sikh immigration. In 1907, more than two thousand Asian Indian men arrived in Canada, most of them Sikhs. More than one thousand Asian Indians immigrated to the United States in 1907, hundreds of whom were Sikh laborers crossing the border from Canada. Just south of the border, the town of Bellingham in Washington State had about 250 Asian Indian immigrants, mostly Sikh, working in its lumber mills by September, 1907.

Prejudices against Chinese, Japanese, Korean, and Filipino immigrants along the West Coast were strong by 1907, and the Asian Indian workers in Bellingham became targets, too. Movements against Chinese immigrants during the nineteenth century were driven by white workers' racism and fear of economic competition with the newcomers. These movements expanded into broad anti-Asian agitation during the twentieth century. In 1905 in San Francisco, the Asiatic Exclusion League formed to block Asian immigrants, particularly those from China and Japan. In Bellingham, the league had eight hundred members by 1907. While the radical Industrial Workers of the World criticized anti-Asian hostility, most unions supported it. On Labor Day, September 2, 1907, hundreds of union advocates marched in Bellingham against the Sikh immigrants. Calling the Sikhs "Hindus" (falsely believing that Asian Indians all practiced the Hindu religion), marchers demanded that mill owners fire all "Hindus" immediately.

Sikh workers reported for work on September 3, but that night roving vigilantes targeted Sikh residences. The next evening, September 4, a mob of 150 men and boys formed and surged through Bellingham, assaulting some Sikhs and forcing others from bunkhouses and mills into the basement of Bellingham's city hall. Up to five hundred participants eventually joined in the coercive roundup. Police officers cooperated, claiming that this calmed the vigilantes and reduced violence.

On September 5, with up to two hundred Sikhs held captive, Bellingham's mayor claimed that the city could protect anyone who wished to stay in Bellingham. However, the obvious failure of the police to stop the previous night's coercion convinced Sikh laborers not to trust the mayor. A Sikh spokesman stated that all "Hindus" would leave Bellingham by September 7. Approximately half went to Canada and half to California.

No attackers were brought to trial, and most white people in Bellingham apparently supported the expulsion, combining racism with economic fears to justify their approval. A few falsely claimed that Sikh men deserved expulsion because they insulted white women, but most argued that by accepting lower pay and inferior housing, immigrant Asian Indians undercut unions' efforts to improve economic benefits for white laborers. Waves of anti-Sikh, anti-Asian Indian protests spread from Bellingham north to Alaska and Canada, and south to towns in Washington State and California. Asian Indian immigrants would not return to Bellingham for many decades after the 1907 expulsion. Immigration from India and other parts of Asia to the United States was stopped entirely during the 1920's, but by the early twenty-first century Bellingham was a more welcoming home for Asian Indian immigrants and recognized the one hundredth anniversary of the Bellingham incident with apologies and commemorations against all anti-immigrant discrimination.

Beth Kraig

FURTHER READING

Allerfeldt, Kristofer. *Race, Radicalism, Religion, and Restriction: Immigration in the Pacific Northwest, 1890-1924.* Westport, Conn.: Praeger, 2003.

Jensen, Joan M. *Passage from India: Asian Indian Immigrants in North America.* New Haven, Conn.: Yale University Press, 1988.

Lee, Erika. "Hemispheric Orientalism and the 1907 Pacific Coast Race Riots." *Amerasia Journal* 33, no. 2 (2007): 19-47.

SEE ALSO: Anti-Chinese movement; Anti-Japanese movement; Asian Indian immigrants; Asiatic Exclusion League; Economic consequences of immigration; Employment; Industrial Workers of the World; Labor unions; Washington State.

BERLIN, IRVING

IDENTIFICATION: Russian-born American songwriter
BORN: May 11, 1888; Temun, Russia
DIED: September 22, 1989; New York, New York

SIGNIFICANCE: After immigrating from Russia as a child, Irving Berlin grew up in New York City, wrote songs that caught the spirit of immigrant New York, and eventually won fame for such mainstream holiday classics as "Easter Parade" and "White Christmas" and, most notably, the exuberantly patriotic "God Bless America."

Born with the name Israel Beilin, Irving Berlin was the eighth child of a Jewish cantor, Moses Beilin, and his wife, Leah. In later life, Berlin's only memory of his native Russia was of his home burning after an anti-Jewish pogrom. Carrying few possessions, his family left Russia and crossed Europe and the Atlantic Ocean to reach New York Harbor's Ellis Island, where the family name was changed to Baline, on September 12, 1893. Berlin was only five years old when his family then settled in the teeming tenements of New York's lower East Side.

When Berlin was thirteen, his father died. By then he was already earning money as a newsboy. He left home to reduce the family's financial pressures and worked as a song plugger and singing waiter at Bowery saloons. He played the piano but used only the black keys. Eventually, he bought a transposing piano that, turned with a crank, allowed him to play in other keys. With a friend, he wrote his first lyric, "Marie from Sunny Italy" (1907). A typographical error on the sheet music changed his name from "I. Baline" to "I. Berlin." Afterward, he went by the name "Irving Berlin."

Berlin's earliest successes were vaudeville songs such as "My Wife's Gone to the Country, Hurrah! Hurrah!" (1909). Many of his songs exploited the kinds of ethnic humor then popular. "Alexander's Ragtime Band" (1911) made him internationally famous. The first all-Berlin review, *Watch Your Step*, starred dancers Irene and Vernon Castle. American entry into World War I in 1916 marked a turning point in his career. Shortly after he became an American citizen in February, 1918, he was drafted into the U.S. Army. He performed his military service by writing a benefit show called *Yip, Yip, Yaphank*

Irving Berlin. (Library of Congress)

that was staged with an all-Army cast. One of the songs he wrote for that show, "Oh! How I Hate to Get Up in the Morning," became a favorite among soldiers.

During this period, Ginger Rogers and Fred Astaire performed Berlin's songs in *Top Hat* (1935) and *Follow the Fleet* (1936). The film *Alexander's Ragtime Band* (1938) contained a collection of his songs. He wrote both words and music for the honest, timeless songs that brought him lasting fame. Among the first was "When I Lost You," (1912), wrung from him by the death of his first wife, Dorothy Goetz, soon after their marriage. Another such song was "Always," his 1926 wedding gift to his second wife, Ellin Mackay, a wealthy Roman Catholic socialite who defied her millionaire father to marry the immigrant Jew. The headline-making marriage lasted until Ellin's death in 1988.

After World War I, as fascism and racism gained ground in Europe, Berlin evidenced his hatred of both and his deep loyalty to America. In his 1933 Broadway review, *As Thousands Cheer*, African American Ethel Waters sang "Supper Time," a bitter lament about lynching. In November, 1938, vocalist Kate Smith introduced Berlin's "God Bless America," which became an immediate and enduring patriotic hit. All the royalties that Berlin earned from the song went to the Boy Scouts and the Girl Scouts.

In 1942, after the United States entered World War II, Berlin created a new Army show, *This Is the Army*, for which he established the first racially integrated U.S. Army unit. The profits from that show and its 1943 film adaptation went to charities, and Berlin himself accepted nothing. Following Broadway performances and a national tour, the middle-aged Berlin took the show's troupe to Great Britain, Italy, and the Pacific theater of the war and continued to perform "Oh! How I Hate to Get Up in the Morning" himself.

Later film hits based on Berlin's music include *Holiday Inn* (1942), *Blue Skies* (1946), *Easter Parade* (1948), *White Christmas* (1954), and *There's No Business Like Show Business* (1954). Postwar Broadway musicals include Ethel Merman's *Annie Get Your Gun* (1946) and *Call Me Madam* (1950), both of which were later adapted to the screen. Berlin retired during the 1960's, recipient of many awards and honors.

Betty Richardson

FURTHER READING

Furstinger, Nancy. *Say It with Music: The Story of Irving Berlin.* Greensboro, N.C.: Morgan Reynolds, 2003.

Jablonski, Edward. *Irving Berlin: American Troubadour.* New York: Henry Holt, 1999.

Leopold, David. *Irving Berlin's Show Business.* New York: Harry N. Abrams, 2005.

SEE ALSO: Citizenship; Economic opportunities; Ellis Island; European immigrants; Jewish immigrants; Music; New York City; Sweatshops.

BERNAL V. FAINTER

THE CASE: U.S. Supreme Court ruling on the civil rights of resident aliens

DATE: Decided on May 30, 1984

> **SIGNIFICANCE:** Striking down a state law prohibiting aliens from working as notary publics, the *Bernal* decision asserted that laws discriminating against resident aliens must be assessed according to the demanding standard of strict scrutiny, thereby requiring a compelling governmental interest in order to be upheld as constitutional.

In a few earlier cases, including *Graham v. Richardson* (1971), the Supreme Court had applied strict scrutiny when examining classifications disadvantageous to aliens legally residing in the country. In *Foley v. Connelie* (1978), however, when approving a statute that barred aliens from working as state po-

lice officers, the majority of the justices endorsed a much less demanding standard of review.

In the case of *Bernal v. Fainter* (1984), the Court voted 8-1 that a Texas statute requiring notary publics to be U.S. citizens violated the equal protection clause of the Fourteenth Amendment. Writing for the majority, Justice Thurgood Marshall asserted that discrimination based on alienage would continue to trigger strict scrutiny. In an attempt to harmonize *Foley* and *Bernal*, Marshall claimed that the former had been based on the "political function" exception, which referred to government-sponsored positions that delegate a high degree of responsibility and discretion to enforce the processes of democratic self-government. In contrast to police officers and teachers, he found that notary publics enforced laws without exercising much discretion or authority.

Thomas Tandy Lewis

FURTHER READING

Bosniak, Linda. *The Citizen and the Alien: Dilemmas of Contemporary Membership.* Princeton, N.J.: Princeton University Press, 2006.

Hull, Elizabeth. *Without Justice for All: The Constitutional Rights of Aliens.* Westport, Conn.: Greenwood Press, 1985.

SEE ALSO: Citizenship; Supreme Court, U.S.

BILINGUAL EDUCATION

DEFINITION: Use of minority and majority language as media of instruction in all or part of the curriculum for non-English-speaking children in elementary schools

> **SIGNIFICANCE:** Civil rights laws and judicial mandates during the 1960's and early 1970's supported the need for bilingual education as a process to instruct large numbers of U.S.-born English learners and immigrant non-English-speaking children from Latin America, Southeast Asia, and other regions.

The influx of immigrant groups into the United States since the early colonial period long required that non-English-speaking newcomer children receive instruction in their home language. During the eighteenth century, school instruction throughout what is now Pennsylvania, Virginia, Maryland, and North and South Carolina was delivered in German, often to the total exclusion of English. Bilingual schools were also provided for the French students in Louisiana and Spanish-speaking children and other groups in early southwestern regions of the United States. Ethnocentric attitudes by English-speaking groups toward immigrants mainly from southern and eastern Europe and later Latin America and Asia displaced what had been a tradition of flourishing bilingual education.

LANGUAGE GROUPS

In early colonial America and through the late nineteenth century, there were no legal restrictions that prevented schools for immigrant students from using native (non-English) languages for instructional purposes. There were laws that required the teaching of English, but no explicit requirements that outlawed teaching in other languages. Communities chiefly in rural agrarian enclaves in early America wielded major control over their schools with little or no intervention from central legislative or administrative agencies. This allowed German settlers, for example, to preserve German schools, as in Pennsylvania, where they represented a third of the colony's population.

After the 1803 purchase of the Louisiana Territory by the United States, Louisianans used French extensively in government affairs and in social circles. Louisiana's 1845 constitution allowed the legislature to operate bilingually. A subsequent 1847 law authorized bilingual (French and English) instruction in the schools. As U.S. punishment for Louisiana's role in the Confederacy, the use of French in government and in the schools was banned. Nevertheless, dialectal variations of the French language could be found during the early twenty-first century among Cajun and Creole communities, just as the Amish people in Pennsylvania continued to use German.

Conquered Spanish-speaking groups in Texas, New Mexico, California, and other southwestern states after the Mexican War ended in 1848 initially experienced the same fate as the French speakers of Louisiana. A school law in New Mexico recognized the use of Spanish and English in the public schools. In 1850, the year California became a state, 18 percent of all education was private and

Roman Catholic. Many of the children were of Spanish and Mexican descent and were taught in the Spanish language by priests.

Soon after Texas became a state in 1845, Czech, German, Polish, and Dutch settlers joined with the more established Spanish-speaking Texans, known as Tejanos, whose roots in the state dated back to the time of Spanish domination. Early German communities are credited with establishing one of the first bilingual schools in Texas, the German-English School, founded in 1858. Located in San Antonio, this school not only was successful in providing instruction in German and English but also later adopted Spanish as a studied language. The small town of Panna Maria, Texas, was home to a large number of Polish immigrants who founded St. Joseph's Catholic School, an early testament to the bilingual tradition. Without a legal structure or central bureaucracy to control curriculum content and language requirements for schools, the Tejanos also were successful in establishing their own community-based educational institutions, such as the Concepción School of Duval County, founded in 1870.

Native American groups, such as the Cherokee, used bilingual materials to such an extent that Oklahoma Cherokees had a literacy rate in English superior to that of the white population of either Texas or Oklahoma. The literacy in native language among this indigenous people is reported to have exceeded 85 percent during the nineteenth century.

AMERICANIZATION MOVEMENT

The advent of centralized control of education as evidenced by the proliferation of state regulatory agencies for education throughout the country during the early twentieth century and the movement toward a nationalistic policy in the United States led quickly to a nationwide imposition of English-only instructional laws. The curriculum that sprang from the 1918 English-only law dictating the use of English in all Texas public schools was the beginning of a statewide effort to Americanize the immigrant groups, including the Spanish-speaking Tejano community. At the same time, there was an attempt to unify statewide education policy. Interestingly, the Texas English-language policy was not aimed at the large Spanish-speaking community but instead at the

German-speaking citizens of the state. German Americans bore the brunt as targets of retaliation throughout the country because of Germany's adversarial stance against the United States in World War I. The huge wave of Italians, Polish, Czechs, and other groups immigrating to the United States from southern and eastern Europe during the Industrial Revolution further exacerbated the rift between the majority population and minority language groups and committed the nation even more aggressively to assimilationist practices.

This pattern of state governments' enactment of English-only laws and efforts to integrate all non-English groups began during the late nineteenth century, when Wisconsin and Illinois approved policies for both public and church-operated schools requiring exclusive English instruction. Foreign language classes were exempted from the rule. Efforts to encourage assimilation became progressively coercive. In extreme imposition of the English-only laws, schools meted out various forms of punishment to nonconforming students. In Texas and other southwestern states and in Indian boarding schools, students caught speaking Spanish or native American languages in the schools were fined or physically punished for violating the English-only rule. These "melting pot" dictums were applied with such vigor that many non-English-speaking children, such as those of Mexican American descent, often had to spend as many as three years in the first grade learning English. Educators too were subject to the punitive provisions of the law. Teachers who violated the policy risked losing their teaching certificates.

RESURGENCE OF BILINGUAL EDUCATION

The English-only rule and other culturally exclusionary acts of the schools were at the heart of grievances driving the Civil Rights movement of the 1960's and 1970's. The hostile conditions of the monolingual schools, for example, were often cited by Chicano and Puerto Rican civil rights activ-

Arab American schoolgirls in a bilingual grade school class in Dearborn, Michigan, in 1995. (Time & Life Pictures/ Getty Images)

ists as inextricably connected with the poor academic achievement, low self-concept, and alienation of many of the minority-language student groups affected by the English-only restrictions. It was during this same period that segregated schools for African American children were declared unconstitutional by the U.S. Supreme Court and equality of educational opportunity for ethnic minority students evolved as a desirable goal for public education. Bilingual education emerged as an alternative to English-only education and was promulgated as a way to promote equity and justice in schools for language-minority students.

The signing of the Bilingual Education Act (Title VII of the Elementary and Secondary Education Act) in 1968 by President Lyndon B. Johnson was pivotal in making possible the return of bilingual education to the public schools. This was the first federal recognition that limited-English-proficient (LEP) children have special educational needs. The act initially targeted Mexican Americans, Puerto Ricans, Cubans, and other Latino minorities. These groups constituted increasingly large, poor, and working-class populations within the school systems of such U.S. urban centers as Los Angeles, New York, San Antonio, and Miami. Judicial support of the Bilingual Education Act was strengthened when in 1974 the U.S. Supreme Court ruled in *Lau v. Nichols* that LEP children could receive instruction in their native language while learning English. Equally significant was the 1982 *Plyler v. Doe* Supreme Court decision that allowed undocumented children "free access to public education."

Immigration into the United States primarily from developing countries since the mid-1980's has heavily affected the public schools and created the need for expanded bilingual and English as a second language (ESL) programs. Aided by the new and more liberal provisions of the 1965 immigration policy, coupled with cycles of national economic prosperity, immigration in the past thirty years has produced profound demographic changes in the United States. In particular, the foreign-born, non-European population has increased significantly.

Although immigrants have come to United States from virtually every corner of the world, Mexico and Spanish-speaking countries in Central America have dominated U.S. immigration. The impact of Latinos has been especially felt in public education. This group accounts for the largest enrollment increase in the schools since the early 1990's. These are children who are, for the most part, limited- or non-English proficient and account for the greatest number of English learners in bilingual and ESL education. While Spanish is the mother tongue of three in four English learners in bilingual and ESL programs, other languages spoken by elementary and secondary students include Vietnamese, Hmong, Cantonese, Korean, Haitian, Russian, Creole, Arabic, Urdu, Tagalog, Mandarin, Serbo-Croatian, Lao, Japanese, Armenian, Polish, and Hindi. California, Texas, New York, and Florida, states with the greatest concentration of immigrants, have each reported more than one hundred different language groups in the schools.

CONTINUING LANGUAGE DEBATE

Increases in the numbers of both documented and undocumented immigrants and concomitant growth of publicly funded services, including bilingual and ESL programs for newcomer group children, have fomented rising opposition to special language programs for and treatment of immigrant groups. English-only campaigns have targeted primarily the large immigrant population of Latinos, seeking to establish English as the official U.S. language and to forbid the use of Spanish and other non-English languages in government and education. Approval of English-only laws has met with some success. Sixteen states and many local municipal and county governments throughout the United States have enacted policies that prohibit the use of languages other than English by government agencies. In some states, these language-restrictive laws were passed during the early twentieth century, during upsurges of nativist sentiments. The rise of modern-day English-only initiatives has stirred anxieties about bilingualism and doubts about the merits of bilingual education. Bilingual education in particular is viewed by the English-only law advocates as an obstacle for immigrant children in learning English, thereby severely retarding their assimilation into mainstream U.S. society.

Proponents for greater linguistic and cultural tolerance, such as the American Civil Liberties Union (ACLU) and language rights groups, argue that the "sink or swim" English-only experience of past immigrants was detrimental to their success in school. In 1911, the U.S. Immigration Service found, for example, that 77 percent of Italian, 60 percent of Russian, and 51 percent of German immigrant children were one or more grade levels behind in school compared to 28 percent of U.S.-born white children. English-only laws, according to the ACLU of Florida, "disparage the immigrants' native languages [and] assault the rights of the people who speak the languages."

One of the principal advocates for immigrant and U.S.-born language-minority students is the National Association for Bilingual Education (NABE). Since its founding in 1976, NABE has confronted political attacks on language-minority communities, such as the English-only movement and anti-bilingual education initiatives. The organization has advocated for strong civil rights policies and aggressive enforcement of the *Lau v. Nichols* decision.

Rudy Rodríguez

FURTHER READING

Blanton, Carlos Kevin. *The Strange Career of Bilingual Education in Texas, 1836-1981.* College Station: Texas A&M Press, 2004. Historical account of Texas's bilingual tradition and how various immigrant groups, including Spanish-speaking Tejano groups, adapted to or resisted government laws to assimilate into the mainstream English-speaking culture.

Crawford, James. *At War with Diversity: U.S. Language Policy in an Age of Anxiety.* Buffalo, N.Y.: Multilingual Matters, 2000. Penetrating discussion of the debate engendered by the English-only movement.

_____. *Educating English Learners: Language Diversity in the Classroom.* 5th ed. Los Angeles: Bilingual Educational Services, 2004. Focuses on the students in bilingual and ESL programs and politics surrounding their education.

González, Josué M. "Coming of Age in Bilingual/Bicultural Education: A Historical Perspective." *Inequality in Education* 19 (February, 1975): 5-17. Overview of the historical development of bilingual education in the United States.

SEE ALSO: Bilingual Education Act of 1968; Chicano movement; Civil Rights movement; Educa-

tion; English as a second language; English-only and official English movements; Language issues; Latin American immigrants; *Lau v. Nichols*; Mexican immigrants; *Plyler v. Doe.*

BILINGUAL EDUCATION ACT OF 1968

THE LAW: Federal legislation that provided funding to school districts to develop bilingual education programs

ALSO KNOWN AS: Title VII of the Elementary and Secondary Education Act of 1965; Public Law 90-247

DATE: Signed into law on January 2, 1968

SIGNIFICANCE: The Bilingual Education Act was the first federal legislation to address the unique educational needs of students with limited English-speaking ability (later called "limited English proficient"). It set the stage for further legislation regarding equality of educational opportunity for language minorities.

From 1921 to 1965, immigration to the United States was significantly restricted by the national origin system, which placed a quota on the number of immigrants from any given country. Due to the specifications of the system, immigration from non-European nations was particularly restricted. In 1965, these restrictions were lifted with the passage of the Immigration and Nationality Act. As a result of this new legislation, there was a significant increase in the number of immigrants from non-European countries, which had a profound impact on the face of the nation. The effects of increased numbers were felt in many societal institutions, and new issues arose with regard to integrating this diverse population into society. The education system in particular experienced a significant shift in immigrant composition. Schools were faced with large numbers of immigrant children who did not speak English as their first language.

In 1967, concerned about the academic performance and attainment of Spanish-speaking children, Senator Ralph Yarborough of Texas proposed a bill that would provide assistance to schools serving large populations of Spanish-speaking children. The bill would eventually be passed as an amendment to the Elementary and Secondary Education Act of 1965 and became officially known as the Bilingual Education Act of 1968. The act in its final form addressed the needs of any child of "limited English-speaking ability" (section 702). Through federal grants, assistance would be provided to school districts that wished to develop bilingual education programs. Funds could be used for program development and research, staff training, and educational resources. Schools serving high populations of low-income children were to be the primary beneficiaries. The goal was to encourage school districts to incorporate native-language instruction. Participation was voluntary, and the government refrained from providing specific guidelines with regard to the types of programs to be developed.

Although the Bilingual Education Act has been amended several times since its passage in 1968, some of the most substantial amendments were enacted in 1974. These amendments were influenced by a Supreme Court ruling that year in *Lau v. Nichols*, a case initiated on behalf of Chinese students in San Francisco's schools. Because they had limited skills in English, the students were performing poorly in school. It was argued that they were therefore receiving an unequal education. The Supreme Court agreed, stating that equal educational opportunity consisted of more than just equal educational treatment. The Bilingual Education Act was amended to address these concerns. The 1974 amendments clarified program goals, more clearly defined bilingual education programs, helped to establish regional support centers, and provided funding for efforts to develop the programs (curricula, staff, and research). The amended act provided new grants for technical assistance, special training programs, and a clearinghouse to disseminate information. The criterion that only low-income students could be beneficiaries was removed.

Amy J. Orr

FURTHER READING

Anderson, Theodore. "Bilingual Education: The American Experience." *The Modern Language Journal* 55, no. 7 (1971): 427-440.

Lyons, James J. "The Past and Future Directions of Federal Bilingual-Education Policy." *Annals of the American Academy of Political and Social Science* 508 (1990): 66-80.

Wiese, Ann-Marie, and Eugene E. Garcia. "The Bilingual Education Act: Language Minority Students and U.S. Federal Educational Policy." *International Journal of Bilingual Education and Bilingualism* 4, no. 4 (2001): 29-48.

SEE ALSO: Bilingual education; Child immigrants; Education; English as a second language; English-only and official English movements; Immigration and Nationality Act of 1965; Language issues; *Lau v. Nichols*; Quota systems.

BIRTH CONTROL MOVEMENT

THE EVENT: National movement to encourage the use of birth control methods

DATE: Emerged after 1914, when term "birth control" was coined

SIGNIFICANCE: Starting with the efforts of Margaret Sanger and the National Birth Control League, attempts to promote family planning through contraceptive use among recently arrived immigrant groups have proven extremely controversial and have closely paralleled the national debates over such divisive issues as eugenics and reproductive rights.

As waves of immigrants from southern and eastern Europe arrived on American shores in the decades leading up to World War I (1914-1918), a backlash arose among native-born intellectuals who feared that this influx would lead to what sociologist Edward Alsworth Ross termed "race suicide." In seminal and widely influential works such as *Social Control* (1901) and *The Old World in the New: The Significance of Past and Present Immigration to the American People* (1914), Ross argued that increased fertility rates among immigrants of Slavic and Mediterranean ancestry, whom he believed to be, on average, less intelligent than Americans of Anglo-Saxon descent, threatened to undermine American national prosperity. The ideas of Ross and fellow eugenicist Charles Davenport heavily influenced President Theodore Roosevelt. From 1901 to 1909, when he was in office, Roosevelt spoke frequently of the danger that allegedly high fertility rates among new immigrants posed to the United States. He argued that women of English descent had a moral obligation to produce more offspring to offset immigrant birthrates. Although later scholarship would find that second-generation immigrants actually had relatively low fertility rates during the early twentieth century, the public perception that American cities were being swamped with the children of recent immigrants led to efforts to decrease the birth rate among these newcomers.

FROM EUGENICS TO BIRTH CONTROL

One woman highly influenced by the work of eugenic theorists was Margaret Sanger, a nurse who worked with immigrants living in New York City's lower East Side. Sanger had witnessed firsthand the toll that multiple, unwanted pregnancies inflicted on the physical and mental health of the women of the Italian and Jewish communities in which she labored. She was particularly disturbed by the widespread incidence of illegal and often fatal septic abortions that she believed stemmed from the unavailability of safe methods of contraption. Sanger coined the term "birth control" in 1914 and began distributing diaphragms to poor immigrant women the following year.

In 1915, Sanger published *Family Planning,* a guide to contraception in pamphlet form. Distributing the pamphlet by mail violated the federal antiobscenity statutes known as the Comstock Laws. In 1921, she formed the American Birth Control League (not to be confused with the unrelated National Birth Control League), which campaigned for legal contraception and made "birth control" available to many immigrant women for the first time.

Sanger's motivations were twofold. She was concerned about the welfare of individual immigrant women and their families, but she was also influenced by eugenicist arguments. Among the stated

Margaret Sanger. (Library of Congress)

goals of her American Birth Control League was to prevent the birth of large numbers of diseased and so-called feebleminded infants to women whose ethnicity rendered their offspring prone to such traits. However, many leading eugenicists initially opposed her work to legalize contraception because they feared that such efforts would result in a greater use of diaphragms among native-born women that would lead to a further decrease in the percentage of American residents of British extraction.

By the 1920's, the failure of such groups as the Eugenics Education Society and the American Eugenics Society to increase birth rates among woman of Anglo-Saxon heritage led them to reconsider their reservations. If native-born American women could not be persuaded to reproduce with greater frequency, they reasoned, then immigrants should be given the means to reproduce less. As a result, many of the same intellectuals who pushed for passage of the restrictive Immigration Act of 1924 also advocated legalizing contraception. Their efforts led to a groundbreaking federal court ruling in *United States v. One Package of Japanese Pessaries* (1936). The Second Circuit Court of Appeals decision ruled that the federal government could not prevent physicians from prescribing contraceptives. After a lengthy legal battle waged by Planned Parenthood, the successor organization to Sanger's American Birth Control League, the U.S. Supreme Court finally legalized contraception for married couples nationwide in its 1965 *Griswold v. Connecticut* decision.

BIRTH CONTROL AFTER WORLD WAR II

As a result of the Supreme Court's *Griswold* ruling, contraceptives became available to adult immigrant women throughout the United States. However, efforts to target birth control specifically at new immigrants have remained controversial. During the 1980's, conservative opponents of increased immigration began citing high fertility rates among Hispanic women as a cause for concern. Some commentators even argued that these women should be encouraged to use birth control.

Family-planning organizations have also frequently been criticized by opponents of contraception for targeting poor, urban women—many of who are recent immigrants—as perpetuating a form of voluntary eugenics among these newcomers. Like some of their Mediterranean and eastern European predecessors, immigrants from Latin America, Africa, the Middle East, and Asia may also bring with them personal ambivalence or doubts about the use of birth control, often stemming from cultural or religious practices in their nations of origin. However, by the early twenty-first century, contraceptives and family planning were being openly advertised in many languages, and their use among new immigrants was becoming increasingly common.

Jacob M. Appel

FURTHER READING

Chelser, Ellen. *Woman of Valor: Margaret Sanger and the Birth Control Movement in America*. New York: Simon & Schuster, 1992. Exhaustively researched biography brings the strong-willed birth control pioneer vividly to life, along with the individuals and movements that influenced her work.

Franks, Angela. *Margaret Sanger's Eugenic Legacy: The Control of Female Fertility*. Jefferson, N.C.: McFarland, 2005. Describes Sanger's ideas— many of which are still debated—about birth control, eugenics, sterilization, and population control.

Gordon, Linda. *The Moral Property of Women: A History of Birth Control Politics in America*. Champaign: University of Illinois Press, 2003. Broad, analytical history of the birth control movement by the author of *Woman's Body, Woman's Right: Birth Control in America* (1990).

Gray, Madeline. *Margaret Sanger: A Biography of the Champion of Birth Control*. New York: Richard Marek, 1979. Excellent, well-researched biography with a revelatory examination of Sanger's later years.

Kennedy, David M. *Birth Control in America: The Career of Margaret Sanger*. New Haven, Conn.: Yale University Press, 1970. Focuses on Sanger's public career in the United States and illuminates American society in the years prior to 1945. Describes the social context in which Sanger worked and the attitudinal, behavioral, and institutional responses she evoked.

Reed, James. *From Private Vice to Public Virtue: The Birth Control Movement and American Society Since 1830*. New York: Basic Books, 1978. Excellent overview of the leading figures in the American birth control movement.

Sanger, Margaret. *Margaret Sanger: An Autobiography*. New York: Dover, 1971. This description of Sanger's life provides few insights but described people who influenced her views on birth control.

_____. *Woman and the New Race*. New York: Brentano's, 1920. Attempts to convince working-class women that control of reproduction is the key to a healthier, more satisfying life and a better world. Advocates rebellion to gain access to contraceptive information.

SEE ALSO: Child immigrants; Eugenics movement; Families; Immigration Act of 1924; Women's movements.

BORDER FENCE

THE EVENT: Construction of barriers to prevent undocumented immigrants and potential terrorists from entering the United States along its southern border
DATE: Construction began in 1994
LOCATION: U.S.-Mexico border

SIGNIFICANCE: The congressional decision in 2006 to build hundreds of miles of additional fencing along portions of the 1,951-mile U.S.-Mexico border touched off a diplomatic dispute with Mexico, angered Latino communities in the United States, and was almost unanimously condemned by human rights organizations, who believed the policy would result in a large number of deaths among immigrants seeking to enter the country via its more dangerous but as yet unfenced stretches of borderland.

The tightening of the border with Mexico was begun during the mid-1990's in response to the drug trade and the growing number of illegal immigrants entering the United States. Containing the latter quickly became a security concern in the aftermath of al-Qaeda's attack on the World Trade Center and Pentagon on September 11, 2001. After five years of congressional debate, the construction of an additional 850 miles of barriers along the U.S.-Mexico border was authorized in the Secure Fence Act of 2006.

FENCING THE BORDER

Although the terminology evokes images of a conventional, high, and possibly barbed-wire fence stretching across the border separating Mexico from California, Arizona, New Mexico, and Texas, the "fence" that has been erected and that remains to be completed is as varied as the landscape along the border. A substantial portion consists of walls as well as border control points and obstacles to vehi-

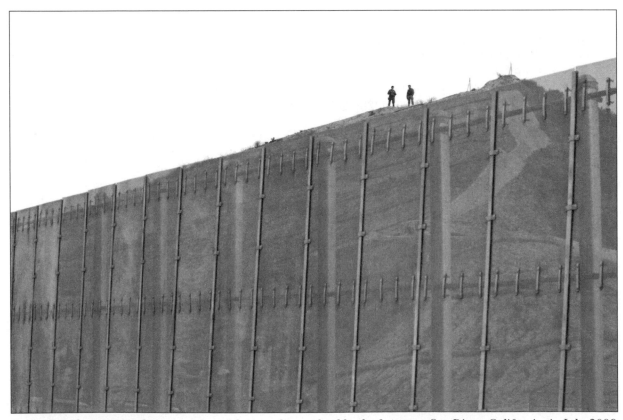

Border Patrol agents stand atop a section of the recently completed border fence near San Diego, California, in July, 2009. (AP/Wide World Photos)

cle movement constructed where major highways link Mexico to such metropolitan areas as San Diego. Other sections include pedestrian barriers—often parallel walls separated by "no-go" zones—but many segments are or will be of a "virtual" electronic variety, using cameras, motion-detection devices, and observer personnel to monitor the border.

To a significant degree, the form of the border fence and its pace and site of construction have been determined by the border landscape. The more desolate and dangerous the area on the U.S. side of the border, the lower the priority to fence it immediately. The first barriers were thus erected near the urban areas that beckoned drug dealers and illegal immigrants. In 1994, the administration of Bill Clinton launched Operation Gatekeeper to construct a barrier along a fourteen-mile stretch south of San Diego. Similarly, most of the nearly five hundred miles of border that were covered by either pedestrian or vehicle border barriers by the end of 2008 lay along the zones nearest to the United States highway network, not the long stretches of desert borderland.

EVALUATING THE OPERATION

Assessments of the success of the fencing operation in controlling illegal immigration have been mixed, although most concede that the U.S.-Mexico border has become one of the most challenging law-enforcement areas in North America. There, bandit gangs in Mexico, volunteer spotters from right-wing groups in the United States, paid smugglers of human cargo (the armed "coyotes"), drug dealers, impoverished Mexicans living in shantytowns just south of the border, Mexican authorities, and 90 percent of the U.S. Border Patrol (nearly ten thousand agents), augmented by National Guard troops, coexist and often collide.

Increased surveillance and fencing on parts of the border has affected the pattern of illegal immigration. Many would-be immigrants have been forced into entering the United States by way of the often lethal, less monitored desert access points, and thousands have died in the fifty-mile trek necessary to reach roadways. For those choosing the less dangerous crossing points, interdiction has become easier given the combination of high physical walls, cameras, and sensors lining those areas. Furthermore, the rate of illegal immigration did

seem to slow in 2008, although it was not clear whether it was a result of the increasing number of fenced miles or the fact that a U.S. economy in recession discouraged many from seeking employment north of the border.

The principal indictment of the fence is that it constitutes too little, too late. By the time the Secure Fence Act was passed, it was conservatively estimated that there were at least 12 million illegal immigrants in the United States, nearly 60 percent of whom were Mexicans. Moreover, the same year that the Secure Fence Act passed, the governors of New Mexico and Arizona declared states of emergency on the grounds that their states were suffering significant financial hardship because the federal government had failed to control the drugs and illegal immigrants entering them from Mexico. Meanwhile, as the illegal immigrants spread across the country, by approximately the same time forty-three states had legislation pending that was designed to limit illegal immigrants' access to employment, education, and social welfare benefits.

Joseph R. Rudolph, Jr.

FURTHER READING

Alden, Edward H. *The Closing of the American Border: Terrorism, Immigration, and Security Since 9/11.* New York: HarperCollins, 2008. Thoughtful and generally critical assessment of the George W. Bush administration's restrictive policies on immigration, concluding with a chapter devoted to the border fence.

Bigelow, Bill. *The Line Between Us: Teaching About the Border and Mexican Immigration.* Milwaukee, Wis.: Rethinking Schools, 2006. Although designed to help teachers explain the nature of life around the border, the book also provides a useful, concise history of Mexican migration. Excellent background reading.

Buchanan, Patrick J. *State of Emergency: The Third World Invasion and Conquest of America.* New York: Thomas Dunne Books, 2006. Thorough, if at times bombastic, statement of the ultraconservative Right's implacable opposition to further immigration from nations to the south of the United States.

Guerette, Rob T. *Migrant Death: Border Safety and Situation Crime Prevention on the U.S.-Mexico Divide.* New York: LFB Scholarly Publishing, 2007. One of the best available summary analyses of the violence and crime surrounding the deadly border zone separating the United States and Mexico and of the risk run by those crossing it illegally.

Romero, Fernando. *Hyperborder: The Contemporary U.S.-Mexico Border and Its Future.* Princeton, N.J.: Princeton Architectural Press, 2007. Well-researched discussion of life along the border and the issues permeating the debate over its future in general and the fence in particular.

See also: Border Patrol, U.S.; Drug trafficking; Homeland Security, Department of; Illegal immigration; Illegal Immigration Reform and Immigrant Responsibility Act of 1996; Mexican immigrants; 9/11 and U.S. immigration policy; North American Free Trade Agreement; Texas.

Border Patrol, U.S.

Identification: Federal law-enforcement agency with the primary responsibility of protecting U.S. borders against unlawful crossings

Also known as: U.S. Customs and Border Protection (CBP)

Date: Established on May 28, 1924

Significance: Since its 1924 creation, the U.S. Border Patrol has served as the primary federal law-enforcement agency responsible for the prevention and detection of illegal immigrants, drugs, and contraband entering the United States along both the Mexican and Canadian borders. After the terrorist attacks of September 11, 2001, the newly formed Department of Homeland Security merged a number of federal law-enforcement agencies with the Border Patrol to create a new combined agency called U.S. Customs and Border Protection (CBP).

The U.S. Border Patrol is a uniformed federal law-enforcement agency that was placed under the control of the Department of Homeland Security in 2001. After the terrorist attacks on the United States during that year, the Border Patrol was combined with three other federal law-enforcement agencies—the U.S. Customs inspection division, the Immigration and Naturalization inspection di-

vision, and the Department of Agriculture's animal and plant inspection service—to form a new federal law-enforcement agency known as U.S. Customs and Border Protection.

Since 2001, the Border Patrol's primary mission has remained to detect undocumented aliens, illegal drugs, and other types of illegal contraband and prevent them from entering the United States. The reorganized Border Patrol has also been responsible for detecting, preventing from entering the country, and apprehending suspected terrorists and their weapons. All these difficult tasks have made the Border Patrol one of the most important federal law-enforcement agencies in the United States, especially in the context of the nation's ongoing struggles against drugs and terrorism.

In the national war on drugs, the Border Patrol has continuously distinguished itself as one of the most effective law-enforcement agencies in the United States. The agency is particularly important in the struggle against rising drug-smuggling efforts along the southwestern border and has become one of the key agencies on the frontline of the war on drugs. In 2007 alone, Border Patrol agents seized more than 14,000 pounds of cocaine and more than 1.8 million pounds of marijuana. The drugs confiscated in that one year had an estimated street value of more than $1.6 billion.

The Border Patrol has also played a key role in apprehending undocumented aliens. In 2007, the agency's agents arrested more than 850,000 people who attempted illegally to enter the United States. Over the next two years, this figure declined, but that was because of improved enforcement methods, improved infrastructure and management, and technological advances.

Historical Overview

In 1904, during Theodore Roosevelt's presidential administration, the U.S. commissioner general of immigration assigned mounted inspectors to patrol the U.S.-Mexican border. The federal government initially hired only seventy-five men to patrol the nearly two-thousand-mile-long southern border of the United States, riding horses that the men personally owned. With occasional exceptions, this work was relatively uneventful over the next decade and a half, but it changed forever at midnight January 16, 1920. At that time, the Eighteenth Amendment to the U.S. Constitution went into effect prohibiting the sale, importation, manufacture, and transportation of all alcoholic beverages.

With the onset of Prohibition, foreign borders became important routes for smugglers willing to stop at nothing to get their illegal products to their destinations. The smuggling of alcohol into the United States became a hugely profitable criminal enterprise during the 1920's. Not surprisingly, dealing with smugglers soon became a major problem for the badly outnumbered mounted border inspectors. To deal with the problem, Congress passed the Labor Appropriation Act on May 28, 1924. That law officially established the U.S. Border Patrol as a federal law-enforcement agency.

In 1925, Congress expanded the mission of the Border Patrol to include protection of Florida's long shoreline and the region along the Gulf coast. The government then recruited 450 new Border Patrol agents and assigned most of them to the long Canadian border to stop the smuggling of illegal liquor into the United States

Border Patrol officers inspecting vehicles entering the United States from Mexico at Nogales, Arizona, in early 2005. Since the Border Patrol was placed under the new Department of Homeland Security in 2003, inspections at border crossings have become more intensive—along both the Mexican and Canadian borders. Inspectors are making increasing use of technology in their work and still use dogs trained to sniff out drugs and explosives. (AP/Wide World Photos)

from the north. Confronted by this strengthened Border Patrol presence on the Canadian border, many bootleggers shifted their smuggling operations to the Mexican border. Many of them used mules to carry alcoholic beverages directly across the Rio Grande. Meanwhile, the federal government also became concerned with increased smuggling of undocumented immigrants into the United States for profit. To deal with all these challenges, the Border Patrol continued to hire more agents.

In 1933, President Franklin D. Roosevelt recombined the Bureau of Immigration and the Bureau of Naturalization into the Immigration and Naturalization Service (INS), under which the Border Patrol officially fell. Late the following year, the

first Border Patrol Academy opened in, El Paso, Texas. In 1940, the Immigration and Naturalization Service was moved from the Department of Labor to the Department of Justice. Immediately afterward, 712 new agents were added, raising their total number to more than 1,500 officers.

During World War II, the Patrol played an integral role in national security by guarding alien detention camps, protecting diplomats, restricting border immigrant entries, and working with the U.S. Coast Guard to secure the nation's borders and coasts against potential enemy combatants. Border Patrol agents had long used both horses and motorized vehicles with radios to patrol the borders. During this period, aircraft were added and quickly became an essential part of Border Patrol security operations.

Meanwhile, the jurisdiction of the Border Patrol continued to expand. In 1952, agents were first permitted, for the first time, to board and search transportation vehicles for illegal immigrants anywhere within the United States, not just along the borders. As the nation continued to grow, so did the staffing levels investigative and patrol efforts of the agency. By the turn of the twenty-first century, the Border Patrol had evolved into one of the nation's most important federal law-enforcement agencies.

MISSION AND OPERATIONS

Throughout its history, the Border Patrol has continued to change dramatically. However, its chief mission has always been to detect and deter aliens attempting to enter the United States illegally. In cooperation with law-enforcement officers from such federal agencies as U.S. Customs, Immigration and Naturalization (INS), and the Department of Agriculture, Border Patrol agents have helped to maintain operational entry points into the United States and to facilitate the entry of legal immigrants and goods while preventing the illegal trafficking of people, drugs, and other types of contraband.

In addition to managing legal entry points along the borders, the Border Patrol has been responsible for patrolling the nearly six thousand miles of the Mexican and Canadian land borders and more than two thousand miles of coastal waters surrounding Puerto Rico and Florida's peninsula. Many agents work in isolated regions, often in difficult terrain and extreme weather conditions.

By the year 2009, the Border Patrol had experienced massive growth. After starting with only a handful of mounted agents who patrolled uninhabited areas along U.S. borders, the agency expanded to employ more than seventeen thousand agents and more than three thousand support personnel. Much of this growth took place after the mid-1990's, as Congress increased the agency's funding to improve border security. Along with its increased funding, the Border Patrol was required to gives its agents nineteen weeks of training at its academy in Artesia, New Mexico, which is affiliated with the Federal Law Enforcement Training Center (FLETC) located in Glynco, Georgia.

The Border Patrol accomplishes its primary mission of preventing immigrants from entering the United States illegally through several means:

- continuous surveillance of international borders and shorelines
- questioning informants and recently apprehended persons
- rapid response to electronic sensor alarms along border fences and aircraft sightings
- interpreting and following human tracks

Other major activities that agents carry out include conducting city patrol and transportation checks, investigating drug and contraband smuggling operations, and conducting traffic checkpoints along highways leading from border areas. During the decade leading up to 2009, agents apprehended nearly 13 million aliens attempting to enter the United States illegally. This number is especially impressive in view of the many deserts, canyons, and mountains straddling the borders. Border Patrol police work differs from that of typical urban police officers in large part because of the added dangers of wildlife and harsh weather conditions. To make accomplishing their difficult mission possible, Border Patrol agents make extensive use of such high-tech equipment as electronic sensors, video monitors, and night vision scopes to detect people crossing the borders. Meanwhile, agents continue to patrol the borders on foot, on horseback, and in various types of vehicles including suburban utility vehicles, snowmobiles, all-terrain vehicles, boats, airplanes, and helicopters. They also use unmanned aerial vehicles operated by remote control computers.

Paul M. Klenowski

FURTHER READING

Andreas, Peter. *Border Games: Policing the U.S.-Mexico Divide.* 2d ed. Ithaca, N.Y.: Cornell University Press, 2009. Scholarly work offering insights into the many political forces involved with U.S.-Mexican border patrol work. Provides details about how corruption and the drug trade have been variables in border policies.

Bullock, Jane, and George Haddow. *Introduction to Homeland Security.* 2d ed. Burlington, Mass.: Butterworth-Heinemann, 2006. Introductory text offering a comprehensive overview of the Department of Homeland Security. Examines the new cabinet department's various agencies, including the Border Patrol, and their missions as they pertain to border security and combating terrorism.

Maril, Robert. *Patrolling Chaos: The U.S. Border Patrol in Deep South Texas.* Lubbock: Texas Tech University Press, 2006. Offers an ethnographic account of Border Patrol work on the frontlines of the U.S.-Mexican border, Documenting the lives of a handful of border patrol agents, Maril gives explicit details of positive and negative aspects of their work, including the element of danger that is unavoidable.

Miller, Connie C. *The U.S. Border Patrol: Guarding the Nation.* New York: Capstone Press, 2008. Concise explanation of the history and mission of the Border Patrol as a law-enforcement entity. Excellent introductory work that provides details about the qualifications and importance of this highly regarded federal law-enforcement agency.

Morgan, Lee. *The Reaper's Line: Life and Death on the Mexican Border.* Tucson, Ariz.: Rio Nuevo, 2006. Firsthand account of work on the frontline of the U.S.-Mexican border by a former Border Patrol agent with three decades of experience. Morgan chronicles true-life tales of both success and horror stories along the border.

Pacheco, Alex, and Erich Krauss. *On the Line: Inside the U.S. Border Patrol.* New York: Citadel Press, 2005. Told from the viewpoint of recently employed Border Patrol agents, this book provides details about the recruitment, training, and daily life of agents, as well as insights into the general problem of illegal border crossings.

White, Richard, and Kevin Collins. *The United States Department of Homeland Security: An Overview.* Boston: Pearson Custom Publishing, 2006. Scholarly but nonetheless accessible examination of the newly formed Department of Homeland Security, providing details about the department's various agencies and the role of the Border Patrol in combating terrorism.

SEE ALSO: Border fence; Bureau of Immigration, U.S.; Citizenship and Immigration Services, U.S.; Coast Guard, U.S.; Drug trafficking; El Paso incident; Homeland Security, Department of; Immigration and Naturalization Service, U.S.; 9/11 and U.S. immigration policy; Patriot Act of 2001.

BORN IN EAST L.A.

THE FILM: Comedy written and directed by Cheech Marin
DATE: Released in 1987

> **SIGNIFICANCE:** Now a cult classic, *Born in East L.A.* features Cheech Marin, formerly of the Cheech and Chong comedy duo, as an American citizen mistakenly deported to Tijuana. The film, which marks Marin's first solo performance, is based on Cheech and Chong's 1985 parody song of Bruce Springsteen's "Born in the U.S.A."

Within its relatively brief eighty-seven-minute running time, *Born in East L.A.* manages to explode an array of stereotypes associated with Hispanic Americans (Chicanos), insensitive Border Patrol officials, predatory immigrant smugglers, and the difficulties of crossing a heavily patrolled border. The film's comic plot is set in motion when Rudy (Marin), a resident of East Los Angeles, is asked by his mother to pick up his cousin, an undocumented Mexican immigrant working at a toy factory in Los Angeles. Absent-mindedly leaving his wallet, with all its identification papers, at home, Rudy arrives at the factory at the moment immigration officers are conducting a raid and arresting undocumented workers. Swept up in the raid and arrested along with dozens of Mexican nationals, Rudy cannot establish his U.S. citizenship and is put on a bus and sent to Tijuana, Mexico, along with the undocumented workers. After he arrives in Mexico, his problems are compounded by his lack of money and inability to speak Spanish. A born and bred English-speaking American citizen, he cannot get back into his own country simply because he lacks documentation and does not match the stereotype of a typical Anglo-American.

After enduring several days in a Mexican jail, Rudy befriends Jimmy (Daniel Stern), an American former convict who gets him a series of menial jobs so he can earn enough money to pay a Mexican "coyote" to smuggle him back to the United States. When that effort fails, Rudy leads scores of Mexicans on a defiant march across the border, where they overwhelm the Border Patrol agents with their numbers. The film's ending adds more than one ironic twist to the means by which Latino immigrants might achieve the American Dream.

Cordelia E. Barrera

FURTHER READING

Chong, Thomas. *Cheech and Chong: The Unauthorized Autobiography.* New York: Simon Spotlight Entertainment, 2008.

Marin, Cheech, et al. *Chicano Visions: American Painters on the Verge.* Boston: Little, Brown, 2002.

Torranes, Thomas. *The Magic Curtain: The Mexican-American Border in Fiction, Film, and Song.* Fort Worth: Texas Christian University Press, 2002.

SEE ALSO: Border Patrol, U.S.; California; Citizenship and Immigration Services, U.S.; Deportation; Ethnic enclaves; Films; *Green Card*; Green cards; Los Angeles; Mexican immigrants; Stereotyping.

BOSTON

IDENTIFICATION: Capital and largest city of Massachusetts and one of the most important cities on the Atlantic seaboard since early colonial times

SIGNIFICANCE: During the nineteenth and early twentieth centuries, Irish and Italian immigrants significantly changed the political, religious, and cultural life of the predominantly Anglo-Saxon Protestant city of Boston. In the early twenty-first century, Roman Catholics make up Boston's largest religious community, and the Irish play a major role in Boston politics. Non-European immigrants have transformed Boston into a racially diverse city with a significant minority population.

From its founding by Puritans in 1630 until 1845, Boston was a port city dominated by what were called the Brahmins: a community of English-descended Protestants. The city was a financial and business center with little indigenous industry or agriculture to attract immigrants. After the American Revolution, prospective settlers of the new country, arriving with dreams of land ownership, bypassed Boston because of its lack of space.

IRISH GREAT MIGRATION

The economic and political environment in Ireland—widespread evictions and the potato famine beginning in 1845—created the conditions necessary for the first large immigrant group to remain in Boston. Irish immigrants were too financially drained by the cost of transportation to move on once they reached Boston. The dramatic influx of Irish immigrants—the Irish population in Boston grew from four thousand in 1840 to more than fifty thousand by 1855—permanently changed the city socially, culturally, and economically. Cheap Irish labor transformed Boston from a commercial to an industrial economy, with the native Bostonians reaping the benefits as owners, while low wages left the Irish crowded into the city's first tenements. There were cultural conflicts with the native Bostonians, especially over religion, since the vast majority of the Irish were Roman Catholic, while the Brahmins were Protestant, and politics, since the Irish tended to be labor-oriented Democrats, while the Brahmins tended to be business-oriented Republicans.

By 1880, a new native-born generation of Irish descendants had a secure place in the community while retaining a distinct group identity. Some Boston neighborhoods such as South Boston and Charlestown continue to be largely Irish in character, with such events as the annual St. Patrick's Day parade becoming a permanent part of Boston's culture. The Catholic Church in Boston is influential and retains an Irish flavor in spite of the presence of Italian, French, and German Catholics. Perhaps most important, by the early twentieth century Boston politics was dominated by the Irish, who contributed such figures as Mayors John F. Fitzgerald and James Michael Curley and President John F. Kennedy.

NORTH END AND THE ITALIAN PRESENCE

The North End, one of Boston's oldest neighborhoods, had been predominantly Irish for two generations. At the end of the nineteenth century, conditions in eastern and southern Europe stimulated two new groups of non-English-speaking immigrants: the Jews and the Italians. By 1895, the North End was dominantly southern Italian, with Russian and Polish Jews close behind in numbers.

The Jewish immigrants considered education essential for social integration and economic advancement. (The North End's Eliot School was two-thirds Jewish in 1906.) They were oriented toward business, opening retail stores and small businesses of all kinds, and moved into the mainstream of commercial and education-oriented Boston fairly rapidly. The North End, which remains Boston's Little Italy, was 90 percent Italian in 1920.

The southern Italians, like the Irish before them, arrived in Boston with little money and few prospects and found work in the factories and on the docks. In the North End, they created a community that was similar to an Italian village. Italian culture—street corner and café life, restaurants and markets specializing in Italian ethnic foods such as pizza and pasta, the religious *feste*, or feasts, with processions and a festival atmosphere on summer evenings—was introduced to Boston. By 1910, the Italian influence in the Massachusetts legislature had instituted the Columbus Day holiday. Since the second half of the twentieth century, several Massachusetts governors and Boston mayors have been of Italian descent. Today, Boston is as Irish and Italian in flavor as it is Brahmin.

LATE TWENTIETH CENTURY DIVERSITY

In 1965, a new Immigration and Nationality Act lifted the restrictive quotas of the 1924 National Origins Act. In Boston, the numbers of foreign-born residents and their children rose dramatically until the immigrant community would make up more than one-third of the population. A substantial number of the new wave of immigrants originated in the Caribbean, Latin America, Africa, and Asia, changing Boston to a racially diverse city. The new immigrants came from a wide variety of countries. Soviet Jews, Vietnamese, Cambodians, Salvadorans, Haitians, Dominicans, Brazilians, and Colombians, as well as Indians, Chinese, Cape Verdeans, and Africans all flocked to a Boston that was known as a center of educational opportunity and economic prosperity.

Susan Butterworth

Immigrant children learning to play American games on the roof of Boston's Washington School in 1915. (Library of Congress)

FURTHER READING

Antin, Mary. *The Promised Land.* New York: Penguin Books, 1997. Reprint of the 1912 autobiography of a young Jewish woman who emigrated from Russia to Boston during the early twentieth century. A primary source documenting conditions and opportunities for immigrants in Boston.

Handlin, Oscar. *Boston's Immigrants, 1790-1880: A Study in Acculturation.* Cambridge, Mass.: Belknap Press, 1991. Updated fiftieth anniversary edition of the classic study. Focus is on the years of the Irish great migration to Boston, from the 1845 potato famine until the decline of Irish immigration in 1880.

Johnson, Violet Showers. *The Other Black Bostonians: West Indians in Boston 1900-1950.* Bloomington: Indiana University Press, 2006. Study of black immigrants from the British West Indies during the first half of the twentieth century.

O'Connor, Thomas. *The Boston Irish: A Political History.* Boston: Northeastern University Press, 1995. Focuses on the rise of the considerable Irish influence on Boston politics.

Puleo, Stephen. *The Boston Italians: A Story of Pride, Perseverance, and Paesani, from the Years of the Great Immigration to the Present Day.* Boston: Beacon Press, 2007. Focuses on Boston's North End and the Italian influence in Boston from immigration to Boston Italian leaders.

Shaw-Taylor, Yoku, and Steven Tuch, eds. *The Other African Americans: Contemporary African and Caribbean Immigrants in the United States.* Lanham, Md.: Rowman & Littlefield, 2007. Discussion of Haitian, Jamaican, Dominican, and African immigrants. Includes an essay on intermarriage and ethnic boundaries among black Americans in Boston.

Ueda, Reed, and Conrad Wright, eds. *Faces of Community: Immigrant Massachusetts, 1860-2000.* Boston: Northeastern University Press, 2003. Includes articles on ethnic politics and the clash of Catholic and Protestant identities in Boston.

SEE ALSO: Antin, Mary; Asian immigrants; Haitian immigrants; Immigration Act of 1924; Immigration and Nationality Act of 1965; Irish immigrants; Italian immigrants; Jewish immigrants; Latin American immigrants; Little Italies; Massachusetts.

BOUTILIER V. IMMIGRATION AND NATURALIZATION SERVICE

THE CASE: U.S. Supreme Court ruling on the immigration of gays and lesbians
DATE: Decided on May 22, 1967

> **SIGNIFICANCE:** Based on congressional intent combined with commonly accepted psychiatric ideas of the time, the Supreme Court approved the Immigration and Naturalization Service's policy of classifying gays and lesbians as ineligible for immigration.

Clive Michael Boutilier was a Canadian citizen who lived in the United States with his parents for several years. When he applied for citizenship in 1963, he admitted to an official of the Immigration and Naturalization Service (INS) that he had been arrested in 1959 on the charge of sodomy. Subsequently, at the request of the INS, he revealed in an affidavit that he had participated in homosexual encounters since the age of fourteen. Based on his affidavit, the Public Health Service classified him as a "psychopathic personality, sexual deviate." In pursuance of the Immigration and Nationality Act of 1952, which barred entry of persons "afflicted with psychopathic personality," the INS instituted deportation proceedings. After his appeal was rejected by the court of appeals, the Supreme Court agreed to review the case.

By a 6-3 vote, the U.S. Supreme Court upheld the INS decision to deport Boutilier. Writing for the majority, Justice Tom C. Clark observed that "Congress has plenary power to make rules for the admission of aliens and to exclude those who possess those characteristics which Congress has forbidden." Following an analysis of the 1952 law, he concluded:

> The legislative history of the Act indicates beyond a shadow of a doubt that the congress intended the phrase "psychopathic personality" to include homosexuals such as petitioner.

In a long and forceful dissent, Justice William O. Douglas presented evidence that many psychologists and psychiatrists disagreed with the notion that homosexuality was pathological or incompatible with good citizenship.

Thomas Tandy Lewis

FURTHER READING

Galloway, Donald. *Immigration Law.* Concord, Ont.: Irwin Law, 1997.

Legomsky, Stephen. *Immigration and the Judiciary: Law and Politics in Britain and America.* New York: Oxford University Press, 1987.

Luibhéid, Eithne. "Sexuality, Migration, and the Shifting Line Between Legal and Illegal Status." *GLQ* 14, nos. 2-3 (2008): 289-313.

SEE ALSO: Constitution, U.S.; Gay and lesbian immigrants; Immigration and Nationality Act of 1952; Immigration and Naturalization Service, U.S.; Immigration law; "Moral turpitude"; Naturalization; Supreme Court, U.S.

BRACERO PROGRAM

DATE: 1942 to 1964
LOCATION: Southwestern states
THE EVENT: Cooperative international program through which the United States imported large numbers of Mexican workers—mainly farmworkers—on a temporary basis
DATE: 1942-1964

SIGNIFICANCE: Initiated because of farm labor shortages caused by American entry into World War II, the bracero program brought Mexican workers to replace American workers dislocated by the war. The program was intended to be temporary, but a growing dependence of American farms on Mexican labor kept it going for nearly two decades after the war ended.

Mexican immigration has historically fluctuated with changing social and economic conditions in both the United States and Mexico. During periods of social unrest, violent uprisings, or bad economic times in Mexico—such as the Mexican Revolution—immigration increased. When the U.S. economy has been in decline, Mexican immigration has decreased. Whatever the circumstances, however, Mexico has long been a source of cheap

temporary labor for the United States. Indeed, until the establishment of the U.S. Border Patrol in 1924, the border between the United States and Mexico was virtually unsupervised. Citizens of both countries crossed it as they pleased, and farmers in the American Southwest recruited seasonal workers from Mexico without government interference or supervision. After the United States entered World War I in 1917, Mexican workers played an important role in keeping American agriculture productive. The bracero program of the 1940's was essentially a more formal and more tightly supervised international agreement to provide an adequate labor force during and after World War II. However, despite the contributions the program made to American agriculture and to the Mexican economy, it had many vocal critics in both countries.

U.S.-MEXICAN RELATIONS

Relations between the Mexico and the United States have never been intimate. Since the time of the 1846-1848 Mexican War, which ended with Mexico losing half its territory to the United States, relations have been strained. Added to this initial source of conflict was the large-scale "repatriation" of Mexicans and Mexican Americans during the Great Depression during the early 1930's, when Mexican workers were indiscriminately rounded up from their workplaces and off the streets on which they lived and summarily sent back to Mexico. Meanwhile, the nationalization by Mexico of its petroleum industry, which resulted in the seizure of property that had been owned by American companies during the 1930's, caused a festering legal dispute between the United States and Mexico.

In addition to these international events involving governments, there was the personal ongoing problem of racist antipathy against Mexicans that was prevalent throughout the American Southwest. A common saying that expressed Mexican feelings toward the United States at that time was "Poor Mexico, so far from God but so close to the United States." Mexicans were generally considered "nonwhites," forced to live in segregated barrios, and limited to employment in low-level jobs. Nevertheless, the prospect of finding better wages in the United States than those in Mexico has always drawn Mexicans north of the border. Consequently, even the state of Texas, which Mexicans have generally considered the most discriminatory of U.S. states, has been one of the most popular destinations for Mexican immigrants.

NEGOTIATING THE AGREEMENT

Before the United States entered World War II at the end of 1941, some Americans were concerned that if their country entered the war, there would again be a need, as there had been during World War I, for foreign workers. Farmers were especially concerned, and they pressured the federal government to make preparations to ensure an adequate farm labor supply in case of entry into the war. When the U.S. government approached the Mexican government about providing workers, its leaders were initially uninterested. This was partly due to the strained relations between the countries that had existed for some time. However, the situation changed after Japan's surprise attack on the U.S. Navy base Pearl Harbor on December 7, 1941. The United States quickly declared war on Japan and Germany, and Mexico, which until then had

been neutral, followed suit by declaring war against the Axis. The Mexican government then saw providing workers for the United States as a tangible means of actively contributing to the Allied war effort.

Mexico still had certain reservations about entering a cooperative program with the United States. American racism against its people was a concern, as was the size of its own labor force at a time Mexico itself was attempting to modernize and industrialize. Another consideration was how the stability of families would be affected if only male workers were allowed to migrate to the United States under the new program. Apart from those concerns, the Mexican government wanted to address four major issues before making an agreement:

- Mexican workers were not to serve in the U.S. military
- Mexican workers were not to be subjected to discrimination on or off the job

Bracero workers registering at the Hidalgo, Texas, labor center in 1959. (AP/Wide World Photos)

- Mexican workers were to be guaranteed transportation to and from their destinations, decent living conditions in the United States, and repatriation at the end of their contract periods, in accordance with Mexican labor laws
- Mexican workers were not to be used to replace American domestic servants or to reduce wage levels

After its concerns were addressed in the negotiations with the U.S. government, the Mexican government considered the benefits that would accrue from a labor agreement. These included providing jobs for poor unemployed men, who might otherwise cause social unrest in Mexico; the acquisition of new skills and knowledge by workers that might later benefit Mexico when the workers returned home; and the infusion of U.S. dollars into the Mexican economy from the remittances workers sent to their families from the United States. For its part, the United States stood to gain workers who would replace American farmworkers who entered military service or left rural areas for better-paying jobs in cities as the war economy expanded.

ESTABLISHMENT OF THE BRACERO PROGRAM

The final agreement that established the bracero program was reached on August 4, 1942, the date on which the program officially went into effect. The agreement acknowledged the sovereignty of Mexico and stated that either government could terminate the program unilaterally by notifying the other party ninety days in advance. The program was to provide the United States with both agricultural and nonagricultural workers.

Although both Mexico and the United States would benefit from the program, the program had many opponents in both countries. American labor unions were among the most vocal opponents. Their leaders argued that there was no significant labor shortage in the United States

---

BRACERO PROGRAM AGREEMENT

The Bracero program was developed as a labor agreement between the governments of Mexico and the United States. General provisions of the "Agreement for the Temporary Migration of Mexican Agricultural Workers to the United States" include the following:

GENERAL PROVISIONS

1. It is understood that Mexicans contracting to work in the United States shall not be engaged in any military service.
2. Mexicans entering the United States as result of this understanding shall not suffer discriminatory acts of any kind in accordance with the Executive Order No. 8802 issued at the White House June 25, 1941.
3. Mexicans entering the United States under this understanding shall enjoy the guarantees of transportation, living expenses and repatriation established in Article 29 of the Mexican Federal Labor Law as follows:

Article 29—All contracts entered into by Mexican workers for lending their services outside their country shall be made in writing, legalized by the municipal authorities of the locality where entered into and vised by the Consul of the country where their services are being used. Furthermore, such contract shall contain, as a requisite of validity of same, the following stipulations, without which the contract is invalid.

I. Transportation and subsistence expenses for the worker, and his family, if such is the case, and all other expenses which originate from point of origin to border points and compliance of immigration requirements, or for any other similar concept, shall be paid exclusively by the employer or the contractual parties.

II. The worker shall be paid in full the salary agreed upon, from which no deduction shall be made in any amount for any of the concepts mentioned in the above sub-paragraph.

III. The employer or contractor shall issue a bond or constitute a deposit in cash in the Bank of Workers, or in the absence of same, in the Bank of Mexico, to the entire satisfaction of the respective labor authorities, for a sum equal to repatriation costs of the worker and his family, and those originated by transportation to point of origin.

IV. Once the employer established proof of having covered such expenses or the refusal of the worker to return to his country, and that he does not owe the worker any sum covering salary or indemnization to which he might have a right, the labor authorities shall authorize the return of the deposit or the cancellation of the bond issued.

4. Mexicans entering the United States under this understanding shall not be employed to displace other workers, or for the purpose of reducing rates of pay previously established.

and thus no justification for a large and continuing influx of immigrant workers. Unions and their members were also convinced that a large influx of migrant workers would depress American wages. Texas growers were also opposed to the final agreement because it promised to make a drastic change in the way they had been accustomed to hiring Mexican workers. Texas growers were among the most prominent supporters of importing Mexican farmworkers, but they did not like the government oversight and guarantees of the bracero program.

VIOLATIONS OF THE AGREEMENT

Another reason that many Americans were upset by the bracero agreement was that it gave guarantees to Mexican workers that domestic workers did not enjoy. In practice, however, many provisions of the program were not honored. Among the many violations and abuses reported were charges that American growers made Mexican workers pay for food, lodging, tools, and blankets they were supposed to receive without charge. Growers were also accused of requiring workers to perform tasks beyond those specified in their contracts. Under the terms of the original agreement, the Farm Security Administration (FSA) was the principal federal government agency responsible for the importation of foreign labor. Aware of the criticisms of the agreement, the FSA attempted to secure better living conditions and pass legislation favorable to American workers, such as those guaranteed to foreign workers.

Violations of the agreement also occurred through the actions of the U.S. government itself. On April 20, 1943, the U.S. Congress passed Public Law 45. Its section 5 could be interpreted as allowing the commissioner of immigration and naturalization, with the approval of the U.S. attorney general, to import Mexican workers without the permission of the Mexican government. For example, in 1948 and 1954, the U.S. government would open the Mexican border to admit thousands of undocumented workers to satisfy the urgent demands of American growers who wanted more and cheaper labor. Meanwhile, the FSA was replaced by the more grower-friendly War Food Administration's Office of Labor to oversee the bracero program. Another serious violation occurred when the wartime bracero workers returned home to

find that the 10 percent of their wages that had been withheld had disappeared. It is unknown who was responsible for this violation.

Because of the history of Texas racism against Mexicans and the frequent abuses of workers practiced by Texas growers, the Mexican government refused to allow its citizens to work in Texas under the bracero program. This turn of events contributed to an increase in the number of undocumented workers who were allowed to cross the border into Texas, where they worked without government oversight or written contracts. In further violation of the agreement that stipulated that only single or unaccompanied men be employed, Texas growers employed men, women, and children. The wages they paid to these undocumented workers were also well below the levels specified by the bracero agreement. In 1947-1948, for example, average incomes for undocumented Mexican workers were less than ten dollars per week.

Both the U.S. and Mexican governments were aware of these violations. In an attempt to correct the problem, an agreement was reached whereby undocumented immigrant workers would be returned to Mexico, where they were to be given physical examinations, fingerprinted and photographed, and provided with identification cards. Each worker would then be given a written work agreement indicating where they would work and the conditions of their employment. They then were returned to the United States, where again they were to be given physical exams, fingerprinted, photographed, and given identification cards that would make them legal immigrants. Meanwhile, the governors of Texas attempted to improve working conditions in their state, and Mexico finally agreed to let workers go there in 1947.

RENEWAL OF THE BRACERO PROGRAM

The original U.S.-Mexican agreement was to end the bracero program in 1947; however, there were numerous extensions. Although most of the braceros worked in agriculture, some did not. For example, from 1942 to 1946, more than 100,000 Mexicans worked for American railroads.

While most of the program's conditions and guarantees were the same for both agricultural and nonagricultural workers, some differences applied. For example, wages were higher for railroad workers, who were allowed to engage in collective bargaining and join unions, although unions were generally reluctant to accept them. The use of these nonagricultural braceros to work in the United States stopped after the war ended. However, the agricultural agreement was renewed on February 21, 1948. A significant change was made in this new agreement, whereby growers, rather than the U.S. government, would be the employers of record. This agreement was renewed again in 1951, during the Korean War.

President Harry S. Truman was sufficiently concerned with the bracero program to establish a commission to study problems connected with it in 1950. However, his commission's recommendations for reforms in the program were ignored by Congress because the program as it was already constituted was popular with growers, and keeping Mexican farm labor cheap helped keep food prices down for consumers. A decade later, President John F. Kennedy moved to terminate the program. Congress nevertheless extended the program an additional year, but it finally ended in 1964. Overall, the program lasted for twenty-two years and was extended or renewed eight times. Braceros were employed in approximately thirty states with most working in California, Texas and Arizona.

Philip E. Lampe

FURTHER READING

Bustamante, Jorge, Clark Reynolds, and Raul Hinojosa Ojeda. *U.S.-Mexico Relations: Labor Market Interdependence.* Stanford, Calif.: Stanford University Press, 1992. Broad survey of the dependence of American agriculture on immigrant Mexican workers.

Copp, Nelson Gage. *"Wetbacks" and Braceros: Mexican Migrant Laborers and American Immigration Policy, 1930-1960.* San Francisco: R and E Research Associates, 1971. Provides detailed accounts of emigration and immigration policies affecting migrant agricultural workers from Mexico.

Craig, Richard B. *The Bracero Program: Interest Groups and Foreign Policy.* Austin: University of Texas Press, 1971. Discusses the political agreement between the United States and Mexico regarding migrant laborers.

Galarza, Ernesto. *Merchants of Labor: The Mexican Bracero Story.* Santa Barbara, Calif.: McNally & Loftin, West, 1978. Discusses the treatment of braceros and the effects of the bracero program in California.

Gamboa, Erasmo. *Mexican Labor and World War II: Braceros in the Pacific Northwest, 1942-1947.* Austin: University of Texas Press, 1990. Detailed history of the life, conditions, and social policy affecting migrant workers from Mexico in Oregon and Washington State.

Gonzalez, Gilbert G. *Guest Workers or Colonized Labor? Mexican Labor Migration to the United States.* Boulder, Colo.: Paradigm, 2005. Study of the state of Mexican labor immigration to the United States into the early twenty-first century.

Ngai, Mae M. *Impossible Subjects: Illegal Aliens and the Making of Modern America.* Princeton, N.J.: Princeton University Press, 2004. General history of the problem of illegal immigration in the United States that includes a chapter covering Operation Wetback and the bracero program.

Valdes, Dennis Nodin. *Al Norte: Agricultural Workers in the Great Lakes Region, 1917-1970.* Austin: University of Texas Press, 1991. Penetrating discussion of the Mexican migration to and settlement in the upper Midwest regions.

SEE ALSO: El Paso incident; Farm and migrant workers; Guest-worker programs; Immigration Act of 1943; Latinos and immigrants; Mexican American Legal Defense and Educational Fund; Mexican deportations of 1931; Mexican immigrants; Operation Wetback; United Farm Workers; World War II.

"BRAIN DRAIN"

DEFINITION: Exodus of highly educated and skilled workers from developing countries to more advanced industrial countries

SIGNIFICANCE: Brain drain oftentimes pulls the best and the brightest from their homelands as workers seek more lucrative job opportunities abroad, where they believe their marketability will be rewarded. Brain drain usually occurs in developing countries where there is religious persecution, political instability, economic turmoil, or civil conflict. The emigrating workers are skilled specialists (researchers, technicians, medical professionals, engineers, and educators) who perform crucial services that contribute to global competitiveness in medical or scientific research, entrepreneurship, and technological advances for the host country.

The London Royal Society coined the term "brain drain" to describe the mass emigration of preeminent scientists from East Germany and the Soviet Union to the United States and Canada after World War II. The advantages of brain drain include knowledge flow, global cooperation, and international mobility, which allows professionals to exchange management experience. However, critics have contended that such an exodus of talented persons has negative consequences for the emigrants' home countries, which are left behind in an economic sense. Migrants from developing countries are likely to stay in advanced countries, since certain fields require expensive equipment and labs that the host countries have, and because such amenities are not always available or accessible in developing countries.

The negative economic consequences of brain drain are substantial. At the beginning of the twenty-first century, one study found that an estimated 20 percent of skilled South Africans had left their homeland and that brain drain cost the country about $250 million annually. India was producing 178,000 software engineers each year, and four of ten programmers worked in the United States. In 1998, the Indian Institute of Technology sent 30 percent of its graduates to the United States. In 2001, the United Nations estimated that India was losing $2 billion per year because of brain drain, a devastating loss for a country in which 40 percent of the adult population is illiterate.

UNITED STATES

The United States attracts more foreign-born professionals than any other country in the world. American colleges and universities have traditionally recruited foreign students in the hope that they may return to make significant contributions to their home countries. However, higher education has been an important means for American companies to recruit such workers. In fact, fewer than one-half of foreign doctoral and postdoctoral students who study in United States return to their home countries after graduation. Surveys showed that 88 percent of doctoral graduates in science

and technology from 1990 to 1991 still resided in the United States five years later, leaving home countries with shortages in the fields of medicine and engineering. Since the early 1990's, approximately 900,000 skilled workers have emigrated from India, China, and Russia under the temporary visa program, and only a few countries have been successful in luring their talented, well-educated young people back home.

REVERSE BRAIN DRAIN

At the beginning of the twenty-first century, the United States began losing scientists and engineers to Asia, confronting a "reverse brain drain," in which individuals legally enter the country to work or study but, due to a limited visa quota and numerous delays in processing, return to their home countries to work for global competitors of the United States. Amid the global recession that began in 2008, these professionals have been returning to countries such as India and China, whose economies are booming, applying their knowledge and experience gained while living in the United States. These countries have learned that the best method for attracting and maintaining professionals is to improve working conditions and career advancement opportunities.

Reverse brain drain could have serious implications for the United States. In 2006, 25.6 percent of all patent applications in the United States listed foreign national as inventors or coinventors, an increase of 18 percent from 1998. The loss of such innovation in the fields of medicine and engineering could be devastating unless the immigration policy for skilled workers is improved. On an annual basis, more than one million skilled immigrants compete for only about 120,000 visas allotted by the United States, fueling the brain drain reversal.

Gayla Koerting

FURTHER READING

Beine, Michel, Frédéric Docquier, and Hillel Rapoport. "Brain Drain and Economic Growth: Theory and Evidence." *Journal of Development Economics* 64 (February, 2001): 275-289. Utilizing a quantitative analysis of data, the authors address the impact of migration on human capital formation for small developing countries. They conclude that migration does foster advancement in educational levels, but because of economic limitations in the native country, such immigrants will not have an incentive to return home.

Cervantes, Mario, and Dominique Guellec. "The Brain Drain: Old Myths, New Realities." *OECD Observer* no. 230 (January, 2002): 40-41. Addresses how native countries cope with the brain drain phenomenon by developing government policies to attract and retain highly skilled workers or researchers.

Cordis Corporation. "Should We Plug the Brain Drain? The Pros and Cons of Scientist Mobility." *Times Higher Education Supplement,* July 20, 2006, 1-2. Summary of a discussion by panelists at the Euroscience Open Forum held in Munich, Germany, debating the costs and benefits of brain drain in the sciences, information technology, and business.

Miyagiwa, Kaz. "Scale Economies in Education and the Brain Drain Problem." *International Economic Review* 32 (August, 1991): 743-759. Argues that brain drain is more detrimental to professionals possessing intermediate-level skills regardless of whether this class chooses to emigrate or to remain in their native countries.

Solimano, Andrés. *Globalizing Talent and Human Capital: Implications for Developing Countries.* Santiago, Chile: CEPAL, 2002. Solimano provides facts, trends, and empirical evidence that emigration of human capital often depends on the country of origin. Poor countries and economies suffer the most from emigration of highly skilled researchers or entrepreneurs. The author also suggests how governments can develop policy initiatives to stem the outflow of talent from these countries.

Wadhwa, Vivek. "The Reverse Brain Drain." *BusinessWeek Online,* August 22, 2007, 22. In this editorial, the author surmises that poor immigration policy, low visa quotas, and numerous delays in this process drive talented foreigners away from the United States to global competitors.

Webber, Alan M. "Reverse Brain Drain Threatens U.S. Economy." *USA Today,* February 23, 2004, p. 13A. The author contends that restrictions on talented foreign researchers migrating into the United States and the outsourcing of jobs formerly held by highly educated Americans overseas has serious implications for the U.S. economy.

SEE ALSO: African immigrants; Argentine immigrants; Australian and New Zealander immigrants; Economic consequences of immigration; Economic opportunities; Education; Emigration; Globalization; Higher education; Return migration; Science.

BRAZILIAN IMMIGRANTS

SIGNIFICANCE: Economic and political instability in Brazil during the late twentieth century prompted unprecedented emigration from the country. Approximately one million Brazilians came to live in the United States. Many of these immigrants took jobs in service industries in northeastern metropolitan areas, southern Florida, and California. Mostly members of the middle and upper classes in their native country, they came primarily from the Europeanized southern areas of Brazil.

The first Brazilians to enter what is now the United States may have been a group of Sephardic Jews who arrived in 1654. Calculating the number of Brazilians in the United States is speculative. With a sparse migration history, they have been ambiguously identified by immigration agencies as "His-

PROFILE OF BRAZILIAN IMMIGRANTS	
Country of origin	Brazil
Primary language	Portuguese
Primary regions of U.S. settlement	Northeast, Florida, California
Earliest significant arrivals	Possibly 1654
Peak immigration period	Late twentieth century
Twenty-first century legal residents*	96,829 (12,104 per year)

*Immigrants who obtained legal permanent resident status in the United States.

Source: Department of Homeland Security, *Yearbook of Immigration Statistics, 2008.*

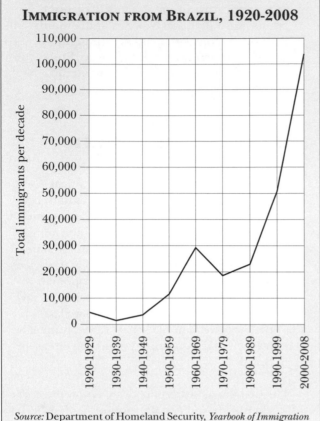

IMMIGRATION FROM BRAZIL, 1920-2008

Source: Department of Homeland Security, *Yearbook of Immigration Statistics, 2008.* Figures include only immigrants who obtained legal permanent resident status.

panic," "Latino," and "South" or "Latin" American. The U.S. Census Bureau first listed a category for Brazilians residents in 1960, calculating under thirty thousand. Until the 1980's, no more than a few thousand entered annually.

The 1980's saw a gargantuan swell of immigrants seeking economic opportunity and fleeing social decay. During that decade, Brazil suffered hyperinflation that paralyzed its economy, causing unemployment to soar. Moreover, an authoritarian military government was replaced by a democratic civilian administration. These factors prompted numerous middle- and upper-class Brazilians to emigrate, primarily to Europe and the United States. By the end of the twentieth century, approximately two million Brazilians had migrated abroad, more than 1 percent of the national population.

Brazil is a country of richly mixed African, Euro-pean, and indigenous ethnicities. However, the Brazilians most likely to emigrate were from the European-heritage southern parts of the country. They settled in northeastern U.S. states with Portuguese-speaking communities, East Coast metropolitan areas with varied job opportunities, and in parts of California and southern Florida with climates similar to those of their homeland. California and Florida tended to attract upper-class Brazilians with professional and artistic ambitions. About 100,000 Brazilians lived in New York City, forming a Little Brazil neighborhood in mid-Manhattan, where the monthly tabloid newspaper *The Brasilians* was launched.

At the beginning of the twenty-first century, approximately one million Brazilians lived in the United States. However, that figure is merely an estimate because as many as one-third of the Brazilian immigrants enter the United States without documentation to evade quota restrictions. One city in central Brazil became notorious for sending clandestine immigrants, who settle mostly in New Jersey and work shoeshine services.

Middle-class Brazilians who have settled in the United States may decline in social status, working in restaurants and housecleaning jobs; but they improve economically relative to Brazil, sending back remittances to their families. Economic and political conditions have greatly improved in Brazil during the twenty-first century so that the impetus for immigrating has declined. At the same time, since the terrorist attacks on September 11, 2001, U.S. immigration and police agents are more vigilant regarding illegal immigrants. Thereby, uncertain legal status and marginal socioeconomic status has prompted many Brazilians to return to Brazil.

Edward A. Riedinger

FURTHER READING

Beserra, Bernadete. *Brazilian Immigrants in the United States: Cultural Imperialism and Social Class.* New York: LFB Scholarly Publishing, 2003.

Jouët-Pastré, Clémence, and Leticia J. Braga. *Becoming Brazuca: Brazilian Immigration to the United States.* Cambridge, Mass.: David Rockefeller Center for Latin American Studies, Harvard University Press, 2008.

Margolis, Maxine L. *Little Brazil: An Ethnography of Brazilian Immigrants in New York City.* Princeton, N.J.: Princeton University Press, 1994.

SEE ALSO: California; Economic consequences of immigration; Economic opportunities; Employment; Florida; Latin American immigrants; New Jersey; New York City; Portuguese immigrants; Push-pull factors; Remittances of earnings.

BRIN, SERGEY

IDENTIFICATION: Russian-born cofounder of Google

BORN: August 21, 1973; Moscow, Soviet Union (now in Russia)

SIGNIFICANCE: Brin teamed up with Stanford University classmate Larry Page to found the Internet company Google, based on its search engine that uses backlinks for ranking. By the early twenty-first century, Google had become the most popular search engine in the world.

Born in Moscow in what was then the Soviet Union, Sergey Brin grew up in a very intellectual Russian Jewish family. His mother was an aeronautical engineer and his father was a mathematician. By the time he was six, anti-Semitism in the Soviet Union had reached such a fevered pitch that his parents decided it was time to leave for their son's sake.

When Brin's family arrived in the United States, his father, who had formerly worked as an economist for the Soviet state planning agency, Gosplan, was able to secure a position teaching mathematics at the University of Maryland. A brilliant student, Brin took classes at the University of Maryland while still in high school. After earning his bachelor's degree, he pursued a doctorate in computer science at Stanford University in Northern California. There he met Larry Page, with whom he designed a practical Internet search engine that they called Google. They both dropped out of Stanford in 1998 to start their company in a friend's garage. Google had its initial public offering six years later.

Brin's experiences have informed both Google's corporate ethos ("Don't be evil") and his determination to make Google profitable. He takes a token salary of one dollar per year, instead depending on the value of his Google stock for his income. In 2009, *Forbes* magazine ranked the thirty-five-year-old billionaire Brin as the twenty-sixth richest person in the world.

Leigh Husband Kimmel

FURTHER READING

Battelle, John. *The Search: How Google and Its Rivals Rewrote the Rules of Business and Transformed Our Culture.* New York: Portfolio, 2005.

Langville, Amy N., and Carl D. Meyer. *Google's PageRank and Beyond: The Science of Search Engine Rankings.* Princeton, N.J.: Princeton University Press, 2006.

Vise, David A. *The Google Story: Inside the Hottest Business, Media, and Technology Success of Our Time.* New York: Macmillan, 2005.

SEE ALSO: Former Soviet Union immigrants; Jewish immigrants; Railroads; Religions of immigrants; Russian and Soviet immigrants.

BRITISH IMMIGRANTS

SIGNIFICANCE: As one of the earliest immigrant groups to North America, the British were responsible for some basic American cultural features, including language, laws, religion, education, and administration. They were also responsible for developing forms of trade and for creating strong American political and cultural links with Great Britain that have survived into the twenty-first century.

British immigration to what is now the United States has run in an unbroken line from 1607 into the twenty-first century. However, it has gone through major transformations over the centuries: The earliest British settlers were the first major immigration group, imposing their culture on newly settled territory; modern British immigrants have become an almost invisible group, whose members assimilate quickly into American culture. Never been culturally homogeneous, British immigrants have been made up of several subgroups. Scotland remained a separate country for the first hundred years of British immigration, and Scottish immigrants developed their own distinctive patterns. In contrast, what is now the independent nation of Ireland was part of the United Kingdom until the early twentieth century, and its immigrants also developed their own immigration patterns, which should be considered separately. Even Welsh immigration had somewhat different features, though statistically these are much more difficult to disentangle from the predominant English patterns.

VIRGINIA COLONIES

The first phase of British—mainly English—settlement in the North American colonies was centered on Virginia and New England, to be followed by Maryland, the Carolinas, and Pennsylvania. After the transfer of the Dutch colonies to British rule, British immigration developed in New York, New Jersey, and Delaware. Lastly came the Georgia settlement. British emigration was not confined to the colonies that would later become the United States, however. Scottish immigration to Nova Scotia (New Scotland) was attempted in the face of French opposition. Newfoundland was settled unsuccessfully by the second Lord Baltimore, who then moved on to Maryland in an attempt to found a Roman Catholic settlement. However, the majority of British emigrants preferred Bermuda and colonies in the West Indies, especially Barbados, and Providence Island, off the coast of Central America, followed by Jamaica, Antigua, and other small islands that the British had wrested from the Spanish.

The main colonies of Virginia and New England developed quite differently in that they attracted very different types of immigrants. The first settlement that became permanent was founded in 1607 in the Jamestown area of Virginia. This was overseen by the Virginia Company of London, and was largely a commercial venture. In the hope of earning quick profits, many settlers who had little experience in farming or building came to Virginia. To these were added convicts whose sentences were commuted to "transportation." Had it not been for a few determined leaders, such as Captain John Smith, the Virginia colony would have foundered on several occasions because of rampant sickness, company inefficiency, and an Indian massacre. After the company finally went bankrupt in 1624, the English crown took over the running of the colony

directly. Meanwhile, new immigrants kept coming. The indenture system was instituted in which young men and women effectively sold themselves into servitude for fixed periods, at the end of which their masters were to give them capital and, at first, some land. Tobacco became the colony's dominant crop.

NEW ENGLAND COLONIES

In contrast, British colonies in New England were founded by more principled immigrants, many of whom left England for religious reasons. The "Pilgrim fathers," landing under the aegis of the Plymouth Bay Company, were basically nonconformists, that is, believing in the separation of church (especially the Church of England) and state. The Puritans, who held for radical reform of the Church of England, settled to the north around Salem and then Boston, under the aegis of the Massachusetts Bay Company and the Council for New England.

In practical and organizational terms, these settlers were highly self-sufficient and quickly began making commercial profits through fishing and furs, then lumber products and even staple foodstuffs. As their settlements developed, they chose to sever as many ties with England as they could, at least until the 1640's, when the Puritan Revolution launched the two-decade Commonwealth era in England. They created their own legal and electoral systems. They were fortunate to have a continuity of good leadership under men such as John Winthrop. Even so, the colonies' growth was slow, with deaths through disease common and many settlers returning to England. In 1640, it is estimated that Massachusetts had only 14,000 English settlers; Virginia had 8,000, and Connecticut, Maryland, and New Hampshire each had fewer than 2,000. By 1660, Boston had no more than 3,000 inhabitants and Virginia's towns even fewer. Backcountry settlements stretched barely one hundred miles inland from the coastal towns.

PLACE-NAMES

It generally falls to the first inhabitants of a land to name its features. Place-names consequently provide valuable evidence about the identities of early inhabitants and particularly whence they originated. Most place-names adopted by English settlers fall into four categories:

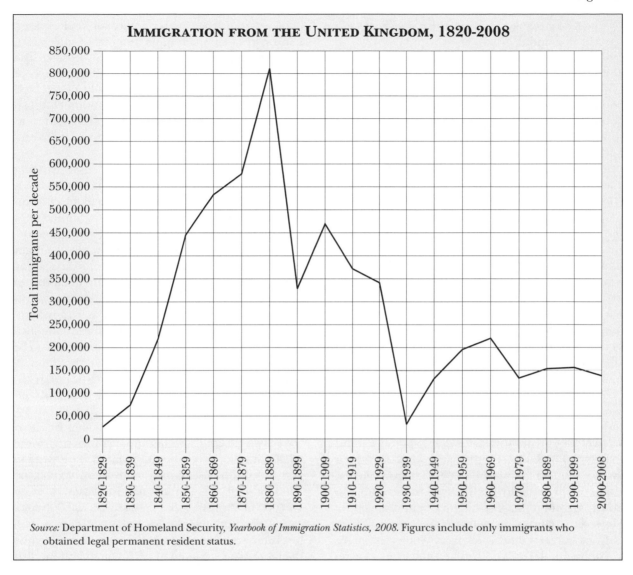

IMMIGRATION FROM THE UNITED KINGDOM, 1820-2008

Source: Department of Homeland Security, *Yearbook of Immigration Statistics, 2008.* Figures include only immigrants who obtained legal permanent resident status.

- names adapted from Native American forms
- names symbolizing their hopes and beliefs
- names honoring eminent persons,
- names borrowed from places in their original homeland

Examples of place-names adapted from earlier Native American names include Massachusetts, Connecticut, and Susquehanna. Names expressing hopes and beliefs include Providence (divine guidance), Salem (peace), and Philadelphia (love). The many places honoring persons include Delaware and Baltimore (both aristocratic founders of colonies), Virginia (after the Virgin Queen, Eliza-

beth I), and Charlotte, Charles Town, Charleston James Town, and Jamestown—all from British monarchs. New York was named after the duke of York, whose brother, King Charles II granted him the land taken from the original Dutch settlers.

However, the fourth category—names borrowed from homelands—is most informative about the origins of the earliest British settlers. Nearly all such names in the early British colonies were taken from names of English places. Indeed, the very name "New England" suggests that a number of these places had the prefix "New." Other examples include New London, New Shoreham, New Jersey, and New Hampshire. The majority of such borrowings, however, were simply the names that were used in England.

The early settlers also brought their English county system with them and used distinctly English names for their new American counties. Many county names were borrowed from the names of counties in eastern England. These include Norfolk, Suffolk, Essex, Cambridge, Haverhill, Boston, and Yarmouth. Such county names are especially evident in the New England colonies. Other borrowings come from southwestern England: Bristol, Gloucester, Somerset, and Barnstaple—the later a major port of exit, as were Plymouth and Weymouth. Another major grouping of names comes from London and southeastern England. Examples include Middlesex, Surrey, Guildford (or Guilford), Hertford (or Hartford), Newhaven, Kent, Isle of Wight, Portsmouth, and Southampton. Other parts of England are also represented by county names such as Chester, Cheshire, Lancaster, and Manchester from the northwest; Cumberland and Westmorland from the north; Litchfield, Birmingham, and Stafford from England's West Midlands.

The absence of Scottish-derived place-names is significant. Welsh place-names are also rare, with only Bangor, Newport, and Swansea being well known. Welsh immigrants tended to prefer settling in colonies in the West Indies, and the Scots did not face the same religious pressures that drove the Puritans out of England. Only a few Scottish names in South Carolina suggest later immigration there. However, a cluster of Welsh names around Philadelphia suggests significant early Welsh settlement there. Examples of Welsh place-names in that region include Bryn Mawr, Haverford, Naberth, Berwyn, and Llanerch.

COLONIAL PERIOD

The English Civil War (1642-1651) temporarily curtailed British emigration to North America. However, the Commonwealth period and the subsequent Restoration period produced large numbers of disaffected emigrants. One of the disaffected groups was the rapidly growing Quakers, who were fiercely persecuted in England. One of the leaders, William Penn, was the son of Admiral William Penn, a friend of Charles II, the restored British monarch. Penn was granted a large tract of land north of Maryland and south of New York and New Jersey. Large numbers of English and Welsh

Quakers took the chance for religious freedom. Penn laid out Philadelphia as a city of toleration. His idealistic hopes were similar to those of the Puritans, but unlike them, he was willing to accept adherents of other faiths, especially persecuted Christians from Europe. For the first time, English immigrants mixed with people from Germany and mingled with previous immigrants from the Netherlands and Sweden.

English immigration continued to all existing twelve colonies, which were soon to be joined by a thirteenth, Georgia. Though some went to Boston and the newly founded Charleston in South Carolina, Philadelphia and its surrounding areas became the most popular. Indenture was still a main means of settling in the colonies, though as slavery grew in the southern plantations, the need for indentured servants lessened there. Transportation of felons still continued, but it was becoming unpopular. During the eighteenth century, one estimate suggests as many as 40,000 prisoners were transported, the growing majority to Maryland. A significant number of immigrants—especially children—were actually kidnapped in Britain and sold in the United States.

In 1689, the British population of New England was about 80,000. The middle colonies had some 40,000 immigrants, not all of whom were British; and the southern colonies more than 80,000. By 1760, immigrant numbers had increased to some 165,000 in Virginia alone, plus some 150,000 African slaves. Other colonies saw similar increases, but immigration into New York was hampered by the large estates owned by early Dutch and English grandees. However, in New England especially, the increase in population was mainly by natural increase, the flow of immigrants declining considerably. One estimate suggests that natural population increases doubled every twenty-five years.

REVOLUTIONARY WAR

The colonies all evolved forms of self-government some were more democratic than others. The growing demands of the British government for revenues, first confined to commerce through the Navigation Acts of the mid-seventeenth century, grew as the costs of wars against North America's other main colonial power, France, escalated. In the end, the colonies revolted over these demands. An inept British government was unable to compromise and the Revolutionary War (1775-1783) ensued, beginning in New England, and then working its way down all the British colonies. Voluntary immigration into British North America virtually stopped during this period; however, large numbers of British soldiers were sent there to fight.

At the cessation of hostilities, a number of settlers who remained loyal to Britain decided to go to Britain or to Canada, which remained under British rule since being wrested from the French in 1763. Estimates of the numbers of postwar emigrants range from 80,000 to 100,000. For a short period of time, therefore, there was a net outward flow of people from the former colonies. By the early nineteenth century, an inward flow had returned, though initially not on the same scale as before the war. Transportation of British felons was diverted from North America to the newly settled Australia, and indenture was ended in 1825.

Figures from the U.S. Census of 1790 suggest that people of English descent made up 60 percent of the total U.S. population, and the Scots some 8 percent. Massachusetts and Virginia each had more than 300,000 of English and Welsh residents, followed by North Carolina with 190,000.

As lands in Tennessee, Ohio, and the Midwest opened to settlers and lands even farther west enticed, more British settlers followed. The English poet John Keats's brother George was one of the new immigrants. The poet's correspondence documents his brother's misfortunes. George Keats and his wife returned to England eventually, after losing most of their money to no less a trader than the famous naturalist John James Audubon. The early Industrial Revolution was also absorbing large numbers of landless British workers into growing British cities, restricting the flow of British emigrants.

NINETEENTH CENTURY SURGE

Precise U.S. immigration statistics began in 1830, making it easier to trace the pattern of British immigration from that date. Overall British immigration was not significant again until 1851. Figures for the years up to that date appear high only because they included Irish immigrants, who made up the bulk of the numbers. After midcentury, however, English immigration made up 10 percent of all European immigration into the United States, with Scottish immigration running at 9 percent of

PROFILE OF BRITISH IMMIGRANTS	
Country of origin	United Kingdom
Primary language	English
Primary regions of U.S. settlement	New England, East Coast, South
Earliest significant arrivals	1607
Peak immigration periods	1620-1760, 1850-1920
Twenty-first century legal residents*	124,917 (15,615 per year)

*Immigrants who obtained legal permanent resident status in the United States, including people from England, Scotland, Wales, and Northern Ireland.
Source: Department of Homeland Security, *Yearbook of Immigration Statistics, 2008.*

the English figures and Welsh at about 4 percent. Both figures conform with the overall composition of Great Britain's population. About 250,000 English immigrated to the United States during the 1850's. That figure grew to 644,680 during the peak decade of the 1880's, when English immigrants constituted 13.6 percent of all European immigrants.

No single destination attracted these new immigrants. The reasons behind the increased immigration rates lay in the huge growth of the British population, deteriorating urban conditions and a slowdown in Britain's Industrial Revolution, which was being overtaken by those of Germany and France. Included in the figures for English immigrants were unknown numbers of Irish who moved on to the United States after first immigrating to England.

SCOTTISH IMMIGRATION

The Scottish experience can be divided into two. The first arises out of the Scots being encouraged to emigrate to Ulster, in Northern Ireland, around 1611, to occupy land taken from the native Irish. These people became known as the Scotch-Irish, and their immigration to the Americas might best be regarded as part of Irish immigration.

The second Scottish group were mainly Presbyterians. During the seventeenth century they enjoyed freedom of religion until the Restoration period after 1660. After that, they endured severe restrictions. However, as Canada came under British control, most Scottish emigrants preferred to go there, perhaps partly because Canada's terrain resembled that of Scotland. There was, however, Scottish emigration as far south as the Carolinas.

Extrapolations of data from the U.S. Census of 1790 suggest that overall Scottish immigration into the United States stood at 8 percent of the total population, with the heaviest groupings in Virginia, the Carolinas, and Pennsylvania. At the same time, Canada remained a popular destination for Scottish immigration, which was hastened by the Highland clearances during the eighteenth and nineteenth centuries. However, significant numbers continued to arrive in the United States. In fact, during the first decade of the twentieth century, when Scotland's economy took a downturn, the 120,469 Scottish immigrants who entered the United States were represented almost one-third the 388,051 English immigrants who arrived during the same period. A peak period of Scottish immigration was during the 1920's, when 159,781 Scots entered the United States; this number matched that of English immigrants during that decade.

WELSH IMMIGRATION

Welsh names can be found in early lists of British emigrants going to the West Indies, but not in lists of emigrants going to the North American colonies. However, significant numbers of Welsh Quakers arrived in Philadelphia at the end of the seventeenth century, as place-name evidence testifies, and to a lesser extent in Rhode Island. Other Welsh groups settled in the Carolinas and Virginia, according to data in the 1790 U.S. Census.

The rapid growth of the coal-mining industry, driven by the Industrial Revolution, absorbed thousands of landless Welsh. Welsh miners would also later be in demand during the California gold rush. The repression of Welsh culture and language by the English during the nineteenth century drove Welsh emigrants to countries such as Argentina, where their traditional sheep-farming could be practiced unhindered. However, smaller numbers came to the United States with other British immigrants throughout the nineteenth and twentieth centuries.

MODERN TRENDS

British immigration to the United States declined slowly during the early decades of the twentieth century at the same time immigration from southern and eastern Europe was increasing. More mindful of the needs of its own empire, Great Britain by then was sending large numbers of people to Canada, Australia, New Zealand, and South Africa. During the U.S. immigration-quota era that began during the 1920's, the British quota was not always filled.

A sudden surge of British immigration after World War II can be partly explained by the number of war brides who came to the United States. These women had met and married American servicemen stationed in the United Kingdom during the war. However, the more significant reason for the increased immigration was the great disparity in standards of living in postwar Britain and the United States. After World War II, the British once again saw America as a land of opportunity. However, as Britain's own standard of living improved, emigration dropped of. By the 1970's, only 2.7 percent of all immigrants entering the United States legally came from Great Britain.

After the 1970's, British immigration held steady at about 20,000 persons per year. According to the 2000 U.S. Census, 824,239 residents of the United States had been born in the United Kingdom, a figure that made the British the ninth-largest immigrant group. Most modern British immigrants have been professionals and skilled workers, including students, teachers and medical personnel, multinational employees, skilled construction workers, and spouses of Americans. British immigrants are nearly invisible in the United States, where they have assimilated quickly. With the growing ease of transatlantic travel, many British immigrants prefer to go back and forth between the United States and Britain instead of opting for American citizenship. In 2004, 139,000 British people entered the United States to become residents, but only 15,000 sought naturalization.

David Barratt

FURTHER READING

Berthoff, Rowland T. *British Immigrants in Industrial America, 1790-1950*. Cambridge, Mass.: Harvard University Press, 1953. Early study of the effects of the Industrial Revolution in both the United

Kingdom and United States, and on British immigration.

Coldham, Peter Wilson. *The Complete Book of Emigrants, 1607-1660*. Baltimore: Genealogical Publishing, 1987. One of the fullest available summaries of all documents relating to English emigration during the seventeenth century, and where they are to be found. Every family name mentioned is indexed.

Daniels, Roger. *Coming to America: A History of Immigration and Ethnicity in American Life*. New York: HarperCollins, 1990. Sets British immigration into a wider context and deals fully with pre-Revolutionary War British immigration.

Erickson, Charlotte J. *Invincible Immigrants: The Adaptation of English and Scottish Immigrants in Nineteenth Century America*. Leicester, England: Leicester University Press, 1972. Important survey of the second peak period of British immigration, with useful data and appendixes.

Gerber, David. *Authors of Their Lives: The Personal Correspondence of British Immigrants to North America in the Nineteenth Century*. New York: New York University Press, 2006. Gerber analyzes letters to see what immigration meant to individuals. Gerber studies the letters as a literary form in which immigrants recorded their experiences.

Waters, Mary C., and Reed Ueda, eds. *The New Americans: A Guide to Immigration Since 1965*. Cambridge, Mass.: Harvard University Press, 2007. This volume's chapter on the United Kingdom by Wendy D. Roth is the most up-to-date account of the continuing British immigration. However, it makes only a limited attempt to separate out the various countries of Great Britain.

Whyte, Donald. *Dictionary of the Scottish Emigrants to the U.S.A.* Baltimore: Genealogical Publishing House, 1972. Fully catalogued list of Scottish immigration and analyses.

SEE ALSO: Canada vs. United States as immigrant destinations; European immigrants; History of immigration, 1620-1783; History of immigration, 1783-1891; Irish immigrants; Massachusetts; Pilgrim and Puritan immigrants; Virginia; War brides.

BUREAU OF IMMIGRATION, U.S.

IDENTIFICATION: Federal government agency established to control immigration in the United States

DATE: Established on March 3, 1891

ALSO KNOWN AS: Bureau of Immigration and Naturalization

SIGNIFICANCE: The Bureau of Immigration was the first federal government entity to standardize immigration operations in the United States, and it enforced legislation passed by the U.S. Congress and reported on the status of immigrants entering the country.

Until late in the nineteenth century, foreign immigration into the United States was overseen by the governments of individual states. The U.S. Congress created a commissioner of immigration in 1864, but that position was abolished only four years later. It was not until 1891 that managing immigration became a federal responsibility. In March of that year Congress established the Bureau of Immigration, charging it with developing policies to systematize immigration processes.

Initially, the bureau was responsible for collecting the tax new immigrants were required to pay on entry to the country. Bureau officials later began collating and publishing rosters of immigrants, enforcing laws that established quotas for immigrants from certain countries, and conducting health inspections to detect communicable diseases among those wishing to enter the United States. One of the bureau's first actions was to begin operating newly created permanent immigrant inspection stations at the nation's borders. The most notable of these was at Ellis Island, which opened in New York Harbor in 1892. The bureau also eventually ran stations in other major ports of entry such as Philadelphia, Boston, New Orleans, and San Francisco, where a facility on Angel Island served as a detention center for Asians whose entry into the country was being contested by federal and California state officials.

The bureau was never adequately funded to perform all its assigned tasks. Over the years, it was shifted among various government departments. In 1903, it became a part of the newly created Department of Commerce and Labor. In 1906, it was

Immigrants awaiting examination at Ellis Island during the early twentieth century. (Library of Congress)

given the additional responsibility of administering federal programs for naturalization and became known as the Bureau of Immigration and Naturalization. In 1914, the agency moved to the Department of Labor and its functions were divided between two agencies—the Bureau of Immigration and the Bureau of Naturalization.

Annual reports from the Bureau of Immigration often served as cautionary tales regarding the future of immigration. Bureau leaders constantly warned about problems caused by the increasing concentration of foreign immigrants in major northeastern cities and about increasing problems of immigration from Mexico. The latter concern prompted Congress to create the U.S. Border Patrol in 1924. The initial mission of this new subsidiary of the Bureau of Immigration was to apprehend immigrants entering the United States illegally; however, its principal initial targets were Chinese attempting to enter the country illegally by going through Mexico because they had been denied legal admission through U.S. ports of entry.

In 1933, the Bureau of Immigration and the Bureau of Naturalization were once again reunited in a single agency, the U.S. Immigration and Naturalization Service (INS), within the Department of Labor. After that date, the term "Bureau of Immigration" became used less frequently. The name had largely disappeared from common parlance by the time the INS was transferred to the Department of Justice in 1940.

Laurence W. Mazzeno

FURTHER READING

Briggs, Vernon M., Jr. *Immigration Policy and the American Labor Force.* Baltimore: Johns Hopkins University Press, 1984.

Smith, Darrell Hevenor, and H. Guy Herring. *The Bureau of Immigration: Its History, Activities, and Organization.* New York: AMS Press, 1974.

Zolberg, Aristide. *A Nation by Design: Immigration Policy in the Fashioning of America.* New York: Russell Sage Foundation, 2006.

SEE ALSO: Citizenship and Immigration Services, U.S.; Commission on Immigration Reform, U.S.;

Ellis Island; History of immigration after 1891; Immigration Act of 1891; Immigration Act of 1903; Immigration Act of 1907; Immigration Act of 1917; Immigration Act of 1921; Immigration Act of 1924; Immigration and Naturalization Service, U.S.; Immigration law.

BURLINGAME TREATY OF 1868

THE TREATY: Formal agreement between the United States and China that allowed substantially increased Chinese immigration to the United States

DATE: July 28, 1868

SIGNIFICANCE: The Burlingame Treaty permitted almost unlimited and unrestricted immigration by Chinese to the United States. It annulled several state laws that had restricted Chinese immigration. Passed at a time when significant domestic opposition to Chinese immigration was emerging, it was the final agreement with China that encouraged immigration before the federal government introduced severe restrictions.

The Burlingame Treaty of 1868 allowed Chinese immigration to the United States with few regulations. Chinese had begun coming to the United States mostly because of the discovery of gold in California, and they also played an important role in constructing railroads. In addition, they served as a source of cheap labor for American businesses. Their numbers gradually increased during the mid-nineteenth century. Around 1850, approximately 10,000 Chinese came to the United States. During the mid-1850's. By 1867, approximately 50,000 Chinese lived in California alone.

The Burlingame Treaty amended the Tientsin Treaty of 1858. The new treaty arose partly out of China's concerns about many U.S. state laws that discriminated against Chinese immigrants. In addition, the Chinese government wanted recognition of its own territorial integrity and national sovereignty. Consequently, the agreement also permitted China to have consuls at American ports who were similar to those of other national powers. Furthermore, the United States wanted more access for its people and products to the Chinese market. The reasons the United States entered into the treaty were primarily economic, and because anti-Chinese sentiment was growing within the

Canton, the only Chinese port open to American trade during the mid-nineteenth century. (R. S. Peale and J. A. Hill)

United States, American participation in the agreement proved politically challenging.

The treaty is named after Anson Burlingame, an American diplomat who served as U.S. minister to China during the 1860's. Because of the respect he earned from the Chinese government, they asked him to lead their own diplomatic mission to the West. The agreement contained a reciprocal provision, which meant that Chinese immigration to the United States would not be heavily regulated. Industrial interests within the United States were strongly supportive of the treaty. The treaty's clause regarding immunities and privileges was strongly endorsed by China in order to prevent discrimination and violence against Chinese living in the United States.

The growing opposition to Chinese immigration was strongest in the western part of the country. American-born workers vehemently objected to the presence of and further immigration by Chinese, whom they perceived as competitors for their jobs. Indeed, anti-Chinese riots occurred in San Francisco in the latter part of the 1870's. In the 1876 national elections, both Democrat and Republican candidates took anti-Chinese immigration stances in their platforms. However, in 1879, when both houses of the U.S. Congress passed a bill to regulate Chinese immigration, President Rutherford B. Hayes vetoed it because it would violate the Burlingame Treaty.

The Burlingame Treaty was eventually annulled by subsequent American legislation. Pressure from various interest groups within the United States led to the passage of multiple acts that gradually reduced Chinese immigration. The Chinese Exclusion Act of 1882 basically prohibited Chinese from coming to the United States. After numerous renewals, its ban was finally lifted in 1943.

Kevin L. Brennan

FURTHER READING

Chen, Jack. *The Chinese of America*. San Francisco: Harper & Row, 1980.

Lee, Erica. *At America's Gates: Chinese Immigration During the Exclusion Era, 1882-1943*. Chapel Hill: University of North Carolina Press, 2003.

Tsai, Shih-shan Henry. *China and the Overseas Chinese in the United States, 1868-1911*. Fayetteville: University of Arkansas Press, 1983.

SEE ALSO: Alien land laws; Angell Treaty of 1880; Anti-Chinese movement; Bayard-Zhang Treaty of 1888; California; *Chae Chan Ping v. United States*; *Chinese Exclusion Cases*; Chinese immigrants; Geary Act of 1892; Gentlemen's Agreement; Immigration Act of 1882.

BURMESE IMMIGRANTS

SIGNIFICANCE: Burmese immigrants are relatively recent arrivals to the United States. Most immigrated after Ne Win seized power in Myanmar in 1962. With eight major ethnic groups, Burmese nationals are diverse in culture, education, and religion. They have suffered under an oppressive government regime, and most of those who have immigrated to the United States have come as refugees. During the year 2008, Burmese immigrants made up nearly 30 percent of all refugees who entered the United States.

Burmese have made up only a small portion of the Asians who have immigrated to the United States, and an overwhelming majority of them have come as refugees. Their homeland, now called Myanmar, is approximately the size of Texas, with the Himalayas along its northern and western borders, and the Indian Ocean and the Bay of Bengal to the south. This geography influenced the development of eight major ethnic groups. During the age of European imperialism, Great Britain fought to colonize the region and came to power there in 1885. The British had a significant impact on the Burmese. The groups who lived in the country's great valley region—Burmans, Mon, Rakhine, and Shan—lived under a British civil system. The ethnic minorities who lived in the mountains—Chin, Kachin, Karen, and Wa—maintained their traditional tribal systems, in which local chieftains retain their authority. This distinction in government systems fostered a gap between the country's ethnic groups, as the valley peoples had opportunities for modern education and Western customs, while the mountain peoples had limited educational opportunities and resources. The peoples in urban centers practiced Theravada Buddhism, while Christian missionaries served in rural areas and converted many Buddhists and animists to Christianity.

During the 1940's, an independence movement arose in colonial Burma under the leadership of Aung San. He wished to unify the ethnic groups but was assassinated in 1947. In January, 1948, Burma achieved its independence but remained in civil unrest for many years. In 1962, Ne Win seized power. Ruling by military force, he imposed a socialist government. He destroyed many rural villages and suppressed ethnic minorities.

Many Burmese who opposed the new regime began emigrating to the United States. This movement began slowly, with approximately 10,000 Burmese arriving in the United States before 1980. The pace of Burmese immigration accelerated during the last two decades of the twentieth century. However, after the terrorist attacks on the United States of September 11, 2001, the numbers fell as the U.S. government tightened on immigrants from Myanmar, whose government was regarded as a terrorism threat. It was not until 2006 that more immigrants began arriving from the region.

BURMESE IN THE UNITED STATES

Most Burmese immigrants have come to the United States as refugees. Many lived in refugee camps on the border with Thailand for significant periods before moving on to the United States. The immigrants have tended to settle in such major metropolitan areas as New York City, Los Angeles, Chicago, and Washington, D.C. Many refugee children have arrived in the United States with no experience of living anywhere other than in the camps and have limited education. In contrast, members of the older generations have been comparatively well educated; approximately three-quarters of them at least have the equivalent of high school diplomas. They have a strong work ethic and are eager to gain employment.

By the year 200, only about 48,000 Burmese immigrants were living in the United States. Because of their small numbers, they have had limited op-

PROFILE OF BURMESE IMMIGRANTS

Country of origin	Myanmar
Primary language	Burmese
Primary regions of U.S. settlement	East Coast, California, Illinois
Earliest significant arrivals	1962
Peak immigration period	1998-present
Twenty-first century legal residents*	1,120 (140 per year)

*Immigrants who obtained legal permanent resident status in the United States.
Source: Department of Homeland Security, Yearbook of Immigration Statistics, 2008.

portunities for cultural networking. Few people outside their group speak Burmese, and the demand for publications in Burmese is limited. Moreover, individual Burmese tend to identify themselves primarily as members of their individual ethnic group, rather than as Burmese or Myanmar nationals.

Tessa Li Powell

FURTHER READING

Barron, Sandy, et al. *Refugees from Burma: Their Backgrounds and Refugee Experiences.* Washington, D.C.: Center for Applied Linguistics, 2007.
Levinson, David, and Melvin Ember, eds. *American Immigrant Cultures: Builders of a Nation.* New York: Macmillan Reference, 1997.
Oberoi, Pia. *Exile and Belonging: Refugees and State Policy in South Asia.* New York: Oxford University Press, 2006.

SEE ALSO: Asian immigrants; Asian Indian immigrants; Cambodian immigrants; Laotian immigrants; Missionaries; Refugee fatigue; Refugees; Thai immigrants; Vietnamese immigrants.

C

Cable Act of 1922

The Law: Federal legislation that changed the status of married immigrant women so that not all of them would automatically obtain the citizenship of their husbands

Date: September 22, 1922

Also known as: Married Woman's Act

Significance: In 1907 a federal immigration law was passed that specifically stated that upon marriage a woman would take the nationality of her husband. The Cable Act changed this, except for women who were American citizens and married men who were ineligible for American citizenship under federal law because of their race.

From the creation of the United States during the late eighteenth century, it was assumed that people would immigrate to the country. The first law setting standards and processes for immigration was passed in 1790. It did not mention gender when it set up the process for Europeans—and only Europeans—to immigrate to America. Although some single women did immigrate and remain single after arriving, an assumption behind the law was that women immigrants would be part of family units and be included when their husbands, who were assumed to be the heads of the households, applied for citizenship. Although this assumption became the normal interpretation of the law, it was only in 1907 when a law was passed that specifically stated that a woman would automatically become a citizen of the country of which her husband was a citizen. This rule applied to non-U.S. citizens marrying Americans and American women marrying non-Americans. When women born in the United States tried to overturn their status in federal courts, they were unsuccessful.

In most cases the undocumented citizenship status of women was not a major issue. However, with the 1920 ratification of the Nineteenth Amendment to the U.S. Constitution, guaranteeing women the right to vote, documentation of the citizenship status of women became much more important. Similarly, the loss of citizenship for American women marrying foreigners became a consideration. Clarifying these issues was one of the earliest national legislative priorities for the recently created League of Women Voters. In addition, there were some cases when male immigrants were denied U.S. citizenship because it would have made citizens of wives who did not meet all the requirements for citizenship.

Effective with the signing of the Cable Act, most women kept their own citizenship regardless of their marital status. This was a major step toward the recognition of women as independent persons, rather than merely as part of family units. However, the rules for immigrant women married to American men were not the same as those for immigrant men married to American women. To obtain citizenship, immigrant women did not have to file as many forms and had a briefer length-of-residence requirement than immigrant men.

Most of the women who had lost their American citizenship between 1907 and 1922 because of their marriages to foreigners could apply for citizenship through the naturalization process. Exceptions to this rule included women married to Asians and Asian American women who had lost their American citizenship through marriage. Throughout the nineteenth century, immigration laws had increasingly restricted the ability of Asians to become U.S. citizens. Reflecting the rule in effect in the 1907 law, the Cable Act specifically excluded American women who married Asians (racially ineligible men) in the new provisions. In 1931 the law was amended to allow U.S. women who married Asians to retain their American citizenship. With other changes in immigration law having been passed since 1922, the Cable Act was formally repealed in 1936.

Donald A. Watt

Further Reading

Gardner, Martha Mabie. *The Qualities of a Citizen: Women, Immigration, and Citizenship, 1870-1965.* Princeton, N.J.: Princeton University Press, 2005.

Lemons, J. Stanley. *The Woman Citizen: Social Feminism in the 1920's.* Charlottesville: University of Virginia Press, 1990.

SEE ALSO: Asian immigrants; Chinese Exclusion Act of 1882; Chinese immigrants; Families; History of immigration after 1891; Immigration Act of 1907; Intermarriage; "Mongrelization"; Naturalization Act of 1790; Women immigrants; Women's movements.

CALIFORNIA

SIGNIFICANCE: California began drawing large numbers of immigrants only since its great gold rush began in 1848. That era brought in large numbers of French, German, Italian, British, Chinese, Filipino, and Mexican immigrants. Since that time, constantly changing immigrant communities have contributed enormously to the state's development.

One of the most populous subnational entities in the world, California is also ethnically very diverse, thanks to a century and a half of heavy immigration. The first major influx of immigrants occurred with the California gold rush, which attracted people hoping to strike it rich from Europe, China, Australia, and the rest of the United States. The first transcontinental railroad, which connected California with the eastern states, was built primarily by Irish and Chinese laborers. During the twentieth century, Filipino and Mexican immigrants began playing a big role in the state's huge agricultural industry.

GOLD RUSH AND THE TRANSCONTINENTAL RAILROAD

On January 24, 1848, James W. Marshall discovered gold at Sutter's Mill, near Sacramento, California. Soon, tens of thousands of immigrants from around the world traveled to California hoping to find wealth in the mines or to take advantage of the burgeoning business opportunities in the free-spending gold rush economy. Most of these immigrants came in 1849. Known as "Forty-Niners," they comprised Australians, New Zealanders, Mexicans, Germans, Italians, Britons, French, Latin Americans, and others. This period also saw the first major influx of Chinese workers into California—both as miners and as merchants and as other types of laborers. Chinese workers would provide a cheap labor pool for the state for decades to follow.

The first transcontinental railroad made immigration to California easier and more attractive. The railroad ran from Council Bluffs, Iowa, and Omaha, Nebraska, to Alameda, California, linking the Atlantic and Pacific coasts by rail for the first time. The railroad was divided into Union Pacific (westward) and Central Pacific (eastward) lines, both of which were built primarily by immigrant labor. The Central Pacific line began with Irish laborers, but due to a labor shortage in California and a downturn in mining, the railroad turned to Chinese miners and other immigrants. More than ten thousand Chinese workers were drafted to railroad work. By the second year of construction, nine of ten railroad workers were Chinese. The work was difficult, as it required carving a track through the rugged Sierra Nevadas; only fifty miles of tracks were laid during the first two years. The work was also dangerous. During one winter season in the late

---

PROFILE OF CALIFORNIA

Region	Pacific coast
Entered union	1850
Largest cities	Los Angeles, San Diego, San Jose, San Francisco, Long Beach, Fresno, Sacramento (capital), Oakland
Modern immigrant communities	Mexicans, Filipinos, Chinese

Population	*Total*	*Percent of state*	*Percent of U.S.*	*U.S. rank*
All state residents	36,457,000	100.0	12.18	1
All foreign-born residents	9,902,000	27.2	26.37	1

Source: U.S. Census Bureau, *Statistical Abstract for 2006.*
Notes: The U.S. population in 2006 was 299,399,000, of whom 37,548,000 (12.5%) were foreign born. Rankings in last column reflect total numbers, not percentages.

1860's, almost half of the three thousand workers tunneling through the summit of the Sierra Nevadas were killed by explosions, avalanches, and other accidents.

Most of the Chinese immigrants were married men who had come to California for mining, agriculture, and other work and intended to return to China. Chinese railroad workers were poorly paid and expected to work twelve hours a day, six days a week, but many managed to set aside enough money to buy land later. The need for railroad workers grew, and the railroad company imported more from China. The newer workers were paid less than those already in California, and all the Chinese immigrants were treated poorly. They were expected to work longer hours than the white laborers, and were often beaten or prevented from seeking other employment. In 1867, approximately two thousand railroad workers in the high Sierras went on strike, asking for more pay and better working conditions. However, their strike was broken within a week.

Despite the important contributions of Chinese laborers to the railroads and other sectors of California's economy, they had few recognized legal rights. In 1877, Pacific General Superintendent Charles Crocker testified before the Joint Special Committee to Investigate Chinese Immigration on the role of Chinese workers in the construction of the Central Pacific Railroad. At the time, there was great concern about the effect of cheap Chinese labor on the U.S. economy and culture, particularly in California. Crocker, who was instrumental in the decision to hire Chinese railroad workers, believed that Chinese labor was necessary to American society and benefited white laborers.

Anti-Chinese sentiment in California grew through the end of the nineteenth century, largely due to depressed wage levels. The Chinese Exclusion Act of 1882 attempted to exclude additional

Cover of an 1877 issue of Harper's Weekly *showing Chinese immigrants arriving in San Francisco.* (Berkeley DIG Library SunSITE)

Chinese laborers from entering the U.S. in an attempt to reduce the supply of cheap labor, made it difficult to reenter the country, and excluded Chinese from U.S. citizenship. This made it difficult for Chinese American communities to balance gender ratios (Chinese men outnumbered Chinese women about 19 to 1 in California), and led many Chinese workers to return to their families in China. Meanwhile, immigrants of other races were not restricted from entry to the United States.

TWENTIETH CENTURY IMMIGRATION

The Immigration Act of 1882 further restricted immigration, barring all immigration from China and restricting immigration from other Asian countries. Consequently, the Chinese American community in California consisted primarily of bachelors. After the San Francisco fire of 1906 destroyed a large number of government records in the city, many Chinese families claimed "paper sons"—immigrants from China whose ties to Chinese living in California could not be documented.

These legal exclusions contributed to the separate lives that Chinese Americans lived during the nineteenth and early twentieth centuries, centering around Chinatowns like that of San Francisco. Chinese nationals residing in the United States were permitted to become citizens in 1943 by the Magnuson Act, but large-scale Chinese immigration did not begin again until 1965.

Throughout the twentieth century, California received an influx of farmworkers, many migrant or undocumented, from Latin American nations. Agriculture, long established in California and already dependent on minorities for labor, turned to Mexican immigrants, particularly for its expanding citrus industry. The citrus industry, which had been established during the late nineteenth century, was able to expand into new markets because of the building of the transcontinental railroad. From about 1890 to 1940, citrus fruits, such as oranges and lemons, were California's main agricultural products. Mexican immigrants, living in largely company-owned villages, formed the backbone of the citrus industry.

During the early twenty-first century, seasonal migrant farmworkers, many of whom were undocumented immigrants from Mexico and other Latin American countries and the Philippines, still formed a significant percentage of California's agricultural worker pool. These migrant farmworkers were typically extremely poor and uneducated and had considerably shorter life expectancies than members of the general population.

Of California's 36.6 million residents in 2004, 9.5 million (26 percent) were foreign-born, with 2.4 million (7 percent) of these estimated to be undocumented immigrants. Nationwide, approximately 11.6 percent of the population consists of foreign-born individuals, and only 4 percent of the population is estimated to consist of undocu-mented immigrants. Through the last decade of the twentieth century, California's major immigrant groups included Mexicans, Filipinos, Chinese, Salvadorans, Vietnamese, and Koreans. Roughly 90 percent of the state's immigrants come from Latin America and Asia, with Asia contributing 40 percent of California's legal immigrants.

Despite California's impressive immigration numbers, the state was becoming a less popular destination for immigrants during the early twenty-first century. Undocumented immigrants in particular were beginning to prefer other states over California, which was home to 45 percent of the nation's undocumented immigrants in 1990, but only 24 percent in 2004. Nevertheless, immigrants have continued to fill a wide variety of roles in the California economy, particularly in construction, agriculture, service, and production industries. Asian immigrants are more likely to fill management and professional jobs than Latin American immigrants. Undocumented immigrants, primarily from Latin America, typically work on farms, in construction, or in cleaning.

Melissa A. Barton

FURTHER READING

Bain, David Howard. *Empire Express: Building the First Transcontinental Railroad.* New York: Viking Adult, 1999. Solidly researched account of the building of the railroad to cross the United States, the western half of which was built largely by Chinese immigrants to California.

Brands, H. W. *The Age of Gold: The California Gold Rush and the New American Dream.* New York: Doubleday, 2002. Readable account of the California gold rush that covers immigrant experiences during that era.

Chang, Iris. *The Chinese in America: A Narrative History.* New York: Penguin Books, 2004. History of Chinese Americans from their arrival in California during the gold rush through the twentieth century.

González, Gilbert G. *Labor and Community: Mexican Citrus Worker Villages in a Southern California County, 1900-1950.* Champaign: University of Illinois Press, 1994. Scholarly account of the rise and fall of the California citrus industry and the Mexican immigrants who worked in it.

Mitchell, Don. *The Lie of the Land: Migrant Workers and the California Landscape.* Minneapolis: University of Minnesota Press, 1996. Hard-hitting examination of how the California agricultural landscape has been built by the labor of migrant workers, including Japanese, Filipino, and Mexican immigrants.

Nahmias, Rick. *The Migrant Project: Contemporary California Farm Workers.* Albuquerque: University of New Mexico Press, 2008. Spectacular photography capturing the lives and labors of modern migrant farmworkers.

SEE ALSO: Alien land laws; Anti-Chinese movement; California gold rush; Capitation taxes; Chinatowns; Chinese immigrants; Farm and migrant workers; Filipino immigrants; Los Angeles; Mexican immigrants; *Oyama v. California*; Proposition 187; San Francisco.

CALIFORNIA GOLD RUSH

THE EVENT: The discovery of gold at Sutter's Mill in California and the subsequent influx of immigrants seeking their fortunes
DATE: 1848-1855
LOCATION: California

SIGNIFICANCE: The California gold rush was a defining moment in the history of westward migration in the United States. It was also an important period in U.S. immigration history. Many immigrant groups, especially the Chinese, began coming to the United States following news of the discovery of gold in California. Initially, the call for citizens was open to all, but as immigrants began coming in larger and larger numbers, laws were established to limit immigration and curtail the rights of those immigrants.

Despite the popular conception of the gold rush as an American event, the demographics of those who participated in it suggest otherwise. John Sutter, who had laid claim to the land on which gold was discovered, was not interested in word of the discovery being made public. He was in the midst of building a lumber mill on the South Fork of the American River on January 24, 1848, when gold was found. He wanted to finish his mill and solidify his claim to the land before hoards of gold

---

PRESIDENT POLK ACKNOWLEDGES CALIFORNIA'S GOLD

On December 5, 1848, President James K. Polk announced to Congress in his state of the union address the discovery of phenomenal amounts of gold in California, thereby giving credibility not only to the gold rush but also to the state itself. His words opened the floodgates to miners from around the world.

It was known that mines of the precious metals existed to a considerable extent in California at the time of its acquisition. Recent discoveries render it probable that these mines are more extensive and valuable than was anticipated. . . .

The effects produced by the discovery of these rich mineral deposits and the success which has attended the labors of those who have resorted to them have produced a surprising change in the state of affairs in California. Labor commands a most exorbitant price, and all other pursuits but that of searching for the precious metals are abandoned. Nearly the whole of the male population of the country have gone to the gold districts. Ships arriving on the coast are deserted by their crews and their voyages suspended for want of sailors. Our commanding officer there entertains apprehensions that soldiers can not be kept in the public service without a large increase of pay. Desertions in his command have become frequent, and he recommends that those who shall withstand the strong temptation and remain faithful should be rewarded.

This abundance of gold and the all-engrossing pursuit of it have already caused in California an unprecedented rise in the price of all the necessaries of life.

---

seekers began coming to his property to search for gold. However, Mormon settler Sam Brannan made sure that word spread, and he had a good reason to do so. He owned a flour mill in the area as well as a newspaper called the *Star,* and when gold was discovered at Sutter's Mill, he opened a store nearby and stocked it with mining implements.

Newspaper articles touting the discovery made this local event into an international incident. "The Discovery of Inexhaustible Gold Mines in California" read one headline, closely followed by these tantalizing details, clearly intended for an international audience: "Tremendous Excitement

Among the Americans: The Extensive Preparations to Migrate to the Gold Region." With such news, the flood of immigrants was inevitable.

The numbers tell the story. Fully one-third of the "forty-niners" were immigrants. Furthermore, the two-thirds who were native-born made up a diverse group: Among their numbers were Native Americans, freed blacks, and even African American slaves. The immigrant groups were equally diverse, coming from Mexico, China, France, Germany, Russia, Ireland, Italy, the West Indies, and even as far away as Australia. The gold rush attracted 30,000 immigrants from France alone. In 1852 alone, twenty thousand Chinese came to California seeking gold; as many as 2,000 Chinese arrived in San Francisco in a single day. Nevertheless, despite all the diversity in ethnicity and nationality, there was little diversity in gender: Nine out of ten of the forty-niners were men.

The gold rush is an early example of a number of attempts to sell the West to any and all that might come and settle and thus populate and tame the wilderness. Like so many other attempts to draw people westward, the reality never lived up to the hype. This became painfully true for Chinese immigrants.

CHINESE IMMIGRANTS

The citizens in southeast China were particularly vulnerable to the lure of easy gold. After China's defeat in the first Opium War with Great Britain (1839-1842), the country was open to foreign trade and foreign domination. The results were devastating to local economies. The Pearl River Delta in the Guangdong Province was particularly hard hit with high rates of unemployment brought on in part by competition from imported goods. In addition, there were peasant riots and interethnic feuding. Because of the coastal location of the province and the frequent presence of

Contemporary editorial cartoon lampooning the motives of the many immigrants flocking to California to join in the gold rush. (Library of Congress)

foreign traders, citizens quickly learned of the gold strike in California. In fact, the Chinese began calling California "Gold Mountain," and Chinese men made their way to San Francisco hoping to find enough gold to solve their family's woes.

As in all gold rushes, the so-called placer phase was short-lived: The gold that was found in abundance near the surface was taken early on, and that which was left was embedded in rock and was very difficult for individual miners to extract. Ultimately, individual miners would be replaced by mining companies. Most of the Chinese who came to America were disciplined, dedicated workers with a strong entrepreneurial spirit. Therefore, they not only worked hard in the gold fields for themselves but also proved to be indefatigable in working for others. This very quality, however, made them a threat to "American" workers, particularly as miners discovered that very few of the people who rushed to California were getting rich.

By 1852, the California state legislature had enacted a foreign miners' tax, something directed primarily toward the large numbers of Chinese and Mexicans who were mining in California. Furthermore, plans that Chinese immigrants had made to bring their families to California for a new life fell victim to increasingly strict anti-Chinese immigration laws. The ultimate expression of anti-immigrant and anti-Chinese hysteria found expression in the Chinese Exclusion Act of 1882, which suspended Chinese immigration for ten years.

Ultimately, those men who had traveled from China to California to find an escape from poverty for their families wound up alone in California. Few records remain of these lonely men, only scattered songs such as the following:

In the second reign year of Haamfung [1852], a trip to Gold Mountain was made.
With a pillow on my shoulder, I began my perilous journey.
Sailing a boat with bamboo poles across the seas,
Leaving behind wife and sisters in search of money,
No longer lingering with the women in the bedroom,
No longer paying respect to my parents at home.

OTHER IMMIGRANT GROUPS

The Chinese were not the only immigrant group that suffered persecution in the gold fields of California. All immigrants were targeted by leg-islation that made their lives much more difficult than those of Americans. They were also targeted by physical violence. For example, a group of French miners who raised a French flag over their claim were forced to abandon their mine. Mexican miners took to the hills and came back to the gold fields merely to raid the mines. The most famous of these was the legendary Hispanic outlaw Joaquín Murieta. His exploits were so notorious that the governor of California offered a reward of one thousand dollars for his head. When Murieta was finally captured and killed in 1853, his head was put in a jug of alcohol and taken from mining camp to mining camp, supposedly as an example. Legends of Murieta abound, growing out of the 1854 book *The Life and Adventures of Joaquin Murieta*, written by John Rollins Ridge. Some portrayed him as a Robin Hood figure, out to help those who were persecuted, and others as a ruthless thug. Some historians question whether he actually existed. He could well have been a composite figure, representing all Hispanic mine raiders.

H. William Rice

FURTHER READING

Brands, H. W. *The Age of Gold: The California Gold Rush and the New American Dream*. New York: Doubleday, 2002. Lively history of the event that Brands describes as having launched "the most astonishing mass movement of people since the Crusades." Does an admirable job of placing the California gold rush in the broadest possible historical perspective.

Caughey, John W. *Gold Is the Cornerstone*. Berkeley: University of California Press, 1948. Brief overview of several significant facets of the gold rush, including the original discoveries, the rush of the forty-niners, and the impact of the gold rush on California and United States history.

Gordon, Mary M., ed. *Overland to California with the Pioneer Line*. Champaign: University of Illinois Press, 1984. Collection of memoirs of participants in various land expeditions to California during the 1840's.

Holliday, J. S. *The World Rushed In: The California Gold Rush Experience*. Norman: University of Oklahoma Press, 2002. First published in 1981, this book examines the California gold rush through the voluminous and often compelling diaries of a single prospector, to which the author connects the letters of hundreds of other gold seekers.

Johnson, Susan Lee. *Roaring Camp: The Social World of the California Gold Rush.* New York: W. W. Norton, 2000. Innovative social history of the California gold rush that explores the event's multicultural dimensions and the collisions among vastly different cultures. Well written and filled with fascinating anecdotal material.

Limerick, Patricia Nelson. *The Legacy of Conquest.* New York: W. W. Norton, 1987. A must for any serious study of westward migration, this book pays particular attention to the roles of overlooked minorities. Chapter 4, "Uncertain Enterprises," concerns the gold rush.

Ward, Geoffrey C. *The West: An Illustrated History.* Boston: Little, Brown, 1996. Chapter 7, "Seeing the Elephant," provides an overview of California's gold rush, paying special attention to the role that immigrants played in the event. The chapter also contains important photographs of mining.

Yung, Judy, Gordon H. Chang, and Him Mark Lai, eds. *Chinese Voices: From the Gold Rush to the Present.* Berkeley: University of California Press, 2006. The introduction to this volume is a succinct account of the Chinese experience during the gold rush and after.

SEE ALSO: Asian immigrants; Australian and New Zealander immigrants; California; Capitation taxes; Chinese Exclusion Act of 1882; Chinese immigrants; Contract labor system; Economic opportunities; Foreign miner taxes; Mexican immigrants; San Francisco.

CAMBODIAN IMMIGRANTS

SIGNIFICANCE: The arrival of thousands of immigrants from Southeast Asia during the mid-to-late 1970's marked a new era in immigration to the United States because of multiple factors. One of the characteristics that defined this new era was the region from which these new immigrants were coming. A second trait of this new era was that the arrival of these immigrants created a strong, negative reaction among Americans against them.

Furthermore, the arrival of these immigrants led to new legislation regarding their status.

The first major influx of Cambodian immigrants who began arriving in the United States during the late 1970's was part of a large group of refugees from Southeast Asia fleeing political instability in their homelands. The most unstable Southeast Asian nation may have been Cambodia. In 1975, the Khmer Rouge came to power in that country and implemented an extreme version of agricultural-based communism. The new government may have killed as many as two million Cambodians in its attempt to reshape society. As a result, thousands of Cambodians fled the country. Vietnam's invasion of Cambodia in 1979 intensified the exodus.

A LONG JOURNEY AND UNWELCOMING ARRIVAL

Many of the Cambodian refugees initially fled to neighboring Thailand. There, they were put in refugee camps in which they endured poor conditions. Although some Cambodians remained in Thailand, thousands eventually were permitted to come to the United States at the beginning of the 1980's. This group was part of a second wave of Southeast Asian immigrants to come to the United States, the first of which had been the massive exodus from Vietnam in 1975. Given the significant influx of immigrants from Vietnam during the last half of the 1970's, the U.S. government was forced to act. In 1975, the federal government passed and signed into law the Indo-China Migration and Refugee Act. The large numbers of refugees coming to the United States from Southeast Asia led the American government to establish a resettlement program, which was created by this piece of legislation.

The U.S. government utilized this resettlement program that was created during the mid-1970's to assist Vietnamese refugees who arrived in the country. Through this program, voluntary agencies helped find sponsors to help support the new immigrants and help them adjust to American society for a limited time. The Cambodian immigrants who arrived a few years later were put through the same program. Between 1980 and 1984, approximately 75,000 Cambodians arrived in the United States.

After arriving in the United States, the difficul-

PROFILE OF CAMBODIAN IMMIGRANTS

Country of origin	Cambodia
Primary languages	Khmer, French
Primary regions of U.S. settlement	California
Earliest significant arrivals	1979
Peak immigration period	Early 1980's
Twenty-first century legal residents*	28,832 (3,604 per year)

*Immigrants who obtained legal permanent resident status in the United States.

Source: Department of Homeland Security, *Yearbook of Immigration Statistics, 2008.*

ties confronting the Cambodian immigrants did not end. They faced strong opposition from many Americans. Much of the opposition was due to the economic problems in the United States at the time. Another aspect of the opposition seemed to be racial.

The large numbers of refugees coming from Southeast Asia led to additional legislation by the federal government. Congress passed the Refugee Act of 1980 to limit the number of refugees who could enter the United States on an annual basis. Although elected officials argued that it was necessary to act in order to put the United States in line with international standards for the treatment of refugees, the numerical cap suggested it had more to do with opposition to immigration primarily linked to the economic problems confronting the United States.

ECONOMIC CHALLENGES

Like many other immigrants from Southeast Asia, Cambodian immigrants have tended to work mostly in low-wage jobs, most notably in the seafood processing industry. Many have looked for work similar to what they did in Cambodia, but some who had professional training have been unable to find corresponding employment in the United States. A relatively large number have opened grocery stores. Cambodian Americans have generally had a difficult time economically in the United States. Unemployment among them is

high. Many of them have lived in poverty and been dependent on government assistance. Their situation has tended to be worse that of other recently arrived ethnic groups in the United States.

Prior to this wave of southeastern immigration, very few people with Cambodian heritage lived in the United States. According to the U.S. Census, approximately 120,000 foreign-born Cambodians lived in the United States in 1990. More than 100,000 of them had come to the country during the 1980's. Most of them lived in California. The second-largest concentration of Cambodians lives in Massachusetts, with between 15,000 and 20,000 Cambodians. Many also live in New York City, Texas, and Pennsylvania. As the political situation in Southeast Asia improved around 1990, few Cambodians continued to immigrate to the United States.

Kevin L. Brennan

FURTHER READING

Barkan, Elliott Robert. *Asian and Pacific Islander Migration to the U.S.: A Model of New Global Patterns.* Westport, Conn.: Greenwood Press, 1992. Descriptive account of modern immigration to the United States and how it has mirrored trends in global migration.

Caplan, Nathan, John K. Whitmore, and Marcella H. Choy. *The Boat People and Achievement in America: A Study of Family Life, Hard Work, and Cultural Values.* Ann Arbor: University of Michigan Press, 1989. Historical overview of the refugee crisis in Cambodia, Laos, and Vietnam during the late 1970's. Also contains numerous individual stories of life in the United States.

Ebihara, May M., Carol A. Mortland, and Judy Ledgerwood, eds. *Cambodian Culture Since 1975: Homeland and Exile.* Ithaca, N.Y.: Cornell University Press, 1994. Collection of articles examining the perceived threat to Khmer culture and efforts to preserve it at home and abroad.

Navarro, Armando. *The Immigration Crisis: Nativism, Armed Vigilantism, and the Rise of a Countervailing Movement.* Walnut Creek, Calif.: AltaMira Press, 2008. Comprehensive history of the politics of immigration to the United States since the colonial era.

Scott, Joanna C. *Indochina's Refugees: Oral Histories from Laos, Cambodia, and Vietnam.* Jefferson, N.C.: McFarland, 1989. Several individual accounts of life in these three Southeast Asian countries immediately after the communists came to power, as well as the escape to foreign refugee camps.

SEE ALSO: Asian immigrants; Burmese immigrants; California; Employment; History of immigration after 1891; Lahiri, Jhumpa; Thai immigrants; Vietnam War; Vietnamese immigrants.

CANADA VS. UNITED STATES AS IMMIGRANT DESTINATIONS

SIGNIFICANCE: The United States and Canada are the two main immigrant destinations in North America. Although similarities exist in terms of their reception of immigrants and immigration patterns, there are important differences both in the reasons that immigrants have chosen the United States or Canada and in immigration policies between the two countries.

Although both the United States and Canada had similar British colonial origins, there were differences in the national origins of those who settled each country. In terms of ethnic diversity among immigrants, Canada did not start to catch up to the heterogeneous United States until the latter part of the twentieth century. In the early twenty-first century, both Canada and the United States are important immigrant destinations for many of the same immigrant groups, but immigration policies and immigrant settlement patterns have often diverged during the history of each country.

COLONIAL SETTLEMENT
The English began planting colonies in North America during the early seventeenth century, while the French established a small but influential presence in Canada. Thus, both English and French culture helped shape Canada, a dual heritage that sets Canada apart from the United States. Also, the British colonies of the future United States drew more immigrants than the British or French colonies in Canada. Many immigrants

heard dismal things about Canada's climate and the poor prospects for acquiring farmland, so they chose to go south instead, where there was good land and better weather.

The demand for labor was greater in the southern British colonies than in Canada, so more indentured servants went south. Because of difficulties with indentured servants running away, English colonists began transporting slaves from Africa to supplement their labor needs. African slaves and their descendants would become a significant population in the United States, but not so much in Canada. The seventeenth and eighteenth centuries also saw many more Germans, Dutch, and Scotch-Irish settle in the American colonies, especially in cities such as New York and Pennsylvania. These immigrants came for economic opportunities that they perceived were greater in the British colonies south of Canada.

WESTERN AND NORTHERN EUROPEAN IMMIGRATION
With its defeat in the French and Indian War in 1763, France lost New France to Great Britain. Thirteen years later, Britain lost American colonies in the American Revolutionary War but retained its Canadian colonies. One of the first major migrations to Canada came from the United States after the revolution, when Loyalists (Americans who remained loyal to the British monarchy), mainly of British ancestry but including a significant population of African Americans, resettled in Nova Scotia and New Brunswick.

By the beginning of the nineteenth century, both the United States and Canada had fairly open immigration policies, and the native-born populations of the countries were generally accepting of immigrants. As both countries expanded west, Canada continued to attract mainly immigrants from the British Isles. Often, immigrants chose to migrate to Canada because the ship passage from England or Ireland was cheaper than the passage to America. During the nineteenth century, thousands of Highland Scots and Irish came to Canada. The Ulster (Protestant) Irish usually stayed in Canada, whereas many of the Roman Catholic Irish traveled to Canada and then simply crossed into the United States. Irish Catholics may have settled in the United States for political reasons, because the United States was not connected to the British

CANADA'S VAST LANDSCAPE

In this extract from the final chapter of Roughing It in the Bush *(1852), English writer and Canadian pioneer Susanna Moodie expresses some of her feelings about her life in Canada and predicts a prosperous future for the new land. Western immigration would be opened by the Dominion Lands Act of 1872 and would thrive in the last decades of the nineteenth century.*

When I say that Canada is destined to be one of the most prosperous countries in the world, let it not be supposed that I am influenced by any unreasonable partiality for the land of my adoption. Canada may not possess mines of gold or silver, but she possesses all those advantages of climate, geological structure, and position, which are essential to greatness and prosperity. Her long and severe winter, so disheartening to her first settlers, lays up, amidst the forests of the West, inexhaustible supplies of fertilising moisture for the summer, while it affords the farmer the very best of natural roads to enable him to carry his wheat and other produce to market. It is a remarkable fact, that hardly a lot of land containing two hundred acres, in British America, can be found without an abundant supply of water at all seasons of the year; and a very small proportion of the land itself is naturally unfit for cultivation. To crown the whole, where can a country be pointed out which possesses such an extent of internal navigation? A chain of river navigation and navigable inland seas, which, with the canals recently constructed, gives to the countries bordering on them all the advantages of an extended sea-coast, with a greatly diminished risk of loss from shipwreck!

Source: Susanna Moodie, *Roughing It in the Bush* (3d ed., London, 1854), chapter 28.

in the United States and because certain factors—such as dissatisfaction with government, religious intolerance, poor job opportunities, or famine—pushed them out. Most chose the United States because they believed that they could earn higher wages, find better farmland, and more freely practice their religious or political beliefs there than anywhere else. The United States was rapidly expanding its territory and economy, and the perception that America was a land of freedom and opportunity was already widespread in many European communities. Canada did not have the same political appeal as the republican government of the United States, where numerous immigrants made a successful career in politics.

IMMIGRATION RESTRICTIONS

During the late nineteenth and early twentieth centuries, both the United States and Canada experienced increased diversity in the national origins of their immigrants, and both federal governments began to limit immigration. The first exclusion laws passed in the United States and Canada limited Chinese immigration. Starting in the 1850's, Chinese laborers began immigrating to the West Coast of the United States and Canada. Because the Chinese were ethnically and culturally distinct from the white population, many Euro-Americans and Euro-Canadians considered them unassimilable. The U.S. Congress passed the Chinese Exclusion Act of 1882, which suspended Chinese immigration for ten years. In a similar action, in 1885 the Canadian government put a heavy head tax on Chinese entering Canada and limited the number of Chinese immigrants that ships could carry to Canada.

During the late nineteenth century, both countries, especially the United States, were receiving thousands of new immigrants from eastern and southern Europe. In the United States, Italians, Greeks, Hungarians, and Jews from Poland and Russia were filling industrial and unskilled jobs in the growing cities of the East and Midwest, while many others, such as Swedes, Norwegians, and Germans, continued to move west, claiming farmland and building small ethnic communities. Many of these immigrants were following chain migration patterns and chose the United States because they already had friends and relatives living in America. Others came because of America's rep-

Empire, or for economic reasons, because they believed they could earn more money and find work more easily in America. Many of the Germans and Scandinavians who went to Canada were also trying to make their way to the United States, where economic opportunities seemed greater and where family members or friends were already settled.

In the United States, the century of immigration began around 1820 with increasing numbers of British, Irish, German, and then Scandinavian immigrants entering the country. Many immigrants left their homelands because they wanted a better life

utation as a land of liberty. At the same time, the Canadian government encouraged farmers from Great Britain to establish farms in the Canadian west. Canada had little success in attracting the same numbers of immigrants flocking to the United States. Still, thousands of Italian and Slavic contract workers came to Canada to work on railroads and in mines, and although many eventually returned home, some settled in Canada. Some Americans went north to settle farms in western Canada, but even more native-born Canadians left for the United States, especially French Canadians who went to the mill towns of New England.

As a result of this new immigration, nativism grew and efforts to restrict immigration increased in the United States and Canada. In the United States, the Immigration Act of 1891 enabled federal authorities to reject entry to those who were diseased, morally objectionable, or whose fares had been paid by others. Five years later, Canada adopted similar restrictive standards. Immigration restriction legislation in the United States culminated in the Immigration Act of 1924 (Johnson-Reed Act), which limited immigration based on a national origin quota system. Canada continued to pursue its Asian exclusion policies and, in 1930, during the Great Depression, suspended all continental European immigration, allowing only British and Americans with sufficient financial resources to immigrate.

IMMIGRATION AFTER WORLD WAR II

In the second half of the twentieth century, increased numbers of immigrants from developing countries in Asia, Africa, and Latin America came to Canada and the United States. After World War II, the two North American countries received many refugees from war-torn European countries, but the United States admitted far more than Canada, whose citizens were still resistant to large-scale immigration from anywhere but Western Europe. The Canadian Immigration Act of 1952 did little to change Canada's restrictive immigration policy, but many entered Canada through a program that enabled immigrants whose relatives lived in Canada to sponsor their entry. In the United States, the Immigration and Nationality Act of 1952 (McCarran-Walter Act) liberalized naturalization procedures and included more provisions for bringing family members. In 1965, the United States eliminated the quota system and placed a cap on immigration from the Western and Eastern hemispheres.

The late twentieth century saw a shift in the origins of immigrants to the United States. Immi-

Refugees from Hungary's failed 1957 revolution boarding a charter plane to Canada, which, like the United States, took in many Hungarian refugees. (Hulton Archive/Getty Images)

153

grants from Asian countries such as China, South Korea, Vietnam, and India came to the United States, spreading out from their traditional area of concentration on the West Coast to the rest of the country. Immigration from Latin America, especially Mexico, increased greatly during the second half of the twentieth century, as did emigration from Africa and the Middle East. Like previous immigrants, Asian, African, Middle Eastern, and Latin American immigrants chose the United States for economic opportunities or because of family already living in the United States. For many, such as Mexican, Cuban, and Puerto Rican immigrants, the United States was closer and easier to reach than Canada.

As late as the 1960's, most immigrants to Canada came from Europe, especially Britain. Changes in immigration policy in 1967 introduced a points system to determine immigrant eligibility and removed all race restrictions on immigration. The 1976 Immigration Act, an overhaul of the 1952 law, established four basic categories of individuals eligible to immigrate: family, assisted relatives, refugees, and independent immigrants. Since the 1970's, Canada has experienced many of the same trends as the United States with regard to immigration, but on a smaller scale. Canada received immigrants from Portugal and Greece as well as from China and British Commonwealth countries such as India, Pakistan, and former British Caribbean colonies.

Many British Commonwealth immigrants chose Canada because it is a fellow Commonwealth country, which facilitates entry into society and government and where established immigrant communities already existed. Haitians and French-speaking immigrants from West Africa came to Quebec because of commonalities in language. In contrast to the United States, Canada has had little immigration from Latin American countries. Because both the United States and Canada have a reputation as wealthy, industrialized countries with free societies, many immigrants in the early twenty-first century choose one country over another based on family and community ties or geographical proximity and ease of entry.

In general, the United States and Canada have had similar immigration policies during their histories, and both countries have accepted large and increasingly diverse numbers of immigrants. From the beginning, however, the United States had a much more diverse population in terms of ethnicity and race than Canada, and many more immigrants have chosen to settle in the United States than in Canada. While the ethnic makeup of the United States was changing drastically at the beginning of the twentieth century, Canada still had a rather homogeneous population made up of people of British and French origin. This was due in part to perceived greater opportunities in the United States and a Canadian government that encouraged farmers to immigrate but did not have a need for industrial laborers. Both countries experienced nativism and immigration restrictions, but the United States liberalized its immigration policies earlier, while Canadians clung to their western European heritage longer, resulting in a more sustained tide of immigration from the developing world to the United States. In the early twenty-first century, both countries are ethnically and racially diverse societies that continue to receive large numbers of immigrants looking for a better life.

Jonathan Keljik

FURTHER READING

Bumsted, J. M. *Canada's Diverse Peoples: A Reference Sourcebook.* Santa Barbara, Calif.: ABC-CLIO, 2003. A textbook-style introduction to immigration and ethnicity in Canada, from the earliest settlers to modern racial and ethnic issues.

Burnet, Jean R., with Howard Palmer. *Coming Canadians: An Introduction to a History of Canada's Peoples.* Toronto: McClelland & Stewart, 1989. A rather celebratory account of Canadian immigration, focusing especially on the social history of immigrant groups during the twentieth century.

Daniels, Roger. *Coming to America: A History of Immigration and Ethnicity in American Life.* Princeton, N.J.: Visual Education Corporation, 1990. A comprehensive summary of the major immigrant groups in the United States, emphasizing numbers, settlement patterns, and socioeconomics.

_____. *Guarding the Golden Door: American Immigration Policy and Immigrants Since 1882.* New York: Hill & Wang, 2004. A good review of U.S. debates and laws on immigration policy and immigrant exclusion up to the early twenty-first century.

Knowles, Valerie. *Strangers at Our Gates: Canadian Immigration and Immigration Policy, 1540-1990.* Toronto: Dundurn Press, 1992. An easy-to-understand survey of Canadian government policies and their effect on immigration and Canadian society.

SEE ALSO: British immigrants; Canadian immigrants; Chinese Exclusion Act of 1882; Emigration; Immigration Act of 1924; Immigration and Nationality Act of 1952; Immigration and Nationality Act of 1965; Irish immigrants; Nativism; Push-pull factors.

CANADIAN IMMIGRANTS

SIGNIFICANCE: Canadian immigration to the United States has historically been episodic, typically paralleling economic fluctuations and shifts in employment opportunities in one or the other of the two neighboring countries. However, during the early twentieth century, many French-speaking Canadians immigrated to the United States to remove themselves from religious and political discrimination.

Immigration into the territory of the future United States from what were once called British North America and French Canada began during the age of exploration and colonization, when international borders were porous. Large-scale migration from French Canada began in 1755, with the expulsion of the Acadian French from Nova Scotia by Great Britain. There was little immigration from British North America after the American Revolution ended in 1783. Immigration to the United States from British North America did not significantly resume until the decade before the U.S. Civil War (1861-1865) and continued to increase until 1890. The migration of French Canadians intensified from 1900 until 1930 to fill assembly lines in New England shoe and textile factories. The last major wave of Canadian immigration to the United States occurred between 1940 and 1990, after which Canadian immigration to the United States steadily declined.

IMMIGRATION BEFORE 1776

Exploration and colonization of the Americas and the region later known as Canada was undertaken by both French- and English-sponsored sea captains and companies. Borders between French Canada, or Quebec, and British-controlled areas of North America were ill defined and porous. Consequently, explorers and settlers moved freely around North America's rivers and lakes. French exploration reached as far south as the mouth of the Mississippi River, Pennsylvania, along the Great Lakes, and Lake Champlain. Geography and climate limited the population north of the Great Lakes to fur trappers and fishermen. Both Great Britain and France had difficulties attracting settlers to these northern regions.

The English colonies in New England and Virginia were the fastest-growing regions in which European immigrants were likely to settle because they afforded greater chances of economic success. In fact, the growing economic prosperity of England's original thirteen colonies did lure an unrecorded number of settlers from the north. In 1745, New Englanders temporarily seized the French settlement and fortress of Louisbourg. Eighteenth century rivalries between Great Britain and France ultimately led to Britain's successful acquisition of Nova Scotia from France and the expulsion of an estimated 18,000 French-speaking Acadians to Britain's Atlantic colonies between 1755 and 1763 and, after France's withdrawal from North America in 1763, to Louisiana. The Acadian French of Louisiana were the first major immigration wave into the future United States from what would eventually become Canada.

IMMIGRATION, 1776-1867

The independence of the United States in 1783 led to the emigration from the United States to British North America of more than 35,000 United Empire Loyalists. Britain's Constitutional Act of 1791 split Quebec into territories named Upper and Lower Canada, each with its own assembly and council elected by its own people. The creation of the Hudson Bay Company to undertake fur trapping and settlement in the western regions of North America was accompanied by the granting of increased political rights for Canadian settlers, thereby lessening the desire of British subjects to go to the United States.

French-speaking Acadians who were expelled from Nova Scotia by the British in 1755. Many of them immigrated to Louisiana, which was then under Spanish rule, and contributed to the development of Cajun culture. (Francis R. Niglutsch)

The unsuccessful attempts by the United States during the War of 1812 to annex Upper and Lower Canada significantly strained relations between the neighboring countries and limited population movements from either direction. The Rush-Bagot Agreements of 1817 and 1818 demilitarized the border between the United States and Canada, permitting free and mostly unrecorded movements of people between the two countries. Low-cost land grants in 1815 to spur Canadian settlement proffered an economic boom that lasted several decades and attracted more than 800,000 immigrants to Canada between 1815 to 1850, in what has been called the Great Migration. Other nineteenth century developments that lessened incentives for Canadian settlers to move to the United States included the discovery of gold in the territory now known as British Columbia in 1858 and the building of canals and railroads connecting the different parts of British North America.

Records kept by Canada's Office of Immigra-

tion Statistics show that only 209 people immigrated to the United States from Upper and Lower Canada and Newfoundland in the year 1820. Over the ensuing decade, 2,277 more Canadians made the move. The rate of British immigration to the United States from those territories increased in the succeeding decades, with 13,624 making the move during the 1830's, 41,723 during the 1840's, and 59,309 during the 1850's, the decade preceding the U.S. Civil War.

IMMIGRATION, 1867-1900

The U.S. Civil War severely strained relations between the United States, Great Britain, and Canada, which was still called British North America. Union blockades of Southern shipping during the war denied British textile factories the cotton they needed to operate. British attitudes toward immigrating to the United States changed after 1865, as the rapid industrialization of the country began generating a higher volume of manufacturing jobs that needed workers. The U.S. Census of 1870 recorded that 478,685 immigrants from British North America were living in the United States. The majority of them settled in Massachusetts, New York State, Michigan, Maine, Vermont, Wisconsin, and Illinois. Each of these states bordered Canada, making frequent movements back and forth easy.

In 1867, the British North American Act officially created the Dominion of Canada. At that time, Canada had four provinces: Ontario, Quebec, New Brunswick, and Nova Scotia. The act created a federal government in Ottawa and provided a process to admit future provinces into the Canadian confederation. Although Canadians continued to move to the United States in succeeding decades, larger numbers of people from other parts of the world were immigrating into Canada to take advantage of inexpensive land in the western regions and to search for gold in the Yukon Territory.

The U.S. Census of 1880 listed 697,509 immigrants from British North America living in the United States, with the states of Massachusetts, Michigan, and New York their principal destinations. In 1890, Massachusetts, Michigan, New York, and Maine were the principal residences of the 978,219 immigrants from Canada and Newfoundland in the United States. Canadians were particularly drawn to U.S. states along the border that were rapidly industrializing.

In 1900, the U.S. Census divided Canadian immigrants into English- and French-speakers. English-speaking immigrants numbered 747,050 and lived principally in Rhode Island, Massachusetts, Michigan, New York, and Illinois, all industrial states. French-speakers numbered 439,950, with Massachusetts, Rhode Island, New Hampshire, and California their principal destinations.

FRENCH CANADIANS IN NEW ENGLAND

Between 1900 and 1950, U.S. Census figures showed a substantial migration of French Canadians to the United States. The 1900 census recorded

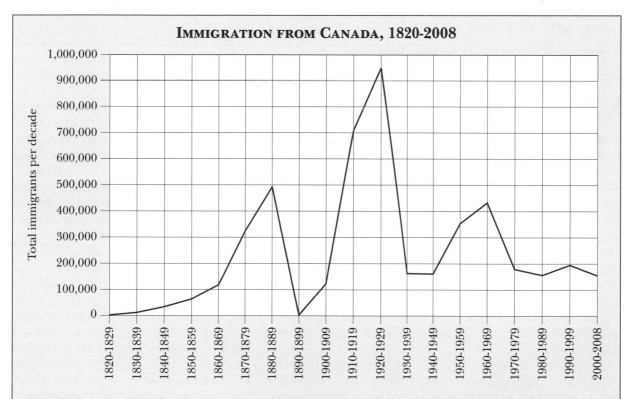

IMMIGRATION FROM CANADA, 1820-2008

Source: Department of Homeland Security, *Yearbook of Immigration Statistics, 2008.* Figures include only immigrants who obtained legal permanent resident status. Data from before 1911 are from British North America; data after 1911 include Newfoundland.

that 439,950 immigrants from Quebec were living in the United States, principally in New England. Many were motivated to emigrate because of a long history of discrimination in employment and educational opportunities under British rule. Moreover, raising money to buy farmland in Canada was becoming increasingly difficult. By contrast, employment opportunities in the United States were expanding in the textile, shoe-making, and lumber industries throughout the Northeast. California's expanding trade with Asia, the lure of mining jobs, and less expensive land to farm lured French Canadians to the West Coast of the United States. The first half of the twentieth century witnessed a large influx of French Canadians into New England, which was home to 371,928 of them in 1910, to 300,703 in 1920, to 342,075 in 1930, and to 381,302 in 1940.

French Canadians also continued to settle in U.S. states bordering Canada, with Massachusetts, New Hampshire, Michigan, Maine, and New York their principal destinations. U.S. Census records from 1910, 1920, and 1930 divided Canadian immigrants into four categories:

- Newfoundlanders (Newfoundland was not part of Canada until 1949)
- Canadians
- Other Canadians
- French-speaking Canadians

During the year 1910, 1,934 Newfoundlanders were living in the United States, along with 784,063 "Other Canadians," and 23,089 listed as Canada along with 371,928 French-speakers. The U.S. Census for 1920 recorded 7,562 Newfoundlanders, 121,805 Canadians, 693,773 Other Canadians, and 300,712 French Canadians. The 1930 U.S. Census, taken during the first year of the Great Depression, listed 25,283 Newfoundlanders, 52,562 Canadians, 872,133 Other Canadians, and 342,072 French-speakers. The increase in Canadians moving to the United States can be explained by the migrants' need to find work during the growing international financial crisis.

After Great Britain entered World War II in 1939, many Canadians were drafted into the military to fight; others went to the United States to find jobs in the expanding American war-based economy. The 1940 U.S. Census counted 21,301 Newfoundlanders, 742,358 "Canadians" ("Other

PROFILE OF CANADIAN IMMIGRANTS

Country of origin	Canada
Primary language	English, French
Primary regions of U.S. settlement	New England, New York, Michigan, California, Louisiana, Washington
Earliest significant arrivals	Seventeenth century (British America), Seventeenth century (New France)
Peak immigration period	1900-1930
Twenty-first century legal residents*	138,712 (17,339 per year)

*Immigrants who obtained legal permanent resident status in the United States.
Source: Department of Homeland Security, Yearbook of Immigration Statistics, 2008.

Canadians" and "Canadians" were combined), and 273,086 French Canadians living in the United States. As Canadian involvement in the war intensified, civilian and military job opportunities increased, and the numbers of Canadians going to the United States declined. The New England states of Massachusetts, Maine, and New Hampshire continued to attract the largest numbers of French-speaking Canadians.

In parts of New England in which French Canadians took up residence, new French-speaking Roman Catholic parishes were created with their own parochial schools, French-language newspapers were published, and French-owned businesses established. Through several generations French Canadian culture was preserved in neighborhoods that were essentially French-speaking enclaves. Members of New England's French-speaking communities continued to move back and forth freely between the United States and Canada, as border-crossing documents have recorded. Most Newfoundlanders who entered the United States between 1910 and 1940 resided in Massachusetts, Maine, New Hampshire, New York, and in 1930 in Arkansas. Canadians other than French-speakers and Newfoundlanders were principally located in

New England, Michigan, Pennsylvania, Colorado, New Jersey, Washington, California, and Texas.

IMMIGRATION AFTER 1945

After World War II ended in 1945, Canadian immigration to the United States began a steady decline. Historically, the movement of Canadians to the United States had been based on the need for jobs and better pay since the seventeenth century. The U.S. Census of 1950 no longer separated immigration statistics for Newfoundland, which had become a Canadian province. That census was also the last to distinguish French-speaking and other Canadians. The number of French Canadians in the United States in 1950 was 159,187. As before, they principally resided in Massachusetts, New York, Michigan, and California. The number of "Other Canadians" in the United States who were recorded in the 1950 census numbered 321,097, with Massachusetts, New York, New Hampshire, and Michigan their principal places of residence. U.S. Census tabulations over the next four decades showed 377,952 Canadian-born residents of the United States in 1960, 413,310 in 1970, 169,030 in 1980, 156,938 in 1990, and 191,987 in 2000.

The decline in Canadian immigration after World War II was caused by a number of factors. After the war, Canada pursued more independent policies in foreign and domestic policies. During the early 1970's, Canada became a haven for Vietnam War protestors from the United States. Meanwhile, increasing numbers of American companies were establishing subsidiaries in Canada that made it less necessary to go to the United States to find automobile and other manufacturing jobs. Canada's less costly universal health care system insured all Canadians for life—a sharp contrast with the health care system in the United States. Canada has increasingly developed its own national identity, separate from those of the United States and Great Britain. Canadian federal legislation has tended to foster policies that reflect Canadian innovations, greater tolerance of diversity, and a global agenda more compatible with the European Union than with the United States. All these developments have tended to make emigrating to the United States less attractive to Canadians.

A parallel decline in the migration of French Canadians to the United States after World War II has been due, in part, to the Canadian government's granting of more political autonomy to French-speaking Quebec. This change has made it easier for French-speaking Canadians to preserve their language, culture, and Roman Catholic faith—all of which would be threatened if they were to move to the English-speaking United States.

At the same time, the decline of the shoe, textile, and logging industries in New England and other U.S. border states has lessened the attractions of emigrating.

TWENTY-FIRST CENTURY TRENDS

Population movements between Canada and the United States have been influenced by the North American Free Trade Agreement (NAFTA) that Canada, the United States, and Mexico signed in 1993. NAFTA significantly reduced trade barriers between Canada and the United States and made it much easier for Canadians to work in the United States on temporary visas. In 2006, 64,633 Canadians were working in the United States on temporary employment visas, and another 13,136 were in the United States as their dependents. In contrast, during that same year, 24,830 U.S. citizens worked in Canada on similar temporary visas.

The U.S. Congress's passage of the Patriot Act in 2001, after the terrorist attacks of September 11, 2001, started a process that increasingly tightened border controls between Canada and the United States. Later amendments to the law for the first time began requiring people crossing the U.S.-Canadian border, in either direction, to carry passports. Heightened security at border crossings has entailed closer scrutiny of travelers and more frequent searches of vehicles, creating unprecedented delays and increased stress—all of which has made border crossings less convenient.

Despite the decline in Canadian immigration to the United States, Canadians have continued to see their southern neighbor as a land of greater economic opportunities, though to a lesser degree than in earlier years. Many Canadian athletes, actors, broadcasters, artists, writers, and corporate executives have continued to work in the United States, where their talents reach larger audiences and markets and where they earn higher incomes than they can in Canada.

William A. Paquette

159

FURTHER READING

Brault, Gerard J. *The French-Canadian Heritage in New England*. Hanover, N.H.: University Press of New England, 1986. Detailed history of New England's third-largest ancestry group.

Doty, C. S. *The First Franco-Americans: New England Histories from the Federal Writers' Project, 1938-39*. Orono: University of Maine at Orono Press, 1985. Comprehensive history of French Canadian immigration and experiences in the United States, based on oral histories collected during the 1930's.

Faragher, John Mack. *A Great and Noble Scheme*. New York: W. W. Norton, 2005. History of the Acadian French, many of whom immigrated to Louisiana.

Hamilton, Janice. *Canadians in America*. Minneapolis: Lerner, 2006. Brief survey of Canadian immigration to the United States, emphasizing the years after 1860.

Ramirez, Bruno. *Crossing the Forty-ninth Parallel*. Ithaca, N.Y.: Cornell University Press, 2001. Detailed study of Canadian immigration to the United States between 1900 and 1930.

Schideler, Janet L. *Camille Lessard Bissonnette: The Quiet Evolution of French-Canadian Immigrants in New England*. New York: Peter Lang, 1998. Narrative of personal histories among New England French Canadians.

Wade, M. *The French Canadians, 1760-1967*. Toronto: MacMillan, 1968. Comprehensive history of French Canadians.

SEE ALSO: Canada vs. United States as immigrant destinations; Hayakawa, S. I.; History of immigration, 1620-1783; History of immigration, 1783-1891; History of immigration after 1891; Jennings, Peter; Louisiana; New York State; North American Free Trade Agreement; Patriot Act of 2001; Vermont.

CANALS

DEFINITION: Canals are artificial waterways constructed across land; navigational canals link bodies of water, whereas water-conveyance canals—such as irrigation canals—move water from place to place

SIGNIFICANCE: During the early history of the United States, the paucity of transportation canals stifled commercial development because farmers only had poor roads over which to move their produce to cities. During the 1820's and 1830's, often called the "Canal Age," the construction of several major canals significantly improved transportation while simultaneously unifying the young country. The backbreaking work of digging these canals was done mostly by Irish and German immigrants. Their work was grueling, poorly paid, and dangerous, resulting in many deaths from accidents and diseases. These immigrants later settled in towns and cities along the canals, while others traveled on the canals to seek their fortune in the American West.

Although scholars have traditionally associated American canal construction with the third and fourth decades of the nineteenth century, several canals were built earlier. George Washington himself, even before he became the first president, managed the Potomac Company, which built a canal linking the Potomac and Ohio rivers in order to open a major route from Virginia to the western territories. Such early canals as those connecting Charleston, South Carolina, and the Santee River, and the Middlesex Canal that linked Boston with the Merrimac River required the efforts of thousands of workers, many of them immigrants. However, their contributions have been largely overshadowed in history by the attention given to the merchants and landholders who sponsored these early canals.

During the Canal Age, the building of canals became massive enterprises, often involving extensive excavations through hundreds of miles of wilderness, large labor forces, and gigantic investments. Scholars have estimated that about 35,000 men participated in these projects, and many of the workers were drawn from a growing pool of immigrant labor. The U.S. Census of 1820 reported that more than 8,000 immigrants had entered the country that year. By 1830, that figure had nearly tripled, and by 1840 it had more than tripled again, to more than 84,000 immigrants. In 1848, 226,000 foreigners, mainly Irish, German, and English, had traveled to the United States seeking jobs, while fleeing political unrest and famine in Europe. A significant proportion of these found employment

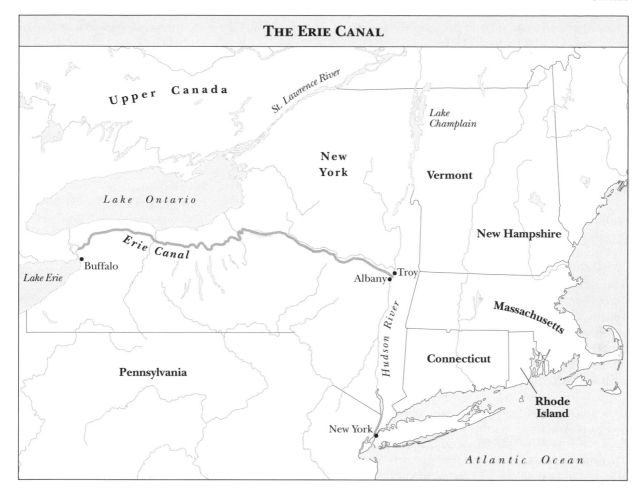

THE ERIE CANAL

in mammoth construction projects, the prime example of which was the Erie Canal.

Financed at public risk through the issuance of bonds, the Erie Canal ran over 360 miles from Albany on the Hudson River to Buffalo on Lake Erie when it was completed in 1825. Scholars differ on the makeup of the workforce that built the canal. Some have emphasized the contributions of local farmers and laborers, while others have stressed that German and especially Irish immigrants did the bulk of the unskilled work. Immigrant workers toiled for twelve or more hours per day in all kinds of weather. Many died of malaria in building the canal through Montezuma Marsh. They were provided with inadequate food and lodging, irregularly and poorly paid, and treated paternalistically by managers, contractors, and engineers who looked down on them. To alleviate their bodily and emotional pains, the immigrant

workers often resorted to whiskey. Nevertheless, they did not labor in vain, as the Erie Canal proved a great commercial success, reducing by tenfold both the costs of shipping freight from Albany to Buffalo and the prices of farm products shipped from the Midwest to the East. It also shortened the time of travel for westbound settlers from six weeks to six days. The longest canal in the world at that time, the Erie Canal also helped transform New York City into the nation's chief port and largest metropolis.

The Erie Canal's success inaugurated a period of intensive canal construction. A canal linking the Ohio River with Cleveland on Lake Erie was completed in 1833, and a waterway between the Chicago and Illinois rivers was built between 1836 and 1848. During the 1830's, a system of more than one thousand miles of canals was constructed in Pennsylvania, helping make Pittsburgh another gateway

161

to the West. All these projects owed much to immigrant workers, the Irish and Germans as well as the Polish and Lithuanians. In the South, canal construction sometimes differed from northern projects. For example, New Orleans, much of which is below sea level and lacks natural outflow, needed drainage canals to create dry from wet lands. These drainage canals and other flood-control projects depended on the labors and French and Irish immigrants as well as on African Americans, both free and enslaved.

The railroads helped bring the Canal Age to an end, because they transported people and goods even faster and more economically than the canals and because they could run in all types of weather, unaffected by drought or winter freezes. Nevertheless, new canals continued to be built. By 1900, more than 4,000 miles of canals operated throughout the United States. President Theodore Roosevelt passionately advocated the construction of a canal in Central America that would link the Atlantic and Pacific oceans. That canal was eventually built across the Panamanian Isthmus, but only after great obstacles had been overcome.

Yellow fever and malaria had doomed earlier efforts, but American doctors were able significantly to reduce deaths from those and other diseases. The international labor force working on the Panama Canal at times numbered as many as 50,000. Many were immigrants from Caribbean islands, but thousands also came from Europe and Asia. While white workers were given the best jobs and were well paid and housed, black workers were poorly paid and segregated in dilapidated barracks. Most of those who died in landslides and explosions and from diseases were black. Although the composition of the canal-construction workforce had changed, the problems that immigrant laborers encountered were much the same as those faced by previous "canalers."

Robert J. Paradowski

FURTHER READING
Bernstein, Peter L. *Wedding of the Waters: The Erie Canal and the Making of a Great Nation.* New York: W. W. Norton, 2005. Engagingly written history of the Erie Canal that considers it in the broad context of nineteenth century American history and demonstrates its impact on national development.

Goodrich, Carter. *Government Promotion of Canals and Railroads, 1800-1890.* New York: Columbia University Press, 1960. A study of federal, state, and local government aid and encouragement of internal improvements, including an enlightening analysis of state efforts.

Hecht, Roger W., ed. *The Erie Canal Reader, 1790-1950.* Syracuse, N.Y.: Syracuse University Press, 2003. Collection of fiction, poetry, essays, and other works about the Erie Canal written over the course of its history.

Meyer, Balthaser H. *History of Transportation in the United States Before 1860.* Reprint. Washington, D.C.: Peter Smith, 1948. Reference work containing facts and information regarding all the major early road, canal, and railroad developments in the nation.

Shaw, Ronald E. *Erie Water West: A History of the Erie Canal, 1792-1854.* Lexington: University Press of Kentucky, 1966. A complete history of the canal from its conception to completion, and its first twenty-nine years of operation.

Way, Peter. *Common Labour: Workers and the Digging of North American Canals, 1780-1860.* New York: Cambridge University Press, 1993. Comprehensive study of canal construction through the mid-nineteenth century.

SEE ALSO: Employment; European immigrants; German immigrants; History of immigration, 1783-1891; Irish immigrants; Italian immigrants; New York State; Pennsylvania; Railroads; Virginia.

CAPITATION TAXES

DEFINITION: Head taxes levied on Chinese immigrants and laborers by the state of California
ALSO KNOWN AS: Chinese Police Tax; Passenger taxes

SIGNIFICANCE: During the 1850's and 1860's, the state of California singled out Chinese immigrants for capitation taxes, which were assessed on individual immigrants. These taxes were subsequently declared unconstitutional by California's state supreme court as interfering with foreign commerce.

In 1849, the first Chinese laborers arrived in California, where they encountered great local resentment. Known derogatorily as "coolies," they were subjected to various discriminatory laws. In 1852, for example, California imposed foreign miner's licensing fees of three dollars per month on Chinese gold miners. Over the next two decades, this fee was steadily increased until it was ruled unconstitutional in 1870. In 1855, a capitation tax of fifty dollars was imposed on every Chinese immigrant to California. Also known as a head tax, a capitation tax is a direct tax on a person, as opposed to a tax on income, merchandise, or an economic transaction.

In the 1857 case of *People v. Downer,* California's state supreme court held the 1855 capitation tax unconstitutional because it intruded with the exclusive power of the U.S. Congress to regulate commerce with foreign nations that was delegated to it by the U.S. Constitution. California responded in 1862 by enacting a law designed to "protect free white labor against competition with Chinese coolie labor, and discourage the immigration of Chinese into the State of California." This new act levied a monthly $2.50 capitation tax on Chinese workers and merchants that was called the Chinese Police Tax.

In June, 1862, a Chinese laborer named Lin Sing brought suit against the San Francisco tax collector Washburn for a refund of the capitation taxes he had paid for the previous two months. After a magistrate and local court ruled against him, Lin Sing appealed to the state supreme court in what was apparently a concerted effort by the state's Chinese community to resist discrimination. In its July, 1862, ruling in *Lin Sing v. Washburn,* California's supreme court ruled the 1862 capitation tax unconstitutional. Citing its own *People v. Downer* precedent, the court found that the 1862 law demonstrated "special and extreme hostility to the Chinese" and likewise violated the foreign commerce powers exclusively vested in the U.S. Congress. The famous future U.S. Supreme Court justice Stephen J. Field dissented from the decision.

The history of these capitation tax cases demonstrates several things. The great hostility to Chinese in California immediately expressed itself in a host of discriminatory laws and taxes. The Chinese community made recourse to the courts to fight this discrimination. California's supreme court showed itself sympathetic to the lawsuits and interpreted the foreign commerce clause of the U.S. Constitution in the most expansive manner in order to void discriminatory taxes. Although racial discrimination at the time was not illegal, the court behaved in a far-sighted manner by linking hostility against a particular ethnic group to other constitutional violations. Nevertheless California continued to enact discriminatory laws against the Chinese, many of which were beyond attack under then current jurisprudence. In addition, as the federal government assumed exclusive control over immigration during the 1880's, it enacted its own discriminatory laws, including the Chinese Exclusion Act of 1882, designed to stop Chinese immigration to the United States.

Howard Bromberg

FURTHER READING

McClain, Charles. *Chinese Immigrants and American Law.* New York: Garland, 1994.

_____. *In Search of Equality. The Chinese Struggle Against Inequality in Nineteenth-Century America.* Berkeley: University of California Press, 1996.

Motomura, Hiroshi. *Americans in Waiting: The Lost Story of Immigration and Citizenship in the United States.* New York: Oxford University Press, 2006.

Sandmeyer, Elmer Clarence. *The Anti-Chinese Movement in California.* Champaign: University of Illinois Press, 1991.

SEE ALSO: Anti-Chinese movement; Asian immigrants; Assimilation theories; California; California gold rush; Chinese Exclusion Act of 1882; Chinese immigrants; Coolies; Economic consequences of immigration; Foreign miner taxes.

CAPTIVE THAI WORKERS

THE EVENT: Government raid of a factory in Southern California where employers held seventy-two Thai workers in slavelike conditions

DATE: August 2, 1995

LOCATION: El Monte, California

SIGNIFICANCE: Thai laborers were forced to toil in a makeshift garment factory in a Los Angeles suburb for more than six years until the operation was busted. Workers were eventually given back pay as well as permanent residency status.

Starting in 1989, seventy-two rural Thai villagers, mostly women, were confined in apartment buildings at El Monte, California, where they were forced to sew garments for less than two dollars per hour, working sixteen-hour-plus workdays, seven days a week. After arriving at Los Angeles International Airport on tourist visas, the laborers were transported to work compounds, and their passports and possessions were confiscated. Promised $1,000 monthly wages and a ten-hour workday, they had signed contracts before their trips pledging to pay back $8,000 to $15,000 in travel and other expenses. Workers' living quarters were infested with cockroaches and rats, and razor wire outside the compound deterred escape. They were denied communication with the outside as well as medical care, and they were forced to pay inflated prices for their food. Although most had no idea that their rights had been violated, at least seven escaped.

Acting on a tip from an escaped worker's friend on August 2, 1995, California and federal government officials, who had gathered sufficient information to obtain a search warrant, broke into the compound and arrested members of the Thai family who ran the factory, except for one who was absent that day and fled after being tipped off by his girlfriend. Federal authorities took the workers into custody until Asian activists had them released from detention.

Suni Manasurangkun and her five sons and two daughters-in-law were in charge of the facility. In 1996, seven defendants pleaded guilty to charges of conspiracy, requiring indentured servitude, and harboring illegal immigrants. Manasurangkun received a seven-year prison sentence. Five were sentenced from two to six years. The seventh, who cooperated with the prosecution, was deported to Thailand, as were the rest after serving their sentences.

A civil lawsuit filed by the Asian Pacific American Legal Center in 1996 against the retail companies that purchased the garments recovered approximately $4 million in back pay, with awards ranging from $10,000 to $80,000 depending on the workers' time in confinement. The center also won permanent residency status for them in 2002.

Most of the freed workers remain in the Los Angeles area, cleaning homes or working in restaurants, massage studios, or garment factories. By 2008, a few had become prosperous owners of busy massage studios or Thai restaurants, and dozens had been granted citizenship.

Michael Haas

FURTHER READING

International Labor Organization. *Human Trafficking and Forced Labour Exploitation Guidance for Legislation and Law Enforcement.* Geneva: Author, 2005.

Kang, K. Connie. "Once Virtual Slaves, Seventy-one Thai Workers Win U.S. Residency." *Los Angeles Times*, November 18, 2002, p. B-1.

Richard, Amy O'Neil. *International Trafficking in Women to the United States: A Contemporary Manifestation of Slavery and Organized Crime.* Reston, Va.: Center for the Study of Intelligence, Central Intelligence Agency, 1999.

Su, Julie A. "Making the Invisible Visible: The Garment Industry's Dirty Laundry." In *Critical Race Theory: The Cutting Edge*, edited by Richard Delgado and Jean Stefancic. 2d ed. Philadelphia: Temple University Press, 2008.

SEE ALSO: Asian immigrants; Contract labor system; Crime; Globalization; Illegal immigration; Los Angeles; Quota systems; Sweatshops; Thai immigrants.

CATHOLIC CHARITIES USA

IDENTIFICATION: Social services organization run by the Roman Catholic Church

ALSO KNOWN AS: National Conference of Catholic Charities

DATE: Founded in 1910

SIGNIFICANCE: Catholic Charities USA is the second-largest provider of social services in the United States, behind only the federal government. Its refugee services wing has been active in helping with refugee resettlement and immigration concerns in the United States since the post-World War II era.

Catholic Charities USA is a network of more than fifteen hundred agencies and organizations nationwide that provide assistance to individuals and families in need of food and housing, social support services (such as employment training and child and senior care), immigration and refugee services, and disaster relief. Local Catholic Charities agencies have provided services to immigrant groups for more than 280 years.

EARLY HISTORY

Although officially founded in 1910, Catholic Charities USA traces its existence back to 1727 to an orphanage founded by the Ursuline Sisters in New Orleans. Throughout the eighteenth and nineteenth centuries, a system of locally organized services usually developed and staffed by Catholic laity and nuns provided housing, subsistence, employment, and legal assistance to French, Irish, and German immigrants. These services were staffed by volunteers and often not subject to oversight by either bishops or clergy at the parish level. The growth of these services reached a peak during the years before the U.S. Civil War, when nativist sentiment (as exemplified by the so-called Know-Nothing Party) grew and Catholic immigrants were suspected of undermining American social and cultural values through their allegiance to the papacy.

Following the Civil War, patterns of immigration shifted in the United States, and large numbers of immigrants from southern and eastern Europe began to arrive. Settling in urban areas in the northeast and midwestern states, these new arrivals, most of whom were Catholic, sought support from Catholic service agencies affiliated with their local parishes. The strain on these agencies' resources led parishes to raise funds through affiliation with groups such as the Leopoldine Society and the Society for the Propagation of the Faith, missionary groups that were skilled at raising money but that lacked the necessary oversight to ensure that those funds reached the new urban immigrant poor. Though some wealthier parishes were able to form benevolent societies to fund orphanages and social service efforts, many urban parishes and dioceses had more needy parishioners (and nonparishioners) than they could effectively serve.

CONSOLIDATION

In an effort to meet the needs of the burgeoning Catholic immigrant populations, many parish or-

ganizations, especially those in large cities, joined ecumenical or even secular "umbrella" charitable groups. During the 1880's and 1890's, groups such as the Associated Charities of Boston and the New York Charity Organization Society were viewed suspiciously by clergy as being "too Protestant," and many Catholics expressed concern that a formal affiliation with the charity arms of other denominations would both hamper the effectiveness of the Catholic parish charities and dilute the theological teachings that Catholic organizations wished to impart. Additionally, reform projects such as Helms House in Brooklyn, New York, were not embraced by church officials, as such projects stressed social reform rather than relief.

In 1910, the heretofore loosely organized Catholic agencies were consolidated as the National Conference of Catholic Charities (NCCC), founded on the campus of Catholic University of America in Washington, D.C. Through this consolidation, revenue could be shared and the "uniquely Catholic" character of the services provided could be maintained. However, consolidation did serve to remove control by the laity and the sisterhood from many charitable enterprises. Such control would not be restored in any significant way until 1939, when Mary Gibbons became president of the NCCC. In 1986, the NCCC became Catholic Charities USA.

POSTWAR YEARS TO THE PRESENT

During the 1950's, in the years following World War II and the Korean War, Catholic Charities USA worked with the U.S. Conference of Catholic Bishops and various dioceses to provide both immigrant and refugee services to Latin Americans, specifically Mexicans, and Haitians seeking residency or asylum in the United States. Along with providing traditional charitable services such as food and housing, Catholic Charities chapters began to provide services to undocumented immigrants as their numbers increased. Indeed, in places such as Arizona and New York, various agencies associated with Catholic Charities USA worked with the Sanctuary movement, a loosely organized ecumenical effort that seeks to help undocumented immigrants remain in the United States.

Also, the organization provided services that included legal assistance for migrant workers in the Southwest and Florida in cases that involved workers' rights, safety, and compensation. Catholic Charities volunteers also assisted in resettlement efforts for refugees from the Sudan, the Balkans, Ethiopia, Cuba, and Vietnam. In many states, Catholic Charities volunteers are authorized to present cases before U.S. Citizenship and Immigration Services (formerly the Immigration and Naturalization Service, or INS) proceedings and immigration courts.

In the early twenty-first century, Catholic Charities USA expanded its advocacy efforts in a variety of areas. The organization lobbied members of Congress and state government officials for low-cost health care for children and those with low incomes, regardless of citizenship. It also advocated for providing adequate funding for programs such as Head Start and the Low Income Home Energy Assistance Program. It lobbied for a temporary worker program, improved access to government services for immigrants, an easier path to citizenship for undocumented immigrants, and a more liberal admission policy for refugees.

William Carney

FURTHER READING

Bane, Mary Jo, Brent Coffin, and Ronald Thiemann. *Who Will Provide? The Changing Role of Religion in American Social Welfare.* Boulder, Colo.: Westview Press, 2000. Examines the shift in focus away from government assistance toward agencies such as Catholic Charities.

Brown, Dorothy M., and Elizabeth McKeown. *The Poor Belong to Us: Catholic Charities and American Welfare.* Cambridge, Mass.: Harvard University Press, 1997. Examination of the role of women in those Catholic agencies that provide services to immigrants.

Oates, Mary. *The Catholic Philanthropic Tradition in America.* Bloomington: Indiana University Press, 1995. Scholarly exploration of Catholic charitable giving with particular attention paid to the groups that became part of Catholic Charities.

SEE ALSO: Employment; Farm and migrant workers; French immigrants; German immigrants; Haitian immigrants; History of immigration, 1620-1783; History of immigration, 1783-1891; Illegal immigration; Religion as a push-pull factor; Sanctuary movement.

CENSUSES, U.S.

THE EVENTS: Official enumerations of the population of the United States undertaken by the federal government every ten years
DATE: Began in 1790

SIGNIFICANCE: Mandated by the U.S. Constitution, the decennial censuses were originally undertaken for the purpose of apportioning congressional seats, electoral votes in presidential elections, and funding of government programs among the states. Over the years, the censuses have collected ever broader and more diverse data on residents of the United States. Data collected by the census are of tremendous value to all studies of U.S. immigration history.

When the Framers of the U.S. Constitution drafted the document that would serve as the foundation of U.S. government and law, they recognized the importance of the government's having complete and accurate demographic data on which to base the apportionment of elective offices and government funding. Consequently, Article I, section 2 of the Constitution was written explicitly to direct that the population of the United States be enumerated at least once every ten years, so the resulting figures would be used to set the numbers of seats apportioned to each state in the U.S. House of Representatives and, by extension, in the Electoral College.

The Constitution was ratified in 1789. The very next year, 1790, the first U.S. Census was taken. Since that date, a new census has been taken in every year whose number ends in a zero. Between official census counts, the United States Census Bureau analyses the data from the previous census and makes population estimates and projections.

RACIAL, ETHNIC, AND NATIONAL CLASSIFICATIONS

During the first half-century of the U.S. Census, from 1790 to 1840, censuses were taken by marshals of the federal judicial districts. Those years were a period of rapid natural population growth, which was increased by growing immigration from Europe and other continents. Early census takers did not ask the people whom they counted about their countries of birth. That omission limited the value of the data they collected in studies of immigration. However, researchers have nevertheless been able to extract useful information on where immigrants came from by studying the family names of the people counted in the raw census records. The seventh U.S. Census, which was taken in 1850, began asking questions about residents' countries of birth.

Terminology used in censuses to classify people by their race, ethnicity, and countries of birth has tended to evolve from census to census. When census takers began asking about countries of birth, they were especially very precise in identifying western European nations and principalities; however, they were less precise in identifying eastern European nations. For example, while they carefully recorded the names of each of the several hundred tiny German principalities from which immigrants came, they ignored the names of some much larger states in the Balkans. The names of the Balkan states of Montenegro and Serbia appeared for the first time in the census of 1910. Immigrants from German-speaking Austria were counted as "Hungarians" until 1870 because Austria was part of the Austro-Hungarian Empire.

Another quirk in mid-nineteenth century census records was the tendency of census takers to assign to immigrants certain nationalities that technically did not then exist. For example, in 1860 they introduced a special "country" of Poland for ethnic Poles, despite the fact that Poland did not then exist as a separate nation. Polish-speaking immigrants from Germany, Austria, and Russian were all officially recorded as coming from "Poland." Another special country created by census takers in 1870 was "Bohemia," which was then part of the Austro-Hungarian Empire. All Czech-speaking immigrants were recorded as having been born in Bohemia.

THE U.S. CENSUS BUREAU

In order to give census taking a more permanent home, the U.S. Congress passed a law in 1902 that established the U.S. Census Bureau as the government agency responsible for overseeing the census. The new bureau was also charged with

Contemporary drawing of a government census taker in 1870. (Library of Congress)

gathering other types of demographic and economic data. As a part of the U.S. Department of Commerce, the bureau has ever since that time served as the primary source of authoritative data about almost every aspect of American demography and the national economy. In establishing the bureau, Congress finally recognized the need for centralizing the gathering of statistical data within one agency.

After 1902, the Census Bureau began growing into a substantial-sized government agency with responsibilities much greater than those of the less permanent offices that it succeeded. Before 1902, the only clear function of the census was to collect population data with which to reapportion congressional seats every decade as the relative sizes of state populations changed.

The first census overseen by the new bureau was that of 1910, which introduced new methods. Under the leadership of Edward Dana Durand, a professional statistician who had become the bureau's director in 1908, the census added numerous new questions, with particular emphasis on labor and industrial matters. The 1910 census required some fundamental procedural changes.

In order to determine the ethnic composition of the nation's immigrant population, the new census form included a question about "mother tongues"—the languages spoken in the ancestral homes of immigrants. That question provided information that would not be learned simply by learning immigrants' countries of birth, as nationality did not always indicate a person's ethnicity. This was particularly true of Jews and members of other ethnic groups from the great multiethnic eastern and central European empires of Russia and Austria-Hungary. Moreover, many individual Slavic immigrants, such as Czechs, Croats, Slovenes, and Slovaks did not want to be counted as "Austrians" or "Hungarians." Czechs started the protests, and members of other Slavic groups soon joined in. The 1920 census asked the same question as the 1910 census about the mother tongues of immigrants and their children. However, the census of 1930 asked only about the mother tongues of the immigrants themselves.

The 1940 census introduced sampling methodology and so they started to ask the question on mother tongue for immigrants and their children and grandchildren on the longer questionnaires.

The 1950 census did not ask the question on mother tongue at all and the 1970 census asked the question on mother tongue again on a longer questionnaire.

CENSUSES AND IMMIGRANT ANCESTRY

At the suggestion of officials of the Bureau of the Census in 1980, Congress replaced the census question about mother tongues with a more open-ended question about ancestry. The new census form asked all respondents to identify their ethnic ancestry. Respondents were asked to answer the question without regard to how many generations removed they were from their ancestral countries of origin or what ties, if any, they had with their ancestral groups. In 1990, respondents were allowed to identify more than a single ancestral group, which slightly few than one-third of the respondents did.

It is interesting to note that information gathered by the 2000 census reflected recent changes in the political map of Europe, after the breakups of the Soviet Union and Yugoslavia. Many more Americans identified as their ancestry nationalities that had recently reappeared on maps of Europe.

Matjaž Klemenčič

FURTHER READING

Anderson, Margo J. *The American Census: A Social History.* New Haven, Conn.: Yale University Press, 1988. Historical account of U.S. census taking that discusses many controversies associated with the censuses.

Choldin, Harvey M. *Looking for the Last Percent: The Controversy over Census Undercounts.* New Brunswick, N.J.: Rutgers University Press, 1994. Critical study of the tendency of censuses to undercount minorities.

Kertzer, David I., and Dominique Arel, eds. *Census and Identity: The Politics of Race, Ethnicity, and Language in National Census.* New York: Cambridge University Press, 2002. Scholarly study of how the U.S. Census has counted members of racial and ethnic minorities.

Perlmann, Joel, and Mary Waters, eds. *The New Race Question: How the Census Counts Multiracial Individuals.* New York: Russell Sage Foundation, 2002. Collection of critical essays on changing racial categories and the social and political effects of these changes in the U.S. Census.

Rodriguez, Clara E. *Changing Race: Latinos, the Census, and the History of Ethnicity.* New York: New York University Press, 2000. Study of the treatment of ethnic minorities in the U.S. Census, with special attention to the counting of Latinos.

Skerry, Peter. *Counting on the Census? Race, Group Identity, and the Evasion of Politics.* Washington, D.C.: Brookings Institution Press, 2000. Analytical study of the problems of accurately counting members of racial and ethnic groups in the U.S. Census.

SEE ALSO: Commission on Immigration Reform, U.S.; Congress, U.S.; Constitution, U.S.; History of immigration, 1620-1783; History of immigration, 1783-1891; History of immigration after 1891; Select Commission on Immigration and Refugee Policy.

CENTER FOR IMMIGRATION STUDIES

IDENTIFICATION: Right-leaning think tank that advocates limiting immigration into the United States and reducing the undocumented population already present

DATE: Established in 1985

SIGNIFICANCE: Through its many publications, public statements and links to conservative legislators, the Center for Immigration Studies has become an influential voice in the congressional debate over immigration policy.

The Center for Immigration Studies (CIS) describes itself as an independent, nonpartisan, nonprofit research organization. It also claims to be the only think tank in the United States devoted exclusively to research and policy analysis of the economic, social, demographic, fiscal and other impacts of immigration on the United States. Its stated mission is to expand the base of public knowledge and understanding of the need for an immigration policy whose first priority is the broad national interest. The center further describes itself as driven by a "pro-immigrant, low-immigration vision that seeks fewer immigrants but a warmer welcome to those admitted." It is not allowed to conduct direct lobbying.

The longtime director of CIS, Mark Krikorian, advocated a policy of "attrition through enforcement," that is, enforcement of immigration laws that would increase the numbers of deportations of undocumented immigrants. He sought not mass deportations that would have an adverse effect on businesses employing undocumented aliens, but rather a steady reduction in the numbers of such aliens already residing in the United States. One of the programs that the center promotes is "E-Verify," a voluntary program begun in 2004 that certifies that companies are hiring only people who are legally entitled to U.S. residence.

HISTORY

CIS was founded in 1985, and its board of directors has usually included several persons affiliated with American universities. Since its beginning the organization has not been without its detractors. The Southern Poverty Law Center, for example, has charged that CIS is one of several organizations established by the anti-immigration activist Dr. John Tanton, who, it claims, espouses a white nationalist and nativist agenda. At least some of the center's funding has been supplied by foundations on the right of the political spectrum. Among the other anti-immigration organizations with which Tanton is reputed to be affiliated are the lobbying group the Federation for American Immigration Reform and its legal arm, the Immigration Reform Law Institute. Other supporters have include the grassroots organizers NumbersUSA, and Project-USA. These groups ostensibly have influence with many conservative politicians on the federal and state levels.

In addition to government crackdowns on employers who hire undocumented workers and the workers themselves, the center advocates greater federal emphasis on border policing. It also opposes awarding amnesty to undocumented workers who, it believes, should be "induced" to return to their native countries. The center has claimed that immigration to the United States declined by about 1.3 million from mid-2007 to mid-2008, a decrease that it attributes to the stricter immigration enforcement policies it supports. Some who oppose the CIS's stance have termed such an assertion arguable because the extent of illegal immigration is not precisely known and the figures the center cites are not statistically provable. Such critics counter that any reduction in immigration could be attributable to the worsening U.S. economy, rather than stricter law enforcement.

Although accused of advocating "restrictionism," the Center for Immigration Studies has attained a measure of credibility with media outlets that frequently quote its statements and statistics. The center receives some respect for including differing opinions in the forums it presents and in its books, reports and papers as well as monthly "backgrounders," usually present a nonconfrontational tone. Director Mark Krikorian, who has stated that "modern America has outgrown mass immigration," has often testified before congressional committees on immigration. He has also engendered some controversy by linking immigration with global warming by arguing that immigration moves people from low-polluting countries to the United States, which is a high-polluting country. He specifically cites the numbers of automobiles driven by undocumented immigrants.

In 2009, Krikorian's critical comments on the way U.S. Supreme Court nominee Sonia Sotomayor pronounced her name also created some stir. Another CIS employee has implicated immigration in the rise of big government because, in his opinion, highly populated societies are more highly regulated societies. Among the other ways that CIS attempts to influence immigration issues is its Edward Katz Award, named for a former board member, which is given to journalists "who best challenge the norm of immigration reporting." Among its recipients is the former CNN commentator Lou Dobbs.

Roy Liebman

FURTHER READING

Briggs, Vernon. *Immigration: The Neglected Orphan of Economic Policy.* Washington, D.C.: Center for Immigration Studies, 1993. A Center for Immigration Studies "backgrounder" report that calls for a halt to mass immigration as a means to aid the American economy.

Hanson, Victor D. *The Universe of the Illegal Alien.* Washington, D.C.: Center for Immigration Studies, 2003. Another CIS "backgrounder" that examines the adverse role undocumented workers play in the life of the United States.

Krikorian, Mark. "Borderline Insanity." *The National Interest*, March 22, 2005, pp. 70-73. The CIS director proposes that a swath of land along the United States-Mexican border be plowed up to produce a mile-wide no-man's-land in which it would become easier to apprehend immigrants attempting to cross the border illegally.

_____. "Enforcement at Work: The Strategy of Attrition Is Bearing Fruit." *National Review*, August 4, 2008, 23. Makes the case that illegal immigration is declining due to stepped-up enforcement and the reality of "self deportation."

_____. "'Give Me the Tools': They Have Them—So Use Them (Immigration Reform in the United States)." *National Review*, July 9, 2007, 20. Urges that current immigration laws be fully and forcefully utilized to prevent further illegal immigration.

_____. *The New Case Against Immigration: Both Legal and Illegal.* New York: Sentinel, 2008. Argues against granting amnesty to undocumented immigrants. Also proposes that standards of skill and merit be applied to prospective new immigrants, and that they be required to learn English.

SEE ALSO: American Protective Association; Commission on Immigration Reform, U.S.; Dillingham Commission; English-only and official English movements; Illegal immigration; Proposition 187; Stereotyping; Xenophobia.

CHAE CHAN PING V. UNITED STATES

THE CASE: U.S. Supreme Court ruling on the exclusion of Chinese immigrants
ALSO KNOWN AS: Chinese Exclusion Case
DATE: Decided on May 13, 1889

SIGNIFICANCE: In addition to recognizing the sovereign power of Congress to exclude any groups from immigration, the decision in this case reaffirmed congressional discretion to abrogate or modify treaties.

Chae Chan Ping, a subject of the emperor of China, worked as an unskilled laborer in San Francisco, California, for about twelve years. In 1887, he went to China for a short visit. Before leaving, he obtained a customs certificate entitling him to return to the United States. On October 1, 1888, Congress amended the 1882 Chinese Exclusion Act with the Scott Act, which included a complete prohibition on the reentry of all Chinese laborers who left the country, even if they had legal certificates to the contrary. The Scott Act was inconsistent with rights guaranteed to Chinese visitors in the 1868 Burlingame Treaty and the 1880 Treaty Regulating Immigration from China. When Ping arrived at the San Francisco port on October 8, 1888, Customs House officials, because of the Scott Act, refused his request to land. After Ping's appeal to the federal district court in California was unsuccessful, the Supreme Court agreed to review the case.

The Supreme Court unanimously upheld the decision of the lower court. Writing the official opinion for the Court, Justice Stephen J. Field wrote that the power to exclude foreigners was an "incident of sovereignty," which was "a part of those sovereign powers delegated by the Constitution." The federal government had the right to exercise this power "at any time when, in the judgment of the government, the interests of the country require it." Conceding that the Scott Act contradicted "express stipulations" in treaties, Field wrote that a treaty, according to the Constitution's supremacy clause, must be deemed as "only the equivalent of a legislative act, to be repealed or modified at the pleasure of Congress." Field also rejected the idea that the right of visitation in a treaty was a form of property protected by the Fifth Amendment.

Thomas Tandy Lewis

FURTHER READING

Chang, Iris. *The Chinese in America: A Narrative History.* New York: Viking Press, 2003.

McClain, Charles J. *In Search of Equality: The Chinese Struggle Against Discrimination in Nineteenth-Century America.* Berkeley: University of California Press, 1994.

SEE ALSO: Burlingame Treaty of 1868; Chinese Exclusion Act of 1882; *Chinese Exclusion Cases*; Chinese immigrants; Congress, U.S.; Constitution, U.S.; Deportation; San Francisco; Supreme Court, U.S.

CHAIN MIGRATION

DEFINITION: Process of movement from immigrants' homelands that builds upon networks of familiar social relationships to construct neighborhood or communities within in the new places of habitation that reflect the cultural norms and societal expectations of the homelands

SIGNIFICANCE: As a result of family members or neighbors contacting others from their home countries for purposes of inspiring them to become their new neighbors in America, chain migration has had a significant impact on the history and growth of immigration to the United States. The virtual replication of "Old World" neighborhoods in America not only has historically allowed recently arrived immigrants to reconstruct familiar communities but has also enabled the new immigrants to survive the rigors of a new and unfamiliar land, by incorporating familiar language, religious worship, and social venues into a sustainable working and living environment.

Chain migration is in many ways a larger sociological process involving the movement of labor around the world. Networks of social connections developed over time between newly arrived immigrants in the United States and peoples in the immigrants' former homes that paved the way for further migration to America. This process made it easier for newcomers to find and secure economic opportunities in the growing industrial, urban, and later agricultural, areas of the United States. When new immigrants arrived, they stood a better chance of achieving prosperity and endured less "shock" to the new American culture. This was because previous migrants had already established culturally familiar communities—with churches, ethnic neighborhoods, social-benefit societies, and foreign-language newspapers—that made even the newest arrivals believe that they were, in essence, "coming home."

EASTERN AND SOUTHERN EUROPEAN CHAIN MIGRATION

During the last few decades of the nineteenth century and the first few decades of the twentieth century, eastern and southern Europeans migrated by the hundreds of thousands to the United States seeking new lives. Many Slavic, Hungarian, and Italian immigrants responded to the dramatic rise in the need for unskilled labor in the American steel industry during the late nineteenth century by accepting manual labor jobs in factories. In addition, steel companies actively contracted for foreign labor, leading to increased migration to steel-producing regions. Many of these newly arrived immigrants would, in turn, write to relatives, neighbors, and friends in their homelands, telling them of the work available in America.

Recently arrived immigrants sometimes returned home themselves and spread the word about the opportunities for unskilled workers in the coal mines and steel plants in the United States. Their letters and conversations inspired many others to follow their examples by migrating to America. When they arrived in their new homes, they often found fellow countrymen who spoke, read, and wrote in their own languages, worshiped in the same churches, and socialized at the same institutions. Moreover, they often found that the immigrants who had preceded them had already built familiar social and community networks, which gave the newcomers a sense of security and the basis for a successful start.

Slovak immigrants who came to the United States during the late nineteenth century provide an important example of successful chain migration. After many of these migrants had settled into jobs, paid off their debts for their passage to America and established themselves in settled working-class communities, they invited their extended family members in Europe to join them in America. As word spread in the home country from the migrants' written and oral contacts, people from neighboring villages followed the initial migrants to the United States and set up similar Slovak communities around many of the same mills and mines that employed large amounts of unskilled labor, from Bethlehem and Philadelphia, Pennsylvania, to cities such as Minneapolis, Minnesota.

Nativist Reactions

By the late twentieth century, chain migration had been viewed negatively by some nativists as having contributed to increased illegal immigration, particularly from Latin America. Holders of this view point to the consequences of the bracero program that brought thousands of Mexican into the country as guest farmworkers during the mid-twentieth century. They argue that the program enabled Mexican immigrants to establish chain-migration patterns that later fostered a dramatic rise in illegal immigration.

James C. Koshan

FURTHER READING

Bell, Thomas. *Out of This Furnace: A Novel of Immigrant Labor.* Pittsburgh: University of Pittsburgh Press, 1976. Originally published in 1941, this historical novel is set in the steel mills and communities of Braddock, Pennsylvania, drawing on three generations of the author's own Slovak family history.

Castile, George Pierre, and Gilbert Kushner, eds. *Persistent Peoples: Ethnic Enclaves in Perspective.* Tucson: University of Arizona Press, 1982. Valuable collection of essays on immigrants living in ethnic enclaves. A good introduction to the subject.

Čulen, Konštantin. *History of Slovaks in America.* St. Paul, Minn.: Czechoslovak Genealogical Society, 2007. Translation of *Dejiny Slovákov v Amerike* (1942), a detailed portrait of Slovak life in the United States before 1914.

Daniels, Roger. *Coming to America: A History of Immigration and Ethnicity in American Life.* New York: HarperCollins, 1990. Popular social analysis of immigration to America since the sixteenth century that includes many obscure facts and personalized accounts.

Jones, Maldwyn Allen. *American Immigration.* 2d ed. Chicago: University of Chicago Press, 1992. Comprehensive history of American immigration that explores all aspects of the newcomers' impact on the United States as well as the overall immigrant influence on American history.

Rechcígl, Miloslav. *Czechs and Slovaks in America.* Boulder, Colo.: East European Monographs, 2005. Collection of essays relating to the history and contributions of Czech and Slovak immigrants and their descendants in the United States.

See also: Dual citizenship; Employment; Ethnic enclaves; Families; Push-pull factors; Religion as a push-pull factor; Return migration; Settlement patterns; Social networks.

CHANG CHAN V. NAGLE

THE CASE: U.S. Supreme Court ruling on immigration law
DATE: Decided on May 25, 1925

> **SIGNIFICANCE:** The *Chang Chan* ruling upheld the application of a law disallowing the entrance of some foreign wives of U.S. citizens.

The Immigration Act of 1924 contained a provision that excluded foreign wives of U.S. citizens from entering the country if they were members of a race ineligible for naturalization. Chang Chan, as well as three other native-born U.S. citizens, had married Chinese women in China prior to the law's enactment. When the four young women arrived in San Francisco on July 24, 1924, they were denied permanent admission. The Supreme Court unanimously held that the women did not have the right to enter the country. In the majority opinion, Justice James Clark McReynolds examined the few exceptions in the law and concluded that none of them applied to this particular case. He wrote that the "hardships of a case, and suppositions of what is rational and consistent in immigration policy, cannot justify a court in departing from the plain terms of an immigration act."

Thomas Tandy Lewis

FURTHER READING
Hyung-chan, Kim, ed. *Asian Americans and the Supreme Court: A Documentary History*. Westport, Conn.: Greenwood Press, 1992.
LeMay, Michael, and Elliott Robert Barkan, eds. *U.S. Immigration and Naturalization Laws and Issues: A Documentary History*. Westport, Conn.: Greenwood Press, 1999.

SEE ALSO: Asian Indian immigrants; *Cheung Sum Shee v. Nagle*; Chinese immigrants; Congress, U.S.; Immigration Act of 1924; San Francisco; Supreme Court, U.S.

CHEUNG SUM SHEE V. NAGLE

THE CASE: U.S. Supreme Court decision on immigration rights
DATE: Decided on May 25, 1925

> **SIGNIFICANCE:** The *Cheung Sum Shee* ruling held that treaty provisions guaranteeing rights for foreign citizens were legally binding unless Congress had clearly and explicitly abrogated those rights.

The Immigration Act of 1924, effective from July 1 of that year, allowed entrance into the United States of alien merchants who came "solely to carry on trade" in pursuance of an existing treaty of commerce and navigation. When Cheung Sum Shee, a Chinese merchant, arrived with his wife and minor children on July 11, 1924, government officials refused their application to land. Their explanation was that the new law did not mention the right of a merchant to bring his family.

When the case reached the Supreme Court, the justices unanimously agreed that the government was obligated to allow the admission of the Shee family. Writing the opinion for the Court, Justice James Clark McReynolds made two factual observations: First, the 1880 treaty with China guaranteed the right of visiting merchants to bring their families with them; second, the Immigration Act of 1924, as well as other laws, had not explicitly abrogated this particular right. He affirmed that an act of Congress

> must be construed with the view to preserve treaty rights unless clearly annulled, and we cannot conclude that, considering its history, the general terms therein disclose a congressional intent absolutely to exclude the petitioners from entry.

Although the members of the Shee family were ineligible for naturalization, there was no limit to the number of years that Shee was permitted to stay in the United States with the purpose of engaging in commerce.

Thomas Tandy Lewis

FURTHER READING
Chang, Iris. *The Chinese in America: A Narrative History*. New York: Viking Press, 2003.

McClain, Charles J. *In Search of Equality: The Chinese Struggle Against Discrimination in Nineteenth-Century America.* Berkeley: University of California Press, 1994.

SEE ALSO: *Chang Chan v. Nagle*; Chinese immigrants; Constitution, U.S.; Supreme Court, U.S.

CHEW HEONG V. UNITED STATES

THE CASE: U.S. Supreme Court decision on treaty rights

DATE: Decided on December 8, 1884

> **SIGNIFICANCE:** In the first of the Supreme Court's Chinese exclusion cases, the *Chew Heong* decision affirmed that a Chinese citizen had the benefit of rights promised in treaties with China unless the treaties had been clearly and explicitly repealed by Congress.

In an 1884 amendment to the Chinese Exclusion Act of 1882, Congress required Chinese laborers residing in the United States to obtain reentry certificates if they left the country with the intention to return. Chew Heong, who left in 1881, returned not long after the amendment went into effect. Lacking the certificate, he was denied permission to land. In response, he challenged the denial in federal court on the ground that it violated privileges guaranteed under a treaty made between the United States and China in 1880.

The Supreme Court, by a 7-2 vote, ruled in Heong's favor. Writing for the majority, Justice John Marshall Harlan addressed two major arguments. First, Heong was qualified to obtain a certificate, and he could not be required to do what had been impossible for him to do. Second, the denial of his right to return contradicted a treaty with China. Unless Congress had unambiguously expressed its intent to repeal the relevant part of the treaty, established rules of construction required the Court to attempt to reconcile the treaty with the legislation.

Thomas Tandy Lewis

FURTHER READING

Chang, Iris. *The Chinese in America: A Narrative History.* New York: Viking Press, 2003.

McClain, Charles J. *In Search of Equality: The Chinese Struggle Against Discrimination in Nineteenth-Century America.* Berkeley: University of California Press, 1994.

SEE ALSO: Chinese Exclusion Act of 1882; *Chinese Exclusion Cases*; Chinese immigrants; Congress, U.S.; Supreme Court, U.S.

Reentry documents carried by a Chinese immigrant in 1891. (NARA)

CHICAGO

IDENTIFICATION: Largest city and major commercial hub in both Illinois and the Midwest

SIGNIFICANCE: From the time of its incorporation during the early nineteenth century, Chicago has attracted many immigrants seeking jobs and business opportunities. With immigrants from Europe, Asia, Latin America, and the Middle East, Chicago has become a center of multiculturalism and enriched the United States with a diverse population.

From the 1840's through the early twentieth century, oppression, religious persecution, a rapid increase in population, and a scarcity of land and employment and the resulting starvation forced many Europeans to leave their native lands in search of employment and the opportunity to improve their lives. Chicago, with its big steel mills, stockyards, and meatpacking plants, attracted a vast number of these immigrants.

NINETEENTH CENTURY TRENDS

During the late nineteenth century, immigrants from Ireland, Germany, Italy, and eastern European countries—especially Poland and Lithuania—made their way to Chicago. Roman Catholicism and Judaism were the predominant faiths of these immigrants, many of whom were fleeing harassment as well as severe hardships in earning a living. The vast majority of these immigrants were poor individuals lacking specific skills. The Irish immigrants, for example, had almost exclusively been tenant farmers. The continental European immigrants were mostly of peasant ancestry and came from small farms. In 1916, with the increase in the number of workers required to meet the needs of the war effort, a considerable number of Mexicans, displaced by the Mexican Revolution, also immigrated to Chicago.

Unskilled and for the most part non-English speaking, Chicago's diverse immigrants took low-paying and often dangerous jobs requiring manual labor in the stockyards, meatpacking plants, and steel mills. They settled in areas close to their work and attempted to recreate the social and cultural life they had known in their homelands. Irish immigrants tended to settle in Bridgeport on the South Side and in Kilglubbin to the north and east of the stockyards in Canaryville.

Lithuanians also settled in areas of Bridgeport, while the Polish lived in Back of the Yards. The Italians created "Little Italies" and the Germans established their own communities. In the meatpacking plants, certain immigrant groups tended to concentrate in specific jobs. For example, the Irish worked primarily in livestock handling. Germans, Poles, and Lithuanians worked mainly on the killing floors, and Mexicans worked in the freezers and hide cellars. Similar ethnic patterns could also be found in the steel mills.

TWENTIETH CENTURY DEVELOPMENTS

The flood of immigrants entering Chicago continued into the first decade of the twentieth century. In addition to the large group of Mexicans who fled the revolution in their home country, large numbers of Lithuanian farmers displaced by industrialization and the advent of commercial farming and Russian Jews fleeing religious persecution settled in Chicago. As concern over the size of the nation's growing immigrant population became greater, the U.S. government enacted a number of laws to restrict the inflow. As in other parts of the country, Chicago then experienced a significantly slower pace of new immigration.

After World War II ended in 1945, the number of immigrants coming to Chicago increased again. With the Soviet Union occupying Eastern European countries, Chicago experienced a resurgence of immigrants from these countries, especially Lithuania. Liberalization of federal immigration laws in 1965 brought large numbers of immigrants from Asian countries, including South Korea, the Philippines, China, and India as well as from many Latin American countries. By the 1990's, three-fourths of Chicago's population growth was attributable to immigration. During the 1990's, the number of Chicago residents who had been born in India doubled. The areas in which the immigrants settled during the late twentieth century also changed. Most early immigrants settled in the city proper, but after 2000, immigrants began settling in the suburbs.

The composition of Chicago's immigrant population changed significantly between the mid-nineteenth century and the early twenty-first century. Irish, German, Italian and Polish immigrants constituted the most numerous foreign-born segments of Chicago's population during the nineteenth and early twentieth centuries. The 2000 U.S. Census found that Mexicans, Poles, and Indians constituted the city's three largest foreign-born groups. Mexicans alone accounted for 40 percent of the foreign-born population. During the 1990's, the numbers of immigrants from sub-Saharan Africa began increasing significantly. The numbers from Nigeria and Ghana alone tripled during the 1990's. However, despite these changes, the presence of Irish, Italians, Poles, Germans, and other early immigrant groups remains visible in the many festivals, ethnic celebrations and cultural attractions that enrich the city.

Shawncey Webb

FURTHER READING

Arredondo, Gabriela F. *Mexican Chicago: Race, Identity, and Nation, 1916-39.* Champaign: University of Illinois Press, 2008. Close study of how Mexican immigrants' revolutionary background affected their reaction to prejudice and how they established their own Mexican identity in Chicago. Excellent for explaining differences in experiences of immigrant groups.

Candeloro, Dominic. *Chicago's Italians: Immigrants, Ethnics, Americans.* Charleston, S.C.: Arcadia, 2003. Traces the contributions of Chicago's Italians to labor unions, politics, and religion, and treats changes brought to the Italian community by World War II.

Koval, John, et al., eds. *The New Chicago: A Social and Cultural Analysis.* Philadelphia: Temple University Press, 2006. Broad study of immigrant groups who arrived in Chicago during the late twentieth and early twenty-first centuries, including the Poles. Also discusses Asian, Latino, and Arab immigrants in work and social roles.

Pacyga, Dominic A. *Polish Immigrants and Industrial Chicago: Workers on the South Side, 1880-1922.* Chi-

An elevated train passes over a Chicago street crowded with demonstrators marching in support of immigrant rights on May 1, 2006, during a nationwide day of immigrant action. (AP/Wide World Photos)

cago: University of Chicago Press, 2003. Excellent discussion of Polish immigrants working in Chicago's steel mills, slaughterhouses, and meatpacking plants. Details how they created ethnic neighborhoods like those of Eastern Europe.

Rangaswamy, Padma. *Namasté America: Indian Immigrants in an American Metropolis.* University Park: Pennsylvania State University Press, 2000. Concentrating on Chicago, Rangaswamy addresses the social conditions, ethnic identity, and ethnic relations of Indian immigrants in urban America.

SEE ALSO: Asian immigrants; Cultural pluralism; European immigrants; Great Irish Famine; Gresham-Yang Treaty of 1894; Hull-House; Illinois; *The Jungle*; Little Italies; Mexican immigrants.

CHICANO MOVEMENT

THE EVENT: Movement in which Mexican Americans defined and took pride in their own identity, asserted their civil rights, and worked toward self-determination by improving their financial, social, and political circumstances

ALSO KNOWN AS: *El Movimiento*

DATE: 1960's and 1970's

LOCATION: Northwestern, southwestern, and parts of the midwestern United States

SIGNIFICANCE: Similar to other movements of this period promoting civil rights, the Chicano movement made society aware of the injustices suffered by Mexican Americans in the United States and spurred social change.

The Chicano movement, also known by Chicanos as *El Movimiento*, was a cultural and political movement that raised awareness of the history of Mexicans and/or Chicanos in North America. The origin of the term "Chicano" is not known, and its definition varies, yet it has been proudly reclaimed by Americans of Mexican ancestry to emphasize their descent from colonial projects. The movement has been analyzed in three parts: the struggle for restoration of land grants, the appeal for Mexican American farmworkers' rights, and the demand for equal access to empowerment via education and politics.

RESTORATION OF LAND GRANTS

During the 1960's, a group of Mexican Americans attempted to reclaim federal land in the United States. This group basied their actions on the Treaty of Guadalupe Hidalgo, which was signed by the United States and Mexico in 1848 to end the Mexican War of 1846-1848. The treaty ceded Mexican lands to the United States and ensured that landowning Mexicans would keep their preexisting property rights in the lands transferred. The United States failed to honor this latter part of the agreement, as it did not recognize Mexicans' original land grants that were given under Spanish and Mexican law. Many Mexicans thus lost their lands.

Leaders of the Chicano movement argued that many Mexican Americans were not immigrants and that the Mexican people legitimately owned parts of the land ceded to the United States. When they failed to secure these lost lands, the Chicanos of the 1960's and 1970's reclaimed Aztlán, the ancestral homeland of an indigenous group from Mexico, the Nahua. Media representations of the Chicano movement are characterized by attention to the integration of various indigenous cultural elements into the movement's struggle.

FARMWORKERS' RIGHTS

The Chicano movement also protested the exploitation of Mexican American migrant farmworkers, who traveled throughout the United States following the crop seasons for wages that kept their families well below the poverty level. Because migrant families were unable to stay in one town for much time, workers' children were limited to two to three years of education before they too would begin to pick produce for growers. Both adults and children were exposed to poisonous pesticides and the harsh sun for long periods of time, among other detrimental conditions.

To put an end to these conditions, Mexican American migrant farmworkers organized. Cofounded in 1962 by Dolores Huerta and César Chávez, the National Farm Workers Association (NFWA), which later evolved into the United Farm

---

"CHICANO"

The origin of the term "Chicano" is unclear; however, some experts believe that the word originated from an improper pronunciation or slang version of "Mexicano." Consequently, the user was viewed by middle-class Mexicans or Mexican Americans as uneducated, poor, and probably "Indian," a pejorative appellation from those of Mexican origin who rejected their indigenous roots. In the Chicano critique of Anglo society, the rejection of Anglo racial and ethnocentric designations also included the repudiation of those in Mexicano communities who accepted anti-Native American and capitalist belief systems. To call the self Chicano is to affirm that which is denounced by Anglo-created racial constructs and ethnocentric depictions. To be Chicano is to affirm and proclaim historic, indigenous origins and to understand that Chicano culture has Spanish-Indian roots in a land invaded and conquered by the European Americans.

Workers (UFW), initiated strikes and boycotted various fruits and vegetables in support of farmworkers' rights. The union workers further protested the growers' employment of undocumented Mexican immigrants as strikebreakers, as it undermined their own efforts toward fair treatment and wages as employees. Though the union had failed in its early attempts to bring about reform, it was strengthened in 1964 when the U.S. government terminated the bracero program, which had allowed the importation of temporary labor from Mexico. This termination resulted in a reduced workforce for growers and enabled the union to effect changes, as the growers became desperate for U.S. farmworkers. In the early twenty-first century, the UFW continues to fight for the rights of both documented and undocumented farmworkers.

EDUCATION AND POLITICS

During the Chicano movement, Chicanos became conscious of the injustices in the educational system. Cognizant of the fact that only 25 percent of Chicanos graduated from high school, students were awakened to the need for reform within what they perceived to be a discriminatory system. Poor quality of education and unequal access to learning resources channeled Chicano students into cheap labor positions like those of their parents. Chicano youths were also being conscripted to fight in the Vietnam War and were dying at a higher rate than others in the military. Nevertheless, their contributions to the United States were not being acknowledged. Governmental systems, Chicanos argued, were keeping generations of Chicanos impoverished and powerless.

Aware of their oppression, these youths became an energetic source of cultural pride, activism, and radicalism. They organized into a conglomerate of various student organizations collectively named the Movimiento Estudiantil Chicano de Aztlán (MEChA). They walked out of high schools and universities, demanding educational reform, including the integration of Mexican American history courses into the curriculum and the hiring of Mexican American teachers and counselors. Other youths formed militant groups such as the Brown Berets.

In order to effect social change, Chicanos saw the need to enter into politics and galvanize the Mexican American community. Growing disenchanted with the Democratic and Republican parties, they saw the need for a third political party that would refuse to compromise with these traditional groups. Chicanos organized the Raza Unida Party (RUP) to bring Mexican Americans' values and needs under one political banner. Though the RUP eventually failed in its initial efforts, it nonetheless paved the way for Chicanos to enter the political arena.

Sara A. Ramírez

FURTHER READING

Acuña, Rodolfo F. *Occupied America: A History of Chicanos.* 6th ed. New York: Pearson Education, 2006. Surveys the history of Chicanos from the Mesoamerican era to the present day and examines the complex intersections of race, gender, and class in Chicano identity.

Cockcroft, Eva Sperling, and Holly Barnet-Sánchez, eds. *Signs from the Heart: California Chicano Murals.* Albuquerque: University of New Mexico Press, 1993. Includes four essays analyzing the educational, historical, and artistic significance of the mural genre inspired by Chicano culture.

García, Alma M., ed. *Chicana Feminist Thought: The Basic Historical Writings.* New York: Routledge, 1997. Recovers the writings of a generation of Chicano feminists who collectively struggled against gender conflicts within the Chicano movement.

Maciel, David R., Isidro D. Ortiz, and María Herrera-Sobek. *Chicano Renaissance: Contemporary Cultural Trends.* Tucson: University of Arizona Press, 2000. Examines the broad range of artistic cultural forms inspired by the Chicano movement, including art, literature, music, television, radio, and cinema. Focuses on the decades following the Chicano movement.

Muñoz, Carlos. *Youth, Identity, Power: The Chicano Movement.* New York: Verso, 1989. Written by a leader of the Chicano movement, this book explores the origins and development of Chicano political protest contextualized within the history of Mexicans and their descendants in the United States.

Rosales, Francisco Arturo. *Chicano! The History of the Mexican American Civil Rights Movement.* Houston: Arte Público Press, 1996. Companion to a documentary of the same name, this text highlights pivotal moments, key issues, and important figures of the Chicano movement and includes historical photographs.

SEE ALSO: Bilingual Education Act of 1968; Bracero program; California; Civil Rights movement; Latinos and immigrants; Mexican American Legal Defense and Educational Fund; Mexican immigrants; New Mexico; Texas; United Farm Workers.

CHILD IMMIGRANTS

DEFINITION: Immigrants who have not yet reached the legal age of majority—usually people under eighteen years of age

SIGNIFICANCE: The estimated five million child immigrants residing in the United States during the first decade of the twenty-first century have presented unique anomalies for those charged with enforcing immigration laws. Children often become the innocent victims of such laws, especially those who belong to families of undocumented aliens. Although these children frequently have lived much of their lives within the United States, they are often deported as illegals and returned to countries whose languages they do not speak and whose customs they do not know.

The United States is a society built by immigrants who flowed into the country in vast numbers during the nineteenth and twentieth centuries. Whether these newcomers were fast or slow to adapt to their new surroundings, they all produced children who, as second-generation immigrants, quickly learned the language and customs of their new surroundings. Their assimilation was accelerated by intermarriage. Assimilation was generally smoother for immigrants from most of Europe, as they bore a general similarity of appearance to the majority population of native-born Americans of European descent. Slower to be assimilated were those who, because of their skin pigmentation and other features, looked different from most of the European immigrants. Asians often created their own ethnic enclaves, and such enclaves as Chinatowns continued to thrive as many as three or four generations after their founders arrived in the United States.

In many of America's large cities, tight-knit ethnic communities were formed by those of similar backgrounds. However, by the second or third generations, the structures of most such communities tended to weaken as their younger members became upwardly mobile and entered professions outside their communities, rather than remaining in the ranks of unskilled laborers that they had formerly occupied.

ACCEPTING AMERICAN WAYS

The most crucial step toward assimilation is learning the language of one's adopted country. In many immigrant families, particularly those from eastern European nations, immigrant parents insisted that only English be spoken in their homes. Consequently, their children tended to gain English fluency quickly.

Many eastern European immigrants arrived at seaports on the East Coast of the United States and settled in such coastal cities as Boston, New York, Philadelphia, and Baltimore. In cities that provided free or inexpensive educations—in some cases, as in New York City, through higher education—the children of immigrants hastened to take full advantage of the educational opportunities available to them. Their assimilation was assured.

CLASSIFICATION OF CHILD IMMIGRANTS

Child immigrants can be classified within a number of categories, ranging from infants adopted from foreign countries by American citizens to the children of aliens, documented and undocumented, who may be seeking citizenship independently or as members of families. Although most legislation on immigration professes respect for family unification, significant problems arise for the children of undocumented aliens.

Under U.S. law, all children born within the United States or in its territories are automatically U.S. citizens. Their birth certificates are proof of their citizenship, even if they are born while their parents are in the United States illegally. If that is the case, their parents remain viewed as undocumented aliens and are, if apprehended, subject to deportation. The citizenship of children thus has little bearing on the parents' status as illegals.

Child immigrants can be classified variously. American citizens often look to foreign countries when they wish to adopt children. In the past, such

Young immigrants at Ellis Island during the early twentieth century. The tags they wear identify the ship on which they arrived. (Library of Congress)

can enter the United States fully documented and with citizenship status.

U.S. citizens who adopt older children holding foreign citizenship can usually obtain U.S. citizenship for these children if they are under eighteen years of age. However, they must present convincing evidence that they are not adopting merely so the children can obtain citizenship. Such practices have been dubbed "adoptions of convenience," which are similar to "marriages of convenience"—those entered into for the sole purpose of obtaining citizenship. The adoptive parents must usually verify that they have supported their adopted children for substantial periods, usually two years, prior to filing their applications for citizenship.

NATURALIZATION OF STEPCHILDREN AND ORPHANS

Stepchildren constitute another category pertaining to child immigration. When American citizens marry spouses whose children are not citizens, they can apply to have their new stepchildren declared U.S. citizens. Stepparents do not necessarily have to adopt their stepchildren to make them eligible for citizenship, but they must demonstrate that they have contributed significantly to the children's support and upbringing for a minimum period of time if the children are declared to have nonorphan status.

When children have orphan status, the requirement for nonorphans is not enforced. An orphan is defined as a child whose natural parents have died, disappeared, or abandoned the child. Such children are eligible for permanent resident status if they are being adopted by U.S. citizens. A child who has lost one parent may be designated an orphan if the surviving parent has not remarried and is incapable of supporting the child in question. The surviving parents must surrender their parental rights in order for their children to be declared orphans.

Adopting single parents must be twenty-five years of age or older to qualify as petitioners for adoption. However, married people need not meet this age requirement. Adopting parents need only

children, who were usually babes in arms at the time of their adoption, did not automatically become U.S. citizens. However, if their adoptions were approved by the appropriate federal government authorities, the adopting parents, on proving their willingness and ability to assume the full responsibilities of parenthood, routinely obtained citizenship for the children they adopted or were about to adopt.

The Child Citizenship Act of 2000 streamlined the process though which adopted children from other countries gain American citizenship. In the past, children who were approved for adoption and removal from their native countries were routinely granted citizenship after entering the United States. Under the provisions of the 2000 law, however, U.S. citizenship is now granted immediately upon the approval of an adoption in the child's native country so that the adopted infant meet the adoption adoptive parent requirements of the states in which they file their petitions to adopt.

TWENTY-FIRST CENTURY LEGISLATION

In October, 2000, President Bill Clinton signed the Intercountry Adoption Act, which adhered to the Hague Convention on International Adoption. This bill was intended to simplify the process for adopting children from foreign countries. Although the new law was a significant step forward, it did not take effect immediately. The federal government first had to establish a Central Adoption Authority, the details of which had to be established and agreed to by all of the participating parties.

In a continuing effort to streamline the adoption of children from foreign countries in 2009, the Families for Orphans Coalition (FACE) supported a bill in both the U.S. Senate and the House of Representatives for legislation to be called the Foreign Adopted Children Equality Act. The bill was sponsored by John Boozman and Diane Wilson in the Senate and by Mary Landrieu and James Inhofe in the House. Under the provisions of this act, citizenship would be granted immediately to all foreign children being adopted by U.S. citizens so they would enter the United States as full-fledged citizens, rather than as petitioners for citizenship. This act would eliminate the need for adopted children in this category to obtain immigration visas in order to enter the United States. Rather, they are declared "citizens from birth." Whereas children who enter the United States on immigration visas, albeit legally, might at some future date be denied scholarships, passports, or entry into the U.S. armed forces, the new status would bestow upon foreign adoptees all the rights and privileges of anyone born in the United States.

Passage of this 2009 bill would eliminate many heartbreaking situations that have afflicted those who entered the United States on immigration visas. Under the old rule, adopted children who have lived virtually their entire lives within the United States could, on being convicted of committing minor juvenile offenses, be deported to their countries of origin. It is estimated that one-half of the adopted children who enter the United States each year, do so on visas that may place them at risk of deportation in the future.

INS PROCEDURES

All persons applying for U.S. citizenship, except for very young children, must undergo interviews conducted by the Immigration and Naturalization Service. At these interviews, applicants are fingerprinted and given two tests, one to demonstrate their ability to speak English and the other to demonstrate their knowledge of basic American government and history. Older applicants are occasionally granted exemptions from the language test. Those who pass the tests are immediately informed that they have passed. Those who do not pass one or both tests may apply to retake the tests at a later date.

CHILDREN BORN ABROAD TO U.S. CITIZENS

Children born in foreign countries to U.S. citizens receive American citizenship immediately if both their parents are already citizens. In cases in which only one parent is a citizen, the children must live in the United States for at least five years—two of which must be after the child reaches the age of fourteen. In the latter situation, full citizenship must be applied for, but granting it is routine.

R. Baird Shuman

FURTHER READING

Alvarez, Julia. *How the García Girls Lost Their Accents.* Chapel Hill, N.C.: Algonquin Books, 1991. Well-written memoir detailing the immigration trials of four sisters fleeing an oppressive regime in the Dominican Republic.

Canter, Laurence A., and Martha S. Siegel. *U.S. Immigration Made Easy.* 10th ed. Berkeley, Calif.: Nolo Press, 2003. Perhaps the most comprehensive quick guide on matters of immigration. An indispensable resource for those seeking accurate information about all aspects of United States immigration. Chapter 6 focuses on child immigration.

Hamilton, John. *Becoming a Citizen.* Edina, Minn.: ABDO Publishing, 2005. Directed at juvenile readers, this volume is lucid in its presentation of such topics as immigrants, eligibility, how to apply for citizenship, and the INS interview process for those seeking American citizenship.

Jones, Maldwyn Allen. *American Immigration.* 2d ed. Chicago: University of Chicago Press, 1992. Although this source is somewhat dated, it presents a striking history of immigration, touching on the most salient laws that deal with the topic.

LeMay, Michael C. *Guarding the Gates: Immigration and National Security*. Westport, Conn.: Praeger, 2006. Challenging contrastive study of how U.S. immigration policy has moved progressively from an open door policy through what LeMay terms, "door ajar," "pet door," "Dutch door," and "storm door" policies.

LeMay, Michael C., and Elliott Robert Barken, eds. *U.S. Immigration and Naturalization Laws and Issues: A Documentary History*. Westport, Conn.: Greenwood Press, 1999. Collection of 150 documents dealing with immigration. These primary sources are presented in their entirety. The book has a helpful glossary and a time line of significant dates.

Suro, Roberto. *Strangers Among Us: Latino Lives in a Changing America*. New York: Vintage Books, 1999. Balanced view of immigration by Latin Americans with a cogent chapter, "Branding the Babies," that deals with young immigrants.

SEE ALSO: Alvarez, Julia; Amerasian children; Bilingual education; *Born in East L.A.*; Deportation; Education; Families; Foreign exchange students; Luce-Celler Bill of 1946; Parachute children; Sweatshops.

CHIN BAK KAN V. UNITED STATES

THE CASE: U.S. Supreme Court decision on the Chinese Exclusion Acts

DATE: Decided on June 2, 1902

> **SIGNIFICANCE:** The decision demonstrated that the majority of the justices sympathized with the vigorous enforcement of the Chinese Exclusion Acts and that they were not disposed to allow minor procedural defects to interfere with the deportation of persons entering the country illegally.

In 1901, Chin Bak Kan, a Chinese laborer, surreptitiously entered the state of New York through Canada. Following Kan's arrest, a U.S. commissioner for the Northern District of New York found him guilty of violating the most recent Chinese Exclusion Act and ordered his immediate deportation to China. Kan appealed the order on procedural grounds, but the U.S. district court approved the deportation.

The Supreme Court unanimously upheld the district court's judgment. Writing the opinion for the Court, Chief Justice Melville Fuller reviewed the history of the Chinese Exclusion Acts and considered the principles of due process utilized in the proceedings. Although finding a few minor defects, he concluded that they did not affect the authority of the commissioner or the validity of the deportation order. The fact that a U.S. commissioner rather than a judge had ordered the deportation was not problematic because the law delegated this power to commissioners. In Fuller's view, the crucial issue was Kan's inability to establish by "affirmative proof, to the satisfaction of such justice, judge, or commissioner, his lawful right to remain in the United States."

Thomas Tandy Lewis

FURTHER READING

Chang, Iris. *The Chinese in America: A Narrative History*. New York: Viking Press, 2003.

McClain, Charles J. *In Search of Equality: The Chinese Struggle Against Discrimination in Nineteenth-Century America*. Berkeley: University of California Press, 1994.

SEE ALSO: Chinese Exclusion Act of 1882; *Chinese Exclusion Cases*; Chinese immigrants; *Chy Lung v. Freeman*; Congress, U.S.; Supreme Court, U.S.

CHINATOWNS

DEFINITION: Ethnic enclaves of cities within which Chinese residents are concentrated

> **SIGNIFICANCE:** American Chinatowns are viewed by some as ethnic ghettos and places of exploitation by an internal Chinese American business elite and by society as a whole. Others see them as a source of economic opportunity and an aid in adjusting to a new environment for newly arrived Chinese. In either case, Chinatowns have been the points of entry into America for most Chinese immi-

grants, and they are an important part of American culture and history.

Thanks to Spain's presence in the Americas and its trade with China, ethnic Chinese have been in America since the sixteenth century. It was not until the mid-nineteenth century, however, that significant numbers began to seek their fortune in *Gam Saan,* or "Gold Mountain," as some called California. It was during this time that the Qing Dynasty was collapsing in China, accompanied by wars and revolutions. In addition, the population of China was exploding. Guangdong and Fujian provinces' population doubled during the nineteenth century, displacing thousands of farmers and merchants, and more than half the Chinese immigrants at that time came from this area. In 1848, gold was discovered in California, and construction of the transcontinental railroad was begun in 1863.

The lure of fortunes in the gold fields and steady work on the railroad brought immigrants by the thousands, who, in order to protect themselves from the mistreatment and discrimination of the greater society, congregated together and insulated themselves. In addition to this self-segregation, laws were passed that prohibited Chinese from buying land or living outside certain areas. These factors combined to create America's Chinatowns, which have served as an American repository of the languages, customs, and culture of one of humankind's oldest civilizations.

History of Chinatowns

The majority of the early Chinese immigrants were either bachelors or men whose families remained in China. These early Chinatowns were seen as bachelor outposts where opium dens and prostitution were common. In most cases, these immigrants did not come to America seeking the cele-

Store in New York City's Chinatown in 1903. (Library of Congress)

brated American Dream but were instead sojourners who hoped to one day return to China with a fortune. Any who may have wanted to pursue the American Dream were faced with the Naturalization Law of 1790, which stated that only "free white persons" could become citizens. These Chinese sojourners usually sent a large part of their earnings to their families in China, and a large number of them wound up penniless and exhausted.

After the transcontinental railroad was completed in 1869, Chinatowns were full of men who were willing to work in worse conditions and for less money than the greater population. Meanwhile, the railroad they had built brought thousands of easterners to the West seeking their fortunes. When these new arrivals found that most of the entry-level jobs had been taken by Chinese men, they declared them a threat and sought protection against the "yellow peril." This anti-Chinese sentiment resulted in the Chinese Exclusion Act of 1882, which suspended Chinese immigration for ten years, with the exception of diplomats, tourists, students, and merchants. The act also denied U.S. citizenship to Chinese already in the country; thus, Chinese men already in America were unable to send for their families. As a result, well into the twentieth century the population of Chinatowns continued to be predominantly made up of single men. The U.S. Census of 1890 showed that there were twenty-seven Chinese men to every Chinese woman in America, and the gender ratio did not reach parity until 1990.

In 1943, when the United States allied with China against Japan in World War II, the Chinese Exclusion Act was repealed. However, the immigration quota was set at 105 Chinese per year, which removed any effectiveness the repeal might have had toward lessening the Chinatowns' gender gap. The War Brides Act of 1945, however, allowed thousands of wives of Chinese American veterans entry into the United States without being a part of the quota. After the Chinese Revolution of 1949, several thousand professionals, students, and government workers were allowed to become citizens through several refugee acts. The Immigration and Nationality Act of 1952 (also known as the McCarran-Walter Act) ended Asian exclusion from immigration to the United States. As a result of these changes, almost 90 percent of Chinese entering the United States from 1947 through 1953 were women.

It was finally the Immigration and Nationality Act of 1965 (also known as the Hart-Celler Act) that made the most significant changes to the demographic profile of America's Chinatowns. Among other significant changes, it permitted family members of Chinese Americans nonquota entry. Chinatowns had at last become a place for families.

By the early twenty-first century, the majority of Chinese immigrants came from non-Cantonese-speaking areas of China, particularly Taiwan, Hong Kong, and other areas of the People's Republic of China. While Cantonese culture is still dominant in most Chinatowns, Mandarin is also spoken and is the most commonly used language in some of the newly established Chinatowns.

Many of the new immigrants are accustomed to a Western lifestyle, speak Mandarin, Fukien, or other dialects, and are more comfortable going directly to middle-class Chinese communities in the suburbs. These satellite Chinese communities are replacing the old Chinatowns as the initial destination for many Chinese immigrants. They have been established across the country, notably in Flushing, Queens, in New York City, and in Monterey Park, San Jose, and Mountain View in California.

It should be noted that although Chinatowns are most often associated with urban centers, in their early days there were many rural and frontier Chinatowns. These rural Chinatowns gradually diminished as the urban Chinatowns grew, particularly between 1910 and 1940.

DISTRIBUTION

San Francisco's Chinatown is the oldest and most famous in the United States, but it is certainly not the only one. By 1990, New York City's Chinatown had overtaken San Francisco's as the largest Chinese American enclave. There are also significant Chinatowns in Oakland and San Jose, California; Los Angeles; Honolulu; Boston; Chicago; and Washington, D.C. Also, while the Chinese American population is still greater in the West, modern trends are to the East.

Chinatown population statistics are inexact due to low participation in the U.S. Census arising from language problems. For example, the 2000 U.S. Census reported the population of San Francisco's Chinatown to be a little over 100,000, but the city conducted a census that claimed an additional

100,000. In addition, the Chinatown population does not always reflect the city's Chinese population. Los Angeles, for example, claimed an ethnic Chinese population near 400,000, while the 2000 U.S. Census declared Los Angeles's Chinatown population to be just under 10,000.

POPULATIONS OF U.S. CHINATOWNS IN 2000

For a variety of reasons, U.S. Census Bureau figures for the populations of Chinatown communities appear to be far below actual figures.

New York City	120,000-160,000
San Francisco	100,000-200,000
Los Angeles	10,000-20,000
Oakland, California	7,000-10,000
Honolulu	2,500-3,000

Source: U.S. Census Bureau.

SOCIAL STRUCTURE

Chinese speakers call Chinatowns *Tangrenjie* (streets of Tang people) and regard them as cities within cities. Entering most Chinatowns can be like entering a different country, as one encounters exotic sights, sounds, and smells. The exotic nature of these communities has always made them places of interest for tourists, novelists, and romanticists. Some of their inhabitants find everything they need to live full lives and seldom leave or interact with outsiders.

Three types of associations, all based on traditional Chinese social organization, have played an important role in the lives of Chinatown inhabitants. Clans, or *tsu*, are organizations based on kinship or family name. Immigrants with family ties are organized to provide aid to each other in time of need. An individual might be provided the benefits of a clan based solely on his or her family name, even if there is no actual blood tie. The role of the clans has largely been taken over by government agencies.

Secret societies, or tongs, are also organized to give assistance to members in need and to push for the interests of their members in Chinatown and in the larger society. Some tongs were very respectable, but they were often thought of as criminal or-

ganizations. Many were involved in illegal activities such as prostitution and drug trafficking, both of which were very lucrative in the predominantly male Chinatowns before World War II. There were constant disputes between these tongs over territory, drugs, and Chinese women, and these led to a series of tong wars during the late nineteenth and early twentieth centuries that terrorized the citizens of Chinatowns from San Francisco to Cleveland.

The benevolent associations, or *hui kuan*, were organized around the places of origin of their members. They not only provided loans and other assistance but also arbitrated disputes among their members and exercised considerable power over them. Over time, the *hui kuan* were consolidated into a national group called the Chinese Consolidated Benevolent Association, more commonly known as the Chinese Six Companies. This new organization took on the role the *hui kuan* had played. These organizations still exist and play significant roles in Chinatowns, especially among immigrants.

FUTURE OF CHINATOWNS

The face of Chinatowns has continued to change, but during the early twenty-first century, the communities still faced problems such as substandard housing, crime, and subsistence wages. These problems were growing with increased immigration. By 2008, more than half the population of San Francisco's Chinatown was foreign-born. Many of the most recent immigrants spoke no English and found themselves trapped in low-paying, dead-end jobs with little time or energy left to learn English or to improve their situation.

At the same time, many new immigrants are highly skilled professionals and international businessmen who avoid the Cantonese-dominated old Chinatowns and turn instead to the middle-class satellite Chinese communities in the suburbs. Called "ethnoburbs" by some, these communities are flush with an influx of foreign capital, particularly from Taiwan, and boast banks, hotels, shopping malls, and office towers. They are much more interactive with the rest of the community than the old Chinatowns.

While Chinese families still keep their differences from the rest of society in many matters, some of the old walls constructed by them and by the greater society are falling. For example, there has been an increase in mixed marriages, something historically resisted by Chinese families. Other evidence, including increasingly favorable attitudes toward ethnic Chinese by Caucasians, lends weight to the idea that Chinese Americans are less likely to remain insulated. These trends have led some sociologists to expect future Chinatowns to be no more than ethnic theme parks. Whatever their future, studies indicate that tourism will play a major role in their survival.

Whether they are destined to continue to be a destination for new Chinese Americans or to become nothing more than tourist attractions or centers of multiculturalism, Chinatowns have established an enduring place in American history.

Wayne Shirey

FURTHER READING

Kinkead, Gwen. *Chinatown: A Portrait of a Closed Society.* New York: HarperCollins, 1992. Presents New York's Chinatown from the perspective of newly arrived immigrants.

Lin, Jan. *Reconstructing Chinatown: Ethnic Enclave, Global Change.* Minneapolis: University of Minnesota Press, 1998. Examines New York's Chinatown and deconstructs the stereotypes associated with the enclave.

Min, Pyong Gap. *Asian Americans: Contemporary Trends and Issues.* Thousand Oaks, Calif.: Pine Forge, 2005. Examination of the Asian American experience, including sections devoted to Chinese Americans.

Yung, Judy. *San Francisco's Chinatown.* Charleston, S.C.: Arcadia, 2006. Excellent collection of vintage photographs showing the history of San Francisco's Chinatown, with an emphasis on daily life.

Zhou, Min. *Chinatown: The Socioeconomic Potential of an Urban Enclave.* Philadelphia: Temple University Press, 1992. Focuses on the immigrant Chinese experience in New York's Chinatown during the 1970's and 1980's.

SEE ALSO: Chinese Six Companies; Ethnic enclaves; Immigration Act of 1943; Immigration and Nationality Act of 1952; Immigration and Nationality Act of 1965; San Francisco; War Brides Act of 1945; "Yellow peril" campaign.

CHINESE AMERICAN CITIZENS ALLIANCE

IDENTIFICATION: Chinese American political organization
ALSO KNOWN AS: Native Sons of the Golden State (1895-1915)
DATE: Chartered in 1915

SIGNIFICANCE: The alliance has provided a unified political voice for American-born Chinese Americans, combating discrimination in immigration, housing, education, and health care and creating social activities for the celebration of Chinese heritage.

American-born Chinese Americans at the end of the nineteenth century had much to overcome. Anti-Chinese sentiment was high among European Americans, and laws such as the Chinese Exclusion Act of 1882 and the Geary Act of 1892 restricted immigration and residency of those born in China. Those of Chinese descent born in the United States faced concern by their elders that they were becoming too assimilated and forgetting their heritage. In 1895, a group of Chinese Americans in San Francisco created the Native Sons of the Golden State (not to be confused with the white nativist organization "Native Sons of the Golden West"), the first chapter in what grew by 1915 to be a national organization, the Chinese American Citizens Alliance. The group sought to find ways for Chinese Americans to overcome anti-Chinese sentiment and participate fully in American life. At first limited to male members, the group accepted its first female members in 1977. The alliance published its own Chinese-language newspaper, the *Chinese Times*, from 1924 to 1988; provided insurance to members denied coverage because of discrimination; organized and supported community projects, including voter registration drives, playground and educational programs, and medical facilities; and encouraged young people to participate in traditional Chinese and American activities.

Cynthia A. Bily

FURTHER READING

Chen, Shehong. *Being Chinese, Becoming Chinese American.* Champaign: University of Illinois Press, 2002.

Lai, H. Mark. *Becoming Chinese American: A History of Communities and Institutions.* Walnut Creek, Calif.: AltaMira Press, 2004.

Ng, Franklin, ed. *The Asian American Encyclopedia.* Tarrytown, N.Y.: Marshall Cavendish, 1995.

SEE ALSO: Anti-Chinese movement; California; Chinese American press; Chinese boycott of 1905; Chinese Exclusion Act of 1882; Chinese immigrants; Chinese laundries; Chinese Six Companies; Geary Act of 1892; Native Sons of the Golden State.

CHINESE AMERICAN PRESS

DEFINITION: News media in Cantonese, Mandarin, and English published for new immigrants from China and for ethnic Chinese communities in the United States

SIGNIFICANCE: The existence of Chinese-language newspapers and other media gives new immigrants access to necessary information in their native language and fosters greater integration of the immigrant and ethnic communities. Chinese-language news media allow for the strengthening of cultural ties within the milieu of a new culture and for easy assimilation into the mainstream without losing cultural and ethnic identity.

Between 1849 and 1882—the year during which a new federal law forbade Chinese immigration—large groups of Chinese male laborers came to California to work in the mining industry and on the transcontinental railroad. While most worked and sent money to relatives in China, some settled in cities and towns in California and established businesses. The establishment of these new Chinese immigrant communities created a need for information in the Mandarin and Cantonese dialects of Chinese, giving rise to the creation of Chinese-language newspapers. The first such paper was the *Golden Hills News*, a weekly published by William Howard in San Francisco for a few months in 1854. It was followed by *The Oriental*, an English and Cantonese weekly published from 1855 to 1857 by William Speer, a Presbyterian missionary who had spent time in China. Although neither of these early papers had Chinese owners, both were edited by recent Chinese immigrants, and a later version of *The Oriental* was owned by ethnic Chinese.

The first Chinese-owned newspaper was the *Sacramento Daily News*, published by Ze Tu Yun from 1856 to 1858. Although none of these individual enterprises lasted more than a few years, San Francisco and Sacramento consistently had Chinese-language papers throughout the period leading up to the Chinese Exclusion Act of 1882, a law barring the immigration of Chinese laborers for ten years and not allowing Chinese-born residents already in the United States to become naturalized citizens. Indeed, despite the racial violence and economic discrimination that the Chinese community suffered in California, a Chinese American press continued to thrive.

MOVE EAST AND COVERAGE OF THE REVOLUTION

With conditions deteriorating for Chinese residents in California after the early 1880's, many immigrants moved to Hawaii, where racial discrimination was not as virulent and work could be found in agriculture. Other immigrants relocated to such midwestern cities as Chicago and St. Louis. Newspapers were published in each place to serve the local Chinese communities. In Chicago, Protestant missionaries and Catholic parishes hired Cantonese- and Mandarin-speaking editors to publish newsletters that served not only to proselytize but also to provide much information about the burgeoning nationalist movement that sought to overthrow the imperial system in China during the early twentieth century. Indeed, the revolutionary movement of Sun Yat-sen in China was funded to a significant extent by donations from wealthy Chinese American businesspeople, many of whom learned about the revolution from the Chinese American newspapers.

The dual focus on Christian evangelization and Chinese nationalism has continued to color the social and political views of Chinese Americans in larger cities into the twenty-first century. In 1883, the *Chinese American*, the Chinese American paper with the widest circulation, was launched in New York City. Meanwhile, even after many Chinese Americans had started moving to the Midwest and the East, significant numbers remained in California where papers such as the *Chinese Free Press*—which was founded in San Francisco in 1903 by Chinese Freemasons—exerted the same influence on public opinion about China's revolution as their midwestern counterparts.

CHINESE POLITICAL INFLUENCE

By the 1920's, most Chinese American newspapers had standardized their formats along the lines established by mainstream English-language newspapers. News reporting within the papers was arranged under local, national, and international headings, and each issue of the papers had an editorial page. During the era of the Chinese Civil War (1927-1950), however, individual papers tended to become formally affiliated with one or the other side in the conflict. Operatives from the Kuomintang and Communist Parties living in the United States exerted significant editorial influence on the content of Chinese-language papers. Papers that sided with—and in some cases received funding from—the Chinese Communist Party were routinely monitored and harassed by the federal government during the 1940's and 1950's. New York City's *China Daily News* and San Francisco's *The China Weekly* were both hounded out of business during the Korean War of the early 1950's.

LATE TWENTIETH CENTURY TRENDS

Not all Chinese American newspapers during the first half of the twentieth century had strong affiliations with Chinese political parties. To serve the growing numbers of newly naturalized Chinese American citizens and ethnic Chinese who resided legally in the United States, independent weekly newspapers arose in many large cities. New York's *Chinese Journal of Commerce* (1928-1944) focused on issues of interest to Chinese American business owners. The *Chinese American Weekly* had a similar focus but featured a state-of-the art pictorial section. The *Hawaii Chinese News*, an English-language paper, was established in 1926 to serve the bilingual Chinese population of the islands. The trend toward English language and bilingual publications continued into the 1960's and 1970's with publications such as Boston's *Sampan* and Houston's *Southwest Chinese Journal*. These newspapers also featured a strong commercial focus. The 1970's also saw the rise of national Chinese newspapers in the United States. Although previous attempts to publish Chinese American newspapers in more than one market had met with limited suc-

cess, publishers in Taiwan and Hong Kong successfully entered the U.S. national market with publications such as the daily *Sing Tao Jih Pao*.

TWENTY-FIRST CENTURY MARKETS

The modern market for Chinese American newspapers and bilingual news published in the United States by news corporations from China reflects the same trends affecting the American news business in general. In the face of competition from the Internet, long-established newspapers are shutting down and those that survive seem to do so because they have invested in a strong online news reporting presence. However, an increase in Chinese immigration to the United States since the 1980's has led to record numbers of start-up ventures for newsweeklies and Chinese-language magazines. Additionally, *China Daily*, an English-language newspaper owned and operated by the Chinese government, serves readers in the United States through its print and online services, as does CCTV, an English-language television and online news service. It may be argued that no other ethnic group in the United States of comparable size has the variety of news reporting venues that the Chinese community has. Indeed, the volatility of the market is belied by the yearly increases in advertising revenues collected by the Chinese American press as an industry.

William Carney

FURTHER READING

Chang, Iris. *The Chinese in America: A Narrative History.* New York: Viking Press, 2003. General study of the political, social, economic, and cultural history of Chinese Americans from the mid-nineteenth century into the early twenty-first century.

Daniels, Roger. *Asian America: Chinese and Japanese in the United States Since 1850.* Seattle: University of Washington, 1988. Scholarly examination of the first two major groups of Asians to come to the United States.

Ling, Huping. *Chinese St. Louis: From Enclave to Cultural Community.* Philadelphia: Temple University Press, 2004. The first comprehensive study of an ethnic community in the Midwest, this groundbreaking work proposes a "cultural community" model to interpret the new type of ethnic community that is defined more by its cultural boundaries than by geographical ones.

Miller, Sally, ed. *The Ethnic Press in the United States: A Historical Analysis and Handbook.* Westport, Conn.: Greenwood Press, 1987. Broad collection of essays on the journalism of many different ethnic communities within the United States.

SEE ALSO: Asian American literature; California; Chinatowns; Chinese Exclusion Act of 1882; Chinese immigrants; Filipino American press; Japanese American press; Television and radio.

CHINESE BOYCOTT OF 1905

THE EVENT: Chinese nationalist movement against the mistreatment of Chinese immigrants in the United States

DATE: Began on July 20, 1905

LOCATION: China, Southeast Asia, the United States

SIGNIFICANCE: The boycott signified the emergence of modern Chinese nationalism and the importance of immigration in Sino-American relations.

Significant Chinese immigration to the United States began during California's gold rush, which began in 1849. By the early twentieth century, the number of Chinese in the United States was more than 100,000. Chinese immigrants were frequent victims of racial discrimination then prevalent in the United States, suffering various mistreatments such as harassment, mob attacks, massacres, and restrictive or exclusionary legislation, local and federal. At the federal level, the U.S. Congress passed a series of exclusion laws in 1882, 1888, 1892, and 1894 that prohibited Chinese laborers from entering the United States. This prohibition was extended to include Hawaii in 1898 and the Philippines in 1900—Chinese laborers in these regions also were not allowed to come to the United States. Meanwhile, the "exempted" groups of Chinese who were permitted to enter the United States—officials, teachers, students, journalists, merchants, and travelers—were often subjected to abuses and humiliations.

The mistreatment of Chinese immigrants, and especially the exclusion laws, triggered furious protests from the Chinese in the United States. They tried to fight injustice and seek remedies, primarily through the legal channel. Having failed to gain protection from the U.S. courts, they looked to their homeland for help. In May, 1905, when the U.S. plenipotentiary William W. Rockhill arrived in Beijing (then known to the West as Peking) for Sino-American treaty negotiations, Chinese merchants and members of the Emperor Protection Society (Baohuang hui) in the United States sent wires and telegrams to various departments of the Chinese government urging it not to sign any treaty that would restrict Chinese immigration. The Chinese in China also were outraged by the American mistreatment of Chinese immigrants and were ready to take actions to support the cause of their Chinese compatriots in the United States.

BOYCOTT BEGINS

On May 10, 1905, the Shanghai Chamber of Commerce board met and decided to call for a boycott of American goods. The chamber sent telegrams urging joint actions to the merchant guilds in twenty-one cities throughout China and received positive and enthusiastic response. Agitated also were students, writers, entertainers, women, and even children, who held meetings pressing for an anti-American boycott. Adding fuel to the popular agitation, a Chinese by the name of Feng Xiawei, who had been wrongly arrested by the Boston immigration officers and later returned to China, committed suicide in front of the American consulate in Shanghai on July 16, 1905, in protest of the injustice he had suffered in the United States. On July 20, the Shanghai Chamber of Commerce held a meeting, announcing commencement of the boycott.

The anti-American boycott in China was a nationwide urban popular and peaceful movement. It spread to most Chinese cities, including those in Jiangsu, Zhejiang, Guangdong, Fujian, Sichuan, Hubei, Jiangxi, Jilin, Zhejiang, Shaanxi, Shandong, and Hebei provinces, and involved people from all walks of life and all social strata—merchants, scholars, students, laborers, women, and children. The Chinese participated in the boycott movement in different ways. Merchants, as the leading group of the boycott, stopped ordering or selling American goods, mostly consumer goods such as cotton textiles, petroleum, matches, cigarettes, flour, and other items in daily use—soap, candles, cosmetics, hardware, and stationery. Students and artists resorted to artistic and literary works—novels, plays, storytelling, songs or ballad-singing, posters, handbills and pamphlets, and speeches—to describe the suffering of Chinese immigrants in the United States, to express their opposition to the Chinese exclusion laws, and to demonstrate their pride in being Chinese. The anti-American boycott in China received support from Chinese communities in other countries and regions such as Hong Kong, Singapore, Thailand, Japan, and the Philippines.

The boycott movement in China reached its climax between July and September of 1905. Afterward, it gradually lost its momentum because of the withdrawal of merchants, especially those who dealt with American goods, and because of the change in the Chinese government's attitude toward the movement from sympathy to suspicion and even hostility. The Chinese government was worried that the boycott would turn into an antigovernment movement. The boycott eventually died out in late 1905 and early 1906.

The boycott of 1905 did not reverse the U.S. immigration policy toward Chinese nationals, and the Chinese Exclusion Act of 1882 remained in effect until 1943. Nevertheless, the movement demonstrated the force of rising Chinese nationalism and helped reinforce the bond between Chinese communities in the United States and their compatriots in China.

Yunqiu Zhang

FURTHER READING
Cassel, Susie Lan, ed. *The Chinese in America: A History from Gold Mountain to the New Millennium.* Walnut Creek, Calif.: AltaMira Press, 2002. Comprehensive history of the impact of Chinese immigration on the United States since the time of the California gold rush.
McKee, Delber L. "The Chinese Boycott of 1905-1906 Reconsidered: The Role of Chinese Americans." *Pacific Historical Review* 55, no. 2 (May, 1986): 165-191. Scholarly analysis of the boycott from a Chinese perspective.
Tsai, Jung-Fang. *Hong Kong in Chinese History: Community and Social Unrest in the British Colony, 1842-1913.* New York: Columbia University Press, 1993. Examination of the unique role Hong Kong has played in China's history from the time it was taken over by Great Britain through the end of China's Qing Dynasty.
Wang, Guanhua. "Between Fact and Fiction: Literary Portraits of Chinese Americans in the 1905 Anti-American Boycott." In *Re/collecting Early Asian America,* edited by Josephine Lee, Imogene L. Lim, and Yuko Matsukawa. Philadelphia: Temple University Press, 2002. Examination of the lives of several of the key figures in the Chinese boycott.
_____. *In Search of Justice: The 1905-1906 Chinese Anti-American Boycott.* Cambridge, Mass.: Harvard University Asia Center, 2001. Full, scholarly study of the boycott by one of the leading authorities on the subject.

SEE ALSO: Anti-Chinese movement; California; Chinese American Citizens Alliance; Chinese American press; Chinese Exclusion Act of 1882; *Chinese Exclusion Cases*; Chinese immigrants; Citizens Committee to Repeal Chinese Exclusion; Geary Act of 1892; Native Sons of the Golden State.

CHINESE EXCLUSION ACT OF 1882

THE LAW: Federal legislation designed to limit Chinese immigration into the United States
DATE: Became law on May 6, 1882

SIGNIFICANCE: The Chinese Exclusion Act of 1882 marked the first time that the United States legislated to block immigration by a specific ethnic or racial group. The law ushered in a new period of American history that was defined by skepticism and occasional hostility toward immigration, especially by immigrants of a non-European race.

The Chinese Exclusion Act of 1882 prohibited all Chinese laborers from entering the United States for a period of ten years. It also banned Chinese immigrants who were already in the United States from becoming U.S. citizens. The legislation permitted a few groups of Chinese to immigrate, but it was aimed primarily at unskilled laborers. An additional provision of the law led to the first significant deportation of a particular group of immigrants. It was the first time that the United States outlawed immigration on the basis of ethnicity.

HISTORICAL BACKGROUND

Anti-Chinese sentiment emerged in the western part of the United States during the latter half of the nineteenth century, when large numbers of Chinese workers arrived to work on the railroads and mines. As the nation expanded west, Americans tended to justify their annexations of Native American and formerly Mexican lands by citing the presumed inferiority of nonwhite peoples. Their negative views of Chinese were similar to their perceptions of Native Americans and Mexicans. The difference was that Chinese were recent immigrants.

Most Chinese immigrants to the United States during the 1850's were laborers. Initially, they worked in gold mines, agriculture, laundries, and the textile industry and played a major role in the construction of western railroads. However, as their numbers increased, a white backlash arose, especially among other American laborers.

Not only were the numbers of Chinese immigrants considered threatening, but they also worked harder than most American laborers and for less money. As a result, pressure mounted on the federal government to reduce immigration from China.

The arguments against Chinese immigration had both economic and social components. The rhetoric of supporters of restricting immigration often stressed the need to help American workers keep their jobs. They argued that immigrants would compete for jobs in the United States with those already in the country. Furthermore, opposition to immigration emphasized negative cultural traits as well. Americans spread rumors that Chinese immigrants gambled and smoked opium. Related to this, many opponents of Chinese immigration stated they were a threat to American moral stan-

---

CHINESE EXCLUSION ACT OF 1882

An Act to Execute Certain Treaty Stipulations Relating to Chinese

Preamble. Whereas, in the opinion of the Government of the United States the coming of Chinese laborers to this country endangers the good order of certain localities within the territory thereof: Therefore,

Be it enacted by the Senate and House of Representatives of the United States of America in Congress assembled, That from and after the expiration of ninety days next after the passage of this act, and until the expiration of ten years next after the passage of this act, the coming of Chinese laborers to the United States be, and the same is hereby, suspended; and during such suspension it shall not be lawful for any Chinese laborer to come, or, having so come after the expiration of said ninety days, to remain within the United States.

SECTION 2. That the master of any vessel who shall knowingly bring within the United States on such vessel, and land or permit to be landed, any Chinese laborer, from any foreign port or place, shall be deemed guilty of a misdemeanor. . . .

SECTION 14. That hereafter no State court or court of the United States shall admit Chinese to citizenship; and all laws in conflict with this act are hereby repealed.

SECTION 15. That the words "Chinese laborers," wherever used in this act, shall be construed to mean both skilled and unskilled laborers and Chinese employed in mining.

Source: The Avalon Project at Yale Law School. Documents in Law, History, and Diplomacy.

---

dards. This situation was exacerbated due to their reputation for living in close-knit communities and attempting to preserve their cultural identity.

The opposition to Chinese immigration became very intense. Other Americans committed violence against them. Some of the worst incidents occurred in Los Angeles in 1870, San Francisco in 1877, Denver in 1880, and Wyoming Territory in 1885. In the latter case, an estimated twenty-five Chinese were killed by gunshot or by being burned to death. Furthermore, local courts declined to punish those responsible for the violence.

As a result of popular opposition to Chinese, elected officials began to act. The initial governmental action taken against the Chinese in the United States was at the state level. California adopted seveal laws that targeted Chinese immigrants. These state laws included such provisions as

Thomas Nast cartoon published in Harper's Weekly *in March, 1882, suggesting that the racially discriminatory principle behind the Chinese Exclusion Act might next be applied to Irish immigrants.* (Library of Congress)

mandating special licenses for Chinese-owned enterprises and prohibiting the naturalization of Chinese immigrants.

Domestic opposition to Chinese immigration made U.S. relations with China more complex. China's government was concerned about anti-Chinese sentiment among Americans and California's discriminatory laws. As a result, the United States and China agreed to two treaties during this period that partially addressed Chinese immigration to the United States. The federal government annulled many of California's discriminatory laws with the Burlingame Treaty of 1868, an agreement with China that essentially permitted unrestricted immigration to the United States. However, as domestic opposition to Chinese immigration continued to grow in the United States, the American government persuaded China to accept some restrictions on Chinese immigrants to the United States in the Angell Treaty of 1880.

CHINESE EXCLUSION ACT AND ITS AFTERMATH

Domestic pressure to restrict Chinese immigration did not abate, so the U.S. Congress passed the Chinese Exclusion Act, which became law on May 6, 1882. In addition to prohibiting the immigration of Chinese laborers, the new law made it more difficult for immigrants who had already come to the United States to reenter the country after they revisited China. As a result of the law, the number of Chinese in the United States dropped significantly. The number of Chinese in the United States reached its nineteenth century peak at 107,488 in 1890. That number fell to 88,863 in 1900. No Chinese immigrants at all were admitted into the United States in 1892.

Restrictions on Chinese immigration became a long-standing U.S. policy. In 1888, the Scott Act forbade Chinese laborers who revisited China from reentering the United States, even if they held official documents permitting their return. In 1892, the Geary Act renewed the ban on Chinese immigration for ten more years. In 1902, the ban on Chinese immigration was extended indefinitely. Not surprisingly, these U.S. actions increased friction with China. Restrictions on Chinese immigration were not lifted until passage of the Immigration Act of 1943 (also known as the Magnuson Act).

Passage of the Chinese Exclusion Act of 1882 led to other attempts at immigration restrictions based on ethnicity. The law also led to the creation of a national immigrant inspection system. Furthermore, this piece of legislation led to the U.S. government's initial efforts to accumulate information regarding the movements of immigrants. The act signaled the emergence of a new era in U.S. history that was defined by skepticism and sometimes hostility toward immigration, especially by those of a different race.

Kevin L. Brennan

FURTHER READING

Chan, Sucheng, ed. *Entry Denied: Exclusion and the Chinese Community in America, 1882-1943*. Philadelphia: Temple University Press, 1991. Collection of articles examining both restrictions placed on Chinese and the contributions they have made to the United States.

Chen, Jack. *The Chinese of America*. San Francisco: Harper & Row, 1980. Historical overview of Chinese immigration to the United States and their changing socioeconomic conditions.

Chua, Lee-Beng. *Psycho-social Adaption and the Meaning of Achievement for Chinese Immigrants*. New York: LFB Scholarly Publishing, 2002. Addresses the social conditions and development of an ethnic identity for Chinese Americans.

Lee, Erika. *At America's Gates: Chinese Immigration During the Exclusion Era, 1882-1943*. Chapel Hill: University of North Carolina Press, 2003. Detailed account of the legal obstacles to Chinese immigration, as well as a rich description of conditions confronting Chinese in the United States while the provisions of the Chinese Exclusion Act were in force.

Tsai, Shih-shan Henry. *China and the Overseas Chinese in the United States, 1868-1911*. Fayetteville: University of Arkansas Press, 1983. Analysis of the relationship between U.S. policy toward Chinese immigration and Sino-American relations.

SEE ALSO: Alien land laws; Angell Treaty of 1880; Anti-Chinese movement; Asiatic Barred Zone; *Chae Chan Ping v. United States*; *Chinese Exclusion Cases*; Chinese immigrants; Congress, U.S.; Geary Act of 1892; Immigration Act of 1882; Page Law of 1875.

CHINESE EXCLUSION CASES

THE CASES: Series of U.S. Supreme Court rulings on the Chinese Exclusion Acts
DATES: 1884-1905

> **SIGNIFICANCE:** When making decisions that dealt with the various Chinese Exclusion Acts, the Supreme Court examined the language of the legislation and attempted to discern the intent of Congress. As a consequence, almost no immigrants from China entered the country from the 1880's until World War II.

The Chinese Exclusion Act of 1882 prohibited most Chinese laborers from entering the country. The Scott Act (1888), the Geary Act of 1892, and the McCreary Amendment of 1893 added additional restrictions. The 1920 revision of the Chinese Exclusion Act of 1882 entirely closed the door on all further immigration, and the door continued to be closed until 1943. In reviewing these laws, the Supreme Court consistently acknowledged that the U.S. Constitution gave Congress the plenary power to decide which foreign persons might be kept out of the country. The Court, however, often had to interpret various aspects of the law, and it also made a number of rulings about the due process standards that applied to the thousands of Chinese who had resided in the country before 1882.

In the first of the cases, *Chew Heong v. United States* (1884), the petitioner had lived in the United States before 1882, but he had visited China before the amendment of 1884 required residents to obtain a reentry certificate. In this instance, the Court decided to allow his reentry. After the Scott Act entirely prohibited reentry, the petitioner in *Chae Chan Ping v. United States* (1889) was a resident who had obtained a reentry certificate before the statute was enacted. In this case, Ping was denied admission. In upholding the Scott Act, the Court recognized that Congress had unlimited power to modify or to abrogate treaties with foreign countries. Writing the majority opinion, Justice Stephen J. Field declared that the United States "considers the presence of foreigners of a different race in this country, who will not assimilate with us, to be dangerous to its peace and security."

While recognizing that minimal standards of due process were required in immigration and deportation proceedings, the Supreme Court put almost no limits on the power of Congress to define which standards and rules applied. When Fong Yue Ting and two other Chinese residents were found not to have required residency certificates, they were ordered to be deported. In the resulting case of *Fong Yue Ting v. United States* (1893), the Supreme Court upheld the deportations and recognized that the government's power to deport foreigners "is as absolute and unqualified as the right to prohibit and prevent their entrance into the country." Likewise, when Congress authorized immigration officials to exclude foreigners from admission without any habeas corpus relief, the Supreme Court upheld this procedure in *Lem Moon Sing v. United States* (1895), which meant that immigration officials no longer had to worry about judges looking over their shoulders. In the case of *United States v. Ju Toy* (1905), the Court even allowed Congress to deny writs of habeas corpus for persons claiming to be U.S. citizens.

Thomas Tandy Lewis

FURTHER READING

Chang, Iris. *The Chinese in America: A Narrative History.* New York: Viking Press, 2003.

Kim, Hyung-chan, ed. *Asian Americans and the Supreme Court: A Documentary History.* Westport, Conn.: Greenwood Press, 1992.

McClain, Charles J. *In Search of Equality: The Chinese Struggle Against Discrimination in Nineteenth-Century America.* Berkeley: University of California Press, 1994.

Salyer, Lucy. *Laws as Harsh as Tigers: Chinese Immigrants and the Shaping of Modern Immigration Law.* Chapel Hill: University of North Carolina Press, 1995.

SEE ALSO: Anti-Chinese movement; *Chae Chan Ping v. United States*; *Chew Heong v. United States*; *Chin Bak Kan v. United States*; Chinese Exclusion Act of 1882; Chinese immigrants; *Chy Lung v. Freeman*; *Fong Yue Ting v. United States*; Geary Act of 1892; *Lem Moon Sing v. United States*; Page Law of 1875; Supreme Court, U.S.

CHINESE FAMILY ASSOCIATIONS

DEFINITION: Organizations composed of Chinese immigrants who share common surnames, ancestors, or places of origin. These associations provide mutual aid, protection and socialization and have been in existence since the first waves of Chinese immigrants came to California during the late 1840's

ALSO KNOWN AS: *Fangs*

SIGNIFICANCE: Chinese family associations, or *fangs*, provided social and financial support to early Chinese immigrants living in hostile environments. Later, as many of these

family groups combined to create larger organizations, they served to make residency and citizenship easier for immigrants and acted as informal chambers of commerce for Chinese businesspeople.

The first wave of Chinese immigration to the United States occurred during the late 1840's and continued through the 1850's. Due to economic problems in southern China, male Cantonese-speaking workers arrived in California to accept jobs in mining, various small industries, and on the transcontinental railroad. Most of them intended to stay only briefly so they could send money back to relatives in China. However, worsening economic conditions in their homeland and plentiful, if low-paying, jobs in the United States extended the stays of many Chinese workers.

CHALLENGES TO IMMIGRANTS

With the completion of the transcontinental railroad and anti-Chinese nativist sentiment rising on the West Coast, Chinese workers responded by starting businesses such as laundries and restaurants—enterprises often viewed as difficult and undesirable by U.S.-born businesspeople. With these businesses generally concentrated in Chinese neighborhoods, generally known as Chinatowns, and with the overwhelming gender imbalance (the vast majority of Chinese immigrant workers were men), Chinese business owners and workers were often viewed as "alien" by native-born Americans and even by members of other better-established immigrant communities. Because of this particular set of circumstances and significant language barriers, Chinese business owners often had little access to the financial and community support systems that other entrepreneurs did. To compensate, they formed family associations, or *fangs*, for mutual aid and support. Membership in these organizations was at first based upon common surnames or common ancestors, but membership in many individual organizations was later broadened to include all immigrants from particular villages or regions.

CONSOLIDATION

Some of the early Chinese family associations were formed in San Francisco. Because of the large numbers of immigrants who settled there, several small associations formed but, due to their size and the anti-Chinese sentiment beginning to grow during the 1870's, many of these associations found it beneficial to combine. Six of the largest associations formed the Chinese Consolidated Benevolent Association, more commonly known as the Chinese Six Companies. This combined family association provided support services for new immigrants as well as arranging small loans for businesses and protection for its members. The organization grew over time and established chapters in other cities.

As economic conditions worsened on the West Coast during the late 1870's, family associations in other cities found it necessary to combine to ensure mutual aid and protection. Anti-Chinese sentiment grew so virulent that the U.S. Congress passed a law called the Chinese Exclusion Act on May 6, 1882, which suspended immigration of Chinese laborers for ten years. It permitted Chinese who had been already in the United States on November 17, 1880, to stay, travel abroad, and return. It also prohibited the naturalization of Chinese and created the "Section 6" exempt status for Chinese teachers, students, merchants, and travelers. Members of the exempt classes would be admitted to the United States upon presentation of certificates from the Chinese government. Many Chinese immigrants and longtime residents, fearing for their livelihood and safety, relocated to cities in the Midwest such as Chicago and St. Louis, and others emigrated to the eastern seaboard.

Even with these new restrictions, Chinatowns were established in midwestern and eastern cities after the early 1880's. There immigrants faced better economic opportunities than were available on the West Coast, but they were still subject to significant anti-Chinese sentiment. Chinese family associations were formed in cities such as Chicago, New York, and Boston. Associations in these cities based membership on more traditional criteria, such as common surnames, ancestors, and home regions. This trend led to the establishment of tong organizations.

Tongs were secret fraternal societies that represented Chinese immigrants lacking connections with groups based on common surnames and native places. In cities such as Chicago, tong organizations vied with the more traditional *fangs* for economic opportunities. The result was that many tongs became involved in organized crime activities in Chinese neighborhoods. In New York City,

however, the tongs and family associations combined in 1886 to provide a mutual aid and social welfare organization for new immigrants. A second combined organization was formed in Brooklyn a few years later. Both of these combined associations served to provide English-language instruction, housing, and job placement services for newly arrived immigrants.

TWENTIETH CENTURY DEVELOPMENTS

By the 1920's and 1930's, China's civil war and the U.S. government's relaxation of Chinese immigration quotas led to a rapid influx in Chinese immigration and an increase in the number of family associations formed in the cities' many Chinatowns. In 1949, communist leader Mao Zedong's victory over the Kuomintang led to another increase in Chinese immigration to the United States. This time, however, most of the immigrants were Mandarin speakers—unlike the earlier Cantonese-speaking immigrants—who swelled the populations of Chinatowns during the 1950's.

Although many of the new immigrants established traditional *fang* associations, there was a greater tendency among these new Chinese immigrants to join long-established combined family associations, as these organizations already had resources needed by new arrivals. However, their full participation in these associations was weakened by the tendencies of Mandarin-speaking immigrants to move out of densely populated urban areas and into the suburbs of large cities. Later Chinese family associations have been formed mostly by ethnic Chinese who have immigrated to the United States from such countries as Malaysia, South Korea, and Vietnam. In contrast to the Mandarin-speaking Chinese nationals, these immigrants have tended to settle in urban centers and participate in combined *fang* associations or in the few remaining "legitimate" tong associations.

William Carney

FURTHER READING

Chang, Iris. *The Chinese in America: A Narrative History.* New York: Viking Press, 2003. Excellent source for stories about specific Chinese family businesses.

Jenkins, Shirley. *Ethnic Organizations and the Welfare State: Services to Immigrants in Five Countries.* New York: Columbia University Press, 1988. Overview of the ways in which Chinese family associations and other ethnic organizations fill the gaps in a country's social safety net.

Jung, John. *Chinese Laundries: Tickets to Survival on Gold Mountain.* Morrisville, N.C.: Yin & Yang Press, 2007. Fascinating historical, social, and psychological study of families in the important laundry business. Well illustrated.

Li, Minghuan. *"We Need Two Worlds": Chinese Immigrant Associations in a Western Society.* Amsterdam: Amsterdam University Press, 1999. Although this book is about the Netherlands, it provides useful insights into the workings of Chinese associations, which have broad similarities in cities around the world.

Liu, Haiming. *The Transnational History of a Chinese Family: Immigrant Letters, Family Business and Reverse Migration.* New Brunswick, N.J.: Rutgers University Press, 2005. Excellent study of a single Chinese immigrant family that has operated an agricultural business through several generations.

Siu, Paul C. P. *The Chinese Laundryman: A Study of Social Isolation.* New York: New York University Press, 1987. The son of a laundryman, the author presents an intimate but scholarly study of Chinese laundries in Chicago from 1870 to 1940.

SEE ALSO: California gold rush; Chinatowns; Chinese American Citizens Alliance; Chinese Exclusion Act of 1882; Chinese Hand Laundry Alliance; Chinese immigrants; Chinese laundries; Chinese secret societies; Chinese Six Companies; Family businesses; Immigrant aid organizations.

CHINESE HAND LAUNDRY ALLIANCE

IDENTIFICATION: Labor union formed to protect Chinese workers in New York City

DATE: Founded in 1933

SIGNIFICANCE: The alliance successfully defeated anti-Chinese legislation in New York City during the 1930's. Although hand laundries no longer exist, the organization continued to support the civil rights of Chinese Americans into the twenty-first century.

Because few jobs were available to Chinese Americans during the late nineteenth and early twentieth centuries, about 25 percent of Chinese American men worked in laundries. The work was difficult, but there was a steady need for it and many Chinese Americans found that they could make a modest living running their own small hand laundry business. When the Great Depression began, New York City alone had more than three thousand laundries run by Chinese Americans, and European Americans, struggling with the poor economy, felt that the Chinese laundries were a threat. A New York City law passed in 1933 required owners of laundries to be U.S. citizens. To provide a unified voice in opposition, the Chinese Hand Laundry Alliance was formed and successfully fought to repeal the law. The group published a newspaper, the *China Daily News*, beginning in 1940, and continued to organize in support of the rights of Chinese Americans and to lobby the federal government in matters of foreign policy.

Cynthia A. Bily

FURTHER READING

Bao, Xiaolan. *Holding Up More Than Half the Sky: Chinese Women Garment Workers in New York City, 1948-92.* Champaign: University of Illinois Press, 2001.

Yu, Renqiu. *To Save China, to Save Ourselves: The Chinese Hand Laundry Alliance of New York.* Philadelphia: Temple University Press, 1992.

Yung, Judy, Gordon H. Chang, and H. Mark Lai. *Chinese American Voices: From the Gold Rush to the Present.* Berkeley: University of California Press, 2006.

SEE ALSO: Anti-Chinese movement; Asian immigrants; Chinese American press; Chinese Exclusion Act of 1882; Chinese immigrants; Chinese laundries; Great Depression; Labor unions; *Yick Wo v. Hopkins.*

CHINESE IMMIGRANTS

SIGNIFICANCE: During the late twentieth century, Chinese became one of the fastest-growing immigrant populations in the United States. By the early twenty-first century, they constituted the largest Asian immigrant group in the United States and could be found throughout the North American continent.

Although most immigration from China to the United States occurred during the twentieth century, the earliest identifiable Chinese immigrants arrived in America during the 1780's. However, the discovery of gold in California in 1848 brought a large wave of Chinese. In the following three decades, about 300,000 Chinese entered the United States to work primarily as miners in gold mines, laundry and grocery operators in urban communities, farm laborers in agricultural areas, or fishermen in fishing villages in California.

PUSH-PULL FACTORS

Similar to their counterparts from other countries, early Chinese immigrants were "pushed" by forces in China and "pulled" by attractions in the United States. The "push" mainly came from natural disasters, internal upheavals, and imperialistic aggressions in China during the 1840's and 1850's. The "pull" resulted from the discovery of gold in California and the economic opportunities in the United States.

The decades of the 1840's and the 1850's in China were full of natural calamities. The major ones were the severe draught in Henan Province in 1847, the flooding of the Yangtze River in the four provinces of Hubei, Anhui, Jiangsu, and Zhejiang, and the famine in Guangxi in 1849. Flood and famine in Guangdong gave way to the catastrophic Taiping Revolution (1850-1864), which devastated the land, uprooted the peasantry, and dislocated the economy and polity.

Moreover, the importation of opium deepened the social and economic crisis. As a result of the Opium War of 1839-1842, opium traffic practically became unrestrained. The volume of imports rose from 33,000 chests in 1842 to 46,000 chests in 1848, and to 52,929 chests in 1850. The year 1848 alone witnessed the outflow of more than ten million taels of silver, which exacerbated the already grave economic dislocation and copper-silver exchange rate. The disruptive economic consequence of opium importation was further compounded by the general influx of foreign goods in the open ports. Canton was particularly hit because it had the longest history of foreign trade and the widest foreign contact. Local household industries were swept away, and the self-sufficient agrarian economy suffered. Those who were adversely affected became potential emigrants.

News of the discovery of gold in California (which the Chinese called *Gam Saan*, or "Gold Mountain") spread like wildfire to every corner of the world and soon attracted thousands of gold seekers to California. Among them were 325 Chinese "forty-niners." During the early 1850's, the number of Chinese increased dramatically: 2,716 in 1851 and 20,026 in 1852. By 1882, when the passage of the Chinese Exclusion Act ended the large-scale Chinese immigration, about 300,000 Chinese were living in the continental United States.

The Chinese gold seekers, referred to by their compatriots as *Gam Saan Haak* ("travelers to Gold Mountain" or "Gold Mountain guests"), were mostly adult males from Guangdong Province. Gold played a significant role in the lives of the early Chinese immigrants, and the majority of these gold seekers worked in the mining areas of California. U.S. Census statistics indicate that almost all the Chinese in the continental United States lived in California in 1860. Most Chinese miners worked in placer claims. They washed the gold-bearing sand in a pan or rocker to let the heavier particles of gold settle at the bottom.

As Chinese miners became ubiquitous in the California hills, white miners felt threatened and demanded that the California legislature eliminate the competition from foreign miners. In May of 1852, the state legislature passed the Foreign Miners' Tax, which required every foreign miner who was ineligible for citizenship to pay a monthly fee of three dollars. Chinese immigrants, the primary targets of the California law, were considered ineligible for citizenship because of a 1790 federal law that reserved naturalized citizenship to "white" persons only.

In addition to mining, the construction of the transcontinental railroad absorbed a large number of Chinese laborers, many of whom were former miners. After the end of the U.S. Civil War, the U.S. government could once again devote its attention to the construction of the transcontinental railroad. The eastern part of the railroad was contracted to the Union Pacific Railroad to build westward from the Missouri River, and the western part of the railroad to the Central Pacific Railroad Company—financed by the "Big Four," Sacramento merchants Leland Stanford, Charles Crocker, Mark Hopkins, and C. P. Huntington, to build eastward from Sacramento. In February, 1865, fifty Chinese workers were hired by the Central Pacific Railroad Company as an experiment. As the Chinese workers performed various tasks of blasting, driving horses, handling rock, and doing pick-and-shovel work, they proved to be effective and reliable workers, and the company began to hire more Chinese. During the peak time of the construction, the Central Pacific Railroad Company hired twelve thousand Chinese, representing 90 percent of its entire workforce.

While the majority of Chinese were digging gold and building railroads, some Chinese families fished for their livelihood in the Monterey Bay region. The completion of the transcontinental railroad in 1869 forced most Chinese railroad workers to become farm laborers in California; many others had to migrate south and east, working in southern plantations or in new booming towns on the East Coast and in the Midwest.

ANTI-CHINESE SENTIMENTS AND EXCLUSION LAWS

The anti-Chinese movement, compounded by the economic depression on the West Coast in the last decades of the nineteenth century, contributed to the redistribution of Chinese immigrants. Economic discrimination in the form of special taxes and levies targeted the Chinese. For example, California's foreign miner taxes discouraged Chinese in particular, and an 1870 San Francisco ordinance taxed laundrymen without horses for their delivery wagon. (The Chinese did not use horses,

MARK TWAIN ON CHINESE IMMIGRANTS

During the 1860's, Mark Twain spent five years working mostly as a journalist in Virginia City, Nevada, and San Francisco, California, where he had ample opportunities to observe many Chinese immigrants. As he shows in this passage that opens chapter 54 of his 1872 book *Roughing It*, he had a high regard for the work ethic and behavior of the Chinese. Elsewhere in *Roughing It* and other writings, he expressed his disdain for the unfair stigmatization of the Chinese and the rough treatment they endured from the Americans who regarded them as an undesirable criminal class.

Of course there was a large Chinese population in Virginia—it is the case with every town and city on the Pacific coast. They are a harmless race when white men either let them alone or treat them no worse than dogs; in fact they are almost entirely harmless anyhow, for they seldom think of resenting the vilest insults or the cruelest injuries. They are quiet, peaceable, tractable, free from drunkenness, and they are as industrious as the day is long. A disorderly Chinaman is rare, and a lazy one does not exist. So long as a Chinaman has strength to use his hands he needs no support from anybody; white men often complain of want of work, but a Chinaman offers no such complaint; he always manages to find something to do. He is a great convenience to everybody—even to the worst class of white men, for he bears the most of their sins, suffering fines for their petty thefts, imprisonment for their robberies, and death for their murders. Any white man can swear a Chinaman's life away in the courts, but no Chinaman can testify against a white man.

so the law effectively discriminated against them.) Furthermore, anti-Chinese sentiment subjected immigrants and their businesses to violent physical attacks and abuse. The anti-Chinese violence generally took three forms: murder, spontaneous attacks and destruction of Chinatowns, and organized effort to drive Asians out of certain towns and cities.

The series of Chinese exclusion laws effectively banned the entry of Chinese into the United States. The passage of the 1882 Chinese Exclusion Act suspended the entry of all Chinese laborers for ten years. Merchants, diplomats, teachers, students, and travelers were exempt, but they still needed documentation. The ban was extended in 1892 and 1902, and made indefinite in 1904. The 1892 Geary Act required all Chinese laborers to register for a certificate of residence. Those who did not register could be arrested or deported. A storm of protest followed, but a test case brought before the U.S. Supreme Court confirmed the constitutionality of the law.

LIVELIHOOD OF CHINESE IMMIGRANTS

During the late nineteenth and early twentieth centuries, the laundering business had been a predominant occupation of the Chinese in the United States. After the 1870's, prejudice against Chinese immigrants from American society effectively cut them out of the rest of the labor market. Persecuted and harassed, the Chinese could not find jobs, and they were forced to rely on their own resources. When they were excluded from the gold mines in the hills, they found an equally lucrative gold mine in the city. In setting up laundries, they did not have to seek out jobs in established industries or incur the risk of heavy capital investment. All they needed for the business were scrub boards, soap, irons, and ironing boards. They would canvass a neighborhood, seek out a low-rent location, and open up a business.

Like laundries, restaurants were one of the most important businesses for the Chinese in the United States. Initially, Chinese restaurants started as a service for the bachelor communities of Chinese immigrants in isolated ranches, logging camps, mining towns, and other areas where Chinese men and women were willing to cook. When the eating places that the Chinese had set up for themselves soon attracted a number of outsiders, the Chinese realized that restaurants were profitable business enterprises well suited to their temperament. During the 1890's, Chinese restaurants sprouted in the United States in many places. Most small Chinese restaurants were run as husband-and-wife businesses; the husband served as cook and dishwasher in the kitchen, while the wife worked as waitress, barmaid, and cashier in the front.

The grocery business ranked as a distant third occupation for Chinese immigrants before the 1940's, although it was one of the major enterprises of the Chinese in some southern and western states. Chinese grocery stores provided Chinese ingredients for cooking and other goods for Chinese communities. Unlike the Chinese restaurants, the Chinese grocery stores found their clientele primarily among Chinese and other Asian immigrants. The stores were mostly located in Chinatowns and Asian communities.

POSTWAR CHINESE IMMIGRATION

Anti-Chinese sentiment abated during World War II, when China became a member of the Grand Alliance and public images of the Chinese gradually changed. A more favorable attitude in America toward China and Chinese Americans continued after the war. Facing pressures from the public and other interest groups, Congress repealed a large number of exclusion laws, which for years had denied Chinese Americans fundamental civil rights and legal protection. On December 17, 1943, Congress passed the Immigration Act of 1943 (also known as the Magnuson Act), which repealed all Chinese exclusion laws that had been passed since 1882, permitted Chinese aliens in the United States to apply for naturalization, and allowed 105 Chinese to immigrate annually.

In spite of the repeal of the Chinese exclusion laws, the Chinese immigrant quota designated by the American government was quite low. This figure was one-sixth of 1 percent of the number of the Chinese in the United States in 1920 as determined by the census of that year. Nevertheless, nonquota immigrants were allowed to immigrate. More Chinese scholars came to teach in the United States—an average of about 137 each year, compared with 10 per year during the previous decade. More important, under the War Brides Act of December 28, 1945, and the G.I. Fiancées Act of June 29, 1946, alien wives and children of veterans and American citizens were permitted to enter the United States as nonquota immigrants. During the three-year op-

PROFILE OF CHINESE IMMIGRANTS	
Country of origin	People's Republic of China
Primary language	Chinese (Mandarin)
Primary regions of U.S. settlement	West Coast, Hawaii
Earliest significant arrivals	1780's
Peak immigration period	Late twentieth century
Twenty-first century legal residents*	527,577 (65,947 per year)

*Immigrants who obtained legal permanent resident status in the United States.

Source: Department of Homeland Security, *Yearbook of Immigration Statistics, 2008.*

eration of the War Brides Act, approximately 6,000 Chinese war brides were admitted. Thus, in 1947 the number of Chinese immigrants entering the United States climbed to 3,191, most of whom came on a nonquota basis.

Many women also immigrated under other laws. The Displaced Persons Act of 1948 and the Refugee Relief Act of 1953 allowed several thousand Chinese women to come to America. The former granted "displaced" Chinese students, visitors, and others who had temporary status in the United States to adjust their status to that of permanent resident. The latter act allotted three thousand visas to refugees from Asia and two thousand visas to Chinese whose passports had been issued by the Chinese Nationalist government, which lost power in mainland China in 1949. On September 22, 1959, Congress passed an act under which more Chinese on the quota waiting list obtained nonquota status. Thus, by 1960 the number of Chinese in the United States, as reported by the 1960 U.S. Census, had reached 237,292. This included 135,549 male and 101,743 female persons, of whom 60 percent were native born.

Among the women who immigrated during this period were many so-called war brides who had hurriedly married Chinese American veterans before the expiration date of the War Brides Act in 1949. In her article "The Recent Immigrant Chinese Families of the San Francisco-Oakland Area," Rose Hum Lee describes the war bride:

> The most publicized case of "getting married quick" was of the ex-soldier who enplaned to China, selected his bride, was married, and landed at the San Francisco airport the evening before his month's leave of absence expired. His bride came later, a practice applying to many others whose admission papers could not be processed rapidly.

Whereas during the 1930's an average of only 60 Chinese women entered the United States each year, in 1948 alone 3,317 women immigrated. During the period from 1944 to 1953, women constituted 82 percent of Chinese immigrants to America. For the first time, the number of Chinese women and families in the United States noticeably increased. The male-female ratio dropped from 2.9:1 in 1940 to 1.8:1 in 1950, and 1.3:1 in 1960.

POST-1965 IMMIGRATION

The Immigration and Nationality Act of 1965 and the consequent influx of new Chinese immigrants contributed to the transformation of Chinese American society. The act abolished the 1924 quota system and set up three immigration principles of family reunification, the need for skilled workers, and the admission of refugees. According to these principles, the visas were allocated among quota immigrants from the Eastern Hemisphere according to seven preferences:

- 20 percent of total annual visas to unmarried children of citizens of the United States
- 20 percent to spouses and unmarried children of permanent residents
- 10 percent to professionals, scientists, and artists with "exceptional ability"
- 10 percent to married children of citizens of the United States
- 24 percent to siblings of citizens of the United States
- 10 percent to skilled and unskilled workers in occupations "for which a shortage of employable and willing persons exists in the United States"
- 6 percent to refugees

The architects of the 1965 act intended to make the immigration policies appear more humanitarian and impartial to applicants on one hand and more beneficial to the United States on the other. The new law allowed 20,000 quota immigrants from every country in the Eastern Hemisphere to be admitted to the United States each year, regardless of the size of the country. It reserved 74 percent (including 20 percent in the first preference, another 20 percent in the second preference, 10 percent in the fourth preference, and 24 percent in the fifth preference) of the total 170,000 visas annually allotted for the Eastern Hemisphere for family reunification.

The lawmakers anticipated that European immigrants would continue to be the cohort of new immigrants, since there was a very small percentage (0.5 percent of the total U.S. population during the 1960's) of Asian Americans in the country. Two occupational preferences (preferences three and six) allowed the U.S. immigration authorities and the Department of Labor to select carefully only applicants with special training and skills who would fill the vacuum in the American job

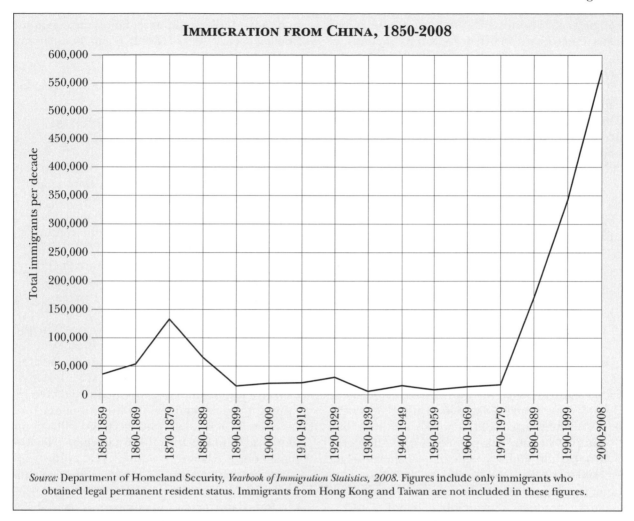

IMMIGRATION FROM CHINA, 1850-2008

Total immigrants per decade

600,000
550,000
500,000
450,000
400,000
350,000
300,000
250,000
200,000
150,000
100,000
50,000
0

1850-1859
1860-1869
1870-1879
1880-1889
1890-1899
1900-1909
1910-1919
1920-1929
1930-1939
1940-1949
1950-1959
1960-1969
1970-1979
1980-1989
1990-1999
2000-2008

Source: Department of Homeland Security, *Yearbook of Immigration Statistics, 2008.* Figures include only immigrants who obtained legal permanent resident status. Immigrants from Hong Kong and Taiwan are not included in these figures.

market. In the years following this act, the Chinese American population increased dramatically. In addition, the male-female ratio finally approached parity.

CHANGING PUSH-PULL FACTORS

The majority of new immigrants came to the United States for economic reasons. The influx of Chinese refugees from Vietnam since 1975 were lured by economic opportunities in America. In addition to laboring immigrants, a large number of professionals (the better-educated and the wealthier from China, Taiwan, Hong Kong, and Southeast Asia) also arrived since 1965. These new immigrants benefited from the 1965 Immigration and Nationality Act, which gave priority to refugees, to those who had close family members in the United

States, and to applicants who had skills, education, and capital.

After the normalization of Sino-American relations in 1979, some Chinese who had family members in the United States were allowed to come to America as immigrants. Since many of them came for economic reasons and were determined to settle, they brought their families as allowed by U.S. immigration policies. Some resigned their professional jobs in China and started from scratch in the United States.

As of 2008, at least twenty-four national-origin groups had been officially tabulated into the U.S. Census. Americans of Chinese and Filipino ancestries are the largest subgroups, at more than 2 million each, followed by Indians, Koreans, Vietnamese, and Japanese, whose numbers surpass 1 million each. The nearly 2.9 million Chinese Americans tend to settle in urban areas and concentrate in the West. According to the 2000 U.S. Census, California by itself accounted for 35 percent of the 4.3 million people of Asian descent living in the United States and also had the largest number of Chinese. The state of New York accounted for 10 percent (1.2 million) of all Asians, second only to California. Chinese were also heavily concentrated in New York.

Huping Ling

FURTHER READING

Chan, Sucheng. *Asian Americans: An Interpretive History.* Boston: Twayne, 1991. A scholarly, comprehensive survey of Americans of Chinese, Japanese, Korean, Filipino, and Asian Indian ancestry from the mid-nineteenth century to the 1980's.

Chang, Iris. *The Chinese in America: A Narrative History.* New York: Viking Press, 2003. A comprehensive account of the political, social, economic, and cultural history of Chinese Americans over a century and a half.

Daniels, Roger. *Asian America: Chinese and Japanese in the United States Since 1850.* Seattle: University of Washington, 1988. Scholarly synthesis encompassing the two pioneer Asian American groups, the Chinese and the Japanese, from 1850 to 1980.

Ling, Huping. *Chinese St. Louis: From Enclave to Cultural Community.* Philadelphia: Temple University Press, 2004. The first comprehensive study of an ethnic community in the Midwest, this groundbreaking work proposes a "cultural community" model to interpret the new type of ethnic community that is defined more by its cultural boundaries than by geographical ones.

_____. *Surviving on the Gold Mountain: Chinese American Women and Their Lives.* Albany: State University of New York Press, 1998. The first comprehensive history of Chinese American women from the mid-nineteenth century to 1990's. Explores topics such as causes of immigration, settlement patterns, family, work, and community.

SEE ALSO: Anti-Chinese movement; Bayard-Zhang Treaty of 1888; Burlingame Treaty of 1868; Cable Act of 1922; California gold rush; Chinese American press; Chinese boycott of 1905; Chinese Exclusion Act of 1882; Chinese family associations; Coolies; Geary Act of 1892; Hong Kong immigrants; Taiwanese immigrants.

CHINESE LAUNDRIES

DEFINITION: Important niche industry for Chinese immigrant families

> **SIGNIFICANCE:** Chinese laundries developed as a major occupation for the first wave of Chinese immigrants who came to the United States during the mid-nineteenth century. Laundries opened throughout the country and became uniquely identified with this ethnic group. The Chinese launderer stereotype appeared in popular culture and media.

Although the first Chinese had arrived in the United States in 1820, the first significant wave of Chinese immigration did not occur until soon after the California gold rush in 1849. With hopes of making a fortune in "Gold Mountain" and then returning to their families in China, thousands of young men left their impoverished villages in southern China to travel to California. They became contract laborers who worked in the gold mines and on the railroads. However, growing anti-Chinese sentiment and restricted urban labor markets forced the increasing numbers of Chinese immigrants to seek other work.

GROWTH OF CHINESE LAUNDRIES

In 1851, Wah Lee opened the first Chinese hand laundry in the United States. His small, leased storefront in San Francisco had a simple sign: "Wash'ng and Iron'ng." Within a few weeks, the business had expanded to twenty washermen working three shifts daily. A laundry was an ideal business for Chinese immigrants, since it required no special skills or venture capital, and Euro-American men considered it undesirable work. Typically, laundry work required long days of exhausting manual labor over kettles of boiling water and hand irons heated on stoves. By the 1870's, Chinese laundries were operating in all towns with Chinese populations.

However, as more groups competed for work, prejudice against Chinese immigrants intensified.

In 1880, 95 percent of San Francisco's 320 laundries operated in wooden buildings. The city passed an ordinance requiring owners of laundries in wooden buildings to obtain a permit. Two-thirds of the laundries were owned by Chinese people, but none of them was granted a permit. Only one non-Chinese owner was denied.

The Chinese Exclusion Act of 1882, the first race-based immigration law, was designed to prohibit Chinese immigration and deny citizenship to Chinese people for a decade. In 1883, 8,031 Chinese people, including immigrants returning from visits to China, entered the United States. However, in 1884 only 279 entered the country, and in 1887, only 10 entered. In 1892, the act was extended for another 10 years, so for decades there were violent crimes and discrimination aimed at the Chinese, but they found safety in Chinatowns. By the early twentieth century, there were Chinese laundries in every major city. The Chinese persevered, taking actions such as forming the Chinese Hand Laundry Alliance in 1933. The Chinese Exclusion Act was repealed in 1943. By then, entire families worked and lived in Chinese laundries, and the new generations of Chinese Americans gradually became assimilated into American society.

CHINESE LAUNDRIES IN POPULAR CULTURE AND MEDIA

From the 1870's through the 1890's, trade or advertising cards were popular for promoting a service, product, or event. The stereotype of Chinese laundrymen was used to advertise laundry-related products, such as detergents, wringers, and soap. For example, the Lavine Soap trade card showed small, cute, pig-tailed Chinese with the product. A silent film of 1895, *The Chinese Laundry Scene*, featured the popular slapstick vaudeville act Robetta

Family-run Chinese laundry in California around 1910. (California State Library)

and Doretto as an Irish police officer and a Chinese laundry worker quarreling.

In 1922, the *Los Angeles Times* ran a "Junior Times" section that included a variety of mechanical paper puppets. Along with policemen, animals, a jack-in-the-box, and other figures was "Lee Ling, Chinese Laundry Man." Shockingly derogatory portrayals occurred in *Laundry Blues*, a Van Beuren cartoon distributed by RKO Radio Pictures in 1930. Because it was so overtly racist, this cartoon was censored and banned.

An ingrained part of popular culture, the old comedic associations were carried into television. A television commercial for Calgon water softener that was popular during the 1970's featured a white woman asking a laundry owner named Lee how he gets his shirts so very clean. He replies, "Ancient Chinese secret." The secret is exposed when Lee's wife sticks her head out from the back room and shouts that they need more Calgon.

The Chinese laundryman stereotype persisted, but by the 1950's the actual traditional Chinese laundries were becoming obsolete. Self-service laundromats proliferated during the 1950's. Generations of children who grew up in laundries pursued higher education and entered other occupations. With the end of the civil war in China in 1949, a new wave of Chinese immigration had begun. These immigrants often came from upper- and middle-class families searching for a better life in America or were well-educated intellectuals pursuing advanced degrees. In 1993, writer Alvin Ang and composer John Dunbar presented the musical *The Last Hand Laundry in Chinatown (A Requiem for American Independents)* as a homage to Chinese laundries.

Alice Myers

FURTHER READING

Chang, Iris. *The Chinese in America: A Narrative History.* New York: Viking Press, 2003. Highly readable chronicle of the Chinese American experience through the twentieth century. Includes details about Chinese laundries and the laundry workers.

Jung, John. *Chinese Laundries: Tickets to Survival on Gold Mountain.* Morrisville, N.C.: Yin & Yang Press, 2007. Comprehensive historical, social, and psychological study that includes personal stories from "children of the laundries," as well as newspaper articles, photographs, and historic documents.

Siu, Paul C. P. *The Chinese Laundryman: A Study of Social Isolation.* New York: New York University Press, 1987. The son of a laundryman, the author presents an intimate but scholarly study of Chinese laundries in Chicago from 1870 to 1940. This classic is a landmark in the exploration of ethnic occupations and the American immigrant experience.

Yu, Renqiu. *To Save China, to Save Ourselves: The Chinese Hand Laundry Alliance of New York.* Philadelphia: Temple University Press, 1992. The complete story of the leftist labor organization that successfully advocated for Chinese laundry workers and other overseas Chinese living in North America.

Yung, Judy, Gordon H. Chang, and H. Mark Lai, eds. *Chinese American Voices: From the Gold Rush to the Present.* Berkeley: University of California Press, 2006. Anthology of personal stories revealing the political, social, and cultural history of the Chinese American experience. Includes the Declaration of the Chinese Hand Laundry Alliance of 1933.

SEE ALSO: Anti-Chinese movement; Chinatowns; Chinese American Citizens Alliance; Chinese Exclusion Act of 1882; *Chinese Exclusion Cases*; Chinese family associations; Chinese Hand Laundry Alliance; Chinese immigrants; Family businesses; Geary Act of 1892; Railroads; *Yick Wo v. Hopkins.*

CHINESE SECRET SOCIETIES

DEFINITION: Clandestine organizations imported to the United States whose origins go back to earlier Chinese history

SIGNIFICANCE: The secret societies founded in China several centuries ago to combat unjust rulers often turned to criminality. During the mid-nineteenth century, following the discovery of gold in California, many members of these societies emigrated to the United States. They frequently retained their ancient mores and brought new types of criminal activities to America that further turned the populace against them.

To the general American public, the best-known Chinese secret societies are the tongs and the triads. Long the subject of countless lurid films and literature, the tongs were a specifically American creation, established by the most poor Chinese immigrants who came to work in the western mining camps and on railroad construction. Their lineages went back to the secret groups formed in China to attempt to overthrow the Qing Dynasty that ruled from the mid-seventeenth century to 1912.

TONGS

Originally merchant associations in U.S. Chinatowns, the tongs were established to provide mutual support and protection against other Chinese organizations and hostile outsiders. Racial prejudice against the Asian immigrants in the western United States was widespread even before the Chinese Exclusion Act was passed in 1882. Early tong activities were benign. However, in the crowded Chinatowns many of these organizations eventually turned to crime. There was generally a shortage of marriageable Chinese women available to the immigrants because of U.S. exclusionary laws, so prostitution and even slavery were profitable, as was gambling.

Intra-Chinese conflicts popularly known as "tong wars" arose out of intense competition for spoils among tong gangs. They were usually fought among warring factions of immigrants and did not involve outsiders. They were particularly prevalent in the Chinatowns of San Francisco, Cleveland, and Los Angeles. These conflict were bloody, as combatants used hatchets, meat cleavers, and machetes as weapons. The wars began to decline during the 1930's, as new generations of American-born Chinese achieved middle-class lifestyles and Christianity took increasing hold.

TRIADS

Like the tongs, the triads are criminal gangs that trace their ancestry to secret societies formed to re-

Federal government photograph of Sun Yat-sen, the future first president of the Republic of China, that was made during his 1909-1910 visit to the United States. The photograph was kept in a file relating to Sun's entry into the United States under the restrictions of the Chinese Exclusion Act. (NARA)

move the Qing Dynasty from power. According to legend, the first such group was begun by Buddhist monks who communicated with secret codes to confound imperial agents and who mastered the martial arts. They adopted the color red as their symbol. Many such triads were established, and they ultimately became criminal organizations. Among the best known of them were the White Lotus Society, the Red Fists, and the Cudgels.

At the beginning of the twentieth century, the triad-like Society of Harmonious Fists (known by the Western powers as the Boxers) attempted to rid China of the foreign powers that were exploiting the country. The so-called Boxer Rebellion of 1900 was the result. The rebellion was eventually crushed, but not until after many deaths had occurred. In the chaos surrounding the fall of the last Chinese emperor a decade later, the triads flourished and were utilized by the warlords who operated almost unchecked in many parts of the country. Among the most prominent triad members were Sun Yat-sen, founder of the modern Chinese republic, and Chiang Kai-shek, who later became president of nationalist China.

With the rise to power in China of the communists under Mao Zedong in 1949, members of the old triads scattered to such places as Thailand, British-ruled Hong Kong, Portuguese-ruled Macao, and San Francisco. Those who had come to the United States in earlier years had often become members of various tongs. While the tongs gradually lessened in importance, the triads built a worldwide criminal network. Smuggling, both of drugs and human beings, remains a large part of their operations as well as extortion, counterfeiting, money laundering, and contract murders.

As late as the early twenty-first century, violent triad-affiliated Chinese American street gangs continued to flourish in New York and along the West Coast, often victimizing other Chinese Americans. They are also believed to have been active in such cities as Las Vegas, Boston, Miami, and Chicago. The triads have been compared to the Italian Mafia in their organization and customs, including the pricking of fingers and a lengthy list of sworn oaths as part of their initiation rite.

Roy Liebman

FURTHER READING

Bolton, K. *Triad Societies: Western Accounts of the History, Sociology and Linguistics of Chinese Secret Societies.* London: Routledge, 2000. Overview of scholarly texts that goes beyond the traditional Western view of the "Chinese Mafia" to discuss Chinese secret societies from the early nineteenth to the mid-twentieth centuries.

Chan, Sucheng, and Madeline Y. Hsu, eds. *Chinese Americans and the Politics of Race and Culture.* Philadelphia: Temple University Press, 2008. Collection of scholarly essays based on archival sources that cover a wide range of topics, including the activities of Chinese immigrants to the United States.

Hanson, Gayle M. B. "Triads and Tongs Team Up to Prey on Asian Populace (Asian Organized Crime in the United States)." *Insight on the News* 13, no. 11 (1997): 18-19. Discusses how China's long tradition of organized crime reached the United States and how gangs operate in American cities.

Huston, Peter. *Tongs, Gangs and Triads: Chinese Crime Groups in North America.* Boulder, Colo.: Paladin Press, 1995. Explores the various types of Chinese secret societies and their frequent involvement in criminal activities with Chinatown street gangs.

Li, Minghuan. *"We Need Two Worlds": Chinese Immigrant Associations in a Western Society.* Amsterdam: Amsterdam University Press, 1999. Although focusing on Amsterdam in the Netherlands, this book provides useful insights into the workings of Chinese associations in major urban centers everywhere.

Posner, Gerald L. *Warlords of Crime: Chinese Secret Societies—The New Mafia.* New York: McGraw-Hill, 1985. Covers the history of triads from their founding during the seventeenth century to their establishment in Western countries and their involvement in crime, particularly the drug trade.

See also: Chinatowns; Chinese family associations; Chinese immigrants; Crime; Criminal immigrants; Ethnic enclaves.

Chinese Six Companies

Identification: National network of benevolent social organizations for Chinese Americans

Date: Established in 1882

Also known as: Chinese Consolidated Benevolent Association

Significance: Begun to promote community cooperation and to protect ethnic identity in the face of discrimination and violence against first-generation Chinese immigrants in the Chinatown district of San Francisco, the Chinese Six Companies quickly grew into a powerful national organization that worked to defend the civil and political rights of Chinese Americans in the face of increasingly anti-Chinese federal legislation enacted by the U.S. Congress between 1880 and 1920.

For the nearly 100,000 Chinese immigrants who came to California during the mid-nineteenth century—mostly to work in the newly opening gold fields—assimilation into the established European American community was never a possibility. Divided from the established Americans by sharp social, cultural, language, and religious differences, as well as obvious physical differences, the Chinese immigrants came to live in tightly closed neighborhoods. The most famous of these was Chinatown in San Francisco. These immigrants were mostly poorly educated men from rural China. After arriving in California, they worked diligently and quickly became an essential element of California's developing economy. The Chinese Six Companies had their roots in this era. Loose confederations of neighbors in the Chinese districts helped arrange work for new immigrants and provided new arrivals with shelter and food.

As the numbers of Chinese immigrants increased and the gold fields were played out, the immigrants extended the range of their economic activities to fishing, food services, farming, service trades (most prominently laundering), and, most famously, helping to build the transcontinental railroad. Meanwhile, violence against these immigrants became more common. They were perceived as threats to the economic livelihood of "real" Americans. By the early 1880's, such resentment and violence had become routine. Within the Chinese neighborhoods of San Francisco, the largest enclave of Chinese immigrants in the United States, neighborhood organizations made up of successful merchants and political activists began to provide a kind of pseudo-government structure to the neighborhoods. At the same time, they promoted pride in their shared ethnic identity. After the original Chinese Consolidated Benevolent Association was chartered in San Francisco in 1882, it was soon followed by five other community organizations which joined to become the Chinese Six Companies.

In the face of an organized effort to use federal legislation to curtail the immigration of Asians generally and the Chinese specifically, the Chinese Six Companies took an increasingly prominent role in publicly defending civil rights for Chinese immigrants. Federal laws initially denied the Chinese immigrants the right to become naturalized citizens, but the controversial 1882 Chinese Exclusion Act virtually ended Chinese immigration. It then fell to the Chinese Six Companies to maintain commu-

nity integrity. The organizations encouraged immigrants to develop urban trades, most notably restaurant management, factory labor (particularly in the thriving garment industry), and import-export businesses. In addition to encouraging employment, these community organizations settled petty disputes, helped develop neighborhood schools, sponsored the building of Buddhist temples, and funded community cultural and social events to preserve the sense of Chinese identity.

Over the decades, as immigration restrictions slowly eased, the Chinese Six Companies continued to grow, chartering councils in more than a dozen cities. As a collective, these companies initiated significant law suits that brought discrimination issues to the U.S. Supreme Court. Locally, they continued to encourage community involvement for Chinese Americans and provided a sense of continuity and ethnic identity to generations long removed from the immigrant experience. The organizations have continued to promote business opportunities for Chinese American neighborhoods and to seek political support for agendas that promote issues key to the Chinese American community.

Joseph Dewey

FURTHER READING

Chang, Iris. *The Chinese in America: A Narrative History.* New York: Penguin Books, 2004.

Kwong, Peter, and Dušanka Miščević. *Chinese America: The Untold Story of America's Oldest New Community.* New York: New Press, 2005.

_____. *Chinese Americans: The Immigrant Experience.* New York: Universe, 2000.

Lee, Erika. *At America's Gate: Chinese Immigration During the Exclusion Era, 1882-1943.* Chapel Hill: University of North Carolina Press, 2007.

SEE ALSO: Anti-Chinese movement; Asian American Legal Defense Fund; California; California gold rush; Chinatowns; Chinese American Citizens Alliance; Chinese Exclusion Act of 1882; Chinese family associations; Chinese immigrants; Coolies; History of immigration, 1783-1891; San Francisco; "Yellow peril" campaign.

CHINESE STUDENT PROTECTION ACT OF 1992

THE LAW: Federal legislation permitting Chinese students and scholars to remain in the United States and apply for permanent residency
ALSO KNOWN AS: Public Law 102-404
DATE: Enacted on October 9, 1992

SIGNIFICANCE: The passage of this law indicated that U.S. immigration policies could be influenced by domestic political developments of other countries.

The history of Chinese students coming to study in the United States could be traced back to the early twentieth century. This history was interrupted in 1949 with the victory of the Chinese Communist Revolution. Between 1949 and 1972, when China and the United States were Cold War enemies and closed to each other, there existed no educational exchanges between the two nations, and hence almost no students from China could be found on American campuses. Only with the normalization of Sino-American relations in 1972, which was marked by President Richard M. Nixon's visit to China, did educational exchanges between the two countries resume.

Such exchanges accelerated during the late 1970's, when Chinese leaders decided to adopt the reform and open policy (in 1978) and the United States and China established diplomatic relations (1979). An integral component of the U.S.-China educational exchange was that Chinese students were allowed to study in the United States. The number of Chinese students in the United States grew steadily and by 1989 reached more than fifty thousand. These students, especially those who were sponsored financially by the Chinese government, were required or expected to go back to China upon graduation. However, their status was changed from student status to immigrant status by a major political event in China—the Tiananmen Square massacre, also known as the June Fourth incident.

Between April 15 and June 4, 1989, large-scale demonstrations occurred in and near the Tiananmen Square in Beijing, with most participants being students and intellectuals. The demonstrators called for deepening economic and political reforms as well as curbing rampant official corruption. Similar demonstrations also took place in many other Chinese cities. The Chinese leadership responded first with denunciation of the protests, then with half-hearted dialogues with student representatives, and finally on June 4, 1989, with military crackdown, killing hundreds (or thousands according to a different estimate) of protesters, mostly students. Following this violence, the Chinese government conducted widespread arrests of protesters and political dissidents and purged liberal-minded officials.

The Chinese government's brutal suppression of the civilian protesters incurred condemnations and various sanctions from the international community, especially from Western nations. Some Western governments, including the United States, also took measures to protect Chinese nationals then residing in their countries from persecution by the Chinese government. On April 11, 1990, President George H. W. Bush issued Executive Order 12711, permitting Chinese students, visiting scholars, and other Chinese who had been in the United States between June 5, 1989, and April 11, 1990, to stay until July 1, 1993. Then, in 1992, the U.S. Congress passed the Chinese Student Protection Act, which had been initiated by California Democratic representative Nancy Pelosi.

This act allowed Chinese nationals who entered the United States before the issuance of Executive Order 12711 (April 11, 1990) to apply for permanent resident status. The stated purpose of this act was to prevent political persecution of Chinese students in the aftermath of the June 4 incident. One provision of the act was that permanent resident status granted to Chinese nationals under the act would be subtracted from the immigration spaces available in later years. Most Chinese students submitted applications and were granted green cards. Though students were supposed to be the beneficiaries of this legislation, some of those receiving green cards were actually illegal immigrants from the province of Fujian who had been smuggled into the United States by "snakehead" gangs. Altogether, more than eighty thousand Chinese nationals became permanent residents because of this act.

The Chinese Student Protection Act of 1992 sent a strong signal to the Chinese government that political persecution of its citizens was unacceptable to the international community and that it must treat them humanely. The act benefited not only the Chinese immigrants admitted under the act but also the United States, given that most of them were well educated and possessed scientific and technological expertise that were much needed in the United States.

Yunqiu Zhang

FURTHER READING

Barth, Kelly, ed. *The Tiananmen Square Massacre.* San Diego, Calif.: Greenhaven Press/Thomson Gale, 2003.

Poston, Dudley L., Jr., and Hua Luo. "Chinese Student and Labor Migration to the United States: Trends and Policies Since the 1980's." *Asian and Pacific Migration Journal* 16, no. 3 (2007): 323-356.

Qian, Ning. *Chinese Students Encounter America.* Translated by T. K. Chu. Seattle: University of Washington Press, 2002.

U.S. Congress. House Committee on the Judiciary. *Chinese Student Protection Act of 1992: Report.* Washington, D.C.: Government Printing Office, 1992.

SEE ALSO: Asian immigrants; Chinese American press; Chinese immigrants; Education; Foreign exchange students; Higher education.

CHY LUNG V. FREEMAN

THE CASE: U.S. Supreme Court decision concerning the authority of the national government
DATE: Decided on October 1, 1875

SIGNIFICANCE: Based on principles of federalism, the *Chy Lung* decision put limitations on the extent to which the states might restrict the admission of persons into the country.

When Chy Lung, a subject of the emperor of China, arrived in San Francisco, immigration officials classified her and twenty other women as "lewd and debauched." In order for the women to be admitted, California law required a bond of five hundred dollars in gold from each of them. Unable to obtain the money, and refusing to return to China, the women were held as prisoners in the custody of San Francisco's sheriff. The state's high court upheld the constitutionality of the statute.

The Supreme Court, however, ruled unanimously that the statute was "in conflict with the Constitution of the United States, and therefore void." Writing the rationale for the decision, Justice Samuel F. Miller explained that Congress, not the states, was empowered to enact legislation concerning the admission of persons from other nations. Although states could make reasonable and necessary regulations concerning paupers and convicted criminals, this particular statute went far beyond what was appropriate, and it had the potential of embroiling the United States in quarrels with foreign nations. Its "manifest purpose," moreover, was simply to obtain money. The Court ordered, therefore, that the women must be released.

Thomas Tandy Lewis

FURTHER READING

Chang, Iris. *The Chinese in America: A Narrative History.* New York: Viking Press, 2003.

McClain, Charles J. *In Search of Equality: The Chinese Struggle Against Discrimination in Nineteenth-Century America.* Berkeley: University of California Press, 1994.

SEE ALSO: Anti-Chinese movement; *Chae Chan Ping v. United States; Chin Bak Kan v. United States;* Chinese Exclusion Act of 1882; Chinese immigrants; *Fong Yue Ting v. United States;* Supreme Court, U.S.

CITIZENS COMMITTEE TO REPEAL CHINESE EXCLUSION

IDENTIFICATION: Private committee established to lobby for repeal of the Chinese Exclusion Act of 1882
DATE: Established on May 25, 1943
ALSO KNOWN AS: Citizens Committee to Repeal Chinese Exclusion and Place Immigration on a Quota Basis

SIGNIFICANCE: Made up of a relatively small group of notable public figures, this ad hoc organization successfully leveraged its influence to persuade other organizations and members of the public to lobby Congress for the repeal of the Chinese Exclusion Act of 1882.

Chinese immigrants first came to the United States during the late 1840's, when a student sponsored by American missionaries arrived in Hartford, Connecticut, to study. He later graduated from Yale University and eventually established a program that sent 120 more male students to study in Hartford. Chinese first came in substantial numbers during California's mid-nineteenth century gold rush, which attracted about 25,000 immigrants from China. Thereafter, tens of thousands, mostly laborers, arrived, seeking employment in the railroad, agricultural, and lumber industries. By the 1870's, Chinese immigrants constituted 10 percent of California's population. Because they competed for jobs with members of other ethnic groups, they encountered active discrimination and persecution by those resenting their willingness to accept lower wages, their abstemious and disciplined habits, and their capacity to work at the most difficult jobs. "We were persecuted for our virtues," one Chinese later remarked. Racial, cultural, and linguistic differences marked the Chinese out for exclusion from white society.

In 1882, the U.S. Congress enacted the Chinese Exclusion Act, which prohibited most Chinese from entering the United States, owning property, or becoming American citizens. The Chinese who were already in the country could not bring in their wives or children. The law was renewed in 1892 and made permanent in 1902. By the time the United States entered World War II, in 1941, Chinese exclusion was the law of land. The Angel Island Immigration Station in San Francisco Bay, which operated from 1910 to 1940, detained arriving Chinese, who were usually sent home after months of harsh interrogation.

BACKGROUND TO THE COMMITTEE

Although American missionaries had attempted to have Chinese exclusion rescinded during the 1920's, an array of economic interests along with social prejudice, including racism, stood in their way. Nevertheless, during the 1930's, a pro-Chinese movement began after the publication of Pearl S.

Buck's *The Good Earth* about the sufferings of ordinary Chinese in rural China caused a sensation in the United States, while earning its author both a Pulitzer Prize and the Nobel Prize for Literature. The book also was made into a feature film that won five Academy Awards, including the award for best picture. Moreover, Henry Luce, the publisher of *Time* magazine, led a campaign of sympathy for China after its brutal invasion by the Japanese army during the 1930's. Wellesley College-educated Madame Chiang Soong Mei-ling, better know as Madame Chiang Kai-shek, the wife of the head of the Chinese nationalist government, began touring the United States appealing for support for the Chinese war cause. Accordingly, by the time Japan launched its sneak attack on Pearl Harbor in December, 1941, and the United States entered World War II, sympathy for China and the Chinese was growing in the United States. On the other hand, opposition to lifting Chinese exclusion remained well entrenched, especially among members of labor unions who feared competition from Chinese workers, and the American public generally opposed large-scale non-western European immigration.

The immediate background to the formation of the Committee to Repeal Chinese Exclusion lay in the war in the Pacific. President Franklin D. Roosevelt, among others, considered it essential for victory that the U.S. alliance with China be preserved and that the Chinese continue fighting against Japan. However, the Japanese government was making frequent, skillful propaganda use of the Chinese Exclusion Act as proof of American moral hypocrisy and U.S. imperial aspirations toward Asia, which Japan argued would be far better off under Japanese rule. Chinese diplomats quietly suggested to Washington that the Exclusion Act was harming their war effort because it lowered Chinese morale. Thus the committee was formed in response to the need to rally public support for repeal as an aid to the American war effort. Such a repeal, supporters said, would also aid a postwar world in which U.S. relations with Asia and trade with China would gain new importance.

MAKEUP AND MISSION OF THE COMMITTEE

The committee was organized by James Walsh, a prominent New York publisher and the husband of Pearl S. Buck. Although the committee was relatively small—with never more than about 240 persons—it was highly influential in organizing support for repeal of the federal law. Meeting first on May 25, 1943, the committee functioned as a pressure group that induced larger forces to lobby Congress for repeal. Although lobbying against the law on moral grounds was decades old, the committee sought to take advantage of the new military situation in the Pacific by making the U.S. alliance with China a central feature.

The committee's members were mostly eastern elites and their allies in other parts of the country who could use their social and professional positions to generate action against the Exclusion Act. Urged by the committee, business groups, for example, lobbied Congress to change the law, arguing that total exclusion and mistreatment of Chinese by customs officials were bad for business. When pressed, members such as Buck emphasized that repeal was necessary as a measure to win the war.

Outcome of the Committee's Work

The committee was instrumental in bringing repeal of the Chinese Exclusion Act. By urging larger groups to lobby Congress for support, it effectively leveraged its limited size. During the late autumn of 1943, only seven months after the committee first met, Congress passed the Immigration Act of 1943, which repealed Chinese exclusion.

Charles F. Bahmueller

Further Reading

Ma, Xiaohua. "A Democracy at War: The American Campaign to Repeal Chinese Exclusion in 1943." *Japanese Journal of America Studies* 9 (1998): 121-142. Account of the politics of repealing Chinese exclusion emphasizing arguments that repeal was required for a successful war effort against Japan.
Riggs, Frederick. *Pressure on Congress: A Study of the Repeal of Chinese Exclusion.* New York: Columbia University Press, 1950. Definitive work on Chinese exclusion that is widely cited by scholars. Gives a detailed account of how lobbying Congress led to the repeal of the discriminatory law.
Skrentny, John D. *The Minority Rights Revolution.* Cambridge, Mass.: Harvard University Press, 2002. Dispassionate account of its subject that seeks understanding of how change occurs rather than denouncing the moral wrongs that impelled it. Locates the repeal of Chinese exclusion within the historical narrative of minority movements for redress of grievances.
Wang, L. Ling-chi. "Politics of the Repeal of the Chinese Exclusion Laws." In *Remembering 1882: Fighting for Civil Rights in the Shadow of the Chinese Exclusion Act.* San Francisco: Chinese Historical Society of America, 2007. Account of the political process that led to repeal of Chinese exclusion with particular attention to pressure-group lobbying.

See also: Anti-Chinese movement; Chinese American Citizens Alliance; Chinese boycott of 1905; Chinese Exclusion Act of 1882; *Chinese Exclusion Cases*; Chinese family associations; Chinese immigrants; Native Sons of the Golden State; Page Law of 1875; World War II.

Citizenship

Definition: Status of being a citizen, or an inhabitant of a country or other political entity, who enjoys its full privileges and rights, including the right to vote, to hold elective office, and to enjoy the full protections of government

Significance: Under the U.S. Constitution and laws of the United States, the status of citizenship entitles possessors, whether native born or naturalized, to all established civil rights and also includes the duty of rendering allegiance to the country.

According to U.S. law, a person can obtain U.S. citizenship in one of two ways: as a result of birth or as a result of naturalization. Birthright citizenship is automatically granted to a person whose parents are citizens (jus sanguinis) and to a person born on U.S. soil (jus soli). Other persons, however, can acquire citizenship only by fulfilling the complex requirements for naturalization, which have changed frequently over the years.

Advantages of Citizenship

U.S. citizens possess a number of constitutional rights that cannot be claimed by noncitizens, even if the latter legally reside within the United States. For example, Article I of the original Constitution specifies that only citizens are qualified to serve in Congress. Article IV, section 2, further recognizes that citizens of each state are entitled to certain "privileges and immunities" in all the states, a clause that the U.S. Supreme Court has interpreted as referring to "fundamental rights" inherent in a free government. The Fourteenth Amendment further prohibits the states from abridging the "privileges or immunities" that accompany U.S. citizenship. Finally, constitutional amendments relating to voting rights apply only to citizens of the country.

Individual state constitutions, as well as federal and state legislation, have placed many additional restrictions on the rights and privileges of noncitizens. Although the U.S. Supreme Court has overturned some of these restrictions as unconstitutional, it has also upheld many of them, including restrictions on foreign travel, welfare benefits, employment in public service, and the buying and selling of property. Noncitizens, moreover, can be deported for a number of reasons, even for certain political activities that American citizens have an unquestioned legal right to pursue without fear of punishment.

Nevertheless, the Constitution and U.S. laws guarantee many rights for noncitizens. All the liberties guaranteed by the Bill of Rights apply to "persons," not just "citizens." Likewise, the Fourteenth Amendment prohibits a state from denying "due process" or "equal protection" to any "person" under its jurisdiction. During the second half of the twentieth century, the Supreme Court's interpretations of the Fourteenth Amendment significantly lessened the number of rights applicable only to citizens. After the landmark decision *Graham v. Richardson* (1971), for instance, the Supreme Court began holding that discrimination in employment on the basis of alienage must be justified by a very strong rationale.

For the most part citizens by naturalization are guaranteed the same legal rights as citizens by birth. Two significant exceptions apply, however. First, the U.S. Constitution explicitly states that only a natural-born citizen can serve as the president. Second, although the Supreme Court held in *Trop v. Dulles* (1958) that birthright citizens could not be involuntarily deprived of their citizenship, the Court subsequently approved the revocation of

naturalization whenever immigrants were found to have falsified information when they entered the country or applied for naturalization.

In addition to legal rights, the status of citizenship is often desired because of its social and symbolic significance. Citizenship provides many persons with a sense of belonging; it has the meaning of full membership within a national community. When persons are classified as "foreigners" or "aliens," citizens tend to look upon them as outsiders, as "them," rather than as "us."

NATURALIZED CITIZENSHIP

In view of the importance of immigration in U.S. history, it is not surprising that the issue of how to become a citizen has often been controversial. The original Constitution, as ratified in 1789, said nothing about birthright citizenship. Consequently, the English common-law rules of jus soli and jus sanguinis continued in force. In contrast, Article I of the Constitution provided the U.S. Congress with unrestricted discretion in establishing "a uniform rule of naturalization." Accordingly, the Congress enacted a law in 1790 that restricted naturalized citizenship to "free white persons." Racial bias was even more evident in the Supreme Court's decision in *Dred Scott v. Sandford* (1857), which held that no persons of African ancestry were eligible for U.S. citizenship, regardless of their locations of birth. Eleven years later, however, this infamous decision was reversed by the Fourteenth Amendment, which specified that the status of citizenship, both state and national, was automatically conferred on all persons born or naturalized within the United States.

CITIZENSHIP CLAUSE OF THE FOURTEENTH AMENDMENT

All persons born or naturalized in the United States and subject to the jurisdiction thereof, are citizens of the United States and of the State wherein they reside. No State shall make or enforce any law which shall abridge the privileges or immunities of citizens of the United States; nor shall any State deprive any person of life, liberty, or property, without due process of law; nor deny to any person within its jurisdiction the equal protection of the laws.

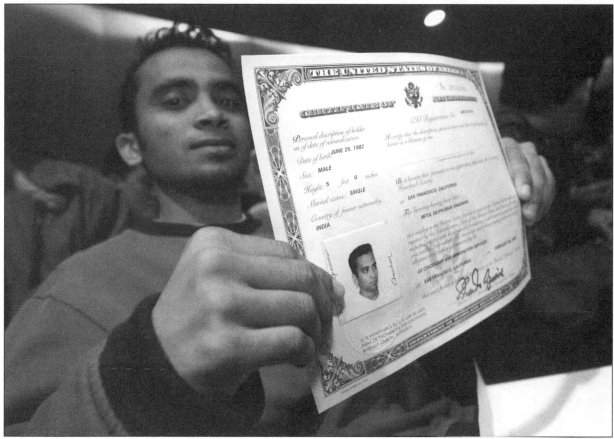

Newly naturalized American citizen holding his certificate of naturalization after a ceremony in San Francisco in which more than 1,400 immigrants were sworn in as citizens. (Getty Images)

Following ratification of the Fourteenth Amendment, there was some debate about the legal status of children who were born in the United States to nonwhite parents ineligible for citizenship. This debate was finally settled in *United States v. Wong Kim Ark* (1898), in which the Supreme Court interpreted the amendment to mean that all such persons automatically acquired citizenship on the basis of the common-law rule of jus soli. The *Wong Kim Ark* decision had no effect on the legal status of nonwhite persons who had already immigrated into the United States. Although the Fourteenth Amendment required each state to provide the "equal protection of the laws" to all persons under its jurisdiction, this clause was not applicable to federal legislation. It was not until passage of the Immigration and Nationality Act of 1952 that Congress finally abolished the last remaining racial restrictions on eligibility for naturalization.

Until 1922, the citizenship status of married women was usually determined by the status of their husbands. Alien women acquired U.S. citizenship when they married Americans, and American women lost their citizenship when they married aliens. The Cable Act of 1922 provided that alien women could no longer become citizens simply through marriage; it also specified that marriage of American women to alien men who were eligible for naturalization would not automatically cause loss of American citizenship. Although the Cable Act continued to take away the citizenship of women who married men ineligible for naturalization, an amendment to the act in 1931 eliminated this discriminatory provision. Finally, on May 24, 1934, President Franklin D. Roosevelt signed an equalization bill that eliminated all discriminatory treatment because of sex or marriage.

Ineligibility because of political opinion has historically been a prominent feature in U.S. naturalization law. In *United States v. Macintosh* (1931), for example, the Supreme Court upheld a requirement that applicants for citizenship must pledge to bear arms in defense of the country, and the majority opinion in the case defined naturalization as "a privilege to be given, qualified, or withheld as Congress may determine." During the Cold War that lasted from the late 1940's until the late 1980's, discrimination was especially virulent against persons who openly espoused prosocialist or procommunist sentiments. Although policies were liberalized after the end of the Cold War, persons with extremist viewpoints continued to be ineligible for naturalization, even though expression of such viewpoints is protected by the First Amendment.

Another important addition to U.S. naturalization law was the Child Citizenship Act of 2000, which allowed many foreign-born, biological, and adopted children of U.S. citizens to acquire citizenship status automatically when they entered the country as lawful permanent residents. To qualify, a child must have at last one parent who is already a U.S. citizen, be under eighteen years of age, and live under the custody of the parent having citizenship. If the child is adopted, the adoption process must be final and complete.

In order for adult immigrants to become naturalized citizens in the early twenty-first century, they generally had to live within the country as permanent residents for five years, during which time they had to demonstrate "good moral character." Disqualifying moral behaviors included drug abuse, prostitution, illegal gambling, terrorism, polygamy, Communist Party membership, advocacy of violent revolution, and lying to immigration officials. Applicants also had to demonstrate an ability to use simple English and pass a test on the history and government of the United States. Finally, applicants had to take an oath promising to give up foreign allegiance, to obey the U.S. Constitution and U.S. laws, and be willing either to fight for the U.S. military or to perform some alternative service useful to the national interest.

Thomas Tandy Lewis

FURTHER READING

Aleinikoff, Thomas A., et al. *Immigration and Citizenship: Process and Policy.* 6th ed. St. Paul, Minn.: West Group, 2008. Standard legal textbook that discusses legislation and court cases relating to all aspects of immigration and naturalization.

Bosniak, Linda. *The Citizen and the Alien: Dilemmas of Contemporary Membership.* Princeton, N.J.: Princeton University Press, 2006. Philosophical exploration of the question of whether a moral justification exists for historical distinctions between citizens and aliens.

Bray, Ilona. *Becoming a U.S. Citizen: A Guide to the Law, Exam, and Interview.* 4th ed. Berkeley, Calif.: Nolo Press, 2008. Practical, clearly written guide explaining the advantages and disadvantages of citizenship and current American rules for naturalization.

Kim, Hyung-chan. *A Legal History of Asian Americans, 1790-1990.* Westport, Conn.: Greenwood Press, 1994. Clearly written book that includes much information about the historical discrimination against Asians in the naturalization process.

LeMay, Michael, and Elliott Robert Barkan, eds. *U.S. Immigration and Naturalization Laws and Issues: A Documentary History.* Westport, Conn.: Greenwood, 1999. Excellent collection of legislative texts, court decisions, and introductory historical essays.

Schreuder, Sally A. *How to Become a United States Citizen.* 5th ed. Berkeley, Calif.: Nolo Press, 1996. Concise guidebook that clearly explains the rules and procedures of the naturalization process.

Schuck, Peter. *Citizens, Strangers, and In-Betweens: Essays on Immigration and Citizenship.* Boulder, Colo.: Westview, 1998. Collection of thoughtful essays on a large variety of topics by a recognized authority on the legal aspects of immigration and naturalization.

Smith, Roger M. *Civic Ideals: Conflicting Visions of Citizenship in U.S. History.* New Haven, Conn.: Yale University Press, 1999. Liberal analysis emphasizing racial and gender discrimination in naturalization laws from the colonial era to the early twentieth century.

SEE ALSO: *Afroyim v. Rusk*; Cable Act of 1922; Citizenship and Immigration Services, U.S.; Constitution, U.S.; Dual citizenship; Naturalization; Naturalization Act of 1790; *Oyama v. California*; *Ozawa v. United States*; Permanent resident status; Resident aliens; *United States v. Bhagat Singh Thind*; *United States v. Wong Kim Ark*.

CITIZENSHIP AND IMMIGRATION SERVICES, U.S.

IDENTIFICATION: Bureau of the U.S. Department of Homeland Security that oversees lawful immigration into the United States

DATE: Began operations on March 1, 2003

SIGNIFICANCE: The mandate given to this federal bureau was to establish immigration services, policies, and priorities that preserve the United States as a nation of immigrants by ensuring that no one is admitted into the country who may threaten public safety.

The United States Immigration and Naturalization Service (INS) was created as part of the Department of Justice in 1891. It was transferred to the Department of Labor in 1940. As a result of the tragic terrorist events and aftermath associated with September 11, 2001, President George W. Bush signed the Homeland Security Act into law on November 25, 2002. This law assigned the INS to the Department of Homeland Security. On March 1, 2003, the INS officially became the Bureau of Citizenship and Immigration Services (BCIS), renamed the U.S. Citizenship and Immigration Services (USCIS), with the charge to oversee lawful immigration to the United States. Eduardo Aguirre was appointed as the first director of the USCIS.

Priorities of the USCIS include the promotion of national security, elimination of immigration case backlogs, and improvement of customer services. It supervises lawful permanent residency, citizenship, employment authorization, intercountry adoptions, asylum and refugee status, replacement of immigration documents, and foreign student authorization. The USCIS adjudicates immigrant visa petitions, naturalization petitions, and asylum and refugee applications. It offers a variety of resources for immigrants, including a comprehensive orientation guide and copies of the Immigration and Nationality Act.

Alvin K. Benson

FURTHER READING

U.S. Citizenship and Immigration Services. *USCIS Issues Citizenship and Naturalization Facts.* Washington, D.C.: U.S. Department of Homeland Security, 2006.

U.S. Citizenship and Immigration Services. Office of Citizenship. *The Citizen's Almanac: Fundamental Documents, Symbols, and Anthems of the United States.* Washington, D.C.: U.S. Citizenship and Immigration Services, 2007.

SEE ALSO: Border Patrol, U.S.; Bureau of Immigration, U.S.; Citizenship; Constitution, U.S.; Homeland Security, Department of; Illegal immigration; Immigration and Nationality Act of 1965; Immigration and Naturalization Service, U.S.; Immigration law; Naturalization.

CIVIL RIGHTS MOVEMENT

THE EVENT: Nationwide social movement to ensure full social and legal equality for all citizens regardless of race or ethnicity

DATE: 1930's-1970's

LOCATION: All parts of the United States but primarily in the South

SIGNIFICANCE: The U.S. government's policies regarding immigration have historically reflected prevailing racial and cultural biases held by Americans with the most power. Therefore, the successes and failures of the Civil Rights movement, in its impact on American consciousness, directly influenced the immigrant experience in America.

The traditional time line for the Civil Rights movement is 1954-1965 or 1968, beginning with the Supreme Court's *Brown v. Board of Education* decision (1954) and ending with either the Voting Rights Act (1965) or the assassination of Martin Luther King, Jr. (1968). However, the growing consensus among historians is that the movement really begins during the 1930's and lasts at least through the Black Power era into the 1970's. Traditionally, historians have examined how the Civil Rights movement played out in the South, where activists challenged Jim Crow laws. However, historians have studied the effects of the Civil Rights movement elsewhere, particularly in the urban North, the Midwest, and the West.

From 1910 through 1930, more than one million African Americans migrated out of the South into northern cities. The migrants left in part to escape the violent Jim Crow-dominated communities that left them disenfranchised following the end of Reconstruction. In the North, blacks found dirty, crowded cities as well as housing and employment discrimination. These tensions were further exacerbated by the influx of more African Americans, as well as other laborers, during World War II to fill labor needs in northern industries. In many places during the war, various immigrant groups and African Americans formed political alliances as they mutually experienced the failures of civil rights liberalism.

PROTEST AND LEGISLATIVE VICTORIES

The large numbers of African Americans in northern cities during the 1950's and 1960's facilitated southern blacks' battle against Jim Crow laws because of northern blacks' proximity to one another and capacity to organize visibly as well as their newfound electoral clout. During this period, many organizations formed with the intention of ending racial discrimination and promoting equality for all American citizens. Groups such as the Congress of Racial Equality, the Student Nonviolent Coordinating Committee, and the Southern Christian Leadership Conference registered black voters, staged sit-ins and marches, and attempted to integrate racially segregated spaces. Three major legal victories were claimed by civil rights activists: The Supreme Court's *Brown* v. *Board of Education* decision began to integrate public schools; the Civil Rights Act of 1964 protected citizens against discrimination based on race, color, or national origin; and the Voting Rights Act of 1965 protected citizens' voting rights regardless of race or color. Additionally, various groups, such as the Black Panthers and the Puerto Rican Young Lords, continued to work for social equality in their communities.

IMMIGRATION AND NATIONALITY ACT OF 1965

The most significant effect of the Civil Rights movement for immigrants was the passage of the Immigration and Nationality Act of 1965. President Lyndon B. Johnson signed this bill into law at the foot of the Statue of Liberty on October 3, 1965. The act diverged in spirit and substance from some of the nation's most restrictive immigration legislation, such as the Chinese Exclusion Act of 1882, the Immigration Act of 1924, and the Immigration and Nationality Act of 1952 (also known as the McCarran-Walter Act). While the 1965 law still provided caps on the numbers of immigrants from certain places throughout the world, it ended discrimination based on national origin. Furthermore, it provided for family reunification, allowing immigrants living in the United States to bring their families into the country. While the prevailing opinion in 1965 was that immigration patterns would not drastically change because of this legislation, the number of immigrants, particularly from previously excluded countries, was much higher than anticipated.

Laurie Lahey

FURTHER READING

Countryman, Matthew J. *Up South: Civil Rights and Black Power in Philadelphia*. Philadelphia: University of Pennsylvania Press, 2007. Examines how the groups most affected by the failure of civil rights liberalism coped in post-World War II Philadelphia.

Graham, Hugh Davis. *Collision Course: The Strange Convergence of Affirmative Action and Immigration Policy in America*. New York: Oxford University Press, 2003. Examines how the Civil Rights Act of 1964 and the Immigration Act of 1965 eventually came into conflict with each other as immigrants and African Americans competed for jobs.

Hall, Jacquelyn Dowd. "The Long Civil Rights Movement and the Political Uses of the Past." *Journal of American History* 91, no. 4 (March, 2005): 1233-1263. A groundbreaking and widely respected article that challenges the traditional frameworks of Civil Rights movement historiography.

Johnson, Kevin R. *The "Huddled Masses" Myth: Immigration and Civil Rights*. Philadelphia: Temple University Press, 2004. Focuses on how discrimination has influenced U.S. legislation regarding immigration by examining the exclusion of groups deemed unfavorable due to sexual orientation, disabilities, political beliefs, race, and so on.

Pulido, Laura. *Black, Brown, Yellow, and Left: Radical Activism in Los Angeles*. Berkeley: University of California Press, 2006. Pulido examines African American, Japanese American, and Chicano interracial relationships in Southern California during the 1960's and 1970's as these groups struggled for equality.

Sugrue, Thomas. *Sweet Land of Liberty: The Forgotten Struggle for Civil Rights in the North.* New York: Random House, 2008. Sugrue studies the Civil Rights movement in the North, where close to one million African Americans migrated during the Great Migration and competed with immigrants for housing and employment.

Varzally, Allison. *Making a Non-White America: Californians Coloring Outside Ethnic Lines, 1925-1955.* Berkeley: University of California Press, 2008. Considers how various immigrant and native-born groups competed and aligned in diverse California neighborhoods during the early years of the Civil Rights movement.

SEE ALSO: Affirmative action; African Americans and immigrants; Chicano movement; Coalition for Humane Immigrant Rights of Los Angeles; Commission on Civil Rights, U.S.; Employment; Japanese American Citizens League; *Lau v. Nichols*; Mexican American Legal Defense and Educational Fund; *Sei Fujii v. State of California*.

CIVIL WAR, U.S.

THE EVENT: Large-scale war fought between the Northern states of the Union and eleven Southern slaveholding states of the Confederacy that declared their secession from the United States

DATE: 1861-1865

LOCATION: Principally in the southern United States

SIGNIFICANCE: Immigrants played leading roles in the Civil War and the reconstruction of the South. Apart from slavery, few issues were as important in Civil War America as immigrants and immigration policy. Immigrant settlement patterns in the earlier decades of the nineteenth century demonstrated an ever-deepening division between the North and the South that would soon explode into open war.

From the founding of the United States through the first quarter of the nineteenth century, white American culture was generally homogenous; most whites were Protestant and could trace their ancestry to Great Britain. The slaves and free blacks in America were notable exceptions, but isolated pockets of non-British and/or non-Protestant whites were also scattered throughout America. The latter included French and Spanish in Louisiana and Florida, Germans in Pennsylvania and parts of the Carolinas, and the descendants of Dutch settlers in New York.

Several of the Founders, including Thomas Jefferson, were ambivalent about immigration and argued that it should be limited to those who were culturally and politically similar to native-born Americans. By the 1850's, however, most immigrants were either non-English speaking or non-Protestant. Local reactions were sometimes extreme. During the 1840's and 1850's, anti-immigrant riots occurred in New Orleans, Philadelphia, Baltimore, Louisville, and St. Louis. In the same decades, antipathy toward immigrants led to the development of the Know-Nothing Party, whose dominant plank was the restriction of immigration.

IMMIGRANTS ON THE EVE OF THE CIVIL WAR

Despite the prejudice and violence, immigration increased more than 500 percent from 1845 until 1855, with about three million immigrants coming to the United States. Almost 90 percent settled in the North or the West, where either jobs or cheap land, or both, were plentiful. German and Hungarian farmers tended to settle in the central and upper Midwest. By 1860, more than 1.25 million Americans of German descent lived in the United States.

Unskilled and semiskilled immigrants from Ireland, Wales, and Italy settled in urban or industrialized areas in Pennsylvania, New York, and New England. These immigrants, particularly the Irish, often found themselves competing against native-born white Americans and free blacks for low-paying jobs. The million Irish immigrants who came to America were survivors of the Great Irish Famine (1845-1852) and could be both tenacious and incredibly brutal, as events in 1862-1863 would show.

From 1830 until 1860, relatively few immigrants settled in the South. The southern political elite opposed homesteading and government spending for infrastructure, such as canal or railroad construction. Further, there was less capital invested in industrial development in the South, thus fewer factory jobs for immigrants. Despite these facts, there were some immigrant communities in the South, especially in the cities. Historian David Gleeson points out that the population of Savannah, Memphis, and New Orleans ranged from 20 to 25 percent Irish. Besides the Irish, New Orleans had an economically strong community of free black immigrants from Haiti.

The vast numbers of immigrants who flooded into the North and West during the nineteenth century provided evidence of a vibrant, blended economy of small farms and urban centers with brisk entrepreneurial and industrial sectors. Far fewer immigrants settled in the South, where the single-crop farming economy was strong, but where job creation was less rapid, and where slave labor limited employment opportunities for unskilled la-

borers. During the Civil War, immigrants provided a source of manpower for the North but proved troublesome as the war dragged on. Finally, after the war, northern and southern politicians contended over immigration policy in their efforts to reconstruct the South.

IMMIGRANTS IN UNIFORM

When the Civil War broke out in 1861, America's standing army consisted of about seventeen thousand troops, stationed mostly along the western frontier. Many of these soldiers resigned to serve in the Confederate armed forces. To expand the northern army and to build the southern one, each national government depended upon militia troops raised by the states.

Fortunately for the states, there were literally hundreds of various semiprofessional military organizations connected haphazardly with various lo-

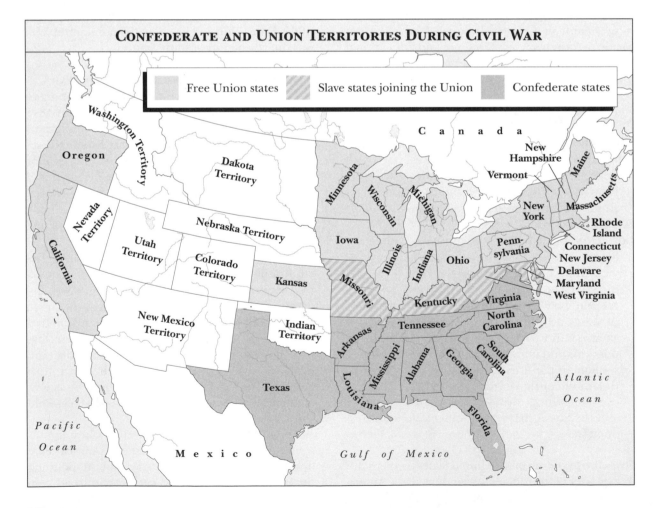

CONFEDERATE AND UNION TERRITORIES DURING CIVIL WAR

Free Union states / Slave states joining the Union / Confederate states

cal governments. In the North, many of these had an ethnic flavor. When war broke out, these drilling societies and irregular companies, native-born or immigrant, were usually integrated into various state militias.

Immigrants could find themselves enrolled in a predominantly ethnic unit in another way. In 1861, most states encouraged local recruiting, allowing hundreds of men from small towns and counties to form their own companies and elect their own officers. Where large immigrant communities existed, new militia companies were predominantly foreign born. For example, the Ninth Ohio Volunteer Infantry consisted almost entirely of German immigrants, many with previous military experience in Germany. The unit's officers followed German military practices and issued commands in German. Similar units were raised in Wisconsin, Missouri, Pennsylvania, and New York. In all, about 200,000 German immigrants served in the Union forces.

About 140,000 Irish-born soldiers served in the Union forces, with about one-third serving in New York State forces. The Army of the Potomac's famous Irish Brigade was made of a number of predominantly Irish units: the 63d, 69th, and 88th New York, the 28th Massachusetts, and the 116th Pennsylvania. Other famous Irish units included the Irish Legion: the 155th, 164th, 170th, and 180th New York, and the Hibernian Guards, a company of the 8th Ohio Volunteers.

New York's units were especially multicultural. One polyglot regiment from New York—the Garibaldi Guards—consisted of roughly three hundred Germans, three hundred Hungarians, one hundred Swiss, one hundred Italians, one hundred French, and one hundred combined Spanish and Portuguese.

Although immigrants also served in the Confederate forces, there were almost no distinctive immigrant units. Immigration patterns before the war explain this difference. Far fewer immigrants lived in the South, and their communities were smaller. A community of a few dozen families could hardly be expected to furnish the hundred volunteers necessary to form a company. In addition, some of the larger immigrant communities—such as the free black immigrants from Haiti in New Orleans—did not volunteer for the Confederacy.

Few immigrants were motivated to enlist by the political rhetoric of either the North or the South. In fact, as historians Richard F. Welch and Susannah U. Bruce point out, immigrants were more often moved to enlist by economic need or loyalty to neighbors, family, and friends who were themselves enlisting. Some Irish immigrants enlisted for military experience, hoping eventually to drive the English out of Ireland. Other immigrants were motivated by fellow expatriates who personally appealed to them to enlist. In 1861-1863, the famous Irish general Thomas Francis Meagher was sent on many recruiting trips throughout New York to exhort Irish volunteers to enlist.

IMMIGRANTS ON THE HOME FRONT

As the war developed, northern strategy demanded ever-increasing numbers of soldiers, yet the U.S. government was faced with increasing public disillusionment over the prosecution of the war, its casualties and costs.

In 1862, northern efforts to win the war were fruitless, marked by increasingly costly campaigns that failed to defeat the Confederacy. Public frustrations with repeated military disasters were intensified by the press. In 1861, many northern newspapers ran hawkish editorials demanding victory at all costs. By 1862, these were replaced by dovish pleading for peace at any price.

In light of defeatism in the press and military disasters in the field, voluntary enlistments plummeted. As a result, individual states in the North resorted to drafts to meet their federal quotas. As one might expect, these worsened an already sour public mood. Immigrant communities throughout the North expressed their frustrations violently. In 1862, there were antidraft riots in four states, including immigrant areas in the coalfields of Pennsylvania and the German American farming communities of Wisconsin. In each case, federal troops had to be sent in to quell the violence.

With lessons unlearned, the U.S. government in 1863 issued a new national draft, which provoked the worst outbreak of civil disorder in the country with the exception of the Civil War itself. For three days, a largely Irish working-class mob plundered New York City, looting, burning, attacking police and city officials, and killing any black person it could find.

The New York City riot demonstrated the intensity of Irish immigrant anger over related issues: an-

Federal troops firing on draft rioters in New York City. (Gay Brothers)

ger over the Emancipation Proclamation of January, 1863, which seemed to demonstrate perceived favoritism toward black people, as well as fear that the newly liberated slaves would flood the North and increase the economic pressure on the Irish. In short, the Irish of New York City—who competed with free black people for the lowest-paying industrial jobs, and who had themselves experienced extensive prejudice—believed that they were being forced to die so that others could be free to come North and take their jobs. Historian Richard Welch points out, in fact, that this had happened as late as June, 1862, when black workers were hired as "scab" laborers during a shipyard workers' strike.

Eventually, the riot was suppressed, and even the most militant immigrants learned that federal draft laws did not target them. In fact, far more of the rural, native-born poor were forced into service than their urban immigrant counterparts.

As one might expect, urban industrial workers were often exempted for economic reasons. The structural challenge faced by the federal government from 1861 until 1865 was to expand the economy while replacing the vast numbers of experienced farmers and workers who were now in uniform. To meet this challenge, the federal government introduced new legislation to promote increased immigration to meet the demands of the wartime economy. In 1862-1863, Congress passed a homestead law and a law allowing immigration for the purposes of labor contracts. Previous versions of these bills had been proposed before the Civil War but had always been blocked by legislators in the South. As a result of these laws, immigration surged once again, with subsequent railroad expansion, as well as increased production of food, textiles, clothing, and military technologies.

THE WAR'S AFTERMATH

Prewar settlement patterns led to the northern and western immigrant communities that sometimes caused chaos in the North, yet which also contributed enormous numbers of soldiers to win the war. After the war, the status of certain immigrant groups increased tremendously in both the North and the South. Immigrants were perceived as a crucial element in various competing strategies for economic recovery in the South.

Northern politicians who loathed the prewar planter aristocracy and feared their return to power passed the Southern Homestead Act of 1866 with the goal of breaking up the larger plantations into small family farms that could be parceled out to new immigrants. Ironically, southern politicians also hoped for increased immigration of northern or western European immigrants. They hoped to increase immigration to the South in order to flood the labor market and drive down wages in the South, thereby bringing the newly liberated slaves once more into economic subservience.

With this goal in mind, most southern states founded commissions to market the region to prospective European immigrants. Although pursued vigorously, these efforts were usually unsuccessful. Of the three million immigrants who came to America from 1865 to 1873, almost none settled in the South. Some historians contend that these efforts failed because they were founded on the unrealistic belief that immigrants would passively accept the sort of living conditions and treatment that slaves had been forced to endure. In 1866, an Alabama planter persuaded a group of thirty Swedish immigrants to settle on his plantation. He fed, housed, and clothed them as he had formerly provided for his slaves. Nevertheles, they all quit within a week.

Michael R. Meyers

FURTHER READING

Anbinder, Tyler. "Which Poor Man's Fight? Immigrants and the Federal Conscription of 1863." *Civil War History* 52, no. 4 (2006): 344-372. Study of conscription records demonstrating that immigrant groups were not unfairly targeted by federal draft laws in 1863.

Bruce, Susannah U. *The Harp and the Eagle: Irish-American Volunteers and the Union Army, 1861-1865.* New York: New York University Press, 2006. Recounts the motives and exploits of Irish immigrants during the war.

Foner, Eric. *Reconstruction: America's Unfinished Revolution, 1863-1877.* New York: Perennial, 1989. One of the best studies of the politics of the era.

Gleeson, David T. *The Irish in the South, 1815-1877.* Chapel Hill: University of North Carolina Press, 2001. One of the few modern studies of southern immigrants.

Kamphoefner, Walter, and Wolfgang Helbich, eds. *Germans in the Civil War: The Letters They Wrote Home.* Translated by Susan Carter Vogel. Chapel Hill: University of North Carolina Press, 2006. Presents the views of German immigrants on the war.

McPherson, James. *Battle Cry of Freedom: The Civil War Era.* New York: Oxford University Press, 1988. Although not specifically about immigrants, perhaps the best single-volume history of the war.

Silverman, Jason H., and Susan R. Silverman. *Immigration in the American South, 1864-1895.* Lewiston, N.Y.: Edwin Mellen Press, 2006. Account of southern efforts to market the region to prospective immigrants.

Welch, Richard F. "The Green and the Blue." *Civil War Times,* October, 2006, 22-30. A short account of the Irish Fenian movement and the war.

Woodworth, Steven E. "The Other Rock." *Civil War Times,* October, 2003, 44-56. An article on the exploits of a German unit during the war.

SEE ALSO: Abolitionist movement; African Americans and immigrants; European immigrants; German immigrants; History of immigration, 1783-1891; Homestead Act of 1862; Irish immigrants; Military conscription; New York City.

CLAIBORNE, LIZ

IDENTIFICATION: Belgian-born American fashion designer and entrepreneur
BORN: March 31, 1929; Brussels, Belgium
DIED: June 26, 2007; New York, New York

SIGNIFICANCE: One of the most successful female entrepreneurs in American business history, Belgian-born Claiborne founded Liz Claiborne, Inc., in 1976.

Born in Brussels, Belgium, Anne Elisabeth Jane Claiborne was the daughter of American-born parents, Omer Villere and Louise Carol Claiborne. Because of the growing threat of World War II, the family returned to the United States in 1939. Claiborne returned to Europe in 1947 to study art in Brussels and Nice, France. Returning to the United States in 1949, she moved to New York City to pursue a career in fashion design. During the 1970's, Claiborne recognized that increasing numbers of women were entering the workforce and that there would be a growing need for affordable

Liz Claiborne on her return to the United States in 1949. (AP/Wide World Photos)

and stylish women's business attire. In 1976, she founded Liz Claiborne, Inc. As the primary designer for the company, Claiborne attributed her sense of style to her European upbringing and her study of art.

In 1980, Claiborne was the first woman to be named Entrepreneurial Woman of the Year by the American fashion industry. In 1986, her company made the Fortune 500 list, giving Claiborne the distinction of being the first female chief executive officer of a Fortune 500 company.

Bernadette Zbicki Heiney

FURTHER READING

Brands, H. W. *Masters of Enterprise: Giants of American Business from John Jacob Astor and J. P. Morgan to Bill Gates and Oprah Winfrey.* New York: Free Press, 1999.

Landrum, Gene N. *Profiles of Female Genius: Thirteen Creative Women Who Changed the World.* Amherst, N.Y.: Prometheus Books, 1994.

SEE ALSO: Belgian immigrants; New York City; Women immigrants.

CLOTILDE SLAVE SHIP

THE EVENT: The last sailing ship rumored to have completed a voyage to West Africa for the purpose of obtaining and transporting a cargo of African slaves to the southern United States prior to the beginning of the Civil War
DATE: 1859
LOCATION: Alabama

SIGNIFICANCE: The case of the *Clotilde* marks the end of successful slave trading by American vessels and is notable both for the evasion of U.S. Navy patrols attempting to interdict such voyages and the eventual failure of the federal government to successfully prosecute those responsible.

The story of the slaving voyage of the schooner *Clotilde* begins in 1858 on a steamboat on the Alabama River when a wealthy shipyard owner named Timothy Meaher, during a discussion of secession and the federal campaign against the importation of Africans as slaves, wagered a group of other Southerners $100,000 that he could accomplish such a feat within two years' time. Beginning in 1794, a series of U.S. laws barred both such importation and the fitting out of vessels intended for use in the slave trade, with government agents in all major ports to search for infractions. Despite the strengthening of legal penalties for individuals engaged in slave trading, the importation of slaves continued, although the bulk of the slave population of the southern states was by this time native born.

Learning that the wars of the kingdom of Dahomey had resulted in a large supply of captives for export at the slave port of Whydah, Meaher chose the *Clotilde* (which he had constructed in 1856) for the expedition because of its speed and cargo capacity: eighty-six feet in length and twenty-three feet wide with a copper-clad hull. One hundred and sixty slaves were purchased and taken aboard in West Africa and transported to a prearranged location on the Alabama River. Widespread rumors of the voyage had alerted the federal authorities, who regarded the slave cargo as contraband and the crew and officers of the ship as pirates. To avoid authorities, Meaher arranged for the slaves to be transshipped to a steamboat and taken up to the canebrake region, where they were hidden for twelve days, while the *Clotilde* itself was set afire and scuttled and the crew smuggled to Montgomery and sent by train to New York City. During this time, Meaher was arrested, charged with illegal importation, and released on bond. Efforts by the federal authorities to locate the slaves proved fruitless, as the sponsors of the voyage were alerted by Meaher and dispersed the group according to the original agreement.

Formal legal proceedings against Meaher and his associates were dismissed in the spring of 1861 because the federal government was unable to prove its case because of the manner in which Meaher had supposedly arranged affairs to mask his involvement. Local opinion varied as to the reality of the entire affair, with the idea that the whole business had been a hoax gaining some acceptance due to lack of agreement as to the precise sequence of events. A second complicating factor was that by the time the trial was to have begun, Alabama had seceded from the Union and the Civil War had been declared, with a federal judge ruling that the locale of the incident was now beyond U.S. jurisdiction. The combination of narrative detail and lack of solid evidence against any of the principals substantiated in a court of law makes the *Clotilde* case a perfect example of the tangled legal obstacles faced by federal authorities in the prosecution of slave traders and their supporters.

Robert B. Ridinger

FURTHER READING

Diouf, Sylviane A. *Dreams of Africa in Alabama: The Slave Ship Clotilda and the Story of the Last Africans Brought to America.* New York: Oxford University Press, 2007.

Lockett, James D. "The Last Ship That Brought Slaves from Africa to America: The Landing of the *Clotilde* at Mobile in the Autumn of 1859." *Western Journal of Black Studies* 22, no. 3 (1998): 159-163.

SEE ALSO: Abolitionist movement; African immigrants; Alabama; Civil War, U.S.; Slave trade.

COAL INDUSTRY

DEFINITION: Rapidly expanding industry that was largely dependent on immigrant labor through its formative period during the nineteenth century Industrial Revolution

SIGNIFICANCE: The American coal industry relied heavily on immigrant labor during the late nineteenth and early twentieth centuries. Immigrant miners exerted a powerful and pervasive influence upon life in coal mining towns and figured prominently in early organized labor movements.

Used as a source of fuel and warmth since ancient times, coal was first mined in the United States in mid-eighteenth century Virginia and was mined on a large scale in the Appalachian Mountains of Virginia and Pennsylvania starting in the mid-nineteenth century. The discovery of large coal deposits in the central Appalachian region of Kentucky, Virginia, and West Virginia during the Civil War and later in the midwestern states and western territories resulted in dramatic expansion of the coal industry and a corresponding increase in the demand for mine labor. In order to fulfill this demand, the coal industry attracted large numbers of immigrant laborers from various countries during its formative period.

IMMIGRANT MINERS

Immigrants to the United States came to the coal mines through a variety of means. Some were attracted by labor agents stationed in major ports of entry who often resorted to elaborate and deceptive descriptions of living and working conditions in the mines. Others followed friends and relatives to coal towns and camps. Early immigrant miners were primarily natives of coal mining regions of Great Britain and Ireland. Wales, a region containing numerous coal mines, was heavily represented, and a continuous influx of Irish labor during the nineteenth century ensured the presence of large numbers of Irish miners in most coal-producing regions.

The ethnic composition of immigrant coal miners changed dramatically toward the end of the nineteenth century as large numbers of eastern and southern European immigrants flooded into coal mining towns and camps. As both demand for mine labor and demands of miners for better pay and working conditions increased, coal mine operators began actively recruiting immigrants from these regions to increase their labor pools and to foster linguistic, religious, and cultural divisions intended to complicate the efforts of miners to organize. These divisions, often exacerbated by the physical separation of ethnic groups within coal mining towns and camps, occasionally resulted in violent clashes.

INTERACTION AND CONFLICT

Although segregation of African American, native-born, and immigrant miners was common

"Breaker boys" in a Kingston, Pennsylvania, anthracite coal mine in 1900. Predominantly immigrants, these boys often worked fourteen- to sixteen-hour days separating slate from the coal after it was taken out of the mine shafts. (Library of Congress)

in coal towns and camps, attitudes toward the social adjustment of eastern and southern immigrants varied. Many coal mine operators preferred that immigrants continue to retain their native languages and customs to foster dependence upon management and segregation from other miners, while others encouraged immigrant miners and their families to learn English and adopt "American" values and customs. Attitudes toward assimilation also varied among immigrant miners; many adamantly preserved their native culture, while others sought rapid assimilation, sometimes Anglicizing their surnames and changing religious affiliations.

Interethnic tension among immigrant miners often complicated life in coal mining camps and towns. Many of these tensions were religious in nature; others, such as conflicts between British miners and later arrivals from Poland, Czechoslovakia, Greece, and other eastern and southern European nations, revolved around ethnicity. Still others, such as the backlash against German immigrants during World War I, were precipitated by popular perceptions of geopolitical events and trends.

ACTIVISM AND REACTION

The rise of organized labor in the United States during the late nineteenth and early twentieth centuries weakened many of these ethnic and cultural barriers by drawing large numbers of immigrant miners into their ranks, but also strengthened existing stereotypes of foreigners as radicals and revolutionaries. Although initially dominated by British miners, the immigrant ranks of coal mining unions had begun accepting, and later actively recruiting, members from other regions of Europe. Immigrants constituted a substantial number of new recruits to the United Mine Workers of America (UMWA) during the 1890's, during which membership in the union increased nearly tenfold.

Traditions of political radicalism already existed in many immigrant mining communities, some of which contained residents who had participated in socialist or anarchist movements in their countries of origin. The real or perceived presence of political radicals within the ranks of immigrant miners provoked harsh reactions from many labor opponents, who exploited fears of foreign influence to provoke clashes between unions and antilabor groups that often erupted into violence.

The entry of the United States into World War I in 1917, the rise of communism in the Soviet Union following the end of the war, and ongoing reports of radical political activity attributed to immigrants produced a backlash against southern and eastern European immigration, resulting in escalated discrimination against these immigrants and legal restrictions upon further immigration, including the Espionage Act of 1917 and the Sedition Act of 1918, the Immigration Acts of 1921 and 1924, and the Alien Immigration Act of 1930. The Immigration Acts in particular resulted in a dramatic decrease in southern and eastern European immigration.

A Lasting Impact

Immigrants exerted a significant and lasting impact upon the coal mining industry in all coal-producing regions of the United States. Before the arrival of immigrants, many communities in these regions were racially, ethnically, and religiously homogeneous, yet by the mid-twentieth century, persons of a variety of geographical and cultural backgrounds had resided in these areas for generations, their customs and folkways a permanent although sometimes obscure part of the local culture. Meanwhile, the influx of immigrants to mines continued on a much smaller scale as coal mines in western states employed increasing numbers of Hispanic immigrants during the late twentieth century.

Michael H. Burchett

Further Reading

Bartoletti, Susan Campbell. *Growing Up in Coal Country.* Boston: Houghton Mifflin, 1996. Social history of Pennsylvania coal camps during the late nineteenth and early twentieth centuries. Discusses the role of immigrants in the social structure of coal camps and in early labor movements.

Corbin, David. *Life, Work, and Rebellion in the Coal Fields: The Southern West Virginia Miners, 1880-1920.* Champaign: University of Illinois Press, 1989. Contains detailed discussion of immigrant labor recruitment to the coal mines of West Virginia and the participation of immigrant miners in labor movements.

Eller, Ronald. *Miners, Millhands, and Mountaineers: Industrialization of the Appalachian South, 1880-1930.* Knoxville: University of Tennessee Press, 1982. Discusses recruiting of immigrant labor and the social structure of coal mining towns and camps.

Shiflett, Crandall. *Coal Towns: Life, Work, and Culture in Company Towns of Southern Appalachia, 1880-1960.* Knoxville: University of Tennessee Press, 1995. General history of coal camps, including discussion of interactions between immigrant and nonimmigrant coal miners.

United States Immigration Commission. *Immigrants in Industry: Bituminous Coal Mining V1 (1911).* Whitefish, Mont.: Kessinger, 2008. Reprint of federal study provides primary source information on immigrants in coal mining.

SEE ALSO: Economic opportunities; European immigrants; Iowa; Iron and steel industry; Kentucky; Labor unions; Mexican immigrants; Molly Maguires; Oklahoma; Pennsylvania; Virginia; West Virginia; World War I.

COALITION FOR HUMANE IMMIGRANT RIGHTS OF LOS ANGELES

IDENTIFICATION: Immigrant support organization
DATE: Founded in 1986
LOCATION: Los Angeles, California
ALSO KNOWN AS: CHIRLA

SIGNIFICANCE: Since its creation, the Coalition for Humane Immigrant Rights of Los Angeles (CHIRLA) has worked as an immigrant advocacy group with Southern California's Los Angeles County. The group provides job-skills training, union organizing, voter registration, and research to challenge anti-immigrant stereotypes. A DVD it produced, *Know Your Rights!*, has become a popular tool among members of immigrant communities.

As the center of a vibrant culture, sprawling Los Angeles County boasts a history full of ethnic diversity drawn from immigrants all over the world. These immigrants and their families have historically faced housing, job, and wage discrimination, and inability to communicate fluently in English has inhibited the ability of many immigrants to assert their rights. CHIRLA was founded to bridge the gap between immigrants and those employing them. Its purpose is to advocate fair wages, increased employment and education opportunities, and the end of negative immigrant stereotypes.

CHIRLA was built on the collaboration of several immigrant-rights lobbying and law groups. These included the Central American Resource Center, the Asian Pacific American Legal Center, the Los Angeles Center for Law and Justice, and the Mexican American Legal Defense and Education Fund. Although CHIRLA has represented members of all immigrant communities in Los Angeles, it has been especially outspoken on behalf of the large numbers of Latin American immigrants, and it maintains a Web site in Spanish and English.

CHIRLA PROGRAMS

Through the implementation of what it calls its California Dream Network, CHIRLA worked alongside other organizations on a movement to pass legislation for undocumented students to pay resident-student tuition rates in California public colleges and universities. Under the title of Proposition AB540, this legislation became law on October 11, 2001. CHIRLA also created a group for student activists, called the Wise Up! program, that cultivates youth leadership for outreach, lobbying, and demonstrations. The membership of Wise Up! was made up primarily of students who, for various reasons, were classified as undocumented even though they had been residents of California since infancy. Trained and organized by CHIRLA, these students worked diligently to promote their eligibility to declare legal residency on college applications.

In 2001, California governor Gray Davis signed AB540 into law, allowing thousands of students access to affordable college education. CHIRLA also worked alongside the Immigrant Legal Resource Center in 2007 to create an online manual, *Living in the United States: A Guide for Immigrant Youth*, that serves as a guidebook for adolescent immigrants. This manual answers questions about deportation, voting rights, obtaining green cards, naturalizing, obtaining Social Security cards, and other topics.

CHIRLA has also represented female domestic workers across Los Angeles. Its Household Workers program was created out of the need to protect domestic workers from wage theft and exploitation by employers and employment agencies. To promote this effort, CHIRLA hired a bus and distributed five thousand copies of a specially created Spanish-language comic book, *Super Doméstica en: El Caso de las Trabajadoras Explotadas* (Super Doméstica in the house of the exploited workers) to women making their way to domestic jobs. The "Super Doméstica" of the book's title is a caped superhero who shows immigrant domestic workers how to obtain their rights.

CHIRLA maintains that domestic workers are an intimate and valued part of American family life and, as such, should be protected with full rights under the law. The Household Workers program often holds rallies to promote public awareness of domestic workers' rights.

IMMIGRATION AND NATIONALITY ACT OF 1965

Section 287(g) of the Immigration and Nationality Act called for the cooperation of state and local law enforcement with federal authorities in the capture of illegal immigrants. CHIRLA has worked with other groups to help protect immigrants from unlawful arrest. To that end, it created a video and fact sheet to help prevent fraudulent seizures in the Los Angeles area. The video, *Know Your Rights!*, depicts a dramatized raid on a factory in which Latinos are working, as well as a scene where a police officer pulls an Asian driver over and impounds her vehicle. In another scene, officers of the United States Immigration and Customs Enforcement (ICE) surprise a Latino couple in their home. The video serves to underline how people should behave when they are taken into custody and how they should avoid providing information that might be used against them. CHIRLA's fact sheet on 287(g) further details the mistakes made by police and ICE officials who have deported people

Coast Guard, U.S.

with mental disabilities and those who have been citizens.

CRITICISMS OF CHIRLA

CHIRLA has been criticized by anti-immigration groups for its creation and maintenance of a support program for day laborers in Los Angeles. Through this program, CHIRLA has encouraged members of the community to come together by inviting citizens, police, business leaders, and day laborers to discuss their issues openly. CHIRLA's program has worked to fight stereotypes of day laborers, who have developed a poor image from congregating on street corners and parking lots while soliciting day jobs.

Groups such as the Federation for American Immigration Reform (FAIR) that encourage citizens to report illegal hiring of immigrants maintain that any support for undocumented day laborers is illegal and should be prosecuted. Although CHIRLA defends the right of day laborers to seek work, anti-immigration groups maintain that these people are loiterers and public nuisances. Despite these stereotypes, CHIRLA continues to advocate for day laborers, working with the National Day Laborer Organizing Network to promote the protection of civil and labor rights.

Shannon Oxley

FURTHER READING

Buiza, Cynthia, ed. *Beyond Myths and Stereotypes: Facts About Immigration and Crime.* Los Angeles: CHIRLA, 2008. Pamphlet that debunks stereotypes of immigrants as criminals.
_____. *Local Law Enforcement and Immigration: The 287(g) Program in Southern California.* Los Angeles: CHIRLA, 2008. Pamphlet underscoring the failures of law enforcement in regard to section 287(g) of the Immigration and Nationality Act of 1965 in Southern California.
Garr, Robin. *Reinvesting in America: The Grassroots Movements That Are Feeding the Hungry, Housing the Homeless, and Putting Americans Back to Work.* Reading, Mass.: Addison-Wesley Longman, 1995. Analysis of community service organizations in the United States that provides background information on CHIRLA.

SEE ALSO: *Born in East L.A.*; Captive Thai workers; El Rescate; Farm and migrant workers; Immigrant

aid organizations; Immigration Reform and Control Act of 1986; Labor unions; Los Angeles; Proposition 187.

COAST GUARD, U.S.

IDENTIFICATION: U.S. maritime military and civilian service
DATE: Founded on August 4, 1790

SIGNIFICANCE: The United States Coast Guard is a unique multimission, maritime agency categorized as one of five branches of the U.S. armed forces. Its major role is to protect the nation's ports and waterways or any maritime region, including international waters, as required or requested to support national security. The Coast Guard specifically looks to protect the public, the environment, and governmental interests by maintaining safe waterways.

The United States Coast Guard (USCG) is tasked with enforcement of maritime law, mariner assistance including search and rescue, and national security of all major waterways, particularly coasts and ports; and interstate bodies of such as lakes, streams, and rivers within the United States; and sometimes in international waters.

The Coast Guard's history can be traced back to August 4, 1790, when the first Congress, under the encouragement of Secretary of the Treasury Alexander Hamilton, authorized the construction of ten vessels to enforce tariff and trade laws while attempting to prevent smuggling, thus predating the nation's first official navy by eight years. Through the early twentieth century, the Coast Guard was known as the Revenue Marine and Cutter Service, until it received its present name in 1915 under an act of Congress combining the maritime service with the new mandate of life-saving operations. This new single maritime armed service would now dedicate its efforts to saving lives at sea and enforcing the nation's maritime laws. Over time as the country grew, more responsibilities were given to the Coast Guard, including operation of the nation's lighthouses and former tasks of the Bureau of Marine Inspection and Navigation, including merchant marine licensing and merchant vessel safety.

227

MISSION AND ROLES

The Coast Guard has always been the smallest of the five U.S. military branches. In 2009, it had just over 40,000 active-duty members, roughly 8,000 reservists, and close to 37,000 civilian and auxiliary employees. However, the Coast Guard is unique because of its vast mission. For example, in times of peace, the Coast Guard can operate as part of the U.S. Department of Homeland Security, serving as the nation's front-line organization for enforcing laws at sea, protecting the marine environment, and saving lives. In times of war, or under the executive order of the president, the Coast Guard can become part of the Department of the Navy. In fact, since 1790 the Coast Guard has participated in every major war or conflict in which the United States has been involved.

The Coast Guard provides unique services to the nation because of its distinctive blend of military, civilian law-enforcement, and humanitarian capabilities. The Coast Guard has five specific roles as they pertain to the American public: search and rescue (SAR) pertaining to recreational boating, commercial fishing, and transportation; homeland security related directly to protection of waterways, ports, and coastlines from enemy combatants; environmental protection of the nation's coasts, waterways, sea habitats, and wildlife; maritime mobility, which is associated with ensuring safe passage of cargo for economical purposes; and maritime law enforcement and security, which focuses on enforcement of water-related federal laws dealing with the smuggling of aliens, illicit drugs, or counterfeit products as well as illegal fishing and boating operations.

Although the Coast Guard carries out all the aforementioned roles on a daily basis, the role of law enforcement and security has been deemed one of its most vital responsibilities. Aside from saving lives at sea on a daily basis, the Coast Guard has played a vital role since the terrorist attacks of September 11, 2001, in protecting and patrolling the nation's ports, coastlines, rivers, and other bodies of water. On average each day, the Coast Guard apprehends seventeen illegal immigrants; seizes one thousand pounds of illegal drugs; boards, inspects and searches roughly two hundred commercial and recreational vessels; and escorts roughly twenty boats that are either passenger vessels, military cargo ships, or boats carrying hazardous or toxic wastes. Because of the security changes instituted after the 2001 attacks, the Coast Guard has become one of the largest active law-enforcement agencies in use in the United States.

Paul M. Klenowski

FURTHER READING

Beard, Tom. *Coast Guard.* Seattle: Foundation for Coast Guard History, 2004. Provides the definitive story of the Coast Guard. Packed with unique historical facts and firsthand accounts of former "Coasties," this book is an excellent reference for those interested in learning more about the Coast Guard as both a military branch and an agency that serves the general public in various capacities.

Bonner, Kit, and Carolyn Bonner. *Always Ready: Today's U.S. Coast Guard.* St. Paul, Minn.: MBI, 2004. A concise look at the evolving mission and goals of the Coast Guard. In particular, specific detail is offered about the role the Coast Guard has carried out for the Department of Homeland Security in the wake of the terrorist attacks on September 11, 2001. Above all, the book is appropriate as a reference for understanding the varying missions of the Coast Guard.

Krietemeyer, George E. *The Coast Guardsman's Manual.* 9th ed. Annapolis, Md.: Naval Institute Press, 2008. This book is issued to new recruits as they enter boot camp for the Coast Guard. Offers a readable history of the Coast Guard, highlighting everything from its military roles to enforcement of maritime law and search and rescue missions.

Ostrom, Thomas P. *The United States Coast: 1790 to the Present.* Rev. ed. Oakland, Oreg.: Red Anvil Press, 2006. Detailed historical overview of the Coast Guard told from the viewpoint of a former member. Provides insight into the significance of the Coast Guard and its various roles in protecting U.S. waterways.

Phillips, Donald T., and James M. Loy. *Character in Action: The U.S. Coast Guard on Leadership.* Annapolis, Md.: Naval Institute Press, 2003. Offers a detailed look into how the Coast Guard has set a standard for creating young leaders.

Rasmussen, R. Kent. "Coast Guard, U.S." In *Magill's Guide to Military History,* edited by John Powell. Pasadena, Calif.: Salem Press, 2001. Concise history of the Coast Guard by a former Guardsman that pays special attention to the service's changing roles and its participation in national military conflicts.

SEE ALSO: Border Patrol, U.S.; Coolies; Drug trafficking; Haitian boat people; Homeland Security, Department of; 9/11 and U.S. immigration policy; Patriot Act of 2001; Transportation of immigrants.

COLOMBIAN IMMIGRANTS

SIGNIFICANCE: Although Colombian immigrants are relative newcomers to the United States, their numbers began increasing greatly during the last decades of the twentieth century. By 2008, Colombians were the largest South American immigrant group in the United States, accounting for 30 percent of all South Americans in the country and 2.65 percent of all documented immigrants.

Since the mid-twentieth century, tumultuous developments in Colombia have spurred large numbers of Colombians to emigrate to the United States. As in many other Latin American countries, Colombia's political instability has played a major role in motivating people to leave the country. Colombia has, in fact, lacked political stability since it became independent from the Spanish Empire in 1819. In 1948, a civil war broke out between conservative and liberal factions within the country. Throughout the 1950's—a period remembered as the *Violencia*—hundreds of thousands of Colombians were killed or displaced from their homes. The election of President Carlose Lleras Restrepo during the late 1960's brought some stability to the country. However, political turmoil returned in 1974, with the defeat of the ruling political party. The 1980's witnessed a dramatic upsurge of Colombia's political, social, and economic problems, due to the unprecedented factor of drug-related crime. The widespread sale and use of illegal drugs, particularly cocaine, was the primary catalyst for the continuing unrest in Colombia.

COLOMBIAN DIASPORA

The early twenty-first century has seen much debate over the actual number of Colombians resid-

ing in the United States. Colombia's own census bureau has estimated that 4.1 million Colombians were living abroad in 2005; about one-half of these people were living in the United States. However, data from the U.S. Census Bureau show only 730,510 Colombians living within U.S. borders during that year. The discrepancy between the Colombian and U.S. government figures is almost certainly due to the high levels of undocumented Colombian immigration into the United States.

The large number of Colombian natives living outside their homeland is evidence of a major diaspora. Historically, the numbers of Colombians who immigrated to the United States did not become significant until about 1948, when Colombia's civil war began. That war caused many rural Colombians to move into Colombia's urban areas. An overabundance of workers in the cities helped cause an economic recession, which in turn increased emi-

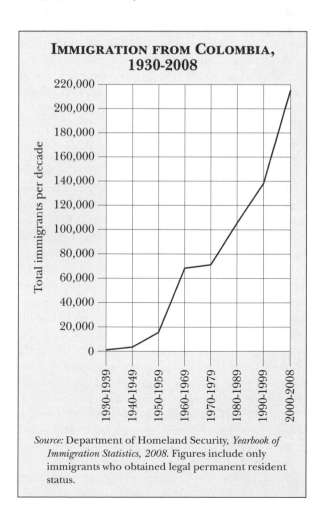

IMMIGRATION FROM COLOMBIA, 1930-2008

Source: Department of Homeland Security, *Yearbook of Immigration Statistics, 2008.* Figures include only immigrants who obtained legal permanent resident status.

gration to the United States. The disruptions of the *Violencia* era and growing social networks of Colombians in the United States also encouraged more Colombians to emigrate.

Through the end of the 1980's, Colombians living in the United States were almost exclusively upper-middle- and upper-class professionals. Migration of these individuals resulted in a massive brain drain from Colombia. During the 1990's, however, less educated Colombian laborers began immigrating to the United States in larger numbers.

The emergence of Colombia's illegal narcotics industry during the 1980's compounded the nation's political and economical problems. Drug-related crime began affecting the lives of everyday Colombians. Through murder, assassination, bombings, and kidnappings, the drug cartels gained so much power that they demanded political control and threatened the very foundation of Colombia's political structure. Growing political instability brought new levels of internal population movements and emigration. Many Colombians fled to Venezuela, Spain, and the United States. Colombia's problems with drug cartels, economic recession, and political instability persisted throughout the 1990's.

COLOMBIAN IMMIGRANTS TO THE UNITED STATES

Escalating violence and political disorder in Colombia have driven increasing numbers of its citizens to seek asylum in other countries, and most asylum seekers have come to the United States. In 2003, 11,600 Colombian immigrants classified as asylum seekers were in the United States, making Colombians the second-largest asylum applicant population. The U.S. government has the option of granting Colombians temporary protective status (TPS). This status is normally reserved for refugees from countries whose citizens are in grave imminent danger. However, that status is rarely granted, and the United States has not acknowledged appeals from human rights organizations and the Colombian government to grant Colombians the status. Colombians attempting to enter the United States must instead secure legal immigrant status—a process all immigrants face but whose difficulty many underestimate. Although many Colombians are granted legal permanent residence status, many others are stuck in an ambiguous, un-

---

PROFILE OF COLOMBIAN IMMIGRANTS

Country of origin	Colombia
Primary language	Spanish
Primary regions of U.S. settlement	New Jersey, South Florida
Earliest significant arrivals	Prob. nineteenth century, but U.S. did not record Colombians until 1930
Peak immigration period	1990's-Present
Twenty-first century legal residents*	201,061 (25,133 per year)

*Immigrants who obtained legal permanent resident status in the United States.
Source: Department of Homeland Security, *Yearbook of Immigration Statistics, 2008.*

---

documented category. In 2000, Colombia was believed to have the fourth-largest number of undocumented residents in the United States.

COLOMBIANS IN THE UNITED STATES

Since they first arrived in the United States in substantial numbers, Colombians have strived to establish their own identity among the numerous Hispanic populations and find their place within mainstream America. However, many immigrants endure the effects of stereotyping and discrimination because of negative American perceptions of Colombia as a drug-trafficking, criminal country, even though a minuscule number of Colombians in the United States engage in illegal activities.

Remittances, the transfers of money from Colombian Americans to relatives in Colombia, are an important part of immigrant life. In 2006 alone, Colombian residents of the United States remitted an estimated $4.2 billion to Colombia to aid relatives and friends. From 1990 to 2004, the dollar value of remittances to Colombia grew 25 percent annually. The increasing number of remittances further illustrates the dramatic rise in migration from Colombia to the United States, and provides evidence of greater interdependence between the two nations and their peoples.

Alexandria J. Murnan

FURTHER READING

Aysa-Lastra, Maria. *Diaspora Philanthropy: The Colombia Experience.* Cambridge, Mass.: Philanthropic Initiative and Global Equity Initiative, Harvard University, 2007. Overview of the Colombian diaspora and the remittances of Colombians in the United States to their homeland. This eighteen-page paper is available online in PDF format.

Collier, Michael W., et al. *The Colombian Diaspora in South Florida: A Report of the Colombian Studies Institute's Colombian Diaspora Project.* Dallas: Latin American Studies Association, 2003. Overview of the effects of the mass exodus from Colombia to South Florida. Available online in PDF format.

González, Juan. *Harvest of Empire: A History of Latinos in America.* New York: Viking Press, 2000. Useful historical overview of the many Hispanic peoples who have immigrated to the United States.

Reuners, David M. *Other Immigrants: The Global Origins of the American People.* New York: New York University Press, 2005. Broad examination of American immigrants that includes a useful chapter on Central and South Americans.

SEE ALSO: "Brain drain"; Censuses, U.S.; Drug trafficking; Ecuadorian immigrants; Latin American immigrants; Remittances of earnings; Stereotyping.

COLORADO

SIGNIFICANCE: Colorado has a unique immigration history that has been affected by its mining, agriculture, and tourism industries. The history of immigrant groups within the state is not limited to those that reside in Denver, but also includes immigrants from Europe, Asia, and Africa who have settled throughout the state.

Colorado's history regarding new immigrants is complicated by the fact that immigrant labor was eagerly welcomed in some areas and strongly opposed in others. After establishing its railroads and utilizing inexpensive labor in its mining industry during the nineteenth century, the state took an anti-immigrant stance. During the 1920's, it sought to reduce or eliminate foreign immigration into the state. However, by the late twentieth century, the state had become dependent on its substantial Hispanic population for labor, and its Hispanic leaders were making a dramatic impact both on Colorado and throughout the United States.

LATE NINETEENTH CENTURY IMMIGRATION

Even before Colorado became a state in 1876, waves of new settlers and immigrants peppered its plains, foothills, and mountains in search of fortune, employment, or simply arable farmland. Even as the state's first railroads were nearing completion during the 1880's, new settlers and miners were already living in Colorado. Many of them had come during the 1859 Pikes Peak gold rush and the formal annexation of the Rocky Mountain region into the United States. By 1880, Colorado had a population of nearly 200,000 people, who included, with sizeable numbers of Scandinavians, Irish and Scots working in the mining, railroad or farming industries. The discovery of silver in 1879 in Leadville continued to draw speculators and miners into the region.

The expansion of coal mining throughout the Colorado basin encouraged new waves of immigrants to move to the state. The exhausting and dangerous work of extracting coal from open-pit mines was often the only employment available to immigrants with limited education and limited access to working capital. Many immigrants from Italy, Germany, and Russia were hired to replace striking workers through the numerous violent clashes that erupted during Colorado's labor wars during the first decade of the twentieth century.

TWENTIETH CENTURY ARRIVALS

Immigration into the region was slowed during the early part of the twentieth century as numerous groups protested and demonstrated against new arrivals into the state. During the early 1920's, the Ku Klux Klan possessed considerable political clout and targeted immigrants, African Americans, and Roman Catholics through intimidation and violence. The Klan reached the peak of its influence in Colorado in 1924, with the election of Klansman Clarence Morely as the state's governor. Through-

---

PROFILE OF COLORADO

Region	Rocky Mountains
Entered union	1876
Largest cities	Denver (capital), Colorado Springs, Aurora, Lakewood, Fort Collins
Modern immigrant communities	Hispanics, Africans

Population	Total	Percent of state	Percent of U.S.	U.S. rank
All state residents	4,753,000	100.0	1.58	22
All foreign-born residents	489,000	10.3	1.3	16

Source: U.S. Census Bureau, *Statistical Abstract for 2006.*
Notes: The U.S. population in 2006 was 299,399,000, of whom 37,548,000 (12.5%) were foreign born. Rankings in last column reflect total numbers, not percentages.

---

out cities such as Denver, Pueblo, Canyon City, and Grand Junction, the organization sought to intimidate followers of the Roman Catholic Church, especially those of Italian descent.

In the years immediately following World War II, there was an influx of immigrants from Lithuania because of the Soviet occupation of that east European nation. However, that influx was limited and not sustained in subsequent years. In addition to the Lithuanian immigration, a sizable number of Germans and Central Americans moved into the area. Many of them were fleeing the aftereffects of the war. Some of the German immigrants were families of former prisoners of war who had been interned in Colorado camps during the war.

The second half of the twentieth century and the early twenty-first century saw a dramatic growth in Colorado's total population, from 1.3 million persons in 1950 to 5 million in 2008. Although the state's population continued to be predominantly white, Hispanic residents constituted about 20 percent of the total population by the turn of the new century. The majority of early Hispanic immigrants worked in various agricultural roles—either as migrant workers during the sugar beet and melon harvests or in meat-processing factories through-

out the northeastern region of the state. Meanwhile, the increasing Hispanic population began to influence regional, state, and national politics with the election of numerous Hispanic leaders to offices. These included Denver mayor Frederico Pena, who served from 1983 to 1991, and U.S. senator Ken Salazar, who was elected in 2004.

During the first decade of the twenty-first century, Colorado's Hispanic population continued to grow rapidly throughout the state. Other groups, however, were also being drawn to Colorado as the state's agriculture and tourist industries expanded. These new immigrants have continued to follow the traditional patterns of Colorado settlement by expanding beyond the urban centers located along the Front Range—the north-south corridor stretching from Fort Collins to Pueblo. Western Colorado, the eastern plains, and the central mountain areas of the state have also become homes to new arrivals. For example, in 2009 meatpacking houses in northeastern Colorado employed 650 Somali immigrants, and another 500 Africans—mostly from Senegal, Nigeria, and Morocco—were working in the resort areas of Colorado's mountains.

Robert D. Mitchell

FURTHER READING

Dorsett, Lyle W. *The Queen City: A History of Denver.* Boulder, Colo.: Pruett Publishing, 1977.

Mehls, Steven F. *The New Empire of the Rockies: A History of Northeast Colorado.* Washington, D.C.: Bureau of Land Management, 1984.

Ubbelohde, Carl. *A Colorado History.* Boulder, Colo.: Pruett Publishing, 1976.

SEE ALSO: Economic opportunities; Employment; History of immigration after 1891; Irish immigrants; Ku Klux Klan; Labor unions; Railroads.

COMMISSION ON CIVIL RIGHTS, U.S.

IDENTIFICATION: Independent, bipartisan federal commission created to monitor civil rights throughout the United States

DATE: Established on September 9, 1957

ALSO KNOWN AS: USCC

SIGNIFICANCE: The U.S. Commission on Civil Rights is a federal commission tasked with protecting the civil rights of all people residing in the United States. It investigates and studies and issues reports on various types of discrimination based on gender, race, religion, age, disability, or national origin. Created as a provision of the Civil Rights Act of 1957, the commission was originally intended to be temporary, but Congress has repeatedly renewed its mandate.

The commission was established as a result of the Civil Rights Act of 1957, which was signed into law by President Dwight D. Eisenhower on September 9, 1957. It originally contained six members, who were appointed by the president and approved by Congress. A 1983 reorganization increased that number to eight. The commission's primary mission was to investigate and to ensure the voting rights of African Americans. Indeed, its very first assignment was to collect evidence of racial discrimination in voting rights in the South. Since its creation, the commission has been restructured under the U.S. Commission on Civil Rights Acts of 1983, 1991, and the Civil Rights Commission Amendments Act of 1994. In addition to its early investigation of minority voting rights, the commission also held hearings on thousands of cases of housing discrimination in major U.S. cities and the implementation of the U.S. Supreme Court's ruling on public school desegregation in its 1954 *Brown v. Board of Education* ruling. The commission's investigations, hearings, and research became foundational components of the federal Civil Rights Acts of 1960 and 1964, the Voting Rights Act of 1965, and the Fair Housing Act of 1968.

The commission performs three basic tasks to protect civil rights:

- investigating citizen allegations of voter discrimination by reason of race, religion, sex, age, disability, or national origin, or by fraud
- collecting and analyzing information relating to discrimination or denials of equal protection of the law under the U.S. Constitution or in the administration of justice
- reviewing federal laws and policies with respect to discrimination and denial of equal rights

In carrying out its tasks, the commission issues public service announcements to discourage discrimination, holds hearings and issues subpoenas for documentation and witnesses at such hearings, and provides investigative reports to the president and his top cabinet officials, including the U.S. attorney general, regarding issues of discrimination. Because the commission has no real enforcement powers, it refers countless complaints to various federal, state, or local government enforcement agencies for appropriate legal action.

In 2009, the commission still had eight commissioners, who serve six-year staggered terms. Four commissioners are appointed directly by the president, two by the president pro tempore of the U.S. Senate, and two by the Speaker of the House of Representatives. To avoid issues related to political ideologies, no more than four commissioners may be from the same political party. Furthermore, each pair of Senate and House appointees cannot be from the same political party. The president, with the consent of the majority of commission members, can designate a chair, vice chair, and staff director. Additionally, the commission appoints fifty-one state advisory committees to serve as watchdogs in the fifty states and the District of Columbia.

Paul M. Klenowski

FURTHER READING

Dulles, Rhea. *The Civil Rights Commission, 1957-1965.* East Lansing: Michigan State University Press, 1968.

Jackson, Donald W., and James W. Riddlesperger Jr. "The Eisenhower Administration and the 1957 Civil Rights Act." In *Reexamining the Eisenhower Presidency,* edited by Shirley Anne Warshaw. Westport, Conn.: Greenwood Press, 1993.

SEE ALSO: Alabama; Civil Rights movement; Japanese American Citizens League; Ku Klux Klan;

Mexican American Legal Defense and Educational Fund; Washington, D.C.; Women's movements.

COMMISSION ON IMMIGRATION REFORM, U.S.

IDENTIFICATION: Federal commission created by the U.S. Congress to conduct a critical, bipartisan investigation of national immigration policies and to recommend changes to Congress

DATE: Operated from 1990 to 1997

ALSO KNOWN AS: Jordan Commission

SIGNIFICANCE: The U.S. Commission on Immigration Reform was the most far-reaching body charged with examining immigration legislation during the last decade of the twentieth century.

In 1990, the U.S. Congress sought to establish a more inclusive immigration policy than existed at that time, one that would correct some of the inequities in current immigration legislation. Barbara Jordan, a Democratic member of the House of Representatives from Texas from 1973 until 1979, was appointed chair of the newly formed commission. Rather than merely attempting to make cosmetic changes in the complex provisions of former immigration policies, under Jordan's guidance, the commission chose fundamentally to rethink policies and to streamline them by focusing on the three stated aims and intentions of earlier immigration laws:

- reuniting immigrant families
- building pools of workers in areas where they were needed
- providing humanitarian respite for those seeking asylum from life-threatening repression in their native countries

COMPOSITION AND MISSION OF THE COMMISSION

When Congress created the commission, it made every attempt to ensure that its membership would be bipartisan. Three of the commission's eight members were appointed by the Republican leadership in both houses of Congress and three were appointed by the Democratic leadership. Two mem-

bers, Shirley Hufstedler and Robert Charles Hill, were appointed by the president of the United States.

The commission was charged with making a critical study of U.S. immigration policies then currently in effect and with making recommendations for sweeping changes in such policies. As was intended, it made interim reports in 1994, 1995, and 1997, prior to submitting its final report in December, 1997. The commission's first interim report emphasized means of controlling illegal immigration, which had reached staggering proportions by the year in which the report was submitted. The commission recommended increased border controls and the hiring of more border police to reduce the flow of illegal immigrants from Mexico into Texas, Arizona, and California.

The second interim report, in 1995, focused on legal immigration, emphasizing the goals of family reunification, employment-based immigration, and the admission of refugees fleeing despotic regimes. The report urged the simplification of immigration categories and recommended that no more than 550,000 legal immigrants be admitted to the United States annually.

The third interim report, in 1997, was much concerned with refugee status and granting asylum, urging international assistance even for refugees who could not legally resettle in the United States. The final report, at the end of 1997, amalgamated the earlier reports and dealt in detail with illegal immigration, legal immigration, and border control. It suggested means of helping refugees who could not resettle in the United States.

IMPACT OF THE COMMISSION

Although the United States is a nation built by immigrants, immigration policy has long been a thorny issue in the country. Early American settlers were prejudiced against Irish immigrants. As the Irish were assimilated into American society, they in turn became prejudiced against southern Europeans, notably Italians. As Italians were assimilated, they had their own prejudices against members of such ethnic minorities as African Americans, Jews, and Latinos.

The Commission on Immigration Reform had to view realistically the prejudices that its reports would elicit in Congress, whose members must take into account the biases of the constituents who elect them to office and keep them there. The commission expressed its official distress with the hordes of undocumented immigrants who were entering the United States and who were not being deported. It urged more stringent enforcement of existing immigration laws. It also recommended that the Immigration and Naturalization Service (INS) be disbanded and its functions be assigned to other government agencies. It recommended that immigration-related employment standards should fall to the Department of Labor, refugee questions should be handled by the State Department, and a new bureau of immigration enforcement should be established within the Department of Justice.

As desirable as many of the recommendations of the commission were to some people, they were never acted upon, and the INS remained intact. Later, such extreme measures as erecting a huge border fence were undertaken, but through the first decade of the twenty-first century, no workable solutions were found to stem the tide of illegal immigration and to deal fairly with immigrants, legal and illegal, many of whom live on society's fringes.

R. Baird Shuman

FURTHER READING

Hing, Bill Ong. *Immigration and the Law: A Dictionary*. Santa Barbara, Calif.: ABC-CLIO, 1999. Comprehensive, alphabetical listing of terms relating to immigration. An outstanding quick reference for those studying immigration.

Joppke, Christian. *Selecting by Origin: Ethnic Migration in the Liberal State*. Cambridge, Mass.: Harvard University Press, 2005. Study that considers international migration in the light of a world composed of individual nation-states.

LeMay, Michael C. *Guarding the Gates: Immigration and National Security*. Westport, Conn.: Praeger, 2006. Thorough consideration of U.S. immigration policies from 1820 through the late 1990's.

LeMay, Michael C., and Elliott Robert Barkan, eds. *U.S. Immigration and Naturalization Laws and Issues: A Documentary History*. Westport, Conn.: Greenwood Press, 1999. Based on documents regarding immigration, the scope of this study is impressive. Highly recommended.

Motomura, Nikoshi. *Americans in Waiting: The Lost Story of Immigration and Citizenship in the United States*. New York: Oxford University Press, 2006. Thorough and up-to-date account of barriers to legal immigration that face people seeking U.S. citizenship.

Smith, Rogers. *Civic Ideals: Conflicting Visions of Citizenship in U.S. History*. New Haven, Conn.: Yale University Press, 1997. Revealing overview of how attitudes toward immigration and immigrants have changed over time in the United States.

Wong, Carolyn. *Lobbying for Inclusion: Rights Politics and the Making of Immigration Policy*. Stanford, Calif.: Stanford University Press, 2006. Interesting account of the role politics play in immigration enforcement and reform.

SEE ALSO: Border fence; Border Patrol, U.S.; Bureau of Immigration, U.S.; Center for Immigration Studies; Deportation; Federation for American Immigration Reform; Immigration and Naturalization Service, U.S.; Immigration law; Immigration Reform and Control Act of 1986; *A Nation of Immigrants*; 9/11 and U.S. immigration policy; Refugees.

CONGRESS, U.S.

SIGNIFICANCE: Since 1875, Congress has played the major role in determining U.S. immigration law and policy. After a century of unrestricted immigration, Congress began passing laws limiting entry of "undesirables" in 1875 and by national origin during the 1880's. The major pieces of immigration legislation in 1924, 1952, 1965, and 1986 reflect the contours of American history and beliefs.

Congressional laws regarding immigration clearly follow the general shape of American history. When the U.S. Congress began restricting immigration during the 1880's, it did so largely in reaction to an outcry against the changing demographics of immigration. Chinese workers were accused of taking American jobs; poor immigrants were seen as coming from the crowded cities of southern and eastern Europe, unlikely to be assimilated in a country made by immigrants from the United Kingdom, France, the Netherlands, Germany and the Scandinavian countries. The attempt to preserve the traditional, pastoral nature of America reached a crescendo during the 1920's as complicated quota systems were instituted to restore the nation's ethnic heritage.

The battle against the race-obsessed Axis nations in World War II spurred the United States to relax its own national origins immigration scheme. However, the emergence of the Cold War gave a new cast to Congress's congressional laws: heightened security against radical influences and the desire to gain skilled workers so as to keep America's edge against the communist powers. The Civil Rights era of the 1960's saw the final abolition of the national origins formula. With the end of the Cold War, the direction of immigration laws changed again. By the 1980's, Congress was most concerned with what to do about the millions of undocumented immigrants who had entered the country outside the elaborate immigration process mandated by Congress.

CONGRESSIONAL POWER OVER IMMIGRATION LAW

Although the U.S. Constitution explicitly grants Congress the power to naturalize foreign-born persons as citizens, it does not explicitly enumerate jurisdiction over immigration as one of the powers of Congress. However, in Article I, section 8, clause 3, the Constitution does grant Congress the power to "regulate commerce with foreign nations." Partly because of this ambiguity, Congress made little attempt to control immigration for the first century of the nation's history. Congress did, however, regulate naturalization—the process of becoming a citizen—for example in the Naturalization Act of 1790, limiting the process to free white persons. As most Americans believed that the United States would be settled by arrivals from foreign nations, this period can be described as one of generally unrestricted immigration. In the period from 1776 to 1875, approximately 11 million immigrants came to the United States. What little regulation there was over immigration came from the individual states.

Comprehensive congressional legislation of immigration began in the last quarter of the nineteenth century. Congressional action in this field can be mostly attributed to two causes—one juridical, the other political. As to the juridical change, the post-Civil War federal government was finding itself possessed of all kinds of powers that had been previously left to the states. As to the political changes, Congress was subjected for the first time to great pressure to restrict immigration, both as to overall numbers and as to national origin. The political battles in Congress and between the federal branches were intense. Over the next seventy-five years, Congress would continue to allow the entry and naturalization of millions of immigrants. However, it would attempt through legislation to shape both the ethnic composition and the beliefs of the new Americans.

The power of Congress over immigration was clarified in the historic Supreme Court case of *Henderson v. Mayor of the City of New York* (1875). In that case, the Court held that the exclusive power over immigration to the United States lay with the federal government. This power was to be exercised by the Congress chiefly through its power to regulate foreign commerce, although other sources of congressional power over immigration also exist in the Constitution. Concurrently with the *Henderson* decision, Congress enacted the Page Law, the first permanent legislation restricting immigration to the United States. This 1875 statute forbade the immigration of convicts and prostitutes. Although this legislation affected a relatively small population, it indicated the pattern of restrictive immigration that Congress would follow for the next seventy-five years: excluding disfavored individuals and groups from the nation's policy of open immigration.

RESTRICTIVE IMMIGRATION

In 1882, Congress extended the immigration exclusions to "lunatics," "idiots," and paupers. In addition, Congress enacted its first exclusion based on national origin. American attitudes toward immigration were undergoing a sea change, reflecting changes in both the nation's beliefs and the immigration population. The frontier was declared closed during the 1890's; the vast internal spaces of the American continent were being closed up. No longer was there a western frontier yearning for massive populations arriving from foreign shores. The destination of early immigrants to the United States had often been the frontier; by the end of the nineteenth century, it had become America's teeming cities. Critics declared this urbanization of the nation, fueled by immigration, a threat to its pastoral, Jeffersonian way of life.

In addition, the composition of the immigrants was changing. During the seventeenth and eighteenth centuries, England and Scotland were the chief sources of immigration. In the first half of the nineteenth century, millions of Irish and Germans were added to the mix, many of whom represented the first large-scale immigration of Roman Catholics to the United States; the nativist movement of the 1840's was the result. By the end of the nineteenth century, however, the patterns of immigration had shifted from northern and western Europe to southern and eastern Europe. In addition, thousands of immigrants were arriving from non-Western nations, such as China and Japan. These hard-working immigrants were seen by many Americans as competing for American jobs and threatening American businesses. Responding to anti-Chinese sentiment in California and the West, Congress passed the Chinese Exclusion Act of 1882, suspending immigration of Chinese laborers for a period of ten years. In 1892, Congress extended the Chinese exclusion for another decade; exclusion would be made permanent in 1904 and be repealed only in 1943. In addition, the 1892 law required all Chinese laborers to obtain "certificates of residence"; without such a certificate, Chinese were subject to deportation.

Through the following decades, Congress passed additional exclusionary laws against Chinese, Japanese, Filipino, and Indian nationals that together constituted an effort to stem an influx of immigrants from Asia. The Dillingham Commission, operating under congressional mandate from 1907 to 1911, proposed more restrictive im-

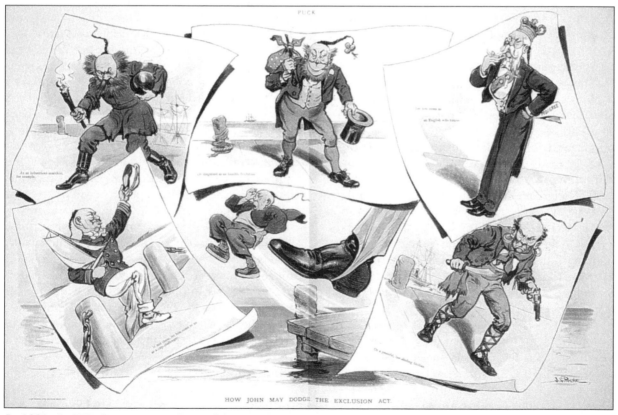

In 1882, the U.S. Congress passed one of the most discriminatory pieces of legislation in U.S. history—the aptly named Chinese Exclusion Act. This early twentieth century illustration from Puck *suggests five ways in which the Chinese man being kicked ("John") might get around the law to enter the United States—as an anarchist, as an Irishman, as an English wife-hunter, as a yacht racer, or as a Sicilian. The joke underlying this cartoon was the fact that all five alternative immigrant types were also unpopular in the United States. In later years, Congress would enact immigration laws restricting additional immigrant groups.* (Library of Congress)

migration so as to exclude immigrants from cultures "alien" to American values and beliefs. In addition, Congress continued to add to the list of excluded undesirables: polygamists in 1891; epileptics and anarchists in 1903; people with physical and mental defects or tuberculosis in 1907; and illiterates, alcoholics, vagrants, and, reflecting dubious psychological theories of the day, people of "psychopathic inferiority" in 1917. The head tax, imposed on every entering immigrant beginning in 1882 and increasing in subsequent decades, deterred immigration of the destitute. Medical examinations, begun in 1891, were designed to keep out the diseased. With increased congressional restrictions came the need for increased administrative resources. In 1891, Congress created the Bureau of Immigration as a division of the Treasury Department to enforce immigration law. (With future administrative reorganizations, this division was eventually renamed the Immigration and Naturalization Service—the INS.)

IMMIGRATION QUOTAS BASED ON NATIONAL ORIGIN

With the end of World War I in 1918, pressure on Congress to pass immigration restriction was revived. In May, 1919, Washington State congressman Albert Johnson, an outspoken restrictionist, became chair of the House of Representatives Committee on Immigration and Naturalization. In 1921, Congress enacted the Emergency Immigration Act, which is also known as the Immigration Act of 1921. The aim of this law was to preserve the ethnic makeup of the United States. The act limited immigration from each nation to 3 percent of the proportion of foreign-born immigrants of that nationality already living in the United States according to the 1910 U.S. Census.

In 1924, Congress passed the Johnson-Reed Act (also known as the Immigration Act of 1924), which made the national origins quota system permanent. Scheduled to take effect in 1927, it limited immigration from outside the Western Hemisphere to 150,000 persons. The act made immigration from regions other than western Europe even more restrictive by reducing the quota from 3 percent to 2 percent of foreign-born persons. In addition, the act substituted the 1890 U.S. Census as the standard, when fewer immigrants had arrived from outside western Europe. Another provision of the

1924 act excluded from immigration aliens who were not eligible for citizenship. As the Naturalization Act of 1790 limited the naturalizing process to white residents, this provision served to exclude Asians. Having passed more restrictive laws, Congress needed to authorize greater enforcement: The 1924 act established the U.S. Border Patrol to police illegal immigration.

Under the complicated provisions of the 1924 act, the year 1929 saw another change in the calculation of national origin. Again reflecting a more nativist sentiment brought on in part by the disillusion of post-World War I America, the new calculation was aimed to prevent further dilution of the nation's Anglo-Saxon majority. The new basis for the national immigration quota was to reflect the national origins of the entire American population as indicated by the census. Under this formulation, 85 percent of the total immigration pool was assigned to northern and western Europe and only 15 percent to eastern and southern Europe.

The onset of World War II in Europe in 1939 was an inopportune moment to limit immigrants from Europe. For example, many Jews who wanted to flee Nazi-occupied territories were denied entry. A humanitarian bill introduced to Congress in 1939 that would allow entry to 20,000 refugee children fleeing Nazi Germany was defeated. Under the Alien Registration Act of 1940, all aliens were required to register with the government. Even as illustrious an immigrant as renowned physicist Albert Einstein faced obstacles under the immigration system. Because of his supposedly radical views, such as his belief in pacifism and a one-world government, several conservative groups lobbied for his expulsion. The Federal Bureau of Investigation (FBI) compiled a 1,500-page dossier on Einstein's suspicious pronouncements and views. Nevertheless, when Einstein acquired American citizenship in 1940, the United States gained one of the great figures of the twentieth century through immigration.

MODERN IMMIGRATION LAW: THE INA

With the calamity of World War II, theories of racial superiority that were used to justify the national origins quota system were discredited. Expressing solidarity with its ravaged wartime ally, the People's Republic of China, Congress in 1943 repealed the Chinese Exclusion Act of 1882 and authorized the eligibility of Chinese for citizenship. Nevertheless, the system of ethnic quotas was not jettisoned. Many congressmen still aspired to shape the immigrant pool so as not to disrupt the melting pot of American society. Congress had been adding piecemeal to the immigration laws for decades: allowing for agricultural workers in 1943; foreign-born spouses in 1946; refugees from persecution in 1948, 1950, and 1953; and exclusion and deportation of communists and subversives in 1950.

In 1952, Congress enacted a comprehensive immigration bill, the Immigration and Nationality Act (INA). The INA, also known as the McCarran-Walter Act, retained the national origins quotas, despite President Harry S. Truman's veto, which Congress overrode. The law continued to favor immigrants from western Europe; in contrast, immigration from the Eastern Hemisphere was limited to about 150,000 persons. However, the law also indicated new directions that American immigration would take.

To some extent, the emphasis on national origins that had dominated congressional immigration policy since its inception was being displaced by a new requirement: professional skills. Immigrants with desirable work skills were granted one-half of the quota places. Another preference was created for parents, spouses, and children of aliens and citizens. For the first time, naturalization was made possible for all immigrants regardless of race. Reflecting the Cold War atmosphere in which the McCarran-Walter Act was enacted, security measures and screening tests for immigrants were tightened. Likewise, the 1965 amendments to the INA (also known as the Hart-Celler Act), enacted in the midst of the Civil Rights era, imported newly won American beliefs of ethnic and racial equality into the immigration system.

In the 1965 amendments, Congress finally rejected the seventy-five-year-old immigration scheme based on national origins, as well as race. Instead, the act emphasized family reunification as the most important factor in immigration admission. Under the act's more generous provisions for the Western and Eastern hemispheres, millions of immigrants from Latin American and Asia were able to enter the country. In 1976 and 1978, Congress eliminated preferential treatment for residents from nations in the Western Hemisphere and enacted

amendments limiting immigration from any one country to 20,000 persons. This was to the obvious disadvantage of people seeking immigration from countries such as Mexico. Under the Refugee Act and the Refugee Education Assistance Act, both of 1980, approximately 125,000 Cubans entered the country and tens of thousands of Vietnamese entered or received permission to stay in the United States.

IMMIGRATION REFORM LEGISLATION

In the century of legislation following the *Henderson v. Mayor of the City of New York* decision, Congress had focused on immigration *restriction*: how many people from which countries should be excluded from immigrating. Beginning in the 1980's, Congress devoted itself to immigration reform: what to do about the millions of people who had entered the country illegally or who had stayed past their visa dates. The centerpiece of this effort was the Immigration Reform and Control Act of 1986 (IRCA). It was passed by Congress with great difficulty, representing a hard-fought compromise between the major groups involved in immigration affairs. The IRCA was one of the most important and controversial pieces of legislation signed into law by President Ronald Reagan.

The most important part of the legislation was the granting of amnesty to the estimated 6 million undocumented aliens in the United States. These aliens, who were not otherwise subject to criminal sanctions and deportation, could become permanent residents or citizens but only under stringent circumstances. For example, an alien seeking legalization had to apply within one year of enactment of the statute, establish a period of continuous residence, and meet most of the requirements for admissibility as an immigrant. The 1986 act had other important provisions as well. For the first time, sanctions were applied against employers who hired undocumented aliens. Because of a fear that such sanctions could lead to discrimination against foreign-born residents who were eligible to work, the IRCA also added numerous antidiscrimination provisions. The IRCA also provided for the legalization of certain seasonal agricultural workers.

By the time the IRCA deadline for amnesty had expired on May 4, 1988, the federal government was already widely criticized for the inadequacies of the bill. Fewer than 2 million people had applied for amnesty. The enforcement mechanisms against hiring illegal workers were considered lax. Employers claimed to be confused as to the new hiring rules. They were in the odd position of having to examine certain documents and ask certain questions so as to determine whether the prospective employee was authorized to work in the United States, but they were forbidden from examining other documents and asking similar questions so as to comply with the antidiscrimination provisions. Workers with foreign accents or even foreign appearances complained that they were being discriminated against by wary employers.

As a result, Congress passed a series of amendments to the IRCA known as the Immigration Act of 1990 ("IMMACT"). Whereas the IRCA dealt mostly with unskilled laborers, IMMACT focused on the legal entry of highly skilled foreign workers. However, debates over illegal immigration continued to dominate congressional oversight in this area. Most of the congressional legislation at the end of the twentieth century and the beginning of the twenty-first century, including the 1996 Illegal Immigration Reform and Immigrant Responsibility Act (IIRIRA), had to do with authorizing and empowering the INS to keep out and deport undocumented aliens. In the wake of the September 11, 2001, terrorist attacks on the United States, Congress abolished the INS and transferred its duties to the newly created Department of Homeland Security.

Howard Bromberg

FURTHER READING

Graham, Otis, Jr. *Unguarded Gates: A History of America's Immigration Crisis.* Lanham, Md.: Rowman & Littlefield, 2004. Controversial work critiquing America's open immigration history.

Huntington, Samuel. *Who Are We? The Challenges to America's National Identity.* New York: Simon & Schuster, 2004. A well-known Harvard professor, Huntington argues for a return to the more restrictive immigration laws that characterized the first half of twentieth century America.

Hutchinson, E. P. *Legislative History of American Immigration Policy, 1798-1965.* Philadelphia: University of Pennsylvania Press, 1981. Chronological and analytical account of U.S. immigration laws, with extensive annotations.

Johnson, Kevin. *Opening the Floodgates: Why America Needs to Rethink Its Borders and Immigration Laws.*
New York: New York University Press, 2007. Examines the cyclical history of U.S. immigration law to argue for open borders.

King, Desmond. *Making Americans: Immigration, Race, and the Origins of the Diverse Democracy.* Cambridge, Mass.: Harvard University Press, 2000. Thoughtful, academic study of the history of immigration law and policy, with detailed chapters on the Immigration Acts of 1924 and 1965. Includes helpful appendix tables showing immigrant numbers by decade and summarizing the major immigration laws in American history.

LeMay, Michael, and Elliott Robert Barkan, eds. *U.S. Immigration and Naturalization Laws and Issues: A Documentary History.* Westport, Conn.: Greenwood Press, 1999. Includes helpfully edited versions of major immigration and naturalization laws enacted by Congress since the nation's origin, as well as major court decisions and executive orders and proclamations. A must for primary research.

Motomura, Hiroshi. *Americans in Waiting: The Lost Story of Immigration and Citizenship in the United States.* New York: Oxford University Press, 2006. An overview of American immigration laws that emphasizes the traditional American preference for generous acceptance and naturalization of immigrants.

SEE ALSO: Constitution, U.S.; History of immigration after 1891; Immigration Act of 1907; Immigration Act of 1917; Immigration Act of 1921; Immigration Act of 1924; Immigration Act of 1990; Immigration and Nationality Act of 1952; Immigration and Nationality Act of 1965; Immigration law; Immigration Reform and Control Act of 1986; Supreme Court, U.S.

CONNECTICUT

SIGNIFICANCE: A New England state originally settled by British Protestants, Connecticut's long immigrant history has been colored by its nearness to one of the primary ports of entry for immigrants, whom it has offered a variety of occupational opportunities. Its immigrant history exemplifies the benefits and problems in a diversified urban society.

Connecticut's earliest immigrants were primarily English and Scottish. However, the early nineteenth century introduced substantial numbers of Germans, many of whom were skilled workers in fields such as furniture manufacturing. Germans tended to establish their own social, musical, and athletic organizations in their new abodes. Many German immigrants were Jews, who contributed significantly to the state's business development, particularly in the state capital, Hartford, which became a notable center of Zionism in the nation. However, the Irish formed the state's largest immigrant group up to the 1850's. They came as weavers, spinners, and unskilled railroad and canal workers. During the second half of the nineteenth century, many of them became police officers, firefighters, omnibus drivers, and railroad conductors.

Around 1850, a growth spurt began in Connecticut's population, partly because of the state's proximity to New York, where the bulk of European immigrants entered the United States. In 1850, Connecticut's immigrant population of more than 38,000 constituted about 10 percent of all state residents, but by 1870, that proportion had risen to nearly 25 percent. Increases in immigrant numbers were particularly noticeable in Hartford and New Haven. Of the 113,000 immigrants living in Connecticut in 1870, more than half were Irish.

LATE NINETEENTH AND EARLY TWENTIETH CENTURY

Immigrants contributed heavily to the growth of Connecticut's labor unions. They also contributed to the frequency of labor strikes, which started prompting state labor laws during the 1880's; however, these laws were seldom enforced rigidly. An economic downturn during the Panic of 1893 and a growing awareness of the potential political influence of Irish Americans contributed to a short-lived but fierce movement to deny political office to Roman Catholics, chiefly because of their supposed allegiance to the pope. There was also a movement

PROFILE OF CONNECTICUT

Region	New England
Entered union	1788
Largest cities	Bridgeport, New Haven, Hartford (capital), Stamford, Waterbury
Modern immigrant communities	Mexicans, Asian Indians, Chinese, Puerto Ricans

Population	Total	Percent of state	Percent of U.S.	U.S. rank
All state residents	3,504,000	100.0	1.17	29
All foreign-born residents	452,000	12.9	1.20	18

Source: U.S. Census Bureau, *Statistical Abstract for 2006*.
Notes: The U.S. population in 2006 was 299,399,000, of whom 37,548,000 (12.5%) were foreign born. Rankings in last column reflect total numbers, not percentages.

to exclude Roman Catholic teachers from public schools. However, the American Protective Association that was behind these movements failed, partly because Catholic voters were already too influential to be suppressed. Meanwhile, new immigrants from southern and eastern Europe began to appear. These included Russians, among whom Jews were even more predominant than among the earlier German immigrants.

The early decades of the twentieth century saw considerable gains in the Italian, Polish, and French Canadian immigrants in Connecticut. The earliest Italian newcomers were chiefly unskilled laborers, but they developed into skilled factory workers, market gardeners, and members of the building trades. They also found work as barbers, cobblers, tailors, and musicians. Many Italians settled in Hartford, New Haven, and Waterbury. The incoming Poles were mainly farmers and tended to remain farmers longer than immigrants from most other nations. However, many Poles worked in textile factories. With one the highest proportions of Polish immigrants among American states, Connecticut had the most Poles of any New England state. Connecticut's French Canadians, who were less numerous than in other New England states, worked mainly in textile factories. Many lived in the most crowded sections of Hartford.

THE 1930'S AND LATER

During the 1930's, the Federal Writers' Project produced a valuable ethnic survey of Connecticut. Many of the people interviewed in this survey explained how kinship and friendship networks had affected their lives. Immediately after arriving in Connecticut, 84 percent of new immigrants lodged with relatives or friends from Europe. Some European immigrants considered domestic jobs in wealthy families to offer the best employment opportunities, but young immigrants tended to prefer factory work. About 40 percent of the women tended lodgers and boarders in rooming houses, washed clothes, did piece work, or assisted husbands in family stores—enterprises that also often employed families' children.

Home-based work had declined by the late 1930's, and more women went into factories or stores or performed personal services, until about 65 percent of the women worked outside their homes. Older children who worked away from home expected to turn over the bulk of their earnings to their parents. The earnings of girls were often spent on their brothers' educations. Parents did not expect their children to become financially independent, but the children often did. Young women in particular discovered new possibilities by being in the workforce, and some became active in labor unions.

MODERN DEVELOPMENTS

By the end of the twentieth century, Connecticut's Latino population was increasing sharply. The vast majority of the state's Latino newcomers are Puerto Ricans, who are already American citizens when they arrive. Mexican immigration has also become important. The heavy population of Latinos, especially in Hartford, where slightly more than half the public schools' students live in homes in which English is not the primary language, has created an important educational problem. Poverty is another issue. A report issued in 2005 found that 15 percent of the state's immigrant population—compared to 9 percent of the general population—fell into the category of families earning less than twenty thousand dollars a year. Immigrants from Asia, primarily India and China, have not been as numerous as Latinos, but they have generally been better educated and more prepared to perform at a high level.

Illegal immigration has become an important political issue in Connecticut. Individual communities have responded to the problem in sharply contrasting ways: either toward providing sanctuary status for undocumented aliens or toward vigorous application of the law. New Haven has undertaken a program of identifying and assisting both documented and undocumented immigrants. This program has been popular in the city center but unpopular in its suburbs. Danbury, which has a large number of undocumented alien residents, has had city detectives work with federal immigration officials to find and remove them.

Robert P. Ellis

FURTHER READING

Andersen, Ruth O. M. *From Yankee to American: Connecticut, 1865-1914.* Chester, Conn.: Pequot Press, 1975. Study of the growth of a cosmopolitan state through an active and varied half-century of immigration.

Blatt, Martin Henry, and Martha K. Norkunas, eds. *Work, Recreation, and Culture: Essays in American Labor History.* New York: Garland Publishers, 1996. Collection of articles that are especially helpful on family relationships and responsibilities among immigrants.

Meyer, David R. *From Farm to Factory to Urban Pastoralism: Urban Change in Central Connecticut.* Madison: University of Wisconsin Press, 1976. Economic history that demonstrates how Connecticut's well-educated citizens appreciated and encouraged newcomers with shrewdness and acquisitiveness.

Roth, David M. *Connecticut: A Bicentennial History.* New York: W. W. Norton, 1979. General history of Connecticut that includes some discussion of how the state's immigrants from many lands have both enriched and complicated life in the New England state.

Van Dusen, Albert E. *Connecticut.* New York: Random House, 1961. Overview of Connecticut with information on the effects of immigrants on business and labor conditions in the state.

SEE ALSO: American Protective Association; Anti-Catholicism; Ellis Island; German immigrants; Irish immigrants; Italian immigrants; Jewish immigrants; Labor unions; Massachusetts; Polish immigrants.

Constitution, U.S.

THE LAW: Foundation document for all legal authority in the United States

DATE: Became effective on March 4, 1789

SIGNIFICANCE: As the fundamental law of the United States, the U.S. Constitution empowers the U.S. Congress to pass federal immigration and citizenship laws providing such laws do not violate the provisions of the Constitution itself, particularly those included in the Bill of Rights and the Fourteenth Amendment.

The U.S. Constitution, which became effective on March 4, 1789, replaced the Articles of Confederation, which had been the governing charter of the United States as a confederation of thirteen independent states since 1781. The people of the newly independent United States had found their confederation of former British colonies was too weak a structure to govern the nation. The new Constitution established the basic institutions of the national government and granted various powers to the legislative, executive, and judicial branches it created. As long as those institutions acted within the scope of their constitutionally granted powers, their enactments were, according to Article VI of the Constitution, the "supreme law of the Land."

One of the areas in which the Articles of Confederation had proven weak and disorganized was the field of immigration and naturalization. Thus, the constitutional Framers authorized Congress, in Article I, section 8, to establish a uniform standard for naturalization and citizenship, subject always to limits placed on Congress by the Constitution itself. Most notably, Congress was not authorized to prohibit the importation of slaves until 1808.

The Framers also limited the office of the president to those who were "natural born" citizens if they were born after the establishment of the United States. By this provision, the Framers generally chose the international legal principle of jus soli (law of the soil) instead of jus sanguinis (law of the blood) as the basis of citizenship in the United States. While this concept of jus soli may seem a natural basis for citizenship to modern Americans, other developed nations, such as Germany and Japan, have continued to grant citizenship only to persons whose parents are ethnic Germans or Japanese respectively. Consequently, immigrants are allowed to reside in Germany and Japan for certain periods, but they can never be-

The U.S. Constitution was first printed in the Pennsylvania Packet, *a daily newspaper, on September 19, 1787.* (Library of Congress)

Constitution, U.S.

come citizens of those countries. Children of immigrants who are born in Germany do not automatically become German citizens; they may naturalize, but only by following a very complicated process when they are between the ages of sixteen and twenty-three. In Japan, children of immigrants may not become citizens no matter how many generations of their ancestors may have resided in Japan.

That the United States was—from the beginning—willing to allow immigrants and their children to become citizens was an almost inevitable outcome of the wide diversity of ethnic groups that settled Great Britain's North American colonies. This decision also affected patterns of immigration repeatedly in American history. Throughout most of the twentieth century, the United States accepted more immigrants than all other nations on earth combined.

Before the U.S. Civil War (1861-1865), the federal government gave a great deal of leeway to the individual states to control naturalization of immigrants, despite the authority that the U.S. Congress had been granted in Article I, section 8 of the Constitution. Members of one class of "immigrants"—African American slaves—were never granted citizenship in the states that permitted slavery. Moreover, many other states that had not permitted slavery also restricted citizenship for African Americans. Because no slaves were legally imported after 1808, all African Americans born in the United States after that date were secondary immigrants. Those African Americans were denied citizenship based on the principle of jus sanguinis, while most other categories of primary and secondary immigrants were governed by the principle of jus soli.

FOURTEENTH AMENDMENT

The Union victory in the U.S. Civil War, preceded by President Abraham Lincoln's 1863 Emancipation Proclamation, changed the status of African Americans forever. On December 6, 1865, the requisite number of states ratified the Thirteenth Amendment ending slavery throughout the United States. However, this change left African Americans in an ambiguous status: They were no longer slaves but were also not yet citizens. The Fourteenth Amendment, which was ratified in 1868, was designed to change that. Its sweeping language also forever changed immigration, natu-

ralization, and citizenship law in the United States.

In an attempt to guarantee first-class citizenship to African Americans wherever they lived in the United States, the Fourteenth Amendment's first section stated:

All persons born or naturalized in the United States and subject to the jurisdiction thereof, are citizens of the United States and of the State wherein they reside.

The Fourteenth Amendment not only ended jus sanguinis as a basis for excluding African Americans from citizenship, it also clearly established jus soli as the basis for citizenship for all African Americans. This language also had sweeping implications for all immigrants, for it meant that all children born in the United States were automatically citizens of the United States regardless of the circumstances of their birth and ethnicity and citizenship of their parents. The Fourteenth Amendment provided one of the broadest and clearest definitions of citizenship granted by any country in the world, but it continues to have curious results.

The language of the Fourteenth Amendment has occasionally prompted individuals to behave in ways that some others find objectionable. For example, children born in the United States are

---

AN al-QAEDA MEMBER AND THE FOURTEENTH AMENDMENT

In 2003, American forces in Afghanistan captured a Saudi Arabian citizen who was a member of the terrorist organization al-Qaeda against whom they were fighting. Initially, the Americans treated the man as they would any other al-Qaeda combatant. However, his status changed radically after they discovered that their captive was also a natural-born American citizen. He had been born in New Orleans, Louisiana, while his Saudi parents were serving as diplomats in the Saudi consulate there. The man himself had no memory of having lived in the United States because his family had returned to Saudi Arabia when he was one year old. Moreover, he had never even returned to the United States, even though he could have entered the country without any legal difficulty because of his American citizenship by right of jus soli.

American citizens and cannot be deported, even if they are the children of immigrant parents who may be subject to deportation. Because deporting parents of American citizens is nearly impossible to do, some noncitizens illegally in the United States have made concerted efforts to bear children while in the country to prevent their own deportation. However, while immigrant parents may not be citizens automatically, their children can seek to have them granted citizenship over time. Anti-immigrant advocates occasionally call for a change in U.S. immigration law without realizing that what they are actually asking is that the U.S. Constitution be amended—a process far more difficult than passing or amending an ordinary law in Congress.

The first section of the Fourteenth Amendment also goes far beyond providing a sweeping definition of citizenship by adding,

> No State shall make or enforce any law which shall abridge the privileges or immunities of citizens of the United States; nor shall any State deprive any person of life, liberty, or property, without due process of law; nor deny to any person within its jurisdiction the equal protection of the laws.

This part of the constitutional amendment protects not only citizens, but also "any person within [a state's] jurisdiction" from arbitrary government action through either the "due process" clause or the "equal protection" clause. This has had profound implications for protecting the status of all immigrants to the United States, especially as interpreted in the latter half of the twentieth century.

INTERPRETING THE FOURTEENTH AMENDMENT

The first test of Fourteenth Amendment protections of immigrants came as Congress attempted to restrict immigration of Chinese immigrants to the United States during the late nineteenth century. Initially, the U.S. Supreme Court interpreted the amendment in a way that protected Chinese immigrants. Such decisions provoked an outcry against the Court and may have contributed to a revision in the Court's interpretation of the Fourteenth Amendment.

In its 1883 decision in the *Slaughterhouse Cases*, the Supreme Court ruled that the Fourteenth Amendment sought only to make African American citizens equal to white citizens and did not af-

fect the rights of aliens in the United States. Consequently, the Court's earlier decisions favoring Chinese immigrants were effectively reversed and Chinese immigration to the United States was drastically curtailed by congressional legislation.

In 1896, the Supreme Court rendered a decision in another case, which seems even more curious in view of the Court's contention in the *Slaughterhouse Cases* that the Fourteenth Amendment protected only the rights of African Americans. In the 1896 case of *Plessy v. Ferguson*, a man named Plessy, who was only one-eighth part African American, was denied the opportunity to ride in a segregated first-class car on a Louisiana train. Plessy sued on grounds that segregated public transportation denied him "equal protection of the laws" under the Fourteenth Amendment. However, the Supreme Court ruled that Plessy would be provided equal protection under the laws so long as the state provided him with transportation facilities equal to those of white passengers, even if those facilities were separate. Together, these two Supreme Court rulings seemed to establish the principle that the Fourteenth Amendment protected the rights of only African Americans.

The *Slaughterhouse* and *Plessy* rulings stood for decades. Gradually, the Supreme Court reversed itself by adopting a doctrine known as selective incorporation. Under this doctrine, selective provisions of the U.S. Bill of Rights were ruled to be so basic to the nature of "due process" that they were incorporated in the language of the Fourteenth Amendment. From the early 1920's and continuing through the 1970's, almost all the most important provisions of the Bill of Rights were selectively incorporated through the Fourteenth Amendment and applied to the states and their subdivisions.

By the early twenty-first century, the first section of the Fourteenth Amendment served as the basis for a broad range of protections extended to both citizens and immigrants in the United States. For example, many states had imposed antimiscegenation laws prohibiting intermarriage between members of different racial groups that had the effect of restricting the right of immigrants to marry whom they chose. These laws persisted until the U.S. Supreme Court used the equal protection clause of the Fourteenth Amendment to void such laws during the 1967 decision in *Loving v. Virginia*. In other states, anti-immigrant groups have sometimes persuaded their state legislatures and governors to enact statutes denying various benefits to immigrants. The federal courts have often voided these state laws as violations of the Fourteenth Amendment. Still other examples of the impact of the U.S. Constitution on the lives of immigrants can be found.

Richard L. Wilson

FURTHER READING

Abraham, Henry J., and Barbara A. Perry. *Freedom and the Court: Civil Rights and Liberties in the United States.* 8th ed. Lawrence: University Press of Kansas, 2004. Classic treatment of American constitutional law that considers immigration issues as civil rights issues under the Fourteenth Amendment.

Craig, Barbara Hinkson. *Chadha: The Story of an Epic Constitutional Struggle.* Berkeley: University of California Press, 1988. This award-winning account of the Supreme Court case *Immigration and Naturalization Service v. Chadha* is a broad look at immigration law in the context of congressional legislation, executive authority, and bureaucratic practice.

Epstein, Lee, and Thomas G. Walker. *Constitutional Law for a Changing America: Rights, Liberties, and Justice.* 6th ed. Washington, D.C.: CQ Press, 2007. Places immigration in the context of constitutional limitations.

Ivers, Gregg. *American Constitutional Law: Power and Politics.* Boston: Houghton Mifflin, 2001. Treats immigration issues among other civil rights issues and provides excerpts from U.S. Supreme Court cases to support the arguments that are discussed.

Kommers, Donald P., John E. Finn, and Gary Jacobsohn. *American Constitutional Law.* Lanham, Md.: Rowman & Littlefield, 2004. Textbook that treats immigration and other constitutional issues from a comparative constitutional perspective, while providing important examples from other countries, most notably Germany.

LeMay, Michael C., and Elliott Robert Barkin, eds. *U.S. Immigration and Naturalization Laws and Issues: A Documentary History.* Westport, Conn.: Greenwood Press, 1999. Exceptionally useful compilation of more than one hundred primary source documents on immigration issues, including U.S. Supreme Court cases, statues, and commentaries, providing a readily accessible source for student research.

Randall, Richard S. *American Constitutional Development: The Powers of Government.* New York: Longman, 2002. Contemporary look at the constitutional issues bearing on immigration.

SEE ALSO: Censuses, U.S.; Citizenship; Congress, U.S.; History of immigration, 1620-1783; History of immigration, 1783-1891; History of immigration after 1891; Immigration and Naturalization Service, U.S.; Immigration law; Naturalization; Supreme Court, U.S.

CONTRACT LABOR SYSTEM

DEFINITION: System used by American industry to attract Asian immigrants

SIGNIFICANCE: During the mid-nineteenth century, a labor shortage in the western United States led to creation of a contract labor system to help the mining and railroad industries attract cheap immigrant labor to the United States. Using labor contracts that paid below-market wages, American industries attracted thousands of Chinese immigrants, angering some Americans who feared immigrant competition and eventually prompting the enactment of federal legislation outlawing foreign contract labor.

The California gold rush that started in 1849 saw the first influx of Chinese and other Asian immigrants into the state as a shortage of American labor forced mining companies to seek out immigrant workers. Chinese immigration to the Western Hemisphere had been begun long before California's gold rush. Spanish emigration companies had recruited cheap Asian labor to work in Peruvian silver mines and Cuban plantations. During the U.S. Civil War (1861-1865), the Lincoln administration pushed through the 1864 Act to Encourage Immigration, which established the U.S. Emigration Office. That office worked with the American Emigrant Company, a private organization that focused on European immigration to respond to the shortage of workers created by the drafting of some one million American men into the Union Army. The law was repealed in 1868, but by that time, a mechanism for recruiting immigrant workers had been established.

RAILROAD WORKERS

Also during 1868, the U.S. and Chinese governments signed the Burlingame Treaty, under which China allowed mass emigration of workers to the United States. At the same time, labor was needed to build the first transcontinental American railroad, a massive engineering and construction feat that required thousands of workers performing dangerous work for limited wages. Immigration agents signed contracts with employers promising specified numbers of immigrant laborers, who would sign contracts to work for at least three years, in return for wages that were low by American standards. This contract labor system was difficult to enforce after the immigrant workers arrived in the United States, where they could leave their jobs relatively easily for better-paying work elsewhere without serious consequences for breaking their contracts.

The railroads recruited tens of thousands of Chinese laborers from China's Pearl River area in Guangdong Province, paying their passage to the United States. Derisively known as "coolies" to many Americans, the Chinese workers did much of the most dangerous work in the construction of the railroad, particularly in helping to blast tunnels through the Sierra Nevada range.

American companies were not the only agencies recruiting contract labor. During the 1870's a group of Chinese American industrialists known as the Six Companies used their close ties to their homeland to attract thousands of Chinese immigrants to San Francisco to work in the Chinese-run industries or to establish their own businesses. Also known as the Chinese Consolidated Benevolent Association, the Chinese Six Companies helped build a Chinese American community that would assist new immigrants find jobs and adapt to their new homeland.

Other Asian countries that sent large numbers of contract laborers to the United States included Japan and the Philippines. Many Japanese laborers were recruited to work on Hawaiian pineapple and sugar plantations. Under the contract labor system, they signed three- to five-year contracts to work in return for wages and free passage to Hawaii. By the end of the nineteenth century, when Hawaii became an American territory, the Japanese were one of the islands' largest minority groups, while native islanders made up only a small minority of the population. Filipinos were also heavily recruited to work in Hawaii. The contract labor system worked more efficiently on the islands than it did

Chinese railroad workers watching a Central Pacific train roll by during the 1870's. (Hulton Archive/Getty Images)

in the continental United States because of the islands' isolation and small geographical area, which limited the ability of immigrant workers to abandon their contract jobs to find work elsewhere.

IMMIGRATION LAWS

In the United States, the influx of low-wage immigrant workers brought in by the contract labor system angered many American labor organizations, such as the Knights of Labor, which lobbied the California and federal governments to restrict or halt all Chinese immigration. The labor groups feared American wages were being depressed by cheap foreign labor and directed their ire at the Chinese. In 1862, California responded to these complaints with the Anti-Coolie Act that imposed a special tax on all Chinese workers. Particular targets of this law were Chinese miners, who were forced to pay a monthly $2.50 tax in order to work in California. Mining companies employing Chinese miners were responsible for collecting the tax and were subject to large fines for noncompliance. The state law targeted Chinese workers on the assumption that raising the costs of immigrant labor would stop mass immigration from Asia. However, the tax had little effect in slowing immigration.

Douglas Clouatre

FURTHER READING

Ambrose, Stephen. *Nothing Like It in the World.* New York: Simon & Schuster, 2001. Examination of the leaders and workers involved in the construction of the transcontinental railroad.

Lee, Erika. *At America's Gates: Chinese Immigration During the Exclusion Era.* Chapel Hill: University of North Carolina Press, 2007. Detailed look at the various federal and state laws passed in the latter half of the nineteenth century and early twentieth century to limit Chinese immigration to the West Coast.

Peck, Gunther. *Reinventing Free Labor.* New York: Cambridge University Press, 2000. Examination of the contract labor system for all immigrants and the legal changes in labor law for immigrants.

Takaki, Ronald. *Strangers from a Different Shore.* Boston: Back Bay Books, 1998. Wide-ranging book that examines the immigration stories of Chinese, Japanese, Filipino, Korean, and Southeast Asian immigrants to the United States.

Zia, Helen. *Asian American Dreams.* New York: Farrar, Straus and Giroux, 2001. Examination of stories about individual immigrant families in the United States dating back to the nineteenth century.

SEE ALSO: Alien Contract Labor Law of 1885; Asian immigrants; Asian Indian immigrants; Asiatic Exclusion League; California gold rush; Chinese immigrants; Credit-ticket system; Guest-worker programs; *Imingaisha*; Indentured servitude; Japanese immigrants.

COOLIES

DEFINITION: Term historically used to describe unskilled, low-wage laborers from Asia

SIGNIFICANCE: Chinese coolies came to the United States both as free immigrants looking for work and as contract workers hired to build America's first transcontinental railroad. They worked in gold mines, on the railroad, and on California levees, and their work ethic set a high standard.

The term "coolie" may have derived from the Hindi *Kuli*, an aboriginal tribal name, or *kuli*, a Tamil word meaning "wages." Europeans used the term to refer to low-status laborers in their Asian colonies. Early nineteenth century Chinese workers in the United States were called "coolies," which soon acquired a pejorative connotation.

Chinese workers in the United States during the 1849 California gold rush soon ran into discrimination. Thugs and bigots victimized them and often set them in conflict against one another. When gold became more difficult to mine, coolies were relegated to shantytowns in San Francisco and Sacramento, earning paltry livings as servants, laundrymen, cooks, truck farmers, peddlers, and construction workers.

In 1865, fifty Chinese immigrants were hired to work on the Central Pacific Railroad roadbeds. Unlike the other workers, most of whom were Irish, the Chinese worked from dawn to dusk in extreme weather. They were so "tireless and unremitting" (as a newspaper from 1869 described) in their work that the railroad sent recruiters to China to bring back thousands more workers. At one time,

Chinese and white miners sluicing for gold at Auburn Ravine in Northern California's Placer County in 1852. (California State Library)

60 percent of the Central Pacific workforce was Chinese. They worked for less pay than white workers and faced serious economic restrictions, but they were still able to make a better living in America than they could in China. Because their exceptionally efficient work ethic and willingness to labor under horrendous conditions made them such valuable workers, California endorsed the Burlingame Treaty of 1868, which granted the Chinese free entry to the United States. In 1880, the treaty was renegotiated and amended to suspend, though not prohibit, Chinese immigration.

Coolies were also involved in the construction of a network of levees in California. During the 1870's, they worked on more than one thousand miles of levees in the Sacramento-San Joaquin River Delta, turning swampland into fertile farmland. By the end of the decade, when the U.S. economy was in a slump and white workers went on strike, Chinese coolies were hired as "scabs," and anti-Chinese sentiment increased. White workers began disparaging Chinese workers even more than before, characterizing them as petty criminals, carriers of leprosy, white slavers, and opium smokers, all willing to work at menial jobs for less pay and under worse conditions than "regular" American workers. Writers and journalists satirized the "heathen Chinee," and some intolerant Americans, including Irish teamster Dennis Kearney, tried to run them out of town and the country. Race riots erupted against the Chinese in California, and several immigrants were lynched.

The federal Chinese Exclusion Act of 1882 barred free immigration of Chinese for ten years, essentially stopping the influx of cheap Chinese laborers, who had proven to be clean, sober workers who worked harder, better, and longer and for less money than other workers. President Chester A. Arthur had vetoed the first Chinese Exclusion Act (which called for a twenty-year immigration suspension) as violating the Burlingame Treaty, but the revised act passed and was extended indefinitely and made permanent in 1902. In 1943, when China allied with America in the war against Japan, the act was finally repealed.

Jane L. Ball

FURTHER READING

Aarim-Heriot, Najia. *Chinese Immigrants, African Americans, and Racial Anxiety in the United States, 1848-82.* Champaign: University of Illinois Press, 2006.

Chen, Yong. *Chinese San Francisco, 1850-1943: A Trans-Pacific Community.* Palo Alto, Calif.: Stanford University Press, 2000.

Steiner, Stan. *Fusang: The Chinese Who Built America.* New York: Harper & Row, 1979.

Teitelbaum, Michael. *Chinese Immigrants.* New York: Facts On File, 2005.

SEE ALSO: Anti-Chinese movement; Asian immigrants; California gold rush; Chinese Exclusion Act of 1882; Chinese immigrants; Nativism; Railroads; San Francisco; Stereotyping; "Yellow peril" campaign.

CREDIT-TICKET SYSTEM

DEFINITION: System by which American employers lent nineteenth century Chinese immigrants travel money at their ports of departure with the understanding that the immigrants' wages in the United States would be garnished to repay the loans

SIGNIFICANCE: During the mid- to late nineteenth century, the fares Chinese immigrants

crossing the Pacific Ocean to the United States paid ranged from fifteen to forty-five dollars—amounts that few Chinese workers could afford. American companies recruiting workers in China advanced money to immigrants to cover their travel expenses. The immigrants often ended up paying these loans several times over, but this so-called credit-ticket system enabled tens of thousands of Chinese to reach the United States.

Before 1850, Chinese migration to the United States was rare. Both China and the United States placed restrictions on emigration that tended to discourage all but a handful of merchants, scholars, and sailors from settling in the United States. When stories concerning a massive gold rush in the United States started circulating in Canton, China, however, foreign travel became a far more desirable proposition. By 1851, drought, war, and social upheaval in China encouraged many young men to abandon their agricultural way of life and seek better opportunities elsewhere; a trend further encouraged in 1860 by the Chinese government reluctantly permitting emigration.

Paying the cost of travel, however, was a difficult problem for the average Chinese worker, even though foreign companies were actively seeking Chinese laborers. In response, the "credit-ticket system" was established. Chinese immigrants received loans to cover their travel costs from hiring agencies employed by foreign companies. After the new immigrants reached their destination, they paid back these loans, plus interest, out of their wages. The Burlingame Treaty of 1868 removed most of the restrictions on Chinese immigration, and the credit-ticket system enabled tens of thousands of Chinese workers to reach California.

The credit-ticket system had some serious faults. Most immigrants preferred using it over becoming indentured or contract laborers because it allowed them to choose their own employment. However, paying off the loans typically required months of labor. With interest and fees, loans of forty dollars could easily rise as high as $160. The money that Chinese immigrants made was never great. Even successful gold miners typically realized only modest incomes, and wages paid to Chinese workers for other kinds of employment, such as railroad work, were low. On average, it took seven months for workers to pay off their debts. Nevertheless, the credit-ticket system remained firmly in place and popular until Chinese immigration was halted by the Chinese Exclusion Act of 1882 and admittance to the United States stopped by the Scott Act of 1888.

Julia M. Meyers

FURTHER READING

Brands, H. W. *The Age of Gold: The California Gold Rush and the New American Dream.* New York: Doubleday, 2002.

Chang, Iris. *The Chinese in America: A Narrative History.* New York: Penguin Books, 2004.

Kuhn, Philip A. *Chinese Among Others: Emigration in Modern Times (State and Society in East Asia).* Lanham, Md.: Rowman & Littlefield, 2008.

Pan, Lynn. *Sons of the Yellow Emperor: A History of the Chinese Diaspora.* New York: Kodansha International, 1994.

Yung, Judy, Gordon Chang, and Him Mark Lai, eds. *Chinese American Voices: From Gold Rush to the Present.* Berkeley: University of California Press, 2006.

SEE ALSO: Anti-Chinese movement; Burlingame Treaty of 1868; California gold rush; Chinese Exclusion Act of 1882; Chinese immigrants; Contract labor system; Coolies; Indentured servitude; Paper sons; Railroads.

CRIME

DEFINITION: Violations of U.S. state and federal laws perpetrated by and on immigrants

SIGNIFICANCE: The development of organized criminal activities among certain ethnic groups has perpetuated the notion that undesirable elements of society have been disproportionately represented among new immigrant populations in the United States. Popular perceptions that newly arrived immigrants are often responsible for rises in crime rates has made it more difficult for immigrants to assimilate. At the same time, the new immigrants themselves have often been victims of criminal activity.

The widespread belief that immigrants are prone to commit crimes at higher rates than members of the general population has affected attitudes and laws throughout the United States since the founding of the republic. As early as the 1790's, the U.S. Congress expressed concern that alien criminal elements were trying to sabotage the new government. Each successive wave of new immigrants has generally been judged to have been morally inferior to members of groups already established in the country. Patterns of systematic discrimination against new immigrants, noticeable as early as the 1830's when practiced against Irish immigrants, were repeated against the Chinese during the latter half of the century, against Italians, Jews, and eastern European immigrants between 1880 and 1920, and again in the late twentieth century against Asians and Latin Americans.

While much anti-immigrant discrimination took the form of laws aimed at controlling entry or restricting economic opportunity, many immigrants also found themselves targets of various hate crimes, including looting, robbery, arson, and murder. At the same time, they often fell prey to criminal elements within their own ethnic groups. Local, state, and federal law-enforcement officials have often been unable—or unwilling—to deal with those committing crimes against law-abiding immigrants.

CRIME FACTORS AMONG IMMIGRANTS

Although immigrants may not have committed crimes at a greater rate than members of ethnic populations already established in the United States, several factors have contributed to making recent arrivals more prone to break the law. First among those factors has been a general unfamiliarity with American law and customs, often exacerbated by the newcomers' inability to speak English fluently. Many immigrants have arrived with little education and few skills, factors that have often kept them in low-paying jobs. Additionally, the high costs of living—sometimes the fault of landlords or shopkeepers who have gouged naive immigrants for rents, goods, and services—have made it difficult for immigrants to work their way out of poverty.

Whenever immigrants have arrived in large numbers from the same countries, they have tended to group together in enclaves that have given them some comfort amid the strange surroundings in their new homeland. The newest immigrants frequently moved into tenements whose squalid living conditions have contributed to high crime rates. Fellow immigrants from their homelands have typically helped them find work, food, clothing, and lodging on a temporary basis. Close cooperation among immigrants has helped newcomers to adjust, but it has also been looked upon with suspicion by those already living in the United States. Moreover, the tendency of recent immigrants to live in close proximity makes newcomers easy targets for those wishing to take advantage of them, and their communities often become places where crime can run rampant. This tendency becomes cyclical: As members of one immigrant group become established and begin moving into the American mainstream, other groups take their place on the lowest rung of the socioeconomic ladder. Members of older immigrant groups typically become the most vocal opponents of the newest arrivals.

IMMIGRANT EXPERIENCES, 1820-1920

The first groups of immigrants to suffer systematic discrimination as criminal populations were the Irish and Germans, who began arriving on the East Coast in great numbers during the 1820's. While many German immigrants moved westward and took up farming, the Irish tended to congregate in major East Coast cities. For example, new arrivals in New York settled in Lower Manhattan, which quickly became notorious for gangs that preyed on both residents and visitors. Law-enforcement officials often refused to act against Irish criminals when their victims were fellow Irish. There were, however, frequent arrests of Irish immigrants. At one point prior to the U.S. Civil War, the Irish made up nearly 60 percent of the inmates of New York City jails; however, most of them had been arrested for petty crimes such as public drunkenness.

Ironically, because many immigrants were also perceived as hard-working and willing to take jobs at low wages, they were often considered threats to those already living in certain areas. As a result, they were often targets of mob violence intended to drive undesirable immigrants out of communities. This was the experience of the Irish in both New York City and Boston during the 1840's and 1850's, and the Chinese in the western United States after the railroads were completed during the 1860's. The same circumstances existed in the East and South at the turn of the twentieth century, when eastern Europeans and sometimes Jews were targeted.

The first wave of many immigrant groups included a disproportionate number of young men, a subgroup within any population who are more prone to be both perpetrators and victims of criminal activity, especially activities such as gambling, public drunkenness, disorderly conduct, prostitution, and drugs. In many cases, young men would travel to America alone so they could establish themselves in jobs before sending for their families. In other cases, the demand for male workers in the United States led to massive numbers of men arriving in the country to take on jobs that those already living in the country could not or would not perform. For example, the wave of Chinese immigration that began during the 1850's brought nearly twenty times the number of young males as it did females to the United States. These men worked in the gold fields and then in railroad construction. When not at work they were often in the gambling dens or houses of prostitution, and unscrupulous entrepreneurs (many of them fellow Chinese) took advantage of the situation by opening establishments where such activities could be pursued.

Throughout the nineteenth century attacks on Chinese communities were routinely carried out by white Americans who distrusted the Chinese and often blamed them for taking away jobs. Victims of intense racial prejudice, the Chinese were subjected to beatings, lootings, arson against homes and businesses, and even murder. They were driven to establish their own separate communities virtually independent of mainstream America. These "Chinatowns" provided much-needed security and economic opportunities, but they also fostered the growth of criminal activity. Organizations known as tongs that had originated in China as mutual-aid societies were imported to the United States and soon existed in nearly every American Chinatown. The tongs opened saloons, gambling houses, opium dens, and brothels, often smuggling from China young women, many of whom were abducted or enticed with false promises of opportunities in America. In response to what was perceived as a threat to public order,

American citizens lobbied the U.S. Congress to take some action. In 1882, Congress passed the Chinese Exclusion Act, which established strict quotas that limited the entry of certain racial and ethnic groups and stopped most Chinese immigration.

A similar pattern emerged among Italian immigrants who came to America by the thousands beginning in the 1880's. There was a common perception in America that most Italian immigrants were criminals. As they had done with the Irish decades earlier, many law-enforcement agencies took a hands-off approach to crimes committed by Italians on other Italian, thereby allowing what was actually only a small criminal element within that community to flourish. Only after crimes became too heinous or were committed outside Italian immigrant communities did city and state officials begin to pay serious attention. Just as happened in southern Italy and Sicily centuries earlier, "protective agencies" sprang up among Italian communities in America. Ironically, although these bodies were created to keep neighbors safe from outside harm, many of them turned to preying on law-abiding citizens. Even more ominously, they evolved from simple street gangs into one of the most notorious criminal organizations in American history: the Mafia.

The growing fear that immigrants were a principal reason for increased crime facilitated passage of a number of laws restricting immigration, especially of specific ethnic or racial groups. In addition to the Chinese exclusion acts, the Emergency Immigrant Act of 1921 and the Immigration Act of 1924 were both aimed at stemming the flow of immigrants from countries perceived to be sending known indigents and criminals to the United States.

GANGS AND ORGANIZED CRIME

From the early decades of the nineteenth century, immigrant communities were breeding grounds for gangs in American cities. Usually made up of young men, these gangs frequently preyed upon their fellow immigrants. Irish gangs roamed port cities such as New York City and Boston from the 1840's through the 1870's, while Chinese gangs plagued many western cities. Italian gangs and, to a lesser extent, Jewish gangs did the same in the East and South beginning in the 1880's.

While gangs were loosely organized and tended to operate principally to provide immediate wealth or status to their members, a more formalized version of criminal activity sprang up in immigrant communities beginning in the late nineteenth century. What came to be known as "organized crime" was different from simple gang activity in that it took on a businesslike structure wherein those who rose to the top of an organization could achieve a certain social status and often were able to distance themselves from their criminal ties and become respectable citizens in their communities. This was often done at the expense of the immigrant communities from which they sprang, however, as fellow members of the same ethnic groups were usually their first victims.

A number of men who had been engaged in criminal activities in Italy were among those who were allowed into the United States during the forty-year period beginning in 1880 when Italian immigration reached its height. In cities where Mafia organizations sprang up, beginning in New Orleans during the 1870's and appearing shortly thereafter in metropolises such as New York, Philadelphia, and Chicago, legitimate protection activities were soon transformed into extortion rackets. Mafia leaders organized prostitution rings and set up various forms of gambling operations—often bilking honest players through various schemes that allowed the Mafia to keep the bulk of the money wagered by bettors. Property damage, bodily harm, and even murder were common forms of retribution practiced against those who protested or attempted to bring in law enforcement to stop Mafia operations. Although systematic efforts by law enforcement to eradicate these criminal groups began as early as the 1890's, relatively little progress was made over the ensuing century.

The Italian Mafia was not the only organized crime operation to prey on immigrant communities. A Jewish Mafia was operating as early as the 1890's in New York, and soon spread to other cities, coexisting with Italian operations or sometimes vying with them for control of various neighborhoods. While the influence of these Mafia organizations waned as the twentieth century progressed and immigrant populations became absorbed into mainstream America, international criminal organizations such as South American drug cartels and Russian and eastern European Mafia-like groups

Suspected members of the Russian mob being escorted by Federal Bureau of Investigation agents after being arrested on extortion charges in 1995. (AP/Wide World Photos)

began operating in the United States, often preying on immigrant communities in which drugs and contraband goods found willing buyers.

TRENDS AFTER 1965

In 1965, the U.S. Congress passed a new Immigration and Nationality Act that radically reformed U.S. immigration and ushered in a new wave of criminal activity associated with immigrant populations. The 1965 law eliminated preferences for European immigrants and broadened opportunities for immigrants from Asia and Latin America. When these new groups began arriving in great numbers, however, the historical pattern of mistrust and blame directed at new immigrants was repeated. People coming from the East and from Central and South America were subjected to the same prejudices as European immigrants had endured decades earlier. The general public blamed

increased crime in various localities on the influx of immigrants, even when statistics suggested these perceptions were wrong.

Some new immigrants did, however, become involved in serious criminal activity. Many of the Vietnamese immigrants who made their way to the United States during the 1970's after the end of the Vietnam War became involved in a cycle of crime that caused serious rifts between them and members of the communities in which they settled. Many of the people who fled Vietnam after the war had little formal education but were hard workers willing to take unskilled jobs in order to survive in their adopted homeland. Many who settled along the Gulf coast took up fishing, a trade many had practiced in Vietnam. The immigrants' industrious work habits, coupled with their unfamiliarity with practices in the region, soon made them targets of a variety of hate crimes. Their boats were burned, their catches were looted, and their families were threatened. On the West Coast, the unwillingness of the established population to embrace Vietnamese immigrants, coupled with the lack of good jobs for immigrants with limited formal education, drove many young Vietnamese into gang life.

GENERATIONAL FACTORS AND GANGS

Studies of immigrant communities settling in the United States during the late twentieth century have repeatedly shown that first-generation immigrants have been less likely to commit crimes than members of the population at large. Second-generation immigrants, however, have often drifted into criminal behavior, largely because they have not been prepared for good jobs or have found it easier to make money by resorting to illegal activities. Young men who drop out of school are especially prone to join gangs that terrorize local neighborhoods, making their own immigrant neighbors their principal victims. This has been especially true in Hispanic and Vietnamese communities, but other ethnic groups have not been immune to gang activity in their neighborhoods.

During the late twentieth century, youth gangs made up of Asians and Latin Americans began operating in the West and Southwest and spread throughout most major metropolises and many smaller American cities. These gangs have generally operated within the finite boundaries of specific neighborhoods, in which they claim exclusive rights to all criminal activities. Robbery and extortion have been the most common crimes committed by gang members, but they have also often employed physical violence. In extreme cases, gang members have resorted to murder when their demands are not met, or when victims have sought help from law enforcement. Gangs have also used murder to deter members from rival gangs from violating their own "turf."

Compounding the problem of gang violence often associated with Latino and Asian immigrants has been the growth of international drug trafficking. During the 1970's an elaborate network run by Central and South America drug cartels began operating in immigrant communities in the United States, typically making use of immigrants as drug runners and pushers. When the federal government began cracking down on this illegal trade during the 1980's, a high percentage of persons arrested for drug violations were found to be illegal immigrants. As a result, federal, state, and local law-enforcement officials began targeting immigrant communities under the assumption that reducing their populations would decrease the numbers of persons involved in crime.

LEGISLATIVE RESPONSES

News stories sensationalizing violence associated with gangs and drug activity have fed stereotypes that immigrants were responsible for rising

In a nine-month investigation code-named "Operation Gilded Cage," more than four hundred federal, state, and local law-enforcement officers searched about fifty San Francisco Bay Area brothels, homes, and businesses, such as this San Francisco massage parlor. In July, 2005, they arrested more than two dozen people on charges of smuggling foreign women into the country through Canada and forcing them to work as prostitutes. (AP/Wide World Photos)

crime rates. Responding to public pressure, legislators have pushed for ever more stringent laws restricting immigration and for providing harsh penalties for immigrants convicted of crimes. One of the more curious statutes to affect the rise of crime among immigrants was the state of California's Proposition 187, which was passed by voter referendum in 1994. Under the provisions of the law created by that initiative, undocumented immigrants were denied all public medical care except emergency treatment, and their children were denied educational benefits. Hospital and school system officials who violated the law were subject to criminal penalties. Additionally, falsifying documents or using false documents to establish legitimacy was made a felony offense. Although many of the provisions of Proposition 187 were later declared unconstitutional, the law's passage provided further proof that the majority of American citizens were increasingly willing to stiffen criminal penalties for anyone entering the United States without proper documentation. Thanks to this attitude, immigrants could be regarded as felons simply by crossing the border without proper documentation.

In 1996, the federal Illegal Immigration Reform and Immigrant Responsibility Act created harsher penalties for both illegal and legal immigrants. Legal immigrants could be arrested and deported for crimes committed as long as a decade earlier. Such crimes included not only traditional felonies such as murder, drug possession and use, or robbery, but also domestic violence and even drunk driving. Suddenly the entire immigrant population was placed under a cloud, as the general populace came to see all immigrants either as criminals or as potential criminals. Meanwhile, federal efforts to increase the size and scope of the Immigration and Naturalization Service led to increased detentions and arrests of both legal and illegal immigrants, further supporting perceptions among American citizens that recent immigrants posed a danger to the health and welfare of the society as a whole.

Laurence W. Mazzeno

FURTHER READING

Freilich, Joshua D., and Graeme Newman, eds. *Crime and Immigration.* Burlington, Vt.: Ashgate, 2007. Collection of twenty-three essays dealing with relationships between immigrant populations and crime in a number of countries, including the United States.

Launer, Harold M., and Joseph E. Palenski, eds. *Crime and the New Immigrants.* Springfield, Ill.: C. C. Thomas, 1989. Essays reprinted from publications on criminology and sociology focusing on issues related to criminal activities associated with immigrant populations that arrived in the United States during the last decades of the twentieth century.

Mangione, Jerre, and Ben Morreale. *La Storia: Five Centuries of the Italian-American Experience.* New York: HarperCollins, 1992. Study of Italian Americans that includes lengthy sections on crimes perpetrated by and upon Italian Americans. Also covers the activities of the Italian Mafia in America.

Martinez, Ramiro, Jr., and Matthew T. Lee. "On Immigration and Crime." In *Criminal Justice 2000.* Vol. 1 in *The Nature of Crime: Continuity and Change.* Washington, D.C.: U.S. Department of Justice, 2000. Examination of the historical relationship between crime and immigrant communities, stressing disparities between public perceptions and empirical data.

Martinez, Ramiro, Jr., and Abel Valenzuela Jr., eds. *Immigration and Crime: Race, Ethnicity, and Violence.* New York: New York University Press, 2006. Useful collection of essays exploring relationships between immigrant populations and criminal activities, focusing on causes of criminal behavior among immigrants. Articles examine individual ethnic groups in a number of major American urban centers. Includes extensive list of sources for further study.

Waters, Tony. *Crime and Immigrant Youth.* Thousand Oaks, Calif.: Sage Publications, 1999. Explains the cultural and sociological factors accounting for criminal activities engaged in by young members of immigrant communities. Includes a chapter on juvenile immigrants in America.

SEE ALSO: Captive Thai workers; Chinese secret societies; Criminal immigrants; Ethnic enclaves; *Godfather* trilogy; Italian immigrants; Ku Klux Klan; Ponzi, Charles; Smuggling of immigrants; "Undesirable aliens."

CRIMINAL IMMIGRANTS

DEFINITION: Aliens who enter the United States with criminal records, or those who commit crimes after arriving in the United States

SIGNIFICANCE: Over time the federal government has passed numerous laws and increased enforcement efforts to thwart the entry of criminal immigrants and to make it easier to deport alien criminals who are in the country, including those who have committed their crimes after arriving. During the late twentieth century, the list of criminal activities for which aliens could be deported was expanded greatly, increasing arrests and detentions and driving up costs to the government for carrying out enforcement activities.

Immigrants who committed crimes in other countries have been entering the United States since the first Europeans began arriving in the colonies during the early seventeenth century. However, many early immigrants were considered "criminals" simply because poverty had driven them to break harsh European laws that made seemingly petty crimes such as stealing bread, pickpocketing, and vagrancy felony offenses. Consequently, many so-called felons who immigrated to America were actually merely petty criminals.

After the United States became independent in 1783, federal government officials were lax in dealing with criminal immigrants. However, the great waves of newcomers arriving from Europe after the 1820's spurred more aggressive efforts, first by the individual states and eventually by federal authorities, to bar persons with criminal records from entering the country and to detain and deport immigrants who committed crimes after arriving in the United States.

NINETEENTH AND EARLY TWENTIETH CENTURY INITIATIVES

National immigration policy was slow to develop after independence. Initially each state was responsible for overseeing foreign immigration. Most states had laws prohibiting criminals from gaining admittance, but these laws were so loosely enforced that many foreigners with criminal records in their home countries entered the United States legally. In 1875, the federal government finally entered the effort to prohibit immigration by criminals by passing the Page Law, which restricted entry of "undesirables," particularly from China. The U.S. Congress took stronger steps in 1882, and in 1891 the federal government empowered the new office of the Commissioner for Immigration to oversee all immigration. This office was specifically directed to take measures to turn away criminals at ports of entry. Generally, aliens found already to have criminal records or to have engaged in criminal activities within one year of their arrival in the United States could be deported. The Immigration Act of 1907 extended the period from one to three years to give the government more time to deal with those discovered to be criminals.

Despite these new laws, lax enforcement continued to permit many immigrants with criminal records—especially those from Italy—to enter the United States. Many criminal Italian immigrants would eventually form the nucleus of what would become known as the Mafia. As the federal government became more aware of the kinds of individuals who were slipping past immigration officials, a serious proposal was made to require all Italian immigrants to obtain certificates of good character from the local police chiefs in their hometowns. This proposal died when government officials realized it was unenforceable. In any case, criminal activity was not restricted to immigrants coming from Italy. Frequently, when persons apprehended in the United States for criminal activities were determined to be recent immigrants, or to have entered the country illegally, they were deported, in addition to other criminal penalties that may have been imposed when they were convicted of their crimes.

HIGH-PROFILE IMMIGRANT CRIMINALS

The U.S. government has often used its power to deport undesirables as a means of ridding the country of notorious criminal immigrants. In some cases, deportation was used to guarantee that the person would no longer be able to pursue criminal activities in the United States. For example, deportation procedures were used to remove a number of important Mafia figures. One of the most notable Mafia figures was Salvatore Luciana, best known in America as Charles "Lucky" Luciano. The first Mafia leader caught engaging in wide-scale sales of illegal drugs, Luciano was returned to Sicily as part of a plea-bargain agreement in 1946. Another key Mafia leader, Carlos Marcello of New Orleans, was deported to Guatemala in the 1950's. However, he later managed to return to the United States to resume his criminal activities.

Another category of criminal immigrants who received significant publicity after World War II were those generically classified as Nazi war criminals. These included officials of the Nazi Party and other persons who helped manage concentration camps in which millions of innocent civilians were massacred during the Holocaust. During the decade following the end of the war, many of these people—including citizens of other countries who assisted the Nazis—managed to slip out of their homelands and escape to other nations. Many of these people evaded detection for decades. In 1973, the first suspected war criminal to be extradited from the United States to Germany to stand trial for war crimes was Hermine Braunsteiner. A guard at Majdanek and other women's prisons, she had married an American serviceman after the war.

In 1979, the U.S. Justice Department established the Office of Special Investigations to help root out Nazi war criminals living in the United States. Among the more famous criminals identified and deported was John Demjanjuk, who had been known during the war as "Ivan the Terrible" for his savage treatment of prisoners at Treblinka. In almost all cases, the U.S. government took the position that anyone who—like Demjanjuk and Braunsteiner—had obtained U.S. citizenship after having participated in the extermination of innocent citizens abroad had done so under false pretenses and was therefore eligible for deportation.

Sicilian-born mobster Charles "Lucky" Luciano leaving a New York court appearance in 1936, when he received a long prison sentence for running a prostitution ring. He was paroled in 1946 on the condition that he return permanently to Sicily. He never came back to the United States but later tried to run criminal activities in the United States from Cuba. (AP/Wide World Photos)

OBSTACLES TO DEPORTATION

Despite strong government efforts to apprehend and deport war criminals, lengthy court battles have frequently permitted many war criminals to remain in the United States for long periods. Additionally, efforts to deport immigrants with criminal records have not always gone smoothly. In 1980, Cuban leader Fidel Castro authorized the emigration of all Cuban citizens wishing to go to the United States. In a mass exodus that became known as the "Mariel boatlift," more than 100,000 Cubans left their homelands on boats from the port of Mariel. Among them were nearly 8,000 known prostitutes, criminals, and persons judged criminally insane whom Castro had released from prison and directed to leave the country. After U.S. authorities became aware of the large criminal element entering the country as a

"IVAN THE TERRIBLE?"

Accused war criminal John Demjanjuk (center) in 1986, after being deported to Israel, where he was convicted of having been the notorious "Ivan the Terrible" in the Treblinka concentration camp during World War II. After his conviction was overturned on the basis of reasonable doubt in 1993, he was returned to the United States, only to face new charges of having served in Nazi death camps. In 2005, the United States tried to deport him again, but no country would accept him. In 2009, however, he was deported to Germany to stand trial on nearly 28,000 counts of being an accessory to murder. (AP/ Wide World Photos)

result of this supposedly humanitarian effort, a massive search was mounted to track down everyone who had entered the country in the boatlift. Federal officials detained thousands of Cubans until their backgrounds could be checked. Eventually most of the Cuban criminals were sent back to Cuba. However, detentions of innocent immigrants—some of whom were detained as long as

five years—led to two riots at prisons in the southern states in which the detainees were held.

ILLEGAL IMMIGRATION AND CRIMINAL ACTIVITY

Although immigrants in the nineteenth and early twentieth centuries were occasionally driven to criminal activity, the ready availability of jobs in America's rapidly expanding industrial economy usually meant that new arrivals could become economically independent relatively quickly. However, similar opportunities were not available to immigrants arriving after World War II, especially during the 1980's and 1990's. By then the American economy had changed radically, and the lack of preparedness among many new immigrants for the new knowledge economy created a permanent underclass willing to work for minimal wages. The presence of this growing group fueled new fears among the general population, who were already skeptical of newcomers who were perceived as contributing little to the country's prosperity. These concerns led to the enactment of a new round of restrictive policies, often couched in terms of weeding out criminal elements among immigrant populations.

During the second half of the twentieth century, the bulk of "criminal" immigrants in the United States were Mexicans. Mexican immigration had been an issue since the early twentieth century. In 1924, the U.S. government took steps to limit immigration from Mexico, passing a law that made it a misdemeanor to gain entry illegally; second attempts at entering illegally after deportation were considered felony offenses. During the 1970's, the federal government began passing tougher laws that treated illegal immigrants as felons. Consequently, thousands of immigrants with no criminal records in their homelands who happened to enter the United States without documentation became instantly branded as criminals upon their arrival. At the same time, the federal government began stronger enforcement efforts to capture, detain, and deport those who had crossed the nearly two-thousand-mile border between Mexico and the United States without proper documentation.

Meanwhile, federal efforts to limit legal immigration from Mexico made possible a flourishing criminal business in human trafficking. Networks sprang up to help thousands of people who could not qualify for legal entry into the United States get across the border, where they could find work in agricultural, construction, and manufacturing businesses desperate for cheap labor. The smuggling of illegal immigrants thus created criminal subcultures on both sides of the Mexican border.

Compounding the problem of illegal immigration from Mexico was the growth in drug smuggling across the border. A number of those crossing into the United States were actively participating in the drug trade, which was built on a sophisticated network run by cartels in Central and South America. During the 1980's the federal government began cracking down on this illegal drug trade, and a high percentage of those arrested for drug violations turned out to be illegal immigrants. Efforts to curb the inflow of drugs into the United States dovetailed with increased efforts to round up and deport illegal immigrants, under the assumption that reducing the number of illegal immigrants in the country would decrease the number of those involved in criminal activities involving illicit substances.

ILLEGAL IMMIGRATION REFORM AND IMMIGRANT RESPONSIBILITY ACT OF 1996

In 1996, the federal Illegal Immigration Reform and Immigrant Responsibility Act further stiffened penalties for both illegal and legal immigrants. Under its provisions, immigrants who had entered the United States legally could be arrested and deported for certain crimes they may have committed as long as a decade earlier. In addition to felonies, crimes for which deportation was permissible were drug use and sale, domestic violence, and even drunk driving. All persons who entered the country without proper documentation were subject to immediate deportation, and immigration officials did not have to obtain permission from judges to carry out this action. Moreover, it became a felony for a deported alien to reenter the United States within ten years of deportation. The Immigration and Naturalization Service was expanded to provide more agents to track down undocumented immigrants, who were handled as criminals.

At the end of the twentieth century, a high percentage of inmates in federal prisons were immigrants who had been arrested and were being held for entering the country illegally, but who had committed no other crime. At the same time, gangs in many metropolitan areas contained large populations of illegal immigrants. While apprehension and deportation of these individuals became a priority for the U.S. government, the porous border between the United States and Mexico made it easy for recently deported persons to sneak back into the United States.

After the terrorist attacks on New York and Washington of September 11, 2001, the U.S. government stepped up efforts to find and deport undocumented aliens, especially those of Middle Eastern descent and Muslims of all nationalities. Although the U.S. Supreme Court reaffirmed the right of immigrants to due process under the U.S. Constitution, provisions of the 2001 Patriot Act strengthened the power of immigration officials wishing to use detention and deportation as tools to rid the country of immigrants judged to be a security risk.

The cost of dealing with criminal activity attributable to immigrants is often hard to calculate. Best estimates in the early years of the twenty-first century indicated that expenses for enforcement operations, court systems, and incarceration facilities were running into billions of dollars annually.

Laurence W. Mazzeno

FURTHER READING

Brotherton, David C., and Philip Kretsedemas, eds. *Keeping Out the Other: A Critical Introduction to Immigration Enforcement Today*. New York: Columbia University Press, 2008. Collection of essays investigating the federal government's attempts to control immigrant populations through a series of laws that consistently expanded the number of crimes for which deportation was permissible.

Finckenauer, James O., and Elin J. Waring. *Russian Mafia in America: Immigration, Culture, and Crime*. Boston: Northeastern University Press, 1998. Describes activities of criminal elements among Russian immigrants, compares their activities to elements in other immigrant groups, and describes efforts of law enforcement to deal with these criminals.

Martinez, Ramiro, Jr., and Abel Valenzuela Jr., eds. *Immigration and Crime: Race, Ethnicity, and Violence*. New York: New York University Press, 2006. Collection of essays exploring the causes for criminality among immigrants. Includes discussions focusing on behavior of specific ethnic groups in several major American urban centers. Provides an extensive list of sources for further study.

Ryan, Allan A., Jr. *Quiet Neighbors: Prosecuting Nazi War Criminals in America*. New York: Harcourt Brace Jovanovich, 1984. Study of the U.S. government's efforts to identify and extradite or deport Nazi war criminals, compiled by a member of the Justice Department's Office of Special Prosecution.

Waters, Tony. *Crime and Immigrant Youth*. Thousand Oaks, Calif.: Sage Publications, 1999. Sociological study that attempts to account for cultural and sociological factors influencing criminal behavior of young members of immigrant communities. Traces the history of crimes committed by youthful immigrants in America.

SEE ALSO: Crime; Deportation; Drug trafficking; *Godfather* trilogy; Illegal immigration; Mariel boatlift; Ponzi, Charles; Russian and Soviet immigrants; Smuggling of immigrants; Stereotyping; "Undesirable aliens."

CUBAN IMMIGRANTS

SIGNIFICANCE: The overwhelming majority of Cubans who have immigrated into the United States have settled in Florida, whose political, economic, and cultural life they have transformed. The first wave of Cuban refugees used the state as a base to oppose the Cuban government. The refugees of the 1960's brought Cuban customs to Florida as well as virulently anticommunist beliefs. The sheer volume of the last wave of Cubans during the 1980's exacerbated already tense racial relations with African American communities, especially in Miami, who felt politically and economically marginalized.

Cuban immigration waves have tended to follow periods of political repression in Cuba. Most Cuban immigrants have settled in Florida, a state only ninety miles from the coast of Cuba. By the year 2008, more than 1.24 million Cuban Americans were living in the United States, mostly in South Florida, where the population of Miami was about one-third Cuban. Many of these Cubans have viewed themselves as political exiles, rather than immigrants, hoping eventually to return to their island homeland after its communist regime falls from power. The large number of Cubans in South Florida, particularly in Miami's "Little Havana," has allowed them to preserve their culture and customs to a degree rare for immigrant groups.

NINETEENTH CENTURY IMMIGRATION

The tradition of Cuban political exiles coming to the United States began during the nineteenth century, when Spain still ruled the island. The first exiles arrived in 1823. Many of them hoped that the United States would annex Cuba, and they supported a failed Cuban revolt against Spain in 1867. During the 1890's, the exiled Cuban nationalist leader José Martí organized a second revolt and sought the support of thousands of fellow Cuban exiles in New York and Florida. During the Spanish-American War of 1898, exiles fought on the American side but opposed the Platt Amendment of 1902 that afterward turned Cuba into a protectorate of the United States. After Cuba finally won its full independence, its government became an oppressive dictatorship. During the late 1920's, Cuban exiles opposed to the government used Miami as a base to plot its overthrow in favor of democratic government.

CASTRO AND IMMIGRATION

In 1959, a communist movement led by Fidel Castro overthrew the government of Fulgencio Batista to take power in Cuba. Castro immediately nationalized businesses and large land holdings, while attacking potential political opponents among the wealthy, entrepreneurs, and Batista supporters. Cubans who did not unconditionally support Castro appeared in media portrayals as enemies of the revolution. As Cubans had often done during past periods of political trouble, many sought temporary exile in the United States. However, unlike the past wave, this group of immigrants benefited from the political atmosphere in the United States fostered by Cold War. Both the Eisenhower and Kennedy administrations enthusiastically supported Castro's enemies as anticommunist freedom fighters.

Between 1959 and 1962, 119,922 Cubans arrived in the United States. These people were primarily of Cuba's elite: executives and owners of firms, big merchants, sugar mill owners, cattlemen, representatives of foreign companies, and professionals. They used whatever means were necessary to get out of Cuba. The most fortunate among them obtained U.S. immigrant, student, and tourist visas; others entered the United States indirectly, through countries such as Canada, where they applied for U.S. visas. About 14,000 unaccompanied minors arrived in the United States in 1960 and 1961 alone through a clandestine U.S. program code-named "Operation Pedro Pan." After 1961, Castro permitted emigrants to take only five dollars with them, while requiring them to surrender all other property to his government.

SETTLING IN THE UNITED STATES

Although thousands of Cuban immigrants arrived in the United States nearly destitute, they were not without resources. Many were already familiar with the United States, which they had often visited for business or pleasure before the Cuban Revolution. Some also had business or personal contacts in the country to help them adjust. In addition, since Cuban culture itself was highly Americanized before 1960, the American way of life was not altogether alien to them. Moreover, as exiles fleeing a common enemy, they arrived with a strong sense of solidarity. In South Florida, where the bulk of exiles waited for Castro's overthrow, those who had arrived earlier tried to ease the shock of the newcomers by advising them on matters such as securing U.S. social security cards, enrolling children in schools, and enlisting in the federally funded Cuban Refugee Program, which provided free medical care and food. The exiles themselves helped one another find jobs and living quarters.

The U.S. government attempted to relocate the newcomers throughout the country. The stated ob-

PROFILE OF CUBAN IMMIGRANTS

Country of origin	Cuba
Primary language	Spanish
Primary region of U.S. settlement	South Florida
Earliest significant arrivals	1823
Peak immigration period	Late nineteenth century, 1960's, 1980's
Twenty-first century legal residents*	245,864 (30,733 per year)

*Immigrants who obtained legal permanent resident status in the United States.

Source: Department of Homeland Security, *Yearbook of Immigration Statistics, 2008.*

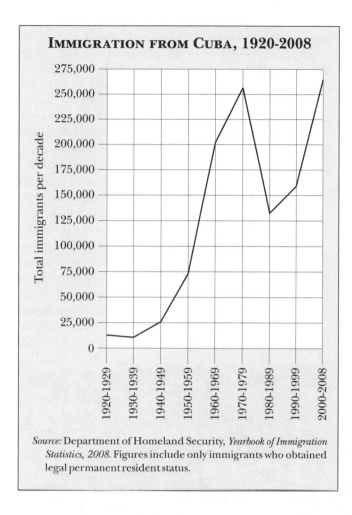

IMMIGRATION FROM CUBA, 1920-2008

Source: Department of Homeland Security, *Yearbook of Immigration Statistics, 2008.* Figures include only immigrants who obtained legal permanent resident status.

LATER IMMIGRATION WAVES

The third wave of Cuban immigration began after the fall of 1965, when Castro announced that all Cubans with relatives living in the United States would be allowed to leave through the port of Camarioca. He invited exiles to come to Cuba by sea to collect their relatives, as commercial flights between Cuba and the United States had been discontinued in the wake of the 1962 Cuban Missile Crisis. Hundreds of Miamians accepted Castro's offer. Within only a few weeks, about 5,000 Cubans left Cuba. Because of the chaotic nature of this exodus, Cuba and the United States negotiated a plan for a more orderly departure through a program the U.S. government dubbed the "Freedom Airlift." These flights continued until 1973, when Castro unilaterally stopped them. By that time, 247,726 more Cubans had entered the United States. This immigrant wave comprised mostly small merchants, craftsmen, skilled and semiskilled workers, and relatives of middle-class Cubans who had immigrated during the early 1960's.

In 1978, the Cuban government began discussions with Cuban exiles over the fates of political prisoners in Cuba. The government agreed to release 3,600 of its prisoners and to promote reunification of families by allowing Cubans living in the United States to visit their families on the island. These visits led to a fourth wave of Cuban immigration. In 1980, a chaotic flotilla of Miamians began sailing to the Cuban port of Mariel to bring their families to the United States in what became known as the "Mariel boatlift." The sailors were forced to carry everyone whom Cuban officials put aboard their boats, including people regarded as social undesirables: prisoners who had committed nonpolitical crimes, mental patients, and homosexuals. However, contrary to popular perceptions in the United States, most of the people who came to the United States in the boatlift were not criminals. The majority were young, working-class men from the mainstream of Cuban society. A significant number of intellectuals were also among these immigrants, some of whom lacked legal immigrant status and consequently spent years in detention in the United States.

jective of the government's resettlement efforts was to lighten the financial burden that the exiles presented to South Florida's strained social institutions. The federal government may have also feared the social and political implications of having a large, increasingly frustrated, and heavily armed exile population concentrated in Miami. In any case, after the exiles realized that Castro's government would not soon fall, many began to take advantage of resettlement assistance offered through the Cuban Refugee Program. Many wound up in New York, New Jersey, Chicago, Boston, and Washington, D.C. They brought conservative political views and quickly established cultural organizations. Meanwhile, a four-square-mile area in Miami's southwest section attracted so many Cubans that it garnered the nickname of Little Havana. The area would become the heart of the exile community and act as a magnet to future Cuban immigrants.

END OF THE COLD WAR

The end of the Soviet Union's economic aid to Cuba in 1989 combined with the U.S. trade embargo to produce another wave of immigrants seeking better economic conditions. This final wave of Cuban immigration began in 1989 and continued into the early twenty-first century. These new arrivals became known as *balseros* because they traveled on makeshift rafts or *balsas*. Castro initially opposed this immigration. However, in 1994, in an apparent effort to reduce domestic political tensions or to force the United States to negotiate an immigration agreement, Castro reversed his three-decade-old policy of arresting people who tried to escape the island by sea. He announced that Cubans would be allowed to leave in small vessels and makeshift rafts if they wished to go to the United States. U.S. president Bill Clinton's administration subsequently negotiated an agreement with Cuba to halt this exodus. The accord suspended the preferential treatment that had been given to Cubans since 1959. No longer would they be treated as refugees from a communist state. Additionally, the U.S. Coast Guard was ordered to send all *balseros* to the U.S. Navy Base in Guantanamo Bay in Cuba. The rafters faced the prospect of being detained indefinitely at Guantanamo if they would not voluntarily return home. Cuban exiles reacted angrily to this change in policy with demonstrations throughout South Florida. Meanwhile, Guantanamo's detainee population reached 32,000 men, women, and children. Most of these undocumented immigrants were young and without resources.

In 1995, the Clinton administration allowed Guantanamo detainees to qualify for entrance into the United States. However, Cubans wishing to immigrate had to follow the same procedures as immigrants from other countries. They were no lon-

Cuban cigar rollers working in Miami's Little Havana neighborhood in 2009. (AP/Wide World Photos)

ger to receive preferential treatment and would be limited to 20,000 visas per year. With the end of the Cold War, immigrants from communist countries no longer mandated special treatment. Meanwhile, Cubans—including Elián González, who became a cause célèbre in the United States—continued to pile onto rafts in the hope of reaching Florida. Cuban exile organizations, such as Brothers to the Rescue, sent planes near or into Cuban airspace in search of rafters. In 1996, the Cuban air force shot down two of the exile planes, sparking an international crisis with the United States. Clinton retaliated by tightening the embargo on Cuba, but his administration's policy on Cuban immigration remained unchanged.

CUBAN LIFE IN THE UNITED STATES

Cuban Americans have made remarkable progress in adjusting to life in the United States. The 1959 wave of immigrants, who were well above average in educational background and business skills, established an economic and cultural base that would ease the adjustment of later immigrants. However, the successes of the Cubans led to friction with African Americans, many of whom felt politically marginalized and shut out of economic advancement. This friction resulted in 1980 in a riot in the Overtown district of Miami that had a 50-percent unemployment rate among African Americans. The riot was triggered by an incident of police brutality but reflected deep anger at persistent police mistreatment and well as neglect of the black community by Miami's predominantly Cuban American political leaders. In the aftermath of the riot, little changed despite promises to fix the underlying causes of the revolt. The Cuban immigrants and their descendants have remained a powerful political and cultural force within South Florida.

Caryn E. Neumann

FURTHER READING

De los Angeles Torres, Maria. *In the Land of Mirrors: Cuban Exile Politics in the United States.* Ann Arbor: University of Michigan Press, 1999. Examines the politics of Cuban exiles during the twentieth century, including a focus on the period after the end of the Cold War.

Fernandez, Alfredo A. *Adrift: The Cuban Raft People.* Houston: Arte Público Press, 2000. Discusses Cuban refugees, including Elián González, who traveled on rafts to reach U.S. soil during the 1990's.

Gonzalez-Pando, Miguel. *The Cuban Americans.* Westport, Conn.: Greenwood Press, 1998. Historical examination of Cuban Americans during the twentieth century with a focus on the post-1959 years.

Landis, Jacquelyn, ed. *The Cubans.* Farmington, Mich.: Thomson Gale, 2005. Collection of essays on early Cuban exiles, political unrest and later waves of immigration, the refugee crisis, and the accomplishments of Cuban Americans.

Ojito, Mirta. *Finding Manana: A Memoir of a Cuban Exodus.* New York: Penguin Books, 2005. Contains accounts from people who participated in the 1980 exodus from Cuba.

Pedraza, Silvia. *Political Disaffection in Cuba's Revolution and Exodus.* New York: Cambridge University Press, 2007. Superb historical study of the role of politics in prompting Cuban immigration.

Perez-Firmat, Gustavo. *Life on the Hyphen: The Cuban-American Way.* Austin: University of Texas, 1994. Explores how tradition and interpretations of tradition have influenced the identities of Cuban Americans.

SEE ALSO: Florida; Florida illegal immigration suit; Freedom Airlift; González case; History of immigration after 1891; Latin American immigrants; Little Havana; Mariel boatlift; Miami.

CULTURAL PLURALISM

DEFINITION: Concept that individual ethnic groups have a right to exist on their own terms within the larger society while retaining their unique cultural heritages

SIGNIFICANCE: As a concept cultural pluralism is an alternative to the "melting pot" view that immigrants should assimilate to American culture by abandoning their own cultures, languages, and other traditions. Cultural pluralists insist that different ethnic groups have enriched the American way of life as immigrants and native-born citizens have learned from one another, thereby broadening their views on art, cuisine, education, history, music, and other aspects of life.

During the late nineteenth and early twentieth centuries, which saw the largest surge of immigrant arrivals in American history, an anti-immigrant backlash took the forms of nativism, xenophobia, and other expressions of prejudice. Criticism of the unfamiliar appearances and behaviors of the newly arrived peoples prompted discriminatory treatment of the new immigrants in education, employment, government programs, housing, and public accommodations. As a result, the advance of industrious and talented immigrants whose efforts could enhance American progress was held back.

A CRITIQUE OF ASSIMILATIONISM

In 1914, sociologist Edward Alsworth Ross, an advocate of scientific racism, published *The Old World in the New: The Significance of Past and Present Immigration to the American People*. This book contained scathing critiques of immigrant peoples such as Italians and Slavs as genetically inferior, arguing their presence in the United States as a rootless proletariat threatened skilled native-born workers and promoted political corruption. Reviewing that book for the leftist magazine *The Nation* in 1915, Horace Kallen critiqued assimilationist theory in an article titled "Democracy Versus the Melting Pot."

Kallen was first and foremost a philosophical pluralist—that is, he believed in the value of differences existing side by side. He opposed orthodoxies as imposing oversimplified straightjackets on the inherent complexity of reality. Philosophical certainty is impossible, according to pluralists, so different theories should be debated and respected rather than having one dominant view overturn another in an endless power struggle among competing narratives or paradigms.

Applying his philosophical views to matters of social reality, Kallen advocated cultural pluralism. He believed that the acceptance of diverse cultures coexisting in the United States strengthened, rather than jeopardized, American solidarity. If one culture insisted on dominating all others, he argued, the result would be continuing disunity and strife. He asserted that assimilationists not only misrepresented the contributions of immigrant groups but also ignored fundamental American constitutional principles of equality and justice.

More to the point, Kallen interpreted Ross and the assimilationists as members of an elite Anglo-Saxon class that was losing its dominance and fighting to protect its prerogatives by means of an undemocratic and unscholarly discourse. The uniqueness of America, Kallen felt, lay in the many streams of immigrants that had been enriching the country for more than a century. He argued that ethnic groups should be free to retain what is valuable in their own social cultural heritages while accepting a common political culture in the form of democratic principles—representative government under a rule of law that protects the liberties of the individual.

CRITIQUES OF CULTURAL PLURALISM

Cultural pluralism has been attacked for justifying cultural separatism—that is, a transformation to a "nation of nations" similar to what is found in Switzerland or a segregated America of ethnically pure residential enclaves. A second critique is that cultural pluralists assume that because ethnic traditions are static they suppress individuality. Third, cultural pluralists are attacked for a belief that ethnic identity is primary and thus more powerful than other identities. Some critics even see Kallen's concept of cultural pluralism as rooted in Jewish ideology.

Cultural pluralists respond that American cultural pluralism thrives in an integrated, not a segregated, society. They accept cultures as internally dynamic, changing and adapting over time with plenty of room for diversity inside each culture. Cultural attachments are seen as important but not exclusive, as Americans must respect those of different cultures in order to enjoy liberty together. Moreover, Kallen's argument is entirely philosophical.

Originally, cultural pluralists had much difficulty distinguishing their views from segregationist rhetoric. In contrast with more politically active multiculturalists, they were incoherent in stating how the political system should treat separatists. By the early twenty-first century, the philosophy of cultural pluralism seemed almost irrelevant as many Americans were by then claiming multiple ethnic and racial backgrounds. That very multiplicity, according to some observers, is a reason for a crisis of identity.

Michael Haas

FURTHER READING

Akam, Everett H. *Transnational America: Cultural Pluralist Thought in the Twentieth Century.* Lanham, Md.: Rowman & Littlefield, 2002. Applies cultural pluralism to modern-day identity politics that pretends to be "post-ethnic."

Baghramian, Maria, and Attracta Ingram, eds. *Pluralism: The Philosophy and Politics of Diversity.* New York: Routledge, 2000. Collection of scholarly essays on a wide variety of aspects of cultural pluralism.

Brooks, Stephen, ed. *The Challenge of Cultural Pluralism.* Westport, Conn.: Praeger, 2002. Collection of essays on cultural pluralism in modern world history. Includes chapters on theoretical aspects of the subject and on pluralism in Canada.

Denton, Nancy A., and Stewart E. Tolnay, eds. *American Diversity: A Demographic Challenge for the Twenty-first Century.* Albany: State University of New York Press, 2002. Collection of papers presented at a conference on ethnic diversity in the United States.

Hollinger, David A. *Postethnic America: Beyond Multiculturalism.* New York: Basic Books, 1995. Criticizes Kallen for depicting the United States as a social federation of ethnic groups, an impossibility in light of ethnic and racial intermarriage.

Kallen, Horace M. *Cultural Pluralism and the American Idea: An Essay in Social Philosophy.* Philadelphia: University of Pennsylvania Press, 1956. Kallen develops his cultural pluralist ideas in this book, which contains comments by Stanley H. Chapman.

_____. *Culture and Democracy in the United States.* New introduction by Stephen J. Whitfield. New Brunswick, N.J.: Transaction Books, 1998. Originally published in 1924, this classic book developed the concept of cultural pluralism.

_____. "Democracy Versus the Melting Pot: A Study of American Nationality." *The Nation* (February 18 and 25, 1915): 190-194, 217-220. Kallen's original statement of the concept of cultural pluralism.

Patterson, Orlando. *Ethnic Chauvinism: The Reactionary Impulse.* New York: Stein & Day, 1977. Assesses Kallen's effort to reconcile philosophical pluralism with cultural pluralism as a failure because group needs inevitably conflict with democratic principles.

Sollors, Werner. "A Critique of Pure Pluralism." In *Reconstructing American Literary History,* edited by Sacvan Bercovitch. Cambridge, Mass.: Harvard University Press, 1986. Criticizes Kallen for advancing group survival of the Jews as a paradigm for all ethnic groups.

SEE ALSO: Anglo-conformity; Assimilation theories; Ethnic enclaves; Hansen effect; Immigration waves; Intermarriage; Jewish immigrants; Melting pot theory; Multiculturalism; Nativism; Xenophobia.

CZECH AND SLOVAKIAN IMMIGRANTS

SIGNIFICANCE: During the late nineteenth and early twentieth centuries, about one-sixteenth of all European Czechs immigrated to America, while the Slovaks made up the sixth-largest group of immigrants during this period of the "new immigration." Eventually, about one-fifth of the entire Slovak nation arrived, trailing only the Poles in numbers among all Slavic immigrant groups in the United States.

The overwhelming majority of Slovak and Czech immigrants arrived in the United States during the fifty years prior to the outbreak of World War I. The first immigrant from the Czech lands, Herrman Augustin, arrived in 1633 and eventually owned a large estate in Maryland; the first known Slovak in America, Andrej Jelik, arrived around the mid-eighteenth century. A small group of religious dissenters from the Czech lands, known as Moravians, arrived before the American Revolution. Members of both ethnic groups fought in the American War of Independence and the U.S. Civil War.

CZECHS AND SLOVAKS BEFORE WORLD WAR I

A few Czech immigrants continued to arrive over the next two centuries after 1633. Following the failed 1848 revolutions in the Habsburg monarchy, the first sizable number of Czechs came to the United States, with a steady flow by the late 1850's, who usually came as family groups initially attracted by the lure of cheap land. Besides farming, by the turn of the century about one-half of Czech immigrants in America lived in urban settings, where they worked as small businessmen and as skilled and unskilled laborers. By the onset of World War I in 1914, approximately 350,000 highly skilled and mostly literate Czechs had settled in the United States.

The Slovaks began to immigrate to America in large numbers during the late 1870's to escape problems of overpopulation and unemployment at home. The overwhelming majority of these poorly educated agricultural workers found work as unskilled laborers in coal mines and heavy industry, especially steel mills, where, by 1909, about 10 percent of all iron- and steelworkers were Slovak. They usually came as single men expecting to earn enough money to return home and purchase land, prior to realizing the new economic benefits of America. By the 1880's, Slovak women began to arrive to satisfy the need for spouses, while married men either returned home or sent funds to bring their families to the United States. More than 60 percent of all Slovak immigrants returned at least once to the old country before the war. It is estimated that 650,000 Slovaks lived in the United States in 1914.

Both groups flourished in the United States. Wherever a community of Czechs and/or Slovaks could be found, thriving ethnic newspapers, fraternal and cultural clubs and organizations, and parishes arose. However, these entities remained separated along Roman Catholic and Freethinker lines for the Czechs, while the Slovaks were even more divided among Roman Catholics, Lutherans, Calvinists, and Byzantine-rite (Uniate or Greek-rite) Catholics.

WORLD WAR I AND AFTERWARD

The start of World War I in August, 1914, effectively cut off Slovak and Czech immigration, but ethnic leaders of both groups in the United States realized that the war presented an opportunity for greater freedoms for their homelands against the Austrian Germans and the Hungarians. Leaders of the American Czechs and Slovaks met in Cleveland, Ohio, in 1915, to propose a common, independent state after the war. In May, 1918, the Pittsburgh Pact updated the Cleveland Agreement, calling for the new joint state. The American Czechs and Slovaks collected hundreds of thousands of dollars for relief efforts of their conationals abroad and the new Czecho-Slovakia/Czechoslovakia, enlisted in foreign armies and the U.S. Army after the United States entered the war in 1917, and actively supported the war effort against the Central Powers. Their work paid off with the proclamation of the Czechoslovak Republic in October, 1918.

Despite the creation of the new country with greater opportunities for ethnic Czechs and Slovaks, immigration resumed after the war. The numbers rose steadily until the immigration laws of the 1920's effectively lim-

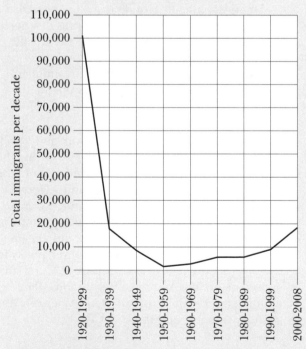

IMMIGRATION FROM CZECHOSLOVAKIA AND THE CZECH AND SLOVAK REPUBLICS, 1920-2008

Source: Department of Homeland Security, *Yearbook of Immigration Statistics, 2008.* Figures include only immigrants who obtained legal permanent resident status. Czechoslovakia existed from 1918 until 1989. Figures for 1990-2008 include immigrants who identified themselves as "Czechs," "Slovaks," and "Czechoslovakians."

ited the total number of immigrants from Czechoslovakia to about three thousand annually. The 1920's and 1930's mark the height of Slovak and Czech cultural life in the United States. However, without the influx of numerous new immigrants, both groups began to acculturate and assimilate, with the second and third generations from the mass immigration period becoming more American. These generations lost interest in the language and the old country ways of their parents and grandparents, preferring to speak English and marrying spouses from other ethnic groups. This trend accelerated after World War II, with people leaving their old ethnic neighborhoods, parishes, and organizations for the suburbs, where the Czech and Slovak Americans retained only aspects of their forefathers' culture, usually concerning holiday celebrations. Although there was a brief surge in immigration after the communist takeover of Czechoslovakia in 1948 and the Soviet invasion of the country in 1968, these immigrants were largely professional people and intellectuals who had little in common with the earlier arrivals.

According to the 1990 U.S. Census, almost 1.9 million Americans professed Slovak ancestry, about 1.2 million Americans claimed Czech roots, while approximately 300,000 considered themselves Czechoslovakian. The 2000 U.S. Census saw a slight decline for the Czech Americans, while the Slovak response was close to 800,000, nearly a 58 percent drop in ten years. This decline probably resulted from "Slovak" being listed as an example category in the 1990 U.S. Census and not the subsequent one, while Czechoslovakian ancestry claims rose by 40 percent, or 140,000 people, in 2000.

Gregory C. Ference

PROFILE OF CZECH AND SLOVAKIAN IMMIGRANTS

Countries of origin	Czech and Slovak republics
Primary languages	Czech, Slovak
Primary regions of U.S. settlement	Northeast, Midwest
Earliest significant arrivals	Mid-seventeenth century
Peak immigration period	1850's-1914
Twenty-first century legal residents*	Czech: 2,632 (329 per year) Czechoslovakia: 6,991 (874 per year) Slovak: 6,500 (813 per year)

*Immigrants who obtained legal permanent resident status in the United States. Note that government immigration figures are categories under "Czech Republic," "Czechoslovakia (former)," and "Slovak Republic."

Source: Department of Homeland Security, *Yearbook of Immigration Statistics, 2008.*

FURTHER READING

Alexander, June Granatir. *Ethnic Pride, American Patriotism: Slovaks and Other New Immigrants in the Interwar Era.* Philadelphia: Temple University Press, 2005. History of interwar America from the perspective of eastern Europeans that focuses on the Slovaks.

Čulen, Konštantin. *History of Slovaks in America.* St. Paul, Minn.: Czechoslovak Genealogical Society, 2007. Translation of *Dejiny Slovákov v Amerike* (1942). Detailed portrait of Slovak life in the United States before 1914.

Habenicht, Jan. *History of Czechs in America.* St. Paul, Minn.: Czechoslovak Genealogical Society, 1996. Translation of *Dejiny Čechův amerických* (1904). Describes the living conditions and experiences of Czechs in the United States from the mid-nineteenth century to 1904.

Kovtun, George J. "Czechs and Slovaks in the United States and Other Countries." In *Czech and Slovak History: An American Bibliography.* Washington, D.C.: Government Printing Office, 1996. Overview of sources in English about American Czechs and Slovaks.

Rechcígl, Miloslav. *Czechs and Slovaks in America.* Boulder, Colo.: East European Monographs, 2005. Collection of essays relating to the history and contributions of Czech and Slovak immigrants and their descendants in the United States.

SEE ALSO: Albright, Madeleine; Austrian immigrants; Censuses, U.S.; Chicago; European revolutions of 1848; Immigration Act of 1921; Immigration Act of 1924; Industrial Revolution; Nebraska; Pennsylvania; Texas.

D

DADA V. MUKASEY

THE CASE: U.S. Supreme Court decision on a principle of immigration law

DATE: Decided on June 16, 2008

SIGNIFICANCE: The *Dada* decision recognized the right of immigrants to pursue motions to reopen their cases after agreeing to voluntary departure, thereby permitting such immigrants to present new facts to immigration officials.

Samson Dada, a citizen of Nigeria, entered the United States in 1998 on a temporary visa. Although he was married to a U.S. citizen, the couple had failed to submit the required documentation to secure Dada a permanent residence visa. When the federal government ordered Dada's removal in 2004, he had the choice of voluntarily departing within sixty days or filing a motion to have his case reconsidered. By agreeing to a voluntary departure, he maintained some reentry privileges, and by skillful maneuvering around bureaucratic rules, he managed to remain in the country almost eight more years. When the government finally ordered his removal in February, 2006, Dada requested that his case be reopened, which would permit him to present new evidence. The government denied the request. Dada then petitioned the court of appeals for relief, which was denied on November 28, 2006. He petitioned the U.S. Supreme Court for a writ of *certiorari*, which was accepted.

By a 5-4 margin, the Supreme Court held that persons must be permitted to withdraw their requests for voluntary departure if they do so before the final deadlines for their departure. However, the decision was not a complete victory for aliens because the Court specifically declined to hold that the deadline for voluntary departure would be stayed while the motion to reopen was pending. Thus, aliens subject to departure continued to have a difficult choice to make. Justice Anthony Kennedy wrote the opinion for the majority. Justice Antonin Scalia wrote a dissenting opinion, insisting that an alien agreeing to depart voluntarily should not have any opportunity to change his mind. Justice Samuel Alito also filed a dissent, arguing that immigration officials should have the discretion of accepting or denying the withdrawal of an agreement to a voluntary withdrawal.

Thomas Tandy Lewis

FURTHER READING

Aleinikoff, Thomas, et al. *Immigration and Citizenship: Process and Policy.* 6th ed. St. Paul, Minn.: West Group, 2008.

Gordon, Charles, Stanley Mailman, and Stephen Yale-Loehr. *Immigration Law and Procedure.* New York: Matthew Bender, 2001.

SEE ALSO: Citizenship; Congress, U.S.; Constitution, U.S.; Immigration law; Supreme Court, U.S.

DALLAS

IDENTIFICATION: Third-largest city in Texas, with an estimated population of slightly fewer than 1,300,000 people in 2009

SIGNIFICANCE: Although usually perceived as a hub of Texas's staple industries of oil and cattle, Dallas has long had a wide diversity of flourishing enterprises, including those in the computer and telecommunication industries. Indeed, the very diversity of the city's thriving economy has attracted so many immigrants—especially from Mexico and Asia—that roughly one quarter of the city's residents are immigrants.

Dallas is home to a large number of Hispanics, especially people of Mexican ancestry, because Texas shares a border with Mexico and was once part of that country. Dallasites of Mexican descent therefore include both recently arrived immigrants and members of families that have lived in Texas for hundreds of years. Approximately 36 percent of the population of Dallas is Hispanic. Although Hispanics live throughout the city, Oak Cliff, a large neighborhood in the southwestern sector of the city, comes close to being an ethnic enclave, as the vast majority of its residents are of Hispanic background. People of Asian descent constitute roughly 3 percent of the city's population. Most of them stem from India, Pakistan, China, Korea, and Vietnam.

The vitality of both the Hispanic and Asian communities of Dallas is exemplified by the city's large number of service businesses and cultural enterprises supported by the two groups. For example, the Greater Hispanic Chamber of Commerce integrates the activities of the large Hispanic business community in the Dallas area, where roughly 13 percent of all businesses are owned and operated by Hispanics. The Dallas Concilio of Hispanic Service Organizations is prominent in efforts pertaining to literacy and education, health care, and race relations. Likewise, there is an equally active Greater Dallas Asian American Chamber of Commerce, which coordinates the efforts of the almost 5 percent of businesses in the city owned by Asians. Many Asian Dallasites are active in various arts. For example, Dallas is home to an annual Asian American Film Festival and to the much-admired Dallas Asian American Youth Orchestra.

Dallas serves to illustrate how issues having little to do with immigration can place a city at center stage when issues pertaining to immigrants are raised. Although long a large, populous, and active city, Dallas is probably most famous throughout the world for two things. First, it is infamous as the city in which President John F. Kennedy was assassinated in November of 1963. Second, it is famous as the setting for one of the most popular television series in history, the prime-time soap opera, *Dallas* (1978- 1991). In popular thought, Dallas has become a crystallization of all things Texan, both exciting and unpleasant. Although Dallas does indeed have a large immigrant population, so do other large cities in Texas. Nevertheless, news reports both in print and on air often tend to draw on Dallas when providing specific details for stories dealing with immigration from Mexico, such as anti-immigration measures and debates on amnesty for illegal immigrants. This trend was most clearly demonstrated in August of 2006, when NBC's *Nightly News* ran a story about how public hospitals were coping with large numbers of undocumented immigrants as patients. The network sent a reporter to Dallas to interview doctors at Parkland Memorial Hospital, where President Kennedy had died in 1963.

Thomas Du Bose

FURTHER READING

Fitzgerald, Ken. *Dallas Then and Now.* San Diego: Thunder Bay Press, 2001.

Hill, Patricia Evridge. *Dallas: The Making of a Modern City.* Austin: University of Texas Press, 1996.

Rozek, Barbara. *Come to Texas.* College Station: Texas A&M Press, 2003.

SEE ALSO: Asian immigrants; Chinese immigrants; Houston; Illegal immigration; Mexican immigrants; Texas.

DANTICAT, EDWIDGE

IDENTIFICATION: Haitian American author
BORN: January 19, 1969; Port-au-Prince, Haiti

SIGNIFICANCE: The leading writer of the Haitian diaspora, Danticat memorably conveys the struggles and identity crises of Haitian immigrants, the grim poverty and political oppression of their homeland, their mistreatment in the United States, and their vibrant language and popular culture.

Edwidge Danticat's father emigrated from Haiti to New York City in 1971, and her mother followed in 1973, leaving Danticat and her brother with her uncle Joseph, a Baptist minister who ran a school. In 1981, Danticat followed her parents, part of the immigration that has made New York City and Montreal the two largest Haitian communities in the Americas.

Danticat spoke Haitian Creole at home; her school language was French. A brilliant student, she received a bachelor's degree in French from Barnard College in 1990 and a master of fine arts degree in creative writing from Brown University in 1993. From 1993 until 1995, Danticat worked on documentary films about Haiti with American filmmaker Jonathan Demme. She was the associate producer of *Courage and Pain* (1996) and *The Agronomist* (2003), about the life and assassination of a crusading Haitian radio journalist. She has taught creative writing at New York University, the University of Texas, and the University of Miami, where she moved with Faidherbe Boyer, whom she married in 2002.

Sometimes called "the voice of Haiti" in the

United States, Danticat has been a forceful advocate for human rights. She has protested against U.S. interference in Haitian affairs, and she helped expose criminal violence by New York Police Department officers against innocent Haitian immigrants in New York, such as Abner Louima and Patrick Dorismond. In the 2004 presidential elections, she campaigned to register Haitian Americans in Miami. Many of them had been disenfranchised by Florida elections officials in 2000.

Danticat's master of fine arts thesis, a novel on the multigenerational trauma caused by mothers "testing" their daughters' virginity, was revised as *Breath, Eyes, Memory* and published by Soho Press in 1994. In 1998, it became Oprah Winfrey's book club Selection of the Month. Danticat's eloquent collection of Haitian folktales, *Krik? Krak!*, published in 1995, was a finalist for that year's National Book Award. Among her other noteworthy contributions to preserving Haitian culture is *After the Dance: A Walk Through Carnival in Jacmel, Haiti* (2002), which vividly creates a sense of place and memorably links the fantastic figures of carnival to Haitian religion, history, and politics.

Danticat's three masterpieces emphasize testimony, with varying degrees of fiction. The powerful saga *The Farming of Bones* (1998) retells from a woman's viewpoint Jacques-Stéphen Alexis's *Compère Général Soleil* (1955), a story of the Dominican dictator Rafael Trujillo's unprovoked massacre of Haitian guest workers in 1937. *The Dew Breaker* (2004) tells of a former Tonton Macoute torturer, the traumatic aftereffects of his crimes, and his moral redemption as he lives quietly in the United States. *Brother, I'm Dying* (2007) records the scarifying experiences of the deaths of Danticat's beloved uncle and father. In 2004, her uncle Joseph, pursued by armed mobs fighting with U.S. peacekeepers, sought political asylum in Miami. He was eighty-one and in ill health. He collapsed and vomited during his intake interview but was considered to be malingering. Immigration officials held him for five days; he died from acute pancreatitis shortly after he was finally taken to the hospital. Danticat was denied permission to see him.

Danticat frequently gives interviews, and she has published stories in more than two dozen magazines—most notably *The New Yorker*. Many of her stories have been anthologized. Her work has been translated into several languages, and she has won a number of literary awards, including the 2005 Story Prize for *The Dew Breaker* and the 2007 National Book Critics Circle Award for *Brother, I'm Dying*. After her first novel appeared, *The New York Times* predicted that she would be one of the thirty artists and writers under thirty most likely to transform American culture over the next thirty years.

Laurence M. Porter

FURTHER READING

Danticat, Edwidge. *Brother, I'm Dying*. New York: Alfred A. Knopf, 2007.

_____. "The Dangerous Job of Edwidge Danticat: An Interview." Interview by Renee H. Shea. *Callaloo* 19, no. 2 (January 17, 1996): 382-389.

Shemak, April. "Re-membering Hispaniola: Edwidge Danticat's The Farming of Bones." *Modern Fiction Studies* 48, no. 1 (Spring, 2002): 83-113.

Wucker, Michele. "Edwidge Danticat: A Voice for the Voiceless." *Americas* 52, no. 3 (May/June, 2000): 40.

SEE ALSO: Anglo-conformity; "Brain drain"; Child immigrants; Families; Films; Haitian immigrants; Higher education; History of immigration after 1891; Literature.

DAVIS, JAMES JOHN

IDENTIFICATION: Welsh-born American politician
BORN: October 27, 1873; Tredegar, South Wales
DIED: November 22, 1947; Takoma Park, Maryland

SIGNIFICANCE: As the secretary of labor under three U.S. presidents, Davis helped to enforce the national origins quotas of 1920's immigration law and advocated additional restrictions on immigration.

Born in 1873, James John Davis was the son and grandson of skilled workers in Welsh iron mills. His family emigrated to Pennsylvania when he was eight. At the age of eleven, Davis became an apprentice in a steel mill; by sixteen, he was a puddler who stirred molten metal. At that time, he joined the ironworkers' union, in which he eventually became a leader.

James John Davis (right) with future U.S. president Herbert Hoover during the early 1920's. (Library of Congress)

After leaving factory work, Davis became rich and achieved a national reputation as director general of the fraternal Loyal Order of Moose. In March, 1921, President Warren G. Harding appointed Davis secretary of labor. As the federal Bureau of Immigration was then an agency of the Department of Labor, Davis was responsible for enforcing the recently enacted national-origins restrictions strictly but humanely. In support of the highly restrictive Immigration Act of 1924 (also known as the Johnson-Reed Act), Davis published articles advocating increased quota restrictions and argued they should be imposed on Mexico and Canada.

In May, 1924, while Davis was still head of the Labor Department, the U.S. Border Patrol was established under the department's jurisdiction. Five years later, Davis felt frustrated by what he called the "patchwork" nature of federal enforcement of immigration laws and urged Congress to codify the immigration laws. He specifically suggested deterring unauthorized entry through the use of deten-

tion facilities and air patrols. He kept his cabinet post under both President Calvin Coolidge and President Herbert Hoover. However, he resigned from the department in 1930 when he was Republican senator from Pennsylvania. He served in the U.S. Senate until 1945, two years before he died.

Howard Bromberg

FURTHER READING

Chapple, Joseph. *"Our Jim": A Biography of James Davis.* Boston: Chapple Publishing, 1928.

Davis, James John. *The Iron Puddler: My Life in the Rolling Mills and What Came of It.* Indianapolis: Bobbs-Merrill, 1922.

_____. *Selective Immigration.* St. Paul, Minn.: Scott-Mitchell, 1925.

Zolberg, Aristide. *A Nation by Design: Immigration Policy in the Fashioning of America.* Cambridge, Mass.: Harvard University Press, 2006.

SEE ALSO: Border Patrol, U.S.; Bureau of Immigration, U.S.; Congress, U.S.; Gompers, Samuel; Immigration Act of 1917; Immigration Act of 1921; Immigration Act of 1924; Immigration law; Iron and steel industry; Pennsylvania.

DELAWARE

SIGNIFICANCE: Aside from the more heavily populated northern tip of the state around Wilmington, Delaware has not been a popular destination for immigrants. The Wilmington area's importance as a transportation hub and corporate center has offered prosperity to immigrants with backgrounds in chemistry, business, and technology. However, less well-educated immigrants have not shared in that prosperity.

Migration to the region that would become the state of Delaware began during the seventeenth century with ventures by Dutch and Swedes up the Delaware River to New Castle. During the eighteenth century, much larger contingents of Scotch-Irish and English settlers arrived, and by 1787, when Delaware became one of the original thirteen states, the area was English-speaking, with some Quakers among the settlers. Smaller numbers of French and Irish settlers also lived in the region. The Irish worked in mills and on the Chesapeake and Delaware Canal, on which construction began in 1804 but did not reach completion until 1829. The canal remained commercially important into the twenty-first century.

PROFILE OF DELAWARE

Region	Atlantic coast
Entered union	1787
Largest cities	Wilmington, Dover (capital), Newark
Modern immigrant communities	Mexicans

Population	Total	Percent of state	Percent of U.S.	U.S. rank
All state residents	854,000	100.0	0.28	45
All foreign-born residents	69,000	8.1	0.18	41

Source: U.S. Census Bureau, *Statistical Abstract for 2006.*
Notes: The U.S. population in 2006 was 299,399,000, of whom 37,548,000 (12.5%) were foreign born. Rankings in last column reflect total numbers, not percentages.

NINETEENTH CENTURY IMMIGRATION

Delaware's nineteenth century immigrants were mainly Irish and German until late in the century. The Irish worked in construction and manufacturing, while many of the Germans were painters, upholsterers, woodworkers, brewers, and saloon keepers. Members of both groups clung to cultural elements from their former homes, but the Germans were unsuccessful in preserving the use of their native language. As in other areas, the Irish became increasingly important in local political life as the century unfolded. By the 1870's and 1880's, the Irish played significant roles in state politics.

Italians, many of whom were masons and construction workers, began to appear late in the century, as did German and Russian Jews fleeing persecution. The bulk of the immigrants settled in New Castle, the northernmost of Delaware's three counties, particularly in Wilmington. In 1900, by 1900 that city's population exceeded 76,000, with the foreign-born constituting about 14 percent of that total. Many immigrants worked in manufacturing of such products as black powder, ships, leather, and textiles.

TWENTIETH CENTURY IMMIGRATION

By 1920, the proportion of immigrants among Delaware's residents reached its historic high, accounting for just under 9 percent of the total population. By 1970, the percentage of immigrants had dropped to 2.9 percent. During the early twentieth century, Italian and Polish immigrants outnumbered Irish and Germans; most of them worked in factory and service areas. Early in the century three powder companies, including the Du Pont Company, moved into the chemical industry. They concentrated the business, scientific, and technological aspects of their business in Wilmington, much of the manufacturing taking place elsewhere. Delaware saw a sharp decline in the number of blue-collar workers and an increasing need for well-educated ones.

Aside from Puerto Ricans, who are technically not foreign immigrants, the largest concentration of late twentieth and early twenty-first century immigrants in Delaware have been Mexicans. In contrast to Mexican immigrants in other states, relatively few of Delaware's Mexican residents are agricultural workers. Retail trade has attracted many, especially restaurant operations. Others have worked in finance, insurance, real estate, and rental and leasing occupations. Nearly two thirds of Delaware's Mexican-born women are in the labor force.

A study of the economic and employment status of Delaware's Hispanics, including Puerto Ricans, completed in 2008 found that one-quarter of them were living in poverty. In Kent and Sussex, the central and southern of the state's three counties, 59 percent of the Hispanic households did not earn enough money to meet the basic needs of the family. This report found construction, restaurant operation, and professional services as the most frequent sources of income. Moreover, nearly one-half of employed Hispanics were judged to be deficient in English-language skills. However, the report also revealed that an overwhelming majority of the state's Hispanic residents were interested in job training and English classes that many of them were not receiving.

Robert P. Ellis

FURTHER READING

Boyer, William W., and Edward C. Ratledge. *Delaware Politics and Government.* Lincoln: University of Nebraska Press, 2009.

Hoffecker, Carol E. *Delaware: A Bicentennial History.* New York: W. W. Norton, 1977.

Munroe, John A. *Colonial Delaware: A History.* Millwood, N.Y.: KTO Press, 1978.

_____. *History of Delaware.* Newark: University of Delaware Press, 1984.

SEE ALSO: English as a second language; Language issues; Maryland; Mexican immigrants; New Jersey; Pennsylvania; Puerto Rican immigrants.

DEPORTATION

DEFINITION: Legal process by which a government expels noncitizens from its country

SIGNIFICANCE: Deportation power gives the federal government a tool to remove immigrants who enter the United States in violation of immigration law or violate standards of behavior, as outlined in immigration law, after lawful entry into the country. Under U.S. law, deportations are civil proceedings administered by the executive branch of the government. Deportees are generally removed to the country of his or her last legal residence.

By almost any measure, deportation is an enormous federal power. Between 1892 and 2000, the U.S. government used this power to expel more than 40 million immigrants from the country. The federal government first began to build its modern deportation policy with the passage of the Chinese Exclusion Act of 1882.

During the early twenty-first century, deportations continued to be based on the basic deportation powers and policies constructed between the late nineteenth and early twentieth centuries. However, by then, the U.S. government was no longer officially using the term "deportation." Instead, it processed deportees under two official procedures called "immigrant removals" and "immigrant returns."

ORIGINS OF DEPORTATION POLICY

The roots of what would become deportation policy in the United States, however, stretch further back in time. During the colonial period and much of the nineteenth century, European and Euro-American communities expelled vagrants and individuals they thought were unable to support themselves. Residents in towns and villages expelled the migrant poor. There was, however, little distinction made between the nationalities of the poor. Membership in the local community was what mattered. American citizens and immigrants alike could be expelled from an American town if they were not municipal members and became public charges. Some American colonies tried sending expelled criminals or poor immigrants back to England, but it was generally too expensive and inefficient to remove undesirable residents to Europe. Consequently, expulsion was never a widespread practice in America during the colonial period. After 1787, several state constitutions authorized the removal of nonresidents, but this power also languished.

In 1798, the U.S. Congress passed two laws called the Alien Friends Act and the Alien Enemies Act. These laws gave the president of the United States a limited power, based on executive order with judicial enforcement, to expel foreigners from the United States. Some Republicans, including Thomas Jefferson, maintained that this expulsion policy was patently unconstitutional; they thought it represented an attempt by the opposing Federalist Party to remove its political enemies from the country. The constitutionality of the two 1798 laws was never tested, and most sections of the Alien Friends Act expired two years after its passage. Before the U.S. Civil War (1861-1865), there was neither the popular will nor, after the election of the Republicans and the dissolution of the Federalist Party, the political will to legitimize the federal removal of immigrants.

U.S. deportation policy developed in tandem with immigration exclusions and citizenship law during the late nineteenth century. As a part of the Chinese Exclusion Act of 1882, Congress first empowered the federal government to deport immigrants. Like all the sections of Chinese exclusion laws, the deportation provision wrote racism into U.S. immigration policy. In 1892, when Congress passed the Geary Act, it significantly expanded the range of immigrants who could be deported under Chinese exclusion and made deportation policy punitive. With this law, the government put the onus of proving lawful residence on every Chinese person within the United States. The Geary Act required that all Chinese workers apply for certificates of residence, which would prove that they were in the country lawfully. When immigrants were found without these certificates in their possession, the government assumed that they were in the United States unlawfully. The certificate of residence requirement made long-term residents who entered the country before 1882 deportable.

Over the next twenty years, Congress wrote immigration laws that gave the federal government the power to deport immigrants from all racial and ethnic heritages—beyond Chinese immigrants. General exclusion laws were passed in 1882 and 1883, but it was not until 1891 that the government synced each excludable category with a deportation provision. By 1903, the list of excludable and deportable immigrants included Chinese workers, contract workers (of all ethnicities), anarchists, prostitutes, and all those the government classed as morally or physically unfit. Included in the list of deportable immigrants were categories that are no

Recently arrived immigrants taking a break in the open-air detention pen atop the main reception center at Ellis Island while awaiting deportation in 1902. (Library of Congress)

longer meaningful today, categories such as vagrants, idiots, and imbeciles.

DEPORTATION, 1882-1965

As the federal government began using its new power to deport, several immigrants challenged their deportations in the courts. Their cases went further than challenging an individual deportation—whether or not the government's case against one immigrant was fair or warranted—to challenge the entire legitimacy of the government's new power of deportation. In 1893, the first deportation case reached the U.S. Supreme Court in *Fong Yue Ting v. United States*. This case disputed the government's ability to deport immigrants under the Chinese exclusion laws generally and under the Geary Act of 1892 specifically.

In *Fong Yue Ting*, the Court found that deportation was simply an extension of the government's power to exclude. The Court wrote that the power to exclude and deport originated from the powers of a sovereign nation and fell within the powers nation-states could use to protect their national security. Relying on the precedent established in *Chae Chan Ping v. United States* (1889; also known as the *Chinese Exclusion Case*), the Court found that the power to exclude and deport fell into the emerging plenary power doctrine.

The Court's decision in *Fong Yue Ting* also dealt with the validity of the process of deportation under the Geary Act. In a decision that distinguished between punishment and protection, the Court upheld the government's deportation power. Something that was protective of national sovereignty, the Court reasoned, could not also be a punishment. The Court, therefore, legitimated the administrative and judicial structures of deportation under Chinese exclusion, dismissing claims that the hearings and appeals process violated Fourth, Fifth, and Sixteenth Amendment rights. The *Fong Yue Ting* precedent still stood during the early twenty-first century, upholding the legitimacy of the civil nature of deportations.

Between the passage of the first deportation law in 1882 and 1924, the U.S. government typically deported a few hundred—at most, a few thousand—people each year. In the Immigration Act of 1924, Congress introduced the national origins system, which led to a number of significant changes in American deportation policy. Under the national origins system, the Bureau of Immigration began deporting thousands more immigrants each year. In 1922, just prior to the passage of the new law, the bureau deported 4,283 immigrants. In 1923, the bureau deported 3,546 immigrants. In 1925, the first year after Congress passed the new law, the government deported 9,402 immigrants. A high point in the deportations under the national origins system came in 1954, when federal officials deported more than one million Mexican immigrants in the campaign known as Operation Wetback.

The Immigration Act of 1924 created the deportable category of "aliens without proper visas," and, by the late 1920's, the Bureau of Immigration was deporting more than half of all deportees under it. Immigrants without proper documentation quickly became the largest class of deportees, above the qualitative provisions included in the immigration laws passed between 1882 and 1920. During the Great Depression of the 1930's, the government used deportation policy, in cooperation with state and local officials, as a part of Mexican repatriation—the forced removal of one million Mexican and Mexican Americans from the United States to Mexico.

A category particularly important during the pre- and post-1924 periods was that of alien radicals. In 1903, Congress first included alien anarchists in the list of inadmissible classes. In immigration laws passed in 1917 and 1919, it expanded the scope of the antiradical provisions. Unsuccessfully, the Bureau of Immigration tried to deport members of the Industrial Workers of the World in a number of cases in the Pacific Northwest during World War I. Then, in the Palmer raids beginning in 1919, the Bureau of Immigration arrested close to three thousand noncitizens, mostly from Russia. In the end, however, immigration agents deported only about three hundred. A broader use of the antiradical provisions occurred during the Cold War, especially after the passage of the Internal Security Act of 1950 and the Immigration and Nationality Act of 1952. The Supreme Court upheld the expansive antiradical provisions in *Harisiades v. Shaughnessy* (1952).

DEPORTATION AFTER 1965

In 1965, Congress ended the national origins system, but under the policies that the government built to replace it, deportations continued to increase. In the Immigration Act of 1997, however, Congress and the Immigration and Naturalization Service (INS) stopped using the term "deportation." In the early twenty-first century, U.S. immigration officials deport immigrants through formal processes, officially called removals, and returns, when immigrants "voluntarily" depart the country after being detained by immigration officials. The Immigration and Customs Enforcement (ICE) in the Department of Homeland Security administers immigrant returns and removals.

Since the 1980's, one of the largest and most significant categories immigration and customs agents have used to remove immigrants is criminal status. In 2006, for example, the government deported 95,752 immigrants under this category, constituting about 35 percent of all removals. Important laws that expanded the grounds for criminal deportations included the Anti-Drug Abuse Act of 1988 and the Illegal Immigration Reform and Immigrant Responsibility Act of 1996. The majority of immigrants found in violation of immigration law, however, are not processed under the formal removal process. Most leave the country through the return process. In 2006, for example, the government removed 272,389 immigrants and returned 1,043,381.

In the early twenty-first century, removals and returns continue to operate under the administrative process of deportation and the court precedents established during the late nineteenth and early twentieth centuries. Immigrants may hire attorneys to represent them, but they must pay for the costs themselves. The decisions of the removal hearing are not "subject to judicial review" on grounds of fact, but only on procedural grounds. Laws do allow for charging some immigrants with criminal violations, but, as had been the case during the late nineteenth and early twentieth centuries, federal law states that a removal hearing is a civil proceeding. Removals as well as returns continue to be classified as protective of national security, and the government's power continues to originate from national sovereignty.

Torrie Hester

FURTHER READING

Balderrama, Francisco E., and Raymond Rodríguez. *Decade of Betrayal: Mexican Repatriation in the 1930's.* Albuquerque: University of New Mexico Press, 1995. Engaging history of the misuse of deportation against both Mexican immigrants and many of their U.S.-born children. Also includes a rich history of repatriates' lives in Mexico following their removal from the United States.

Daniels, Roger. *Guarding the Golden Door: American Immigration Policy and Immigrants Since 1882.* New York: Hill & Wang, 2004. Provides a strong overview of deportation as a part of a broader immigration policy between 1882 and 2004.

Kanstroom, Daniel. *Deportation Nation: Outsiders in American History.* Cambridge, Mass.: Harvard University Press, 2007. Done by a legal historian, this work provides an overview of deportation as a part of a larger history of forced migrations in the United States.

Lee, Erika. *At America's Gates: Chinese Immigration During the Exclusion Era, 1882-1943.* Chapel Hill: University of North Carolina Press, 2003. Provides a rich social and legal history of deportation in a broader study of Chinese exclusion.

Lytle-Hernandez, Kelly. "The Crimes and Consequences of Illegal Immigration: A Cross-Border Examination of Operation Wetback, 1943-1954." *Western Historical Quarterly* 37 (Winter, 2006): 421-444. Award-winning article that examines the actions of both the United States and Mexican governments in the deportation of more than one million Mexican immigrants.

Neuman, Gerald L. *Strangers to the Constitution: Immigrants, Borders, and Fundamental Law.* Princeton, N.J.: Princeton University Press, 1996. Modern scholarly work that provides insight into immigrant removals during the colonial period and the limited deportation power built into the Alien and Sedition Acts of 1798.

Ngai, Mae M. *Impossible Subjects: Illegal Aliens and the Making of Modern America.* Princeton, N.J.: Princeton University Press, 2004. Modern scholarly study that examines immigration exclusions and deportations between 1924 and 1965.

SEE ALSO: Alien and Sedition Acts of 1798; *Chae Chan Ping v. United States*; Criminal immigrants; *Fong Yue Ting v. United States*; Mexican deportations of 1931; "Moral turpitude"; Operation Wetback; Red Scare; *Wong Wing v. United States*; *Zadvydas v. Davis.*

DILLINGHAM COMMISSION

IDENTIFICATION: Joint congressional committee formed to study immigration

DATE: Operated from 1907 to 1911

ALSO KNOWN AS: U.S. Immigration Commission

SIGNIFICANCE: The forty-one volumes of statistical material on immigration eventually published by the Dillingham Commission contained a wealth of information that provided support for limiting immigration, thereby helping lead to passage of the Emergency Immigration Act of 1921 and the Immigration Act of 1924.

During the late nineteenth century, the United States underwent a period of rapid industrialization that required an expanding work force. Immigration supplied much of the new labor needs, and the country's foreign-born population grew rapidly between 1880 and 1914. Although most Americans thought of themselves as belonging to a nation of farms and small towns, the newest arrivals were predominantly big-city dwellers. New York, Boston, Pittsburgh, and Chicago held the largest immigrant settlements in the United States. By 1910, 79 percent of immigrants from southern and eastern Europe and 68 percent of those from northern and western Europe lived in American cities. The numbers of immigrants from southern and eastern Europe had also been increasing most rapidly, a matter of concern to some native-born Americans. In 1860, only 1.2 percent of foreign-born residents of the United States had come from the southern and eastern countries; by 1910, that proportion had grown to 37.5 percent of the foreign-born.

BACKGROUND TO THE COMMISSION

Densely concentrated in the growing cities and distinctly alien in the eyes of many American officials and older American citizens, the new immigrants seemed to represent a problem to groups such as the Immigration Restriction League of Boston. The trend in political and social thinking known as Progressivism contributed to concerns over immigration, because many Progressives believed that solving social problems such as alcoholism, poverty, urban slums, and poor education re-

quired improving the human stock of the United States, and they saw continuing immigration as contributing to civic decay. Creating a culturally more unified nation was part of the Progressive ideology. Some political leaders argued that immigrants were flooding into the country in such great numbers that the newcomers could not be assimilated. Progressives also believed that social problems could be solved by the careful scientific analysis of experts.

The desire to bring immigration under control led the U.S. Congress to pass the Immigration Act of 1907. This legislation updated earlier immigration laws and—consistent with Progressive goals ofimproving the American population—excluded persons classified as physically and mentally defective. Section 39 of the 1907 law established a nine-member commission, made up equally of members of the Senate, members of the House of Representatives, and presidential appointees. The task of the commission was to undertake a full examination of the issue of immigration and to prepare a detailed report of its findings, with recommendations for future action, for the U.S. Congress.

MAKEUP AND MISSION OF THE COMMISSION

The U.S. senators on the U.S. Immigration Commission established in 1907 were Republican William P. Dillingham of Vermont, Republican Henry Cabot Lodge of Massachusetts, and Democrat Asbury Latimer of South Carolina. After Latimer died in 1908, he was replaced by Mississippi Democratic senator LeRoy Percy. Dillingham chaired the commission, which became known by his name. New Jersey Republican Benjamin F. Howell, New York Republican William S. Bennet, and Alabama Democrat John L. Burnett made up the trio of members from the House of Representatives.

President Theodore Roosevelt appointed three experts to guide the investigation. Jeremiah Jenks, who later summarized the commission's findings in a book he coauthored with W. Jett Lauck, was a professor, academic researcher, attorney, and respected writer on social and political issues. Charles P. Neill was a former professor of political economy who had entered into public administration. The president's third appointee, William Wheeler, was a prominent California businessman.

Members of the commission were generally suspicious of immigration from the beginning, and their preconceptions guided their investigations. Nevertheless, they engaged in detailed and intensive research. In May, 1907, Dillingham, Bennet, Burnett, Howell, Latimer, and Wheeler went to Europe with a commission staff to study the sources of European immigration to the United States. They visited most of the countries that had sent immigrants to the United States and interviewed 108 former immigrants who had returned to their home countries. Within the United States, the commission amassed and organized a vast range of statistics on immigration and immigrants under the direction of Neill and Jenks. The commission also sponsored the research of anthropologist Franz Boas, who looked at the changes thought to have occurred in the bodies of immigrants and their children. Boas argued that these changes could be taken as physical evidence of the degree of assimilation of immigrants in American society.

FINDINGS OF THE COMMISSION

The Dillingham Commission concluded its work in 1911. Its official final report filled forty-one volumes and formed a virtual encyclopedia of immigration. The commission presented its conclusions and recommendations in the first volume. The most notable conclusion was that the heavy southern and eastern European immigration of recent years had posed a serious danger to American society by bringing in large numbers of people who were dramatically different from the older stock of European Americans and who could not be assimilated. The report recommended much more restrictive immigration policies. It also suggested literacy tests to raise the education levels of new settlers.

The Immigration Problem, the summary book based on the report first published by Jenks and Lauck in 1911, is still available in many libraries. It offers an excellent portrait of immigration in the early twentieth century and an illuminating example of how American officials of that era saw immigration.

The findings of the Dillingham Commission helped steer American legislation. In 1917, Congress passed a new law that not only barred all immigrants from a vast zone in Asia but also expanded categories of admissible preexisting immigrant communities and made literacy a requirement for admission for all immigrants above the age of sixteen. In 1921, the Congress enacted the Emergency Immigration Act, which attempted to limit numbers of southern and eastern Europeans by pegging the number of immigrants permitted from each country at 3 percent of the number of people from that country who had been living in the United States in 1910. The Immigration Act of 1924 made American policy even more restrictive by setting the national quotas at 2 percent of the number of people from each country living in the United States in 1890.

Carl L. Bankston III

FURTHER READING

Gould, Lewis L. *America in the Progressive Era, 1890-1914.* Harlow, England: Pearson, 2001. Stimulating history of the United States during the era of its heaviest immigration from Europe—the same era during which the Dillingham Commission undertook its investigation.

Jenks, Jeremiah W., and W. Jett Lauck. *The Immigration Problem: A Study of American Immigration Conditions and Needs.* 6th ed. New York: Funk & Wagnalls, 1926. One-volume summary of the Dillingham Commission's official forty-one volume report containing the most important findings of the commission.

Zeidel, Robert F. *Immigrants, Progressives, and Exclusion Politics: The Dillingham Commission, 1900-1927.* De Kalb: Northern Illinois University Press, 2004. Objective modern scholarly study of the work of the Dillingham Commission that assesses its role in bringing about the restrictive immigration laws of the following years.

SEE ALSO: Center for Immigration Studies; Congress, U.S.; History of immigration after 1891; Immigration Act of 1907; Immigration Act of 1917; Immigration Act of 1921; Immigration Act of 1924; Language issues; Literacy tests; Progressivism; Select Commission on Immigration and Refugee Policy.

DISASTER RECOVERY WORK

DEFINITION: Large-scale relief efforts to repair damage left by fires, floods, hurricanes, and other natural disasters

SIGNIFICANCE: Disaster recovery work in the United States has become an occupation heavily populated with both documented and undocumented immigrant laborers, the latter of whom are usually paid significantly less than documented workers. During the early twenty-first century, many immigrant disaster recovery workers were victims of exploitation and in some situations were exposed to harmful toxins from which they contracted unnecessary chronic illnesses.

As a labor-intensive industry, disaster recovery work demands hard physical labor to perform tasks ranging from heavy lifting, brickwork, and pipe laying to sewage cleanup and refuse clearance. Although these jobs are physically taxing, many of them require little training and consequently are given to unskilled workers. Hours of disaster-relief workers tend to be long, with shifts averaging from twelve to fourteen hours at a stretch. Since the inception of the bracero program for Mexican farmworkers during the early 1940's, disaster-relief jobs have often been filled by Mexican and other Latino laborers who have stayed on in the United States after completing their bracero contracts.

Many of these immigrant workers have suffered exploitation in the form of wage theft and poor working conditions. This is partly because it is difficult to maintain in disaster areas the kinds of workplace standards mandated by the federal Occupational Safety and Health Administration (OSHA). Moreover, immigrant workers are often hesitant to report cases of exploitation for fear of being deported. Language barriers also pose obstacles to many of those suffering mistreatment.

The exploitation of immigrants working in disaster relief has been widespread over a very long period. However, it has only been since the late twentieth century that it has become a well-documented phenomenon, thanks to worker rights organizations working to empower, protect, and assist immigrant workers. Two of the biggest disasters of the twenty-first century provide useful case studies.

SEPTEMBER 11, 2001, TERRORIST ATTACKS

The terrorist attacks on the Pentagon and New York City's World Trade Center of September 11, 2001, had a great impact on immigrant families living near the affected areas. In New York City, the smoke-filled air that clung for months after the World Trade Center towers collapsed contributed to debilitating, long-term lung problems among disaster relief workers and members of immigrant communities living in the lower East Side of Manhattan. Health services have been provided to New York City police and fire department personnel who developed symptoms of 9/11-related lung problems. However, no special health services were provided for immigrant workers who contracted illnesses while working at Ground Zero.

Numerous class-action lawsuits have been filed on behalf of more than eight thousand workers who developed lung problems from inhaling air with high levels of lead, asbestos, benzene, and mercury. Filed against both the firms that employed the workers and the city itself, which claimed that the air was safe, these lawsuits ask for damages for three levels of injuries.

- Level 1: chronic coughing, apparently caused by prolonged exposure to macerated cement in the air surrounding Ground Zero
- Level 2: scarring of lung tissue and chronic respiratory illness
- Level 3: cancer.

Toxins in the air around the collapsed buildings have been shown to cause blood cancer, lymphatic cancer, and multiple myeloma. Those seeking damages in the class-action suit face thousands of dollars of debt in unpaid hospital bills and doctors' fees.

Although anti-immigrant sentiments throughout America were higher during the period directly following 9/11, many immigrants responded as relief workers, often as unpaid volunteers, to assist in the clean-up efforts. Undocumented Latino workers, as well as undocumented workers from Poland, Russia, and China assisted in the dangerous cleanup effort at Ground Zero. Many were given only paper masks, and some women—used because of their generally smaller physical sizes—cleaned air ducts with virtually no protective gear. Many undocumented workers who assisted in the relief work have been wary of coming forward to claim damages in the class-action lawsuit, assuming that they have no right to access the funds. They have continued to suffer from debilitating illnesses in silence. Many cannot afford their health care treatments, and attorney fees are even more difficult to arrange for many.

Immigrant workers from El Salvador, Mexico, Nicaragua, Honduras, and other Latin American countries made up most of the labor force that rebuilt the Pentagon building after the September 11 attack. Many of these workers were in the country on temporary visas and worked for American contracting businesses in the Arlington, Virginia, area. Some of these immigrants did potentially harmful work in asbestos removal, and some complained of incidents of wage theft.

New Orleans and Hurricane Katrina

When Hurricane Katrina hit the Gulf coast region in 2005, flooding brought noxious sediment from the canal breaches and deposited toxins throughout the city of New Orleans, displacing thousands of residents from their homes and jobs. When migrant workers arrived looking for work, they found numerous jobs in refuse removal. Much of this work was done in dangerous waste zones, involving hazardous tasks such as pressure-washing black mold and removing canal sediment that contained high levels of arsenic. These jobs required protective gear that some workers complained they were not given. In addition, undocumented workers claimed to receive significantly less money for the same jobs done by documented workers, while some claimed they were paid nothing at all.

Shannon Oxley

Further Reading

Bradford, Marlene, and Robert S. Carmichael, eds. *Natural Disasters.* 3 vols. Pasadena, Calif.: Salem Press, 2000. Comprehensive reference work covers natural disasters of all types throughout world history. The set is organized by types of disasters, with overview essays and case studies of individual disasters.

Brinkley, Douglas. *The Great Deluge: Hurricane Katrina, New Orleans, and the Mississippi Gulf Coast.* New York: William Morrow, 2006. Useful guide to understanding the immense problems faced by New Orleans and other Gulf coast communities during and after Hurricane Katrina.

Bullard, Robert D., and Beverley Wright. *Race, Place, and Environmental Justice After Hurricane Katrina.* Boulder, Colo.: Westview Press, 2009. Revealing look at the roles of different ethnic communities in the rebuilding of the Gulf coast after Hurricane Katrina struck.

Pielke, R. A., Jr., and R. A. Pielke, Sr. *Hurricanes: Their Nature and Impacts on Society.* New York: John Wiley & Sons, 1997. Informative and well-written book by father and son meteorologists. Focuses on the United States, integrating science and social policies in response to these storms.

Rosner, David, and Gerald Markowitz. *Deadly Dust: Silicosis and the On-Going Struggle to Protect Workers' Health.* Ann Arbor: University of Michigan Press, 2006. Provides a description of the industrial lung problems similar to those faced by recovery workers after 9/11.

See also: Health care; Homeland Security, Department of; Mexican immigrants; Natural disasters as push-pull factors; Push-pull factors; Remittances of earnings.

Displaced Persons Act of 1948

The Law: Federal legislation designed to help resettle thousands of Europeans who had been displaced from their homes by World War II
Date: Enacted in 1948

> **Significance:** Under this law, refugees became for the first time a major factor in U.S. immigration, and the administration of this law would influence subsequent policies on refugees, notably those from communist countries, including Hungary, Cuba, and Vietnam.

When World War II in Europe came to an end in 1945, an estimated 7 to 11 million displaced persons were still living in Germany, Italy, and Austria. President Harry S. Truman called upon Congress to enact legislation that would allow some of these wartime refugees to enter the United States. Along with the Citizens Committee on Displaced Persons, a prorefugee lobbying group working for legislation to bring displaced persons to the United States, the Truman administration supported admitting a number of European refugees over and above the existing immigration quotas for that region of the world. The law passed in 1948 authorized the entry of 200,000 displaced persons over the next two years but within the quota system. When the act was extended for two more years in 1950, it increased displaced-person admissions to 415,000.

Harry S. Truman. (Library of Congress)

Among numerous restrictions on immigration imposed by the law, the act stipulated that only applicants who had been in resettlement camps by the end of 1945 would be eligible for American visas. It also gave preference to relatives of American citizens and insisted that all applicants must present guarantees by sponsors that housing was waiting for them and they would not displace American workers. More important than these restrictions, however, was the fact that the legislation authorized the U.S. Displaced Persons Commission to administer the program, instead of the U.S. State Department or the Immigration and Naturalization Service (INS). This enabled President Truman to appoint three commissioners known to be sympathetic to refugees to administer the program. Consequently, the program used less severe screening and security measures than similar programs of earlier decades.

Refugees admitted to the United States under this program were also aided by voluntary social service agencies, accredited by the Displaced Person Commission. Most of these agencies were created by religious and ethnic groups, who gave assurances that the admitted refugees would not become "public charges" and that they, the agencies, would help oversee the resettlement of the refugees. Among these relief organizations were the National Catholic Welfare Council, the National Lutheran Council, the Church World Service, and the United Service for New Americans. They sponsored the majority of persons brought to the United States under the Displaced Persons program.

By the end of 1952, slightly more than 400,000 persons were admitted to the United States under the authority of the Displaced Persons Act. More than 70 percent of them were refugees from Eastern Europe and the Soviet Union. Nearly 75 percent came to the United States within family groups, and about 16 percent, or 63,000 persons were Jewish. The people admitted under this program represented nearly one-half the 900,000 legal immigrants admitted to the United States from 1949 to 1952. For the first time in American history refugee immigration became an important component of immigration.

John Boyd

FURTHER READING

Bon Tempo, Carl J. *Americans at the Gate: The United States and Refugees During the Cold War.* Princeton, N.J.: Princeton University Press, 2008.

Genizi, Haim. *America's Fair Share: The Admission and Resettlement of Displaced Persons, 1945-1952.* Detroit: Wayne State University Press, 1993.

Zolberg, Aristide. *A Nation by Design: Immigration Policy in the Fashioning of America.* Cambridge, Mass.: Harvard University Press, 2006.

SEE ALSO: Anti-Semitism; Congress, U.S.; *Fedorenko v. United States*; History of immigration after 1891; Immigration law; Jewish immigrants; Quota systems; Refugee Relief Act of 1953; Refugees; World War II.

DOMINICAN IMMIGRANTS

SIGNIFICANCE: Although the West Indian island nation of the Dominican Republic had a close relationship with the United States through much of the twentieth century, significant Dominican immigration into the United States did not begin until the latter part of the century. By the turn of the twenty-first century, Dominicans had become one of the fastest-growing immigrant populations and ranked as the fourth-largest Hispanic group in the United States, after Mexicans, Puerto Ricans, and Cubans.

The first West Indian landfall of explorer Christopher Columbus in 1492, the island of Santo Domingo was colonized by Spain. Later, the French took control of the western part of the island, which became the separate nation of Haiti. By enslaving Arawak, Taino, and African peoples, the Spanish and French produced valuable sugar cane, tobacco, indigo, cotton, and coffee crops on the island's plantations. By the eighteenth century, the island was the most prosperous colony in the West Indies. Modern Dominicans trace their origins to colonial intermixtures of Native Amerindians, Africans, and European settlers.

U.S. INVOLVEMENT IN THE DOMINICAN REPUBLIC

During the early nineteenth century, Spanish Santo Domingo was almost constantly in upheaval. Between 1805 and 1844, it experienced two Haitian invasions, a popular revolt that led to independence, and a return to Spanish rule. After the country became fully independent in 1844 as the Dominican Republic, it was beset by an ongoing civil war that produced twenty different governments in as many years. Meanwhile, Americans became involved in the island nation when U.S. president Andrew Jackson sought a Caribbean naval base and later, when President Ulysses S. Grant considered annexation. The island's position along sea-lanes essential to U.S. commerce, its proximity to the proposed Panama Canal, and its emergence as a profit-

able sugar cane exporter were among its strategic assets.

Burdened with foreign debt, the Dominican Republic yielded to the United States in 1905, when Theodore Roosevelt used a corollary of the Monroe Doctrine to appoint an American to run the Dominican customs office. By that time, U.S. investors controlled the Dominican sugar industry. Ostensibly concerned with the island's debt to European creditors during World War I, the United States occupied the Dominican Republic from 1916 through 1930. During those years, the U.S. government oversaw the installation of constitutional government and took control of the country's finances, allowing U.S. banks and sugar investors to advance their local business interests. Four years after the assassination of Dominican dictator

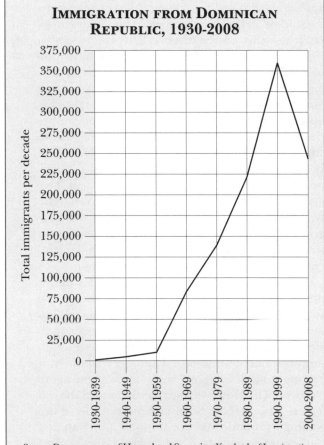

IMMIGRATION FROM DOMINICAN REPUBLIC, 1930-2008

Source: Department of Homeland Security, *Yearbook of Immigration Statistics, 2008.* Figures include only immigrants who obtained legal permanent resident status.

Rafael Trujillo in 1961, the United States again occupied the Dominican Republic in response to the overthrow of President Juan Bosch.

PUSH-PULL FACTORS

From 1910 through the 1940's, when U.S. involvement in the Dominican Republic was strongest, a small number of Dominican immigrants entered the United States seeking employment. Most resided in New York City. Much like many other Caribbean migrants, Dominicans typically came to the United States as secondary migrants after first working in Puerto Rico, Cuba, Panama, or elsewhere. Many Dominicans helped build the Panama Canal or did agriculture work in American-ruled Puerto Rico during the early twentieth century, but it is difficult to estimate how many of these people afterward entered the United States. It is, however, known that Harlem became home to thousands of West Indians from the Greater Antilles island group, of which the Dominican Republic is part, during the second decade of the century. Some New York City neighborhoods in Queens trace Dominican settlement to the 1920's.

Caribbean immigration was indirectly promoted with the passage of the Immigration Act of 1924, which restricted new immigration from Eastern Hemispheric but not Western Hemispheric nations. After 1930, the Dominican Republic's oppressive Trujillo regime restricted Dominican emigration. Only 1,150 Dominicans immigrated to the United States between 1931 and 1940, and 5,627 arrived between 1941 and 1950—the first decades for which U.S. Immigration and Naturalization Service has data on Dominican immigration.

A larger wave of Dominican immigration began after 1950. During the 1950's, 9,987 Dominicans—mostly political exiles—entered the United States legally, an average of 990 per year. During the 1960's, the total was more than nine times greater when more 93,000 immigrants arrived. After Trujillo's 1961 assassination and a 1963 coup in which the democratically elected president Juan Bosch was deposed, immigration to the United States averaged 9,330 people per year.

Dominicans began to find entry into the United States more difficult in 1968 when the Immigration and Nationality Act of 1965 put a limit on the number of immigrants permitted from the Western Hemisphere. Nevertheless, Dominican immigra-

PROFILE OF DOMINICAN IMMIGRANTS

Country of origin	Dominican Republic
Primary language	Spanish
Primary regions of U.S. settlement	New York, New Jersey, Florida, New England
Earliest significant arrivals	Late nineteenth century
Peak immigration period	1990's
Twenty-first century legal residents*	225,849 (28,231 per year)

*Immigrants who obtained legal permanent resident status in the United States.
Source: Department of Homeland Security, *Yearbook of Immigration Statistics, 2008.*

tion continued to grow during every decade. The peak year was 1994, when 51,221 Dominicans entered the United States. In 2009, the U.S. Office of Immigration Statistics reported that 31,879 Dominican immigrants had obtained permanent resident status during the previous year, when 22,562 (71 percent) of that total were new arrivals. The remaining 9,317 Dominicans received status adjustments during 2008. These figures do not include undocumented Dominican immigrants, whose numbers may be several times greater than official counts of documented immigrants.

Political violence and repressive governmental policies were push factors during the Trujillo years. During the 1960's, U.S. foreign policy became a pull factor. Fearing the spread of communism from nearby Cuba, the United States invaded the Dominican Republic in 1965, helping to stabilize a pro-Western government, and encouraging increased U.S. immigration in order to quell political differences on the island. Political factors motivated much of the Dominican immigration through the 1970's, but economic factors became paramount after 1980.

During the 1970's, the Dominican economy sharply declined. Urban residents desiring middle-class lifestyles were challenged by their homeland's shortages of well-paying jobs and reliable transportation, water, and electrical services. Meanwhile, inflation and shortages placed even basic groceries out of reach of many Dominicans. From the 1980's

FAMOUS DOMINICAN AMERICANS

By the end of the twentieth century, a growing number of Dominican Americans were winning fame in the United States. In view of the fact that baseball has become the national sport of the Dominican Republic, it is not surprising that Dominicans have been especially prominent in Major League Baseball in the United States. Among the many star Dominican players are Tony Fernandez, Juan Marichal, Sammy Sosa, Manny Mota, and Felipe, Jesus, and Matty Alou. The oldest of the Alou brothers, Felipe was not only the first prominent Dominican player in the major leagues, he was also later the first Dominican to manage major league clubs. His son, Moisés Alou, has carried on the family tradition in baseball.

Other prominent Dominican Americans have included authors Julia Alvarez and Junot Díaz, fashion designer Oscar de la Renta, and U.S. assistant attorney general for civil rights Thomas E. Perez.

through the first decade of the twenty-first century, most Dominicans who have come to the United States have done so in the hope of finding decent work opportunities and living wages. Some do not intend to stay permanently, hoping instead to save enough money to return home to start new businesses or simply to live more comfortably.

UNIQUE CHARACTERISTICS

A large portion of Dominican immigrants send part of their U.S. earnings to their families in the Dominican Republic. Their remittances have made an important contribution to the Dominican economy. Patricia Pessar's analysis of a 1981 survey of Dominicans in New York City shows that both male and female Dominican immigrants have worked as semiskilled and unskilled laborers in the manufacturing sector. Many Dominican men worked in the service sector, sometimes as managers and proprietors of small businesses, and as skilled craft and blue-collar workers. Many of the women worked as clerical or domestic workers.

Surveys of Dominican immigrants during the 1980's indicated that more than half of Dominican immigrants were female and either were married or were divorced heads of households. They also saw a high concentration of female Dominican garment workers. In New York City, a profusion of

Dominican small businesses emerged during the 1980's and 1990's. These included grocery stores, beauty shops, travel agencies, and small manufacturing plants that did subcontracting work for larger manufacturers. As Dominicans have experienced greater economic success in the United States, many of those who once planned to return to their homeland have decided to remain in the United States, partly in order to be near their American-born children.

Linda A. Winterbottom

FURTHER READING

Hernández, Ramona, and Francisco L. Rivera-Batiz. *Dominicans in the United States: A Socioeconomic Profile, 2000.* New York: CUNY Dominican Studies Institute, 2003.

Pessar, Patricia. "The Dominicans." In *New Immigrants in New York*, edited by Nancy Foner. New York: Columbia University Press, 1987. Essay analyzing the Dominican immigrant stream based on survey data from the late 1970's and early 1980's.

_____. *A Visa for a Dream: Dominicans in the United States.* Boston: Allyn & Bacon, 1995. Exploration of the emigration process for Dominican immigrants, their aspirations, and family and community life in New York City.

Ricourt, Milagros. *Dominicans in New York City: Power from the Margins.* New York: Routledge, 2002. Narrative study of the political and ethnic identity of Dominican New Yorkers.

Torres-Saillant, Silvio, and Ramona Hernández. *The Dominican Americans.* Westport, Conn.: Greenwood Press, 1998. Thorough study of the Dominican immigrant community's emergence and the creation of a distinctive Dominican American culture.

Watkins-Owens, Irma. *Blood Relations: Caribbean Immigrants and the Harlem Community, 1900-1930.* Bloomington: Indiana University Press, 1996. Study focused on the presence of Caribbean immigrants in Harlem during the early twentieth century.

SEE ALSO: Alvarez, Julia; Economic consequences of immigration; Economic opportunities; Garment industry; Immigration and Nationality Act of 1965; Latin American immigrants; New Jersey; New York City; Rhode Island; West Indian immigrants.

DRUG TRAFFICKING

DEFINITION: Importation and sale of narcotic and other drugs legally defined as controlled substances

SIGNIFICANCE: Drug trafficking and immigration are strongly correlated because most of the illegal drugs that enter the United States originate outside the country. Thousands of undocumented immigrants from various countries work as couriers, smuggling narcotic and other banned drugs into the United States.

The drug trade in illegal drugs began reaching epidemic proportions during the 1990's. Scholars have estimated that profits from international drug trafficking were nearing $10 trillion dollars annually by the twenty-first century. The United States is meanwhile the most lucrative market for international drug traffickers, with tons of illegal drugs smuggled into the country every day. Many of the couriers who are paid to bring in the drugs are themselves illegal immigrants.

Illegal drug trafficking has become a global black market consisting of the farming, processing, distribution, and sale of illegal narcotics. Most countries throughout the world prohibit trade, except under license, of many types of illegal drugs. The illicit drug trade operates much like other illegal underground markets. Drug gangs and cartels specialize in the separate processes along the supply chain, sometimes involving multiple countries. The cartels vary in size, ethnic and racial membership, organizational structure, and country of origin. Supply chains range from low-level street dealers to mid-level street gangs and couriers, up to multinational drug empires. Illegal drugs can be grown and processed almost anywhere: in the wilderness, on farms and plantations, in residential gardens, inside residential homes, and in labs secreted inside such structures as abandoned city buildings in major urban districts or rural mobile home parks. The most common element connecting these places of production is that all the locations must remain secret to avoid detection by law enforcement. Much of the twenty-first century illegal drug cultivation and processing takes place in developing nations; however, some is done in such developed nations as the United States, Canada, Germany, and France. Consumption of illegal drugs is widespread globally and has been regarded as having reached epidemic proportions within the United States.

Although consumers of illegal drugs avoid taxes by buying their drugs on black markets, the high costs of illegal narcotics comes from the money necessary to protect trade and trafficking routes from law enforcement. Those who carry the drugs from country to country tend to be undocumented migrants who work as low-level employees for known drug cartels. Illegal immigrants are recruited and used on a daily basis to transport drugs over national borders, especially into the United States. Mexico is particularly well known for the growing, processing, and distribution of various illegal narcotics including marijuana, cocaine, heroin, and methamphetamines. Because the U.S. demand is huge, Mexican drug cartels can easily recruit Mexicans and Central Americans seeking better lives in the United States to carry the contraband north when they attempt to enter the United States. When these people succeed in crossing the border, they may choose either to continue to transport drugs for the cartel or to remain in the United States illegally. Although most illegal immigrants who come to the United States are not involved in drug trafficking, thousands are.

SOURCES OF ILLEGAL DRUGS

Many diverse groups traffic and dispense illegal drugs in the United States. Criminal gangs operating in South America smuggle thousands of pounds of cocaine and heroin into the United States via a variety of entry points, including land routes through Mexico, offshore routes along Mexico's east and west coasts, open-sea routes through the Caribbean Islands, and air routes. Violent criminal drug gangs operating out of Mexico transport millions of pounds of various narcotics into the U.S annually. Some of these groups began smuggling and distributing drugs such as cocaine, heroin, and marijuana across the U.S.-Mexican border during the mid-1970's. After successfully distributing drugs in western and midwestern American states, Mexican drug cartels have begun expanding their markets into southeastern, eastern, and northeastern states.

Other countries have also gained footholds in

the U.S. drug market. Israeli and Russian drug cartels along with other western European drug traffickers have been using illegal immigrants to traffic a drug known on the street as "ecstasy" in the United States. This drug is usually manufactured in underground labs in both eastern and western Europe, whence it is transported to the United States, usually in commercial airliners. Criminal gangs located in Southeast and Southwest Asia smuggle thousands of pounds of heroin into the United States every year. Using New York City and Philadelphia as their primary distribution points, these gangs move heroin up and down the eastern United States with the help of illegal immigrants.

Drug Trafficking and Illegal Immigration

Drug smuggling and money laundering have been practiced for hundreds of years, but globalization has raised drug trafficking to a multi-trillion dollar international business. U.S. authorities have witnessed and felt the deleterious effects of both the narcotics trade and the illegal immigrants who transport the drugs into the country. The illegal drug market in the United States is one of the most lucrative in the world. Consequently, the country attracts the most merciless, sophisticated, and insistent drug traffickers. Federal, state, and local law-enforcement agencies face intimidating challenges in protecting the national borders.

According to early twenty-first century U.S. Customs Service figures, 70 million people enter the United States on more than 700,000 commercial and private flights every year. Another 6.5 million arrive by sea, and millions more arrive by land. Nearly 120 million vehicles cross U.S. land borders with Canada and Mexico. More than 90,000 merchant and passenger ships dock at U.S. ports, carrying 10 million shipping containers loaded with more than 400 million tons of cargo. Another 160,000 small vessels visit many U.S. coastal towns. There are thus ample methods for transporting illegal narcotics into the United States.

Roadblock set up by U.S. border officials checking for drugs on Interstate-5 near San Diego, California, in early 2009. (AP/Wide World Photos)

According to federal government figures, roughly 12 million illegal immigrants were living in the United States in 2008. About 75 percent of all illegal immigrants who made the United States their new home between 2000 and 2008 came from Mexico. By the end of 2008, California alone had about 3 million illegal immigrants residing within its boundaries. On the frontline of illegal immigrant and drug trafficking is the United States Border Patrol. Along with legal entry points, the Border Patrol is responsible for patrolling nearly 6,000 miles of both the Mexican and Canadian land borders and more than 2,000 miles of coastal waters surrounding Puerto Rico and the Florida peninsula.

On average, more than 500,000 illegal immigrants were arrested every year during the early twenty-first century, either while they were in the United States or while they tried to cross the border. In 2007 alone, Border Patrol agents arrested more than 850,000 people attempting to enter the country illegally. Because the federal government estimates that only 10-20 percent of all illegal immigrants are apprehended, as many as 4 million undocumented immigrants may enter the country undetected every year. Federal officials have also estimated that nearly 80-90 percent of illegal drugs entering the United States come from Mexico. Most of these drugs are smuggled in by illegal immigrants.

In 2005, federal law-enforcement seizure counts for cocaine and marijuana alone were astounding. The government stated that 1.13 million pounds of cocaine and 6.9 million pounds of marijuana with a total estimated street value of more than $80 billion dollars was seized. Additionally, federal law-enforcement officials estimated that only 20 percent of the drugs coming into the country is seized.

Because of increasing drug-smuggling activities along the southwestern border, the Border Patrol has also become a frontline agency in the war on drugs. Between October, 2006, and February, 2007, Border Patrol agents seized 299,154 pounds of marijuana—an amount averaging more than a ton a day. These totals represented a 31 percent increase over the same period during the previous fiscal year, when the amount of marijuana seized shattered previous records. Using the federal law-enforcement seizure rate of 20 percent, federal agents and officers fail to seize close to 4 million

pounds of marijuana a year. By the end of 2007, Border Patrol agents seized modest amounts of both cocaine (14,000 pounds) and marijuana (1.8 million pounds). The total street value of drugs confiscated by the Border Patrol in 2007 alone was placed around $1.6 billion. However, the estimated total street value of cocaine and marijuana that actually made it into the United States during that fiscal year was placed around $100 billion.

Paul M. Klenowski

FURTHER READING

Bailey, Bruce, and William Walker, eds. *Drug Trafficking in the Americas.* Miami, Fla.: University of Miami, North/South Center Press, 1994. Compilation of various research efforts of both North and South American scholars on the illicit drug trade and its effects on both continents. Each chapter provides a different perspective on the problem, including the use of illegal immigrants as drug couriers.

Bhattacharyya, Gargi. *Traffick: The Illicit Movement of People and Things.* London: Pluto Press, 2002. Broad overview of global trafficking in contraband, with a particularly emphasis on drugs, counterfeit products, and people. The author candidly explains how the world's official economy has become dependant on illegal trade, without which globalization cannot access cheap labor, reach vulnerable new markets, or finance development in poor countries.

Decker, Scott, and Margaret Chapman. *Drug Smugglers on Drug Smuggling: Lessons from the Inside.* Philadelphia: Temple University Press, 2008. Scholarly work offering firsthand accounts of drug smugglers. Drawing on numerous interviews with convicted drug traffickers, the authors provide powerful insights into the dark underworld of drug trafficking, including the use of illegal immigrants as drug "mules."

Friman, H. Richard, and Peter Andreas, eds. *The Illicit Global Economy and State Power.* Lanham, Md.: Rowman & Littlefield, 1999. Detailed look at the global economic impact of illegal commerce throughout the world, with considerable detail on drug trafficking profits and the trade's ties to some national governments.

Morgan, Lee. *The Reaper's Line: Life and Death on the Mexican Border.* Tucson, Ariz.: Rio Nuevo Press, 2006. Firsthand account of life on the front line of the U.S.-Mexican border. With more than two decades of experience as a U.S. Border Patrol and U.S. Drug Enforcement Agency officer, Morgan chronicles various true-life tales of both success and horrific failures along the border, providing revealing insights into bribery, corruption, and other crimes involving government agents, American politicians, and Mexican and American drug lords.

Naim, Moises. *Illicit: How Smugglers, Traffickers, and Copycats Are Hijacking the Global Economy.* New York: Anchor Books, 2007. Uncensored look at the global impact of the drug trade during the previous decade. Special attention is given to the people who are recruited to smuggle drugs across international borders, especially in the United States.

SEE ALSO: Border fence; Border Patrol, U.S.; Coast Guard, U.S.; Colombian immigrants; Coolies; Criminal immigrants; Homeland Security, Department of; Illegal immigration; 9/11 and U.S. immigration policy; Patriot Act of 2001; Smuggling of immigrants.

DUAL CITIZENSHIP

DEFINITION: Simultaneous possession of two or more citizenships

> **SIGNIFICANCE:** Since its founding, the United States has declared itself to be a country whose greatest strengths lie in its open-armed acceptance of immigrants; however, it has traditionally discouraged its citizens from forming or retaining ties to other nations, including the holding of dual citizenship.

National governments tend to bestow citizenship in two ways. The first is recognizing citizenship by right of birth—provided certain conditions have been met relating to place of birth and the possession of citizenship by one's parents. The second way is by acquiring citizenship through a naturalization process that begins with stating one's intention of becoming a permanent resident. In the first case, citizenship is obtained automatically at an eligible child's birth. In the second case, citizenship is finally obtained by taking an oath of loyalty to the nation, sometimes with the added requirement of formally renouncing any ties to other nations.

In some countries, merely being born in the country automatically confers citizenship through the principle of jus soli, a Latin phrase meaning "right of the soil." This is the case within the United States, where the Fourteenth Amendment to the U.S. Constitution clearly spells out this guarantee:

> All persons born or naturalized in the United States and subject to the jurisdiction thereof, are citizens of the United States and of the State wherein they reside. No State shall make or enforce any law which shall abridge the privileges or immunities of citizens of the United States . . .

Dual citizenship cases may arise when noncitizens give birth to children in the United States or its territories. Because of the Fourteenth Amendment guarantees, the children may be entitled to U.S. citizenship; at the same time they possess the citizenship of their parents that is conferred by right of descent. In many countries, being born to citizens may automatically confer citizenship in the parents' country, regardless of their place of birth. The United States recognizes a limited form of this method, which called jus sanguinis (right of blood). The United States permits citizenship to be conferred on children provided that their citizen parents have, at some time, resided in the United States.

Dual citizenship may be acquired by alien adults who wish to naturalize in the country in which they reside and either can not or choose not to renounce their existing citizenship. The United States requires immigrants who naturalize as citizens to swear an oath in which they renounce their former national ties. However, many other countries do not consider such an oath to be legally binding and therefore continue to recognize the naturalized Americans as their own citizens, too.

HISTORICAL TREATMENT OF DUAL CITIZENS

The U.S. State Department has historically regarded dual citizenship as an undesirable status. In the past, the federal government sometimes vigorously punished dual citizens by expelling them, even though such policies were unconstitutional. The case of *United States v. Wong Kim Ark* (1898) was an early example of U.S. policy in such circumstances.

The child of Chinese immigrants working in California, Wong Kim Ark was born in San Francisco around 1870. After a visit to China in 1895, he was refused reentry to the United States by U.S. customs officials on the grounds that he was a subject of the emperor of China by the principle of descent, and the Chinese exclusion laws prevented Chinese subjects from becoming naturalized American citizens. Hence, Wong was not really a U.S. citizen. Fortunately for Wong, however, his case found its way to the U.S. Supreme Court, which ruled that the citizenship clause of the Fourteenth Amendment, although originally intended to secure citizenship for freed African American slaves, applied to *all* persons born in the United States, regardless of their race or national origin.

Similarly, naturalized U.S. citizens' actions were scrutinized for behavior contrary to the U.S. State Department's expectations of loyalty. In the case of *Afroyim v. Rusk* (1967), for example, a man named Beys Afroyim discovered that he had been stripped of his U.S. citizenship when he was unable to renew his U.S. passport. A naturalized U.S. citizen since 1926, Afroyim traveled to Israel in 1950. There, he apparently obtained Israeli citizenship, as he voted in a 1951 Israeli election. Although the U.S. State Department's case against Afroyim did not state that Afroyim intended to renounce U.S. citizenship when he acquired Israeli citizenship, the fact of his voting in an Israeli election in 1951 was apparently enough to demonstrate that intent. Afroyim sued to retain his U.S. citizenship. After a lengthy legal battle, the Supreme Court ruled that he was still a U.S. citizen because the citizenship clause made citizenship a constitutionally protected right regardless of how it was obtained.

DUAL CITIZENSHIP AFTER 1965

According to a section of the Immigration and Nationality Act of 1965, demonstrating loyalty to another country might cause one to lose U.S. citizenship. Ways in which a person might demonstrate loyalty to another country include seeking naturalization, reciting an oath of loyalty, or serving as an officer in a foreign army. Nevertheless, these conditions have been specified to the point that naturalization by itself (with or without a loyalty oath) may not be sufficient evidence to prove "intent" to renounce U.S. citizenship. This means that citizenship can only be lost when the person in question "intends" to give up his or her citizenship—that is, declares before consulate witnesses that one wishes to renounce U.S. citizenship.

Julia M. Meyers

FURTHER READING

Bauman, Robert E. *The Complete Guide to Offshore Residency, Dual Citizenship and Second Passports.* New York: Sovereign Society, 2000. A former member of the U.S. House of Representatives from Maryland, Bauman discusses the procedures for obtaining dual citizenship.

Faist, Thomas. *Dual Citizenship in Global Perspective: From Unitary to Multiple Citizenship.* New York: Palgrave Macmillan, 2008. Faist explains that while national loyalty used to be the foundation for citizenship, dual and multiple citizenship have increasingly challenged such exclusivity.

Hansen, Randall, and Patrick Weil. *Dual Nationality, Social Rights and Federal Citizenship in the U.S. and Europe: The Reinvention of Citizenship.* Oxford, England: Berghahn Books, 2002. Comparison of the politics and migration policies of Germany and the United States.

Kymlicka, Will. *Multicultural Citizenship: A Liberal Theory of Minority Rights.* New York: Oxford University Press, 1996. Discusses dual citizenship in light of multicultural pressures on political and cultural policy.

Spiro, Peter J. *Beyond Citizenship: American Identity After Globalization.* New York: Oxford University Press, 2008. Investigation into the changing nature of American identity that touches on the changing nature of citizenship and nationality in an increasingly globalized culture.

SEE ALSO: *Afroyim v. Rusk*; Chinese Exclusion Act of 1882; *Chinese Exclusion Cases*; Citizenship; *Green Card*; Green cards; Naturalization; *United States v. Wong Kim Ark*.

DUTCH IMMIGRANTS

SIGNIFICANCE: Commercial enterprises constituted the first organized wave of immigration from the Netherlands to North America during the early seventeenth century and led to the founding of Fort Nassau, which was only the second permanent European settlement in North America. Continuing Dutch immigration waves have produced both complete assimilation of the immigrants from the Netherlands into North American culture, and also continuing pockets of a persistent hyphenated "Dutch-American" culture.

Three major immigration waves have brought Dutch-speaking people from the Netherlands to North America. During the first third of the seventeenth century, the Dutch West Indies Company sponsored exploring and colonizing voyages to the New World. The second wave, subsequently known as the "Great Migration," began during the 1840's, triggered by religious tensions in the homeland. The final wave of Dutch immigration followed the end of World War II, encouraged by the government of the Netherlands in order to help relieve pressing economic problems in the homeland.

EARLY DUTCH IMMIGRATION

The Dutch maritime empire of the early seventeenth century was a global one, with colonies stretching from Asia to Brazil. The explorations of Henry Hudson, who sailed up the river named after him in 1609, was one major participant of this vast commercial expansion. In 1614, the Netherlands States-General granted a charter to found Fort Nassau, which was only the second European settlement in what would become British North America, after British Jamestown. In 1721, the Dutch West Indies Company stock company was founded to promote trade between Europe and North America. During this earliest period, immigrants to North America included the nationals of many countries. Although Henry Hudson himself was an Englishman, he claimed lands in what was to become the United States in the name of his Dutch sponsors. The Pilgrims, too, although they sailed to America from the Netherlands, were English.

Immigrants spread outward from the first trading posts, founding New Amsterdam (later New York City) in 1625. New Amsterdam served as a defensive bulwark that helped keep immigrants from other European countries from settling in the region, and as a center for both trade and warfare with local Native American communities.

It soon became clear that a flow of additional immigrants would be needed to support continued commercial growth. Therefore, beginning in 1629, the Dutch West Indies Company encouraged immigration by offering land purchases along major rivers to investors who were willing to sponsor sizable numbers of immigrants. This so-called patroon system (similar to later *padrone* systems) of settlement was not successful. Other efforts to attract immigrants followed, such as shipping children from Dutch orphanages across the Atlantic to serve as contract workers in New Netherland. Despite all such efforts, the settlement's population remained low, which was one reason the British were able to seize the region from the Dutch with relative ease in 1664. The British takeover halted further immigration from the Netherlands. Nevertheless, Dutch language and culture continued to be commonplace in the Hudson and Mohawk River valleys even decades later.

NINETEENTH CENTURY IMMIGRATION

Economic hardships including potato and rye crop failures in the Netherlands during the 1840's,

PROFILE OF DUTCH IMMIGRANTS

Country of origin	Netherlands (Holland)
Primary language	Dutch
Primary regions of U.S. settlement	Northeast, Midwest
Earliest significant arrivals	1609
Peak immigration periods	1880's, 1940's-1950's
Twenty-first century legal residents*	11,586 (1,448 per year)

*Immigrants who obtained legal permanent resident status in the United States.
Source: Department of Homeland Security, *Yearbook of Immigration Statistics, 2008.*

were among the motivations for the second wave of Dutch immigration to the New World. However, religious tensions in the Netherlands constituted its most significant motive force and resulted in its longest-lasting effects. Immigration was significantly encouraged by a "seceder" movement within the official Dutch Reformed Church in the Netherlands. Starting fairly early during the nineteenth century, some congregations and individuals rejected what they perceived as a liberalization of the Dutch church, a moving away from its deep commitment to Calvinism. The Dutch government responded by attempting to repress the seceder movement by breaking up the movement's meetings, billeting soldiers in the homes of separatist families, and imposing fines on its pastors. Official state hostility continued until 1848.

In 1834, the Dutch seceders officially broke from the Netherlands state religion. Some of their congregations, led by their pastors, emigrated as groups to the United States during the 1840's and 1850's. Many, perhaps most, settled in the Midwest, founding such towns as Oostburg and Holland (now Cedar Grove), in Wisconsin. In Michigan, they settled in the western part of the Lower Peninsula, founding the communities of Holland and Zeeland. Pella, Iowa, is a final example of what became a host of new Dutch immigrant-founded communities. These communities continued many of the traditions of their homeland for generations. Indeed, all the communities discussed here continued to retain traces of their Dutch origins into the twenty-first century. As late as 1990, more than one-third of the citizens of Holland, Michigan, were of Dutch descent. As farmland in the United States grew both less plentiful and more expensive near the end of the nineteenth century, newly arrived Dutch immigrants began to settle in such American cities as Chicago and Grand Rapids.

CHURCH SCHISMS

During their first two waves of immigration, the Dutch brought with them to the New World a strong loyalty to the Dutch Reformed Church, which had its roots in the Reformation of the sixteenth century. In colonial times, some of their New World congregations favored keeping close ties with the church in the Netherlands, but others sought greater independence from their homeland. The latter eventually prevailed. In 1792, the Dutch Reformed Church in the United States became an independent denomination, the Reformed Protestant Dutch Church. Subsequent doctrinal and procedural differences within the newly independent church in North America continued to influence the speed and degree of Dutch assimilation into mainstream American culture.

Throughout the mid-nineteenth century, some congregations in the Midwest broke from the newly established Reformed Protestant Dutch Church in America. Members of these congregations regarded themselves as remaining more loyal to the 1834 secession that had encouraged nineteenth century Dutch immigration to America; they saw themselves as more committed to continuing some of the traditions of Calvinism. These tensions led to yet another separation in 1857 that created the Christian Reformed Church. Parallel developments in the old country helped to account for the fact that the new Christian Reformed denomination would attract the majority of Dutch immigrants during the peak years of the second wave of immigration, from 1880 until 1920. The two

HOLLAND, MICHIGAN

In 1847, more than seven hundred Dutch seceders settled near a Native American village close to Lake Michigan. No actual fighting erupted between the settlers of what would become the town of Holland, Michigan, and inhabitants of the Native American village, but only two years after the Dutch arrived, the Native Americans moved out of the area, resettling far to the north, never to return. They left because the Dutch settlers had brought smallpox into the region, and because settler-owned livestock trampled their vegetable gardens.

Immigration to Holland, Michigan, from the Netherlands continued throughout the nineteenth century, becoming what was termed the "followers immigration," so-named because many people were inspired to immigrate by the exchange of personal letters between new settlers and their Old World relatives—an example of chain migration. Members of the followers immigration at first joined their New World relatives but soon spread out to found more than one hundred new towns.

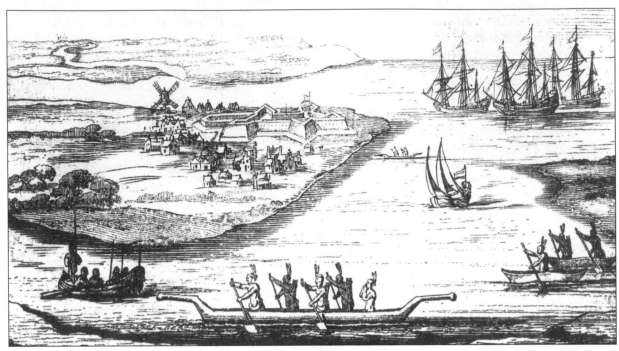

Contemporary view of New Amsterdam about twenty-five years after the Dutch settled Manhattan Island. (Library of Congress)

branches of Dutch Calvinist-based New World church denominations were later joined by two more, the Protestant Reformed Church and the Netherlands Reformed Congregations.

By the early twenty-first century, the Reformed Church in America had adopted such typical American Protestant traits as membership in the National Council of Churches and the World Council of Churches, while the Christian Reformed Church continued to emphasize its loyalty to somewhat more conservative practices. One of its distinguishing characteristics is its emphasis on Christian elementary and secondary schooling, rather than public schooling. Its generally conservative position is also exemplified by the fact that well into the twentieth century, Dutch-owned stores in western Michigan closed on Sundays. Moreover, it was not until 2008 that purchasing beer and wine was legal in Ottawa County, Michigan, the home of Holland and Zeeland.

Twentieth Century

During the twentieth century, all immigration to the United States was limited by new federal national origin-based quota legislation. Nevertheless,

World War II prompted a third and final wave of Dutch arrivals in the United States. Because the population of the Netherlands had suffered so greatly during the war, the Dutch government actively encouraged its own citizens to emigrate. In 1949, it even began offering travel subsidies. At the same time, it successfully. government to exempt Dutch citizens from U.S. immigration quotas.

Dutch Immigrants to Canada

Dutch immigration to Canada has historically been closely tied to Dutch immigration to the United States. A trickle of Dutch immigrants began arriving in Canada during the late eighteenth century. Some of the immigrants simply moved north across the U.S. border because they had been Loyalists fighting on the side of the British during the American War of Independence. By the late nineteenth century, much of the farmland in the United States was either unavailable or expensive, while at the same time the Canadian government was offering free or inexpensive land to new immigrants.

The volume of Dutch immigration to Canada rose after the end of World War II. The Dutch and

Canadian governments cooperated to encourage this postwar immigration. Canada was having a labor shortage, while there was surplus labor in the Netherlands. Many new arrivals landed in Canada in family groups, sponsored by relatives who were already settled. Strong Dutch-Canadian communities grew around church membership.

Summary

Historically, the Dutch in North America have focused on theological rather than political disputes, despite the paradoxical fact that three U.S. presidents are direct descendants of the first wave of Dutch immigrants (Martin Van Buren, Theodore Roosevelt, and Franklin D. Roosevelt). The sole exception to this relative lack of political organizing was an effort of Dutch Americans to support the Afrikaner (Boer) republics against Great Britain during the South African (Boer) War of 1899-1902.

A cohesive subculture has continued to exist among some geographically localized descendants of immigrants from the Netherlands. Although the majority of Americans of Dutch extraction have assimilated completely into mainstream Anglo-American culture, some residents of these local communities have preserved and built upon institutions that to a greater or lesser extent relate to the tenets and practices of their Calvinist-inspired religion. A variety of other kinds of ties to the Netherlands continue as well, especially in the form of such tools of communication as newspapers and publishing houses, and even television and radio programming. For example, a western Michigan Public Broadcasting System television station aired a long-running series titled *Thinking of Holland*. Another kind of continuity is represented by the Dutch Immigrant Society, based in Grand Rapids, Michigan. Familiarly known by its initials as "the DIS," it operates charter flights to Amsterdam that

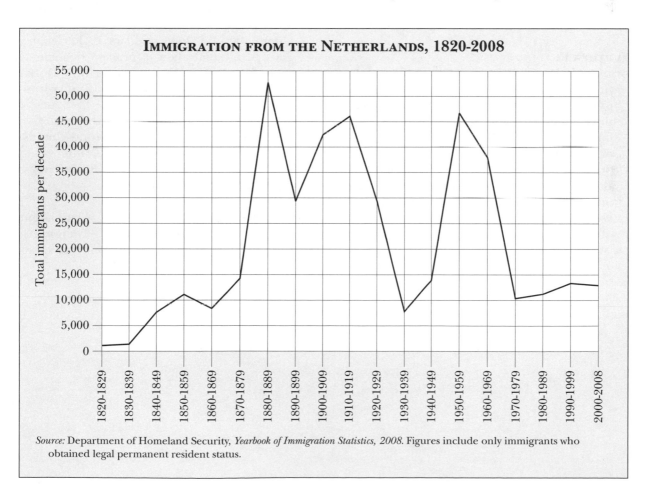

Source: Department of Homeland Security, *Yearbook of Immigration Statistics, 2008*. Figures include only immigrants who obtained legal permanent resident status.

are filled with Dutch Americans hoping to rediscover their roots or to visit relatives in the homeland.

The term "Hollander" brings to the foreground a rare example of the negative stereotyping of Dutch Americans. In some contexts "Hollander" has the pejorative meaning of "cheapskate" as exemplified in a phrase such as "Dutch treat." Far more frequently, stereotypes that refer to the Dutch heritage of some North Americans are positive in nature. This positive image manifests in the generalized "Dutchness" animating annual "tulip festivals" scattered across North America. Founded as a way to commemorate Dutch traditions, the festivals have developed into tourist attractions. Pella, Iowa, has its Tulip Time; Baldwin, Wisconsin, has "Let's Go Dutch Days"; and Woodburn, Oregon, has the "Wooden Shoe Tulip Festival." Holland, Michigan's annual Tulip Festival was even visited by the Netherlands' Queen Juliana in 1952 and by Queen Beatrix in 1982.

Barbara Roos

FURTHER READING

Brinks, Herbert, ed. *Dutch-American Voices: Letters from the United States, 1850-1930.* Ithaca, N.Y.: Cornell University Press, 1995. Excellent collection of letters from nineteenth century Dutch immigrants to friends and relatives in the Netherlands.

De Jong, Gerald F. *The Dutch in America, 1609-1974.* Boston: Twayne, 1975. Broad survey of Dutch immigration to the United States, from the earliest settlements through the first three quarters of the twentieth century.

De Klerk, Peter, and Richard De Ridder, eds. *Perspectives on the Christian Reformed Church: Studies in Its History, Theology and Ecumenicity.* Grand Rapids, Mich.: Baker Book House, 1983. Collection of essays on a variety of aspects of the many schisms within the Dutch Reformed Church.

Kessler, Henry H., and Eugene Rachlis. *Peter Stuyvesant and His New York.* New York: Random House, 1959. Biography of the Dutch founder of New Amsterdam that provides insights into the early colony.

Rink, Oliver A. *Holland on the Hudson: An Economic and Social History of Dutch New York.* Ithaca, N.Y.: Cornell University Press, 1986. Useful general survey of the Dutch settlement of New York.

Shorto, Russell. *The Island in the Center of the World: The Epic Story of Dutch Manhattan and the Forgotten Colony That Shaped America.* New York: Random House, 2004. Good, up-to-date study of early Dutch America.

Stellingwerff, Johan, comp. *Iowa Letters: Dutch Immigrants on the American Frontier.* Translated by Walter Lagerwey, edited by Robert P. Swierenga. Grand Rapids, Mich.: William B. Eerdmans, 2004. Large collection of primary documents that offers fascinating glimpses into Dutch immigrant life on the nineteenth century frontier.

Swierenga, Robert. *Dutch Chicago: A History of the Hollanders in the Windy City.* Grand Rapids, Mich.: Wm. B. Eerdmans, 2002. Interesting microstudy of Dutch immigrants in the largest city in the American Midwest.

SEE ALSO: Canada vs. United States as immigrant destinations; Chicago; European immigrants; Families; Michigan; New York City; New York State.

E

Economic consequences of immigration

Significance: Any understanding of the factors encouraging immigration to the United States must rest on an understanding of the economic conditions motivating immigrants, as well as the effects of their presence in the United States. Though the groups coming to the United States have changed over time in their place of origin as well as the role they assumed after arriving, economic factors have generally been the primary driving forces behind both immigration and responses of U.S. residents to immigrants.

During the seventeenth and eighteenth centuries, as England was building what would become the British Empire, its leaders were driven by the doctrine of mercantilism. English colonies were to serve as sources of raw materials that would be processed and turned into marketable goods in the home country. The raw materials that North America had to offer, notably tobacco and later cotton, were in high demand in England. It was therefore in England's interest to encourage production of these and other labor-intensive natural products. It was also in England's interest to populate its American colonies to meet the consequent labor needs. Immigration was promoted by those whose potential profits required as many settlers as possible.

Some settlers went to the colonies on their own, particularly as the restructuring of English agriculture during the eighteenth century deprived many who lacked title to land in Great Britain of the opportunity to make adequate livings. Those who lacked the capital to make the voyage to America could become indentured servants, paying off the costs of their transportation through several years of contractually bound labor. Indentured servitude was most common in the southern colonies during the seventeenth century. After it became clear that northern Europeans had trouble performing hard physical labor in the South's hot climate, indentured European servants were replaced by enslaved Africans.

Throughout the British North American colonies, populations grew through high rates of natural increase and immigration of people despairing of ever owning enough land in Britain to support their families. The earliest immigrants settled close to the Atlantic coast, but through the seventeenth and eighteenth centuries, inland regions began to fill up. Meanwhile, increasing numbers of non-English immigrants, especially members of German religious groups such as the Amish sought greater freedom in America. These people brought with them both devotion to their communities and a willingness to work hard to expand their communities' agricultural output. Many British immigrants dreamed of climbing the social ladder by becoming craftsmen or traders, especially in New England, where the poor agricultural potential of much of the land propelled the most ambitious immigrants into trades.

Nineteenth Century Immigration

From the end of the American Revolution in 1783 to the outbreak of World War I in 1914, the population of the United States increased from about 3 million people to around 100 million. Much of that increase was from natural population growth, but as many as 45 million immigrants are believed to have come to the United States during that long period. While spreading out across the landscape from the Atlantic Ocean to the Pacific, immigrants helped to make possible the dynamic economy that characterized the United States at the beginning of the twentieth century.

Most of the early immigrants came from the British Isles, especially the large number of Irish who left in the wake of the potato famine of the late 1840's. Despite their lack of experience in anything but hard-scrabble farming, many of these immigrants settled in cities, especially New York and Boston. They came during a time when the Industrial Revolution was changing the way economic value was generated, and they and their descendants provided the labor force for the new, mass-producing industries. They provided much of the labor for the Erie Canal and for the numerous railroads that began to cross the nation, joining the East and West coasts.

Most new immigrants to the United States hoped to achieve prosperity, but many, such as this early twentieth century Italian clam seller, had to start humbly. (Library of Congress)

As America emerged from being primarily a producer of raw materials to a producer of manufactured goods, immigrants provided the labor force for the new industries. This was particularly true when immigration shifted from the farmers of nineteenth century Germany and Scandinavia to the displaced peasants of eastern Europe. Many of the latter wound up in industrial cities, such as Pittsburgh, where the steel industry dominated, and its labor force was predominantly composed of Slavic immigrants. Eastern European immigrants also ran the spinning and weaving machinery in New England's textile mills. Without this supply of immigrant labor the capitalists behind the nation's industrial growth would not have been able to achieve what they did.

Despite their central role in American industrialization, new immigrants were not always welcome. The notorious Boston signs proclaiming "No Irish Need Apply" were indicative of the often hostile American attitude toward recent immigrants. Another indication of the unwelcoming attitude of many Americans to immigrants was the apparent indifference of many factory owners to the terrible and often dangerous conditions under which their immigrant employees worked. The lethal fire that killed 146 predominantly immigrant workers in New York City's Triangle Shirtwaist Factory in 1911 was dramatic proof of that indifference. The large numbers of eastern and southern European immigrants who entered the United States during the decade leading up to World War I was a catalyst for the negative reaction that led to new immigration laws during the 1920's, which attempted to restrict immigration to the northern Europeans who had dominated the earlier arrivals.

TWENTIETH CENTURY

Immigration dropped off markedly during World War I as Europe was convulsed by the conflict. In America, the period and the isolationist culture that it spawned hardened attitudes of the native-born population toward immigrants. In 1924, the U.S. Congress passed an immigration act that for the first time limited the total number of immigrants who could come to the United States. It also limited the countries from which they could come by setting numerical quotas based on the numbers of foreign nationals who had been living in the United States in 1890.

The national origin quotas were finally ended by the Immigration and Nationality Act of 1965. In their place came the concept of "family unification" under which the family members of current citizens were given preference. The 1965 immigration law also for the first time included immigration quotas for those originating in the Western Hemisphere. The law's sponsors hoped that it would have the same effect as the 1924 national origin restrictions. However, it instead encouraged the immigration of relatives of immigrants already in the United States who had secured citizenship. Later changes to the law authorized admitting more refugees, but these were now coming primarily from Asia rather than Europe. More major changes were introduced in 1986, under the Immigration Reform and Control Act, one of whose most controversial provisions was a system under which illegal immigrants could secure legal status.

TWENTY-FIRST CENTURY CONTROVERSIES

By the turn of the twenty-first century, the issue of what sort of immigration policy was appropriate had taken center stage in the United States. The presence of large numbers of illegal immigrants, mostly from Latin America, aroused substantial concern that these people might be taking jobs from native-born Americans. Although it was technically illegal, even under the 1986 law, for employers to hire undocumented immigrants, illegal immigrants provided a substantial supply of labor for industries—the hotel, construction, and building

maintenance industries in particular—that had low margins and in which labor costs played crucial roles in profitability.

Defenders of immigrants asserted that many of the jobs they took were jobs Americans shunned. Books appeared supporting both sides of the issue. For example, George Borjas argued in *Friends or Strangers: The Impact of Immigrants on the U.S. Economy* (1990) that statistical analysis showed that the presence of immigrants, including those illegally in the United States, had a very small negative effect on the wages of American citizens. On the other side, in *Mass Immigration and the National Interest: Policy Directions for the New Century* (2003), Vernon Briggs, Jr., argued that the presence of perhaps as many as 12 million illegal immigrants had a profound effect on the national economy.

By the first decade of the twenty-first century, so many illegal immigrants were living in the United States that the issue became a matter of national policy. Alan Greenspan, the chairman of the Federal Reserve Board, weighed in on the topic in his testimony in 2003 before a U.S. Senate committee on aging. Immigration was essential, according to Greenspan, to ensure an adequate supply of active workers to support the Social Security System that would otherwise buckle under the weight of all the retired baby boomers by the year 2030.

The issue moved onto center stage in the political contests of the first decade of the twenty-first century. President George W. Bush outlined a fairly elaborate procedure through which undocumented workers, largely from Mexico, could win legal authorization to be in the United States. His plan envisaged vigorous enforcement of the ban on hiring undocumented immigrants and proposed the construction of a fence across parts of the U.S.-Mexican border. However, Bush's plan failed to secure sufficient support to pass through Congress.

In his memoir, *The Age of Turbulence* (2007), Alan Greenspan attributes the issue of immigration to the ever-increasing globalization of the economy. He argued that whatever depressive effect immigration had on American wage levels was outweighed by the fact that the United States had become part of a world economy in which labor costs must be determined by the economies of all parts of the world. The important point for the United States, he stressed, was to attract the most skilled workers the world produced and to allow them to work either in the United States or abroad. That approach, he argued, was the true road to economic prosperity in the future.

Nancy M. Gordon

FURTHER READING

Borjas, George J. *Friends or Strangers: The Impact of Immigration on the U.S. Economy.* New York: Basic Books, 1990. Argues that immigration does not impact either wages or employment of native-born Americans to any significant degree.

Briggs, Vernon M., Jr. *Mass Immigration and the National Interest: Policy Directions for the New Century.* Armonk, N.Y.: M. E. Sharpe, 2003. Argues that immigration does indeed impact negatively many American workers.

Glazer, Nathan, and Daniel Patrick Moynihan. *Beyond the Melting Pot: The Negroes, Puerto Ricans, Jews, Italians, and Irish of New York City.* 2d ed. Cambridge, Mass.: MIT Press, 1970. Study of the diverse ethnic communities of North America's largest city and challenges the notion that assimilation occurs in many groups.

Greenspan, Alan. *The Age of Turbulence.* New York: Penguin Books, 2007. The former chairman of the Federal Reserve Board speaks his mind on a number of issues related to immigration.

Joppke, Christian, and Ewa Morawska, eds. *Toward Assimilation and Citizenship.* New York: Palgrave Macmillan, 2003. Collection of articles by scholars on immigration issues, focusing particularly on recent immigration.

Smith, James P., and Barry Edmonston, eds. *The New Americans: Economic, Demographic and Fiscal Effects of Immigration.* Washington, D.C.: National Academy Press, 1997. Another collection of articles that focuses on recent immigration issues.

Tilly, Charles. "Transplanted Networks." In *Immigration Reconsidered: History, Sociology and Politics,* edited by Virginia Yans-McLaughlin. New York: Oxford University Press, 1990. Broad discussion of the early phases of American immigration.

SEE ALSO: "Brain drain"; Economic opportunities; Employment; Farm and migrant workers; Guest-worker programs; Indentured servitude; Industrial Revolution; Labor unions; Remittances of earnings; Sweatshops.

ECONOMIC OPPORTUNITIES

DEFINITION: Opportunities to find better employment, to own land, and to trade and build businesses that have attracted immigrants to the United States

SIGNIFICANCE: Throughout the history of the United States, quests for economic betterment have been a driving force behind the decisions of immigrants to come to the United States. Most immigrants remain permanently after they arrive, but an estimated 30 percent of them eventually return to their original homelands. Most who return do so after saving the amounts of money they have set as their goals.

Before the late eighteenth century American Revolution, the vast majority of immigrants to what became the United States came from the British Isles. Although many of these early immigrants sought new homes in which they would create communities that shared their religious beliefs without government hindrance, they also sought something else that had become difficult to obtain in their homeland: ownership of freehold land—land without overlords. Some immigrants came hoping to become big landlords themselves and profit from producing crops not readily available in England, such as tobacco, for which the climate and soil of colonies such as Virginia were particularly suitable. By the eighteenth century, a new economic motive helped drive immigration: opportunities to prosper from the international trade in which the American colonies were beginning to participate.

Another sizeable contingent of immigrants came involuntarily—Africans imported as slaves. Although they came unwillingly, their labor made possible the development of large landholdings in British North America's southern colonies, thereby helping many European immigrants to realize their own dreams of becoming agricultural entrepreneurs. Along with these involuntary immigrants were many Europeans who voluntarily endured indentured servitude because they lacked the capital to finance their own transportation to America. Unlike the African slaves, however, their indentures were for only limited periods of time. In some colonies, during the seventeenth century, they were given small freeholds themselves after they had worked off their indentures.

By the time of the American Revolution, the lands up and down the eastern seaboard, between Massachusetts and Georgia, had become well settled, and a more diverse society was beginning to develop. The first cities to emerge were nearly all seaports, which offered many economic opportunities for employment and trade. Colonial society was then still overwhelmingly made up of people earning their livings from cultivating the land, but it also included many people who made their livings by providing services to the urban dwellers that were needed to support international trade.

EARLY NINETEENTH CENTURY

U.S. Census records of immigration into the United States began in 1820, but estimates from the years between the Revolution and about 1815 show that immigration was slowing down. However, it accelerated during the 1820's and continued until the U.S. Civil War began in 1861. The acquisition from Great Britain of most of the land between the Appalachian Mountains and the Mississippi River meant that the United States had a vast, undeveloped region that would be open to agriculture. After most of the Native American peoples were driven out, the land was largely unoccupied and began attracting settlers from coastal areas eager to buy superior farming land from the federal government cheaply. It also opened up land for new waves of immigrants from Europe.

The first great wave of immigrants to come were the Irish, most of whom were young men who were coming to work. One of the first great projects to employ Irish immigrants was New York State's Erie Canal, on which construction began in 1817. By the 1820's, the majority of Erie Canal workers were Irish, many of whom were saving money to purchase their own land so they could become independent farmers. Some succeeded, but the vast majority did not, instead remaining wage laborers in the numerous small businesses that were emerging around the canal.

Most of the Irish immigrants, particularly those who came during the time of the Great Irish Famine of the late 1840's, eventually settled in the growing cities. Not a few found work in the textile mills that emerged first in New England. Indeed, the mills drew heavily on Irish immigrants after they began by recruiting local farm girls as their first employees. The Irish proved to be a relatively reliable source of unskilled and semiskilled labor.

Meanwhile, changing economic developments in Europe impelled people from other countries to emigrate. Many European farmers were becoming unable to make their livings from the ever smaller

Vietnamese-Chinese grocery store in New York City's Lower Manhattan. (Smithsonian Institution)

plots of land that members of each succeeding generation inherited. Moreover, it was becoming increasingly difficult for them to supplement their meager farm income with seasonal labor in the form of handwork as spinners and weavers. Emigration to go to America offered the hope of finding opportunities while none existed at home. Significant numbers of farmers left peasant villages in southwestern Germany and traveled to America. Many of them settled in the midwestern states of the Old Northwest—Ohio, Indiana, Illinois, Michigan and Wisconsin. Like the Irish, they tended to congregate in communities made up primarily of fellow European immigrants, giving their neighborhoods a distinctively German character.

LATE NINETEENTH CENTURY

The U.S. Civil War put a temporary brake on immigration, but after it ended in 1865, the flood of immigration resumed. Rapidly developing industrialization saw the expansion of railroads, the building of large steel plants, and the exploitation of coal mines on unprecedented scales. All these and other developments drew great numbers of Europeans to the United States. Among the new immigrants were many Norwegians who, like the Germans, sought to exploit the agricultural lands of the Midwest and gave Minnesota and the rest of the Upper Midwest its heavily Scandinavian character. Other immigrants were beginning to come from eastern Europe, where the creation of large agricultural estates was diminishing opportunities for peasants to acquire land for themselves. This wave of immigrants peaked in 1907, a year during which more than six million new immigrants entered the United States.

A major technological development that contributed to the increased flow of immigrants was the shift from sailing vessels to steam-powered ships. Prior to the Civil War, the overwhelming majority of immigrants crossed the Atlantic Ocean in sailing vessels, but this changed shortly after the war, making oceanic travel faster, cheaper, safer, and more comfortable. Europeans willing to travel in steerage class could cross the Atlantic for as little as twenty-five dollars. Companies that owned the steamships drummed up business by actively recruiting people in Europe to go to America.

During this same period, the ethnic mix of immigrants was changing. By this time, Italians, Poles, Greeks, Slavs from the Balkans, and, in particular, large numbers of Jews from eastern Europe were making up the bulk of immigrants to the United States. As with the Irish before the war, members of each of these groups tended to cluster together in ethnic enclaves in the cities and towns where most of them settled. It was not uncommon for American employers seeking workers to contract with members of these communities to get them to pass the word to their fellow countrymen in their homelands that jobs were available.

The outbreak of World War I in 1914 put a stop to the great flood of immigration. Meanwhile, however, that flood had engendered a backlash among many native-born Americans. Aside from laws specifically prohibiting Chinese immigrants on the West Coast, the first comprehensive immigration legislation was passed in 1891. This law created the Bureau of Immigration within the Department of the Treasury and sought to prohibit immigrants that suffered from disabilities. It was only after World War I, however, that group restrictions were imposed to discourage immigration from countries other than those of western and northern Europe. A major exception was made for Mexican agricultural workers, who were brought into the United States on a season basis under the bracero program begun in 1943. It was never intended that these workers would stay permanently in the United States, and they were carefully policed and returned to Mexico at the end of their contractual periods. In addition, the lack of employment opportunities during the Great Depression years of the 1930's ensured that few would want to come.

LATE TWENTIETH CENTURY IMMIGRATION

Federal rules governing U.S. immigration changed dramatically after passage of the federal Immigration and Nationality Act of 1965, Under the new rules, family unification became a primary goal, and most new immigrants came from countries in the Western Hemisphere, particularly those in Latin America. During the 1970's, substantial numbers of Vietnamese and other Asians began immigrating. With this next ethnic mix, the traditional emphasis on assimilation was somewhat modified, partly because members of second and later generations of earlier immigrants had shown that members of immigrant families gradually abandon the cultures from which they originate.

Greater tolerance was now shown for immigrants who retained their old cultures, so long as they also learned to speak English.

The latest waves of immigrants, however, have tended to remain longer in low-wage jobs requiring only limited skills. Nevertheless, controversies have arisen during periods of economic downturns as some people have argued that immigrant workers are depriving American citizens of industrial jobs. Meanwhile, another controversy over the "off-shoring" of manufacturing jobs to Latin America and Asia has arisen, and this, too, has cooled down the welcoming of new immigrants.

Nancy M. Gordon

FURTHER READING

Bodnar, John. *The Transplanted: A History of Immigration in Urban America.* Bloomington: University of Indiana Press, 1985. Major work on the experience of immigrants in transitioning to American capitalism, emphasizing employment opportunities.

Borjas, George J. *Friends or Strangers: The Impact of Immigrants on the U.S. Economy.* New York: Basic Books, 1990. Examination of the effect of U.S. immigration laws on the employment of immigrants. Also looks at job competition among members of different immigrant groups.

Hareven, Tamara K., and Randolph Langenbach. *Amoskeag: Life and Work in an American Factory-City.* New York: Pantheon Books, 1978. Collection of interviews with a host of immigrant workers at a textile mill in New England.

Millman, Joel. *The Other Americans: How Immigrants Renew Our Country, Our Economy, and Our Values.* New York: Viking, 1997. Exploration of immigrant entrepreneurship, showing how many immigrant business people have helped save declining communities.

Morawska, Ewa. *Toward Assimilation and Citizenship.* New York: Palgrave, 2003. Broad study of recent immigration trends that pays special attention to the cultural factors surrounding them.

Smith, James, and Barry Edmonston, eds. *The New Americans: Economic, Demographic and Fiscal Effects of Immigration.* Washington, D.C.: National Academy Press, 1997. The product of a yearlong study by a panel of social scientists examining the effects of California's Proposition 187 and welfare reform in 1996, this volume provides insights into the impact of immigration on American society in general and on the national economy in particular.

Wyman, Mark. *Round Trip to America: The Immigrants Return to Europe, 1880-1930.* Ithaca, N.Y.: Cornell University Press, 1993. Detailed discussion of immigrants who returned to their home countries after sojourns in the United States.

SEE ALSO: Coal industry; Economic consequences of immigration; Employment; Ethnic enclaves; Family businesses; Great Irish Famine; Industrial Revolution; Iron and steel industry; Natural disasters as push-pull factors; Sweatshops.

ECUADORIAN IMMIGRANTS

SIGNIFICANCE: Ecuadorians constitute the eighth-largest Latino group in the United States, according to the 2000 U.S. Census. About 70 percent of the 600,000 Ecuadorians counted in the census live in the New York City metropolitan area. Many are undocumented workers.

Most Ecuadorians living in the U.S. are economic refugees. During the 1960's and 1970's, small num-

PROFILE OF ECUADORIAN IMMIGRANTS

Country of origin	Ecuador
Primary language	Spanish
Primary regions of U.S. settlement	New York State
Earliest significant arrivals	1970
Peak immigration period	1990-present
Twenty-first century legal residents*	96,571 (10,730 per year)

*Immigrants who obtained legal permanent resident status in the United States.
Source: Department of Homeland Security, *Yearbook of Immigration Statistics, 2008.*

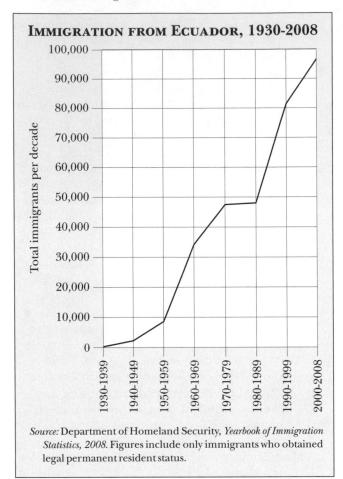

IMMIGRATION FROM ECUADOR, 1930-2008

Source: Department of Homeland Security, *Yearbook of Immigration Statistics, 2008.* Figures include only immigrants who obtained legal permanent resident status.

tives in the United States. Moreover, the Ecuadorian financial crisis made it impossible for many young Ecuadorian men to obtain the prerequisites for manhood—land ownership, marriage, and the establishment of independent households—within their homeland. Migration to the United States has provided young immigrants with both incomes and the status of acquiring North American styles of speech, fashion, and attitude.

Census figures show a 99 percent increase in the numbers of Ecuadorians who entered the United States between 1980 and 2000. In contrast to many immigrants from neighboring Mexico, Ecuadorians do not move back and forth across the U.S. border frequently. After Ecuadorians arrive in the United States, they frequently wait several years to summon the courage and save the money to return to Ecuador. Many reach the United States by flying to Panama, where they find overland guides to help them cross the U.S. border. They generally leave children behind in Ecuador.

The Ecuadorians in the United States include a disproportionately large number of undocumented workers. Most of them are poor peasants with limited resources, who come from Ecuador's Azuay-Canari region in the rural Andes. Many work in the low-paying, unskilled service and manufacturing sectors of the New York City economy, particularly in restaurants and the garment industry. One scholar estimates that 95 percent of Ecuadorian garment workers are paid in cash, with no deductions taken out. Eighty percent of these workers are identified as undocumented, with little job security.

Caryn E. Neumann

bers of Ecuadorians began entering the U.S. on tourist and work visas. Many of these early migrants intended to return to Ecuador after spending a year or two earning money. However, after passage of the Immigration Reform and Control Act in 1986 conferred legal status on undocumented migrants, many of these immigrants decided to obtain U.S. citizenship and remain.

After several decades of fairly slow immigration, the numbers of Ecuadorian immigrants to the United States jumped dramatically during the 1990's. A drop in Ecuadorian petroleum revenue combined with a 60 percent inflation rate to devalue the Ecuadorian currency, the sucre, leaving many Ecuadorian families impoverished. To survive, many families sent young members—typically young men—to the United States to earn U.S. dollars. Many of these families have made ends meet only because of the remittances sent by their rela-

FURTHER READING

Cordero-Guzman, Hector R., Robert C. Smith, and Ramon Grosfoguel, eds. *Migration, Transnationalization, and Race in a Changing New York.* Philadelphia: Temple University Press, 2001.

Miles, Ann. *From Cuenca to Queens: An Anthropological Story of Transnational Migration.* Austin: University of Texas Press, 2004.

Pribilsky, Jason. *La Chulla Vida: Gender, Migration, and the Family in Andean Ecuador and New York City.* Syracuse, N.Y.: Syracuse University Press, 2007.

SEE ALSO: Colombian immigrants; Economic consequences of immigration; Economic opportunities; Immigration Reform and Control Act of 1986; Latin American immigrants.

EDUCATION

IDENTIFICATION: Formal and informal learning opportunities for immigrants from childhood through adulthood

SIGNIFICANCE: Schools are important sociopolitical entities within American communities. As such, they are a key arena where conflicting views about immigrants regarding identity, linguistic and cultural diversity, assimilation, accommodation, and other issues play themselves out. Many issues remain unresolved, and new issues continue to surface as the ever-changing landscape of immigration superimposes itself over the education systems of the United States.

Formal and informal education has always been important to immigrants as they have entered the United States, adjusted to the U.S. culture and way of life, and sought to advance their personal and family goals. Throughout the long history of the United States, educational institutions and public and immigrant attitudes toward education have adapted to reflect the economic and political changes of each era.

EDUCATION IN THE YOUNG REPUBLIC

The period from the Revolutionary era of the late eighteenth century through the early nineteenth century witnessed a diverse set of institutions and means by which Americans were educated. Most education was informal during this period and was undertaken principally by males within the context of occupational apprenticeships. The bulk of Americans possessed only rudimentary literacy skills, such as the ability to sign their own names and read a few simple words. European American families who were well-to-do hired tutors to teach their children; more advanced formal education was reserved for young men. Formal schools were rare, and only the privileged were eligible and able to attend them. Many of the early schools operated only intermittently, as they depended upon the uncertain availability of teachers. Books were treasured by the literate class but were both expensive and in short supply. Only a few people in colonial times, such as Cotton Mather, Benjamin Franklin, James Madison, and Thomas Jefferson, could accumulate libraries that could command respect from visiting well-heeled Europeans.

The second wave of immigration, from 1820 to 1860, saw immigrants primarily from Ireland and Germany. These Europeans brought with them books and literacy skills that they were eager to pass on to their children. Upon settling into new territories in the movement westward, as well as taking up abode within the small cities of the growing nation, they quickly established schools with their own languages as the media of instruction. Norwegians and Germans were particularly associated with this trend. Irish Catholics established Catholic schools in the parishes in which they came to reside. Many of these schools endured for long periods of time. During the 1920's, for example, Detroit, Michigan, alone had a network of some sixty Catholic schools educating nearly 50,000 pupils, most of whom were first- and second-generation Irish immigrants.

Within that same time period, Horace Mann, Henry Barnard, and others began to advance what became known as the Common School Movement. Citing the ideals of Jacksonian Democracy, proponents argued that the United States needed public schools that were free to all if the nation was to capitalize on its vast natural resources, preserve its democratic institutions, and serve as an example of new possibilities to the rest of the world.

As the nineteenth century unfolded, the numbers of immigrants continued to increase. In 1850 alone, some 2.2 million foreign-born immigrants entered the United States. At midcentury, foreign-born residents constituted 9.7 percent of the nation's total population. In 1849, the president of Middlebury College speculated that the huge mass of humanity arriving on America's shores could foreshadow the downfall of the nation, just as Huns and Goths had settled within the confines of the Roman Empire and ultimately weakened it because of their failure to assimilate and become "true" Romans.

Mann, Barnard, and others argued that schools were the ideal institutions within society to take up the important task of turning immigrants into Americans as well as providing the means for the poor to advance their prospects within society, working from the foundation of a solid education. It could no longer be left to chance that the varied, loosely organized system of informal learning would inculcate the skills and values that were necessary for the young and dramatically growing nation. Teachers and pundits of the time noted that schools also needed to instruct in personal health and hygiene, as many immigrants exhibited undesirable grooming habits. The metaphor of the "melting pot" gained currency, drawing upon the notion that when steel and other useful metal alloys were made, the combination of several different metals produced new metals considerably stronger than any individual component alone. By extension of this metaphor, socializing and educating the teeming numbers of immigrants and the

poor would help make the nation stronger and more unified.

This notion was seriously challenged by the unfolding tragedy of the U.S. Civil War (1861-1865), which swept vast numbers of immigrants into armies on both sides of the conflict and caused more American deaths per capita than any other military conflict in U.S. history. Nevertheless, the war reinforced in people's minds the necessity of binding the nation together again and intensifying the national spirit of its inhabitants after hostilities ceased. New immigrants had to be rapidly assimilated into the American way of life and the values and mores of society. Schools were vital to this process of Americanization, even though teachers often complained about the unruly immigrant students, overcrowded conditions in urban schools, and the overwhelming amount of attention that needed to be given to promoting socialization skills,

Young Chinese immigrant students in New York City, 1910. (Library of Congress)

teaching the English language, and improving personal health and hygiene.

Biculturalism was seen as distinctly un-American. There was no general sense that maintenance of facility in languages other than American English was valuable or desirable. Blatant public condemnation of immigrants or entire sets of people from particular parts of the world were common in the newspapers, magazines, and books of the period and from learned professors as well as from common folk. Many anti-immigrant ideas were tied to erroneous views about racial differences accounting for differences in innate mental capacities and fixed personality traits associated with distinct ethnicities. Ethnic stereotyping was rampant. Teachers were not immune to commonly received wisdom, some of which was taught to prospective teachers as they prepared for their important life work.

LATE NINETEENTH AND EARLY TWENTIETH CENTURIES

Immigration to the United States increased rapidly after the Civil War. The years between 1860 and 1914 saw the majority of new immigrants arriving from southern and eastern Europe, in contrast to the mostly British and northern European immigrants of earlier periods. Chinese and Japanese immigrants also began arriving on the West Coast, as the rulers of both those Asian nations finally gave in to pressure from the United States and other Western nations to permit their subjects to emigrate. Farming and railroads associated with the opening of the West provided ideal conditions for the United States to accommodate the large number of new arrivals and for these immigrants to have a major role in opening up the region to settlement. Wealthy Chinese merchants in California established academies and schools during the 1880's and 1890's. Japanese immigrants, who were more likely to be Christians than Daoists or Buddhists, started Japanese schools in Hawaii and the western United States.

The pattern of Japanese immigrants' assimilation into American society was distinctly different than that of the Chinese, in part because of the emperor's embracing of Western ways, including American science and technology. Japanese students were far likelier to attend American schools than their Chinese counterparts. At the same time,

events unfolding in Asia through this period had a substantial impact in how these two cultures interacted with each other in their new nation, as well as with other cultures. For example, the Sino-Japanese War of 1894-1895, Russo-Japanese War of 1905, Japanese invasion and annexation of Korea in 1910, and conflicts between China and Japan that continued through World War II, all affected relationships and rivalries among these groups, especially in the western United States.

Meanwhile, in the cities of the eastern United States, and to a much lesser degree in the South, poor immigrants arriving from southern and eastern Europe presented new challenges to the process of Americanization. Public officials commented openly about the depravity, defiance, and criminal tendencies that these immigrants allegedly manifested. Worries about the political radicalism of immigrants led to a sharp suppression of dissent, and immigrants were schooled in the ways of American democracy. Instruction was conducted solely in English. Any maintenance of their native facilities in reading, writing, and speaking was left to the informal world of learning that ethnic communities could organize and encourage.

Immigrant students' names were Anglicized as part of this process. Students were strongly admonished to drop ethnic customs, shed their foreign accents, and suppress expressing themselves in their own native tongues.

In response to a perceived need, many schools began opening their doors to the community for evening adult classes in English, government, vocational education, and the naturalization process during the later nineteenth century. By 1906, the U.S. government was requiring English competency as part of the process of naturalization and citizenship procedures. Schools were becoming de facto social centers and homogenization sites for urban U.S.

Meanwhile, the U.S. Congress was becoming increasingly interested in the process of immigration and its impact on the nation. In December of 1908, investigators for the U.S. Senate's committee on immigration compiled statistics for thirty-seven cities across the United States. They documented the presence of sixty separate nationalities and found that within cities, huge percentages of residents had fathers who were born abroad.

Vast numbers of immigrant children during this

period of massive influx of immigrants were denied entry into urban schools due to overcrowded conditions. Although some degree of literacy and aptitude for mathematics was required during this period, most students, regardless of their ethnic backgrounds, received only grade school educations. A study of New York City public schools in 1911 found these high school graduation rates for students of various ethnic backgrounds:

- British, 10.8 percent
- German, 15 percent
- Russian, 16 percent
- Irish, 0.1 percent

Although immigrants and others needed enough education to hold jobs in the developing industrial economy, few immigrants attained the higher levels of literacy, math ability, or advanced subject matter knowledge that would become the norm after the mid-twentieth century. World War I (1914-1918) highlighted even more starkly for Americans the importance of forging an American identity for all immigrants, as ethnic groups attacked one another with a vengeance across Europe in a war that would ultimately involve the United States. There was considerable concern at the time that these deep European rivalries would erupt into violence on U.S. city streets.

After World War I, many U.S. states passed laws declaring English as the official state language. Some of these laws were so restrictive that Robert Meyer, a Nebraska parochial schoolteacher was brought up on charges because he taught his immigrant students in German. In its *Meyer v. Nebraska* decision in 1923, the U.S. Supreme Court ruled the Nebraska language law overreaching, holding that teachers could control their own curriculum and that parents had rights to determine the best educational interests of their children.

LATE TWENTIETH CENTURY CHANGES

A major wave of immigration that began in 1965 has continued to the present in the twenty-first century. Most of these new immigrants have been persons of Hispanic and Asian ancestry. In 2007, slightly more than one in five of all school-age children in America spoke a language other than English at home. Of these children, one in four reported having difficulty in speaking English.

Many immigrant children in schools have par-

ents who engage in seasonal work or are members of families that move frequently because of rising rents or changing sociopolitical situations in their homelands. Indeed, high rates of student mobility among many immigrant school populations present considerable challenges to the ability of schools to provide adequate educations. Transnational migration, sojourning workers, and "parachute children" who live on their own while attending American schools are all part of the complex contemporary mosaic of immigrants and education.

LANGUAGE ISSUES

The metaphor of the melting pot has given way to a new metaphor of the "salad bowl" that suggests an essential unity in the midst of considerable diversity. Bilingual education, which arose as a formal response of the educational system in the light of the fourth wave of immigration coupled with the achievements of the Civil Rights movement, led to changes in laws, regulations, and public perceptions about the desirability of preserving competencies in native languages and developing more successful approaches to full English-language competencies. The Bilingual Education Act was passed in 1968 as part of the updating of the Elementary and Secondary Education Act (ESEA). Coupled with Title I funding under ESEA that was targeted to educationally deprived children, this legislation opened up increased possibilities for schools to support immigrant children's education.

Three conflicting fundamental views about how to handle non-native speakers of English within formal educational systems have emerged. The first view sees language as a barrier to acquisition of English and generally takes a remedial approach to the problem. A second view sees language as a right tied to the individual (although it has been difficult to translate this view into effective educational policy). A third view that has gained momentum in the globalized economy, sees the acquisition and maintenance of multiple languages as a positive asset for both individual persons and the future of the United States. At varying times at national, state, and local levels these views have asserted themselves politically, ranging from English-only movements led with great success by S. I. Hayakawa and John Tanton in twenty-three states to the passage of English-only legislation approved by voters in California in 1998, in Arizona in 2000, and in Massachusetts in 2002.

During the same period, some other states, including New Mexico, Oregon, and Washington, declared themselves to be multilingual states and required their schools to reflect this orientation in their curriculum and assessment procedures. The federal No Child Left Behind Act of 2001, the successor to the Improving America's Schools Act (IASA) that had superseded the original Elementary and Secondary Education Act of 1968, removed all references to bilingual instruction. Moreover, the Office of Bilingual Education within the U.S. Department of Education was renamed the Office of English Language Acquisition, Language Enhancement, and Academic Achievement for Limited English Proficient Students as part of a new wave of educational accountability at the federal level.

The U.S. Supreme Court has also been active in this arena, for example, its 1974 decision in *Lau v. Nichols* ruled that the San Francisco school district had to provide instruction in the Chinese language for Chinese pupils who did not speak English. In *Plyler v. Doe* (1982), the Court ruled that schools could not deny undocumented immigrant children access to free public education. Since the last decades of the twentieth century, state education departments and school districts have struggled to fulfill various requirements imposed or rescinded by federal or state legislative or judicial actions.

MULTILINGUALISM

Concerns about American security since the terrorist attacks of September 11, 2001, raised new issues related to language acquisition by American students and highlighted continued angst about immigrants within American society. In many ways, formal educational policies regarding language and culture in American schools closely resemble those of nations such as France, Portugal, Turkey, Japan, and Syria. They are less like the officially multilingual societies and educational systems of nations such as Canada, Israel, Singapore, Paraguay, Switzerland, and Belgium. Some nations, such as India and South Africa, and the European Union as a whole, eschew identification of any specific languages as hallmarks of their national identities.

The special challenges presented by education of a diversity of immigrant peoples have contributed significantly to American education generally. For example, addressing immigrant needs has helped to promote the expansion of kindergartens, vocational education, civics education, adult education programs, summer schools, compulsory attendance laws, and an expansion of foreign-language courses in school systems.

Dennis W. Cheek

FURTHER READING

Donato, Rubén. *Mexicans and Hispanos in Colorado Schools and Communities, 1920-1960.* Albany: State University of New York Press, 2007. Historical examination of the descendants of Spanish troops and Mexicans in Colorado with special attention to the role of the schools over the period.

Feliciano, Cynthia. *Unequal Origins: Immigrant Selection and the Education of the Second Generation.* New York: LFB Scholarly Publishing, 2006. Sociological study that demonstrates Asians are the most highly educated group of immigrants entering the United States.

Gándara, Patricia, and M. Cecilia Gómez. "Language Policy in Education." In *Handbook of Education Policy Research,* edited by Gary Sykes, Barbara Schneider, and David N. Plank. New York: Routledge, 2009. Overview of the various issues in this complex arena by two leading authorities.

Jeynes, William H. *American Educational History: School, Society, and the Common Good.* Thousand Oaks, Calif.: Sage Publications, 2007. Standard history of American education that sets immigration issues within a larger framework of changes within schools and American society.

Portes, Alejandro, and Rubén G. Rumbaut. *Legacies: The Stories of the Immigrant Second Generation.* Berkeley: University of California Press, 2001. Results of a large research study of second-generation immigrant children in Miami and San Diego including family and school life, language, identity, and achievement.

Rong, Xue Lan, and Judith Preissle. *Educating Immigrant Students in the Twenty-first Century: What Educators Need to Know.* 2d ed. Thousand Oaks, Calif.: Corwin Press, 2009. Wide-ranging guide for teachers and others regarding factors influencing learning, successful transitions, working with families, and appropriate teaching and assessment strategies.

Suárez-Orozco, Carola, and Marcelo M. Suárez-Orozco. *Learning in a New Land: Immigrant Students in American Society.* Cambridge, Mass.: Belknap Press, 2008. Study of four hundred recently arrived immigrant children from the Caribbean, China, Central America, and Mexico over five years. Full of poignant stories, challenges, and differentiated outcomes.

Sudem, Garth, Jan Krieger, and Kristi Pikiewicz. *Ten Languages You'll Need Most in the Classroom: A Guide to Communicating with English Language Learners and Their Families.* Thousand Oaks, Calif.: Corwin Press, 2008. Highly specific information and suggestions for teaching immigrant children whose first languages are Spanish, Russian, Vietnamese, Arabic, Tagalog, Haitian Creole, Navajo, Hmong, Cantonese, or Korean.

SEE ALSO: Bilingual education; Bilingual Education Act of 1968; English as a second language; Foreign exchange students; Hayakawa, S. I.; Higher education; Language issues; *Lau v. Nichols*; Parachute children; *Plyler v. Doe.*

EINSTEIN, ALBERT

IDENTIFICATION: German-born American physicist
BORN: March 14, 1879; Ulm, Germany
DIED: April 18, 1955; Princeton, New Jersey

SIGNIFICANCE: The greatest physicist of the twentieth century, Albert Einstein found refuge from Nazi threats in the United States, where he became a symbol of scientific genius and internationalism.

Albert Einstein was born into a middle-class Jewish German family in 1879. He found German schooling stultifying and in 1895 went to study in Switzerland. He renounced his German citizenship in 1896, when he was only sixteen. During the first two decades of the twentieth century, Einstein transformed modern science with his theoretical work on the photoelectric effect, Brownian motion, quantum energy, light, gravity, relativity of

Albert Einstein. (Library of Congress)

space and time, and conversion of matter into energy ($E = mc^2$).

In 1914, Einstein returned to Germany as a professor at the University of Berlin, winning the 1921 Nobel Prize in Physics. Einstein's fame brought him lectureships throughout the world; it also made him the focus of attacks in an increasingly anti-Semitic and militaristic Germany. Fearing for his safety, he and his wife, Elsa, immigrated to the United States on October 17, 1933, where Einstein accepted a position at the Institute for Advanced Study in New Jersey. Although some Americans opposed Einstein's immigration for his "radical" views, Einstein embraced the opportunities and freedom of his new nation. He cowrote a famous letter to President Franklin D. Roosevelt in 1939 advising him of the possibilities of developing an atomic bomb. On June 22, 1940, Einstein took his American citizenship test and gave a talk for the government's *I Am an American* radio series; he was naturalized on October 1, 1940. After World War II, Einstein advocated nuclear disarmament and international cooperation. He died in 1955.

Howard Bromberg

FURTHER READING

Isaacson, Walter. *Albert Einstein: His Life and Universe.* New York: Simon & Schuster, 2007.

Sayen, Jamie. *Einstein in America: The Scientist's Conscience in the Age of Hitler and Hiroshima.* New York: Crown, 1985.

Schweber, Silvan. *Einstein and Oppenheimer: The Meaning of Genius.* Cambridge, Mass.: Harvard University Press, 2008.

SEE ALSO: Anti-Semitism; Citizenship and Immigration Services, U.S.; Congress, U.S.; German immigrants; Jewish immigrants; Naturalization; New Jersey; Science; Swiss immigrants; World War II.

EL PASO INCIDENT

THE EVENT: Dispute over the wages of bracero workers that led to agents of the U.S. Border Patrol allowing four thousand Mexicans to enter the United States illegally to harvest the cotton crop

DATE: October, 1948

SIGNIFICANCE: The complicity of agents of the U.S. government to contravene an agreement with Mexico by allowing Mexican farmworkers to enter the United States was another black mark in the administration of the bracero programs that damaged U.S.-Mexican relations.

Two bracero agricultural labor programs brought Mexicans to work on American farms and railroads. The first, which operated from 1917 to 1921, left some of the 80,000 Mexican participants in the program disillusioned and in debt to American employers from whom they had bought things at company stores. When the United States proposed to inaugurate a new bracero program during the 1940's, the Mexican government insisted that the U.S. government guarantee minimum wages and working conditions in the new program, which would involve almost five million Mexican workers between 1942 and 1964. At first, many American farmers resisted hiring braceros, fearing that the thirty-cents-per-hour minimum wage they would have to pay them in 1942 would also have to be paid to American farmworkers, who were not covered by minimum-wage laws.

Between 1942 and 1946, the U.S. government was the "employer" of record of the braceros, and it was responsible for paying the workers' wages if the farmers did not pay them. After 1946, however, the American farmers became the official employers. The Mexican government had established recruitment centers in the interior of Mexico to which these farmers had to go to select workers. The farmers also had to pay transportation costs of the Mexican workers to their farms. The farmers preferred to recruit workers along the border, so they could select them without Mexican government involvement and save money on transportation costs. Consequently, many Mexicans moved close to the U.S. border to increase their chances of getting American jobs.

The minimum wages and conditions of work for braceros were renegotiated annually. An agreement for the 1948 program was reached in February, 1948, but in October of that year, Texas cotton growers offered bracero workers a piece rate of $2.50 for each one hundred pounds of cotton they picked. The Mexican government, which insisted that the minimum payment be $3.00 discouraged its citizens from crossing the border to work until the American growers raised the piece rate.

Cotton farmers in Texas and New Mexico warned U.S. Border Patrol agents that they risked losing their crop without braceros, so local U.S. officials agreed to open the border. The farmers then sent supervisors to the plazas of Ciudad Juárez where the would-be braceros were waiting, directing them to a shallow crossing spot in the Rio Grande, where they promised trucks would be waiting to transport them to the cotton fields. Between October 13 and 18, 1948, some four thousand Mexican workers crossed the Rio Grande, were registered by the Border Patrol, and were immediately turned over to American farmers, who trucked them to cotton fields. The Mexican government formally protested. After the harvest was completed and the workers had been returned to Mexico, the U.S. government formally apologized. However, the U.S. government did not discipline any of the officials involved in the illegal border crossings.

Philip L. Martin

El Rescate

FURTHER READING

Cohen, Deborah. "Caught in the Middle: The Mexican State's Relationship with the United States and Its Own Citizen-Workers, 1942-1954." *Journal of American Ethnic History* (Spring, 2001): 110-132.

Garcia y Griego, Manuel. "The Importation of Mexican Contract Laborers to the United States, 1942-64." In *Between Two Worlds: Mexican Immigrants in the United States*, edited by David G. Gutierrez. Wilmington, Del.: Jaguar Books, 1996.

Martin, Philip. *Importing Poverty? Immigration and the Changing Face of Rural America.* New Haven, Conn.: Yale University Press, 2009.

SEE ALSO: Border Patrol, U.S.; Bracero program; Farm and migrant workers; Mexican deportations of 1931; Mexican immigrants; Operation Wetback; Texas.

EL RESCATE

IDENTIFICATION: Nonprofit resource center providing free legal and social services
DATE: Founded in 1981
LOCATION: Los Angeles, California

> **SIGNIFICANCE:** By providing free legal and social services to Salvadorans and other Central American immigrants, as well as refugees and immigrants from other Latin American countries living in Los Angeles, California, El Rescate has been an important force for social justice and human rights.

When a civil war began in El Salvador in 1980, refugees arrived in the United States in great numbers; by the early twenty-first century, more than two million Salvadorans were living as exiles, mostly in the United States. To ease their transition, Los Angeles church organizations and members of the Santana Chirino Amaya Refugee Committee formed El Rescate (the rescue) in 1981. Its first project, the Monsignor Romero Clinic, provided free health care to refugees. Soon the group provided basic housing and free legal assistance to help refugees complete the paperwork necessary for achieving legal immigrant status, represented refugees seeking political asylum, supported victims of discrimination and abuse, and offered other forms of legal aid.

During the 1980's, it was difficult for Central American refugees to obtain legal refugee status because President Ronald Reagan's administration argued that its Central American allies protected the human rights of their citizens. El Rescate opened a secret office in El Salvador in 1985 to document human rights abuses in that country. The information was broadly disseminated and helped El Rescate persuade U.S. legislators that Salvadorans deserved refugee status.

When the civil war ended in 1992, many Salvadorans decided to settle in California, but most retained strong ties to those back home. Approximately one million Salvadorans lived in the United States at that time, compared with a population of about six million in El Salvador. El Rescate shifted its focus from refugee services, expanding to offer financial services for immigrants and permanent residents, including credit cards, phone cards, payroll services, and the Comunidades Federal Credit Union; assistance with sending money to relatives in Central America; and small loans and workshops to help immigrants become financially secure. The group also provided literacy tutoring and helped clients gain access to health care services. Its primary beneficiaries were Salvadorans, but refugees from other parts of Central America and other Latino immigrants in the Los Angeles area were also served.

In 1997, President Bill Clinton signed the Nicaraguan Adjustment and Central American Relief Act (NACARA), which provided immigration benefits and relief from deportation to certain Salvadorans, Nicaraguans, Cubans, and Guatemalans, as well as refugees from the former Soviet Union. A year later, El Rescate campaigned successfully for amendments that allowed more Salvadorans and Guatemalans to receive assistance. During the twenty-first century, El Rescate also sponsors community and social events, and it has joined with other Salvadoran organizations to sponsor an annual International Convention of Salvadoran Communities Residing Abroad. It hosts weekly *charlas* (public presentations) on legal issues and sponsors a Web site promoting community events.

Cynthia A. Bily

FURTHER READING

Coutin, Susan Bibler. *Legalizing Moves: Salvadoran Immigrants' Struggle for U.S. Residency.* Ann Arbor: University of Michigan Press, 2003.

Hamilton, Nora, and Norma Stoltz Chinchilla. *Seeking Community in a Global City: Guatemalans and Salvadorans in Los Angeles.* Philadelphia: Temple University Press, 2001.

Howland, Todd. "How El Rescate, a Small Nongovernmental Organization, Contributed to the Transformation of the Human Rights Situation in El Salvador." *Human Rights Quarterly* 30, no. 3 (August, 2008): 703-757.

Ruíz, Vicki, and Virginia Sánchez Korrol. *Latinas in the United States: A Historical Encyclopedia.* Bloomington: Indiana University Press, 2006.

SEE ALSO: California; Citizenship and Immigration Services, U.S.; Guatemalan immigrants; Health care; Latin American immigrants; Los Angeles; Nicaraguan immigrants; Refugees; Salvadoran immigrants.

ELLIS ISLAND

IDENTIFICATION: Immigrant reception center in New York Harbor

DATE: Opened on January 1, 1892; closed on November 12, 1954

SIGNIFICANCE: The first official immigration station and long the busiest in the United States, Ellis Island was the entry point for more than 12 million newcomers. By the early twenty-first century, more than 40 percent of the people living in the United States could trace their ancestry to immigrants who were processed through Ellis Island.

Ellis Island was once the site of the nation's busiest immigrant processing center. Called Kioshk, or Gull Island, by the Indians, the island was renamed Oyster Island when the Dutch acquired the property in the 1630's. During the British colonial period, it went by the names Dyre's Island, Bucking Island, Anderson's Island, and Gibbet Island. Manhattan merchant Samuel Ellis held title to the land during the American Revolution, and his heirs sold what became known as Ellis Island to New York State in

1808. Later that same year, the property was acquired by the federal government. Originally 3.3 acres, the island was expanded to 27.5 acres mostly by landfill from ballast removed from ships. Though the federal government maintains control over the island, a long-standing dispute between New Jersey and New York was finally resolved in 1998, when the two states agreed to share jurisdiction.

Before 1890, when the federal government assumed responsibility for immigration control and designated Ellis Island as the first federal immigrant processing station, individual states were responsible for processing immigrants. Until that year, Castle Garden, located in Battery Park at the southern tip of Manhattan, served as the immigration absorption center for New York. Between 1855 and 1890, more than 8 million immigrants, mostly from northern and western Europe, passed through Castle Garden.

On January 1, 1892, Annie Moore, a fifteen-year-old from Ireland, became the first immigrant registered at Ellis Island, which was larger and more isolated than the cramped Castle Garden. By the time the facility ceased operations, on November 12, 1954, it had processed more than 12 million immigrants from a wide range of origins, including southern and eastern Europe. During 1907, its peak year, 1,004,756 immigrants passed through the island. The highest volume recorded for any single day was 11,747, on April 17, 1907.

Although the United States also maintained immigration stations in Boston, Philadelphia, New Orleans, Galveston, San Francisco, and elsewhere, Ellis Island was by far the busiest. During a period of unprecedented dislocation, it was a barometer of the massive immigration from Europe that was transforming American culture.

ARRIVAL AND INSPECTION

The majestic Statue of Liberty was the first inspiring sight that greeted most ship passengers arriving in New York Harbor at the conclusion of a long voyage across the Atlantic. Half a mile north, however, most immigrants were soon forced to disembark at Ellis Island, which for some was the only piece of American soil on which they were able to set foot. Would-be immigrants were screened on Ellis Island, and during the course of the immigration station's existence, approximately 2 percent of passengers were denied admission into the United

States. Since it was assumed that passengers arriving in first- and second-class accommodations had sufficient resources to avoid becoming public charges, they were provided the courtesy of a brief shipboard inspection. However, those with medical or legal problems were forced, along with third-class and steerage passengers, to get off at Ellis Island and submit to a series of mental and physical tests designed to screen out undesirables.

Inspectors were particularly vigilant about preventing the spread of tuberculosis. Those who were determined to be seriously ill or insane or who possessed criminal records were deemed unworthy to enter the United States. For those who had endured at least a month at sea within the miserable confines of steerage only to be forced to return from whence they came, the famous immigration station earned its popular nicknames "Island of Tears" and "Heartbreak Island." During the island's history, thirty-five hundred immigrants died in its hospital facilities.

Agents of the United States Public Health Service and the Bureau of Immigration carried out inspections, which took place in the Registry Room (also known as the Great Hall) and usually lasted three to five hours. The total time required to process a new arrival was usually one to three days. Dormitories and dining halls were built to accommodate the newcomers during their stay on Ellis Island. Legend has it that, either deliberately or through misunderstanding, Ellis Island officials Americanized many quaint foreign names. However, hundreds of translators were on hand to facilitate communication, and officials simply copied information from the questionnaires that passengers had filled out themselves during embarkation.

LAST YEARS OF ELLIS ISLAND

During World War I, the volume of immigration to the United States decreased, and Ellis Island was used to intern suspected enemy aliens. The restrictive Immigration Act of 1924 reduced traffic

View of Ellis Island reception center seen by arriving immigrants during the first decade of the twentieth century. (Library of Congress)

through the processing center to a trickle. During World War II, seven thousand German, Italian, and Japanese nationals, classified as enemy aliens, were detained on Ellis Island, which was also used as a training base for the U.S. Coast Guard. In 1954, a Norwegian sailor named Arne Peterssen became the last immigrant processed through the immigration station, and the island ceased its operations.

Steven G. Kellman

FURTHER READING

Brownstone, David M., Irene M. Franck, and Douglass L. Brownstone. *Island of Hope, Island of Tears: The Story of Those Who Entered the New World Through Ellis Island—In Their Own Words.* New York: Rawson, Wade, 1979. The authors assemble and comment on testimony by dozens of immigrants from a variety of backgrounds.

Conway, Lorie. *Forgotten Ellis Island: The Extraordinary Story of America's Immigrant Hospital.* New York: Smithsonian Books, 2007. A study of the medical facilities, policies, and history of the immigration station.

Moreno, Barry. *Encyclopedia of Ellis Island.* Westport, Conn.: Greenwood Press, 2004. More than four hundred alphabetically arranged entries as well as a chronology and a bibliography provide a thorough source of information about Ellis Island.

Novotny, Ann. *Strangers at the Door: Ellis Island, Castle Garden, and the Great Migration to America.* Riverside, Conn.: Chatham Press, 1971. An illustrated history of Ellis Island and its changing role in immigration to the United States. One chapter is devoted to celebrity immigrants.

Pitkin, Thomas M. *Keepers of the Gate: A History of Ellis Island.* New York: New York University Press, 1975. Originally prepared as a report for the National Park Service, a study of the island's history and its prospects, as of 1975, as a museum site.

Yans-McLaughlin, Virginia, and Marjorie Lightman. *Ellis Island and the Peopling of America: The Official Guide.* New York: New Press, 1997. Designed for high school students, this book, enriched by documents and charts, surveys the evolution of official policy and popular reactions toward immigration.

VISITOR INFORMATION

Ellis Island opened as a public museum on September 10, 1990. Visitors to New York City can reach the island on boats that also dock at Liberty Island, the site of the Statue of Liberty. The Statue of Liberty-Ellis Island Foundation maintains a Web site at www.ellisisland.org that enables visitors to research family immigration records. Ellis Island is administered, along with the Statue of Liberty National Monument, by the National Park Service.

SEE ALSO: Angel Island Immigration Station; Bureau of Immigration, U.S.; European immigrants; Hamburg-Amerika Line; History of immigration after 1891; Immigration waves; Infectious diseases; Intelligence testing; Name changing; New York City; Statue of Liberty.

EMIGRATION

DEFINITION: Outward movement of citizens from their native countries to other countries

SIGNIFICANCE: The fact that large numbers of Americans have emigrated to other countries is not often openly acknowledged because immigration of foreigners to the United States has always received more media attention. However, American emigrants provide many of their adopted countries with productive new citizens who strengthen their new homes while reducing the number of the talented and skilled people living and working in the United States.

Americans have always found reasons to leave the United States for other countries. As early as the days of the American Revolution, thousands of people who sided with Great Britain in the conflict emigrated to Britain after it ended. Since then, groups and individuals who have found conditions in the United States disagreeable or who have become enamored of foreign societies or cultures have chosen to make their homes abroad. Some have become citizens of their new homelands, but many have become disenchanted and returned to the United States.

The first settlers of British North America were all immigrants accustomed to the idea of relocating. Consequently, when many of them found their new country and its inhabitants too different culturally or too hostile to feel comfortable, they returned to their European homelands. As late as the early decades of the twentieth century, this trend continued. Between 1900 and 1930, about 30 million people immigrated to the United States, and 10 million people emigrated. Between 1931 and 1940, another 600,000 people left the country, while it was being devastated by the Great Depression.

After 1957, the U.S. government stopped keeping emigration records. Because Americans living abroad have not been required to register with American consulates since that date, the numbers of Americans who have emigrated are difficult to tabulate. Nevertheless, because America is home to people from 168 different countries, it is not surprising that second- and third-generation Americans have occasionally chosen to go to their forebears' homelands and put down roots in places as varied as the Netherlands, Saudi Arabia, Australia, Panama, Egypt, and Sri Lanka.

EMIGRATION TO EUROPE

Since the era of the Revolutionary War, in the late eighteenth century Americans have found much in Europe to lure them, particularly the compatible cultures and societies. Most early American citizens were themselves only first- or second-generation Americans, so they were not far removed from their ancestral homelands. English settlers went back to England, French settlers to France, and German settlers to German states. During the late nineteenth century, 35 percent of the Croatians, Serbs, and Poles who had immigrated to America returned home. About 40 percent of Greeks and more than 50 percent of the Italians, Hungarians, and Slovaks did.

Many individual American writers and artists felt a special cultural pull to Europe. Some scholars attribute this to a "colonial complex"—an attitude that the Continent, with its long cultural history and achievements, was undeniably superior in most ways to the "upstart" new nation that had been hewn out of a primitive land. Before the U.S. Civil War (1861-1865), when the first American literary giants were writing, many of them went to Europe. Examples included Nathaniel Hawthorne, Washington Irving, James Fenimore Cooper, Ralph Waldo Emerson, and Henry Wadsworth Longfellow. Some went to immerse themselves in European culture. Others went for personal or financial reasons. Some remained in Europe through the rest of their lives. Others returned to the United States only reluctantly, after periods of exile ranging from a few months to several years.

Wars disrupted many European countries through much of the nineteenth century, making parts of them less attractive destinations for Americans wishing to emigrate. The onset of the U.S. Civil War of the 1860's and the upheavals among European governments kept Europe in turmoil for much of the century. However, as European visual artists continued to develop intriguing new styles and techniques, American artists such as Mary Cassatt, Benjamin West, and James Whistler went to Europe to study and work in the latter years of the century.

After World War I, some Americans were attracted to French and British receptiveness to Americans with artistic, musical, and literary talent. Writers such as Ernest Hemingway, T. S. Eliot, F. Scott Fitzgerald, Gertrude Stein, and Ezra Pound moved there to enjoy Europe's comparatively free and permissive lifestyles. African Americans such as entertainer Josephine Baker and writer Langston Hughes, and veterans of the war found French society less racist and segregated than that of the United States.

During the Great Depression, some Americans were lured to the Soviet Union, believing they would find better wages, free medical care and free schooling there, a prosperity not foreseeable in the United States at the time. However, emigrants did not learn until too late that Americans who went to the Soviet Union were considered the "flotsam and jetsam of the Depression." They were soon treated badly, not only by Soviet citizens but also by U.S. diplomatic personnel. Many had their passports taken away, removing any chance they had of leaving the country. Many were consigned to the Soviet labor camps known as gulags.

The aftermath of World War II found many emigrant American artists, jazz and rock musicians, and writers continuing to choose Europe. American fashion designers were particularly attracted to the famed French and Italian fashion houses,

W. E. B. Du Bois (holding cane) with Ghanaian president Kwame Nkrumah in 1962. Never fully comfortable in the United States, the distinguished African American scholar and socialist activist emigrated to Ghana, the first black African colony to gain its independence from European colonial rule, when he was in his nineties. When he was refused a new American passport shortly before he died, he and his wife became Ghanaian citizens. However, Du Bois never renounced his American citizenship. (AP/Wide World Photos)

where they hoped their working and studying would enhance their own credentials. Some American actors whose film careers were less successful than they had hoped moved to Europe, especially to Italy, Germany, and England, where they became bigger stars in foreign films. Some late twentieth century celebrities, such as Lorraine Bracco, Tina Turner, Gwyneth Paltrow, Johnny Depp, Chaka Khan, and Madonna, have found Europe an inviting place to live because the European media are less intrusive into their private lives.

EMIGRATION TO AFRICA AND ASIA

During the early nineteenth century, freed American slaves were allowed, in fact, encouraged to emigrate to Africa's west coast. The establish-ment during the 1820's of colonies in what would become the independent nation of Liberia held out the promise to former slaves of better lives than they might enjoy in the United States. More than 13,000 African Americans had settled in Liberia by 1870. During the 1920's, smaller numbers of African Americans were enticed to go there by Marcus Garvey's back-to-Africa movement. During the 1940's, Morocco became an attractive destination for such African American writers as Paul Bowles and Claude McKay. After the abolition of apartheid and democratization of the Republic of South Africa during the early 1990's, that nation became an attractive destination for American émigrés, largely because of its English-speaking population and vast economic potential.

Cultural and language restrictions have been among the reasons that American emigration to Asian countries has been limited. Some Asian countries have also had immigration policies that exclude foreigners. Even as British were nationals making homes in many Asian countries during the era of the British Empire, Americans were not inclined to follow suit in any large numbers. Christian missionaries from the United States worked in many of the countries, notably China, for many decades. Novelist Pearl S. Buck was a child of missionaries to China during the early twentieth century. She lived a good portion of her life there. Since the late twentieth century, China's government has allowed foreigners to work, study, or travel in China, but it has not permitted permanent immigration. Foreign workers have been required to live close to their places of work in order to limit their exposure to and possible influence on the rest of the country.

Japan, though more flexible than China in permitting Americans to reside in the country for longer periods of time, has continued to discriminate against non-Japanese residents. Nevertheless, many Americans have lived there in various capacities since the end of World War II. In 2004, the 51,851 Americans living in Japan constituted 2.4 percent of all registered foreigners in the country—a figure that made them the sixth-largest group of foreign residents.

India has seen a surge of American immigrants. Most are young college graduates looking to study or work there. In 2009, approximately 800 Americans were interning in Indian information technology companies. Most older Americans living in the country are managers of subsidiary companies who train Indian employees. Many Americans in India are second-generation Indian Americans who have returned to their parents' native land with job skills that assist the growing Indian economy. Other Indian Americans in India are motivated by a desire to live where they are not in the minority and do not have to deal with various levels of discrimination.

EMIGRATION TO CANADA AND MEXICO

Many American citizens dissatisfied with their lives in the United States choose to emigrate to neighboring countries to make it easy to return. Should they change their minds about emigrating or should conditions at home improve, they can simply get in their cars and drive back to the United States. Moreover, Canada and Mexico provide havens with climates and cultures not greatly different from those in the United States.

Before the U.S. Civil War, many fugitive slaves and free blacks headed north to Canada's comparative safety. During the late 1960's and early 1970's, a period of divisiveness in the United States caused by the fundamental differences over American involvement in the Vietnam War, young Americans of all political stripes went to Canada in large numbers to avoid conscription into the military or to dramatize their protest against the political climate in the United States. Records of the numbers of Americans who went to Canada during the war are incomplete because not all Americans who entered Canada registered themselves. However, it is estimated that between 50,000 and 100,000 Americans, mostly draft avoiders, entered Canada during that period. War protestors and draft avoiders were not the only Americans to emigrate to Canada during that time. From 1968 until 1978, more than 400,000 Americans became Canadian residents. During the decade following those years, the numbers of American emigrants to Canada fell to 5,000 per year.

In later decades, gay and lesbian Americans, opponents of the U.S. invasion of Iraq in 2003, and people seeking a better health care system or the right to use medical marijuana legally have found Canada a more receptive environment. For example, Canada has allowed more rights to same-sex partners than most American states. Canada is also preferred by some environmentally conscious Americans because it signed the Kyoto Protocol in support of international efforts to save the world's environment, which the United States declined to do.

Americans who have emigrated to Canada have tended to be well educated and under the age of forty. They are generally skilled and speak English—both traits that make them highly eligible for permanent residence status when they apply. Canada's population is only a little larger than one-tenth the size of the population of the United States, but its surface area is about the same size as that of the United States, so it has plenty of room for a larger population. Nevertheless, in 2001, American-born émigrés to Canada constituted only 4.6 percent of Canada's foreign-born population.

For potential American emigrants, Mexico offers many of the same advantages as Canada. It also has the additional advantage of a warmer year-round climate. Americans seeking to lower their living costs and to enjoy a less-hectic lifestyle have been emigrating to Mexico for many years. Indeed, Mexico has been rated as one of the ten destination countries best suited for American emigrants because of its nearness to the United States and its low cost of living.

Before the late twentieth century, most of the emigrants were older Americans living on fixed incomes. In the United States, many of these people would have been living close to the poverty level, but in Mexico they were comparatively well off. For example, it has been estimated that American retirees can maintain standards of living in Mexico equivalent to levels about 50 percent higher than those their incomes would afford them in the United States.

Because American retirees who relocate to Mexico generally settle in communities in which other American expatriates have already settled, they generally find English spoken almost as much as Spanish, and local businesses cater to American tastes. Transitions to living in Mexico thus may become as comfortable as relocating to another American community, with the additional advantages of much lower rent and medical care costs. Between 1990 and 2000, the numbers of Americans living in Mexico grew by 84.3 percent. By 2001, more than 75,000 American retirees were living in Mexico, and all American-born residents made up 63.2 percent of Mexico's foreign-born population.

Jane L. Ball

FURTHER READING

Anhalt, Diana. *A Gathering of Fugitives: American Political Expatriates in Mexico, 1948-1965*. Santa Maria, Calif.: Archer Books, 2001. Discusses the Americans who moved to Mexico during the McCarthy era to escape political persecution.

Campbell, James T. *Middle Passages: African American Journeys to Africa, 1787-2005*. New York: Penguin Books, 2007. Although this book is primarily about African American travelers in Africa, portions of the book also discuss the motivations of African Americans who have permanently emigrated to Africa. These motivations have ranged from nostalgia for the African past to religious to economic reasons.

Finifter, Ada W. "American Emigration." *Society* 3, no. 5 (July, 1976): 30-36. Examines the reasons why some Americans emigrate. These reasons have included general dissatisfaction with the American political system and feelings of being marginalized because of holding unpopular political views.

Gaines, Kevin. *American Africans in Ghana: Black Expatriates and the Civil Rights Era*. Chapel Hill: University of North Carolina Press, 2006. Examines how African Americans sought freedom from the discrimination experienced in the United States by settling in the newly independent Ghana.

Tzouliadis, Tim. *The Forsaken: An American Tragedy in Stalin's Russia*. New York: Penguin Books, 2008. Well-researched and well-written discussion of the brutal conditions in the Soviet Union experienced by Americans who went there during the years of the Great Depression.

SEE ALSO: Canada vs. United States as immigrant destinations; Dual citizenship; Garvey, Marcus; Gay and lesbian immigrants; Great Depression; Liberia; Literature; Missionaries; Return migration; Universal Negro Improvement Association.

EMPLOYMENT

DEFINITION: Occupations and conditions of immigrant laborers in the United States

SIGNIFICANCE: Often called a nation of immigrants, the United States has borne witness, from the time of its earliest European settlements to the twenty-first century, that immigrant groups have significantly contributed to its survival, development, and prosperity. Although some scholars argue that low-skilled immigrants have helped to reduce American wage levels and overburden public services, most agree that immigrants have been essential to the country's industrialization as well as to its economic, scientific, technological, and cultural growth.

More than thirteen thousand years ago, well before the arrival of the first Europeans, America was the destination of people from Asia. Those ancient immigrants spread out throughout the Western Hemisphere and diversified into about 750 distinct cultures that developed an immense variety of means of employment that enabled them to survive in arctic, temperate, and tropic regions. After Christopher Columbus's four voyages of discovery to what Europeans called the New World around the turn of the sixteenth century, the increasing numbers of Spanish immigrants settled in South, Central, and North America. The earliest Spanish arrivals concentrated on exploiting gold and silver resources, but later immigrants came to work the land with imported horses, cattle, pigs, sheep, and goats. They also introduced new crops, such as European wheat, Asian rice, and African bananas. These modern immigrants also found that such New World plants as corn, tomatoes, potatoes, and tobacco could be cultivated as valuable crops.

EARLY BRITISH IMMIGRANTS

Tragic failures of early English settlements in North America convinced English investors that, to succeed, colonies required skilled husbandmen and artisans. With the hope for a better life, many English immigrants came freely to work in New England as well as in the middle and southern colonies, but other immigrants, such as African slaves, British convicts, and indentured servants, came less freely or with no freedom at all. Most worked on plantations producing rice, tobacco, and indigo, or on farms producing wheat, corn, and cattle. While the English dominated North American immigration of the seventeenth century, during the eighteenth century other European immigrants arrived in large numbers. For example, in Pennsylvania, by 1776, the majority of settlers were non-English, and German workers had helped create a very successful iron industry.

Indentured servants, after their four to seven-year contracts had been fulfilled, often received fifty acres of land, which they proceeded to farm. By the time of the Revolutionary War (1775-1783) the numbers of Irish immigrants nearly equaled those of the Scotch-Irish, and many of them worked as unskilled laborers. Scholars have estimated that, at that time, African immigrants, mostly slaves, numbered about 360,000; English immigrants about 230,000; with smaller numbers of Scotch-Irish, Irish, and German immigrants.

AMERICAN REVOLUTION TO U.S. CIVIL WAR

Late eighteenth and early nineteenth century immigration patterns tended to resemble those of the colonial period. Most immigrants came to farm lands that were much less expensive than those in Europe, while a small but significant minority came as artisans skilled in such professions as carpentry, metal working, textile production, and iron-making. For example, Samuel Slater, who had mastered methods of manufacturing cotton cloth in England, immigrated to Rhode Island where, during the 1790's, he built the first American factories manufacturing cotton cloth. This technology quickly spread throughout New England, and immigrant workers were employed in large numbers in these cotton and in woolen mills.

After the United States won its independence, its leaders held contrasting views about the roles that immigrants should play in the new country. President Thomas Jefferson, for example, hoped that immigrants would contribute to his vision of a nation of self-sufficient farmers. In contrast, Secretary of the Treasury Alexander Hamilton wanted immigrants to work in cities and factories. However, both Jefferson and Hamilton agreed on the importance of attracting artisans with advanced skills from Europe.

From the 1820's to the 1830's European immigrants to the United States increased from about 150,000 per year to about 600,000. At the same time, the governments of their home countries tried to limit emigration, particularly of skilled artisans. However, the strong attractions of low-priced land and a labor shortage in America provided incentives for English and Irish to cross the Atlantic to pursue their occupations as farmers, blacksmiths, weavers, masons, shoemakers, and tailors. Mechanical expertise was especially highly valued in the United States. Different immigrant groups tended to settle in different sections of the country. In general, many more settled in the North than in the South, a situation that pleased certain southerners, who were suspicious of immigrants and satisfied with their slave system. English and Scottish immigrants tended to have the best educations and technical training, and they naturally settled in such cities as Boston, New York, and Philadelphia, in which they were able to pursue their specialized work. Skilled laborers also found work outside cities. For example, Scottish quarrymen mined granite in New England, and Welsh miners dug coal in the Middle Colonies.

Irish immigrants tended to be poorer in education, skills, and money than others, leading them to take manual jobs such as digging the Erie Canal and constructing roads and turnpikes. In cities such as Boston, the Irish became the dominant foreign-born group, and some obtained skilled jobs as carpenters and printers, but most men worked as laborers and most women as domestics. Other Irish women worked in the textile mills of Lowell, Lawrence, and Fall River, Massachusetts. An occasional Irishman became extraordinarily successful, such as James McCreery, who immigrated to the United States in 1845 and became wealthy selling Irish lace.

The Great Irish Famine of 1845-1849 and the political revolutions in continental Europe in 1848 accelerated immigration to the United States. Many of the more than two million Irish men and women who came were forced into low-paying menial jobs. The men worked on construction projects in the cities and on railroads in the countryside; the women worked as servants, laundresses, and dressmakers. On the other hand, the 1.5 million German immigrants, sometimes called "Forty-eighters," had greater numbers of artisans and trained professionals than the Irish. However, unskilled German workers did help construct canals and railroads along with their Irish counterparts. Many Germans also found work as shoemakers, tailors, and butchers. In 1850, half of Philadelphia's Germans were employed in jobs that required skills. Sometimes, as in Germantown, Pennsylvania, they created communities where Germans had jobs at every level, from mayor to day laborer. German immigrants also settled in such cities as Chicago, Milwaukee, and Cincinnati, and in such states as Wisconsin and Missouri. There many of them found work as brewers and bakers, while a minority, about 25 percent, became farmers.

Other events that influenced immigration were the 1848 discovery of gold in California and the admission of California into the Union two years later. These events stimulated immigration from Mexico, South America, China, and Europe. Particularly notable were the large numbers of Chinese, some who came at their own expense, while others arrived indebted to merchants who had paid for their ocean passage. Although some Chinese panned for gold, most worked at menial jobs in the gold miners' camps, where they were denigratingly called "coolies." As gold production declined, Chinese workers traveled to towns and cities of the West, where they ran laundries, opened restaurants, and worked as laborers on construction projects.

U.S. CIVIL WAR TO 1900

Even before the U.S. Civil War began in 1861, many immigrants had entered the U.S. Army. During the war, the numbers of immigrant military personnel grew so much that eventually more than one-half of all Union enlisted men were immigrants. The military forces of both the North and South energetically recruited Irish, German, and Italian immigrants. However, because foreign-born residents of the North vastly outnumbered those of the South, the Union army had many more immigrant soldiers. Moreover, because soldiers—immigrant as well as native-born—needed food, clothing, and weapons, more immigrant workers were needed to produce these necessities, leading to the liberalization of immigration laws.

The federal Alien Contract Labor Law of 1864 permitted employers to recruit groups of workers overseas. By that date, immigration into the United States had declined, and many immigrant workers were serving in the military, hence the need for recruitment. Despite the fact that nearly 500,000 foreign-born immigrants volunteered to fight for the Union, the federal Draft Law of 1863 prompted violent resistance among many immigrants, particularly the Irish in New York City and Germans in Milwaukee, Wisconsin. Nevertheless, the North's ultimate victory owed much to its immigrant troops. However, these immigrants hoped that their loyal military service would result in improved employment opportunities after the war, but quickly became disillusioned as newly freed African Americans and more recently arriving immigrants competed with them for precious jobs.

One of the characteristics of the postwar period was the settlement and economic development of regions from the Mississippi River to the Pacific Ocean. More than 25 million new immigrants entered the United States during the thirty-five years after the war; they played important roles in these developments. German immigrants, the largest group of the nineteenth century, participated, along with Poles, Lithuanians, and Irishmen, in such midwestern enterprises as meatpacking, mining, iron and steel making, and the manufacture of furniture and bicycles. Builders of the transcontinental railroad recruited Chinese workers, who eventually numbered more than 10,000, to carve out mountainsides, lay tracks, and construct bridges. After the Central Pacific was linked to the Union Pacific in 1869, many Chinese became agricultural workers. By the 1880's, according to one estimate, as many as 90 percent of California farmworkers were Chinese. Japanese immigrants began coming in large numbers to California during this same time, and Japanese farmers, who employed new immigrants, often extended-family members, as sharecroppers, had particularly productive enterprises.

During the late decades of the nineteenth century, the pattern of immigration from Europe changed. By then, immigrants from Britain, Germany, Spain, and France were greatly outnum-

bered by those people from southern and eastern Europe. Although most came from rural backgrounds, these Italians, Greeks, Poles, and Russians mainly sought employment in northern and midwestern cities, in which they became unskilled factory workers in industries such as steelmaking. In 1886 Andrew Carnegie—himself an immigrant from Scotland—praised these immigrants as "a golden strand" that made possible the dramatic progress in American manufacturing. However, later critics pointed out that Carnegie's exploitation of these cheap laborers contributed to the immense profitability of his steel business.

Hundreds of thousands of Italians, mostly men, spread throughout the Northeast and Midwest, where they worked in factories and mines or served as barbers and bootblacks. Others became involved in massive projects such as digging aqueduct tunnels and helping build New York City's Grand Central Station and the Brooklyn Bridge. The famous bridge itself was designed by a German

Young immigrants working in a Fall River, Massachusetts, mill in 1912. (Library of Congress)

Confined to substandard tenement housing in major eastern cities and severely restricted in employment opportunities, many Italian immigrant families took garment work into their homes and employed their children. The mother and her three eldest children in this picture earned a total of about two dollars a week—when work was available—around 1913, while the father sought day work on the street. (Library of Congress)

immigrant, John Augustus Roebling, and was completed by his son. Other immigrants who arrived in New York City around that time who achieved fame in their chosen fields included Irving Berlin, a Russian Jew who went on to become one of America's greatest songwriters. Many other Russian Jews entered the garment trade.

1900 TO WORLD WAR I

As the U.S. population was increasing naturally during the early twentieth century, the numbers of immigrants increased even more dramatically, peaking in 1914. While restrictive legislation had drastically reduced Chinese and Japanese entrants, immigration from southern and eastern Europe accelerated. Even with the introduction of labor-saving machinery, the coal, steel, and railroad busi-

nesses, all of which were expanding, needed workers. For example, in Birmingham, Alabama, noted for its booming iron and steel industry, about half of the laborers were immigrants. The ethnic make-up of immigrants differed from region to region. In New York State, for example, Russians were the largest immigrant group, at over 558,000, followed by Italians, Germans, and Irish. By the time of World War I, Chicago had more Poles, Lithuanians, Serbo-Croats, Swedes, and Norwegians than any other American city. Certain ethnic groups, such as Italians, Greeks, and Turks, made use of *padrones*, foreign-born labor brokers who exploitatively obtained jobs and housing for immigrants.

Most Italians got jobs in construction, mines, or railroads (only 15 percent obtained positions as skilled workers). Other immigrants got jobs in the new and prospering automobile industry. Henry Ford made finding employment easier for unskilled workers by introducing a system of assembly-line mass production in which, he claimed, workers could be taught their jobs in a few days. In fact, by 1914, unskilled workers, many of them immigrants, constituted more than 90 percent of the workers at a Ford plant.

The number of Mexican immigrants officially entering the United States rose from 49,000 in the new century's first decade, to 219,000 in the second, and 459,000 in the third, though actual numbers were well in excess of these due to illegal immigration. Most of these immigrants settled in California, Arizona, and Texas, where they cultivated, harvested, and packed fruits and vegetables.

Because immigrants often occupied low-paying positions that involved boring and sometimes dangerous manual labor, they tended to leave their jobs in droves. In 1913, one Ford factory experienced a 416 percent turnover rate, and the turnover rates for the mining and steel industries were routinely near 100 percent per year. Many immigrant workers began to agitate for national labor unions to improve work conditions, pay, and benefits. Immigrant women workers were also part of this movement. In 1909, garment workers in New York City, most of them Italian and Jewish immigrants, organized a movement dubbed the "Uprising of the 20,000," which did lead to higher wages and better conditions in some business. However, conditions were not improved in New York City's Triangle Shirtwaist Company, which ran an operation on the tenth floor of a Lower Manhattan building. In 1911, a devastating fire in the building resulted in the deaths of 146 immigrant women, many of them young, who had been locked into their workplace. This tragedy called national attention to the exploitation of immigrant workers.

WORLD WAR I THROUGH WORLD WAR II

Immigration into the United States diminished during the four years of World War I (1914-1918) to a little more than 1 million entrants—a figure slightly greater than 25 percent of the previous five years' immigration. Members of certain ethnic groups, particularly Germans, suffered from the chauvinistic and xenophobic sentiments fostered by the war. Some American nativists tried to prevent the admission of immigrants with radical political and labor views, such as socialists. In response, the U.S. Congress further restricted immigration by passing a law requiring a literacy test for immigrants. However, because of protests from fruit and vegetable growers, many Mexican immigrant workers were exempted from the literacy test because they were essential in harvesting food for American civilians and the military.

After the war, the Industrial Workers of the World (IWW, or "Wobblies," as they were nicknamed) sponsored strikes, and the IWW did include immigrants from the mining, agricultural, and meatpacking industries. State and federal governments used raids and deportations to try to control labor unrest. After much debate Congress passed the Immigration Act of 1924, one of whose goals was to limit immigration from southern and eastern Europe in favor of immigrants from the northern and western countries of Europe. The Great Depression, which started in 1929, created incentives for further restrictions on immigration because many native-born workers were losing their jobs. The new measures worked: During the 1930's only about 500,000 immigrants entered the United States, compared to more than 4.1 million during the 1920's.

The rise of Adolf Hitler's Nazi Party to power in Germany created many Jewish refugees, but isolationist, nativist, and anti-Semitic attitudes by many Americans led political leaders to remain largely unresponsive to their plight, though some "illustrious immigrants," such as Albert Einstein, Edward Teller, and Bruno Walter found fulfilling work that enhanced American life. After Germany's annexation of Austria in early 1938 and the Kristallnacht pogrom in November of that year, during which many German Jewish businesses and synagogues were destroyed, U.S. policy toward Jewish German and Austrian immigrants became more liberal, and about 85,000 were admitted during a short period after these events. However, after World War II began in Europe in 1939, U.S. refugee policy became increasingly restrictive, with catastrophic consequences for Europe's Jews.

Meanwhile, because of the American need for workers on farms and in defense plants, the United States forged an agreement with Mexico that facilitated the organized recruitment of Mexicans for seasonal agricultural work and full-time factory work in such defense industries as airplane manufacture in California. The resulting bracero program allowed each Mexican state to provide the names of workers to the U.S. Department of Labor, which then assigned workers to various employers. The program was so popular in Mexico that the numbers of Mexicans wanting this work always far outnumbered those who actually got American contracts.

WORLD WAR II TO 1965

Immediately following the end of World War II in Europe and Asia in 1945, a huge problem confronted the world's leaders—millions of displaced people. President Harry S. Truman issued a directive allowing the immediate admission of 41,000 displaced persons into the United States, and Congress passed the Displaced Persons Act in 1948 that provided for the admission of over 100,000 of them in a four-year period. Some scholars consider this act revolutionary, because through it Congress actually weakened restrictive and exclusionary policies. This liberalization continued in 1956 when President Dwight D. Eisenhower authorized the admission of 38,000 Hungarian immigrants who had fled their country after an abortive anticommunist revolt.

During the two decades following the war, several million immigrants entered the United States, but the nature of immigration changed yet again, as did the types of employment that the new immigrants sought and found. By this time, nearly one-half the immigrants were coming from countries in the Western Hemisphere. After Fidel Castro established a communist government in Cuba, about 650,000 Cubans, many of them well educated and professionally trained, entered the United States. Growing numbers of immigrants from Mexico and other Latin American countries created serious problems because illegal entrants constituted large and unmanageable numbers. Some U.S. employers actually encouraged illegal immigration. By hiring undocumented workers, they could circumvent laws governing minimum wages, work hours, and contracts. In 1954, more than 1 million illegal immigrants were caught and returned to their native countries. Despite this deterrent and the immigrants' exploitation by their U.S. employers, undocumented workers continued to come from Mexico, Central and South America, and the Caribbean. A higher ratio of female to male immigrants characterized this new wave of immigration, with many women finding work in the garment industry and as domestics.

AFTER 1965

A central goal of the Immigration and Nationality Act of 1965 was to remove racial and ethnic discrimination from the system, just as the Civil Rights Act of 1964 had outlawed discrimination in jobs and housing. Nevertheless, changing circumstances often alter laws, and the Vietnam War created so many refugees during the 1970's that political leaders felt duty-bound to allow them to enter the United States. They arrived in two waves, the first consisting largely of educated, English-speaking Vietnamese, who got jobs in industry or went into business for themselves, whereas the "boat people" were largely without marketable skills and, once in the U.S., were forced mostly into menial jobs.

Other Asian immigrants fared much better. For example, those coming from India and the Philippines were often already well educated and possessed professional skills that made getting jobs relatively easy. In fact, the 1965 immigration law had the greatest influence on Asian immigration, which rapidly rose by 500 percent. So many doctors, engineers, and scientists left India, Korea, and the Philippines that politicians in these countries became concerned about a "brain drain." Some scholars believe that this new immigration has indeed contributed to widening the gap between developed and developing countries.

During the 1980's, more than 1.6 million Mexicans entered the United States legally, but many more entered illegally. Those who became agricultural workers were often subjected to poor working conditions, wages, and housing. César Chávez, an American labor leader who helped found the United Farm Workers union, tried to remedy these abuses through boycotts and strikes. Mexicans, both legal and illegal, dominated the growing, cultivating, harvesting, packing, and transportation of grapes, though policies on wages and working conditions were set by business leaders far from the scene. After much conflict and controversy, Chávez was able to gain recognition for his union, with consequent improvements in the lives of both Chicanos and Latin American immigrants.

Employment

SUMMARY

Statistical evidence indicates that, throughout the history of the United States, immigrants have experienced large variations in their occupational achievements. During some periods, immigrant groups have been forced to take low-paying and poor-quality jobs, and many even returned, disappointed, to their native countries. However, many of those who remained eventually got better jobs at higher rates of pay. Some studies have shown that newly arrived immigrants have higher rates of unemployment and tend to work at much lower-paying jobs than native-born Americans with similar levels of education and job skills. However, the same studies have also shown that immigrant employment rates and job status reach the levels of native-born workers after several years of residence.

The controversy over immigrants and employment has continued into the twenty-first century, with some believing that immigrants lower wages and become a drain on American taxpayers, while others insist that immigrants do not adversely affect the wages of American citizens, even those in unskilled jobs. A study of illegal immigration has shown that undocumented workers contribute as much as $10 billion to the U.S. economy each year. Furthermore immigrants have more often than not achieved the American goal that allows people of various backgrounds to rise as far as their talents and energies will take them.

Robert J. Paradowski

FURTHER READING

Borjas, George J. *Friends or Strangers: The Impact of Immigrants on the U.S. Economy.* New York: Basic Books, 1990. Analysis of the influence of immigration laws on the employment of immigrants, as well as the competition among members of different immigrant groups for jobs. Illustrated with tables. Notes and index.

Fermi, Laura. *Illustrious Immigrants: The Intellectual Migration from Europe, 1930-1941.* Chicago: University of Chicago Press, 1971. The author, who accompanied an illustrious immigrant, Enrico Fermi, to the United States, divides her book into two parts: "Arrival" and "Achievement." She details the role played by dictatorships in driving talented refugees to America and shows how, despite difficulties, refugees made major contributions to science, mathematics, and the arts. Reference notes and an index of persons.

Glenn, Evelyn Nakano. *Unequal Freedom: How Race and Gender Shaped American Citizenship and Labor.* Cambridge, Mass.: Harvard University Press, 2002. This historical study covers the period from Reconstruction to World War II, and the difficulties encountered by immigrants in finding employment are very much a part of her story. Notes and index.

Jones, Maldwyn A. *Destination America.* New York: Holt, Rinehart and Winston, 1976. This extensively illustrated volume centers on "the greatest mass migration in history"—the settling of millions of Europeans in the United States during the previous 150 years. He makes use of personal as well as published accounts, and the need to find meaningful employment is one of his chief themes. Further reading section and an index.

Karas, Jennifer. *Bridges and Barriers: Earnings and Occupational Attainment Among Immigrants.* New York: LFB Scholarly Publishing, 2002. Part of the New Americans series, this book emphasizes immigration and employment in the United States from 1965 to 2000. Several helpful tables of data, bibliography, and index.

Millman, Joel. *The Other Americans: How Immigrants Renew Our Country, Our Economy, and Our Values.* New York: Viking Press, 1997. Study analyzing what immigrants do in America by showing how certain of them have formed successful businesses, rescued declining communities, and, in general, improved themselves while improving America. Notes and index.

Portes, Alejandro, and Rubén G. Rumbaut. *Immigrant America: A Portrait.* Berkeley: University of California Press, 1990. This study uses various primary sources to help understand recent immigration to the United States, including how immigrants find employment and become part of the American economy. Notes, bibliography, and index.

SEE ALSO: Affirmative action; Economic opportunities; Great Depression; Green cards; Guest-worker programs; Immigrant advantage; Labor unions; Sweatshops; Women immigrants; World War I; World War II.

Empresario Land Grants in Texas

DEFINITION: Tracts of land granted to settlers, known as empresarios, by Mexico to encourage settlement in Texas while it was part of Mexico

SIGNIFICANCE: By issuing empresario grants, Mexico hoped to attract settlers from around the world. Some Europeans did immigrate to Texas, but most settlers were from the United States. Rather than assimilate as loyal Mexican citizens, the American settlers remained a foreign element, and many of them were instrumental in leading the Texas Revolution in 1835-1836.

During the Spanish colonial era in Mexico, Texas was on the far northern fringe of the Spanish empire, and there was little effort to settle the region. In 1820, Moses Austin, a miner and businessman from Missouri, traveled to San Antonio de Béxar, the provincial capital of the Texas region, to meet with governor Antonio Mária Martínez about bringing American settlers into the region. Austin eventually received permission to bring in three hundred American families but died shortly after returning to Missouri.

In 1821, Mexico became independent of Spanish control. Stephen F. Austin, the son of Moses Austin, made an arrangement with the new Mexican administration that was similar to the one his father had worked out with the Spanish. Settlers entering Mexico were required to become Mexican citizens and had, at least nominally, to profess Roman Catholicism, the established religion of Mexico. Each American settler was given a generous land grant—either 170 acres suitable for cultivation or more than 4,000 acres of grazing land.

Austin led the first settlers into Texas in December, 1821. In 1824, the Mexican government passed a law formalizing these colonization efforts, offering land and tax exemptions to foreign settlers. Mexico hoped that these settlers would create a kind of buffer between Mexico and the United States and also deal with the hostile Indians in the region. Most of the American settlers, however, saw their Mexican citizenship as a mere formality and still considered themselves to be Americans.

The vast majority of the settlers who came into Texas were from the United States, but European immigrants established a few colonies, including two of the most successful—San Patricio and Refugio, both near the Gulf coast. In August of 1828, James McGloin and John McMullen were allowed to bring in two hundred Irish Catholic families, who created the San Patricio colony. The Irish settlers were actually recruited in New York City; however, many of them had only recently arrived from Ireland. In 1831, James Power and James Hewetson were given permission to bring in another two hundred Irish families, and these people founded the Refugio colony.

In 1830, about seven thousand Americans were living in Texas. By then, the Mexicans realized that allowing Americans to colonize the province had been a mistake, as the settlers largely resisted assimilation. New laws were passed forbidding further American migration into Texas, but illegal immigration continued. By the time of the Texas Revolution in 1835-1836, about thirty thousand Anglo-American settlers and about three thousand African American slaves were living in the region.

Mark S. Joy

FURTHER READING

Anderson, Gary Clayton. *The Conquest of Texas: Ethnic Cleansing in the Promised Land, 1820-1875.* Norman: University of Oklahoma Press, 2005.

Cantrell, Gregg. *Stephen F. Austin: Empresario of Texas.* New Haven, Conn.: Yale University Press, 1999.

Davis, William C. *Lone Star Rising: The Revolutionary Birth of the Texas Republic.* New York: Free Press, 2004.

SEE ALSO: Alien land laws; Dallas; Houston; Mexican immigrants; Mexican Revolution; Texas; Texas Cart War; Westward expansion.

ENGLISH AS A SECOND LANGUAGE

DEFINITION: Language-instruction programs for young learners and adults whose native languages are not English

ALSO KNOWN AS: ESL

SIGNIFICANCE: As an instructional tool to help language-minority students develop English-language skills, the English as a second language program came into popular usage during the late 1950's. It is the most common language education program used by American schools to facilitate the integration of limited- or non-English-speaking students into mainstream general education. For adult second-language learners, ESL education helps the individual to enhance his or her opportunities for employment in the English-speaking workplace.

English-language education for non-English speakers has gone through various phases of development since the early twentieth century. English-only requirements as an integral aspect of the national movement to Americanize all non-English-speaking immigrants proved ineffective in helping language-minority children acquire the necessary English literacy skills to succeed in school. Since the early ESL programs of the late 1950's, many changes have occurred in the methods of English-language education to accommodate the various needs of immigrant and U.S.-born second-language learners. Although ESL teaching techniques vary, the programs' primary aim is the same: to help students develop knowledge and skills in the four major domains of the language—listening, speaking, reading, and writing.

Immigrants in a U.S. Department of Labor English class in a Ford Motor Company factory in Detroit, Michigan, during the early twentieth century. (Library of Congress)

EARLY ENGLISH-LANGUAGE DEVELOPMENT PROGRAMS

At the turn of the twentieth century, in the midst of one of the largest waves of immigration into the United States, mainly from southern and eastern Europe, President Theodore Roosevelt urged that all newcomers learn English: "We should provide for every immigrant . . . the chance to learn English; and if after say five years he has not learned English, he should be sent back to the land from whence he came." The national push for the rapid assimilation into American culture of all non-English-speaking populations, as reflected in President Roosevelt's proclamation, provided the catalyst for the enactment of laws by state legislative bodies requiring English as the sole language of communication in both government affairs and education. This further spurred the growth of special curricula to help U.S.-born and immigrant language-minority children learn English. In many cases, educators in Indian Boarding Schools and in the segregated Mexican schools of the Southwest and other school settings applied these laws with so much force that students who were caught speaking their mother tongues were punished, sometimes physically, and parents admonished for not encouraging their children to speak English.

Lacking in a solid theoretical base and knowledge of how first languages are learned, much less the processes of second-language development, the initial English-language education programs for limited- or non-English-speaking children had to rely in both content and methodology on the traditional English-language arts curriculum designed for native English speakers. The coercive "sink or swim" aspect of the nascent programs further deterred many of the language-minority children from effectively learning English and achieving in school. The process was analogous to trying to fit a square peg into a round hole.

ORIGINS OF ESL EDUCATION

The foreign language programs in the secondary schools and colleges established the effectiveness of the audio-lingual technique in teaching French, German, Spanish, and other world languages to English speakers learning a second language. These foreign language programs, as well as the ESL audio-lingual programs implemented during the late 1950's and early 1960's, were influenced by advances in the fields of structured linguistics and behavioral psychology.

The initial ESL programs evolved from the premise that language is habit-forming. Based on the theory, it was further believed that through the use of various forms of student repetition of structured language patterns modeled by the teacher, second-language learners would eventually internalize the receptive and speaking skills of English as a fundamental first step to learning how to read and write in the same language. The rigid curriculum of the ESL programs found some degree of success with adult learners, who were more motivated than young learners, to develop the language. These more mature learners realized that the ability to speak English was crucial to their success in the workplace. The constant drilling and repetition exercises associated with the audio-lingual approach was less appealing for elementary and secondary school second-language learners.

NEW FORMS OF ESL

The inadequacy of the audio-lingual programs, as well as the growth in the enrollment of a new generation of English-language learners different in many ways from those immigrant and nonimmigrant populations served by the earlier models of ESL, has resulted in the expansion of English-language education. These new programs offer many instructional options to accommodate the varied needs of the learners. Recent immigrant students, for example, and the large number of first-generation immigrant students present distinctive challenges to educators based on the learners' differing levels of English proficiency and prior education. Recent immigrant students with previous schooling in their home countries have greater ease in learning English and possess the basic knowledge and skills to cope with the academic demands of American schools.

Children and adolescents who are new arrivals without previous formal education present the greatest challenge. These students do not have the cognitive/academic skills underlying literacy in their first language, much less English. Even children who come to the United States as young children or are born in this country of parents who are poor and illiterate experience adjustment and learning difficulties in school. Children born in the United States of immigrant parents (also first-generation immigrant students) may be more fluent in English than in their heritage (home) language, or they may be more proficient in their native language than in English. Some of these first-generation immigrant students may even be balanced bilinguals, meaning they have equal proficiency in the heritage language and English.

The more modern programs of ESL attempt to respond to the myriad, complex needs and characteristics of recent arrivals as well as first-generation immigrant students, including refugee and undocumented children. The curriculum requirements and learning expectations of the ESL programs are also influenced by federal and state legislative and judicial mandates designed to promote fair and equitable treatment for ethnic minority students. These mandates include those promulgated by the No Child Left Behind Act of 2001, state school reform requirements, and Supreme Court decisions such as the *Lau v. Nichols* (1974) and *Plyler v. Doe* (1982). Studies in the field of psycholinguistics, along with the legislative and judicial requirements, support planning and delivery of ESL education in less stressful and more flexible learning environments planned in accordance with the English-language proficiency level of each learner. The programs provide for more varied opportunities for meaningful participation by students than in earlier models of ESL. These programs are also intended to reduce the influence of factors that create stress for students and obstruct their success in school, including cultural incompatibilities, poverty, fear of deportation, and traumatic conditions associated with the refugee experience.

One type of ESL education is provided in the Newcomer Centers that originated in California schools. The Newcomer (or Welcome) Center is a school-within-a-school-type program for recent immigrant students. These centers typically operate in middle and high schools, preparing new arrivals for transition to mainstream education. English-language development is provided within class environments that are nurturing and supportive of language and cultural diversity.

For language-minority children in elementary grades, ESL teachers immerse the learners in a variety of English-language activities. These are age-appropriate and allow the learners to progress through various stages of English production similar to first-language development processes: for example, nonverbal responses, one-word utterances, and finally more complete and meaningful production of language. Further support to ESL is offered by teachers of science, mathematics, social studies, reading, and other subjects taught at all grade levels of elementary and secondary schools. These content-area teachers incorporate ESL techniques in their instruction, allowing for second-language learners (especially intermediate and advanced ESL students) to develop English-language skills while learning subject matter. The push toward greater accountability in schools and standards-driven education has accelerated the need for immigrant students to develop English sooner and more efficiently without sacrificing the requirements of the curriculum designed for all learners.

Rudy Rodríguez

FURTHER READING

Crawford, James. *Educating English Learners: Language Diversity in the Classroom.* 5th ed. Los Angeles: Bilingual Educational Services, 2004. Focuses on the students in bilingual and ESL programs and the politics surrounding their education.

Eagle-Rodríguez, Cynthia, ed. *Achieving Literacy Successs with English Language Learners: Insights, Assessment, Instruction.* Worthington, Ohio: Reading Recovery Council of North America, 2009. Collection of papers on understanding the challenge of educating second-language learners, developing English literacy, and assessment processes.

González, Josué M. "Coming of Age in Bilingual/Bicultural Education: A Historical Perspective." *Inequality in Education* 19 (February, 1975): 5-17. Overview of the historical development of bilingual and ESL education in the United States.

SEE ALSO: Bilingual education; Education; English-only and official English movements; European immigrants; Language issues; Latin American immigrants; *Lau v. Nichols*; Nativism; *Plyler v. Doe*; Xenophobia.

ENGLISH-ONLY AND OFFICIAL ENGLISH MOVEMENTS

DEFINITION: Efforts by federal and state governments, lobbyists, organizations, or private citizens to make English the "only" or "official" language for use in public or governmental situations in the United States

SIGNIFICANCE: Although some Americans see these movements as patriotic or well-intended, other Americans perceive such efforts to be anti-immigrant or racist. These movements tend to experience their greatest popularity during times of economic hardship, massive immigration, or war. At the same time, they represent a desire by members of the English-speaking majority in the United States to create national cohesiveness under the banner of the English language.

HISTORY OF ENGLISH-ONLY MOVEMENTS

Although sentiments against non-English-speaking residents in America can be found in the words of the English colonists and the nation's first political leaders, the history of English-only movements in the United States can be traced back to the nineteenth century in California. The 1849 California constitution called for the publication of the future state's laws in both English and Spanish, yet by 1855 English became the official language in the state's schools. When the state constitution was rewritten a generation later, all governmental proceedings were ordered to be held and recorded in English only.

German immigrants, who settled in the Midwest during the late nineteenth century, spoke German in their homes, churches, and public places. In some regions, public schools taught classes in both English and German, while in other regions only private schools that were usually run by churches did so. Nativist and anti-Roman Catholic elements opposed the use of German in public places. During the late 1880's, laws requiring instruction solely in English in both public and private schools were enacted in Illinois and Wisconsin.

As the U.S. economy expanded and immigrant workers flowed into the United States during the early years of the twentieth century, the English-only movement grew. Funded by businessmen who feared possible revolutionary violence among newly arrived immigrants, the movement ranged from the benign efforts of the Young Men's Christian Association (YMCA) teaching English to workers in the evenings to the more aggressive drives undertaken by the "Americanization" campaign led by the anticommunist National Americanization Committee.

After the Spanish-American War (1898), English was made the official language of public education in the newly acquired colonies, Puerto Rico and the Philippines. Attempts to prohibit the teaching of Japanese, Chinese, and Korean in private schools in California and Hawaii were voided by the Ninth Circuit Court of Appeals in 1926. Anti-German-language sentiment continued through World War II; in addition, legislation prohibiting public use of the Japanese language was enacted in response to public demand.

LATE TWENTIETH CENTURY MOVEMENTS

From 1981 until 1990, more immigrants arrived in the United States than in any other ten-year period since the decade that began in 1901. Movements scapegoating immigrant groups began to experience a renaissance. One organization, called U.S. English, was founded in 1983 by Senator S. I. Hayakawa of California and Dr. John Tanton, a Michigan ophthalmologist, environmentalist, and population-control activist. Within four years of the organization's founding, proposals designating English as the official language of the United States were considered by forty-eight of the fifty states. Voters passed several English-only measures, and numerous legislatures followed suit.

In 1986, a memorandum written by Tanton containing derogatory remarks regarding Latinos was made public. In response, retired CBS newsman Walter Cronkite and political columnist Linda Chavez resigned from the organization's board. That year, two other organizations, English First and the American Ethnic Coalition, were formed by Larry Pratt and Lou Zaeske, respectively. In a blow to the movement, U.S. district judge Paul Rosenblatt struck down Arizona's Official English amendment in 1990 as unconstitutional, ruling that it violated free speech guarantees under the First Amendment. During the legislative session of the 103d Congress (1993-1995), no fewer than four

California senator S. I. Hayakawa in 1981. A Canadian immigrant of Japanese heritage and a former educator, Hayakawa was one of the leading proponents of making English the official language of the United States. (Time & Life Pictures/Getty Images)

bills were introduced that would have made English the official language of the United States.

As the twenty-first century began, another wave of anti-immigrant sentiment swept across the United States. Although this movement claimed to be against illegal immigration only, both documented and undocumented Spanish-speaking residents of the United States faced increased official and unofficial harassment from authorities and private citizens. Once again, there were calls to make English the official language of the United States. Laws were passed in some states forbidding the use of Spanish in the workplace and in schools, even informally. In 2007, a bill sponsored by members of both major political parties for the English Language Unity Act was introduced into the U.S.

House of Representatives. The language of the bill was designed to make English the official language of the United States. It was still working its way through the legislative process in late 2009.

Ron Jacobs

FURTHER READING

Crawford, James. *At War With Diversity: U.S. Language Policy in an Age of Anxiety.* Clevedon, England: Multilingual Matters, 2000. Collection of essays providing a clear and lively account of language politics in the United States. Crawford discusses the history of legislation attempting to make English the official language of the United States, as well as the debate around the issue.

_____, ed. *Language Loyalties: A Source Book on the Official English Controversy.* Chicago: University of Chicago Press, 1992. This collection of readings is a reasonably balanced guide to the issues in the English-only debate. While it mostly addresses the movement to make English the official language that began during the 1980's, the primary source documents herein are important for their content and historical value.

Gonzalez, Roseann Dueñas, with Ildikó Melis, eds. *Language Ideologies: Critical Perspectives on the Official English Movement.* Vol. 2, *History, Theory, and Policy.* Urbana: National Council of Teachers of English, 2001. A collection of essays that addresses the history and issues involved in the debate over teaching English-only in American classrooms. The essays are written by a number of people representing different backgrounds, although the overwhelming consensus is that English-only classrooms are not beneficial to students or society.

King, Robert D. "Should English Be the Law? Language Is Tearing Apart Countries Around the World, and the Proponents of 'Official English' May Be Ready to Add America to the List." *The Atlantic Monthly* 279, no. 4 (April, 1997): 55-64. King discusses the English-only movement of the 1980's and 1990's and examines the possible conflicts that could arise if English were made the official language of the United States. He takes an instructive look at other nations where linguistic differences have caused conflicts that broke into war or were resolved through compromise.

Ricento, Thomas, ed. *An Introduction to Language Policy: Theory and Method.* Malden, Mass.: Blackwell, 2005. Aimed at the higher education market, this book provides the reader with the important debates in the English-only controversy. Encompassing a wide range of opinions, it is a useful sourcebook on the subject.

SEE ALSO: Americanization programs; Anglo-conformity; Anti-Chinese movement; Anti-Japanese movement; Bilingual education; Bilingual Education Act of 1968; English as a second language; German immigrants; Hayakawa, S. I.; Language issues.

ESPIONAGE AND SEDITION ACTS OF 1917-1918

THE LAW: Federal legislation that made it illegal to speak out against the government during World War I

DATES: Espionage Act enacted on June 15, 1917; Sedition Act enacted on May 16, 1918

SIGNIFICANCE: Enacted soon after the United States entered World War I in 1917, the Espionage Act prohibited individuals from expressing or publishing opinions that would interfere with the U.S. military's efforts to defeat Germany and its allies. A year later, the U.S. Congress amended the law with the Sedition Act of 1918, which made it illegal to write or speak anything critical of American involvement in the war.

While the Espionage Act dealt with many uncontroversial issues such as punishing acts of spying and sabotage and protecting shipping, the act, as amended by the Sedition Act, was extremely controversial for many immigrants who were opposed to war, the military draft, and violations of their free speech rights. Specifically, the Espionage Act made it a crime willfully to interfere with U.S. war efforts by conveying false information about the war, obstructing U.S. recruitment or enlistment efforts, or inciting insubordination, disloyalty, or mutiny.

The Sedition Act made the language of the Espionage Act more specific by making it illegal to use disloyal, profane, or abusive language to criticize the U.S. Constitution, the government, the military, the flag, or the uniform. The government had the authority to punish a wide range of speech and activities such as obstructing the sale of U.S. bonds, displaying a German flag, or giving a speech that supported the enemy's cause. Persons convicted of violating these laws could be fined amounts of up to ten thousand dollars and also be sentenced to prison for as long as twenty years.

Under the Espionage and Sedition Acts, the U.S. postmaster general had the authority to ban the mailing of all letters, circulars, newspapers, pamphlets, packages, and other materials that opposed the war. As a result, about seventy-five newspapers either lost their mailing privileges or were pressured to print nothing more about the war. These publications included German American or German-language newspapers, pacifist publications, and publications owned by the American Socialist Party and the Industrial Workers of the World.

No one was convicted of spying or sabotage under the Espionage Act during World War I. However, more than two thousand people were arrested for sedition. One thousand of them—including many immigrants—were convicted. The U.S. Supreme Court upheld the constitutionality of the Espionage and Sedition Acts, ruling that the government had the authority to punish speech that would create a "clear and present danger."

The Espionage Act was intended to be in effect only during wartime, but the law continued to be invoked following the end of World War I during the Red Scare of 1919-1920 and again after World War II during the Cold War. The Sedition Act was repealed in 1921, but major portions of the Espionage Act remained in effect as part of U.S. law.

Eddith A. Dashiell

FURTHER READING

Kohn, Stephen M. *American Political Prisoners: Prosecutions Under the Espionage and Sedition Acts.* Westport, Conn.: Praeger, 1994.

Manz, William H., ed. *Civil Liberties in Wartime: Legislative Histories of the Espionage Act of 1917 and the Sedition Act of 1918.* Buffalo, N.Y: W. S. Hein, 2007.

Stone, Geoffrey R. *Perilous Times: Free Speech in Wartime from the Sedition Act of 1798 to the War on Terrorism.* New York: W. W. Norton, 2004.

SEE ALSO: Alien and Sedition Acts of 1798; Constitution, U.S.; History of immigration after 1891; Immigration Act of 1903; Immigration Act of 1917; Loyalty oaths; Red Scare; World War I.

ETHIOPIAN IMMIGRANTS

SIGNIFICANCE: After passage of the 1965 Immigration and Nationality Act, Ethiopians became the third-largest national group of African immigrants to immigrate to the United States. Most arrived in the United States after Congress passed the Refugee Act of 1980.

Ethiopia and its people have long held a special meaning in America. Once known as Abyssinia, Ethiopia stood for black pride and black independence as far back as the 1760's. Already possessing strong biblical associations, the name "Ethiopia" became an iconic symbol of African independence throughout Europe's twentieth century colonization of Africa. Some educated African American slaves such as the poets Phillis Wheatley and Jupiter Hammon occasionally identified themselves as "Ethiopians" during the era of the American Revolution. The tendency of black intellectuals to describe themselves as "Ethiopians" stems from the European custom—derived from biblical usage—of applying "Ethiopian" to all peoples from the African interior. This usage, which dates back to the ancient Greeks, can make it difficult to separate immigrants from the actual Northeast African nation of Ethiopia from the masses of African Americans.

The first Ethiopian immigrants to reach North America probably arrived as slaves sometime during the seventeenth century. However, the bulk of voluntary immigrants to the United States came after 1974, when a repressive regime toppled the ancient monarchy and took control of the Ethiopian government. The ensuing exodus from Ethiopia, a landlocked nation on the northeastern Horn of Africa, resulted from political turmoil as well as famine and drought. Many refugees fled initially to settlement camps in the neighboring Sudan before moving on to the United States. Impoverished, the Sudan offered few economic opportunities, while the United States held out the hope of a prosperous future. Until Somalis surpassed them in 1994, Ethiopians were the largest group of Africans to immigrate under the provisions of the Refugee Act of 1980.

Ethiopian immigrants to the United States have differed from many other immigrant ethnic groups in that they typically arrived with a basic command of British English and tended to settle in disparate neighborhoods, instead of gathering in ethnic enclaves. The consequent lack of cohesive immigrant communities has complicated their efforts to maintain language and cultural ties to their homeland. Also, racism has been a new experience, with many exposed to the color line for the first time in the United States.

Most Ethiopian immigrants are Coptic Christians and Muslims, and their religions

IMMIGRATION FROM ETHIOPIA, 1930-2008

Source: Department of Homeland Security, *Yearbook of Immigration Statistics, 2008.* Figures include only immigrants who obtained legal permanent resident status.

PROFILE OF ETHIOPIAN IMMIGRANTS

Country of origin	Ethiopia
Primary language	Amharic
Primary regions of U.S. settlement	Los Angeles, New York City
Earliest significant arrivals	Seventeenth century
Peak immigration period	1980's
Twenty-first century legal residents*	8,004 (1,000 per year)

*Immigrants who obtained legal permanent resident status in the United States.
Source: Department of Homeland Security, Yearbook of Immigration Statistics, 2008.

have served as sources of comfort in the New World, with churches and mosques serving as community centers, health centers, and social services providers. During the early twenty-first century, the population of Ethiopia was almost evenly divided between Christians and Muslims, a split that is reflected among the immigrants to America. Ethiopia has also long had a significant Jewish population, but most of its Jews emigrated to Israel, while the bulk of other refugees fled to the United States. Ethiopians in America have subsequently established the Ethiopian Orthodox churches as well as the Bilal Ethiopian mosques.

Caryn E. Neumann

FURTHER READING

Getahun, Solomon Addis. *The History of Ethiopian Immigrants and Refugees in America, 1900-2000.* New York: LFB Scholarly Publishing, 2006.

Olupona, Jacob K., and Regina Gemignani, eds. *African American Religions in America.* New York: New York University Press, 2007.

Scott, William R. *The Sons of Sheba's Race: African-Americans and the Italo-Ethiopian War, 1935-1941.* Bloomington: Indiana University Press, 1993.

SEE ALSO: African Americans and immigrants; African immigrants; History of immigration after 1891; Immigration and Nationality Act of 1965; Refugees.

ETHNIC ENCLAVES

DEFINITION: Usually urban areas, within which culturally distinct minority communities maintain ways of life largely separate from those of the generally larger communities that surround them

SIGNIFICANCE: Ethnic enclaves have long played, and continue to play, significant and normally peaceful roles in bridging the periods between the arrivals of new and culturally different immigrant groups and their assimilation into United States society. At the same time, they have also, to some degree, prolonged assimilation periods, and their presence has sometimes been perceived as an inflammatory refusal on the immigrants' part to join the American nation.

One of the most enduring self-images of United States society is that of the melting pot—that is, the notion that the United States is a country into which immigrants from multiple points of origin have come, intermingled, intermarried, and produced new citizens endowed with a rich, intermixed cultural heritage. It is an image that has served the country well, providing, as it did, the philosophical foundations for the widespread acceptance of the culturally pluralistic, or multicultural, nation that emerged in the United States during the second half of the twentieth century.

The melting pot image also rests on a firm empirical base, albeit mostly on the frontier, where immigrant groups often spread out, where marriageable partners from within the same "Old World" communities were often hard to find, and where the harshness and dangers of life necessitated collaboration across ethnic and cultural lines. In the coastal cities where the immigrants arrived, however, and in the urban areas across the country where ethnic groups settled in large numbers, a different pattern prevailed. In big cities, neighborhoods with revealing names such as "Little Italy," "Germantown," and "Chinatown" often sprang up. These communities led day-to-day internal lives quite apart from those of the broader, usually English-speaking communities around them and the other ethnic enclaves that sometimes abutted them. Comforting in origin and resilient over time, significant portions of many of these early ethnic enclaves have survived into the twenty-first century across the United States. They have been joined by new ethnic enclaves being created, especially in suburbs, by more recently arrived immigrants from Asia and Latin America.

CULTURE SHOCK AND ETHNIC ENCLAVES

The factors that produced, and continue to lead to the emergence of these ethnic neighborhoods are varied and, in some instances, idiosyncratic. One pervasive element, however, has doubtless been the normal human desire to remain within one's comfort zone and associated reluctance to move precipitously outside one's cultural community in one's new homeland. It is one of the standard reactions to minority status across time and space, and where enough members of a person's point of origin to sustain the development of an ethnic neighborhood are living, ethnic enclaves have arisen among immigrant countries throughout the world.

Other factors also work to foster and sustain such enclaves. None is more common or significant than the two-sided nature of the culture shock that groups from differing ethnic backgrounds experience when they first encounter one another. For newcomers, immersion in a foreign culture, adjusting to a different economic setting—such as urban rather than rural—and perhaps encountering a different dominant language and a different religion can all combine to produce a strong desire to recreate a more familiar environment. The recreation of the remembered homeland by incoming immigrants, often from a single village or province, provides a secure environment to which to return after a daily bath in the outside culture. Such a setting can even serve as a cocoon within which a day-to-day life not too distant from that of the land of origin can be preserved, in which a familiar religion can be practiced, in which an immigrant entrepreneur class can develop, and in which the process of assimilating to the new world can be eased.

Meanwhile, encounters with the newly arrived can also result in a culture shock to the host culture, whose members may resent the immigrants' "otherness" and ways of life and even fear that the new immigrants' willingness to accept wages below prevailing market rates may threaten their own economic status. In extreme cases, new organizations may emerge to oppose the immigrants' presence and even visit violence upon them to "keep them in their place." American history holds no shortage of such organizations. Outstanding examples included the post-Civil War Know-Nothing Party and the Ku Klux Klan, whose bigotry extended far beyond harassing freed slaves to target Jews and Roman Catholics as well. However, even nonviolent forms of rejection, such as restrictive housing covenants designed to keep unwanted ethnic and racial groups out of existing neighborhoods, also played a role in the creation and endurance of ethnic enclaves in twentieth century America. In such environments, ethnic neighborhoods became more than cultural and economic oases. They also became both sanctuaries from violence and secure homelands within a hostile world.

Unemployed Chinese men in San Francisco's Chinatown district around the year 1900, when the city had the largest concentration of Chinese immigrants in North America. (Library of Congress)

LIFE WITHIN ENCLAVES

As immigrants moved inland from their coastal points of arrival, ethnic enclaves became common in cities throughout the country. Their presence remained strong during the early twenty-first century, though often in less heavily populated centers, and have sometimes taken the forms of small restaurant or tourist districts, rather than the mini-worlds of cultural distinctiveness they constituted a century earlier. At least a score of United States cities, and another half-dozen in Canada and Mexico, contain Chinatowns. Little Indias exist in at least a dozen U.S. cities, Germantowns and Little Italies are almost ubiquitous parts of urban America, and even Greektowns can be found in North American cities as diverse and spread out as Baltimore, Chicago, Denver, Toronto, Omaha, and Vancouver.

Although culturally distinct, these older ethnic enclaves have nonetheless exhibited significant structural similarities. For example, religion has played a strong role in the founding of most of these enclaves and a leading role in the origins of some. For Roman Catholics, Jews, and immigrants from Asia and the Middle East who have found themselves in predominantly Protestant environments upon arrival, neighborhood churches, synagogues, and temples often became the social as well as religious centers of enclaves.

At least equally important, the ethnic enclaves were sustained by economic cores. Their businesses were generally owned and operated by members of the community, with many of them catering to their communities' particular tastes and needs, while providing jobs for their members. Indeed, inside the enclaves, discrimination often favored community members over outsiders in the sense that social norms sheltered the housing, investment, and labor markets of the enclaves from outsider competition. Consequently, ethnic enclaves often provided their members with economically secure footings from which to venture into the broader society. At the same time, to the extent that they became restaurant zones or otherwise attracted outsiders, ethnic enclaves fostered interaction between their members and others within secure environments. In so doing, they encouraged their own members to learn English sooner rather than later, thus facilitating the process of interethnic interaction within the linguistic polyglots that were late nineteenth century U.S. cities and, ultimately, the assimilation of the ethnic groups into the wider society.

TWENTY-FIRST CENTURY ENCLAVES

The history of the United States as an immigrant nation continues to unfold—sometimes over the opposition of such conservative groups as those fearing the "Re-Mexicanization" of the American Southwest—as asylum seekers, refugees, and both documented and undocumented immigrants continue to enter the country. Meanwhile, the process of forming new ethnic enclaves in receiving cities within the United States and Canada has continued.

The arrival of new immigrants is rapidly transforming the ethnic character of the American nation. Latinos have already replaced African Americans as the country's largest ethnic or racial minority, and the arrival of large numbers of Koreans, Vietnamese, and others from Southeast Asia in the last third of the twentieth century recast the Asian American profile, which previously had been dominated by Chinese and Japanese immigrants. Like their predecessors, members of these new groups have established their own ethnic neighborhoods, albeit increasingly in suburban areas, rather than the inner city enclaves created by the immigrants arriving from Europe and Asia during the nineteenth century. Indeed, for all the talk of cities like Los Angeles taking on a "third world" personality because of their large numbers of immigrants from non-European areas, their ethnic enclaves are often being established in areas once far removed from the inner-city ethnic neighborhoods of the nineteenth and early twentieth century.

In Washington, D.C.'s commuter landscape in Virginia, for example, places such Manassas Park are growing quickly into areas in which ethnic minorities constitute local majorities. Moreover, as was true in the past, stores within these enclaves have emerged to offer goods not readily available in the wider, outside community. Examples include shops selling news publications, video discs, and compact music discs in foreign languages. In many of these communities, particularly those of Hispanic residents, foreign-language radio and television stations provide stories in greater detail on life and politics in the country of origin than what is available in the broader community's media outlets.

Joseph R. Rudolph, Jr.

FURTHER READING

Abrahamson, Mark. *Urban Enclaves: Identity and Place in America.* 2d ed. New York: Worth Publishers, 2005. Sociological study of ethnic enclaves that is especially useful for advanced research.

Bohon, Stephanie. *Latinos in Ethnic Enclaves: Immigrant Workers and the Competition for Jobs.* New York: Garland, 2001. Focusing on the ethnic enclaves of Latinos in four American cities, this study is valuable both as a snapshot of major recent immigrant communities and as an examination of the competition among members of various Latino communities rooted in the struggle for jobs.

Castile, George Pierre, and Gilbert Kushner, eds. *Persistent Peoples: Ethnic Enclaves in Perspective.* Tucson: University of Arizona Press, 1982. Older but widely available and still valuable collection of essays on enclaves. A good basic introduction to the subject.

Jendian, Matthew A. *Becoming American, Remaining Ethnic: The Case of Armenian Americans in Central California.* New York: LFB Scholarly Publishing, 2008. Focuses on the oldest Armenian community in the western United States; however, the true value of this immensely interesting book lies in its treatment of the multidimensional nature of assimilation in American society.

Keyes, Charles F. "The Dialectics of Ethnic Change." In *Ethnic Change,* edited by Charles F. Keyes. Seattle: University of Washington Press, 1981. Authoritative source on the definition of ethnic enclaves, and a useful introduction to the topic offered in the form of an anthology on ethnic groups coping with their minority status.

Logan, John R. *The New Ethnic Enclaves in America's Suburbs.* Albany, N.Y.: Lewis Mumford Center for Comparative Urban and Regional Research, 2001. Census-based and statistics-laden study of the changing patterns of residency in the United States between 1990 and 2000. Also available online.

Ryon, Roderick N. *Northwest Baltimore and Its Neighborhoods, 1870-1970: Before "Smart Growth."* Baltimore: University of Baltimore and the City of Baltimore, 2000. Exceptionally interesting account of ethnic enclaves and their gradual transformation in Baltimore, Maryland, a major port city during the nineteenth century.

SEE ALSO: Assimilation theories; Chain migration; Chinatowns; Immigration waves; Little Havana; Little Italies; Little Tokyos; Melting pot theory; Settlement patterns; Social networks.

EUGENICS MOVEMENT

THE EVENT: Broad-based pseudoscience movement seeking to influence immigration law by invoking eugenic ideas to limit immigration to members of ethnic groups whom eugenicists consider biologically superior

DATE: Late nineteenth century to 1920's

SIGNIFICANCE: The eugenics movement had a significant influence on U.S. immigration policy. Politicians, reformers, and civic leaders imbued with a sense of Americanism and scientific justification enacted laws to limit immigration to what they regarded as "desir-

English statistician Francis Galton, the founder of the eugenics movement. (Library of Congress)

THE QUESTION OF EUGENICS

In a 1904 scholarly article, Francis Galton defined "eugenics" as "the science which deals with all influences that improve the inborn qualities of a race; also with those that develop them to the utmost advantage." Twenty-one years earlier, however, Galton had introduced the term "eugenic," albeit in a footnote to his 1883 book on the human faculty. His definition is excerpted here.

I do not propose to enter further into the anthropometric differences of race, for the subject is a very large one, and this book does not profess to go into detail. Its intention is to touch on various topics more or less connected with that of the cultivation of race, or, as we might call it, with "eugenic" questions, and to present the results of several of my own separate investigations. . . .

[footnote:] That is, with questions bearing on what is termed in Greek, *eugenes*, namely, good in stock, hereditarily endowed with noble qualities. This, and the allied words, *eugeneia*, etc., are equally applicable to men, brutes, and plants. We greatly want a brief word to express the science of improving stock, which is by no means confined to questions of judicious mating, but which, especially in the case of man, takes cognisance of all influences that tend in however remote a degree to give to the more suitable races or strains of blood a better chance of prevailing speedily over the less suitable than they otherwise would have had. The word *eugenics* would sufficiently express the idea; it is at least a neater word and a more generalised one than *viriculture* which I once ventured to use.

Source: "Eugenics: Its Definition, Scope, and Aims" (1904), and *Inquiries Into Human Faculty and Its Development* (1883).

tive breeding. Eugenicists—those who subscribed to this theory—believed that heredity largely determined success and development. Consequently, they encouraged the breeding of people with the most desirable traits while discouraging the perpetuation of those with the least desirable traits. According to their theories, eliminating unfit members of society would result in a more enlightened civilization.

Within the United States, the opportunities and challenges of the early twentieth century brought the eugenics movement to the forefront of progressive reform efforts, specifically related to limiting the influx of immigrants. After the U.S. Civil War ended in 1865, increasing numbers of Asians and eastern and southern Europeans came to the United States in search of brighter futures. Many well-established American citizens opposed the growing foreign population and demanded a return to the core Anglo-American Protestant values and the stock of people upon which they believed the United States had been built. Publication of Madison Grant's *The Passing of the Great Race* in 1916 had a strong influence on popular audiences. Grant presented data that, he argued, proved that the northern European races that had founded the United States were of superior hereditary stock.

Eugenics, rising xenophobia, and the progressive spirit of the early twentieth century resulted in new restrictive rules in U.S. immigration policy. Advocates of the eugenics movement pressed state and federal governments to take action to foster eugenics goals. Eugenicists succeeded in influencing the passage of state laws supporting intelligence testing and the forced sterilization of persons deemed unfit to bear eugenically sound offspring. The federal Immigration Act of 1924, spearheaded by Washington congressman and Eugenics Research Association president Albert Johnson, established an immigrant quota system based on country of origin. Eugenicists believed that the limitations would rescue the hereditary stock of

able" types. The intersection of scientific theory on heredity, the tendency of progressive reformers to control their environment, the popularity of nativist groups, and struggling immigrant laborers created a perfect storm for changing immigration policy and attitudes during the early years of the twentieth century. The eugenics movement set out to define the "real Americans" in society and decide who should inherit the nation's future.

During the late nineteenth century, scholars and scientists applied naturalist Charles Darwin's evolutionary theory of natural selection to social, political, and economic development. The consequent derivative theory that became known as "social Darwinism" served as the backbone ideology of the eugenics movement. During the 1880's, Darwin's cousin Francis Galton coined the term "eugenics," which he defined as the theory of hereditary improvement of the human race by selec-

the nation from so-called inferior races. Congress adjusted the quotas several times, but the basic law remained in effect until 1965.

The eugenicists' plan for "race betterment" attracted many followers during the first decades of the century. Prominent and influential figures, including Presidents Theodore Roosevelt and Woodrow Wilson, birth control advocate Margaret Sanger, and inventor Alexander Graham Bell, supported eugenics. However, after the 1920's, the influence of the eugenics movement on immigration policy and attitudes declined. Through the ensuing decades, eugenics groups remained active, but their message of eliminating the "unfit" in society mirrored the discredited racist and genocidal policies of Nazi Germany.

Aaron D. Purcell

FURTHER READING

Black, Edwin. *War Against the Weak: Eugenics and America's Campaign to Create a Master Race.* New York: Four Walls Eight Windows, 2003.

Engs, Ruth Clifford. *The Eugenics Movement: An Encyclopedia.* Westport, Conn.: Greenwood Press, 2005.

Kline, Wendy. *Building a Better Race.* Berkeley: University of California Press, 2001.

Pickens, Donald K. *Eugenics and the Progressives.* Nashville, Tenn.: Vanderbilt University Press, 1968.

SEE ALSO: Birth control movement; Congress, U.S.; Immigration Act of 1924; Immigration law; Infectious diseases; Intelligence testing; "Mongrelization"; Nativism; Progressivism; Quota systems; Xenophobia.

EUROPEAN IMMIGRANTS

SIGNIFICANCE: Although the territory of the United States was originally settled in ancient times by the Asian ancestors of modern Native Americans, European immigrants of the seventeenth through early twentieth centuries dominated the landscape and brought with them the culture and institutions to which other modern immigrants have had to adapt.

European immigration to the New World of the Western Hemisphere had its origins in the Age of Exploration that began with Spanish and Portuguese voyages of discovery in the fifteenth and sixteenth centuries. The creation of European colonies in the Americas, as expressions of political power and as business opportunities, stimulated both forced and free migration from Europe. European immigration has been almost constant since the early seventeenth century, but it has waxed and waned with changing economic, social, demographic, and political conditions on both sides of the Atlantic Ocean.

HISTORICAL ORIGINS OF TRANSATLANTIC MIGRATION

Transatlantic migration can be seen as an extension of long-standing patterns of movement within Europe that stretch back to the Middle Ages. Due to better technology, improved farming practices, and a warming of the climate, medieval populations expanded, putting pressure on existing arable land. Encouraged by rulers, nobles, and kings, who would often remit certain feudal duties, peasant populations migrated to virgin lands. This occurred within the core regions of western Europe, but there were significant movements of population from Germany and Flanders into less populated areas of central and eastern Europe. Due to persecutions that stemmed from the onset of the bubonic plague during the mid-fourteenth century, Jewish populations migrated to Poland and Lithuania, where they received improved treatment and a measure of religious freedom.

As urban areas across the continent grew during the early modern period, they increasingly drew populations from the countryside. During the early modern period populations displaced by war or religious persecution also migrated throughout Europe. These included French Huguenots who moved to England, and Irish and Scottish Roman Catholics who left the British Isles for the Continent.

Migration within Europe was a necessary precursor to transatlantic migration. Studies of immigrants from the colonial period onward have indicated that a majority of individual European immigrants had some previous migration experience, either regionally or within Europe, prior to coming to North America. In a study of the British colonies in North America after the Seven Years' War (also known as the French and Indian War; 1756-1763), Bernard Bailyn found that one-third of all immigrants to North America came from London or its surrounding counties and one-quarter directly from London itself. Of these immigrants, many were relatively recent arrivals in the British capital city. Two-thirds of these immigrants were Scots, many of whom came as a result of political and economic disruptions in the Highland regions.

Internal migrations within Europe increased the likelihood of individuals making longer and more permanent journeys for several reasons. First, it gave them access to new economic opportunities and altered their economic worldviews. Most local peasant and subsistence economies in Europe prior to migration were perceived as zero-sum games in which those who attained greater material wealth did so only at the expense of their neighbors. Migration changed this view and opened up the possibility of expanding one's material universe and realizing economic possibilities that were previously unattainable.

MARKET ECONOMIES AND INDUSTRIALIZATION

The process of European immigration to the New World is closely tied to economic and social changes in Europe that were well underway by the eighteenth century. In England, the process of enclosure took open land away from peasant-tenant farmers, often to create pasture land for raising sheep, encouraged by the growth of the profitable wool trade. Although this movement began during the late medieval period, it accelerated during the seventeenth and eighteenth centuries. Dispossessed peasants were sometimes compensated with less desirable pieces of land, but many migrated to cities or to rural areas to work as wage laborers. The common saying was that England was a land where sheep eat men. In Ireland, Scotland, and parts of Germany, efforts to modernize farming had a similar effect that, coupled with wars and political upheaval, resulted in the growth of a class of landless or land-poor people in need of wage labor.

By the mid-eighteenth century, the growth of European industrialization drew many out of the countryside and into factories, mills, and mines. This process affected western Europe most directly, but its indirect effects were felt throughout the Continent. By the nineteenth century, industrialization was evident throughout central Europe and even in Russia and the Balkans by the end of the century. This movement drew large numbers of peasants out of rural villages and into cities, but the new industrial jobs provided by this economic change could not keep pace with the expanding size of the rural population or with the number being displaced from the land. Rural populations continued to grow throughout the nineteenth century because of the cessation of major war, the introduction of new crops such as the potato, and improved health and sanitary conditions. This put additional land pressure on the rural populations, something that was exacerbated in some areas by inheritance patterns in which land was divided evenly among peasants' heirs.

In central and eastern Europe, the movement of peasants was kept in check throughout the seventeenth century by quasi-feudal laws that bound the peasants to the land. Throughout the nineteenth century, however, these laws were gradually done away with in an effort to modernize agriculture. The peasants were emancipated in Prussia in 1807, Austria-Hungary in 1848, Russia in 1863, Romania in 1864, and the Balkans after 1878 as Ottoman control receded.

The usual method of peasant emancipation was to convert labor duties into cash rents and—much like the earlier enclosure movement in England—to restrict peasant access to pastures, woodlands, or other resources once used in common. As one Polish scholar put it, "peasant emancipation took the shackles off the peasants' feet—and took the shoes as well." The result was a sudden need for money in village economies where cash had rarely been used. This impelled peasants to migrate in search of work, and as they did so they found not only the ability to pay rents but the possibility of bettering their economic status.

Those living close to industrial areas in Europe were usually attracted to those regions. Peasants living in more remote areas, however, were more likely to travel overseas, especially to the United States. This was the result of a clear-sighted economic strategy and improving transportation technology, especially railroads and steamships. Over time the speed of travel grew and its costs shrank—not only in the price of tickets but also in the time and other expenses saved. This made the New

World more attractive as a destination. Given the higher wages offered in America, the benefits of peasants traveling to America grew accordingly.

ATTRACTION OF THE NEW WORLD

North America's abundance of resources and its relatively smaller and less densely concentrated population began attracting immigrants during the early seventeenth century. By the time of the American Revolution (1775-1783), the average American had more personal freedom and a better standard of living than counterparts in Europe, even in the better-off countries of western Europe. Throughout its history, average wages in the United States have always been higher than in Europe. Moreover, due to Indian removal policies and westward expansion during the nineteenth century, the United States offered an abundance of farm and grazing land that was both relatively inexpensive and highly productive.

America attracted three main types of immigrants. The first are "settler immigrants," who come with the intention of settling permanently in the New World. They usually bring all or most of their immediate and extended family members and thus cut their strongest ties to their home villages. Historically this pattern was often associated with those who came to America with the specific intention of taking up farms. Bringing additional family members was beneficial as an additional source of farm labor. The majority of settler immigrants from Europe during the nineteenth and early twentieth centuries were from northern and western Europe.

Labor seekers are the second type of immigrants—those who come to find jobs that pay good wages. Labor-seeking immigrants have made up and continue to make up the largest numbers of immigrants to the United States. Typical labor-seeking immigrants are men aged between sixteen and forty-five who come for unskilled or semi-skilled work. A significant number of women also come as labor-seeking immigrants. However, in most European immigrant streams, with the notable exception of Ireland, men have historically predominated. Labor-seeking immigrants may come for limited periods of time and then return. In the case of European immigrants, this has resulted in very high return rates from some countries. Among southern Italian immigrants, return rates as high as 40 percent were not unknown. The largest groups of labor-seeking immigrants from Europe during the nineteenth and early twentieth centuries were from eastern and southern Europe.

Refugees or those fleeing some form of religious or political persecution constitute the third type of immigrants. These immigrants—despite their prominence in the public consciousness—have represented by far the least common form of immigration. Political or religious immigrants range from seventeenth century dissenters to victims of Nazi or Soviet terror during the 1940's and 1950's.

COLONIAL IMMIGRATION

The first significant European immigration to the New World came from the British Isles with the first communities formed in New England during the 1620's. A smaller number of English also settled in Virginia and the Chesapeake region. Throughout the seventeenth century and early eighteenth centuries, immigrants arrived in a slow trickle from the British Isles along with some Germans and Swiss in Pennsylvania, Dutch and Flemish in New York, and about six hundred Swedes and Finns in Delaware and Pennsylvania. A scattering of Sephardic Jews, French Protestants, and Poles

---

PROFILE OF EUROPEAN IMMIGRANTS

Countries of origin	All European nations
Primary languages	English, German, French, Italian, Polish, and many others
Primary regions of U.S. settlement	Throughout the country
Earliest significant arrivals	1607
Peak immigration period	1820-1914
Twenty-first century legal residents*	1,162,269 (145,284 per year)

*Immigrants who obtained legal permanent resident status in the United States.

Source: Department of Homeland Security, *Yearbook of Immigration Statistics, 2008.*

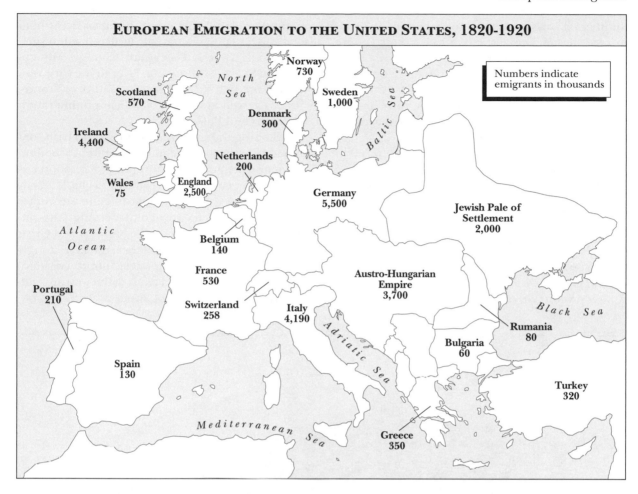

EUROPEAN EMIGRATION TO THE UNITED STATES, 1820-1920

Numbers indicate emigrants in thousands

Norway 730
Scotland 570
Sweden 1,000
Denmark 300
Ireland 4,400
Netherlands 200
Wales 75
England 2,500
Germany 5,500
Jewish Pale of Settlement 2,000
Belgium 140
France 530
Austro-Hungarian Empire 3,700
Portugal 210
Switzerland 258
Italy 4,190
Rumania 80
Bulgaria 60
Spain 130
Turkey 320
Greece 350

North Sea
Baltic Sea
Atlantic Ocean
Adriatic Sea
Black Sea
Mediterranean Sea

could also be found. The majority of English settler immigrants came to New England as members of religious dissenter groups. In Virginia and the Chesapeake region, a significant number of indentured servants from throughout the British Isles were transported to serve as labor on tobacco plantations.

Between the Seven Years' War and the American Revolution, immigration to the British colonies grew dramatically, rising to approximately 15,000 per year. Germans and Swiss made up the largest single group, numbering about 125,000, followed by Protestant Irish (55,000), Scots (40,000), and English (30,000). In addition to the transportation of about 85,000 enslaved Africans, the new immigration greatly increased the population of the middle and southern colonies in the years before the outbreak of the Revolutionary War.

During the Revolutionary War and in the de-cades of economic readjustment and wars in Europe that followed American Independence, immigration decreased dramatically, especially from its traditional sources in the British Isles, though some German immigrants continued to arrive. During the conflict, a significant number of Europeans with military experience arrived to provide critical assistance to the American colonists, with French, Germans, Poles, and Hungarians the most prominent among them.

IMMIGRATION, 1820-1880

Immigration began to increase once again during the 1820's in response to the end of the Napoleonic Wars, the western expansion of the United States, and the growth of the American economy. In 1820, 8,385 European immigrants arrived in the United States. Ten years later, arrivals reached 23,322. During the 1840's and 1850's, immigration numbers skyrocketed, reaching a peak of 427,833 in 1855 alone. Thereafter, poor economic conditions and the onset of the U.S. Civil War in 1861 again reduced European immigration dramatically. However, it never fell below 100,000 immigrants per year. Immigration grew once more, peaking in 1866 and again in 1873, when arrivals again topped 400,000 per year.

Among immigrants arriving before the Civil War, three groups predominated: Irish, Germans, and English. Irish immigrants were the most numerous during the 1840's and early 1850's. The Great Irish Famine, repressive English land policies in Ireland, and generally backward economic conditions pushed many Irish to the New World, where they found work as laborers. From the mid-1850's, German immigration dominated arrivals. A high proportion of Germans came as settler immigrants and took up homes and farms in the Midwest and Great Lakes states as well as in cities such as St. Louis, Detroit, Cincinnati, Chicago, Milwaukee, and St. Paul, Minnesota. Prior to the Civil War, there was also a steadily growing influx of Scandinavians as well as the first significant immigration of Czechs and Poles.

Following the Civil War, Germans and Irish continued to arrive in large numbers, but new nationalities also began to appear on American shores as well: Norwegians, Swedes, Danes, Czechs, Hungarians, and Poles. Immigration after the war represented the last great wave of settler immigrants who arrived to look for farms in the Midwest and Great Plains. Thereafter, good land became increasingly difficult to acquire, though agricultural colonization continued in the arid lands of the west and cut-over regions of the Great Lakes.

European immigrants arriving at Ellis Island in 1902. Located in New York Harbor, Ellis Island was the primary port of entry for European immigrants between 1892 and 1954. (Library of Congress)

344

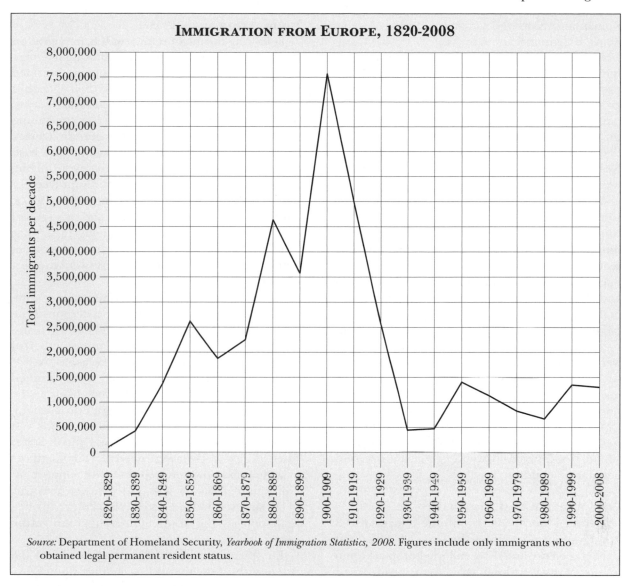

IMMIGRATION FROM EUROPE, 1820-2008

Source: Department of Homeland Security, *Yearbook of Immigration Statistics, 2008.* Figures include only immigrants who obtained legal permanent resident status.

IMMIGRATION, 1880-1924

Beginning in the 1880's and continuing through the passage of restrictive immigration laws in 1924, the largest wave of immigration in history arrived on North America's shores. The largest number of arrivals came in the period from 1900 to 1914. Arrivals fell off sharply during World War I. The largest number of immigrants came in 1907, when approximately 1.3 million arrived during that year alone.

Although immigrants continued to arrive from western Europe and Scandinavia, this wave of immigration was dominated by east-central and southern European. Beginning in the eastern marches of the German Empire, "immigration fever" spread eastward into Austria-Hungary, Romania, and the western regions of Russia. Italy also sent massive numbers of immigrants, and while many came from northern Italy, southern Italians and Sicilians dominated Italian arrivals. From east-central Europe, Poles were the largest single group, arriving from the German, Russian, and Austrian empire. Jews were a close second—although many came from Austria-Hungary, Germany, and Romania, Russian Jews formed the largest contingent. A host of smaller groups also came—Hungarians, Lithuanians, Ukrainians, Carpatho-Rusins, Slovaks, Czechs,

Romanians, Slovenes, Croatians, Serbs, Macedonians, Bulgarians, and Greeks.

In contrast to earlier waves of immigrants, the Europeans who came between 1880 and 1924 were predominantly labor-seeking immigrants. However, some did come within family units and some did settle on farms. It was primarily industrial work that drew them to the United States, and they settled in the areas of heaviest industrial activity—New York, New Jersey, Pennsylvania, and the Midwest and Great Lakes states.

Wage labor immigrants from east-central and southern Europe provided the workforce for America's industry, and by the turn of the century dominated both heavy and light industry in most sectors. Jews and Italians were prominent in the needle trades. Poles, Italians, Slovaks, Ukrainians, and Hungarians dominated coal mining and steel making. Poles were the largest group in auto manufacturing, and Poles and Lithuanians predominated in meatpacking. Finns and southern Slavs were the largest groups in copper and other hard-rock mining. The prominence of these groups made them a significant force in the industrial labor movement of the 1930's. The success of the Congress of Industrial Organizations (CIO) and the United Auto Workers (UAW) depended on the support of immigrant workers and their second-generation children.

POST-WORLD WAR II IMMIGRANTS

Between World War II and the reform of U.S. immigration laws in 1965, the United States admitted between two and three million European immigrants. Many were political refugees, with Jewish Holocaust survivors the most prominent among them. There were also significant numbers of Poles—victims of Nazi and Soviet genocide and persecution as well as former members of the Polish armed forces in exile who were unable to return home due to communist oppression. Refugees from the Soviet Union who were in Germany were also granted entry—with Balts and Ukrainians the most numerous. Another often overlooked immigration that resulted from the war was the arrival of war brides of U.S. servicemen. An estimated 100,000 arrived during and after the war. Hungarian freedom fighters were another refugee group from Europe that arrived after the failed Hungarian uprising against Soviet rule.

IMMIGRATION SINCE 1965

Following the major reform of U.S. immigration laws in 1965, a steady flow of immigration from Europe developed. Family reunifications, the need for work, political oppression, and the collapse of communism during the 1980's and 1990's have been some of the major factors in this continuing stream. Some traditional sending countries continued to provide large numbers of immigrants. Irish immigrants arrived in the United States during the 1970's and 1980's until the dramatic improvement in Ireland's economic situation during the 1990's. Dissidents from the Soviet Union and its so-called satellite nations figured prominently in arrivals prior to 1989. Jewish refuseniks from the Soviet Union and Polish Solidarity activists were the best known.

Following the fall of Eastern Europe's communist governments during the last decade of the twentieth century and the wars and ethnic cleansing in the former Yugoslavia, a large number of Russians, Jews, Ukrainians, and Poles, as well as Romanians and Bosnians arrived in the United States. These new immigrants were likely to be better educated than earlier eastern European immigrants. They followed employment trends and could be found throughout the United States where skilled workers were needed. Older patterns of settlement, however, continued to be important. For example, Russian Jews settled in New York City in the largest numbers, and by 2000 Poles had once again become the largest immigrant group in Chicago.

European immigration has continued into the first decade of the twenty-first century, when Europeans were still making up between 15 and 20 percent of the immigrants admitted to the United States. This pattern appeared likely to continue into the foreseeable future.

John Radzilowski

FURTHER READING

Bailyn, Bernard. *The Peopling of British North America: An Introduction.* New York: Vintage, 1986. Useful study of early British immigration to North America.

Daniels, Roger. *Coming to America: A History of Immigration and Ethnicity in American Life.* Princeton, N.J.: Visual Education Corporation, 1990. Comprehensive survey of the major immigrant groups in the United States, emphasizing numbers of immigrants, their settlement patterns, and socioeconomic issues.

Erickson, Charlotte. *American Industry and the European Immigrant, 1860-1885.* Cambridge, Mass.: Harvard University Press, 1957. Excellent study of the employment of European immigrants during the Civil War and postwar eras.

_____. *Invincible Immigrants: The Adaptation of English and Scottish Immigrants in Nineteenth Century America.* Leicester, England: Leicester University Press, 1972. Important survey of the second peak period of British immigration, with useful data and appendixes.

Greene, Victor R. *A Singing Ambivalence: American Immigrants Between Old World and New, 1830-1930.* Kent, Ohio: Kent State University Press, 2004. Comparative study of the different challenges faced by members of eight major immigrant groups—Irish, Germans, Scandinavians and Finns, eastern European Jews, Italians, Poles and Hungarians, Chinese, and Mexicans—through one of the longest peak periods of immigration.

Meltzer, Milton. *Bound for America: The Story of the European Immigrants.* New York: Benchmark Books, 2001. Very readable history of European immigration to the United States, written for young adult readers.

SEE ALSO: Austrian immigrants; Belgian immigrants; British immigrants; Czech and Slovakian immigrants; Dutch immigrants; European revolutions of 1848; Former Soviet Union immigrants; French immigrants; German immigrants; Greek immigrants; Hamburg-Amerika Line; Hungarian immigrants; Irish immigrants; Italian immigrants; Jewish immigrants; Pilgrim and Puritan immigrants; Polish immigrants; Portuguese immigrants; Russian and Soviet immigrants; Scandinavian immigrants; Spanish immigrants; Swiss immigrants; Yugoslav state immigrants.

EUROPEAN REVOLUTIONS OF 1848

THE EVENTS: Series of similarly motivated nationalist uprisings and full-scale revolutions that swept through central Europe, at the conclusion of which many participants and supporters emigrated to the United States

DATE: 1848-1849

LOCATION: Western and central Europe

SIGNIFICANCE: Europe's revolutions of 1848 did not fulfill their goals for most participants and, as a result, many participants and supporters felt that the future in their European homelands was particularly bleak. This sense of disillusionment, along with fear of persecution for their actions during the uprisings, led many to leave Europe in search of a better political environment. A majority of them chose to emigrate to go to the United States.

During the 1840's, Europe was swept up in a whirlwind of political and social turmoil. Among the forces leading to this development liberalism, frustrated nationalism egged on by the Romantic movement, the tensions of burgeoning industrialism, and an agricultural revolution. The popular uprisings challenged the conservative order of Europe, characterized by monarchical-autocratic governments, hierarchical society, and aversion to ethnic determinism.

COURSE OF EVENTS

The years directly following the 1815 Congress of Vienna, which settled the Napoleonic Wars, saw a series of liberal and national outbreaks against the restored governments across Europe. In every instance the chief architect of the peace settlement, Klemens von Metternich, and his allies were able to put down the insurrections and restore conservative rule. However, nothing was done to alleviate the fundamental pressures that had created those disturbances, and they continued to grow until 1848. These forces were many, and an economic depression that began in 1846 and got steadily worse over the next two years combined with the dislocations caused by the ongoing agricultural and Industrial Revolutions, increased demands for

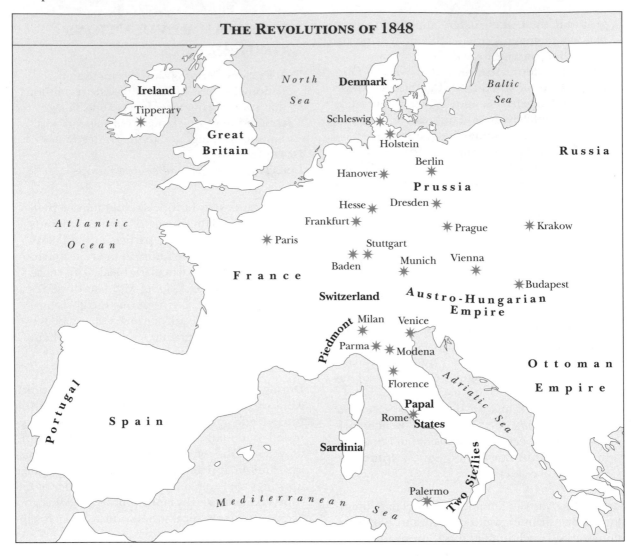

THE REVOLUTIONS OF 1848

ethnic determinism, and the strong rise of liberalism.

The traditional home to European revolution, Paris, lit the match of revolutionary fire in February, 1848. An uprising ousted the monarchy of Louis Philippe and created the Second French Republic, which adopted universal manhood suffrage and a guarantee of the right to work. This success set off a chain reaction of revolution throughout Europe. Insurrections broke out in the major European cities of Vienna, Milan, Berlin, and Budapest and throughout the Habsburg Empire and in the numerous Italian and German states.

There were minor differences among the revolutionary movements in the various countries, as each uprising had its own local concerns. However, their general patterns were essentially the same. During the spring of 1848, the revolutionary cause was going well throughout Europe. A republic replaced the monarchy in France, rulers in the Italian and German states as well as the Habsburg emperor were forced either to abdicate or to grant liberal constitutions, and the Italian and Germanic states found themselves on the path to unification. Within the multiethnic Habsburg Empire, many ethnic groups, most notably the Magyars and the Czechs, were given autonomy. This series of revolutionary successes appeared to have broken the hold of conservative Europe and appeared poised to begin a new chapter in European history.

During the summer, however, the political inexperience of the revolutions' leaders became apparent as each movement went through a series of internal crises. The divisions between the leaders of liberal and nationalist causes led to clashes among the social classes. These were most evident in the bloody street fighting in Paris in what became known as the June Days. Bitter jealousy among leaders in the Italian states weakened their military campaign against Italy's Austrian rulers. In the German states, delegates to the Frankfurt Assembly wasted precious time arguing about boundaries and minute details of the Germany they hoped to create. While all this infighting was dividing the revolutionaries and sapping their strength, the conservative powers were recovering their strength and regaining their authority. Most liberal reforms that had been granted were rescinded, and military force was used to overthrow the incipient nationalist republics that had arisen, such as the Magyar Republic that Louis Kossuth had built in Hungary.

By 1851, virtually all of Europe was politically back to where it had been before the outbreaks in 1848. Dreams of unifying Italy and Germany had been crushed, and the heyday of liberalism was over. In the final analysis, the revolutions of 1848 were long on ideals but short on practicality. From the beginning, they suffered from divisions in leadership and confusion in strategy. Many of their leaders had a passion for criticism and opposition but little talent for organization. As a result, the revolutions fell victim to the more experienced conservative authorities and the bullets and bayonets of Prussian, Russian, and Habsburg armies. Those who had harbored optimism for the future in the spring of 1848 were now disillusioned and angry. Many chose to seek their fortunes elsewhere and turned their attention across the Atlantic.

IMMIGRATION TO THE UNITED STATES

Emigration from Europe seemed to be the only answer for many of the former revolutionaries. Several feared reprisal by the restoration authorities and faced criminal charges including high treason. Others felt that the future in their homelands was too bleak to bear. The majority of these immigrants were Germans, and the United States provided sanctuary. Approximately sixty thousand German "Forty-eighters" joined other groups of Europeans

in this period of mass immigration, which also included a large group of Irish immigrants after Ireland's failed 1848 rebellion against the British crown.

The influx of Germans led to an increase in nationalistic activities of previous German immigrants and tended to retard their assimilation into the American mainstream. The revolutionary struggles rekindled interest in the homeland and cultural traditions that had been abandoned upon entering the United States. Immigrant organizations underwent a transformation and increased in power and membership. Many put political pressure on the United States to intervene in the affairs of Europe. This political activism increased as revolutionaries came to the United States. Also, the immigrant press came of age in this era as, first, old immigrants demanded news from the Old World, and after their arrival, new immigrants brought a professionalism and enthusiasm for a German-language press. Between 1848 and 1852, the number of German-language newspapers in the United States doubled to 150.

The surge in ethnic pride and radical politics led to an increase in nativist feelings among native-born Americans. The nativists argued that instead of showing gratitude to the nation that gave them asylum, many of the exiles were openly critical of the United States and trying to remake the United States to meet their political and cultural desires. Others claimed that America was going to be used as a staging ground for a war with conservative Europe.

Regardless of the nativist reaction, the German Forty-eighters brought with them more than radical political ideas. Many of the immigrants were artisans who contributed considerably to the arts and crafts world of America. Among the Forty-eighters were also a number of medical professionals who brought their European training with them. They also brought with them appreciation of great masters of music such as Ludwig van Beethoven and Wolfgang Amadeus Mozart and the classical dramas of Friedrich Schiller, Johann Wolfgang von Goethe, and William Shakespeare.

Perhaps the most identifiable contribution was in the realm of education. One of the best schools in Maryland, F. Knapp's German and English Institute, was founded by a Forth-eighter who had been convicted of high treason in Germany in 1850. The kindergarten movement in the United States began with German immigrants of this era. Forty-eighter politicians such as Carl Schurz played a substantial role in American politics during the 1850's, and German immigrants played a role in the U.S. Civil War. It was the sacrifices on that battlefield by the German immigrants that quelled most of the nativist argument against them by the 1870's.

Amanda J. Bahr-Evola

FURTHER READING

Brancaforte, Charlotte L., ed. *The German Forty-eighters in the United States.* New York: Peter Lang, 1990. Collection of eighteen essays covering a wide range of topics, including a reappraisal arguing that many Forty-eighter immigrants were not radicals or revolutionaries.

Rapport, Mike. *1848: Year of Revolution.* New York: Basic Books, 2009. Covers each of the revolutions and discusses the implications for later events in European history.

Robertson, Priscilla Smith. *Revolutions of 1848: A Social History.* Princeton, N.J.: Princeton University Press, 1952. Classic work on the 1848 revolutions that focuses on the roles of various social classes and the impact of the failed uprisings for each of the classes.

Sperber, Jonathan. *The European Revolutions, 1848-1851.* New York: Cambridge University Press, 1994. Comprehensive coverage of the events, written in a highly readable narrative. Excellent introduction.

Wittke, Carl. *Refugees of Revolution: The German Forty-eighters in America.* Philadelphia: University of Pennsylvania, 1952. Classic work on the experience of the Forty-eighters in the United States. Heavy emphasis on biography.

Zucker, A. E., ed. *The Forty-eighters: Political Refugees of the German Revolution of 1848.* New York: Columbia University Press, 1950. Lays out the political beliefs of the German immigrants and how they evolved in the United States.

SEE ALSO: Austrian immigrants; Czech and Slovakian immigrants; German American press; German immigrants; Hungarian immigrants; Linguistic contributions; Nativism; Political parties; Schurz, Carl.

EXETER INCIDENT

THE EVENT: Anti-Filipino riot in a farming community in California's San Joaquin Valley, where there had been a long-standing feud between Filipino field-workers and their white counterparts

DATE: October 24, 1929

LOCATION: Exeter, California

SIGNIFICANCE: This racially motivated attack on Filipino farmworkers was one of the first of several similar attacks in central California's agricultural centers. It led to another, larger attack in Watsonville, which in turn prompted a decline of Filipino immigration to California and encouraged California farmers to turn to Mexican laborers to work their fields.

One of the causes of anti-Filipino prejudice in California was economic. While American workers were generally unwilling to perform "stoop labor" in agricultural fields, Filipinos, who had replaced Chinese and Japanese farmworkers in California, were willing to work ten-hour days for less than two dollars, six days a week. This was only about half of what union factory workers were paid during the late 1920's. The Filipinos cut asparagus, planted cauliflower, and—much to the ire of white workers—harvested Kadota figs and Emperor grapes—both jobs that had formerly been reserved for white workers.

In addition to providing economic competition for white farmworkers, Filipinos socialized with white women making them targets on both counts. With a ratio of approximately forty Filipino men to each Filipina woman in California, Filipino men frequented taxi-dance halls, where they could dance with white women. In October of 1929, when a number of Filipino men escorted white women to a street carnival in the town of Exeter, white men pelted them with rubber bands. In the fight that ensued, a white man was stabbed and a riot broke out. Instead of maintaining public safety, the local police chief responded by leading into the agricultural fields a band of three hundred white vigilantes, who attacked the Filipino workers with simple farm tools, beating and stoning them. About fifty Filipinos were injured, and more than two hundred were driven from their camp.

AFTERMATH OF THE EXETER INCIDENT

The following year, memories of the Exeter incident contributed to more anti-Filipino rioting in Watsonville, a town near California's coast. The Watsonville riots only made the situation worse for Filipino workers. One inflammatory event involved an alleged attempt to sell a sixteen-year-old white girl to a Filipino man; a picture of the man embracing the girl made the newspapers. The subsequent opening of another taxi-dance hall in nearby Palm Beach further inflamed racist passions. After a series of Filipino run-ins with local law enforcement, a local judge was quoted as saying that if the present situation were to continue, there would be "forty thousand half-breeds" in California within ten years. The judge also charged that Filipino workers were both impregnating white women and crowding whites out of their jobs—thereby linking sex and economics.

Politicians added fuel to the fire when they presented a Filipino exclusion bill in both the U.S. House of Representatives and the U.S. Senate. These events culminated in a series of battles between whites and Filipinos that ended on January 23, 1930, when a Filipino man named Fermin Tobera was killed by random gunshots. His body was returned to Manila, the capital of the Philippines, where it lay in state. Afterward, Tobera became a nationalist icon in his country's struggle to win independence from the United States.

Despite other racist attacks in California, in such farming communities as Salinas, Stockton, and Gilroy, most of the Filipino workers in California remained in the state. Later in 1930, they staged a successful strike in the Salinas lettuce fields. Eventually, Filipino laborers were replaced by Mexican braceros, who then became new targets of American racism.

Thomas L. Erskine

FURTHER READING

DeWitt, Howard A., ed. *Violence in the Fields: California Filipino Farm Labor Unionization During the Great Depression.* Saratoga, Calif.: Century Twenty-One Publishing, 1980.

Melendy, H. Brett. "Filipinos in the United States." *Pacific Historical Review* 43 (November, 1974): 520-547.

Min, Pyong Gap, ed. *Asian Americans: Contemporary Trends and Issues.* 2d ed. Thousand Oaks, Calif.: Pine Forge Press, 2006.

SEE ALSO: Anti-Filipino violence; Farm and migrant workers; Filipino immigrants; History of immigration after 1891.

F

FAMILIES

SIGNIFICANCE: U.S. immigration laws have emphasized the goal of family reunification, making it relatively easy for relatives of immigrants already in the United States to enter the country. However, after arriving, immigrants must use their own resources to adapt and survive. Families are a significant source of social, economic, and emotional support.

Before 1882, the U.S. government imposed few restrictions on foreign immigration. With the passage of the Chinese Exclusion Act in 1882, Congress began a pattern of ever more restrictive immigration laws that were in force into the 1960's. Despite their restrictions, however, each immigration law granted special exemptions to family members. For example, the Immigration Act of 1924 imposed quotas limiting the numbers of immigrants from specified countries, but it allowed two exceptions for family members. Wives were permitted to immigrate to join their immigrant spouses; however, husbands of immigrant wives were not granted the same exemption. Also, unmarried children under the age of eighteen of parents who were U.S. citizens were admitted without limitation from countries in the Western Hemisphere.

POST-WORLD WAR II CHANGES

During the 1940's, immigration restrictions were eased to support American wartime allies and to assist refugees. The Immigration and Nationality Act of 1952 eliminated racial and gender discrimination but otherwise left the national quota system unchanged into the 1960's. By that time, the Civil Rights movement had begun to change public attitudes about racial minorities. Nevertheless, some political conservatives continued to support immigration quotas to preserve what they regarded as racial and ethnic balance. However, cosmopolitan attitudes, expanding cultural awareness regarding discrimination, and liberalism of the 1960's led to replacing immigration quotas based on nationalities with quotas based on hemispheres.

The Immigration and Nationality Act of 1965, also known as the Hart-Celler Act, ended the practice of using national quotas to regulate immigration to the United States from non-Western countries. After receiving overwhelming support in Congress, the act was signed into law by President Lyndon B. Johnson on October 3, 1965, and went into effect on July 1, 1968. The law permitted up to 120,000 immigrants per year from the Western Hemisphere and 170,000 from the Eastern Hemisphere, with a limit of 20,000 from any single country. However, while the law allowed for 290,000 total immigrants, the actual numbers of immigrants who entered the United States was higher, as the law continued to allow exceptions for family members. Family reunification visas were unlimited.

In contrast to earlier immigration laws that emphasized the national origins of immigrants, the 1965 immigration law emphasized the goals of family reunification and bringing in skilled immigrants. The law awarded visas first to unmarried adults whose parents were U.S. citizens, followed by spouses and offspring of permanent residents and skilled professionals, scientists, and artists. Initially, parents of American citizens could enter regardless of the law's quotas. However, in 1976, the law was amended to require children be at least twenty-one years old before their parents were permitted to immigrate. Before then, pregnant mothers could enter the United States illegally, have children who automatically became citizens, and then claim citizenship for themselves as the mothers of American citizens.

The 1965 law provided an impetus for increased immigration through the next four decades, especially from non-European countries. Most of the 22.8 million people who immigrated to the United States between 1966 and 2000 were family members of recent immigrants.

CHAIN MIGRATION

Chain migration plays an important role in reuniting families and facilitates the assimilation of new immigrants. It occurs when recent immigrants maintain connections with family and friends in their home countries. After individuals have immigrated to their new country and established them-

352

selves, other members of their families and friends often follow. Typically, husbands, unmarried sons and daughters of working age, or young, married, childless couples migrate first.

Chain migration occurs because early immigrants establish patterns of residency, and help recruit, support, and socialize new immigrants, most often family members. Many immigrants choose residential and occupational destinations because of kinship ties in the area. The flow of information about job opportunities in the new country encourages others to migrate and leads to ethnic concentrations such as Scandinavians in the midwestern United States and Germans in Pennsylvania.

Ethnic enclaves first arose in American cities as products of chain migration from such European countries as Ireland, Germany, Scotland, England, and Italy during the nineteenth century. In some cases, entire European communities regrouped in the United States, where they preserved their family ties and traditions within their new enclaves. This process continued well into the twentieth century. During the 1980's, for example, Filipino immigration increased dramatically, and at least three-quarters of new Filipino immigrants were sponsored by family members already in the United States.

Later immigrants from Mexico and Central American nations had similar patterns of chain migration. Immigrants generally choose as their destinations communities that offer a familiar culture and family connection. Gateway cities, where immigrants first enter the United States, such as Los Angeles, Miami, and New York, attract disproportionate numbers of ethnic families because well-established social institutions, churches, and schools are already in place to provide social and economic support.

Some critics have charged that the family provisions of the Immigration and Nationality Act of 1965 tended to shift control of who was allowed to immigrate into the United States in the hands of foreigners through its kinship formulas. They have also charged that the law tends to discourage immigrants from assimilating into American society by encouraging chain migration. However, others

Family of Russian immigrants on their arrival in New York Harbor in 1921. (Library of Congress)

have argued that the law's family priority system and subsequent chain migration has actually helped immigrants to adapt and succeed, thereby strengthening American society. Immigrant families often form close-knit, extended family units whose members help raise one another's children and cooperate economically.

IMMIGRANT FAMILIES

Historically, the success of immigrant groups has been closely tied to the ability of their members to establish strong families in the United States. Immigrant families demonstrate striking diversity. Their members migrate for different reasons, with different kinds of resources, and from vastly different homelands. Nevertheless, they all face similar challenges, including ethnic prejudices and discrimination and economic exploitation that limits occupational and educational opportunities. Immigrant families tend to fare better in their new homes than the people they leave behind. However, they generally have lower income levels and experience greater poverty than native-born American families. Male heads of immigrant families tend to be employed at wage levels similar to those of native-born families, but their employment is more likely to be part-time or seasonal. Many of their occupations are concentrated in such service industries as restaurants and laundries. Foreign-born women tend to have higher unemployment rates than native-born women.

The close family ties that typify many immigrant groups have fostered surprisingly good levels of health, despite the immigrants' generally lower incomes and the often unhealthful and dangerous conditions in their countries of origin. For example, immigrant Mexican women tend to have low infant mortality rates and to bear babies with healthy birth weights, despite the fact that they typically come from great poverty. This apparent paradox has been explained, in part, by the close family ties that Mexican immigrants enjoy. However, the longer immigrants reside in the United States, the poorer their health becomes. This deterioration may be the result of changes in their diets and lifestyles. Moreover, immigrant families often experience difficulty obtaining access to health care because of language barriers, uncertainties about their legal immigration status, and their working in occupations offering no health benefits.

ELDERLY IMMIGRANTS

Immigrant families face generational conflicts complicated by the immigration process. The Immigration and Nationality Act of 1965 allowed many late-life immigrants to reunite with family members. About two-thirds of elderly immigrants are parents of U.S. citizens. Older immigrants tend to be poorer and less likely to speak English than younger ones. Because many immigrants maintain strong family ties, many older parents live with their adult children. Given this familism, parents provide their adult children high levels of emotional and child-care support, allowing younger family members more opportunities for wage-earning. However, because intercultural expectations can differ greatly, the presence of older parents in households may contribute to family conflicts. For example, many older immigrants expect their children to remain submissive and deferential, even as adults—traits less valued in the United States than in many other countries. Elderly immigrants who arrive in the United States expecting to live with their children and become involved in their day-to-day lives experience high levels of depression when they are disappointed in their hopes.

GENDER ROLES AND IMMIGRANT FAMILIES

After passage of the Immigration and Nationality Act of 1965, many new immigrants to the United States came from patriarchal societies in which men were expected to dominate their families and that had well-defined divisions of labor between husbands and wives and between parents and children. Many immigrants from Latin America, Asia, the West Indies, and the Middle East view paid labor as undesirable for women. They believe that having women work outside their homes can contribute to a loss of ethnic identity because it symbolizes the failure of husbands to provide for their families. In practice, however, many immigrant women must work outside their homes because of the husbands' difficulties in finding adequate employment. When women enter the work force, it contributes to "Americanizing" families and undermining traditional immigrant family structures.

One of the greatest challenges that immigrant families face is dealing with having their women enter the paid workforce. Labor force participation does not empower immigrant women within their families as it does for native-born women. Many immigrant families attempt to preserve their traditional family arrangements, even when wives must work. Consequently, many immigrant women live double lives, asserting independence and power in the workforce, while deferring to the patriarchal gender hierarchies at home. These dual roles allow immigrant women to give their families economic, social, and political power as they adapt to new circumstances.

Barbara E. Johnson

FURTHER READING

Benokratis, Nijole V. "The Changing Ethnic Profile of U.S. Families in the Twentieth Century." In *Contemporary Ethnic Families in the United States*, edited by Nijole V. Benokratis. Upper Saddle River, N.J.: Prentice Hall, 2002. General introduction to immigration, ethnicity, and families; includes discussions of the effects of immigration laws; patterns of immigration by country, race, age, and sex; and residential and socioeconomic patterns of immigrant groups.

Fix, Michael, Wendy Zimmerman, and Jeffrey S. Passel. *The Integration of Immigrant Families in the United States.* Washington, D.C.: Urban Institute, 2001. Policy paper on how immigrant families are changing and adapting and how government policies might address immigrant family needs more effectively.

Guendelman, Sarah. "Immigrant Families." In *All Our Families New Policies for a New Century*, edited by Mary Ann Mason, Arlene Skolnick, and Stephen D. Sugarman. 2d ed. New York: Oxford University Press, 2003. Describes immigrant families and discusses strategies for helping immigrant families adapt to life in the United States.

Pyke, Karen. "Immigrant Families in the United States." In *American Families A Multicultural Reader*, edited by Stephanie Coontz. 2d ed. New York: Routledge, 2008. Overview of the great wave of immigration after 1965; discusses theoretical perspectives on immigration research, patterns of immigration by age and sex, and areas for further study.

Shields, Margie K., and Richard Behrman. "Children of Immigrant Families." *The Future of Children* 14, no. 2 (Summer, 2004): 4-14. Overview of issues facing children in immigrant families. Addresses social and economic strengths and weaknesses of immigrant families.

SEE ALSO: Amerasian Homecoming Act of 1987; Chain migration; Child immigrants; *I Remember Mama*; Immigration and Nationality Act of 1965; Marriage; Paper sons; Parachute children; Picture brides; War brides; Women immigrants.

FAMILY BUSINESSES

DEFINITION: Establishments run and staffed by family members and within which entire families may work

SIGNIFICANCE: Family businesses have played an important role in the lives of immigrants to the United States. These businesses have enabled immigrants to establish themselves, first as members of their ethnic neighborhoods and secondly, as members of the American community in which they live. Family businesses have also contributed to the preservation of the ethnic heritage and culture of immigrants and have enriched multiculturalism in the United States.

The majority of European immigrants who arrived in the United States during the nineteenth century found work in the burgeoning new industries of the country. Meatpacking plants, steel mills, the garment industry, coal mining, and railroad construction provided a large number of jobs, most of which required few if any special skills. Many of these jobs required strenuous manual labor in harsh working conditions for as long as ten to twelve hours a day. Some were dangerous, posing constant risks of serious injury and possibly even of death. At the same time, they typically paid low wages, and bosses occasionally would not even pay non-English-speaking immigrants. In these conditions, enterprising immigrants lived as frugally as they could, saved money, and joined with other family members to start small businesses using such skills as they had and small investments. Not only did husbands, wives, and children work in these family businesses but also brothers, sisters, cousins, and even grandparents. Most such businesses were located within the ethnic neighborhoods in which the immigrants lived.

FOOD BUSINESSES AND NONFOOD BUSINESSES

Family businesses were most typically associated with food. Residents of predominantly Irish, German, Polish, Lithuanian, Italian, and Greek communities provided ready markets for products that reminded them of their homelands and for shops where they conducted their transactions in their native languages. Restaurants, bakeries, grocery stores, candy stores, and taverns all provided both the familiar foods of home and opportunities to interact with friends and neighbors in familiar atmospheres.

The food industry also provided business opportunities for those lacking the funds to open stores or restaurants. Greek and Italian immigrants were particularly resourceful in creating small business enterprises that did not require storefronts by selling their wares from pushcarts and temporary stands along the streets of their ethnic neighborhoods. Many sold local specialties of the particular regions from which they emigrated. Others sold fruits and vegetables that they raised in small garden plots.

Immigrants also established businesses not related to food, such as sewing and laundry and dry cleaning services. When they saved sufficient capital, many immigrants who had been skilled tradesmen in their home countries opened cobbler shops, small cigar-making shops, and tanneries, as well as cabinet-making shops, metal and woodworking shops, and barbershops. Italians in particular established businesses in the construction trades. European Jewish immigrants became involved in the garment industry as tailors and dressmakers.

Encouraged by their success in their local neighborhoods, the Italian pushcart vendors soon started sending family members with carts of fruits and vegetables into adjacent residential neighborhoods. Immigrant street vendors also set up stands in major commercial areas of the cities in which they lived to sell their wares to larger markets.

FROM SMALL SHOPS TO LARGE COMMERCIAL VENTURES

Immigrant family businesses did not simply remain small storefronts or home-based service businesses. Many Italian immigrants who began as pushcart vendors of fruits and vegetables transformed their businesses into wholesale produce firms with fleets of delivery trucks. Such businesses typically remained family owned and managed, while also employing many nonfamily members. German bakers expanded their businesses. Some opened chains of bakeries, others set up wholesale bread companies. Many Jewish immigrants expanded small tailoring and dressmaking shops into large garment factories.

As they became more affluent, immigrants from virtually all immigrant groups founded businesses in profitable market sectors. Immigrants owned steel mills, breweries, flour mills, and other businesses. These businesses tended to stay family owned, as they were passed down to succeeding generations of family members. Many of these businesses grew from single commercial entities to become large corporations with facilities throughout the United States. By the middle of the twentieth century, firms founded by immigrant families were a major part of the mainstream of American business.

ASIAN AND LATIN AMERICAN FAMILY BUSINESSES

At the same time that European immigrants were settling in the eastern and midwestern states, Chinese immigrants were arriving in California to work in the gold mines and to work as laborers building the transcontinental railroad. This growing influx of Chinese workers created markets for familiar Chinese products, especially foodstuffs. Family-owned and operated Chinese restaurants and grocery stores soon began opening, with husbands, wives, children, and other family members all involved. Other family-owned and operated businesses appeared as well. Herbalists opened shops in which family members knowledgeable in the medicinal properties of herbs saw patients, while other family members prepared the herbal medicines—often within family kitchens.

The booming population of miners from around the world and the growing number of tourists in San Francisco and other California towns created additional business opportunities for Chinese immigrants. The need for laundry services provided a major business sector in which Chinese-owned and operated businesses prospered. Curio shops also enjoyed immense success in the West. Immigrants with families still in China imported carved ivory and jade items to sell in their shops. However, Chinese immigration experienced a major setback in 1882, when the U.S. Congress en-

Members of a Chinese family posing in front of their New York City grocery store. (Smithsonian Institution)

acted the Chinese Exclusion Act. This was an era when anti-Chinese sentiment was growing in the West. By the early twentieth century, 80 percent of the Chinese living in the United States had fled to large metropolitan cities where they lived together in an area known as Chinatowns and continued to operate family businesses.

In the latter half of the twentieth century, immigrants not only from China but also from Korea, Vietnam, India, and many other Asian countries came to the United States. Family businesses, especially in the food sector, continued to offer opportunities for financial success. Although the United States increasingly was by then becoming a country of large conglomerate commercial enterprises, Asian immigrant families still managed to find success in starting ethnic-based enterprises.

Early immigrants from Mexico and other Latin American countries, like the Asian and European immigrants, settled in large cities and established ethnic neighborhoods. These neighborhoods provided the opportunity for successful family businesses that served the needs of the communities. During the later years of the twentieth century and the early years of the twenty-first century, many Hispanic immigrants, especially from Mexico, also settled in rural areas in which Hispanic populations were smaller and more dispersed. However, as the United States has continued to evolve into a multicultural society, families in these immigrant communities have found many opportunities to establish restaurants and food stores that provide the traditional foods of their native countries.

CHANGING TRENDS

During the early history of U.S. immigration, family structures were not significantly changed within families that worked together in businesses. However, by mid-twentieth century, the roles that parents and children assumed in these businesses began to have a significant impact on family relationships. For example, children of non-English-speaking immigrants began to play more important roles in the businesses as parents relied increasingly on the children's better English-language skills. The American-educated children assumed more of the tasks requiring interaction with clientele and vendors. Consequently, the parent-child roles within many immigrant families have undergone reversals, with the younger generation taking greater control.

By opening family businesses, immigrants have played an important role in the development of the American business sector. Although immigrant businesses were originally staffed predominantly by family members, many of them evolved into large enterprises that have employed large workforces. As family businesses have grown, they have offered employment opportunities to other immigrants, particularly those in the same ethnic groups as the owners of the businesses.

While various immigrant groups were instrumental in the creation of a broad range of business activity such as the garment industry, trucking and manufacturing, immigrant family business has been the most visible as a factor in the food service business. Ethnic restaurants have become an integral part of the American landscape.

Shawncey Webb

FURTHER READING

Aldrich, Howard, Robert Ward, and Roger Waldinger, eds. *Ethnic Entrepreneurs: Immigrant Business in Industrial Societies*. n.p.: BookSurge Publishing, 2006. Self-published new edition of a book originally issued by Sage Publishing in 1990. Collection of studies of influences on the establishment of businesses by immigrants around the world and the forces affecting their transformations. Two chapters address ethnic businesses in the United States.

Chang, Iris. *The Chinese in America: A Narrative History*. New York: Viking Press, 2003. Very good source for Chinese immigrant history with interesting stories about Chinese family businesses.

Colli, Andrea. *The History of Family Business, 1850-2000*. New York: Cambridge University Press, 2002. Not limited to immigrant family businesses but an excellent discussion of what a family business is.

Liu, Haiming. *The Transnational History of a Chinese Family: Immigrant Letters, Family Business, and Reverse Migration*. New Brunswick, N.J.: Rutgers University Press, 2005. Excellent study of an immigrant family in business throughout several generations. Examines asparagus farming as a family business.

Portes, Alejandro, and Rubén G. Rumbaut. *Immigrant America: A Portrait*. 3d ed. Berkeley: University of California Press, 2006. This book does not specifically focus on family business but does discuss immigrants in relation to the American economy and presents a good general view of the immigrant experience in the United States.

Rath, Jan. *Immigrant Business: The Economic, Political and Social Environment*. New York: Palgrave Macmillan, 2000. Explores factors that enable some immigrant businesses to become part of the mainstream economy and why economic, political, and social factors cause others to remain outside the mainstream.

Vo, Linda Trinh, and Roger Bonus, eds. *Contemporary Asian American Communities: Intersections and Divergences*. Philadelphia: Temple University Press, 2002. Excellent study of the Asian community in America and how it has changed. Chapter 10 addresses the important role of children in Asian family businesses.

SEE ALSO: Alien land laws; California gold rush; Chinatowns; Chinese Exclusion Act of 1882; Chinese laundries; Economic opportunities; Families; Foodways; Garment industry; San Francisco.

FARM AND MIGRANT WORKERS

DEFINITION: Mostly seasonal agricultural workers, many of whom are temporary immigrants

SIGNIFICANCE: The supply of farm labor has become one of the most significant issues in

U.S. immigration policy. During the early twenty-first century, the U.S. Department of Labor's National Agricultural Worker Survey reported that 77 percent of all workers on American crop farms had been born abroad, that almost half the foreign-born workers had been in the United States for fewer than five years, and that more than half were not legally authorized to work in the United States.

Commercial farms in the western United States have long depended on workers from other countries. Most foreign farmworkers stay only long enough to earn target amounts of money and then return to their home countries. Some do remain in the United States, but their American-educated children rarely follow their parents into the fields. Consequently, much of the American agricultural industry has remained on a immigration treadmill, needing constantly to recruit new foreign workers willing to accept seasonal jobs.

Farmworkers have loomed large in U.S. immigration debates. During the mid-twentieth century, the U.S. government two made exceptions to policies blocking the entry of low-skilled foreigners in order to admit Mexican farmworker in the braccro programs. The first program brought legal Mexican workers to southwestern American farms between 1917 and 1921, a migration that afterward continued practically unimpeded, despite the formation of the U.S. Border Patrol in 1923. The second program admitted almost five million Mexican workers between 1942 and 1964 and established networks between rural Mexico and rural America that afterward continued to draw Mexican farmworkers north.

From the mid-1990's into the early twenty-first century, about one-half of workers employed on American crop farms have not been legally authorized to work in the United States. After 2000, both farm employers and worker advocates agreed that the best way to deal with unauthorized workers in agriculture would be to legalize their immigration status and simultaneously make it easier for farmers to hire temporary foreign workers legally. In 2006, a bill called the Agricultural Job Opportunity Benefits and Security Act (AgJOBS) was included in the comprehensive immigration reform bill approved by the U.S. Senate in May, 2006. However, it was rejected in June, 2007. While running for president in 2008, Barack Obama endorsed AgJOBS, but no progress was made in getting the bill passed during the first year of his administration, largely because of resistance from opponents of giving amnesty to undocumented immigrants.

WAVES OF IMMIGRANTS

During the late nineteenth century, as irrigation transformed the valleys of the western states into open-air greenhouses that produced fruits and vegetables, finding enough people to work the fields became a problem. Most leaders expected some of the immigrants then coming to the United States from eastern and southern Europe to travel by rail to California and other western states to become family farmers. Some did; however, most of the farmworkers in western states during the late nineteenth century were immigrants who were barred from most nonfarm employment. These included Chinese immigrants who had helped to construct the transcontinental railroad, only to be driven out of cities afterward.

Chinese workers were willing to work seasonally because they had few other options. The fact that they were paid low wages and were paid only when they worked kept costs of agricultural production down and increased the value of farmland. This made it more difficult for European immigrants who entered the West on the railroad to buy land so they could become family farmers. Most of the large farms established by land grants and speculation during the gold rush era were not broken up into family-sized units. Instead, large-scale farmers who had cooperated in the development of irrigation facilities and in dealings with railroad monopolies also cooperated to find new sources of foreign workers. After the Chinese Exclusion Act of 1882 virtually stopped Chinese immigration, the American farmers turned to Japan. They attracted thousands of Japanese farmworkers to California, until the so-called Gentlemen's Agreement of 1907 between the United States and Japan stopped Japanese immigration.

During World War I, farmers persuaded the U.S. government to exempt Mexicans from restrictions imposed by the Immigration Act of 1917 to slow European immigration. On May 23, 1917, the U.S. Department of Labor, which then included the Bureau of Immigration, approved the request of western farmers "to admit temporarily otherwise inadmissible aliens" to work in agriculture and on railroads. This began the first bracero program. Under this program, almost 80,000 Mexican farmworkers came to the United States before the program was halted in 1921. Most of these people worked in cotton and sugar beet fields.

In 1931, as the Great Depression was worsening, many Mexicans who had settled in the United States were sent back to Mexico in order to open jobs for American workers. The reduction of Mexican workers in the West and dust bowl conditions in midwestern states brought a new wave of migrant farmworkers to the western states. For the first time, most newcomers to the western agricultural labor force were English-speaking American citizens. Their experiences as seasonal farmworkers would be memorialized in John Steinbeck's 1939 novel, *The Grapes of Wrath*. That book and the film adapted from it helped provide an emotional impetus for farm labor reforms.

Farm labor reformers were divided between those such as University of California economist Paul Taylor, who wanted to break up big farms and turn farmworkers into small farmers, and those such as writer Carey McWilliams, who wanted the U.S. government to recognize large farms as open-air factories and apply factory labor laws to them. Taylor opposed treating agriculture as other industries. Perhaps ironically, he was the husband of photographer Dorothea Lange, whose famous "Migrant Mother" photograph famously captured the desperate poverty of Depression-era migrant farmworkers.

Mexican farmworkers leaving Chihuahua City, Mexico, to work in the bracero program in Texas during the 1950's. (AP/ Wide World Photos)

The standoff among farm labor reformers met strong opposition from farmers who opposed both land reform and labor laws. Meanwhile, American entry into World War II in 1941 set the stage for a new bracero program to supply farmworkers as Americans mobilized for war. The new program began on a small scale during the war years but eventually expanded to admit almost 500,000 Mexican workers a year into the United States during the 1950's. Operation Wetback slowed unauthorized migration in 1954-1955, so the federal government made it easier for farmers to hire legal bracero workers.

UNIONIZATION OF FARMWORKERS

In 1964, the U.S. Congress ended the bracero program, convinced that bracero workers were holding down wages and retarding opportunities for American farmworkers. That view appeared to be vindicated in 1966, when the Mexican American farmworker César Chávez took over the leadership of a Filipino grape pickers' union, which he helped win a 40 percent wage increase for grape harvesters. The union succeeded, in part, because bracero workers were not available to break strikes.

Chávez then helped found the United Farm Workers (UFW) union, which flourished through the next fifteen years, while unauthorized immigration remained low. In 1975, the union's mostly Mexican American members persuaded the state of California to enact an agricultural labor law that applied factory labor laws to farms, as Carey McWilliams had proposed doing during the 1930's. Under UFW contracts, entry-level wages for farmworkers rose to twice the level of federal minimum wages during the late 1970's. Some people predicted that unionization would sweep American agriculture, making the UFW one of the largest American labor unions. However, a combination of factors reduced the power of the UFW during the 1980's; one was rising rates of unauthorized immigration. There were few federal sanctions on the hiring of undocumented immigrants until passage of the federal Immigration Reform and Control Act (IRCA) of 1986 was enacted. Some farmers tired of dealing with UFW demands encouraged their Mexican supervisors to become labor contractors by recruiting friends and relatives in Mexico. As these labor contractors began supplying more workers to farms, the UFW supplied fewer.

UFW leaders thought that the 1986 immigration reform law would strengthen their union as previously undocumented immigrant workers would become union supporters in return for union assistance. However, the UFW helped only a few of the one million foreigners whose immigration status was legalized the 1986 law's agricultural provisions. The new upsurge of unauthorized immigration that accompanied IRCA doomed union efforts to raise wages. IRCA's legalization provisions allowed one-sixth of the adult men in rural Mexico to work in the United States legally, but it did not provide for the workers' families. Framers of the act evidently hoped that the Mexican workers would be satisfied to commute between their Mexican homes and the American farms, but this view proved wrong. During the recession of 1990-1991, many of the Mexicans whose immigration status had been legalized under IRCA brought their families in the United States, thereby increasing public costs for schooling, health care, and other serves. The resulting anti-immigrant backlash among citizens in California helped spur a state ballot initiative called Proposition 187, which California voters approved by a wide margin in November, 1994. Had not implementation of Proposition 187 been blocked by the courts, the measure would have created a state-funded system to ensure that undocumented immigrants did not gain access to state-funded services.

By the time of César Chávez's death in 1993, UFW membership had fallen to less than 10 percent of its 70,000-member peak of the early 1970's. Competition with undocumented immigrant farmworkers encouraged American farmworkers to look for jobs in nonagricultural sectors. Meanwhile, the children of both legal and unauthorized farmworkers educated in the United States did not follow their parents into the fields, contributing to the dependence of American farmers on fresh immigrants from abroad.

IMMIGRATION REFORM

IRCA helped to spread immigrant farmworkers throughout the United States, eventually making Mexican-born farmworkers almost as common in states such as Iowa and North Carolina as in California. Farmers acknowledged that many of the workers they hired were undocumented and lobbied Congress to create a new guest-worker program during the mid-1990's. However, farmworker advocates persuaded Congress not to approve such a program. Their hand was strengthened by President Bill Clinton, who issued a statement in June, 1995, expression his opposition to any program that would bring thousands of foreign workers into the United States for temporary farm labor.

The pattern of farmworker advocates blocking farm employer requests for a new guest worker program continued through the year 2000. In response to the election of Mexican president Vincente Fox and U.S. president George W. Bush during that year, worker advocates and employers agreed to repeat the IRCA agricultural provisions, which legalized unauthorized farmworkers and made it easier for farm employers to obtain legal guest workers. The IRCA guest-worker provisions were not used because so many unauthorized workers were available.

The AgJOBS bill embodying the compromise between workers and employers was reintroduced repeatedly after 2000 but was unsuccessful despite strong bipartisan support. As a counter to AgJOBS, George W. Bush's administration proposed a new guest-worker program, called H-2A, as it prepared to leave office in early 2009, despite objections from incoming President Barack Obama and Democratic leaders in Congress. The revised H-2A program achieved many of the changes sought by farm employers in AgJOBS, but without legalizing undocumented immigrants.

U.S. immigration and enforcement policies have played a major role in determining the composition of the agricultural workforce and the wages of farmworkers. Farmworkers have continued to be mostly relatively recent arrivals from abroad. Most of them have seen working for wages on American farms as their first step up the American job ladder. Few immigrant farmworkers who have remained in the United States have been able to rise to the middle class. Their hope has been that their children, educated in the United States, will eventually achieve the upward mobility that originally drew them to the United States.

Philip L. Martin

FURTHER READING

Ganz, Marshall. *Why David Sometimes Wins: Leadership, Organization, and Strategy in the California Farm Worker Movement.* New York: Oxford University Press, 2009. A former UFW organizer, Ganz credits the UFW's "strategic capacity" for winning contracts with grape and lettuce growers during the late 1960's, using marches, fasts, boycotts, and espousing nonviolence to win the struggle with growers. He credits Chávez for union victories during the 1960's and 1970's but also blames him for the union's decline during the 1980's.

Gonzalez, Gilbert G. *Guest Workers or Colonized Labor? Mexican Labor Migration to the United States.* Boulder, Colo.: Paradigm, 2005. Historical study of Mexican farmworkers in the United States that examines the subject in the context of American dominance over Mexico.

Martin, Philip. *Importing Poverty? Immigration and the Changing Face of Rural America.* New Haven, Conn.: Yale University Press, 2009. An up-to-date study of the employment of foreign-born workers in American agriculture, this volume explores the effects of such workers in selected states, assessing efforts to enact immigration reforms between 2000 and 2009.

_____. *Promise Unfulfilled: Unions, Immigration, and Farm Workers.* Ithaca, N.Y.: Cornell University Press, 2003. One of the fullest studies of the rise and fall of the UFW, this volume stresses that the changing structure of agriculture and rising unauthorized migration in the 1980's were likely more important than changing UFW leadership and the shift from Democrats to Republicans in making appointments to California's Agricultural Labor Relations Board.

Nahmias, Rick. *The Migrant Project: Contemporary California Farm Workers.* Albuquerque: University of New Mexico Press, 2008. Richly illustrated book capturing the lives and labors of modern migrant farmworkers.

Pawel, Miriam. *The Union of Their Dreams: Power, Hope, and Struggle in César Chávez's Farm Worker Movement.* New York: Bloomsbury Press, 2009. History of the UFW emphasizing the union's decline after the early 1980's. Also explores links among the many UFW organizations run by Chávez's children and relatives.

Shaw, Randy. *Beyond the Fields: César Chávez, the UFW, and the Struggle for Justice in the Twenty-first Century.* Berkeley: University of California Press, 2008. Study of the UFW emphasizing the union's importance as a training school for a generation of activists.

SEE ALSO: Bracero program; California; El Paso incident; Filipino immigrants; Guest-worker programs; Labor unions; Mexican deportations of 1931; Mexican immigrants; Texas; United Farm Workers.

FEDERATION FOR AMERICAN IMMIGRATION REFORM

IDENTIFICATION: Nonprofit organization dedicated to preventing high levels of immigration to the United States
DATE: Established on January 2, 1979
ALSO KNOWN AS: FAIR

SIGNIFICANCE: Recognized as the leading anti-immigration group in the United States, the Federation for American Immigration Reform (FAIR) has received support from numerous celebrities and politicians and claims membership from both conservative and liberal party supporters, whose donations make possible the high visibility FAIR receives through its many advertising campaigns. FAIR specifically supports improving the security of America's borders, documenting all noncitizen residents, and implementing a documentation-verification system.

A nonprofit, nonpartisan organization, FAIR was started by John Tanton, the founder of several anti-immigration groups in the United States. He built FAIR upon the principle that high levels of immigration increase overpopulation and pollution that damage the environment. FAIR also maintains that high immigration hurts the national economy by raising unemployment levels due to the influx of job candidates. FAIR has consistently condemned companies that have hired undocumented workers, who FAIR charge take jobs that should go to American citizens. In addition, FAIR maintains that the welfare system has been flooded due to the congestion of workers and lack of jobs.

GOALS

FAIR's purpose is not to halt immigration completely, but to reduce its rate to about 30 percent of its current annual levels. It has outlined a number of principles for immigration reform:

- limiting immigration rates
- rejecting amnesty and guest-worker programs
- setting minimum wages for jobs—such as those in agribusiness—that draw undocumented immigrants
- penalizing employers who hire illegal immigrants
- restricting offers of asylum
- increasing border patrols

FAIR'S opposition to certain immigration reform proposals has contributed the defeat of some measures in Congress. A notable example was the so-called H1B Visa program, which was designed to attract more high-technology workers during the 1990's. Arguing that high-tech companies wished to hire foreign workers only because they could be paid cheaper wages, FAIR led a campaign to defeat this bill. FAIR also complained that the bill had no stipulation requiring companies to hire American workers first, which would have meant that Americans might lose out on high-paying jobs to cheaper foreign workers.

FAIR has also supported other congressional bills that have not been made into law. Its Web site reports regularly on current immigration legislation, including a call by the organization's president, Dan Stein, urging Congress to pass H.R. 1940, the Birthright Citizenship Act of 2007. This bill sought to eliminate the automatic granting of U.S. citizenship to all persons born in the United States, regardless of their parents' legal status. Stein supported the proposal on the grounds that it would eliminate the problem of "anchor babies," a derogatory term for children born in the United States to illegal immigrants. The bill sought to amend immigration law to grant citizen status only to children born with at least one parent who was a U.S. citizen. The bill was introduced in the House of Representatives in April, 2007, but was never moved to a vote in either the House or the Senate.

CRITICISMS OF FAIR

FAIR has faced its share of controversies, particularly criticisms that it has used racist and unfair tactics in its ad campaigns. For example, the group's inflammatory attack on Michigan senator Spencer Abraham was condemned as a smear cam-

---

FAIR WEB SITE

FAIR maintains a large and frequently updated presence on the World Wide Web. Its official Web site, at www.fairus.org, provides up-to-date commentaries on immigration bills under consideration in the U.S. Congress and offers detailed analyses of current immigration issues and how they affect different facets of American life, from national security and jobs to environmental issues. One of the site's many features is a time line called "Chronology of Terror," which provides a year-by-year analysis, since 1990, of how known international terrorists have taken advantage of residence in the United States before committing violent acts abroad and within U.S. borders.

---

paign when it displayed a picture of Abraham standing alongside the al-Qaeda leader Osama bin Laden, while denouncing him for his efforts to block Section 110 of the Enhanced Border Security and Visa Reform Act of 2001. That section proposed the creation of a database for all border entry points that would record the arrivals and departures of all noncitizens. Senator Abraham claimed that this would cause undue delays at the already congested borders, particularly in his own state of Michigan, where delays of two-four hours at the Detroit-Windsor border were common. When Abraham was up for reelection against FAIR's founder John Tanton in 2000, FAIR ran advertisements opposing him. These ads depicted Abraham, who happens to be of Lebanese Arab descent, as a terrorist supporter.

Tanton himself has been labeled a racist, and FAIR was classified as a hate group by the Southern Poverty Law Center in 2007. Other organizations that Tanton has founded include NumbersUSA, a body with the same basic objectives as FAIR. He also founded the Social Contract Press, a publishing company that specializes in anti-immigration books.

FAIR has also come under attack for its receipt of donations from the Pioneer Fund, an organization that supports eugenics research. Other criticisms have been aimed at remarks made by Dan Stein, which have been labeled anti-Catholic and xenophobic. FAIR has also been criticized for utilizing scare tactics in its campaign advertisements, which indicate that the level of immigration is so dangerously high that it might threaten America's ability to survive.

Shannon Oxley

FURTHER READING

Baumgarten, Gerald. *Is FAIR Unfair? The Federation of American Immigration Reform (FAIR)*. New York: Anti-Defamation League, 2000. Fifteen-page report offering an objective analysis of FAIR policies. Available in PDF format on the Anti-Defamation League's Web site, www.adl.org.

Jones, Maldwyn A. *American Immigration*. 2d ed. Chicago: University of Chicago Press, 1992. Impartial historical summary of immigration in the United States.

Riley, Jason L. *Let Them In: The Case for Open Borders*. New York: Gotham Books, 2008. Offers rebuttals to anti-immigrationists and argues for a practice of regulating cross-border labor flows rather than stopping them and maintains that the United States has more to gain than to lose from immigrants seeking a better life.

SEE ALSO: Eugenics movement; Immigration Reform and Control Act of 1986; Language issues; Refugees; Welfare and social services.

FEDORENKO V. UNITED STATES

THE CASE: U.S. Supreme Court decision concerning denaturalization

DATE: Decided on January 21, 1981

> **SIGNIFICANCE:** The *Fedorenko* decision established that the citizenship of a naturalized citizen may be revoked in cases when individuals intentionally provided false information to enter the country or to obtain materialization.

Following World War II, Feodor Fedorenko, who was born in Ukraine, obtained a visa to enter the United States under the Displaced Persons Act of 1948 (DPA), which did not apply to anyone who had voluntarily assisted the enemy or had participated in persecuting civilians. Fedorenko became a naturalized citizen in 1970. A decade later, witnesses testified that he had concealed his service as an armed guard at Treblinka, a Nazi extermination camp, and that he had committed atrocities against inmates. Fedorenko claimed that the German army had forced him to serve in the camp, although he admitted that he had never tried to escape. The government brought denaturalization action under the Immigration and Nationality Act of 1952, which requires revocation of citizenship that was procured by "willful misrepresentation." Ruling in favor of Fedorenko, the district court held that because his service in the camp had been involuntary, his misrepresentation was not material to his admission.

Reversing the ruling by a 7-2 margin, the Supreme Court ordered Fedorenko's denaturalization based on the fact that the language of the DPA made him ineligible to receive a visa. Speaking for the majority, Justice Thurgood Marshall criticized the district court for ignoring the clear and explicit wording of the DPA. Once the district court determined that either immigration or naturalization had resulted from willful misrepresentation, it had no discretion to excuse Fedorenko's conduct. The DPA, moreover, referred to the objective fact of persecuting others, so that even if he had acted under duress, the DPA would not have allowed him to enter the country. In 1984, Fedorenko was deported to the Soviet Union, where he was executed by a firing squad two years later.

Thomas Tandy Lewis

FURTHER READING

Bosniak, Linda. *The Citizen and the Alien: Dilemmas of Contemporary Membership.* Princeton, N.J.: Princeton University Press, 2008.

LeMay, Michael, and Elliott Robert Barkan, eds. *U.S. Immigration and Naturalization Laws and Issues: A Documentary History.* Westport, Conn.: Greenwood Press, 1999.

SEE ALSO: Citizenship; Congress, U.S.; Constitution, U.S.; Deportation; Displaced Persons Act of 1948; Holocaust; Immigration law; World War II.

FENIAN MOVEMENT

THE EVENTS: Series of violent, revolutionary, and ultimately unsuccessful struggles against British control of Ireland that were transatlantic in scope
DATE: 1848-1867
LOCATION: New York, Canada, Ireland, and Great Britain
ALSO KNOWN AS: Irish Revolutionary Brotherhood (IRB)

SIGNIFICANCE: The Fenians began a secular nationalistic revolutionary tradition in Ireland that aimed at freeing Ireland from British control. The armed Fenian risings were ultimately ineffective, but they helped to inspire later nationalists. Irish immigrants in America provided men, arms and money to fight in Ireland and some even launched an invasion of British Canada.

The Fenian movement was founded in Dublin, Ireland, on St. Patrick's Day in March, 1848. The American Fenian movement emerged one year later in New York City. The organization took its name from a legendary ancient Irish warrior. Two recent events inspired the movement: the failed rebellion of a group called Young Ireland in 1848 and the sufferings caused by the Great Irish Famine of the 1840's. Members of the movement, who were predominantly Roman Catholic, believed that only armed resistance could free Ireland from British rule. However, the Roman Catholic Church itself disapproved of the movement because of its reliance upon violence and because of its opposition to secret societies in general. Consequently, the movement began a secular tradition in Irish nationalist movements.

The movement operated clandestinely, drawing on Continental revolutionary models, with secret cells. Nevertheless, British-paid spies often penetrated the movement. The public side of the movement was aided by publication of a popular radical newspaper and large gatherings at important funerals in Ireland. By 1864, the Fenians had at least 50,000 members in Ireland and similar numbers in North America.

Fenians in the United States were asked to furnish money, arms, and men for the struggle in Ire-

Battle between Fenians and a Canadian militia unit near Ridgeway, Ontario, on June 2, 1866. (Library of Congress)

land and to organize an attack on British Canada. After the U.S. Civil War ended in 1865, American Fenians were able to provide legions of experienced military officers and soldiers from recently demobilized Irish immigrant veterans of the war. However, the Fenian schemes were hampered by factional bickering that rose within the American movement. Many Fenian leaders shuttled between Ireland and New York. Almost one-half of the most prominent thirty-nine Fenian leaders emigrated to the United States, either permanently or temporarily.

Meanwhile, relations between the governments of the United States and Canada had still not recovered from American anger at the Confederate incursions from Canada into New England during the Civil War. Consequently, when armed Fenians preparing to invade Canada massed along Vermont's Canadian border and the Niagara Falls region in 1866, U.S. authorities were not firm in restraining them.

The grandiose plan of the Fenians was to use Irish veterans of the U.S. Civil War to seize all of Canada and hold it hostage until Great Britain recognized Irish independence. About 1,500 armed Irishmen actually did cross the Niagara River into Canada in June, 1866. They were met by Canadian militia, who gave battle before fleeing. This single battle left about twenty Canadians and Fenians dead. Soon, the Fenians themselves fled. Those who returned into New York State were promptly arrested. They were equally promptly released, as the Irish vote was important in New York politics.

The Fenians attempted several risings in Ireland that were aborted by informed British authorities. The most notable Fenian rising during the nineteenth century occurred in Ireland in 1867, but it failed when a ship bringing arms and men from the United States arrived too late to assist rebels attempting to seize a cache of British arms. The Fenian leaders involved in the scheme were arrested. Afterward, only scattered guerrilla fighting broke out in Ireland.

During the twentieth century the Fenian devotion to violence and guerrilla warfare would serve as examples for the generation that did wrest Irish independence from Britain. The famous Easter Rebellion of 1916 has been cited as the Fenian underground surfacing once more.

Henry G. Weisser

FURTHER READING

Coohill, Joseph. *Ireland: A Short History.* 3d ed. Oxford, England: Oneworld Publications, 2008.

Fry, Peter, and Fiona Somerset. *A History of Ireland.* New York: Routledge, 1991.

Kee, Robert. *The Green Flag: A History of Irish Nationalism.* New York: Penguin Books, 2000.

Welch, Richard F. "The Green and the Blue." *Civil War Times* (October, 2006): 22-30.

SEE ALSO: Anti-Catholicism; Great Irish Famine; History of immigration, 1783-1891; Irish immigrants; Molly Maguires; New York City; New York State.

FIANCÉES ACT OF 1946

THE LAW: Federal legislation permitting American servicemen to bring their foreign-born fiancés into the United States
DATE: Enacted on June 29, 1946
ALSO KNOWN AS: G.I. Fiancées Act

SIGNIFICANCE: An extension of another piece of post-World War II legislation, the War Brides Act of 1945, the Fiancées Act granted the fiancés of American servicemen a special exemption from previously established immigration quotas that allowed them to enter the United States.

Following the War Brides Act of 1945, which allowed foreign spouses and children of American servicemen to enter the United States without regard to previously established immigration quotas, the U.S. Congress passed the Fiancées Act on June 29, 1946, extending immigration exemption to foreign women engaged to marry American soldiers.

In 1946, nearly 45,000 foreign-born women entered the United States under the provisions of this act. However, foreign-born fiancés who did not marry the American men who sponsored them after arriving in America were subject to deportation. Most women who immigrated in this manner were of European origin, from nations such as Great Britain, France, and Italy. However, many women of Asian origin also entered the United States under the provisions of this act, including large numbers of Chinese, Japanese, and Filipino women who would have been otherwise unable to immigrate due to strict quotas on Asian immigration. The act was scheduled to expire on July 1, 1947, but was extended to December 31, 1948, after which those with pending applications were allowed five months to enter the United States.

Aaron D. Horton

FURTHER READING

Bankston, Carl L., and Danielle Antoinette Hidalgo, eds. *Immigration in U.S. History.* 2 vols. Pasadena, Calif.: Salem Press, 2006.

Hutchinson, E. P. *Legislative History of American Immigration Policy, 1789-1965.* Philadelphia: University of Pennsylvania Press, 1981.

Lowe, Lisa. *Immigrant Acts: On Asian American Cultural Politics.* Durham, N.C.: Duke University Press, 1994.

SEE ALSO: Green cards; Intermarriage; Mail-order brides; Marriage; "Marriages of convenience"; Picture brides; Quota systems; War brides; War Brides Act of 1945; Women immigrants; World War II.

FILIPINO AMERICAN PRESS

DEFINITION: Newspapers, magazines, and other printed materials published within the United States for Filipino American and Filipino immigrant readers

SIGNIFICANCE: Filipino American newspapers and magazines have featured stories not only about Filipinos living in the United States but also about events of interest in the Philippines, demonstrating the desire among many Filipino Americans to stay connected with their ancestral homeland. These publications help foster a sense of community empowerment and collective identity among Americans of Filipino descent.

Since the 1920's, numerous periodicals have been produced by and for the Filipino American community, providing news of particular interest to Filipino immigrants, while fostering a sense of collective identity and cultural pride. One of the first Filipino American publications, the *Philippine Mail*, circulated among the immigrant community in California during the 1920's and 1930's, providing stories of interest about Filipinos living in the United States and elsewhere.

NEWSPAPERS

From his San Francisco garage, Alex Esclamado began publishing *The Manila Chronicle*, named after a publication banned at the time by dictator Ferdinand Marcos in the Philippines, in 1961. His weekly publication later became the *Philippine News* and developed into one of the most widely read Filipino American newspapers in the United States. It provides a broad array of original content dealing with such issues as immigration, health, and culture, as well as news from the Philippines.

In 1972, Libertito Pelayo, a former reporter for *The Manila Times*, founded the *Filipino Reporter*, a weekly based in New York City. This paper has provided news and editorials on a variety of subjects, including politics, immigration, sports, and entertainment. The *Philippine News* and the *Filipino Reporter* have become the most widely known and distributed Filipino American newspapers, but numerous smaller publications have also served the Filipino American community. Due to California's large number of Filipino immigrants, the state is home to the majority of these publications, which include the *Filipino Guardian*, the *Asian American People's Journal*, and *Manila Mail*. Newspapers in other regions include the *Filipino-American Bulletin* in Washington, D.C., the *Hawaii-Filipino Chronicle* in Hawaii, *The Filipino Express* in New Jersey, and *Basta Pinoy* in Florida. Most Filipino American newspapers also provide online editions, and many are online-only.

MAGAZINES

Although not as numerous as newspapers, several magazines also cater to the Filipino American community. Early examples have included *The Republic*, published in California between 1924 and 1933, and the Seattle-based *The Filipino Forum*. During the first decade of the twenty-first century, the most widely known and distributed Filipino American magazine was *Filipinas*, a monthly based in Cali-

fornia that began publication in Ma, 1992. Mona Lisa Yuchengco, the magazine's founder and a prominent activist in the Filipino American community, claimed during a 2003 interview in the *San Francisco Chronicle* that she founded the magazine not only because she "wanted Filipinos to have pride in who they were as a people, where they came from, their culture and heritage" but also in order to "pass on that pride to non-Filipinos who wanted to know more about us." *Filipinas* offers a wide range of articles dealing with many aspects of Filipino American life, including history, business, entertainment, food, travel, and immigration issues. Another notable magazine is *Poptimes*, an online-only publication dedicated to covering Filipino American music, with articles, artist bios, album reviews, and concert schedules.

Aaron D. Horton

FURTHER READING

Bautista, Veltisezar. *The Filipino Americans from 1763 to the Present: Their History, Culture, and Traditions.* Farmington Hills, Mich.: Bookhaus, 1998.

Root, Maria P. P., ed. *Filipino Americans: Transformation and Identity.* Thousand Oaks, Calif.: Sage Publications, 1997.

Sterngrass, Jon. *Filipino Americans (The New Immigrants Series).* New York: Chelsea House, 2007.

SEE ALSO: Asian American literature; Asian immigrants; Chinese American press; Cultural pluralism; Family businesses; Filipino immigrants; Japanese American press; Television and radio.

FILIPINO IMMIGRANTS

SIGNIFICANCE: During the late twentieth century, Filipinos became one of the fastest-growing immigrant populations in the United States. By the early twenty-first century, they constituted the third-largest Asian immigrant group in the United States, after Asian Indians and Chinese, and could be found living throughout the North American continent.

Although most immigration from the Philippines to the United States occurred during the twentieth century, the earliest identifiable Filipino immigrants arrived in America during the 1830's. At that time, hunters and trappers of Filipino origin settled in the region of Louisiana below New Orleans, which was then the busiest port in the United States after New York City. At that time, the Philippine Islands were a Spanish colony, and these first Filipino immigrants appear to have reached New Orleans on Spanish ships. As late as the 1930's, descendants of these early Filipino immigrants, popularly known as "Manila men," maintained a settlement along the mouth of the Mississippi River and supported themselves by shrimping, fur-trapping, and fishing.

AMERICAN INVOLVEMENT IN THE PHILIPPINES

At the end of the nineteenth century, the Philippines came under the political dominance of the United States, a development that would eventually contribute to a large Filipino American population. When the United States fought Spain in the Spanish-American War in 1898, Filipino rebels were engaged in their own war against their Spanish rulers. When Assistant Secretary of the Navy Theodore Roosevelt ordered the U.S. Navy to attack the Spanish at Manila, the Philippines' capital, the United States established contact with Filipino insurgents. After the United States defeated Spain, the U.S. government did not withdraw its armed forces from the occupied former Spanish colonies, which included the Philippines, Cuba, and Guam. Instead, the United States sent troops to the Philippines to subjugate Filipinos unwilling to accept American rule, and the United States set up its own colonial government.

U.S. governor-general William Howard Taft, who later became president of the United States, was among many Americans who believed that educational programs could help to direct the development of the Philippines and establish ties between the United States and its new colonial subjects. American teachers were sent to the Philippines, and Filipino students known as *pensionados* were brought to the United States. About 14,000 government-subsidized Filipino students studied in the United States between 1903 and 1938.

PUSH-PULL FACTORS

During the decade following the arrival of the first *pensionados*, Filipino immigration to the United States increased dramatically. The Filipino

PROFILE OF FILIPINO IMMIGRANTS

Country of origin	Philippines
Primary language	Tagalog, English
Primary regions of U.S. settlement	West Coast, Hawaii
Earliest significant arrivals	1830's
Peak immigration period	1965-2008
Twenty-first century legal residents*	469,033 (58,629 per year)

*Immigrants who obtained legal permanent resident status in the United States.
Source: Department of Homeland Security, *Yearbook of Immigration Statistics, 2008.*

American population increased from fewer than 3,000 persons in 1910 to more than 26,000 in 1920 and more than 100,000 in 1930. These new immigrants were drawn to America primarily by the demand for labor.

During the early twentieth century, American industry grew rapidly and agriculture increasingly became a large-scale enterprise, requiring growing numbers of hired workers. Farming became more regionally specialized as advances in refrigeration and transportation made it practical to grow fruits and vegetables on large regional farms for export to distant parts of the United States. To meet the need for labor, farmers in California and canning factories in Alaska began recruiting Filipino workers. In 1920, the West Coast of the United States alone was home to an estimated 5,600 Filipinos. By 1930, this number had grown to 45,372. Filipino migrant workers provided much of the seasonal labor for fruit and vegetable farms in California, Oregon, and Washington, where they harvested asparagus, grapes, strawberries, carrots, lettuce, potatoes, and beets.

Hawaii, then an American territory, was the destination for many Filipino agricultural workers. American sugarcane planters in Hawaii rapidly expanded their exports during the first decade of the twentieth century and needed workers for the fields. In 1906, A. F. Judd, an attorney representing the Hawaii Sugar Planters Association (HSPA) arrived in the Philippines to recruit workers for the sugarcane fields and to make the legal arrangements to bring them to Hawaii. However, relatively few agricultural workers left the Philippines for Hawaii until 1909. During that year, unrest among the Japanese, who until then had made up the majority of laborers in the Hawaiian sugarcane fields, prompted plantation owners and managers to increase their recruiting efforts among Filipinos. When Japanese plantation workers went on strike, Hawaiian planters concluded that they needed a new and more easily controlled labor source.

The peoples of the Philippines speak many different languages, although there are a few widely spoken major languages, such as Tagalog, Ilocano, and several closely related dialects of Visayan. The linguistic diversity among the Filipino immigrants helped the Hawaii planters to avoid the labor problems they had experienced with the linguistically homogeneous Japanese. By being careful to recruit workers from different regions of the Philippines, they limited communication among Filipino field-workers. Between 1909 and 1914, about

4,000 Filipinos made the voyage from the Philippines to Hawaii each year. Their numbers decreased after 1915, when the Philippine legislature passed laws regulating the recruitment and treatment of Filipino workers. The numbers picked up again during the 1920's, however. By 1925, around half of all plantation workers in Hawaii were Filipinos. By the early 1930's, Filipinos made up about three-fourths of all Hawaii plantation workers.

FROM THE 1930's TO 1965

The wave of Filipino immigrant labor to the United States that began in the first decade of the twentieth century became a trickle in 1934. During that year, the U.S. Congress passed the Tydings-McDuffie Act, which transformed the political status of the Philippines into a commonwealth—the first step toward independence for the Philippines. Under the law's provisions Filipinos were no longer considered American nationals, and immigration from the Philippines was limited to fifty persons per year. When World War II reached the Philippines in 1942, Japan occupied the Philippine

Filipino farmworkers in California during the 1930's. (Library of Congress)

Islands, bringing even this limited flow of migration to the United States to a temporary halt.

After World War II, the United States recognized the full independence of the Philippines. However, the U.S. government still maintained a presence in the Philippines that contributed to new forms of migration. In 1946, the U.S. Congress passed the Luce-Celler Bill, which increased the Philippines' immigration quota from fifty to one hundred persons per year. Spouses of U.S. citizens were not counted within this quota, however, and they became a major part of Filipino immigration. Meanwhile, the United States retained large military bases in the Philippines, ensuring an ongoing presence of large numbers of mostly male American military personnel, some of whom interacted socially with Filipino women. Many Filipino-American marriages resulted from these contacts. Between 1946 and 1965, as many as one-half of all immigrants from the Philippines arriving in the United States were wives of U.S. servicemen.

In 1948, the U.S. Congress passed the Education Exchange Act, another piece of legislation that promoted the immigration of a new category of Filipinos who would join the growing Filipino American population. The 1948 law enabled foreign nurses to spend two years in the United States for study and professional experience. Differences between American and Filipino living standards lured many Filipino nurses to remain in the United States after they completed their training, and the large demand for nurses in the United States made it relatively easy for them to find work.

POST-1965 IMMIGRATION

The 1960 U.S. Census counted 105,000 people living in the United States who had been born in the Philippines. At that moment, Filipinos constituted the second-largest immigrant group in the United States, only slightly behind immigrants born in Japan. As American restrictions on immigration from Asia were relaxed after 1965, the historical ties between the Philippines and the United States set the stage for a new wave of Filipino migration.

When Congress passed the Immigration and Nationality Act of 1965 (also known as the Hart-Celler Act), the United States adopted a new immigration policy that dropped the former quota system of immigration that had been biased in favor of immigrants from northern and western Europe.

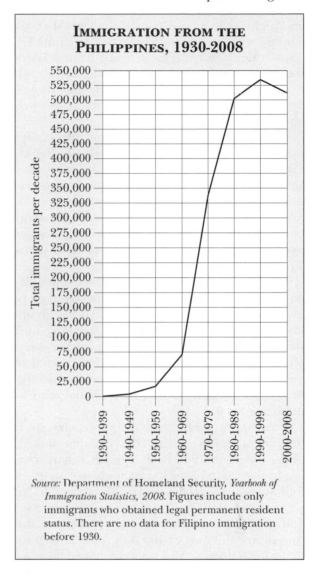

IMMIGRATION FROM THE PHILIPPINES, 1930-2008

Source: Department of Homeland Security, *Yearbook of Immigration Statistics, 2008.* Figures include only immigrants who obtained legal permanent resident status. There are no data for Filipino immigration before 1930.

The new basis for admitting immigrants was a set of preferences, with immigrants migrating to reunite with family members in the United States given the highest priority classifications, followed by immigrants with needed job skills. The new immigration policy opened immigration to the United States to many parts of the world, and the numbers of immigrants began climbing dramatically.

Thanks to the historical links between the United States and the Philippines, Filipinos were in a particularly good position to take advantage of the change in American immigration law. Because the Philippines remained a relatively low-income country—even though it had many well-educated and highly skilled people—and the United States was one of the world's most prosperous nations, Filipino interest in emigrating to the United States was great. Moreover, many potential immigrants already had skills that were in demand in the United States and some familiarity with the English language and American culture.

Many post-1965 immigrants from the Philippines were highly skilled professionals. Before 1960, fewer than 2 percent of the people of Filipino ancestry residing in the United States had professional occupations, compared to 6 percent of all Americans. By contrast, two decades later, about one-quarter of all Filipinos in the United States were professionals. By the twenty-first century, this figure had risen to nearly one-third.

The United States had a particularly strong demand for medical workers that Filipinos could supply because the American occupation of the Philippines had established American training and standards in the islands. As a consequence, nurses, physicians, medical technicians, and other medical professionals were heavily overrepresented among the occupational fields of Filipino immigrants to the United States.

Nurses, who had already begun moving from the Philippines to the United States after passage of the 1948 Education Exchange Act, began arriving in the United States in even greater numbers following the passage of the Health Professions Assistance Act in 1976. This piece of legislation required professionals to have firm job offers from American employers before they could immigrate to the United States. This law was followed by active cooperation of immigration officials with American hospitals in recruiting nurses. Again, the special historical connections between the United States and the Philippines meant that the Philippines was training nurses ready for work in the United States, making that Asian country an ideal recruiting ground for immigrants.

CHANGING PUSH-PULL FACTORS

During the 1960's, the American military presence in the Philippines continued and even grew along with American involvement in the Vietnam War. By 1980, one quarter of all married Filipino American women had husbands who had served in the U.S. military during the Vietnam War period. The popular identification of the Philippines as a source of wives also expanded into civilian American society, so that marriages arranged by mail between women in the Philippines and men in the United States were becoming common during the 1970's. By the early 1990's, an estimated 19,000 so-called mail-order brides were leaving the Philippines each year to join husbands and fiancés abroad, with the United States their primary destination.

As the Filipino American population increased, a growing number of residents of the United States had immediate relatives in the Philippines. Because the 1965 change in immigration law had made family reunification the category that allowed the most immigrants, this meant that each new immigrant opened the way for others. The result was an exponential growth in the Filipino American population throughout the last decades of the twentieth century and the first decade of the twenty-first century. In 2007, the U.S. Census Bureau estimated that 2.5 million people of Filipino descent were living in the United States, ranking Filipino Americans only slightly behind Asian Indian Americans and a little further behind Chinese Americans.

In 2007, more than 72,500 people from the Philippines were admitted to legal permanent residence in the United States, and nearly 39,000 people born in the Philippines became naturalized U.S. citizens. By this time, Filipino Americans were living in communities across the United States, but the single largest concentration could be found in California's Los Angeles-Long Beach-Santa Ana metropolitan area, in which an estimated 380,000 Filipinos resided in 2007.

Carl L. Bankston III

FURTHER READING

Bankston, Carl L. "Filipino Americans." In *Asian Americans: Contemporary Trends and Issues*. Edited by Pyong Gap Min. 2d ed. Thousand Oaks, Calif.: Pine Forge Press, 2006. Sociological survey of modern Filipino American communities throughout the United States.

Bulosan, Carlos. *American Is in the Heart: A Personal History*. 1946. Reprint. Seattle: University of Washington Press, 1974. Memoir of perhaps the best-known Filipino American writer, who came to the United States as an immigrant field-worker during the 1930's.

_____. *On Becoming Filipino: Selected Writings of Carlos Bulosan*. Edited by Epifanio San Juan, Jr. Philadelphia: Temple University Press, 1996. Additional writings by Bulosan documenting the Filipino American immigrant experience.

Espiritu, Yen Le. *Homebound: Filipino American Lives Across Cultures, Communities, and Cultures*. Berkeley: University of California Press, 2003. Study of how Filipino immigrants have adapted to American culture and society built around interviews with more than one hundred Filipino Americans.

Karnow, Stanley. *In Our Image: America's Empire in the Philippines*. New York: Random House, 1989. History of the American conquest and occupation of the Philippines and efforts to impose American culture and institutions on the island nation.

Okamura, Jonathan Y. *Imagining the Filipino American Diaspora: Transnational Relations, Identities, and Communities*. New York: Garland, 1998. Exploration of Filipino immigration that examines the subject in the context of Filipino emigration to more than 130 countries around the world.

SEE ALSO: Alaska; Anti-Filipino violence; California; Exeter incident; Filipino American press; Filipino Repatriation Act of 1935; Hawaii; Immigration and Nationality Act of 1965; Indonesian immigrants; Luce-Celler Bill of 1946; Mail-order brides; Malaysian immigrants.

FILIPINO REPATRIATION ACT OF 1935

THE LAW: Federal legislation designed to help Filipino immigrants return to their homeland
DATE: Signed into law on July 10, 1935

SIGNIFICANCE: This federal law provided free transportation for Filipino residents of the continental United States who wished to return home but could not afford to do so. The act was backed by both humanitarians concerned about the condition of Filipinos, many of whom were unemployed or destitute during the Great Depression, and anti-Asian exclusionists who wanted Filipinos out of the United States.

As a territory of the United States from the time of the 1898 Spanish-American War until the year following the end of World War II, the Philippines was a major source of immigration into the United States. Between 1935 and 1940, during the Franklin D. Roosevelt administration, the Filipino Repatriation Act permitted the U.S. government to pay the transport costs of Filipinos who wanted to return home but lacked the financial means to do so. The law was not widely used; only about 2,200 people were granted money under its provisions during the five years the law was in effect.

HISTORICAL BACKGROUND

The first Filipino immigrants to arrive in America, called "Manila men," escaped slave labor on Spanish ships sailing to Mexico during the seventeenth and eighteenth centuries and took up work fishing and shrimping near New Orleans. Immigration increased rapidly following the Spanish-American War in 1898, when the Philippines became a U.S. colony. Filipinos entered the country on U.S. passports and were not considered to be aliens.

Some of the early immigrant Filipinos, called *pensionados*, were Muslim students who were supported by the federal Pensionado Act of 1903. Several attended Harvard, Stanford, Cornell, and the University of California in Berkeley. Many of these students started Filipino student groups that remained active into the twenty-first century. Some returned home and convinced others to seek education in the United States. While some were successful, others were forced by lack of money to work in California as migrants, in Hawaii sugar plantations (as *sakadas*, or contract workers), and in Alaska fish canneries.

By 1930, men made up 94 percent of the Filipino immigrant workforce, who hoped to save enough money to return home and buy homes and land. As the Great Depression intensified, many of these plans were scuttled. Some of the Filipino workers also became involved in union organizing, which provoked some agricultural enterprises and other employers to call for their expulsion. In the meantime, some U.S. cities, notably in California, became home to sizable communities, with dance halls, restaurants, Roman Catholic churches, grocery stores, churches, clothing stores, and other shops.

Films

The Filipino Repatriation Act of 1935 followed the Tydings-McDuffie Act (known officially as the Philippine Independence Act), which was enacted on March 24, 1934. The Tydings-McDuffie Act established the Philippines as a commonwealth and provided for self-government, to be followed by Filipino independence after ten years. Actual independence was delayed two years by World War II. The law was passed after Philippine political activist Manuel L. Quezon (after whom the Philippines' former capital city was named) led a Philippine Independence Mission to Washington, D.C., to advocate for his country's independence.

In a bow to the nativist lobby, the Tydings-McDuffie Act also reclassified all Filipinos living in the United States as aliens under immigration law. Filipinos thus no longer were allowed to freely immigrate into the United States. As aliens, Filipinos also were barred from owning land or businesses in the United States. In 1943, however, they were allowed to lease land, much of which had been owned by Japanese Americans before they were sent to internment camps in 1942. The act also imposed a fifty-person-per-year limit on Filipino immigration to the United States. The quota was unrealistically low, and immigration continued at levels much higher than the legal quota.

RESULTS OF THE LAW

The Filipino Repatriation Act provided free one-way transportation only for single adults. Such grants were supplemented in some instances by private fund-raising (such as that of the California Emergency Relief Association) that paid passage for Filipino children who had been born in the United States so that they could return with their parents. Both the Tydings-McDuffie and the Filipino Repatriation acts halted reunification of families under U.S. immigration law, forcing many to remain separate for a number of years.

The Filipino Repatriation Act was declared unconstitutional by the U.S. Supreme Court in 1940, after 2,190 Filipinos had been returned to the Philippines. Filipino immigration to the United States continued, with a resurgence in the late 1960's. The large number of Filipino workers outside the country has even helped to spawn an acronym, OFWs (overseas Filipino workers), and a political movement, Gawad Kalinga, which has provided a sense of community and basic services to millions of expatriate Filipinos worldwide. Many Filipino immigrants have worked with the U.S. military in war zones, from World War II to the Iraq War of 2003, earning broad-based support for their continued immigration to the United States.

Bruce E. Johansen

FURTHER READING

Lawsin, Emily Porcincula. "Pensionados, Paisanos, and Pinoys: An Analysis of the Filipino Student Bulletin, 1922-1939." *Filipino American National Historical Society Journal* 4 (1996). History of early Filipino university-student communities in the United States.

Martinez, Eric V. "The Anti-Filipino Watsonville Race Riots: 1930." *Filipino American National Historical Journal* 4 (1996). Labor-organizing tensions and cultural differences led to riots that provoked some of the nativist sentiment that was reflected in the Filipino Repatriation Act of 1935.

"Philippine Flop." *Time*, October 3, 1938. Reporting on the Filipino Repatriation Act of 1935 indicating that 1,900 Filipinos had returned to the Philippines in three years.

Stern, Jennifer. *The Filipino Americans.* New York: Chelsea House, 1989. Wide-ranging history of Filipinos in the United States, including provisions affecting immigration.

SEE ALSO: Anti-Filipino violence; Asian immigrants; Congress, U.S.; Deportation; Filipino immigrants; Great Depression; History of immigration after 1891; Immigration law; Japanese American internment; Luce-Celler Bill of 1946.

FILMS

DEFINITION: Motion pictures depicting immigrant experiences in America

SIGNIFICANCE: The images of ethnic immigrants in Hollywood feature films change with changing attitudes and also help in producing changes in their audience's attitudes. For the most part, ethnic images early on were used for comic effect, but over the years the immigrants' images and their plights have been more realistically and sympathetically portrayed on the screen.

Of the films made during the early silent era only a few dealt explicitly with immigration. One of the first was *The Italian* (1915), which offered a realistic portrayal of Italian immigrants pursuing the American Dream. In the film Beppo Donnetti travels to America to make enough money to satisfy his fiancé's father and have her join him in New York. They have a son, who becomes ill; and Beppo does not have enough money for medicine. After he fails to get money and support from Corrigan, a local politico, he gets into trouble and spends five days in jail. When he is released, he finds out that his son has died. So much for the American Dream.

Charles Chaplin's *The Immigrant* (1917) took a slightly different tack. Although his character's ethnicity is not identified, Chaplin's Little Tramp has been identified by some critics as Jewish. Chaplin himself was not Jewish, but he always refused to deny being Jewish. In what is a comedy with a happy ending there are, nevertheless, realistic touches, especially dealing with Ellis Island officials, that are critical of the United States.

Another silent film of note is John Ford's *Four Sons* (1928), a film dealing with the problems a Bavarian mother faces in her hometown when one of her sons, who has emigrated to the United States, fights for the Americans in World War I. The film is interesting not only because it has little in common with Ford's later films but also because it presents a cultural clash from a non-American point of view.

At the end of the silent era *The Jazz Singer* (1927), starring Al Jolson in blackface, appeared. The plot involves a young Jew who does not want to follow in his cantor father's footsteps, but desires instead to appear in a secular world of show business. The film, like several others featuring Jews, involves cultural conflicts and the gradual movement away from past traditions.

EARLY SOUND ERA

Where Is My Child? (1937) continued the theme of Jewish travails and suffering in the immigration experience. In this film a widowed Jewish mother, destitute and newly arrived in New York City, places her son in an orphanage. After he is adopted, she regrets her decision and then spends the next twenty years of her life searching for her son. Although there is a happy ending, the film demonstrates that there is a price to be paid for the advantages of living in the United States: Health, family ties, and religion all are weakened.

In a lighter vein the Marx Brothers' film *Monkey Business* (1931) presents the brothers as stowaways on an American-bound ship. Although the brothers are not identified as Jews, the humor in the film, which is decidedly Jewish, pokes fun not only at the immigration procedures at Ellis Island, where the brothers impersonate Maurice Chevalier, but at the conventions and values of white Anglo-Saxon American society.

My Girl Tisa (1948) starred Lilli Palmer as a young immigrant who works hard to save money to bring her father to the United States, only to be duped by her travel agent, exploited, and intimidated by the owner of the sweatshop in which she works. She is threatened with deportation before she is rescued by none other than President Theodore Roosevelt at Ellis Island. There she also miraculously meets her father. The film is essentially a comedy, but it offer at least a superficial exploration of problems related to Ellis Island and immigration procedures, such as the fear of being deported, language problems, tough working conditions, and political bosses who exploit their constituents.

The many Latin Americans who have immigrated to the United States have inspired a number of films about border crossings. One of the first of these is *Border Incident* (1949). A noir film about smuggling and exploiting illegal immigrants, it focuses on how undocumented aliens are knifed, robbed, and abandoned by their smugglers, who are ultimately brought to justice. *Wetbacks* (1956) also deals with smuggling aliens into the United States but has them arriving on fishing vessels. Once again, the smugglers are apprehended.

The most upbeat of the immigration-themed films during this period was *I Remember Mama* (1948) about a family of Norwegian immigrants living in San Francisco, California. Most of the action in the film occurs after 1910 and involves matriarch Marta Hanson's struggles with a child's illness, a son's struggle to finance his education, and various problems with her extended family, which includes a cantankerous Uncle Chris. Narrated by Marta's novelist daughter, the film tends toward sentimentalism but was nevertheless an enormous hit with both audiences and critics and inspired a popular television series of the same name.

THE 1970'S AND LATER

There were few significant films about immigration during the 1960's, but beginning with the 1970's there were dozens of films involving not only Jews, Mexicans, and Italians but also Indians, Hondurans, Iranians, and Swedes.

Perhaps the best 1970's film about Jewish immigrants is Joan Micklin Silver's *Hester Street* (1975) about life in the Jewish ghetto of the lower East Side of New York City. In the film, Jake comes to New York and is "Americanized," abandoning his Jewish traditions. When Gitl, his wife, joins him a year later, she brings with her the Old World clothes, hairstyle, traditions, and values, all of which Jake has renounced. Jake has fallen for Mamie, a Jewish woman who is also Americanized, and Gitl has to fend for herself. She and Jake take in a boarder named Bernstein, who studies the Torah and retains his Jewish culture. Gradually, he and Gitl, who divorces Jake, get together, but both couples are affected by their residence in the United States. Jake and Mamie are more obviously Americanized, but even Gitl and Bernstein are changing. The film deals realistically with sweatshops, the ghetto, poverty, and cultural conflicts, but it suggests that assimilation, though it entails the loss of some customs and traditions, is possible and even healthy.

Director Barry Levinson's *Avalon* (1990), an autobiographical film about his Jewish family from Eastern Europe, received more critical and box office support. The Krichinsky family settles in Baltimore, becomes prosperous because of their hard work, and eventually assimilates into American culture. Although the family is never explicitly identified as Jewish, Christmas gifts are called "holiday" gifts, and the grandmother's funeral is conducted in a cemetery in which the star of David can be seen on gravestones. Although the family, whose members live close to one another, comes into money through their successful appliance store, some of its members become disillusioned with the American Dream. Two male members of the family change their names, signaling a break from the past. Growing affluence, changing attitudes toward the elderly, and the increasing influence of television are responsible for the drift away from old values and the past. However, what happens to the Krichinskys happened to the entire nation. One critic called the film, which received several awards, Levinson's "bittersweet mosaic." Levinson, who also wrote the film's screenplay, won a Writer's Guild of America award for best original screenplay.

NEGATIVE AND POSITIVE STEREOTYPES

Thanks to films such as Francis Ford Coppola's *Godfather* trilogy (1972, 1974, and 1990), the Italian immigrant experience has become popularly associated with the Mafia and Sicilians. After the first *Godfather* film was released in 1972, there were many protests about the anti-Italian feelings that it was alleged to have created. The second film describes the arrival of the Sicilian Corleone family in New York and concerns the family's rise to gangland prominence in the United States. The films depict poverty in the Italian ghettos, clashes between Italian and Anglo-American cultures, police corruption, and political patronage. The films garnered many awards, including Oscars for best picture, actor, supporting actors, screenplay, and director, and the first film was rated as one of the best one hundred films by the American Film Institute.

After becoming settled in America, Italian immigrants encountered problems not only in assimilation, but also in exploitation: *Blood Red* (1988) recounts the difficulties Italians faced in Northern California. *Wait Until Spring, Bandini* (1990), focuses on a family's struggles in 1925 Colorado. *Tarantella* (1995) depicts a different challenge: how assimilated Italian Americans become reconciled to their Italian pasts. Director Martin Scorsese, whose own body of work has presented a kind of kaleidoscopic history of the entire Italian immigrant experience, has called Italian director Emanuele Crialese's *Nuovomondo* (2009; released as *The New World* in the United States) the film that best balances the Old World values of Sicily against the New World of the United States. Crialese's film depicts the superstitions of Sicily and the rigorous Ellis Island tests to determine just who is "fit" to pass through the "Golden Door."

The Scandinavians, Irish, and Chinese have been more fortunate than the Italians in the ways in which their emigration experiences have been portrayed on the screen. Perhaps because Amy Tan's novel *The Joy Luck Club* (1989) was a best seller being widely read in book clubs, the film adapted from her book in 1993 was a successful rendering of the fates of four Chinese women who immigrated to the United States. Their emotional and cultural "baggage" is reflected in the relationships they have with their daughters, who have assimilated into the American mainstream.

The Manions of America (1981) is the "rags-to-riches" story of an immigrant who left Ireland during the potato famine and established himself and his family in a new country. Nicole Kidman and Tom Cruise appeared in a similar story in *Far and Away* (1992). Not all the films about Irish immigrants were as positive. *Gangs of New York* (2002), Martin Scorsese's violent film about rival gangs in New York City's Five Corners, depicts the grinding poverty, the political exploitation of the Irish, and their forced induction into the Union Army during the Civil War.

Jim Sheridan's *In America* (also 2002) focuses on modern immigrants from Ireland to the United States through Canada and offers viewers a more complex cast of characters. Despite some problems the family encounters, the film is ultimately uplifting. An example of stereotyping Irish immigrants is provided by James Cameron's ponderous *Titanic* (1997), in which the Irish passengers traveling across the Atlantic in steerage are depicted as the good people, in sharp contrast to the their wealthy, snobbish, and ruthless Anglo-Saxon counterparts aboard the doomed passenger liner.

The Swedes may have fared best. Jan Troell's *The Emigrants* (1972) with a cast headed by Liv Ullmann and Max von Sydow, traces a family's decision to leave Sweden through their eventual settling in Minnesota. Troell followed this film, which won major awards for acting and directing, with *The New Land* (1973). The latter film continued the family's story of survival in their new land, where members

Corleone family posing during the wedding scene early in the first Godfather *film. The Godfather, Don Corleone (Marlon Brando) is the second man from the right. One of the acknowledged strengths of the* Godfather *films is their rich depictions of Italian American families.* (Hulton Archive/Getty Images)

of the family faced Indian attacks and were involved in the U.S. Civil War.

BORDER SETTINGS

The U.S.-Mexican border has been the subject of many Hollywood films. The cowboy film hero Hopalong Cassidy (William Boyd) appeared in *Border Patrol* in 1943. However, the emphasis on exploitation switched to problems with American corruption at the border. For example, Tony Richardson's *The Border* (1982) presents actor Jack Nicholson's struggles with the criminal element within his own law-enforcement agency.

The Three Burials of Melquiades Estrada (2005) concerns racism within the U.S. Border Patrol. In this film a racist Border Patrol agent kills a Mexican attempting to cross into the United States illegally. The murdered man's friend forces the killer to return his victim's body to his hometown in Mexico. During their ensuing journey, the racist agent begins to comprehend the implications of his act and may even find redemption. The film is more concerned with the killer and the victim's friend than it is with the actual burial ground, which may not be really found.

Under the Same Moon (2007) also concerns the U.S.-Mexican border. However, this somewhat sentimental film, which resembles *Central Station* (1998) in its plot involving the reunion of a boy with a parent, is, despite some danger in crossing the border, a realistic look at the economic plight of undocumented aliens working in the United States and the courage and compassion of Mexicans. The evolving friendship between the boy and a cynical loner who helps him find his mother is one of the highlights of the film. Each proves willing to sacrifice himself for the other near the end of the film.

CULTURE CLASHES

In a more somber vein, the cultural clash depicted in *House of Sand and Fog* (2003) is the tragic tale of an Iranian immigrant, played by Ben Kingsley, who wants to live out the American Dream by buying a house being sold cheaply because of its unpaid taxes so he can "flip" it for a profit. His purchase, which is, strictly speaking, legal is at the expense of a young woman who thought she was inheriting the house free and clear. Her determination to regain the house and the Iranian's desire to

keep what is legally his results in the death of his son and the suicides of both him and his wife.

Another tragic film involving a cultural clash is director Clint Eastwood's *Gran Torino* (2009), which was overlooked by the Motion Picture Academy. The film features Eastwood as Walt, an eighty-year-old retiree and Korean War veteran whose speech is choked with ethnic slurs and misunderstandings. His neighbors are Hmong, the Southeast Asian hill people who aided the United States during the Vietnam War and are now assimilating to American ways. Eventually, Walt is drawn into the Hmong community and befriends the shy son who does not want to join a gang of Hmong hoodlums. After he catches the boy trying to steal his Gran Torino automobile, Walt takes him under his wing. He teaches the boy how to use tools, gets him a job, and teaches him how to "speak American"—that act is at once amusing, pathetic, and degrading. When members of the Hmong gang continue to harass his neighbors, Walt goes to their aid. The grateful Hmong community, with their food (including beer) and hospitality win Walt over. To free his neighbors from gang harassment, Walt will not adopt the Hmong way, which would include violent revenge. Instead, he concocts a carefully planned scheme that induces the gang to gun him down when he has no weapon. As he lies in a Christ-like crucifixion pose, the police take the members of the gang away. At his funeral, members of his own estranged family sit on one side of the church; the Hmong, his extended family, fill the other side. In his will Walt leaves his Gran Torino to his surrogate son rather than to his spoiled granddaughter. Walt's redemptive sacrifice saves the people he initially scorned.

While many of the immigration films focus on Ellis Island, the poverty of the ghettos, the exploitation of immigrants, and the problems of assimilation and do tend to stereotype immigrant groups, later films are more sympathetic and realistic in the ways in which individual immigrants are portrayed. The characters have different customs, but they are also real people with many of the same problems native-born Americans face.

Thomas L. Erskine

FURTHER READING

Girgus, Sam B. *America on Film: Modernism, Documentary, and a Changing America.* New York: Cambridge University Press, 2002. Demonstrates how American films both reflect and produce stories about national ideologies and identities.

Hamilton, Marsha J., and Eleanore S. Black. *Projecting Ethnicity and Race: An Annotated Bibliography of Studies on Imagery in American Film.* Westport, Conn.: Praeger, 2003. Indispensable, comprehensive guide to films about ethnicity and race, including immigration issues.

Mangione, Jerre, and Ben Morreale. *La Storia: Five Centuries of the Italian-American Experience.* New York: Harper, 1993. Interesting account of how post-World War II Hollywood films fueled prejudice against Italians by resurrecting the Italian Mafia image of the 1890's.

Puleo, Stephen. *The Boston Italians: A Story of Pride, Perseverance, and Paesani from the Year of the Great Immigration to the Present Day.* Boston: Beacon Press, 2008. Touches on films about Italian immigrants.

Rogin, Michael. *Blackface, White Noise: Jewish Immigrants in the Hollywood Melting Pot.* Berkeley: University of California Press, 1998. Discusses how Jewish studio heads evaded the issue of anti-Semitism by eliminating Jews from the screen. They allowed Jews to play African Americans but not themselves.

Torranes, Thomas. *The Magic Curtain: The Mexican-American Border in Fiction, Film, and Song.* Fort Worth: Texas Christian University Press, 2002. Contains an invaluable list of films dealing with the border crossing between Mexico and the United States.

Winokur, Mark. *American Laughter: Immigrants, Ethnicity, and the 1930's Hollywood Film Comedy.* Basingstoke, England: Palgrave Macmillan, 1996. Finds and discusses immigration and ethnic aesthetics in the films of Charlie Chaplin, the Marx Brothers, and William Powell/Myrna Loy films.

SEE ALSO: Border Patrol, U.S.; *Born in East L.A.*; *Godfather* trilogy; *Green Card*; *I Remember Mama*; *The Immigrant*; Literature; Melting pot theory; Rockne, Knute; Stereotyping; Television and radio.

FLANAGAN, EDWARD J.

IDENTIFICATION: Irish-born American social activist and humanitarian
BORN: July 13, 1886; Leabeg, County Roscommon, Ireland
DIED: May 15, 1948; Berlin, Germany

SIGNIFICANCE: Father Flanagan was an early and vocal advocate of child-care reform whose experiences as a Roman Catholic parish priest among the impoverished immigrants in Omaha, Nebraska, convinced him that addressing such catastrophic social conditions could only begin with taking in homeless boys and educating them. His idea grew into Boys Town, one of the most successful social engineering projects of the twentieth century.

Born in rural west central Ireland, Edward Joseph Flanagan, the eighth of eleven children, was a gifted, if frail, child who often devoted the long hours of tending his family's sheep and cattle to reading and prayer. Although poor, his parents were determined to provide Edward with education sufficient for him to become a priest. When he turned eighteen, he immigrated to the United States, his parents convinced that America offered educational opportunities not available in Ireland. In 1906, Flanagan completed his undergraduate work at Maryland's prestigious Mount St. Mary's College. He then enrolled in St. Joseph's Seminary in New York City, but persistent respiratory problems compelled him to return to Ireland and then recommence his education first at Rome's Gregorian University and ultimately at the Jesuit-run University of Innsbruck, Austria, where in 1912 he was ordained.

Because he had worked briefly as an accountant for a meatpacking firm in Omaha, Nebraska—a job secured for him by Omaha's bishop, an early sponsor of his studies—Flanagan accepted a pastoral appointment at St. Patrick's Parish in one of the city's most impoverished neighborhoods. After the catastrophic drought of 1913, migrant farmworkers, largely German and Irish immigrants, were left without work. Flanagan worked tirelessly for five years to provide the homeless men shelter and food, but he became convinced that long-term correction of the problem had to begin with saving the youth, specifically the boys he saw wandering the streets. In 1917, with a ninety-dollar loan from a pawnbroker, Flanagan opened an orphanage for boys, determined to provide them not only food and shelter but also education, vocational training, and moral instruction.

The number of boys grew so quickly that by 1921 Flanagan had purchased a farm ten miles west of Omaha and turned it into The City of Little Men, his model for what would eventually become Boys Town. The experimental community accepted homeless boys between the ages of ten and sixteen (550 residents at any one time). The community, guided by Flanagan's philosophy that there was no such thing as a bad boy, received enormous media attention: It was the subject of a 1938 Oscar-winning film in which Spencer Tracy played Flanagan, and Flanagan himself had a weekly radio show. Within a decade, Boys Town was welcoming boys from more than thirty-five states.

Flanagan received numerous humanitarian awards and became internationally known for his research into child care, particularly his visionary theories on how introducing community interaction, moral guidance, and social responsibility to abandoned children were critical in creating well-adjusted adults. After World War II, the War Department asked Flanagan to serve on a blue-ribbon panel sent to the Far East to study the care of war orphans. While in Germany on a similar commission, Father Flanagan died of a heart attack. President Harry S. Truman attended the funeral conducted on the grounds of Boys Town.

Joseph Dewey

Father Flanagan celebrates Christmas with residents of Boys Town, Nebraska. (The Granger Collection, New York)

FURTHER READING

Graves, Charles P. *Father Flanagan: Founder of Boys Town.* Champaign, Ill.: Garrard, 1972.

Ivey, James R. *Boys Town: The Constant Spirit.* Charleston, S.C.: Arcadia, 2000.

Lonnborg, Barbara A., and Thomas J. Lynch. *Father Flanagan's Legacy: Hope and Healing for Children.* Boys Town, Nebr.: Boys Town Press, 2003.

SEE ALSO: Child immigrants; Families; Farm and migrant workers; German immigrants; History of immigration after 1891; Irish immigrants; Nebraska.

FLORIDA

SIGNIFICANCE: Newcomers to Florida, from both other countries and other parts of the United States, have tended to settle in clusters, while maintaining their ethnic identities and their ties to their birthplaces. As a result, Florida is often viewed as an artificial entity, made up of regional groups that differ markedly from one another both culturally and politically.

When the first Europeans arrived in what would become the state of Florida during the sixteenth century, they found the Panzacola, Chatot, and Apalachicola Native American tribes in the western panhandle, the Apalachee and Timucua in the east, and the Calusa and Metecumbe in the south. Two centuries later, Creeks moved south into Florida, where they became known as Seminoles. By the twenty-first century, few Native Americans were left in the state. Those who had not succumbed to diseases brought in by the Europeans were either killed in battle or shipped west under the U.S. government's policy of Indian removal during the nineteenth century.

PROFILE OF FLORIDA

Region	Southeast coast
Entered union	1845
Largest cities	Jacksonville, Miami, Tampa, St. Petersburg, Hialeah, Orlando, Fort Lauderdale, Tallahassee (capital)
Modern immigrant communities	Cubans, Haitians, Mexicans, Brazilians

Population	Total	Percent of state	Percent of U.S.	U.S. rank
All state residents	18,090,000	100.0	6.04	4
All foreign-born residents	3,426,000	18.9	9.12	4

Source: U.S. Census Bureau, *Statistical Abstract for 2006*.
Notes: The U.S. population in 2006 was 299,399,000, of whom 37,548,000 (12.5%) were foreign born. Rankings in last column reflect total numbers, not percentages.

Spanish explorers discovered and named Florida in 1565. That same year, they founded St. Augustine, making it the first European city in the United States. In 1698, Pensacola became a permanent settlement in the panhandle. When control of Florida passed to the British in 1763, Florida was divided into two colonies: East Florida, with its capital at St. Augustine, and West Florida, governed from Pensacola. The Spanish promptly left St. Augustine, and English and Scottish immigrants moved in. Those with the means to do so established huge plantations nearby.

Less prosperous Europeans from Minorca, Greece, and Italy were brought in as indentured servants, and there were also a great many black slaves. Because Florida remained loyal to Great Britain during the late eighteenth century American Revolution, Tories from coastal cities such as Savannah, Georgia, and Charleston, South Carolina, found refuge in St. Augustine. By the time the United States acquired Florida in 1821, the region's white population was primarily British or Anglo-American. However, there were also a number of Jewish settlers in St. Augustine and in Pensacola.

Even before the Civil War (1861-1865), Florida had been promoted as a place where ailing northerners could come to regain their health. By the end of the century, Florida had become fashionable. Refugees from the cold weather of the northern states and Canada spent their winters in Florida, built homes there, and often retired there. During the 1930's, many Jewish Americans from New York City began settling in Miami and Miami Beach. In 1959, Cubans fleeing from Fidel Castro's new communist regime began to arrive there. By 1980, 60 percent of the Miami population was Cuban. Because most of these exiles were well educated, they contributed significantly to the growth of the city, notably through banking and business dealings with Latin America.

During the late 1950's, Haitians in flight from a repressive regime began coming to Florida. The first of them to arrive were mostly members of the middle and upper classes. Despite encountering racial discrimination, they soon adjusted to their new country. However, by the 1970's, though some Haitians were still granted asylum, boatloads of undocumented Haitians were being routinely intercepted, denied asylum, and sent home.

At the end of the twentieth century, almost 20 percent of the total population of Florida had been born in foreign countries. Many of the new immigrants came from Brazil, Nicaragua, El Salvador, Colombia, and the Dominican Republic. However, they were greatly outnumbered by Mexicans, who by 2006, ranked second behind Cubans among the state's foreign-born communities. By that year, Florida ranked fourth among all U.S. states in the size of its foreign-born population.

Rosemary M. Canfield Reisman

FURTHER READING

Gannon, Michael. *Florida: A Short History.* Rev. ed. Gainesville: University Press of Florida, 2003.

Mormino, Gary Ross. *Land of Sunshine, State of Dreams: A Social History of Modern Florida.* Gainesville: University Press of Florida, 2005.

Shell-Weiss, Melanie. *Coming to Miami: A Social History.* Gainesville: University Press of Florida, 2009.

Waters, Mary C., and Reed Ueda, eds., with Helen B. Marrow. *The New Americans: A Guide to Immigration Since 1965.* Cambridge, Mass.: Harvard University Press, 2007.

SEE ALSO: Colombian immigrants; Cuban immigrants; Florida illegal immigration suit; Georgia; Haitian immigrants; Jewish immigrants; Little Havana; Mariel boatlift; Mexican immigrants; Miami; West Indian immigrants.

FLORIDA ILLEGAL IMMIGRATION SUIT

THE EVENT: Florida governor Lawton Chiles sued the federal government for nearly $1 billion to reimburse his state for the costs of its handling of illegal immigrants

DATE: 1994

LOCATION: Florida

SIGNIFICANCE: Although the Florida lawsuit was eventually dismissed, the case was important because it represented the first time a state sued the federal government for costs associated with illegal immigrants. The state alleged that the growing number of illegal immigrants in Florida was the result of flawed federal immigration policies that imposed an unfair economic burden on the state.

In 1994, Florida became the first state to sue the federal government for reimbursement of the costs of services to immigrants. Florida's long coastline had historically provided popular entry points for large numbers of immigrants bound for the United States from West Indian and Central American countries such as Cuba, Haiti, and Nicaragua. Florida also experienced several mass influxes of immigrants, including the so-called Mariel boatlift, in which as many as 125,000 refugees may have fled Cuba through the port of Mariel in response to a temporary Cuban suspension of restrictions on emigration before Fidel Castro again closed his country's borders. At that time, U.S. immigration policy allowed the Cuban immigrants to stay in the United States.

Lawton Chiles was elected governor of Florida in 1990. By 1993, it was estimated that 345,000 undocumented immigrants were living in Florida who had cost the state $884 million in public services. Governor Chiles repeatedly asked the federal government to reimburse the state for money spent on the immigrants. He was part of a group of governors who wrote a letter to President Bill Clinton asking for federal assistance to states with large immigrant populations.

Frustrated by the failure of the federal government to respond, Chiles sent a letter to Florida state attorney general Bob Butterworth on December 31, 1993, asking him to sue the federal government and the U.S. Immigration and Naturalization Service. Butterworth filed the suit in behalf of Florida on April 12, 1994, in the U.S. District Court for the Southern District of Florida, Miami division. The suit charged that the state of Florida had incurred unfair expenses in services to immigrants as a result of the federal failure to enforce U.S. immigration policies properly.

On August 5, 1994, the number of refugees attempting to flee Cuba again rose dramatically when Fidel Castro instructed his country's coast guard to allow Cubans to leave the country. With thousands of new immigrants reaching Florida on makeshift rafts, arriving in need of food, clothing, and medical attention, Governor Chiles again appealed to the federal government for help. On August 20, 1994, President Clinton directed that Cuban refugees should be sent to camps at the American naval base at Guantánamo Bay on Cuba, instead of granting them asylum in the United States.

On December 20, 1994, U.S. district judge Edward B. Davis dismissed Florida's lawsuit on the grounds that federal assistance to states for immigration expenses was a political question, not a legal issue. The state then appealed its case to the U.S. Court of Appeals for the Eleventh Circuit. However, the appellate court affirmed the district court's decision on November 8, 1995, and dismissed the claims of the state. The U.S. Supreme Court declined to review the case when it denied a petition for writ of *certiorari* on May 13, 1996.

Heather R. Love

FURTHER READING

Boulard, Garry. "Immigration: Left to the States." *State Legislatures* 32, no. 9 (October-November, 2006): 14-17.

Copeland, Emily. "When Backyards Are Borders: The Debate over Immigration Issues in Florida, 1994-1996." In *The Ethnic Entanglement: Conflict and Intervention in World Politics*, edited by John F. Stack and Lui Hebron. Westport, Conn.: Greenwood Press, 1999.

Garcia, Maria Cristina. *Havana USA: Cuban Exiles and Cuban Americans in South Florida, 1959-1994.* Berkeley: University of California Press, 1996.

SEE ALSO: Cuban immigrants; Florida; Illegal immigration; Immigration and Naturalization Service, U.S.; Immigration law; Immigration waves; Mariel boatlift.

FOLEY V. CONNELIE

THE CASE: U.S. Supreme Court decision on rights of immigrants
DATE: Decided on March 22, 1978

SIGNIFICANCE: Upholding a state law that discriminated against aliens, the Supreme Court in the *Foley* decision departed from a previous decision based on strict scrutiny, thereby making it much more likely that similar policies would be upheld.

A legally admitted resident alien, Edmund Foley applied for a position as a New York State trooper. A state law, however, provided that only U.S. citizens could be appointed to the state's police force. When Foley was denied the right to take the competitive examination, he went to court to argue that the law violated the equal protection clause of the Fourteenth Amendment.

In a 6-3 decision, the Supreme Court emphasized that the states had exercised a "historical power to exclude aliens from participation in its democratic political institutions," and that the police function was "one of the basic functions of government." In contrast to the landmark precedent case *Graham v. Richardson* (1971), the Court did not assess the law according to the demanding standard of strict scrutiny. In contrast to classifications based on race, the majority of the justices accepted the premise that a classification based on alienage was acceptable so long as there was a rational relationship between the classification and a valid governmental interest. In a subsequent decision, *Ambach v. Norwick* (1979), the Court used the same standard of review in upholding alienage restrictions for teachers in the public schools.

Thomas Tandy Lewis

FURTHER READING

Bosniak, Linda. *The Citizen and the Alien: Dilemmas of Contemporary Membership.* Princeton, N.J.: Princeton University Press, 2008.

Epstein, Lee, and Thomas Walker. *Constitutional Law for a Changing America: Rights, Liberties, and Justice.* 6th ed. Washington, D.C.: CQ Press, 2006.

SEE ALSO: *Bernal v. Fainter*; Citizenship; Congress, U.S.; Constitution, U.S.; Immigration law; Supreme Court, U.S.

FONG YUE TING V. UNITED STATES

THE CASE: U.S. Supreme Court decision concerning deportation of Chinese immigrants
DATE: May 15, 1893

SIGNIFICANCE: Upholding the constitutionality of the Geary Act of 1892, the controversial *Fong Yue Ting* decision recognized that the U.S. Congress had almost unlimited discretion to establish all aspects of the nation's immigration policy, including the rules and procedures for alien registration and deportation.

Because Fong Yue Ting was an immigrant laborer born in China to Chinese parents, he was ineligible for U.S. naturalization. He wanted to continue living in the United States but did have the certificate of residence that was required by the Geary Act. Following his arrest by a federal marshal, a district judge of New York ordered his immediate deportation without a hearing of any kind. Fong appealed the action, claiming that he had applied for a certificate but could not supply the "credible white witness" required by the Geary Act. Because he had only Chinese acquaintances, he argued that the law's requirement was unfair, but a federal court of appeals quickly rejected his argument. Eventually, his case reached the U.S. Supreme Court.

By a 6-3 vote, a divided Supreme Court upheld the rulings of the two lower courts. Writing on behalf of the majority, Justice Horace Gray cited a large number of court precedents and authoritative books on international law. He declared that the power of "every sovereign nation" to deport noncitizens was "as absolute and unqualified as the right to prohibit and prevent their entrance into the country." There was no reason, therefore, why Congress might not add requirements for immigrants already residing in the country. Although the three dissenting justices did not deny congressional authority to enact new requirements, they insisted that the due process clause of the Fifth Amendment mandated that any person residing in the country be given an opportunity to challenge a deportation order in a judicial hearing.

Thomas Tandy Lewis

FURTHER READING

McClain, Charles. *In Search of Equality: The Chinese Struggle Against Discrimination in Nineteenth-Century America.* Berkeley: University of California Press, 1996.

Salyer, Lucy. *Laws as Harsh as Tigers: Chinese Immigrants and the Shaping of Modern Immigration Law.* Chapel Hill: University of North Carolina Press, 1995.

SEE ALSO: Asian immigrants; *Chinese Exclusion Cases*; Citizenship; Congress, U.S.; Constitution, U.S.; Deportation; Geary Act of 1892; Immigration law; Supreme Court, U.S.

FOODWAYS

DEFINITION: Foods preferred by immigrant groups, together with the circumstances under which they are produced, cooked, and consumed

SIGNIFICANCE: What people eat, when, and with whom—their "foodways"—are largely determined by their cultures. As circumstances allowed, immigrant groups brought their food preferences and eating customs with them to the United States, allowing them to maintain a sense of identity and cohesion.

What Americans think of as "their" food is an amalgam of numerous culinary traditions. Particular foodstuffs, recipes, methods of preparation, and styles of presentation have been contributed to the mixture by dozens of ethnic groups, but few of the "ways" survived intact. Interactions with a new environment and with an alien and often hostile culture produced a synthesis of old and new, a synthesis that changed as one generation replaced another.

Until relations turned antagonistic, Native Americans aided European settlers on the East Coast of North America and traded with them. Although European immigrants had found a landscape and climate somewhat similar to their own, they survived in large part thanks to the three major crops that the Native Americans shared with them—squash, beans, and corn.

ENGLISH, DUTCH, AND IRISH IMMIGRANTS

The English and the Dutch were the most important ethnic groups to settle along the eastern coast of what would become the United States, with the former eventually attaining political dominance. The first English settlers were males drawn from social classes with little experience of hunting, fishing, or cooking. Although much of their food did not survive the sea journeys, they brought cattle, swine, poultry, and honeybees with them and introduced wheat, barley, rye, and fruit trees.

The diet of New Englanders was plain, featuring cod and corned (preserved) beef. Popular dishes included succotash (a mixture of beans and corn) and baked beans prepared with salt pork and maple syrup. The English also learned from Native

Americans to combine lobsters, shellfish, and vegetables in communal clambakes. They drank beer, often brewed from corn, and cider made from apples and pears. In time, rum made from West Indian sugarcane and tea from China became popular. As women joined the settlements, they were expected to take over the cooking, most of which was done over open fires.

English settlers in the warmer southern colonies enjoyed a richer diet than those in the north, eating more pork than beef and in some cases adopting the foods eaten by their slaves. Wealthy landowners also depended upon slaves and servants to prepare their food, often in buildings separate from the living quarters. Like the residents of New York (but unlike those of New England), southerners celebrated Christmas as a day of feasting and merrymaking.

Although they too relied on corn, Dutch settlers in New Netherland (part of which would become the English territory of New York) raised a wider range of fruits and vegetables than the English and ate richer foods. One distinctive dish was *hutespot*, salt beef or pork cooked with root vegetables and added to corn porridge. The Dutch also had a greater preference for cakes and cookies.

A wave of poverty-stricken Irish immigrants began to appear in the United States during the 1840's, driven by a blight that destroyed their principal food crop, potatoes. Although they too spoke English and were assimilated relatively quickly, these immigrants brought a cuisine less elaborate than that of the English. The dish that many people think of as particularly Irish, corned beef and cabbage, is an elaboration of a much plainer everyday dish. Alcohol played an important role in Irish culture, and, for Irish males at least, taverns fulfilled many of the same social purposes that eating establishments played among other groups.

A reflection of the growing popularity of diverse immigrant foods, this West Coast restaurant chain offers noodle dishes prepared with recipes based on American, Italian, Cuban, Thai, and other Asian cuisines. (AP/Wide World Photos)

CENTRAL, EASTERN, AND NORTHERN EUROPEAN IMMIGRANTS

Germans were the most numerous ethnic group migrating to the United States during the nineteenth century. Most settled in the Midwest, with many of them growing their own food and raising dairy cattle. German Americans cooked potato dishes and introduced such foods as sauerkraut and frankfurters. Those settling in the nation's growing towns and cities often opened delicatessens, which have since become a fixture of urban American life. Bakeries and breweries were important, as was the consumption of beer in communal settings such as beer gardens. A typical link with the home country was Oktoberfest, a beer festival originally held in Munich but copied in German communities around the world. Poles and other eastern Europeans brought foodways that resembled those of the Germans, preferring sauerkraut, noodle dishes, and pierogi (dumplings filled with potatoes, cheese, and cabbage).

Many Jews settling in the United States were central or eastern European, and their foodways drew upon national traditions as well as Jewish religious tenets. Because Orthodox Jews observe strict dietary laws, avoiding pork for example, most Jewish immigrants settled where religiously sanctioned kosher foods were available. Thus, Jewish marketplaces became the culinary and cultural centers of Jewish communities, offering fruits and vegetables, fish, and the meat of animals slaughtered according to religious law. The women of the house prepared deboned fish with egg, onion, and flour, called gefilte fish, served on Sunday mornings.

Many delicatessens were run by Jews and specialized in kosher food, one of the first being that established by H. Schulz in Brooklyn in 1882. Such "delis" proved popular with non-Jews as well, and they sprang up in many communities, large and small. In time, the kosher food trade grew so large that dozens of Yiddish-language periodicals devoted to it were established, including *Der Groseriman*, which began publication in 1909 in New York City.

Along with Germans, Scandinavian immigrants living in cities opened bakeries and soon dominated the industry. Those settling in the Midwest outside cities missed the seafood that formed a major component of their diet in Europe but found substitutes in nearby streams and rivers. As circumstances allowed, Scandinavians served a buffet meal at holidays called *smorgasbord* by Swedes, *koldtbord* by Norwegians, and *kolde bord* by Danes. With time, they imported a characteristic dish to be served at Christmas called lutefisk, dried cod preserved using what was originally a mixture of lye and water. Scandinavian immigrants celebrated Saint Lucia Day on December 13 (near the winter solstice) to welcome the return of daylight. To mark the event, Swedes served sweet buns known as Saint Lucia buns, while Norwegians served cookies flavored with ginger or cinnamon and called *pepperkake*.

FRENCH, CAJUN, AND SOUTHERN EUROPEAN IMMIGRANTS

The French were the major European immigrant group to settle in what would become Louisiana. During the eighteenth century, they were joined by other immigrants of French ancestry from Canada known as Cajuns and whose Cajun cuisine, strongly influenced by French cooking, would become regionally important. Closely related Creole cuisine developed around the port of New Orleans. Besides French, it combined African, Native American, and Spanish elements and involved rice, game, chicken, smoked pork, and crawfish. Mardi Gras ("Fat Tuesday") was celebrated for the first time in the New World in 1699 in New Orleans. Later, the festival, which involves parades, consumption of Cajun and Creole dishes, and a general spirit of revelry, spread to many other cities.

Most Italians immigrated to the United States during the decades immediately before and after the beginning of the twentieth century, living and working in cities. Many were men who saved their pay, lived penuriously, and eventually returned home, where they shared stories of America's abundance. Most Italian immigrants were able to eat much better in the United States than they had at home, purchasing imported cheese and pasta and adding meat, fish, and fresh vegetables. As Italian immigrants were thus able to imitate the eating habits of their native country's tiny upper class, food played a prominent role in their culture.

Thanks to enterprising immigrant restaurateurs, a distinctive Italian American cuisine soon arose. Authentic Italian pizza had begun as a flat piece of bread sprinkled with salt and flavored with

Mexican food has become so pervasive throughout the United States that Mexican food shops and restaurants can be found in every state. These women are making authentic tamales in a store in Detroit's Mexican Town. (AP/Wide World Photos)

a little oil, but the more elaborate product familiar to most Americans originated in the Little Italy district of New York City at the beginning of the twentieth century. Many other foods served in "Italian" restaurants were scarcely Italian but became popular nevertheless.

Initially, most Greeks who came to America were men who expected to work, save their money, and return home. They often lived in boardinghouses with other Greek men, eating communal meals of familiar food—a pattern shared by Romanians and Basque-speaking immigrants from Spain. Typical dishes involved grains, spiced meats, and fresh vegetables cooked in olive oil. After the first decade of the twentieth century, the pattern of Greek immigration came to include entire families intent on remaining in the United States. The lives of Greek immigrants revolved around Eastern Orthodox churches, which began staging public food festivals as a means of raising money while allowing their

members to celebrate their heritage. These festivals also attracted other Eastern Orthodox immigrants such as Serbs.

LATIN AMERICAN AND CARIBBEAN IMMIGRANTS

Most Latin American and Caribbean immigrants brought with them cuisines combining Native American and European elements. In the case of immigrants from Mexico, the European element was Spanish. Mexican immigrants' proximity to their native country made it relatively easy to obtain ingredients not ordinarily raised in the United States, and in communities with significant populations of Mexican immigrants, specialty groceries and bakeries supplied Mexican foods and served as informal social centers.

The staples of the Mexican immigrant diet were tortillas and beans. The former, flat pieces of bread made from corn or wheat, were eaten plain, rolled and filled with cheese or spiced meat to make enchiladas, folded and fried crisp as tacos to hold similar fillings, and so on. Beans were boiled, then often crushed and fried in fat. Mexican cooking made use of chili peppers of varying hotness as well as salsas (sauces) made from chilies and spices such as cumin. Mexican Americans used what were regarded as less desirable cuts of meat in stews and versions of the spicy Spanish sausages known as chorizos. Chile—a stew made from beef or pork cooked slowly with chilies and tomatoes—evolved numerous regional variations in the Southwest and became a staple of the American diet.

Mexican immigrants (as well as those from Central America) prepared tamales—corn dough packed around a meat or cheese filling, wrapped in corn husks, and steamed—for consumption at Christmas. As was the case with other aspects of food preparation, the time-consuming process of preparing the tamales fell to women.

Haitian immigrants in Louisiana and Atlantic coast ports at the end of the eighteenth century brought with them a cuisine combining Caribbean, European (particularly French), and African elements, with rice, squash, corn, and black-eyed peas predominating. A favorite dish was *pois et riz*, a mixture of kidney beans and rice. Meats included chicken, goat, and pork, all cooked with hot peppers and spices. Haitian immigrants made patties of black-eyed peas for consumption on New Year's Eve.

Cuban cooking reflected Spanish as well as Caribbean and African influences. After the Cuban Revolution of 1959, many Cubans settled in nearby Florida, where they reproduced a Cuban cuisine based on red beans, black beans, rice, and pork. The last was usually cooked in a *sofrito*, or sauce, of olive oil, lemon juice, onion, and spices. Corn was cooked in stews and soups and ground for tamales.

AFRICAN IMMIGRANTS

Most African Americans are descendants of Africans transported involuntarily from the western shores of Africa to the southern United States as slaves. Drawn from numerous cultures, they brought a variety of foodways with them but adopted ingredients and cooking methods from their masters and from Native Americans. Living in an agrarian society, most grew private gardens and were allowed to hunt and fish. They frequently shared communal cooking facilities, and, at least under slavery, men and women shared cooking responsibilities.

African American foodstuffs came to include many ingredients that had been introduced into the South by European or American traders. Some foods, such as rice and black-eyed peas, came directly or indirectly from Africa itself. Okra was also of African origin, and it became a key ingredient in the meat and vegetable stew enjoyed by both African Americans and Cajuns as gumbo. Peanuts were originally carried by the Portuguese from Peru to Africa before being reintroduced into the New World. The sweetness of many African American dishes may be a result of the introduction of sorghum and sugarcane into the South, where it was harvested by slaves for the production of molasses and sugar.

African Americans adopted corn for bread and grits and cooked native catfish and such small game as opossum, raccoon, and squirrel. Cuts of meat such as oxtails, hog jowls, and tripe that were discarded or deemed less than desirable by their masters were also widely used. Dandelions and the tops of beets, turnips, and other vegetables were boiled as greens, and the cooking liquid (rich in vitamins and minerals) esteemed as "pot likker." During the 1960's, the resulting complex cuisine became known as "soul food."

Unlike slaves, Africans migrating voluntarily to the United States during the twentieth century usually found an infrastructure in place that allowed them to buy foodstuffs and prepared foods similar to what they had known in their native countries.

Although slaves generally adopted Christianity and observed such Christian holidays as Christmas, a distinctly African American celebration, Kwanzaa, was created in 1966 by Ron Karenga. Running from December 26 through January 1, the celebration was based loosely on African harvest festivals and included a *karamu* (feast) held on the evening of December 31.

EAST AND SOUTHEAST ASIAN IMMIGRANTS

Due to growing anti-Chinese prejudice and the desire of Chinese immigrants themselves to maintain their cultural identity, Chinese immigrants in nineteenth century California lived in myriad Chinatowns, neighborhoods in which they opened their own groceries and restaurants. They continued to consume traditional foods, leading to the importation of millions of tons of rice. Stir-fried dishes were preferred as a means of saving fuel, and most ate with the traditional Chinese utensils, chopsticks. Because most Chinese, like most peoples of Asian origin, are lactose intolerant, they did not eat dairy products.

Chinese Americans developed a new cuisine for non-Chinese diners. Inexpensive dishes such as chow mein were created by immigrant Chinese cooks, but despite, or perhaps because of, their inauthentic nature, they proved to be popular with non-Chinese diners. At the same time, many Chinese restaurants continued to supply authentic dishes to their ethnic customers. What Americans think of as the traditional conclusion to a Chinese meal, the fortune cookie, is said to have been invented in Los Angeles by an immigrant named David Jung, the founder of the Hong Kong Noodle Company, during the second decade of the twentieth century.

Many Japanese immigrant families worked as agricultural laborers, frequently contracting with landowners to share profits from the crops they tended. Besides working in the fields, women were expected to prepare all the food, purchasing rice, soy products, and fish from Japanese importers. Japanese Americans grew their own vegetables such as napa cabbage and daikon, a type of large white radish.

Asian immigrants celebrated the Mid-Autumn Festival and Lunar New Year (Tet) with dancing, the exchange of food and gifts, and ceremonies honoring their ancestors. Chinese Americans prepared mooncakes, rich pastries traditionally containing lotus seed paste and the yolks of salted duck eggs, for the Mid-Autumn Festival, while Vietnamese Americans produced a version known as *bánh trung thu*. During Tet, Vietnamese Americans cooked an elaborate rice, meat, and vegetable dish known as *banh chung* that they exchanged with other families and placed on their ancestors' altars. To celebrate their New Year, Japanese immigrants ate *mochi*, or roasted rice cakes, which for them symbolized strength. Other foods consumed during the New Year celebration and regarded as symbolically important were eggs, red fish, and fish roe. As is the case with many other groups, such festivals eventually became a means for immigrants who had given up traditional foodways to remember and reaffirm their heritage.

ARAB IMMIGRANTS

The first major wave of Arab immigrants came to the United States during the late nineteenth century from the area at the eastern end of the Mediterranean known as Greater Syria. Most were Christians and tended to settle in neighborhoods known as Little Syrias that had their own specialized grocery stores. A second wave of Arabs arrived after World War II. Most of them were Muslims. Like Jews, Muslims observe a strict set of dietary rules, avoiding all pork products and alcohol. Their preferred beverage is green tea, usually sweetened.

Like Greeks and other Mediterranean peoples, Arabs ate a diet based on grains, olive oil, cheese, and vegetables such as zucchini and eggplant. Mutton and beef were the favored meats and were often grilled as shish kebabs or mixed with cracked wheat to become kibbe (meatballs). Eggplants were often cooked and mashed with oil to become baba ghanoush, while chickpeas underwent the same process with lemon juice to become hummus; both spreads were served with *khubz*, flat breads known as pita in the United States. Meals often began with appetizers called meze.

Initially, Christian Arabs celebrated Christmas on January 7, eating *mamoul* and sweet *ka'ak* (cookies and pastries stuffed with dates, walnuts, or pistachios). During Lent, Christian Arabs abstained from consuming eggs, meat, and dairy products. Easter called for a large, rich meal, often featuring ham as the main course.

Muslims observed Ramadan during the ninth month of the Muslim calendar, a period that for most adherents involved avoiding food, drink, and tobacco from sunrise to sunset. The meal that broke the fast was also regarded as important, although here, as was the case with many other immigrant groups, regional differences were maintained in the New World. To break their fast, Palestinian immigrants consumed dates along with water or apricot juice, while Yemeni immigrants ate *asida*, wheat dough cooked with chicken or lamb broth. Desserts might include milk pudding, *qatayef* (a kind of folded crepe filled with cheese or nuts), and baklava.

Grove Koger

FURTHER READING

Counihan, Carole, ed. *Food in the USA: A Reader.* New York: Routledge, 2002. Collection of essays, several of which deal with immigrant foodways, their evolution, and their impact on American cuisine.

Diner, Hasia R. *Hungering for America: Italian, Irish, and Jewish Foodways in the Age of Migration.* Cambridge, Mass.: Harvard University Press, 2001. Readable survey of the foodways carried to America by three important groups of European immigrants. Photographs, extensive notes.

Gabaccia, Donna R. *We Are What We Eat: Ethnic Food and the Making of Americans.* Cambridge, Mass.: Harvard University Press, 1998. Includes chapters on immigrant foodways, ethnic entrepreneurs, and ethnic cookbooks. List of sources, extensive notes.

Hall, Robert L. "Food Crops, Medicinal Plants, and the Atlantic Slave Trade." In *African American Foodways: Explorations of History and Culture,* edited by Anne L. Bower. Champaign: University of Illinois Press, 2007. Analysis of the specific food and medicinal plants brought to the southern American colonies by enslaved African Americans. Extensive bibliographical notes.

Keller, Linda, and Kay Mussell, eds. *Ethnic and Regional Foodways in the United States: The Performance of Group Identity.* Knoxville: University of Tennessee Press, 1984. Essays discussing general aspects of immigrant foodways as well as those of several specific groups. Illustrations, tables, bibliography.

SEE ALSO: Arab immigrants; British immigrants; Chinese immigrants; Family businesses; German immigrants; Greek immigrants; Irish immigrants; Italian immigrants; Japanese immigrants; Jewish immigrants; Mexican immigrants.

FOREIGN EXCHANGE STUDENTS

DEFINITION: Foreign students admitted to a country as nonimmigrant residents to attend institutions of higher learning, as other students from their host country attend schools in the visiting students' home countries

SIGNIFICANCE: Exchange students undertake formal studies at postsecondary institutions to increase their cultural exposure, expand their learning opportunities, and improve their language skills. These experiences enrich human societies by building greater understanding among peoples of different cultures and nationalities and often lead to collaborations that benefit organizations, institutions, and disciplines over time.

Since ancient times young people have traveled to other lands to acquire new languages, improve their existing language skills, broaden understanding of foreign customs, access historical sites and geography, and reflect about the meaning of these experiences. The rise of universities and particularly their expansion within the modern era, has created a context for these experiences to become more formalized. Under organized exchange student programs, students spend time in other countries with structured educational aims in mind for set periods of time and report back to supervisors within their home institutions.

POST-WORLD WAR I DEVELOPMENTS

The calamity of World War I caused many world leaders and educators to consider ways in the postwar period to increase understanding among people at all levels of society, but especially among current and future leaders of governments, business, and academia. The Carnegie Foundation of New York provided thirty thousand dollars to create the International Institute of Education (IIE) in New York City for the express purpose of fostering educational exchanges between the United States and other nations. By 1921, this institute had designed a special student visa that would simplify the process by which foreign students could enter the United States for formal study, and it was lobbying the U.S. Congress to approve the visa. The institute was also undertaking the first survey of American academic institutions to gather their views on adopting new programs and approaches for dealing with foreign students. The institute would go on to become a key global hub of information and coordination for foreign student exchange activities and a vital source of information collected from around the globe.

World War II touched every continent and resulted in catastrophic loss of life and demonstrated the potential capacity of humankind to destroy the

HIGH SCHOOL STUDENT EXCHANGE PROGRAMS

In cooperation with their global counterparts, American high schools participate in many formal student exchange programs. These programs are generally limited to students between the ages of fifteen and eighteen and are organized and run by nonprofit organizations with the collaboration of high schools. The Council on Standards for International Educational Travel serves as a nonprofit body that promulgates standards and provides an annual list of programs operating out of the United States that meet its criteria for listing on full, provisional, or conditional status. The 2009 list provides contact details for more than seventy exchange-student organizations. The largest exchange programs in America are those of the American Field Service Intercultural Programs, Student Exchange Alliance, Center for Cultural Interchange, Academic Year in America, Rotary International, and National 4-H. Tens of thousands of American high school students annually participate in programs that may last for a full academic year, a single semester, or only summer session. However, the exact number of high school students in these programs is not monitored by any central body.

globe. Once again, the end of hostilities heightened public interest in improving understanding among nations. Private organizations such as the Rockefeller Foundation, Ford Foundation, and the Carnegie Foundation of New York joined with the United Nations and its affiliates such as the United Nations Educational, Scientific, and Cultural Organization (UNESCO), as well as government agencies such as the U.S. State Department, to promote formal student exchange programs among American universities and their overseas counterparts. New organizations were launched during this period. They include the National Association of Foreign Student Advisors, established in 1948. The latter body eventually grew to over 10,000 individuals from more than 150 nations under its revised name, NAFSA: Association of International Educators.

FOREIGN STUDENTS IN THE UNITED STATES

Foreign students enter the United States by obtaining any one of three types of visas:

- F-1 visa for full-time academic education
- J-visa for cultural exchange for informal learning of professionals as well as student travel and work programs
- M-visas for nonacademic courses of study, such as vocational training

J-visas are often colloquially called "Fulbrights"; however, that name properly refers only to a specific program, not to all programs that merit J-visas.

During the academic year of 2007-2008, a total of 623,805 foreign students registered for full-time study at American universities. This figure represented an increase of 7 percent over the prior year and a substantial increase over the 481,280 students who had registered during the 1997-1998 academic year. Between 1997 and 2008, foreign students accounted for 3.5 percent of all students enrolled in American institutions of higher learning. Their numbers have been split about equally between undergraduate and graduate students. The states of California, New York, Texas, Massachusetts, Illinois, Florida, and Pennsylvania—in that order—have had the highest enrollments. During the 2007-2008 academic year, six countries provided 54 percent of all the foreign students in the United States: India, China, South Korea, Japan, Canada, and Taiwan.

AMERICAN STUDENTS OVERSEAS

The numbers of American students going abroad for both short- and long-term study increased 8 percent in 2006-2007 to an all-time high of 241,791. That figure represented almost 1.6 percent of all American students enrolled in higher education during that academic year. Thirty-six percent of the students studying abroad were in semester-long programs, while 55 percent elected short-term programs. Almost 30 percent of entering freshmen at four-year colleges in the fall of 2008 indicated an interest in studying overseas. This positive trend seemed to be due to increases in the numbers of foreign-study programs, greater awareness that globalization requires knowledge and experience with other cultures, and the demands of a highly competitive job market. Some universities, especially private liberal arts colleges, make a full semester of overseas study a graduation requirement; many more require at least some formal overseas exposure. Great Britain, Italy, Spain, and France have been the most popular destinations for American students, but by the early twenty-first century, students were demonstrating increased interest in going to China, Japan, South Africa, and India.

EARLY TWENTY-FIRST CENTURY DEVELOPMENTS

After the terrorist attacks on the United States of September 11, 2001, and other international incidents of terrorism, government monitoring of foreign students increased significantly, and many nations instituted more rigid requirements for student visas. The United States put in place a national monitoring system run by the Student and Exchange Visitor Program (SEVP). Although members of the national security community have remained concerned about the effectiveness of this system in monitoring possible terrorist activity, higher education institutions have come to accept that it is a worthwhile if cumbersome burden in a more complex global environment.

Dennis W. Cheek

FURTHER READING

Bhandari, Rajika, ed. *Higher Education on the Move: New Developments in Global Mobility.* New York: Institute of International Education, 2009. Authoritative treatment of global mobility of students, professors, and researchers and their financing.

Haddal, Chad C. *CRS Report for Congress. Foreign Students in the United States: Policies and Legislation.* Washington, D.C.: Congressional Research Service, 2009. Regularly updated report for Congress on foreign students that provides demographic data and information about what foreign students are studying and where.

Institute of International Education. *Expanding Study Abroad Capacity at U.S. Colleges and Universities.* New York: Author, 2009. Part of a continuing series of Study Abroad White Papers that deals with various topics related to overseas study for Americans.

_____. *Open Doors 2008: Report on International Educational Exchange.* New York: Author, 2009. Definitive annual report published since 1948 that compiles and provides commentary on all relevant educational statistics from a global perspective.

SEE ALSO: Au pairs; Chinese Student Protection Act of 1992; Congress, U.S.; Education; English as a second language; Higher education; 9/11 and U.S. immigration policy; Parachute children; Passports.

FOREIGN MINER TAXES

DEFINITION: Discriminatory taxes imposed by the state of California on Mexican and Asian miners

SIGNIFICANCE: In the absence of federal laws that discriminated against immigrants, the state of California sought to favor immigrants of European origin by enacting special taxes that targeted the state's Mexican and Chinese miners.

After the discovery of gold in northern California in 1848, a major gold rush drew waves of immigrants to the state's new mining industry. Although the U.S. government officially encouraged the importation of Chinese laborers during the 1840's and 1850's, the Chinese who arrived on American shores encountered fierce racial animosity, as did miners from Latin America. Employers liked the Mexicans and the Chinese because they were inexpensive workers. However, many white workers felt threatened by the competition. The Irish and German miners, undoubtedly prompted as much by economics as by racism, were particularly outspoken about their dislike of those whom they regarded as "foreigners" in the mines.

Responding to the demands of the Irish and Germans, the state of California enacted the Foreign Miners' Tax in 1850. The tax was designed to discourage immigration by removing an economic incentive for moving to the United States or remaining in the country. The law, primarily directed at forcing Latinos out of the mines, required all persons who were not native born or who had not become American citizens under the Treaty of Guadalupe Hidalgo, which had settled the Mexican War, to pay twenty dollars for licenses allowing them to mine. An exception covered California's Native Americans.

The law did prove successful in its aim. Mexican miners balked at the exorbitant charge and refused to pay it. Twenty U.S. dollars in 1850 was the equivalent of almost five hundred dollars in 2008.

Chinese mine workers traveling on a railroad handcart in California. (Asian American Studies Library, University of California at Berkeley)

After Mexican workers exited the mines, the Chinese remained as the largest nonwhite group of miners. As a result, anti-Chinese sentiment rose throughout the 1850's. In the absence of restrictive federal immigration laws, the state asserted control over immigrants. The next foreign miner tax, enacted in 1852, targeted the Asians. The anti-Chinese legislation would ultimately culminate in the federal Chinese Exclusion Act of 1882, which barred entry of Chinese workers in the United States altogether.

Despite their discriminatory treatment, both Mexican and Asian miners continued to play critical roles in the development of California. Apart from contributing to the population growth that allowed California in 1850 to become the first territory in the far West to achieve statehood, these "foreign" miners brought critical skills. The Mexicans, largely from the area of Sonora, possessed considerable experience and knowledge of mining techniques. They introduced the stair-step separator,

known as the sluice box. They also utilized methods of dragging to crush ore. The Chinese did not have the same degree of mining experience but many displayed considerable resourcefulness in turning profits on mines that had been abandoned because of the difficulty in finding ore.

Caryn E. Neumann

FURTHER READING

Brands, H. W. *The Age of Gold: The California Gold Rush and the New American Dream.* New York: Doubleday, 2002.

Calderon, Roberto R. *Mexican Coal Mining Labor in Texas and Coahuila, 1880-1930.* College Station: Texas A&M University Press, 2000.

Hing, Bill Ong. *Making and Remaking Asian America Through Immigration Policy, 1850-1990.* Stanford, Calif.: Stanford University Press, 1993.

Holliday, J. S. *The World Rushed In: The California Gold Rush Experience.* Norman: University of Oklahoma Press, 2002.

SEE ALSO: Anti-Chinese movement; Asian immigrants; California; California gold rush; Capitation taxes; Chinese immigrants; Snake River Massacre; Westward expansion.

FORMER SOVIET UNION IMMIGRANTS

SIGNIFICANCE: Immigration to the United States from several of the former Soviet countries is a relatively recent development, but some of the others have long histories of sending people to the United States.

Arising out of the Russian Revolution that began in 1917, the Soviet Union expanded into the largest nation in the world in land area and became a world superpower after World War II. In theory at least, it was a voluntary union made up of fifteen autonomous Soviet socialist republics, but it was dominated by Russia, by far the largest of the republics in both population and area. Under the strains of the Cold War and the pressures of the modern world economy, the Soviet Union collapsed in 1991 and separated into its constituent republics, each of which became an independent nation.

The fifteen Soviet socialist republics that made up the Soviet Union all became independent after the breakup of the union in 1991. They can be divided into five groups:

- Slavic states: Russian Federation, Ukraine, and Belarus
- Baltic states: Estonia, Latvia, and Lithuania
- Caucasus states: Armenia, Azerbaijan, and Georgia
- Central Asian republics: Kazakhstan, Uzbekistan, Turkmenistan, Kyrgyzstan, and Tajikistan
- Moldova

None of these states is ethnically homogeneous, and several are home to large ethnic minorities—notably ethnic Russians. Several of the countries have been troubled by separatist movements and quasi-autonomous regions within them.

HISTORICAL BACKGROUND

During the late nineteenth century, peasant emancipation and the expansion of a market economy began to affect the western regions of the Russian Empire, sparking the emigration of ethnic Poles, Jews, Ukrainians, Lithuanians, Latvians, Finns, and ethnic Germans. Emigration to America was heaviest from the areas bordering the German and Austrian empires in the west and was much lighter from regions to the east. Prior to World War I (1914-1918), transatlantic immigration of ethnic Russians and Ukrainians from eastern and central Ukraine was limited. Opportunities for settlement in southern Russia and Siberia drew many people eastward in a wave of internal migration. Nevertheless, during the first decade of the twentieth century more than 1.5 million immigrants from the Russian Empire arrived in the United States. Despite a halt in immigration during World War I, another 1.1 million immigrants came during the following decade.

Ukrainian immigration to the United States has been significant since the 1880's. At that time most Ukrainian immigrants came from the provinces of Galicia and Bukovina in the eastern reaches of the Austro-Hungarian Empire. Following the failure to establish an independent Ukrainian nation after World War I and the subsequent Soviet repression, culminating in the terror-famine of the early 1930's, many Ukrainians active in the independence movement left their homeland. Alongside Ukrainians were Rusins (or Carpatho-Rusyns), members of small east-Slavic speaking communities in the eastern Carpathian region. Ukrainian and Rusin immigrants settled in industrial regions of the United States, such as New Jersey, Pennsylvania, and the Great Lakes states. Large numbers also settled on Canada's western prairies.

Polish, Jewish, and Finnish immigrants were the largest groups from the former Russian Empire, but most came from regions that after 1922 were outside the Soviet Union. Jews from central Belarus or central Ukraine were an exception. Aside from these groups, Lithuanians and Latvians came to the United States during this era, the former greatly outnumbering the latter. Both groups settled in industrial regions of the Northeast and Great Lakes states. Russian Germans from Ukraine and the Volga regions also arrived during this period, settling in the Great Plains and Midwest.

Small number of Estonians and Belorussians also arrived in the United States. Following the Russian Revolution and the defeat of anticommunist forces, a small number of so-called "White" Russians settled in the United States.

SOVIET UNION DURING WORLD WAR II

World War II (1939-1945) displaced large numbers of Soviet citizens from their homelands as well as citizens of the three Baltic states, Poland, and Romania. During the war, many people were taken as slave laborers by Germany's Nazi regime to work in factories and farms. Others became prisoners of war or victims of Nazi persecution, and still others were refugees who fled the fighting as well as violence, genocide, and ethnic cleansing that were integral features of the war on the eastern front. Following the Yalta accords of early 1945 that recognized Soviet domination of Eastern Europe, significant portions of Poland, Romania, and all the Baltic states were annexed by the Soviet government, which imposed a regime of terror on the remaining inhabitants.

Postwar legislation put in place to ease earlier national-origin quotas in light of the refugee crisis allowed a significant number of former Soviet citizens into the United States, especially people from the Baltic republics, Belorussians, and Ukrainians. After the end of the national origin quotas in 1965, a trickle of Soviet citizens arrived in the United States during the era of U.S.-Soviet détente, often under family reunification provisions. The so-called refuseniks were a small but important group of anti-Soviet immigrants. Many Soviet immigrants of Jewish ancestry sought to emigrate to Israel or the United States but were denied by the Soviet government, which viewed them with suspicion and prejudice.

Harsh treatment of Soviet Jews became a major human rights issue for Americans during the 1970's. The Jackson-Vanik amendment to the U.S. Trade Act of 1974 penalized the Soviet Union and other countries that restricted the right of emigrants peacefully to leave their homelands. The law effectively pressured the Soviet government into releasing a steady flow of emigrants, primarily dissidents and members of minority religious communities—Jews, evangelical Christians, and Roman Catholics. The majority of these immigrants settled in the United States. The most famous Soviet immigrant of this period was the Nobel Prize-winning writer Aleksandr Solzhenitsyn, who settled in Cavendish, Vermont.

Following the rise of the Solidarity movement in Poland and the subsequent peaceful revolu-

Many refugees from the Soviet Union who could not obtain Soviet passports, traveled under League of Nations passports such as this one, which was issued shortly after Joseph Stalin took power in the Soviet Union. (Library of Congress)

tions in east-central Europe, communism began to collapse in the Soviet Union, despite the reform efforts of Mikhail Gorbachev, the president of the Soviet Union. In 1991, a failed coup against Gorbachev brought an end to the Soviet Union and all of the constituent republics declared independence. The newly independent states, including Russia, continued to send significant numbers of immigrants to the United States.

From the mid-1980's until 2008, more than 1 million legal immigrants were admitted to the United States. from countries of the former Soviet Union, including the three Baltic republics. The three Slavic countries of the FSU contributed the majority of these immigrants. Of the three, Ukraine has provided the most, calculated both in raw numbers and as a percentage of the country's total population. Among the five Central Asian republics, Uzbekistan, the most populous of the group, has sent the most immigrants, followed by Kazakhstan. A significant portion of immigrants from the Central Asian republics appear to have been ethnic Russians. Likewise, immigrant streams from Ukraine and Belarus appear to have included numerous Russians. Immigrants from nearly all the states of the former Soviet Union outside Russia itself speak Russian, and those who speak Russian as their primarily language are in the great majority in several of the countries, most notably Belarus.

JEWISH IMMIGRANTS

A high proportion of immigrants from the former Soviet Union have been Jewish in heritage. Their precise number is unknown, but estimates have ranged as high as 700,000 immigrants throughout history. Approximately one-half of these immigrants have settled in the greater New York City metropolitan area. Other important centers of immigration have included Philadelphia, Miami, Chicago, San Francisco, and Los Angeles.

Jewish American organizations have taken the lead role in sponsoring and assisting Jewish arrivals from the former Soviet Union. Data from these organizations indicate that former Soviet Jewish émigrés are older on average than most other immigrant populations. One study found that more than one-third of Jewish immigrants from the former Soviet Union living in the New York area were at least fifty-five years old. Significantly, nearly two-thirds of all Jewish immigrants from the former Soviet Union have close relatives in Israel, indicating the divided destinations of Jewish family migration during the post-Soviet period.

CHARACTERISTICS OF POST-SOVIET IMMIGRANTS

Post-Soviet émigrés have tended to be better educated than the older waves of immigrants from the former Russian Empire. One study in 2003 found that 34 percent of Ukrainian immigrants in the United States had university educations, compared to 23 percent of non-Ukrainian immigrants. The same study found these immigrants outperforming Ukrainian immigrants to Canada, and other immigrants in the United States in terms of earnings and acquisition of English.

Due to their different socioeconomic standing and experiences in the former Soviet Union, most post-Soviet immigrants have tended to form their own organizations and develop their cultural and social activities apart from established communities. Jewish immigrants from the former Soviet Union have tended to be secularized and often religiously nonobservant. Although efforts have been made to change that, and Jewish American social service agencies continue to play an important role in serving Jewish immigrants, especially the elderly, the majority of these immigrants remain apart from the community mainstream. A similar situation exists among non-Jewish immigrants, such as Ukrainians, who have not joined existing Ukrainian American organizations in large numbers.

The growth of the Russian-speaking population in the United States during the two decades since the collapse of the Soviet Union has spurred the growth of Russian-language media. In 2008, nearly thirty Russian-language and bilingual newspapers and magazines were published within the United States. All but one—New York City's daily *Novoye Russkoye Slovo*— were weeklies and biweeklies; most were published in the greater New York area. There were also several cable television channels broadcasting in Russian and a New York-area Russian radio network. Most Russian-language television programming is produced in Russia. The growth of new media among new immigrants from the former Soviet Union has been somewhat hampered by competition with ready Internet access to homeland newspapers and the streaming of radio and video broadcasts.

PROFILE OF FORMER SOVIET UNION IMMIGRANTS

Countries of origin	Armenia, Azerbaijan, Belarus, Estonia, Georgia, Kazakhstan, Kyrgyzstan, Latvia, Lithuania, Moldova, Russia, Tajikistan, Turkmenistan, Ukraine, Uzbekistan
Primary language	Russian
Primary regions of U.S. settlement	Throughout the United States, with largest concentration in New York
Earliest significant arrivals	1870's
Peak immigration periods	1900-1919, 1990's
Twenty-first century legal residents*	391,577 (48,947 per year)

*Immigrants who obtained legal permanent resident status in the United States.

Source: Department of Homeland Security, Yearbook of Immigration Statistics, 2008.

Typically well educated, sophisticated, knowledgeable about computers and international finance, and apparently enjoying the covert support of Russian security agencies, members of the Russian mafia have posed major threats to American law enforcement, despite the arrests and convictions of a few notable racketeers. These groups have also been involved in drug trafficking and prostitution and developed ties to organized crime groups from other ethnic and racial backgrounds. Some youth gang activities have also been observed, including Armenian gangs, such as "Armenian Power" in the Los Angeles area.

The apparent growth of the Russian economy during the middle of the first decade of the twenty-first century, due to high oil prices, has somewhat reduced emigration from Russia. However, emigration from Ukraine, Moldova, and the Central Asian republics has remained fairly steady. In 2009, it appeared likely that post-Soviet countries would continue to send immigrants to the United States into the foreseeable future.

John Radzilowski

FURTHER READING

Altshuler, Stuart. *The Exodus of the Soviet Jews.* Lanham, Md.: Rowman & Littlefield, 2005. Detailed study of Jewish immigrants from the Soviet Union.

Finckenauer, James O., and Elin J. Waring. *Russian Mafia in America: Immigration, Culture, and Crime.* Boston: Northeastern University Press, 1998. Examination of the criminal activities of Russian immigrants, who are compared to criminal members of other immigrant groups.

Foner, Nancy, ed. *New Immigrants in New York.* New York: Columbia University Press, 2001. Collection of sociological essays on seven modern immigrant groups, including Soviet Jews, that addresses how they have interacted with New York City.

Gloecker, Olaf, Evgenija Garbolevsky, and Sabine von Mering, eds. *Russian-Jewish Emigrants After the Cold War.* Waltham, Mass.: Brandeis University Center for German and European Studies, 2006. Collection of conference papers on Jewish immigrants from Russia in the United States.

Shasha, Dennis, and Marina Shron. *Red Blues: Voices from the Last Wave of Russian Immigrants.* New York: Holmes & Meier, 2002. Study of Soviet im-

Another important contribution of first-generation immigrants from the former Soviet Union has been widespread entrepreneurship. Small to medium-size start-up firms are common and most cities with any sizeable community of recent Russian or Ukrainian émigrés supports at least a few ethnic delicatessens and gift shops.

CRIME

Alongside such positive aspects of post-Soviet immigration to the United States, there have also been growing problems of crime and violence. Russian and post-Soviet organized crime groups with ties to Russian-based mafia and Russian security services have become a major problem in the United States. During the late 1980's, the Brighton Beach section of Brooklyn was a notorious area for Russian mafia activities, which often preyed on fellow immigrants in various extortion schemes. Since that time, organized Russian crime operations have expanded throughout the United States.

migration to the United States based on a collection of interviews with immigrants documenting their experiences in America. Includes a foreword by Steven J. Gold.

SEE ALSO: Brin, Sergey; Canada vs. United States as immigrant destinations; European immigrants; Jewish immigrants; Polish immigrants; Russian and Soviet immigrants.

FRANKFURTER, FELIX

IDENTIFICATION: Austrian-born law professor, political activist, and U.S. Supreme Court justice
BORN: November 15, 1882; Vienna, Austria
DIED: February 22, 1965; Washington, D.C.

SIGNIFICANCE: As a professor at Harvard, Frankfurter got involved in a number of causes. He became a close adviser of Franklin D. Roosevelt. As a U.S. Supreme Court justice, 1939-1962, he was the leading advocate of the philosophy of "judicial restraint."

Felix Frankfurter was born in Vienna, Austria, in 1882. When he arrived in the United States at the age of twelve, he spoke no English. However, he quickly acclimated himself to his new country and graduated from a combined high school and college program at nineteen. He then entered Harvard Law School, graduating first in his class three years later.

Frankfurter joined the Harvard Law faculty in 1914. His was not a cloistered existence. He was active in the American Zionist movement for many years. While at Harvard, he struggled against such postwar excesses as the execution of the two radical political immigrants, Nicola Sacco and Bartolomeo Vanzetti. As a professor, he strongly opposed attempts to limit admission of applicants of Jewish background to Harvard.

After Franklin D. Roosevelt became president, Frankfurter was very active as an adviser on personnel, policy, and legal issues. In 1939, Roosevelt nominated Frankfurter for a position on the United States Supreme Court, and Frankfurter

U.S. Supreme Court justice Felix Frankfurter. (Library of Congress)

became one of three foreign-born individuals to serve there. There, he was an articulate supporter of "judicial restraint," the philosophy that courts should defer to the other branches of government. He served until 1962 and died in 1965.

David M. Jones

FURTHER READING

Domnarski, William. *The Great Justices, 1941-54: Black, Douglas, Frankfurter, and Jackson in Chambers.* Ann Arbor: University of Michigan Press, 2006.
Hirsch, H. N. *The Enigma of Felix Frankfurter.* New York: Basic Books, 1981.
Parrish, Michael. *Felix Frankfurter and His Times.* New York: Free Press, 1982.

SEE ALSO: American Jewish Committee; Austrian immigrants; Education; *Galvan v. Press*; Jewish immigrants; Sacco and Vanzetti trial.

FREEDOM AIRLIFT

THE EVENT: U.S.-supported airlift of more than 260,000 Cuban emigrants to the United States

DATE: December, 1965-April, 1973

LOCATION: Cuba and United States

SIGNIFICANCE: The airlift of hundreds of thousands of Cuban migrants to the United States increased the size and political strength of the Cuban American community while furthering the Cold War foreign policy goals of the United States.

Relations between Cuba and the United States soured after the 1959 Cuban revolution created a communist government headed by Fidel Castro. The failed Bay of Pigs invasion in 1961 and the tense Cuban Missile Crisis of October, 1962, worsened relations so badly that the administration of U.S. president John F. Kennedy severed diplomatic ties with Cuba and led an international effort to isolate Cuba politically and economically. The United States also opened its borders to refugees from Cuban communism, offering Cubans preferential immigration options that made immigration easier for them than for other Latin Americans. Many of the Cubans who then came to the United States were well-educated members of the professional classes who hoped the communist government would soon fall so they could return home.

By the mid-1960's, Cuba's economic isolation had created hard times that led to rising public discontent. In the autumn of 1965, Castro announced a new emigration policy, opening the port of Camarioca to Cubans living in the United States who wished to retrieve their relatives by boat. As Cubans flocked to the port to leave their island nation, the United States and Cuba entered negotiations to manage the migration in an orderly fashion. The Cuban government opened a six-month period during which its citizens, with the exception of political prisoners and draft-age men, could register for emigration. Beginning on December 1, 1965, the United States organized and funded a massive airlift of Cubans to the United States, offering flights to Miami twice a day, five days a week. The resulting airlift continued until the spring of 1973, transporting more than 260,000 Cubans to the United States.

GOALS

Policy makers in the United States hoped that the mass exodus would accomplish three Cold War goals:

- drain talent and expertise from Cuba, disrupting social conditions and weakening Castro's regime
- symbolize the dysfunction of communism, as hundreds of thousands of Cubans demonstrated their preference for the political and economic conditions in the United States
- emphasize alternatives to Cuban communism, thereby potentially promoting active resistance to Castro within Cuba

In practice, the effects of the airlift were somewhat more complex. Many members of Cuba's professional classes did leave their homeland. However, over time, the majority of emigrants tended to come from poorer and less well-educated backgrounds. The "brain drain" in Cuba did occur to some extent, but the airlift also reduced political pressures on Castro within Cuba, as dissidents and opponents to Castro's revolution were free to leave.

By the early 1970's, attitudes toward the airlift had shifted. Some members of the U.S. Congress opposed footing the bill for such an expensive operation, a position that hardened as the new immigrants were increasingly seen as requiring extensive social and economic support after they arrived in the United States. At the same time, a thaw in U.S. relations with the Soviet Union contributed to a softening of some hard-line attitudes toward Cuba. Meanwhile, within Cuba itself, nearly all original registrants for the boatlift and airlift were gone, and outgoing flights continued only intermittently until the airlift officially ended on April 6, 1973. The next major migration from Cuba to the United States would not occur until the Mariel boatlift of 1980. It would prove to be a shorter-term, less expensive, and more politically unpopular operation.

Sarah Bridger

FURTHER READING

Arboleya, Jesus. *Havana-Miami: The U.S.-Cuba Migration Conflict.* Melbourne, Vic.: Ocean Press, 1996.

Colomer, Josep M. "Exit, Voice, and Hostility in Cuba." *International Migration Review* 34, no. 2 (Summer, 2000): 423-442.

García, María Cristina. *Havana USA: Cuban Exiles and Cuban Americans in South Florida, 1959-1994.* Berkeley: University of California Press, 1996.

Pedraza, Silvia. *Political Disaffection in Cuba's Revolution and Exodus.* New York: Cambridge University Press, 2007.

SEE ALSO: "Brain drain"; Congress, U.S.; Cuban immigrants; González case; Little Havana; Mariel boatlift; Miami; Push-pull factors; Transportation of immigrants; Welfare and social services.

FRENCH IMMIGRANTS

SIGNIFICANCE: French immigration to the United States has been episodic, generally paralleling religious, political, and economic upheavals in France.

French settlement in the United States began during the age of exploration and colonization of the seventeenth century in Louisiana and intensified with the expulsion from France of the Huguenots or French Protestants during the eighteenth century. Migration from French Canada in 1755 originated with the expulsion of the Acadian French from Nova Scotia by Great Britain. Voluntary migration of French Canadians intensified from 1900 until 1930 to New England to work on the assembly lines of shoe and textile factories. Haitian migration to New York City increased during the 1980's because of economic and political upheavals. French migration to the United States can also be documented from the French-speaking nations of Belgium, Switzerland, West Africa, and French Polynesia.

FRENCH IMMIGRATION BEFORE THE REVOLUTION

French interest in the Americas was stimulated by the earlier voyages of the Spanish, Portuguese, and English. During the seventeenth century, explorers sailing under the French flag navigated the waters of the Gulf of Mexico and the Atlantic Ocean and founded settlements along the Mississippi River in what would become Louisiana and along the St. Lawrence River in New France or Quebec, with much smaller settlements at Beaufort, South Carolina, and Jacksonville, Florida.

Emigration from France was strictly regulated by law. French settlers in the New World were usually trappers, soldiers, or clerics until 1685, when King Louis XIV revoked the Edict of Nantes stripping the Protestant Huguenots of their political rights unless they converted to Roman Catholicism. In response, many Huguenots opted to emigrate to North America. Among France's most skilled artisans, the Huguenots were well-educated members of the wealthy middle class. Their departure crippled the French economy but led to the creation of prosperous settlements at New Rochelle, Staten Island, Harlem, and New Paltz in what would become the state of New York. Huguenot families also settled in Massachusetts, Pennsylvania, Virginia, and South Carolina, Conflicting accounts make it difficult to provide accurate figures on the numbers of Huguenots who settled in the future United States. Estimates range from as few as 3,000 to as many as 15,000 before the first U.S. Census in 1790.

NINETEENTH CENTURY IMMIGRATION

The first U.S. Census in 1790 listed 11,307 residents of French origin. New York, Pennsylvania, South Carolina, and Maryland had the largest numbers of French-speaking residents. Other states with significant French populations included North

---

PROFILE OF FRENCH IMMIGRANTS

Country of origin	France
Primary language	French
Primary regions of U.S. settlement	Louisiana, New England, New York
Earliest significant arrivals	Seventeenth century
Peak immigration periods	1840's-1920's, 1950's-1960's
Twenty-first century legal residents*	31,288 (3,911 per year)

*Immigrants who obtained legal permanent resident status in the United States.
Source: Department of Homeland Security, *Yearbook of Immigration Statistics, 2008.*

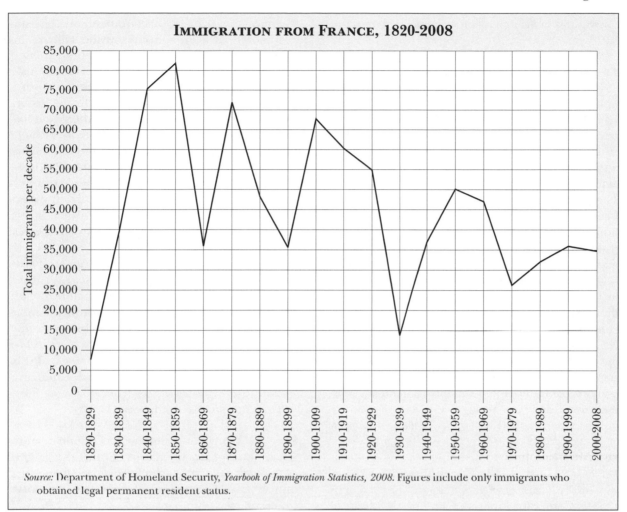

IMMIGRATION FROM FRANCE, 1820-2008

Source: Department of Homeland Security, *Yearbook of Immigration Statistics, 2008.* Figures include only immigrants who obtained legal permanent resident status.

Carolina, Virginia, Vermont, Connecticut, Massachusetts, Rhode Island, New Hampshire, and what was then the territory of Maine.

Between 1819 and 1870, 245,812 French immigrants arrived in the United States. Their numbers steadily rose—from 8,868 during the 1820's to 45,575 during the 1830's. The next two decades witnessed further increases of French immigrants: 77,262 during the 1840's and 76,358 during the 1850's. The increased numbers of French immigrants during each of those decades reflect the disorders caused by political revolutions in France in 1830, 1848, and 1852.

During the 1860's, the decade in which the U.S. Civil War was fought, the number of new French immigrants declined to 37,749. The 1870 U.S. Census counted 115,260 U.S. residents born in France,

with the largest numbers in New York, Ohio, Louisiana, Georgia, and Pennsylvania. The loss of the French province of Alsace-Lorraine to Germany in 1871 increased the number of French Alsatians, particularly French Jews, who went to the United States. Nevertheless, the 1880 U.S. Census saw a decline in the number of French-born residents of the United States to 104,143. By this time, California had replaced Ohio among the five states with the most French residents.

The 1900 census showed a further decline in the size the French-born population, whose numbers had dropped to 102,535. The largest communities were in New York, Colorado, Illinois, Pennsylvania, and Louisiana. Between 1875 and 1914, France's politics and national economy was stabilizing, and most French emigrants chose to see economic opportunities in French colonies in North Africa and Southeast Asia.

TWENTIETH CENTURY PATTERNS

Immigration from France declined during the upheavals brought by World War I (1914-1918) and World War II (1939-1945). After 1945, Europe experienced an economic recovery that further discouraged emigration to the United States, and new immigration was most likely to be motivated by marriages between French and American citizens. The postwar French immigrants who came to the United States generally had high levels of education and significant job skills.

In 1980, the U.S. Census began collecting information on national ancestry and found that 13 million American citizens regarded themselves as having French ancestry. More than one-quarter of these people lived in the Northeast. A similar percentage in north-central and southern states claimed French ancestry, but in the West only 19 percent claimed French heritage. The individual states with the most residents claiming French ancestry were California, Louisiana, Michigan, Massachusetts, and New York.

William A. Paquette

FURTHER READING

Brasseaux, Carl A. *The Foreign French: Nineteenth-Century French Immigration into Louisiana.* Lafayette: Center for Louisiana Studies, University of Southwestern Louisiana, 1990. Survey of the complex ethnicity of Louisiana, which was founded as a French colony and still retains much of its French heritage.

Houde, Jean-Louis. *French Migration to North America, 1600-1900.* Translated by Hubert Houle. Chicago: Editions Houde, 1994. Broad historical survey of French migration to Canada and the United States.

Kaiser, Hilary. *French War Brides in America: An Oral History.* Westport, Conn.: Praeger, 2008. Collection of oral histories, detailing the experiences of fifteen French women who married American servicemen and came to the United States. Three stories come from World War I, the rest from World War II.

McDermott, John Francis, ed. *Frenchmen and French Ways in the Mississippi Valley.* Champaign: University of Illinois Press, 1969. Collection of scholarly articles on the contributions of French explorers and immigrants to the Mississippi region.

Robbins, Albert. *Coming to America: Immigrants from Northern Europe.* New York: Delacorte Press, 1981. Broad survey of the history of immigration to the United States from northern European nations including France.

SEE ALSO: Belgian immigrants; Canadian immigrants; European immigrants; *Green Card*; History of immigration, 1620-1783; History of immigration, 1783-1891; History of immigration after 1891; Louisiana; Swiss immigrants.

ENCYCLOPEDIA OF
AMERICAN
IMMIGRATION

ENCYCLOPEDIA OF
AMERICAN
IMMIGRATION

Volume 2
Galvan v. Press—Pakistani immigrants

Edited by
Carl L. Bankston III
Tulane University

SALEM PRESS
Pasadena, California　　Hackensack, New Jersey

Editor in Chief: Dawn P. Dawson

Editorial Director: Christina J. Moose *Research Supervisor:* Jeffry Jensen
Project and Development Editor: R. Kent Rasmussen *Photo Editor:* Cynthia Breslin Beres
Manuscript Editor: Tim Tiernan *Production Editor:* Andrea E. Miller
Indexer: R. Kent Rasmussen *Design and Graphics:* James Hutson
Acquisitions Editor: Mark Rehn *Layout:* William Zimmerman
Editorial Assistant: Brett S. Weisberg

Frontispiece: Eastern European immigrants bound for the United States around the turn of the twentieth century. (The Granger Collection, New York)

Cover photo: (The Granger Collection, New York)

Library of Congress Cataloging-in-Publication Data

Encyclopedia of American immigration / edited by Carl L. Bankston III.
    p.   cm.
Includes bibliographical references and index.
    ISBN 978-1-58765-599-9 (set : alk. paper) — ISBN 978-1-58765-600-2 (vol. 1 : alk. paper) —
ISBN 978-1-58765-601-9 (vol. 2 : alk. paper) — ISBN 978-1-58765-602-6 (vol. 3 : alk. paper) —
1. United States—Emigration and immigration—History. I. Bankston, Carl L. (Carl Leon), 1952-
JV6450.E66 2010
304.8'73003—dc22

2009054334

First Printing

PRINTED IN THE UNITED STATES OF AMERICA

CONTENTS

CONTENTS

COMPLETE LIST OF CONTENTS

VOLUME 1

VOLUME 2

Volume 3

ENCYCLOPEDIA OF
AMERICAN
IMMIGRATION

G

GALVAN V. PRESS

THE CASE: U.S. Supreme Court decision concerning deportation

DATE: Decided on May 24, 1954

> SIGNIFICANCE: In the context of the Cold War, the *Galvan* decision upheld the authority of the U.S. government to order the deportation of persons who had been members of the Communist Party, even if there was no good evidence that they had understood the party's advocacy of violent revolution.

The McCarran Internal Security Act of 1950 included a provision for deporting any alien who was a member of the Communist Party at any time after entering the United States. Juan Galvan, an alien born in Mexico, had lived in the United States for more than thirty years. In 1948, he admitted to the Immigration and Naturalization Service (INS) that from 1944 to 1946 he had been a member of the Communist Party, but at a later hearing in 1950, he denied having ever joined the party. After a witness claimed otherwise, the hearing officer concluded that he had been a party member and ordered his deportation for that reason. Galvan's petition for a writ of habeas corpus was rejected by both the District Court and the Court of Appeals for the Ninth Circuit.

By a 7-2 margin, the U.S. Supreme Court upheld both the statute and the deportation order. Speaking for the majority, Justice Felix Frankfurter discussed three main issues. First, the use of the word "member" in the statute did not just refer to persons who had joined the party fully conscious of its violent goals. Second, the INS had obtained sufficient evidence to reasonably conclude that Galvan had been a member of the party. Finally, based on the "broad power of Congress over the admission and deportation of aliens," Frankfurter wrote that there was no good reason to conclude that the statute violated constitutional principles of due process. Justice Hugo L. Black and William O. Douglas wrote strong dissenting opinions.

Thomas Tandy Lewis

FURTHER READING

Belknap, Michal. *The Supreme Court Under Earl Warren, 1953-1969*. Columbia: University of South Carolina Press, 2005.

Stevens, Richard. *Reason and History in Judicial Judgment: Felix Frankfurter and Due Process*. New Brunswick, N.J.: Transaction, 2008.

SEE ALSO: Citizenship; Congress, U.S.; Constitution, U.S.; Deportation; Due process protections; Frankfurter, Felix; Immigration law; McCarran Internal Security Act of 1950; Supreme Court, U.S.

GARMENT INDUSTRY

DEFINITION: Industry encompassing all aspects of clothing manufacturing

> SIGNIFICANCE: Fueled by immigrant labor since the massive surge of Jewish and Italian immigrants to New York City during the decades surrounding the turn of the twentieth century, the American garment industry was long a major economic portal to recently arrived immigrants. It was especially important to Jews from the Russian Empire, Italians from the south of their native land, Chinese, Latin Americans, and Southeast Asians. The industry has provided immigrants with jobs, entries into their new culture, and business opportunities.

Before the massive migration of the early twentieth century, most wholesale garments were made in workshops owned by German Jews of earlier immigrations. The Jews who arrived during the early twentieth century already had a long history of garment work in their native countries, largely because Jews observed religious restrictions on certain materials in their clothes, so they preferred to make their own garments. The influx of poor Russian Jews to the United States happened to coincide with a surging American demand for factory-made clothes, and new production systems were emerging. Small contractors rented workshops within the New York tenements in which the immi-

grants lived. These contractors, most of whom were themselves Russian Jewish immigrants, had more success than large manufacturers in recruiting labor, as the workers whom they recruited were usually from their own Russian hometowns. Job opportunities for these immigrants were often limited by language difficulties and economic necessity, and the Russian contractors could push their laborers to greater efforts of productivity than large manufacturers. This tendency to use small workshops for small-scale contracting long remained a feature of the garment industry.

EARLY LABOR ORGANIZATION

In 1900, the International Ladies' Garment Workers' Union (ILGWU) was organized at a conference of New York City East Side delegates and representatives of the American Federation of Labor. Their goal was to improve the wages and working conditions of the city's thousand of garment workers, most of whom were young female immigrants. In 1909, the new union called a strike against the more than five hundred shirtwaist manufacturers in New York. Settlement of the strike in early 1910 significantly improved working conditions but did not attain the recognition of the union that the ILGWU had demanded. Nevertheless, membership in the local union had grown to ten thousand members, and many immigrants had achieved a new sense of dignity and confidence on the picket lines. The settlement did not, however, improve conditions at all garment-making facilities. In March, 1911, 146 mostly immigrant workers were killed in a fire at the Triangle Shirtwaist Factory. The tragedy did, however, have the beneficial effect of attracting public and government attention to the dangerous conditions in many garment workplaces.

Meanwhile, the New York garment industry remained robust. It expanded during the 1920's, but by the 1930's other cities in the United States were attracting sizable concentrations of garment manufacturers. By the 1940's, Boston, Philadelphia, Chicago, and Baltimore had become important

Garment factory in Jersey Homesteads (now Roosevelt), New Jersey, in 1936. (Library of Congress)

garment centers. In 1941, only 39 percent of all American clothing manufacturers were located in New York City. A decade later, the South and then the Far West became productive centers of industry growth. By then, the importation of foreign-made clothing was rapidly increasing in the United States. Initially, Japan and Hong Kong were the only important supplies of clothes to the United States. Eventually, however, virtually every country throughout the world with a developed garment industry found a share of the U.S. market. Due to higher labor and capital costs at home, U.S. manufacturers found it difficult to compete, and the industry shrank.

RENEWAL OF THE GARMENT INDUSTRY

Although Russian Jews and Italians had dominated the garment industry in New York since 1914, many immigrants wanted something better for their children and dissuaded them from pursing similar employment. Their withdrawal from the industry opened opportunities to other groups of immigrants, such as Puerto Ricans and Africans. Between 1930 and 1936, about 30 percent of gainfully employed Puerto Rican workers in the United States were either garment or hand-sewing workers. However, most of them worked at home until the 1940's and early 1950's, when they began to enter the garment workshops in great numbers.

Despite the differences in when they arrived, the reasons for their immigration, their prior experiences, and their different cultures, African and Puerto Rican women workers had experiences in the garment industry similar to those of their Jewish and Italian predecessors. The Puerto Rican and African women were generally relegated to the lowest-paid unskilled and semiskilled jobs in the industry. However, they earned even lower pay than their Jewish and Italian counterparts who had done the same jobs. The period during which African and Puerto Rican workers entered New York City's garment industry was an important factor in causing this disparity, as New York's garment industry was already on its way from being one of the highest-paid industries to becoming one of the lowest paid.

In 1969, New York City's economy had a sudden downturn and vacancy rates in industrial buildings soared. In the Lower Manhattan district bordering New York's Chinatown, rents dropped dramatically and many Chinese entrepreneurs started their own garment factories. As their Jewish and Italian predecessors had done, the Chinese organized ethnic business associations. However, they started from a stronger base, drawing on greater collective resources. Chinese owners from Hong Kong recruited other immigrants from Hong Kong, while new immigrants from mainland China tended to hire immigrants from the mainland.

The tremendous number of Asian and Latin American immigrants to the West Coast during the 1970's and 1980's created a boom in Los Angeles's garment trades. Immigrants from Southeast Asia, El Salvador, and Guatemala found opportunities for work in the city's garment workshops, and ethnic networking assured immigrant owners of a certain reservoir of trust and dependability. Garments made in Los Angeles took their place among those made in New York, and the rise of the garment industry allowed West Coast clothing designers who were once obscure to become nationally, and even internationally, known.

DECLINE OF THE GARMENT INDUSTRY

The North American Free Trade Agreement is a trilateral trade pact created by the leaders of Mexico, Canada, and the United States that went into effect in 1993. One of the most powerful and wide-reaching international treaties in the world, it reduced trade and investment barriers among the three North American nations through a gradual and methodical process. Its goal was to reduce tariffs among Mexico, Canada, and the United Sates over a period of years, making it easier to trade goods across national borders. *Maquiladoros*, or small Mexican factories, sprang up along the border on the Mexican side, and many jobs from the American garment industry were lost to these factories. Especially disturbing to the workers was the fact that their jobs were exported partly to take advantage of low wages and environmental standards.

Another blow to the garment industry was the World Trade Organization, which defines the rules of trade among nations at a near-global level. Created in early 1995, it had 153 nation members that account for more than 95 percent of the world's trade. The stated aim of the organization was to promote free trade and stimulate economic growth, but American labor unions condemned the labor-rights records of developing countries. They claimed that the more the World Trade Organiza-

tion promoted globalization, the more labor rights would suffer. After China joined the World Trade Organization in 2001, it would eventually double its exports to the United States. China had a strong competitive edge in clothing manufacture because of its government's exploitation of the millions of rural Chinese who migrated to China's cities in search of work—much like Europeans had flocked to the United States a century earlier.

ILLEGAL IMMIGRATION AND THE GARMENT INDUSTRY

During the last decades of the twentieth century, more and more illegal immigrants were arriving in the United States by clandestinely crossing the U.S. border with Mexico. Mexican agricultural workers had long crossed the border to work in seasonal American farming industries, but most had returned home when their harvesting work was finished. In contrast, many workers from Mexico and Central American nations were entering the United States illegally in the hope of finding steady, permanent jobs that would permit them to stay. Many of these people found steady jobs in the Los Angeles garment industry.

The problem of illegal immigrants became a topic of public discussion, and attempts were made by the federal government to improve border security. However, many U.S. employers were becoming dependent on undocumented workers, who were willing to work for lower pay than American workers. In August of 2007, the U.S. Department of Homeland Security announced a controversial new immigration enforcement policy. It issued a "No-Match" regulation intended to help employees ensure that their workers are legal, and to help the government identify and crack down on employers who knowingly hire illegal immigrants. This new policy caused a great deal of consternation within Los Angeles's multibillion-dollar garment industry. Some manufacturers threatened to move their operations offshore.

In October of 2007, a U.S. district court judge issued a preliminary injunction that prevented the Department of Homeland Security from carrying out its new policy. The judge who ruled in the case of *AFL-CIO v. Chertoff* accepted the plaintiffs' argument that such a rule would cause thousands of employers to bear significant expenses and would likely lead to unfair terminations of many workers

because of errors in the Social Security database that was to be used to identify undocumented immigrants.

In late 2008, when the United States was entering into a severe recession and Congress was debating the implementation of a massive economic stimulus package, the U.S. House of Representatives passed a bill with a provision to ensure that new jobs go to Americans and not to illegal immigrants.

Sheila Golburgh Johnson

FURTHER READING

Bacon, David. *Illegal People: How Globalization Creates Migration and Criminalizes Immigrants.* Boston: Beacon Books, 2008. Shows the human side of globalization, exposing the way it uproots people in Latin America and Asia, driving them to emigrate.

Gordon, Jennifer. *Suburban Sweatshops: The Fight for Immigrant Rights.* Cambridge, Mass.: Belknap Press, 2005. A record of the Workplace Project founded by the author in 1992 to help immigrant workers in the underground suburban economy of Long Island, New York. This book discusses new possibilities for labor organizing, community building, and participatory democracy.

Green, Nancy L. *Immigrants: Ready-to-Wear and Ready-to-Work—A Century of Industry and Immigrants in Paris and New York.* Durham, N.C.: Duke University Press, 1997. Compelling comparative study of the garment industries in France and the United States that analyzes the garment industry from the point of economic, social, cultural, political, and gender history.

Louie, Miriam Ching Yoon. *Sweatshop Warriors: Immigrant Women Workers Take on the Global Factory.* Cambridge, Mass.: South End Press, 2001. Examination of transnational sweatshops through the eyes of Korean, Chinese, and Mexican women forced to leave their homelands to take exploitative labor jobs in the world's sweatshops.

Woloch, Nancy, ed. *Early American Women: A Documentary History, 1700-1900.* Belmont, Calif.: Wadsworth, 1992. Collection of more than seventy-five primary sources, almost all written by women. Each chapter begins with a generic history.

SEE ALSO: Asian immigrants; Captive Thai workers; Chinese family associations; Family businesses; International Ladies' Garment Workers' Union; Jewish immigrants; New York City; Sweatshops; Triangle Shirtwaist fire; Women immigrants.

GARVEY, MARCUS

IDENTIFICATION: Jamaican immigrant, social activist, and journalist
BORN: August 17, 1887; St. Ann's Bay, Jamaica
DIED: June 10, 1940; London, England

SIGNIFICANCE: The first person of African descent to galvanize black people throughout the world with the idea of returning to Africa, Garvey founded the Universal Negro Improvement Association (UNIA), which sought to deliver African Americans from injustice, encourage racial self-improvement, and promote a back-to-Africa movement. He also started the Black Star Line shipping company to help promote black economic independence and to provide transportation back to Africa.

Born in the British Caribbean colony of Jamaica in 1887, Marcus Garvey was the son of sharecroppers. At the age of fourteen, he moved to Jamaica's capital city, Kingston, where he became a printer. There he learned the journalism trade, which would later enable him to set up newspapers that he would use to organize and address workers who were victims of racial injustice. He traveled throughout Central America, South America, and Europe and witnessed the living conditions of people of African descent around the world. Eventually, he returned home to Jamaica and started the UNIA, a racial uplift organization for all peoples of African descent.

Disappointed by the lack of support from the black community in Jamaica but determined to continue this path of liberating his people from oppression and inequality, he went to the United States, hoping to gain some financial support from the African American educator Booker T. Washington. Garvey arrived in the United States in 1916, after Washington had already died but nevertheless found an eager audience for his message that he had not found in Jamaica. In New York City's Harlem district, his black nationalist ideas were accepted, as he promoted the back-to-Africa movement and established the shipping company the Black Star Line.

As Garvey traveled throughout the United States, he witnessed the living conditions of African Americans and spoke and met with African American leaders. The economic disaster of World War I, racial discrimination, lynching, and the injustices faced by African Americans opened the door to a leader willing to speak up and support racial pride and economic independence. Over the next half dozen years, Garvey built the largest mass movement of black people in

Marcus Garvey. (Library of Congress)

the world, finding his strongest support in the Caribbean, Central America, and the United States. However, his Black Star Line fell short of success as a result of negligence and the need for financial resources. In 1922, J. Edgar Hoover of the federal government's Bureau of Investigation (forerunner of the Federal Bureau of Investigation) started investigating Garvey for financial fraud. In 1925, Garvey was sentenced to federal prison on mail-fraud charges. Two years later, he was deported to Jamaica, never to return to the United States. Eventually, he returned to England, where he died in 1940. By then, his UNIA was only a fraction of its former size.

Garvey was very influential at a time when there was a need for leadership for descendants of Africans. He was effective because he sought to improve the self-esteem and condition of black people all over the world. His published speeches and letters address issues of injustice and offer suggestions for the elevation of self-esteem based on racial pride and economic independence.

Diana Pardo

FURTHER READING

Cronon, Edmund David. *The Black Moses: The Story of Marcus Garvey and the Universal Negro Improvement Association.* Madison: University of Wisconsin Press, 1969.

Garvey, Marcus. *Selected Writings and Speeches of Marcus Garvey.* Edited by Bob Blaisdell. New York: Dover, 2004.

Grant, Colin. *Negro with a Hat: The Rise and Fall of Marcus Garvey.* New York: Oxford University Press, 2008.

Hill, Robert A., ed. *The Marcus Garvey and Universal Negro Improvement Association Papers.* 9 vols. Berkeley: University of Califorina Press, 1983-1996.

SEE ALSO: African Americans and immigrants; Economic opportunities; Emigration; Liberia; Universal Negro Improvement Association; West Indian immigrants.

GAY AND LESBIAN IMMIGRANTS

SIGNIFICANCE: U.S. immigration law has historically excluded openly gay and lesbian individuals on various bases, ranging from classifications of them as morally or medically unfit to their perceived social and political threats to the desirable character of American society. This practice began to be challenged during the 1950's and was eliminated in 1990 by congressional repeal of a statutory provision barring entry to persons determined to be psychopathic personalities or sexual deviants.

The original regulatory purpose of U.S. immigration law was to deal with the management of easily recognized and defined ethnic, racial, and social groups, with existing provisions applied (with varying degrees of accuracy and success) to populations that did not fall within these categories. In the case of gay and lesbian immigrants, the underlying concept of homosexuality did not exist as such until the end of the nineteenth century. Prior to that time, U.S. immigration officials had to utilize certain sections of federal laws originally intended to address questions of public welfare and health concerns to bar homosexuals from immigrating.

STATUTORY BARS TO IMMIGRATION

The federal Page Law of 1875 provided for the exclusion of people who had been convicted of crimes involving "moral turpitude," was interpreted as including sodomy, while an 1885 statute barred persons who were judged incapable of taking care of themselves and would thus become "public charges" supported by the state. Homosexuals were considered by immigration officials to be both mentally and physically degenerate—a combination that would render them unable to function in society. This approach was applied to identified gay and lesbian people until 1917, when a ruling from the federal government's solicitor of labor invalidated its application to "moral perverts," unless actual proof of their lack of means of support existed.

The most problematic aspect of excluding persons of same-sex orientation was identifying them so that extant laws could be applied. While in many urban gay communities certain items of dress and certain social mannerisms and behaviors were used by homosexuals to signal their sexual orientation nonverbally, the fashions of these codes varied widely from country to country and were not known to most U.S. immigration personnel. Only those individuals who admitted their sexual histories after being legally admitted to the United States were subject to deportation. An example of this is the case of a young Greek immigrant who, in the course of an investigation on charges of breaking and entering in 1912, confessed that he had been sexually active with men in St. Louis, Missouri. He was deported to Argentina.

The Immigration Act of 1917 kept the older exclusionary bases of medical and moral grounds, adding new language referring to "constitutional psychopathic inferiority." This term reflected the intent of the discarded public charge category by preserving the idea that sexual inversion was the result of a permanent psychological defect, which, instead of forcing the state to support homosexual immigrants, would drive these immigrants to prey upon American youth. Between 1917 and American entry into World War II in 1941, roughly three dozen people per year were deported under this provision.

The expanded Immigration and Nationality Act of 1952 kept the older language of federal immigration laws, rephrasing it to cover people suffering from mental disorders or psychopathic personalities. Despite the absence of anything language in the law specifically targeting homosexuals, the Immigration and Naturalization Service (INS) interpreted its text as prohibiting the immigration of identifiable homosexuals, and it began deporting dozens of gay people each year. The morally suspect character of homosexuals was not forgotten, with a requirement that immigrants be of "good moral character" taken from an earlier immigration law and used to deny applications for citizenship to gay and lesbian foreigners.

CHALLENGES TO RESTRICTIVE LAWS

The 1950's and 1960's witnessed legal challenges to the exclusionary policy, notably the case of *Rosenberg v. Fleuti* (1963), which held that the term "psychopathic personality" was too vague for general application, a judgment that led to an amendment of the 1952 act through the explicit addition of the term "sexual deviation." The Canadian plaintiff in *Boutilier v. Immigration and Naturalization Service* (1967) presented psychiatric testimony attesting to his lack of pathology. He appealed his case to the U.S. Supreme Court but was nonetheless eventually deported.

Immigration law and policy were early targets of the American gay rights movement, which was sparked by the Stonewall riots in New York City in 1969 and assisted by an erosion of the legal, medical, and psychiatric beliefs used to support and rationalize existing legislation during the 1970's. The removal of homosexuality from the list of recognized mental illnesses by the American Psychiatric Association in 1974 led to a letter to the INS from the Public Health Service in 1979 stating that immigrants would no longer be examined for "psychopathic personalities" as grounds for exclusion. In 1976, the INS had issued a confusing announcement stating that while entry would not be denied to anyone who had been a "practicing sexual deviant," immigration officials would reserve the right to deny full citizenship to people convicted of homosexual acts. This policy persisted until 1980, when the INS instructed its personnel not to ask about applicants' sexual orientations. However, the INS continued to exclude immigrants who admitted to being homosexual. In 1983, that policy that was invalidated by the U.S. Supreme Court's ruling in *Hill v. Immigration and Naturalization Service*. In 1990, the section of the INS statutes mandating the exclusion of people determined to be sexual deviants or psychopathic personalities was repealed.

LATE TWENTIETH AND EARLY TWENTY-FIRST CENTURY ISSUES

Although sexual orientation stopped being used as a basis for immigrant exclusion during the 1990's, that decade witnessed the rise of new issues for lesbians and gay men applying for entry and citizenship. These issues centered on definitions of family, acquired immunodeficiency syndrome, and quests for political asylum. Immigrants applying for U.S. residency under family petitions were required to be legally recognized spouses, children, siblings, or parents of American citizens. The refusal of U.S. immigration law to recognize the va-

lidity of same-sex partnerships—even those recognized by other nations, such as Canada—bars both same-gender partners who have formally wed and individuals who have established relationships with American citizens and wish to join their partners in the United States.

The same-sex marriage issue was further complicated when the Defense of Marriage Act was signed into law on September 21, 1996. This controversial piece of legislation defined marriage in the United States as limited to the unions of a man and a woman. It thus explicitly relieved the federal government from recognizing same-sex marriages as valid relationships. In early 2000, Representative Jerrold Nadler of New York introduced in the House of Representatives a bill for a law to be called the Permanent Partners Immigration Act. That bill called for the addition of the term "permanent partner" to all sections of federal immigration laws relevant to married couples. The bill was referred to the House Judiciary Committee and subsequently to the Subcommittee on Immigration and Claims, which took no action. Later attempts to reintroduce the bill also failed. When it was introduced again in early 2007 as the Uniting American Families Act, it gained bipartisan support but was still not passed through 2009.

In 1987, U.S. senator Jesse Helms of North Carolina introduced an amendment to a law to prohibit the entry of immigrants testing positive for the human immunodeficiency virus (HIV), which can lead to the acquired immunodeficiency syndrome (AIDS). The amendment was justified as a public health measure, but it was been not uniformly applied and has been attacked by many American and international health organizations. Reforms in the Immigration Act of 1990 reforms gave the secretary of health and human services discretion to decide what diseases would be used as grounds for exclusion of immigrants, but in 1993 a second amendment was passed by Congress specifically excluding persons infected with HIV. The spread of AIDS beyond the gay and lesbian community has widened the impact of this portion of immigration law with uncertain results.

Granting political asylum to persons who can demonstrate legitimate and clear fears of persecution in their home nations has long been a part of U.S. immigration law. However, the application of this principle to gay and lesbian immigrants has re-

quired a shift in perspective. The concept of regarding homosexuals as members of a persecuted minority who should be classified as refugees and be eligible for asylum in the United States came into use only during the last decades of the twentieth century. An early, if unintentional, example of this was the influx of several thousand gay Cubans to the United States as part of the Mariel boatlift in 1980.

In 1994, a ruling from the Board of Immigration Appeals declared a Cuban gay man to be eligible for asylum, followed by a directive from Attorney General Janet Reno that immigration officials were to consider lesbians and gays under the rubric of a "social group" as stated in the existing regulations. This placed openly gay and lesbian people in a stronger position to request asylum than those who concealed their sexual orientations. The situation was further complicated with the introduction in 1997 of a one-year filing deadline, making any gays or lesbians who had arrived in the United States prior to April 1, 1997, ineligible to file for asylum.

LGBT ACTIVISM

The growth in federal agencies involved with lesbian, gay, bisexual, and transgender (LGBT) immigration has been matched by the rise of LGBT activist organizations dedicated to advocacy and reform. The oldest such organization is the New York-based Immigration Equality, which was founded in 1994 as the Lesbian and Gay Immigration Rights Task Force. Lambda Legal, the Human Rights Campaign, and the International Lesbian and Gay Association have also made immigrant rights a priority of their civil rights work. Chief among the strategies proposed has been the creation of a pool of same-sex couples facing challenges to their own immigration status to serve as lobbyists in an effort to get the American Families Act passed and signed into law.

Other goals have included expanding the number of law firms who agree to accept LGBT immigration cases on a pro bono basis, educating both immigration judges and asylum officers on the legal rights of LGBT immigrants and asylum applicants, and raising awareness in corporate America of the impact that excluding skilled personnel on the basis of sexual orientation has on the national labor pool.

The use of an immigrant's HIV status as the basis

for denial of admission to America has remained problematic into the twenty-first century, despite the development of drugs that have made AIDS a manageable condition. Immigrants wishing to obtain HIV waivers are required to provide documentation attesting that they have received counseling on AIDS and its manner of transmission and do not constitute a public health threat to the United States. Qualifying for the waiver is also essential for obtaining permanent residency, even when prospective immigrants already have employers willing to sponsor their applications for legal permanent residence.

Robert B. Ridinger

FURTHER READING

Andriote, John-Manuel. *Victory Deferred: How AIDS Changed Gay Life in America.* Chicago: University of Chicago Press, 1999. Excellent analysis of the devastating impact of acquired immunodeficiency syndrome in the United States during the 1980's and 1990's.

Badgett, M. V. Lee. *When Gay People Get Married: What Happens When Societies Legalize Same-Sex Marriage.* New York: New York University Press, 2009. Study of how same-sex marriages have influenced societies that also includes some discussion of immigration issues.

Canaday, Margaret. "Who Is a Homosexual? The Consolidation of Sexual Identities in Mid-Twentieth-Century American Immigration Law." *Law and Social Inquiry* 28, no. 2 (2003): 351-386. Interesting essay on the problem of defining homosexuality that provides insights in the difficulties that immigrants historically faced.

Eskridge, William N. "Immigration, Asylum, and Deportation Law and Policy." In *Encyclopedia of Lesbian, Gay, Bisexual and Transgender History in America*, edited by Marc Stein. New York: Charles Scribner's Sons, 2004. Broad discussion of the manifold legal issues surrounding gay immigrants.

Luibhéid, Eithne. "Sexuality, Migration, and the Shifting Line Between Legal and Illegal Status." *GLQ: A Journal of Gay and Lesbian Studies* 14, nos. 2-3 (2008): 289-313. Up-to-date exploration of legal problems that gay immigrants confront.

SEE ALSO: Acquired immunodeficiency syndrome; *Boutilier v. Immigration and Naturalization Service*; History of immigration after 1891; Immigration Act of 1917; Immigration Act of 1990; Immigration and Nationality Act of 1952; Mariel boatlift; Marriage; "Moral turpitude"; Stereotyping.

GEARY ACT OF 1892

THE LAW: Federal legislation designed to limit Chinese immigration to the United States
DATE: Became law on May 5, 1892

SIGNIFICANCE: Enacted to reinforce and extend provisions of the Chinese Exclusion Act of 1882, the Geary Act prevented further immigration from China and required established Chinese residents of the United States to carry certificates of residence. The act grew out of an assumption that low-wage Chinese laborers were responsible for the economic downturn in the last quarter of the nineteenth century.

The Chinese Exclusion Act, passed in 1882, put a ten-year federal moratorium on the immigration of Chinese laborers, and increased restrictions on Chinese immigrants already living in the United States. When the act expired in 1892, a new bill was proposed by California Democratic congressman Thomas J. Geary. Geary's bill extended the immigration moratorium for ten additional years and required existing Chinese immigrants to obtain official certificates of residence from the Internal Revenue Service. Immigrants found without these certificates faced up to one year of hard labor followed by deportation. Bail was not permitted for immigrants arrested for being in the country illegally, and only a "credible white witness" could testify on behalf of an accused Chinese immigrant. The Geary Act was upheld by the U.S. Supreme Court in 1893, in *Fong Yue Ting v. United States*. In 1902, the act was extended indefinitely, but Congress eased restrictions during the 1920's and finally removed them in 1943.

Cynthia A. Bily

FURTHER READING

Ancheta, Angelo N. *Race, Rights, and the Asian American Experience.* Piscataway, N.J.: Rutgers University Press, 2006.

Kim, Hyung-chan. *Asian Americans and the Supreme Court: A Documentary History.* Westport, Conn.: Greenwood Press, 1992.

Motomura, Hiroshi. *Americans in Waiting: The Lost Story of Immigration and Citizenship in the United States.* New York: Oxford University Press, 2006.

SEE ALSO: Asian immigrants; Asiatic Exclusion League; Bayard-Zhang Treaty of 1888; Chinese Exclusion Act of 1882; Chinese immigrants; Congress, U.S.; Deportation; *Fong Yue Ting v. United States*; History of immigration after 1891; McCreary Amendment of 1893.

GENTLEMEN'S AGREEMENT

DATE: Signed on March 14, 1907

THE TREATY: Informal agreement between the governments of Japan and the United States that limited Japanese immigration to the United States to nonlaborers, laborers already settled in the United States, and members of their families

SIGNIFICANCE: In the wake of Japanese military victories over the Chinese and the Russians as well as following the turmoil of the San Francisco earthquake of 1906 and a resultant segregation order by the San Francisco Board of Education against Japanese and Korean schoolchildren, President Theodore Roosevelt's federal government negotiated a Gentlemen's Agreement with Japan that defused threats of war, ended the segregation order, and limited Japanese immigration.

After Japan's Meiji Restoration began in 1868, Japanese emigrants began to seek their fortunes in California. After the passage of the Chinese Exclusion Act of 1882, labor shortages drew increasing numbers of Japanese immigrants both to Hawaii (especially after its annexation in 1898 by the United States) and to California, especially the San Francisco Bay Area. Japanese victories in the Sino-Japanese War (1894-1895) and the Russo-Japanese War (1904-1905) established the previously closed country as a world power, even as California and other West Coast states began to extend antimiscegenation laws to bar marriages between whites and "Mongolians."

SAN FRANCISCO EARTHQUAKE AND AFTERMATH

Unlike the earlier Chinese immigrants who were mostly male and lived in or near the Grant Street Chinatown, Japanese Americans in San Francisco lived throughout the city. Before the 1906 earthquake, there were ninety-three Japanese children in twenty-three different elementary schools. Also, anti-Asian sentiment was being redirected from the Chinese to the Japanese by statements from San Francisco mayor Eugene Schmitz; a series of articles in the *San Francisco Chronicle* describing the "yellow peril"; and the Asiatic Exclusion League, which was organized by one hundred San Francisco unions in 1905 in order to extend the Chinese Exclusion Act to cover Japanese and Koreans, boycott Japanese workers and Japanese-owned businesses, and segregate Japanese and Korean students from public schools.

The San Francisco earthquake of April 18, 1906, destroyed municipal records that had inflamed fears concerning the incursion of the supposedly more aggressive, clever, and acquisitive Japanese. On October 11, 1906, as temporary and rehabilitated public schools were ready to reopen, the San Francisco Board of Education ordered the segregation of Japanese and Korean schoolchildren with the already segregated Chinese. Although the few Koreans complied with the order, Japanese parents objected strenuously. The Japanese government lodged a formal protest, claiming that the order violated the treaty of 1894. President Theodore Roosevelt, who had received a Nobel Peace Prize earlier in 1906 for helping to negotiate the treaty that ended the Russo-Japanese War, articulated his sincere "regard and respect for the people of Japan" in his December 3, 1906, state of the union address. Roosevelt subsequently called San Francisco government and board of education officials to Washington and facilitated the negotiation of what has since been termed the Gentlemen's Agreement of 1907.

LEGACY OF THE GENTLEMEN'S AGREEMENT

The Gentlemen's Agreement forced the rescinding of the board of education order. In return, the Japanese government agreed not to issue

President Theodore Roosevelt. (Library of Congress)

ment led to the Immigration Act of 1924, effectively halting all further Japanese immigration to the United States until the passage of the Immigration and Nationality Act of 1952.

Richard Sax

FURTHER READING

Chan, Sucheng. *Asian Americans: An Interpretive History.* Boston: Twayne, 1991. Comprehensive social and political history of four principal Asian immigrant cultures (Chinese, Japanese, Filipino, Korean) includes treatment of diplomatic and legal landmarks and struggles.

Daniels, Roger. *The Politics of Prejudice: The Anti-Japanese Movement in California and the Struggle for Japanese Exclusion.* Berkeley: University of California Press, 1999. Details issues of regionalism and racial politics in late nineteenth and early twentieth century California.

Esthus, Raymond A. *Theodore Roosevelt and Japan.* Seattle: University of Washington Press, 1967. Chronological history that describes how statesmanship kept the United States and Japan on diplomatic terms even as Japan waged war with the Russians, annexed Korea, and negotiated the informal Gentlemen's Agreement with the United States.

Kiyama, Henry, and Frederik Schodt. *The Four Immigrants Manga: A Japanese Experience in San Francisco, 1904-1924.* Berkeley, Calif.: Stone Bridge Press, 1999. Manga (graphic novel) treatment of four Japanese immigrants to San Francisco, humorously poking fun at the quirky and culturally obtuse behavior of their employers from the perspective of student-workers.

Neu, Charles E. *Troubled Encounter: The United States and Japan.* Malabar, Fla.: R. E. Krieger, 1979. Diplomatic study of Japanese-U.S. relations from beginning of the Meiji Restoration (1868) through the late twentieth century. Details how the Gentlemen's Agreement of 1907 was a precursor to more draconian immigration measures of 1924 that exacerbated relations between the two countries.

_____. *An Uncertain Friendship: Theodore Roosevelt and Japan, 1906-1909.* Cambridge, Mass.: Harvard University Press, 1967. Describes Roosevelt's complex relationship with the Japanese government during the latter years of his second term as well as the legacy leading into the di-

any new passports for Japanese citizens who sought to work in the United States. However, parents, children, and wives of Japanese laborers already in the United States could still immigrate to the United States. Also, critics of the agreement noted the loophole that Japanese laborers could still freely immigrate to the territory of Hawaii, and the "picture bride" industry subsequently developed, in which single male Japanese laborers in the United States could select a Japanese bride from the old country solely on the basis of mailed photographs. The provisions of the Gentlemen's Agreement allowed immigrant Japanese communities to develop complex family networks in a manner that the previous male-only Chinese communities never achieved. There were 90 Japanese-owned businesses in San Francisco in 1900 and 545 by 1909, despite the negative financial ramifications of the 1906 earthquake. According to the 1900 U.S. Census, there were 72,257 citizens of Japanese heritage living in the United States (42 percent in California); by 1920, there were 138,834 (70 percent in California). Continuing anti-immigration senti-

plomacy policies of the William Taft administration.

Takaki, Ronald. *Strangers from a Different Shore: A History of Asian-Americans.* Boston: Little, Brown, 1989. Historical study of Asian Americans with significant treatment of the settling of Japanese America and resultant ethnic stereotyping, prejudice, and state and federal legal issues.

SEE ALSO: Alien land laws; Amerasian children; Anti-Japanese movement; Asiatic Exclusion League; California; Immigration Act of 1924; Immigration and Nationality Act of 1952; Japanese immigrants; San Francisco; "Yellow peril" campaign.

GEORGIA

SIGNIFICANCE: Georgia was originally settled by immigrants from various parts of Europe. Later, slaves were brought in from Africa and the Caribbean. During the century following the Civil War, Georgia's population declined, but during the late twentieth century, Asian immigrants arrived in the state, followed by large numbers of Mexicans.

The original inhabitants of Georgia were several Native American tribes: the Apalache in the south, the Yamasee along the coast, and Cherokees and Creeks throughout the entire region. In 1526, Spain made its first attempt to plant a colony on the eastern seaboard; it is now believed that the Spanish settlement was not located in South Carolina, as had been thought, but on the Georgia mainland. However, many of the early Spanish settlers fell ill and died, and the survivors abandoned the colony, leaving few permanent traces of their presence behind. During the first half of the seventeenth century, the Spanish built forts and established missions in Georgia, but they were not able to maintain their ascendancy against the British, who soon laid claim to the Carolinas, Georgia, and part of Spanish Florida.

In 1731, the British crown granted a charter to a group of men led by General James Edward Oglethorpe, whose purpose was to establish a new colony called Georgia, in which there would be no slavery, no hard liquor, and no Roman Catholics. Oglethorpe offered land and supplies to poor laborers from England. Georgia was also a safe haven for those fleeing persecution by the Roman Catholic Church, among them German Lutherans and Moravians and French Huguenots. In 1733, forty-two Jews arrived in Savannah, most of them Sephardic Jews driven out of Portugal. In 1736, the colonists were joined by Scottish Highlanders, many of them Jacobites whose property had been confiscated after the rebellion of 1715. Lutherans from Salzburg, Germany, established the town of Ebenezer, upriver from Savannah, and Moravians also settled there, though they later moved north. Scots founded New Inverness (now Darien) on the Altamaha River.

Because of frequent attacks by the Spaniards and Indians, along with restrictions that made trade difficult and the establishment of large plantations impossible, most of the original colonists had left Georgia by 1743. However, after the original prohibition against slavery was rescinded in 1750, the colony attracted prosperous settlers, many of whom became planters and merchants.

PROFILE OF GEORGIA

Region	Southeast coast
Entered union	1788
Largest cities	Atlanta (capital), Augusta, Columbus, Savannah, Athens
Modern immigrant communities	Koreans, Asian Indians, Mexicans

Population	Total	Percent of state	Percent of U.S.	U.S. rank
All state residents	9,364,000	100.0	3.13	9
All foreign-born residents	860,000	9.2	2.29	9

Source: U.S. Census Bureau, *Statistical Abstract for 2006.*
Notes: The U.S. population in 2006 was 299,399,000, of whom 37,548,000 (12.5%) were foreign born. Rankings in last column reflect total numbers, not percentages.

During the next few years, large numbers of slaves were brought into Georgia from Africa and from the Caribbean. By the 1830's, however, the once wealthy planters were in economic trouble, in large part because their intensive cotton cultivation had ruined the soil. Many of them uprooted their households and moved west to Alabama and Mississippi, taking their slaves with them.

Meanwhile, after 1815, Irish colonists fleeing poverty and oppression had been coming to Georgia. Though at first their lack of education held them to menial jobs, they developed strong communities and became a political force. Savannah later became known for its annual Irish festival.

After the Civil War (1861-1865), the hard-pressed planters made their land available for sharecropping, but tenants could barely survive on what they made, and the whites who went to work in the new cotton mills fared no better. As one of the poorest states in the Union, Georgia attracted few immigrants. Only metropolitan Atlanta offered some opportunities, at least for whites; the rest of the state remained in the grips of poverty, which was only intensified during the Great Depression of the 1930's. After World War II, many black and some white Georgians fled to the North, where they could earn better wages as factory workers.

During the 1970's, immigrants from Korea and Vietnam began settling in Georgia, where many of them opened shops. Well-educated Asian Indians arrived to fill vacancies in medical and professional fields. During the 1980's, a new wave of Latin American immigrants flooded into Georgia. By 2006, according to the Migration Policy Institute, 32.2 percent of the foreign-born population of Georgia came from Mexico. About half of them were undocumented immigrants. Their lack of education forced them into low-paying jobs with no health benefits, and they had to rely on government welfare programs. They often faced resentment from native-born Americans, and they became easy targets for criminals.

Rosemary M. Canfield Reisman

FURTHER READING

Cobb, James C. *Georgia Odyssey.* 2d ed. Athens: University of Georgia Press, 2008.

Coleman, Kenneth, ed. *A History of Georgia.* 2d ed. Athens: University of Georgia Press, 1991.

Mohl, Raymond A. "Globalization, Latinization, and the *Nuevo* New South." In *Other Souths: Diversity and Difference in the U.S. South, Reconstruction to Present,* edited by Pippa Holloway. Athens: University of Georgia Press, 2008.

Murphy, Arthur D., Colleen Blanchard, and Jennifer A. Hill, eds. *Latino Workers in the Contemporary South.* Athens: University of Georgia Press, 2001.

SEE ALSO: African Americans and immigrants; Asian immigrants; Austrian immigrants; British immigrants; Crime; Florida; French immigrants; German immigrants; Irish immigrants; Jewish immigrants; Mexican immigrants; South Carolina.

GERMAN AMERICAN PRESS

DEFINITION: German-language newspapers catering to German immigrants

SIGNIFICANCE: As German immigrants reached the United States and began settling in the interior of the country, the German American press catered to their need for news and information, providing stories about their adopted homeland while keeping in touch with Germany. The German American press became one of the largest and most powerful ethnic presses in the country, aiding German politicians at both state and national levels.

Ethnic presses in the United States were a major force in American journalism during the nineteenth century, when mass European immigration was bringing millions of non-English speakers into the United States. The German-language press was one of the most influential of the ethnic presses. The first German newspaper in the British colonies was published by Benjamin Franklin in 1732. However, his *Philadelphische Zeitung* lasted only a few months, and other German language dailies had similarly short life spans. In 1735, John Peter Zenger was publishing the *New York Weekly,* a German American paper, when he was charged with libel. His trial expanded freedom of the press by making it more difficult for government officials to sue for libel.

Meanwhile, developments in Europe invigorated the German American press as political turmoil accelerated German emigration. The revolutions of 1848 and subsequent government crackdowns drove millions of central Europeans from the continent. As German émigrés arrived in North America, they found newspapers such as the *New York Staats-Zeitung*, a major daily established in 1834, already flourishing and ready to cater to German speakers hungry for news about their adopted homeland.

A GROWING PRESENCE

As new German immigrants settled throughout the United States, their daily newspapers followed. By the 1850's, Cincinnati alone had four German-language newspapers, and St. Louis had three. The most influential of these papers were St. Louis's *Anzeiger des Westens*, or *Western Informant* and the *Cincinnati Volksblatt*. Both papers supported the abolitionist movement and the Republican Party, which formed during the mid-1850's. In Illinois, the *Staats Zeitung* was the official Republican voice in the German community, and it gained prominence during the 1860 presidential campaign.

As the circulations of German-language papers topped one hundred thousand in cities such as Chicago and New York, German American politicians used the papers as campaigning tools. Carl Schurz, a German-born Republican who became a political reformer and secretary of the interior for President Rutherford B. Hayes, used his part ownership in the *St. Louis Westliche Post* to promote his own political career. German-language newspapers also closely followed the military exploits of German American generals, such as Franz Sigel. With their large readerships and captive audiences of German immigrants who were not yet familiar with English, the papers became a force in politics and were courted by politicians eager to communicate with their German constituents.

The German American press also aided in the rise of major newspaper magnates, who used ethnic newspapers to expand their overall readership. For example, Joseph Pulitzer published the St. Louis *Westliche Post* along with his *St. Louis Post-Dispatch*, providing a gateway as German immigrants adopted English and switched their loyalty to English-language newspapers.

DECLINE OF THE PRESS

European turmoil during the 1870's and 1880's drove more Germans to emigrate to North America, increasing demand for German-language papers. New York City alone had more than a half-dozen such papers, while many rural communities with German settlers had their own German papers. However, as German immigration waned, and second- and third-generation German Americans adopted English, the German papers saw their readerships decline. Rural papers were the first to shut down. During the early years of the twentieth century, mergers left most large cities with only one or two German-language dailies each.

American entry into World War I in 1917 proved to be the end of the German American press's influence in American politics. Much of the fall of the papers may be attributed to the German entrepreneur George Vierek, who established a pro-German newspaper called *The Fatherland* in August, 1914, at the time the war was starting in Europe. The circulation of the paper grew rapidly, as German Americans sought news about the course of the war. Vierek used his newspaper as a propaganda machine for the German government, receiving reports from the German Information Service. His paper defended the German government against charges of war crimes and brutality against civilians. It also attacked British influence in American foreign policy, taking particular aim at the Wilson administration when it tilted in favor of the Allies. Many German newspapers supported the candidacy of Charles Evans Hughes during the 1916 presidential election, believing that he was less likely than President Woodrow Wilson to lead the United States into the war against Germany. Their endorsements of Hughes would not be forgotten by Wilson after he won the November, 1916, presidential election and took the country into the war the following April.

In 1918, Wilson signed the Trading with the Enemy Act, which regulated all trade with Germany and its allies. Such trade included news reports passed on to the German-language press. Onerous regulations were imposed requiring costly record keeping by the newspapers as they were forced to record all their contacts with the German government.

Such regulations weakened the German lan-

guage press, while growing distrust of the loyalty of German speakers led to the demise of half of the German newspapers during the early 1920's. The end of large-scale German immigration and the general economic turndown of the Great Depression reduced the circulation of the German newspapers, leaving only a few in the largest American cities such as New York. By the turn of the twenty-first century, fewer than two dozen German American newspapers were still publishing. These included Chicago's *Amerika Woch*, New York's *Staats Zeitung*, and the *Florida Journal*.

Douglas Clouatre

FURTHER READING

Fleming, Thomas. *The Illusion of Victory*. New York: Basic Books, 2003. Discusses how the Wilson administration used the national emergency to attack ethnic groups including Germans suspected of supporting their homeland during World War I.

Gross, Ruth. *Traveling Between Worlds*. College Station: Texas A&M Press, 2006. Study of German immigration into the United States that includes coverage of such institutions as churches and the press.

Heinrich-Tolzmann, Don. *The German American Experience*. Amherst, N.Y.: Humanity Books, 2000. Wide-ranging study of how Germans who emigrated to the United States became an integral part of their new country's cultural and political system.

Keller, Phyllis. *States of Belonging*. Cambridge, Mass.: Harvard University Press, 1979. Examines several German intellectuals, including publishers of German American newspapers and journals.

Miller, Sally, ed. *The Ethnic Press in the United States*. Westport, Conn.: Greenwood Press, 1987. Shows how immigrant presses were an important part of arrivals to United States, including the active German American press.

SEE ALSO: Austrian immigrants; European revolutions of 1848; German immigrants; History of immigration, 1783-1891; Italian American press; Pulitzer, Joseph; Spanish-language press; World War I.

GERMAN IMMIGRANTS

SIGNIFICANCE: The first non-English-speaking immigrant group to enter the United States in large numbers, Germans played major roles in American economic development, the abolitionist movement, U.S. military forces, and other spheres during the nineteenth century, and German immigrants continued to make important contributions to the United States during the twentieth century.

Most German immigration to the United States occurred during the nineteenth century, but Germans began arriving as early as 1608, when they helped English settlers found Jamestown, Virginia. Germans also played an important role in the Dutch creation of New Amsterdam, which later became New York City, during the early 1620's. Other early German immigrants helped to settle North and South Carolina. By the nineteenth century, German immigrants were advancing farther inland to states such as Nebraska, Ohio, Illinois, Missouri, Wisconsin, Kansas, Minnesota, and Texas.

EARLY IMMIGRATION, 1608-1749

Two forces were paramount in prompting early German immigration: heavy taxation and German laws of primogeniture, which permitted only the eldest sons in families to inherit their fathers' land. These forces, along with seemingly constant and disruptive German wars, gave many young Germans strong motivations for emigrating to a new country, where they could hope to own their land and prosper with minimal government hindrance.

The first American region in which large numbers of Germans settled was Pennsylvania. Germantown, near what is now Philadelphia, was the first of many permanent German settlements in the British colonies—many of which had the same name. After Germantown was founded in 1683, German immigration to Pennsylvania grew more rapidly. By the mid-eighteenth century, Pennsylvania's approximately 50,000 German immigrants made up about 40 percent of the colony's entire population. Amish and Mennonite religious communities and the creation of the perhaps inaptly named "Pennsylvania Dutch" established Pennsyl-

PROFILE OF GERMAN IMMIGRANTS

Country of origin	Germany
Primary language	German
Primary regions of U.S. settlement	Pennsylvania, New York, Missouri, Minnesota, Ohio, Illinois, Nebraska
Earliest significant arrivals	1608
Peak immigration periods	1840's-1920's, 1950's
Twenty-first century legal residents*	63,214 (7,901 per year)

*Immigrants who obtained legal permanent resident status in the United States.
Source: Department of Homeland Security, Yearbook of Immigration Statistics, 2008.

vania as a primary stronghold for German immigration. Pennsylvania was also becoming a base from which Germans migrated to other colonies, including what is now northern West Virginia, most of Maryland, parts of North Carolina, and the western regions of Virginia and South Carolina.

Taking their name from *Deutsche*, the German word for "German," the Pennsylvania Dutch were the primary builders of Philadelphia and many of its neighboring communities in what became a six-county region that would be known as "Pennsylvania Dutch Country." Pennsylvania's Amish communities have kept alive German culture through their rejection of modern technology, their continued wearing of early German farming attire, and their ability to speak both old and modern forms of German. German farmers, craftsmen, and indentured servants helped develop Pennsylvania.

LATE EIGHTEENTH CENTURY DEVELOPMENTS

During the late eighteenth century, the Industrial Revolution began transforming the economies of the many German states from agricultural to manufacturing bases, making it more difficult for farmers to prosper. The lure of apparently unlimited farmland in North America, coupled with news from successful immigrants to provide a powerful lure to emigrate. From the late eighteenth

century through much of the nineteenth century, millions of Germans went to the United States. Many of them were farmers who brought skills that contributed significantly to the agriculture of the Midwest, and many settled and helped build cities such as Milwaukee and Cincinnati.

The success of many early German immigrants in agriculture helped draw many German-born businessmen to the United States, where some of them built beer breweries that prospered alongside local agriculture. Some the best-known American breweries, such as Pabst, Anheuser-Busch, Schlitz, Blatz, and Miller, were started by Germans.

Because Philadelphia was at the center of American opposition to British colonial rule, it is not surprising that Germans played an important role in the American Revolution that led to the independence of the United States. By the late eighteenth century, many German immigrants had deep roots in North American and were eager to help fight for independence. However, Great Britain's use of German mercenaries against Americans helped give German Americans a bad name.

Known as Hessians because most of them were from the German state of Hesse, as many as 30,000 German mercenaries may have fought for Great Britain, and they may have constituted as many as one-third of all British combat troops in the Revolutionary War. These Germans fought ruthlessly against the Americans, but they paid a heavy price in casualties. Nearly one-quarter of them died from illnesses, and another quarter may have died in combat. It is not known exactly how many of the German troops remained in the United States after the war, but their number seems to have been high. Moreover, many Hessian mercenaries prospered after the war, thanks to the fact that the new U.S. government lacked the funds to send them back to Europe.

German immigrants who fought on the American side were also recognized for their valor and loyalty. Some held high commands. A particularly well-known German general in the war was Baron Friedrich Wilhelm von Steuben, who volunteered his services as a trained Prussian general to the American cause free of pay. Von Steuben was especially valuable in teaching discipline and drill to revolutionary soldiers, few of whom had any formal military training. The colonial troops were initially ridiculed by British troops for their inability

to hold line and their eagerness to retreat. Von Steuben helped transform the untrained men into efficient soldiers. Steubenville, Ohio, was later named in his honor.

FIRST CENTURY OF AMERICAN INDEPENDENCE, 1783-1900

Through the half-century following the Revolutionary War, German immigration increased steadily. Many of the new arrivals settled in such major cities as New York and Philadelphia, but independence from Great Britain allowed the United States to open up the West to settlers, greatly expanding agricultural opportunities for Germans and other immigrants.

Although much of the prosperity that German immigrants enjoyed in North America was based on their success in agriculture, Germans played a leading role in opposing slavery, which provided most of the farm labor in southern U.S. states. Some of the German leaders in the American abolitionist movement were political refugees from the many failed revolutions of 1848 in Europe who came to the United States filled with liberal ideals.

After the U.S. Civil War began in 1861, German immigrants again played a prominent role in the fighting. Some Germans fought for the Confederacy during the war, but the overwhelming majority of Germans involved in the conflict fought on the Union side. Indeed, nearly one-quarter of all Union Army troops were German Americans, about 45 percent of whom had been born in Europe. Among the most outstanding German officers in the Union Army were Carl Schurz, Max Weber, Louis Blenker, and Franz Sigel. Many Germans who fought for the Union brought considerable military experience. A slave state that remained in the Union, Missouri had a large German population that supplied many soldiers to the Union cause. After the war ended in 1865, German immigration continued to rise at a rate faster than that of any other immigrant group into the early twentieth century.

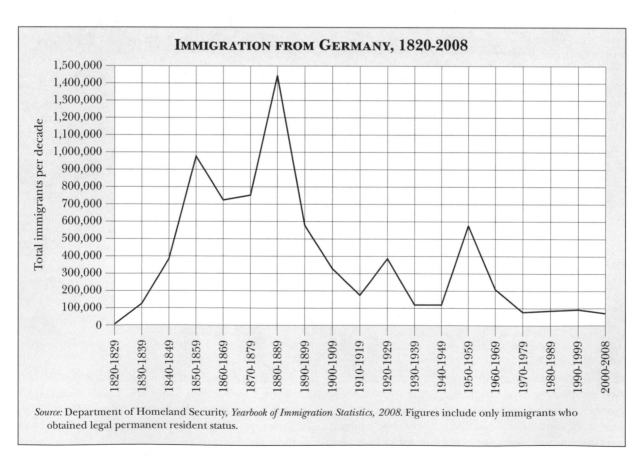

Source: Department of Homeland Security, *Yearbook of Immigration Statistics, 2008.* Figures include only immigrants who obtained legal permanent resident status.

TWENTIETH TO TWENTY-FIRST CENTURIES

German immigration to the United States continued to grow until 1914, when World War I began in Europe. The U.S. declaration of war against Germany in 1917 began the first period of anti-German sentiment since the Revolutionary War, when Great Britain used German soldiers against Americans. Anti-German fever during the war caused many Americans to vilify German Americans, especially those known still to speak German, and recently arrived German immigrants. Only a small number of German Americans openly supported Germany's position in the war. Many of them were imprisoned for sedition or attacked by mobs.

During the war, former U.S. president Theodore Roosevelt went as far as to say neutrality was not an option and dual loyalty could not exist.

Rising anti-German sentiment saw many German names disappear from the names of businesses, schools, and even public streets. Indeed, World War I helped accelerate the obliteration of German subcultures within the United States. Many German-language magazines and newspapers stopped publishing. German Americans avoided speaking German in public, and school systems stopped teaching German. Many German Americans anglicized their own surnames: "Mueller" became "Miller," "Schmidt" became "Smith," and "Franz" became "Franks." Fear of American hostility, not the war itself, did much to destroy visible traces of German culture in the United States.

American entry into World War II in 1941 renewed American animosity toward Germans. Anti-German and anti-Japanese campaigns began shortly after Japan launched its sneak attack on

German immigrants on the steerage deck of the immigrant ship Friedrich der Grosse. *When World War I began in August, 1914, the U.S. government seized the ship, which happened to be laid up in New York harbor. After the United States entered the war in 1917, the Navy used the ship, renamed USS* Huron, *to transport troops across the Atlantic. Over the next two years, the ship completed fifteen round-trip voyages.* (Library of Congress)

Pearl Harbor on December 7, 1941. The United States had still not fully recovered from anti-German animosity during World War I, and the new war against Germany's already reviled Nazi regime renewed American distrust of Germans. Using the Alien and Sedition Acts of 1798, the U.S. government legally detained more than ten thousand German Americans during the war. German businesses suffered vandalism and many Germans were attacked by American mobs. Meanwhile, the Holocaust in Europe led to another increase in German immigrants following the war. Most of these people were German Jews who had suffered greatly under the Nazi regime.

An ironic aspect of the war was the fact that the supreme Allied military commander and future president of the United States, Dwight D. Eisenhower was himself of German descent. Some of his ancestors had been members of the Pennsylvania Dutch communities. The war also brought to the United States the great German theoretic physicist Albert Einstein and German rocket expert Wernher von Braun, who would later help shape the American space program.

After memories of World War II receded and Eisenhower became a popular U.S. president, German heritage lost some of the negative stigma it had acquired over the previous decades. This development was aided by growing American distrust of the Soviet Union and the beginning of the Cold War. With an ominous new international threat looming, Americans were becoming less inclined to worry about differences among their own subcultures.

Despite early twentieth century anti-German movements, many traces of German culture have survived into the twenty-first century. These can be seen in product names such as Bayer, Heinz, Chrysler, Busch, and Budweiser, and in such now thoroughly American items of cuisine as hot dogs (frankfurters) and pretzels. In addition to foods and beers, German culture has provided the American educational system with the concept of kindergarten, which was regularly practiced in Germany following the increased immigration during the early nineteenth century. Other German contributions to American culture include two-day weekends, gymnasiums, Christmas trees, and theme parks.

Keith J. Bell

FURTHER READING

Brancaforte, Charlotte L., ed. *The German Forty-eighters in the United States.* New York: Peter Lang, 1990. Eighteen essays covering a wide range of topics, including a reappraisal that many of the immigrants were not radicals or revolutionaries.

Creighton, M. *The Colors of Courage: Gettysburg's Forgotten History: Immigrants, Women, and African Americans in the Civil War's Defining Battle.* New York: Basic Books, 2006. Depicts the forgotten heroism of Germans and other immigrant peoples in one of the bloodiest battles in American history.

Fogleman, Aaron Spencer. *Hopeful Journeys: German Immigration, Settlement, and Political Culture in Colonial America, 1717-1775.* Philadelphia: University of Pennsylvania Press, 1996. Details the everyday struggles of common German immigrants to the colonies during the eighteenth century and includes many individual stories.

Heinrich-Tolzmann Don. *The German American Experience.* Amherst, N.Y.: Humanity Books, 2000. Thought-provoking examination of how German immigrants have blended into American society.

Kamphoefner, Walter, and Wolfgang Helbich, eds. *Germans in the Civil War: The Letters They Wrote Home.* Translated by Susan Carter Vogel. Chapel Hill: University of North Carolina Press, 2006. Fascinating collection of documents presenting the firsthand views of German immigrants who fought in the U.S. Civil War.

Kennedy, David M. *The American People in World War II: Freedom from Fear, Part II.* New York: Oxford University Press, 1999. This book places immigration issues in the broad context of America at war and looks at American attitudes toward German immigrants.

Spalek, John, Adrienne Ash, and Sandra Hawrylchak. *Guide to Archival Materials of German-Speaking Emigrants to the U.S. After 1933.* Charlottesville: University of Virginia Press, 1978. Invaluable handbook for historical and genealogical research into German/Austrian immigration during the mid-twentieth century. Especially strong on Holocaust-related immigrants.

Tolzmann, Don Heinrich. *The German-American Experience.* New York: Humanity Books, 2000. Comprehensive study of German immigrants in the United States, with sections on politics and na-

tivism, German rural and urban communities, and German-speaking communities.

Trumbauer, L. *German Immigration.* New York: Facts On File, 2004. Details personal stories of German immigrants to the United States and the key players in the formation of the country.

Wittke, Carl. *Refugees of Revolution: The German Forty-eighters in America.* Philadelphia: University of Pennsylvania, 1952. A classic work on the experience of the Forty-eighters in the United States. Heavy emphasis on biography.

SEE ALSO: Austrian immigrants; Civil War, U.S.; Einstein, Albert; German American press; History of immigration, 1620-1783; History of immigration, 1783-1891; History of immigration after 1891; Holocaust; Prisoners of war in the United States; Schurz, Carl; Strauss, Levi; World War I; World War II.

GLOBALIZATION

DEFINITION: Transformation occurring as movements of people, goods, and ideas among countries and regions increase greatly

SIGNIFICANCE: Many countries, including the United States, are undergoing serious demographic transformations as a result of changing global migration patterns. Immigrants bring with them customs, practices and behavior patterns different from those of the receiving countries. Branches of the original culture are recreated in host countries, particularly within urban ethnic enclaves. Although multiethnicity is common in large urban communities, it can be threatening to native-born citizens.

In many ways the nature of migration has changed. Individuals migrate among countries for more than economic reasons. The creation of global culture brought about by a revolution in mass communications has encouraged foreign influences through media. Globalization of communication technology has helped to influence migration. By creating linkages between receiving and sending countries, communication technology has provided means by which news and information is readily available almost everywhere. This developed has helped to foster increasing immigration into the United States. Information about job opportunities is readily spread; earlier immigrants help later immigrants with housing, employment, and networking opportunities. Successful transitions from one country to another encourage still more immigration that may continue even after the original reasons for immigrating are no longer present.

Acculturation occurs when the attitudes and behaviors of individuals from one culture are affected by contact with a different cultures. In order for acculturation to occur, a relative cultural equality must exist between the giving and receiving cultures. Acculturation differs from assimilation, which occurs when the cultural characteristics of a minority group become lost within a larger culture. The acculturation process affects a variety of behaviors, values, and beliefs. For individual immigrants, the amounts of time they have spent in their host countries and their ages when they immigrate have been shown to correlate with their likelihood of acculturation and are good indicators of an individual's level of acculturation in the absence of more detailed information. Three dimensions of acculturation have been defined: assimilation, biculturalism, and observance of traditionality. Biculturalism is the ability to live in both worlds, with denial of neither. Observance of traditionality is the rejection of the dominant culture.

Sandra C. Hayes

FURTHER READING

Aneesh, A. *Virtual Migration: The Programming of Globalization.* Durham, N.C.: Duke University Press, 2006.

Bacon, David. *Illegal People: How Globalization Creates Migration and Criminalizes Immigrants.* Boston: Beacon Books, 2008.

Reimers, David M. *Other Immigrants: The Global Origins of the American People.* New York: New York University Press, 2005.

Spiro, Peter J. *Beyond Citizenship: American Identity After Globalization.* New York: Oxford University Press, 2008.

SEE ALSO: "Brain drain"; Chain migration; Drug trafficking; Economic consequences of immigration; Ethnic enclaves; Foreign exchange students; Garment industry; Health care; "Immigrant"; Mexican immigrants.

GODFATHER TRILOGY

IDENTIFICATION: Francis Ford Coppola's films based on Mario Puzo's 1969 novel *The Godfather*, about the family of a Sicilian immigrant who builds a criminal empire in New York that one of his sons inherits

DATES: Released in 1972, 1974, and 1990

SIGNIFICANCE: The winner of nine Academy Awards and dozens of critical and film-industry awards, and with *The Godfather* (1972) and *The Godfather: Part II* (1974) voted among the ten best American films ever, the trilogy occupies an iconic place in American cinema and culture. Viewed by hundreds of millions in and outside the United States, its portrayal of Sicilian immigrants, New York's Little Italy, and the organized crime underworld vie in many viewers' minds with historical truth.

In a 1963 testimony to the Congressional Hearing on Organized Crime, Joe Valachi, a "soldier" in the Genovese crime family, was the first mobster to publicly acknowledge the existence and power of the Mafia. His testimony, broadcast on radio and television and published in newspapers, was devastating for the mob, already reeling from the 1957 Apalachin exposure when New York State police had accidentally uncovered a meeting of several Mafia bosses from all over the United States. However, while the Italian crime syndicate stretching across the United States was no longer invisible to the public, few Americans gave it a second thought. Together with Mario Puzo's novel, the *Godfather* blockbusters changed that.

The Godfather (1972) opens in 1945. A decision not to enter the narcotics trade brings Vito Corleone, Italian Mafia family boss, onto a violent collision course with other New York crime families. Peace ensues only after a series of assassinations, instigated by his youngest son, Michael, who takes over the "business" after his father's death and removes the crime family to Las Vegas. The plot of *The Godfather: Part II* (1974) is complex and ambitious (the film runs two hundred minutes). Now a billionaire reaping the benefits of legalized gambling in Las Vegas, during the late 1950's Michael Corleone expands his criminal base, buys political clout, and successfully fends off a federal indictment, while competing against an aging Jewish boss from Miami (modeled after Meyer Lansky). Running in parallel is the story of his father who, as a boy, arrived at Ellis Island from Sicily in 1901, only to rise as a crime lord ("Don") in Little Italy. The much weaker *Godfather: Part III* (1990) picks up the story in 1979 and essentially reprises the plot of the first film, with the aging Michael passing the reins to the crime empire amid a new wave of machinations and assassinations.

The films are steeped in the Italian immigrant experience in the United States. Italian dialogue

Marlon Brando (right) as Don Corleone, with his son, played by Al Pacino. (Museum of Modern Art, Film Stills Archive)

(with subtitles) is ubiquitous, in *Godfather: Part II* amounting to almost half of the film. Scenes of baptism, first communion, wedding, family dinners, and other aspects of Italian Roman Catholic religion and culture are painstakingly recreated. Street life during the early decades of New York, the annual Feast of San Gennaro, and other traditions combine with extensive footage from rural and small-town life in Sicily to enrich the film's gangster plot and give it an authentic feel of the immigrant experience, not to mention a criminal underworld twist to the American Dream of "rags to riches."

Peter Swirski

FURTHER READING

Jones, Jenny M. *The Annotated God-father: The Complete Screenplay.* New York: Black Dog & Leventhal, 2007.

Messenger, Christian K. *The Godfather and American Culture: How the Corleones Became "Our Gang."* Albany: State University of New York Press, 2002.

Puzo, Mario. *The Godfather.* New York: New American Library, 1978.

SEE ALSO: Anglo-conformity; Crime; Criminal immigrants; Drug trafficking; Ellis Island; Films; Italian immigrants; Labor unions; Literature; Little Italies; New York City.

GOLDEN VENTURE GROUNDING

THE EVENT: After a freighter named the *Golden Venture* grounded off Queens, New York, 276 undocumented Chinese passengers were taken into custody by federal authorities

DATE: June 6, 1993

LOCATION: Rockaway Peninsula, Queens, New York

SIGNIFICANCE: The *Golden Venture* incident raised public awareness of the fact that dur-

A police rescue boat attempts to remove the last passengers from the Golden Venture *as men who have already been rescued watch in the foreground.* (AP/Wide World Photos)

ing the 1990's thousands of Chinese immigrants were entering the United States without legal documentation. Federal authorizes prosecuted the *Golden Venture* crew and parties responsible for the smuggling attempt and detained the would-be immigrants.

When the *Golden Venture* grounded, some passengers dove off the ship into the sea. During the rescue procedure ten people drowned or died of hypothermia and six others escaped. Those surviving were sent to detention centers, where 90 percent of them applied for political asylum. Public opinion on how to treat these survivors ranged from humanitarian appeals for full exoneration to calls for their immediate deportation.

The fates of individual survivors varied. The juveniles were transferred to court custody; some were given political asylum in the United States or South America, but many were deported. In February, 1997, President Bill Clinton awarded humanitarian paroles to the fifty-three remaining detainees, but this gesture did not alter their legal status.

After they were freed, they were left to pursue their own destinies in America. More than half of those who had been deported are believed to have later returned to the United States.

During the several years that the detainees were incarcerated in York County prison, some of them created more than ten thousand intricate paper sculptures that were later exhibited throughout the United States.

Cynthia J. W. Svoboda

FURTHER READING

Chin, Ko-Lin. *Smuggled Chinese: Clandestine Immigration to the United States.* Philadelphia: Temple University Press, 1999.

Kwong, Peter. *Forbidden Workers: Illegal Chinese Immigrants and American Labor.* New York: New Press, 1997.

SEE ALSO: Border Patrol, U.S.; Chinese immigrants; Citizenship; Deportation; Due process protections; Illegal immigration; Immigration and Naturalization Service, U.S.; Immigration law; New York State; Smuggling of immigrants; Transportation of immigrants.

GOLDMAN, EMMA

IDENTIFICATION: Lithuanian-born American anarchist and feminist

BORN: June 27, 1869; Kovno, Lithuania, Russian Empire (now Kaunas, Lithuania)

DIED: May 14, 1940; Toronto, Ontario, Canada

SIGNIFICANCE: A forceful voice for the nascent anarchist movement in the United States, Goldman founded the magazine *Mother Earth* and crisscrossed the United States lecturing about anarchy and supporting anarchists, immigrant and labor groups, women, and others oppressed by the government and institutionalized capitalism.

In 1885, Emma Goldman, having rejected her brutal father, the prospect of domestic life, and state-sanctioned oppression of radicals and Jews, emigrated from Russia to the United States. In the immigrant communities of New York, she experienced sweatshop life, worker oppression, and an unhappy marriage. Inspired by the persecution of eight anarchists involved in the Haymarket riot of 1886, Goldman joined the American anarchist movement that in its early stages attracted European, Russian, and Jewish immigrants.

Notoriety attended Goldman's advocacy of birth control, the poor, and antimilitarism. She engaged in public demonstrations and hunger strikes. Jailed on several occasions, she worked tirelessly for others accused of challenging the government, the law, and social norms. With Alexander Berkman, she conspired to murder company manager Henry Clay Frick during the Homestead, Pennsylvania, standoff between Carnegie Steel and the Amalgamated Association of Iron and Steel Workers in 1892. In 1901, she was blamed—but not convicted—for inciting Leon Czolgosz to assassinate President William McKinley. In 1906, she began publishing *Mother Earth*, a magazine promoting anarchy.

Although Goldman's own philosophy of anar-

Emma Goldman riding a public streetcar in 1917. (Library of Congress)

chy shifted over time, her enduring tenet was individual freedom of expression. Despite numerous struggles in America, Goldman embraced the country's essential belief in the individual. She was deported in 1919 for her antiwar efforts, but President Franklin D. Roosevelt allowed her return in 1934. She died in 1940 and was buried in Chicago.

Jennie MacDonald Lewis

FURTHER READING

Chalberg, John C. *Emma Goldman: American Individualist*. Edited by Mark C. Carnes. 2d ed. New York: Pearson Longman, 2008.

Goldman, Emma. *Red Emma Speaks: An Emma Goldman Reader*. Edited by Alix Kates Shulman. 3d ed. Amherst, N.Y.: Prometheus-Humanity Books, 1996.

SEE ALSO: Birth control movement; Deportation; Former Soviet Union immigrants; Immigration Act of 1903; Jewish immigrants; Labor unions; Red Scare; Sacco and Vanzetti trial; "Undesirable aliens"; Women's movements.

GOMPERS, SAMUEL

IDENTIFICATION: English-born American labor activist
BORN: January 27, 1850; London, England
DIED: December 13, 1924; San Antonio, Texas

SIGNIFICANCE: Undeniably one of the leading figures in labor history, Gompers was already an ardent unionist prior to leaving London for New York City in 1863. The giant union he cofounded in 1881, the American Federation of Labor, was based on the pragmatic principles he had learned in England.

At a young age, Samuel Gompers was immersed in working-class culture, toiling as an apprentice

Samuel Gompers and his wife, Sophia, in 1908. (Library of Congress)

shoemaker and cigar maker in London. Upon his arrival in the United States, he rose quickly through the ranks of union leadership and became an American citizen in 1872. His decision to immigrate was based on a desire for higher wages and freedom from European anti-Semitism, as he had been born a Jew. In 1881, he cofounded what became the American Federation of Labor (AFL) and, except for one year, served as president until his death. He rose to the rank of first vice president of the Cigar Makers' International Union in 1896.

Gompers displayed his British cultural origin by repudiating the class hatred that plagued continental unions. The beliefs he had embraced in England—for example, that union policy should be practical and nationalistic—served him well in the United States. By accepting only skilled labor, he guaranteed substantial bargaining clout. However, he strongly supported immigration restrictions because he felt that immigrants bidded down the price of labor, a view many saw as hypocritical. Also, his policies were of little use to unskilled laborers, who were excluded from the AFL.

Thomas W. Buchanan

FURTHER READING

Gompers, Samuel. *Seventy Years of Life and Labor.* 1925. Reprint. Ithaca, N.Y.: ILR Press, 1984.
Sloane, Arthur A. *Hoffa.* Cambridge, Mass.: MIT Press, 1991.

SEE ALSO: British immigrants; Davis, James John; Industrial Workers of the World; Jewish immigrants; Labor unions.

GONZÁLEZ CASE

THE EVENT: Asylum petition and legal custody battle of a young boy who dramatically escaped drowning during his mother's attempt to reach the United States on a small boat ignited a political feud

DATE: November 25, 1999-June 28, 2000

SIGNIFICANCE: What may have been the world's most closely watched custody battle became a cause célèbre that reached the U.S. Supreme Court, strained U.S.-Cuba relations, and had future political repercussions.

On Thanksgiving Day in 1999, a five-year-old Cuban boy named Elián González was found clinging to a rubber inner tube floating off the coast of South Florida. Five days earlier, the boy had left Cárdenas, Cuba, on a seventeen-foot boat with his mother and twelve others hoping to reach the United States. When the vessel sank during a storm, Elián and a young couple were the only survivors.

After the U.S. Coast Guard turned Elián over to the Immigration and Naturalization Service (INS), INS agents paroled Elián to the family of his great-uncle Lázaro González, who were living in Miami's Little Havana district. Meanwhile, Cuban president Fidel Castro charged that the boy had been "kidnaped" and demanded that he be returned to his father in Cárdenas. Castro threatened that if Elián were not returned to Cuba within seventy-two hours, he would cancel the U.S.-Cuba negotiations on migration that were scheduled to be held in Havana. Massive Cuban protest rallies were staged daily in front of the U.S. Interests Section in Havana.

U.S. President Bill Clinton's administration rejected Castro's ultimatum and declared that a Florida family court would rule on Elián's custody. However, that plan was reversed on December 9, when Deputy U.S. Attorney General Eric Holder stated that Elián's fate would be settled by the INS itself. The U.S.-Cuba migration talks were then held on December 13, as originally scheduled.

Six days afterward, the U.S. government ended a six-day hostage standoff in a Louisiana jail by secretly negotiating with Cuba to settle the deportation demands of six criminals who had arrived in Florida during the 1980 Mariel boatlift. The return of Elián was speculated to be part of the deal. Two weeks later, INS commissioner Doris Meissner rejected a political asylum petition filed on Elián's behalf and Attorney General Janet Reno upheld the right of Elián's father to have custody. The great-uncle of Elián who had received temporary custody of Elián in state court then challenged the INS ruling in federal court.

On April 12, 2000, Reno ordered the Florida relatives to surrender Elián. The family defied her and obtained an injunction keeping the boy in America. Ten days later, Reno authorized a predawn raid by 151 heavily armed federal agents who battered in the door of Elián's relatives' home and seized him. The boy was then reunited in Washing-

Havana taxi passing a public poster calling for Elián González's return to his homeland in early 2000. (AP/Wide World Photos)

ton, D.C., with his father, who had arrived in the capital city two weeks earlier.

On June 1, the Eleventh U.S. Circuit Court of Appeals ruled that the INS had acted properly in denying Elián asylum but ordered that the boy remain in the United States pending the appeal of his great-uncle's case. Three weeks later, the court reaffirmed its decision, which was challenged by the Miami family in the U.S. Supreme Court on June 26. Two days later, the Court declined to intervene, and Elián and his father immediately returned home to a hero's welcome in Cuba.

The Clinton administration's handling of the González case greatly angered the large and strongly anti-Castro Cuban American community in Florida. When Clinton's vice president, Al Gore, ran for president in November, 2000, Florida's Cuban Americans voted heavily against him. Their votes may have cost Gore the presidency. He lost narrowly, and the election hinged on Florida. Two

years later, Reno ran for governor of Florida and lost in the primary.

In 2003, Elián's father, whom Castro had decorated as a national hero, won a seat in Cuba's National Assembly after running unopposed. Elián frequently appeared at political rallies with Castro, whom he called a friend and "father." A museum was dedicated to Elián in his hometown and he is portrayed on a statue in front of the U.S. Interests Section in Havana. In 2008, Elián joined Cuba's Young Communist Union.

Antonio Rafael de la Cova

FURTHER READING

De los Angeles Torres, Maria. *In the Land of Mirrors: Cuban Exile Politics in the United States.* Ann Arbor: University of Michigan Press, 1999.

Diaz, Guarione M. *The Cuban American Experience: Issues, Perceptions, and Realities.* St. Louis, Mo.: Reedy Press, 2007.

Fernandez, Alfredo A. *Adrift: The Cuban Raft People.* Houston, Tex.: Arte Público Press, 2000.

SEE ALSO: Cuban immigrants; Due process protections; Families; Florida; Immigration and Naturalization Service, U.S.; Little Havana; Mariel boatlift; Miami; Presidential elections; Supreme Court, U.S.; Washington, D.C.

GOSPEL SOCIETY

IDENTIFICATION: Christian-based support organization for Japanese immigrants
DATE: 1877-1906
LOCATION: San Francisco, California
ALSO KNOWN AS: Fukuinkai

SIGNIFICANCE: Founded in San Francisco by Japanese Christian students, the Gospel Society was the first immigrant association established by Japanese in the United States. The organization played an integral part in helping many new Japanese immigrants adjust to life in America while pursuing their studies. It was also instrumental in shaping the development of Japanese Protestant Christianity.

At the end of the nineteenth century, many Japanese immigrants arrived in the San Francisco area after being told that it was possible to work and study in the area. The Gospel Society was formed by recent converts to Methodism and Congregationalism to assist these often penniless students. The first meeting place was an austere, windowless room in the basement of the Chinese Methodist Episcopal Mission in the city's Chinatown. Every Saturday night, thirty-five members assembled for Bible study and debate. For a fee of thirty-five cents per month, the society provided community support, room and board, and help with job searching. Over the years, a variety of splinter groups emerged, including a group that formed the First Japanese Presbyterian Church of San Francisco. In 1886, the group moved out of the Chinese Mission basement with the newly established Japanese Methodist Episcopal Mission. Despite the success of the Japanese Mission, the Gospel Society remained an autonomous student residence until the great San Francisco earthquake of 1906.

Joy M. Gambill

FURTHER READING

Ichioka, Yuji. *The Issei: The World of the First Generation Japanese Immigrants, 1885-1924.* New York: Free Press, 1988.

Yoshida, Ryo. "Japanese Immigrants and Their Christian Communities in North America: A Case Study of the Fukuinkai, 1877-1896." *Japanese Journal of Religious Studies* 34, no. 1 (2007): 229-244.

SEE ALSO: California; Issei; Japanese American Citizens League; Japanese immigrants; Missionaries; Religions of immigrants; San Francisco.

GRAHAM V. RICHARDSON

THE CASE: U.S. Supreme Court decision on rights of resident noncitizens
DATE: Decided on June 14, 1971

SIGNIFICANCE: The *Richardson* decision was the first in a series of rulings that struck down discriminatory state laws denying public benefits to noncitizens.

Carmen Richardson, a legally admitted resident alien, had been living in Arizona since 1956. When she became totally disabled in 1964, she applied for welfare benefits that were administered by the state with federal subsidy. Her application was denied because of an Arizona statute requiring a person either to be a citizen or to have resided in the country for fifteen years. After the district court decided in Richardson's favor, the state's commissioner of public welfare, John Graham, appealed the case to the Supreme Court. Until that time, the Court had usually upheld laws that discriminated against noncitizens.

The Supreme Court unanimously ruled that the Arizona law was unconstitutional and that Richardson was entitled to benefits. Writing the opinion for the Court, Justice Harry A. Blackmun made four major points. First, from the perspective of equal protection, alienage, like race, is a suspect classification, because aliens are a discrete and po-

litically weak minority. As a result, all governmental discrimination based on alienage must be justified by the standard of strict scrutiny, requiring a compelling governmental interest. Second, the Arizona law was contradictory to the federal Social Security Act of 1935, and that federal law overrides state law. Third, immigrants admitted into the country had the "right to enter and abide in any state," with the same rights for public assistance as citizens. Finally, Congress possessed plenary power to establish regulations concerning the admission of immigrants into the country, and it had already put restrictions on the admissibility of paupers. The opinion left unanswered the extent to which Congress might have more discretion in distinguishing between the privileges of aliens and citizens.

Thomas Tandy Lewis

FURTHER READING

Greenhouse, Linda. *Becoming Justice Blackmun: Harry Blackmun's Supreme Court Journey.* New York: Henry Holt, 2005.

O'Brien, David M. *Constitutional Law and Politics.* 7th ed. New York: W. W. Norton, 2008.

SEE ALSO: *Bernal v. Fainter*; Citizenship; Congress, U.S.; Constitution, U.S.; Due process protections; *Foley v. Connelie*; Immigration law; *Plyler v. Doe*; Supreme Court, U.S.

GREAT DEPRESSION

THE EVENT: Severe worldwide economic downturn that intensified anti-immigrant nativism within the United States

DATE: 1929-1941

> **SIGNIFICANCE:** Immigration was a thorny issue during the Depression. Legislation was already in place barring certain ethnic groups from entering the United States, and immigration remained restricted during the era owing to economic factors. Many refugees fleeing Nazi persecution were denied entrance to the United States because of ethnic quotas.

Beginning in the 1880's, nativists, who favored the interests of native-born Americans over those of immigrants, succeeded in securing legislation that restricted immigration. The first legislation directed against a specific ethnic group, the Chinese Exclusion Act of 1882, prohibited the entry of Chinese laborers into the United States, and it was not until 1943 that the act was repealed. With the passage of the Immigration Act of 1891 and the opening of Ellis Island the following year, the federal government assumed full control over immigration, and the United States continued its restrictive immigration and naturalization policy. The Immigration Act of 1917 banned immigration from most Asian countries and introduced a literacy test for all immigrants over the age of sixteen. The Immigration Acts of 1921 and 1924 significantly limited immigration from southern and eastern Europe by assigning a quota for each nationality based on past U.S. Census data. In 1929, the year of the stock market crash that precipitated the Depression, the national origins system established by the Immigration Act of 1924 went into effect. Canadians and Latin Americans were exempt from the quota system.

MEXICAN REPATRIATION

Because the Immigration Act of 1924 specifically excluded Asian immigration, the United States turned to Mexico as its primary source of cheap labor during the late 1920's. With its proximity to the United States, Mexico supplied thousands of both legal and undocumented workers to labor on farms and ranches and in construction and mining in the Midwest and Southwest. These immigrants joined Mexican Americans, some of whom were descendants of Mexicans who had entered the United States following the Mexican War of 1846-1848. At the time of the Depression, several hundred thousand people of Mexican ancestry were living in the United States.

Rampant job losses caused by the Depression generated anti-Mexican sentiment, which had grown following World War I and had since redoubled with the massive number of Mexicans who immigrated during the mid-1920's. As the Depression deepened, government authorities determined that the expense would be less to return Mexicans to Mexico than to keep them on the welfare program.

With the cooperation of the Mexican government, the United States repatriated about one-half million Mexicans between 1929 and 1935. Some of the people sent back to Mexico were actually U.S.

Dust Bowl conditions in the Plains states of the Midwest sent many poor American farmers on the road to find agricultural work in the Far West. The resulting influx of migrant American workers severely limited the number of jobs available for foreign workers. (Library of Congress)

citizens with long-established residences and others who were tricked or forced to go. Indicative of their historical pattern of immigration and deportation, Mexicans were welcomed back to the United States a decade later, when they were invited to fill the gaps in the American workforce as the United States mobilized for World War II.

ROOSEVELT ADMINISTRATION

After Franklin D. Roosevelt became president in 1933, he made no significant changes in the immigration policy he inherited from his predecessor, Herbert Hoover. In the midst of anti-immigration popular sentiment, Roosevelt supported the immigration quotas established by the Immigration Acts of 1921 and 1924 but, lacking Hoover's nativist

zeal, succeeded in drastically lowering the number of deportations. By providing relief through the New Deal, Roosevelt decreased the annual number of deportees from nearly 20,000 in 1933 to fewer than 9,000 in 1934 and maintained that number until the 1940's.

As the Depression wore on, immigration into the United States declined significantly. The average annual number of immigrants for 1931-1940 was 6,900—a mere trickle compared to the 1.2 million total for the year 1914 alone. Despite the decrease in immigration, however, public sentiment against immigrants, particularly Filipinos, continued to increase. The massive number of Filipino immigrants who arrived during the 1920's, the targets of violent attacks by U.S. citizens, continued to

vex immigration restrictionists. Proclaimed by federal courts as American nationals following the Spanish-American War in 1898, when the Philippines became a U.S. colony, Filipinos entered the United States without restriction. The Tydings-McDuffie Act of 1934 provided for Philippine independence in ten years (but actually delayed until 1946) and also conferred alien status on Filipinos residing in the United States. The legislation created an annual quota of fifty immigrants per year.

During World War II, thousands of Jewish refugees fled Nazi persecution, and a number of them were refused asylum in the United States because of its restrictionist immigration policy. At the time, the United States made no distinction between immigrants and refugees; thus, both groups were subject to immigration quotas. During the early years of his administration, Roosevelt, though aware of Adolf Hitler's inhumane regime, made no effort to liberalize immigration laws, though some of his close advisers urged him to do so. Moreover, the annual German immigration quota was not being filled; according to Roosevelt's critics, the thousands of unfilled quota spaces could have been allocated to German Jewish refugees. The United States did not pursue a rescue policy for Jewish victims until 1944.

Mary G. Hurd

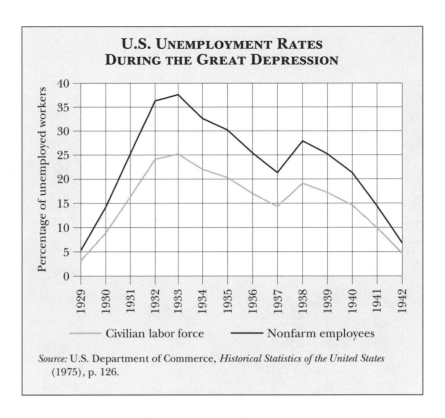

U.S. UNEMPLOYMENT RATES DURING THE GREAT DEPRESSION

Source: U.S. Department of Commerce, *Historical Statistics of the United States* (1975), p. 126.

FURTHER READING

Chomsky, Aviva. *"They Take Our Jobs!" and Twenty Other Myths About Immigration.* Boston: Beacon Press, 2007. In debunking the most common misconceptions about immigration, Chomsky provides informative discussions on history, law, and racism.

Daniels, Roger. *Coming to America: A History of Immigration and Ethnicity in American Life.* 2d ed. New York: HarperPerennial, 2002. Daniels examines individual racial groups entering the United States, their patterns of immigration, and the reactions of U.S. citizens to these groups.

Krikorian, Mark. *The New Case Against Immigration: Both Legal and Illegal.* New York: Sentinel, 2008. Krikorian argues that since economic, societal, and even technological changes in the United States hinder the assimilation of immigrants, the United States should permanently reduce immigration.

Mills, Nicolaus, ed. *Arguing Immigration: The Debate over the Changing Face of America.* New York: Simon & Schuster, 2007. Contains a wide variety of opinions on immigration from the standpoints of politics, economics, and race and ethnicity.

Rauchway, Eric. *The Great Depression and the New Deal: A Very Short Introduction.* New York: Oxford University Press, 2008. Analyzes Roosevelt's New Deal policies to combat the Great Depression.

SEE ALSO: Anti-Filipino violence; Anti-Semitism; Asian immigrants; Bracero program; Emigration; Filipino Repatriation Act of 1935; German immigrants; Holocaust; Immigration Act of 1917; Immigration Act of 1924; Mexican deportations of 1931; Push-pull factors.

GREAT IRISH FAMINE

THE EVENT: Devastating potato blight that caused mass starvation
DATE: 1845-1852
LOCATION: Ireland

SIGNIFICANCE: One of the single-most influential events in U.S. immigration history, Ireland's great potato famine induced a massive wave of Irish emigration to Great Britain, Canada, and the United States, where Irish immigrants quickly became the nation's second-largest ethnic group. Most of the immigrants settled in the large urban centers of New York, Boston, Philadelphia, and San Francisco.

The hsitory of Irish immigration to the United States goes back well before the nineteenth century, but the Great Irish Famine that began during the late 1840's brought the greatest number of Irish immigrants to America. Before the famine began, Ireland was already a desperately poor country. The only European country controlled by another country, it had been ruled by Great Britain for many centuries. Ireland had virtually no significant manufacturing sector. Most Irish were farmers who worked tiny plots of land, paying stiff rents to British landlords and living in primitive mud and stone huts.

By 1844, Ireland's population had swelled to 8.4 million, most of whom had lives built around potatoes. In 1845, the Phytophthora fungus, believed to have arrived from America, infected Ireland's potato crops and quickly spread throughout the country. Great Britain's response was minimal, but as the fungus ravaged the crops every year, successive British governments determined that providing aid to the Irish would only create greater dependency. By 1851, British neglect had contributed to the deaths of 1.1 million people who perished from starvation or from famine-related diseases. Meanwhile, another 1.5 million Irish people were immigrating to North America and England.

ARRIVAL IN AMERICA

Most refugees from Ireland's famine arrived in the United States nearly destitute. They settled in cities, where they had few skills needed in the industralizing urban economies. About 650,000 Irish immigrants arrived in New York alone. Because of their outdated clothing and distinctive accents, they were easily identified and made victims of various unscrupulous schemes. Landlords promising comfortable rooms left them in overcrowded, vermin-infested tenements. Others, promising railroad and boat passage to other parts of the nation, sold them phony tickets.

The immigrants took whatever unskilled jobs they could find, working on the docks, pushing carts, or digging canals and laboring on the railroads. Their lives were so harsh that their mortality rates remained high. For example, 60 percent of children born to Irish immigrants in Boston died before the age of six. Adult immigrants lived an average of only six years after their arrival in the United States. When these immigrants arrived, they were a comparatively docile and law-abiding population. However, many of them turned to crime out of boredom, desperation, and anger. Young Irish immigrants in New York City formed criminal gangs, and the area known as Five Points became a cauldron of all manner of criminal activity.

IRISH STEREOTYPES

Invidious stereotypes of the Irish were quickly imported from Britain. Cartoons on both sides of the Atlantic depicted the Irish as brutish, simian, bellicose, and always drunk. With employment opportunities limited, the Irish turned to crime and drink, which only exacerbated the public perception of them as troublemakers and public scourges. As suspicions increased, a common sentiment was expressed in the "No Irish Need Apply" signs that limited their economic and social opportunities.

In an overwhelmingly Protestant country, the Roman Catholic Irish were further reviled. During the 1850's, such prejudice was institutionalized in the creation of the Know-Nothing Party, a nativist political group that sought to curb immigration and the spread of Roman Catholicism. The party's largest victory came in 1854, when it elected candidates to every state office in Massachusetts.

With the outbreak of the U.S. Civil War, many Irish immigrants served valiantly in both armies; however, because of their tenuous social position, many Irish were targets for military conscription. Resentment of such practices erupted in 1863 in

the New York draft riots, when Irish created a major civil disruption over having to fight in a war to free slaves whom they regarded as competition for the few jobs the Irish could secure.

The Irish also imported some of their secret societies that were established to undermine British rule in their homeland. One of these was the Molly Maguires, who were active in the coalfields of Pennsylvania during the 1870's. They were alleged to have used coercion and intimidation against owners and other miners; historians, however, disagree on the extent of their criminality.

ASSIMILATION

Fearing discrimination and abuse, the Irish banded together in their parishes and led major efforts to build churches, parochial schools, and major private universities where they and their children felt comfortable. Catholicism, a minor religion before the arrival of the Irish, grew to become the largest single denomination by the early twentieth century, and much of that growth and visibility was due to the devotion of the Irish.

Systematically marginalized by a hostile culture, the Irish quickly realized that citizenship and their vote were among their most powerful weapons. The Irish understood the efficacy of ward politics, starting small and local and eventually taking over city halls and state governments. The Irish were also eager to take civil service jobs that offered relative security. There were certainly abuses, the most egregious being the Tammany Hall corruption in New York, but the Irish soon dominated Massachusetts politics, the apogee of which came with the election of John F. Kennedy to the presidency in 1960 and the creation of the closest thing to a political dynasty in the United States. In the twenty-first century, the Irish can be found in all professions and are among the most successful ethnic groups in America.

David W. Madden

As this 1880 cover of Harper's Weekly *shows, the problem of insufficient food continued to afflict Ireland well after the great potato blight.* (Library of Congress)

FURTHER READING

Gribben, Arthur, ed. *The Great Famine and the Irish Diaspora in America.* Amherst: University of Massachusetts Press, 1999. A collection of twelve essays commemorating the 150th anniversary of the famine that considers life in Ireland, historical perceptions of the events, and the creation of the Irish American identity.

Laxton, Edward. *The Famine Ships: The Irish Exodus to America.* New York: Henry Holt, 1996. A careful, detailed history of the often unseaworthy

"coffin ships" that transported destitute Irish to Canada and America.

Miller, Kerby. *Emigrants and Exiles: Ireland and the Irish Exodus to North America.* New York: Oxford University Press, 1985. The most authoritative study of Irish immigration to Canada and America and the ways in which the displaced transplanted their culture to the New World.

Miller, Kerby, and Paul Wagner. *Out of Ireland: The Story of Irish Emigration to America.* Washington, D.C.: Elliott & Clark, 1994. A photoessay companion to the 1995 PBS documentary of the same name that considers not only the famine but also the entire experience of Irish immigration to America.

Woodham-Smith, Cecil. *The Great Hunger: Ireland, 1845-1849.* London: Penguin Books, 1991. One of the most authoritative histories of the causes and results of the famine, considering its political, economic, and social consequences.

SEE ALSO: Anti-Catholicism; California gold rush; Canada vs. United States as immigrant destinations; Fenian movement; History of immigration, 1783-1891; Irish immigrants; Molly Maguires; Natural disasters as push-pull factors; New York City; Push-pull factors.

GREEK IMMIGRANTS

SIGNIFICANCE: Although Greeks have accounted for a relatively small percentage of the total immigrants to the United States, they have formed strong ethnic communities that have kept alive their language, traditions, and religion. Persons of Greek ancestry account for 0.4 percent of the current population of the United States.

Significant numbers of Greeks did not begin immigrating to the United States until the 1880's. However, the first Greek immigrants arrived during the 1820's, when the Greek war of independence from the Ottoman Empire left Greece with a large foreign debt, and the lack of industrialization forced inhabitants to look elsewhere for employment.

After the Turks captured Constantinople in 1453, Greece became part of the Ottoman Empire.

PROFILE OF GREEK IMMIGRANTS	
Country of origin	Greece
Primary language	Greek
Primary regions of U.S. settlement	East Coast states, Midwest
Earliest significant arrivals	1824
Peak immigration periods	1900-1917, 1970's
Twenty-first century legal residents*	7,429 (929 per year)

*Immigrants who obtained legal permanent resident status in the United States.
Source: Department of Homeland Security, *Yearbook of Immigration Statistics, 2008.*

Inspired by the late eighteenth century revolutions in North America and western Europe, as well as their own sense of Greek nationalism, a group of Greek loyalists planned a rebellion against the Ottoman state. They gained the support of numerous countries, including Great Britain, France, and Russia. Greece became an independent nation after signing the Treaty of Adrianople in 1832.

IMMIGRATION BEGINS

Following the end of its war of independence, Greece faced a number of internal economic challenges. The country was slow to industrialize through the nineteenth century. As late as 1879, more than 80 percent of its people still lived in rural communities. Currants were Greece's chief export product, and their price declined so much that many Greek farmers went bankrupt and were unable to pay their taxes. This poor economic climate prompted many Greeks to emigrate.

With the encouragement of the Greek government, young men began leaving the country during the late nineteenth century in the hope of gaining employment in the United States. Large-scale Greek immigration to the United States began in 1880, with the largest numbers immigrating during the early twentieth century. Between 1900 and 1920, more than 350,000 Greeks immigrated to the United States. About 95 percent of the immigrants who came between 1899 and 1910 were men. In

Emigrants boarding small boats in Patras, Greece, on their way to the steamship that will take them to America in 1910. (Library of Congress)

In Chicago, some moved into the lunch business, working from street carts that sold inexpensive fare to factory workers. After the Chicago city council banned the sale of food on city streets, the immigrants turned to opening permanent establishments. Using mainly family members for labor and requiring little start-up money, the restaurant business was the first stable economic base for Greeks in America. By 1919, one of every three restaurants in Chicago was operated by a Greek.

A major unifying force for the Greek community in America was the church. The first Greek Orthodox Church in the United States, the Holy Trinity of New Orleans, was founded in 1864. By 1918, nearly 130 Orthodox churches had been founded across the country. Local community organizations called *kinotis* raised the necessary funds to establish the churches. Many Greeks sought the close-knit communities they had in their home country, and the churches provided the immigrants with forums in which to share their common beliefs. During the early twenty-first century, Greek Orthodox churches have continued to serve as cultural and social centers for many Greek communities within the United States.

keeping with Greek tradition, these men often worked to secure dowries for their sisters back home. In 1905 alone, Greek immigrants remitted more than four million dollars to their families in Greece. Most did not intend to stay in the United States.

GREEKS IN THE UNITED STATES

Upon arriving in the United States, most Greek immigrants found jobs in various industries. In New England, for example, they worked in textile mills. A particularly large Greek community formed in Lowell, Massachusetts, where many Greek men worked in the mill. In Utah and Colorado, Greeks found work in copper and coal mines. In California they worked in railroad gangs. Many were victimized by *padrones*, labor brokers who recruited immigrants for jobs in exchange for the immigrants' wages.

Around the turn of the twentieth century, Greek immigrants began going into business for themselves. They opened shoeshine parlors, candy shops, and, most notably, restaurants. Their first restaurants served native cuisine to fellow Greeks.

LATE TWENTIETH CENTURY IMMIGRATION

Prior to 1965, the United States had established quotas restricting immigration from certain countries and ethnic groups. The quotas favored immigrants from northern and western European countries. The Immigration Act of 1924 had imposed harsh restrictions on non-western European immigrant groups. Under that law, only one hundred Greeks per year were allowed entry into the United States.

In 1965, the Democratic-controlled U.S. Congress passed the Immigration and Nationality Act. Whereas previous immigration acts had imposed quotas by country, the 1965 act established hemi-

spheric quotas, and distributed visas based on job skills and family reunification. Many Greek Americans used the new law to bring members of their families to the United States. Between 1960 and 1980, more than 170,000 Greeks immigrated to the United States, many with family reunification visas.

During the first decade of the twenty-first century, approximately 1.4 million persons of Greek ancestry were living in the United States. They resided in all fifty states, with the greatest numbers living in large cities such as Chicago, New York City, and Detroit. Many Greek immigrants have assimilated into American culture, but have remained strongly connected to Greek traditions, religion, and ethnicity.

Bethany E. Pierce

FURTHER READING

Contopoulos, Michael. *The Greek Community of New York City: Early Years to 1910.* New Rochelle, N.Y.: Aristide D. Caratzas, 1992. History of one of the largest concentrations of Greek immigrants in any American city.

Moskos, Charles. *Greek Americans: Struggle and Success.* 2d ed. New Brunswick, N.J.: Transaction Publishers, 1989. Scholarly study of Greeks in America through the 1980's.

Orfanos, Spyros D., ed. *Reading Greek America: Studies in the Experience of Greeks in the United States.* New York: Pella, 2002. Collection of essays examining a variety of issues surrounding Greek immigrants.

Saloutos, Theodore. *The Greeks in the United States.* Rev. ed. New York: Greekworks.com, 2007. Comprehensive study of Greek immigrants. Includes an introduction by Charles Moskos, and historiographical essay by Alexander Kitroeff.

Scourby, Alice. *The Greek Americans.* Boston: Twayne, 1984. Broad study of Greek Americans with background information on Greek history, several chapters on immigrants, and a chapter on changes in Greek American family structures.

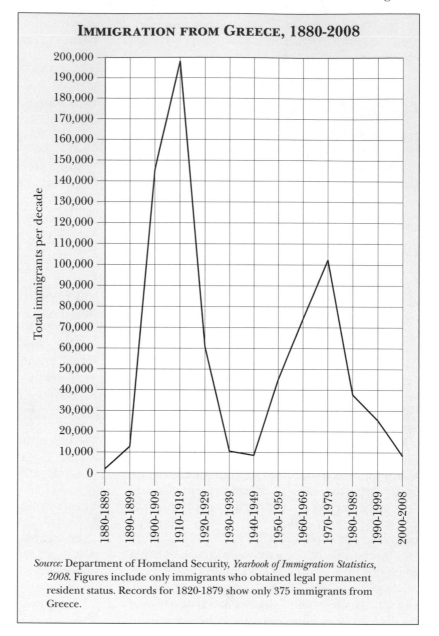

IMMIGRATION FROM GREECE, 1880-2008

Source: Department of Homeland Security, *Yearbook of Immigration Statistics, 2008.* Figures include only immigrants who obtained legal permanent resident status. Records for 1820-1879 show only 375 immigrants from Greece.

SEE ALSO: Congress, U.S.; Economic opportunities; History of immigration after 1891; Huffington, Arianna; Immigration Act of 1921; Immigra-

tion and Nationality Act of 1965; Italian immigrants; Quota systems; Turkish immigrants; Yugoslav state immigrants.

GREEN CARD

IDENTIFICATION: Film, written by Peter Weir, about a French immigrant to the United States who enters into a marriage of convenience

DATE: Released in 1990

> **SIGNIFICANCE:** *Green Card* tells the story of an American woman and a French immigrant living in New York City who enter into a marriage of convenience for different reasons. Complications develop when Immigration and Naturalization Service agents seek evidence that their marriage has been undertaken solely to enable the immigrant husband to obtain his green card.

Green Card opens by introducing a young American woman named Brontë (Andie MacDowell) who cannot obtain a lease on an upscale New York apartment unless she is married. At the same time, a French waiter named Georges (Gérard Depardieu) who needs a green card to work in the United States and become a citizen seeks an American wife so he can get that card. After a mutual friend brings Georges and Brontë together, the couple get married and then say goodbye to each other immediately after the ceremony.

The amicably estranged couple's troubles begin when two Immigration and Naturalization Service (INS) inspectors randomly, it is presumed, investigate them to determine whether they have satisfied the immigration laws concerning the green card and their lawful permanent residence. Audiences unaware of federal immigration regulations might see these government agents as intruders. However, the film makes it clear that the INS is obligated to investigate green card petitioners to deter fraudulent behavior.

As nearly a year passes by, both characters go through changes in their lives as they come together to learn more about each other's habits and behaviors so they can make the INS inspectors think they have entered their marriage in good faith. Each of them must provide, as the law states,

general and specific supporting evidence that Georges's obtaining of his green card has not been fraudulent, and they must have a common residence. The rest of the film shows them trying to learn about each other. As they grow closer, they behave more deceitfully toward their friends and relatives. Georges knows, and the audience learns, that his ability to obtain permanent resident status can be lost if they are found out—and the law allows for his immediate removal from the United States and the possibility of his being permanently banned. Eventually, the government deports Georges. However, love wins out as the film ends, as Brontë prepares to go to France to join her husband, who is waiting for her.

James F. O'Neil

FURTHER READING

Bray, Ilona M. *Fiancé and Marriage Visas: A Couple's Guide to U.S. Immigration.* 5th ed. Berkeley, Calif.: Nolo, 2008.

Gania, Edwin T. *U.S. Immigration Step by Step.* 3d ed. Naperville, Ill.: Sphinx; Sourcebooks, 2006.

Motomura, Hiroshi. *Americans in Waiting: The Lost Story of Immigration and Citizenship in the United States.* New York: Oxford University Press, 2006.

Wernick, Allan. *U.S. Immigration and Citizenship: Your Complete Guide.* 4th ed. Cincinnati: Emmis Books, 2004.

SEE ALSO: Citizenship and Immigration Services, U.S.; Deportation; Films; French immigrants; Green cards; Immigration law; Intermarriage; Marriage; "Marriages of convenience"; Resident aliens; Yugoslav state immigrants.

GREEN CARDS

DEFINITION: Identification cards issued by the federal government to aliens who qualify for permanent resident status and therefore have the right to live and work in the United States for indefinite periods

> **SIGNIFICANCE:** Immigrants without green cards have no legal right to reside permanently or to work in the United States. In addition to facing possible criminal charges and deportation by the federal government,

undocumented aliens who attempt to work in the country are vulnerable to abuse from their employers and other unscrupulous persons because they cannot seek redress from the U.S. legal system.

Every alien who resides in the United States must be registered with the U.S. government, and those who wish to reside permanently are legally required to obtain green cards. Not every alien who applies for a green card receives one. The U.S. Congress decided that a highly skilled immigrant workforce is needed to sustain the nation's economic progress and gave priority status to immigrants with exceptional talents, such as acclaimed actors, musicians, and painters. Immigrants with advanced academic degrees also receive priority.

Immigrants who qualify as priority workers are not required to go through the complicated and time-consuming procedure of obtaining labor certification to obtain their green cards. Formal certification procedures require prospective employers of applicants to demonstrate that no Americans or already established permanent residents are ready, willing, and able to take the jobs offered to the new immigrants at the wages that prevail. Labor certification is designed to guarantee that the employment of new immigrants will not adversely affect the wages and working conditions of workers who are already resident in the areas in which the jobs are performed.

GREEN CARD FRAUD

U.S. Citizenship and Immigration Services imposes requirements for immigrants not applied to U.S. citizens because immigrants lack the protections of American citizenship. Aliens over the age of eighteen who are permanent residents must at all times carry valid green cards or risk being found guilty of a misdemeanor. Immigrants who leave the United States for periods of more than six months risk losing their green cards on the principle that long absences from the country may betray lack of interest in residing in the United States. Immigrants can also lose their green cards by failing to report changes of address or for committing crimes.

Immigrants can obtain green cards by marrying American citizens or permanent resi-

dents. One of the best-known provisions of immigration law, this principle has often led to abuses. During the early 1980's, the Immigration and Naturalization Service reported that as many as one-half of all petitions for green cards based on marriages were fraudulent, as they were entered into solely for the purpose of obtaining green cards. In 1986, Congress responded to these concerns by passing the Immigration Marriage Fraud Amendments to eliminate as many "paper marriages," or "marriages of convenience," as possible. American citizens and permanent residents who conspire with would-be immigrants to evade immigration laws by means of fraudulent marriages can be charged with federal crimes. Permanent residents convicted of this crime can be deported. Both permanent residents and U.S. citizens convicted of the crime can serve jail time, be fined, or both. Immigrants who are proven guilty of fraud permanently lose all chance of ever living legally in the United States.

When applications for new or renewed permanent resident cards are denied, applicants are sent letters detailing the reasons. Immigrants cannot appeal negative decisions. They can, however, submit motions to have their denials reconsidered when new facts can be presented or their denials can be shown to have been based on incorrect applications of law or immigration policy.

OBTAINING GREEN CARDS

A primary goal of U.S. immigration law is to help keep immigrant families together. Consequently,

---

WHY GREEN?

Despite their popular name, "green cards" have not always been green. Officially known as Alien Registration Receipt Cards, they were first introduced during the 1940's, when the federal government issued them on green plastic. During the 1960's and 1970's, however, the government issued the cards on blue stock. During the 1980's, the cards became white stock, and during the 1990's they were pink.

Through all these color changes, the cards have always included their owners' photographs, federal registration numbers, dates of birth, and ports of entry into the United States. The cards are generally issued for periods of ten years, but they can be renewed indefinitely.

immediate relatives of American citizens are guaranteed green cards. Immigrants who overstay their visas or work without authorization can still qualify for green cards if they are the minor children of legal residents or the parents of adult American citizens. Classes of immigrants who cannot qualify for green cards after they are in the United States include stowaways, aliens who have failed to follow deportation orders, or those who have failed to appear at scheduled removal proceedings or asylum interviews.

The federal Immigration Act of 1990 permitted a total of 675,000 immigrants to obtain green cards each year, and each individual country can send up to 25,620 immigrants to the United States. Demand for visas in some countries, notably Mexico and the Philippines, typically greatly exceeds supply, requiring applicants from those countries to wait for years to obtain immigration documents from the United States.

Each year, the U.S. State Department conducts a free Diversity Visa lottery that is also known as the "green card lottery" to distribute applications randomly for 50,000 green cards. Winners of the lottery are given the opportunity to apply for visas but no guarantees that they will receive them. Lottery entrants must be from eligible countries—which vary from year to year—and have at least twelve years of education or two years of skilled work experience. The lotteries have become the targets of scam artists who claim that they can increase would-be immigrants' chances of winning the lottery for a price.

Caryn E. Neumann

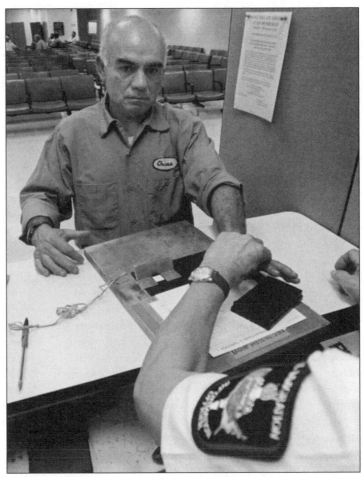

Salvadoran immigrant being fingerprinted by a Los Angeles Immigration and Naturalization Service officer while renewing his green card in 1999. (AP/Wide World Photos)

FURTHER READING

Anosike, Benji O. *How to Obtain Your U.S. Immigration Visa for a Temporary Stay: The Non-Immigrant Visa Kit.* Newark, N.J.: Do-It-Yourself Legal Publishers, 2003. Detailed, practical manual explaining almost every imaginable procedure in obtaining documentation to immigrate legally.

Bray, Ilona M. *Fiancé and Marriage Visas: A Couple's Guide to U.S. Immigration.* 5th ed. Berkeley, Calif.: Nolo, 2008. How-to book that provides a good, easy-to-follow guide to immigration policies on marriage issues, including the awarding of green cards.

Cortes, Luis, Jr. *A Simple Guide to U.S. Immigration and Citizenship.* New York: Atria Books, 2008. Useful and up-to-date manual for immigrants working to become U.S. citizens.

Farrell, Mary H. J. "For Immigrants Trying to Obtain the Coveted Green Card, Marriage May Be a Treacherous Strategy." *People Weekly,* February 25, 1991, 93-96. Interesting article on legitimate and fraudulent marriages entered into for the purpose of obtaining green cards.

Lewis, Loida Nicolas. *How to Get a Green Card: Legal*

Ways to Stay in the U.S.A. 6th ed. Berkeley, Calif.: Nolo, 2005. Practical handbook offering step-by-step guidance on obtaining green cards.

SEE ALSO: Deportation; Due process protections; Employment; Families; Illegal immigration; Immigration and Naturalization Service, U.S.; Immigration law; "Marriages of convenience"; Passports; Permanent resident status; Resident aliens.

GRESHAM-YANG TREATY OF 1894

THE LAW: U.S.-Chinese agreement that suspended immigration of Chinese laborers to the United States for ten years but allowed conditional readmission of immigrants who were visiting China
DATE: Signed on December 7, 1894
ALSO KNOWN AS: Sino-American Treaty of 1894

SIGNIFICANCE: The Gresham-Yang Treaty did away with the terms of the Scott Act of 1888 and placed exclusion and registration laws passed since 1882 on a proper treaty basis. Proposed renewal of the treaty caused China to call for a boycott of American goods and the U.S. Congress to extend exclusion indefinitely.

The Scott Act of 1888 excluded virtually all Chinese from entering the United States, including those who had traveled from the United States to visit China. It was superseded in 1894 by the Gresham-Yang Treaty, which stipulated total prohibition of immigration of Chinese workers into the United States for the next ten years, with the promise that immigrants who were visiting China could be readmitted. Readmission was allowed only if returning Chinese immigrants had family living in America or property or debts owed to them of at least one thousand dollars. The treaty exempted Chinese officials, students, and merchants.

In 1904, China refused to renew the Gresham-Yang Treaty and asked to negotiate a less harsh agreement. Chinese merchants called for a boycott of American goods. Unrest over the mistreatment of Chinese immigrants in America changed the po-

litical landscape in China by fueling political participation of the Chinese populace. The administrations of U.S. presidents William McKinley and Theodore Roosevelt showed little concern over China's repeated protests and warnings. When China denounced the Gresham-Yang Treaty in 1904, the U.S. Congress extended exclusion indefinitely.

Alvin K. Benson

FURTHER READING
Cassel, Susie Lan, ed. *The Chinese in America: A History from Gold Mountain to the New Millennium.* Walnut Creek, Calif.: AltaMira Press, 2002.
Lee, Erika. *At America's Gates: Immigration During the Exclusion Era, 1882-1943.* Chapel Hill: University of North Carolina Press, 2007.

SEE ALSO: Alien Contract Labor Law of 1885; Anti-Chinese movement; Burlingame Treaty of 1868; Chinese Exclusion Act of 1882; *Chinese Exclusion Cases;* Chinese immigrants; Contract labor system; Geary Act of 1892; McCreary Amendment of 1893; Taiwanese immigrants.

GROVE, ANDREW

IDENTIFICATION: Hungarian-born chief executive officer of Intel
BORN: September 2, 1936; Budapest, Hungary

SIGNIFICANCE: The third person hired by the cofounders of the Intel Corporation, the Hungarian-born Grove rose relatively quickly to the company's top management position.

Born in Hungary's capital city, Budapest, András Gróf grew up in the town of Bácsalmás near the border with present-day Serbia. His early childhood was darkened by the virulent anti-Semitism of Nazi Germany, then the "liberation" by the Soviet Union that quickly turned into an oppressive regime. When he was four, he contracted scarlet fever and lost most of his hearing.

After Hungary's failed uprising against the Soviet Union in 1956, the twenty-year-old Gróf fled to the United States, where he Americanized his surname to Grove. He earned a doctorate in chemical engineering from the University of California in

Berkeley in 1963 and was subsequently hired at Fairchild Semiconductor by Robert Norton Noyce, whom he followed to the microchip maker Intel. Grove often collided with Noyce's personnel policy, which he considered excessively liberal, and he eventually took over the day-to-day managerial functions, driving his employees hard but winning their respect because he drove himself just as hard. From 1987 to 1998, he served as Intel's chief executive officer, and from 1979 to 1997 he served as president. After nominally retiring from Intel, he continued to advise the company and remained a respected figure throughout Silicon Valley.

Leigh Husband Kimmel

FURTHER READING

Jackson, Tim. *Inside Intel: Andy Grove and the Rise of the World's Most Powerful Chip Company.* New York: Dutton, 1997.

Tedlow, Richard S. *Andy Grove: The Life and Times of an American.* New York: Portfolio, 2006.

Yu, Albert. *Creating the Digital Future: The Secrets of Consistent Innovation at Intel.* New York: Free Press, 1998.

SEE ALSO: Hungarian immigrants; Jewish immigrants; *A Nation of Immigrants*; Pulitzer, Joseph; Railroads; Religion as a push-pull factor; Tesla, Nikola.

GUATEMALAN IMMIGRANTS

SIGNIFICANCE: Civil war, natural disasters, and economic hardships combined to cause Guatemalan immigration to the United States to begin a rise during the 1960's that has continued to grow into the twenty-first century. Guatemalans have become the second-largest Central American immigrant community after Salvadorans.

Before 1930, the U.S. Census did not break down Central American immigration by countries, but in any case, overall immigration from that region was small. According to the U.S. Census, only 423 Guatemalans were formally admitted into the United States during the 1930's. The number of Guatemalan immigrants remained low until the 1960's, when a significant increase began to occur. The

---

PROFILE OF GUATEMALAN IMMIGRANTS

Country of origin	Guatemala
Primary language	Spanish
Primary regions of U.S. settlement	California, Texas, Illinois, New York, Florida, Washington, D.C.
Earliest significant arrivals	Early twentieth century
Peak immigration period	1980's-2008
Twenty-first century legal residents*	138,021 (17,253 per year)

*Immigrants who obtained legal permanent resident status in the United States.
Source: Department of Homeland Security, *Yearbook of Immigration Statistics, 2008.*

---

majority of Guatemalan immigrants have arrived in the United States since the mid-1980's.

During the 1980's, the number of Guatemalans granted legal permanent resident status reached almost 60,000, continuing a growth pattern that started during the 1960's. The numbers of immigrants have continued to rise, with 145,111 Guatemalans granted legal permanent resident status between 2000 and 2008. The 2000 U.S. Census listed the total number of Guatemalan immigrants living in the United States as 480,665. Of that number, 111,375 were naturalized U.S. citizens and 369,290 were listed as "not a U.S. citizen." However, these numbers tell only a part of the story, as the majority of Guatemalan immigrants are undocumented aliens. The number of actual Guatemalan immigrants in the United States in 2008 was estimated to be as high as 1.3 million people.

PUSH-PULL FACTORS

Factors that have contributed to Guatemalan immigration into the United States have included Central American civil unrest, natural disasters, and economic problems. A thirty-six-year civil war began in Guatemala in 1960, when the right-wing military rose up against the increasingly liberal government. The war left thousands dead and

drove tens of thousands to flee to Mexico and the United States. During the 1980's, Guatemala's indigenous communities endured the worst of the war's violence, as they were suspected by the military of aiding the rebel forces. Because the U.S. government backed the right-wing Guatemalan leaders, it denied personal petitions for political asylum from Guatemalans during that period. The refusal to grant protected status prompted some religious groups in the United States to form the Sanctuary movement, an activist movement that aided undocumented immigrants from Guatemala and El Salvador.

A series of natural disasters in Guatemala left thousands of families without homes, land, or work, driving many of them to emigrate. In 1976, an earthquake destroyed much of Guatemala City and its environs, leaving 26,000 dead, 76,000 injured, and thousands more homeless. In 2005, Hurricane Stan caused torrential rain and mud-slides that killed as many as 2,000 people in Guatemala and devastated entire villages.

A low standard of living, poor health care, and unfair land distribution have all contributed to Guatemalan immigration to the United States. Guatemala has the highest infant and child mortality rate, the lowest life expectancy, and the worst malnutrition problem in Central America. During the early twenty-first century, more than 60 percent of Guatemala's people were living in poverty. The majority of the adult working population were engaged in migrant farm labor for the coffee, sugar, and cotton plantations.

For Guatemalans attempting to emigrate to the United States, the journey north is difficult, dangerous, and expensive. Fees for guides facilitating illegal entry into the United States can be as high as fifteen hundred U.S. dollars. Rape, robbery, injury, and death are some of the dangers in migrating north.

TRANSNATIONAL GUATEMALAN IMMIGRANT COMMUNITIES

The largest Guatemalan immigrant community in the United States is in Los Angeles; it is estimated at more than 100,000 people. Other large Guatemalan immigrant communities have arisen in Houston, Chicago, New York City, Washington, D.C., southern Florida, San Francisco, Miami, New Orleans, and the Phoenix-Tucson area in Arizona. These communities tend to be transnational; as their members work to create new lives for themselves in the United States, they continued to maintain ties with their home communities. Many Guatemalan immigrants send financial remittances to relatives in their Guatemalan hometowns that constitute a substantial portion of the latters' incomes. In 2005, immigrants sent more than $3 billion to relatives in Guatemala.

A special problem arising from Guatemalan immigration has been the spread of gang culture from the United States to Guatemala. Beginning during the 1990's the U.S. government began targeting undocumented immigrants in the penal system for deportation. Many of these deportees have been in the United States so long that they have no memory of having lived in Guatemala. After they return to their original homeland, they tend to continue their criminal activities.

Elizabeth Ellen Cramer

IMMIGRATION FROM GUATEMALA, 1930-2008

Source: Department of Homeland Security, *Yearbook of Immigration Statistics, 2008.* Figures include only immigrants who obtained legal permanent resident status.

FURTHER READING

Bacon, David. *Communities Without Borders: Images and Voices from the World of Migration.* Ithaca, N.Y.: ILR Press, 2006. Through candid photos and oral histories, this book tells the story of transnational communities made up of Guatemalan and Mexican migrants and of their struggles for better working conditions, improved health care, and the retention of their cultures.

Fink, Leon, and Alvis E. Dunn. *The Maya of Morganton: Work and Community in the Nuevo New South.* Chapel Hill: University of North Carolina Press, 2003. Study of how indigenous Guatemalan Mayans have battled unfair labor practices in the poultry plants of their new home in North Carolina.

Foxen, Patricia. *In Search of Providence: Transnational Mayan Identities.* Nashville, Tenn.: Vanderbilt University Press, 2007. Tells the story of a community of the K'iche Mayan Indians— members of the largest indigenous group in Guatemala—who have settled in Providence, Rhode Island.

Hamilton, Nora. *Seeking Community in a Global City: Guatemalans and Salvadorans in Los Angeles.* Philadelphia: Temple University Press, 2001. Drawing on her twenty years of work with the Central American community in Los Angeles, Hamilton tells of the immigrants' experiences with war and poverty in their homelands and of the creation of their new home in the United States.

Stolen, Kristi Anne. *Guatemalans in the Aftermath of Violence: The Refugees' Return.* Philadelphia: University of Pennsylvania Press, 2007. Looks at Guatemalan immigration patterns in the aftermath of the Civil War.

SEE ALSO: El Rescate; History of immigration after 1891; Honduran immigrants; Immigration lawyers; Latin American immigrants; Push-pull factors; Refugees; Salvadoran immigrants; Sanctuary movement.

GUEST-WORKER PROGRAMS

DEFINITION: Government-sponsored programs permitting the temporary importation of workers in specific occupations

SIGNIFICANCE: Guest-worker programs in the United States, such as the mid-century bracero program, have often met with controversy due to variable labor conditions and their perceived effect on American wages and job availability.

Guest-worker programs import laborers from other countries into the United States for temporary employment. Early variants of such programs included indentured servitude during the colonial period, when European immigrant workers agreed to fixed terms of labor in exchange for transportation and other costs. The recruiting of Chinese railroad workers and other forms of contract labor during the mid-nineteenth century were also forms of indentured servitude; they were eventually outlawed by the Foran Act of 1885. Another form of indentured servitude was the nineteenth century Italian *padrone* system, which was facilitated by labor contractors with transatlantic ties. These early forms of indentured servitude did not always require that the laborers return to their home countries at the end of their terms of service, but many indentured laborers did.

The best-known guest-worker arrangement in the United States was the bracero program, which imported millions of Mexican agricultural laborers between 1942 and 1964. The imposition of this program required the repeal of the Foran Act, but growers' associations successfully convinced the U.S. Congress that manpower shortages during World War II required new sources of farm labor. The program ended in 1964 amid increased scrutiny by labor regulators and in face of competition from the widespread mechanization of agricultural work.

During the early twenty-first century, President George W. Bush's proposal to expand guest-worker programs met with significant criticism across the political spectrum. As late as 2009, the United States continued to maintain limited guest-worker programs for agricultural, low-skilled, and skilled

labor, through the issuance of "H" type temporary work visas.

Sarah Bridger

FURTHER READING

Bustamante, Jorge, Clark Reynolds, and Raul Hinojosa Ojeda. *U.S.-Mexico Relations: Labor Market Interdependence.* Stanford, Calif.: Stanford University Press, 1992.

Griffith, David. *American Guestworkers: Jamaicans and Mexicans in the U.S. Labor Market.* University Park: Pennsylvania State University Press, 2006.

Jordan, Don. *White Cargo: The Forgotten History of Britain's White Slaves in America.* New York: New York University Press, 2008.

Ngai, Mae M. *Impossible Subjects: Illegal Aliens and the Making of Modern America.* Princeton, N.J.: Princeton University Press, 2004.

SEE ALSO: Alien Contract Labor Law of 1885; Bracero program; Contract labor system; Economic consequences of immigration; Employment; Farm and migrant workers; Federation for American Immigration Reform; Indentured servitude; Mexican immigrants.

Meyer Guggenheim. (The Granger Collection, New York)

GUGGENHEIM, MEYER

IDENTIFICATION: Swiss-born American industrialist
BORN: February 1, 1828; Lengnau, Switzerland
DIED: March 15, 1905; Palm Beach, Florida

SIGNIFICANCE: Originally an impoverished Jewish peddler from Switzerland, Guggenheim built a worldwide mining conglomerate after immigrating to the United States.

Born during the early nineteenth century in a Jewish ghetto in the Aargau canton of Switzerland, Meyer Guggenheim worked as a traveling peddler in Switzerland and Germany. In 1848, Guggenheim immigrated to the United States at the age of twenty and settled in Philadelphia. In 1854, he married Barbara Meyers, whom he had met on the Atlantic voyage; they would have ten children.

Guggenheim's remarkable rise in the world of industry bore several marks of his immigrant background. His success as a peddler of stove polish and instant coffee to Pennsylvania Dutch miners and farmers was helped by his native command of German. After acquiring capital through his grocery store, lye factory, and railroad speculation, Guggenheim relied on Swiss relatives to supply imported laces and embroideries at great profit. Free from the restrictions he faced as a Jew in Europe, Guggenheim tenaciously built an American business dynasty. He groomed his seven sons to advance his enterprises, sending them to schools in Zurich and Paris. Upon their return, he formed M. Guggenheim's Sons in 1877, giving each son an equal share in the partnership.

Guggenheim acquired silver mines and smelting operations in Colorado, expanding into Monterrey, Mexico, in 1890. By the turn of the century, M. Guggenheim's Sons dominated the Ameri-

can Smelting and Refining Trust and mining interests worldwide. Soon the Guggenheims relocated to mansions in New York City. Meyer Guggenheim died in 1905. The philanthropy that his descendants pursued during the twentieth century reflected Guggenheim's cosmopolitan perspective and determination to make a permanent legacy in his adopted country.

Howard Bromberg

FURTHER READING

Davis, John H. *The Guggenheims (1848-1988): An American Epic.* New York: Shapolsky, 1988.

Unger, Irwin, and Debi Unger. *The Guggenheims: A Family History.* New York: HarperCollins, 2005.

SEE ALSO: Anti-Semitism; Family businesses; Jewish immigrants; Marriage; New York City; Pennsylvania; Philadelphia; Swiss immigrants.

H

HAITIAN BOAT PEOPLE

THE EVENT: Attempts by Haitian asylum seekers to reach the United States on small boats
DATE: Late 1970's to early twenty-first century
LOCATION: Waters off the coast of South Florida

SIGNIFICANCE: Defining the Haitian boat people as economic rather than political refugees allowed the United States to refuse asylum to thousands of Haitians and raised serious questions about human rights standards and treatment of refugees in the United States.

Large-scale Haitian immigration to the United States began during the 1970's when Haitians, attempting to escape Jean-Claude "Baby Doc" Duvalier's dictatorship, sailed for the United States. Before 1977, about 7,000 boat people had arrived in the United States; by 1979, 8,300 more had arrived. U.S. policy decided that Haitians were not political refugees but economic immigrants, seeking jobs and better living conditions, making them ineligible for asylum. Thus, no Haitians were given refugee status, and every Haitian landing in the United States was subject to immediate deportation. The 1980 Mariel boatlift, in which 125,000 Cubans and 40,000 to 80,000 Haitians tried to immigrate to the United States, caused President Jimmy Carter to reevaluate U.S.-Haitian policies. He created a class of immigrant, the "Cuban/Haitian entrant (status pending)," allowing Haitians who had entered up to October 10, 1980, to apply for asylum. Any Haitian entering after that date was faced with incarceration and deportation.

In 1981, President Ronald Reagan reinforced the policy and began interdiction of Haitian boats. For the next ten years, U.S. Coast Guard ships returned any seized boat carrying Haitian refugees to Port-au-Prince, Haiti. Interviews were supposed to be conducted on board, and anyone with a legitimate request was to be granted asylum. However, during that period, only twenty-eight applications for asylum were granted out of approximately twenty-five thousand. Many reported never having actually been interviewed at all.

In 1991, the numbers of asylum seekers dropped when Jean-Bertrand Aristide, the first democratically elected president of Haiti, took office. How-

Haitian sailboat loaded with 155 people awaiting a U.S. Coast Guard cutter to pick them up off the coast of Miami, Florida, in June, 1994. (AP/Wide World Photos)

ever, within months a violent military coup ousted Aristide, leading to the murders of fifteen hundred Aristide supporters and precipitating a new immigration crisis. By 1992, tens of thousands of Haitians attempted to sail to the United States for political asylum. However, President George H. W. Bush claimed that because there were no human rights violations going on in Haiti, the United States could not recognize Haitian refugees as political asylum seekers. In 1992, thirty-seven thousand Haitians were repatriated or incarcerated in holding facilities such as Guantanamo Bay, Cuba.

Human rights groups condemned the American refusal to accept Haitian refugees even after the fall of Aristide. Citing numerous murders of repatriated Haitians, violations of Haitians' civil rights, and imprisonment and harassment upon repatriation, these groups tried to change the status of the Haitian boat people to political refugees. Human rights groups asserted that the United States was in violation of the 1951 Convention and subsequent 1967 Protocol Relating to the Status of Refugees, and President Bush was found to be in violation of the Refugee Act of 1980. However, by defining Haitians as economic relief seekers and not refugees, the United States was allowed to maintain its repatriation policy.

Taking office in 1993, President Bill Clinton had opposed Bush's repatriation/interdiction policy and promised that he would be generous toward Haitian refugees. Coast Guard personnel remarked that seven hundred new boats were built by Haitians awaiting Clinton's presidency. However, in a reversal of opinion, Clinton reinstated Bush's policy.

In 1993, the U.S. Supreme Court agreed that only those refugees who actually make it to U.S. soil on their own could be considered for refugee status and that anyone interdicted would be repatriated. This controversial policy, along with continued interdiction at sea, remains in effect in the early twenty-first century.

Leslie Neilan

FURTHER READING

Gaines, Jena, and Stuart Anderson, eds. *Haitian Immigration.* Broomal, Pa.: Mason Crest, 2003.

Garrison, Lynn. *Voodoo Politics: The Clinton/Gore Destruction of Haiti.* Los Angeles: Leprechaun Press, 2000.

Haines, David W., ed. *Refugees in America in the 1990's: A Reference Handbook.* Westport, Conn.: Greenwood Press, 1996.

SEE ALSO: Bureau of Immigration, U.S.; Coast Guard, U.S.; Commission on Immigration Reform, U.S.; Cuban immigrants; Dominican immigrants; Florida; Haitian immigrants; Infectious diseases; Mariel boatlift; Refugees; Transportation of immigrants.

HAITIAN IMMIGRANTS

SIGNIFICANCE: Although Haitians are citizens of the second-oldest republic in the Western Hemisphere, an island nation located only seven hundred miles from the United States, they have experienced unique difficulties in finding acceptance as immigrants and have become one of the most abused groups of immigrants in modern American history. Black-skinned, French- and Creole-speaking, and generally very poor, Haitians have been slow to assimilate into American society.

A comparatively small Caribbean nation whose people are virtually all descendants of African slaves, Haiti occupies the western third of the island of Hispaniola, which it shares with the Dominican Republic. Immediately to its west is the larger island of Cuba, and the much smaller island of Puerto Rico lies to the east of Hispaniola. After a 1697 treaty between France and Spain split the island into French and Spanish colonies, France began developing its western portion as the colony of Saint-Domingue. Saint-Domingue proved a deadly home to European settlers, but over the course of the next century, African slave labor made it a prosperous sugar- and coffee-producing colony. During the 1790's, the black workers on whose backs the colony's prosperity was built rose up in revolt. After a decade of bloody wars, the slaves ousted the French and established the independent nation of Haiti in 1804.

Over the next two centuries, Haiti never gained full political stability and became one of the poorest nations in the world. Nevertheless, its popula-

tion continued to grow. By the twentieth century, its limited arable land could not easily feed all its people, and emigration to other countries became an increasingly attractive option for many Haitians.

TWENTIETH CENTURY PRESSURES

During the early twentieth century, many rural Haitians began moving to the cities, causing such overcrowding that many city residents sought better living conditions abroad. Some went east, overland to the adjacent Dominican Republic, and some went to French-speaking African countries and to French Canada. Many others emigrated to the nearby United States. Mostly from Haiti's small middle and upper classes, these emigrants were generally well educated—some had attended schools in France—and most found new homes and good jobs abroad.

During the 1950's and 1960's, Haitian emigration increased after President Francois "Papa Doc" Duvalier declared himself ruler for life and deprived his citizens of privileges and rights they had enjoyed under earlier regimes. The best-educated Haitians—doctors, lawyers, teachers, and engineers—who opposed Duvalier were special targets of his animosity. They left the country in large numbers, creating a serious "brain drain" that the country could ill afford. Indeed, so many qualified doctors left between 1957 and 1963 that only three of the 264 graduates of Haiti's lone medical school remained in Haiti.

From 1957 until his death in 1971, Duvalier continued his repressive regime. As the country's economy deteriorated, more Haitians fled to America, where the sympathetic U.S. government welcomed them. During only three decades, the United States issued more than one million entry visas to Haitians. Many were given to semiskilled workers who ostensibly wanted only to visit relatives already in the United States. However, many of these people overstayed their allotted time limits with the intention of gaining permanent residence status.

By the 1960's, immigrants to the United States were coming not only from Haiti's cities but also from its villages and small towns. After arriving, these immigrants tended not to venture far from where they first set foot in America. As a result, they congregated in South Florida, where large Haitian communities arose in Miami and other South Florida cities. As the numbers of French- and Creole-speaking Haitians increased, the welcoming attitudes of the U.S. government and the American public cooled. However, after Lyndon B. Johnson became president in 1963, he focused on domestic issues and the expanding Vietnam War and regarded Haitian immigration as little more than a minor annoyance.

LATE TWENTIETH CENTURY BOAT PEOPLE

The less welcoming attitude of Americans did not, however, reduce Haitian interest in coming to the United States. Poverty, political repression, and crime were making life in Haiti increasingly difficult. Impediments placed in the way of emigrants by both the Haitian and U.S. governments simply forced the emigrants to become more inventive. During the 1970's, Haitians began trying to reach the United States on small, often unseaworthy boats, risking drowning at sea. During the 1980's, the exodus of Haitians by boat was so great that many people were using almost any craft that would float to reach South Florida. The distance they had to travel was several times greater than that required by Cubans sailing small boats to Florida.

The Haitians using small boats to emigrate were generally from the poorest classes—those who could not afford airfares or government exit visas. Because they arrived in the United States with no kind of documentation that would allow them to enter legally, they tried to enter surreptitiously.

PROFILE OF HAITIAN IMMIGRANTS

Country of origin	Haiti
Primary language	French
Primary regions of U.S. settlement	South Florida, East Coast
Earliest significant arrivals	Early 1950's
Peak immigration periods	1980's-2008
Twenty-first century legal residents*	166,890 (20,861 per year)

*Immigrants who obtained legal permanent resident status in the United States.

Source: Department of Homeland Security, *Yearbook of Immigration Statistics, 2008.*

Those who successfully entered the United States then had to live underground until they could legitimize their presence. The U.S. Immigration and Naturalization Service estimated that about 55,000 Haitian boat people safely reached the United States after 1980, but it also admitted as many as another 45,000 may have escaped detection. The number of would-be immigrants who perished at sea can only be conjectured. About 85 percent of the boat people settled in Miami.

Most of the Haitian immigrants who came during the 1980's were related to Haitians already living in the United States when they arrived. These immigrants were generally literate with some job skills and were consequently able to contribute to their new communities. However, as the total number of these exotic black immigrants increased, a backlash against them developed in the United States. As with many earlier immigrant groups in America, the Haitians were accused of placing new burdens on America's already overburdened welfare systems and of taking jobs from American citizens.

During 1981 alone, nearly 1,000 Haitian boat people arrived in South Florida every month. Some came indirectly, after first passing through the Bahamas. The U.S. government tried to reduce the flow of illegal immigrants through an agreement with the Haitian government that allowed it to interdict Haitian boats before they neared the Florida coast and return Haitian immigrants to Haiti.

HAITIANS IN THE UNITED STATES

Haitians are culturally distinct from other West Indians, most of whom speak Spanish or English. French is the official language of Haiti, but many rural Haitians speak only Haitian Creole, which isolates them linguistically. After Haitians settle in the United States, they tend not to identify with other nonwhite immigrant groups or even with African Americans.

Most Haitians are devout Christians, both Roman Catholics and Protestants, whose Christian religious rituals typically incorporate special island features. A large majority of recently arrived Haitians in South Florida attend weekly services at churches, which—like their island counterparts—play more than a spiritual role by helping the sick and the poor. Haitians have great respect for reli-

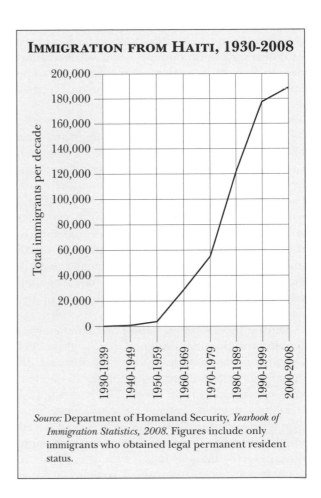

IMMIGRATION FROM HAITI, 1930-2008

Source: Department of Homeland Security, *Yearbook of Immigration Statistics, 2008.* Figures include only immigrants who obtained legal permanent resident status.

gion and members of the clergy. This respect was evident when Haiti made a former priest, Jean-Bertrand Aristide, its first democratically elected president in 1991, after the Duvaliers were ousted from power.

Black, non-English speaking, and culturally exotic, Haitian immigrants have experienced innumerable instances of prejudice and discrimination in the United States. Most are of African descent, so historically they faced the same discriminatory Jim Crow laws and racist attitudes as black Americans. However, even after strong civil rights laws and softening American attitudes toward racial minorities began making life in America more equitable for nonwhite peoples, Haitian faced new forms of discrimination. The slowness with which they have assimilated is doubtless partly due to their own reluctance to abandon Haitian customs and the insistence of many of them on continuing to speak Haitian Creole, at least among themselves. Their

retention of voodoo rituals and other traditional religious and medical practices, as well as their frequent return visits to Haiti, have all helped brand them as "different."

During the 1970's and 1980's, a new negative stereotype was attached to the Haitian immigrants: They were accused of being disease carriers. Initially, tuberculosis was said to be endemic among the Haitian population. An even worse condemnation came later, when Haitians were officially "identified" as acquired immunodeficiency syndrome (AIDS) carriers. This designation was later removed by the U.S. Centers for Disease Control and Prevention, but the U.S. Food and Drug Administration refused to accept blood donations from all persons of Haitian descent during the late 1980's.

During the 1980's, about 800,000 people of Haitian descent were living in the United States. They included naturalized citizens; legal immigrants; nonimmigrants, such as students, temporary workers, tourists, Haitian government personnel, and employees of international organizations; undocumented aliens; persons on transitional status; and refugees requesting political asylum. Those seeking refugee status came by the thousands during the four years of military rule in Haiti, from 1991 to 1994, following the exile of "Baby Doc" Duvalier. The situation in Haiti being so horrendous, many were granted refugee status and resettled in areas all around the nation.

TWENTY-FIRST CENTURY TRENDS

In 2004, nearly 450,000 foreign-born Haitians were living in the United States. Florida and New York were home to most, followed by Massachusetts, New Jersey, Connecticut, Maryland, Washington, D.C., Pennsylvania, Georgia, Illinois (particularly Chicago), and California. Miami, Florida, had an ethnic enclave called "Little Haiti." New York City had Haitian enclaves in East Flatbush, Brooklyn, Elmont, and Long Island. Queens is also a favored location for those Haitians with the means to purchase single-family homes, the preferred type of residence. Boston also has a Haitian enclave.

In these and other areas, Haitians have set up many businesses that cater to the special needs of their fellow countrymen. Along with barbershops and car services, they operate restaurants specializing in Haitian cuisine. Haitians able to support themselves and their families in America tend not to forget their allegiance to their homeland and relatives they have left behind. They are estimated to remit as much as 600 million dollars a year to relatives in Haiti. These remittances have become an important part of the Haitian national economy.

Jane L. Ball

FURTHER READING

Foner, Nancy, ed. *American Arrivals: Anthropology Engages the New Immigration.* Oxford, England: James Currey, 2004. Discusses health care, education, and issues of cultural values and practices among immigrants, including Haitians, and how they adapt to American society.

Gaines, Jena, and Stuart Anderson, eds. *Haitian Immigration.* Broomal, Pa.: Mason Crest, 2003. Overview of Haitian immigration since the 1960's, the conditions in Haiti causing emigration, and adjustments and problems faced. Written for readers aged twelve and older.

Schiller, Nina, and Georges Fouron. *Georges Woke Up Laughing: Long-Distance Nationalism and the Search for Home.* Durham, N.C.: Duke University Press, 2001. Recounts the Haitian immigrant experience in America, the daily struggles for survival for both the immigrants and those left behind. Combines history, autobiography—coauthor Fouron is a Haitian immigrant—and ethnography.

Shaw-Taylor, Yoku, and Steven Tuch, eds. *The Other African Americans: Contemporary African and Caribbean Immigrants in the United States.* Lanham, Md.: Rowman & Littlefield, 2007. Comparative study of Haitian, Jamaican, Dominican, and African immigrants in the United States.

Shell-Weiss, Melanie. *Coming to Miami: A Social History.* Gainesville: University Press of Florida, 2009. History of immigration to Miami since 1880 that examines the struggles of Haitians, Cubans, and other Latin American peoples to achieve citizenship and labor rights in the United States.

Stepick, Alex, and Nancy Foner. *Pride Against Prejudice: Haitians in the United States.* Boston: Allyn & Bacon, 1998. Describes the struggles of Haitian immigrants, the causes and consequences of their immigration, and how family, community, and culture help them maintain their pride while coping with prejudice and economics.

Zéphir, Flore. *Haitian Immigrants in Black America: A Sociological and Sociolinguistic Portrait.* Westport, Conn.: Greenwood Press, 1996. Provides multiple perspectives on Haitian immigration experiences, based on hundreds of interviews with Haitian immigrants, especially as they reveal how they cope with America's system of racial classification and how they view themselves as a distinct ethnic group.

SEE ALSO: Acquired immunodeficiency syndrome; Danticat, Edwidge; Dominican immigrants; Florida; Haitian boat people; *Immigration and Naturalization Service v. St. Cyr*; Miami; Quota systems; Religions of immigrants; *Sale v. Haitian Centers Council*; Settlement patterns.

HAMBURG-AMERIKA LINE

IDENTIFICATION: Transatlantic passenger shipping company

DATE: Established in 1847

LOCATION: Based in Hamburg, Germany

ALSO KNOWN AS: Hamburg Amerikanische Packetfahrt Actien Gesellschaft (HAPAG); Hamburg-Amerika Linie; Hamburg-America Line, Hamburg-American Line

SIGNIFICANCE: From 1881 until 1914, the Hamburg-Amerika Line was the largest shipping line in existence. It transported hundreds of thousands of emigrants from Germany, Scandinavia, and eastern Europe to the United States, Canada, Latin America, and other destinations around the world.

The German city of Hamburg lies on the Elbe River, a navigable waterway that empties into the North Sea. Also accessible by railroad from the east and south, Hamburg became the most important emigration port in continental Europe during the last decades of the nineteenth century, outstripping its rival German port, Bremen, during the 1890's. Hamburg became the point of embarkation not only for German and Scandinavian emigrants, but also for Russian and Polish Jews, many of whom were fleeing persecutions that had started in czarist Russia in 1881.

By 1914, when World War I interrupted shipping, the Hamburg-Amerika Line had a fleet of 175 active steamships, several of which could carry one thousand passengers each. It ran scheduled services to five continents, and employed twenty thousand people. Its steamships crossed the North Atlantic in a little over one week. Most immigrants to the United States traveled by the lowest-cost class, which was known as "steerage." Such passengers were accommodated between decks in closely packed bunks. However, despite their crowding, they were relatively comfortable, and the shipping line provided them with three meals a day. The cost of a typical adult steerage ticket was equivalent to about twenty U.S. dollars—a price that decreased slightly as the demand rose. Children's fares were the adult fares. Ships arriving in New York docked at company piers in Hoboken, New Jersey, from which passengers were ferried to the immigrant processing stations—Castle Garden between 1855 and 1891 and Ellis Island afterward.

Under the directorship of Albert Ballin, the son of a German-Jewish mercantile family, the shipping company expanded its reach into eastern Europe during the 1890's, sending agents to recruit passengers, sell them rail and steamship tickets, and connect them with temporary lodging at the embarkation port. Ballin's agents set up health inspection checkpoints at the frontiers of the German state and arranged "disinfection" routines for emigrants prior to their eventual embarkation. This latter procedure was done because passengers found to be carrying contagious diseases could be turned back at U.S. ports of immigration, leaving the shipping company to pay for return to Europe.

As the flow of emigrants needing accommodation began to overwhelm the capacity of Hamburg's hotels and hostels, Ballin arranged for the construction of an emigrant village, the *Auswandererhallen* (emigrant halls), to be built on Veddel Island in the Elbe, on the outskirts of Hamburg. Able to accommodate as many as five thousand people at one time, the village provided dormitories, kosher and nonkosher dining halls, shops, a bandstand, and houses of worship, including a synagogue. It also had facilities for quarantine and further health inspections. When sailing day arrived, the passengers loaded their belongings onto tenders, which transported them down the Elbe to Cuxhaven, the city's deep-water outport, where giant transatlantic ships awaited their boarding.

German emigrants boarding a ship at the port of Hamburg. (NARA)

Between 1850 and 1938, approximately 5 million people emigrated from Europe aboard Hamburg-Amerika Line ships. During World War II, Germany's Nazi government expunged Albert Ballin's name and contributions from the historical record. The emigrant village he had built was demolished in 1962. During the 1970's, the Hamburg-Amerika Line merged with the Norddeutscher Lloyd of Bremen to establish the modern Hapag-Lloyd shipping company. Hapag's detailed passenger records, covering the period 1850-1934, have survived and are housed in the Hamburg State Archive, and Ballin's reputation has been restored. Twenty-first century American tourists may visit BallinStadt, a re-creation of the *Auswanderer* village on Veddel Island and a center for family history research.

Karen Manners Smith

FURTHER READING

Baines, Dudley. *Emigration from Europe, 1815-1930.* New York: Cambridge University Press, 1995.

Fry, Henry. *The History of North Atlantic Steam Navigation.* London: Sampson Low, Marston, 1896.

Groppe, Hans-Hermann, and Ursula Wöst. *Via Hamburg to the World: From the Emigrants' Halls to BallinStadt.* Translated by Paul Bewicke and Mary Tyler. Hamburg, Germany: Ellert and Richter Verlag, 2007.

Page, Thomas W. "The Transportation of Immigrants and Reception Arrangements in the Nineteenth Century." *Journal of Political Economy* 19, no. 9 (1911): 732-749.

SEE ALSO: Austrian immigrants; Ellis Island; European immigrants; German immigrants; Hungarian

immigrants; Infectious diseases; Jewish immigrants; Pacific Mail Steamship Company; Polish immigrants; Russian and Soviet immigrants; Transportation of immigrants; World War I.

HAMPTON V. MOW SUN WONG

THE CASE: U.S. Supreme Court decision on the rights of aliens

DATE: Decided on June 1, 1976

> **SIGNIFICANCE:** The *Hampton* decision took an expansive view of noncitizens' right to public employment and severely restricted the extent to which the federal government and federal agencies might refuse to employ noncitizens.

Mow Sun Wong was an alien immigrant residing lawfully and permanently in the United States. When he applied for a position with the U.S. Civil Service Commission, his application was rejected solely because of the agency's policy of employing only American citizens. Many federal agencies maintained the same policy. In a class-action suit, Wong and four other resident aliens accused the agencies of unconstitutional discrimination. The Supreme Court had previously struck down such discrimination when practiced by state governments. Although the district court upheld the federal agencies' policy, the court of appeals reversed and held that the policy of excluding all aliens without a special justification violated the principle of equal justice under the law, which had been established as a component of the due process commanded by the Fifth Amendment.

By a 5-4 vote, the Supreme Court agreed with the court of appeals. Writing for the majority, Justice John Paul Stevens presented a long, nuanced discussion of the issues. Although endorsing the idea that the "overriding national interests may [often] provide a justification for a citizenship requirement in the federal service," Stevens repudiated the notion that "any agent of the national government may arbitrarily subject all resident aliens to different substantive rules from those applied to citizens." Whenever the national government deprives a person of "an aspect of liberty," it must explicitly refer to that interest and show that

the deprivation directly promotes that interest. Distinguishing between mandating a rule and passively accepting it, moreover, Stevens observed that Congress had allowed but never commanded the Civil Service Commission to refuse to employ aliens legally residing in the country.

Thomas Tandy Lewis

FURTHER READING

O'Brien, David M. *Constitutional Law and Politics.* 7th ed. New York: W. W. Norton, 2008.

Schwartz, Bernard, ed. *The Burger Court: Counter-Revolution or Confirmation?* New York: Oxford University Press, 1998.

SEE ALSO: Chinese immigrants; Citizenship; Congress, U.S.; Constitution, U.S.; Due process protections; Immigration law; Supreme Court, U.S.

HANSEN EFFECT

DEFINITION: Groundbreaking theory in European American immigration studies

> **SIGNIFICANCE:** In 1938, shortly before he died, social historian Marcus Lee Hansen revolutionized the understanding of the assimilation of immigrant generations into American life by suggesting that assimilation and ethnic identity within the so-called melting pot of America were far more complex than had been assumed.

At the turn of the twentieth century, immigrant studies within American academia were restricted by a lack of perspective and hard data. The great era of European immigration had not quite ended and historians generally considered the influx of poorly educated, lower-class Europeans into East Coast cities more as a pressing social problem than as a historical phenomenon. Establishment historians drew upon an Anglo-Saxon model to define America, arguing that Anglo-Saxon—that is, northern and western European—families had initially settled the New World, expressed by the New England town system. That tradition—specifically Protestant religious structures, patriarchal communities, and competitive economic markets—created the industrial order, the political dynamic

of a constitutional government, and the economic class system that had come to define America.

Scholars paid little attention to immigrants from southern and eastern Europe. When historian Frederick Jackson Turner revolutionized the concept of American history during the late nineteenth century by shifting the focus from New England to the frontier, a new impetus was given to studying the impact of immigrants in shaping the American character. Turner argued that in confronting the frontier, immigrants necessarily shed their European customs and forged a kind of American identity.

At issue then was the process of assimilation itself. One of Turner's history students at Harvard University was Marcus Lee Hansen (1892-1938), a Wisconsinite of northern European descent from the rural Midwest. Hansen came to appreciate the complexity of the question of immigration studies. For more than four years during the early 1930's, he gathered data in Europe and the Plains states and came to theorize that the melting pot model was inadequate to explain the experience of American immigrants because ethnic identity was not entirely surrendered to the collective identity. In a historical society pamphlet titled *The Problem of the Third Generation Immigrant* (1938), Hansen formulated his thesis: That the third generation, the grandchildren, wished to recover the ethnicity of their grandparents.

According to Hansen's thesis, the first generation, as foreign born, inevitably maintained the language and customs of their Old World identity. Their children sought to assimilate into the American identity and deliberately distanced themselves from the customs and language of the Old World. However, the grandchildren sought to recover the original ethnic identity. What the son wanted to forget, the argument went, the grandson wished to remember. Hansen proposed that assimilation and ethnic identity could actually be part of the same process, that the third generation could adapt to their New World environments without sacrificing ethnic identity. Ethnicity was then a generational process, with each generation struggling with the implications of its cultural heritage. Thus assimilation was best studied within, rather than across, generations.

Because Hansen died of renal failure while still in his forties, he was never able to examine the experience of nonwhite immigrants and the special problems posed by Native Americans. However, his theory, as a challenge to the melting pot, gained interest. This was particularly true after World War II, when America's international reputation suffered during the prolonged Cold War, the Korea and Vietnam conflicts, civil rights unrest, and a series of national political scandals. Within that heated environment, Hansen's thesis was embraced as an early, albeit indirect, proponent of multiculturalism and the celebration of diversity.

Joseph Dewey

FURTHER READING

Bayor, Ronald H. *Race and Ethnicity in America: A Concise History.* New York: Columbia University Press, 2003.

Daniels, Roger. *Coming to America: A History of Immigration and Ethnicity in American Life.* New York: Harper, 2002.

Hansen, Marcus Lee. *The Problem of the Third Generation Immigrant.* Rock Island, Ill.: Augustana Historical Society, 1938.

Takaki, Roger. *Debating Diversity: Clashing Perspectives on Race and Ethnicity in America.* New York: Oxford University Press, 2002.

Zlner, Mette. *Re-imagining the Nation: Debates on Immigrants, Identities and Memories.* New York: Peter Lang, 2000.

SEE ALSO: Anglo-conformity; Assimilation theories; Cultural pluralism; European immigrants; Families; History of immigration after 1891; Identificational assimilation; Melting pot theory; Migrant superordination; Push-pull factors.

HAWAII

SIGNIFICANCE: Hawaii is one of only four U.S. states in which residents of European ancestry do not form a majority, and it is home to large Asian immigrant communities, including Japanese, Chinese, Filipino, and Koreans. Many of Hawaii's native-born citizens are descendants of Chinese, Filipino, and Japanese immigrants who came during the nineteenth and early twentieth centuries to work the islands' sugar cane plantations, and

immigration from Asia has continued into the twenty-first century.

Hawaii was originally settled by Polynesian islanders. Western traders first arrived during the late eighteenth century, bringing with them Chinese sailors, who began settling in Hawaii in 1789. These early Asian settlers, who were virtually all male, intermarried with Hawaiian women and assimilated into Hawaiian culture. Intermarriage between Chinese immigrants and native Hawaiians was common well into the nineteenth century.

In 1887, American and European businessmen in Hawaii forced King Kal kaua I to abdicate his power by signing a constitution that gave voting rights exclusively to wealthy Americans, Europeans, and the few native Hawaiians who had achieved significant wealth. The new constitution disenfranchised the islands' many Asian immigrants. Kal kaua's sister, Queen Liliuokalani, was deposed when she attempted to regain sovereignty for Hawaiians. In 1900, the United States annexed Hawaii as a U.S. territory.

SUGAR CANE INDUSTRY

During the late nineteenth and early twentieth century, white plantation owners imported numerous workers from Asia. Initially, most of these workers were from China and Japan. The first labor recruits came from China in 1850; by 1887, 26,000 Chinese were working on Hawaii's sugar cane plantations, but about 38 percent of them eventually returned to China. Between 1868 and 1924, 200,000 Japanese workers came to Hawaii; eventually, about 55 percent of them returned to Japan. During this same period, 7,300 Korean workers came to Hawaii; 16 percent eventually returned home. Asians were not, however, the only labor immigrants. Almost 13,000 Portuguese workers had also been imported by 1899, and 5,000 Puerto Ricans by

Japanese sugar plantation workers in Hawaii around 1890. (Hawaii State Archives)

1901. Meanwhile, the white plantation owners established a hierarchical system that kept workers divided by ethnic groups to make it difficult for them to organize.

Recruitment campaigns in the Philippines brought the first Filipinos to Hawaii in 1906. Called "Hawayanos," these first Filipino immigrants were Tagalog-speaking sugar cane workers. Like the earlier Asian immigrant workers, Filipinos came to Hawaii to earn money to take home. The numbers of Filipino workers immigrating to Hawaii increased dramatically over the next fifteen years, from 150 in 1907 to approximately 3,000 per year between 1911 and 1920. By the 1930's, Filipino workers outnumbered Japanese in the sugar plantations, even though 7,300 of them were repatriated to the Philippines during the Great Depression.

Sugar cane plantation owners preferred Filipino workers because they worked for the lowest wages. Moreover, as Filipinos were technically considered U.S. nationals because the United States administered the Philippines, they were not restricted by federal laws that barred importation of workers from other Asian countries. The Filipino workers could also be used as levers in labor disputes again Japanese plantation workers.

Filipino immigrants to Hawaii were typically rural and poorly educated, and were often unaware of their legal rights. The harsh conditions they endured on the sugar plantations were unexpected, and linguistic differences between different Filipino groups and from the Japanese and Chinese plantation workers meant that communication among immigrant workers was difficult. However, after Hawaii became a U.S. territory in 1900, immigrant workers enjoyed more rights and were no longer effectively indentured. Consequently, labor costs rose, and workers began to unionize.

Pablo Manlapit, who came to Hawaii as a laborer in 1909, became the first Filipino lawyer in the United States during the 1920's. He helped organize the Filipino Labor Union in Hawaii and advocated for the rights of Filipino workers. He also worked with the Japanese Federation of Labor

PROFILE OF HAWAII				
Region	South Pacific Ocean			
Entered union	1959			
Largest cities	Honolulu (capital), Hilo, Kailua			
Modern immigrant communities	Chinese, Japanese, Filipinos			
Population	*Total*	*Percent of state*	*Percent of U.S.*	*U.S. rank*
All state residents	1,285,000	100.0	0.43	42
All foreign-born residents	210,000	16.3	0.56	26

Source: U.S. Census Bureau, *Statistical Abstract for 2006.*
Notes: The U.S. population in 2006 was 299,399,000, of whom 37,548,000 (12.5%) were foreign born. Rankings in last column reflect total numbers, not percentages.

(later the Hawaiian Federation of Labor) during a sugar workers' strike in 1920. His work as a labor agitator led to his being deported to the mainland United States in 1924. He returned to Hawaii in 1933 and continued to agitate, but his deportation to the Philippines two years later ended his career in the Hawaiian labor movement.

Hawaii's rich multicultural mix of immigrant workers led to the creation of a Hawaiian form of Creole English, sometimes called "Hawaiian Pidgin." It combined native Hawaiian, English, Japanese, Chinese, Ilocano, Tagalog, and Portuguese vocabulary, allowing plantation workers of all ethnic backgrounds to communicate with one another. Hawaiian Creole was still being spoken during the early twenty-first century.

JAPANESE AMERICANS AND WORLD WAR II

The United States entered World War II at the end of 1941, immediately after Japan launched a sneak attack on the great Pearl Harbor naval base in Hawaii. By that time, roughly one-third of Hawaii's population, about 150,000 people, were Japanese or of Japanese descent. In contrast to the Japanese residents of the western states of the United States, almost all of whom were interned throughout the war, only about 1 percent of Hawaii's Japanese residents were interned. The federal government declared martial law in Hawaii after the Pearl Harbor attack, but attempting to intern one-third of the islands' population would have been a logistical nightmare and caused an economic disaster.

Nevertheless, Hawaii hosted two internment camps: Sand Island, in Honolulu Harbor, and Honouliuli, on the southwestern shore of Oahu. Some Japanese immigrants in Hawaii were sent to internment camps on the mainland.

POSTWAR IMMIGRATION

During the 1990's, an influx of nearly 50,000 new immigrants brought Hawaii's total foreign-born population to 212,000, accounting for about 48 percent of the state's overall population increase. Between 1985 and 2000, approximately 4,800 immigrants from newly independent Micronesia and the Marshall Islands moved to Hawaii. This led the Hawaiian government to sue the federal government for inadequately reporting the impact on Hawaii of unrestricted immigration from these territories to Congress.

Melissa A. Barton

FURTHER READING

Ch'oe, Yong-ho, ed. *From the Land of Hibiscus: Koreans in Hawai'i, 1903-1950*. Honolulu: University of Hawaii Press, 2007. Collection of scholarly essays on Korean immigration to Hawaii and immigrant culture.

Duus, Masayo Umezawa. *The Japanese Conspiracy: The Oahu Sugar Strike of 1920*. Translated by Beth Cory, adapted by Peter Duus. Berkeley: University of California Press, 1999. Narrative account of the 1920 sugar strike by Japanese and Filipino workers originally written for Japanese readers.

Kerkvliet, Melinda Tria. *Pablo Manlapit: A Filipino Labor Leader in Hawai'i*. Honolulu: University of Hawaii Press, 2002. Historical account of one of Hawaii's most controversial labor leaders, who fought for the rights of sugar cane workers before World War II.

Odo, Franklin. *No Sword to Bury: Japanese Americans in Hawai'i During World War II*. Philadelphia: Temple University Press, 2004. Tells the story of Japanese American college students barred from serving in World War II and of their immigrant community.

Patterson, Wayne. *The Korean Frontier in America: Immigration to Hawaii, 1896-1910*. Honolulu: University of Hawaii Press, 1988. Useful survey of the earliest years of Korean immigration to Hawaii.

Young, Nancy Foon. *The Chinese in Hawaii: An Annotated Bibliography*. Honolulu: University of Hawaii Press, 1973. Comprehensive bibliography of material on Chinese Americans in Hawaii up to the date of its publication.

SEE ALSO: Anti-Japanese movement; Chinese immigrants; Filipino immigrants; *Imingaisha*; Immigration Convention of 1886; Japanese immigrants; Korean immigrants; Portuguese immigrants; Puerto Rican immigrants; World War II.

HAYAKAWA, S. I.

IDENTIFICATION: Japanese Canadian immigrant, college president, and U.S. senator
BORN: July 18, 1906; Vancouver, British Columbia, Canada
DIED: February 27, 1992; Greenbrae, California

SIGNIFICANCE: A notable scholar of semantics, Hayakawa also had a political career. He represented California in the U.S. Senate, where he launched a movement to establish English as the official language of the United States by introducing the English Language Amendment in 1981.

Born in Vancouver in 1906, Hayakawa was the son of a Japanese immigrant to Canada. After completing high school in Winnipeg, he continued his education at the University of Manitoba and McGill University in Montreal, earning a master of arts degree in English in 1928. In 1935, he completed his doctorate in English and American literature at the University of Wisconsin.

Hayakawa taught English at the University of Wisconsin from 1936 to 1939 and at the Illinois Institute of Technology from 1939 to 1947. As a Canadian immigrant, he was not subject to internment during World War II. Because of wartime restrictions, Hayakawa had to wait until 1954 to become a U.S. citizen.

In 1955, Hayakawa became a professor of English at San Francisco State College (now known as San Francisco State University). He was promoted to college president in 1968. Hayakawa was elected to the U.S. Senate as a Republican in 1976. He introduced the first English Language Amendment in 1981. After leaving the Senate in 1983, he

S. I. Hayakawa (right) with President Richard M. Nixon in 1969, when Hayakawa was president of San Francisco State College. (Time & Life Pictures/Getty Images)

founded U.S. English, an organization that promoted English as the official language of the United States. Hayakawa died in 1992.

John David Rausch, Jr.

FURTHER READING

Baron, Dennis. *The English-Only Question: An Official Language for Americans?* New Haven, Conn.: Yale University Press, 1990.

Gallegos, Bee, ed. *English: Our Official Language?* New York: H. W. Wilson, 1994.

Tse, Lucy. *"Why Don't They Learn English?" Separating Fact from Fallacy in the U.S. Language Debate.* New York: Teachers College Press, 2001.

SEE ALSO: Asian immigrants; Bilingual education; Canadian immigrants; Education; English as a second language; English-only and official English movements; Higher education; Japanese immigrants; World War II.

HEAD MONEY CASES

THE CASE: U.S. Supreme Court decision on immigration law

DATE: Decided on December 8, 1884

SIGNIFICANCE: The *Head Money Cases* expanded the powers of Congress to control immigration, to use taxation in regulating commerce, and to repeal treaties with foreign countries.

Before the 1880's, individual U.S. states exercised the primary role in the admission of immigrants. In the Immigration Act of 1882, Congress moved to assume greater control over immigration policy. In order to obtain funds to compensate the states for the burden of financing needy immigrants, Congress approved a federal head tax of fifty cents on every immigrant. Owners of passenger ships

challenged the constitutionality of the tax on the grounds that the tax was not applied uniformly throughout the United States, that the law was not passed to provide for common defense or general welfare, and that the tax conflicted with foreign treaties previously approved by the Senate.

The U.S. Supreme Court unanimously rejected each of the three arguments against the head tax. Speaking for the Court, Justice Samuel F. Miller explained, in the first place, that a fee was uniform because it "operates precisely alike in every port of the United States where such passengers can be landed." Second, the head tax was not to be considered as an exercise of the taxing power, but rather it was a "mere incident of the regulation of commerce," designed to mitigate "the evils inherent in the business of bringing foreigners to the United States." Finally, because the U.S. Constitution recognized treaties and federal statutes to be of equal authority, Congress had almost an unlimited discretion to modify or disregard treaties.

Thomas Tandy Lewis

FURTHER READING

Fairman, Charles. *Mr. Justice Miller and the Supreme Court, 1862-1890.* Clark, N.J.: Lawbook Exchange, 2003.

LeMay, Michael, and Elliott Robert Barkan, eds. *U.S. Immigration and Naturalization Laws and Issues: A Documentary History.* Westport, Conn.: Greenwood Press, 1999.

SEE ALSO: Citizenship; Congress, U.S.; Constitution, U.S.; Due process protections; History of immigration after 1891; Immigration law; Supreme Court, U.S.

HEALTH CARE

DEFINITION: Professional medical and mental health services

SIGNIFICANCE: The access of recently arrived immigrants to health care in the United States has often been limited by cultural and language barriers, lack of information, and economic disparities. Thus, alternative medicines and traditional healers have become important parts of immigrant health care. Immigrants' struggle for health care has continued into the twenty-first century, with ongoing efforts to incorporate immigrants and refugees into the American health care system.

Concern about the possible threats to public health that might be brought into the United States by new immigrants has long been a concern of U.S. immigration law. The Immigration Act of 1891 required medical inspections of immigrants before they left their home countries and immediately after their arrival in the United States. Subsequent immigration acts during the 1890's and the early twentieth century barred diseased immigrants from the United States and expanded the categories of excludable immigrants.

Although the actual number of people who were deported for medical conditions around the turn of the twentieth century was quite small, memoirs and oral histories from that era reflect immigrants' fear of medical inspection processes and physicians at American ports. In Ellis Island, through which about 70 percent of immigrants entered the United States during that time period, U.S. Public Health Service officers examined new immigrants. With hundreds of newcomers arriving daily at the reception center, detailed and thorough examinations were often impossible, and physicians relied on various clues to weed out immigrants with physical or mental defects. Immigrants found to be suffering from contagious and dangerous diseases who could not earn their livings due to their physical or mental conditions were detained for more thorough inspections and afterward often deported to their home countries, unless they recovered. Developments in medical technology, such as X rays for tuberculosis and Wasserman tests for syphilis, aided inspections of immigrants between 1882 and the mid-1920's.

THE AMERICAN HEALTH CARE SYSTEM

Immigrants from the Old World found the American health care system cold, distant, and frightening. Their cultural identities were often threatened by American hospitals and reform-minded individuals, who introduced them to new means of treatment and care but did not consider cultural confusions the immigrants might have experienced. Immigrants and their families did not want to commit themselves to hospitals because

they were worried about possible long separations and even possible deaths through hospitalization.

Immigrants also received health care at dispensaries, alms houses, and private charities, which served diverse groups of people. Immigrant hospitals and medical facilities were built to provide health care with attention to immigrants' cultural and medical needs. Reform-minded individuals and communities also partook in the establishment of various medical facilities for immigrants, in which Western medical practices and traditional cures were often combined. Immigrants also looked for alternative means of care and treatment from traditional healers within their own ethnic communities. One such example was ethnic pharmacies, where they could find more familiar and accessible treatments for their ills.

IMMIGRANT HEATH CARE PROBLEMS

As late as the early twenty-first century, many immigrants were still experiencing the same kinds of health care problems that immigrants had experienced a century earlier. Their suspicions of American health care providers and hospitals have not gone away. In particular, immigrants with no prior exposure to Western medical facilities are likely to fear encounters with the American health care system. Moreover, various immigrant groups have experienced inequalities in receiving health care. They lack information regarding where and how to get appropriate health care in their new home. Language and cultural barriers prevent them from seeking health care services and increase their distrust of American hospitals and other medical institutions. Although hospitals are required to provide interpretation and translation services for non-English-speaking immigrants, they are not always equipped to fulfill such needs. The geographical inaccessibility of medical facilities has also prevented economically disadvantaged newcomers from getting proper care.

Another important problem for immigrants has been the lack of health insurance, which is partly attributable to their lower levels of education and poverty rates. Lack of health insurance has posed special problems for immigrant workers, who are typically more likely to get injured at work and to get injured more seriously than their native-born counterparts. This has been particularly true for Hispanic immigrant laborers, many of whom per-

form demanding physical work. When they are injured at work, they typically hesitate to take time off for medical treatment for fear of losing their jobs. Undocumented immigrant workers are even more reluctant to seek medical treatment, fearing exposure of their illegal immigration statue and possible deportation. Even insured immigrants and their families have less access to health care than insured native-born American citizens for nonfinancial reasons such as unfamiliarity with the American health care system.

MENTAL HEALTH CARE

Because of the stresses that many immigrants encounter in adjusting to life in the United States, their psychological well-being has become an important social and policy issue. Traumatic experiences in home countries, cultural and language barriers, and discrimination can all combine to aggravate the mental health problems of immigrants. While mental health care has been increasingly utilized in the United States, many immigrants are still unwilling to use such services because of their cultural norms and beliefs. In many Asian countries, for example, stigmas attached to mental illness inhibit people from seeking medical help.

Many immigrants are also handicapped by not having information about the availability of mental health care services. Moreover, the scarcity of mental health care providers who understand the cultural norms and languages of immigrant groups has prevented many immigrants from receiving proper care. Research has shown that immigrants often manifest their mental health problems in ways different from those of native-born Americans. For example, Asian immigrants are more likely than Americans to manifest mental distress through somatic symptoms. Medical health care providers who do not understand ethnic-specific symptoms of mental illness may not be able to offer timely medical interventions.

The mental health of Southeast Asians who have taken refuge in the United States since the 1960's has drawn special attention from health professionals and social workers. For example, Hmong refugees from the war-torn country of Laos are known to have suffered from posttraumatic stress disorder even before their arrival in the United States. However, due to their cultural and language differences and the lack of American medical pro-

fessionals familiar with Hmong culture and language, these immigrants have generally not received proper treatment and care.

The languages of some immigrant cultures do not have words for mental illness, but this does not mean that the people themselves are immune from mental distress. Thus, Southeast Asian refugees frequently use traditional healers and therapies. When administered in conjunction with Western medical practices, such measures are of great benefit to mentally stressed immigrants. American health care professionals have consequently become increasingly aware of the importance of understanding cultural and ethnic differences and finding ways to provide better care for immigrants and refugees.

CULTURAL NEGOTIATIONS IN HEALTH CARE

Understanding cultural differences of immigrants is crucial to providing appropriate health care services. As was the case during the early twentieth century, immigrant hospitals and medical facilities in major American cities have continued to serve not only members of their own ethnic groups but also those of other immigrant groups. Immigrants are also active in cultural negotiations. In general, they have received less health care than native-born Americans, but they have tried hard to improve their conditions. In addition to visiting American hospitals for medical care, they have also utilized traditional and ethnic care systems within their immigrant communities, often receiving good results by using both systems. Increasingly, American health professionals have accepted alternative drugs and therapy systems brought to the United States by immigrants. They have shown greater respect for various measures adopted by immigrants to treat their minds and bodies and been willing to work with non-Western medical practitioners. Growing numbers of ethnic medical professionals who understand cultural and ethnic differences of immigrant patients have been making available better health care services for immigrants.

WELFARE POLICIES AND IMMIGRATION

Policy issues regarding heath care of immigrants have interested many Americans. Again, as was the case during the early twentieth century, concerns that immigrants may bring diseases into the country and drain taxpayer dollars to pay for their care have persisted into the twenty-first century. The federal Personal Responsibility and Work Opportunity Reconciliation Act and the Illegal Immigration Reform and Immigrant Responsibility Act of 1996 both restricted Medicaid eligibility of immigrants, except in emergencies, during their first five years of residence in the United States.

California's Proposition 187, which eliminated all public services except emergency health care for undocumented immigrants, helped start nationwide debates on health care and immigrants. Despite government efforts to restrict health care for undocumented immigrants, there have been continuing efforts to provide immigrants with health care, regardless of their legal status. State- and community-based programs, such as free clinics and nonprofit institutions, have served immigrants, both documented and undocumented. Educational efforts to inform immigrants of available resources have been launched as well.

Immigrants and refugees in the United States have often been misunderstood and unfairly stigmatized as potential health menaces. During the early twentieth century, Jewish immigrants from eastern Europe were blamed for spreading trachoma, the eye disease that eventually led to blindness. Italian immigrants were associated with polio epidemics. In late nineteenth century San Francisco, Chinese immigrants were accused of bringing bubonic plague. During the 1930's, Mexicans in Los Angeles were expelled for tuberculosis. During the 1970's tuberculosis reemerged as the immigrant disease in many American urban centers. During the 1980's and 1990's, Haitian immigrants were widely associated with acquired immunodeficiency syndrome (AIDS). As a consequence, a large number of Haitians in the United States lost their jobs, housing services, and other opportunities due to their perceived association with the disease.

In addition to being stereotyped without concrete evidence, immigrants and refugees—in particular, those who are undocumented—have been blamed for draining health care resources of the United States. However, their cultural values and ethics have made positive contributions to American society as well. Various efforts to promote cultural understanding and knowledge of the immigrant population have been going on in spite of

numerous problems that have threatened the health care access of immigrants in the United States.

Ji-Hye Shin

FURTHER READING

Conway, Lorie. *Forgotten Ellis Island: The Extraordinary Story of America's Immigrant Hospital.* New York: Collins, 2007. History of the Ellis Island Hospital with photographs and vignettes from the early twentieth century.

Fadiman, Anne. *The Spirit Catches You and You Fall Down: A Hmong Child, Her American Doctors, and the Collision of Two Cultures.* New York: Farrar, Straus and Giroux, 1997. Accounts of a Hmong refugee family and various parties involved in providing care and treatment for Hmong refugees in America.

Hoy, Suellen. *Chasing Dirt: The American Pursuit of Cleanliness.* New York: Oxford University Press, 1996. History of American attitudes toward cleanliness that includes Americanization efforts toward immigrants and minority groups.

Kraut, Alan M. *Silent Travelers: Germs, Genes, and the "Immigrant Menace."* Baltimore: Johns Hopkins University Press, 1995. Synthesis of immigration history and the history of medicine that provides an overview to public health, diseases, and health care of immigrants during the nineteenth and twentieth centuries.

Kretsedemas, Philip, and Ana Aparicio, eds. *Immigrants, Welfare Reform, and the Poverty of Policy.* Westport, Conn.: Praeger, 2004. Analysis of how welfare policy is implemented and experienced at the local level by immigrants and minorities.

Markel, Howard. *When Germs Travel: Six Major Epidemics That Have Invaded America and the Fears They Have Unleashed.* New York: Vintage, 2004. Study that examines six epidemics—tuberculosis, bubonic plague, trachoma, typhus, cholera, and AIDS—to explore American public health efforts in relation to immigration.

SEE ALSO: Acquired immunodeficiency syndrome; Disaster recovery work; Ellis Island; Illegal Immigration Reform and Immigrant Responsibility Act of 1996; Immigrant aid organizations; Immigration Act of 1891; Infectious diseases; Intelligence testing; Proposition 187; Welfare and social services.

HELSINKI WATCH

IDENTIFICATION: Nongovernmental human rights organization

DATE: Founded in 1978; absorbed into Human Rights Watch in 1988

SIGNIFICANCE: Helsinki Watch was a U.S.-based group made up of private citizens devoted to monitoring compliance with the Helsinki Final Act, an international agreement signed in 1975 by thirty-five countries pledging to respect basic human and civil rights. The organization focused on human rights abuses in the Soviet Union, Eastern European nations, and the United States, documenting violations of the Helsinki Final Act in lengthy research reports and frequent press releases.

Helsinki Watch was conceived as an organization focused primarily on Eastern European human rights activists, working both to influence government policy and to keep the repression of dissidents under an international spotlight. Helsinki Watch, and in particular its executive director, Jeri Laber, sought to garner public support and attention for the plight of repressed or imprisoned individuals by issuing press releases, writing op-ed pieces, and speaking out publicly. Over time, Helsinki Watch became well known for the quality and comprehensiveness of its research reports, which were relied upon by policymakers, diplomats, and others interested in Helsinki compliance. Finally, Helsinki Watch sought to influence diplomats through direct contact, making itself a permanent, visible presence at international meetings.

Helsinki Watch and its staff worked with ethnic interest groups focused on Eastern Europe as well as organizations concerned about the plight of Soviet Jews. Dissidents who had emigrated from the Soviet Union and Eastern Europe often worked closely with Helsinki Watch, offering firsthand accounts of human rights violations to the organization's researchers. Helsinki Watch pursued a range of objectives, including advocating for those who wished to emigrate from the Soviet Union and Eastern Europe, in particular for reasons of religious freedom or family reunification. In 1988, Helsinki Watch, along with committees devoted to

monitoring human rights abuses elsewhere in the world, became part of a larger organization, Human Rights Watch, which is devoted to human rights internationally.

Sarah B. Snyder

FURTHER READING

Laber, Jeri. *The Courage of Strangers: Coming of Age with the Human Rights Movement.* New York: PublicAffairs, 2002.

Neier, Aryeh. *Taking Liberties: Four Decades in the Struggle for Rights.* New York: PublicAffairs, 2003.

SEE ALSO: El Rescate; Jewish immigrants; New York City; Russian and Soviet immigrants; West Indian immigrants.

HENDERSON V. MAYOR OF THE CITY OF NEW YORK

THE CASE: U.S. Supreme Court decision on federal power over immigration
DATE: Decided on October 1, 1875

SIGNIFICANCE: Based on Congress's exclusive authority to regulate international commerce, which included the landing of passengers, the *Henderson* decision had the effect of striking down all state laws regulating immigration.

The attempt of states to impose various kinds of taxes on immigrants and other passengers entering the United States was a controversial issue for many decades during the nineteenth century. In several decisions, including *Cooley v. Board of Wardens of the Port of Philadelphia* (1852), the Supreme Court held that the commerce clause prohibited the states from passing laws that placed a burden on Congress's power to maintain national uniformity in regulating international commerce. As the number of immigrants increased in the post-Civil War years, many Americans were concerned about an alleged "flood of pauperism emigrating from Europe." The states of New York and Louisiana required ships to post a bond on each entering passenger in order to indemnify the states for the costs associated with immigrants needing financial assistance. The two states argued that the bonds were not a regulation of commerce but rather a legitimate exercise of their "police power."

The U.S. Supreme Court unanimously ruled that the required bonds violated the U.S. Constitution because they interfered excessively with foreign commerce. Writing the opinion for the Court, Justice Samuel F. Miller explained that whenever a state statute "invades the domain of legislation which belongs exclusively to the Congress," such a statute is unconstitutional and therefore void. Although Miller acknowledged that the payment of bonds was somewhat related to the police power of the states, he nevertheless found that charging such a requirement made it impossible for Congress to maintain one uniform system of rules for the landing of passengers and immigrants in all ports throughout the United States. As a result of the *Henderson* decision, all the immigration legislation of the seaboard states was held to be unconstitutional. In response, the states abolished their immigration commissions, and private philanthropic organizations assumed most of the burden of assisting needy immigrants. The decision encouraged the federal government to pass sweeping new immigration laws in 1882.

Thomas Tandy Lewis

FURTHER READING

Fairman, Charles. *Mr. Justice Miller and the Supreme Court, 1862-1890.* Clark, N.J.: Lawbook Exchange, 2003.

LeMay, Michael, and Elliott Robert Barkan, eds. *U.S. Immigration and Naturalization Laws and Issues: A Documentary History.* Westport, Conn.: Greenwood Press, 1999.

SEE ALSO: Citizenship; Congress, U.S.; Constitution, U.S.; Due process protections; History of immigration, 1783-1891; Immigration law; *New York v. Miln*; *Passenger Cases*; Supreme Court, U.S.

HIGHER EDUCATION

DEFINITION: College-level, graduate school, and professional-school level education

SIGNIFICANCE: International scholars and students have made great contributions to the United States—economically, in helping to advance science and technology, and in increasing international understanding. However, as global competition for highly educated and skilled people has increased, fewer international scholars are choosing to come to the United States. This development could handicap the United States in future global competition, especially in the fields of science and technology. At the same time, making access to U.S. universities easier for foreign students threatens to create problems for domestic students and create security problems.

Since the 1940's, the United States has led the world in attracting international scholars and students to its institutions of higher learning. Definitions vary, but international students are persons who are not American citizens or permanent residents, who have temporary visas, and who are enrolled full-time at American universities, either to pursue a degree or to attend at least one semester as exchange students. International scholars are persons who are not American citizens or permanent residents, who have temporary visas, and who are engaged full-time in research or teaching programs at American institutions.

NUMBERS AND TRENDS

Data on international students and scholars are reported in the annual "Open Doors" report of the Institute of International Education (IIE). The IIE has conducted the annual census of international students and scholars in the United States since its founding in 1919. Since 1954, it has published "Open Doors" reports, which are based on surveys sent to more than two thousand accredited U.S. institutions.

From 1954-1955 through 2007-2008, the number of international students in the United States increased more than 1,800 percent—from 34,323 to 623,805. The latter number represents a 7 percent increase over the figure for 2006-2007. In 2008, international students represented about 3.5 percent of all college students in the United States. Their numbers have increased during every academic year, except those between 2002-2003 and 2005-2006, when their numbers dropped by about 4 percent. This drop was largely due to stricter visa restrictions and increased scrutiny of foreign students and scholars put in place in the United States following the September 11, 2001, terrorist attacks. In 2006-2007 and in 2007-2008, enrollments rebounded. Since 2001-2002, Asian countries have sent more students to the United States than any other region of the world, with India sending the most. In 2007-2008, fully 61 percent of all international students came from Asia, with India, Japan, China, and South Korea accounting for approximately 40 percent of the total.

According to United Nations Educational, Scientific, and Cultural Organization (UNESCO) reports, the United States ranked first in the world in attracting international students in 2008, when it hosted 20 percent of international students. The top ten U.S. states, which accounted for slightly more than 60 percent of all international students in the United States in 2007-2008, are, in descending order, California, New York, Texas, Massachusetts, Florida, Illinois, Pennsylvania, Michigan, Ohio, and Indiana.

In 2007-2008, 48.8 percent of international students in the United States were at the graduate level. According to the IIE, these international students represent 12 percent of all graduate students in the United States. In the fields of science and engineering, the international student percentage goes up to 30 percent, and for doctorates awarded in science and engineering it increases to 43 percent.

About 50 percent of recent international graduate students in the United States come from the nations of India, China, and South Korea. The drop-off in applications and admissions of international students to graduate school in the United States following the September 11, 2001, attacks was greater than that for all international students. However, the Council of Graduate Schools (CGS) found that a rebound in enrollments began in 2005-2006, with an increase of 1 percent, followed by a 7 percent increase in 2006-2007, and a 3 percent increase in 2007-2008. Enrollments still lagged slightly behind the figures from before the decline.

DOCTORAL STUDENTS

International students who earn doctoral degrees have a special importance; they often remain in the United States after they complete their formal studies and make crucial contributions to research and science. The Survey of Earned Doctorates by the National Opinion Research Center (NORC) estimates that in 2007, 16,947 international students received doctorates in the United States, representing 38.1 percent of all doctorates awarded in the country. The increase in foreign doctorates has been steady and substantial, as in 1977 foreign students received only 4,854 doctorates, representing 15.5 percent of all doctorates.

The proportion of international students earning American doctoral degrees ranged from a low of 13 percent in education to a high of 68 percent in engineering. International students also received 53 percent of all American doctorates awarded in the physical sciences. Students from Asia have earned about 68 percent of doctorates awarded to international students in the United States since the 1990's, with China leading all other nations.

INTERNATIONAL SCHOLARS

The "Open Doors" report on international scholars reported that 106,123 foreign scholars were teaching and doing research in the United States in 2007-2008, an increase of 8 percent over 2006-2007 and of 70.2 percent over 1996-1997. Of these scholars, 65.6 percent were men, a decrease of 8.6 percent since 1996-1997. The vast majority, 71.0 percent, were primarily involved in research. Another 12.0 percent were in teaching, 9.7 percent in research and teaching equally, and 6.9 percent in other work.

The biological and biomedical sciences had more international scholars than any other fields. Health sciences (17.7 percent), engineering (12.8 percent), and physical sciences (12.1 percent)

President John F. Kennedy at the White House with students from Nigeria, Pakistan, Iran, Colombia, Morocco, and other countries who came to the United States to study at American colleges and universities in 1961. (AP/Wide World Photos)

ranked second, third, and fourth; U.S. social sciences and history were a distant fifth at 4.1 percent. In 2007-2008, the 23,799 scholars from China constituted 22.4 percent of all international scholars in the United States, more than any other nation. India was a distant second at 9.4 percent. Overall that year, 41.1 percent of international scholars were from China, India, and South Korea. Harvard was by wide margin the number one destination with 3,712 international scholars, Stanford University being second with 2,824. Seven of the top ten destination universities were in California.

STAY RATES

International scholars, students, and graduates who have remained in the United States have contributed greatly to research labs, universities, and other high-tech institutions. However, there is virtually no information on stay rates for international undergraduate degree recipients or for scholars who arrive here with doctorates. The annual Oak Ridge Institute for Science and Education report, "Stay Rates of Foreign Doctorate Recipients," covers doctorates in science (including economics and social sciences) and engineering. The most recent report was issued in 2007, including data through 2005.

Stay rates are looked at in terms of one, two, five, and ten years. The 2007 report found the two-year stay rate was 40 percent in 1989; it increased to 71 percent in 1992, declined after the 2001 terrorist attacks, and rebounded to 66 percent by 2005. The five-year stay rate for those getting doctorates in 2000 was an all-time high of 68 percent, and the ten-year stay rate in 2005 was 62 percent. Five-year stay rates from 2000 to 2005 for the four countries with the most doctorate recipients were as follows: China (92 percent), India (85 percent), Taiwan (50 percent), and South Korea (42 percent). Five-year stay rates also varied by degree field, with computer and electrical engineering highest at 76 percent, and physical sciences, computer science, and life sciences all running close seconds at 73 percent. The lowest stay rate was economics (44 percent). This report is optimistic about the chances of current foreign doctoral students remaining in the United States, pointing out the recent rebound in stay rates, the high long-term stay rates, and a similar turnaround in recent graduates who say they wish to stay.

MOST POPULAR FIELDS OF STUDY AMONG INTERNATIONAL STUDENTS, 2007-2008

	Field	Percent
1	Business and management	19.6
2	Engineering	17.0
3	Physical and life sciences	9.3
4	Social sciences	8.7
5	Mathematics and computer sciences	8.2
6	Fine and applied arts	5.6
7	Health professions	5.1
8	Intensive English language	4.6
9	Education	3.1
10	Humanities	3.1
	Other	15.7

Source: UNESCO

NORC's Survey of Earned Doctorates asks international graduates whether they plan to stay in the United States. Past research indicates most of the recipients who state they plan to stay actually do so. The percentage of foreign doctoral recipients planning to stay had reached an all-time high of 71.7 percent in 2001, declined after the terrorist attacks, and rebounded in 2005, with the percentage saying they planned to stay at 74.7 percent in 2006. That year's doctoral recipients from China (89.8 percent) were most likely to say they intended to stay, followed closely by Bulgaria (88.9 percent), India (88.1 percent), and Iran (88.0 percent). The lowest percentage was Chile (30.1 percent), with South American countries having generally lower percentages. The 2006 survey found that graduates in chemistry (90 percent), biological/biomedical sciences (88 percent), and electrical engineering (87 percent) were most likely to say they planned to stay, while graduates in education (43 percent), social sciences (60 percent), and humanities (62 percent) were least likely.

CONTRIBUTIONS

NAFSA: Association of International Educators conservatively estimated that foreign students and their dependents contributed approximately $15.5 billion to the U.S. economy during the 2007-2008 academic year. The figures for the previous two academic years were only slightly lower.

Several recent studies have found that in terms of scientific publications, citations, and patents, international students and scholars have made exceptional contributions to the United States, proportionately greater than those made by U.S.-born scientists. In many fields of science and engineering, foreign students make up the majority of doctorate recipients. Foreign scholars and graduates fill important positions in universities, high-tech industries and research establishments.

International students and scholars enrich American campuses and businesses by adding diversity and providing American students and scholars with greater understanding and knowledge of foreign cultures and governments. Even after international scholars leave, many of them continue to collaborate with scholars in the United States. Many return to their home countries to become respected scientists and leaders, bringing with them positive attitudes toward the United States and fostering mutual understanding, respect, and cooperation.

ISSUES AND PROBLEMS

For many years, the high quality of educational and research opportunities in the United States has resulted in a brain drain of talented students and scholars from other nations. Due to increasing global competition for these people from both developing and developed nations, this trend has slowed and appeared to be reversing in 2009. Two reports from the Ewing Marion Kauffman Foundation from that year found that fewer foreign students expressed a desire to remain permanently in the United States than in the past, and that more perceived the United States to be declining as a land of opportunity. Greatly improved opportunities in many developing countries, particularly those of India and China, may well influence stay rates of graduates and scholars.

Developed nations have also increased their efforts to retain and attract international students and scholars. In particular the forty-six European Higher Education Area (EHEA) countries have initiated the Bologna Process to make academic standards and quality assurance standards of its nations more comparable and compatible, resulting in greater mobility among nations and increased collaboration.

The majority opinion, particularly in academia

and research institutes, is that having fewer international scholars and students studying and working in the United States would be detrimental to the scientific and technological innovation crucial to the success of the U.S. economy. There is a counter opinion, mostly articulated by the Center for Immigration Studies, that having too many foreign-born scholars and students in the United States is counterproductive. They contend that NAFSA greatly exaggerates the economic contribution of foreign students and that the United States is damaging its long-term competitiveness by displaying a preference for foreign over domestic students.

Critics have further argued that U.S. scholars, researchers, and students are denied opportunities and discouraged from choosing careers in science and engineering because of foreign-born competitors. The negative impact is argued to be particularly great on minority students. They also propose that student visas are an ideal way for terrorists to enter and stay in the United States and that foreign scholars might take part in espionage for their governments and businesses. While the decline in the U.S. economy that began in 2008 has resulted in some U.S. firms reducing their hiring of foreign scholars and students due to fear of political backlash, the federal government and U.S. universities have continued to work to increase their number.

Jerome L. Neapolitan

FURTHER READING

Committee on Policy Implications of International Graduate Students and Postdoctoral Scholars in the United States, Board on Higher Education and Workforce, National Research Council. *Policy Implications of International Graduate Students and Postdoctoral Scholars in the United States.* Washington, D.C.: National Academy Press, 2005. This book explores the impact of international students and scholars on the United States, particularly educational institutions.

Gürüz, Kemal. *Higher Education and International Student Mobility in the Global Knowledge Economy.* Albany: State University of New York Press, 2008. Examines how the international mobility of students has changed over time.

Institute of International Education. *Higher Education on the Move: New Developments in Global Mobility.* Leetsdale, Pa.: IIE Books, 2009. Collection of eight articles, each by a different author, explor-

ing recent changes in higher education, the world economy, and governmental changes.

_____. *Open Doors 2008: Report on International Educational Exchange.* Leetsdale, Pa.: IIE Books, 2009. Annual report that provides a statistical analysis of international students and scholars at U.S. academic institutions. Much of the data and analysis are available at the Open Doors Web site (http://opendoors.iienetwork.org).

Wadhwa, Vivek, Anna Lee, Richard Freeman, and Alex Salkeyer. *Losing the World's Best and Brightest.* Kansas City, Mo.: Kauffman Foundation, 2009. Report arguing that the United States may be on the verge of experiencing a reverse brain drain.

See also: "Brain drain"; Chinese Student Protection Act of 1992; Economic consequences of immigration; Education; Foreign exchange students; Hayakawa, S. I.; Homeland Security, Department of; Multiculturalism; Science.

History of immigration, 1620-1783

Significance: Immigration from Europe and Africa to America during the seventeenth and eighteenth centuries created the population that existed at the time the United States came into existence. The groups that made up this original population contributed greatly to the events and traditions that would shape the nation throughout its history.

The colonies that became the United States were founded as British outposts, and most of the European immigrants to those colonies were from Great Britain. However, the early British settlers came as distinct groups to different geographic areas. In addition, early American immigrants included people from other places in northern Europe, as well as involuntary immigrants from Africa.

Early English Immigration to New England, 1620-1642

Jamestown, in Virginia, was founded in 1607 and is generally regarded as the first permanent English settlement in North America. However, the 1620 establishment of Plymouth Bay Colony in Massachusetts by the religious immigrants known as the Pilgrims may be regarded as the beginning of large-scale migration from Europe to the territory that would eventually become the United States. The Pilgrims came from English dissenters against the Church of England, known as Separatists, who believed that they should separate themselves from the state Church entirely. In order to follow their separate faith without persecution from English authorities, communities of Separatists went into exile in Holland. However, it was difficult for the English religious refugees to find any work other than in the hardest and lowest-paying occupations, and their economic situations were often precarious. Also, the intensely religious exiles were suspicious of Dutch culture, and they worried about their children losing their English customs. Their leaders managed to get England's King James I to agree to allow them to resettle in America, and they obtained support from financial speculators in the London Virginia Company in return for granting the company a large portion of the crops to be produced in the New World.

On September 16, 1620, the *Mayflower* sailed from Plymouth, England, with 102 emigrants, forty-one of whom were Separatists. Two months later, they arrived at Cape Cod in modern Massachusetts. After tense encounters with Native Americans, they resettled at Plymouth Bay in December. They had a difficult struggle to establish themselves, but eventually, with new arrivals, the colony at Plymouth became one of the bases of the new American population.

An even greater contribution to the American population, in sheer numbers, began with the Puritans, who believed in purifying the established church, a decade after the voyage of the *Mayflower.* In 1630, seventeen ships left England for America. The most famous of these was the *Arabella*, on which the Puritan leader John Winthrop sailed. Mainly stemming from the area of East Anglia in England, the Puritans left during a time when Archbishop William Laud was attempting to eliminate Puritan influences from the Church of England and King Charles I was attempting to rule without calling Parliament into session. The decade of the 1630's, leading up to the English Civil War (1642-1651), was a time of economic depres-

The Mayflower. (R. S. Peale and J. A. Hill)

sion, as well as a period in which the Puritans were out of favor in the English church and state.

The years 1630 to 1640 are known as the Great Migration. The largely Puritan immigrants from England settled in New England, north of the settlement at Plymouth Bay, in a stretch of land known as the Massachusetts Bay Colony. The major centers of the new colony were the eastern coastal Massachusetts towns of Boston and Salem. During the Great Migration, an estimated two hundred ships reportedly carrying approximately 20,000 people arrived in Massachusetts. Although migration to New England dropped dramatically after the Great Migration, the descendants of the people who entered Massachusetts in those years settled much of the northeastern region of the United States and later spread westward throughout the country.

ENGLISH SETTLEMENT IN VIRGINIA, 1642-1675

In the South, the tiny Virginia colony that had barely maintained its existence during the years that Massachusetts became a center of European settlement began to expand rapidly just as the Great Migration ended in the North. In 1642, only 8,000 colonists lived in Virginia. At the beginning of that year, Sir William Berkeley became governor of Virginia, a post he would hold until 1676. Berkeley began a campaign to draw some of England's elite to Virginia. This campaign was assisted by the rise of the Puritans to power and the execution of King Charles I in 1649. Many of the future leaders that Virginia provided to the United States and to the Confederacy were descendants of these aristocratic immigrants.

The largest portion of Virginia's early immigration, though, came from the humblest section of the English population. About three-quarters of the new arrivals in Virginia during the middle to late seventeenth century came as indentured servants, people bound to serve masters without wages for specified periods of time for the price of their passage. The early immigration patterns of Virginia, then, made it a highly unequal society from the very beginning. By 1660, Virginia had a population of about 30,000 people. Neighboring Maryland, also populated largely by indentured servants, held about 4,000 in that year.

QUAKER IMMIGRATION, 1675-1725

The Society of Friends, popularly known as the Quakers, is a Christian religious group that emphasizes the inward experience of faith and the equality of people. It was founded during the mid-seventeenth century, and the Quakers' rejection of social hierarchy led to their persecution in England. Soon after the denomination was established, Quaker immigrants were arriving in America. In 1675, large-scale migration began when the first ship of Quaker passengers reached Salem in West Jersey. Other ships followed, docking in Delaware Bay.

The number of Quakers arriving in the Delaware Valley was so great that by 1750 they made up the third-largest religious denomination in the American colonies. Their growth had been assisted by Quaker leader William Penn's efforts to create a Quaker region in America to which members of the faith in England would be encouraged to relocate. In 1681, he managed to obtain a charter from King Charles II for 45,000 square miles, which the king dubbed Pennsylvania. In 1682, Penn arrived in his colony on the ship *Welcome*. Under his leadership, Pennsylvania drew not only Quaker immigrants but also members of other persecuted reli-

gious groups attracted by the policy of religious toleration.

SCOTTISH, SCOTCH-IRISH, AND ENGLISH IMMIGRATION, 1715-1775

People from the north of England, Scotland, and northern Ireland made up much of the migration to the western frontier regions of the early American colonies, especially to the rugged mountainous areas. The northern Irish migrants were mainly Scotch-Irish, descendants of people from Scotland who had moved to Ireland in earlier centuries. Most of the Irish in America before the nineteenth century were actually Scotch-Irish.

Northern Irish migration peaked between the 1750's and the early 1770's, with an estimated 14,200 people from northern Ireland reaching America from 1750 to 1759, 21,200 from 1760 to 1769, and 13,200 in the half-decade leading up to the American Revolution. Most of the Scots migration took place from 1760 to 1775, when about 25,000 new arrivals came to the colonies. The counties of North England, bordering Scotland, experienced a series of crop failures that were especially severe in 1727, 1740, and 1770. Each of these crop failures resulted in famine that sent successive waves of immigrants to America. Together, the Scottish, Scotch-Irish, and North English immigrants probably made up 90 percent of the settlers in the back country of America. Arriving after the lands along the eastern coast had been taken, these hardy individuals made up the original American frontier folk.

DUTCH, SWEDISH, AND GERMAN IMMIGRATION, 1630-1783

The most significant groups of European immigrants to the colonies of North America before the revolution came from the northern lands of Holland, Germany, and Sweden. The Dutch attempted to found their first colony during the late 1620's, when Dutch trading interests established the col-

Late nineteenth century depiction of Peter Minuit negotiating with Algonquian Indians to purchase the island of Manhattan in 1626. (Francis R. Niglutsch)

ony of New Netherland, with New Amsterdam as its capital. During the mid-seventeenth century, officials in Holland began actively encouraging migration to their colony, so that the population of New Netherland grew from about 2,000 people in 1648 to about 10,000 in 1660. Only about half of these were actually Dutch, though, and the rest consisted mainly of Belgians. In 1664, the British seized New Netherland and changed its name to New York. People with Dutch names and ancestry continued to make up a small but important part of the New York population, particularly among the elite of the area.

Swedes arrived on the northeastern coast in 1637 and founded a colony on Delaware Bay in 1638. Peter Minuit, a former director-general of the Dutch colony of New Netherland who had been born in the German state of Westphalia, led this initial Swedish settlement. New Sweden included areas of the modern states of New Jersey, Maryland, Pennsylvania, and Delaware along the Delaware River. Tensions with New Netherland led to a Dutch takeover of New Sweden in 1654, but the Dutch continued to recognize the colony as a self-governing settlement of Swedes. In 1681, following the British takeover of all the northeastern lands, William Penn received a charter for Pennsylvania, ending the distinctly Swedish identity of the region.

By the time the United States won its independence, Germans made up the largest national origin group in the country, aside from the groups stemming from the British Isles. In the year 1683, Dutch and German people in religious minorities purchased land in Pennsylvania, north of Philadelphia, and founded Germantown. One of the largest migration waves from the lands of Germany began when Protestants from the Palatine area of Germany fled political disorder and economic hardship in their homeland in 1709. After making their way to Holland and then England, about 2,100 Palatine Germans reached America in 1710, settling mainly in New York.

During the early eighteenth century, other German colonists settled in Virginia, the Carolinas, and Massachusetts. Pennsylvania, though, became the main center of German settlement, in part because the Quaker tradition of the state offered religious tolerance to German Lutherans, Mennonites, Amish, and other religious movements.

Probably about half the Germans who arrived in Pennsylvania between 1725 and the American Revolution came as redemptioners, who paid for their passage by working for a certain number of years. In all, an estimated 84,500 Germans reached the thirteen American colonies between 1700 and 1775. After the revolution, an estimated 5,000 German mercenary soldiers, mostly from the state of Hesse, who had been fighting for the British and been taken prisoner by the Americans, remained in the new country.

AFRICAN INVOLUNTARY IMMIGRATION, 1640-1783

African immigration to North America dates back to the time of the first European arrivals. During the entire period of American colonial history, involuntary immigrants arrived as slaves from Africa, mainly West Africa. Between 1700 and 1775, an estimated 278,400 Africans reached the original thirteen colonies that became the United States.

Slave importation to the coastal states of the South grew rapidly during the late seventeenth century and the first half of the eighteenth century because of the growth of the tobacco and rice economies. Imports of slaves to tobacco-growing Virginia reached 7,000 per decade for the 1670's through the 1720's and then nearly doubled to 13,500 per decade until the 1750's. South Carolina, where rice had become an important crop, began importing slaves at about the same level as Virginia during the early eighteenth century and then increased to more than 20,000 during the 1720's. While slave importation began to slow in Virginia during the later eighteenth century, it continued at about 17,000 per decade in South Carolina from the 1750's to the 1790's. By the time of the first U.S. Census in 1790, as a result of involuntary immigration and the increase of native-born slaves, people of African ancestry made up one-fifth of the American population.

Carl L. Bankston III

FURTHER READING

Fischer, David Hackett. *Albion's Seed: Four British Folkways in America.* New York: Oxford University Press, 1989. Intended to trace the cultural contributions of different segments of British society to America, this book is also one of the best general works on the places of origin and settle-

ment of people from Britain in America during the colonial period.

Fogleman, Aaron Spencer. *Hopeful Journeys: German Immigration, Settlement, and Political Culture in Colonial America, 1717-1775*. Philadelphia: University of Pennsylvania Press, 1996. Excellent account of colonial German migration that divides its attention between the lands left behind in Europe, explaining why the Germans left, and the new world they found in America. It also contains informative tables on colonial immigration in general, as well as German immigration in particular.

Moore, Susan Hardman. *Pilgrims: New World Settlers and the Call of Home*. New Haven, Conn.: Yale University Press, 2007. Through looking at the life histories of the approximately one-third of English immigrants to America from 1640 to 1660 who returned to England, this book looks at motives for both migration and return.

Weaver, John C. *The Great Land Rush and the Making of the Modern World, 1650-1900*. Montreal: McGill-Queen's University Press, 2003. General work on how European colonization of other lands transformed world economy and society.

SEE ALSO: British immigrants; Canadian immigrants; Constitution, U.S.; German immigrants; History of immigration, 1783-1891; History of immigration after 1891; Massachusetts; Pilgrim and Puritan immigrants; Slave trade; Virginia.

HISTORY OF IMMIGRATION, 1783-1891

SIGNIFICANCE: The first century of American independence saw great population growth, particularly from the new immigration of Germans and Irish, as the federal government gradually developed a coherent national immigration policy.

During the nineteenth century, the U.S. government began collecting statistical information on immigration and took its first steps toward formulating a national immigration policy. Although immigration did not attain the levels it would reach toward the end of that century, economic opportunities in the new nation and problems in other countries attracted many immigrants who settled new regions and helped build the country's infrastructure.

EVOLUTION OF FEDERAL IMMIGRATION POLICY

Until the first quarter of the nineteenth century, the new federal government was content to leave control over immigration policy to the individual states. The first major federal law to deal specifically with immigration—and not naturalization—was the Steerage Act of 1819. This statute gave the federal government information on immigration by requiring that all vessels reaching American shores deliver passenger lists to customs officials, who were required to send copies to the U.S. State Department, which, in turn, submitted the lists to Congress. The Steerage Act also limited the numbers of passengers on arriving and departing ships.

Congress did not move to impose federal controls over entry into the country until the second half of the nineteenth century. Several of the earliest federal immigration laws were directed against Chinese immigrants, who had begun arriving in the United States in significant numbers during the 1850's. These Asian immigrants came to be seen as undesirable because their culture differed from that of the predominantly white majority population and because of the competition they offered other workers. An 1862 federal law prohibited the transportation of Chinese "coolies," or manual laborers, by American ships. Twenty years later, that anti-Chinese law was followed by the Chinese Exclusion Act of 1882. The latter law suspended all immigration of Chinese laborers for ten years, barred Chinese immigrants from naturalizing as American citizens, and established provisions for their deportation. The principle of excluding Chinese immigrants was later indefinitely extended and not repealed until 1943.

Meanwhile, the first attempt to centralize control of immigration in general in the hands of the federal government came in 1864 with a law that authorized the president to appoint an immigration commissioner under the secretary of state. That law established provisions for contracts in which immigrants could be bound to use their wages to pay off the cost of their transportation to the United States. That law was repealed in 1868.

In 1875, the U.S. Supreme Court ruled that state laws regulating immigration were unconstitutional because they were inconsistent with the exclusive power of the U.S. Congress to regulate foreign commerce. In March of that same year, Congress passed a law prohibiting the entry of classes of undesirable immigrants. Congress also made it illegal to transport Asian workers to the United States without their free consent, forbade contracts to supply Chinese "coolies," and gave customs officials the duty of inspecting immigrants. This was followed by the Immigration Act of 1882, which set up state boards under the U.S. secretary of the Treasury as a way of controlling immigration. This law also added new categories of excluded undesirable immigrants and set a tax on new arrivals in the United States. The creation of the Office of the Superintendent of Immigration in the Department of the Treasury in 1891 and the designation of New York Harbor's Ellis Island as the location for the first national immigrant reception center in 1890 began the modern, federally controlled period in American immigration history.

EARLY NINETEENTH CENTURY IMMIGRANTS

The earliest decades of the new nation saw relatively little new immigration. During the 1780's, while the nation was governed under the Articles of Confederation, the loosely joined states went through difficult economic times, and the future of the independent country seemed too insecure to encourage new immigration. However, even as the nation began settling into a more stable form after adoption of the U.S. Constitution in 1789, immigration was still well below the levels it would later reach. Europe's Napoleonic Wars, which lasted until 1815, and the War of 1812 between Great Britain and the United States made it difficult for emigrants to leave Europe. During the three-decade period between 1789—when the United States adopted its new Constitution and form of government—and 1820, fewer than 500,000 new immigrants arrived in the United States.

During that same period, the same political conditions that made leaving European more difficult also motivated some Europeans to emigrate. For example, during the 1790's, English radicals and Irish opposed to English rule fled their homelands to America. The Revolution in France brought new French arrivals at the end of the eighteenth century. Other French-speaking immigrants fled slave uprisings in Haiti and other West Indies colonies around the same time. These French-speaking newcomers settled mainly in coastal cities, notably in Charleston, New York, Baltimore, and Philadelphia, as well as in New Orleans, which became part of the United States in 1803 as a result of the Louisiana Purchase.

The most numerous non-English-speaking immigrants in the United States at the time of independence were Germans. Germans also constituted one of the significant immigrant groups at the opening of the nineteenth century. Many of those Germans came from what is now the southwestern part of Germany, which was then a poor area. Bad German harvests in 1816-1817 set in motion a flood of emigration out of that region. Although many of the emigrants moved east, to Russia, about 20,000 people from southwestern Germany came to America to escape famine.

IMMIGRATION AFTER THE STEERAGE ACT

The year 1820 is the first year for which detailed immigration statistics for the United States are available, thanks to the Steerage Act of the previous year. During 1820, 8,385 immigrants arrived in the United States. Most, 43 percent, came from Ireland. The second-largest group, 29 percent, came from Great Britain. Hence, almost three-quarters of all immigrants who arrived in the United States during that year came from the British Isles alone. The next-largest groups came from the German states, France, and Canada. During the 1820's, French immigrants moved ahead of Germans as the second-largest group after people from the British Isles. The second half of that decade also saw a steep rise in overall immigration, with the numbers of arrivals rising from slightly fewer than 8,000 in 1824 to more than 22,500 in 1829.

People from Ireland, who already constituted the greatest single immigrant group during the 1820's, were drawn to the United States by both continuing poverty in their original homeland and the growing demand for labor in America. For example, New York State's Erie Canal, which was under construction from 1818 to 1825, drew heavily on immigrant Irish labor. That project began a long history of Irish immigrant labor helping to build the American transportation infrastructure. The rapid commercial success of the Erie Canal

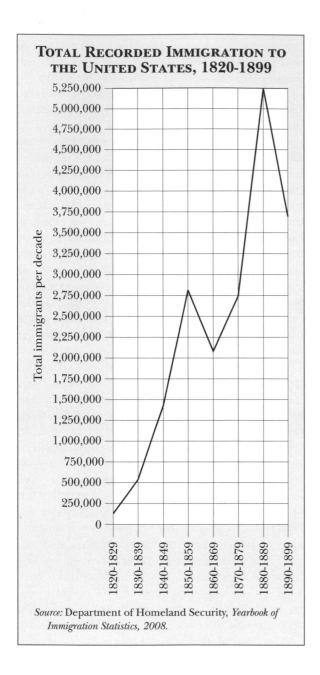

TOTAL RECORDED IMMIGRATION TO THE UNITED STATES, 1820-1899

Source: Department of Homeland Security, *Yearbook of Immigration Statistics, 2008.*

arrivals jumped suddenly from 22,633 in 1831 to 60,482 in 1832 and continued at levels roughly equal to that of 1832 through the rest of the decade.

The 1840's saw yet another surge in the tide from Europe, with 1,713,251 newcomers reaching U.S. shores from 1841 to 1850. This figure was almost triple that of the 1830's and twelve times that of the 1820's. Once again, the most important sources of new immigrants were Ireland (780,719 people) and Germany (434,626). Next highest was the United Kingdom, with 267,044 immigrants. This wave of the 1840's occurred mostly toward the end of the decade, with overall numbers rising from 78,615 in 1844 to 114,371 the following year, and reaching 297,024 in 1849.

At the approach of the mid-nineteenth century, some immigrants were drawn by the availability of land in the vast reaches of North America. Economic development also offered opportunities beyond agriculture for newcomers. Industrialization created jobs in mills and as manual laborers in cities. The expansion of railroads was another major force attracting immigrant labor. In 1830, the United States had a total of only 23 miles of railroad tracks. Only one decade later, this figure had grown to 2,818 miles. It rose to 9,021 miles in 1850 and 30,626 miles in 1860. Immigrants from Ireland played a particularly significant role in laying new railroad tracks.

Economic hardships and political disorders in the sending countries also helped stimulate emigration to the United States. The most significant event was the Great Irish Famine of 1845-1851, which was caused by a devastating potato blight. Irish were already the most numerous immigrants, and the famine drove even more of them to leave their homeland in the hope of finding relief in North America. In the various German states—which would not be united under a single government until 1871—a wave of failed revolutions in 1848 created a flood of political refugees who swelled the ranks of German Americans.

IMMIGRANT POPULATION AT MIDCENTURY

By the middle of the nineteenth century, first-generation immigrants made up one-tenth of the total population of the United States. The 1850 U.S. Census showed that the United States—including Minnesota, New Mexico, Oregon, and

stimulated the building of more canals in other parts of the country, increasing the need for immigrant labor.

The rate of immigration quadrupled during the 1830's, from a total of 143,439 arrivals between 1821 and 1830 to 599,125 between 1831 and 1840. New immigrants came from a wide variety of European countries, but most of the 1830's expansion was driven by a dramatic growth in arrivals from Ireland (207,381) and Germany (152,454). New

Utah, which were not yet states—was home to 2,240,581 foreign-born people. This figure constituted 10 percent of the total U.S. population, including persons held in slavery. Among the states and territories, New York had the largest immigrant population at midcentury, with 655,224 foreign born, who constituted more than 21 percent of the state's total population. Fifty-five percent of New York's immigrant residents were Irish; Germans constituted another 17 percent, and immigrants from England, Scotland, and Wales made up an additional 17 percent. The vast majority of all these immigrants were concentrated in the New York City area.

New York State had the largest number of immigrants in 1850, but it also had the largest total population, and there were other states with higher proportions of immigrants. The highest percentages of immigrants lived in the state of Wisconsin (36 percent of the white population) and the territory of Minnesota (33 percent). Other states with high proportions of immigrants included California (24 percent) and Louisiana. The latter was a slave state in which 26 percent of white residents and 13 percent of all residents were foreign born in 1850.

Wisconsin was home to a large number of German-speaking immigrants, who made up about one-third of all the state's immigrants. Some of these Germans, especially those from the southern German state of Bavaria, had settled in Milwaukee. Aside from the Bavarians, Wisconsin's Germans tended to be farmers who settled in rural areas. Minnesota was about to draw large numbers of immigrants from Scandinavia in the years after the U.S. Civil War. However, in 1850, a majority of the foreign-born residents of the territory came from Canada, with smaller proportions of Irish (18 percent of immigrants) and Germans (12 percent).

California's large immigrant population in 1850 consisted mainly of people from Mexico. In the 1850 U.S. Census, Mexicans made up about 36 percent of the state's foreign born. This was a heritage of California's historic connection with Mexico. Other California immigrants came mainly from Ireland (15 percent of foreign born) and Germany (10 percent). California also had smaller percentages of immigrants from all over the world. Many immigrants were drawn to the state by the discovery of gold in 1849, but most people who flocked there at the beginning of the gold rush came from other parts of the United States. However, the state's gold rush was about to stimulate a great wave of international immigration that would increase California's foreign-born residents to 39 percent of the total population in 1860.

Louisiana held the largest concentration of immigrants in the South in 1850. New Orleans, as the largest port in the South and the second largest in the nation after New York, was a natural place of entry for people from other countries. As elsewhere, the Irish made up the largest immigrant group in Louisiana. An estimated 26,580 Louisianans, or nearly 38 percent of immigrants, were Irish-born in 1850. The Irish who arrived after 1830 were most often poor peasants who settled in the area known as the City of Lafayette, which was later incorporated into New Orleans and is still identified as the Irish Channel, and provided much of the labor for digging the city's system of canals.

Many of the immigrants in both Louisiana and neighboring Texas in 1850 were Germans, who had entered the United States through New Orleans. Of the one in ten Texans who were foreign born at midcentury, over two-thirds came from Germany. These German Texans settled chiefly in the southeastern part of the state.

Most of the southern slave-holding states had low rates of immigration during the first half of the nineteenth century. The slave economy did not hold out the opportunities of the other, industrializing parts of the country. However, Maryland, one of the northernmost southern slave states, was home to an estimated 59,500 immigrants in 1850. This was the largest number of foreign-born people in any southern state except Louisiana, and it accounted for nearly 12 percent of Maryland's entire free population. As in Louisiana, Maryland's early foreign-born population was primarily the consequence of mid-nineteenth century immigration from Germany and Ireland, since Germans made up the majority (55 percent) of immigrants in the border state in 1850 and the Irish made up one-third. These immigrants were heavily concentrated in the port city of Baltimore, where Germans had begun to arrive during the eighteenth century. Irish immigration was stimulated by the potato famine of the 1840's and supported by railroad work on the Baltimore-based B&O Railroad. Southwest Baltimore, in particular, became an Irish commu-

nity during the nineteenth century. The B&O Railroad also opened piers for immigration at Locust Point in 1868, making Baltimore a primary point of entry for immigrants to the United States.

LATE NINETEENTH CENTURY

Immigration continued to climb through much of the third quarter of the century, with people from Germany and Ireland making up most of the new arrivals. For the first time, though, immigrants from China, pushed by political and economic problems in the home country and by opportunities created by the California gold rush and jobs on a railroad that was expanding across the country, began to enter the United States in significant numbers. From 1841 to 1850, only thirty-five newcomers to the United States came from China. During the 1850's, this figure shot up to 41,397. The

Editorial cartoon from a late nineteenth century California newspaper expressing the fear that the United States would be overwhelmed by foreign immigrants—particularly the Irish and Chinese immigrants caricatured in the cartoon. (Library of Congress)

numbers of Chinese immigrants reached 64,301 between 1861 to 1870 and then almost doubled to 123,201 between 1871 and 1880. Chinese immigration began to drop following the Chinese Exclusion Act of 1882, decreasing to 61,711 between 1881 and 1890 and continuing to drop in the following decades.

As the nation faced and entered Civil War, overall immigration dipped, reaching low points of fewer than 92,000 immigrants in both 1861 and 1862. Even during the war, however, immigration began to rise again. Immigrants served on both sides during the war, but far more served in the Union army than the Confederate because the North had a much greater immigrant population. The image of the Irish, who had long been subject to suspicion and prejudice in the United States, suffered when poor immigrant workers from Ireland were the most active and violent participants in riots that broke out in cities such as New York and Boston in July, 1863, in reaction to the military draft.

The Civil War was enormously destructive, but it also helped to stimulate the national economy and to push the nation toward more industrialization. In 1869, the railroad tracks connecting the East and West Coasts were finally completed, helping to create a single nation-wide economy. The mining of coal, the primary fuel of the late nineteenth century, drew more workers, as total output of coal in the United States grew from 8.4 million short tons in 1850 to 40 million in 1870. Pennsylvania and Ohio, important areas for coal mining, increased their immigrant communities, notably attracting people from Wales, an area of the United Kingdom with a long mining tradition. By 1870, Ohio had 12,939 inhabitants born in Wales and Pennsylvania had 27,633, so that these two states were home to over half the nation's Welsh immigrants.

The railroads encouraged settlement of the farmlands of the Midwest and made possible the shipment of crops to the spreading cities. Scandinavians were among the immigrant groups that arrived to plow the newly accessible lands. Minnesota held 35,940 people born in Norway, or close to one-third of America's Norwegian immigrants by 1870. Minnesota was also home to the second-largest population of Swedes in America, with 20,987. Another midwestern state, Illinois, had attracted 29,979 Swedes by 1870. Another 10,796 Swedes had settled in Iowa, adjoining Illinois on the north-

west and just south of Minnesota. About two-thirds of America's Swedish-born population could be found in Illinois, Minnesota, and Iowa.

As the nation entered the 1880's, it entered into a remarkable period of economic expansion that would make the United States into one of the world's greatest industrial powers by the time of World War I (1914-1918). It also began a dramatic rise in immigration as part of this economic expansion. Numbers of immigrants increased from 2,812,191 in the decade 1871 to 1880 to 5,246,613 from 1881 to 1890, in spite of the exclusion of Chinese immigrants following 1882. Sources of immigration also began to shift, from the northern and western European countries to southern and eastern European countries, so that immigration from Italy grew from 11,725 during the 1860's to 307,309 during the 1880's and immigration from Russian and Poland grew from 4,539 to 265,088. The United States was beginning the great immigration wave of the end of the nineteenth and the beginning of the twentieth centuries.

Carl L. Bankston III

FURTHER READING

Brancaforte, Charlotte L., ed. *The German Forty-eighters in the United States.* New York: Peter Lang, 1990. Eighteen essays covering a wide range of topics, including a reappraisal that many of the immigrants were not radicals or revolutionaries.

Gleeson, David T. *The Irish in the South, 1815-1877.* Chapel Hill: University of North Carolina Press, 2001. One of the few modern studies of southern immigrants.

Laxton, Edward. *The Famine Ships: The Irish Exodus to America.* New York: Henry Holt, 1998. Drawing on research in Ireland and compilations of stories passed down to descendants of Irish immigrants in America, the author tells the histories of Irish immigrants during the years of the great potato famine.

Mahin, Dean B. *The Blessed Place of Freedom: Europeans in Civil War America.* Washington, D.C.: Potomac Books, 2003. Comprehensive examination of the views of European immigrants and visitors on America during the U.S. Civil War and of their participation on both sides in the fighting.

Silverman, Jason H., and Susan R. Silverman. *Immigration in the American South, 1864-1895.* Lewiston, N.Y.: Edwin Mellen Press, 2006. Account of

southern efforts to market the region to prospective immigrants.

Van Vugt, William E. *Britain to America: Mid-Nineteenth Century Immigrants to America.* Champaign: University of Illinois Press, 1999. Offers a portrait of immigration from the islands of Great Britain to the United States from 1820 to 1860.

Weaver, John C. *The Great Land Rush and the Making of the Modern World, 1650-1900.* Montreal: McGill-Queen's University Press, 2003. General work on how European colonization of other lands transformed the world economy and society.

SEE ALSO: California gold rush; Canals; Chinese Exclusion Act of 1882; German immigrants; Great Irish Famine; History of immigration, 1620-1783; Immigration Act of 1882; Irish immigrants; Know-Nothing Party; Philadelphia anti-Irish riots; Railroads.

HISTORY OF IMMIGRATION AFTER 1891

SIGNIFICANCE: The period from the end of the nineteenth century to the early twenty-first saw the federal government taking control over immigration policy. It also saw the two greatest immigration waves in the nation's history, as well as a period of highly restrictive immigration laws during the decades between those two waves.

During the century following the first U.S. Census in 1790, the population of the United States grew by nearly 60 million people, from just under 4 million to almost 63 million. During the next century, between 1890 and 1990, the population grew by close to 186 million, adding about three times as many people in the second century as in the first. By 2007, the nation had added another 45 million in just seventeen years. A large part of the country's population growth, throughout its history, had occurred through immigration.

ERA OF FEDERALLY CONTROLLED IMMIGRATION

Until the end of the nineteenth century, immigration to the United States was under the loose control of the individual states. In 1875, the U.S. Supreme Court ruled that state laws regulating immigration were unconstitutional because they were inconsistent with the exclusive power of the U.S. Congress to regulate foreign commerce. This recognition of the exclusive power of Congress over immigration opened the way to immigration policy and therefore to the establishment of procedures and locations for federal control of immigration. The construction of the Ellis Island federal immigration facility during 1891 symbolized the beginning of the modern period in American immigration history.

The Office of the Superintendent of Immigration, originally in the Department of the Treasury, took charge of immigration issues in that same year, 1891. This became the Bureau of Immigration in 1895. The bureau was transferred to the Department of Commerce and Labor in 1903 and became the Bureau of Immigration and Naturalization in 1906. This was moved to the Department of Labor in 1913 and split into the Bureau of Immigration and the Bureau of Naturalization. In 1933, these bureaus were joined as the Immigration and Naturalization Service (INS), which President Franklin D. Roosevelt moved to the Department of Justice in 1940. In 2003, President George W. Bush established the Department of Homeland Security and reorganized the INS as the U.S. Citizenship and Immigration Services (USCIS) under the authority of this new department.

FIRST MODERN IMMIGRATION WAVE

The growth of the American population through immigration was primarily a result of the growth of the American economy, which provided new opportunities. That economy had been growing rapidly throughout the first half of the nineteenth century. The U.S. Civil War caused disruption, but it also stimulated production in the North, and it ultimately created a more politically and economically unified nation. The completion of the transcontinental railroad in 1869 meant not only that people could travel relatively quickly from the East Coast to the West Coast but also that goods from one part of the country could be shipped and sold to other parts of the country. This completion of the transportation infrastructure spurred rapid industrialization in the decades following the Civil War. By 1890, the United States had outstripped

the leading industrial nations of Europe to become the world's foremost producer of manufactured goods. The quickly developing industrial economy required workers, and the availability of jobs drew immigrants to American shores in unprecedented numbers.

As a result of the flow of new workers into the country, the nation's new industrial working class rapidly became disproportionately foreign born. The Dillingham Commission, set up by Congress in 1907 to study the perceived immigration problem, looked at twenty-one industries and found that 58 percent of the workers in these industries were immigrants. The commission found that immigrants were particularly significant in construction work, railroads, textiles, coal mining, and meatpacking.

Transportation systems had linked the United States, and they also made it easier to reach North America from Europe. Train systems in Europe by the late nineteenth century enabled Europeans to reach their own coastal cities. The replacement of sailing ships by steamships cut travel time over the ocean from one to three months during the 1850's to ten days by the 1870's.

During the first decade of the period of federal control of immigration, 1891 to 1900, 350,000 newcomers reached the United States. In the decade after, from 1901 to 1910, this number more than doubled to 800,000 new arrivals. Although the absolute number of foreign-born people was greater at the end of the twentieth century, immigrants made up a larger proportion of the American population during the late nineteenth and early twentieth centuries, when 15 percent of Americans were immigrants. Because of continuing immigration, moreover, by 1910 another 15 percent of native-born Americans were children of two immigrant parents and 7 percent of native-born Americans had at least one immigrant parent, so that immigrants and children of immigrants made up more than one-third of the U.S. population.

The large immigrant population of the United States came from places that had sent few people in earlier years. America's population at its beginning consisted mainly of people from northern and western Europe and people of African heritage, and newcomers in the first century of the nation's existence continued to come primarily from northern and western Europe. As recently as 1882, 87 percent of immigrants came from the northern and western European countries. By the end of the century, though, economic hardship in southern Europe and political oppression combined with poverty in eastern Europe, together with the improved transportation, led to a geographic shift.

By 1907, 81 percent of immigrants to the United States came from southern and eastern Europe. According to the statistics of the Dillingham Commission, of the 1,285,349 foreign-born people who arrived in the United States in 1907, 285,943 (22 percent) came from the Russian Empire and 338,452 (26 per-

Ship carrying European immigrants to Ellis Island, c. 1905. (The Granger Collection, New York)

cent) came from the Austro-Hungarian Empire. Eastern European Jews, fleeing persecution in the two empires, made up many of these arrivals. Italy alone sent 285,731 people (22 percent of total U.S. immigrants) during that year, most of them coming from impoverished southern Italy.

The southwestern part of the United States had been part of Mexico until the middle of the nineteenth century, and many Spanish-speaking people of the same ethnic backgrounds as Mexicans lived in that part of the country. However, the United States had been attempting to anglicize the Spanish-speaking parts of the country since it took possession of this area. After the Mexican Revolution began in 1910, refugees from south of the Rio Grande began to move northward. Between 1910 and 1920, more than 890,000 legal Mexican immigrants arrived in the United States.

Increasing numbers of immigrants arriving from countries that were alien to many native-born Americans and to English-speaking officials raised concerns in the public and among policy makers. Many of those reaching American shores settled in low-income sections of the growing cities in the traditionally rural nation. Perceptions of immigration as a social problem led to a string of new laws, resulting, by the 1920's, in highly restrictive immigration policies.

LEGISLATIVE RESPONSES TO THE FIRST WAVE

At the beginning of the federal period in American immigration history, Congress passed the Immigration Act of 1891, which enabled federal inspectors to examine people on arrival and to reject entry to those who were diseased, morally objectionable, or whose fares had been paid by others. The year after that, Congress renewed the Chinese Exclusion Act of 1882, which had banned new Chinese immigration and Chinese eligibility for citizenship. Thus, federal legislative responses to immigration from the beginning were guided by the idea of keeping out undesirable immigrants and by the idea that some national origin groups were less desirable than others. The Immigration Act of 1903 not only consolidated earlier legislation, it also barred those who were politically objectionable, such as anarchists. Extending this line of action, a new immigration act in 1907 added more categories of people to the list of those to be excluded, and it restricted immigration from Japan.

The Immigration Act of 1917 expanded exclusions still more by identifying illiterates, people entering for immoral purposes, alcoholics, and vagrants as classes that would not be allowed into the country.

Following World War I, Congress enacted laws that would reduce immigration dramatically for three decades. The Immigration Act of 1921, also known as the Emergency Immigration Act, attempted to reduce southern and eastern European immigration by limiting the number of immigrants from any country to 3 percent of the number of people from that country living in the United States in 1910. In 1924, a new immigration act carried the quota concept further by limiting immigrants from any country to 2 percent of the number from that country living in the United States in 1890.

Restrictive legislation brought a drop in immigration. The Great Depression of the 1930's helped to maintain low immigration, since massive unemployment meant that the United States had fewer jobs to offer. Foreign-born people obtaining legal permanent residence status in the United States decreased from a high of 8,202,388 in the peak years 1909-1919 to 699,375 in 1930-1939.

LEGISLATIVE CHANGES

Immigration continued to be low during the World War II years, but there were some indications of a loosening of American immigration law. The United States and China, then under the Chinese Nationalist government, were allies against Japan, and this alliance encouraged American lawmakers to pass the Immigration Act of 1943, which repealed the Chinese Exclusion Act of 1882 and allowed Chinese to become naturalized citizens, although only 105 Chinese were actually allowed to immigrate each year. Worker shortages in the United States due to the war led the U.S. government to establish the bracero program in 1942 to bring in Mexican agricultural laborers.

The Immigration and Nationality Act of 1952, also known as the McCarran-Walter Act, retained the national origin criterion of 1924. It set an overall ceiling for immigrants and within that ceiling gave each country a cap equal to 1 percent of the individuals of that national origin living in the United States in 1920. The new immigration law, enacted at the height of the Cold War, placed new

ideological restrictions on immigration, denying admission to foreign communists. The McCarran-Walter Act also added a series of preferences to the national origins system. The preference system became the basis of a major shift in American immigration policy in 1965.

The Hart-Celler Act, also known as the Immigration and Nationality Act of 1965, revised the McCarran-Walter Act and turned U.S. immigration policy in a new direction. Acting in the spirit of recent civil rights legislation, Congress removed the national origins quota system and instead emphasized the preference system. Family reunification became the primary basis for admission to the United States, followed by preferences for people with valuable skills.

The Immigration and Nationality Act of 1965 went into effect in 1968, and its liberal provisions made possible another great wave of immigration at the end of the twentieth century. Along with those classified as immigrants, the United States also received large numbers of refugees, leading to the passage of the Refugee Act of 1980 to accommodate this additional group of arrivals. By the end of the twentieth century, new concerns over immigration, especially growing undocumented immigration, led the nation to attempt to control the flow across the borders.

In an effort to respond to undocumented immigration, Congress enacted the Immigration Reform and Control Act of 1986, which granted amnesty to immigrants who had entered illegally before 1982 but made it a crime to hire undocumented immigrants. Ten years later, the Illegal Immigration Reform and Immigrant Responsibility Act of 1996 made it easier to deport undesirable immigrants, and it increased the size and activities of the U.S. Border Patrol.

Hmong refugees learning about life in the United States in a cultural orientation class in a Thailand refugee camp in 2004. A great change in U.S. immigration patterns that began during the late twentieth century was a huge increase in the numbers of Asians coming to the United States. (Getty Images)

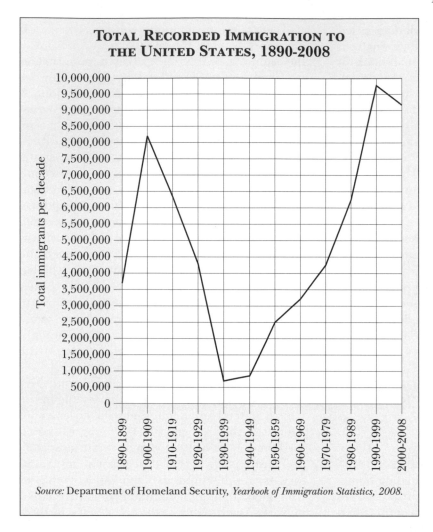

Total Recorded Immigration to the United States, 1890-2008

Total immigrants per decade

10,000,000
9,500,000
9,000,000
8,500,000
8,000,000
7,500,000
7,000,000
6,500,000
6,000,000
5,500,000
5,000,000
4,500,000
4,000,000
3,500,000
3,000,000
2,500,000
2,000,000
1,500,000
1,000,000
500,000
0

1890-1899
1900-1909
1910-1919
1920-1929
1930-1939
1940-1949
1950-1959
1960-1969
1970-1979
1980-1989
1990-1999
2000-2008

Source: Department of Homeland Security, *Yearbook of Immigration Statistics, 2008.*

SECOND MODERN IMMIGRATION WAVE

The 1965 change in immigration policy helped produce the greatest immigration wave in U.S. history in terms of sheer numbers of immigrants reaching American shores. After decreasing since the 1920's, the foreign-born population of the United States suddenly began to grow during the 1970's, increasing from 9,619,000 (4.7 percent of the total population) in 1970 to 14,080,000 (6.2 percent) in 1980, reaching 19,767,000 in 1990 (7.9 percent), and then 31,108,000 (11.1 percent) in 2000. By 2007, the foreign-born population had reached an estimated 38,060,000, or 12.6 percent of all people in the United States.

The places of origin of America's immigrants also changed. While earlier immigrants had come primarily from Europe, those in the post-1965 immigration wave came mainly from Latin America and Asia. From 1820 to 1970, 79.5 percent of immigrants had arrived from countries in Europe, 7.7 percent from countries in the Americas other than Canada, and only 2.9 percent from Asia. During the period 1971 to 1979, only 18.4 percent of immigrants to the United States were from Europe, while 41 percent came from countries in the Americas and 34.1 percent came from Asia. Latin Americans and Asians continued to make up most of this wave of immigration. As a result, only 13 percent of foreign-born people living in the United States in 2007 had come from Europe, while 27 percent had been born in Asia and 54 percent had been born in Latin America. Mexicans had become by far America's largest immigrant group, constituting 31 percent of all immigrants in the United States in 2007.

The heavy immigration from Mexico was a consequence of economic problems in that country, as well as a result of opportunities and relatively liberal immigration policies in the United States. More than 70 percent of Mexico's export revenues came from oil at the beginning of the 1980's. As the price of oil declined beginning about 1982, Mexico had less revenue coming in, provoking a debt crisis, and the country's already existing problems of poverty became worse. Legal immigration from Mexico began to move upward rapidly, from a little over 621,000 in the decade 1970-1979 to over one million during the 1980's.

The Immigration Reform and Control Act of 1986 encouraged some undocumented Mexicans in the United States to remain by offering amnesty, and it encouraged others to move into the United States on a long-term basis by intensifying control of the border, making it more difficult to move

back and forth. The longer-term orientation led many workers to move further north, away from the border. In 1994, a second economic shock hit Mexico, with the devaluation of the peso, which caused dramatic inflation and a decline in living standards. In response to the economic problems, legal migration grew even more during the 1990's, with more than 2.75 million Mexicans entering the United States. From 2000 to 2005, the United States received an average of 200,000 legal permanent residents from Mexico every year.

Illegal immigration also grew at a rapid pace, with the largest number of illegal immigrants arriving from Mexico. Undocumented immigration into the United States rose from an estimated 130,000 undocumented immigrants each year during the 1970's to an estimated 300,000 per year during the 1980's, and their numbers continued to go up. By January, 2007, the estimated undocumented immigrant population of the United States was 11,780,000. A majority (59 percent) were from Mexico, and 11 percent were from the Central American nations of El Salvador, Guatemala, and Honduras, having arrived by way of Mexico.

REFUGEES

The United States classifies "refugees," or people admitted to the United States because of conflict, natural disaster, or persecution in their homelands, separately from "immigrants," people admitted to legal residence in the country. Refugees have, however, been a significant part of the immigration wave that began during the late twentieth century. U.S. refugee policies began before the 1965 change in immigration law. In 1948, Congress enacted the Displaced Persons Act to admit people who had been uprooted during World War II. The beginning of the Cold War gave added motivation to the American refugee program, and the Refugee Relief Act of 1953 granted admission to people fleeing countries that had fallen under communist domination. The Soviet occupation of Hungary in 1956 resulted in new refugees, and the Refugee Escape Act of 1957 explicitly defined refugees as people fleeing communism. In theory, though, refugees were to be counted under the per-country ceiling established by the McCarran-Walter Act, and the added numbers were charged against future ceilings or admitted under special presidential paroles.

America's anticommunist refugee program expanded after Fidel Castro took power in Cuba at the beginning of 1959 and Cubans opposed to Castro, who soon declared himself a communist, began to flee their island nation. President John F. Kennedy's administration established a program of assistance for Cubans, and this program was institutionalized by the Migration and Refugee Assistance Act of 1962. The first wave from Cuba left the island nation between 1959 and 1962. A second wave followed from 1965 to 1974, when the Cuban and U.S. governments agreed to arrange flights between the two countries for Cubans who wished to leave. The Cuban refugee flow slowed substantially after the halting of the flights. In 1980, though, the Cuban government faced internal unrest. This led to a third wave of Cuban refugees. Hoping to ease public unrest on the island, the Cuban government decided to open the port city of Mariel to unrestricted emigration. Vessels from Mariel brought more than 125,000 refugees from Cuba to the United States over a six-month period.

Following the end of the Vietnam War in 1975, Southeast Asian refugees began to resettle in the United States. Largely in response to movement of Southeast Asian refugees, the U.S. Congress passed the Refugee Act of 1980, which was the most comprehensive piece of refugee legislation in U.S. history. As a result, hundreds of thousands of refugees from Vietnam, Cambodia, and Laos were resettled in North America during the early 1980's. In 1980, more than 170,000 people from these three countries entered the United States. The flow of refugees continued so that by the year 2007, the United States was home to an estimated 1.5 million people who described their ethnic background as Vietnamese, close to 220,000 people who described themselves as Cambodian, 200,000 people who identified as Laotian, and more than 200,000 who identified as Hmong, a minority group from Laos.

Carl L. Bankston III

FURTHER READING

Alexander, June G. *Daily Life in Immigrant America, 1870-1920.* Westport, Conn.: Greenwood Press, 2007. Detailed study of the diverse immigrants who arrived in the United States during one of the nation's great immigrant waves. It approaches the topic through thematic chapters that look not only at daily lives but also distribu-

tion and settlement patterns, temporary and permanent residency, and individual and family migrations.

Martínez, Rubén. *The New Americans.* New York: New Press, 2004. Written as a companion book to a PBS television miniseries, this presents five portraits of new immigrants to the United States.

Shanks, Cheryl. *Immigration and the Politics of American Sovereignty, 1880-1990.* Ann Arbor: University of Michigan Press, 2001. An exploration of how political trends and issues in the United States have shaped American immigration policy over time.

Suro, Roberto. *Strangers Among Us: How Latino Immigration Is Transforming America.* New York: Alfred A. Knopf, 1998. Readable portrait of late twentieth century Latino immigrant life with discussions of how the nation has been changing as a result of large-scale Latino immigration.

Waters, Mary C., and Reed Ueda, eds. *The New Americans: A Guide to Immigration Since 1965.* Cambridge, Mass.: Harvard University Press, 2007. Collection of descriptive essays on the various immigrant groups that have made up the post-1965 immigration wave and on the key topics concerning this wave.

SEE ALSO: Asian immigrants; Dillingham Commission; Ellis Island; History of immigration, 1620-1783; History of immigration, 1783-1891; Immigration Act of 1917; Immigration Act of 1924; Immigration and Nationality Act of 1952; Immigration and Nationality Act of 1965; Immigration waves; Refugees; World War II.

HMONG IMMIGRANTS

SIGNIFICANCE: The Hmong are one of the most recent Asian immigrant groups to come to the United States. Their main home is in the northern mountain regions of Laos. The Hmong and other Laotian immigrants were helped by the passage of the Indochina Migration and Refugee Assistance Act of 1975 in their efforts to relocate after the Vietnam War ended.

PROFILE OF HMONG IMMIGRANTS

Countries of origin	Laos and Vietnam
Primary language	Hmong
Primary regions of U.S. settlement	California, Michigan, Minnesota, Wisconsin
Earliest significant arrivals	Mid-1970's
Peak immigration period	1970's-1980's
Twenty-first century legal residents*	30,000 (estimated; 3,750 per year)

*Immigrants who obtained legal permanent resident status in the United States.
Source: U.S. Census Bureau.

The Hmong people have no significant history of immigration to the United States before 1970. By the year 2000, Hmong immigrants numbered around 170,000 according to U.S. Census data. When they began migrating to the United States, they were encouraged by various settlement agencies to disperse throughout the country. However, because of their kinship patterns and collectivist nature, they instead tended to congregate within communities where other Hmong lived. Consequently, 89 percent of these immigrants settled in California, Wisconsin, Minnesota, and Michigan.

AMERICAN INVOLVEMENT WITH THE HMONG

During the Vietnam War, Hmong villagers worked alongside the U.S. Central Intelligence Agency (CIA) in their fight against the North Vietnamese in what has been called a "secret war" in Laos. Their assistance on what was supposed to be neutral territory resulted in problems for Hmong veterans on several different levels. After the South Vietnam capital of Saigon fell to North Vietnamese forces and the war ended, Laos was taken over by Pathet Lao communist forces, and the Hmong were targeted for reprisals because of their support of U.S. involvement in Southeast Asia. At risk of severe retaliation from the Lao government, Hmong and other Laotian exiles escaped to Thailand, where they were placed in refugee camps. Upon resettlement to the United States, the Hmong immigrants

achieved refugee status largely because of their war efforts on behalf of the Americans as well as their need to escape the communist regime in Laos.

IMMIGRATION AFTER 1975

In response to the plight of Indochinese communities such as the Hmong after the Vietnam War, the U.S. Congress enacted legislation to enable Southeast Asian refugees to come to the United States. Many immigrants from that region were well educated and possessed valuable job skills. In contrast, however, a large part of the Hmong immigrants were poorly educated and were unskilled workers, as most had been farmers in their home country, and other aspects of the Hmong economy were not highly advanced. These factors, among others, influenced group assimilation processes even though American officials and citizens were initially supportive of Hmong migration.

Between 1981 and 1986, only a few thousand Hmong refugees came to the United States. Admissions picked up between 1987 and 1994, when more than 50,000 Hmong entered the country. From 2004 until 2006, pressure from human rights groups contributed to the resettlement to the United States of an additional 15,000 Hmong immigrants from a refugee camp in Thailand. Afterward, immigration from northern Laos to the United States slowed.

HMONG IN THE UNITED STATES

Hmong communities in the United States have stabilized. U.S. government estimates indicate that between 170,000 and 186,000 Hmong were living in the United States by 2008. However, estimates from nongovernment sources have suggested that there may actually be between 250,000 and 300,000. About 60,000 Hmong reside in the state of Minnesota, with about 30,000 in the Minneapolis-St. Paul area alone. The first Hmong refugees came from a subsistence and agrarian background, but later waves of immigrants came with some knowl-

Shaman conducting a traditional good-luck ritual for members of a Hmong family preparing to leave a Thai refugee camp for the United States in 2004. (Getty Images)

edge of technology and Western culture. Overall, the American Hmong population was young and highly urban by the year 2009. In fact, the Minneapolis-St. Paul area has the largest Hmong urban population in the world. The majority of Hmong Minnesotans have already become second- or third-generation American-born citizens.

With a relatively short history in the United States, the Hmong still struggle with cultural identity issues. The initial culture shock that occurred during their first wave of immigration resulted in a slower assimilation rate than was anticipated, even though some younger Hmong Americans adapted relatively quickly. The Hmong have not abandoned their collectivist family structures and this has helped them achieve a level of economic stability. Like those of Vietnamese immigrants, Hmong families often pool resources and incomes in order to buy homes, businesses, and cars.

In Minnesota, Hmong residents generate more than $100 million in revenues annually and entrepreneurs have successfully revitalized the University Avenue area of St. Paul. Even though the first wave of Hmong immigrants was not as prepared to cope with the technologically advanced capitalistic society of the United States, over the years they have become upwardly mobile, a situation that indicates a positive future.

Dianne Dentice

FURTHER READING

Barr, Linda. *Long Road to Freedom: Journey of the Hmong*. Bloomington, Minn.: Red Brick Learning, 2004. Account of the plight of Hmong refugees during the early twenty-first century.

Faderman, Lillian, and Ghia Xiong. *I Begin My Life All Over: The Hmong and the American Immigrant Experience*. Boston: Beacon, 1998. Collection of thirty-five Hmong immigrant narratives that emphasizes generational differences.

Keown-Bomar, Julie. *Kinship Networks Among Hmong-American Refugees*. New York: LFB Scholarly Publishing, 2004. Thorough sociological study of Hmong immigrants.

Mote, Sue Murphy. *Hmong and American: Stories of Transition to a Strange Land*. Jefferson, N.C.: McFarland, 2004. Another collection of Hmong immigrant narratives.

Parrillo, Vincent. *Strangers to These Shores*. 9th ed. Boston: Allyn & Bacon, 2008. General treatment of race and ethnic relations with a section on Laotian immigration that emphasizes Hmong immigrants.

Schaefer, Richard T. *Racial and Ethnic Groups*. 11th ed. Upper Saddle River, N.J.: Prentice Hall, 2007. General textbook on American ethnic groups that includes a case study of a Hmong community in Wausau, Wisconsin.

Sherman, Spencer. "The Hmong in America: Laotian Refugees in the Land of the Giants." *National Geographic* (October, 1988). Well-illustrated description of Hmong communities in North Carolina and California.

SEE ALSO: Asian immigrants; Immigration waves; Indochina Migration and Refugee Assistance Act of 1975; Laotian immigrants; Minnesota; Refugees; Tennessee; Thai immigrants; Vietnam War.

HOLOCAUST

THE EVENT: Systematic attempt by Germany's Nazi regime to exterminate European Jews
DATE: Late 1930's to mid-1940's
LOCATION: German-occupied European countries

SIGNIFICANCE: During World War II and the years leading up to it, European Jews were the principal victims of German chancellor Adolf Hitler's genocidal policies. Many fled eastern and western Europe, attempting to enter the United States.

Between 1933, which saw the Nazis' rise to power, and Germany's 1945 surrender that ended World War II, more than 345,000 Jews emigrated from Germany and Austria. Many of them initially fled to countries that were later occupied by Germany, and these Jews subsequently left again or were murdered. Although about 85,000 Jewish refugees reached the United States between March, 1938, and September, 1939, far greater numbers were seeking refuge. However, when U.S. president Franklin D. Roosevelt was inaugurated in 1933, the United States was preoccupied with the challenges of the Great Depression—high unemployment and widespread social disillusionment—which contributed to public resistance to any relaxation of im-

migration quotas. Another factor in opposing specifically Jewish immigration was anti-Semitism. Anti-Jewish sentiment was on the rise during the 1920's; it increased dramatically during the early 1930's and reached its peak in America during the late 1930's and early 1940's.

FAILED ATTEMPTS TO HELP THE JEWS

In 1939, the United States refused to admit more than 900 refugees who had sailed from Hamburg, Germany, on the SS *St. Louis.* After being turned away from Cuba, the ship appeared off the coast of Florida. After the United States denied it permission to land, the *St. Louis* returned to Europe. Great Britain, France, the Netherlands, and Belgium each accepted some of the passengers as refugees. Of the ship's 908 passengers, 254 are known to have died in the Holocaust. The event was widely publicized.

News of the true extent of the Holocaust began to reach the United States only in 1941—the year in the United States entered World War II. Nevertheless, the U.S. Department of State placed even stricter limits on immigration due to national security concerns. The threat of enemy subversion during the war was a legitimate concern, but the State Department exaggerated the problem and used it as a reason for cutting in half the already small immigration quotas. In 1943, 400 Jewish rabbis marched on Washington, D.C., to draw attention to what was happening to Holocaust victims. Only a handful of politicians met with the marchers, but one of them, Senator William Warren Barbour of New Jersey, proposed legislation that would have permitted 100,000 Holocaust refugees to enter the United States temporarily. Barbour's bill failed to pass, and another, similar bill, introduced in the House of Representatives by Representative Samuel Dickstein of New York, also failed to pass.

In 1944, President Roosevelt, pressured by government officials and the American Jewish community, took action. He established the War Refu-

Jewish refugees aboard the St. Louis *arriving in Belgium in June, 1939, after they were turned away from Cuba. More than one-quarter of the refugees eventually died in the Holocaust.* (AP/Wide World Photos)

gee Board to facilitate the rescue of refugees in imminent danger. The American Joint Distribution Committee and the World Jewish Congress worked with the board to help rescue many thousands of Jews in Hungary, Romania, and other European nations. However, government funding for the board was so small that 91 percent of its work was funded by American Jewish organizations. The board conducted a monthlong campaign to persuade Roosevelt to offer temporary shelter to large numbers of refugees, but it yielded only one result. In the spring of that year, Roosevelt established Fort Ontario, New York, as a free port for refugees. However, only a few thousand were allowed to enter, and these were people from liberated countries who were under no immediate threat of deportation to Germany. Roosevelt's response to Holocaust immigration was strongly influenced by political concerns. During an era of strong anti-immigration sentiment, any move to increase immigration might well have cost him votes in elections.

CHANGE IN IMMIGRATION POLICIES

Harry S. Truman, Roosevelt's successor as president of the United States from 1945 to 1953, favored an immigration policy that was liberal toward displaced persons, but Congress failed to act on his proposals. On December 22, 1945, Truman issued an executive order, called the Truman Directive, requiring that existing immigration quotas be designated for displaced persons. Although total U.S. immigration figures did not increase, many more displaced persons were admitted to the United States. Between the end of 1945 and early 1947, about 22,950 displaced persons entered the United States under the new Truman Directive. About 16,000 of these refugees were Jewish.

Before existing immigration quotas could be increased, congressional action was necessary. Pressured intensely by lobbying on the part of the American Jewish community, Congress passed legislation in 1948 to admit about 400,000 displaced persons to the United States. Nearly 80,000 of those who arrived, or about 20 percent, were Jewish. Other immigrants included Christians from eastern Europe and the Baltic nations who had worked as forced laborers under the Nazi regime. American entry laws favored agricultural workers to such a degree, however, that Truman found

the new law discriminatory to Jews, few of whom were agricultural workers. By the 1950's, Congress amended the law, but by that time most of the Jewish displaced persons in Europe had entered the new state of Israel, which was established on May 14, 1948.

Thanks in large part to the influx of Jews during and after the Holocaust, the United States emerged as the largest and most culturally innovative Jewish center in the world after World War II. Smaller centers of Jewish population worldwide soon turned to the vigorous Jewish establishments in the United States for help and support. By the first decade of the twenty-first century, Jews in the United States had risen to leadership positions in government, the media, entertainment, popular culture, business, labor relations, law, and the arts.

Sheila Golburgh Johnson

FURTHER READING

Abzug, Robert H. *America Views the Holocaust, 1933 to 1945: A Brief Documentary History.* New York: Palgrave Macmillan, 1999. This book tries to shed light on such grave questions as what Americans knew about the Holocaust and how they responded as it unfolded.

Breitman, Richard, and Alan M. Kraut. *American Refugee Policies and European Jewry, 1933-1945.* Bloomington: Indiana University Press, 1987. Carefully documented study that argues that U.S. policy regarding the Holocaust was the product of preexisting restrictive immigration laws and the attitude of U.S. State Department leaders who were committed to a narrow defense of American interests.

Novick, Peter. *The Holocaust in American Life.* Boston: Houghton Mifflin, 1999. Historical overview of American attitudes toward the Holocaust. A highly controversial book that argues against misuses of Holocaust history and tries to show how contemporary consciousness was formed by political conditions.

Wyman, David S. *The Abandonment of the Jews: America and the Holocaust, 1941-1945.* New York: Pantheon, 1984. Contends that British and American political leaders turned down many proposals that could have saved European Jews from death in German concentration camps.

_____. *Paper Walls: America and the Refugee Crisis, 1938-1941.* Amherst: University of Massachu-

setts Press, 1968. Study of the obstacles that the U.S. Congress erected to prevent the immigration of Jews during the Holocaust.

SEE ALSO: American Jewish Committee; Anglo-conformity; Anti-Semitism; Center for Immigration Studies; Congress, U.S.; Films; German immigrants; Jewish immigrants; Quota systems; Refugee Relief Act of 1953; Refugees; World War II.

HOMELAND SECURITY, DEPARTMENT OF

IDENTIFICATION: Federal cabinet-level department created to consolidate immigration and domestic security functions
DATE: Established on March 1, 2003

> **SIGNIFICANCE:** Formed in the wake of the September 11, 2001, terrorist attacks on the United States, this well-funded cabinet department of the federal government has exemplified a governmental response to improve the coordination and effectiveness of efforts to combat the ongoing war against terrorism. It has greatly increased the number of illegal immigrants apprehended each year in the United States.

On March 1, 2003, the Department of Homeland Security (DHS) was founded to address concerns with terrorism that were greatly heightened after the 9/11 attacks. Its creation was widely acknowledged to have prompted the largest federal government reorganization since World War II, and its creation had great implications for evolving immigration policy and practice. Two of the largest agencies that had previously been dealing with immigration issues, the Immigration and Naturalization Service and the U.S. Customs Service, were among the approximately one hundred former federal departments absorbed into the new department. Other DHS branches concerned with immigration control had been created after September 11, 2001. A prominent example is the Transportation Security Administration (TSA), whose chief mandate was to ensure airport and airline safety.

KEY IMMIGRATION-RELATED ACTIVITIES OF THE DHS

The DHS subdivision with primary responsibilities for administrative functions and decisions that affect the immigrant population is the U.S. Citizenship and Immigration Services (USCIS). The former Immigration and Naturalization Service and U.S. Customs Service were merged to form the Immigration and Customs Enforcement (ICE) agency. With more than 17,200 employees and an annual budget near $5 billion—more than 20 percent of the entire DHS budget—it is the largest DHS investigative agency. The ICE mission statement emphasizes its fight against the smuggling of goods and the entry of terrorists and other criminals into the United States. Additional priorities include combating arms and drug trafficking, fraud, pornography and related sex crimes, and white-collar crime.

ICE cooperates with corresponding agencies in many foreign countries, helped by more than fifty branch offices around the world. It has five main organizational divisions:

- Office of Detention and Removal Operations
- Office of Investigations
- Office of Federal Protective Service
- Office on Intelligence and the Office of International Affairs
- forensic document laboratory

The forensic document laboratory is an important subdivision established in 1978 but now run by ICE. Its work is focused on discovering identity and travel document fraud. Its staff includes handwriting and fingerprint specialists as well as forensic chemists. Staff members often serve as expert court witnesses, and they maintain an extensive library of relevant documents. Personnel from the laboratory provide consultative and training services to related professionals in the United States and abroad and issue intelligence alerts concerning recently detected fraudulent documents.

The DHS is charged with the responsibility of maintaining the National Security Entry-Exit Registration System (NEERS), which was established in 2002 by congressional order to monitor the more than 35 million nonimmigrants visiting the United States on a temporary basis for work, study, or tourism. These visitors are required to register with DHS authorities and must provide the DHS with

written notification prior to changing their residences, jobs, or schools after they have been in the United States for more than one month. Noncompliance can lead to arrest, fines, and possible deportation. One of the main databases is the Student and Visitor Information System (SEVIS), which tracks foreign students in the United States and provides notification if they do not attend their classes.

The actual activities of ICE have been quite varied. The number of illegal immigrants who have been deported has steadily increased since the agency's formation—from 166,000 in 2004, for example, to 186,000 in 2006. There has also been a large-scale effort to apprehend fugitive aliens who seek to avoid deportation orders. ICE established

"fugitive operations teams" that give priority to apprehending illegal immigrants involved in violent crimes. By 2009, one hundred such teams were operating across the United States. In fiscal year 2008, they made more than 34,000 arrests and reversed a previous trend of yearly increases in the numbers of fugitive aliens. The intelligence hub of this initiative is the Fugitive Operations Support Center (FOSC), which was established in Vermont in 2006. This unit has made use of computerized databases and close contacts with other law-enforcement agencies to increase detection and apprehension rates.

ICE runs an extensive immigration detention custody system with 370 facilities either owned by the DHS or, more commonly, operating under

Secretary of Homeland Security Janet Napolitano speaking at a press conference held at the Port of Miami in May, 2009. Behind her are representatives of the Federal Emergency Management Agency, U.S. Customs and Border Protection, U.S. Coast Guard, and U.S. Immigration and Customs. (AP/Wide World Photos)

service contracts with the DHS. This system has a 32,000-bed capacity, and a detention standards unit monitors compliance with national regulations originally promulgated in 2000 by the former Immigration and Naturalization Service. ICE personnel reviewed these standards and modified them to reflect a performance, outcome-based perspective. The goal is to foster consistency across facilities in areas such as the conditions of confinement, access to lawyers, and overall operations safety.

Spurred on by the 9/11 attacks, the DHS instituted a large-scale tracking program—called U.S. Visitor and Immigration Status Indication Technology—to monitor the millions of nonimmigrant foreign nationals who visit or pass through the United States each year. Designed for use at all land ports-of-entry, it runs fingerprints and pictures through databases of criminals and those on security "watch lists." It also records the dates the visitors enter and leave the country.

CONTROVERSIES

Much of the early twenty-first century controversy swirling around DHS handling of immigration affairs can be seen as a reflection of what some have noted to be a general orientation of "hyper vigilance" in confronting terrorism. This refers to a governmental policy of pursuing even the smallest indications of possible threats to national security, even though the vast majority of such interventions ultimately turn out to be false positives. The "one-percent doctrine" states that even a probability of another 9/11-type attack as small as 1 percent merits full preventive response measures, often at great public expense. Some have noted that this approach is reflective of a general sense of moral panic, especially following 9/11, and an unbridled desire on the part of the public at large to "feel safe," in a very deep-rooted psychological sense.

The implications of such a perspective for immigration policy and practice are profound. The tactics of the DHS have been criticized as relying unfairly on the immigration status and countries of origin of immigrants. For example, immigration raids carried out in airports and utility company plants deemed to be of "high risk" for terrorist acts have often focused in a blanket way on workers of specific ethnicities, without regard to their individual likelihoods of actual guilt. In some airports, groups of Hispanic support personnel have been arrested on the grounds that their undocumented immigration status makes them more liable to terrorist recruitment and coercion.

Approval rates for applications from asylum seekers have steadily declined since the inception of the DHS, and the decision making has at times seemed to proceed on a global country-by-country (instead of on an individual applicant) basis. For example, during the early twenty-first century, more than 60 percent of Iraqi and Cuban applications for asylum were approved, while fewer than 10 percent of those from Haiti and El Salvador were given asylum.

The decreasing approval rates are coupled with a decrease in application rates, and both can be traced to tough, seemingly blanket-type approaches to detention decisions. During various periods between 2003 and 2008, all applicants from thirty-three countries that had an al-Qaeda presence were automatically detained. This practice was carried out in spite of international regulations that mandated detention decision making on an individual, case-by-case basis and a presumption against detention for those with pending asylum applications.

These applications of "guilt by association"-type processing have raised the controversial specter of racial profiling, an alleged police practice that, when exposed, has been roundly reviled by both liberal and conservative critics. This in turn is fueled by an increasing practice of privatization with the fields of corrections and security. The DHS has spent many millions of dollars on lucrative contracts to private agencies involved in augmenting border patrols and running detention centers. Just as the privatization of prisons has raised grave concerns regarding accountability and the protection of human rights, so has its role in DHS operations. This is especially troublesome considering the fact that most of the detainees are being held for alleged immigration violations, not for violent or even for property crimes. Nationally, the number of detainees has quadrupled between 1995 and 2008, when it was estimated that 30,000 immigrants were incarcerated on any given day.

In one Rhode Island detention center formerly under contract to the DHS, for example, it was alleged in a federal lawsuit that a thirty-four-year-old Chinese computer engineer with no prior criminal record was denied medical care for what ultimately

turn out to be a fatal liver cancer illness. During the period of his detention, he was taken screaming in pain to Connecticut for a mandatory meeting with ICE officials, and on the return trip guards are said to have thrown him down and dragged him by his arms and legs, breaking his back in the process. The DHS subsequently canceled its contract with this facility and several of its guards were fired or otherwise disciplined, but lengthy confinement persists for many immigrants who have pending proceedings.

In large measure, the persistence of immigrant detention wings of local jails and even entire facilities occupied by immigrants reflects a financial incentive. Even in an extremely difficult economic climate, the DHS budget for detainees in the New England region alone increased by ten million dollars between 2006 and 2008, and the national budget in 2008 was $1.7 billion. It has been estimated that financially strapped local corrections facilities can receive more than ninety dollars per day for each immigrant detainee. This translates into a lucrative source of inmates to fill all available empty beds, while injecting much needed capital into the sagging economies of most of the communities housing jails and prisons. The facilities themselves have been able to use the added revenue to undertake major renovations and expansions that would never have been possible if public funding were their sole income stream. The overall detention issue is exacerbated by open-ended periods of confinement for most detainees. Unlike their indigent criminal counterparts, they are not entitled to public counsel representation at the hearings themselves.

HIGHLIGHTS OF IMMIGRATION-RELATED DHS ACTIVITIES

Despite all inherent operational difficulties and strong political pressures influencing long-range agency policy and goals, the DHS activities in the area of immigration law enforcement have been largely successful. In terms of apprehending fugitives from deportation orders, for example, two four- and five-day operations in February, 2009, resulted in more than two hundred arrests in four southern states. The nationwide number of such arrests doubled between 2006 and 2008. During the same month, ICE attorneys won prison terms for two members of a human smuggling ring oper-

ating between Canada and Detroit. This "for profit" enterprise had attempted to send a twenty-three-year-old Albanian national and his mother from Canada to the United States across the frozen Detroit River on Jet Skis. However, the Jet Skis overturned and the Albanian man drowned. This type of incident highlights the importance of a vigorously functioning agency that should be afforded a certain degree of autonomy in its operations. In light of the issues raised earlier, however, it is clear that there is a need for considerable oversight in terms of how the DHS runs its immigration-related programs and operations. This supervision, if well planned and executed, can also have positive benefits for the agency internally, in terms of overall employee satisfaction and morale.

Clearly, there is strong potential for the DHS to build on its past track record of successful enforcement, while directly addressing the internal and external controversies that have accompanied its development and growth.

Eric Yitzchak Metchik

FURTHER READING

Ackleson, Jason. "Constructing Security on the U.S.-Mexico Border." *Political Geography* 24 (2005): 165-184. Scholarly, theoretically based analysis of the evolution of U.S. policy regarding border security with Mexico.

Bullock, Jane, and George Haddow. *Introduction to Homeland Security*. 2d ed. Burlington, Mass.: Butterworth-Heinemann, 2006. Introductory text offering a comprehensive overview of the Department of Homeland Security that explains the department's various agencies and their responsibilities.

Kerwin, Donald. "The Use and Misuse of 'National Security' Rationale in Crafting U.S. Refugee and Immigration Policies." *International Journal of Refugee Law* 17, no. 4 (2005): 749-763. Insightful due process-oriented analysis of U.S. immigration policies, as affected by changed priorities after the September 11 attacks.

Kettl, Donald F. *System Under Stress: Homeland Security and American Politics*. Washington, D.C.: Congressional Quarterly Press, 2004. Excellent introductory reading for those seeking to place post-9/11 changes in immigration policy into the broader context of U.S. counterterrorism policy.

Lehrer, Eli. "The Homeland Security Bureaucracy." *The Public Interest* (Summer, 2004): 71-85. Detailed survey of DHS organizational components and capacities.

McEntire, David A. *Introduction to Homeland Security: Understanding Terrorism with an Emergency Management Perspective.* Hoboken, N.J.: John Wiley & Sons, 2009. Extensive survey of all aspects of Department of Homeland Security tasks.

Smith, Michael W. "Denial of Asylum: Is There Organizational Justice Under the Department of Homeland Security?" *International Journal of the Diversity* 6, no. 3 (2006): 61-69. Data-oriented analysis of asylum denial rate elevations during the past decade.

Ting, Jan C. "Immigration and National Security." *Orbis* (Winter, 2006): 41-52. Details national policies that have facilitated the increase in illegal immigrants in the United States, as well as the relationship of this phenomenon to the terrorist threat.

Uehling, Greta Lynn. "The International Smuggling of Children: Coyotes, Snakeheads, and the Politics of Compassion." *Anthropological Quarterly* 81, no. 4 (2008): 833-871. Case study and interview-based analysis of the problem of unaccompanied, illegal immigrant children in the United States.

White, Richard, and Kevin Collins. The *United States Department of Homeland Security: An Overview.* Boston: Pearson Custom Publishing, 2005. Scholarly but nonetheless accessible examination of the newly formed Department of Homeland Security, providing details about the department's various agencies and the role of the Border Patrol in combating terrorism.

SEE ALSO: Aviation and Transportation Security Act of 2001; Border Patrol, U.S.; Citizenship and Immigration Services, U.S.; Coast Guard, U.S.; Deportation; Disaster recovery work; Illegal immigration; Immigration law; Muslim immigrants; 9/11 and U.S. immigration policy; Patriot Act of 2001; Smuggling of immigrants.

HOMESTEAD ACT OF 1862

THE LAW: Federal legislation making public land available to settlers for free
DATE: Signed into law on May 20, 1862

SIGNIFICANCE: The Homestead Act accelerated settlement of western lands in the United States. Initiated in response to pressure for the disposition of public lands, the act transferred ownership of property to U.S. citizens or immigrants willing to establish residence on the land and to make improvements and cultivate crops. A significant number of beneficiaries of the act were immigrants from Europe.

Support for the concept of distributing public land began during the early years of the United States. A precursor to the Homestead Act, the Pre-emption Act of 1841, legitimized squatting by permitting farmers to grow crops on public land that could later be purchased from the government. Despite growing pressure to open western lands, concern over economic and political issues generated opposition to homesteading. For example, eastern factory owners believed that homesteading would lure away immigrants who were an important source of cheap labor. Opposition also came from plantation owners in southern states concerned about increasing the number of small farms whose owners were not likely to support slavery. Homesteading legislation was passed by the U.S. House of Representatives in 1852, 1854, and 1859 but each time was defeated in the U.S. Senate.

The principle of dispersing public land became a major tenet of the Republican Party during the late 1850's as a means of preventing the spread of slavery into western lands. In 1860, homesteading legislation was approved by both houses of Congress but vetoed by President James Buchanan. However, the secession of southern states at the outbreak of the U.S. Civil War brought an end to major opposition. The Homestead Act was signed into law by President Abraham Lincoln on May 20, 1862, and took effect on January 1, 1863.

The central provision of the act was to enable adult heads of households to claim 160 acres each of surveyed public land. To be eligible to file claims on the land, homesteaders had to be U.S. citizens

or have submitted declarations of intent to become citizens. Title to homesteaded properties could be obtained after five years of residence on the land, provided that the claimants made improvements, including construction of houses and wells and cultivation of at least ten acres.

The opportunity to acquire free land became an important factor attracting immigrants who sold assets in their home countries to purchase passage and supplies needed upon arrival in the United States. However, leniency in administration of the homesteading program allowed many people who knew little about farming to claim land—a fact that contributed to the failure of some farms. The harsh environment also created hardships for new immigrants. While 160 acres of humid land in eastern states could support a family, the same acreage west of the hundredth meridian was often too arid to sustain crops in the absence of irrigation. With few trees available in some areas, settlers built sod homes to provide shelter from wind, hailstorms, and winter blizzards.

By 1900, title to about 80 million acres of land had been distributed to 600,000 farmers. In some cases, homestead property was later acquired by speculators who had lent money needed by homesteaders to purchase equipment and supplies. Speculators also acquired land through phony claims or by purchasing abandoned farms. In 1976, the Homestead Act was repealed through passage of the Federal Land Policy Management Act in all states except Alaska, where homesteading ended in 1986.

Thomas A. Wikle

FURTHER READING

Davis, Charles. *Western Public Lands and Environmental Politics.* Boulder, Colo.: Westview Press, 2001.
Diamond, Henry L., and Patrick F. Noonan, eds. *Land Use in America.* Washington, D.C.: Island Press, 1996.
Porterfield, Jason. *The Homestead Act of 1865.* New York: Rosen, 2005.

SEE ALSO: Civil War, U.S.; Economic consequences of immigration; Emigration; Families; History of immigration, 1783-1891; Land laws; Nebraska; Oklahoma; Political parties; Westward expansion.

HOMESTEADER QUALIFICATIONS

The first section of the Homestead Act of 1862 spelled out the qualifications for claiming land.

Be it enacted by the Senate and House of Representatives of the United States of America in Congress assembled, That any person who is the head of a family, or who has arrived at the age of twenty-one years, and is a citizen of the United States, or who shall have filed his declaration of intention to become such, as required by the naturalization laws of the United States, and who has never borne arms against the United States Government or given aid and comfort to its enemies, shall, from and after the first January, eighteen hundred and sixty-three, be entitled to enter one quarter section or a less quantity of unappropriated public lands, upon which said person may have filed a preemption claim, or which may at the time the application is made, be subject to preemption at one dollar and twenty-five cents, or less, per acre; or eighty acres or less of such unappropriated lands, at two dollars and fifty cents per acre, to be located in a body, in conformity to the legal subdivisions of the public lands, and after the same shall have been surveyed: Provided, That any person owning and residing on land may, under the provisions of this act, enter other land lying contiguous to his or her said land, which shall not, with the land so already owned and occupied, exceed in the aggregate one hundred and sixty acres.

HONDURAN IMMIGRANTS

SIGNIFICANCE: Honduran immigration into the United States is a relatively recent phenomenon, but the 81 percent increase of Hondurans coming into the country during the first decade of the twenty-first century, was the largest of any immigrant group. Their numbers rose from approximately 160,000 in 2000 to 300,000 in 2008.

Until the fourth decade of the twentieth century, U.S. Census data did not count immigrants from individual Central American nations. In any case,

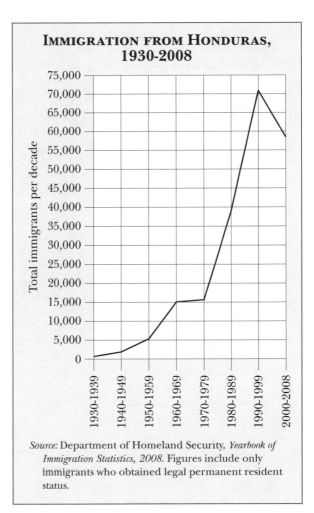

the numbers of Hondurans immigrating to the United States before 1930 was small, and even during the decade of the 1930's, only 679 Hondurans entered the country legally. The numbers of immigrants remained low into the 1960's, when a significant increase began. During that decade, 15,078 Hondurans were granted legal permanent resident status in the United States. By the last year of the twentieth century, an average of more than 7,100 new immigrants per year were coming from Honduras. The 2000 U.S. Census recorded a total of 282,852 Hondurans living in the United States legally. However, these numbers do not include the large numbers of undocumented immigrants. By the year 2008, it was estimated that nearly 1 million Hondurans resided in the United States. Of that number, as many as 70 percent were estimated to be in the country illegally.

Many of the most recent Honduran immigrants to enter the United States legally have been granted temporary protected status because of the devastation in Central America left by Hurricane Mitch in 1998. That status was extended several times, including an extension to July of 2010; it grants work authorization and protection from deportation but does not assure permanent residency. As many as 80,000 Hondurans came to the United States under temporary protected status.

IMMIGRATION FROM HONDURAS, 1930-2008

Source: Department of Homeland Security, *Yearbook of Immigration Statistics, 2008.* Figures include only immigrants who obtained legal permanent resident status.

PROFILE OF HONDURAN IMMIGRANTS

Country of origin	Honduras
Primary language	Spanish
Primary regions of U.S. settlement	California, Washington, New York, Ohio, Illinois, Texas, Nebraska
Earliest significant arrivals	Early twentieth century
Peak immigration period	1980's-2008
Twenty-first century legal residents*	52,534 (6,567 per year)

*Immigrants who obtained legal permanent resident status in the United States.
Source: Department of Homeland Security, *Yearbook of Immigration Statistics, 2008.*

PUSH-PULL FACTORS

A combination of economic hardship and natural disasters has led to the increase in Honduran immigration. Most Hondurans are small-scale farmers with average income of only $1,700 per year. During the first decade of the twenty-first century, it was estimated that 59 percent of all Hondurans were living below the poverty line. Approximately 20 percent of adults were illiterate, and 25 percent of the children were chronically malnourished.

The 1998 arrival of Hurricane Mitch in Central America proved to be one of the worst natural disasters ever to hit Honduras. The hurricane caused great additional economic hardships in what was already a desperately poor country. Entire fruit fields were destroyed, resulting in the departure of many multinational fruit companies that were

important employers. Record amounts of rainfall caused mudslides that wiped out entire villages. Back roads and bridges were destroyed, and as much as 70 to 80 percent of the national transportation infrastructure was ruined. Seven thousand people died, and more than 20 percent of the entire population were left homeless after the hurricane. During the months directly following the hurricane, the U.S. Border Patrol reported a 61 percent increase in captures of Hondurans trying to cross the border into the United States.

HONDURANS IN THE UNITED STATES

Honduran transnational communities strive to maintain ties with their hometowns while creating new homes for themselves in the United States.

The flow of migrants has a direct impact on Honduran communities in both countries, creating an exchange of cultures that changes both. Honduran residents of the United States account for 40 percent of all tourism revenue in Honduras.

Many Hondurans work in the United States in order to send remittances to relatives still in Honduras. In 2007, the Honduran foreign ministry reported that $2.8 billion in remittances were sent to Honduras by workers in the United States. Remittances directly affect the receiving families, lifting many of them out of poverty. They also add to the economic disparity in communities, creating a clear distinction between those who receive them and those who do not. However, some observers feel that remittances can create a dependence on

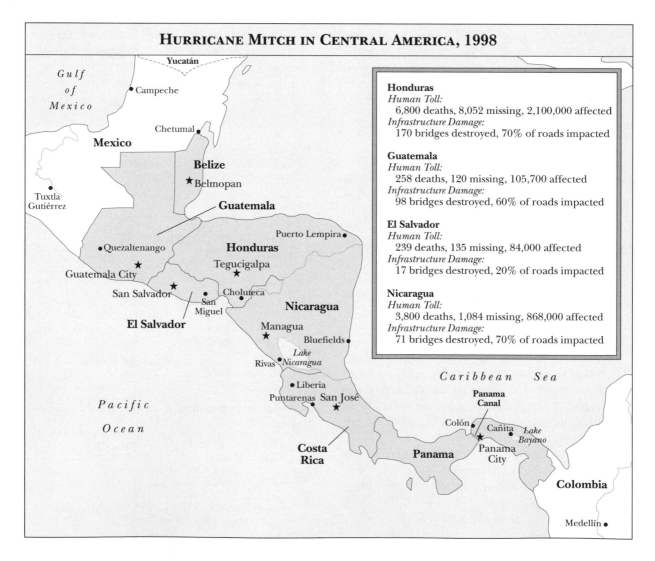

HURRICANE MITCH IN CENTRAL AMERICA, 1998

Honduras
Human Toll:
  6,800 deaths, 8,052 missing, 2,100,000 affected
Infrastructure Damage:
  170 bridges destroyed, 70% of roads impacted

Guatemala
Human Toll:
  258 deaths, 120 missing, 105,700 affected
Infrastructure Damage:
  98 bridges destroyed, 60% of roads impacted

El Salvador
Human Toll:
  239 deaths, 135 missing, 84,000 affected
Infrastructure Damage:
  17 bridges destroyed, 20% of roads impacted

Nicaragua
Human Toll:
  3,800 deaths, 1,084 missing, 868,000 affected
Infrastructure Damage:
  71 bridges destroyed, 70% of roads impacted

charity that does little to improve the economic development of Honduras.

Hondurans who try to travel to the United States to find work face difficult and dangerous journeys that require passing through Guatemala and Mexico. Peril and discomforts include rape, exposure to severe heat in desert areas, long separations from family, robbery, accidents, and even murder. Engaging professional guides known as "coyotes" can cost as much as five thousand dollars. It has been estimated that only 25 percent of the approximately 80,000 Hondurans who have tried to reach the United States each year since 1998 have succeeded.

Many of the Hondurans who have immigrated to the United States have flourished. However, a less positive result of Honduran immigration has been the development of youth gangs. During the 1990's, the U.S. government targeted undocumented residents in the penal system for deportation. Many of these former criminals were also gang members who recommended their gangster lifestyle upon return to Honduras, creating transnational ties with gangs in the United States.

Elizabeth Ellen Cramer

FURTHER READING

Duffy, Maureen P., and Scott Edward Gillig. *Teen Gangs: A Global View.* Westport, Conn.: Greenwood Press, 2004. Discusses teen gang activity in fourteen countries, including Honduras.

González, Juan. *Harvest of Empire: A History of Latinos in America.* New York: Viking Press, 2000. General history of Latin American immigration into the United States, including that from Central and South American nations.

Nazario, Sonia. *Enrique's Journey.* New York: Random House, 2006. True story about an eleven-year-old Honduran boy's epic journey to the United States to find the mother who went north to find work when he was only five years old. Based on a prize-winning series of stories first published in the *Los Angeles Times*, for which Nazario was a feature writer.

Salgado, Sebastião, and Lélia Wanick Salgoda. *Migrations: Humanity in Transition.* New York: Aperture, 2001. Photojournalistic work depicting displaced populations of the world, including Hondurans in the aftermath of Hurricane Mitch.

Schmalzbauer, Leah. *Striving and Surviving: A Daily Life Analysis of Honduran Transnational Families.* New York: Routledge, 2005. Focusing on Honduran families in the United States, this volume investigates the role of the family in transnational communities.

SEE ALSO: El Rescate; Farm and migrant workers; Guatemalan immigrants; History of immigration after 1891; Illegal immigration; Latin American immigrants; Louisiana; Push-pull factors; Salvadoran immigrants; Sanctuary movement; Smuggling of immigrants.

HONG KONG IMMIGRANTS

SIGNIFICANCE: Immigrants from the Chinese port city of Hong Kong have differed from earlier Chinese immigrants in a variety of distinctive ways. Their arrival in the United States has drastically transformed the nature of Chinese American communities.

Located along the South China coast, Hong Kong became a British colony during the mid-nineteenth century. During a century and a half of European

PROFILE OF HONG KONG IMMIGRANTS

Country of origin	China
Primary languages	Chinese (Cantonese), English
Primary regions of U.S. settlement	West Coast, East Coast cities
Earliest significant arrivals	1960's
Peak immigration period	1970's-1990's
Twenty-first century legal residents*	35,761 (4,470 per year)

*Immigrants who obtained legal permanent resident status in the United States.
Source: Department of Homeland Security, *Yearbook of Immigration Statistics, 2008.*

colonial rule, Hong Kong culture became so different from that of the rest of China that the concept of a "HongKonger" identity arose during the 1970's. During the early 1980's, the People's Republic of China determined to take Hong Kong back from Great Britain. As European imperialism was no longer popular throughout the world, Britain eventually agreed to restore Chinese sovereignty to Hong Kong in 1997. The prospect of China's communist government assuming control of strongly capitalist Hong Kong triggered the emigration of between 500,000 and 750,000 residents of Hong Kong to other countries, including the United States.

CHARACTERISTICS OF HONG KONG IMMIGRANTS

During the 1980's and the 1990's, many of the people who emigrated from Hong Kong settled in the United States. In contrast to the peasants and contract laborers who had earlier immigrated from China to the United States, members of the late twentieth century wave of Hong Kong immigrants were primarily middle-class professionals and businesspeople, many of whom were very prosperous. More than 70 percent of the Hong Kong immigrants to the United States fell into the skilled worker and business immigrant categories. Moreover, 90 percent of them arrived in the United States already capable of conversing in English. Some observers have called these immigrants "yacht people," a facetious term that distinguishes the prosperous Hong Kongers from the desperately poor Vietnamese boat people.

In contrast to professional immigrants from other countries who have used migration as a vehicle for upward mobility, many of Hong Kong's immigrants have experienced loss of social status, reduced incomes, damage to their career development, and downward mobility in the United States. Hong Kong's emigrants might be regarded as reluctant exiles because most of them have left their homeland for political reasons, not for economic gain. Fearing they would lose political freedoms, their prosperous lifestyles, and their physical assets after communist China took over Hong Kong, many Hong Kong emigrants were anxious to obtain passports of other countries before 1997, calculating that foreign citizenship would protect them from Hong Kong's new communist regime.

Another unusual characteristic of Hong Kong emigration was its speed. Large-scale migrations of

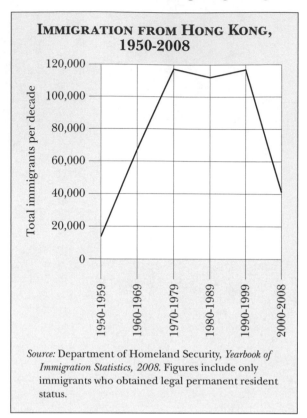

IMMIGRATION FROM HONG KONG, 1950-2008

Source: Department of Homeland Security, *Yearbook of Immigration Statistics, 2008.* Figures include only immigrants who obtained legal permanent resident status.

professional people generally take place over long time spans. In contrast, Hong Kong's middle-class migration was highly compressed. Its emigrants felt compelled to obtain foreign passports before 1997, figuring it would be too late for them to do so after the communist takeover in 1997. Consequently, the overwhelming bulk of Hong Kong immigrants to the United States arrived between the late 1980's and the late 1990's.

Another unusual characteristic of Hong Kong immigrants that set them apart from other professional immigrants was their attitude about remaining in the United States. Whereas middle-class professionals generally prefer to settle permanently after arriving in the United States, Hong Kong immigrants tended to have a "sojourner" mentality. Their paramount aim was to secure citizenship in other countries as a kind of political insurance for their futures in Hong Kong itself. With foreign passports, they could return to Hong Kong knowing that they could later leave at any time, should serious trouble arise under the coming communist government. Indeed, many Hong Kong immigrants

Seattle, Washington, restaurant owner from Hong Kong watching a parade of demonstrators marching toward the city's federal building to protest U.S. immigration policy changes in 2006. (AP/Wide World Photos)

returned to Hong Kong even before they applied for naturalization in other countries; these people sometimes stayed overseas only long enough to meet the minimal residence requirements required to secure their foreign passports.

A final characteristic of Hong Kong immigrants has been their strong sense of Hong Kong Chinese identity. They keep in touch with friends and relatives in Hong Kong and closely monitor political changes occurring there. The social lives of many Hong Kong Chinese in the United States are typically built around networks of friends who are also from Hong Kong. They speak Cantonese in their American homes, dine regularly in Chinese restaurants, regularly buy overseas editions of Hong Kong newspapers, and watch television programs on the Cantonese-language Jade Channel.

IMPACT ON CHINESE AMERICAN COMMUNITIES

The arrival of a large number of Hong Kong immigrants has helped to transform Chinese American communities. Like middle-class white Americans, middle-class Hong Kong immigrants generally seek superior housing and living conditions. Consequently, they tend to live outside the old Chinatowns. The residential patterns of Hong Kong immigrants gave birth to many new suburban Chinatowns during the 1980's and 1990's. Whereas old Chinatowns were mostly located in city centers, the new Chinatowns were attached to newly suburban communities. Old Chinatowns are cohesive residential communities with strong ethnic organizations, but the new Chinatowns were merely clusters of shops established to service ethnic consumer demands for Hong Kong and Taiwanese immigrants.

Because middle-class Hong Kong immigrants are resourceful, they like to purchase properties for investment and speculation. Their investments have triggered rapid rises in property values within both the old and new Chinatowns, as well as nearby neighborhoods. Some established white residents have complained that the intrusion of Chinese shops into their residential areas has changed the character of their neighborhoods.

Alvin Y. So

FURTHER READING

Chabot, Richard, Oi Man Chan, and Alvin Y. So. "Hong Kong Chinese in Hawaii: Community Building and Coping Strategies." In *Reluctant Exiles?*, edited by Ronald Skeldon. Armonk, N.Y.: M. E. Sharpe, 1994. Discusses community building efforts of Hong Kong immigrants in Hawaii.

Kwong, Peter. "New York Is Not Hong Kong: The Little Hong Kong That Never Was." In *Reluctant Exiles?*, edited by Ronald Skeldon. Armonk, N.Y.: M. E. Sharpe, 1994. Examination of the various social problems that Hong Kong immigrants have created in New York City.

Li, Wei, ed. *From Urban Enclave to Urban Suburb: New Asian Communities in Pacific Rim Countries.* Honolulu: University of Hawaii Press, 2006. Collection of articles on Asian immigrants in Pacific Rim countries, including the United States.

Skeldon, Ronald. *Emigration from Hong Kong.* Hong Kong: Chinese University of Hong Kong Press, 1994. Provides much useful information on the background of Hong Kong immigrants.

Tsai, Jung-Fang. *Hong Kong in Chinese History: Community and Social Unrest in the British Colony, 1842-1913.* New York: Columbia University Press, 1993. Study of the early history of British colonization of Hong Kong.

Wong, Bernard P. "Hong Kong Immigrants in San Francisco." In *Reluctant Exiles?*, edited by Ronald Skeldon. Armonk, N.Y.: M. E. Sharpe, 1994. Detailed account of how the Hong Kong immigrants have settled in San Francisco.

SEE ALSO: Asian immigrants; Asian Indian immigrants; "Brain drain"; Chinatowns; Chinese immigrants; Immigration and Nationality Act of 1965; Page Law of 1875; Parachute children; Taiwanese immigrants.

HOUSTON

IDENTIFICATION: Largest and most cosmopolitan city in Texas

SIGNIFICANCE: Often thought of as a "boomtown" of recent origin, Houston is actually comparatively old by American urban standards. It has become a major economic center of the United States and sports a panoply of communities reflecting trends in immigration throughout American history, from a large and longstanding Hispanic presence to new arrivals from West Africa. Houston is in the top five of American cities in regard to the number of businesses owned and run by Hispanics.

The fourth most populous city in the United States, Houston was home to roughly 2,200,000 people in 2009. Of these, approximately 38 percent were Hispanic, mostly people of Mexican origin. Because Texas shares a long frontier with Mexico and was once part of that country, Houstonians of Mexican background, as with Texans in general, may be either recent immigrants, the descendents of people who fled north during periods of political unrest or financial instability in Mexico during the late nineteenth or early twentieth century, or members of families who have resided in the area for centuries. In addition to Hispanics of Mexican background, some Hispanics in Houston are of Cuban, Puerto Rican, and South American descent. Almost one-half million illegal immigrants are estimated to live in the Houston area. Most of them are of Hispanic background, but many are of Asian origin.

Much smaller in numbers than the Hispanic presence, though certainly prominent and vital, is the Asian community of Houston. The first Asians to come to Houston were the Chinese, who arrived during the early 1870's to work on local railroad lines. The number of Chinese in the city remained small until the 1960's, when political upheavals in China—from the Cultural Revolution of that decade on the mainland to the return of Hong Kong to the Beijing government in the late 1990's—led to increased emigration from China.

By the year 2000, almost 25,000 people of Chinese descent lived in Houston. A complexity of immigrant ethnic identity is highlighted by the use of the term "Chinatown" in Houston. Two different regions of the city have been labeled, both officially and unofficially, as "Chinatowns." The more important of these is a long strip along Bellaire Boulevard where many Chinese businesses, shops, churches, and homes are found. However, the American concept of "Chinatown," derived both from examples in other cities and from popular culture such as films, tends to be one of a tightly defined ethnic enclave in which Chinese Americans

both live and work. The Bellaire strip in Houston contradicts this concept in significant ways: First, although there are some homes along the Chinatown strip, businesses predominate there. Second, a number of these businesses are owned and operated by both non-Asians and Asians of other ethnicities, such as Indians, Koreans, Japanese, and Vietnamese. These latter ethnic groups are also prominent in Houston, especially Indians and Vietnamese. In fact, Houston has the third-largest Vietnamese community in the United States, with approximately 33,000 residents at the turn of the twenty-first century.

A small but growing immigrant group in Houston is that of Nigerians. The city's Nigerian community, estimated at 40,000 residents, is one of the largest in the United States. In 2003, the large numbers of Nigerians in Houston who were involved in energy-related enterprises prompted Lee Brown in 2003 to visit West Africa to establish closer ties between that region's petroleum industries and those in Houston.

Thomas Du Bose

FURTHER READING

Borjas, George J. *Mexican Immigration to the United States.* Chicago: University of Chicago Press, 2007.

Powell, William Dylan. *Houston Then and Now.* San Diego, Calif.: Thunder Bay Press, 2003.

Siegel, Stanley. *Houston: A Chronicle of the Bayou City.* Sun Valley, Calif.: American Historical Press, 2005.

SEE ALSO: African immigrants; Asian immigrants; Chinese immigrants; Dallas; Empresario land grants in Texas; Illegal immigration; Mexican immigrants; Texas; Vietnamese immigrants.

HUFFINGTON, ARIANNA

IDENTIFICATION: Greek-born author and journalist
BORN: July 15, 1950; Athens, Greece

> **SIGNIFICANCE:** One of the most politically influential immigrants of the early twenty-first century, Huffington has established herself as a centrist within a variety of media, includ-

Arianna Huffington in early 2009. (Getty Images)

ing the World Wide Web, and named one of *Time* magazine's one hundred most influential people in 2006.

Born Arianna Stassinopolus in the capital of Greece, Arianna Huffington developed a slant toward conservative viewpoints as she grew up in her native country. However, her views shifted toward a more centrist stance after she settled in the United States, and she has called herself a progressive populist. Coming from a line of Greek journalists, she made her way to the United States in 1980 after studying at Cambridge University in England. There she lived with the English author and journalist Henry Levin, who is said to have influenced her work and political positions. At Cambridge, she was the first foreign student to hold the position of president of the Cambridge Union Society.

During the 1980's, Huffington's political activities leaned more to the right and introduced her to

Michael Huffington, an American politician whom she would marry in 1986. She was instrumental in supporting her husband's political career until they divorced in 1997. After becoming an American citizen, Arianna began to pursue her own career and made a swing back to more liberal views on most subjects. In 2003, she ran as an independent candidate in California's special gubernatorial election that another immigrant, Arnold Schwarzenegger, won. Although she officially withdrew from the election before it was held, her name remained on the ballot, and she finished fifth in a field of more than one hundred candidates.

Huffington's move to the news media's fourth dimension, cyberspace, came about after she had published several articles in *The National Review* and made appearances on television and public radio. In 2005, she launched her *Huffington Post* blog site on the World Wide Web. The countless blog entries she has posted there have covered events ranging from presidential politics to the dinner habits of elites and common people alike. She has also authored a number of books, ranging from biographies to messages on spirituality.

Other activities that have kept Huffington in the public's attention have included her political roundtable program on National Public Radio, *Left, Right, and Center,* which presents civil discussions of political events shaping the world. Her Detroit Project is a grassroots campaign designed to encourage American auto manufacturers to build vehicles that reduce American dependency on foreign oil. She has stated that she wants Detroit to build cars "that get Americans to work in the morning, without sending us to war in the afternoon."

Karel S. Sovak

FURTHER READING

Huffington, Arianna. *Fanatics and Fools.* New York: Miramax, 2004.
_____. *On Becoming Fearless . . . In Love, Work, Life.* Boston: Little, Brown, 2008.
_____. *Pigs at the Trough.* New York: Crown, 2003.

SEE ALSO: Greek immigrants; Jennings, Peter; Pulitzer, Joseph; Schwarzenegger, Arnold.

HULL-HOUSE

IDENTIFICATION: Settlement house for the poor founded by Jane Addams and Ellen Gates Starr

DATE: Established in September, 1889

LOCATION: Chicago, Illinois

> **SIGNIFICANCE:** Hull-House provided numerous services for the poor, many of whom were immigrants, that helped immigrants to learn about American culture and life.

The settlement house movement started in England in 1884 to provide education and assistance to the disadvantaged, while also training teachers and social workers. The first settlement house in the United States was established in 1889 in New York's lower East Side. At first staffed by men, women's settlement houses soon followed, giving young educated women an opportunity to use their knowledge and talents. In 1889, Jane Addams and Ellen Gates Starr established the most famous of the settlement houses, Hull-House, in Chicago's West Side. Settlement houses, especially in the United States and Canada, were especially important in serving immigrants who came to the cities in great numbers for work. These immigrants were

---

HULL-HOUSE SERVICES FOR IMMIGRANTS

- medical aid
- child care
- legal aid
- food assistance
- clothing assistance
- financial assistance
- clubs and activities for both children and adults
- English-language classes
- citizenship classes
- cultural classes in the humanities
- lecture and concert series
- University of Chicago Extension classes for credit
- vocational instruction in sewing, basket weaving, millinery, embroidery, crafts, cooking, and dressmaking

typically part of the urban poor and experienced terrible living conditions.

Although Hull-House was not the first settlement house, it became the model for virtually all others that followed. In 1889, Chicago was the second-largest city in the United States and the sixth largest in the world for industry. It offered abundant job opportunities that attracted large numbers of immigrants. Of Chicago's one million residents in 1888, approximately 78 percent were either foreign born or the children of foreign-born parents. Because of the number of potential workers, the wages were low and poverty widespread, especially among unskilled workers.

Hull-House was established on Halsted Street in the middle of an immigrant neighborhood in the Nineteenth Ward, an area considered a slum. The thirty-block area surrounding Hull-House was home to at least eighteen different nationalities that represented twenty-six different ethnic groups, including Italians, Germans, Irish, Poles, Russian Jews, Bohemians, French Canadians, and Greeks. The neighborhood contained manufacturing, small houses, apartment buildings, and tenements. City services could not keep pace with the population growth and so this neighborhood experienced the typical problems of lack of sanitation services, polluted water supply, and overcrowded, rundown housing.

Hull-House was designed to specialize in assisting immigrants, who were among Chicago's neediest residents. Its goal was to add American culture to the immigrants' native cultures, not to replace them. Serving as a neighborhood center, the settlement house provided a wide range of services. Single working women were allowed to live at the house, where they helped with day-to-day activities. Many immigrants were anxious to become Americanized and eagerly sought English and citizenship classes.

Hull-House. (University of Illinois at Chicago, University Library, Jane Addams Memorial Collection)

In addition to the social services and educational offerings, the women in the settlement house movement began to fight for social reform after witnessing at first hand the struggles of the poor. The Working People's Social Science Club offered free weekly public lectures on economic and social issues of interest to working-class people, and broke down the barriers between the middle and working classes. Activists worked to improve the overcrowded public schools, poor sanitation, health care, child labor, housing conditions, and working conditions of women and girls. Additionally, the activists worked to protect immigrants from exploitation, advocating for immigrants' rights and workers' compensation.

Virginia L. Salmon

FURTHER READING

Addams, Jane. *Twenty Years at Hull-House.* Edited by Victoria Bissell Brown. New York: Bedford/St. Martin's, 1999.

Bryan, Mary Lynn McCree, and Allen F. Davis, eds. *One Hundred Years at Hull-House.* Bloomington: Indiana University Press, 1990.

Deegan, Mary Jo. *Race, Hull-House, and the University of Chicago: A New Conscience Against Ancient Evils.* Westport, Conn.: Praeger, 2002.

Glowacki, Peggy, and Julia Hendry. *Hull-House.* Charleston, S.C.: Arcadia, 2004.

Knight, Louise W. *Citizen: Jane Addams and the Struggle for Democracy.* Chicago: University of Chicago Press, 2005.

SEE ALSO: Americanization programs; Chicago; Child immigrants; Citizenship; Education; Progressivism; Settlement houses; Welfare and social services; Women immigrants.

HUNGARIAN IMMIGRANTS

SIGNIFICANCE: Although most Hungarians who emigrated to the United States arrived between 1890 and the start of World War I in 1914, the most significant Hungarian immigration took place during the 1930's. The spread of fascism and Nazism in Europe forced thousands of highly educated scientists, scholars, artists, and musicians to leave

PROFILE OF HUNGARIAN IMMIGRANTS

Country of origin	Hungary
Primary language	Hungarian
Primary regions of U.S. settlement	East Coast
Earliest significant arrivals	Early 1850's
Peak immigration period	1880's-1914
Twenty-first century legal residents*	10,494 (1,312 per year)

*Immigrants who obtained legal permanent resident status in the United States.
Source: Department of Homeland Security, *Yearbook of Immigration Statistics, 2008.*

Hungary and Central Europe to find safe haven in America.

Although Hungarian presence in North America reaches back to 1583, when Stephen Parmenius of Buda reached American shores, the first significant Hungarian political immigration took place in the early 1850's. Following the defeat of the Hungarian Revolution of 1848-1849, several thousand Hungarians found haven in the United States. Most of them came with the intention of returning to Europe to resume their struggle against the Austrian Empire, but a new war of liberation never materialized. However, many émigrés repatriated to Hungary after the Austro-Hungarian Compromise of 1867, which transformed the Austrian Empire into the dualistic state of Austria-Hungary. Before their repatriation, however, close to one thousand Hungarians—25 percent of all Hungarians then in the United States—had served in the Union Army during the Civil War. Almost one hundred of them served as officers; among them were two major generals and five brigadier generals. Many other Hungarians never repatriated and instead joined the ranks of American professionals, businessmen, and diplomats. They were able to do so because over 90 percent of them came from the ranks of the upper nobility and the gentry, and were thus learned enough, with sufficient so-

cial and linguistic skills, to impress contemporary Americans.

EARLY TWENTIETH CENTURY ARRIVALS

The next significant wave of Hungarian immigrants were the turn-of-the-century "economic immigrants." These were mostly peasants and unskilled workers who came in huge numbers, primarily as guest workers, to work in steel mills, coal mines, and factories. Of the nearly two million immigrants from Hungary during the four decades leading up to World War I, about 650,000 were true Hungarians, or Magyars. The remaining two-thirds were Ruysins, Slovaks, Romanians, Croats, Serbs, and Hungarian Germans. Of the 650,000 ethnic Magyars, close to 90 percent were peasants or unskilled workers who had recently emerged from the ranks of the peasantry. They were drawn to America by the work opportunities that did not exist at home. Even though Hungary itself was then being urbanized and industrialized, its development was not sufficient to employ all the peasants who were being displaced from the countryside. In the course of time, about 75 percent of these "guest workers"—two-thirds of whom were young men of marriageable age—transformed themselves into permanent immigrants. They established families in the United States and became the founders of Hungarian churches, fraternal associations, and scores of local, regional, and national newspapers geared to their educational levels.

The mass European immigration that occurred during the four decades before the outbreak of World War I came to an end in 1914. Although it resumed at a slower pace after the war, the federal immigration quota laws of 1921, 1924, and 1927 put an end to this immigration, especially for those from southern and eastern Europe. This decline of immigration was furthered by the collapse of the stock market in 1929 and the resulting Great Depression. Consequently, fewer than thirty thousand Hungarians immigrated to the United States during the 1920's.

GREAT INTELLECTUAL IMMIGRATION AND WORLD WAR II

The next wave of immigrants, known as the "Great Intellectual Immigration," appeared during the 1930's, in consequence of Adolf Hitler's

HUNGARIANS AND THE BOMB

Hungarian émigrés constituted the most significant immigration faction among those involved in the so-called Manhattan Project that developed the atomic bomb during World War II. Laura Fermi, the widow of the Italian Nobel laureate Enrico Fermi, once asserted that the Manhattan Project's "scientific brain power was furnished by three Hungarians and one Italian." The lone Italian was Enrico Fermi himself; the three Hungarians were Leo Szilard, Eugene Wigner, and Edward Teller. Teller has also been called the "Father" of the American hydrogen bomb.

rise to power in Germany in 1933 and the resulting rapid increase of anti-Semitism and antiliberalism. Although only about fifteen thousand Hungarians immigrated during the 1930's, this period brought thousands of highly educated scientists, writers, artists, composers, and other professionals to the United States. Ethnic Magyars constituted only a small segment of this Intellectual Immigration, but their impact was so great and widespread that many people began to wonder about the "mystery" of Hungarian intellectual talent. The impact of this immigration on the United States was felt through the rest of the twentieth century. Several Hungarian scientists played a major role in the development of the atomic bomb during World War II. Others, such as John von Neumann, were later in the forefront of the birth of the computer, and several became Nobel laureates.

COLD WAR ERA

The post-World War II period saw the coming of several smaller immigrant waves that may have brought as many as another 130,000 Hungarians to the United States. These immigrants included about 27,000 displaced persons who represented the cream of Hungary's upper-middle-class society. Most of them left Hungary after the war for fear of the Soviet domination of their homeland. Postwar immigrants also included about 40,000 so-called Fifty-Sixers, or "Freedom Fighters," who left Hungary after the suppression of the anti-Soviet and anticommunist Hungarian Revolution of 1956.

The next three decades saw a trickle of continuous immigration of about 60,000 immigrants who

escaped from Eastern Europe. The collapse of communism and Soviet rule in 1989-1990 altered the situation. With the freedom to emigrate restored, and the attractive opportunities in the United States, many highly trained Hungarians came in quest of greater economic opportunities. One German scholar called these postcommunist immigrants "Prosperity Immigrants"—people who during the Soviet era had lost much of the idealism and ethical values of their predecessors. What most of them wanted was primarily economic success. While searching for affluence in the United States, they contributed their know-how to American society, which valued and rewarded them accordingly.

By the early twenty-first century, the immigrant churches, fraternals, newspapers, and other institutions of immigrant life were in the process of disappearing. Few of the new Hungarian immigrants have shown an inclination to support the traditional institutions that were important to their predecessors. Given this reality, and the unlikelihood that there would be another major immigration from Hungary, it seemed only a question of a few years before all of these institutions would vanish. According to the 2000 U.S. Census, 1.4 million Americans claimed full or primary Hungarian descent. Of these, 118,000 (8.4 percent) still used Hungarian as a language of communication within their families. By contrast, 1.8 million claimed Hungarian ancestry in 1980, and 180,000 were still speaking Hungarian at home).

Steven Béla Várdy

FURTHER READING

Fermi, Laura. *Illustrious Immigrants: The Intellectual Migration from Europe, 1930-1941.* Chicago: Uni-

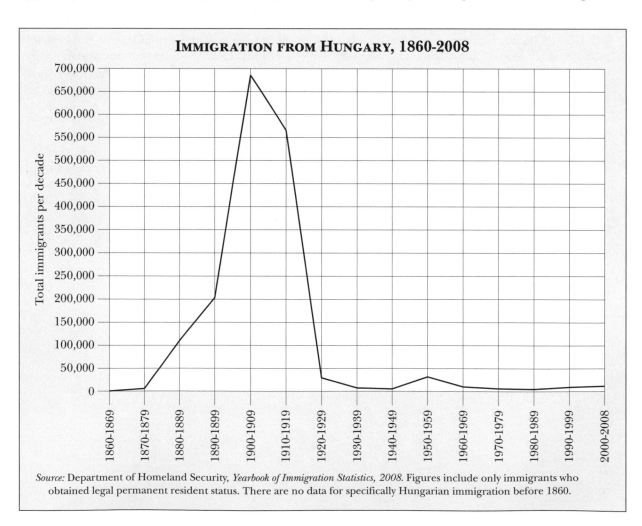

IMMIGRATION FROM HUNGARY, 1860-2008

Source: Department of Homeland Security, *Yearbook of Immigration Statistics, 2008.* Figures include only immigrants who obtained legal permanent resident status. There are no data for specifically Hungarian immigration before 1860.

versity of Chicago Press, 1969. The wife of Nobel laureate Enrico Fermi, who built the first experimental nuclear reactor, Laura Fermi provides an intimate internal view of those whom she calls Europe's "illustrious immigrants," who include such prominent Hungarians as Leo Szilárd, Eugene Wigner, and Edward Teller.

Lengyel, Emil. *Americans from Hungary.* 1948. Reprint. Westport, Conn.: Greenwood Press, 1974. Written by a prominent Hungarian American journalist, this volume is the earliest English-language synthesis of Hungarian American history and draws heavily on earlier Hungarian-language publications.

Puskás, Julianna. *Ties That Bind, Ties That Divide: One Hundred Years of Hungarian Experience in the United States.* Translated by Zora Ludwig. New York: Holmes & Meier, 2000. Scholarly, statistics-filled synthesis of Hungarian American history by a native Hungarian scholar who devoted much of her life to researching "economic" emigrants to the United States of the early twentieth century. Volume says little about post-World War II political immigrants.

Széplaki, Joseph. *Hungarians in America, 1583-1974: A Chronology and Fact Book.* Dobbs Ferry, N.Y.: Oceana, 1975. Short but useful summary of Hungarian American history by a librarian who was not a professional historian.

Várdy, Steven Béla. *Historical Dictionary of Hungary.* Lanham, Md.: Scarecrow Press, 1997. First comprehensive encyclopedic work on Hungarian history in English.

_____. *The Hungarian Americans.* Rev. ed. Safety Harbor, Fla.: Simon Publications, 2001. The first English-language synthesis of Hungarian American history by a trained Hungarian American historian.

_____. *The Hungarian Americans: The Hungarian Experience in North America.* New York: Chelsea House, 1989. Short, heavily illustrated work. Based to a large degree on the first edition of the work but also includes the Canadian Hungarian Americans. Contains an introductory essay by Daniel Patrick Moynihan.

_____. *Magyarok az òjvilágban.* Budapest: Magyar Nyelv és Kultúra Nemzetkšzi Társasága, 2000. This 840-page book on Hungarians in the New World, published by the International Association of Hungarian Language and Culture, is the largest synthesis of Hungarian American history yet published. Although still not available in English, this Hungarian edition contains a thirty-five-page English summary.

SEE ALSO: Austrian immigrants; Czech and Slovakian immigrants; European immigrants; European revolutions of 1848; Grove, Andrew; Polish immigrants; Pulitzer, Joseph; Science; Yugoslav state immigrants.

I

I REMEMBER MAMA

IDENTIFICATION: Film about a fictional Norwegian American family living in early twentieth century San Francisco

DATE: Released in 1948

SIGNIFICANCE: Director George Stevens's *I Remember Mama* offers an amiable portrayal of early twentieth century Norwegian immigrants, revealing their daily challenges, lighthearted moments, and career aspirations. Guided by a foreign-born matriarch who embraces America as she resolves problems with simple, "Old Country" wisdom, the story's Hanson family works together to manage health care and education on a tight budget and deal with problems arising from marriage, illness, eccentric relatives, and a penniless boarder.

Drawing on author Kathryn Forbes's novel *Mama's Bank Account* and playwright John Van Druten's 1944 stage adaption of the book, *I Remember Mama* utilizes an intimate narrative structure to frame the immigrant story. The film opens with Katrin (Barbara Bel Geddes), the eldest Hanson daughter—who has become a writer—typing the final words of her memoir in the attic of the Hanson's San Francisco home. At first, Katrin serves as narrator, reading from her memoir and guiding the audience back in time. Later, she joins the story as a much younger Katrin. The vignettes that follow are set mostly within the family home and feature both nuclear and extended family members, including bossy, whiny, and timid aunts, a blustery great-uncle, and a literary lodger. Meanwhile, Katrin gradually comes of age. The film ends with the family sitting around the kitchen table, with grown-up Katrin, having just received a check for the sale of her first published story, reading "Mama and the Hospital" aloud to the family.

Each time Mama reveals something about her past to Katrin in a candid conversation, she offers insights into the goals and assimilation issues of many immigrants. Family, not riches, wooed Mama and Papa from Norway. Aunts Trina, Sigrid, and Jenny had settled in San Francisco before they arrived, following Uncle Chris (Oskar Homolka), the head of the Scandinavian American clan, who ranches outside the city. Mama has become an American citizen, and her American-born children speak fluent English, without their elders' foibles or foreign accent. Going against the grain of her stodgy Norwegian sisters, Mama calls herself a San Francisco woman.

Like many immigrants, Mama and Papa Hanson and their children, Lars, Katrin, Christine, and Dagmar, stretch their limited money by making

Irene Dunne scrubbing a hospital floor in I Remember Mama. (Time & Life Pictures/Getty Images)

tough sacrifices. Every Saturday they gather to-gether to apportion Papa's carpentry earnings for the landlord, grocer, and vital needs. To fund Lars's education, Papa gives up tobacco, and the siblings take on light work; to buy Katrin's gradua-tion gift, Mama sells a family heirloom so she will not have to tap into the family bank account. How-ever, after Katrin receives her first publication check, Mama admits that the bank account has been a fictional safety net to prevent the children from worrying.

Mama's role in the immigrant family is both tra-ditional and pivotal. She supports, encourages, and makes peace among loved ones, often solving problems with her domestic skills. For example, she enters a hospital's off-limits, postsurgical recov-ery ward in which Dagmar is a frightened patient by scrubbing the floors to pass as a maid. She boosts Katrin's writing career by trading a secret home-land recipe for a celebrity writer's advice and refer-ral. Along the way, Mama helps the family adapt Norwegian customs to America. For example, she smoothes the way for the spinster Trina to wed with neither parents nor a dowry. On porches and over cups of coffee, she curbs teasing, snubbing, and bullying behavior as life and traditions change.

I Remember Mama was popular with post-World War II Americans, first as a play, subsequently as a film, and eventually as a television series broadcast by CBS-TV from 1949 to 1957. Four of the film's ac-tors (including Irene Dunne, who plays Mama) earned Academy Award nominations for their per-formances. Set in a West Coast city that was a portal to America for many newcomers, the landmark film brought widespread and positive attention to immigrant family life.

Wendy Alison Lamb

FURTHER READING

Hoobler, Dorothy, and Thomas Hoobler. *The Scan-dinavian American Family Album.* New York: Ox-ford University Press, 1997.

Zempel, Solveig. *In Their Own Words: Letters from Norwegian Immigrants.* Minneapolis: University of Minnesota Press, 1991.

SEE ALSO: California; Education; Families; Films; Health care; Marriage; San Francisco; Scandina-vian immigrants; Television and radio; Women im-migrants.

IDAHO

SIGNIFICANCE: Idaho's limited immigration contrasts dramatically with the immigration rates of other regions in which large numbers of immigrant groups have developed and be-come ingrained in the local communities. In 2008, 92 percent of the state's residents were classified as "white."

Before the United States expanded into the West, the region that would become the state of Idaho was populated by Native Americans belonging to the Bannock, Lamni, Nez Perce, Coeur d'Alene, and Gosiute nations. After the first waves of Ameri-can settlers moved into the region during the early part of the nineteenth century, new immigration into Idaho slowed down considerably. The reasons for Idaho's relative lack of immigration are many. The most prominent reasons include the state's lack of both a dominant agricultural base that at-tracts farmworkers and major urban centers that provide employment opportunities in service in-dustries and jobs for unskilled labor.

LATE NINETEENTH CENTURY IMMIGRATION

Most immigrants who entered Idaho after it be-came a U.S. state in 1890 were farmers who were able to take advantage of the region's nitrogen-rich soil, which made possible rapid crop cultivation. Limited numbers of new immigrants from Ger-many, England, and Russia did arrive during the nineteenth century. Some found employment in the mining and logging industries; however, many of these immigrants did not remain in the state. They instead tended to move on to California, Alaska, and Canada. Those who did remain in Idaho typically transitioned into the lucrative agri-cultural farming and ranching industries. Idaho's African American population before the turn of the twentieth century never exceeded five hun-dred persons, and the numbers of Asian Americans were similar.

TWENTIETH CENTURY ARRIVALS

During the twentieth century, Idaho remained a secondary destination for new immigrants. As late as 1940, the state registered only 5,855 foreign-born residents. The majority of Idaho's residents had

relocated from eastern regions of the United States, particularly Missouri and Iowa. However, foreign immigration remained limited because of limited employment opportunities within the state, which were due to the lack of the types of heavy industries that needed large labor pools.

The only significant immigrant groups to move into the region during the early twentieth century were Canadian farmers from the neighboring province of Alberta and a very small number of people from the Basque region of Spain. The Basques—who never exceeded more than 1,000 people—typically worked as sheepherders in Idaho's hills and as general laborers for both the fledgling logging and mining industries. Many of these Spanish settlers came from the Spanish province of Bizkala. The presence of this minority population continues to be evident in Idaho's Basque restaurants and in an annual Basque festival held in Boise.

During the twenty-first century, Idaho saw a dramatic growth in population that made it one of the fastest-growing states in the union. Most new residents came from neighboring states, including a significant number from California who were attracted to Idaho's climate, employment opportunities in the technology sector, and its relatively low cost of living. Consequently, the state experienced an annual population growth of more than 13 percent between 2000 and 2006. Among these new Idaho residents were a growing number of Hispanic residents, who constituted about 10 percent of the state's population by 2009. Most of these immigrants settled in and around Boise and Twin Falls, both of which have Spanish-language media outlets.

Despite these changes, immigration into Idaho has remained limited. This may be in part due to

PROFILE OF IDAHO

Region	Northwest
Entered union	1890
Largest cities	Boise (capital), Nampa, Pocatello, Idaho Falls
Modern immigrant communities	Canadians, Hispanics, Basques

Population	Total	Percent of state	Percent of U.S.	U.S. rank
All state residents	1,466,000	100.0	0.49	39
All foreign-born residents	82,000	5.6	0.22	39

Source: U.S. Census Bureau, *Statistical Abstract for 2006.*

Notes: The U.S. population in 2006 was 299,399,000, of whom 37,548,000 (12.5%) were foreign born. Rankings in last column reflect total numbers, not percentages.

Idaho's reputation as a region that is unwelcoming of various minority or ethnic groups. This image reached a level of national notoriety during the 1990's with the highly visible actions of white-power groups, such as the Aryan Nations, and numerous highly publicized confrontations between armed militia groups and isolationists and federal law-enforcement agencies.

Robert D. Mitchell

FURTHER READING

Malone, Michael P. C. *Ben Ross and the New Deal in Idaho.* Seattle: University of Washington Press, 1970.

Peterson, Frank Ross. *Idaho, A Bicentennial History.* New York: W. W. Norton, 1976.

Weatherby, James Benjamin, and Randy Stapilus. *Governing Idaho: Politics, People and Power.* Caldwell, Idaho: Caxton Press, 2005.

SEE ALSO: Chinese immigrants; Economic opportunities; Employment; History of immigration after 1891; Italian immigrants; Labor unions; Montana; Railroads; Utah.

IDENTIFICATIONAL ASSIMILATION

DEFINITION: Late stage of assimilation in which members of a minority group, such as newly arrived immigrants, develop a sense of peoplehood based exclusively on their host society

SIGNIFICANCE: Sociologist Milton Gordon's concept of identificational assimilation helps to explain how minority groups develop a sense of peoplehood, an important stage in the assimilation of U.S. immigrants.

In his 1964 book *Assimilation in American Life*, Milton Gordon created a synthesis that delineates the multiple dimensions of assimilation, according to the various indicators of the process. He identified seven stages in which assimilation takes place: cultural, structural, marital, identity, prejudice, discrimination, and civic. These steps are not causally distinct but describe different dimensions of the same underlying process: they are subprocesses of assimilation. Gordon placed great emphasis on the first two stages—acculturation and structural assimilation. In his analysis, acculturation could occur without the other types of assimilation, and it could last indefinitely. In addition, each of the subprocesses may take place in varying degrees.

The seven stages in Gordon's synthesis offer a composite multidimensional index of assimilation that could be used to determine the extent of a group's assimilation according to both individual- and group-level criteria. Thus, Gordon's framework provides specifications for empirical indicators of assimilation, which contributed to the development of quantitative research in sociology during the 1960's.

GORDON'S FRAMEWORK

The fourth stage in Gordon's multidimensional scheme is identificational assimilation, which occurs when members of the minority group, usually newly arrived immigrants, develop a sense of peoplehood based exclusively on the host society, acquiring the memories, sentiments, and attitudes of people of the core culture. This step of assimilation became more popular in later discussions of assimilation with regard to both the descendants of European immigrants and members of the new immigrant groups.

In Gordon's framework, ethnic identity is not an undifferentiated concept. He distinguishes between historical identification and participational identity. Historical identification is a function of past and current historical events and derives from a sense of "interdependence of fate"—in sociologist Kurt Lewsin's words—which typically extends to the ethnic group as a whole. Participational identity refers to the sense of belonging to a subculture: Its members participate frequently in it and share close behavioral similarities with each other; they are also likely to be people from the same ethnic group and social class.

FURTHER RESEARCH AND CRITICISM

In 1985, Milton Yinger noted that among the several types of assimilation, the identification stage was perhaps the least well conceptualized and measured. In 1983, Richard Alba and Mitchell Chamlin tried to measure ethnic identification using a survey in which they asked people to specify the country of origin of their ancestors. In 1988, Barbara Tomaskovis-Devey and Donald Tomaskovis-Devey did similar research and established that identificational assimilation is an approximate measure of ingroup marriage in the last generation and of the intensity of current ethnic identification. In 1990, J. Allen Williams and Suzanne T. Ortega used the same conceptualization to study the fourth stage of assimilation—they asked respondents to specify if thinking of themselves as a person from the country they named was very, somewhat, or not very important to them.

Some scholars find Gordon's identificational assimilation to be ambiguous because it does not clarify if it applies to individuals or groups. Although the measurement has been applied to individuals, the overall hypothesis has been interpreted as applying to groups. Scholars like Richard Alba, Victor Nee, and Elliott Barkan find the strength of Gordon's framework in its clear articulation of some of the key dimensions of assimilation, viewed as a composite concept. They also recognize that the dimensions of assimilation can be arranged in stages to the advantage of quantitative researchers in sociology.

Elitza Kotzeva

FURTHER READING

Alba, Richard, and Victor Nee. *Remaking the American Mainstream: Assimilation and Contemporary Immigration.* Cambridge, Mass.: Harvard University Press, 2005. Sociologists Alba and Nee advance their arguments about the similarities between the immigrants of the previous century and those of the twenty-first century by providing a thorough overview of theory and history of assimilation and immigration in the United States.

Fuchs, Lawrence H. *The American Kaleidoscope: Race, Ethnicity, and the Civic Culture.* Hanover, N.H.: Wesleyan University Press, 1990. Fuchs traces the assimilation of different immigrant groups into the American mainstream during the eighteenth and nineteenth centuries to show that immigrants contribute to the ethnic diversity and civic unity of American society rather than to its divisiveness.

Gordon, Milton Myron. *Assimilation in American Life: The Role of Race, Religion, and National Origins.* New York: Oxford University Press, 1964. Seminal sociological text on assimilation in which Gordon introduces his innovative ideas on the different stages of assimilation and the stratification of American society.

Jacoby, Tamar. *Reinventing the Melting Pot: The New Immigrants and What It Means to Be American.* New York: Basic Books, 2004. Divided in five parts, the essays in the book examine the process of assimilation from a variety of perspectives and explore the new ways of thinking about America as a melting pot.

Kazal, Russell A. "Revisiting Assimilation: The Rise, Fall, and Reappraisal of a Concept in American Ethnic History." *American Historical Review* 100, no. 2 (April, 1995): 437-471. Article tracing the emergence and centrality of assimilation in the work of sociologists and concluding that a new definition of assimilation is needed.

Kivisto, Peter. *Incorporating Diversity: Rethinking Assimilation in a Multicultural Age.* Boulder, Colo.: Paradigm Publishers, 2005. Presents a set of canonical texts on assimilation theory together with writings on current immigration issues in an attempt to revise the classical perspective for the contemporary situation.

Salins, Peter D. *Assimilation, American Style.* New York: Basic Books, 1997. Examines the process of assimilation and the impacts of immigration on contemporary American society.

SEE ALSO: Anglo-conformity; Assimilation theories; Cultural pluralism; Hansen effect; Melting pot theory; Migrant superordination; Name changing.

ILLEGAL IMMIGRATION

DEFINITION: Undocumented entry into the United States in circumvention of U.S. immigration laws

SIGNIFICANCE: Although a self-professed nation of immigrants, the United States has historically shown ambivalence toward newcomers who enter the country illegally. Despite massive government efforts to curb illegal immigration, an estimated 12 million people who entered the country illegally were living in the United States during the early twenty-first century, when some sectors of the national economy would have been devastated without their labor.

The reception of illegal immigrants in the United States has ranged from open arms in a number of cities that have officially declared themselves immigrant sanctuaries to nativist hostility. Some politicians have regularly demonized illegal immigrants for their purported contributions to crime. The federal government's immigration laws contain exceptions for economic need or political persecution, but the government also maintains a large border-police apparatus that catches only a fraction of those who try to cross the borders without permission.

A SPECIAL PROBLEM

An important aspect of illegal immigration in the United States that is almost uniquely American lies in the Fourteenth Amendment to the U.S. Constitution. Its definition of citizenship makes all persons born within the United States American citizens, regardless of the citizenship of their parents. Few other countries are similarly generous in awarding citizenship, but the U.S. principle has given rise to a difficult problem in combating illegal immigration: Many children are born in the

United States to parents who are in the country illegally.

According to a 2008 study for the Pew Hispanic Center, 73 percent of all children of undocumented immigrants—the majority of whom are Hispanic—have been born in the United States and are thus American citizens. Consequently, when government immigration raids deport illegal immigrants who are parents, they often separate parents from their citizen children. This poses a contradiction in American immigration principles, as separating family members runs counter to the stated U.S. immigration goal of family unification. Immigration raids that have led to the deportation of parents while leaving their American-born children homeless have occasionally provided federal immigration agencies with public-relations embarrassments.

DEMOGRAPHICS OF ILLEGAL IMMIGRATION

Between 1990 and 2006, the numbers of immigrants who entered the United States illegally increased rapidly. After 2006, the rate stabilized, in part because depressed economic conditions in the United States reduced employment opportunities, and in part because of more stringent security controls, including a doubling of the number of U.S. Border Patrol agents working along the Mexican border, from 9,000 to 18,000.

According to early twenty-first century U.S. Census estimates, three-quarters of undocumented immigrants in the United States were Hispanic. A majority, 59 percent, had come from Mexico, with 11 percent from Asia, 11 percent from Central America, 7 percent from South America, and smaller percentages from other areas. According to estimates of the Pew Foundation Hispanic Center, of the 12.7 million Mexicans living in the United States in 2007, roughly 55 percent were in the country illegally. Illegal populations in 2006 were estimated at 2.8 million in California, 1.6 million in Texas, 980,000 in Florida, and about half a million each in New York, Arizona, Illinois, and New Jersey.

The main motivation for crossing the border has long been the quest for better employment. Undocumented immigrants, who have generally outnumbered legal immigrants, can be found in many sectors of the economy. Various surveys, including one by National Public Radio and another by *USA Today*, indicate that 3 to 4 percent of undocumented immigrants are employed in farmwork, 21 to 33 percent in service industries, 16 to 19 percent in construction and related jobs, 12 percent in sales, 15 to 16 percent in production industries, 10 percent in management, and 8 percent in transportation.

CHANGING ECONOMIC CONDITIONS

By 2005, the tide of immigration into the United States had slowed substantially, at least for a time, as increasing numbers of Mexicans and other Hispanics left the United States to return to their home countries. Between August, 2007, and August, 2008, the number of Mexicans immigrating to the United States declined by 25 percent, according to Mexico's own census figures. In 2008, the amount of money that Mexican immigrants remitted from the United States to relatives in Mexico declined by $1 billion.

By 2008, the numbers of arrests at U.S. borders had declined for three consecutive years, dropping to levels not witnessed since 1973, when the total population of the United States was much lower. In 2008, the U.S. Border Patrol reported making 724,000 arrests, 17 percent fewer than in 2007. Ninety-seven percent of these arrests took place on the southern border, and 91 percent of the persons arrested were Mexicans. The number of border arrests actually had peaked two decades earlier, in 1986, at 1.7 million. The Border Patrol credited tighter security, including the construction of fences along parts of the border, for the long-term decline.

SUPPORTERS OF ILLEGAL IMMIGRATION

A number of American communities—including the three largest cities in the United States—have declared themselves as "sanctuary cities." Their governments have instructed city employees, usually including police, to avoid cooperating with federal immigration authorities seeking illegal immigrants. Opponents say that sanctuary city measures violate federal law because the cities are in effect creating their own immigration policies, an area of law that only the U.S. Congress has authority to change. City authorities in many of these urban areas have countered by saying that undocumented immigrants have brought them more benefits than they have cost. Illegal immigrant workers pay about $7 billion per year into the Social Security system from which they will receive no benefits. According

to a paper in *The Tax Lawyer*, a peer-reviewed journal of the American Bar Association, illegal immigrants pay more in taxes than they cost in social services.

During the early twenty-first century, members of a group calling itself No More Deaths patrolled the Mexican border to offer medical aid, food, and water to immigrants crossing the desert regions during hot weather. The organization's aim is to reduce deaths and serious injuries that plague many who make the difficult crossing.

OPPONENTS OF ILLEGAL IMMIGRATION

On the other side of the issue, groups such as the Federation for American Immigration Reform (FAIR), cite other studies asserting that illegal immigrants cost American governments more than the workers pay in taxes. According to this view, illegal immigration degrades public education, health care, and other services for citizens, with the heaviest burdens falling on the poor.

The Minuteman Project has lobbied Congress for increased enforcement of immigration laws as some local people, including white supremacists, have formed posses to prevent immigrants from crossing parts of the border. Sometimes these vigilante groups have assaulted people they believe to be illegal immigrants. Other people have complained that the large number of illegal immigrants have been ruining U.S. public lands on and near the border. For example, Arizona's Fish and Wildlife Service reported finding forty-five abandoned cars on the state's Buenos Aires wildlife refuge and nine tons of garbage during only two months in 2002. Park officials reported that fires set by immigrants flared out of control often enough to char more than 68,000 acres and cost $5.1 million to extinguish.

Undocumented Mexican farm workers waiting to be sent back to Mexico at Calexico in 1972, during a period when an estimated 300,000 Mexicans were entering the United States illegally every year in search of employment. (NARA)

IMMIGRATION SCAMS

The intense desire of impoverished foreigners to work in the United States legally has spawned many criminal activities that prey on would-be immigrants. Creators of these schemes have developed many ruses, all with the attitude that their victims are unlikely to complain to legal authorities. "Coyotes" routinely conduct many people across southern borders for fees ranging in the thousands of dollars per person. Entire cargo ships of illegal immigrants have arrived from Asia and unloaded people at sea after charging each of them tens of thousands of dollars. So-called Mohawk "warriors" have brought immigrants into the United States from Canada through the Akwesasne (St. Regis) reservation on the U.S.-Canadian border. These crossings have often occurred during the winter months, when the St. Lawrence River is frozen over.

On May 27, 2009, twelve Uzbekistani nationals were arrested in Kansas City, Missouri, on charges of recruiting hundreds of prospective workers from Jamaica, the Philippines, and the Dominican Republic, with promises of obtaining for them H-2B visas so they could do seasonal work legally in the United States. However, after they arrived in the country, the workers were held in debt bondage for years and charged fees for work uniforms, food, and rent as they performed menial labor in hotels and office buildings in and near Kansas City. The traffickers, having created a company they called Giant Labor Solutions, collected the workers' paychecks and turned the workers into virtual slaves.

In and near New York City, pastors of a supposed Pentecostal church in Queens, La Iglesia Roca de la Salvación Eterna, asserted that they possessed a special allocation of green cards earmarked for members of church congregations, for paperwork and an $8,000 to $16,000 processing fee. More than 120 illegal immigrants, most of them from Ecuador, were defrauded out of more than $1 million before the bogus pastors were arrested in early 2009. Many of the immigrants lost their life savings in the scam.

Bruce E. Johansen

FURTHER READING

Buchanan, Patrick J. *State of Emergency: The Third World Invasion and Conquest of America.* New York: Thomas Dunne Books/St. Martin's Press, 2006. Visceral discourse asserting that continued illegal immigration will ruin the U.S. economy and culture.

Conover, Ted. *Coyotes: A Journey Through the Secret World of America's Illegal Aliens.* New York: Vintage Books, 1987. Compelling account of the dangers of crossing the United States-Mexico border from the street level, with an emphasis on the "coyotes" who guide illegal immigrants into the United States for fees.

Frank, Thomas. "Modern Slavery Comes to Kansas." *Wall Street Journal,* June 17, 2009, p. A11. Account of a human-trafficking ring that recruited illegal workers with promises of work visas and then held them in debt bondage.

LeMay, Michael C. *Illegal Immigration: A Reference Handbook.* Santa Barbara, Calif.: ABC-CLIO, 2007. Encyclopedic reference work on many issues pertaining to illegal immigration and related subjects.

Ngai, Mae M. *Impossible Subjects: Illegal Aliens and the Making of Modern America.* Princeton, N.J.: Princeton University Press, 2004. Detailed study of illegal immigration into the United States from 1924 to 1965.

Semple, Kirk. "Green Cards, Belief, and Betrayal at a Storefront Church." *The New York Times,* June 17, 2009, p. A17-A18. Detailed account of how 120 illegal immigrants were defrauded of more than $1 million by fake preachers who promised them green cards.

Urrea, Luis Alberto. *The Devil's Highway: A True Story.* Boston: Little, Brown, 2004. Detailed account of a harrowing journey of would-be immigrants across the U.S.-Mexico border in 2001, during which at least fourteen people died.

Williams, Mary E., ed. *Immigration: Opposing Viewpoints.* Farmington Hills, Mich.: Greenhaven Press, 2004. Collection of essays presenting opposing viewpoints on the questions of whether immigration should be restricted, how serious a problem immigration is, how the United should address illegal immigration, and how U.S. immigration policy might be reformed. Also contains a directory of organizations devoted to immigration issues.

SEE ALSO: Border fence; Citizenship and Immigration Services, U.S.; Deportation; Florida illegal im-

migration suit; Illegal Immigration Reform and Immigrant Responsibility Act of 1996; Mexican American Legal Defense and Educational Fund; Sanctuary movement; Sweatshops.

ILLEGAL IMMIGRATION REFORM AND IMMIGRANT RESPONSIBILITY ACT OF 1996

THE LAW: Federal law designed to reduce illegal immigration and to apprehend undocumented aliens
DATE: Signed into law on September 30, 1996
ALSO KNOWN AS: IIRIRA

SIGNIFICANCE: The Illegal Immigration Reform and Responsibility Act, or IIRIRA, was enacted to prevent the flow of undocumented aliens into the United States. The law stipulated such initiatives as increased border patrol staffing for border surveillance, enhanced enforcement and penalties against alien smuggling, tougher sanctions for illegal immigrants caught inside the U.S. borders, and increased restrictions on alien employment, benefits, and assistance programs.

On September 30, 1996, President Bill Clinton signed the Illegal Immigrant Reform and Immigrant Responsibility Act into law. Before the law was passed in Congress, two sets of immigration bills had been considered in each house of Congress. One was dedicated to controlling illegal immigration, the second to managing legal immigration. If the legal-immigration bill had passed, it would have radically reduced the numbers of employment and family immigrants allowed into the United States. The other bill focused specifically on stronger border enforcement, apprehension, and deportation. Eventually, the two bills were combined in each house, only to be split again later, after arguments arose over the language of the bill's component parts. The reason for combining the bills centered on the notion that the controversial legal-immigration bill would have an easier time passing if it were connected to the more popular illegal-immigration bill. After much debate, the legal-immigration bills in each house were defeated. However, several items from them concerning legal immigration ended up in the final draft of the illegal-immigration bill. The final bill was coupled with another piece of legislation not related to immigration issues; it concerned the finances of the day-to-day operation of the entire federal government—an issue that made its immediate passage crucial.

The illegal-immigration bill that ultimately became IIRIRA 96 was divided into six broad areas and focused primarily on stronger enforcement efforts and penalties for person who attempt to enter illegally, smuggle immigrants into the country, or live inside U.S. borders without proper documentation. The six major areas of the new law included:

Six of forty-nine Salvadorans whose attempt to enter the United States illegally in 1999 failed. They are shown at El Salvador's international airport after being returned to their homeland on a plane chartered by the U.S. government. (AP/Wide World Photos)

- Title I: Improvements to border control, facilitation of legal entry, and interior enforcement
- Title II: Enhanced enforcement and penalties against alien smuggling and document fraud
- Title III: Inspection, apprehension, detention, adjudication, and removal of inadmissible and deportable aliens
- Title IV: Enforcement of restrictions against employment
- Title V: Restrictions on benefits for aliens
- Title VI: Miscellaneous provisions

One of the most controversial items in the bill, Title III, addressed the issue of undocumented aliens already inside U.S. borders. In particular, the government enacted rules calling for permanent restrictions or bans on undocumented aliens found in violation of certain legal rules. For example, the act states that any person who has been in the United States illegally for at least 180 days, but less than one year, must remain outside the United States for three years unless granted a pardon. Moreover, any person who has been in the United States illegally for more than one year must reside outside the United States for ten years unless a pardon is granted. Any such person who returns to the United States prematurely without the specified pardon will not be permitted to apply for a waiver for reentry for an additional ten years. Additionally, the language of the law applies regardless of whether a person has a spouse or children who are U.S. citizens.

Paul M. Klenowski

FURTHER READING

Hayes, Helene. *U.S. Immigration Policy and the Undocumented: Ambivalent Laws and Furtive Lives.* Westport, Conn.: Praeger, 2001.

Newton, Lina. *Illegal, Alien, or Immigrant: The Politics of Immigration Reform.* New York: New York University Press, 2008.

SEE ALSO: Border fence; Commission on Immigration Reform, U.S.; Due process protections; Illegal immigration; Immigration Act of 1990; Immigration law; Immigration Reform and Control Act of 1986; Select Commission on Immigration and Refugee Policy; Smuggling of immigrants.

ILLINOIS

SIGNIFICANCE: Illinois has had an immigration history more complex than that of many states. Its early history was characterized by movements of Native Americans and influxes of people from other parts of the United States. During the nineteenth century, the state began drawing large numbers of European immigrants to its farmlands and cities, and the twentieth century brought in new waves of immigrants from Latin American countries and Africa.

Illinois's early immigration history made it a microcosm of the north-south split within the United States as a whole. After the nation gained its independence, many southerners migrated to Illinois from Kentucky (which provided Abraham Lincoln's family), Virginia, and Tennessee. The Blackhawk War of 1832 drove most of the few remaining Native Americans out of northern Illinois, and then new arrivals from New England and New York State began dominating Illinois's commerce and politics. By 1860, the state was divided between those who approved of slavery and favored secession and those who favored abolition and preserving the Union. Illinois remained in the Union during the Civil War, but some of its southern counties remained sympathetic to the Confederacy. As late as the twenty-first century, northern and southern accents could still be observed around the state.

NINETEENTH CENTURY TRENDS

Illinois's first great influx of foreign immigrants came after 1830 with the arrival of Germans, many of whom settled across the Mississippi River from St. Louis, Missouri. Mostly classically educated, these Germans were dubbed "Latin Farmers." The aftermath of Europe's many failed revolutions in 1848 brought another wave of German immigrants known as "Forty Eighters."

During the second half of the nineteenth century Illinois's population increased by more than 20 percent every decade. A large part of this increase was due to foreign immigrants, especially Germans and Irish, along with smaller numbers of Swedes and British. Germans settled throughout most of the upper Mississippi Valley, from St. Louis

in the south to Wisconsin in the north, and they also settled in Chicago and other areas in the northern part of Illinois.

Irish immigrants tended to concentrate in Illinois's cities and along the railroads and assimilated rapidly. Swedes tended to cluster in groups. In 1847, they founded a commune at Bishop Hill, near Galva. They also settled in towns such as Rock Island and Rockford, and many of them farmed. Rock Island's Augustana College originated as a Swedish institution.

The population of Illinois's largest city, Chicago, was more than half foreign born by 1860. Germans made up one-fifth of the total, followed by a slightly smaller number of Irish and even smaller numbers of Swedes. In 1870, Chicago's population of just over 300,000 included more than 50,000 Germans and more than 40,000 Irish. By 1900, Swedes made up 9 percent of Chicago's population. These groups were soon joined by a large influx of African Americans from southern states.

TWENTIETH CENTURY TRENDS

After 1920, immigrants to Illinois came from new sources, especially in Chicago. In 1900, 30,150 Italians were living in Chicago. By 1920, that figure had risen to 109,458. Poles had an established community along Chicago's Milwaukee Avenue by 1900, and they numbered almost 140,000 by 1920. World War II brought refugees who helped swell Chicago's Polish community, which fostered Polish-language newspapers, Polish-language Roman Catholic masses, and other Polish institutions, all of which were still strong into the early twenty-first century. World War II also brought a new wave of German refugees.

Mexican immigration into Illinois began just before 1920. Many of these immigrants were fleeing the violence of the Mexican Revolution, which started in 1910. At the same time, American entry into World War I drew many American workers away from Illinois's farms and factories to serve in the armed forces and war-related industry. Mexican workers took many of their places in both agricultural fields and factories. Mexicans and other Hispanic immigrants concentrated in the Chicago area. Hispanic components of Chicago's population were so important by the 1960's that bilingual signs were appearing in city trains. By the 1990's, some Chicago neighborhoods, such as Pilsen, were predominantly Spanish-speaking and were electing Hispanic representatives to the city council and the U.S. Congress. By the last decade of the twentieth century, Illinois meatpackers were facing such a shortage of workers that they were actively recruiting workers in Latin America and Africa.

By 2006, Illinois's estimated population of 12,832,000 included 1,773,000 foreign-born residents. The state's rich ethnic mix was reflected in its linguistic diversity. More than 10 percent of the state's people spoke Spanish at home, and tens of thousands of families were speaking Polish, German, Tagalog, Italian, Chinese, Korean, French, Russian, or Greek in their homes.

Timothy C. Frazer

FURTHER READING

Arredondo, Gabriela F. *Mexican Chicago: Race, Identity, and Nation, 1916-39.* Champaign: University of Illinois Press, 2008. Analysis of how the revolutionary background of Chicago's Mexican im-

---

PROFILE OF ILLINOIS

Region	Midwest
Entered union	1818
Largest cities	Chicago, Rockford, Aurora, Naperville, Peoria, Springfield (capital)
Modern immigrant communities	Mexicans, other Hispanics, Africans

Population	Total	Percent of state	Percent of U.S.	U.S. rank
All state residents	12,832,000	100.0	4.29	5
All foreign-born residents	1,774,000	13.8	4.72	5

Source: U.S. Census Bureau, *Statistical Abstract for 2006.*
Notes: The U.S. population in 2006 was 299,399,000, of whom 37,548,000 (12.5%) were foreign born. Rankings in last column reflect total numbers, not percentages.

migrants influenced their adjustment to American life.

Candeloro, Dominic. *Chicago's Italians: Immigrants, Ethnics, Americans.* Charleston, S.C.: Arcadia, 2003. Traces the contributions of Chicago's Italians to labor unions, politics, and religion, and treats changes brought to the Italian community by World War II.

Daniels, Roger. *Coming to America: A History of Immigration and Ethnicity in American Life.* New York: HarperCollins, 1990. Thorough but readable treatment of groups of immigrants from the seventeenth century through the 1980's.

Frazer, Timothy C., ed. *"Heartland" English.* Tuscaloosa: University of Alabama Press, 1987. Collection of essays describing the impact immigrants and settlement had on the spoken English of several midwestern states, including Illinois.

Pacyga, Dominic A. *Polish Immigrants and Industrial Chicago: Workers on the South Side, 1880-1922.* Chicago: University of Chicago Press, 2003. Study of Polish immigrants who labored in Chicago factories and attempted to create neighborhoods like those of their homeland.

SEE ALSO: Abolitionist movement; Bilingual education; Chicago; German immigrants; Great Irish Famine; Irish immigrants; Italian immigrants; Language issues; Mexican immigrants; Polish immigrants.

IMINGAISHA

DEFINITION: Japanese-based corporate organizations that recruited emigrant workers for Hawaii's sugar cane industry during the late nineteenth and early twentieth centuries

SIGNIFICANCE: The workers sent to Hawaii by the *imingaisha* began an era of organized Japanese economic emigration that reversed imperial Japan's long-standing restrictions on population movement outside the country and marked the beginning of the Japanese community in the United States.

During the latter part of the nineteenth century, the expansion of the sugar cane industry in the independent kingdom of Hawaii created a demand for foreign workers because the islands' native population were unable to keep up with the new demands for manpower. Of the many nationalities considered for recruitment, the Japanese were seen as most desirable. However, the Japanese government's legal restrictions on emigration posed significant obstacles.

After the failure of several unsanctioned attempts by private individuals to bring Japanese workers to Hawaii during the 1860's, an agreement was reached between Japan and the kingdom of Hawaii permitting workers to emigrate under imperial sanction while governed by ministry officials. After this initial period of Japanese government-sponsored emigration ended in 1894, a new system was set in place to address concerns of possible exploitation of Japanese workers. By that time, Hawaii's monarchy had been replaced by a republican government. In 1898, the U.S. government would annex the islands and make them an American territory. Meanwhile, the independent Hawaiian government was concerned about the danger of allowing so many Japanese workers to enter the islands that they would shift the balance of racial and ethnic groups in the population.

The new arrangement was built on fifty-one independent private corporations that were created to maintain the flow of contract workers (and the economic benefits to Japan their remittances provided), with the five earliest such firms appearing between 1891 and 1894. The original imperial ordinance of 1894 governing the trade in workers was expanded and became law on April 29, 1896, as *Imin hogoho*, the Emigration Protection Law. It defined *imin* as persons who emigrated to foreign countries other than China or Korea for the purpose of labor, and whatever members of their families accompanied or later joined them abroad. Typical *imingaisha* firms operated by negotiating with the owners of more than fifty separate Hawaiian sugar plantations to establish their manpower needs. They then sent recruiters to rural Japanese villages in selected prefectures to contract predominantly male workers, arranging their transportation to Hawaii, while making profits on the entire enterprise.

The Japanese government saw the emigrants as helping to address both the unemployment problems of rural Japan, while providing a new source of income to assist in the nation's modernization

efforts. The degree of popularity of this form of overseas labor can be seen in the fact that the companies eventually transported some 124,000 Japanese workers to Hawaii. The change of Hawaii from an independent republic to an American territory on July 7, 1898, led to the extension of an 1885 U.S. law prohibiting foreign contract employment (a measure originally intended to interdict Chinese laborers) to Hawaii, over the protests of the sugar planters, who tried unsuccessfully to have their workforce exempted from this law.

Paradoxically, the end of the *imingaisha* era came when these same workers' complaints against them for violating the Emigration Protection Law resulted in the formation of the Japanese Reform Association in 1905, while many workers started coming to Hawaii unbound by labor contracts, thereby simply bypassing the organized emigration process completely. The 1907 Gentlemen's Agreement between the United States and Japan banned the movement of Japanese from Hawaii to the mainland but also eliminated the issuance of passports for laborers intending to enter the American market.

Robert B. Ridinger

FURTHER READING

Jung, Moon-Ho. *Coolies and Cane: Race, Labor, and Sugar in the Age of Emancipation.* Baltimore: Johns Hopkins University Press, 2008.

Moriyama, Alan Takeo. *Imingaisha: Japanese Emigration Companies and Hawaii, 1894-1908.* Honolulu: University of Hawaii Press, 1985.

Okihiro, Gary Y. *Cane Fires: The Anti-Japanese Movement in Hawaii, 1865-1945.* Philadelphia: Temple University Press, 1992.

Van Sant, John E. *Pacific Pioneers: Japanese Journeys to America and Hawaii, 1850-1880.* Champaign: University of Illinois Press, 2000.

SEE ALSO: Asian immigrants; Contract labor system; Farm and migrant workers; Gentlemen's Agreement; Hawaii; Immigration Convention of 1886; Issei; Japanese immigrants.

"IMMIGRANT"

DEFINITION: Broad term for a person who has moved from an original homeland to another state or country

SIGNIFICANCE: Although the United States was created through immigration and has absorbed a steady stream of newcomers from many lands throughout its history, the term "immigrant" remains an often unclear or ambiguous word for many Americans, as does its relationship to a number of kindred words and phrases. Within the United States, "immigrant" has both specific legal denotations and popular connotations that differentiate it from terms such as "migrant," "refugee," and "alien."

The roots of the English word "immigrant" go back to the Latin verb *migrare*, which meant precisely what its direct descendant "migrate" means in modern English: to move from one locality to another. Thus, movements of people or animals from one place to another are usually called "migrations," and people who periodically move from one country or region to another are spoken of as "migrants."

The Latin prefix *in-* has several uses and connotations. One is what is sometimes called in linguistics illative force, that is, the suggestion of going into a new place or state of being. Another use of *in-* is intensive in nature; it can lend forcefulness to the word to which it is prefixed. Therefore, "immigration" (in which *in-* has become *im-*) implies not only a change in location but also suggests that the change is a significant one, more than likely a permanent one. This, then, is then the definition of "immigrant" in both legal and lexicographical terms: a person who moves from one country to another to take up residence there. However, the term connotes merely a physical change in location, not any change in political allegiance or legality. Consequently, an immigrant may be a naturalized citizen of the United States, a resident alien who lives in the country but maintains citizenship in the home country and who has proper documentation in the form of a visa and green card, or an "illegal immigrant" who has no such documentation or whose documents are outdated. Resident

aliens are sometimes also referred to as "landed immigrants" or "permanent residents."

Of the various words associated with, or similar to, "immigrant," "immigrant" itself is the broadest term, the generic word for a person who has changed the country of his or her residence. "Alien," from a Latin root meaning "other" or "strange," designates any person from another country and can theoretically be applied to a person from a country other than the United States who is still in that country. A "refugee" is legally defined in the United States as someone who has come to the country to avoid persecution in the country of origin on the basis of such issues as race or religion. Therefore, one person can be—and sometimes is—an alien, an immigrant, and a refugee simultaneously.

The U.S. Citizenship and Immigration Services recognize and define various subcategories of immigrants and immigration. One populous subcategory is that of family-based immigrants, people from other countries who are spouses, fiancés, children, parents, and siblings of U.S. citizens. Another large subcategory is that of employment-based immigrants. These are people who possess job skills and professional expertise that have been deemed especially desirable or needed in the United States—as well as their families. A variation of this latter group is known as investor immigrants: immigrants who are granted visas to begin new businesses in the United States, especially in parts of the country where the economy is sluggish.

Thomas Du Bose

FURTHER READING

Beasley, Vanessa. *Who Belongs in America?* College Station: Texas A&M Press, 2006.

Borjas, George J. *Heaven's Door: Immigration Policy and the American Economy.* Princeton, N.J.: Princeton University Press, 2001.

SEE ALSO: Citizenship; Families; Illegal immigration; Immigration law; *A Nation of Immigrants*; Permanent resident status; Refugees; Resident aliens.

THE IMMIGRANT

IDENTIFICATION: Silent comedy about poor European immigrants arriving in New York during the early twentieth century
DATE: Released in 1917

> **SIGNIFICANCE:** Directed and cowritten by groundbreaking film artist Charles Chaplin, *The Immigrant* depicts obstacles and triumphs associated with the immigrant experience. In 1998, the U.S. Library of Congress selected *The Immigrant* for preservation in the National Film Registry.

Distributed by the Mutual Film Corporation and filmed on location at the Chaplin Studios in Hollywood, California, *The Immigrant* stars Charles Chaplin and Edna Purviance as unnamed immigrants, apparently—but not definitely—of Eastern European origin. The film develops various motifs, often exaggerated for comic effect, based on the harsh realities that a generation of European immigrants to the United States experienced.

The first part of the twenty-minute film takes place aboard a ship, where Chaplin, in his iconic "Tramp" persona, plays a steerage-class passenger who suffers from seasickness and endures the torments of card-playing thieves and pickpockets. Edna Purviance is also among the deck passengers. The voyage ends when the ship enters New York Harbor, and its passengers see the Statue of Liberty. Thrilled by their first glimpse of the most famous symbol of American freedom, the steerage passengers rush to the side of the ship to get a closer look. However, at that moment, they are roughly roped in by immigration officials, who pull them back, as if they were merely so many farm animals. The Tramp expresses his defiance of this exercise of authority by kicking one of the officers in the rear.

The second half of the film depicts the Tramp and Purviance's chance meeting in a restaurant. Money issues and a surly waiter (Eric Campbell) complicate the scene. In the end, however, the American Dream proves true: An artist spots the penniless couple and offers them a job. The film is notable for its command of contemporary filmmaking techniques, editing, and fluid plotline.

Cordelia E. Barrera

Charlie Chaplin's Tramp character (left) and fellow steerage-class passengers relishing their first look at the Statue of Liberty. (The Granger Collection, New York)

FURTHER READING

Chaplin, Charlie. *Charlie Chaplin: Interviews.* Edited by Kevin J. Hayes. Jackson: University Press of Mississippi, 2005.

_____. *My Autobiography.* 1964. New York: Penguin Books, 1992.

Lyons, Timothy J. *Charles Chaplin: A Guide to References and Resources.* Boston: G. K. Hall, 1979.

Robinson, David. *Chaplin: His Life and Art.* Rev. ed. New York: Penguin Books, 2001.

Schickel, Richard, ed. *The Essential Chaplin: Perspectives on the Life and Art of the Great Comedian.* Chicago: I. R. Dee, 2006.

SEE ALSO: California; Crime; European immigrants; Films; Hamburg-Amerika Line; Pacific Mail Steamship Company; Statue of Liberty; Stereotyping; Transportation of immigrants; Women immigrants.

IMMIGRANT ADVANTAGE

DEFINITION: Term used within sociology to describe distinctions among minority groups within a larger society and those peoples who immigrate to these societies voluntarily from other nations

SIGNIFICANCE: Immigrants who are considered members of ethnic groups already residing within the United States often have advantages over native-born members of those groups.

Members of resident minority groups are often "marginalized," living on the fringe of society, often in poverty, lacking education, occupational skills, political power, or the means to integrate into the mainstream. These groups, much like immigrant groups, are frequently made up of ethnic and racial minorities. However, compared with marginalized groups, immigrants have numerous advantages and often become successful, productive members of a society.

One of the primary advantages that many immigrants have is that most people who immigrate to a new country typically do so by choice and therefore arrive already motivated to succeed. Another advantage is that they often have the resources needed to relocate to a new country. National immigration services typically work at keeping out low-skilled and poorly educated immigrants.

A third advantage is that immigrants to the United States tend to believe in the "melting pot" ideal and want to join the mainstream society and learn the new language. To become citizens of the United States, for example, immigrants must speak, read, and write English and pass an examination on U.S. history and government. Therefore, although immigrants may start on the lowest rungs of the economic ladder, they often move up more quickly than members of marginalized resident minorities. In many cases, their rise is accelerated by their ability to take advantage of affirmative action programs that were originally designed to benefit native-born members of disadvantaged minorities.

Rochelle L. Dalla

FURTHER READING

Barone, Michael. *The New Americans: How the Melting Pot Can Work Again.* Washington, D.C.: Regnery, 2001.

Cook, Terrence E. *Separation, Assimilation, or Accommodation: Contrasting Ethnic Minority Policies.* Westport, Conn.: Praeger, 2003.

Jacoby, Tamar, ed. *Reinventing the Melting Pot: The New Immigrants and What It Means to Be American.* New York: Basic Books, 2004.

SEE ALSO: Affirmative action; African Americans and immigrants; Assimilation theories; Civil Rights movement; Employment; Hansen effect; "Immigrant"; Melting pot theory; "Middleman" minorities; Migrant superordination; "Model minorities."

IMMIGRANT AID ORGANIZATIONS

DEFINITION: Charitable organizations established within immigrant communities, often church affiliated, to provide financial assistance and other support to members of the communities

SIGNIFICANCE: Immigrant aid organizations played an important role in helping immigrants to establish themselves in the United States. Not only have they offered much-needed financial assistance to immigrants, many of whom have been employed in low-wage jobs, but they also have given immigrants a sense of belonging and created a sense of home by providing social activities and traditional holiday celebrations.

During the eighteenth, nineteenth, and twentieth centuries, the vast majority of immigrants coming to the United States from Europe, Latin America, and Asia were poor working-class individuals who came seeking economic opportunities and better lives for themselves and their families. Farmers, laborers, and tradespeople who have lacked formal educations have found themselves in a new country in which customs are different, working conditions are often far from ideal, and the legal system is unfamiliar. The situation of new immigrants has been made more difficult by the fact many do not speak English when they arrive, and they have missed the cultural ambiance that they had left in their native lands.

Within the various ethnic communities or groups, organizations were soon formed to help individuals through both financial assistance and moral support. Early organizations helped those in their group who were ill and in need of medical care and those who were at times unable to find work and provide for their families. The concept of self-help was a major part of these organizations. Members paid either set dues or whatever they could afford. These funds were typically used to assist members with expenses incurred in childbirth, weddings, and funerals. Aid organizations eventually began offering health and life insurance at low rates. Some organizations even established banks to provide loans to members. Many organizations

were also active in maintaining traditions of the home countries by sponsoring festivals and traditional holiday celebrations. Many of these organizations have remained active into the twenty-first century. as aid societies or social organizations or both.

ETHNIC-BASED ORGANIZATIONS

The first immigrant aid organization formed in the United States was the Charitable Irish Association of Boston, which was founded in 1737. Originally, its members had to be Irish Protestants, or of Irish ancestry, and had to live in Boston. However, by 1742, the majority of the members were Irish Catholics living in Boston. The Ancient Order of Hibernians (AOH) formed organizations to aid Irish Catholic immigrants in almost all the areas of the United States in which Irish immigrants settled. The Hibernians were present in New York City, in Savannah, Georgia, and in Philadelphia.

The AOH was also active in the anthracite coal-mining region of Pennsylvania where it was purported to be associated with the Molly Maguires, a militant Irish Catholic mineworkers group that attempted to improve their working conditions by the use of intimidation and force. While members of the Molly Maguires were also members of the AOH, the latter organization itself eschewed violence, was benevolent, and provided financial assistance to members who were ill or impoverished.

The large Mexican immigrant population that was first located in the southwestern United States brought with it from Mexico a strong sense of community. *El pueblo*, the place where one lives, had a major significance in the Mexican mindset. Community aid organizations known as *mutualistas* were a part of the culture of their homeland. The membership of the *mutualistas*, which have remained very active into the twenty-first century, has varied and continues to do so. Members have included Mexicans, Mexican Americans, and non-Mexicans. The *mutualistas* provide not only financial assistance and tra-

ditional social activities but also support to members who experience workplace or political discrimination.

The Italian immigrants who came to the United States also created mutual aid organizations to provide financial assistance to the ill and impoverished. However, unlike the Irish, who emphasized nationality and religion, and the Mexicans, for whom *el pueblo*, or the community, was most important, the Italians established their societies on a narrower base. Their organizations based membership either on the families to which members belonged or the regions of Italy from which the immigrants came.

Flyer from an organization dedicated to protecting Italian immigrants from being exploited upon their arrival in America. (Center for Migration Studies)

OTHER IMMIGRANT ORGANIZATIONS

The mutual aid organizations established by the vast number of Chinese immigrants brought to the California area as laborers in the gold mines and for railroad construction were even more complex in their determination of membership. However, they also reflected the traditions and culture of the home country. Three distinct types of Chinese mutual aid associations were established. The clan associations received members having the same surname, and the tongs had a broader membership and included immigrants from different clans and districts. Membership in the *huikuan* or *huiguan* was open to all those speaking the same dialect, coming from the same district, or belonging to the same ethnic group. Other European groups such as the Belgians, Germans, and Poles also established aid organizations based on nationality.

Shawncey Webb

FURTHER READING

Candeloro, Dominic. *Chicago's Italians: Immigrants, Ethnics, Americans.* Chicago: Arcadia Press, 2003. Traces development of Italian contributions to Chicago in labor unions, politics, and religion.

Gutiérrez, David G. *Walls and Mirrors: Mexican Americans, Mexican Immigrants and the Politics of Ethnicity.* Berkeley: University of California Press, 1995. Excellent history of Mexicans and their descendants in the United States with a strong emphasis on the Mexican immigrants' maintenance of their culture and the role of *mutualistas.* Also good presentation of role of labor and political organizations.

Portes, Alejandro, and Rubén G. Rumbaut. *Immigrant America: A Portrait.* Berkeley: University of California Press, 2006. Excellent for understanding the problems and difficulties shared by immigrant groups and the need for immigrant aid organizations.

Pozzetta, George, ed. *Immigrant Institutions: The Organization of Immigrant Life.* New York: Routledge, 1991. Collection of useful articles on Italian, Jewish, and Japanese aid organizations. Many articles emphasize the roles of ethnic newspapers and of saloons as gathering places.

Reimers, David. *Other Immigrants: The Global Origins of the American People.* New York: New York University Press, 2005. Good discussion of the problems faced by non-European immigrants, with

some attention to the aid organizations that were formed.

SEE ALSO: Association of Indians in America; Chinese family associations; Chinese secret societies; Coalition for Humane Immigrant Rights of Los Angeles; El Rescate; Ethnic enclaves; Health care; Mexican American Legal Defense and Educational Fund; Social networks; Sociedad Progresista Mexicana; Welfare and social services.

IMMIGRATION ACT OF 1882

THE LAW: First comprehensive immigration law enacted by the U.S. Congress
DATE: Enacted on August 3, 1882

SIGNIFICANCE: Setting the basic course of United States immigration law and policy, the Immigration Act of 1882 established categories of foreigners deemed "undesirable" for entry and gave the U.S. secretary of the treasury authority over immigration enforcement.

The 1882 Immigration Act was the first comprehensive immigration law enacted by the federal government. As such, it would have enormous consequences for future immigration legislation. The act built the framework for federal oversight over immigration and delineated categories of "undesirables" who would be barred entry to the United States. Through the first century of American independence, immigration had been relatively open, with only occasional oversight and restrictions imposed by individual states. By the 1870's, however, increasing pressure was brought to bear against immigrants, especially Chinese laborers in California. In 1875, Congress passed the Page Law, which served to reduce immigration of women from Asia. Overall immigration continued to increase, however, with the year 1882 seeing the largest number of immigrants in American history: 788,992 persons. In response, Congress passed two historic immigration acts. The first was the Chinese Exclusion Act of 1882, suspending immigration of Chinese laborers.

The second was the Immigration Act of 1882, which was enacted on August 3 of that year. This act

was the first comprehensive immigration law to deal with federal oversight and categories of exclusion. As to oversight, the law gave power over immigration enforcement to the secretary of the treasury, who was already responsible for overseeing customs in U.S. ports. The Treasury Department was mandated to issue regulations for the orderly admission of immigrants and to collect a "head tax" of fifty cents for each arriving immigrant to defray administrative expenses.

The Treasury secretary was authorized to enter into contracts with individual states to administer immigration entry. As to categories of those deemed undesirable, the act prohibited the entry of "any convict, lunatic, idiot, or any person unable to take care of himself or herself without becoming a public charge." Carried over from the immigration rules of several states, the "public charge" doctrine served to bar arriving foreigners who could not show the financial ability to support themselves. Foreigners denied entry were returned to their starting points at the expense of the ship owners. Interestingly, the act made an exception for foreigners convicted of political offenses, reflecting the traditional American belief that the United States is a haven for those persecuted by foreign tyrants.

The specifics of the Immigration Act of 1882 would soon be amended, but the contours of federal oversight and categorical restrictions that it established would remain. In 1891, Congress established exclusive federal control over immigration through a superintendent of immigration, the forerunner of the Bureau of Immigration and Naturalization. States would no longer play a role in the official administration of immigration affairs.

In 1903, Congress, alarmed by the 1901 assassination of President William McKinley and by the specter of political radicalism and anarchism, acted to end the 1882 law's exemption for political offenses, forbidding immigration of persons "opposed to organized government." The exclusion of those likely to become public charges remained a fixed element of American immigration law, presenting a potential obstacle to poorer immigrants. In 1917, 1921, and 1924, Congress added exclusions by national origins to the list of undesirables. National origins quotas would be the centerpiece of immigration policy in the decades to follow. The specifics of the Immigration Act of 1882 had been

altered; however, its focus on federal oversight and exclusion by categories had set the framework for immigration law for the following century.

Howard Bromberg

Further Reading

Daniels, Roger. *Guarding the Golden Door: American Immigration Policy and Immigrants Since 1882.* New York: Hill & Wang, 2004.

Gunderson, Theodore. *Immigration Policy in Turmoil.* Huntington, N.Y.: Nova Science, 2002.

See also: Alien Contract Labor Law of 1885; Bureau of Immigration, U.S.; Chinese Exclusion Act of 1882; Congress, U.S.; Immigration Act of 1891; Immigration Act of 1903; Immigration Act of 1917; Immigration Act of 1921; Immigration Act of 1924; Immigration law; Page Law of 1875.

Immigration Act of 1891

The Law: Federal legislation that increased government regulation of immigration
Date: Enacted on March 3, 1891

> **Significance:** Beginning in 1882, responsibility for administering U.S. immigration law, excluding the Chinese exclusion law, rested with the individual states. In the Immigration Act of 1891, the U.S. Congress assigned responsibility for enforcing immigration policy to the federal government in an effort to increase the effectiveness of immigration law. The act also expanded the list of excludable and deportable aliens.

In the light of several concerns over immigration law, Congress passed the Immigration Act of 1891, which included provisions intended to secure closer inspection and provide more effective enforcement of immigration law. The 1891 act centralized responsibility for enforcement of immigration law in the federal executive branch, tightened regulation along the land borders, and expanded the list of excludable and deportable immigrants.

Of paramount importance to Congress in 1891 was the centralization of enforcement under the executive branch of the federal government. Under the Immigration Act of 1882, the secretary of

the treasury was responsible for executing the provisions of the act, but he did not hire and directly oversee the agents who would regulate immigration. The law mandated that state governors determine which state agency or officials would be responsible for enforcing federal immigration law. After the governor identified the agency, the secretary of the treasury then entered into contract with that state agency. By this law, the national government had broad authority over immigration restriction. While the secretary of the treasury was nominally responsible for immigration regulation, most of the responsibility rested with the states because the state agency responsible for enforcement immigration restriction continued to be state-based.

In the Immigration Act of 1891, Congress made the secretary of the treasury responsible for prescribing rules for inspection of the nation's coastal ports and its borders with Canada and Mexico. The 1891 act created the Office of Superintendent of Immigration. The new executive or bureaucratic office would comprise three clerks and a superintendent appointed by the president, who all worked under the jurisdiction of the secretary of the treasury. By 1894, this federal bureaucracy had become the Bureau of Immigration. The 1891 act, therefore, charged officers of the U.S. government, who were employed directly by the Office of Superintendent of Immigration, with carrying out the inspection and deportation of immigrants. Local or state officials would no longer directly enforce immigration restrictions. The superintendent of immigration was responsible for hearing appeals from aliens, but Congress assigned jurisdiction over cases arising out of the act to the circuit and district courts of the United States.

While the Immigration Act of 1882 regulated coastal borders, it did not regulate the contiguous borders, and immigrants crossing either the U.S.-Canadian or the U.S.-Mexican border entered the nation largely without inspection. Reports estimated that, in six months before the passage of the Immigration Act of 1891, as many as fifty thousand immigrants entered the United States from Canada without inspection. With the Immigration Act of 1891, Congress began tightening regulation of the U.S.-Mexican and the U.S.-Canadian borders.

The 1891 act also extended the federal government's power to deport immigrants beyond Chinese workers and contract laborers. The act listed all the existing categories of excludable immigrants: "idiots," the insane, paupers, and polygamists; persons liable to become a public charge; people convicted of a felony or other crime or misdemeanor involving moral turpitude; and sufferers "from a loathsome or dangerous" contagious disease. This act connected each of these excludable categories with a deportation provision, so that all these categories were now both excludable and deportable.

Torrie Hester

FURTHER READING

Daniels, Roger. *Guarding the Golden Door: American Immigration Policy and Immigrants Since 1882.* New York: Hill & Wang, 2004.

Hutchinson, Edward Prince. *Legislative History of American Immigration Policy, 1798-1965.* Philadelphia: University of Pennsylvania Press, 1981.

Salyer, Lucy. *Laws Harsh as Tigers: Chinese Immigrants and the Shaping of Modern Immigration Law.* Chapel Hill: University of North Carolina Press, 1995.

SEE ALSO: Alien Contract Labor Law of 1885; Bureau of Immigration, U.S.; Congress, U.S.; Deportation; Geary Act of 1892; History of immigration after 1891; Illegal immigration; Immigration Act of 1882; Immigration Act of 1903.

IMMIGRATION ACT OF 1903

THE LAW: Federal legislation that increased government regulation of immigration
DATE: Enacted on March 3, 1903

SIGNIFICANCE: The Immigration Act of 1903 expanded the federal government's power to regulate immigration. In this piece of legislation, Congress codified immigration law and refined the existing classes of inadmissible immigrants. Of even greater significance to the history of immigration was the act's creation of two new inadmissible classes: The first covered immigrants involved in prostitution, and the second dealt with anarchists.

Much of the Immigration Act of 1903 dealt with preexisting immigration law. In this new act, Congress codified immigration law and increased the tax on immigrants entering the United States, excluding Canadians and Mexicans. The law refined the federal regulation of poor immigrants by amending the contract labor and public charge provisions; it also extended the time limit on deporting aliens in most inadmissible classes from one to three years. In addition, Congress added prostitutes and those associated with prostitution, as well as anarchists, to the list of excludable or inadmissible classes of immigrants.

None of the immigration laws passed between 1875 and 1902 explicitly provided for the deportation of prostitutes. The Page Law, passed in 1875, only made the importation of prostitutes a felony and, in practice, provided for tougher screening of Chinese women in Hong Kong. Before 1903, the federal government did deport a small number of Chinese women suspected of prostitution, but it deported them as manual laborers in violation of the Chinese exclusion laws rather than as prostitutes. Under the Immigration Act of 1903, however, Congress empowered the Bureau of Immigration to exclude people involved in prostitution and to deport prostitutes as well as procurers of prostitutes, if they were immigrants too.

The Immigration Act of 1903 made immigrants excludable on political grounds for the first time by adding anarchists to the list of inadmissible classes. Responding to public fears about anarchists, which were heightened by the assassination of President William McKinley in 1901, Congress included a provision in the law that made anarchists or those who advocated violence against government excludable and deportable. John Turner, a British-born labor activist and self-proclaimed anarchist who was in the United States organizing workers, was one of the first people affected by the antianarchist provision of the Immigration Act of 1903. He challenged the constitutionality of the new anarchist provision in the U.S. courts. The U.S. Supreme Court upheld the anarchist provisions in the 1904 case *Turner v. Williams*. Congress would later refine and expand the anarchist provision, which immigration authorities used in the Palmer raids following World War I and against communists during the Cold War.

Torrie Hester

FURTHER READING
Chan, Sucheng. "The Exclusion of Chinese Women, 1870-1943." In *Entry Denied: Exclusion and the Chinese Community in America, 1882-1943.* Philadelphia: Temple University Press, 1991.
Langum, David J. *Crossing over the Line: Legislating Morality and the Mann Act.* Chicago: University of Chicago Press, 1994.
Preston, William, Jr. *Aliens and Dissenters: Federal Suppression of Radicals, 1903-1933.* Champaign: University of Illinois Press, 1963.

SEE ALSO: Congress, U.S.; Espionage and Sedition Acts of 1917-1918; History of immigration after 1891; Immigration Act of 1891; Immigration Act of 1907; Immigration Act of 1917; Immigration law; Industrial Workers of the World; Page Law of 1875; Progressivism; Women immigrants.

IMMIGRATION ACT OF 1907

THE LAW: Federal legislation regulating immigration
DATE: Signed into law on February 20, 1907

SIGNIFICANCE: This law created the Dillingham Commission to collect data used in future immigration laws, further narrowed Asian immigration, limited Muslim immigration, and expanded the definition of undesirable women immigrants.

In 1905, amid continuing concerns over increased immigration, President Theodore Roosevelt called upon the U.S. Congress to increase protection from unwanted immigration, especially in the nation's largest cities, and to codify earlier legislation. Roosevelt and Congress sought to exclude immigrants who would not make good citizens. In February, 1907, Congress passed a new immigration act that expanded previous immigration restrictions by prohibiting Asians from entering the United States through the territory of Hawaii, doubled the immigration head tax to four dollars per person, broadened the excludable classes of immigrants to include contract labor and subversive and presumably immoral groups, and required ships to allow minimum amounts of deck space for each

passenger and to provide manifests of their departing aliens.

Section 39 of the new law created the U.S. Immigration Commission—better known as the Dillingham Commission—to investigate immigration problems and their impact on the nation. The commission provided detailed reports to future Congresses regarding the need for refining immigration laws. The commission called on Congress to put the economic well-being of U.S. citizens above the needs of corporations that relied heavily on uneducated immigrants for cheap labor. The commission also favored further limiting immigration, implementing an alien literacy test, and continuing the Chinese exclusion policy and restricting Japanese and Korean immigration. The commissioners argued that Congress should limit the admission of unskilled aliens and implement a quota system.

The Immigration Act of 1907 was notable for several key innovations regarding immigration policy. Section 12 required ships with alien passengers departing the United States to provide complete lists of their passengers by name, age, sex, nationality, occupation, and place of residence in the United States. The information gathered through this law provided the first statistical documentation on alien departures. To combat the practice of polygamy and the keeping of concubines, the act expanded on the Immigration Act of 1891, which denied entry to polygamists, to include any persons who espoused these practices. The Ottoman Empire viewed these provisions as an attack on Islamic religious practices.

Women were a particular target of the 1907 law, which broadened the definition of prostitutes to include women arriving in the United States for any immoral purposes. The vague language of the law was used to exclude women in arranged marriages, especially those of Asian origin, and allowed for their deportation. Responding to concerns of progressive reformers, the act tightened laws targeting immigrant women suspected of being recruited to work as prostitutes. It also permitted the deportation of women who lived in known houses of prostitution or who had practiced prostitution within three years of their entering the United States. This was the first statutory provision authorizing deportation based on criminal conduct within the United States.

Linda Upham-Bornstein

FURTHER READING

Abrams, Kerry. "Polygamy, Prostitution, and the Federalization of Immigration Law." *Columbia Law Review* 105, no. 3 (2005): 641-716. Examination of the role marriage played in the development of immigration laws regarding women and Muslims.

Cott, Nancy F. *Public Vows: A History of Marriage and the Nation.* Cambridge, Mass.: Harvard University Press, 2000. Thoroughly researched account of the evolution of marriage in American legal and social practice.

Hutchinson, Edward P. *Legislative History of American Immigration Policy, 1798-1965.* Philadelphia: University of Pennsylvania Press, 1981. Survey of congressional actions on immigration, examining specific elements of those policies.

SEE ALSO: Congress, U.S.; Dillingham Commission; History of immigration after 1891; Immigration Act of 1891; Immigration Act of 1903; Immigration Act of 1917; Immigration law; Progressivism; Return migration; Women immigrants.

IMMIGRATION ACT OF 1917

THE LAW: Federal law imposing major new restrictions on categories of people allowed to immigrate

DATE: Went into effect on May 1, 1917

> **SIGNIFICANCE:** The Immigration Act of 1917 was the first federal law to impose a general restriction on immigration in the form of a literacy test. It also broadened restrictions on the immigration of Asians and persons deemed "undesirable" and provided tough enforcement provisions.

Through the first century of American independence, immigration into the United States was largely unrestricted. This open-door policy began to change during the 1870's and 1880's, with the introduction of federal legislation aimed at barring two classes of immigrants: Asian laborers to California and immigrants deemed physically and mentally "undesirable." In 1882, for example, Congress passed the Chinese Exclusion Act to bar the immigration of Chinese workers and a general immigra-

President Woodrow Wilson, with his wife, Edith, at his second inauguration in 1917. Wilson twice vetoed the Immigration Act of 1917, only to see Congress pass it over his objections. (Library of Congress)

tion act to bar the immigration of persons judged likely to become "public charges."

The general Immigration Act of 1882 also imposed a "head tax" of fifty cents on each immigrant. The U.S. Congress, which was constitutionally empowered to exercise exclusive jurisdiction over immigration, continued to increase restrictions through the late nineteenth and early twentieth centuries. The head tax was increased to four dollars by the Immigration Act of 1907. The Chinese Exclusion Act was amended and tightened in legislation enacted in 1884, 1888, 1892, and 1902. In the Gentlemen's Agreement of 1907, Japan agreed to bar its citizens from emigrating to the United States. The Immigration Act of 1891 added more categories of people to the list of "undesirable aliens," including persons with contagious diseases and polygamists. The Immigration Acts of 1903, 1907, and 1910 added rules to exclude persons with mental and physical defects, persons with tu-

berculosis, and anarchists. However, congressional provisions to add a literacy requirement to the immigration laws were vetoed by Presidents Grover Cleveland in 1896, William Howard Taft in 1913, and Woodrow Wilson in 1915.

PROVISIONS OF THE 1917 LAW

The Immigration Act of 1917 updated and codified much of the previous immigration legislation, thereby effectively repealing the Immigration Acts of 1903, 1907, and 1910. President Wilson vetoed the law, but Congress overrode his veto and the act went into effect on May 1, 1917. A long and comprehensive piece of legislation, the act contained thirty-eight subsections and took up twenty-five pages in the Congressional Session Laws.

The law was significant in five major areas; it

- increased the head tax
- expanded categories of "undesirable aliens"
- excluded South Asian immigrants
- added a literacy requirement
- contained new enforcement provisions

The new law increased the head tax levied on every adult immigrant to eight dollars and required liens to be was placed on passenger ships for nonpayment. The law's expansion of categories of "undesirables" who would be barred from entry reflected new theories of comparative psychology. The act excluded so-called "idiots, imbeciles, and feeble-minded persons;" persons of "constitutional psychopathic inferiority;" "mentally or physically defective" persons; the insane; alcoholics; persons with epilepsy, tuberculosis; or contagious diseases; paupers and vagrants; criminals; prostitutes; anarchists; polygamists; political radicals; and contract laborers.

The Immigration Act of 1917 also barred most immigration from Asia. Chinese immigrants were already barred by the Chinese Exclusion Acts and the Japanese by the Gentlemen's Agreement. In addition, the act created the "Asiatic Barred Zone," which encompassed India, Afghanistan, Persia (now Iran), Arabia, parts of the Ottoman Empire and Russia, Southeast Asia, and the Asian-Pacific islands.

Reflecting public hostility to southern and eastern European immigrants, the act required all adult immigrants to demonstrate an ability to read. Any language sufficed. Finally, the act contained

extensive provisions for enforcement. Penalties were imposed on any persons or corporations who encouraged or assisted the immigration of persons barred by the act or contract laborers. The act required all ships carrying immigrants to provide detailed information about each passenger's name, age, sex, physical description, literacy, nationality, destination, occupation, mental and physical health, and criminal record. Immigration inspectors, medical examiners, and Boards of Special Inquiry were authorized to carry out these regulations and decide on the admissibility of immigrants.

IMPACT OF THE LAW

The act of 1917 represented a further tightening of the immigrant restrictions begun by Congress during the 1870's. Although the 1880's witnessed the exclusion of "undesirables" and Chinese and the imposition of a head tax, the 1917 act greatly expanded these restrictions. The list of undesirables was couched in vague terms of mental and physical health, and could thus be interpreted in almost unlimited ways. The eight-dollar head tax was a significant levy on impoverished immigrants. The literacy requirement, which had been vetoed by three presidents, appeared to be a significant impediment to many immigrants. Heavy penalties and fines were imposed on any persons who seemingly assisted immigration in violation of the law. This expansion of restrictions can be explained, in part, by the rise of psychological and eugenics theories categorizing inferior individuals and races and nativist sentiments exacerbated by World War I.

The restrictions culminating in the 1917 act ultimately proved to be more qualitative than quantitative. In fact, the first two decades of the twentieth century saw the greatest numbers of immigrants up to that time: 8,795,386 people entered the United States between 1901 and 1910, and another 5,735,811 entered between 1911 and 1920. In the fiscal year between July, 1920, and June, 1921, more than 800,000 immigrants entered the country. Only about 1,450 persons were actually excluded by the literacy test. The 1917 act prefigured but differed from the immigration quotas that would be imposed by new immigration laws during the 1920's. These quotas greatly restricted immigration for the first time in American history and did so in an attempt to preserve the ethnic heritage of the United States as it was perceived at the turn of the century.

Howard Bromberg

FURTHER READING

Daniels, Roger. *Guarding the Golden Door: American Immigration Policy and Immigrants Since 1882.* New York: Hill & Wang, 2004. General history of immigration restrictions. Notes that the 1917 law represented the first major categorical restriction of immigration in American history.

Hing, Bill Ong. *Defining America Through Immigration Policy.* Philadelphia: Temple University Press, 2004. Chapter 3, on the 1917 literacy test, sees its origins in American animosity toward Italian and Jewish immigrants.

King, Desmond. *Making Americans: Immigration, Race, and the Origins of the Diverse Democracy.* Cambridge, Mass.: Harvard University Press, 2000. Scholarly study of the history of immigration that describes the 1917 act as replacing the tenet of individual selection for admission with group criteria.

Lee, Erika. *At America's Gates: Chinese Immigration During the Exclusion Era, 1882-1943.* Chapel Hill: University of North Carolina Press, 2003. Highlights the creation of the Asiatic Barred Zone as a milestone in restricting Asian immigration.

Shanks, Cheryl. *Immigration and the Politics of American Sovereignty, 1890-1990.* Ann Arbor: University of Michigan Press, 2001. Historical study of the relationship between immigration law and policy and notions of American sovereignty. Portrays the Asiatic Barred Zone as the predecessor of the quota laws of the 1920's and the literacy test as motivated by exclusionary rather than educational sentiments.

SEE ALSO: Asian immigrants; Asiatic Barred Zone; Chinese Exclusion Act of 1882; Chinese immigrants; Congress, U.S.; History of immigration after 1891; Immigration Act of 1882; Immigration Act of 1891; Immigration Act of 1903; Immigration Act of 1907; Immigration law; Literacy tests.

IMMIGRATION ACT OF 1921

THE LAW: Federal legislation limiting the immigration of aliens into the United States

DATE: Enacted and signed into law on May 19, 1921

ALSO KNOWN AS: Johnson Act; Emergency Quota Act of 1921

SIGNIFICANCE: The first federal law in U.S. history to limit the immigration of Europeans, the Immigration Act of 1921 reflected the growing American fear that people from southern and eastern European countries not only did not adapt well into American society but also threatened its very existence. The law specified that no more than 3 percent of the total number of immigrants from any specific country already living in the United States in 1910 could migrate to America during any year.

On May 19, 1921, the same day on which the law was passed by the U.S. Congress, recently inaugurated President Warren G. Harding signed the Emergency Quota Act into law. The premise of the act had been debated in the Congress for several years. Indeed, a version of the bill had passed during the previous session of Congress only to fall victim to a pocket veto by the ailing President Woodrow Wilson during the last days of his administration

The bill was a product of the Dillingham Commission, which had been chartered in 1907 and was chaired by Representative William P. Dillingham of Vermont. It represented several versions, the latest of which had been created by Representative Albert Johnson of Washington. Although concerns about undesirable immigration to the United States had been discussed for decades, and action had been taken to prevent the immi-

gration of most Asians, fears springing out of the aftermath of World War I again bestirred those who would close the floodgates of immigration.

According to federal officials scattered throughout European consulates, literally millions of Europeans hoped to emigrate to the United States in the aftermath of World War I (1914-1918). Some of these would-be immigrants could be considered as coming from the "desirable" classes of western and northern European nations, but it appeared that the vast majority of the potential immigrants would be coming from southern and eastern Europe.

Many Americans held the perception that individuals from southern and eastern Europe could not be assimilated properly into the culture of the United States. Their languages, customs, and religions were thought to be too different from those

Contemporary cartoon portraying the effectiveness of the Immigration Act of 1921 in reducing the flow of European immigrants to the United States to a mere trickle. (The Granger Collection, New York)

of preceding generations of immigrants for full-scale integration into American culture. The fear was that these newer immigrants would always be "hyphenates," or citizens who would call themselves, or be called by others, by such hyphenated names as "Polish-Americans," "Greek-Americans," and "Italian-Americans."

Beyond the fear of being swamped by unassimilable immigrants from eastern and southern Europe was the fear that these immigrants' increasing numbers would depress wages for American workers. In addition, some people feared the potential of the rising political power of the new class of immigrants. To counter the tide of uneducated, working-class immigrants, professionals were allowed to enter the United States with few restrictions, regardless of their nations of origin.

As signed into law, the 1921 bill required that no more than 3 percent of the number of persons from a nation living in the United States, as recorded in the census of 1910, could be admitted to the country in the forthcoming year. Taken to its ultimate understanding, the law allowed only about 357,000 people to immigrate to the United States during the 1922 fiscal year. Based on the 1910 population figures, the bill effectively limited emigration of northern and western Europeans to approximately 175,000 individuals. As this figure reflected almost precisely the numbers of immigrants from these regions during the years leading up to 1921, the bill had little impact on northern and western European immigration. The bill imposed no limitations on immigration from the Western Hemisphere.

The impact of the 1921 law on southern and eastern Europe was much different. Again basing its quotas on 1910 population figures, the bill effectively limited nations in these regions to about 175,000 individuals. However, in contrast to western and northern Europeans, immigrants from southern and eastern Europe had contributed approximately 685,000 persons during each of the years immediately prior to the passage of the 1921 law.

The bill was intended to be in effect for only a single year; however, it was not replaced until 1924. The significance of the 1921 bill lies in the fact that it was the first time Americans had actively and legally sought to limit European immigration.

Kimberly K. Porter

FURTHER READING

Briggs, Vernon M. *Mass Immigration and the National Interest: Policy Directions for the New Century.* Armonk, N.Y.: M. E. Sharpe, 2003.

Higham, John. *Strangers in the Land: Patterns of American Nativism.* New Brunswick, N.J.: Rutgers University Press, 1963.

Shanks, Cheryl. *Immigration and the Politics of American Sovereignty, 1880-1990.* Ann Arbor: University of Michigan Press, 2001.

SEE ALSO: Congress, U.S.; Dillingham Commission; European immigrants; History of immigration after 1891; Immigration Act of 1903; Immigration Act of 1907; Immigration Act of 1917; Immigration Act of 1924; Immigration law.

IMMIGRATION ACT OF 1924

THE LAW: Federal legislation that set immigration quotas for individual countries that were based on the number of foreign nationals living in the United States in 1890

DATE: Signed into law on May 26, 1924

ALSO KNOWN AS: National Origins Act; Johnson-Reed Act; Asian Exclusion Act

SIGNIFICANCE: The act represented the first major attempt to restrict immigration into the United States. The establishment of a quota system limited immigration from southern and eastern Europe (primarily Jewish and Slavic) while allowing significant immigration from northern and western Europe. Asians were specifically excluded from immigration.

The Immigration Act of 1924 was a continuation of the Immigration Act of 1917 and attempted to fix loopholes in immigration restriction established by the earlier law. In the decades prior to 1917, what was effectively unlimited immigration resulted in nearly ten million people legally entering the United States. Many of these people came from eastern Europe and Russia. The onset of World War I significantly reduced the ability of Europeans to enter the United States. The war itself, and the subsequent entry of the United States into the war in April, 1917, resulted in a nationalistic fervor

within the American population that in turn resulted in modifications to existing immigration laws. The effect was to severely alter the demographics of those permitted to enter the country.

IMMIGRATION ACT OF 1917

Previous immigration laws, particularly those that governed immigration from Japan—Chinese were already barred, the result of the Chinese Exclusion Act of 1882—were largely restrictive solely on the basis of a "Gentlemen's Agreement": Since 1907, Japan had voluntarily restricted emigration of its citizens to the United States. The major concern of the Immigration Act of 1917 was the large influx of eastern Europeans, many of them illiterate, as well as "Asiatics"—the term used for Asians. In February, 1917, the act was passed over the veto of President Woodrow Wilson and became law. Provisions of the act included the exclusion of "undesirables" such as criminals, those deemed insane or "idiots," and alcoholics. The most controversial portion of the act, creating an "Asiatic Barred Zone," kept out immigrants from eastern Asia, particularly those from India. The Philippines were not included since the islands were an American possession, nor was Japan included.

Other provisions increased the "head tax" to eight dollars. Finally, a literacy test was imposed on future immigrants. Any persons over the age of sixteen would have to be literate. However, this particular provision was relatively loose in its restrictions. As long as a husband was literate, neither his wife nor other family members had to be literate as well. The literacy test proved to be of no more than minor significance. During the last year in which the act was law—July, 1920, to June, 1921—only some fourteen hundred immigrants were denied entry as a result of illiteracy, compared with more than one million who attempted to enter. Nevertheless, the act of 1917 represented the first broad attempt to restrict immigration into the United States.

IMMIGRATION ACT OF 1921

The recognition that more than 800,000 immigrants had been admitted to the United States during 1920-1921 illustrated the loose restrictions imposed by the immigration law of 1917. Of particular concern was the fear that many of these immigrants from Russia or eastern Europe, many of them Jewish, were Bolsheviks or other kinds of radicals. The Red Scare (1919-1920) represented a symptom of the growing concern that revolutions taking place in Europe could spread to American shores. The Immigration Act of 1921, while merely a stopgap until more encompassing legislation could be passed, reflected that fear. Unlike the 1917 law, the 1921 act limited the annual number of immigrants from each country to 3 percent of that nation's nationals present in the United States according to the 1910 U.S. Census. Total immigration was set at 357,000 persons.

THE 1924 LAW

Introduced by Congressman Albert Johnson in the House of Representatives and David Reed in the Senate, the Immigration Act of 1924 was intended to permanently restrict the immigration numbers from "undesirable" areas of the world—particularly from Russia and eastern Europe.

In addition to having fears about radicalism, congressional leaders were concerned about the large influx of workers willing to work for substandard wages; not surprisingly, among the supporters of the bill were the leaders of the growing unions among American workers. The fear of "cheap labor" was largely directed toward eastern Europeans. During World War I, large numbers of Latin American workers, particularly from Mexico, had entered the United States to supplement the labor force related to war industries or farming, especially in the sparsely populated Southwest. The importance of these workers was reflected in their exemption from the quota system as established by the act. In the years prior to implementation of the act, immigrants from Latin America represented approximately 30 percent of total immigration.

Changes in the demographics of the United States in the years between 1880 and 1920 played perhaps the most significant role in defining the language of the bill. The perception had been that the United States had been settled largely by western European stock, primarily Protestant, and nearly entirely white. Black people, freed from slavery only in recent generations, and mostly uneducated and living in poverty, were either excluded or simply ignored in the argument.

By the 1920's, nearly one-third of the American population consisted of immigrants and their families. The birthrate among this segment of the population suggested that the proportion of the

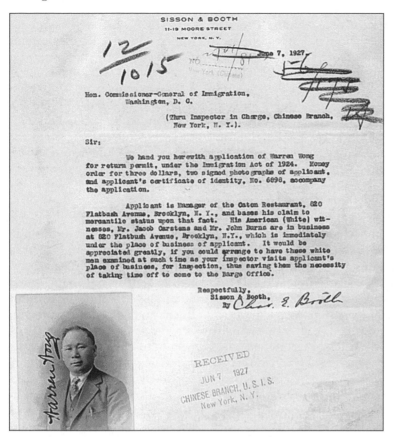

Application for the readmission to the United States of a Brooklyn restaurateur who had returned to China for a visit. The letter cites the terms of the Immigration Act of 1924. (NARA)

population they represented would continue to increase. Moreover, intelligence tests administered to U.S. Army recruits during World War I were interpreted to mean that southern and eastern Europeans were of lesser intelligence than northern Europeans. The mythology of the superiority of the Nordics, or northern and western Europeans, was addressed in a popular book written by the American anthropologist Madison Grant, *The Passing of the Great Race* (1916). Grant argued that both physical and mental characteristics of eastern European immigrants were below the standards of the dominant Protestant stock. Unless restrictions were placed on this population—and a program of eugenics was considered as a portion of such control—both the quality of life and the characteristics of a Protestant-dominated society would suffer. Limits to immigration represented the clearest support for Grant's arguments. The effect on Asian

or African immigration was even greater. The 1924 act excluded Asians "and their descendants" as well as descendants of "slave immigrants."

The greatest influx of immigrants from eastern Europe had occurred in the two to three decades prior to the start of World War I in 1914. Thus, the basis for the quota was changed from the U.S. Census of 1910 to that of 1890, when far fewer southern and eastern Europeans had resided in the United States. Furthermore, the quota was reduced from 3 percent to 2 percent of the number of foreign-born persons of each nationality resident in the United States in 1890. By 1929, the 2-percent quota was replaced by a total annual immigration cap of 150,000.

Other changes were meant to increase the monetary cost to potential immigrants, another means to restrict the poor. The head tax was increased to nine dollars, while requirements for both visas and photographs were implemented. The cost of the visa was nine dollars. This meant that families with several children might have to pay fifty dollars or more, on top of the cost of travel by ship, which might have been ten to twenty dollars per passenger. The significance of the visa was not only at the port of entry. In this manner, consulates at the country of origin also had a mechanism to regulate who was permitted to immigrate to the United States. Since members of the consulate determined which applicants could obtain visas, they exercised significant discretion as to who would be acceptable. In theory, only "desirables" would be issued such visas.

CONSEQUENCES OF THE ACT OF 1924

The most immediate impact of the new law was the restriction of eastern Europeans, particularly Jews, from entering the United States. Between 1880 and 1924, approximately two million European Jews entered the country. In the year after

passage of the new immigration law, fewer than 10,000 European Jews were able to enter on an annual basis. Similar effects were observed among other eastern Europeans. Between 1921 and 1929, the average number of Poles entering the United States was reduced from an annual average of 95,000 to fewer than 10,000. The number of German immigrants, however, because of reduced restrictions—and a larger quota—increased during this period to a high of 45,000 annually, a number exceeded by British subjects to 50,000 annually. Between 1924 and the years immediately following World War II, total immigration was below three million people.

The long-term effects on European Jewry proved particularly devastating. With the limited quotas, European Jews in general, and French, Polish, and German Jews in particular, were largely unable to obtain visas during the years leading up to World War II, during which some six million Jews died at the hands of the Nazis. While Jewish refugees such as Albert Einstein were often epitomized as examples of the openness of American society to European refugees, the reality was that only several thousand Jews, mostly the highly educated, were able to enter the United States.

The national quotas were slightly modified in 1929. However, the system as established by the act of 1924 remained largely in place until 1952. Family members of U.S. citizens were not included in quota numbers, while women were not afforded equal status until the changes of 1952.

Richard Adler

FURTHER READING

Daniels, Roger. *Coming to America: A History of Immigration and Ethnicity in American Life.* New York: HarperPerennial, 2002. History of immigration beginning with the earliest settlements. The significance of various immigration acts and restrictions is explored.

_____. *Guarding the Golden Door: American Immigration Policy and Immigrants Since 1882.* New York: Hill & Wang, 2004. Synopsis of the evolution of immigration policies since the 1880's. Highlighted are specific laws associated with major immigration legislation.

Higham, John. *Strangers in the Land: Patterns of American Nativism, 1860-1925.* New Brunswick, N.J.: Rutgers University Press, 2002. Examines the history of nativism and its significance to the sociology and economics of the developing United States.

LeMay, Michael, and Elliott Robert Barkan, eds. *U.S. Immigration and Naturalization Laws and Issues: A Documentary History.* Westport, Conn.: Greenwood Press, 1999. Collection of documents that covers the history of immigration laws beginning with the colonial period. Relevant court cases are discussed.

Lowe, Lisa. *Immigrant Acts: On Asian American Cultural Politics.* Durham, N.C.: Duke University Press, 1999. Explores the significance of the Asian community in America, its history and response to prejudice.

Wenger, Beth. *The Jewish Americans: Three Centuries of Jewish Voices in America.* New York: Doubleday, 2007. Immigration, challenges, and growth of the Jewish community in America. Includes the effects of laws regulating immigration on the Jewish population.

SEE ALSO: Asian immigrants; Congress, U.S.; European immigrants; Gentlemen's Agreement; History of immigration after 1891; Immigration Act of 1907; Immigration Act of 1917; Immigration Act of 1921; Immigration and Nationality Act of 1952; Immigration law; Jewish immigrants; Quota systems.

IMMIGRATION ACT OF 1943

THE LAW: Federal legislation that lifted a government ban on Chinese immigration
DATE: Signed into law on December 17, 1943
ALSO KNOWN AS: Chinese Exclusion Repeal Act of 1943; Magnuson Act

SIGNIFICANCE: At the height of World War II, when the United States needed to promote goodwill with China, Congress repealed an 1882 federal immigration statute restricting all Chinese from entering the country and considerably eased the process of naturalization for those Chinese already residing in America.

Beginning with the discovery of gold in California in 1848, Chinese immigrants flooded into the state, driven from their home by waves of civil unrest and

Congressman Warren G. Magnuson in December, 1944. (Time & Life Pictures/Getty Images)

catastrophic famines. Even as the prospect of gold mining diminished, these immigrants found ready work building the transcontinental railroad, a massive engineering project that involved brutal work conditions in inhospitable environments. More than seventeen hundred miles of track were laid in six years, thanks largely to Chinese immigrant labor. Once the work was completed in 1869, however, as the Chinese immigrants returned to California urban areas and began working menial jobs, largely food service and laundry, they became the subject of nearly a decade of discrimination and violence driven by heated (and xenophobic) rhetoric that defined their presence as an economic hardship. In addition, because these immigrants did not share the language or religion of Americans, they were viewed with a keener hostility than were European immigrants.

By 1882, more than 300,000 Chinese had emi-grated—a number viewed with alarm—fueling the passage of the 1882 Chinese Exclusion Act, which essentially closed America to any Chinese immigrants and denied citizenship to any Chinese already residing in the United States. It was the first time Congress had ever prohibited specific immigration. Initially, the ban was to last for ten years, but it was extended and ultimately made permanent in 1902. Numerous lawsuits unsuccessfully challenged the act as discriminatory, racist, and a violation of the Fourteenth Amendment.

Lifting the ban on Chinese immigration reflected political expediency during World War II. In the middle of a difficult land war in the Far East, with Japan using America's anti-Chinese sentiments as propaganda in an effort to derail China's alliance with the Allied Powers, the U.S. War Department moved to have the Chinese Exclusion Act rescinded. Sponsored by Washington State Democratic representative (later six-term senator) Warren G. Magnuson, himself a veteran of naval service in the Far East theater earlier in the war, the Immigration Act of 1943 proposed lifting the ban on Chinese immigration, setting a quota on the number of visas to be granted annually at 105. (The policy at the time was to allow annually 2 percent of that immigrant population already living in America.)

The token quota did not mollify those who feared the economic and cultural impact of any surge of Far East immigrants: Chinese immigrants could pursue entry into the country through other nations. To assuage such xenophobic fears, Congress determined that for the Chinese, immigration status would be determined not by country of origin (as it was for Europeans) but rather by ethnicity. Thus, if a Chinese family living in the Philippines applied for entry, they would be counted as Chinese.

President Franklin D. Roosevelt backed the compromise. It passed both houses of Congress and was signed on December 17, 1943. It would take more than twenty years of immigration reform legislation, culminating in the 1965 Immigration and Nationality Act, to eliminate the quota system.

Joseph Dewey

FURTHER READING

Chang, Iris. *The Chinese in America: A Narrative History.* New York: Viking Press, 2003.

Lee, Erika. *At America's Gate: Chinese Immigration During the Exclusion Era, 1882-1943*. Chapel Hill: University of North Carolina Press, 2007.

Yung, Judy, Gordon Chang, and Him Mark Lai, eds. *Chinese American Voices: From the Gold Rush to the Present*. Berkeley: University of California Press, 2006.

SEE ALSO: Angel Island Immigration Station; Anti-Chinese movement; Asian immigrants; Chinese Exclusion Act of 1882; Chinese immigrants; Congress, U.S.; Fiancées Act of 1946; Geary Act of 1892; History of immigration after 1891; Immigration Act of 1924; *United States v. Ju Toy*; World War II.

IMMIGRATION ACT OF 1990

THE LAW: Federal legislation that increased quotas for legal immigration into the United States

DATE: Enacted on November 29, 1990

SIGNIFICANCE: This legislation has been seen as a return to the pre-1920's open door immigration policy of the United States. It allowed for an increase in the number of legal immigrants into the United States and waived many of the conditions that had previously restricted immigration of certain groups. The act allowed for sanctuary in the country and increased the numbers of work visas and visas awarded to immigrants hoping to become permanent residents of the United States.

The Immigration Act of 1990 allowed for an increase of those seeking immigrant visas. Such visas are given for numerous reasons, but are primarily granted to foreign workers seeking permission to work or become permanent residents of the United States. This category includes persons sponsored by American employers and by family members already in the United States, and priority and skilled workers, including college professors, athletes, and professionals in the arts, sciences, and medical fields.

The primary goal of the Immigration Act was to supplement the depleting skilled worker class of the United States. Many leaders in government feared that illegal immigration was flooding the workforce with unskilled and non-English speaking workers who threatened slowly to push skilled labor jobs out of the United States to other nations with less stringent labor laws, such as Mexico and India. The act allowed for an increase from roughly the 50,000 immigrant visas per year of the past to 140,000 visas by the end of the fiscal year 1991 for skilled positions. For the majority of these positions, employers or employees were to submit documentation showing that no skilled American workers were available for the jobs offered to immigrants. Some opponents of the law argued that this important requirement was often ignored by American employers seeking cheaper labor.

In addition to allowing skilled immigrant laborers into the United States, the act allowed for the creation of additional visas to be granted via a lottery system. This lottery system became important for immigrants from countries not regarded by the U.S. government as reliable providers of skilled and priority labor. To allow for an increase in immigrants from previously nonpriority countries, the 1990 law eased the requirements for English-language competency during the immigration phase and simplified the previously lengthy process for seeking permanent residence in the United States. Although standards were generally lowered, the United States still placed a cap on the total numbers of immigrants allowed per year. The cap was 675,000-700,000 through the first five years the law was in effect, and it remained steady at afterward. At the same time, to avoid overrepresentation from any single country, a limit of 48,000 was placed on the total number of immigrants from one nation.

The first several years after passage of the law saw a steady increase in skilled labor immigrants. The 1990 act was the first major overhaul in U.S. immigration law since the 1960's, and its passage prompted increased numbers of both skilled and nonskilled laborers from other nations to immigrate. The largest increases in legal immigration came from Mexico and the Philippines. Other nations that saw increases in numbers of immigrants during the first five years the law was in effect were India, Canada, China, and many African countries.

IMPACT OF THE LAW

The Immigration Act of 1990 was enacted primarily to increase skilled labor positions in the

United States. As a result, the medical fields (such as doctors), the arts, sciences, education (including professors), and athletes all experienced increases in the number of skilled positions in the United States. In an attempt to lure and keep these skilled workers in the country, other laws pertaining to deportation and exclusion were weakened.

This weakening of other laws, as well as new rules and regulations for accepting nonimmigrant visas, accepting immigrants of previously disallowed countries, and the increase in temporary work visas, allowed nonskilled workers to find many loopholes in the new immigration law. This unexpected event produced both positive and negative effects. First, the increase in skilled workers allowed the United States to compensate for the depletion of skilled workers in many fields. However, the parallel increase in nonskilled laborers aggravated problems already evident in the country, notably an overflow of non-English speaking, nonskilled workers. Meanwhile, the positive and negative effects of the law increased the need for policing the nation's borders and ports of entry. The overall effect of the act increased border patrol spending, safety, and procedures for handling high-priority cases for the country.

Keith J. Bell

FURTHER READING

Geyer, Georgia Anne. *Americans No More.* New York: Atlantic Monthly Press, 1996. Critical examination of the impact of the Immigration Act of 1990, which Geyer describes as the "most comprehensive reform of our immigration laws in sixty-six years."

LeMay, Michael C., and Elliott Robert Barkan, eds. *U.S. Immigration and Naturalization Laws and Issues: A Documentary History.* Westport, Conn.: Greenwood Press, 1999. Broad history of U.S. immigration laws supported by extensive extracts from actual documents.

National Immigration Project. *Immigration Act of 1990 Handbook: The Complete Practical Guide to the 1990 Act.* 9 vols. New York: Clark, Boardman, Callaghan, 1991-1999. Massively detailed guide to the 1990 law.

Shanks, Cheryl. *Immigration and the Politics of American Sovereignty, 1890-1990.* Ann Arbor: University of Michigan Press, 2001. Scholarly study of changes in federal immigration laws from the late nineteenth century through the Immigration Act of 1990. Pays particular attention to changing quota systems and exclusionary policies.

SEE ALSO: Congress, U.S.; Economic consequences of immigration; Guest-worker programs; History of immigration after 1891; Illegal Immigration Reform and Immigrant Responsibility Act of 1996; Immigration and Nationality Act of 1965; Immigration and Naturalization Service, U.S.; Immigration law; Select Commission on Immigration and Refugee Policy.

IMMIGRATION AND NATIONALITY ACT OF 1952

THE LAW: Federal legislation that removed restrictions on Asian immigration while also tightening government control over suspected subversive organizations and individuals

DATE: Enacted on June 27, 1952

ALSO KNOWN AS: McCarran-Walter Act

SIGNIFICANCE: This federal law upheld the national origins quota system established by the Immigration Act of 1924, which gave preference to individuals of northern and western European lineage. It also created a system of preferences for skilled workers and relatives of citizens and permanent residents, repealed the last of the existing measures to exclude Asian immigration, and enacted strict security provisions over suspected subversives and "undesirable aliens."

Named for its congressional sponsors and passed by Congress over President Harry S. Truman's veto, the McCarran-Walter Act, or Immigration and Nationality Act of 1952, reaffirmed the quota system designed during the 1920's that favored northern and western Europeans. At the same time, however, it also removed a racist restriction—"aliens ineligible for citizenship"—that had been used against Asian immigration for generations, while keeping the small number of quotas in place. It gave first preference to highly qualified immigrants with skills urgently needed in the United

PREFERENCES UNDER THE 1952 LAW

- First: highly qualified professionals with desirable skills
- Second: parents of U.S. citizens
- Third: spouses and unmarried adult children of resident aliens
- Fourth: other relatives, brothers, sisters, and married children of resident aliens

States, along with the spouses and children of such immigrants. Other preferences depended on family relationships.

The law's quota numbers for European immigrants were raised slightly from the 1920 base of 154,000, to 158,000, and northwestern Europe was allocated 85 percent of these slots, with Great Britain (65,000), Germany (26,000) and Ireland (18,000) receiving two-thirds of the total. The number for Asian nations was set at 2,000 visas annually. No quota restrictions were placed on spouses and minor children of U.S. citizens and on immigrants from the Western Hemisphere. During the ensuing decades, the law would have a significant impact on immigration from Mexico and other Latin American nations. The legislation also made deportation easier and provided for fines and imprisonment for any person convicted of harboring an undocumented alien.

The legislation also sought to raise legal barriers, even preventing temporary visitor visas, against suspected subversives and persons regarded as "undesirable aliens." Section 212(a) of the law listed thirty-one categories of inadmissible aliens, including those

> who write or publish . . . or who knowingly circulate, distribute, print, or display, any written or printed matter, advocating or teaching opposition to all organized government, or advocating or teaching . . . the economic, international, and governmental doctrines of world communism.

President Truman and his supporters thought that any political litmus test of that nature was against America's traditions of freedom of thought and expression, and political belief.

During the 1970's and 1980's, a number of high-profile cases highlighted the "undesirable aliens" section of the McCarran-Walter Act. Under this provision, visas were denied to such "undesirable aliens" as Colombian novelist and Nobel laureate Gabriel García Márquez, British author and later Nobel laureate Doris Lessing, Chilean poet and Nobel laureate Pablo Neruda, British author Graham Greene, and Canadian writer Farley Mowat. All these distinguished persons were denied normal visas to enter the United States because they did not meet the ideological-exclusion provisions of the Immigration and Nationality Act of 1952.

John Boyd

FURTHER READING

Bon Tempo, Carl J. *Americans at the Gate: The United States and Refugees During the Cold War.* Princeton, N.J.: Princeton University Press, 2008.

Daniels, Roger. *Guarding the Golden Door: American Immigration Policy and Immigrants Since 1882.* New York: Hill & Wang, 2004.

Tichenor, Daniel J. *Dividing Lines: The Politics of Immigration Control in America.* Princeton, N.J.: Princeton University Press, 2002.

SEE ALSO: Congress, U.S.; History of immigration after 1891; Hull-House; Immigration Act of 1924; Immigration and Nationality Act of 1965; Immigration law; Luce-Celler Bill of 1946; McCarran Internal Security Act of 1950; "Undesirable aliens."

IMMIGRATION AND NATIONALITY ACT OF 1965

THE LAW: Federal legislation that eased restrictions on non-European immigration
DATE: Signed into law on October 3, 1965
ALSO KNOWN AS: Hart-Celler Act

SIGNIFICANCE: This first major change in U.S. quota policy greatly altered the ethnic makeup of immigrants entering the United States during the late twentieth and early twenty-first centuries and prompted a massive increase in total immigration.

During the 1920's, the federal government set fixed immigration quotas for each country of origin. During the very late nineteenth century and the early twentieth century, the United States had experienced heavy immigration from southern and eastern Europe. Because earlier European American settlers had come mostly from northern and western Europe, many policy makers believed that the more recent immigrants would not fit easily into American society. Accordingly, Congress passed immigration laws in 1921 and 1924 that set quotas for the numbers of immigrants from each region who would be admitted into the country. These quotas were based on the numbers of immigrants who had arrived during earlier eras. The quota system therefore favored northern and western European immigrants.

IMMIGRATION AND NATIONALITY ACT OF 1952

The Immigration and Nationality Act of 1952, also known as the McCarran-Walter Act, retained the national-origin criterion of the 1920's. It also added an overall limit to the numbers of immigrants from each country who would be admitted and within that limit gave each country a cap equal to 1 percent of the persons of that national origin who had been living in the United States in 1920. The 1952 law also added a series of preferences to the national origins system. The first basis rested on an economic criterion, giving first preference to immigrants with valuable skills. Other preferences, however, rested on the social norm that family relationships should enjoy a special status. For example, parents of existing U.S. citizens constituted the second preference, spouses and children

President Lyndon B. Johnson signing the Immigration and Nationality Act of 1965, which substantially changed U.S. immigration policy toward non-Europeans. Johnson made a point of signing the legislation near the base of the Statue of Liberty, which had long stood as a symbol of welcome to immigrants. Lower Manhattan can be seen in the background. (Lyndon B. Johnson Library Collection/Yoichi R. Okamoto)

of resident aliens the third, and other relatives the fourth.

In 1965, Congress amended the 1952 immigration law. In part, this change was a response to the Cold War politics of the time. American lawmakers were concerned about competition with communist nations and believed that more open immigration policies would reflect well on the reputation of the United States abroad. A major stimulus to this new legislation was the opposition to racially discriminatory laws arising during the Civil Rights era. Michigan's Democratic senator Philip Hart, one of the sponsors of the 1965 reform, declared that the effort to maintain the American creed and to protect the American political heritage required that American immigration policy become more consistent with democratic moral and ethical principles.

The new immigration bill was initially introduced in the House of Representatives by New York Democratic representative Emmanuel Celler, and Hart cosponsored it in the Senate. Massachusetts Democratic senator Edward Kennedy was one of the strongest advocates for the new immigration law. President Lyndon B. Johnson also strongly favored the legislation. Other lawmakers objected that the proposed change would lead to a massive increase in immigration and that many new arrivals would be from nations other than the European countries that had historically provided most of America's immigrants. Both President Johnson and Senator Kennedy argued, in response, that the law would bring few changes in either the numbers or the origins of immigrants. The House of Representatives approved the bill by a vote of 326 to 69 and the Senate by 76 to 18. On October 3, 1965, President Johnson signed it into law at the foot of the Statue of Liberty, an important icon to immigrants.

PROVISIONS OF THE 1965 LAW

When the act went into effect on July 1, 1968, it established an annual ceiling of 170,000 immigrants from the Eastern Hemisphere, with each country in the Eastern Hemisphere limited to 20,000 immigrants. At the same time, however, the law initially permitted the entry of children, parents, and spouses of American citizens without limitations. Consequently, nearly three-quarters of the 20,000 immigrants permitted from each Eastern Hemisphere country were to be admitted on the basis of family reunification. Another 6 percent were to be accepted as refugees from repressive communist regimes and 20 percent because they had special skills or other qualifications. Immigrants from the Western Hemisphere were limited to 120,000 per year, initially without the system of preferences.

Although the 1965 act was later amended several times, family reunification has continued to be the primary basis for immigrant admission. The first preference for quota immigrants is unmarried children, of any age, of U.S. citizens. Spouses of resident aliens and unmarried children of residents fall into the second preference. In practice, this means that after unmarried children of U.S. citizens who have applied for U.S. residence in a given year have been granted visas, the next quota slots are filled first by spouses and unmarried children of noncitizen alien residents. The third preference goes to professionals and persons of exceptional ability in the arts and sciences who intend to work for American employers. Married children, of any age, of U.S. citizens receive the fourth preference. The fifth preference goes to noncitizen sisters and brothers of U.S. citizens. Skilled and unskilled workers coming to take jobs for which American workers are in short supply are classified as the sixth preference.

Amendments to the law have allowed some immigrants outside the quota categories to be admitted without yearly numerical limitations. The greatest number of these are spouses of American citizens. Others, such as political refugees, can also enter the United States without being counted as part of the overall ceiling.

CONSEQUENCES OF THE LAW

Contrary to the predictions of Senator Kennedy and President Johnson, the 1965 immigration law was followed by both an enormous increase in immigration and changes in the countries of origin. From 1971 to 1980, 4,493,000 immigrants were admitted into the United States, an increase of 1,171,000 over the years from 1961 to 1970. The increase in numbers accelerated in the decades that followed. By 1990, of the estimated 21,596,000 foreign-born people living in the United States, about 43 percent had arrived during the 1980's. By the year 2007, more than 38 million immigrants

lived in the United States, accounting for about 12 percent of the country's total residents.

Meanwhile, the primary countries of origin shifted from Europe to Latin America and Asia. By the late 1990's, about one-half of all immigrants in the United States were coming from Latin America and about one-quarter from Asia. During the last three decades of the twentieth century, immigration was the primary source of demographic change and population growth in the United States. As a result, scholars in this field use the term "post-1965 immigration" to refer to the new trends that followed the change in law.

Carl L. Bankston III

FURTHER READING

Capaldi, Nicholas, ed. *Immigration: Debating the Issues.* Amherst, N.Y.: Prometheus Books, 1997. Collection of essays examining current U.S. immigration policy and its effects from a variety of perspectives.

Isbister, John. *The Immigration Debate.* West Hartford, Conn.: Kumarian Press, 1996. Extended essay on issues arising from changing federal immigration policy by an economist who is himself an immigrant and the son of a former deputy minister of citizenship and immigration in the Canadian government.

LeMay, Michael C. *Anatomy of a Public Policy: The Reform of Contemporary American Immigration Law.* Westport, Conn.: Praeger, 1974. Scholarly exploration of changes in U.S. immigration policy with particular attention to the Immigration Act of 1965.

LeMay, Michael C., and Elliott Robert Barkin, eds. *U.S. Immigration and Naturalization Laws and Issues: A Documentary History.* Westport, Conn.: Greenwood Press, 1999. Collection of more than one hundred primary documents—ranging from court cases and laws to editorials—on modern immigration issues. Includes edited versions of the Immigration Act of 1965 and other laws that make them easy for students to understand.

Shanks, Cheryl. *Immigration and the Politics of American Sovereignty, 1880-1990.* Ann Arbor: University of Michigan Press, 2001. Study of the history of U.S. immigration policy showing how government criteria for admitting immigration have shifted from race to political ideology, wealth, and job skills.

Waters, Mary C., and Reed Ueda, eds. *The New Americans: A Guide to Immigration Since 1965.* Cambridge, Mass.: Harvard University Press, 2007. Study of modern trends in U.S. immigration that assesses the impact of the Immigration Act of 1965 on American society and government policy.

SEE ALSO: Asian immigrants; Congress, U.S.; History of immigration after 1891; Immigration Act of 1921; Immigration Act of 1924; Immigration and Nationality Act of 1952; Immigration law; Latin American immigrants; Quota systems.

IMMIGRATION AND NATURALIZATION SERVICE, U.S.

IDENTIFICATION: Department of Justice agency formerly responsible for upholding all immigration laws

DATE: Operated from 1933 until March 1, 2003

ALSO KNOWN AS: INS

SIGNIFICANCE: The U.S. Immigration and Naturalization Service was long the primary federal agency responsible for the protection and enforcement of laws guiding the immigration and naturalization processes. It was also responsible for investigating, arresting, prosecuting, and deporting aliens who entered the United States illegally. After the agency was dissolved in 2003, its functions were distributed among three new federal agencies.

Through its seventy-year history, the U.S. Immigration and Naturalization Service, or INS, was the branch of the U.S. Department of Justice that handled both legal and illegal immigration matters. During the eighteenth and early nineteenth centuries, the U.S. population expanded exponentially with immigrants pouring into the country from all over the world. These early immigrants entered the country without having to carry documents or meet the requirements of immigration law.

GOVERNMENT REORGANIZATION

In 1891, the federal government created the U.S. Bureau of Immigration within the Department of the Treasury to oversee the administration of immigration law. After going through several administrative reorganizations and cabinet department shifts, the bureau was combined with the previously separate Bureau of Naturalization into the Immigration and Naturalization Service within the Department of Labor. Put in charge of controlling all aspects of illegal immigration into the United States, this new agency oversaw the U.S. Border Patrol.

In 1940, President Franklin D. Roosevelt transferred the INS from the Department of Labor to the Department of Justice. Over the ensuing decades, the duties and responsibilities of the INS continued to evolve. The agency experienced a dark period during World War II, when it was put in charge of operating and maintaining internment camps and detention centers for enemy aliens and sympathizers. Through the balance of the twentieth century, the agency concentrated on cracking down on illegal immigration resulting from weak border patrol and surveillance efforts. As new laws were enacted, the INS and Border Patrol became essential tools in the fight against domestic and foreign terrorism while continuing to regulate the flow of legal immigrants into the United States.

STRUCTURE OF THE INS

After being reassigned to the Department of Justice, the INS was restructured internally. Its top administrators were commissioners appointed by the president of the United States. The commissioners reported directly to the U.S. attorneys general. A comparatively large bureaucratic agency, the INS comprised four main subdivisions: programs, field operations, policy and planning, and management. Its Programs Division handled all functions pertaining to enforcement and investigations, including arrest, detention, and deportation of undocumented immigrants as well as the regulation and processing of all legal aliens attempting to enter the country.

The Field Operations Division was accountable for the oversight of numerous INS field offices both at home and abroad. It was responsible for the implementation of policies and delegated tasks for its three regional offices. In turn, administrators from these regional offices oversaw thirty-three districts and twenty-one border-area offices throughout the United States. Globally, the Field Operations Division was also tasked with directing the INS's Office of International Affairs headquarters that provided oversight for sixteen offices in other countries. Additionally, the division worked directly with the United Nations, the U.S. Department of State, and the U.S. Department of Health and Human Services to ensure that human and civil rights of all who entered the United States, both legally and illegally would, be safeguarded.

The third major division of the INS, the Office of Policy and Planning, oversaw coordinating, housing, and distributing all information related to immigration-related services. This division was also responsible for official communications with other cooperating federal agencies and the general public, along with all research and evaluation efforts.

The fourth office of the INS was the Management Division, which provided key administrative services to all field offices, both at home and abroad. These services included offices tasked with such items as information resource and technical management, finance, human resources, and clerical support.

DISBANDMENT

On March 1, 2003, the INS was officially disbanded. Most of its original functions and responsibilities were delegated to three new federal agencies to be housed in the newly created Department of Homeland Security, a new federal department created in response to the aftermath of the terrorist attacks of September 11, 2001. All border divisions of the former INS, which included patrol, investigation, prosecution, and deportation of all illegal immigrants, were combined with branches of the U.S. Customs Service to form a new agency called U.S. Customs and Border Protection.

Paul M. Klenowski

FURTHER READING

Andreas, Peter. *Border Games: Policing the U.S.-Mexico Divide.* Ithaca, N.Y.: Cornell University Press, 2001. Academic work that offers insights into the many political elements behind the patrolling of the U.S. border with Mexico.

Boehm, Randolph, et al., eds. *Records of the Immigration and Naturalization Service.* Bethesda, Md.: University Publications of America, 1995. Re-

vealing collection of official documents that provides a unique look at the INS throughout its history.

Cohen, Steve. *Deportation Is Freedom! The Orwellian World of Immigration Controls.* Philadelphia: Jessica Kingsley, 2005. Critical analysis of the implementation of U.S. immigration laws, with particular attention to the work of the Immigration and Naturalization Service.

Galan, Mark, and Edward Dixon. *Immigration and Naturalization Service.* New York: Chelsea House, 1990. Part of a series on federal agencies designed for young readers, this brief book covers the historical foundations of the INS and traces the evolution of the agency's changing responsibilities.

Juffras, Jason. *Impact of the Immigration Reform and Control Act on the Immigration and Naturalization Service.* Santa Monica, Calif.: RAND Corporation, 1991. Brief study of the impact of the 1986 federal immigration law on the INS in eight major cities.

Weissinger, George. *Law Enforcement and the INS: A Participant Observation Study of Control Agents.* Lanham, Md.: University Press of America, 1996. Drawing on interviews with INS investigators, this study describes the structure of the INS in its social context.

IMMIGRATION AND NATURALIZATION SERVICE V. CHADHA

The Case: U.S. Supreme Court decision concerning the use of legislative vetoes on immigration rulings

Date: Decided on June 23, 1983

Significance: Based on the constitutional principles of separation of powers and bicameralism, the *Chadha* decision prohibited legislation authorizing one house of Congress from overriding a decision made by the executive branch.

One section of the Immigration and Nationality Act of 1965 authorized the attorney general to allow particular deportable aliens to remain in the United States, but the act also provided the option of a "legislative veto," which authorized a single chamber of Congress to invalidate the decision of the Immigration and Naturalization Service (INS). From 1932 until 1983, Congress included legislative vetoes in almost three hundred laws. The use of the procedure was considered an effective way of retaining legislative control over the president and regulations of the executive agencies.

Born in Kenya to Indian parents and holding a British passport, Jagdish Rai Chadha had studied in the United States with a student visa. When his visa expired, neither Great Britain nor Kenya would accept him, so he applied for permanent residence in the United States. Based on Chadha's character and "extreme hardship," the INS approved his application, but the House of Representatives voted to veto the decision.

By a 7-2 vote, the U.S. Supreme Court held that the U.S. Constitution did not authorize the use of the legislative veto. With this ruling, the Court struck down more congressional enactments than it had previously in its entire history. Speaking for the majority, Chief Justice Warren E. Burger wrote that "explicit and unambiguous provisions of the Constitution prescribe and define the respective functions of the Congress and of the Executive." Any valid congressional mandate, he explained, must include passage by both houses of Congress, followed by presentment to the president, whose veto could be overridden only by a two-thirds vote in both houses. In a vigorous dissent, Justice Byron R. White argued that if Congress could delegate powers to the executive branch, it should be able to place limitations on these powers.

Thomas Tandy Lewis

Further Reading

Craig, Barbara H. *Chadha: The Story of an Epic Constitutional Struggle.* Berkeley: University of California Press, 1988.

Maltz, Earl. *Chief Justiceship of Warren Burger, 1969-*

1986. Columbia: University of South Carolina Press, 2000.

SEE ALSO: Citizenship; Congress, U.S.; Constitution, U.S.; Due process protections; Immigration law; Supreme Court, U.S.

IMMIGRATION AND NATURALIZATION SERVICE V. LOPEZ-MENDOZA

THE CASE: U.S. Supreme Court decision on the constitutional rights of undocumented immigrants
DATE: Decided on July 5, 1984

> **SIGNIFICANCE:** The *Lopez-Mendoza* decision upheld very minimal application of Fourth Amendment rights to deportation proceedings, thereby allowing immigration officials to use some improperly acquired evidence when deciding whether noncitizens should be expelled from the country.

In 1976 and 1977, Immigration and Naturalization Service (INS) officials arrested Adan Lopez-Mendoza and Elias Sandoval-Sanchez, respectively, at their place of employment. Authorities disregarded rules based on the Fourth Amendment's prohibition against unreasonable searches and seizures. After both men admitted to INS officials that they had unlawfully entered the country from Mexico, their deportation was ordered in separate proceedings. On administrative appeal, the Board of Immigration Appeals (BIA) affirmed the orders, ruling that because a deportation proceeding is a civil action, the mere fact of an illegal arrest is irrelevant to a deportation order. The Ninth Circuit Court of Appeals reversed the ruling and held that the confessions, as fruit of an unlawful arrest, should be suppressed as customary in the exclusionary rule.

By a 5-4 majority, however, the U.S. Supreme Court held that the Fourth Amendment and the exclusionary rule do not apply in deportation proceedings. Writing for the majority, Justice Sandra Day O'Connor made four major arguments. First, the BIA was correct in asserting that the protec-

tions in criminal trials do not apply to civil actions. Second, the INS maintains an adequate oversight program for monitoring compliance with Fourth Amendment requirements. Third, deportation hearings, unlike criminal trials, have the function of stopping the continuation of an illegal situation, and the social costs of releasing a defendant whose mere presence in the country violated the law would be excessive in comparison to the minimal benefits of the exclusionary rule in such contexts. Finally, O'Connor affirmed that the federal courts continued to have the authority to exercise judicial review of any egregious actions of immigration officials. Justices William J. Brennan and Byron R. White both wrote strong dissenting opinions.

Thomas Tandy Lewis

FURTHER READING

Aleinikoff, Thomas A., et al. *Immigration and Citizenship: Process and Policy.* 6th ed. St. Paul, Minn.: Thomson/West, 2008.
McFeatters, Ann C. *Sandra Day O'Connor: Justice in the Balance.* Albuquerque: University of New Mexico Press, 2006.

SEE ALSO: Citizenship; Congress, U.S.; Constitution, U.S.; Deportation; Due process protections; Illegal immigration; Immigration law; Supreme Court, U.S.

IMMIGRATION AND NATURALIZATION SERVICE V. ST. CYR

THE CASE: U.S. Supreme Court decision on deportation procedures
DATE: Decided on June 25, 2001

> **SIGNIFICANCE:** The *St. Cyr* decision held that recent federal legislation did not eliminate the federal courts' jurisdiction to consider habeas corpus petitions from resident aliens who were deportable because of felony convictions.

In 1996, Enrico St. Cyr, a lawful resident alien from Haiti, pleaded guilty to selling controlled substances in Connecticut. As a result, immigration of-

ficials brought deportation proceedings against him. Two complex federal statutes of 1996, the Anti-terrorism and Effective Death Penalty Act (AEDPA) and the Illegal Immigration Reform and Immigrant Responsibility Act (IIRIRA), severely restricted the jurisdiction of the federal courts to exercise "judicial review" over immigration officials' deportation proceedings and deportation orders. Despite the statutes, St. Cyr petitioned a U.S. district court for a writ of habeas corpus, and the petition was granted.

The major issue before the U.S. Supreme Court was whether the district courts continued to have habeas corpus jurisdiction over deportable aliens, as it did before enactment of the AEDPA and IIRIRA. In a 5-4 opinion, the Court ruled in the affirmative. Arguing that the relevant wording was ambiguous, Justice John Paul Stevens argued that the terms "judicial review" and "habeas corpus" had distinct legal meanings and that denial of the opportunity of habeas corpus relief would perhaps be unconstitutional. He wrote: "if an otherwise acceptable construction would raise serious constitutional problems and an alternative interpretation is fairly possible, the statute must be construed to avoid such problems." In a strong dissent, Justice Antonin Scalia that the privilege of habeas corpus relief was not guaranteed in the U.S. Constitution and that the plain language of the two statutes stripped the district courts of jurisdiction to entertain petitions from deportable aliens.

Thomas Tandy Lewis

FURTHER READING

Gordon, Charles, Stanley Mailman, and Stephen Yale-Loehr. *Immigration Law and Procedure.* New York: Matthew Bender, 2001.

Phelan, Margaret, and James Gillespie. *Immigration Law Handbook.* 2d ed. New York: Oxford University Press, 2005.

SEE ALSO: Citizenship; Congress, U.S.; Constitution, U.S.; Deportation; Due process protections; Immigration law; Supreme Court, U.S.

IMMIGRATION CONVENTION OF 1886

THE TREATY: Hawaiian-Japanese protocol that protected Japanese agricultural workers in the independent Hawaiian Islands

DATE: 1886

ALSO KNOWN AS: Treaty of Immigration

> **SIGNIFICANCE:** As a landmark agreement between two sovereign nations designed to protect the human rights of Japanese immigrants relocating to the kingdom of Hawaii, the Immigration Convention reflected less a lofty humanitarian imperative than a pragmatic economic necessity, as it guaranteed a steady stream of cheap immigrant laborers for Hawaii's sugar plantations.

By the 1840's, sugar cane was the primary agricultural export of the kingdom of Hawaii. Sugar planting was labor-intensive; crops required year-round maintenance, and plantation work was grueling under the best circumstances—backbreaking work and long hours in scorching temperatures. Initially, uneducated native Hawaiians provided most of the labor. However, when news of the California gold strikes reached the islands during the late 1840's, waves of native Hawaiians headed to the mainland looking for easy riches, and leaving the islands' sugar plantations in need of cheap labor. At that time, Japan was itself emerging from nearly two centuries of self-imposed isolation from the West, and leaving its new Meiji government was ready to pursue Westernization. In 1867, Japan signed an accord with the government of Hawaii to send Japanese laborers to work the sugar plantations. On June 19, 1868, the first immigrants, 153 men, landed in Hawaii.

With little agricultural background and none in the exacting work of harvesting sugar efficiently, the Japanese workers were quickly unsettled by their experiences on the islands. Hampered by language differences, the Japanese workers were routinely whipped to get them to work more efficiently, and they suffered from high rates of accidents. In addition, the Japanese workers had difficulty adjusting to the tropical climate. Indeed, their working conditions recall the antebellum

slave plantation system of a generation earlier in the American South. Many of the first immigrants wanted to return to Japan, and word quickly spread about the harsh conditions. The Japanese government launched an investigation into the allegations of cruelty. During the late 1870's, it threatened to stop sending workers to Hawaii.

Despite these problems, Japanese immigration to Hawaii continued to rise, largely because of Japan's own economic problems caused by the country's rush to industrialize. By the early 1880's, an estimated 28,000 Japanese laborers worked Hawaii's sugar plantations. Because plantation work was shunned by native Hawaiians, the islands' government understood that it needed to address the concerns of the Japanese government. In 1886, the Hawaiian government intervened on behalf of the Japanese workers at the urging of Katsunosuke Inouye, a special commissioner sent by Japan to investigate plantation conditions. The ensuing accord, the Immigration Convention, redefined the Japanese plantation workers as wards of the government and the planters as agents of the government, thus putting the practices on the plantations under direct government control and scrutiny.

The agreement represented an unprecedented act of intervention by a government to protect the human rights of an immigrant population. However, although the new directive provided a system for reporting abuses and a protocol for accountability, it was largely voided within a year. Nevertheless, Japanese immigration to the islands continued to increase because of bad economic conditions in Japan. By the turn of the twentieth century, nearly 60,000 Japanese worked on the islands.

Joseph Dewey

FURTHER READING

Jung, Moon-Ho. *Coolies and Cane: Race, Labor, and Sugar in the Age of Emancipation.* Baltimore: Johns Hopkins University Press, 2008.

Okihiro, Gary Y. *Cane Fires: The Anti-Japanese Movement in Hawaii, 1865-1945.* Philadelphia: Temple University Press, 1992.

Van Sant, John E. *Pacific Pioneers: Japanese Journeys to America and Hawaii, 1850-1880.* Champaign: University of Illinois Press, 2000.

SEE ALSO: Anti-Japanese movement; Asian immigrants; Asiatic Exclusion League; Gentlemen's Agreement; Hawaii; History of immigration, 1783-1891; *Imingaisha*; Immigration Act of 1882; Japanese immigrants; "Yellow peril" campaign.

IMMIGRATION LAW

DEFINITION: Branch of law that deals with the entry and settlement of alien nationals in the United States

SIGNIFICANCE: The gatekeeper of the borders of the United States, federal immigration law determines who may enter the country, how long they may stay, their status, their rights and duties while in the United States, and how they may become resident aliens or American citizens.

Under the U.S. Constitution, the U.S. Congress has complete authority over immigration. The courts have generally found issues regarding immigration to be nonjusticiable, and presidential power extends only to refugee policy. States have limited authority regarding immigration.

HISTORY

Primarily because of the need for labor and the spacious frontier, there was unrestricted immigration during the first one hundred years of the U.S. government's existence. After the Civil War, federal law began to reflect restrictions on the immigration of certain groups, and in 1875 Congress passed a law barring convicts and prostitutes from admission. These were among the first of many "quality control" exclusions based on the nature of the immigrants. The list of unacceptable types of immigrants continued to grow in subsequent legislation. The Immigration Act of 1882, considered the first-general federal immigration act, added "lunatics," "idiots," and those likely to become public charges to the exclusionary list. For the first time, the act also imposed a head tax on every arriving immigrant, which served to defray administrative expenses. As numbers of immigrants increased steadily, immigration was regarded as a threat to the economy, and Congress expanded the list of "undesirables," adding the diseased, paupers, and

polygamists. Immigrants were required to take a physical examination to determine whether they were diseased.

The Bureau of Immigration was established in 1891. The forerunner of the Immigration and Naturalization Service (INS), the bureau was responsible for inspecting immigrants at all ports of entry into the United States. At the turn of the twentieth century, there was a sharp increase in immigration, which Congress attempted to control by excluding more classes of immigrants: epileptics, the insane, beggars, anarchists, the feebleminded, the tubercular, and those with a mental or physical defect that might affect their ability to earn a living. The quality controls were not easily enforced, however, and huge numbers of immigrants entered the United States from countries in southern or eastern Europe. Because the earlier quality control exclusions did little to restrict the flow of immigrants, groups favoring restrictions on immigration advocated literacy as an entrance requirement. A literacy bill was not passed, however, and a joint congressional-presidential commission to study the impact of immigration on the United States concluded that the country no longer benefited from a liberal immigration policy and should impose further restrictions, including literacy.

In 1921, Congress passed the Emergency Immigration Act, which established national immigration quotas. The Immigration Act of 1924 capped the number of permissible immigrants from each country, but this resulted in more surreptitious border crossing. Complex formulas resulted in unequal quotas that favored immigrants from northern and western Europe. The Great Depression essentially closed the country to immigration, while the post-World War II economic upswing brought an increase in immigration as President Harry S. Truman issued a directive admitting forty thousand war refugees.

MODERN IMMIGRATION LAW

The Immigration and Nationality Act (INA) of 1952, also known as the McCarran-Walter Act, eliminated racial restrictions on immigration but retained nationality-based quotas and created the Immigration and Naturalization Service to enforce the caps. When Congress passed the INA, it defined "alien" as any person lacking citizenship or status as a U.S. national. There are different categories of aliens, including resident and nonresident, immigrant and nonimmigrant, and documented and undocumented (or illegal), depending upon whether the alien has proper records and identification for admission into the United States. Those documents include a visa or valid passport, border-crossing card, permanent resident card, or reentry permit.

The need to curtail illegal immigration motivated Congress to enact the Immigration Reform and Control Act of 1986, which tightened criminal sanctions for those who hire illegal immigrants. The act also denied welfare benefits to undocumented aliens and legitimized certain aliens through an amnesty program. The Immigration Marriage Fraud Amendments of 1986 aimed to eliminate the practice of marrying to obtain citizenship. The Immigration Act of 1990 equalized the allocation of visas worldwide, and the Illegal Immigration Reform and Immigrant Responsibility Act of 1996 changed certain language dealing with the process of alien entry into the United States.

Every person in the United States, including American citizens, has an immigration status that falls under one of these major categories:

- U.S. citizens—persons born within the United States or born abroad to U.S. citizens, or who have naturalized
- lawful permanent residents—green card holders eligible to reside in the United States permanently and apply for naturalization
- asylees and refugees—persons granted asylum in the United States and persons who enter as refugees and who have not yet been granted permanent residence
- nonimmigrants—persons who enter the United States temporarily for specific purposes, such as tourism, study, short-term work, or business
- temporary protected status—persons who have obtained status as citizens of countries designated by the U.S. Congress to receive protected status because of armed conflicts, natural disasters, or other unusual circumstances
- out of status—persons who enter the United States lawfully on nonimmigrant visas that have either expired or had their terms violated
- undocumented aliens—persons who enter the country without inspection—usually from Canada or Mexico—or with a fraudulent passport

POST-9/11 IMMIGRATION REFORM

The terrorist attacks of September 11, 2001, on New York City and Washington, D.C., intensified efforts to confront problems dealing with America's moral commitment to immigrants. President George W. Bush proposed a series of sweeping measures designed to combat terrorism, including the strengthening of borders. The Uniting and Strengthening America by Providing Appropriate Tools Required to Intercept and Obstruct Terrorism (USA PATRIOT) Act was passed quickly and signed into law in October of 2001. The Patriot Act expanded the electronic surveillance powers of government and thus allowed greater intrusion on Americans' civil rights. It provided for greater surveillance of aliens and increased the power of the attorney general to identify, arrest, and deport aliens.

The Patriot Act broadened the definition of "terrorist" to include anyone who endorses or provides financial support to a terrorist organization, or who actually participates in terrorist activities. To identify possible terrorists, U.S. consulates are required to check visa applicants' names against "lookout lists" prior to issuing a visa, resulting in increased time for many noncitizens seeking admission to the United States and causing some people to be denied admission because they were incorrectly identified as terrorists.

In another reaction to the 2001 attacks, Congress enacted the Homeland Security Act in November of 2002, which established a new cabinet department—the Department of Homeland Security—to coordinate the antiterrorist activities of the government and reorganize immigration policy. Functions of the now abolished INS were divided among several agencies within the Department of Homeland Security. The federal government placed more than 300,000 aliens scheduled for deportation on a criminal list, more than doubled the number of border patrol agents, provided high-tech equipment to detect weapons that could be smuggled across Canadian or Mexican borders, enhanced the tracking of visitors to the United States, and gave the attorney general greater authority to expel anyone suspected of terrorist connections.

Americans have been deeply divided over immigration policy, and no consensus has emerged, although most people agree that policies had to be strengthened after the 2001 terrorist attacks. Opponents of these measures argue that these steps curtail civil liberties, particularly those of Muslims; supporters counter that the measures are important and significant tools in the war on global terrorism. Among other steps authorized in the name of national security, the government required special registration of certain Arab and Muslim noncitizens; arrested, detained, and interrogated large numbers of Arab and Muslim noncitizens; and engaged in their selective deportation. Special registration requirements were imposed by the executive branch on the ground that the political branches of the federal government had plenary power over immigration. Throughout history, harsh measures have been taken against unpopular groups in the name of national security. The internment of persons of Japanese ancestry during World War II is the best-known example.

Although early twenty-first century immigration laws are generally neutral on their face and do not discriminate on the basis of race, they have racially disparate effects. For example, ceilings on immigrant admissions from a single country in any year apply to all countries but have a disproportionate impact on prospective immigrants from Mexico as well as noncitizens from other developing nations such as China, India, and the Philippines because demand for immigration from those countries exceeds their annual ceilings. Increased border enforcement on the U.S.-Mexican border has had a disproportionate impact on Mexican citizens and undocumented Mexican migrant workers. Statistics from early 2006 indicated that the United States had no record of as many as twelve million undocumented immigrants, more than half of whom were of Mexican origin and representing more than double the approximately five million undocumented immigrants of the early 1990's. Because there has been a dramatic increase in the undocumented immigrant population, it can be concluded that enhanced border enforcement has largely failed.

The Intelligence Reform and Terrorism Prevention Act of 2004 overhauled the government's intelligence operations and created a director of national intelligence, answerable directly to the president, who was responsible for integrating the activities of fifteen agencies responsible for gathering intelligence information. Major provisions of the act include strengthening visa application requirements, creating a visa and passport security

program within the State Department, establishing more stringent passport requirements for travel within the Western Hemisphere, developing a system to track people entering and leaving the United States, and increasing U.S.-Mexican border security. The number of detention beds for those awaiting deportation was increased, minimum standards were established for issuing driver's licenses and birth certificates and for documents required for boarding airplanes, criminal penalties for alien smuggling were increased, and the General Accounting Office was required to study weaknesses in the asylum system. By 2009, all U.S. citizens and foreign nationals entering or leaving the United States by air, sea, or land to or from Canada, Mexico, Bermuda, the Caribbean, or Central or South America were required to have a valid passport.

Marcia J. Weiss

FURTHER READING

Jasper, Margaret C. *The Law of Immigration.* 3d ed. New York: Oxford University Press, 2008. Almanac that explores immigration law, the rights and obligations of aliens, and the process of citizenship through naturalization. A useful reference for the layperson that contains sample documents and an extensive glossary.

Johnson, Kevin R., and Bernard Trujillo. "Immigration Reform, National Security After September 11, and the Future of North American Integration." *Minnesota Law Review* 91, no. 5 (2007): 1369-1407. Scholarly article with numerous references outlining security problems and possible solutions in the post-9/11 era.

Powell, John. *Immigration.* New York: Facts On File, 2007. Contains essential information for researching the issue of immigration, including chronology, glossary of terms, biographical data, and an extensive and fully annotated bibliography including periodicals and Web documents, microforms, CDs, and film resources.

Weissbrodt, David, and Laura Danielson. *Immigration Law and Procedure in a Nutshell.* St. Paul, Minn.: Thomson/West, 2005. Excellent introduction to immigration law containing summaries and references to court cases, the Constitution, and pertinent statutes.

SEE ALSO: Bureau of Immigration, U.S.; Congress, U.S.; Constitution, U.S.; Homeland Security, De-

partment of; Immigration Act of 1882; Immigration Act of 1917; Immigration Act of 1921; Immigration Act of 1924; Immigration Act of 1990; Immigration and Nationality Act of 1965; McCarran Internal Security Act of 1950; 9/11 and U.S. immigration policy; Patriot Act of 2001; Quota systems; Supreme Court, U.S.

IMMIGRATION LAWYERS

DEFINITION: Attorneys who specialize in representing immigrants

SIGNIFICANCE: As the complexities and restrictions of U.S. immigration law have increased, the legal profession's subspecialty of immigration lawyers has flourished, extending in some cases to social-cause lawyering.

During the era of relatively open immigration that existed in the United States until the last quarter of the nineteenth century, there was little need for specialized immigration lawyers. However, as the federal government began enacting immigration restrictions during the 1870's, a new field arose in the legal profession: lawyers who specialized in helping immigrants navigate the increasing stream of regulations and restrictions emanating from the federal government.

IMMIGRATION LAWYERS ON ELLIS ISLAND

During the 1890's, the U.S. Congress established exclusive oversight over immigration to the United States. It established official immigration reception stations on Ellis Island in New York Harbor in 1892 and on Angel Island in California's San Francisco Bay in 1910. These immigration facilities were staffed by federal officials enforcing the restrictions enacted by Congress in a series of immigration acts. Immigrants responded by beginning to turn, in large numbers, to lawyers to assist them in the immigration process.

Given the almost plenary power vested in immigration officials at that time, early immigration lawyers played a mostly advisory role. Becoming expert in the administrative processes required for immigration, lawyers coached their clients on what to say to customs officials and tried, usually in vain, to appear as counsel for their clients in immigra-

tion proceedings. However, in cases that went before the immigration Boards of Special Inquiry that were authorized in 1893 to make determinations as to the entry of aliens, lawyers played more active roles.

Records have survived from about 424 appeals of decisions made by Boards of Special Inquiry in New York during the 1890's. In 277 cases—about two-thirds of the total—the immigrants involved were represented by attorneys. Of the 277 cases involving attorneys, five of the attorneys appeared in five or more appeals each, thus demonstrating a nascent immigration bar. The most notable of the five attorneys was Henry Gottlieb of the firm of MacKinley & Gottlieb, who handled eighty-five of the appeals. A lawyer named John Palmieri handled the second-greatest number of appeals, thirty-seven. Given that the 1890's represented the first great wave of Jewish and Italian immigration to New York, it is safe to conclude that Gottlieb spe-

cialized in helping Jewish immigrants and that Palmieri helped Italian immigrants.

SOCIAL CAUSE IMMIGRATION LAWYERING

Both immigration and federal immigration legislation steadily increased during the first decades of the twentieth century. With these increases came growth in the numbers of immigration lawyers. What had been part-time legal work for general practitioners was increasingly becoming full-time work for lawyers specializing in immigration cases. With this increased specialization came two developments.

The first development was the immigration bar's looking to promote its own professionalization and expertise. The American Immigration Lawyers' Association (AILA) was founded in 1946 as a national, nonprofit organization dedicated to the practice and teaching of immigration law. In 1975, it had about 600 members. By 1985, its member-

Immigration lawyer, Jessica Salsbury, hugs a domestic worker to celebrate the passage of legislation protecting the rights of domestics at a Montgomery County Council meeting in Rockville, Maryland in 2008. (AP/Wide World Images)

WORK PERFORMED BY IMMIGRATION LAWYERS

- Analyze the facts in the case of someone desiring to immigrate
- Explain all benefits for which immigrants may be eligible
- Recommend the best way to obtain legal immigrant status
- Complete and file appropriate applications
- Keep up with new laws affecting their clients
- Speak for clients in discussions with federal immigration officials
- Represent clients in court
- File necessary appeals and waivers

Adapted from: American Immigration and Lawyers Association, "A Guide to Consumer Protection and Authorized Representation," Washington, D.C.: AILA, 1998.

ship had grown to about 1,800 lawyers. In 2009, the association claimed more than 11,000 lawyers and law professors as its members, with thirty-six chapters and more than fifty national committees.

In the second development, some immigration lawyers began to look upon their specialty as an opportunity for social-cause lawyering. The AILA itself established in 1987 the American Immigration Law Foundation (later renamed the American Immigration Council) as a charitable organization to advocate on behalf of immigrants and to promote public awareness of immigration issues. One of the most successful examples of social-cause lawyering was that of immigration lawyers securing the right to asylum of refugees from the violence engulfing Central America during the late 1980's and early 1990's.

In alliance with members of the Sanctuary movement, immigration lawyers filed politically oriented lawsuits such as *Orantes-Hernandez v. Meese* (1988), *American Baptist Churches v. Thornburgh* (1991), and *Mendez v. Reno* (1993). After years of litigation, these lawyers helped secure the right of Salvadorans and Guatemalans to obtain asylum status in the United States, even though the governments of El Salvador and Guatemala were nominally allies of the United States, receiving extensive American support. Other groups that advocated on behalf of immigration rights and accessible borders included the American Civil Liberties Union, the Fair Immigration Reform Movement,

the Mexican American Legal Defense and Educational Fund, the National Immigration Forum, and the National Immigration Law Foundation.

PRACTICING IMMIGRATION LAW FOR PROFIT

Obtaining residency in the modern United States can be an arduous process, and most aliens seeking residency require legal services. Many lawyers have generously devoted their time to assisting immigrants for reduced fees or even no fees at all. However, as the size of the legal profession in the United States has boomed, and as more avenues have been opened for solicitation and profit-making by lawyers, the immigration bar has become plagued by allegations of corruption, scandal, and exploitation. In 1985, several high-profile immigration lawyers were convicted and disbarred. In 2003, for example, immigration lawyer Samuel Kooritzky was sentenced to ten years in federal prison for engaging in immigration fraud through his Capital Law Centers. In 2005, the federal Executive Office for Immigration Review disciplined fifty-four immigration lawyers.

Howard Bromberg

FURTHER READING

Anthes, Louis. *Lawyers and Immigrants, 1870-1940: A Cultural History.* Levittown, N.Y.: LFB Scholarly Publishing, 2003. This volume in the publisher's Law and Society series traces the connections among law, lawyers, immigrants, and cultural issues. Anthes researched the practice of immigration lawyers on Ellis Island.

Salyer, Lucy. *Laws Harsh as Tigers: Chinese Immigrants and the Shaping of Modern Immigration Law.* Chapel Hill: University of North Carolina Press, 1995. History of Chinese immigration that Salyer shows to be central to the shaping of immigration law, with a detailed account of the administration of immigration law on Ellis Island.

Sarat, Austin, and Stuart Scheingold, eds. *Cause Lawyers and Social Movements.* Stanford, Calif.: Stanford University Press, 2006. Collection of essays on lawyering activists. The essay by Susan Coutin recounts efforts of lawyers working to obtain asylum rights for Central Americans.

Serrill, Michael. "A Booming but Tainted Specialty." *Time*, July 8, 1985. Account of growth of immigration law practice, with both respected human rights advocates and fraudulent and corrupt lawyers.

Warner, Judith, ed. *Battleground Immigration.* Westport, Conn.: Greenwood Press, 2009. Compendium of immigration-related topics, with material on the role of lawyers in forming political perspectives on immigration.

SEE ALSO: Angel Island Immigration Station; Asian American Legal Defense Fund; Deportation; Ellis Island; Immigration law; Mexican American Legal Defense and Educational Fund; New York City; Sanctuary movement.

IMMIGRATION REFORM AND CONTROL ACT OF 1986

THE LAW: First federal law to impose sanctions on American employers who hired undocumented alien workers, while also providing amnesty for a specific category of aliens

DATE: Enacted on November 6, 1986

ALSO KNOWN AS: Simpson-Mazzoli Act; Simpson-Rodino Act; IRCA

SIGNIFICANCE: The Immigration Reform and Control Act (IRCA) was designed to balance public concerns about increasing illegal immigration with business's need for cheap labor and the need to address issues of racial and ethnic discrimination. The final bill focused less on restricting the numbers of immigrants than on putting existing undocumented aliens on the path to citizenship and on deterring further illegal immigration by strengthening border control and employer sanctions.

During the late 1970's, national economic problems and the increased visibility of both documented and undocumented immigrants led the U.S. Congress to focus on immigration reform. Fears traditionally associated with waves of immigration, such as the loss of jobs to lower-wage earners and

unassimilated enclaves of newcomers, led Congress to create the Select Commission on Immigration and Refugee Policy in 1979. The commission reviewed existing immigration laws and produced a report in March, 1981. Two recommendations became the focal point of the Immigration Reform and Control Act of 1986: strengthening sanctions on employers who hired undocumented aliens and improving access to American citizenship for undocumented aliens within the United States.

Immigration reform was championed by Wyoming senator Alan Simpson and Missouri representative Roman Mazzoli. Several versions of the bill they based on the recommendations of the Select Commission languished in Congress throughout the early 1980's. A fragile coalition of civil rights-oriented immigrant advocacy groups and free market business groups who wanted cheap labor helped to overcome opposition from groups who supported restricting immigration to pass the Immigration Reform and Control Act in November, 1986.

IRCA had two major components. The first provided amnesty to illegal immigrants already in the United States. Long-term undocumented immigrants who could prove residency in the United States continuously since before January 1, 1972, were permitted to apply for permanent status that would lead to American citizenship. Aliens residing illegally in the country after January 1, 1982, were given the opportunity to apply for temporary status that could possibly lead to permanent residency. Congress also bowed to the pressure of agricultural interests and placed undocumented workers who had worked in the United States for three months during the fiscal year ending May 1, 1986, on the road to permanent-resident status.

The second component of IRCA focused on deterring future illegal immigration. For the first time, federal law made employers responsible for verifying and keeping records of the work-eligibility status of all employees they hired after November 6, 1986. Employers who hired undocumented immigrants faced fines of up to ten thousand dollars and six-month prison terms for each undocumented employee in their workforces. Congress also strengthened nondiscrimination provisions of the law to placate immigrant-advocacy groups who were concerned that businesses would stop hiring legally documented immigrants who happened to

have "foreign-sounding" names. The final provision aimed at deterring immigration focused on improving border patrolling to prevent illegal passage into the country.

IRCA provided a mix of amnesty for undocumented immigrants already in the United States and provisions designed to deter future illegal immigration. However, by focusing on resolving the problem of undocumented aliens, the legislation did not address the issue of limiting future immigration. Ultimately those in favor of an expansive American immigration policy triumphed over immigration-control advocates. The legislation affected approximately three million undocumented workers. However, its deterrence provisions had relatively little effect on stemming the tide of illegal immigration after 1986.

J. Wesley Leckrone

FURTHER READING

Hing, Bill Ong. *Defining America Through Immigration Policy*. Philadelphia: Temple University Press, 2004.

Zolberg, Artistide R. "Reforming the Back Door: The Immigration Reform and Control Act of 1986 in Historical Perspective." In *Immigration Reconsidered: History, Sociology, and Politics*, edited by Virginia Yans-McLaughlin. New York: Oxford University Press, 1990.

SEE ALSO: Amerasian Homecoming Act of 1987; Border Patrol, U.S.; Congress, U.S.; Gay and lesbian immigrants; History of immigration after 1891; Immigration Act of 1990; Latin American immigrants; Select Commission on Immigration and Refugee Policy.

IMMIGRATION WAVES

THE EVENTS: Periods that experienced large and enduring increases in immigration to the United States

SIGNIFICANCE: With each immigration wave that the United States has experienced, the culture and context of life in the United States have changed considerably. Such changes have continued into the twenty-first century.

The first immigrants to settle in what is now the United States were the ancient ancestors of modern Native Americans. The precise routes of those first North American immigrants are disputed, but there is no uncertainty about the fact that every human being on the continent is either a recent immigrant or a descendant of earlier immigrants. Since the first immigrants came here from Asia more than thirteen thousand years ago, there have been four large and easily recognizable modern waves of immigrants into the United States.

During the seventeenth century, the first wave of European colonists began arriving. Most of them came from England and northern Europe. This wave peaked shortly before the American Revolution of 1776-1783. The second wave lasted about fifty years, through the mid-nineteenth century, and brought mostly Irish and Germans to the United States. That period was followed by the third wave, which lasted about forty years and brought in millions of Asians and southern and eastern Europeans. Finally, after U.S. immigration law abolished quotas based on nationalities in 1965, the fourth major wave began. It has continued into the first decade of the twenty-first century and has been the largest immigration wave in U.S. history. The majority of immigrants it has brought into the United States have come from Mexico, Central America, and the Caribbean islands of the West Indies.

NATIVE AMERICAN ORIGINS

Whether they came by way of a land bridge between Alaska and Siberia or crossed the ocean in junks or on rafts, it is generally agreed that the first Americans arrived on the continent at least thirteen thousand years ago. Some authorities put that date back as far as fifty thousand years. The ancestors of modern Native Americans either entered North America in more than one location or they migrated widely after arriving. Their descendants were eventually spread out over North, Central, and South America and the West Indies and had a total pre-Columbian population of between 10 and 50 million people.

As these first Americans adapted to the changes in their environment brought about by significant climate change and their own travels, they developed rich cultures, and many had what some people have viewed as an almost ideal way of life. Al-

Immigrants registering at New York City's Castle Garden reception center in 1866. (Library of Congress)

though the frequent presence of wars, slavery, and many other social injustices mar that idealistic view, the more human scale of the problems and the closeness to nature make the life of the early Americans very attractive to many citizens of the modern world.

FIRST MODERN IMMIGRATION WAVE, 1609-1775

Quests for adventure, flights from religious persecution, and hopes for brighter economic futures induced almost one-half million Europeans to leave their homeland and come to America between 1609 and 1775. Many of these new arrivals were indentured servants, under contract to work for masters from four to seven years merely to pay the costs of their transatlantic passage. The first black Africans to come to America during this period also came as indentured servants. However, almost all the Africans who followed came as chattel slaves.

Most immigrants who came during the seventeenth century were from England, with smaller numbers from France, Germany, Ireland, Italy, and other countries. By the turn of the eighteenth century, they had raised the population of Great Britain's North American colonies to 250,000. After 1700, the numbers of immigrants from Ireland, Scotland, and Germany increased dramatically,

while those from England decreased. Between 1700 and the start of the American Revolution in 1775, the colonial population almost doubled, to 450,000. During that period, the principal port of entry was Philadelphia, but immigrants also entered through Baltimore, Maryland, and Charleston, South Carolina.

SECOND IMMIGRATION WAVE, C. 1820-1870

After a lull in immigration during the American Revolution and wars in Europe, a second wave of immigrants began arriving around 1820. Most of these newcomers entered the United States through New York City, instead of Philadelphia. In 1855, Castle Garden was opened at the southern tip of Manhattan Island in New York City as the nation's first immigration station.

A majority of immigrants arriving on the East Coast during this second wave were Irish and Germans. A potato famine hit Ireland during the 1840's, and as much as one-third of the immigrants during this time were Irish fleeing that famine. The newly arrived Irish tended to remain near the East Coast. Many of them arrived penniless and lacked the resources to travel further inland. Almost equal numbers of Germans arrived during the same period. However, unlike the Irish, they tended to continue inland. Many of them bought farms in the Midwest.

Gold was discovered in California in 1848, and the transcontinental railroad was begun in 1862. Both the lure of gold and the prospect of work on the railroad brought a wave of Chinese immigrants to the West Coast of the United States that dried up in 1882, only after the U.S. Congress enacted the Chinese Exclusion Act that year. That law made immigration for practically all ethnic Chinese illegal. Meanwhile, most Chinese immigrants entered the United States through the port of San Francisco. Most of them were single men who planned to make their fortunes and return to China. However, a large proportion of them ended up spending the rest of their lives in the United States, where most of them worked in low-paying jobs.

In response to fears of native-born Americans about job competition, concerns about religious and political differences, and simple, blatant racism, a political party was formed called the America Party or the Know-Nothing Party. During the 1850's, supporters of this party and other nativist movements demanded laws that would reduce immigration, particularly from Asia. The state of California, where most of the Chinese immigrants worked, enacted its own laws to discourage Chinese immigration. During the 1870's, the United States suffered an economic depression at the same time Germany and Great Britain were enjoying relative prosperity. Thanks to the combination of restrictive legislation and economic problems, immigration went through another period of decline.

THIRD IMMIGRATION WAVE, 1881-1920

During the 1880's, American states seeking to increase their populations and railroad companies seeking laborers began sending agents across the Atlantic to recruit immigrant workers. By the late nineteenth century, transoceanic transportation had become significantly cheaper and less arduous, making it easier for poor Europeans to immigrate to the United States. The period between about 1881 and 1920 brought more than 23 million new immigrants from all parts of the world, but mostly from Europe, to the United States. The first decade of this period saw most of the immigrants coming from northern and western Europe; after 1890, the majority came from southern and eastern Europe. Meanwhile, restrictive U.S. immigration laws continued to keep the numbers of immigrants from Asia very small.

Like the Chinese immigrants of the previous wave, many of the new immigrants from southern and eastern Europe encountered a good deal of hostility in their new homeland. Again feeling threatened by job competition, and concerned about racial, religious, and political differences, native-born Americans directed their new hostility primarily against Jewish immigrants, Roman Catholics, and Japanese. Before long, a general distrust and resentment of all new immigrants began to grow. Anti-immigrant sentiment found its way into federal government, and the U.S. Congress enacted a new series of restrictive immigration laws between 1917 and 1924. The Immigration Act of 1917, for example, required immigrants to demonstrate their ability to read and write. The same law also created the "Asiatic Barred Zone" to halt immigration from most of Asia.

Nevertheless, despite their chilly reception, immigrants continued to pour into the United States in search of better lives. In 1921, the U.S. Congress passed a new immigration law that set ceilings on the numbers of immigrants permitted from individual countries. Using a formula designed to slow immigration from southern and eastern Europe, the new law had the effect of ensuring that most new immigrants would come from northern and western European nations.

Immigration into the United States was further curtailed by the onset of the Great Depression of the 1930's. During the Depression years, more people emigrated from the United States than immigrated. Between 1931 and 1940, only about one-half million new immigrants arrived in the United States. After the United States entered World War II at the end of 1941, the federal government made its immigration laws less restrictive, particularly for citizens of the country's wartime ally China. Nevertheless, the third great immigration wave was already over.

FOURTH IMMIGRATION WAVE, AFTER 1965

In 1965, passage of the federal Immigration and Nationality Act ended the system of quotas based on nationality. In their place was a new, far less restrictive quota system based on hemispheres. The new system permitted 120,000 immigrants per year from the Western Hemisphere and 170,000 from the Eastern Hemisphere. In 1978, even these quotas were replaced by a single, worldwide quota of

290,000 immigrants per year from all parts of the world. From 1992 to 1994, this figure was raised to 700,000 immigrants before being reduced to 675,000 in 1995. None of these quotas placed any limits on the numbers of immediate family members of U.S. citizens who could enter the country. As a consequence, the actual numbers of immigrants who entered the United States legally were higher than the quota figures.

During the first decade of the twenty-first century, the United States was still in the midst of the largest wave of immigration in its history. One million immigrants entered the country legally every year. By the first decade of the twenty-first century, fully one-tenth of all residents of the United States were foreign born. In addition to these approximately 30 million legal immigrants in the country, the U.S. Census estimated that about 8.7 million immigrants were in the country illegally. Most new immigrants, both legal and illegal, were Hispanics from Mexico, the Caribbean, and Central America. Between 1990 and 2000, the Hispanic population of the United States increased 63 percent—from 22.4 million to 35.3 million residents. Indeed, the largest and longest-enduring movement of laborers between any two countries in the world has been from Mexico to the United States.

Wayne Shirey

FURTHER READING

Foner, Nancy. *From Ellis Island to JFK: New York's Two Great Waves of Immigration.* New Haven, Conn.: Yale University Press, 2000. Comparison of the great wave of Jewish Russian and Italian immigrants to New York City around 1900 with the late twentieth century wave of immigrants from Asia, Latin America, and the Caribbean.

Katz, Michael B., and Mark J. Stern. *One Nation Divisible: What America Was and What It Is Becoming.* New York: Russell Sage Foundation, 2006. Examines the effect of large-scale immigration on American society and the economy.

Lippert, Dorothy, and Stephen J. Spignesi. *Native American History for Dummies.* Hoboken, N.J.: Wiley, 2007. Despite its title, this volume offers a very intelligent discussion of the immigration of the earliest Americans.

Waters, Mary C., and Reed Ueda, eds. *The New Americans: A Guide to Immigration Since 1965.* Cambridge, Mass.: Harvard University Press, 2007.

Collection of descriptive essays on the various immigrant groups that have made up the post-1965 immigration wave and on the key topics concerning this wave.

SEE ALSO: Economic consequences of immigration; Great Irish Famine; History of immigration, 1620-1783; History of immigration, 1783-1891; History of immigration after 1891; Illegal immigration; Immigration and Nationality Act of 1965.

IN RE TIBURCIO PARROTT

THE CASE: U.S. district court decision on racial discrimination
DATE: Decided in 1880

SIGNIFICANCE: In the *Parrott* ruling, a U.S. district court in California prohibited the application of a constitutional amendment that would have prohibited the employment of Chinese persons in the state.

In 1880, section 19 of the new California constitution prohibited the employment of "any Chinese or Mongolian," and it also authorized the legislature to enact laws to this effect. Irish teamster Dennis Kearney held large rallies to promote anti-Chinese sentiments, and a resulting criminal statute made the employment of Chinese a misdemeanor. The president of a silver mining company, Tiburcio Parrott, believing the law was unconstitutional, refused to discharge his Chinese employees. Arrested and charged, he petitioned a U.S. district court for a writ of habeas corpus, which was granted.

Two district judges, Ogden Hoffman and Lorenso Sawyer, held that both the constitutional provision and the statute were inconsistent with rights guaranteed in the Burlingame Treaty with China (1868) and therefore violated Article VI of the U.S. Constitution. Because treaties were part of the "supreme law of the land," their provisions were superior to state constitutions and state statutes. Although this was a major victory for the Chinese of California, the state legislature responded by passing discriminatory laws, restricting where the Chinese might live and prohibiting them from obtaining licenses in various businesses.

Thomas Tandy Lewis

FURTHER READING

Kens, Paul. "Civil Liberties, Chinese Laborers, and Corporations." In *Law in the Western United States*, edited by Gordon M. Bakken. Norman: University of Oklahoma Press, 2000.

McClain, Charles J. *In Search of Equality: The Chinese Struggle Against Discrimination in Nineteenth-Century America.* Berkeley: University of California Press, 1994.

SEE ALSO: Anti-Chinese movement; Burlingame Treaty of 1868; California; Capitation taxes; Chinese immigrants; Citizenship; Due process protections; Immigration law; Supreme Court, U.S.

INDENTURED SERVITUDE

DEFINITION: Form of contract labor that binds employees to work for specified periods of time, usually in satisfaction of debts

SIGNIFICANCE: During the colonial period of British North America, a high proportion of British working-class immigrants to the American colonies came as indentured servants. Precise figures are unavailable, but it is estimated that 40 to 75 percent of white immigrants experienced a period of unfree labor in colonial times. The British indenture system ceased to operate after the American Revolution, but debt-slavery of migrants continued under institutions such as the Chinese credit-ticket system.

The term "indentured servitude" is distinguished from slavery by its temporary nature. The term also refers to labor contracts in which a heavily indebted worker is effectively prevented from changing employers or retaining wages beyond a subsistence level. Indentured servitude as a North American institution dates from the earliest days of the colonial period. This form of bondage preceded African slavery and existed side by side with it up until the American Revolution. When the Americas ceased to be the property of Great Britain, the formal mechanisms for recruiting or forcing individuals into indentures and shipping them across the Atlantic no longer operated, although an internal indenture system continued to operate at the state level for many decades.

In its strictest sense, indentured servitude refers to a contract transferring ownership of an individual to his or her employer for a fixed term. Indentured servants ceased to be autonomous agents. They had no control over place of residence or conditions of employment and could not marry without the owner's consent. Their persons could be bought and sold. Although colonial law and terms of contracts granted them some rights and protections, laws protecting the owners' property rights were more uniformly enforced than those promoting the welfare of the property.

The term "indentured servant" often evokes images of domestic servants. Indeed, the majority of female indentured servants, who constituted about 20 percent of all indentured immigrants during the seventeenth and eighteenth centuries, probably fell into this category. Male indentured servants were more likely to be agricultural laborers. Skilled tradesmen entered the system when they fell afoul of the law.

COLONIAL AMERICA

In theory, an indenture was a voluntary contract, at least for adult males. In practice, most contracts involved an element of coercion or deception. Just under half of the 307,400 migrants from the British Isles to the thirteen colonies between 1680 and 1775 came as free citizens. Seventeen percent were criminal convicts, and 33.7 percent were indentured servants. The convicts, who had been convicted of felonies, served their sentences of transportation as indentured servants to private individuals rather than in state-managed labor camps.

British law also allowed involuntary apprenticeship of orphans, illegitimate children, and children whose families could not support them. Such forced apprenticeship might include transportation across the Atlantic. English poor laws dictated that adults who were capable of supporting themselves, but had no visible means of support, could be compelled to work. Vagrants, beggars, prostitutes, and able-bodied paupers could be forcibly indentured. For the most part, people who made a conscious choice to immigrate to the colonies for economic gain or to take advantage of greater religious and political freedom borrowed money for

relocation costs, calculating (correctly) that a person with any skill or education could redeem the debt in a shorter period and be free in the interim.

For some members of the British underclass, forcible relocation and involuntary labor provided a door of opportunity, but these were a minority. One-third of those transported did not survive until the end of their indentures. During the seventeenth century, contracts often provided for a modest land grant upon completion of service, but by 1700 good land had become scarce, and a newly freed servant who had no developed skills had few resources to begin a new life. Some settled on the frontier in Appalachia. Others remained with their old employers as ostensibly free laborers. To a large extent, their descendants remained a permanent underclass of poor whites, landless or tied to unproductive land, poorly educated, and little attached to cultural norms that had not served their forebears. Some, especially those who still had strong family ties, returned to England.

Life for indentured servants was often bleak and grueling. They worked from dawn to dusk, six days a week. In contrast to black slaves, who were encouraged to raise families, they were expected to remain celibate, and under large employers usually lived under communal conditions resembling military barracks. In theory, the indentured servant had a contractual right to adequate food, clothing, and shelter; in practice, an unscrupulous employer, having no long-term investment in his captive employee, could stint on necessities. Complaints through the civil court system rarely resulted in redress.

In Puritan New England, Sundays included a hefty dose of religious instruction to correct the presumed low moral character of transported ruffians. To some extent justified, the widespread prejudice among free settlers against indentured laborers became a self-fulfilling prophecy. Expecting teenagers and young adults of either sex to remain celibate for years on end, and to refrain from petty property crime when no legal avenue of obtaining money or goods beyond the employer's meager ration existed, was simply unrealistic. Some of the runaways featured in frequent newspaper advertisements were true runaways, but a fair proportion consisted of young men out on a spree.

An owner could flog his servants if they misbehaved. Serious breaches of contract, including running away, were punished by extension of the indenture contract. Women were liable to sexual exploitation, either by their owners or by fellow servants. Societal perception that women of this social class were inherently immoral meant that protestations of rape or seduction fell on deaf ears. If a woman became pregnant, the law automatically added three years to her indenture contract to compensate for loss of labor to the owner.

German immigrants who settled in Pennsylvania during the eighteenth century came to America under a system resembling indentured servitude, with, however, significant differences. Immigrant brokers recruited laborers in Germany, contracting to transport them to America for a set fee, and sold the debt to the American employer. Called redemptioners, these immigrants were obliged either to work for that employer until the debt was paid off or to find another source for the funds. Although brokers charged excessive fees and misrepresented the opportunities for high-paid employment, and a redemptioner could end up working for little net remuneration for years, without any realistic prospect of changing jobs, he was still a free man. A similar system operated in Ireland, where the absence of poor laws prevented coerced indenture through the court system.

AFTER THE AMERICAN REVOLUTION

After Britain recognized the independence of the thirteen colonies in 1784, the flow of legally indentured servants and transported convicts from the British Isles stopped, though not because of the U.S. Constitution or any legislative act in the United States. Britain used these people as a resource to develop its colonial possessions, and was loath to relinquish any of them to an independent state and potential rival. Anyone transported through the justice system after 1784 ended up in Canada, the West Indies, or Australia. Parliament enacted some laws restricting the activities of immigrant brokers and military recruiters during the early nineteenth century, as well as limiting the ability of people with certain critical skills to leave the country voluntarily. The laws restricting voluntary emigration were largely ineffective.

Immigrant brokers continued to operate in Germany and Ireland during the early nineteenth century. European countries with their own expanding empires (France, Spain, Portugal, Holland) or

frontiers (Russia) discouraged emigration to the United States.

Railroad building and continued westward expansion created a huge demand for labor that neither voluntary immigration from Europe nor involuntary internal migration could satisfy. To make up the deficit, the growing nation looked to China as a source of cheap workers. On paper, the Chinese "coolies" appeared to be voluntary migrants enlisted by brokers in China to work for American employers who paid the broker and shipping agent and collected the debt from the Chinese employees' wages. In practice, most were forced into service in China and placed in occupations and regions in the United States where alternative employment was impossible, leaving them at the employer's mercy. This credit-ticket system, which brought 350,000 Chinese laborers to the American mainland between 1840 and 1882, embodied many features of the old indentured labor system. In contrast to earlier European immigrants, however, the Chinese were never encouraged to become permanent settlers or citizens and were prohibited from doing so after 1882.

Military service can be viewed as a form of indentured servitude. During the U.S. Civil War, recruiters for the Union Army operated in some of the German states, enlisting German nationals for a cash bonus on joining and American citizenship and a land grant if they survived the war. Young men from Ireland and other countries where open foreign recruiting was prohibited were met at the docks with the same promise. Availability of an unlimited supply of foreign recruits was a nontrivial factor in the Union's victory over the South.

INDENTURED SERVITUDE IN TWENTIETH AND TWENTY-FIRST CENTURY AMERICA

After World War I, the United States became much more selective in the numbers, classes, and nationalities of immigrants it would accept as permanent residents and potential future citizens. Accepting an exclusive and restrictive contract with a single employer in return for payment of resettlement costs is no longer a possible avenue for becoming an American, except as a means of getting a toehold.

At the same time, the U.S. Citizenship and Immigration Services (formerly the Immigration and Naturalization Service) recognizes a number of classes of temporary workers whose conditions of employment approach indenture. In addition to legal guest workers, there were, in 2004, an estimated six million undocumented foreign nationals working in the United States, some proportion of whom paid hefty fees to the agents who smuggled them into the country and connected them with their present employers. These undocumented workers risk deportation if they complain about working conditions or attempt to change jobs.

Among types of legal labor contracts embodying aspects of involuntary servitude that affect foreign nationals, labor activists have singled out the H-2 visa program, special dispensations for employees of foreign embassies and consulates, and garment sweatshops operating in the Mariana Islands, a U.S. possession.

In 2007, 120,000 workers were admitted to the United States on H-2 visas to take temporary unskilled jobs for specific employers. Charges against the program include exorbitant fees exacted from workers and employers who seize documents, holding the workers effectively prisoner, and fail to provide contractual working conditions. Employees of embassies are governed by the laws of the parent country, which may tolerate virtual slavery. The status of the Mariana Islands as a U.S. territory, their proximity to Asia, and the vagaries of American import laws have allowed multinational corporations to set up garment factories in Saipan, import contract workers from China and Southeast Asia who live as virtual prisoners, and proudly stamp the products as "Made in the USA." Unlike the immigrant garment workers who toiled in New York sweatshops in the early twentieth century, these women have no chance of attaining the benefits of American life.

Martha A. Sherwood

FURTHER READING

Jordan, Don. *White Cargo: The Forgotten History of Britain's White Slaves in America.* New York: New York University Press, 2008. A mixture of statistical and anecdotal material that highlights the involuntary nature of most indenture contracts. Illustrated.

Lancaster, R. Kent. "Almost Chattel: The Lives of Indentured Servants at Hampton-Northampton, Baltimore County." *Maryland Historical Magazine*

94, no. 3 (Fall, 1999). Scholarly study of indentured workers at an iron foundry, 1750-1800, based on company records.

Morgan, Kenneth. *Slavery and Servitude in Colonial America: A Short History.* New York: New York University Press, 2001. Extensive statistical information and discussion of legal status of immigrants.

Wokeck, Marianne. *Trade in Strangers: The Beginnings of Mass Migration to America.* University Park: Pennsylvania State University Press, 1999. Scholarly study of eighteenth century German and Irish immigration, principally to Pennsylvania.

Zipf, Karin. *Labor of Innocents: Forced Apprenticeship in North Carolina, 1715-1919.* Baton Rouge: Louisiana State University Press, 2005. Describes institutionalized involuntary servitude of poor women and teenagers in colonies, when it was a feature of immigration, and in nineteenth century America.

SEE ALSO: Alien Contract Labor Law of 1885; British immigrants; Civil War, U.S.; Contract labor system; Coolies; Credit-ticket system; Economic opportunities; Guest-worker programs; Pilgrim and Puritan immigrants; Slave trade.

INDIANA

SIGNIFICANCE: Because of Indiana's history and geographical location, its population has a higher percentage of people who originated in the American South than any other midwestern state. Indeed, Indiana is politically, culturally, and linguistically the most "southern" midwestern state. In contrast, international immigration has had less of an impact in Indiana than in most other states. In 1880, only 7.8 percent of the state's residents were foreign born, compared to 23.0 percent in Illinois and 14.0 percent in Ohio.

PROFILE OF INDIANA

Region	Midwest
Entered union	1816
Largest cities	Indianapolis (capital), Fort Wayne, Evansville, South Bend, Gary
Modern immigrant communities	Mexicans, Germans

Population	Total	Percent of state	Percent of U.S.	U.S. rank
All state residents	6,314,000	100.0	2.11	15
All foreign-born residents	264,000	4.2	0.70	22

Source: U.S. Census Bureau, *Statistical Abstract for 2006.*

Notes: The U.S. population in 2006 was 299,399,000, of whom 37,548,000 (12.5%) were foreign born. Rankings in last column reflect total numbers, not percentages.

After the United States won its independence in 1783, most of what would become the state of Indiana was considered the property of Native Americans, as stipulated by the 1795 Treaty of Greenville. However, between 1800 and 1810, Indians made land cessions in the extreme southern part of Indiana and again in 1838, when the Potawatomi people were forcibly removed from the state, in defiance of earlier treaty provisions, and removed to Kansas. Their removal made desirable land available to Kentuckians and other southern American settlers before many international immigrants arrived.

EUROPEAN IMMIGRANTS

The first substantial group of overseas immigrants to enter Indiana were Swiss, who settled in Switzerland County, along the Ohio River in the extreme southeast part of the state. Swiss surveyors arrived in 1796, and a colony was founded at Vevay in 1803. Vevay still held a Swiss wine festival as late as 2008.

Germans formed the largest immigrant group to come to Indiana before the late twentieth century, but they were not as numerous there as in many other states. Germans began a colony at New Harmony in 1814. However, they were gone by 1825, and their land was sold to Robert Owen and a group of British utopians. Political problems in

Germany in 1848, together with the scarcity of agricultural land, led to the arrival of more Germans later. Many of these immigrants settled in the southeastern part of the state, near the Swiss. That part of the state was so heavily populated by German speakers that a traveler reported leaving a boat at Madison in 1846 and going north for almost eighty miles without hearing a word of English spoken. German immigrants were most prominent in Indiana's Ripley and Dubois Counties but were outnumbered by American southerners and Ohioans.

In later decades, Indiana's German residents began moving toward the state's cities. In 1850, Germans constituted 14 percent of the population of Indianapolis, where Germans became enough of a political force to make public school instruction in German optional. In Fort Wayne, skilled German workers were recruited for local industries. By the late nineteenth century, that city's population was said to be 80 percent German. German organizations—Turners Clubs and singing societies—were still active in 2000 in Indiana.

Other Indianans of German extraction were not international immigrants. Long-established Amish communities maintained a separate existence and spoke the German dialect called Pennsylvania Dutch. According to the 2000 U.S. Census, that dialect was spoken at home by almost eight thousand Indiana residents.

LATE TWENTIETH CENTURY AND MEXICAN IMMIGRATION

In 1960, only 2 percent of Indiana's residents were foreign born, and most of these were Germans. However, the state's immigrant mix began to change during the 1970's. Failures in Mexico's economy drove many Mexicans north in search of work, and some of these people found their way to Indiana. Although fewer Mexican immigrants came to Indiana than to other midwestern states, they brought a fundamental change to the state's ethnic composition. By the year 2000, foreign-born residents constituted only 3 percent of Indiana's nearly 6,100,000 residents. However, the 185,555 residents whose primary language at home was Spanish outnumbered German speakers by more than four to one.

Timothy C. Frazer

FURTHER READING
Blakely, George T. *Creating a Hoosier Self-Portrait: The Federal Writers' Project in Indiana, 1935-42.* Bloomington: Indiana University Press, 2005.
Carmony, Donald F. *A Brief History of Indiana.* Indianapolis: Indiana Historical Bureau, 1966.
Haller, Charles R. *Across the Atlantic and Beyond: German and Swiss Immigrants to America.* Bowie, Md.: Heritage Books, 1993.

SEE ALSO: German immigrants; Illinois; Kentucky; Ku Klux Klan; Mexican immigrants; New Harmony; Ohio; Rapp, George; Swiss immigrants.

INDOCHINA MIGRATION AND REFUGEE ASSISTANCE ACT OF 1975

THE LAW: Federal legislation establishing a resettlement assistance program for Southeast Asian refugees
DATE: Enacted on May 23, 1975

SIGNIFICANCE: Strongly supported by President Gerald R. Ford and opposed by those who feared an influx of Southeast Asian refugees after the end of the conflict in Vietnam, the Indochina Migration and Refugee Assistance Act allowed some 200,000 Cambodians and Vietnamese to enter the United States under a special "parole" status and provided financial assistance for their resettlement.

After Saigon fell to the North Vietnamese at the end of the Vietnam War in 1975, thousands of people tried to flee Southeast Asia. Although many Americans feared that a large number of refugees would deflate wages and create a social burden, Congress passed the Indochina Migration and Refugee Assistance Act of 1975, which permitted refugees from Cambodia and Vietnam to enter the country and provided $455 million for resettlement. In 1976, the act was amended to include refugees from Laos. Nonprofit groups, including the U.S. Conference of Catholic Bishops, Civitan International, and the International Rescue Committee, sponsored families, providing food, clothing, and shelter until they could support themselves.

Initially, the U.S. government placed refugees in scattered locations, hoping to prevent the formation of large enclaves. Once families' lives stabilized, however, they tended to move near each other, with many settling permanently in Texas and California.

Cynthia A. Bily

FURTHER READING

Bloemraad, Irene. *Becoming a Citizen: Incorporating Immigrants and Refugees in the United States and Canada.* Berkeley: University of California Press, 2006.

Kelly, Gail Paradise. *From Vietnam to America: A Chronicle of the Vietnamese Immigration to the United States.* Boulder, Colo.: Westview Press, 1977.

Strand, Paul, and Woodrow Jones, Jr. *Indochinese Refugees in America: Problems of Adaptation and Assimilation.* Durham, N.C.: Duke University Press, 1985.

SEE ALSO: Amerasian Homecoming Act of 1987; Asian immigrants; Cambodian immigrants; Congress, U.S.; Hmong immigrants; Laotian immigrants; Refugees; Vietnamese immigrants.

INDONESIAN IMMIGRANTS

SIGNIFICANCE: Although the Southeast Asian nation of Indonesia has one of the largest populations in the world, it has sent comparatively few immigrants to the United States. However, the numbers of Indonesian immigrants began increasing rapidly during the 1980's, and their heavy concentration in Southern California gave them considerable visibility.

Indonesia is made up of a large number of populated islands located south of Southeast Asia's Malay Peninsula. It has the largest population of any nation in Southeast Asia and is home to a diverse variety of ethnic and linguistic groups. The most numerous of these groups are the Javanese, who constitute about 45 percent of Indonesia's total population. Partly because it was a Dutch colony until 1949, Indonesia has had fewer political, eco-

PROFILE OF INDONESIAN IMMIGRANTS

Country of origin	Indonesia
Primary language	Indonesian
Primary regions of U.S. settlement	Southern California
Earliest significant arrivals	Early 1950's
Peak immigration period	1980's
Twenty-first century legal residents*	25,281 (3,160 per year)

*Immigrants who obtained legal permanent resident status in the United States.
Source: Department of Homeland Security, *Yearbook of Immigration Statistics, 2008.*

nomic, and cultural ties to the United States than many other Asian nations.

Some of the earliest American immigrants of Indonesian origin were people of mixed European and Indonesian ancestry. These mixed-background migrants left Indonesia during the late 1940's during the nation's struggle for independence. Many of them went first to the Netherlands before moving to the United States. During the mid-1950's, U.S. government scholarships enabled some Indonesian students to study in the United States. During the 1960's, political and economic turmoil in Indonesia prompted some emigration to the United States by Indonesians, especially ethnic Chinese from the archipelago.

By 1980, an estimated 26,700 Indonesian-born immigrants lived in the United States. About one-fourth of them had arrived in the United States before 1960 and close to one-third had arrived between 1960 and 1964. During the 1980's, immigration from Asia increased greatly. By 1990, the total number of foreign-born people from Indonesia in the United States doubled, reaching more than 53,600. This figure increased to close to 77,000 in 2000 and reached an estimated 86,000 by 2007.

Despite this rapid growth, Indonesian migration still remained much lower than immigration from many other parts of Asia. Even in the heavy migration years from 1999 to 2008, a time during which migrants from Asia made up about one-

BARACK OBAMA AND INDONESIA

Although Indonesia's ties with the United States have historically been limited, the Southeast Asian nation has a special connection with the forty-fourth president of the United States. Between the ages of six and ten, future U.S. president Barack Obama lived in Jakarta, Indonesia, while his mother was married to an Indonesian man. Obama attended two schools in Indonesia and learned to speak some Indonesian—the only language other than English that he speaks. While he was in Indonesia, his mother gave birth to a daughter, Maya Soetoro, by her Indonesian husband. Obama's half sister holds dual American and Indonesian citizenship. She later completed her education in the United States and became a teacher in Hawaii. Adding to her family's rich ethnic mix, she married the Canadian-born son of Malaysian Chinese immigrants to Canada and became Maya Soetoro-Ng.

nesian food. Indonesian Americans employed outside the restaurant industry are most heavily represented in professional and technical occupations.

Carl L. Bankston III

FURTHER READING

Takaki, Ronald. *Strangers from a Different Shore.* Boston: Back Bay Books, 1998.

Taylor, Jean Gilman. *Indonesia: Peoples and Histories.* New Haven, Conn.: Yale University Press, 2003.

Vickers, Adrian. *A History of Modern Indonesia.* New York: Cambridge University Press, 2005.

SEE ALSO: Asian immigrants; California; Filipino immigrants; Los Angeles; Malaysian immigrants; Muslim immigrants; Thai immigrants; Vietnamese immigrants.

INDUSTRIAL REVOLUTION

THE EVENT: Era during which the economies of Western countries began moving away from primarily agricultural bases to industrial and commercial bases

DATE: Nineteenth century

SIGNIFICANCE: The shift from economies based largely on subsistence agriculture to economies based on industry and trade created a vast number of unskilled and semi-skilled jobs that helped to attract immigrants to the United States.

quarter of all new legal immigrants to the United States, only about 3,000 immigrants per year came from Indonesia. This figure was dwarfed by the averages of more than 60,000 Chinese and 54,000 Filipinos arriving every year.

In 2007, California was home to about 40,000 people who had been born in Indonesia. This figure accounts for nearly one-half of all Indonesians in the United States. The single-largest concentration of these immigrants was in the Los Angeles/Long Beach metropolitan area, where about 17,500 Indonesians lived. Another 6,000 had settled in the Riverside-San Bernardino area. Other Indonesians were scattered around the country, with the greatest numbers found in Washington, D.C. (about 5,000 Indonesians in 2007), the New York-New Jersey area (about 4,300), and Southern California's Orange County metropolitan area (about 3,600).

Restaurants have been an important source of employment for Indonesians, about 12 percent of whom were employed in commercial eating and drinking places during 2007, according to U.S. Census data. Indeed, roughly one of every eight Indonesian Americans worked as a cook, waiter, or waitress. The Los Angeles area, in particular, has had a significant number of restaurants owned by Indonesian immigrants and specializing in Indo-

The demographic revolution that began in the Western world during the eighteenth century and accelerated during the nineteenth and twentieth centuries made it imperative to develop employment for the increasing numbers of people in the developing nations. During the long period that became known as the Industrial Revolution, large numbers of Europeans moved from rural areas into cities where jobs in new industries were to be found. Many of these people crossed the Atlantic Ocean looking for work and joined native-born Americans who were moving into cities.

CHANGING SOURCES OF ECONOMIC GROWTH

As late as the eighteenth century, the great bulk of people in Europe and North America were still

supporting themselves and their families through their individual labor, mostly on farmlands. They relied on human and animal power to grow and harvest plant food crops and raise livestock that would sustain their lives. In some places, individual farmers made their farms more efficient by harnessing wind and hydraulic power. They had sailing vessels propelled by wind, and grain mills and lumber mills powered by waterwheels and windmills. Coal, petroleum, and electrically powered machines were still largely unknown.

The early nineteenth century saw human beings beginning to harness a new form of power: steam, which could make machines work faster and with greater power. As the century wore on, steam power was made to run trains, ships, and factory machines. By the end of the century, electricity was be-

ing harnessed to run machines even more efficiently, and new kinds of motors were being made to run off petrochemical fuels, such as gasoline.

These new forms of machinery did not suddenly spring into use. They required many years of experimentation and adaptation to reach high levels of efficiency. Steam-powered train, ferry, and shipping services began operating during the first decades of the nineteenth century, but they did not become commercially significant until around mid-century. Meanwhile, factories were beginning to adapt steam-powered machines to manufacturing. A key element of the process of modernizing manufacturing was the introduction of standardization of parts.

The importance of standardization was especially evident in the manufacture of guns, an indus-

Contemporary magazine illustration of the New York headquarters of I. M. Singer & Co. in 1857. Singer was a primary manufacturer of sewing machines, which played a major role in the Industrial Revolution and made possible the employment of many thousands of immigrants. (Library of Congress)

try that played an important role in developing the technique. Armories in Springfield, Massachusetts, and Harpers Ferry, Virginia (later in West Virginia), helped pioneer in the development of machine tools, jigs, and templates that made possible the production of multiple identical parts. Standardized parts made assembly faster and more economical and made replacement parts much easier and cheaper to obtain. Standardization was later introduced into the manufacturing of many other products for which there was increasing demand, such as clocks, sewing machines, farm machines, and transportation equipment. Before the Industrial Revolution, complicated devices such as guns, tools, and clocks had been made by hand by workers trained by long experience to produce individual parts, one at a time. Making the parts and assembling them both required high levels of skills. After techniques for manufacturing identical, and thus fully interchangeable, parts were perfected, the finished products could be assembled relatively easily by semiskilled and sometimes even unskilled workers—many of whom were recent immigrants to the United States.

CREATION OF INDUSTRIAL AMERICA

After the mid-nineteenth century, the development of machine-powered mass-manufacturing techniques powered the American economy. It had begun in the textile industry, whose mills had provided jobs for large numbers of the Irish immigrants who were then beginning to enter the United States. However, mass manufacturing extended well beyond the textile industry and became, in a sense, self-generating. As increasingly large factories required ever greater quantities of materials to operate, their needs spurred the development of other industries. For example, the railroads required steel in huge quantities for their thousands of miles of rails and for the trains themselves. The steamships and ferries that were beginning to move passengers and cargoes at previously unimagined speeds needed giant foundries to manufacture the plates that formed them and the engines that powered them.

The immense demands for the iron alloys from which to fashion the new machines created a steel industry whose size was empowered by the Bessemer process that was invented in 1855 but only widely adopted after the U.S. Civil War (1861-

1865). The Bessemer process made possible the vast steel mills of Pittsburgh and other cities, and the steel industry in turn contributed to the great expansion of the coal-mining industry, which was also beginning to supply great amounts of fuel to railroads and steamships. Through the late nineteenth century, coal mining employed huge numbers of unskilled immigrant laborers.

One of the ultimate achievements of the Industrial Revolution was the creation of assembly-line production that Henry Ford introduced to automobile manufacturing during the early twentieth century. To the system of interchangeable parts, assembly lines added the advantage of simplifying the tasks performed by individual workers to make large-scale manufacturing more profitable. Simplification of workers' tasks opened many jobs to unskilled immigrant workers.

Nancy M. Gordon

FURTHER READING

Hounshell, David A. *From the American System to Mass Production, 1800-1932.* Baltimore: Johns Hopkins University Press, 1984. Traces the development of engineering technology that underlay the Industrial Revolution.

Mayr, Otto, and Robert C. Post, eds. *Yankee Enterprise: The Rise of the American System of Manufactures.* Washington, D.C.: Smithsonian Institution Press, 1981. Collective review of the factors that created the Industrial Revolution in America.

Mokyr, Joel. *The Lever of Riches: Technological Creativity and Economic Progress.* New York: Oxford University Press, 1990. Recounts how technological innovation drove the Industrial Revolution.

Singer, Charles, et al., eds. *The Late Nineteenth Century, 1850 to 1900.* Vol. 5 in *A History of Technology.* New York: Oxford University Press, 1954-1958. Part of a classic multivolume work tracing the role played by technology in history.

Stiles, T. J. *The First Tycoon: The Epic Life of Cornelius Vanderbilt.* New York: Alfred A. Knopf, 2009. Biography of one of the major players in the ferry, shipping, and railroad industries during the nineteenth century that provides fascinating coverage of technological advances in each of the industries that Vanderbilt developed.

Temin, Peter, ed. *Engines of Enterprise: An Economic History of New England.* Cambridge, Mass.: Harvard University Press, 2000. Collection of essays

by a number of scholars that examine the role played by industrial technology in New England's economy.

SEE ALSO: Coal industry; Economic consequences of immigration; Economic opportunities; European immigrants; European revolutions of 1848; Immigration waves; Iron and steel industry; Settlement patterns.

INDUSTRIAL WORKERS OF THE WORLD

IDENTIFICATION: Global labor union
DATE: Founded in June, 1905
LOCATION: Chicago, Illinois
ALSO KNOWN AS: Wobblies

SIGNIFICANCE: The Industrial Workers of the World was the first large labor union in the United States to organize as an industrial union instead of according to craft. It focused a large part of its organizing efforts on newly arrived immigrant workers, whom other union organizations ignored or overtly discriminated against.

The Industrial Workers of the World (IWW) was founded in Chicago in 1905 by unionists opposed to the policies of the American Federation of Labor (AFL), in particular its refusal to organize unskilled workers. Founding members included William D. "Big Bill" Haywood of the Western Federation of Miners, Daniel De Leon of the Socialist Labor Party, and Eugene V. Debs of the Socialist Party. Unlike most union and leftist political organizations in the United States during the early twentieth century, the IWW recognized the importance of organizing all workers regardless of race, gender, national origin, or craft. This realization stemmed from its philosophy of international worker solidarity as expressed in the IWW slogan, "One Big Union." Although many of the workforces involved in IWW organizing drives were made up primarily of European immigrants, internationalist immigrant organizing was important given the separation of communities along ethnic lines.

Other unions, especially those affiliated with Samuel Gompers and the AFL, considered immigrant workers competition for what were considered "American" jobs. The IWW sought to overcome the artificial separations enforced by governmental, economic, and religious authorities in order to create a sense of common struggle. Strikes among miners and textile workers that were organized with the help of the IWW included women, children, and men of all backgrounds and were usually successful, at least in terms of creating class solidarity, based in part on the union's opposition to the "owning classes" of all nations.

In the eastern United States, the IWW organized among textile workers (often the most exploited members of the workforce), many of whom were of southern European origin. In places such as Lawrence, Massachusetts, and other mill towns, the IWW represented multiple nationalities to create a strong, unified strike against the textile mill owners. In the western United States, the IWW was one of the first major national labor organizations to organize Asian workers. In doing so, the union stood in contrast not only to the AFL but also to radical political groups such as the Socialist Party. Asian workers were separated not only by their language differences but also by their physical and cultural differences. Consequently, they faced both de facto and de jure discrimination and the threat of deportation. The IWW worked to defend these workers' rights while organizing. In 1912, after Italian organizers Arturo Giovannitti and Joseph Ettor were arrested in the Lawrence strike, it was the IWW that led the campaign to free the men. The U.S. government responded with mass deportations of immigrants associated with the union.

In its heyday during World War I, the IWW claimed more than 100,000 members. By the first decade of the twenty-first century, it was a much smaller organization. The union has continued to organize among immigrants and other underrepresented workers and advocate for immigrant rights.

Ron Jacobs

FURTHER READING

Foner, Philip S. *History of the Labor Movement in the United States.* Vol. 4. New York: International Publishers, 1965.
Thompson, Fred W., and John Bekken. *The Indus-*

trial Workers of the World: Its First One Hundred Years—1905 Through 2005. Foreword by Utah Phillips. Chicago: Industrial Workers of the World, 2006.

SEE ALSO: Economic opportunities; Employment; Espionage and Sedition Acts of 1917-1918; Garment industry; Gompers, Samuel; Industrial Revolution; International Ladies' Garment Workers' Union; Labor unions; Massachusetts; United Farm Workers.

INFECTIOUS DISEASES

DEFINITION: Communicable human diseases caused by pathogenic microorganisms

SIGNIFICANCE: During North America's colonial era, immigrants from Europe and Africa imported many contagious diseases that wreaked havoc on not only Native American populations but also nonimmunized colonists. Successive waves of disease-carrying immigrants during the nineteenth century set off epidemics ranging from cholera to plague, despite ever more effective public health measures, and encountered effective anti-immigrant sentiment and action. During the early twenty-first century, visitors as well as immigrants posed threats to U.S. public health as carriers of new diseases and new strains of old diseases.

Every person and every community lives in an environment filled with bacteria, viruses, fungi, and parasites, many of which carry pathogens potentially lethal to humans. People who live for many years in the same area and with the same neighbors develop effective immune system defenses against the commonly occurring pathogens. Sometimes they pass their immunity along to subsequent generations genetically. When a new pathogen is inserted into a community by changes in the environment or the intrusion of new people, the effects may be devastating, as existing members of the community may have limited or no developed biological defenses. Unlike noninfectious diseases such as diabetes or cancer, an infectious disease can be passed among members of a community by the actions of carriers of pathogens. These carriers might include tainted foods or water; insects, parasites, and their droppings; and infected people. During the centuries before germ theory made modern medicine an effective counter to most infectious diseases, there was little understanding of pathogens and carriers, and little that any human community could do to defend against them.

COLUMBIAN EXCHANGE

The early history of European and African settlement in the Western Hemisphere provides a depressingly long list of epidemics and pandemics. Many of these occurred on a large geographical scale, sparked by the contact of Native American communities with immigrant men and women who carried deadly pathogens to which the carriers themselves were immune or highly resistant. In turn, these intruders were susceptible to Native American diseases, one example of which may have been syphilis. It seems that some infected Spanish explorers contracted that sexually transmitted disease (STD) and spread it after their return to Europe. For their part, Native Americans died by the thousands of imported Old World diseases such as measles, mumps, smallpox, typhus, and influenza. This biological interaction is sometimes referred to as part of the "Columbian Exchange," taking its name from the Italian explorer Christopher Columbus.

Although early immigrants from Europe and Africa tended to share resistance to a wide range of pathogens, later generations, long removed from their homelands and isolated from certain diseases in the New World, tended to lose their natural defenses to the Old World diseases. When new immigrants arrived from the Old World, even from the same cities and regions as the ancestors of second- or third-generation colonists or slaves, their reinfusion of disease-causing pathogens could and often did trigger outbreaks—even epidemics—among the settled immigrants populations. Perhaps ironically, however, this was least likely to occur in large cities such as New York, Boston, and Philadelphia, in which steady streams of new immigrants kept levels of exposure and resistance relatively high among the urban populations.

Some imported diseases, such as mosquito-borne malaria and yellow fever, were initially and inadvertently inserted into humid coastal environ-

ments in the New World that were well suited to the insects by Spanish slavers and their human cargoes. While the African immigrant populations were generally resistant to the potentially deadly diseases, both Native Americans and Europeans proved to be highly susceptible. The insects became carriers when they sucked the blood of human carriers. In regions where human carriers diminished in number, as along the northern Atlantic coastline (thanks in part to the practice of quarantine), the incidence of the disease dropped off. Fresh arrivals of African or Caribbean slaves along the southern U.S. coasts, however, helped maintain high incidence levels. Even before Walter Reed and other researchers untangled the true nature of yellow fever during the early twentieth century, Americans sought strict limitations on immigrants and even trade from Cuba and other island sources of the disease whose carriers set off recurrent outbreaks.

Epidemics During the Age of Sail

Traditional Western medicine had long associated disease with filth, a lack of basic hygiene, and, by the later eighteenth century, poverty. From the 1820's, ships from Europe brought trickles and then floods of immigrants from Ireland and central Europe. Many of these people were both poverty-stricken and sick with opportunistic diseases such as typhus, influenza, and typhoid fever. Cramped and unsanitary quarters, lack of clean clothing, and poor nutrition shipboard exacerbated weak constitutions and undermined the healthy. Rightly fearful of the spread of infectious diseases, civic and state authorities in North America maintained quarantines and isolation facilities at major ports for sick or suspect passengers. Although a single case of influenza might be gotten over with no lasting effects, chronic conditions such as STDs and Hansen's disease (leprosy) presented almost no possibilities of cure. Those who suffered from such maladies would be turned away, to find refuge elsewhere. They might then attempt to enter the country illicitly or simply return to their homelands.

Even due diligence could fail, especially with emerging diseases. Cholera had first broken out of its homeland in eastern India in 1817, but America was spared the ensuing first pandemic. The second pandemic proved less accommodating, and Irish immigrants brought the waterborne disease with

them to Canadian and U.S. port cities in 1832. New York City lost 3,000 residents in July and August, and New Orleans suffered 4,340 fatalities during three weeks in October. Eventually spreading to the western frontier, cholera killed an estimated 150,000 people in North America between 1832 and 1849. The year 1866 saw the final epidemic of cholera in the United States, when eastern and Gulf port cities counted 50,000 deaths.

The popular conception of Roman Catholic Irish immigrants as lazy, poor, and disease-ridden was reinforced by the huge numbers of penniless refugees who appeared as the potato famine (1845-1852) ravaged their homeland. A British government report in 1856 noted that malnutrition and starvation among the Irish were accompanied by many other medical conditions, including infectious diseases: "fever, scurvy, diarrhea and dysentery, cholera, influenza and ophthalmia." Despite the availability of vaccines, smallpox "prevailed epidemically," and typhus was nearly endemic in crowded Irish cities. Each year, hundreds of thousands of Irish died and one-quarter million Irish emigrated. Although British port authorities were supposed to screen out emigrants carrying diseases before they departed, this task was often left to American officials. As a result, many emigrants died on ships, earning the passenger vessels the nickname "coffin ships." Despite screening and quarantine procedures, many disease carriers still managed to enter the United States, and many of them settled in already overcrowded and unsanitary ethnic enclaves in American cities, inducing outbreaks as well as increased public health structures and efforts to combat the increasingly complex disease regimes.

Public Health and Anti-Immigrant Sentiment

The fact that a significant percentage of immigrants were Roman Catholic and, to a growing extent, Jewish, as well as poor and suffering from diseases, fed the fears and prejudices of nativist and other anti-immigrant groups. During the last decades of the nineteenth and first decades of the twentieth centuries, groups such as the Immigration Restriction League harnessed the ideas of new medical pseudosciences in their attempts to limit the diversity of immigrants. They blamed the perceived prevalence of certain diseases among east-

U.S. Health Service officers inspect Japanese immigrants as they arrive on the West Coast of the United States in the early 1920's. (NARA)

ern and central European immigrants, especially typhus and tuberculosis (TB), on natural genetic dispositions.

Tuberculosis was once widely considered to be a genteel or sensitive person's disease. However, as it spread among the working classes in large U.S. cities, it became associated with poverty, squalor, and ethnic minorities, and sufferers were rounded up for isolation. A major outbreak in 1892 in New York City led to passage of the National Quarantine Act of 1893. San Francisco's bubonic plague outbreak in 1900-1901 was very likely sparked by stowaways aboard a visiting Japanese freighter. However, its first known fatality was a Chinese immigrant who lived in a very poor Chinese neighborhood. Residents of Chinatown, fearing both mobs and the government, hid subsequent cases of plague until the outbreak could no longer be concealed. Anti-Chinese sentiment then flashed across the city, and there were calls to eradicate the Asian American

neighborhood. Cooler heads prevailed, however, and modern antiplague measures kept the number of fatalities to only 122.

The popular linkage of disease and immigrants remained a major factor in U.S. public policy. Along the U.S.-Mexican border, perfunctory visual inspections for obvious signs of diseases were replaced by mandatory flea-dip baths for large numbers of very poor laborers and immigrants who sought work or refuge from the dislocations of the Mexican Revolution after 1917. The worldwide influenza pandemic that followed World War I may have killed more than 40 million people, including 675,000 Americans—a fatality rate that was five times the annual average for that disease. Like the war itself, the pandemic underlined the metaphorical shrinkage of the world and the increasing immediacy of threats that included disease. This sentiment resulted in the federal immigration restriction acts of 1921 and 1924.

MODERN HEALTH THREATS

Twentieth century science and technology complicated ideas about the relationship between immigrants and infectious diseases. Medical researchers have found cures or effective treatments for a wide variety of potentially deadly diseases. While Americans generally have access to these, many are beyond the reach of potential immigrants. At the same time, jet aircraft have made intercontinental travel swift and relatively cheap. Visitors and U.S. travelers abroad, as well as immigrants, can and do enter America as carriers of a wide variety of pathogens.

Those who enter a country illicitly, or choose to remain undocumented, often avoid public health screening and surveillance officials who might identify them as carriers and treat their conditions. Instead, such individuals threaten members of the communities in which they settle. By the end of the twentieth century, tuberculosis was making an alarming resurgence across the globe, especially in developing countries in Asia and Africa. The United States has one of the world's lowest levels of incidence of the disease, but neighboring Mexico's rate is ten times higher. TB presents a problem that is being echoed by other diseases: the natural evolution of drug-resistant varieties that threaten to make the American pharmaceutical arsenal obsolete.

Sexually transmitted diseases, including HIV/AIDS, can be treated, but immigrant communities are often resistant to public health measures. The worldwide spread of HIV/AIDS means that immigrants from Africa or Haiti are not alone suspect. The incidences of forms of hepatitis, malaria, dengue fever, and even leprosy were on the rise across the United States during the early twenty-first century, with health practitioners often noting the prevalence of the foreign-born among their victims. Since many modern-day immigrants find work in agricultural and food preparation and service sectors, the possibilities are good for spreading diseases beyond local communities. The failure effectively to screen those who cross America's borders also opens the door for incidences of bioterrorism, as it raises the potential for other types of terrorism as well.

Joseph P. Byrne

FURTHER READING

Apostolopoulos, Yiorgos, and Sevil Sönmez, eds. *Population Mobility and Infectious Disease.* New York: Springer, 2007. Collection of analytical articles on the variety of forms of population movement and the roles they have played in the spread of disease in the early twenty-first century.

Duffy, John. *Epidemics in Colonial America.* Baton Rouge: Louisiana State University Press, 1953. Older book that remains the standard text on the causes, courses, and effects of epidemic disease in Britain's North American colonies.

Grob, Gerald N. *The Deadly Truth: A History of Disease in America.* Cambridge, Mass.: Harvard University Press, 2002. Broad overview that goes beyond imported disease and effects of disease on immigrants to chronic and occupational problems from the colonial era to the end of the twentieth century.

Markel, Howard. *Quarantine! East European Jewish Immigrants and the New York Epidemics of 1892.* Baltimore: Johns Hopkins University Press, 1997. Study of the role of Jewish immigrants in the outbreaks of cholera and typhus, the ethnically based initial responses, and the role of the events in the passage of the 1893 screening and quarantine act.

_____. *When Germs Travel: Six Major Epidemics That Have Invaded America Since 1900 and the Fears They Have Unleashed.* New York: Pantheon Books, 2004. Chronicle of the historical outbreaks of tuberculosis, plague, typhus, cholera, HIV/AIDS, and trachoma in a very readable set of analytical narratives.

Shah, Nayan. *Contagious Divides: Epidemics and Race in San Francisco's Chinatown.* Berkeley: University of California Press, 2001. Study of San Francisco's large Chinese community that emphasizes the city's bubonic plague outbreaks and the roles of and influences on popular attitudes toward Asian immigrants.

SEE ALSO: Acquired immunodeficiency syndrome; African immigrants; Ellis Island; Eugenics movement; Globalization; Great Irish Famine; Haitian boat people; Health care; Smuggling of immigrants; Sweatshops; Transportation of immigrants; "Undesirable aliens"; World migration patterns.

INTELLIGENCE TESTING

DEFINITION: Use of psychometric standards concerning verbal and nonverbal abilities as part of legislation guiding decisions regarding authorized entry of foreigners into the United States

SIGNIFICANCE: The nascent science of intelligence testing developed in confluence with growing support for more severe controls on the acceptance of foreign-born entrants to the United States. Proponents of this view were able to highlight some of the early studies of psychologists conducting intelligence testing research as part of their efforts to pass restrictive immigration legislation, even in the face of presidential vetoes.

Intelligence testing has a long, honored tradition in the United States. It originated in France, where psychologist Alfred Binet was the first researcher to categorize student performances on specific reasoning tasks in terms of what he called their "mental ages" between 1904 and 1908. When he judged that students' mental ages were substantially lower than their chronological ages, he concluded that the test result argued for special remedial programs for the students. In 1912, the German psychologist William Stern defined "intelligence quotient," or "IQ," as a ratio of mental age divided by chronological age, multiplied by 100. What began in Europe as an earnest attempt to identify the needs of students with learning disabilities became a source of labeling with serious consequences in twentieth century America.

In 1910, the American psychologist Henry H. Goddard translated Binet's work into English. Goddard invented the label "moron" for any adult with a mental age between eight and twelve and advocated that those with IQs below 70 should not be allowed to have children. This perspective fit in well with a budding eugenics movement in the United States that advocated genetic engineering to raise intelligence levels, while reducing poverty and criminality. Lewis Terman, a professor at Stanford University, adapted the Binet scale and its measured intelligence quotient into its most commonly used form. Like Goddard, however, he was heavily influenced by biological determinism and

at least initially supported the idea that there were racial differences in human intelligence that reflected differing biological makeups. He recanted this view in 1937, but not before the stage was set for changes in important immigration legislation in the United States that reflected his earlier orientation toward the understanding of intelligence.

INTELLIGENCE TESTING AND IMMIGRATION LAW

The psychological work with the closest influence on later immigration policy was performed by Robert Yerkes of Harvard University. In 1917, when the United States entered World War I, he created the Army Mental Tests and oversaw their administration to 1.75 million Army draftees. Two versions of the tests, "Alpha" and "Beta," provided written and pictorial modalities so that illiterate servicemen could be tested as well. Carl Brigham, a Princeton University psychologist, analyzed the data that were collected and concluded that native-born draftees had higher IQ scores than immigrants. Moreover, a "Nordic" (northern European) subgroup had higher scores than those from southern and eastern Europe.

Brigham's work was attacked on methodological grounds, and he recanted his conclusions in 1930. However, he published his findings in 1923, the year before the federal Immigration Act of 1924 greatly restricted foreign entry to the United States. This act initially used the 1890 census as a basis for establishing strict quotas not to exceed 2 percent of those from each country included in the census. It greatly reduced the number of southeastern Europeans allowed into the country and had an impact that would be acutely felt during World War II, when entry was largely denied to European Jews seeking a safe haven from extermination in the Nazi Holocaust. Although detailed analyses of empirical work supporting immigration restrictions do not appear in the congressional hearings concerning this law, the acceptance of biological determinism and the discriminatory treatment of minorities may well have contributed to its passage.

LATER PERSPECTIVES

Relatively soon after the Immigration Act of 1924 was passed, the popularity of using racial theories of intelligence as guideposts to immigration law and policy waned. There was an increasing realization that test performances reflected familiarity

with American culture and language more often than they did an assessment of native intelligence. Meanwhile, members of the psychology-research establishment became more ethnically diverse, and during the aftermath of World War II there was more of an interest in explaining prejudicial attitudes. This was accentuated by a eugenics-oriented policy carried to horrific extremity by the German Nazi regime in Europe.

While the current intelligence testing community is much more sensitive to issues of cultural bias and attempts to develop "culture-fair" or "culture-free" instruments, elements of biological determinism have persisted. The Human Genome Project, which some people have claimed has important implications for controlling psychological disorders related to crime and homelessness, is a prominent example.

In addition, the early twenty-first century U.S. "war on terrorism," with its restriction of basic civil liberties, perpetuates an orientation toward selecting out undesirables in order to eliminate their perceived threat. Instead of classifying would-be immigrants as "feebleminded" on the basis of intelligence tests of questionable validity, there has developed a tendency to employ modern biometric technology that enforces even more restrictive policies to bolster homeland security.

Eric Yitzchak Metchik

FURTHER READING

Elliott, Stuart, Naomi Chudowsky, Barbara Plake, and Lorraine McDonnell. "Using the *Standards* to Evaluate the Redesign of the U.S. Naturalization Tests: Lessons for the Measurement Community." *Educational Measurement: Issues and Practice* 25, no. 1 (Fall, 2006): 22-26. Methodological critique of attempts by the U.S. Citizenship and Immigration Services to revise naturalization tests.

Perdew, Patrick R. "Developmental Education and Alfred Binet: The Original Purpose of Standardized Testing." In *2001: A Developmental Odyssey*, edited by Jeanne L. Higbee. Warrensburg, Mo.: National Association for Developmental Education, 2001. Comprehensive review of the historical evolution of intelligence testing in the United States, including its relationship to biological determinism and immigration law and practice.

Resta, Robert G. "The Twisted Helix: An Essay on Genetic Counselors, Eugenics, and Social Responsibility." *Journal of Genetic Counseling* 1, no. 3 (1992): 227-243. Examination of the historical implications of the eugenics movement and its most recent manifestations.

Samelson, Franz. "From 'Race Psychology' to 'Studies in Prejudice': Some Observations on the Thematic Reversal in Social Psychology." *Journal of the History of the Behavioral Sciences* 14 (1978): 265-278. Analysis of historical reasons for change in social psychological research, from studies of alleged racial differences in intelligence to causal models explaining racial prejudice.

Snyderman, Mark, and R. J. Herrnstein. "Intelligence Tests and the Immigration Act of 1924." *American Psychologist* 38, no. 9 (1983): 986-995. Critical analysis of the alleged link between viewpoints of psychologists conducting intelligence research and the passage of the Immigration Act of 1924 that greatly restricted immigration.

SEE ALSO: "Brain drain"; Eugenics movement; Higher education; Immigration Act of 1924; Immigration law; Language issues; Literacy tests; "Mongrelization"; Quota systems; Stereotyping.

INTERMARRIAGE

DEFINITION: Marriage unions between citizens and noncitizens

SIGNIFICANCE: Many Americans believe they have the right to marry whomever they wish and to live with their spouses in the United States, even when their marriages are to residents of other countries. This belief and the practice of intermarriage between immigrants and American citizens have helped shape American immigration policy and influenced the composition of American society.

Under early twenty-first century U.S. immigration policies, valid marriages of citizens of the United States of America with foreign-born persons give the citizens the right to petition for permission for

their spouses to enter the United States. After approval is given by the U.S. Citizenship and Immigration Services, noncitizen spouses may apply for a K-3 visa. This preferential nonimmigrant category has a relatively short waiting period, permits the applicants to apply for work in the United States, and provides the opportunity for permanent resident status. This category of immigration has become a major vehicle for new immigrants to the United States, thanks to the fact that family reunification has become a basic goal of U.S. immigration policy.

HISTORICAL PATTERNS OF IMMIGRATION

U.S. immigration policy, and ultimately the laws pertaining to marriage between aliens and citizens, has evolved in response to the American experience with earlier immigration, fear of change, and a number of major events that have affected U.S. history. Most early immigrants to what is now the United States came from northern and western Europe. After new immigrants arrived, they, in turn, brought in family members who added more permanence to the developing society. However, many immigrants also intermingled with Native Americans and people from countries other than those from which they themselves came. The federal Naturalization Act of 1790 focused on the majority immigration group and, as such, applied exclusively to free white people. During the mid-nineteenth century, Chinese workers, many of them gold prospectors and railroad workers, arrived in the United States. Negative American reactions to the presence of this distinctly different group prompted the U.S. Congress to enact the Chinese Exclusion Act of 1882, which prevented Chinese from becoming naturalized citizens. During the late nineteenth and early twentieth centuries, Japanese and other immigrants were also prohibited from becoming naturalized citizens. However, an 1855 law gave citizenship to foreign-born women who married American men.

During the mid-nineteenth and early twentieth centuries, the pool of immigrants entering the United States grew more diversified and included large numbers of people from southern and eastern Europe. In response to this new immigration, Congress enacted a series of restrictive laws that resulted in a U.S. quota system based on early migration patterns. These laws banned members of specific ethnic groups from immigrating, including those who were spouses of U.S. citizens.

During the 1940's, some American military personnel who went overseas during World War II wanted to return home with their spouses from other countries. Under public pressure, Congress amended immigration laws for this purpose. The 1945 War Brides Act and the 1946 Fiancées Act relaxed immigration restrictions by permitting many foreign spouses and children to immigrate to the United States. Previously excluded populations were still banned from immigrating, but in 1947, the Soldiers Bride Act changed that by allowing formerly barred spouses to enter the United States. Japanese, Filipino, Korean, and other foreign-born spouses of American service personnel then began entering the United States under a nonquota system. The Immigration and Nationality Act of 1952 continued the quota system but granted some Asians immigration privileges and made family reunification a choice method for migration. Nonquota immigrants who came to the United States under this law left open quota slots for other immigrants.

CHANGES FOLLOWING THE IMMIGRATION ACT OF 1965

The Immigration and Nationality Act Amendment of 1965 brought sweeping changes to immigration policy, including the elimination of the quota system. Family reunification was now among the highest preferences for legal migration and put foreign spouses second in line after children of American citizens. This new amendment opened the door for foreign-born immigrants from nations that were barred in 1924. Consequently, Latin American and Asian immigration surged dramatically.

During the early 1970's, American citizens gained the right to petition for their fiancés to be issued nonimmigrant K-1 visas, which permitted fiancés to visit the United States for periods of up to ninety days they actually married. By this time, family reunification was a driving force in qualifying for immigration, but it was causing consternation among some Americans who feared that sham marriages, or "marriages of convenience," would proliferate as a means of avoiding the stricter immigration regulations applying to other categories of immigrants. As a result, the Immigration and Mar-

riage Fraud Amendments (1986) made permanent residency a conditional status that required later proof of marriage validity. Ten years later, the Illegal Immigration Reform and Immigrant Responsibility Act of 1996 codified the responsibilities of American citizens who sponsor aliens.

In 2000, the Legal Immigration Family Equity Act, or LIFE Act, amended the rules for K-1 visas by permitting citizens and permanent residents to bring their spouses and children to the United States under a long-term resident category. Although this amendment raised some concerns regarding the potential for dramatic increases in immigration, it was also seen as a method of easing family dislocations, improving immigrant assimilation, and aiding social and cultural integration.

Throughout American history, men have used long-distance correspondence to find spouses, also known as mail-order brides, in other countries. Modern technology—most notably the World Wide Web and the Internet—and marriage brokers have increased this practice as a legitimate method of migrating to the United States.

Cynthia J. W. Svoboda

FURTHER READING

Bean, Frank D., and Gillian Stevens. *America's Newcomers and the Dynamics of Diversity.* New York: Russell Sage Foundation, 2003. Study of recent immigration and its impact on American society.

Constable, Nicole. *Romance on a Global Stage: Pen Pals, Virtual Ethnography, and "Mail Order" Marriages.* Berkeley: University of California Press, 2003. Research on the practice in which American men use introduction agencies to find Chinese and Filipina wives.

Cott, Nancy F. *Public Vows: A History of Marriage and the Nation.* Cambridge, Mass.: Harvard University Press, 2000. Wide-ranging study of the legal and social institution of marriage in the United States.

Gordon, Linda W. "Trends in the Gender Ratio of Immigrants to the United States." *International Migration Review* 39, no. 4 (Winter, 2005): 796-818. Provides information on recent immigration and the immigration laws that pertain to spousal migration.

Jasso, Guillermina, and Mark R. Rosenzweig. *The New Chosen People: Immigrants in the United States.*

New York: Russell Sage Foundation, 1990. Analysis of marriage and family reunification among immigrants in the United States.

SEE ALSO: Amerasian children; Cable Act of 1922; Child immigrants; Families; Filipino immigrants; Mail-order brides; Marriage; "Marriages of convenience"; War brides; War Brides Act of 1945.

INTERNATIONAL LADIES' GARMENT WORKERS' UNION

IDENTIFICATION: Industrial labor union
DATES: 1900-1995
ALSO KNOWN AS: ILGWU

SIGNIFICANCE: The International Ladies' Garment Workers' Union improved working conditions for garment makers, most of whom were immigrants. Under the leadership of David Dubinsky, himself an immigrant, the union became recognized as one of the most powerful labor unions in the United States.

The International Ladies' Garment Workers' Union (ILGWU), originally formed by the amalgamation of seven unions, at first consisted mostly of eastern European Jewish immigrants, although a few of the original two thousand members were of Irish descent. For years, the union was characterized by internal strife, mainly among the immigrants, many of whom were anarchists, socialists, or members of other radical groups; each group wanted to dominate the union. Still, the union grew.

From 1909 to 1911, large-scale strikes occurred in the garment industry. Most of the people in the picket lines were Jewish women, though a number of Italian immigrants also joined the lines. As a result of the strikes, clothing manufacturers agreed to deal directly with the ILGWU. Part of the settlement of the strikes involved the Protocol of Peace, which led to improved working conditions, increased wages, and shorter workdays for garment industry workers. The agreement was a departure from the strife that many of the immigrant members had brought to the union.

Official seal of the International Ladies' Garment Workers' Union. (The Granger Collection, New York)

The ethnic makeup of the ILGWU changed over the decades. In 1919, many Italian women's unions were chartered as part of the ILGWU, and an even larger number of Italian immigrants joined the union during the 1930's. Also during that decade, immigrants from Asian countries such as Syria, Lebanon, and Armenia entered the garment trade and eventually joined the ILGWU. Later, thousands of Latin American workers, including Puerto Ricans and Mexicans, entered the garment trade and became ILGWU members.

The union thrived under the leadership of David Dubinsky, a Polish immigrant who moved to New York City in 1911, where he worked as a cloak cutter and soon joined the ILGWU. During the 1920's, the communists tried to take over the union, but the moderates, led by Dubinsky, stopped them. Dubinsky became union president in 1932 and remained in that position until he retired in 1966. While he was union president, ILGWU membership grew significantly, especially during the Great Depression and the 1940's. By 1942, the ILGWU had about 300,000 members. Many historians have argued that under Dubinsky's leadership, the ILGWU became one of the most effective American labor unions. By the 1960's, however, the number of garment workers in the United States was begining to decline as a result of cheaper clothing

imports and the offshoring of factories. After Dubinsky's retirement, the ILGWU started to lose membership.

By 1995, the union had only about 125,000 members. That year, it united with the Amalgamated Clothing and Textile Workers' Union to form the Union of Needletrades, Industrial and Textile Employees (UNITE!), representing more than 250,000 members. During its time, the ILGWU bettered working conditions for thousands of immigrants in the garment industry. It improved the sanitation, safety, and comfort of the workplace and won living wages and respect for workers.

Richard Tuerk

FURTHER READING

Bender, Daniel E. *Sweated Work, Weak Bodies: Anti-Sweatshop Campaigns and Languages of Labor.* New Brunswick, N.J.: Rutgers University Press, 2005.

Danish, Max D. *The World of David Dubinsky.* Cleveland: World Publishing, 1957.

Wolensky, Kenneth C., Nicole Wolensky, and Robert P. Wolensky. *Fighting for the Union Label: The Women's Garment Industry and the ILGWU in Pennsylvania.* University Park: Pennsylvania State University Press, 2002.

SEE ALSO: Garment industry; Great Depression; Industrial Workers of the World; Irish immigrants; Italian immigrants; Jewish immigrants; Labor unions; Mexican immigrants; Puerto Rican immigrants; Sweatshops; Triangle Shirtwaist fire; Women immigrants.

IOWA

SIGNIFICANCE: The interactive relationship between the land, immigration, and settlement patterns in the Iowa region has influenced its history, culture, and institutions. Many of the ethnic languages have faded with the third generations of immigrants, but the core values of family and community remain an ideological stronghold in Iowa.

Iowa's first settlers came from the eastern and Old Northwest states of Ohio, Pennsylvania, New York, Indiana, Kentucky, and Virginia. These groups of-

ten resided and lived in one other state before finally moving on to Iowa. Because there was a lack of timber in many parts of the state, many settlers constructed sod houses.

By the mid-nineteenth century, settlers were pouring into the region. Iowans began to plan the first railroad in the state with the development of the Illinois Central. while the Chicago and Northwestern eventually reached Council Bluffs near Omaha. Council Bluffs became the main eastern hub for the Union Pacific. A few years later, the Chicago, Milwaukee, St. Paul, and Pacific completed a line across the state for trading and shipping products and crops. The state eventually had five railroad lines, which contributed significantly to the growth of the agricultural sector for immigrant farmers.

Hoping to attract more foreign-born settlers, state government officials government arranged the publication of a booklet titled *Iowa: The Home for Immigrants* (1870). Promoting the social, political, educational, and physical attributes of the state, the ninety-six-page booklet was issued in English, Dutch, and Swedish editions. In 1870, the state's population rose from 675,000 to 1,194,000. Germans constituted the largest ethnic group. Many Germans took up such professions as shopkeepers, newspaper editors, schoolteachers, bankers, and craftsmen. Other groups whom Iowa attracted from Europe included Swedes, Danes, Hollanders, and Britons. Members of these groups tended to concentrate within specific counties. For example, Scandinavians settled in Winneshiek and Story counties, Swedes in Boone County, and Danes in southwestern Iowa.

TWENTIETH CENTURY DEVELOPMENTS

After 1900, a coal mining industry began to emerge in Buxton, located in the state's northern Monroe County. Many southern and eastern immigrant groups went into the industry's low-skilled jobs because they did not require much training. Italian men often immigrated to the United States alone, working in the coal industry until they saved enough money to send for their families. By 1925, Iowa's coal industry was beginning a steady decline. By the mid-1950's, only a few underground mines remained in the state. After World War II, the state's economy improved with a rise in the manufacturing sector, which manufactured such products as appliances, fountain pens, food products, and farm implements.

The late twentieth century saw an influx of Hispanic immigrants in Iowa. Many of them were undocumented. In May, 2008, federal immigration authorities raided Agriprocessors, Inc, the nation's largest kosher meatpacking plant. and rounded up 389 illegal immigrants, who faced deportation. The raid also found that the plant used underage workers and abused Iowa labor laws in other ways.

Gayla Koerting

PROFILE OF IOWA

Region	Midwest
Entered union	1846
Largest cities	Des Moines (capital), Cedar Rapids, Davenport, Sioux City
Modern immigrant communities	Hispanics

Population	Total	Percent of state	Percent of U.S.	U.S. rank
All state residents	2,982,000	100.0	0.99	30
All foreign-born residents	112,000	3.8	0.29	36

Source: U.S. Census Bureau, *Statistical Abstract for 2006.*
Notes: The U.S. population in 2006 was 299,399,000, of whom 37,548,000 (12.5%) were foreign born. Rankings in last column reflect total numbers, not percentages.

FURTHER READING

Dinnen, Steve. "How an Immigration Raid Changed a Town: Tiny Postville, Iowa, Struggles to Regain Its Footing One Year After the Largest Immigration Sweep in U.S. History." *Christian Science Monitor,* May 31, 2009.

Iowa: The Home for Immigrants—Being a Treatise on the Resources of Iowa. Des Moines, Iowa: Mills, 1870.

Michaud, Marie-Christine. *From Steel Tracks to Gold-Paved Streets: The Italian Immigrants and the Railroad in the North Central States.* New York: Center for Migration Studies, 2005.

Stellingwerff, Johan. *Iowa Letters: Dutch Immigrants*

on the American Frontier. Translated by Walter Lagerwey. Grand Rapids, Mich.: William B. Eerdmans, 2004.

SEE ALSO: American Protective Association; Farm and migrant workers; Illinois; Kansas; Mississippi River; Missouri; Nebraska; Railroads.

IRANIAN IMMIGRANTS

SIGNIFICANCE: Iranian immigration to the United States is a recent phenomenon and has taken place primarily since 1975. The Islamic fundamentalist revolution of the late 1970's that transformed Iran into a theocratic state was a major world event that increased Iranian migration to the United States and created some negative stereotypes of Iranians among Americans. Some large Iranian American communities have developed, most notably in the region of Los Angeles.

The first recorded immigrants from Iran to the United States arrived during the 1920's, when 208 people from Iran (or Persia, as the country was then generally known) came to the United States. Their numbers increased over the next four decades but still remained comparatively small. Immigration and Naturalization Service data show only 9,059 people coming from Iran during the 1960's. In the 1970's through the 1990's, Iranian immigration shot up dramatically. Between 1970 and 1979, 33,763 Iranians immigrated legally to the United States. During the 1980's, this figure went up to 98,141 and decreased only slightly, to 76,899, during 1990's. Between 2000 and 2008, 67,915 new residents came from Iran.

By 1980, the Iranian-born population of the U.S. amounted to 130,000 people, compared to only about 24,000 a mere ten years earlier. More than 70 percent of this 1980 population had arrived during the second half of the 1970's, so they were an extremely new group. They were concentrated on the West Coast, with four out of ten Iranian residents of the United States living in California alone and one out of five living in the Los Angeles-Long Beach metropolitan area. The Iranian-born population continued to expand into the twenty-first century, growing from slightly more than 204,000 in 1990 to more than 290,000 in 2000 and to about 328,000 in 2007.

REVOLUTION AND IMMIGRATION

Much of the immigration from Iran to the United States resulted from political unrest in Iran and as a consequence of people fleeing the Iranian Revolution of 1978-1979 and the creation of the Islamic Republic in 1980. As a state devoted to the majority religion of the Shia form of Islam, the Iranian republic has been intolerant of minority religions. While an estimated 98 percent of Iranians are Shia Muslims, immigrants to the United States have disproportionately contained adherents of Iran's minority religions, which include Sunni Muslims, Zoroastrians, Jews, Baha'is, and Christians. Between the time of the revolution and 1990, the easiest way for an Iranian to obtain legal permission to enter the U.S. was by obtaining refugee status. Even after that time, Iranian refugees entered the United States at a rate of about 2,700 per year. From 1990 to 2008, nearly 50,000 people from Iran were admitted to the United States as refugees. However, not all these people were included in the official immigration statistics, because they were all accepted as refugees receiving legal permanent resident status.

Another important way that Iranians have entered the United States has been to come as stu-

PROFILE OF IRANIAN IMMIGRANTS

Country of origin	Iran
Primary language	Farsi
Primary regions of U.S. settlement	California
Earliest significant arrivals	1920's
Peak immigration period	1979-2008
Twenty-first century legal residents*	93,195 (11,649 per year)

*Immigrants who obtained legal permanent resident status in the United States.
Source: Department of Homeland Security, *Yearbook of Immigration Statistics, 2008.*

dents and then apply for legal residence. Generally, Iranians who have sought student or other types of visas have usually gone to Turkey first, became the United States closed its embassy in Iran after 1979. Before the revolution, Iran went through a rapid period of development, so that it has many well-educated people. In addition, many Iranian high school students had already studied English by the early 1970's, and knowledge of this language has made it easier for Iranian students to gain admission to American colleges and universities.

The period of tension between the United States and Iran immediately following the revolution created some problems for Iranians living in the United States. With the tacit approval of their new government, Iranians seized the American embassy in the capital of Tehran. They held Americans captive there for 444 days, creating an international crisis that contributed to U.S. president Jimmy Carter's electoral defeat in 1980 and caused strong anti-Iranian sentiments to sweep across the United States. The U.S. responded by instituting an "Iranian Control Program," which scrutinized the immigration status of nearly 60,000 people studying in the United States. In addition, even Iranian immigrants who were opposed to the new government in their country sometimes experienced open expressions of public hostility.

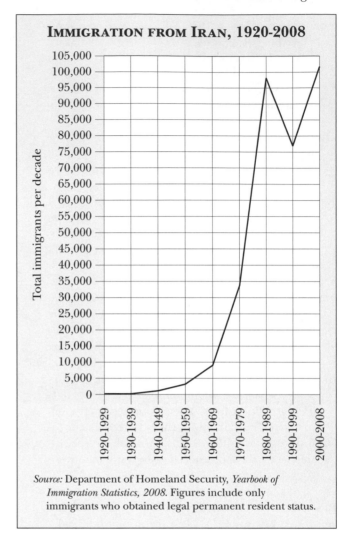

IMMIGRATION FROM IRAN, 1920-2008

Source: Department of Homeland Security, *Yearbook of Immigration Statistics, 2008.* Figures include only immigrants who obtained legal permanent resident status.

IRANIANS IN THE UNITED STATES

By 2007, the geographic concentration of Iranian immigrants had grown greater. About 60 percent of them lived in California, with more than one-third of Iranian-born people in the United States living in the Los Angeles-Long Beach metropolitan area and another 7 percent in nearby Orange County. Outside California, the largest numbers of Iranians could be found in Texas (home to about 6 percent) and in New York State (also about 6 percent). However, there were at least some Iranians in most of the states.

Because of their generally high levels of education, Iranians in the United States have tended to work in white-collar, professional occupations. In 2007, more than one-fifth of them worked as managers, officials, or proprietors. Other common oc-

cupations included salespeople, professional and technical workers, and physicians and surgeons. The most common industrial concentrations were in educational services or medical services. However, compared to native-born American women, Iranian women have shown relatively low labor force participation. In 2007, only about half of Iranian-born women in the United States were in the labor force.

Carl L. Bankston III

FURTHER READING

Ansari, Maboud. *The Making of the Iranian Community in America.* New York: Pardis Press, 1992. Useful overview of the growth of the Iranian immigrant community in the United States.

Bozorgmehr, Mehdi. "Iran." In *The New Americans: A Guide to Immigration Since 1965,* edited by Mary C. Waters, Reed Ueda, and Helen B. Marrow. Cambridge, Mass.: Harvard University Press, 2007. Best available short overview of Iranian immigration, written by a highly respected authority on this topic.

Dumas, Firoozeh. *Funny in Farsi: A Memoir of Growing Up Iranian in America.* New York: Villard, 2003. Warmly personal memoir of the experiences of an Iranian American.

Karim, Perssis, and Mehid M. Khortami, eds. *A World in Between: Poems, Stories, and Essays by Iranian-Americans.* New York: George Braziller, 1999. Anthology of literary works by Iranian immigrants that illustrate the experiences of Iranians in the United States.

Naficy, Maid. *The Making of Exile Cultures: Iranian Television in Los Angeles.* Minneapolis: University of Minnesota Press, 1993. Examination of how Iranian television has influenced group identity in the large ethnic community in Los Angeles.

Sharavini, Mitra K. *Educating Immigrants: Experiences of Second Generation Iranians.* New York: LFB Scholarly Publishing, 2004. Emphasizes the importance Iranian immigrants place on education for their children and looks at the relative success of Iranian ancestry students in American schools.

SEE ALSO: Arab immigrants; California; Israeli immigrants; Los Angeles; Muslim immigrants; Pakistani immigrants; Refugees; Religions of immigrants.

IRISH IMMIGRANTS

SIGNIFICANCE: During the early nineteenth century, Ireland was one of the main sources of immigration to the United States. Irish immigrants provided much of the labor for American cities and transportation systems and helped to establish Roman Catholicism in the United States.

The first identifiable wave of Irish migration to the United States began in 1729, when a poor harvest and a depression in the linen trade created economic hardship in Ireland. By 1784, just after the American Revolutionary War, an estimated 400,000 Irish lived in the new United States. During the six decades leading up the U.S. Civil War (1861-1865), the Irish became one of the nation's largest and most recognizable minority groups. Despite a decline in migration from Ireland in the twentieth century, Irish immigrants and their descendants have continued to play an important part in American history.

EARLY IRISH IMMIGRATION

The majority of the Irish in America before the nineteenth century were those who later became known as Scotch-Irish, descendants of people from Scotland who had moved to the northern part of Ireland in earlier centuries. These northern Irish were mainly Protestant, and distinctions between the them and other Irish immigrants came into popular usage in the nineteenth century when much larger numbers of Roman Catholic Irish began to arrive. Northern Irish migration peaked between the 1750's and the early 1770's, with an estimated 14,200 people from Northern Ireland reaching America during the 1750's, 21,200 during the 1760's, and 13,200 during the first of the 1770's, leading up to the American Revolution. Most of the pre-Revolutionary War immigration from Ireland took place between 1760 and 1775, when about 25,000 new arrivals came to the colonies.

The first U.S. Census in 1790 may have underestimated the proportion of the population that was of Irish background. However, in 1931 scholars who studied the linguistic and national background origin of the American people at the time of that first U.S. Census estimated that about one out of every ten Americans in 1790 was of Irish ancestry, including both Protestants and a smaller numbers of Catholics. The 1931 estimates indicated that people of Irish ancestry could be found in all parts of the new nation, but that they made up the largest proportions of populations in the South. According to these figures, in 1790, people of Irish background made up 15 percent of residents in Georgia, 14 percent in South Carolina, 12 percent in Kentucky and Tennessee, and 11 percent in Virginia and North Carolina. As immigration from Ireland and other parts of Europe increased during the first half of the nineteenth

century, however, the new immigrants tended to settle in the North and in the most urbanized parts of the country, rather than in the rural South.

EARLY NINETEENTH CENTURY IMMIGRATION

Movement from Ireland to the United States continued into the nineteenth century and began to increase in response to new opportunities. Notably, the U.S. began to build up its first transportation infrastructure, in the form of canals. The Erie Canal in New York State, perhaps the best known of these waterways, was under construction from 1818 to 1825. That project drew heavily on immigrant Irish labor, beginning the long history of building the American transportation infrastructure with Irish workers. The success of the Erie Canal stimulated the digging of canals in other parts of the country, creating a growing demand for workers who were willing to endure the hard labor required in canal building. Somewhat later, the Illinois & Michigan Canal, created between 1837 and 1848, employed hundreds of Irish laborers. To the south, Irish workers dug the canal system of swampy New Orleans.

Reliable data on how many Irish reached American shores date only from 1820. In 1819, the United States passed the Steerage Act. It gave the U.S. government information on immigration by requiring that all vessels reaching American shores deliver passenger lists to customs officials, who then sent copies to the U.S. State Department. That department would, in turn, submit the lists to Congress. As a result, 1820 became the first year in which the U.S. systematically collected data on new arrivals. During that same year, the Irish made up the single largest immigrant group, accounting for 43 percent of all arrivals to the United States.

Irish immigration continued at high levels throughout the decades leading up to the Civil War. The numbers of Irish immigrants rose from 51,617 during the 1820's to 170,672 during the 1830's, increasing still further to 656,145 during the 1840's. During the decade of the 1850's, the number of people arriving in the United States from Ireland reached its historical peak at 1,029,486.

One reason that the flow from Ireland increased during these years was that the demand for their labor continued to rise. The railroads made up the second major part of the American transportation

PROFILE OF IRISH IMMIGRANTS	
Countries of origin	Ireland, United Kingdom
Primary language	English
Primary regions of U.S. settlement	All regions
Earliest significant arrivals	1729
Peak immigration period	1830's-1920's
Twenty-first century legal residents*	12,379 (1,547 per year)

*Immigrants who obtained legal permanent resident status in the United States.
Source: Department of Homeland Security, *Yearbook of Immigration Statistics, 2008.*

system, after the canals. In 1830, the United States had only 23 miles of railroad. Only one decade later, this figure had grown to 2,818 miles. It increased to 9,021 miles in 1850 and then to 30,626 miles in 1860. Immigrants from Ireland, in particular, laid these miles of tracks.

The Irish were also pushed out of their native land by poverty and hunger as the middle of the century approached. The Potato Blight created famine in Ireland in the years 1845 to 1850. Continuing hardship, in addition to the existence of established Irish communities around the United States, pushed immigration from Ireland to its record level in the 1850's.

By the middle of the nineteenth century, Irish Americans were an urban and working class group. Only 16 percent of people born in Ireland lived on farms in the United States in 1850, compared to well over one-half of all Americans. A majority of the Irish in the United States (53 percent) lived in urban areas, at a time when urban areas were home to only 15 percent of the people in the nation. While only about 15 percent of all workers in the country were listed as laborers by occupation, about half the Irish natives in the census of that 1850 were so identified.

Anti-Irish feeling among other groups in the United States resulted, in part, from the concentration of many Irish immigrants in lower-income districts of cities, which caused the Irish to be associ-

ated with urban slums. Prejudice against this group also resulted from religious differences. Most Irish immigrants who arrived after 1830 were Roman Catholics. The established population of the United States was mainly Protestant. Suspicion of Catholics in general and of Irish Catholics in particular led to the creation of a number of anti-Catholic organizations. The Native American Party, later renamed the American Party and popularly known as the "Know-Nothing" Party, was the most prominent of these. Fear that floods of Catholics from Ireland and other locations threatened to overwhelm the native-born, Protestant population produced widespread victories for this anti-immigrant and anti-Catholic party in elections across the nation in 1855 and 1856.

IRISH IMMIGRANTS DURING THE U.S. CIVIL WAR

By 1860, a year before the Civil War broke out, well over 1.5 million people born in Ireland were living in the United States; they constituted about 6 percent of the country's total population and about 40 percent of its foreign-born population. New York State held the greatest number of Irish immigrants. Its 500,000 Irish residents made up about 13 percent of its entire population. More than 200,000 Irish immigrants lived in New York City alone, and Brooklyn, then still separate from New York City proper, was home to another 60,000.

Massachusetts had the second-largest number of residents who had been born in Ireland in 1860. Its nearly 200,000 Irish immigrants accounted for just over 16 percent of the whole population of the state. The city of Boston in Massachusetts held nearly 50,000 Irish-born people One out of every five of the people in tiny Rhode Island in 1860 had come from Ireland.

Although most of the Irish immigrants settled in the northeast, they could be found in almost all U.S. states. The southern states that were about to secede from the Union were home to about 100,000 Irish-born people. Louisiana alone was home to more than 26,000 people from Ireland during the last year before the war. The Irish were living on both sides of the divide when the Southern states attempted to secede from the Union, but they were more heavily represented in the North. An estimated 150,000 Irish served in the Union Army, while about 30,000 are believed to have fought for the Confederacy.

The best-known Irish fighting force during the Civil War was the New York Irish Brigade, which saw service from the time of the Battle of Bull Run in July, 1861. Nearly forty other Union regiments had "Irish" in their names. On the Confederate side, Irish fighting forces included the First Virginia Battalion and the Tenth Tennessee Regiment. Irish immigrants and descendants of Irish immigrants also served as individual soldiers in most of the other forces of both sides.

The heavy representation of the Irish in the Civil War was not always voluntary. Both sides drafted soldiers, drawing most heavily among poorer people, such as the Irish. In the North, the Enrollment Act of 1863 enabled any drafted person who paid a fee of three hundred U.S. dollars to hire a substitute draftee. Many low-income Irish immigrants believed that they were fighting on behalf of rich men.

Congress passed the Enrollment Act at a time when many Irish in northern cities were already becoming disenchanted with the war. Irish soldiers had suffered heavy casualties by 1863. As urban laborers, Irish workers were also competing with black workers. When President Abraham Lincoln announced the Emancipation Proclamation on January 1, 1863, many of these workers began to believe that the primary goal of the war was to free black slaves, rather than to preserve national unity. When local authorities used black workers to break a mainly Irish dock strike in New York in the spring of 1863, the anti-war and anti-black feelings of many New York Irish intensified.

On July 10, 1863, government officials posted the first list of draftees under the Enrollment Act. In New York, it seemed evident that the Irish wards were supplying more conscripts than other parts of the city. In response, protesters marched on the city recruiting station. The protests turned into riots, during which blacks became especially targeted. The rioters burned the Colored Orphan Asylum and beat up and lynched a number of New York's black residents. During the week that followed, more than one hundred riot victims died, and another 1,500 suffered serious injuries. The New York draft riots ended only after Union troops returned from the Battle of Gettysburg to reestablish order, and the city voted $2.5 million to buy exemptions.

Despite the draft riots and the resentment they

revealed, Irish immigrants fought in every battle of the Civil War. With the end of the war, the United States entered a new period of rapid industrialization and soon began welcoming a great tide of new immigrants. The Irish continued to be a significant part of immigration after the Civil War; however, the vast numbers of immigrants coming from other countries meant that Ireland no longer dominated international movement to the United States as it had done before the Civil War.

IMMIGRATION DURING AND AFTER THE GREAT WAVE

The Civil War was enormously destructive, but it also helped to stimulate the American economy and to push the United States toward more industrialization. As the nation entered the 1880's, it en-

tered into a remarkable period of economic expansion that transformed the United States into one of the world's greatest industrial powers by the time of World War I (1914-1918). It also began a dramatic rise in immigration as part of this economic expansion. Sources of immigration also began to shift, from northern and western European countries to southern and eastern European countries.

During this great immigration wave, immigrants continued to arrive from Ireland in significant numbers, but these numbers never again reached their peak of the 1850's. Irish migration actually began to decrease gradually around the turn of the twentieth century, even as overall numbers of immigrants to the United States were rapidly growing. As Irish immigration slowed, the Irish-born population of the United States gradually decreased

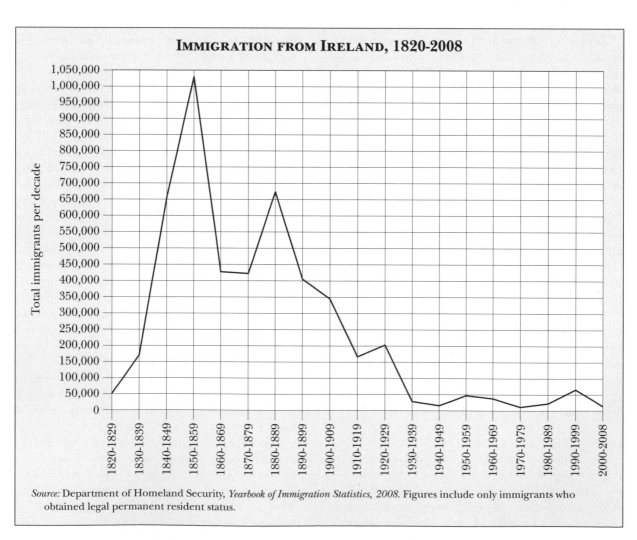

Source: Department of Homeland Security, *Yearbook of Immigration Statistics, 2008.* Figures include only immigrants who obtained legal permanent resident status.

from its maximum of about 1,870,000 people in 1880.

The heavy immigration of earlier years still meant that many locations in the United States had large Irish communities at the opening of the twentieth century. By 1900, the Irish-born population of the New York City metropolitan area had grown to an estimated 366,000 people. Another 650,000 residents of the New York area were children of Irish immigrants. Nearly 200,000 of the people in metropolitan Boston were from Ireland, and another 320,000 were children of Irish immigrants. In many cities across the United States, the existence of Irish American communities provided a basis for ethnically based politics and economic activity. The Kennedy family, which later produced America's first Roman Catholic president in the person of John F. Kennedy, arose from the Irish community of Boston.

Between 1900 and 1909, only 4.2 percent of new immigrants came from Ireland, compared to 43 percent one-half century earlier. The proportion of foreign-born people living in the United States who were from Ireland dropped from 44 percent in 1850 to 15.8 percent in 1900 and about 7.2 percent in 1920. In 1880, 10 percent of all Americans had at least one parent who had been born in Ireland. By 1910, this figure had dropped to 5.7 percent. Nevertheless, the latter figure meant that even as late as 1910, after decades of heavy southern and eastern European immigration, more than one of every twenty people in the United States was the child of an Irish immigrant. People from Ireland or with family links to Ireland still made up a substantial part of the American population in the early twentieth century.

The great wave of immigration came to an end when the United States adopted restrictive immigration policies during the 1920's. Afterward, the overall number of immigrants decreased steadily until the late 1960's. Irish immigration also dropped sharply, both in absolute numbers and as a percentage of all new arrivals.

IMMIGRATION AFTER 1965

During the last three decades of the twentieth century, the United States began welcoming a new great wave of immigrants. This was in large part a consequence of the liberalization of American immigration law in 1965. However, Ireland's contri-

bution to this new wave was relatively small. During the 1970's, people from Ireland made up only 0.2 percent of immigrants to the United States. During the 1980's, they made up only 0.4 percent.

The government of Ireland helped to keep this migration at a relatively low level. The nation's leadership had become concerned about the loss of young people from Ireland's relatively small population during the middle of the twentieth century. During the early 1960's, the government in Dublin persuaded the administration of U.S. president John F. Kennedy to reduce the number of American visas available to potential Irish migrants. In addition, the Immigration and Nationality Act of 1965 gave first preference to immigrants who had immediate family members living in the United States. Because Irish immigration had been relatively small for decades and was then limited by agreement between the two nations, the number of people in Ireland with parents, children, or siblings living in the United States was small.

Irish immigration surged in the 1990's after Connecticut congressman Bruce Morrison sponsored a special green card lottery system for visas that became known as "Morrison visas." New legal residents from Ireland jumped from 4,767 in 1990 to 12,226 in 1991 as Morrison visas became available. However, the Morrison lottery ended after only three years and Irish immigration began to decrease again. The temporary increase in arrivals did not change the historical trend of a decreasing Irish-born population in the United States. By 2007, fewer than 170,000 people born in Ireland were living in the United States, less than one-tenth the number of the Irish-born residents during the late nineteenth century, even though the total American population was much larger at the beginning of the twenty-first century than it had been a century earlier.

Despite the comparatively small numbers of immigrants from Ireland at the end of the twentieth century and beginning of the twenty-first century, the long history of Irish settlement had created a distinctive Irish American identity. According to census estimates made between 2005 and 2007, by the first decade of the twenty-first century more than 22 million Americans, or 7.5 percent of the total population, gave their first ancestry as "Irish"; close to 14 million, or 4.6 percent, gave "Irish" as their second ancestry. Close to 4 million people

gave Scotch-Irish as their first ancestry and another 1.5 million gave that as their second ancestry. Altogether, more than 41 million Americans, 14 percent of the total population, traced at least part of their heritage to the Emerald Isle during the early twenty-first century.

Carl L. Bankston III

FURTHER READING

Dolan, Jay P. *The Irish Americans: A History.* New York: Bloomsbury Press, 2008. History of Irish Americans from the early eighteenth through the early twenty-first centuries. The author examines Irish American history by focusing on the four themes of politics, religion, labor, and nationalism.

Griffin, William D. *The Irish Americans: The Immigrant Experience.* New York: Beaux Arts Editions, 2001. Lavishly illustrated history of Irish Americans, with more than two hundred black-and-white and color paintings and photographs.

Ignatiev, Noel. *How the Irish Became White.* New York: Routledge, 1996. Influential work that argues that the Irish were an oppressed social class and were even seen as members of a distinct race before the Civil War. Ignatiev maintains that the Irish became recognized as "white" in large part by embracing the antiblack racism of other Americans.

Laxton, Edward. *The Famine Ships: The Irish Exodus to America.* New York: Henry Holt, 1998. Based on research in Ireland and compilations of stories passed down to Irish immigrant descendants in America, the author tells the histories of Irish immigrants from 1846 to 1851.

Lee, J. J., and Marion R. Casey, eds. *Making the Irish American: History and Heritage of the Irish in the United States.* New York: New York University Press, 2006. Massive compilation of articles on the Americanization of the Irish, containing both original research and classic articles on this topic. An excellent resource on Irish settlement in America.

McCarthy, Cal. *Green, Blue and Grey: The Irish in the American Civil War.* Cork, Ireland: Collins Press, 2009. Detailed history of Irish soldiers fighting on both sides in the Civil War.

Miller, Kerby, and Patricia Mulholland Miller. *Journey of Hope: The Story of Irish Immigration to America.* San Francisco: Chronicle Books, 2001. Uses letters, journals, and diaries of immigrants to recount the history of Irish immigration and the experiences of Irish immigrants in America.

SEE ALSO: Anti-Catholicism; Boston; British immigrants; Civil War, U.S.; European immigrants; Fenian movement; Flanagan, Edward J.; Great Irish Famine; History of immigration, 1783-1891; Know-Nothing Party; Molly Maguires; Philadelphia anti-Irish riots.

IRON AND STEEL INDUSTRY

DEFINITION: Enterprises involved in the mining of iron ore, its smelting and processing, its conversion to steel, and its distribution to other industries

SIGNIFICANCE: Immigrants to the United States were in many ways responsible for the rise and success of the nation's large iron and steel industry. Most important, their labor made it possible for the significant growth and prosperity of steel manufacturing in America during the late nineteenth and early twentieth centuries.

The growth of the iron and steel industries in the United States has seen a corresponding rise in the employment of European immigrants in the manufacturing of these products. Before 1880, workers in iron and steel facilities of the United States had derived primarily from northern and western Europe, particularly from Great Britain. These mostly English, Welsh, and Scottish ironworkers, engineers, and other metalworkers arrived in the United States during the early to mid-nineteenth century. These skilled migrants, after having weighed their opportunities, chose to emigrate from the British Isles to take advantage of rising opportunities in America, which included the option of owning farmland. Not only did they sustain the development of the American iron industry, they also accelerated the implementation of new technological aspects in its production. Many of these immigrants worked and settled among the diverse iron industries located in Pennsylvania, the largest iron-producing state through much of the nineteenth century.

Pittsburgh, Pennsylvania, steelworkers in 1905. (The Granger Collection, New York)

LATE NINETEENTH CENTURY IMMIGRANTS

The iron and steel industry continued to progress after the U.S. Civil War, and an increasing need for labor corresponded to this growth. During the late nineteenth and early twentieth centuries in particular, steel companies increasingly employed various eastern and southern Europeans in the production and fabrication of steel products. These immigrants included large numbers of Slovaks, Hungarians, and Ukrainians who performed unskilled work in the mills and furnaces in the northern United States, particularly around such cities as Pittsburgh, Pennsylvania.

During this period, the size and scale of manufacturing facilities increased dramatically. The use of more machinery prompted producers to recruit additional unskilled laborers from eastern Europe. About 30,000 new steelworkers were working in American factories by 1900. The motivation of many of these new arrivals was to make enough money to return to Europe and live well in their native villages and towns. The majority migrants who eventually stayed hoped for advancement from the lowest-paid and hardest jobs in the mills to better positions. Many of these men came alone and lived in the boardinghouses and company towns operated by mill owners. As their economic condition improved, they sent for their families, who gradually displaced earlier northern and western European immigrants and their descendants in the steel factories and communities. Meanwhile, they existed a well as they could while working long, hazardous hours with low pay.

STRUGGLE TO UNIONIZE

Many native-born American workers believed that immigrants and their families would not fight against workplace and community injustice on their own accord, and that they would not strike or organize for better working conditions against an overwhelmingly powerful industry. Consequently, craft unions belonging to the American Federation of Labor were reluctant to recruit foreign-born laborers because of skill and ethnic prejudice. However, immigrant workers and their families proved many observers wrong with their participation during the Homestead, Pennsylvania, strike of 1892 and their spontaneous 1909 uprising against Pressed Steel Car in McKees Rocks, Pennsylvania. In the latter conflict, immigrant leaders seized the initiative and recruited organizers from the newly formed Industrial Workers of the World. They won some measure of success, until company officials set native-born against foreign-born workers and broke the unity of the strike.

Later struggles, especially the steel strike of 1919, witnessed even larger immigrant participation, despite successful corporate employment of nativist prejudice and armed force. It was the formation of the Steelworkers' Organizing Committee and the support of the Congress of Industrial Organizations during the 1930's, along with a government that did not support the use of armed intervention,

that led to the second and third generations of workers enjoying the fruits of unionized labor into the 1960's.

LIFE IN THE STEEL COMMUNITIES

Second- and third-generation immigrants and their families built more comfortable lives in steel communities such as Johnstown and Pittsburgh, Pennsylvania. and Youngstown, Ohio, from the 1940's through the 1960's. However, as succeeding generations were assimilating into American society, the nation also experienced a severe economic malaise beginning during the early 1970's that corresponded with corporate decisions to relocate entire steel facilities away from the northern United States. This deindustrialization of the steel industries during the 1970's and 1980's led to the wholesale closing of steel production in Youngstown and Pittsburgh that caused devastating unemployment. This, in turn, forced subsequent generations of immigrant children to struggle to survive in what was left of the industry in their communities or to search for other work elsewhere, away from their ancestral homes. Many of the hard-hit communities remained economically devastated into the twenty-first century. Some have survived to host other forms of employment and newer generations of ethnic families. All, however, still bear the imprints of their original immigrant communities.

James C. Koshan

FURTHER READING

Bell, Thomas. *Out of This Furnace: A Novel of Immigrant Labor.* Pittsburgh: University of Pittsburgh Press, 1976. Originally published in 1941, this classic historical novel is set in the steel mills and communities of Braddock, Pennsylvania, and based on Bell's family of largely Slovak heritage. It covers three generations, from the 1880's through the 1940's.

Brody, David. *Steelworkers in America: The Nonunion Era.* Champaign: University of Illinois Press, 1998. First published in 1960, this informative and well-researched account of iron and steel workers during the early decades of the twentieth century continues to fill in the gaps of the history of pre-unionized steelworkers and their struggles before the 1930's.

Hinshaw, John. *Steel and Steelworkers: Race and Class Struggle in Twentieth-Century Pittsburgh.* Albany: State University of New York Press, 2002. Analytical approach to the unfolding social problems engendered by working in the Pittsburgh steel industry and its effects on subsequent working-class families and communities as the industry declined.

Kleinberg, S. J. *The Shadow of the Mills: Working-Class Families in Pittsburgh, 1870-1907.* Pittsburgh, Pa.: University of Pittsburgh Press, 1989. Narrative work focusing on the lives of mill workers and their families away from the shop floors that utilizes primary sources to build a portrait of working-class life.

Krause, Paul. *The Battle for Homestead, 1880-1892: Politics, Culture, and Steel.* Pittsburgh, Pa.: University of Pittsburgh Press, 1992. Far-reaching, archival- based book on the struggles surrounding the community of Homestead that also provides the necessary context for understanding the infamous strike of 1892.

SEE ALSO: Alabama; Coal industry; Czech and Slovakian immigrants; Economic consequences of immigration; Economic opportunities; Employment; Goldman, Emma; Industrial Revolution; Industrial Workers of the World; Labor unions; Ohio; Pennsylvania.

ISRAELI IMMIGRANTS

SIGNIFICANCE: The state of Israel was established only in 1948, and much of its own population growth has come about through Jewish emigration from the United States and Europe. This makes analyses of migration *from* Israel to the United States uniquely complex. Many ostensible immigrants to the United States from Israel have been Jews who originated in the United States, emigrated to Israel, and later returned to North America. Some of these same returnees have even returned to Israel again. The subject is also complicated by the fact that immigrants to the United States from Israel have included Muslim and Christian Palestinians, who may or may not have been Israeli citizens. Moreover, some Palestinian immigrants who were

legally Israeli citizens may not have identified with the Jewish state.

The number of immigrants to the United States whose last country of residence was Israel has grown steadily over the decades. From 1950 to 1959, 21,376 legal migrants from Israel were admitted into the United States. During the 1960's, that figure increased to 30,911 and in the 1980's to 43,669. After a slight dip to 41,340 during the 1990's, a total of 47,873 new immigrants arrived from Israel between 2000 and 2008. Estimates from U.S. Census data indicate that numbers of people born in Israel, or Palestine, in the United States grew from 94,500 in 1990 to 123,000 in 2000 and reached 154,000 in 2007.

According to the sociologist Steven J. Gold, a widely recognized authority on Israeli immigrants, Jewish Israelis in the United States have shown a number of distinctive characteristics. They have tended to have high levels of education and to work in professional fields, most notably in educa-

PROFILE OF ISRAELI IMMIGRANTS

Country of origin	Israel
Primary languages	Hebrew, English
Primary regions of U.S. settlement	California, New York State
Earliest significant arrivals	1950's
Twenty-first century legal residents*	36,516 (4,565 per year)

*Immigrants who obtained legal permanent resident status in the United States.

Source: Department of Homeland Security, *Yearbook of Immigration Statistics, 2008.*

tional services. According to early twenty-first century U.S. Census figures, about one-quarter of Israeli immigrants have been managers, officials, and proprietors. Other common occupations have been in sales, teaching, and professional and technical jobs. However, most Jewish Israeli immigrants have come to the United States in order to escape political unrest in the Middle East, not to seek improved economic opportunities. Consequently, although they have generally adapted well to American life and generally speak English fluently, a substantial number of them have avoided describing themselves as "Americans" and have expressed a desire eventually to return to Israel. Many continue to speak Israel's national language, Hebrew, at home.

Jewish Israelis live throughout the United States, but they are most heavily concentrated in New York City and Los Angeles. These two cities alone contain about half of all Jewish Israelis living in the United States. Other popular destinations for many Israeli immigrants have included Michigan, Florida, and Illinois. Israeli immigrants are frequently drawn to large established Jewish neighborhoods, such as Brooklyn and Queens in New York City and West Hollywood and the San Fernando Valley in the Los Angeles area.

Carl L. Bankston III

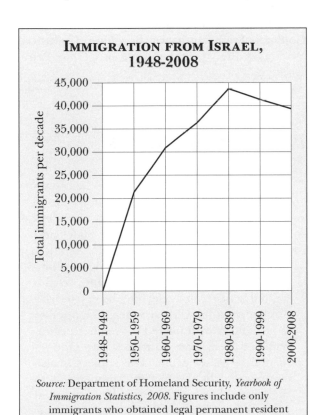

IMMIGRATION FROM ISRAEL, 1948-2008

Total immigrants per decade

Source: Department of Homeland Security, *Yearbook of Immigration Statistics, 2008.* Figures include only immigrants who obtained legal permanent resident status.

FURTHER READING

Gold, Steven J. *The Israeli Diaspora.* Seattle: University of Washington Press, 2002.

Gold, Steven J., and Bruce A. Phillips. "Israelis in the U.S." In *American Jewish Yearbook, 1996.* New York: American Jewish Committee, 1996.

O'Brien, Lee. *American Jewish Organizations and Israel.* Washington, D.C.: Institute for Palestine Studies, 1986.

Sobel, Zvi. *Migrants from the Promised Land.* New Brunswick, N.J.: Transaction Books, 1986.

Telushkin, Rabbi Joseph. *The Golden Land: The Story of Jewish Immigration to America.* New York: Harmony Books, 2002.

Worth, Richard. *Jewish Immigrants.* New York: Facts On File, 2005.

SEE ALSO: *Afroyim v. Rusk*; American Jewish Committee; Anti-Defamation League; Anti-Semitism; Arab immigrants; Dual citizenship; Emigration; Holocaust; Jewish immigrants; Los Angeles; Muslim immigrants; New York City.

ISSEI

IDENTIFICATION: First-generation Japanese immigrants

SIGNIFICANCE: During the mid-nineteenth century, after more than two centuries as a closed nation, Japan began permitting emigration to the United States. The Issei, the first generation of immigrants in the United States, quickly became a crucial element in the development of Pacific states' agricultural economies. However, because they were Asians and maintained tight-knit cultural neighborhoods with other Issei, they were perceived as a threat and faced bigotry as well as discriminatory legislation. Consequently, most Issei never had all the benefits of immigration enjoyed by members of many other immigrant groups.

The first Japanese to enter what is now the United States came to Hawaii in 1885, when the islands were still an independent kingdom. These first immigrants were mostly well-educated working-class men. Many were students and accomplished artisans who were interested in learning at first hand Western agricultural techniques and economic practices so they could help modernize their eco-nomically distressed homeland when they returned to Japan, which was then emerging from two centuries of rigid military rule that had closed off the nation from the international community. These immigrants were welcomed by the Hawaiian government as cheap labor to maintain the islands' extensive sugar cane and pineapple plantations.

These Issei immigrants quickly extended their range, as subsequent waves of migrants went to the Pacific Coast states, most notably California. There, the Issei faced significant challenges. They did not share the language, customs, religions, or history of the established first- and second-generation European immigrants. They were therefore viewed with considerable hostility even as their hard work and the quiet temperaments, derived from their Buddhist training in stoic endurance, made them important contributors to the economic success of the Pacific region. They were especially important in farming, fishing, mining, and railroad construction. By 1910, nearly 180,000 Issei were working in the Pacific coastal areas.

That influx, perceived to be just the beginning by conservative anti-Asian xenophobes, led to popular sentiments that Asian "hordes" would take away jobs belonging to Americans. Indeed, Asian immigrants faced violence as well as a coordinated campaign of bigoted rhetoric from organized labor. Ultimately they faced harsh government restrictions. For example, the controversial 1882 Chinese Exclusion Act was the first national legislation that prohibited a specific ethnic group from immigrating. Ironically, this law initially encouraged Japanese immigration, as the American labor force needed to replace the Chinese. However, the act also denied all Asian immigrants the right to become American citizens, thus ensuring that the Issei would be perpetual aliens in the United States.

In 1907, President Theodore Roosevelt negotiated the so-called Gentlemen's Agreement with Japan in which the Japanese government agreed to issue passports only to military personnel, diplomats, and merchants, thus eliminating working-class immigrants from Japan. In 1910, California passed the Alien Land Law, which prohibited "aliens" from purchasing farmland at a moment when Issei controlled roughly one-half million acres in the state. Anti-japanese sentiments were not nationally held; indeed, Japanese art and cul-

ture was a Jazz Age fad. However, the U.S. Congress enacted the Immigration Act of 1924, which aimed at ending all Japanese immigration.

After imperial Japan launched a surprise attack on the U.S. naval base at Pearl Harbor in Hawaii in December, 1941, bringing the United States into World War II, the federal government interred nearly one-third of the Issei living along the West Coast of the United States. Denied the right to vote or own land, segregated into ethnic schools, and branded as untrustworthy aliens, the Issei had only their Nisei children who were born in the United States to enjoy the benefits of American citizenship and economic prosperity.

Joseph Dewey

FURTHER READING

Ichioka, Yuji. *The Issei: The World of the First Generation Japanese Immigrants, 1885-1924.* New York: Free Press, 1988.

Nakane, Kazuko. *Nothing Left in My Hands: The Issei of a Rural California Town, 1900-1942.* Berkeley, Calif.: Heyday Books, 2009.

Tamura, Linda. *The Hood River Issei.* Champaign: University of Illinois Press, 1994.

SEE ALSO: Anti-Japanese movement; Asian American Legal Defense Fund; Asian immigrants; Asian Pacific American Labor Alliance; Gentlemen's Agreement; Immigration Act of 1924; Japanese American Citizens League; Japanese American internment; Japanese immigrants; Little Tokyos; "Yellow peril" campaign.

ITALIAN AMERICAN PRESS

DEFINITION: American news publications targeted at Italian American and immigrant Italian communities

SIGNIFICANCE: Newspapers, magazines, and journals designed to appeal to the Italian community in America, often published in Italian, provided new immigrants and succeeding generations important information about both the United States and Italy, helping immigrants acclimate to their new homeland while remaining in touch with their roots.

News vehicles for Italian immigrants in America were available as early as 1836, when *El Correro Atlantico* appeared in New Orleans. New York City had its first Italian-language paper, *L'Eco d'Italia*, in 1850, and even before the great influx of Italians into the United States between 1880 and 1920 several other major cities could boast of having one or more publications that catered to this ethnic group.

Because Italian immigrants generally clustered together in neighborhoods that were dubbed "Little Italies," it was easy for publishers to distribute their newspapers to waiting audiences, most of whom were poor and ignorant of American customs. Many publications contained stories about events in Italy as well as news about America, enabling immigrants to stay in touch with the old country while adjusting to their new home. Such publications were also convenient media in which employers could advertise job openings. Newspapers also served as forums for individuals to vent their frustrations about life in what they called *La Merica* that to many was proving less rosy than they had anticipated.

CHARACTERISTICS OF THE ITALIAN AMERICAN PRESS

The explosion of Italian immigration to America after 1880 saw a concurrent rise in Italian American news publications. New York City alone had dozens of small Italian papers, and cities such as Boston, Philadelphia, Chicago, Pittsburgh, and San Francisco also had multiple news organs. Many of these publications competed with one another for the same readers, however, and fierce competition ensured that many would be short-lived. Most readers were working-class men and women to whom the papers delivered a great deal of news and opinions on labor issues. The better-financed papers tended to promote conservative interests. For example, Carlo Barsotti's *Il Progresso Italo-Americano* in New York, Charles Baldi's *L'Opinione* in Philadelphia, and Mariano Cancelliere's *La Trinacria* in Pittsburgh were decidedly promanagement. These conservative papers even went so far as to carry management advertisements for strikebreakers when unions conducted work stoppages.

At the same time, quite a number of papers were controlled by various unions and workers' rights groups; for example, the International Workers of the World used *La Questione Sociale* and later *L'Era*

Editor of an Italian-language newspaper in New York correcting proofs in 1943. (Library of Congress)

Nuova as propaganda tools to influence Italian workers. Publications such as *Il Proletario* in Philadelphia and *La Plebe* in Pittsburgh advocated for workers' rights and promoted civil disobedience, a stance that got them in trouble with authorities on occasion. A typical government tactic used to stymie these radical organs was to have the U.S. Post Office declare them seditious and refuse to grant their publishers mailing privileges, thereby curtailing circulation. Nevertheless, between 1880 and 1940, more than a hundred radical papers appeared. Their impact on the working classes was significant.

RISE OF FASCISM

The passionate interest of Italians in their homeland was at the root of the greatest contro-

versy involving the Italian American press. Beginning during the 1920's Italian American papers ran articles and editorials praising the Fascist Italian dictator Benito Mussolini, whose efforts they thought would unite Italy and bring justice and prosperity to the peasantry. Chief among Mussolini's Italian American supporters was Generoso Pope, a businessman who bought several newspapers, including the New York papers *Il Progresso Italo-Americano* and *Corriere d'America*, both of which enjoyed wide circulation. Pope had personal access to both Mussolini and U.S. president Franklin D. Roosevelt and used his newspapers to promote the Fascist agenda. He was not alone, however. Most mainstream publications, including many supported by the Roman Catholic Church, were ardent Fascist supporters—until Mussolini's bellicose

imperialist ventures in Africa and Spain during the mid-1930's turned American opinion against him. Even then, some Italian papers ran articles critical of Mussolini in their English-language sections while continuing to print favorable pieces about him in Italian.

Support for Mussolini was not universal, however. In Detroit, *La Voce de Popolo* editor Monsignor Joseph Ciarrocchi ran articles exposing the Italian dictator's propaganda campaign being waged in America. Many left-leaning publications were highly critical. One of the most vocal anti-Fascist publications was *Il Martello*, owned and edited by Carlo Tresca, a lifelong activist who had fought for workers' rights since arriving in the United States in 1904. Frequently, those publishing unfavorable material on Mussolini before the outbreak of World War II were intimidated or even assaulted by pro-Fascist elements in the United States. After the United States entered World War II against Japan, Germany, and Italy at the end of 1941, open support for Fascism in the Italian American press was replaced by calls for the overthrow of Mussolini's regime.

POSTWAR PRESS

By the end of World War II in 1945, many Italian Americans had begun to assimilate into the mainstream culture. Dwindling populations in Little Italies and waning interest among second- and third-generation Italian Americans in their ancestral home and language led to a decline in publications targeted specifically at their ethnic interests. Nevertheless, a number of magazines and journals published by various civic groups such as the Italy-America Society and the National Italian-American Foundation enjoyed wide readership into the twenty-first century. Most of these publications promoted pride in the Italian American heritage and celebrated customs from the old country that had become part of the larger melting-pot culture of the United States.

Laurence W. Mazzeno

FURTHER READING

Diggins, John N. *Mussolini and Fascism: The View from America.* Princeton, N.J.: Princeton University Press, 1972. Discusses the fascination of Italian Americans with Mussolini, explains the role of the mainstream Italian American press in promoting a favorable view of him, and describes efforts of anti-Fascist publications to counter positive Fascist images.

Mangione, Jerre, and Ben Morreale. *La Storia: Five Centuries of the Italian-American Experience.* New York: HarperCollins, 1992. Extensive history of Italian immigration to America, outlining contributions of Italian Americans to the United States. Includes a brief commentary on the role of the Italian American press.

Moreno, Barry. *Italian Americans.* Hauppauge, N.Y.: Barron's Educational Series, 2003. Describes the history and customs of Italian immigrants; briefly sketches the role of the Italian American press within these communities.

Park, Robert E. *The Immigrant Press and Its Control.* New York: Harper, Collins, 1922. Provides a sense of the concerns mainstream America had with ethnic newspapers, including those published by Italian Americans, which were perceived as potentially subversive to American values.

Pericone, Nunzio. *Carlo Tresca: Portrait of a Rebel.* New York: Palgrave Macmillan, 2005. Biography of the activist and newspaper editor influential in promoting the cause of labor and combating favorable views of fascism within the Italian American community.

SEE ALSO: Ethnic enclaves; German American press; Immigration waves; Italian immigrants; Labor unions; Little Italies; Spanish-language press.

ITALIAN IMMIGRANTS

SIGNIFICANCE: The late nineteenth and early twentieth centuries saw a large-scale influx of Italian immigrants to the United States. Most of them settled in East Coast cities such as New York and Philadelphia. By the early twenty-first century, people of Italian heritage constituted 6 percent of the total American population and ranked as the fifth-largest ethnic group in the United States.

Italians began immigrating to North America during the early colonial period, but massive Italian immigration began only during the late nineteenth century. The new immigrants faced prob-

Italian immigrants arriving at Ellis Island in 1911. (Library of Congress)

lems similar to those encountered by earlier waves of foreign immigrants, such as the Irish. Most of them tended to gravitate to the eastern cities, in which they created "Little Italies." Their assimilation progressed slowly and was often hampered by the perception that many Italians were members of the criminal Mafia. By the late twentieth century, however, Italian Americans occupied prominent positions in most sectors of American life.

EARLY IMMIGRATION

Immigration from Italy to the United States was only a trickle before the 1880's. The British colonies contained small pockets of Italians, who brought Italian horticulture and winemaking to North America as early as the seventeenth century. During the late eighteenth century Revolutionary War era and in the early days of the independent American republic, political philosopher Filippo Mazzei was probably the most prominent Italian in the United States. He was a close friend of Thomas Jefferson and had a plantation near Jefferson's Vir-

ginia home. The two men conversed in Italian, and Mazzei is believed to have given Jefferson the phrase "that all Men are created equal," which Jefferson famously rendered "all Men are created equal" in the Declaration of Independence.

Later Italian immigrants were important in the development of the early wine industry in California. During the nineteenth century, Italian artists and musicians made significant contributions to art, architecture, and music, especially opera. However, their numbers were small until late in the century.

LATE NINETEENTH CENTURY IMMIGRATION

The political unification of Italy in 1879 did not bring better lives to the majority of Italians, who began to emigrate in large numbers to Brazil, Argentina, and the United States. Life for the new immigrants was difficult in all these countries, but Italians continued to emigrate. Many hoped to accumulate enough money to return to Italy to buy land and lead better lives in their homeland. Most

sent remittances to family members in Italy in the meantime. By 1900, about 500,000 Italians were living in the United States, mostly in New York, Pennsylvania, New Jersey, and New England. About 150,000 Italians lived in New York City alone, and Philadelphia and Chicago also had growing Italian communities.

TWENTIETH CENTURY TRENDS

Anti-Italian sentiments among native-born Americans grew along with the burgeoning numbers of Italian immigrants. Propaganda against the Italian immigrants usually focused on fears of the Mafia. Throughout the United States, Italian immigrants were targets of violence, even lynching, by anti-immigrant nativist groups that were alarmed by the new wave of immigration. To help mitigate their difficult situations, Italians established mutual aid societies that provided services ranging from medical care to funerals to members. Many immigrants cities got moral support from living in Little Italies, in which they were surrounded by fellow countrymen (*paesani*) and could enjoy many of the trappings of the culture of their homeland. Italian grocery stores and other services helped in the transition, especially among those still unable to speak English.

Some immigrants returned to Italy, but most remained in the United States permanently. Male heads of families generally arrived in the United States first. As they became established, they sent

for the rest of their families. Over time, notions of returning to Italy faded. Occasionally, however, some family members remained in the United States while others returned to Italy, traveling back and forth whenever possible. This was especially true after World War II.

Immigrants who came to the United States during the twentieth century, especially after World War I (1914-1918), enjoyed a brief period of relative prosperity. However, the Great Depression of the 1930's proved an especially difficult time. By then, Italy was under Benito Mussolini's Fascist rule, so returning to Italy was out of the question for many immigrants. In 1939, Italy followed Nazi Germany into World War II and became a declared enemy of the United States.

ITALIAN RELIGION AND CULTURE

Historically, most Italians have been Roman Catholics, and immigrants have continued in that religious faith in the United States. However, early Italian immigrants were not entirely comfortable in American Catholic churches, which were dominated by Irish American clergy. In cities in which Italians were concentrated, the immigrants gravitated toward predominantly Italian parishes, which tried to keep alive the Italian language and culture.

Although a majority of Italian Americans have remained Catholics, they have not occupied a place in the leadership of the American church that reflects their numbers. Some Italian American men and women entered the Catholic clergy and religious orders but not in the same numbers as Irish Catholics have done. Consequently, the American church has continued to have a predominantly Irish imprint. Despite the large numbers of Italians in New York City, there has never been an Italian American cardinal in the city's archdiocese.

Not all Italians were or are Catholic. Some have joined Protestant churches in small communities lacking Catholic churches. Others have left the Roman Catholic Church after getting divorced and remarrying—practices on which Catholics frown. By the early twenty-first century, Italian Americans were prominent in a variety of Protestant denominations.

FAMILIES

An important center of Italian immigrant life has been the family. Family members have tended

PROFILE OF ITALIAN IMMIGRANTS	
Country of origin	Italy
Primary language	Italian
Primary regions of U.S. settlement	Northeast
Earliest significant arrivals	Seventeenth century
Peak immigration period	1880's-1920's
Twenty-first century legal residents*	21,028 (2,629 per year)

*Immigrants who obtained legal permanent resident status in the United States.

Source: Department of Homeland Security, *Yearbook of Immigration Statistics, 2008.*

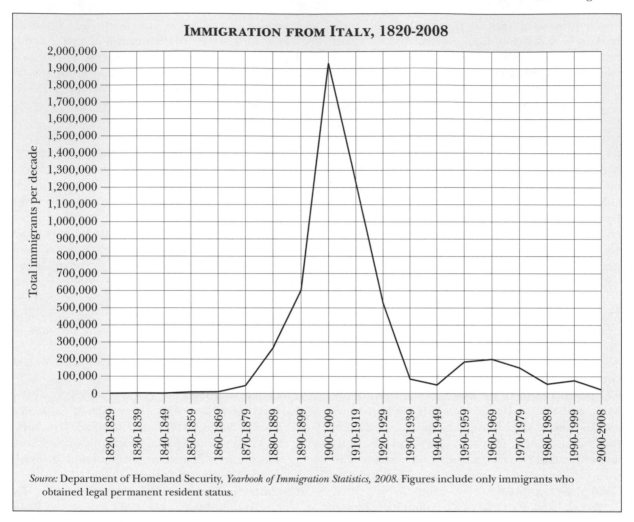

IMMIGRATION FROM ITALY, 1820-2008

Source: Department of Homeland Security, *Yearbook of Immigration Statistics, 2008.* Figures include only immigrants who obtained legal permanent resident status.

to live near one another, especially with the big cities' Little Italies. Italian youths were encouraged to marry not only within the Roman Catholic faith but also within the Italian community. Marrying outside the Italian community was rare among early immigrants, but it became more common after several generations had passed. First-generation immigrant families strongly discouraged marriage with "Americans"—the general designation for anyone not of Italian descent.

The Americanization of an Italian family is a subtheme of Francis Ford Coppola's *Godfather* film trilogy. The films trace the evolution of an Italian family from the youthful Vito Corleone's initiation into the harsh criminal world of New York City's Little Italy to his son Michael Corleone's lavish lifestyle in the Far West, showing how the family's cus-

toms and lifestyle changed. After a poverty-stricken beginning as an immigrant orphan, Vito eventually prospered but hung onto a traditional Italian lifestyle. In contrast, Michael lived like an American millionaire on a large estate with few signs of Italian culture.

Women played a major role in Italian immigrant families and in the workplace. Although men were usually the first to come to the United States, many Italian women also immigrated alone, either as single women seeking better lives or as heads of households. When whole families immigrated together, the women tended to assume matriarchal roles within the families, allowing their husbands to retain their traditional Italian roles as family heads. Some women did part-time piecework at home for wages, while others worked in factories,

entered domestic service, or, together with their husbands and other family members, operated small businesses. Some families ran small grocery stores, or similar establishments, attached to their homes.

The Italian immigrant culture encouraged education as a central part of the goal of achieving better lives. Consequently, Italian Americans have had higher-than-average graduation rates from high schools and average to above-average rates of completion of higher degrees. The Italian family culture subscribed to the concept of the "American Dream," and encouraged their children to pursue education as a way of getting ahead in the new society. Families in the Little Italies tended to be competitive and were proud to boast of their children's achievements.

ITALIAN STEREOTYPES

Few European immigrant groups have faced as much ethnic prejudice as Italians. Epithets such as "wop," "dago," and even "*Eye*-talian" have been only surface manifestations of anti-Italian sentiments. The popular tendency to associate Italians with the Mafia and other criminal elements was long widespread. The federal Immigration Act of 1924 limited the number of southern and eastern Europeans who could migrate to the United States. The measure can be seen as at least partly motivated by anti-Italian sentiment.

The conviction of Nicola Sacco and Bartolomeo Vanzetti for robbery and murder in 1927 has often been cited as an example of anti-Italian xenophobia because the evidence used against them was weak. Their long trial process was highly politicized. Instead of concentrating on the evidence concerning the crimes of robbery and murder, the trial focused on the defendants' anarchist political views, which probably played a greater role in their conviction and eventual execution than the actual evidence in their case.

As time passed and Italians moved into the American cultural mainstream, groups such as the Italian American Civil Rights League (formerly the Italian American Anti-Defamation League) and the National Italian-American Foundation worked to combat negative stereotypes. The fact that criminals in films and television dramas often had Italian surnames contributed to the stereotypes. However, the *Godfather* films that seemed to

romanticize the Mafia also made the American public more aware of the warmth of Italian family life and family values. By the early twenty-first century, stereotyping of Italians was declining, even though the popular cable television series *The Sopranos* was keeping alive public perceptions of criminal Italians.

ITALIAN CONTRIBUTIONS TO AMERICAN CUISINE

The art of cooking has always been part of the Italian domestic landscape. From their earliest arrivals, Italian immigrants have brought vineyards and other forms of horticulture to the United States. Later immigrants, particularly those from southern Italy, also contributed such dishes as pizza, spaghetti, meatballs, and lasagna to the American cuisine. Many immigrants opened restaurants within Italian neighborhoods, and some of these acquired national reputations. Italians have also contributed espresso, cappuccino, and lattes to American coffeehouses.

Norma Corigliano Noonan

FURTHER READING

Brodsky, Alyn. *The Great Mayor: Fiorello LaGuardia and the Making of the City of New York*. New York: St. Martin's Press, 2003. Biography of New York City's famous Italian mayor that emphasizes his role in the city's development.

Cannistrero, Philip, and Gerald Meyer, eds. *The Lost World of Italian American Radicalism*. Westport, Conn.: Praeger, 2003. Collection of essays about the various facets of Italian radicalism, especially after World War I.

Ciongoli, A. Kenneth, and Jay Parini. *Passage to Liberty: The Story of Italian Immigration and the Rebirth of America*. New York: Regan Books, 2002. Glossy and engaging history of Italians in America, going back to the eras of Christopher Columbus and Filippo Mazzei.

Guglielmo, Thomas A. *White on Arrival: Italians, Race, Color, and Power in Chicago, 1890-1945*. New York: Oxford University Press, 2003. History of Chicago's Italian community that focuses on racial aspects of the Italian experience, from characterizations of Italians by themselves and other groups to their relations with the African American community.

Iorizzo, Luciano J., and Salvatore Mondello. *The Italian Americans*. 3d ed. Youngstown, N.Y.: Cam-

bria Press, 2002. Well-written scholarly history of the evolution of the Italian American community in the United States.

Poe, Tracy N. "The Labour and Leisure of Food Production as a Mode of Ethnic Identity Building Among Italians in Chicago, 1890-1940." *Rethinking History* 5, no. 1 (2001): 131-148. Study of Italians in Chicago that focuses on food, culture, and residential patterns.

Vecchio, Diane C. *Merchants, Midwives and Laboring Women: Italian Migrants in Urban America.* Champaign: University of Illinois Press, 2006. Brief history of Italian immigrant women in the United States.

Vecoli, Rudolph J. "European Americans: From Immigrants to Ethnics." *International Migration Review* 6, no. 4 (Winter, 1972): 403-434. Analysis of the historiography of European immigration that reviews the approaches of some of the major immigration historians, revealing the interpretations that evolved over time.

SEE ALSO: Anti-Catholicism; Argentine immigrants; Atlas, Charles; European immigrants; Films; *Godfather* trilogy; History of immigration after 1891; Immigration waves; Italian American press; Little Italies; Ponzi, Charles; Sacco and Vanzetti trial; Tammany Hall.

J

Japanese American Citizens League

IDENTIFICATION: Voluntary organization formed to protect and promote the rights of Japanese Americans

DATE: Established in 1929

ALSO KNOWN AS: JACL

> **SIGNIFICANCE:** The Japanese American Citizens League was founded to protect the civil rights of Japanese Americans but quickly became a champion of all civil rights issues affecting people of all backgrounds.

The Japanese American Citizens League (JACL) was founded in California in 1929 in response to the anti-immigration fervor and legislature that was gaining popularity and support. The organization's mission was to protect the civil rights and liberties of all people, regardless of their race, ethnicity, nationality, or gender.

Early twentieth century California had the largest Japanese American population of any state in the United States. It also had more than one hundred statutes limiting the rights of residents of Japanese ancestry. Groups such as the Grange and the Native Sons of the Golden State used their power both at the state level and in the U.S. Congress to pass legislation that limited the rights and political participation of Japanese and Japanese American citizens. Far more extreme were organizations such as the Asiatic Exclusion League, whose purpose was to purge the West of all Asian residents, including those born in the United States. Although the organization was inexperienced, the JACL challenged not only anti-Asian organizations but also the discriminatory congressional legislation that limited Asian rights.

The importance of the JACL came to a head on December 7, 1941, after the attack on Pearl Harbor. Hours after the attack, U.S. government officials raided offices and homes of Japanese in Hawaii and along the West Coast of the United States, imprisoning many leaders of the Japanese community, including senior JACL members. Junior members of the organization then had to defend their colleagues and fellow citizens under a climate of fear and anger toward all things Japanese. The JACL ensured that the interned were protected and enjoyed a reasonable level of physical comfort. It also kept the Japanese American community aware of developments through its newspaper, *Pacific Citizen*, and won the right for Japanese Americans to serve in the U.S. armed forces during World War II.

Following the release of internees after World War II ended in 1945, the JACL continued to be a champion for civil rights. In 1946, the group began a painstaking campaign to repeal California's alien land law, which prohibited Asian immigrants from owning land in the state. This was followed by the formation of the Leadership Conference on Civil Rights in 1948 and support of the federal Evacuation Claims Act during the same year in its quest for compensation for Japanese who had been interned during World War II. JACL's work on the Immigration and Nationality Act of 1952 allowed women to gain entry into the democratic process, and the organization lobbied strongly for the passage of the federal Civil Rights Act of 1964.

In 1978, the JACL launched an investigation into the losses suffered by Japanese and Japanese Americans who had been sent to relocation camps. The organization supported the formation of a government commission, which was sponsored by President Jimmy Carter, to study the issue. In 1982, the commission declared that the federal government's actions during the war had been unconstitutional and recommended payment of a monetary redress. The redress was awarded under the Civil Liberties Act of 1988, providing compensation and a presidential apology to victims.

During the early twenty-first century, the JACL continued to lobby for civil rights. One of the issues that it has championed is the right for humans to marry, including marriage for same-sex couples.

Sara Vidar

FURTHER READING

Gruenewald, Mary Matsuda. *Looking Like the Enemy: My Story of Imprisonment in Japanese American In-*

ternment Camps. Troutdale, Oreg.: NewSage Press, 2005.

Harth, Erica. *Last Witnesses: Reflections on the War-time Internment of the Japanese.* New York: Palgrave Macmillan, 2003.

Japanese American Citizens League. *The Journey from Gold Mountain: The Asian American Experience.* San Francisco: JACL, 2006.

SEE ALSO: Anti-Japanese movement; Asian American Legal Defense Fund; Asian Pacific American Labor Alliance; Asiatic Barred Zone; Asiatic Exclusion League; California; Japanese American internment; Japanese American press; Japanese immigrants; World War II.

JAPANESE AMERICAN INTERNMENT

THE EVENT: Federal government's forced evacuation and relocation of Japanese Americans living on the West Coast to internment camps during World War II

DATE: 1942 to 1945

LOCATION: Relocation centers in western states between California and Arkansas

SIGNIFICANCE: In February, 1942, President Franklin D. Roosevelt issued Executive Order 9066, which authorized U.S. military officials to remove persons from areas of the American mainland designated as military zones. More than 110,000 Japanese Americans were considered security risks and forced to dispose of their West Coast homes, businesses, and property and move into ten desolate relocation camps from California to Arkansas. The internment deprived the affected Japanese Americans of their civil liberties as U.S. citizens or residents.

As the start of World War II, about 120,000 Japanese Americans resided in the United States. Most lived in California and other Pacific coast states. The 40,000 first-generation immigrant Japanese, or Issei, were generally over the age of fifty and excluded from citizenship by the Immigration Act of 1924. The 80,000 second-generation Nisei were un-

der age eighteen, and most were American citizens.

Immediately after the Japanese attack on Pearl Harbor on December 7, 1941, the U.S. government detained 2,000 Japanese Americans who were considered security risks. The shock of the Pearl Harbor attack; the Japanese military takeover of Guam, Hong Kong, Manila, and Singapore; and reports of Japanese atrocities in the Philippines created an atmosphere of hysteria on the West Coast. Many Americans feared that a bombing attack on the West Coast might be next. They also believed that Japan had resident spies living on the coast and feared that Japanese Americans would aid their racial brothers. Numerous inflammatory and invariably false reports of Japanese attacks on the American mainland flashed through coastal communities. However, no reports of attacks on the American mainland were authenticated until the Japanese shelled an oil refinery near Santa Barbara, California, on February 22, 1942, and the Oregon coast near Fort Stevens on June 21. Neither attack did much damage.

The biggest impetus for internment came with the release in late January of a government investigation of the Pearl Harbor attack. The report, compiled by U.S. Supreme Court justice Owen Roberts, claimed without documentation that Hawaii-based espionage agents, including Japanese American citizens, had aided the Japanese striking force. The press and interest groups further spread fear and prejudice that denied the constitutional rights of Japanese Americans.

EVACUATION ORDER

Assistant Secretary of War John McCloy was responsible for a military decision on the fate of Japanese Americans and ordered Colonel Karl Bendetsen to prepare a final recommendation for General John DeWitt, chief of the Army's Western Defense Command. In early February, DeWitt officially requested authority to remove all Japanese Americans from the West Coast because they belonged to an "enemy race" whose loyalty was suspect. Secretary of War Henry Stimson, Attorney General Francis Biddle, Assistant Attorney General James Rowe, and Edward Ennis, director of the Alien Enemy Control Unit, questioned the internment on racial grounds as unconstitutional and unnecessary. Stimson warned that removal of Japa-

nese Americans on a racial basis would "tear a tremendous hole in our constitutional system." Biddle told Stimson that the Justice Department would not evacuate any American citizen.

The internment strategy was finalized on the evening of February 17, 1942, in the living room of Biddle's Washington home. Biddle had told Stimson that afternoon that he no longer opposed internment after being assured that the Army, not the Justice Department, would handle the mass roundup and detention programs. McCloy persuaded Biddle to participate in publishing the executive order and confronted Rowe and Ennis, who were furious about Biddle's reversal of position on internment. Despite having reservations, Stimson advised Roosevelt that DeWitt should be authorized to proceed.

On February 19, President Roosevelt signed Executive Order 9066, which authorized U.S. military officials to remove any and all persons from areas of the United States designated as military zones. The order did not apply to persons living outside the Western Defense Command. No explicit reference to Japanese Americans was necessary. The secretary of war was authorized to establish detention centers to protect West Coast military facilities from sabotage and espionage. The original order did not specify what should happen to the evacuees or exclude voluntary withdrawal. Japanese Americans were encouraged to leave the prohibited Pacific coast military zone voluntarily. About 15,000 moved in with midwestern or eastern relatives or friends. Roosevelt established the War Relocation Authority (WRA) to administer the voluntary resettlement and designated Milton Eisenhower as its director. Many inland states warned that the eastward movement of Japanese immigrants posed problems. The governors of Wyoming, Idaho, and Kansas adamantly opposed resettlement of Japanese Americans.

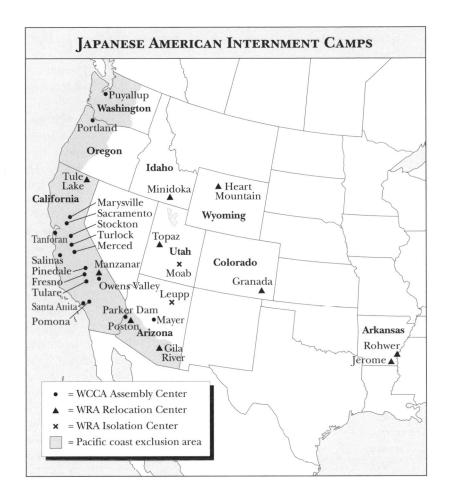

JAPANESE AMERICAN INTERNMENT CAMPS

- ● = WCCA Assembly Center
- ▲ = WRA Relocation Center
- ✕ = WRA Isolation Center
- ▢ = Pacific coast exclusion area

EVACUATION AND INTERNMENT

On March 27, 1942, the Army stopped voluntary withdrawal and began evacuating the remaining Japanese Americans. Within weeks, more than 100,000 Japanese Americans were given forty-eight hours to dispose of their businesses, homes, and property and report to makeshift assembly centers at fairgrounds and racetracks. At Santa Anita Race Track in Arcadia, California, detainees were jammed into hastily converted horse stalls until they could be transferred to permanent relocation centers.

The War Department moved internees to ten inland internment camps from California to Arkansas. All ten sites were located on barren, federally owned land, usually Indian reservations. The first evacuees were sent in June to Manzanar, California—a desolate, 6,000-acre site surrounded by guard towers, searchlights, machine-gun installations, and barbed-wire fencing. The internees en-

dured boiling summer heat and frigid winter cold and sandstorms, confined without any recognition of their constitutional rights.

Each family was crammed into a spartan, 20-by-20-foot uninsulated cabin. The residents tried to live as normally as possible, organizing farm plots, markets, schools, newspapers, and police and fire departments. Eisenhower, deeply troubled by the involuntary internment, resigned as WRA director. In 1943, many internees bristled when Dillon Meyer, Eisenhower's replacement, forced all internees to undergo interrogation to establish their loyalty to the United States. About 8,500 internees, mostly young Nisei men, refused to forswear allegiance to the Japanese emperor or indicate willingness to serve in the U.S. military forces; they were deemed disloyal and sent to a camp at Tule Lake, California. About 3,000 of those considered loyal were recruited into the 442d Regimental Combat Team, an all-Japanese military unit that battled bravely in Italy.

Many internment camps operated through the remainder of the war. The WRA found homes and jobs for 17,000 Japanese Americans in 1943. Late that year, Biddle pressed Roosevelt for accelerated releases of internees from the camps. Secretary of Interior Harold Ickes warned Roosevelt in June, 1944, about the negative historical legacy of the detention centers. Stimson favored freeing the loyal Japanese Americans after the 1944 presidential election. The WRA had relocated about one-quarter of the internees by August, 1945.

Constitutional Challenges

War Department officials observed anxiously as several lawsuits challenged the constitutionality of the relocation program. Surprisingly, only three cases involving Japanese Americans contesting the internment orders reached the U.S. Supreme Court. The three challengers came from varied backgrounds. Minoru Yasui, a lawyer and Army Reserve officer, broke the curfew order in Portland, Oregon. Gordon Hirabayashi, a Quaker pacifist and college student in Seattle, Washington, violated the curfew and exclusion orders on religious grounds. Fred Korematsu, a twenty-three-year-old American-born Nisei shipyard welder, dodged the exclusion order in San Leandro, California, and hoped to escape the West Coast with his Italian American friend.

In each case, the U.S. Supreme Court ruled that the war powers granted to the president and Congress by the U.S. Constitution eclipsed the due process and equal protection claims of the three Japanese Americans. On June 24, 1943, the Court rendered unanimous decisions in *Hirabayashi v. United States* and *Yasui v. United States* supporting the government's stance on the curfew orders (and avoiding the coerced evacuation and compulsory internment issues). In the former case, Justice Frank Murphy, however, warned that the relocation program tested constitutional powers by substantially restricting the personal liberty of American citizens based on the accident of race or ancestry.

An Army document defending the evacuation became an issue in *Korematsu v. United States* (1944). Colonel Bendetsen, DeWitt's deputy, drafted the *Final Report: Japanese Evacuation from the West Coast, 1942*. The 618-page report listed "military necessity" as DeWitt's official explanation for the internment program. Justice Department lawyers initially saw the report in January, 1944, when preparing their briefs for the *Korematsu* case. The *Final Report* stirred a spirited debate between the Justice and War departments. Bendetsen cited hundreds of examples of subversive activities on the West Coast in 1942 to defend the forced evacuation as both militarily necessary and constitutional. The Justice Department, however, soon discovered that Bendetsen had distorted his facts about a raid by the Federal Bureau of Investigation (FBI) turning up more than sixty thousand rounds of ammunition and many rifles, shotguns, and maps that had come from a sporting goods store and about espionage involving supposedly illicit radio transmissions.

The Justice Department attorneys, in a footnote, sought to disavow the *Final Report* when arguing the *Korematsu* case. They questioned both the military's factual assertions that the evacuation was a military necessity and the allegations of espionage, sabotage, and treason by the Japanese Americans. McCloy insisted that the footnote be deleted because it would shatter the consensus the Supreme Court had patched together in the other two cases and would probably prompt the Court to rule the entire relocation program unconstitutional. The top Justice Department officials yielded to McCloy's pressure after two days of spirited debate and deleted the footnote, depriving the Court

of grounds upon which to challenge the *Final Report* assertions. The Court otherwise might have ruled in Korematsu's favor.

In the *Korematsu* case, the Supreme Court on December 18, 1944, upheld the detention program. The case provided the greatest challenge to the constitutionality of the evacuation program. Justice Hugo L. Black's majority opinion affirmed Korematsu's original conviction for violating the evacuation decree but carefully avoided ruling on the legality of his subsequent internment. Black argued that strict scrutiny must be given to all legal restrictions that curtail the civil rights of a single racial group and decided that military necessity provided ample grounds to believe that the government's actions met the strict scrutiny test. Justices Roberts, Murphy, and Robert Jackson sharply dissented. Jackson protested that the Court majority was affirming the principle of racial discrimination.

The previous day, the West Coast military authorities rescinded DeWitt's original evacuation order and permitted the remaining camp residents to reenter the Western Defense Command. Beginning in January, 1945, those Japanese Americans who had passed loyalty test screenings were gradually released from the camps. Several thousand who were considered disloyal were detained until after World War II ended.

LEGACY OF SHAME

The internment of Japanese Americans left a legacy of shame. The Japanese American internees suffered about $400 million in property losses because of the evacuation. In 1948, Congress paid them a paltry $37 million in reparations. Four de-

Internees eating a meal at the Manzanar Relocation Center in California's eastern Sierras. (NARA)

cades later, it responded to calls for redress by passing the Civil Liberties Act of 1988, which awarded $20,000 in reparations to each detainee who was still alive. Meanwhile, the Commission on Wartime Relocation and Internment of Civilians reviewed the factors that led to Executive Order 9066 and examined its consequences. In 1983, the commission concluded that "race prejudice, war hysteria, and a failure of political leadership" by the Roosevelt administration led to Executive Order 9066 and a "grave injustice" to Japanese Americans.

The commission's findings and newly discovered evidence from government files prompted legal efforts to remove the criminal records of the wartime defendants. A federal judge rescinded Korematsu's conviction, holding that the Supreme Court had approved Roosevelt's order on the basis of "unsubstantiated facts, distortions, and misrepresentations" to the Court by high-ranking officials. In 1998, President Bill Clinton bestowed the Presidential Medal of Freedom, the nation's highest civilian honor, on Korematsu. The detention undermined the cultural authority of the elderly Issei, liberated their Nisei children from provincial tradition and cultural isolation, and expedited the Nisei's assimilation into the larger society. Younger Japanese Americans rapidly ascended the ladder of social mobility and became among the best-educated Americans, with incomes substantially above the national average. Roosevelt's Executive Order 9066 created what the American Civil Liberties Union (ACLU) termed "the greatest deprivation of civil liberties by government in this country since slavery." Roosevelt mobilized the country for ultimate victory in World War II, but the internment program remains a stigma on his wartime record.

The Japanese internment decried American ideals of justice. The ceaseless uneasiness of government officials with their own policy and the cautious manner with which the Supreme Court treated the evacuation cases testify to the awkwardness with which American culture dealt with the internment incident. The internment of Japanese Americans refuted the nation's best image of itself as a tolerant, inclusive, fair-minded melting pot society—a vision long nourished in American lore and one strongly reaffirmed by the World War II conflict.

David L. Porter

FURTHER READING

Commission on Wartime Relocation and Internment of Civilians. *Personal Justice Denied.* Washington, D.C.: Government Printing Office, 1983. The commission concluded that "race prejudice, war hysteria, and a failure of political leadership" resulted in "grave injustice" to the Japanese Americans.

Daniels, Roger. *Prisoners Without Trial: Japanese Americans in World War II.* New York: Hill & Wang, 1993. Describes and analyzes the decision to remove Japanese Americans from the West Coast, their confinement, their reaction to their unjust treatment, and the repercussions of the internment.

Hayashi, Brian Masaru. *Democratizing the Enemy: The Japanese American Internment.* Princeton, N.J.: Princeton University Press, 2004. Questions whether racism, wartime hysteria, and a failure of political leadership fully explain the U.S. government incarceration of Japanese Americans and offers revealing new interpretations of their internment.

Irons, Peter. *Justice at War: The Story of the Japanese American Internment Cases.* Berkeley: University of California Press, 1993. Well-researched work examining the *Yasui*, *Hirabayashi*, and *Korematsu* court cases, exposing the government's coverup of data that could have disproved its claims of "military necessity" for evacuation and internment.

Ng, Wendy. *Japanese American Internment During World War II: A History and Reference Guide.* Westport, Conn.: Greenwood Press, 2002. This reference work provides six thematic essays on the history and meaning of the Japanese internment, short biographies of the major personalities in the internment, and a selection of primary documents.

Tateishi, John, ed. *And Justice for All: An Oral History of the Japanese American Detention Camps.* New York: Random House, 1984. This poignant, bitter, inspiring oral history gives the personal recollections and experiences of thirty Japanese Americans who were part of the only group of American citizens ever confined to detention camps in the United States.

War Department. *Final Report: Japanese Evacuation from the West Coast, 1942.* Washington, D.C.: Government Printing Office, 1943. This report, re-

quested by John DeWitt, lists "military necessity" as the official government explanation for the evacuation and internment.

SEE ALSO: Anti-Japanese movement; Asian American literature; Hawaii; Japanese American press; Japanese immigrants; Japanese Peruvians; Loyalty oaths; Oregon; Prisoners of war in the United States; World War II.

JAPANESE AMERICAN PRESS

DEFINITION: Publications issued in both Japanese and English languages that cater primarily to Japanese immigrants and their descendants

SIGNIFICANCE: The Japanese American press provided a means whereby Japanese Americans dealt with the prejudicial treatment they received in America. The idea that the Nisei, or second-generation Japanese Americans, should embrace "Americanism" received major impetus. Newspapers also provided an outlet for incarcerated Issei, or first-generation Japanese immigrants, and Nisei during World War II.

The golden era of the Japanese American ethnic press occurred during the 1920's and 1930's, when the ethnic populations in West Coast cities had grown large enough to support several competing newspapers. The Los Angeles *Rafu Shimpo* provided local and regional news to a large West Coast readership, while the competing but shorter-lived *Doho* gave emphasis to progressive, pro-labor news and opinion. The San Francisco press included the *Nichi Bei Shinbun* and the *Shin Sekai*. Under publisher Kyutaro Abiko, *Nichi Bei* published both San Francisco and Los Angeles editions during the 1920's. However, a labor strike closed the latter paper in 1931. *Nichi Bei* was the highest-circulation Jap-

anese American newspaper. The East Coast press included New York City's *Japanese American News*.

The Japanese-language papers also published articles in English, but not on a regular basis until 1925, in *Nichi Bei*. By this time, the publishers realized the need to cater to English-speaking Nisei. Other English-language sections soon appeared, followed by English-language weeklies, including *Japanese American Weekly*, introduced by Abiko in 1926, and the Seattle-based *Japanese American Courier*, introduced in 1928. Although the *Courier* achieved only a fraction of the circulation of the Japanese-language papers, its editor, James Yoshinori Sakamoto, exerted considerable influence and was instrumental in the development of the Japanese American Citizens League.

Japanese American residents of Manzanar Relocation Center reading newspapers produced within the internment camp during 1943. (Library of Congress)

Several newspapers, especially Sakamoto's *Courier*, fostered the attitude that an ethic of hard work and loyalty would lead to the eventual absorption of Japanese Americans into the mainstream of American life. The press was far from unified in reacting to the times, however. Whereas the Issei press heavily supported Japan in the Sino-Japanese War that began in July, 1937, *Doho* criticized Japan for creating havoc in Asia. Differences of opinion also split the Japanese-language and English-language staffs within individual newspapers.

The Japanese press suffered severely in the aftermath of the Japanese attack on Pearl Harbor on December 7, 1941. U.S. military officials desired total suppression of Japanese-language publishing, while civilian authorities merely urged its control. Nevertheless, all Japanese American papers on the West Coast were shut down by mid-May, 1942. In contrast, the inland press, including the *Rocky Nippon*, *Colorado Times*, *Utah Nippo*, and the relocated *Pacific Citizen*, continued and to some degree thrived during the war. Newspapers also quickly developed within internment camps.

Although officially sanctioned, internment camp newspapers enjoyed some autonomy. The *Manzanar Free Press*, for example, was headquartered in the Office of Official Reports and was subject to censorship by the camp director. In practice, however, the paper's editors received little interference. The director even authorized a Japanese-language edition during the paper's second year. While barred from directly criticizing federal policies that had led to the mass Japanese American incarceration, *Free Press* editors were allowed to print factual stories on legal challenges to those policies. The *Free Press* was circulated by mail to all the internment camps.

The Japanese American press was restored to vitality by the end of the war, with the new *Nichi Bei Times* established in 1946 to reconnect individuals separated by incarceration. As had the *Nichi Bei Shinbun*, the *Times* became the leading U.S. Japanese American newspaper.

Mark Rich

FURTHER READING

Hosokawa, Bill. *Nisei: The Quiet Americans.* New York: William Morrow, 1969.

Mizuno, Takeya. "The Federal Government's Decisions in Suppressing the Japanese-Language Press, 1941-42." *Journalism History* 33, no. 1 (2007): 14-23.

Ng, Wendy. *Japanese American Internment During World War II: A History and Reference Guide.* Westport, Conn.: Greenwood Press, 2002.

Yoo, David K. *Growing Up Nisei: Race, Generation, and Culture Among Japanese Americans of California, 1924-49.* Champaign: University of Illinois Press, 2000.

SEE ALSO: Anti-Japanese movement; Chinese American press; Filipino American press; Japanese American Citizens League; Japanese American internment; Literature; Little Tokyos; San Francisco; Television and radio.

JAPANESE IMMIGRANTS

SIGNIFICANCE: From the 1880's, Japanese immigration to Hawaii and the western states made the Japanese one of the largest Asian ethnic groups in the United States. Though mostly blocked by legislation between 1924 and 1965, some Japanese immigration continued through those years. Japanese Americans completely integrated and became very successful in government, business, the sciences, and cultural enterprises.

The first immigrants from Japan began to arrive in the Hawaiian Islands between 1885 and 1895, following on the heels of the Chinese Exclusion Act of 1882. Plantation owners who were forbidden from hiring Chinese workers hired thousands of Japanese citizens to work in the sugar cane and pineapple fields. About half of these Japanese eventually migrated to California, Oregon, and Washington State. More than 100,000 Japanese people made the journey across the Pacific to Hawaii before 1900, making the Japanese the dominant immigrant group in the islands. The new Meiji emperor of Japan had opened up the country and finally allowed citizens to emigrate. The working conditions were not good in Hawaii, but Japanese laborers were lured to the islands by the prospects of earning ten times more than was possible in their home country.

LIFE IN HAWAII

During the 1880's, Hawaii was technically still a monarchy but was mostly controlled by American businessmen and plantation owners who farmed sugar cane, coffee, and pineapple on large estates throughout the islands. This required huge workforces. The native Hawaiians had fled or died out due to the diseases brought by American and European missionaries and white settlers, thus creating a labor market for the Chinese and Japanese. As a part of its new openness to foreign trade, the Meiji government formulated an agreement with Hawaii that made it easier for agricultural workers to leave Japan to work in the plantations. The agreement took the form of a labor contract that allowed American plantation owners to pay for transportation costs to Hawaii. The Japanese were required to work for up to a year to repay the debt.

In 1885, approximately 30,000 Japanese workers immigrated to Hawaii. The first-generation Japanese born outside America were known as the Issei. They had few chances for education or good-paying jobs at home and hoped to save some of the money they earned working in Hawaii. Almost all the Japanese immigrants to Hawaii worked the sugar cane fields and were paid low wages. Some returned to Japan after one year, but many stayed in Hawaii until the opportunity arose to immigrate to the West Coast of the United States.

PROFILE OF JAPANESE IMMIGRANTS

Country of origin	Japan
Primary language	Japanese
Primary regions of U.S. settlement	Hawaii, West Coast
Earliest significant arrivals	1880's
Peak immigration period	1900-1920's
Twenty-first century legal residents*	62,096 (7,762 per year)

*Immigrants who obtained legal permanent resident status in the United States.
Source: Department of Homeland Security, Yearbook of Immigration Statistics, 2008.

The number of Japanese moving to Hawaii through labor contracts and also through repayment arrangements made between immigrants and their home villages greatly increased during the last years of the nineteenth century. The official census of Hawaii counted 12,610 Japanese citizens in 1890, and that number had increased to more than 60,000 by the turn of the century. The new Japanese residents of Hawaii set up communities that resembled Japanese villages around the boundaries of plantations. The influx of Japanese to the islands was mutually beneficial because it provided jobs to those displaced by the Meiji Restoration. The thousands of new workers helped increase the productivity of the sugar cane and pineapple fields. The working conditions were unsurprisingly not good: The plantation workers spoke only English and treated the Japanese workers like horses or cattle, forcing them to get up at 4:00 A.M. to begin working the fields at 6:00 A.M., seven days a week.

In 1900, Hawaii became a U.S. territory, which meant that it would be governed by U.S. law, under which contract labor arrangements were illegal. When the Japanese who came to Hawaii under such a contract finished their obligation with the plantation owner, they were free to return to Japan. Many chose to go to California to look for better opportunities, while about one-third decided to remain in Hawaii and continue in agricultural labor. Since the majority of Japanese workers were men, some had to wait for future wives to be sent from Japan through arranged marriages, which were still common during the early years of the twentieth century. Some women traveled to Hawaii to join brothers or husbands already working there.

The longer the Japanese stayed in Hawaii, the more likely they were to marry and have children, thereby increasing the size of their community. As fear of the immigrants increased, in 1908 Japanese workers staged protests against the long hours and harsh conditions, demanding better wages and safer working conditions. The strike did not change the plantations' working conditions but served as a testament to increased immigrant political power and community action. With little prospect of change in Hawaii, Japanese workers left the islands to search for better jobs, mostly in California. About 40,000 Japanese traveled from Hawaii in

the years after the labor strike of 1908, becoming the first large group of Japanese immigrants to reach the mainland.

JOURNEY TO THE MAINLAND

By 1908, a labor shortage had been created by anti-immigrant laws such as the Chinese Exclusion Act of 1882, which prohibited Chinese from becoming U.S. citizens, making it easy for the Japanese workers to find jobs. Chinese workers had taken many of the lowest-paying jobs in railroad construction, farming, logging, mining, and fishing, but now those jobs were available to new immigrants. Some Japanese looked for work in cities such as San Francisco and Los Angeles, but many had grown up on farms in Japan or Hawaii, so they decided to pursue agricultural work. They were especially keen on the possibility that they might eventually be able to buy the land themselves. The large and productive valleys of California presented unlimited possibilities.

Japanese workers, like the Chinese before them, soon developed the reputation for accepting physically demanding work for low pay. They took to the fields and factories, working long hours and putting up with challenging conditions. Farmworkers who harvested produce were paid by the bushel of produce picked. Japanese workers proved that they could earn twice the pay of others because they were quick and efficient. They came from a small country with limited farm resources, so they were accustomed to getting the most produce from the lowest-quality farmland. In California, where the land was fertile and abundant, Japanese farmers could outproduce other farmers with techniques such as growing strawberries between rows of grapevines. They were also good at saving their earnings, so eventually farmworkers could combine their individual savings and buy land for the benefit of one another.

PRESSURE BUILDS TO EXCLUDE JAPANESE

The Japanese immigrants' willingness to work long hours and work together in order to purchase farmland made them one of the most successful ethnic groups, but some Americans resented their success. Some people felt that the Japanese were taking away jobs from white Americans. Labor unions such as the American Federation of Labor (AFL) refused to allow Japanese workers to join their organizations. Businesspeople and farmers were afraid of the Japanese workers' success, and they began to pressure the government to take action. In 1905, the Asiatic Exclusion League (AEL) was formed in California to prevent more immigrants from coming to the United States from Japan. The AEL and other racist groups pressured President Theodore Roosevelt to stop further immigration, but Roosevelt did not want to needlessly irritate the Japanese government. Roosevelt vetoed several new laws modeled after the 1882 Chinese Exclusion Act, but he did accept the Gentlemen's Agreement with Japan in 1907, which prohibited male workers from emigrating to Hawaii or the mainland. While new immigration was banned, the agreement allowed the Japanese to send family members (children, wives, or parents) of workers already living in the United States to join them.

More anti-Japanese laws were passed in the years after the Gentlemen's Agreement because of ethnocentrism and negative attitudes about immigrants from places other than northern Europe. The Immigration Restriction League (IRL) was led by Prescott Hall, who argued that people from northern Europe were energetic, free, and progressive while southern Europeans, Jews, and Asians were downtrodden, primitive, and lazy. These racist attitudes were common during the early twentieth century. Both the AEL and the IRL posited that the Japanese were taking away unskilled, low-paying jobs from Euro-Americans, but in fact the industrious Japanese were rapidly leaving agricultural work and beginning to own land and lease it to others.

In 1913, however, California enacted its first Alien Land Law, which made it illegal for noncitizens to purchase land. A Japanese immigrant named Takao Ozawa resented this law and fought against it all the way to the U.S. Supreme Court, which declared in 1922 that naturalized citizenship was limited to whites and African Americans. However, children of Japanese immigrants born in the United States would be considered citizens. The Immigration Act of 1924 prevented almost all immigration from Japan for three decades. Despite these barriers, Japanese immigrants continued to work hard and prosper, combining resources to create social organizations such as savings and loans, banks, and social assistance groups. The slew

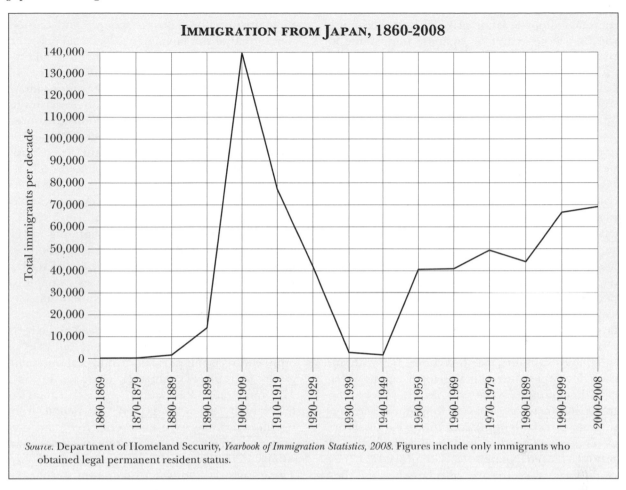

IMMIGRATION FROM JAPAN, 1860-2008

Source. Department of Homeland Security, *Yearbook of Immigration Statistics, 2008.* Figures include only immigrants who obtained legal permanent resident status.

of anti-Japanese laws was not completely effective because the new laws did not apply to those born in the United States.

WORLD WAR II AND JAPANESE IMMIGRANTS

During the 1930's, as the United States struggled through the Great Depression, Japan's government became increasingly militaristic. With Emperor Hirohito on the throne, Japanese leaders elevated the traditional Shinto religion, transformed the emperor into a religious figure, and demanded total obedience to the state. Japan turned away from the path of modernization and democracy, spreading a doctrine of world domination and propaganda about its racial superiority. Japan's army invaded China's Manchuria region in 1931 to begin a path of destruction that would not end until the atomic bombs were dropped on Hiroshima and Nagasaki in August, 1945. After the Jap-

anese surprise attack on Pearl Harbor on December 7, 1941, the United States declared war on Japan and its allies, including Adolf Hitler's Germany and Benito Mussolini's Italy.

Like other Americans, the Japanese Americans in the western states viewed the rise of the military government in 1930's Japan with savage indignation, and they could not understand the godlike reverence for Hirohito. After many years of anti-Japanese laws in California, some people were still suspicious of the Japanese citizens who worked hard, owned houses and farms, and attended churches and schools like other Americans. Soon after Pearl Harbor, western states enforced curfews that required Japanese Americans to stay inside their homes between 8:00 P.M. and 6:00 A.M. The Federal Bureau of Investigation (FBI) went to work arresting suspicious "enemy aliens" who might be leaders in the Japanese community such as Shinto

and Buddhist priests, businesspeople, teachers, and professionals. In 1942, California fired all state employees of Japanese ancestry without reason or due process of law. Most were American citizens with rights guaranteed by the U.S. Constitution. Secretary of War Henry Stimson believed that Japanese American citizens were more loyal to their race than to their adopted country.

In February, 1942, President Franklin D. Roosevelt issued Executive Order 9066, which empowered the military to remove any persons from any area in the country where national security was at risk. Even though the executive order did not mention the Japanese by name, it was effectively designed to contain Japanese Americans in California, Oregon, and Washington State. Roosevelt's order displaced some 120,000 Japanese Americans from their homes, relocating the immigrants to internment camps for the duration of the war. About 70,000 of this group were U.S. citizens. Most of the Japanese were surprised by the forced resettlement because they thought of themselves as Americans. The Army's Western Defense Command set up makeshift assembly centers at old fairgrounds, horse racetracks, rodeo grounds, and farm labor camps, from which internees were later transferred to permanent detention camps in scattered locations throughout the United States, from Manzanar, California, to Rohwer, Arkansas.

As the tide of World War II began to change and the Allies won battles in Europe and in the Pacific, Americans started to reconsider the internment camps and their view of Japanese Americans. Many Japanese Americans stayed in the camps from 1942 until the end of 1944, but some took a loyalty test and were allowed to leave as long as they resettled away from the West Coast. Some Japanese Americans were disgusted by the loyalty tests and refused to submit to them since they were already legal citizens.

FROM THE 1950's THROUGH THE 1970's

With the tragic conclusion of World War II, a difficult period for Japanese Americans ended. The Evacuation Claims Act of 1948 allowed Japanese Americans who had lost property during the internment to claim 10 percent of every dollar lost, but this small amount of compensation was difficult to obtain. During the 1950's, many Japanese immigrants had dispersed to other cities, but the majority still lived in Los Angeles, San Francisco, and San Jose, which had their own Little Toykos. The largest group of new Japanese immigrants was made up of "war brides," women who had married American soldiers during the occupation of Japan. In some ways, the war brides had a more difficult

Japanese immigrants awaiting processing at the federal government's immigrant reception center on San Francisco Bay's Angel Island during the 1920's. (NARA)

time than the first Japanese immigrants because they lacked a social network and moved to places where few if any Japanese people were living.

During the early 1960's, John F. Kennedy called for reform of exclusionary immigration policies, namely those of the Immigration Act of 1924. After Kennedy's assassination in 1963, President Lyndon B. Johnson carried out Kennedy's wishes with the enactment of the Immigration and Nationality Act of 1965, which resulted in more than doubling Japanese immigration to the United States from less than 2,000 to about 4,500 per year. The Civil Rights movement, led by Martin Luther King, Jr., also influenced Japanese Americans, as they began to question the violation of their rights by the government during the 1940's. Some Japanese Americans published memoirs about their experiences in the internment camps and made a pilgrimage to Manzanar. Bowing to pressure from Japanese Americans, Gerald R. Ford signed a proclamation in 1976 admitting that internment had been a "national mistake."

LATE TWENTIETH AND EARLY TWENTY-FIRST CENTURIES

According to the 1980 U.S. Census, more than 600,000 Japanese Americans were living in the United States, still mostly in the western states. Third- and fourth-generation Japanese Americans were well integrated into American society. Surveys revealed that about half of the married Japanese Americans living in large California cities were married to non-Japanese. Japanese Americans were successful in many professional careers and were represented at many levels of local, regional, and national politics. In 1980, Congress established the Commission on Wartime Relocation and Internment of Civilians to hold hearings, allowing many Japanese Americans to speak about their experiences in the internment camps for the first time. In 1988, President Ronald Reagan signed a bill that gave payments of $20,000 to each surviving Japanese American detainee, and the law also provided money for education of their descendants. Although it took more than forty years, justice was finally realized.

The 2000 U.S. Census documented about 800,000 citizens who claimed Japanese ancestry. Most Japanese who came to the United States during the late twentieth century tended to be either university students or high school students who stayed about five years, or Japanese businessmen, who stayed for a shorter time. In the early twenty-first century, the number of Japanese immigrants to the United States is relatively small compared with the influx in the early twentieth century, but the impact of Japanese culture has been tremendous. In the late twentieth and early twenty-first centuries, Japanese corporations started to build factories in the United States as car companies such as Honda, Toyota, and Nissan became increasingly popular. Japanese consumer electronics companies such as Sony, Hitachi, Toshiba, and Panasonic became household names in America. Japanese popular culture, including anime and manga, and Japanese cuisine also became widely popular with Americans. The rapid acceptance of Japanese culture is all the more astonishing given the rampant racism and anti-immigration laws of the 1920's and 1930's. Japanese Americans have become one of the most assimilated and successful groups of immigrants in the United States.

Jonathan L. Thorndike

FURTHER READING

Daniels, Roger. *Asian America: Chinese and Japanese in the United States Since 1850.* Seattle: University of Washington Press, 1988. Well-written, scholarly account of the experiences of Japanese and Chinese immigrants in America.

Duus, Peter, ed. *The Twentieth Century.* Vol. 6 in *The Cambridge History of Japan.* New York: Cambridge University Press, 1989. Essays discuss the rise of Japanese nationalism and the push toward colonial expansion and World War II.

Gordon, Andrew. *A Modern History of Japan: From Tokugawa Times to the Present.* New York: Oxford University Press, 2003. An excellent overview of Japan in relation to world history and immigration.

Ingram, W. Scott. *Japanese Immigrants.* New York: Facts On File, 2005. Juvenile book with good-quality photographs and sidebars about Japanese culture and individuals' stories.

Jansen, Marius B., ed. *The Nineteenth Century.* Vol. 5 in *The Cambridge History of Japan.* New York: Cambridge University Press, 1989. Standard scholarly work that chronicles Japan's transformation from a feudal society to a modern democratic state during the Meiji Restoration.

Takaki, Ronald. *Strangers from a Different Shore: A History of Asian Americans*. Boston: Little, Brown, 1989. An account of the systematic racism and discrimination that Chinese, Japanese, and later immigrants from East Asia and Southeast Asia faced in the West.

SEE ALSO: Anti-Japanese movement; Asiatic Exclusion League; Gentlemen's Agreement; Gospel Society; Issei; Japanese American Citizens League; Japanese American internment; Japanese Peruvians; Little Tokyos; North American Free Trade Agreement; *Ozawa v. United States*; "Yellow peril" campaign.

JAPANESE PERUVIANS

IDENTIFICATION: Peruvians of Japanese descent who were deported to the United States during World War II

SIGNIFICANCE: Although Peruvians would elect a Japanese man, Alberto Fujimori, the president of their country in 1990, earlier generations of Peruvians resented and distrusted the Japanese living in their country. In an effort to send all its Japanese people to Japan during World War II, the Peruvian government began shipping them to the United States, where most of the deportees were interned for the duration of the war, along with many Japanese Americans.

During the late nineteenth and early twentieth centuries, the deteriorating economic situation in Japan prompted many young Japanese to migrate to the Americas. When the Japanese were legally barred from entering the United States, they turned their attention to South American nations. In 1899, the first Japanese began settling in Peru.

Although initially hired by Peruvian agricultural landowners, many Japanese immigrants eventually migrated to Peru's cities to work as small-scale merchants. South Americans did not wholeheartedly welcome the Japanese immigrants, however. This distrust and hostility deepened during the 1930's, partly because of the perceived affluence of the Japanese during the Great Depression and partly because of Japan's aggressive empire building.

During the 1930's and early 1940's, the Peruvian government enacted discriminatory laws directed against Japanese immigrants.

In May, 1940, rumors that the Japanese in Peru's capital city, Lima, were planning to take over the country led to anti-Japanese riots. Anti-Japanese sentiments combined with the December, 1941, Japanese attack on Pearl Harbor, the U.S. naval base in Hawaii, to lead the administration of President Manuel Prado y Ugarteche to view the internment of Japanese as both politically popular and expedient. However, in order to intern more than six thousand people, the government would need money that it did not want to spend. Prado found it easier and cheaper to send the Japanese to the United States.

On the grounds of "military necessity," Peru deported about 1,800 first-generation Issei and second-generation Nisei to the United States. The first ship, the *Etolin*, left Callau in April, 1942, with 141 male Japanese Peruvians. No legal charges had been brought against any of these people, none of whom had criminal records. Designated as prisoners of war, the deportees were taken to temporary camps in Panama before debarking in New Orleans, Louisiana. From there, they were sent to internment camps in Texas and Montana.

Engaged in a version of ethnic cleansing, the Peruvian government expected that the Japanese whom it was deporting would eventually be sent to Japan. Meanwhile, U.S. secretary of state Cordell Hull and U.S. Armed Forces chief of staff George C. Marshall supported the collection of Japanese Peruvians, anticipating that they might be exchanged for American civilians interned in Japanese-occupied territories in Asia. No internees were ever exchanged, but 342 of the Japanese Peruvians did return to Japan in 1942. A lack of shipping hampered Peru's internment program from its start and limited the number of deportees to 1,800.

After World War II ended in 1945, and U.S. internment camps were closed, about 100 Japanese Peruvians who had been interned in the United States returned to Peru. About 300 remained in the United States. The rest went to Japan.

Caryn E. Neumann

FURTHER READING
Kikumara-Yano, Akemi, ed. *Encyclopedia of Japanese Descendants in the Americas: An Illustrated History*

of the Nikkei. Walnut Creek, Calif.: AltaMira Press, 2002.

Masterson, Daniel M., and Sayaka Funada-Classen. *The Japanese in Latin America.* Champaign: University of Illinois Press, 2004.

SEE ALSO: Anti-Japanese movement; Asian immigrants; Japanese American internment; Japanese immigrants; Latin American immigrants.

JENNINGS, PETER

IDENTIFICATION: Canadian-born American television journalist

BORN: July 29, 1938; Toronto, Ontario, Canada

DIED: August 7, 2005; New York, New York

SIGNIFICANCE: As an immigrant news broadcaster, Jennings was exceptionally conscious of America's place in the world community. With his international focus, he led his American Broadcasting Company (ABC) network to top ratings and coauthored two books that illumine the American experience.

Peter Jennings was the son of Elizabeth Osborne and Charles Jennings. His father was Canada's first network television news anchor and later a Canadian Broadcasting Corporation executive. Peter himself was initially so little motivated by formal education that he dropped out of high school. After obtaining some media experience in Canada, he moved to New York when he was given the opportunity to become American television's youngest network news anchor. Feeling unprepared for that assignment, he instead turned to international reporting, at which he excelled. In 1971, he established the first American television news bureau in any Arab country. Six years later, he became ABC's first chief foreign correspondent and was respected for his preparation, research, and eagerness to meet people of all backgrounds.

In 1978, Jennings became part of a three-person

Peter Jennings during the early 1980's. (AP/Wide World Photos)

ABC anchor team for *World News Tonight.* In 1983, he became the program's sole anchor. His documentaries and other specials often covered international problems. As an immigrant and traveler, he was increasingly fascinated by the uniqueness of America, which he described as the only nation founded on ideas written into a constitution. With Todd Brewster he wrote *The Century* (1998), exploring the impact of twentieth century events upon Americans. In 2002, he followed that book with *In Search of America,* an exploration of how constitutional ideals still shape American identity. Both books accompanied television documentary series.

In 2003, Jennings became an American citizen. Through the last two years of his life, he held dual Canadian/American citizenship.

Betty Richardson

FURTHER READING

Darnton, Kate, Kayce Freed Jennings, and Lynn Sherr, eds. *Peter Jennings: A Reporter's Life.* New York: Public Affairs, 2007.

Fensch, Thomas. *Television News Anchors: An Anthology of Profiles of the Major Figures and Issues in United States Network Reporting.* Woodlands, Tex.: New Century, 2001.

SEE ALSO: Canadian immigrants; Dual citizenship; Huffington, Arianna; Pulitzer, Joseph; Television and radio.

JEWISH IMMIGRANTS

IDENTIFICATION: Adherents of Judaism and their ethnic kin who derived from many different European nations, particularly those in eastern Europe

SIGNIFICANCE: By the turn of the twenty-first century, about 5.1 million Jews were living in the United States, primarily in larger cities and their suburbs. Most Jews are considered part of the U.S. middle class, and do every type of work. A high percentage are business executives, professionals, or skilled workers, and many are in the fields of art, literature, and theater. Among Jews' primary concerns are education and philanthropy.

Jews were present in what is now the United States as early as the colonial period of the seventeenth century. The earliest Jewish communities consisted of Sephardic Jews of Spanish and Portuguese ancestry, who had migrated to Brazil before moving on to North America in 1654 aboard a ship named *Sainte Catherine.*

Early settlers in New Amsterdam confronted religious prejudice and discrimination by Governor Peter Stuyvesant, who did not wish them to remain. The Jews petitioned the Dutch West Indies Company, however, and were permitted to settle in the area. Governor Stuyvesant made life difficult for them by restricting their rights and exempting them from military service. However, the Jews were not denied the opportunity to practice their religion in private. The first Jewish congregation in North America, Shearith Israel (Remnant of Israel) dates from April 26, 1655.

After Dutch-ruled New Amsterdam fell to the British and became New York City in 1664, Jewish religious services continued in homes until 1695, when the Jewish immigrants were given permission to build a synagogue. This was finally accomplished in 1728. English became the standard language of these immigrants, and until the early 1820's Jewish immigrant religious practices reflected the Sephardic tradition, and Shearith Israel was regarded as the "mother synagogue." Sephardic rituals were also adopted by Ashkenazi Jews from Germany and Poland.

COLONIAL LIFE

Business was the occupation of the early Jewish settlers. Some were traders and craftsmen; others were wealthy merchants. Eventually, some of them were not satisfied to remain in New York and left for other colonies. Jewish settlements were established in Rhode Island, where Newport became the center of the country's whale oil, candle, and soap industries. By the start of the American Revolution in 1775, Newport had become the most important center of Jewish life in the country. Of the approximately 1,500 Jews in the colonies at that time, the largest concentration—about 200—lived in Newport, where they established what would become the oldest surviving synagogue in the United States.

The lifestyles of colonial Jews generally mirrored those of their neighbors, except in their ritu-

Editorial cartoon in an early 1881 issue of Frank Leslie's Illustrated Newspaper *showing "Columbia" welcoming Jewish refugees from German persecution.* (Library of Congress)

als and religious practices. Following kosher dietary laws, keeping proper Jewish homes, observing holidays, and educating children constituted significant challenges for Jews living outside the large cities. By the end of the eighteenth century, only about 3,000 Jews lived in the entire United States. More than half of them lived in the South. Georgia elected the country's first Jewish governor, Daniel Emanuel. Jews were becoming assimilated into American society and were continuing to thrive, but through intermarriage with Christians and religious conversions, their numbers were actually declining.

With the Louisiana Purchase in 1803, the country's boundaries expanded, and a number of Ashkenazi immigrants went westward. Jews helped to found St. Louis, Nashville, Detroit, and Cincinnati. Many of the Ashkenazi Jews who arrived during the early nineteenth century settled in the large cities of the East where they first landed, but some traveled inland to smaller cities such as Rochester, Pittsburgh, Chicago, and Cincinnati. Because they were generally poor and uneducated with little English-speaking ability, these immigrant tended to live close together in cities and ply trades that

did not require special knowledge or education, such as garment-making and peddling.

NINETEENTH CENTURY TRENDS

Jewish immigration began increasing significant during the mid-nineteenth century, Between 1840 and 1860, the Jewish population of the United States rose to about 200,000, due in large part to an influx of immigrants from central Europe seeking refuge from the strife surrounding the failed revolutions of 1848, worsening economic conditions, and anti-Jewish legislation in many of the German-speaking states. These new immigrants were generally better educated and more financially secure than earlier Jewish immigrants, and brought with them higher culture, a tradition of charity, and reform Jewish practices to their new homes. Among these new immigrants were trained physicians who opened Jews Hospital (later known as Mount Sinai Hospital) in New York City, beginning a tradition of Jewish-sponsored hospitals in American cities. Founded to provide places in which Jewish physicians could work, these hospitals evolved into well-respected community institutions for all members of society. Other Jews eventually became govern-

ment officials in their communities, as well as industrialists and financiers. Many Jewish merchants became successful department store moguls.

By 1880, approximately 250,000 Jews were living in the United States. Many of them were highly educated and largely secular German Jews. Reformers among these immigrants became the foundation of the emerging reform Jewish movement in the United States. Rabbi Isaac Mayer Wise, who had been born in Bohemia in 1819, is credited with founding the reform movement, creating the Union of American Hebrew Congregations, and establishing the rabbinical school Hebrew Union College in Cincinnati, Ohio.

Other immigrants during that era came from the poor rural Jewish populations of Russia, Poland, Lithuania, and Ukraine, fleeing religious persecution in eastern Europe. The primarily Yiddish-speaking Ashkenazi Jews had little in common with the upper-class German Jews, who remained segregated in worship and business dealings. The Ashkenazi Jews founded their own Orthodox synagogues and tended to associate mainly with other members of their own community.

MASS EXODUS

During the nineteenth century, most Russian Jews lived in confined areas as laborers and small merchants. Anti-Semitism, suspicion, and hatred were ever present, and deadly government-sponsored pogroms against Jews created a permanent atmosphere of fear among Russian Jews. The goal of the Russian government was to force one-third of all Russian Jews to leave Russia, another third to convert to Christianity, and the final third to starve to death. In response to this catastrophic government plan, Russian Jews flooded European port cities, from which they sailed to America.

After reaching the United States, many Russian Jews gravitated to New York City's lower East Side, where newcomers sought out others from their Russian village and regions. Eventually, the lower East Side became a melting pot of Yiddish speakers. Similar developments occurred in smaller cities, such as Boston and Philadelphia. To aid new immigrants, *Landsmanschaften*, organizations based on geographic ties to home villages, assumed the role of extended family and provided health insurance, interest-free loans, and medical and burial assistance. Despite their difficulties in becoming assimilated into the new culture, the newly arrived Jews wrote letters to relatives and friends with glowing accounts of America, urging them to follow them there.

Between 1881 and 1890, 3.7 percent of all immigrants to the United States were Jews. By the first decade of the twentieth century, Jews constituted more than 10 percent of all immigrants, and by 1920, 23 percent of the world's Jews lived in the United States. Two million Jews had arrived from eastern Europe alone by 1924. As distrust of immigrants grew after World War I, the Immigration Act of 1921 and the national origins quota system established by the Immigration Act of 1924 severely restricted immigration from southern and eastern Europe after that time.

YIDDISH CULTURE AND ITS DEMISE

A dialect of German written in Hebrew characters, the Yiddish language united Jewish immigrants of all classes and backgrounds. Immigrants were comforted by its familiarity in the cities and the theater, in newspapers and vaudeville. Performers such as Groucho Marx, Jack Benny, Walter Winchell, George Jessel, and Molly Picon, among many others, had their start in vaudeville and went on to success in radio and television. More than twenty Yiddish newspapers, the best known of which was the *Jewish Daily Forward*, were published in New York City alone.

Because the borders of the United States were effectively closed to new Jewish immigrants, the earlier immigrants were becoming Americanized and assimilated more quickly. Consequently, Jewish ghettoes, the Yiddish press, and the Yiddish theater steadily declined. Growing anti-Semitism attacked Jews, their patriotism, and their character. During the 1920's, some prestigious universities established quotas limiting the numbers of Jewish students they would admit. Jewish graduates also faced discrimination as they attempted to attend graduate and professional schools; some were forced to attend foreign medical schools or change their career goals. Some changed their names, hiding their Jewish backgrounds to gain admission to restricted institutions. Blatant discrimination in housing existed, as did discrimination in employment, private clubs, and private schools.

Nevertheless, Jews made their mark in many areas. Jewish Americans achieved success in enter-

tainment. Levi Schubert, Albert Zukor, Marcus Loew, and Louis B. Mayer founded theaters and film production companies; Jewish composers/songwriters George and Ira Gershwin and Irving Berlin achieved phenomenal success. Business entrepreneur Helena Rubenstein founded a giant cosmetics company, and Rose Schneiderman, a labor activist and political leader seeking to improve working conditions, was the only woman appointed by President Franklin D. Roosevelt to the labor advisory board of the National Recovery Administration. Baseball star Hank Greenberg, the first baseman for the Detroit Tigers, broke several long-standing records and was inducted into the Baseball Hall of Fame.

THE EUROPEAN HOLOCAUST

After Adolf Hitler became chancellor of Germany in 1933, he began to put anti-Semitic policies into effect and vowed to exterminate the entire Jewish race. Concentration camps were opened at Dachau, Buchenwald, and Sachsenhausen. The plight of the Jews in Germany grew steadily worse, and many European Jews were convinced that their only chance for survival was to emigrate to the United States. Restrictive U.S. immigration laws were in effect, however, and immigrants had to prove that they either had sufficient resources to sustain themselves in the United States or had families to support them.

Austrian Jews were also forced from their homes and sent to a camp called Mauthausen after Germany occupied Austria in 1938. On November 9-10, 1938, Nazi troops destroyed Jewish homes and synagogues and brutally beat and murdered Jews during *Kristallnacht* (night of the broken glass). The event spurred U.S. president Franklin D. Roosevelt to ease immigration restrictions and permit more Jewish immigrants to enter the United States. Between 1938 and 1941, more than 100,000 European Jews immigrated to the United States.

After Poland fell to the Nazis in September 1939, Jews were forced to leave their homes and move into large cities. Many died from lack of food or proper housing; others were taken to the Auschwitz concentration camp, which opened in 1940. Nazi troops continued to march across Western Europe, conquering many nations. In early 1942, Nazi officials met and discussed what they called the "Final Solution to the Jewish Ques-

tion"—a genocide that had as its goal the total extermination of the Jews. Other concentration camps were erected in Poland in which guards used poisonous gas to execute inhabitants.

By the middle of 1942 confirmed reports came out of Poland about the mass executions of Jews by the Nazis. Jewish charitable organizations worked to aid and transport the Polish Jews; in 1944 the War Refugee Board bribed Nazi officials to release 200,000 from the concentration camps. A total of approximately 6 million Jews were slaughtered during the Holocaust.

AFTER WORLD WAR II

New U.S. laws enacted after the war greatly increased the number of displaced persons permitted to enter the United States. Between 1946 and 1952, more than 80,000 Jews came to America. Assisted by the Hebrew Immigrant Aid society and the National Council of Jewish Women, the immigrants received temporary housing, food, clothing, medical care, and instruction in English. As laws outlawing discrimination in housing were passed during the 1950's, Jews moved to urban suburbs, established new temples and synagogues, and started new religious schools and community centers. During the last two decades of the twentieth century and the first years of the twenty-first century, approximately 400,000 new Jewish immigrants came to the United States, many to seek educational opportunities.

Marcia J. Weiss

FURTHER READING

Diner, Hasia. *The Jews of the United States, 1654-2000.* Berkeley: University of California Press, 2004. Survey of American Jewish history that emphasizes religious issues, while also covering economic and cultural issues.

Finkelstein, Norman H. *American Jewish History.* Philadelphia: Jewish Publication Society, 2007. Introduction to the historical, cultural, and religious heritage of American Jews. Contains numerous photographs, maps, and charts.

Friedman, Saul A. *No Haven for the Oppressed: United States Policy Toward Jewish Refugees, 1938-1945.* Detroit: Wayne State University Press, 1973. Examination of anti-Semitic hostility toward Jews fleeing from the Holocaust during Germany's Nazi era.

Howe, Irving. *World of Our Fathers: The Journey of the East European Jews to America and the Life They Found and Made.* New York: Simon & Schuster, 1976. Story of the eastern European Jews who came to America and their efforts to retain their Yiddish culture.

Telushkin, Rabbi Joseph. *The Golden Land: The Story of Jewish Immigration to America.* New York: Harmony Books, 2002. Tells the story of Jewish immigration to America through removable documents and artifacts.

Wenger, Beth. *The Jewish Americans.* New York: Doubleday, 2007. Comprehensive history of Jews in the United States. Includes numerous first-person accounts of the Jewish experience and numerous photographs.

Worth, Richard. *Jewish Immigrants.* New York: Facts On File, 2005. Concise history of Jewish immigration written for young readers. Well illustrated.

SEE ALSO: American Jewish Committee; Anti-Defamation League; Anti-Semitism; Berlin, Irving; Einstein, Albert; Former Soviet Union immigrants; Garment industry; Holocaust; Israeli immigrants; Name changing; Polish immigrants; World War II.

JORDAN V. TASHIRO

THE CASE: U.S. Supreme Court decision concerning privileges in treaties

DATE: Decided on November 19, 1928

SIGNIFICANCE: One of a series of rulings relating to the tension between U.S. treaties with Japan and California's alien land laws, the *Tashiro* decision gave a broad and liberal interpretation of the privileges guaranteed by treaties, emphasizing the common meanings of the words in a 1911 commerce treaty.

The U.S.-Japanese Treaty of Commerce and Navigation of 1911 authorized citizens of Japan to participate in commerce, which included everything "incident to or necessary for trade upon the same terms as native citizens." The treaty put significant limits on the extent to which California was able to enforce the discriminatory Alien Land Law, passed in 1913. In interpreting the treaty, the Supreme Court had ruled that the treaty protected the right to operate a pawnbroker business but that it did not extend to manufacturing or agricultural production.

K. Tashiro and other citizens of Japan residing in California petitioned the state government for the incorporation of a Japanese hospital in Los Angeles. State officials refused to consider the petition on the grounds that treaty rights did not extend to the operation of a business corporation. Tashiro and his associates challenged the refusal in state court. When the court agreed with Tashiro's position, the secretary of state of California petitioned the Supreme Court for a writ of certiorari, which was granted.

The Supreme Court unanimously upheld the ruling of the lower court. Writing the opinion of the Court, Justice Harlan F. Stone followed the precedent of liberally construing the privileges enumerated in treaties, and he concluded that the ordinary meanings of the words in the 1911 treaty necessarily included three relevant privileges: (1) conducting a business in corporate form, (2) providing medical services for a fee, and (3) leasing an appropriate amount of land needed for the purpose of a commercial business.

Thomas Tandy Lewis

FURTHER READING

Hyung-chan, Kim, ed. *Asian Americans and the Supreme Court: A Documentary History.* Westport, Conn.: Greenwood Press, 1992.

LeMay, Michael, and Elliott Robert Barkan, eds. *U.S. Immigration and Naturalization Laws and Issues: A Documentary History.* Westport, Conn.: Greenwood Press, 1999.

SEE ALSO: Alien land laws; California; History of immigration after 1891; Japanese immigrants; Supreme Court, U.S.

THE JUNGLE

IDENTIFICATION: Novel by Upton Sinclair about an immigrant Lithuanian family in Chicago and the corrupt meatpacking industry

DATE: First published in 1906

SIGNIFICANCE: In preparation for the writing of *The Jungle*, Sinclair visited Chicago meat-

Upton Sinclair. (Library of Congress)

French naturalists such as Émile Zola, the socialist Sinclair borrowed the concept of the individual rendered powerless by immense natural and socio-political forces that reduce humans to animals caught in a trap.

The Jungle begins with the wedding reception of Jurgis Rudkus and Ona Lukoszaite, who postponed marrying to save for this expensive but cherished ritual in their culture. Soon the scene will seem a poignant reminder of lost happiness as the family is ground down by drudgery, deception, and death. Jurgis will witness the deaths of his father, Antanas, then Ona along with their second child, and eventually their toddler son, who drowns in a mud puddle. In addition to these losses, Jurgis comes to recognize the full dimensions of the jungle metaphor, or its variant, the slaughterhouse. The immigrants are lambs drawn to the slaughter by oppressive capitalism, exploiting them as "wage-slaves," fleecing them of their hard-earned wages and savings, then condemning them to death by starvation, accident, or disease, just as callously as the meatpackers butcher animals for meat.

Although a mediocre novel as a work of literature, *The Jungle* was a best seller that is still widely read in the twenty-first century, and it became a primary force behind the passage of the Pure Food and Drug Act of 1906, which led in turn to creation of the Food and Drug Administration.

Earl G. Ingersoll

FURTHER READING

Musteikis, Antanas. "The Lithuanian Heroes of *The Jungle.*" *Lithuanus* 17, no. 2 (1971): 27-38.

Øverland, Orm. "*The Jungle*: From Lithuanian Peasant to American Socialist." *American Literary Realism* 37, no. 1 (2004): 1-23.

Subacius, Giedrius. *The Lithuanian Jungle.* Amsterdam, Netherlands: Rodopi, 2006.

SEE ALSO: Chicago; Former Soviet Union immigrants; Goldman, Emma; Literature; Presidential elections.

packing plants disguised as a worker in order to experience at first hand the brutal working conditions and the contamination of the meat products for America's dinner tables. Although his intention was to bring attention to the plight of exploited workers, public outcry focused on the unsanitary conditions of the meat industry and led to the passage of federal food-inspection laws.

Upton Sinclair's muckraking novel *The Jungle* offers a devastatingly bleak picture of the lives of Lithuanian immigrants lured from their homeland to the dark heart of America—Chicago and the meatpacking industry that destroys them physically and spiritually. From nineteenth century

K

KANSAS

SIGNIFICANCE: Kansas's central position on migration and cattle trails and railroads during the nineteenth century made it a region through which large numbers of immigrants passed on their way west. Many of them went no farther.

The first European to lead an exploration of the region that would become the state of Kansas was Francisco Vásquez de Coronado in 1541. Three centuries later, the Santa Fe Trail was cut across the territory to facilitate the transporting of manufactured goods, silver, and furs from neighboring Missouri to New Mexico. Abilene, Kansas, became the final destination for cattle drives following the Chisholm Trail. Railroads soon followed. Cattle loaded onto railcars were carried to Chicago meatpacking plants. By 1880, 8,720 miles of railroad tracks crisscrossed the state.

The first permanent white settlers began dribbling into the territory during the 1830's. The pace of their settlement accelerated after the passage of the Kansas-Nebraska Act in 1854. By the mid-1850's, both abolitionists from the New England states and proslavery settlers from Missouri poured into Kansas to compete for dominance in the struggle to determine whether the territory would become a free or a slave state. Second-generation pioneers coming from Ohio, Indiana, and Illinois tended to settle in the middle section of the territory, while its upper southern region was settled mostly by those coming from Missouri, Kentucky, and southern Indiana. This mix of settlers with violently opposing views on slavery brought an era of chaos and violence that became known as "Bleeding Kansas." Eventually, however, the abolitionists prevailed, and Kansas entered the Union as a free state on January 29, 1861.

After the Civil War (1861-1865), many military veterans, along with European immigrant groups, settled and constructed homesteads in Kansas. Swedes constituted a major concentration near Lindsborg, which is south of Salina. Germans settled west of Maryville; German-Russian Mennonites north of Newton; German-Russian Catholics near Hays; and Czechs west of Ellsworth.

TWENTIETH CENTURY DEVELOPMENTS

More English-speaking immigrants from Ireland, Wales, and Scotland settled in southeast Kansas than in any other Great Plains state, but Germans have remained the largest European immigrant component of the state's population. Farmers in Kansas have led the United States in wheat, sorghum, and sunflower production, but the state's agricultural industry has faced the problem of finding farmworkers, as young Kansans have moved from the rural areas into the cities. Not surprisingly, Johnson County, which contains metropolitan Kansas City, has become the state's fastest-growing county. Meanwhile, the need for farmworkers has contributed to an increase in foreign immigration.

During the late twentieth century, the Hispanic population had an increasing impact on the demographics of the Great Plains.

PROFILE OF KANSAS

Region	Midwest
Entered union	1861
Largest cities	Wichita, Overland Park, Kansas City, Topeka (capital)
Modern immigrant communities	Mexicans, Central Americans

Population	Total	Percent of state	Percent of U.S.	U.S. rank
All state residents	2,764,000	100.0	0.92	33
All foreign-born residents	173,000	6.3	0.46	31

Source: U.S. Census Bureau, *Statistical Abstract for 2006.*
Notes: The U.S. population in 2006 was 299,399,000, of whom 37,548,000 (12.5%) were foreign born. Rankings in last column reflect total numbers, not percentages.

Meatpacking and construction companies began to recruit and hire Mexicans and Central Americans in large numbers to offset union forces by paying the immigrants lower wages. In 2006, Kansas had 173,000 foreign-born residents, who constituted 6.3 percent of the total population of the state. Hispanics are most numerous around the southeast portion of the state. The large influx in Latin American immigrants has brought with it an increase in the numbers of undocumented aliens in the state. U.S. immigration officials have responded with raids on plants employing immigrants that have resulted in mass deportations. During the first decade of the twenty-first century, legislatures in both Kansas and neighboring Nebraska began grappling with economic and social issues that have arisen from illegal immigration. Both states have seen proposals for major changes in the document-verification systems used by companies to stop unscrupulous hiring practices.

Gayla Koerting

FURTHER READING

Blouet, Brian W., and Frederick C. Luebke. *The Great Plains: Environment and Culture.* Lincoln: University of Nebraska Press, 1979.

Gjerde, Jon. *The Minds of the West: The Ethnocultural Evolution of the Rural Middle West, 1830-1917.* Chapel Hill: University of North Carolina Press, 1979.

Webb, Walter Prescott. *The Great Plains.* New York: Ginn, 1931.

Wishart, David J., ed. *Encyclopedia of the Great Plains.* Lincoln: University of Nebraska Press, 2004.

SEE ALSO: Czech and Slovakian immigrants; German immigrants; Iowa; Latin American immigrants; Missouri; Nebraska; Scandinavian immigrants.

KENTUCKY

SIGNIFICANCE: Kentucky has taken in fewer foreign immigrants than more urban states. Most nineteenth and twentieth century immigration was urban or, in the case of Kentucky's eastern coal region, industrial in nature. However, during the last decade of the twentieth century and the first decade of the

next century, immigration to Kentucky began to increase; undocumented Hispanic workers have come in unprecedented numbers.

Although early immigration to Kentucky was dominated by people of Scotch-Irish and English ancestry, immigrants from other parts of Europe were represented as well. Germans—particularly settlers who came by way of Pennsylvania—were not uncommon, and significant numbers of Welsh, French Huguenot, and other groups also came. As early as the 1780's, Dutch settlers from Pennsylvania arrived in Kentucky and near Harrodsburg erected an archaic Dutch Reformed Church meeting house of timbered wattle and daub that still survives. Slaves, too, migrated to frontier Kentucky, and in their veins ran the blood of various, mostly West African, ethnicities.

After 1848, famine and political unrest drove large numbers of Germans and Irish to the United States. While most headed for the Northeast or joined the growing tide of settlement in the American Midwest, a number entered the urban centers of the South. In Kentucky, this meant the Ohio River cities of Covington, Newport, and Louisville. Louisville especially received large numbers of Irish and Germans. In 1850, members of these groups constituted 11,000 of the city's total white population of 36,224. In Louisville, a combination of raw xenophobia, anti-Catholicism (many of the newcomers were Roman Catholics) and the popularity of a short-lived national nativist movement called the Know-Nothing Party finally erupted in the "Bloody Monday" antiforeign riots on election day, August 6, 1855. Twenty-two people were killed and much property was destroyed, but the incident was not to be repeated in Kentucky.

As occurred in a number of other southern states during the late nineteenth century, some Kentuckians feared that the state was not receiving sufficient immigration to support its economic growth. The state legislature took action, creating an immigration commission in 1880. The commission launched a campaign to attract northern Europeans to the state and met with some success. A number of Swiss, Germans and Austrians did arrive. By 1885, these newcomers had established a sprinkling of small colonies, spanning the region between Lyon County in western Kentucky to Lau-

rel in the east. Although none of these settlements thrived as much as hoped, some have survived into the twenty-first century as small communities.

TWENTIETH CENTURY DEVELOPMENTS

As American industry began tapping in earnest the vast timber and mineral resources of the eastern Kentucky mountains during the early twentieth century, new immigrants entered the state. Indeed, as coal mines and company towns arose during the first two decades of the century, Hungarians, Poles, Italians, Yugoslavs, and a veritable Ellis Island of other groups entered the Kentucky coal fields. These immigrants never outnumbered native-born white miners in the region, but they become a large contingent. Immigrants, along with African Americans, were typically assigned the dirtiest and most dangerous of jobs. By 1930, immigrants had begun to leave Kentucky's depressed coal fields, but a handful stayed and their descendants were absorbed into the local culture.

Into the twenty-first century, Kentucky's population has remained predominantly white and native born. Nonetheless, during the 1990's, Kentucky experienced the nation's third-fastest growth in immigrant population. By 2000, about 2.5 percent of Kentucky's total residents were documented immigrants. Immigrants from Vietnam and China were among the two fastest-growing groups to enter the state during this period. Most of these new immigrants did not come to Kentucky directly from their original homelands but instead migrated from elsewhere in the United States. They were evidently hoping to make their livelihoods in a less crowded state.

Hispanics have long worked as laborers in Kentucky. They have had a particularly long-standing presence in central Kentucky's famous thoroughbred horse industry. During the 1990's and early twenty-first century, Latin Americans began entering Kentucky in unprecedented numbers. By 2006, Mexicans alone accounted for nearly one-quarter

PROFILE OF KENTUCKY

Region	Eastern central United States
Entered union	1792
Largest cities	Lexington-Fayette, Louisville, Owensboro, Bowling Green
Modern immigrant communities	Vietnamese, Asian Indians, Mexicans

Population	Total	Percent of state	Percent of U.S.	U.S. rank
All state residents	4,206,000	100.0	1.40	26
All foreign-born residents	112,000	2.7	0.29	35

Source: U.S. Census Bureau, *Statistical Abstract for 2006.*

Notes: The U.S. population in 2006 was 299,399,000, of whom 37,548,000 (12.5%) were foreign born. Rankings in last column reflect total numbers, not percentages.

of the state's foreign-born population. By this period, a large but unknown number of illegal immigrants—mostly from Mexico but also from other Latin American countries—had entered the Kentucky workforce. Most worked in agriculture, agricultural processing and the service sector. While these undocumented workers are not as numerous as those in some other southern states, their numbers have been sufficiently large to attract political controversy.

Jeremiah Taylor

FURTHER READING

Barrett, Tracy. *Kentucky.* 2d ed. New York: Marshall Cavendish Benchmark, 2008.

Cantrell, Doug. "Immigrants and Community in Harlan County, 1910-1930." *Register of the Kentucky Historical Society* 86 (1988): 119-141.

Klotter, James C., ed. *Our Kentucky: A Study of the Bluegrass State.* 2d ed. Lexington: University Press of Kentucky, 2000.

Ray, Celeste, ed. *The New Encyclopedia of Southern Culture.* Vol. 6. *Ethnicity.* Chapel Hill: University of North Carolina Press, 2007.

SEE ALSO: British immigrants; Coal industry; Economic opportunities; European immigrants; German immigrants; Irish immigrants; Know-Nothing Party; Mexican immigrants; Ohio; Swiss immigrants.

KISSINGER, HENRY

IDENTIFICATION: German-born U.S. secretary of state

BORN: May 27, 1923; Fürth, Bavaria, Germany

SIGNIFICANCE: As national security advisor and secretary of state under Presidents Richard M. Nixon and Gerald R. Ford, Kissinger helped shape American foreign policy during the latter half of the Vietnam War.

The son of a middle-class Bavarian Jewish family, Henry Kissinger fled to the United States with his family in 1938 after it became clear that Nazi Germany's hostility toward Jews was no ordinary pogrom to be weathered. In the United States he changed his first name from Heinz to Henry and succeeded in school even while working long hours to help support his family. Drafted into the U.S. armed services in 1943, he worked as an interpreter during the Allied occupation of Germany, where he helped track down and prosecute former Gestapo agents. After the war ended in 1945, he returned to school and earned a doctoral degree in political science at Harvard University in 1954. He later joined the faculty of Harvard and went on to make his mark as an authority on international relations. The books he wrote in that field offered penetrating insights on American nuclear policy that attracted attention at very high levels.

In 1969, President Richard Nixon wooed Kissinger away from academia to accept an appointment as national security advisor. Nixon was so satisfied with Kissinger's work that he elevated Kissinger to secretary of state, making him the nation's top diplomat and the primary shaper of U.S. foreign policy. Although disliked by critics of the Vietnam war, Kissinger survived the Watergate scandal of the early 1970's and remained at his posts under Gerald R. Ford. After Ford lost the presidential election of 1976, Kissinger retired from public service. He became an elder statesman, offering advice to Republican politicians and conservative think tanks.

Leigh Husband Kimmel

FURTHER READING

Berman, Larry. *No Peace, No Honor: Nixon, Kissinger and Betrayal in Vietnam.* New York: Free Press, 2001.

Dallek, Robert. *Nixon and Kissinger: Partners in Power.* New York: HarperCollins, 2007.

Hanhimäki, Jussi. *The Flawed Architect: Henry Kissinger and American Foreign Policy.* New York: Oxford University Press, 2004.

Kissinger, Henry A. *Ending the Vietnam War: A History of America's Involvement in and Extrication from the Vietnam War.* New York: Simon & Schuster, 2003.

SEE ALSO: Albright, Madeleine; Anti-Semitism; German immigrants; Holocaust; Jewish immigrants.

Henry Kissinger. (© The Nobel Foundation)

KNOW-NOTHING PARTY

IDENTIFICATION: Nativist, anti-Roman Catholic political organization

DATE: 1852-1860

ALSO KNOWN AS: Native American Party; National Council of the United States of North America

SIGNIFICANCE: During the nineteenth century, the United States experienced an influx of Roman Catholic immigrants from Europe. These immigrants differed from earlier European immigrants, most of whom had been Protestants. Religious differences between Protestant Americans and Roman Catholics created economic, social, and political strains as the United States became a more diversified country. The Know-Nothing movement emerged in opposition to Catholic immigration.

During the 1830's and 1840's, the United States witnessed an influx of immigrants from Europe. From 1831 to 1840, approximately 538,000 individuals migrated to the United States; one-third of these were Catholics. The decade of the 1840's saw another 1.7 million immigrants come to the United States. Approximately 50 percent of these immigrants were Catholic, primarily from Ireland and Germany. By 1850, approximately 10 percent of the U.S. population was Roman Catholic. Many native-born Protestant Americans began to fear that the United States was being overwhelmed by Catholic immigrants, and some even believed that the pope wanted to colonize the United States in order to extend his authority.

KNOW-NOTHING MOVEMENT

As more and more Catholics came to the United States, they settled in the cities of the North. These immigrants were generally unskilled workers who competed with working-class Protestants for low-wage jobs. Ten-

sions between the two groups were compounded by the Panic of 1837, as jobs became scarce and the wages of the working class suffered. Also, as Catholics settled in the cities, disputes arose concerning public aid to parochial schools. At the same time, Catholic parents resisted paying taxes for public schools to which they were unwilling to send their children. Amid growing anti-Catholic sentiment, the Know-Nothing movement would emerge and capitalize on the decline of the major parties—the Whigs and the Democrats—during the 1850's.

During the 1840's, several nativist organizations were established in reaction to Catholic immigration. In 1852, these groups merged to form the National Council of the United States of North America, which later became known as the Know-Nothing Party. Members referred to the organization as the Supreme Order of the Star-Spangled Banner. Membership in the society was limited to native-born citizens who were twenty-one years of

KNOW-NOTHINGISM IN BROOKLYN.
"None but citizens of the United States can be licensed to engage in any employment in this city."
Brooklyn Board of Aldermen.

Editorial cartoon from an 1881 issue of Frank Leslie's Illustrated Newspaper *lampooning a nativist policy of Brooklyn's municipal government.* (Library of Congress)

age or older; Protestant, born of Protestant parents, or raised under Protestant influence; and not married to a Catholic. The stated purpose of the organization was to protect American citizens in the legal and proper exercise of their civil and religious rights, to use legal methods to resist the Catholic Church and other foreign influences against American institutions, and to elect only native-born Protestant Americans to public office. The organization also advocated a twenty-one-year residency requirement for citizenship. It developed an elaborate ritual with signs, handshakes, and passwords, and members were required to maintain the secrecy of the group and its activities. When questioned about the organization, members would answer "I don't know"—hence the byname. The group's secrecy was eventually shed, however, as it rose to political prominence.

POLITICAL ACTIVITIES

By 1855, the party had established state councils in approximately thirty-three states, and the movement claimed one million members. Initially, the organization secretly endorsed candidates from one of the major parties; however, by 1854 it had founded its own party and begun to nominate candidates. It held its first open national convention in New York City during that same year and officially abandoned its fraternal secrecy. The apex of the Know-Nothing Party was in 1854 and 1855. During this time, the party elected mayors in Boston, Chicago, and Philadelphia, as well as governors in Rhode Island, New Hampshire, Connecticut, Massachusetts, California, and Kentucky. In Massachusetts, the Know-Nothing Party received 63 percent of the vote and won every state senate seat and all but 3 of the 378 state house seats. In addition, Know-Nothing candidates were elected to all eleven Massachusetts seats to the House of Representatives. It was estimated that at least fifty-one members of the Thirty-fourth U.S. Congress were members of the Know-Nothing Party.

In February, 1856, delegates met in Philadelphia before the nominating convention of their rennamed national party, the American Party. However, members split over the issue of slavery, and delegates from Ohio, Pennsylvania, Illinois, Iowa, and the New England states walked out. The remaining delegates persuaded former President Millard Fillmore to be their party's candidate for president. Fillmore, however, disavowed anti-Catholicism and transformed the American Party from a nativist organization to an anti-Democratic and prounion party. In the election of 1856, Fillmore received just over 20 percent of the vote and carried only one state, Maryland. Following the election, the American Party and the Know-Nothing movement quickly disappeared. While several enclaves remained in border states until 1860, anti-Catholicism was relegated to secondary importance as the issue of slavery became the major concern of the American people.

William V. Moore

FURTHER READING

Bennett, David H. *The Party of Fear: From Nativist Movements to the New Right in American History.* Chapel Hill: University of North Carolina Press, 1988. Discusses the background to nativism and has several chapters on the Know-Nothing movement and party.

Lipset, Seymour Martin, and Earl Raab. *The Politics of Unreason: Right-Wing Extremism in America, 1790-1970.* New York: Harper & Row, 1970. Uses status politics to explain right-wing movements, including the Know-Nothing movement.

Mulkern, John R. *The Know-Nothing Party in Massachusetts: The Rise and Fall of a People's Movement.* Boston: Northeastern University Press, 1990. Analysis of the Know-Nothings in Massachusetts.

Richardson, Darcy G. *Others: Third Party Politics From the Nation's Founding to the Rise and Fall of the Greenback-Labor Party.* New York: iUniverse, 2004. Includes information on the nativist movement and the emergence of the Know-Nothing Party.

Voss-Hubbard, Mark. *Beyond Party: Culture of Antipartisanship in Northern Politics Before the Civil War.* Baltimore: Johns Hopkins University Press, 2002. Includes an analysis of nativist culture as well as the Know-Nothing movement.

SEE ALSO: American Protective Association; Anti-Catholicism; Employment; Great Irish Famine; History of immigration, 1783-1891; Ku Klux Klan; Nativism; Philadelphia anti-Irish riots; Religions of immigrants; Xenophobia.

KOREAN IMMIGRANTS

SIGNIFICANCE: Until the late twentieth century, Korean immigration to the United States was relatively small. However, the Korean War of 1950-1953 prompted a major wave of immigration from South Korea, and the liberalization of American immigration laws during the 1960's brought an even larger wave of immigrants. By the turn of the twenty-first century, Koreans were one of the fastest-growing ethnic groups in the United States. By the year 2008, about 1.5 million people of Korean descent were residing in the country, and Koreans constituted the fifth-largest Asian immigrant group in the United States, after Chinese, Filipinos, Asian Indians, and Vietnamese.

In 2003, Korean American communities throughout the United States celebrated the centennial anniversary of Korean immigration. However, the history of Korean immigrants in America actually started during the late nineteenth century. In 1882, Korea and the United States signed a treaty of amity and commerce that permitted Koreans to immigrate to the United States. Afterward, close political, military, and economic relations between the two countries helped shape Korean immigration to the United States. After the 1882 treaty, Korean diplomats, political exiles, students, and merchants began visiting, but they did not settle in the country. The first significant wave of Korean immigrants came to the American territory of Hawaii as sugar cane plantation workers in 1903.

KOREAN IMMIGRATION TO HAWAII

During the late nineteenth century, famine and poverty had driven many rural Koreans to urban centers, where they were exposed to Christianity and Western cultural influences. During that period, Korea was feeling the pressure of Chinese and Japanese efforts to dominate its government, and many Koreans were becoming more sympathetic to the idea of emigrating. Meanwhile, friendly political and economic relations between Korea and the United States were opening the possibility of having Korean workers go to the U.S. territory of Hawaii. This idea was facilitated by both Hawaiian planters and American missionaries in Korea. The Chinese Exclusion Act of 1882 had contributed to a labor shortage in Hawaii. Hawaiian sugar cane planters relied mostly on Japanese laborers. However, as labor unrest among the Japanese increased in Hawaii, the planters contemplated the possibility of bringing in laborers from other Asian countries and invited Koreans to come to Hawaii as strikebreakers.

Horace Allen, an American medical missionary working in Korea, played a significant role in initiating Korean immigration to Hawaii. During a visit in the United States in 1902, he met with Hawaiian planters and afterward used his political influence as a missionary to send Koreans to Hawaii. Few Koreans were initially willing to go to Hawaii, so missionaries in Korea personally recruited workers from among their own Christian congregations. In contrast to the Japanese and Chinese workers who had come from confined geographical areas in their home countries, early Korean immigrants had diverse geographical backgrounds, and nearly half of them were Christian converts. In December, 1902, 56 men, 21 women, and 25 children left Korea on the SS *Gaelic*. They arrived in Honolulu, Hawaii, on January 13, 1903. Over the next two years, nearly 7,500 Koreans went to Hawaii to work on sugar cane plantations.

KOREAN IMMIGRATION, 1905-1945

That first wave of Korean immigration came to an abrupt end in 1905, when the Korean government received reports of mistreatment of Korean laborers in Mexico and stopped permitting its people to go to either Mexico or the United States. Japan's government also pressured the Korean government to close its emigration bureau because it was concerned with the condition of its own citizens who were working in Hawaii. In 1907, the United States and Japan signed a Gentlemen's Agreement that stopped immigration of Japanese laborers to the United States. By that time, Korea was effectively ruled by Japan, so Korean workers were also banned from emigrating. After Korea was forcibly annexed by Japan in 1910, Korean immigration to the United States virtually halted.

Most of the early Korean immigrants were engaged in agricultural labor in Hawaii on three-year contracts. After their contracts expired, many Koreans went from Hawaii to the mainland United

States or returned to Korea. Some of those who made their way to the United States found success in the West Coast states, where they bought farms and started agricultural enterprises. However, California's Alien Land Law of 1913 prevented all Asian immigrants, including Koreans, from owning land and limited their leases in California. Some of the Koreans who left Hawaii worked on railroads on the West Coast, and some of these people were recruited to work as farm laborers.

Between 1907 and 1924, a small number of picture brides, students, and political exiles from Korea were admitted to the United States. Approximately 1,100 picture brides joined their prospective husbands between 1910 and 1924, when the new U.S. Immigration Act instituted discriminatory quotas based on national origins. This new law greatly reduced immigration from southern and eastern Europe and virtually ended it from Asia. Even after 1924, however, small groups of Korean political exiles and students continued to arrive in the United States, fleeing from the Japanese colonial rule in their homeland.

The U.S. government was sympathetic toward Korean political refugees from Japanese rule and admitted them to the United States as nonquota immigrants. Between 1925 and 1940, about 300 Korean students entered the United States on Japanese-issued passports. Most of them remained in America after completing their studies because they feared persecution by the Japanese government if they returned to Korea. Many of them participated in organizations and demonstrations for Korean independence. Female immigrants, though small in number, also took part in the efforts. As many of the early Korean immigrants were Christians, churches became important gathering places for them and helped fulfill not only their religious but also political and social needs.

KOREAN IMMIGRATION, 1945-1965

After World War II ended in 1945, the Japanese were ousted from Korea, which was effectively partitioned between the Soviet Union and the United States. The United States occupied the southern part of the Korean Peninsula until 1948, when the Republic of Korea was established under president Syngman Rhee. Meanwhile, the Soviet Union helped set up a communist government in the north.

PROFILE OF KOREAN IMMIGRANTS

Country of origin	North and South Korea
Primary language	Korean
Primary regions of U.S. settlement	California and New York State
Earliest significant arrivals	1880's
Peak immigration period	1965-2008
Twenty-first century legal residents*	189,144 (23.643 per year)

*Immigrants who obtained legal permanent resident status in the United States.
Source: Department of Homeland Security, *Yearbook of Immigration Statistics, 2008.*

As the Korean War broke out in 1950, the United States supplied military and economic assistance to South Korea and eventually negotiated the peace settlement with the Soviet Union. After an armistice was declared in 1953, Korea remained divided at the thirty-eighth parallel. The United States continued to provide military and economic aid to South Korea with the goal of containing the spread of communism in Asia. South Korea also depended heavily on U.S. aid to finance its postwar reconstruction.

The Korean War was both directly and indirectly responsible for the immigration of Koreans to the United States. Many people, traumatized by the war experience and looking for political and economic stability, left the war-ravaged country. Because of its close ties to Korea, the United States became the primary destination of many emigrants. The most visible groups of Korean immigrants to the United States after the war were wives of American servicemen, war orphans, and professional workers and students. These people differed from earlier Korean immigrants in many ways, especially in the proportion of women immigrants. The earlier wave of Korean immigration had a ratio of about ten men to every woman. After the arrival of "picture brides" during the 1910's and 1920's, the Korean immigrant population became 66 percent male during the 1930's. During the second wave of

Korean immigration, however, women accounted for more than 70 percent of all Korean immigrants to the United States.

The U.S. War Brides Act of 1945 allowed wives of American soldiers to enter the United States as nonquota immigrants. Korean war brides began to arrive in the United States during the Korean War and continued to come afterward as nonquota immigrants. Every year from 1953 until the end of the decade, about 500 Korean war brides were admitted to the United States. Passage of the Immigration and Nationality Act of 1952 repealed racial exclusion and relaxed the national quota criteria. Although the law was not fully liberalized, it opened a window of opportunity for many Koreans to come to the United States. Along with the wives of American servicemen, babies of servicemen and war orphans entered the United States as nonquota immigrants. Direct products of the Korean War, these typically forlorn-looking people dominated popular images of Korea in the United States during the 1950's. In 1955, Harry and Bertha Holt, American evangelists from Oregon, popularized the adoption of Korean orphans and the abandoned babies of American servicemen. Between 1955 and 1977, American families adopted about 13,000 Korean orphans. Every year during the 1980's, Americans adopted 7,000 to 8,000 Korean children. In contrast to popular images of Korean war orphans, many of the adoptees were not true orphans at all but were children who had been given up for adoption because of Korean racial prejudice against mixed-race babies or because their unwed or impoverished mothers could not afford to raise them.

Along with the military brides and adoptees who came to the United States from Korea were students and professional workers. Between 1945 and 1965, about 6,000 Korean students came to the United States to seek higher education at colleges and universities. After completing their studies some returned to South Korea to work as academicians and professionals, but many became permanent residents in the United States. This period of Korean immigration provided a steppingstone for the third wave of Korean immigrants. Many of the Koreans who immigrated to the United States before 1965 were naturalized as American citizens and were thus able to sponsor relatives who followed them under the family reunification preferences of the Immigration and Nationality Act of 1965.

IMMIGRATION AFTER 1965

The U.S. Immigration and Nationality Act of 1965 (also known as the Hart-Cellar Act) eliminated national origins quotas and gave priority to immigrants with skills. In addition, the law allowed the spouses, unmarried minor children, and parents of U.S. citizens to enter as nonquota immigrants. With the passage of the 1965 law, the third and largest wave of Korean immigration began. While early immigrants were mostly farmers, most post-1965 immigrants have come from urban, middle-class backgrounds and have exhibited considerable diversity in their occupations and social classes.

After 1965, South Korea's own government began actively encouraging emigration as a means to reduce the pressures of its growing population and

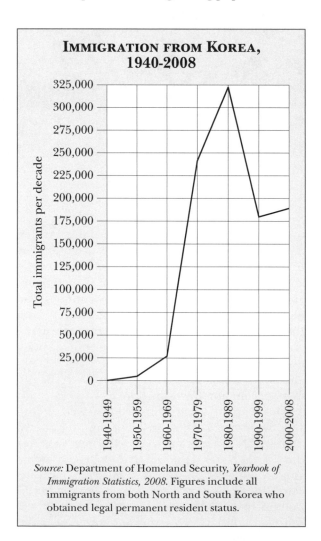

IMMIGRATION FROM KOREA, 1940-2008

Source: Department of Homeland Security, *Yearbook of Immigration Statistics, 2008.* Figures include all immigrants from both North and South Korea who obtained legal permanent resident status.

Residents of Los Angeles's Koreatown watching a parade with floats supporting political candidates in South Korea's presidential elections during the late 1980's. (Korea Society/Los Angeles)

to reap economic benefits from emigrants earning money abroad. Industrialization and modernization in Korea motivated its people to move to cities and to other countries, such as the United States and Germany, to find better opportunities and higher-paying jobs. Moreover, remittances from the immigrants have played a significant role in the growing Korean economy. The close military, political, and economic ties between the United States and South Korea have favored America as the primary destination for many Koreans.

The Korean immigrants who arrived before 1965 were not a highly visible group because of their small numbers and sparse distribution across the United States. However, with the rise of immigration after 1965, Korean immigrants have become one of the fastest-growing immigrant groups in the United States. Between 1970 and 1990, the Korean population in the country rose from

70,000 residents to almost 800,000. By the year 2000, that number had grown to 1.1 million.

KOREAN BUSINESS VENTURES IN THE UNITED STATES

During the 1960's, South Korea rose from the ravages of the war and gained economic strength and stability, aided by U.S. economic support and export-oriented economic policies. The living standards of South Koreans improved, and higher education expanded rapidly. During the early 1960's, only about 6 percent of Korean Americans were classified as professionals and managers. The immigrants who have come to the United States since 1965 have been more highly educated and had more professional job skills than their predecessors. However, despite their educational attainments and technical skills, many new immigrants found themselves confined to the lower rungs of

the occupational ladders in their fields and prevented from practicing their professional skills due to language barriers and their unfamiliarity with American customs. In response, many of them turned to self-employment, running liquor stores, greengroceries, and other small shops in urban centers throughout the United States. Unfamiliar with the American banking system, many Koreans have joined Korean-run rotating credit associations.

Korean immigrants have done well as small merchants throughout the United States. During the 1980's, they began winning praise as a hardworking, law-abiding "model minority." However, their economic success and educational attainments did not always reflect the reality of their lives, and tended to conceal mounting troubles within their Korean American communities. During the 1980's and 1990's, tensions between Korean merchants and the largely black and Hispanic clientele of their innercity stores began rising. In New York City, Washington, D.C., Philadelphia, and Chicago, African Americans launched protest demonstrations and boycotts against Korean businesses, which they believed were exploiting their communities. These tensions reached an exploding point in Los Angeles in April, 1992, when much of the city erupted into rioting after the white police officers who had savagely beaten the black motorist Rodney King were acquitted of wrongdoing. The devastating riots exposed racial and economic hostilities between African Americans and Korean immigrants. During three days of violent rioting, fifty-eight people were killed and more than one billion dollars in property damage was done. A disproportionately large number of Korean stores were destroyed during the rioting, and the media brought to the fore tension and conflicts between Korean immigrants and African Americans.

The Los Angeles riots revealed deeply ingrained racism and economic disparities in American society and Korean ethnic communities. However, in the aftermath of the riots, Koreans made efforts to resolve the conflicts and form alliances with other minority groups. Meanwhile, Korean immigrants discovered greater solidarity within their own community. Like members of other Asian communities, Koreans have been noted for shunning involvement in political organizations and activities.

However, after the riots, they became more outgoing, and national organizations began playing more important roles in Korean immigrant communities.

Ji-Hye Shin

FURTHER READING

Abelmann, Nancy, and John Lie. *Blue Dreams: Korean Americans and the Los Angeles Riots.* Cambridge, Mass.: Harvard University Press, 1995. Study of race relations of Korean Americans analyzed through the Los Angeles riots of 1992.

Hurh, Won Moo, and Kwang Chung Kim. *Korean Immigrants in America: A Structural Analysis of Ethnic Confinement and Adhesive Adaptation.* Rutherford, N.J.: Fairleigh Dickinson University Press, 1984. Overview of Korean immigration to the United States from a sociological perspective.

Kim, Hyung-Chan, and Wayne Patterson, eds. *The Koreans in America, 1882-1974.* Dobbs Ferry, N.Y.: Oceana, 1974. Chronology and fact book that examines the history of Korean immigration to the United States.

Kim, Nadia Y. *Imperial Citizens: Koreans and Race from Seoul to LA.* Stanford, Calif.: Stanford University Press, 2008. Study with a global framework to examine racial ideas Koreans had prior to and after their immigration to the United States.

Lee, Mary Paik. *Quiet Odyssey: A Pioneer Korean Woman in America.* Seattle: University of Washington Press, 1990. First-hand account of a Korean woman who immigrated to Hawaii as a young child with her family. It narrates early years of Korean immigration in the United States.

Min, Pyong Gap. *Caught in the Middle: Korean Communities in New York and Los Angeles.* Berkeley: University of California Press, 1996. Sociological study of post-1965 Korean immigrants in the United States that focuses on lives and challenges of Korean merchants.

SEE ALSO: Alaska; Amerasian children; Chinese immigrants; Gentlemen's Agreement; Hawaii; Immigration and Nationality Act of 1952; Immigration and Nationality Act of 1965; Japanese immigrants; Korean War; Missionaries; "Model minorities"; Push-pull factors.

Korean War

The Event: Unresolved military conflict between North and South Korea that drew the United States and communist China into the fighting

Date: June 25, 1950-July 27, 1953

Location: Korean Peninsula

Significance: The Korean War caused a massive displacement of people in both North and South Korea that left many thousands of Koreans in need of new homes. The close military, political, and economic ties between the United States and South Korea's government during and after the war facilitated the immigration of large numbers of Korean war refugees, war brides, and war orphans to America.

From the early twentieth century until the end of World War II in 1945, Japan ruled Korea as a colony. Japan's defeat in the war ended its control over Korea, but the Korean Peninsula was then politically divided at the thirty-eighth parallel. The northern portion of the peninsula was occupied by the communist Soviet Union, and the southern portion was occupied by the United States. In 1948, each part of Korea established its own independent government: the Democratic People's Republic of Korea in the north, and the Republic of Korea in the south. Vast differences in the political ideology of the communist north and the Western-leaning south generated friction that eventually escalated into a full-scale war that would involve both the United States and the People's Republic of China.

The Korean War officially began on June 25, 1950, when North Korea launched a surprise attack across the thirty-eighth parallel in an attempt to reunify the peninsula under its rule. Under United Nations (U.N.) auspices, the United States sent combat troops and military assistance to South Korea. Despite massive American and Chinese involvement, the conflict became a stalemate, and the United States eventually played a leading role in negotiating an armistice that ended the fighting on July 27, 1953. The settlement reestablished the thirty-eighth parallel as the border between North and South Korea. With the war technically never officially ended, the so-called demilitarized zone surrounding the border was heavily guarded by both sides and remained tense into the twenty-first century.

Meanwhile, the war itself had a devastating impact on the peoples of both North and South Korea. Particularly hard hit were large numbers of women and children who lost their families and were left without any means to support themselves.

Korean Immigration During the 1950's

Both during and after the war, many people fled from both North and South Korea to other countries, including China and the United States. The close military and political ties between South Korea and the United States led the majority of emigrants to choose America. Even North Korean refugees who lacked strong family or regional ties in South Korea generally preferred to go to the United States. A small number of Korean prisoners of war, who refused to be repatriated to either North or South Korea were sent to the United States as well. In fact, the war opened opportunities to all Koreans to emigrate to America. Wives of American servicemen and orphans represented the largest groups of Korean immigrants during and immediately after the war.

Wives of American Servicemen

The military relations between the United States and South Korea created a new group of immigrants: war brides. After the war, the United States continued to station large numbers of American troops throughout South Korea. Many American service personnel married Korean women. U.S. immigrant quotas based on national origin remained in force, but the Korean wives of American servicemen could enter the United States legally as nonquota immigrants under the term of the Immigration and Nationality Act (McCarran-Walter Act) of 1952.

From 1953 until 1960, about 500 Korean war brides arrived in the United States annually. In Korea, these women were ostracized by their relatives and neighbors for marrying non-Koreans. After they reached the United States, many of them encountered prejudice from Americans who stereotyped them as prostitutes and barmaids. Married to white and black Americans, most of these women

had little contact with other Korean immigrants. Out of touch with fellow Koreans and handicapped by limited English-language skills and unfamiliarity with American culture, they led culturally isolated lives. Consequently, many of their marriages did not last long. Because many of them came from lower-class backgrounds and had limited educations and few professional skills, they generally found it hard to support themselves and their children after their marriages failed. Nevertheless, most of these war brides became American citizens, and they would later sponsor the immigration of other Korean family members under the terms of the family reunification preferences of the Immigration and Nationality Act of 1965.

G.I. Babies and War Orphans

Other products of the Korean War were the births of thousands of so-called G.I. babies fathered by U.S. service personnel and the orphaning of thousands of Korean children. During the 1950's, these children became another major category of Korean immigrants to the United States. They also formed the first wave of Korean adoptees in America. G.I. babies and war orphans included children of both white and black American fathers and Korean mothers and orphans of Korean fathers and mothers. Despite the popular images of Korean War orphans at the time, many of the children adopted by American parents were not actually orphans. Most were given up by their natural parents for various reasons. Some were abandoned because of Korean racial prejudice against mixed-race babies. Others were give up by unwed mothers and by families too poor to care for them.

The number of Korean children needing parents was so great that the South Korean government created a special agency to place them for overseas adoption. This effort gained wide publicity when Harry and Bertha Holt, American evangelists in Oregon, adopted eight Korean children in 1955 and started their own international adoption service. Between 1955 and 1977, 13,000 Korean children were adopted by American families.

The Korean immigrants who came to America after the Korean War were noted for their remarkable heterogeneity. However, most Korean immigrants from that period were directly or indirectly connected with the U.S. military and American economic involvement in the Korean War. For many Americans, the Korean War was a quickly forgotten war, but it left a lasting imprint on both American and Korean society.

Ji-Hye Shin

Further Reading

Bergquist, Kathleen Ja Sook, et al., eds. *International Korean Adoption: A Fifty-Year History of Policy and Practice.* New York: Haworth Press, 2007. Collection of multidisciplinary essays on Korean adoption with several articles on Korean adoptees in the United States.

Blair, Clay. *The Forgotten War: America in Korea, 1950-1953.* New York: Times Books, 1987. Well-researched and comprehensive examination of the origins and conduct of the Korean War.

Edwards, Paul M. *The Korean War.* Westport, Conn.: Greenwood Press, 2006. Part of Greenwood's Daily Life Through History series, this book by a Korean War veteran and prolific scholar details the experiences of the individual troops fighting in Korea.

Hastings, Max. *The Korean War.* New York: Simon & Schuster, 1987. Detailed examination of military operations of the nations involved in the Korean War, from a British military historian. Includes a chronology of the war.

Hurh, Won Moo. *The Korean Americans.* Westport, Conn.: Greenwood Press, 1998. Historical, cultural, and socioeconomic study of Korean Americans.

Keller, Nora Okja. *Fox Girl.* New York: Penguin Books, 2002. Novel about a group of Korean children abandoned after the Korean War and their coming-of-age experiences near American military bases in Korea.

Oh, Arissa. "A New Kind of Missionary Work: Christians, Christian Americans, and the Adoption of Korean G.I. Babies, 1955-1961." *Women's Studies Quarterly* 33, nos. 3-4 (2005): 161-188. History of Korean adoption in America that examines adoption as a new missionary work shared by Christians and Christian Americanists.

Yuh, Ji-Yeon. *Beyond the Shadow of Camptown: Korean Military Brides in America.* New York: New York University Press, 2002. First detailed study of Korean military brides in the United States and their oral histories.

KU KLUX KLAN

IDENTIFICATION: Secretive white nativist organization

DATE: First formed in 1866

SIGNIFICANCE: Founded in the American South by a Confederate general to suppress the freedoms of African American former slaves, the Ku Klux Klan disbanded after only five years but reemerged in 1915 as a secret fraternal organization dedicated to racial purity. Throughout its intermittent existence, it has been actively opposed to the immigration of nonwhite peoples.

Thomas Nast cartoon published by Harper's Weekly *in 1874 vilifying the Ku Klux Klan's mistreatment of African Americans.* (Library of Congress)

Months after the formation of the Ku Klux Klan in Tennessee, former Confederate general Nathan Bedford Forrest became the organization's first "grand wizard." During the Klan's first brief incarnation, its southern Democrat members warred against the Reconstruction policy of the federal government. They particularly resented what they regarded as the policy of allowing citizens without substantial property assets to control the manner in which propertied citizens used their own possessions. Meanwhile, they terrorized newly freed African Americans, lynching them and burning their homes to discourage them from voting.

The original Klan had disappeared by the time Reconstruction ended during the 1870's. However, it reappeared in Atlanta, Georgia, in 1915, and began directing its hate campaigns against new immigrants in the name of "Americanism."

The Klan enjoyed its greatest popularity during the 1920's, when many Americans were growing uneasy about the great surge in immigration from eastern and southern European countries. The Klan added its voice to others charging that Italian, Irish, and Polish Catholics; Russian and Slavic Jews; and Asians were threatening to destroy the white Anglo-Saxon Protestant base of the American population. Klan hate literature depicted Roman Catholics and Jews as threats to traditional religious American values and American racial purity. Klan literature found Asians particularly easy to stereotype and denigrate; like African Americans, Asians simply looked different.

Klan propaganda against these immigrant groups attracted millions of new members across the United States. However, the Klan's membership was strongest in the South, from Florida to Texas, and in the Midwest, especially in Indiana. Members came from all strata of white male society.

The Klan's program reflected the anti-immigrant feelings of many Americans during the 1920's, the decade during which the federal

government added restrictions to immigration from southern and eastern Europe to those already in force against Asian immigration. In 1924, the Klan helped elect eleven state governors and sixteen congressmen, and in 1928 it helped defeat the Roman Catholic presidential candidate Alfred E. Smith.

After again fading away during the 1930's, the Klan made its third appearance in 1946 and remained active into the twenty-first century. In its most recent incarnation, the Klan has worked to improve its public image while continuing to campaign against immigration into the United States.

A. W. R. Hawkins III

FURTHER READING

Blee, Kathleen M. *Women of the Klan.* Berkeley: University of California Press, 1991.

MacLean, Nancy. *Behind the Mask of Chivalry.* New York: Oxford University Press, 1994.

Trelease, Allen W. *White Terror: The Ku Klux Klan Conspiracy and Southern Reconstruction.* Baton Rouge: Louisiana State University Press, 1971.

SEE ALSO: African Americans and immigrants; Anti-Catholicism; Anti-Defamation League; Anti-Semitism; Crime; Jewish immigrants; Nativism; Xenophobia.

L

LABOR UNIONS

DEFINITION: Worker organizations formed to seek improvements in their members' wages, benefits, and working conditions

SIGNIFICANCE: During the eras when American labor unions were most powerful, the majority of immigrants to the United States were members of the working class, and many immigrants played major roles in labor organizations. Many immigrants have joined national, industry-based unions; others have created race-specific labor unions. Historically, the racial heterogeneity of the American labor force has been a source of both conflict and solidarity.

Since the end of the U.S. Civil War in 1865, an incredibly diverse mix of races has taken part in the labor movement that has helped to shape the United States. During the Reconstruction era after the war, emancipated African American slaves and their descendants joined the ranks of agricultural and industrial laborers. Meanwhile, the numbers of immigrants flooding into the United States was rising to unprecedented levels. From the last decades of the nineteenth century until 1924, more than 25 million new immigrants, primarily from Asia and Europe, poured into the nation in response to the call for laborers to fill positions in expanding factories, mines, and mills. The later decades of the twentieth century saw even more immigrant laborers join those previous arrivals, but most of these immigrants were from other parts of the world, primarily Mexico, the West Indies, Central and South America, Pacific Rim nations, and South Asia.

HETEROGENEITY IN THE AMERICAN LABOR FORCE

Cultural and racial heterogeneity has long been the unique hallmark of laborers in the United States, but this very diversity has had both negative and positive consequences for the American labor movement as a whole. Individual immigrant groups have sometimes asserted their racial identities in their struggles for recognition in the American working class. This tendency has generated conflicts among workers from different immigrant groups. Many employers, seeking to marginalize their employees to keep wages down, have inflamed those racial tensions to reduce their employees' ability to organize.

At the same time, however, racial and ethnic identification can be a powerful mobilizing force. Immigrant laborers have sometimes realized that their commonality of work experience can bridge their unique cultural understandings, creating points of mobilization for protection and advancement. Both the tendency toward interracial conflict and the tendency toward racial solidarity have coexisted within some of the key national American labor unions, and the ebb and flow of those tendencies have affected their immigrant membership even into the early twenty-first century.

KNIGHTS OF LABOR, THE AFL, AND THE CIO

The Noble Order of the Knights of Labor (KOL) was organized in 1869 with the goal of uniting all those who worked for wages into a single, huge national union that would produce and distribute goods on a cooperative basis. Recognizing the need for broad-based labor solidarity to achieve this goal, the Knights of Labor offered membership to men and women of all races.

Through the 1870's and 1880's, KOL leader Terence Powderly traveled throughout the United States to recruit members. His campaign was successful to the extent that he helped establish more than thirty cooperative enterprises. Peak membership in the KOL included about 70,000 African American workers and 40,000 Asians and Europeans. The organization's multiethnic solidarity helped to improve the conditions of Missouri Pacific Railroad workers in 1885. KOL-led work stoppages ultimately forced railroad mogul Jay Gould to restore the wages he had cut the previous year, and he begrudgingly recognized his employees' union.

Formed in 1886 to organize craft unions encompassing laborers in specific trades, the American Federation of Labor (AFL) was much more racially restrictive and divisive than the Knights of Labor.

In his own membership recruitment campaigns, AFL leader Samuel Gompers appealed only to the elite male members of the working class—the most skilled workers. During the late nineteenth century, few members of minority groups fit that description, and even those who did were excluded from membership. Although Gompers himself was an immigrant from England, he believed that if the AFL allowed members of certain immigrant groups to join, the federation would become caught up in racial controversy. Convinced that his organization had more imperative and concrete issues on its agenda, he avoided racial entanglements by simply prohibiting minority workers from joining the AFL.

The AFL's "aristocracy of labor" continued to deny membership to unskilled and semiskilled immigrant labor through the 1930's. Persistent racist and nativist ideologies led many AFL leaders to see immigrant groups as individual nationalities whose differences were potentially subversive to the American labor movement, rather than as potentially valuable allies in the advancement of labor's interests.

In 1935, John L. Lewis and seven other top AFL leaders broke from the AFL to form the Congress of Industrial Organizations (CIO). These men believed that their new union would make itself strongest by welcoming semiskilled and unskilled workers of all races, who had been ignored by the AFL. The CIO made good use of the more than 1.8 million workers whom it brought under its umbrella. In 1937, successful sit-down strikes against General Motors, Chrysler, and U.S. Steel won the CIO recognition as the bargaining agent for millions of workers previously regarded as unorganizable.

AFRICAN AMERICAN WORKERS

Even before the CIO split from the AFL in 1935, labor organizer A. Philip Randolph had organized the many African Americans working on the nation's passenger railroads into a powerful union. His Brotherhood of Sleeping Car Porters won significant concessions from the Pullman Company during the 1930's and later provided a solid base from which black workers could challenge racial discrimination on a variety of fronts. In 1941, his union helped persuade President Franklin D. Roosevelt to issue an executive order forbidding employment discrimination by defense contractors. Seven years later, Randolph and his union helped persuade President Harry S. Truman to issue an order outlawing racial segregation in the American armed forces.

During the 1960's, African Americans began working to extend connections between labor activism and civil rights. They began at the local level with strikes by sanitation workers in Memphis, Tennessee, and hospital workers in Charleston, South Carolina. Undertaken by previously unorganized, heavily exploited, poverty-wage workers, these actions for higher wages and safer working condi-

Cover of an 1886 magazine depicting a convention of the Knights of Labor in Richmond, Virginia. (The Granger Collection, New York)

tions gained the attention and support of larger national industrial unions, including the United Auto Workers and the United Steelworkers. However, despite the success of the individual strikes, white workers have supported African American labor actions only halfheartedly, reflecting the continued divide between race relations and working-class solidarity.

HISPANIC WORKERS

Responding to the demand for manual laborers after the United States entered World War II, the United States and Mexico instituted the bracero program in 1942. Thousands of impoverished Mexicans, lured by higher wages, headed north to thin sugar beets, pick cotton, and weed and harvest cucumbers, tomatoes, and other crops on American farms. As experienced farm laborers, the more than 350,000 braceros who crossed the border annually helped to develop North American agriculture. The bracero program contract between the United States and Mexico was ended in 1964, pressured by Latino labor activist César Chávez's description of the program as "legalized slavery."

The son of migrant farmworkers, Chávez helped to raise awareness of the plight of braceros and other agricultural workers, and became the head of the United Farm Workers union (UFW) after it formed in 1965. Until his death in 1993, he used strikes and national boycotts against fruit- and vegetable-raising agribusinesses to win wage and working conditions concessions for mostly migrant agricultural laborers. The UFW later became an independent affiliate of the AFL-CIO and helped win passage of a California law recognizing the right of farmworkers to engage in collective bargaining. By the 1980's, about 45,000 farmworkers labored under the protection of UFW contracts, and the union was bargaining on behalf of farmworkers in states across the country.

The majority of farmworkers who have benefitted from UFW labor organizing have been Mexican Americans and Mexicans. Workers from other Hispanic groups, particularly Puerto Ricans and Cubans, have found representation in another major union that protects such service employees as janitors, nursing home aides, hospital aides, security guards, and building service maintenance. Although the membership of the Service Employees International Union (SEIU) is largely Hispanic, the union itself is not a race-specific organization. It merely happens that the majority of public service sector jobs are filled by Hispanic workers, many of whom are foreign immigrants. The SEIU has united more than 1.5 million workers and has become the North American union with the largest number of immigrant members.

ASIAN WORKERS

To an extent that may have been greater than that experienced by any other ethnic group, Asian immigrants have historically been excluded from American labor organizations. This has been true even though Asian immigrants have worked in some of the most dangerous occupations that laborers have faced. For example, the early mining industry in the Far West was one of the first to employ the Chinese, who dug for gold, hauled coal, and worked with explosives. Chinese immigrants also helped to build the railroad lines that connected the West to eastern markets and did some of the most dangerous work with explosives to excavate tunnels. Japanese immigrants also worked on the railroads, first in construction, and later as porters and foremen.

Despite the difficult and often dangerous work that Chinese and Japanese laborers performed, these immigrants were resented and badly treated by native-born American workers and employers. State laws were passed to limit their rights, and federal laws were enacted to limit further Asian immigration. Asian workers responded by organizing at the community level and embracing wider cultural and racial demands for justice and dignity. They also formed their own race-based unions.

Since the early 1990's, one of the most active Asian unions has been the Asian Pacific American Labor Alliance (APALA). This organization was founded in 1992 to address the special needs of Asian and Pacific Islander garment factory workers, hotel and restaurant workers, longshoremen, nurses, and supermarket workers, and to connect those local alliances to the national American labor movement. The APALA has actively promoted the formation of AFL-CIO legislation to create jobs, ensure national health insurance, and reform labor law. It has also supported national governmental action to prevent workplace discrimination against immigrant laborers and to prosecute perpetrators of racially motivated crimes.

The successful creation of race-specific labor unions and the inclusion of immigrant groups in the larger project that is the American labor movement have not resolved the debate about the role of immigrant and minority workers in American labor. However, these developments have helped ensure a continuing discussion about issues that have captured the attention of labor organizers since the late nineteenth century—higher wages, safer working conditions, increased respect—and have raised awareness of the importance of immigrant groups toward realizing those goals for all workers.

Cynthia Gwynne Yaudes

FURTHER READING

Asher, Robert, and Charles Stephenson, eds. *Labor Divided: Race and Ethnicity in United States Labor Struggles, 1835-1960.* Albany: State University of New York Press, 1990. Collection of case studies exploring how racial heterogeneity in the American labor movement has created the potential for both divisiveness and unity.

Briggs, Vernon M. *Immigration and American Unionism.* Ithaca, N.Y.: Cornell University Press, 2001. Evaluates the effects that immigration has had on union membership throughout American history and adds to the current debate about how industries should deal with documented and undocumented immigrant workers.

Milkman, Ruth. *Organizing Immigrants: The Challenge for Unions in Contemporary California.* Ithaca, N.Y.: Cornell University Press, 2000. Analyzes recent California labor history and evaluates prospects for organizing among immigrant labor in America's most populous state.

Ness, Immanuel, ed. *Immigrants, Unions, and the New U.S. Labor Market.* Philadelphia: Temple University Press, 2005. Collection of case studies of worker collective action that explains why and how immigrant workers organize.

Walker, Thomas J. Edward. *Pluralistic Fraternity: The History of the International Worker's Order.* New York: Garland Press, 1991. Examines the seemingly unique ability of communist-backed labor organizations to create worker solidarity across racial and national lines.

SEE ALSO: Asian Pacific American Labor Alliance; Bracero program; Coal industry; Economic consequences of immigration; Employment; Goldman, Emma; Industrial Workers of the World; International Ladies' Garment Workers' Union; United Farm Workers.

LAHIRI, JHUMPA

IDENTIFICATION: British-born American author of Asian Indian descent

BORN: July 11, 1967; London, England

SIGNIFICANCE: Lahiri's focus on cultural displacement highlights the Asian Indian immigrant experience from an intergenerational perspective. Her Pulitzer Prize-winning short-story collection, *Interpreter of Maladies* (1999), concentrates on Indian immigrants searching for cultural connections and love. At a personal level, Lahiri considers herself American, but feels somewhat displaced herself, having been raised with a keen sense of her Indian heritage.

Born Nilanjana Sudeshna Lahiri in London, England, to parents from Bengal, India, Jhumpa Lahiri moved to the United States at the age of three and grew up in Rhode Island. She became an American citizen at the age of eighteen. Immersed in immigrant culture, she also spent a great deal of time in India, where her family made frequent visits to relatives in Calcutta (now called Kolkata).

Lahiri began writing in childhood to stave off the loneliness of feeling like an outsider because she looked different from her classmates. She wrote fiction throughout college. After graduating from Barnard College in 1989 with a bachelor's degree in English literature, she went on to earn three master's degrees and a doctorate from Boston University. Her fiction won both accolades and awards after she finished her doctoral degree.

While Lahiri was still in school, she began consciously examining the immigrant experience, though she was initially seeking to understand her own identity. She used fiction to illustrate the Asian Indian immigrant experience, ranging from conflicts between Hindu and Christian lifestyles to an Indian immigrant's loneliness and longing for "home." She collected her stories into a book, *Interpreter of Maladies* (1999), which won the Pulitzer Prize in 2000. The title story is about an interpreter

for an Indian physician who literally interprets the doctor's diagnoses for patients. Three of the nine stories are set in India, and the other six are set in the United States and feature Indian immigrants. Her work concentrates on cultural displacement, Hindu family structures, and the Westernization of second- and third-generation immigrants.

American reviewers have almost universally praised Lahiri's work for its depictions of the Indian American experience. Her work also had an immediate popular appeal in the United States, where the literature of other Indian Americans such as Bharati Mukherjee appealed more to academics and intellectuals. Critics in India, by contrast, have given her work a mixed reception, and some have criticized her for writing flat Indian characters, saying that she writes better about the general Indian immigrant experience.

Lahiri followed *Interpreter of Maladies* with a novel, *The Namesake*, in 2003, and again drew widespread critical acclaim. The novel concentrates on the issues faced by second-generation Indian immigrants and the importance of names to identity. Her second short-story collection, *Unaccustomed Earth* (2008), also focuses on Indian immigrants, concluding with three linked short stories focusing on both American and Indian customs regarding love, including arranged marriages.

Lahiri has proved to be one of the strongest voices for Indian American immigrants of several generations, capturing their unique struggles to achieve an American identity without surrendering their Indian culture.

Jessie Bishop Powell

FURTHER READING

George, Sheba Mariam. *When Women Come First: Gender and Class in Transnational Migration.* Berkeley: University of California Press, 2005.

Kafka, Phillipa. *On the Outside Looking In(dian): Indian Women Writers at Home and Abroad.* New York: Peter Lang, 2003.

SEE ALSO: Anglo-conformity; Asian American literature; Asian Indian immigrants; Association of Indians in America; Families; History of immigration after 1891; Intermarriage; Lim, Shirley Geok-lin; Literature; Mukherjee, Bharati; Sidhwa, Bapsi.

LAND LAWS

DEFINITION: Federal legislation pertaining to the transfer of public lands to private ownership

SIGNIFICANCE: From the time that the United States was established as an independent nation in 1783, the U.S. Congress has passed land laws defining the procedures by which new territory can pass from public ownership to individual ownership. While agriculture was a major source of employment during the nineteenth century, the acquisition of land became a fundamental inducement to immigrants to come to the United States. Many were pushed off their lands in Europe as population rose dramatically during the late eighteenth and throughout the nineteenth century. Owning land individually became in the eyes of many immigrants the pathway to a secure future.

When European immigrants first came to what became the United States, they brought with them a concept of land ownership fundamentally different from that held by the aboriginal Native American inhabitants. The concept of individual ownership, in Europe restricted by the surviving elements of feudal society, stood in sharp contrast to the concepts prevailing among the Indian tribes, which favored communal ownership with individual rights to use land temporarily. However, striving for land over which they had full control had propelled the first European discoveries in America. Although titles to New World lands were first vested in the monarchs whose subjects "discovered" them, as governments developed into their more modern forms, they found themselves constrained by shortages of funds during an era when possession, or control, of land was considered the primary measure of wealth. As governments sought to expand their territories, they began to use the granting of ownership to pieces of land as a means to collect revenue.

ORIGINS

Some of the major grievances that eighteenth century North American colonists had about British rule concerned government restrictions on their freedom to settle and farm lands in the vast

open spaces between the Atlantic seaboard colonies and the Mississippi River to the west. Great Britain, which had acquired control over those western lands when it defeated France in the French and Indian War (1756-1763), had tried to block settlement by individuals migrating from the colonies along the Atlantic Coast. In its Proclamation of 1763, the British government forbade new settlements in lands west of the Alleghenies that were reserved for use of Native Americans. Attempts by settlers from the coastal colonies to move into that western area became one of the bones of contention in the American Revolution (1775-1783). After the war, the United States gained title to the area in the 1783 peace treaty with Great Britain. Settling in the region then became a priority for the new nation.

Within the British North American colonies, which had ben populated overwhelmingly by immigrants from Great Britain, laws pertaining to land ownership were determined largely by the individual colonial governments. Although it was technically vested in the British monarch, land ownership was quickly devolved to those who managed the colony in America—either as a company such as the Massachusetts Bay Colony, or as individuals, who through wealth or connections, secured from the British monarchs grants of land in North America. These agents in turn passed over control either to large landowners or to new communities, as was the case in Massachusetts. The latter tended to pass subordinate control to new settlements with provisions for dividing the allotted lands to early settlers.

Homesteaders crossing the Plains during the 1880's, looking for land in the West. (Getty Images)

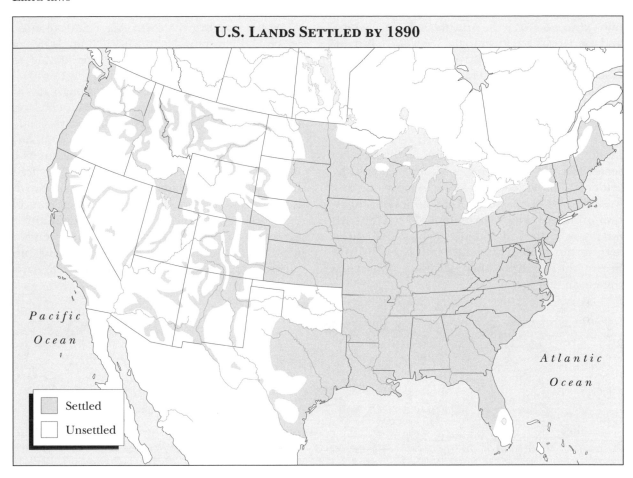

U.S. LANDS SETTLED BY 1890

Pacific Ocean

Atlantic Ocean

Settled
Unsettled

LAND LAWS OF THE UNITED STATES

One of the earliest problems faced by the new Congress of the United States was how to organize the distribution of land west of the Alleghenies. In 1784, Congress appointed a committee, of which Thomas Jefferson was the leading member, to draw up a plan. The proposal the committee produced set forth the outlines of the plan that followed in the Land Ordinance of 1785. The plan required several things:

- resolution of Indian claims to the land through treaties with local tribes
- surveying of the land into rectangular townships six miles on a side, each township to be then subdivided into 36 sections, one mile square and comprising 640 acres
- reservation of some of the land for military bounties granted during the Revolution
- subsequent sale of the land to private individuals

This subdivision of the United States into units of thirty-six square miles was followed throughout the settlement of the west. When Congress was passing the Land Ordinance of 1785, it added some new wrinkles. It reserved one section of each township to be offered for sale for the schools of the future community; it ruled that the secretary of war could claim some of the sections for payment to veterans of the Revolutionary War; it provided that the townships would be distributed to the various states on whom would fall responsibility for selling the land by sections or as whole townships; and it required that sales should be conducted through public auctions after at least seven (later reduced to four) of the survey (range) lines had been run. By 1787, relatively few sales had actually occurred, so Congress then authorized the sale of large aggregates to wealthy individuals who were prepared to take on the task of finding settlers to work the lands.

PEOPLING OF THE WEST

Although settlers from the seaboard colonies poured into the new Ohio Territory, formal settlement was held up by the slow progress of the survey lines and by the need to secure treaties from the Indians then resident in Ohio. Several unsuccessful clashes with tribes that resisted the flood of settlers led, finally, to the conclusive victory of an American force at the Battle of Fallen Timbers in 1794. In the ensuing Treaty of Greenville, the Indian tribes then resident in northwest Ohio ceded all their Ohio lands to the United States. The conditions of the Land Ordinance continued to be fulfilled in future years as more victories over the Indian tribes and cession of their rights by treaty were met.

It is not known how many immigrants were attracted to the United States by the availability of public land because U.S. immigration records were not kept until 1821. However, there is little doubt that the prospect of securing large plots of land at minimal costs drew many immigrants from Europe. Initially most came from the British Isles, including Ireland, but as the nineteenth century wore on, many more came from continental Europe. Early sales of public lands were intended for citizens of the United States, but over the course of the nineteenth century sales were opened to immigrants who began the naturalization process, thereby affirming their intention to become American citizens. Although U.S. debts from the Revolution and the War of 1812 had been paid off with the proceeds from land sales by the 1830's, Congress continued to seek revenue from further sales.

The large number of land laws passed by Congress indicates that the federal government continued to view selling public lands as a major source of revenue. One obstacle to sales was quickly changed: the need to bid at a single, central auction place. As early as the year 1800, Congress designated several on-the-ground sites for land auctions in Ohio—Cincinnati, Chilicothe, Marietta, and Steubenville. Afterward, auctions were held near the sites of the land being sold. Special officials were appointed to handle the sales, and rules spelled out how payments were to be made to the U.S. Treasury. Initially, land was sold for one to two dollars per acre under four-year payment plans. In later years, the prices and payment systems were regularly changed. In 1820, Congress acknowledged that a great deal of land had been occupied by "squatters" and al-

lowed them to "preempt" title to the lands they occupied by paying part of their costs in advance of the auctions.

Meanwhile, Congress often tied land grants to other government programs. For example, by the mid-nineteenth century, its policy of awarding lavish land grants to railroads was becoming notorious. Congress granted large tracts of land to the railroads in the hope that the railroads would pass the land along to settlers. In the 1862 Homestead Act, Congress gave both citizens and prospective citizens a "preemption" right, enabling them to settle on public lands and secure title to those lands after five years for payments of two dollars per acre. The Timber Act of 1873 gave settlers up to ten years to claim title to the land they occupied if they planted substantial numbers of trees on the land. Homesteaders willing to develop desert lands in the West that were unsuitable for agriculture could buy title to their lands for only twenty-five cents per acre.

By the 1890's, Congress was beginning to recognize that public lands suitable for homesteading were becoming scarce, restricting purchasers to those who had not previously claimed land under the Pre-emption or Homestead Acts. It was still unclear to what extent the availability of public land was drawing foreign immigrants. During the early nineteenth century, the attraction of land was no doubt great, and immigration from Germany and Scandinavia undoubtedly was encouraged by the availability of cheap land.

Much of the public land was actually taken up by speculators who had no intention of settling it themselves; they planned to sell it to latecomers. News also got out that the costs of turning public land into useful farms could be high, which meant that immigrants with limited capital would have difficulty developing any land they could afford to purchase. Most immigrants who came to the United States to farm probably arrived during the first half of the nineteenth century; however, major settlement of Wisconsin and Minnesota did not begin until after the U.S. Civil War. Many Europeans who immigrated during the 1850's and 1860's settled in the Upper Midwest.

The goal that propelled many immigrants to come to the United States was the prospect of acquiring land for themselves. The federal land acts strengthened that resolve, by making vast tracts of

land available at low cost to those prepared to settle and take up farming. Creating farms out of wild lands, however, was not an easy task, and many immigrants who tried failed. Consequently, many immigrants who left farms in Europe to farm in the United States wound up as industrial workers in cities.

Nancy M. Gordon

FURTHER READING

Dunham, Harold J. "Some Crucial Years of the Land Office, 1875-1890." In *The Public Lands: Studies in the History of the Public Domain*, edited by Vernon Carstensen. Madison: University of Wisconsin Press, 1968. Long the primary source of material on the public lands, the many useful articles remain relevant.

Freund, Rudolf. "Military Bounty Lands and the Origins of the Public Domain." In *The Public Lands: Studies in the History of the Public Domain*, edited by Vernon Carstensen. Madison: University of Wisconsin Press, 1968. Close study of the vexing problem that Congress faced in dealing with military bounty lands.

Rasmussen, R. Kent, ed. *Agriculture in History*. 3 vols. Pasadena, Calif.: Salem Press, 2010. Collection of essays on specific historical events, including many relevant to U.S. land issues.

Rasmussen, Wayne D., ed. *Agriculture in the United States: A Documentary History*. 4 vols. New York: Random House, 1975. Reprints the land laws of the United States, mostly contained in volume 1.

Rohrbough, Malcolm J. *The Land Office Business: The Settlement and Administration of American Public Lands, 1789-1837*. London: Oxford University Press, 1968. Exhaustive account of how American public lands were sold to settlers.

SEE ALSO: Alien land laws; Economic opportunities; Empresario land grants in Texas; European immigrants; History of immigration, 1783-1891; Homestead Act of 1862; National Road; Railroads; Settlement patterns; Westward expansion.

LANGUAGE ISSUES

DEFINITION: Issues concerning the special problems that non-English-speaking immigrants face in the United States and legislative attempts to address these problems

SIGNIFICANCE: Language issues affect all aspects of an immigrant's life in the United States. The ability to speak English correlates highly with the ability to function well. Access to information, health care, and cultural assimilation are often dependent on an immigrant's ability to speak English.

Since its very beginning, the United States has been a country of many languages. Native Americans spoke at least fifty-five distinct languages, and as immigrants arrived they continued to speak the languages of their home countries. Even though the English language became paramount, there long was a general tolerance of other languages. After the Mexican War, when Mexico ceded large tracts of land to the United States in February of 1848, Mexico and the United States signed the Treaty of Hidalgo, which gave American citizenship to all Mexican nationals who remained in the ceded lands. The treaty also guaranteed certain civil, political, and religious rights to these new Spanish-speaking American citizens. Along with those protections, it was assumed that the former Mexican nationals would keep their language. There were suggestions to restrict this freedom in the early years of the country, but laws of this kind were considered a threat to civil liberties.

In later years, however, various events began to change this tolerant attitude. For example, California's gold rush attracted to the West Coast easterners who ignored the language guarantees of the Mexican-American treaty. In the East, anti-Roman Catholic attitudes and fear of foreign radicals supported a feeling of "national superiority." It was God's design, many thought, that Americans were a chosen people and that foreigners had no place in the United States. A famous late nineteenth century editorial cartoon by Thomas Nast, depicted Roman Catholic bishops as crocodiles swimming ashore with the intention of destroying the public school system.

The onset of World War I brought language issues further to the fore. A great number of American citizens had come from Germany. Many had kept their native language, and German was used in their schools. However, with the onset of the war, those who spoke German were regarded with suspicion as unpatriotic and somehow less than totally "American." In a speech that former president Theodore Roosevelt delivered in 1917, the year that the United States entered the war, he said:

> We must have but one flag. We must also have but one language. That must be the language of the Declaration of Independence, of Washington's Farewell Address, of Lincoln's Gettysburg Speech and Second Inaugural. We cannot tolerate any attempt to oppose or supplant the language and culture that has come down to us from the builders of this Republic with the language of any European country. The greatness of this nation depends on the swift assimilation of the aliens she welcomes to her shores. Any force which attempts to retard that assimilative process is a force hostile to the highest interests of our country. . . . We call upon all loyal and unadulterated Americans to man the trenches against the enemy within our gates.

Two years later, President Woodrow Wilson gave a speech in which he warned against those who continued to speak the languages of their original homelands or to practice their former customs. Wilson complained about what he called "hyphenated" Americans, stating that

> any man who carries a hyphen about him carries a dagger which he is ready to plunge into the vitals of the Republic. If I can catch a man with a hyphen in this great contest, I know I will have got an enemy of the Republic.

By 1919, fifteen U.S. states had decided to make English the sole language of instruction in all their primary schools—both public and private. In some states, bills were introduced that would have prohibited the teaching of foreign languages in elementary schools. These legislative efforts were, in part, expressions of public fear of foreign influences. From 1920 to 1964, American citizenship gradually became dependent upon the ability to read and write the English language, which was increasingly becoming the language of government and education. One result of this tendency was that minority language speakers began to hide their ethnic origins and to forget their ancestral languages. Millions of people were taught to be ashamed of their ancestral languages, their parents, and their foreign origins. Even people whose ancestors who had come to America before the Revolutionary War were told that they could not keep their mother tongues and still be good American citizens. Speaking more than a single language was regarded as a sign of divided allegiance.

FOREIGN WORKERS

At various times in its history, the United States has imported people from other countries to work. For example, thousands of workers were brought from China to do menial work during the California gold rush after 1848. Even more were brought to work on the transcontinental railroad, which was completed in 1869. Like the members of many immigrant groups, Chinese immigrants have tended to stay together within their own ethnic communities and speak their own language. A popular modern argument against permitting foreign immigration is that newcomers tend to isolate themselves within their own communities and refuse to learn the local language.

After the United States signed the Geneva convention relating to the status of political refugees in 1980, the nation opened its borders more widely to new immigrants. Russians, Bulgarians, Vietnamese, Mexicans, and many others entered the United States to find work. Some immigrants have entered the United States seeking asylum because of dangerous situations in their home countries. These people are at greater risk of deportation if they can not speak English because of their restricted ability to explain their situations to immigration officials. Immigrant victims of crime also often face greater dangers because of language barriers.

EDUCATION

In 1968, the Bilingual Education Act became the first piece of federal legislation that addressed the issue of minority language speakers. The bill was introduced in 1967 by Texas senator Ralph Yarborough to provide school districts with federal funds to increase language skills in English. It was

originally intended for Spanish-speaking students, but in 1968 it was merged into the Bilingual Education Act, or Title VII of the Elementary and Secondary Education Act (ESEA). This law gave public school districts the opportunity to provide bilingual education programs to remedy the high rates of school failure. However, its real goal was to direct speakers of other languages into English-speaking programs. The bill provided federal funding for resources for educational programs, teacher training, development of materials, and parent involvement projects.

A central question that needed to be resolved was whether immigrants should learn to speak English before beginning to learn other subjects, or should children begin their formal educations in their own languages so they would not be too old to participate in grade-level activities by the time they developed proficiency in English. The federal law gave individual school districts the freedom to choose whichever approach they believed warranted, so long as their programs were designed to meet the special educational needs of the students. However, President Reagan slashed the funding for bilingual education by $35.4 million. Many native English speakers believed that the national interest is served when all members of society can speak English. In 2006, the U.S. Senate passed an amendment to the Comprehensive Immigration Reform Act designating English as the official national language. However, the amendment never became law.

HEALTH CARE

The Civil Rights Act of 1964 ensured that federal money would not go to any institution that discriminates on the basis of race, color, or national origin. In addition, the U.S. Department of Health and Human Services has stated that health care organizations must offer and provide language assistance services, including bilingual staff members and interpreter services at no cost to people with limited English proficiency. Despite this federal law, as many as twenty-three million people in the United States may be at risk of receiving substandard health care merely because they are not fluent in English. This is due in part to conflicts in understanding. Thirty states have designated English as their official language and require all state services to be conducted in English. When state laws conflict with federal laws, health care professionals can be at a loss in knowing how to react. State laws cannot override the entitlement of the federal Civil Rights Act.

Lack of communication between immigrants and health care providers because of language differences can cause great harm to persons seeking health care. When doctors do not speak their patients' languages and interpreters are not available, misunderstandings can lead to misdiagnoses, incorrect treatments, the inability of patients to understand instructions for medications and therapy, and inability to obtain information about financial assistance. In such situations, many immigrants are understandably reluctant to seek needed medical care. In extreme situations, misunderstandings between medical professionals and non-English-speaking patients can lead to deportation, financial loss, or even death.

TECHNOLOGY

Another area in which language issues make life more difficult for non-English-speaking immigrants is the field of information technology, known popularly as IT. As IT has played a growing role in workplaces, immigrants in general and Hispanics in particular are often at a disadvantage when they search for jobs. More than one-half of immigrants from Latin America have fewer than twelve years of education and are consequently often inadequately educated to work with modern computers and electronic communications. For example, a great majority of pages on the World Wide Web are in English, making them difficult for people with limited English proficiency to understand.

Another difficulty is that many Hispanics do not have social networks that greatly value information technology. Even among native speakers of English, poor language skills can be a barrier to information technology usage. A study of former Soviet-bloc countries also reveals that workers who can speak English are more likely to work with computers and earn more money because of it. In addition to having greater access to better-paying jobs, it has become increasingly important for immigrants to be able to use the Internet for daily living in the United States. Indeed, the World Wide Web can be especially valuable to immigrants as a source of information on immigration law and legal assistance.

CULTURAL ATTITUDES AND LANGUAGE SUPPRESSION

During the early twentieth century, many Americans began accepting the idea that people who could not speak English could not be true, patriotic Americans. The large number of immigrant Italians, German Jews, and Slavic peoples entering the United States from eastern and southern European countries evoked fears among American citizens that new immigrants were not learning English quickly enough, and therefore not assimilating into American culture. In 1911, the Dillingham Commission, led by Senator William P. Dillingham of Vermont, proposed a reading and writing test as a method for barring undesirable aliens from entering the country. The federal Immigration Act of 1924 introduced strict immigration rules that explicitly excluded members of ethnic and racial groups deemed to be genetically inferior. This law sharply restricted the flow of eastern and southern Europeans and totally excluded Asians. It was the first permanent limitation on immigration to the United States.

By the early twenty-first century, most immigrants appeared to believe it was in their own interest to learn to speak English. By this time, members of most Hispanic immigrant families were learning English within two generations, whereas in the past it took about three generations. Consequently, many children of first-generation families now speak English as their primary language.

Winifred O. Whelan

FURTHER READING

Kibler, Amanda. "Speaking Like a 'Good American': National Identity and the Legacy of German-Language Education." *Teachers College Record* 110, no. 6 (June, 2008): 1241-1268. Survey of the history of German language teaching in the United States, showing how it flourished before World War I and declined afterward.

Ono, Hiroshi, and Madeline Zavodny. "Immigrants, English Ability, and the Digital Divide." *Social Forces* 86, no. 4 (June, 2008): 1455-1479. Study showing how immigrants are both financially and culturally disadvantaged by their limited access to information technology, which is overwhelmingly in English.

Pöllabauer, Sonja. "Interpreting in Asylum Hearings: Issues of Role, Responsibility and Power." *Interpreting* 6, no. 2 (2004): 143-80. Findings of a study undertaken in Graz, Austria, where immigrants were asking for asylum in the United States. Translators and interpreters were found to shorten and paraphrase statements, leave out certain information, and otherwise distort the evidence given by the asylum seekers.

U.S. Commission on Civil Rights. *The Excluded Student: Educational Practices Affecting Mexican Americans in the Southwest.* Washington, D.C.: Government Printing Office, 1972. Study revealing how the educations of Spanish-speaking students in southwestern states have been damaged by language differences.

Youdelman, Mara K. "The Medical Tongue: U.S. Laws and Policies on Language Access." *Health Affairs* 27, no. 2 (March/April, 2008): 424-433. Article providing statistics on state laws that deal with language access in health care facilities, and how states are held accountable for providing interpreters and translators.

SEE ALSO: Anglo-conformity; Bilingual education; Education; English as a second language; English-only and official English movements; Hayakawa, S. I.; *Lau v. Nichols*; Linguistic contributions; Literacy tests; Multiculturalism; Name changing.

LAOTIAN IMMIGRANTS

SIGNIFICANCE: Significant numbers of Laotian immigrants first came to the United States in the wake of the Vietnam War. They have often been lumped together with Vietnamese refugees, but the Laotians have differed in generally having less education, fewer skills, and more assimilation challenges. The Hmong, who fought against communism in Laos, are often included among Laotian immigrants, but these mountain people come from throughout Southeast Asia.

Laos is situated in the center of the Indochinese peninsula at the heart of the Mekong Basin, with Vietnam to the east. The location of the country ensured that it would become caught up in the turmoil of the Vietnam War during the 1960's and early 1970's, when its own people were also fighting

Laotian refugee children at a refugee camp in Thailand in 1979. (AP/Wide World Photos)

a civil war. As the United States withdrew from Southeast Asia in 1975, Laotian refugees began to make their way to America. The U.S. government labeled all refugees as "Indochinese" regardless of their countries of origin. As a result, Laotians have been lumped together with the much larger number of Vietnamese refugees who poured into the United States. Consequently, some of the available government information does not represent the pattern of Laotian immigration.

The Laotian refugees came in two major waves, which included ethnic Chinese, Lao minorities (chiefly Lao Theung and Mein), and the Hmong among their numbers. The first wave, from 1975 to 1977, consisted largely of boat people and overland refugees who had spent considerable and often harrowing time in refugee camps in Southeast Asia. Many of these people were Hmong who had fled Laos for refugee camps in Thailand after the communist government of the Pathet Lao took control in December, 1975.

The second wave, consisting largely of Lao minorities who began to arrive in the United States in 1978, resulted from attempts by the new Lao government to consolidate its control over ethnic minorities who had fought earlier for the U.S. Central Intelligence Agency. In 1978, the U.S. government offered "parolee" status to Hmong and other Laotians who had been employees of the U.S. government, with priority given to people who had been persecuted by communists. The 1980 Refugee Act gave the refugees resident-alien status and enabled more Laotians to enter the United States.

The Laotian immigrants who arrived as the result of the Vietnam War tended to be less educated than previous Southeast Asian immigrants. The 20,000 or so Hmong who arrived during the late 1970's were, for the most part, illiterate. The Hmong and Laotian ethnic minorities tended not only to be illiterate, but also to have skills in few fields other than slash-and-burn agriculture. The fact that the Hmong and Mein peoples had no writ-

PROFILE OF LAOTIAN IMMIGRANTS

Country of origin	Laos
Primary language	Lao
Primary regions of U.S. settlement	California, upper Midwest
Earliest significant arrivals	1978
Peak immigration period	1978-1980
Twenty-first century legal residents*	13,953 (1,699 per year)

*Immigrants who obtained legal permanent resident status in the United States.
Source: Department of Homeland Security, *Yearbook of Immigration Statistics, 2008.*

ten language further complicated their ability to adjust to life in the United States. The refugees tended to be young, with most coming as part of large family groups.

By the end of the 1980's, about 266,000 Laotians had immigrated to the United States. Most settled in California but a significant number have established lives in the upper Midwest, chiefly in Minnesota.

Caryn E. Neumann

FURTHER READING

Goudineau, Yves, ed. *Laos and Ethnic Minority Cultures: Promoting Heritage.* Paris: UNESCO, 2003.

Kelly, Gail P. "Coping with America: Refugees from Vietnam, Cambodia, and Laos in the 1970's and 1980's." *The Annals of the American Academy of Political and Society Science* 487 (September, 1986): 138-149.

Lee, Joann Faung Jean. *Asian Americans in the Twenty-first Century: Oral Histories of First- to Fourth-Generation Americans from China, Japan, India, Korea, the Philippines, Vietnam, and Laos.* New York: New Press, 2008.

SEE ALSO: Asian immigrants; Burmese immigrants; History of immigration after 1891; Hmong immigrants; Indochina Migration and Refugee Assistance Act of 1975; Thai immigrants; Vietnam War; Vietnamese immigrants.

LATIN AMERICAN IMMIGRANTS

SIGNIFICANCE: Throughout U.S. history, Latin Americans have immigrated in waves to North America. Halfway through the first decade of the twenty-first century, about 44 million residents of the United States traced their ancestry to Hispanic immigrants; of these, about 17.7 million had been born in Latin American nations. Early Hispanic immigrants tended to congregate in western and southwestern states in the U.S. However, by the turn of the twenty-first century, Latin American immigrants were settling throughout the entire country—in large urban centers, suburban areas, and small towns—and they were becoming one of the fastest-growing ethnic groups in the United States.

In response to changing historical conditions, immigration from Latin America to the United States ebbed and flowed through the nineteenth and twentieth centuries. The late twentieth century surge in Hispanic immigration was a product of many factors, including the increasing economic globalization of labor markets, the long shared border between the United States and Mexico, and increasingly attractive economic opportunities for immigrants in the United States.

Any consideration of "Latin American" immigration must keep in mind the wide diversity and heterogeneous nature of the many Hispanic, or Latino, peoples living in the United States. Immigrants have come to the United States from nineteen Spanish- and Portuguese-speaking countries of the Western Hemisphere, bringing with them a wide variety of cultural backgrounds. They have settled in almost every region of the United States, doing so under a variety of circumstances and for different reasons.

PRE-TWENTIETH CENTURY TRENDS

During the eighteenth and nineteenth centuries, most Hispanics lived in the southwestern region of what is now the United States. This region constituted the northern part of Spain's New World empire until Mexico became independent in 1821. Afterward, it was part of Mexico until the Mexican War of 1846-1848, when the region passed

PROFILE OF LATIN AMERICAN IMMIGRANTS

Countries of origin	Mexico and nations of Central America, South America, and the Caribbean islands
Primary languages	Spanish, Portuguese
Primary regions of U.S. settlement	Southwest, New York State
Earliest significant arrivals	Sixteenth century
Peak immigration period	1965-2008
Twenty-first century legal residents*	3,301,935 (366,881 per year)

*Immigrants who obtained legal permanent resident status in the United States. Figures do not include Puerto Ricans.

Source: Department of Homeland Security, *Yearbook of Immigration Statistics, 2008*. See also articles on immigrants of individual nations and the West Indies.

to the United States. Most of the Hispanic residents of the region remained after 1848 and became American citizens. Initially, Mexicans and other Hispanics continued their historical patterns of moving back and forth between Mexico and the American Southwest in order to work and conduct trade, but they had to cross a new international border to do so. That border would later become the major crossing point for new Hispanic immigration into the United States.

Around the turn of the twentieth century, the United States began receiving Hispanic immigrants from other countries. After the Spanish-American War of 1898, small numbers of Puerto Ricans and Cubans began coming to the eastern United States to work temporarily and later return home. These two patterns of nineteenth century immigration would frame, to a large extent, the continued movement of Latin Americans into the United States during the twentieth century.

TWENTIETH CENTURY DEVELOPMENTS

Immigration from Latin America continued steadily into the twentieth century, a pattern due to changing political and economic conditions in Latin America. During the first decades of the century, Latin Americans came to the United States in search of work. As jobs grew scarce in their own countries, U.S. economic stability drew them into the large urban centers of the Northeast, Midwest, and Southwest. While immigration levels dipped slightly during the Great Depression of the 1930's, they began to rise again immediately after World War II ended in 1945. At that time, the U.S. government began playing an active role instituting policies to encourage an already cyclical migration pattern in which Latin Americans traveled to the United States on a temporary basis to earn money and later return to their home countries. As a result, the already existing movement from regions such as Mexico and the Caribbean continued, with the majority of immigrants being men who worked to support families whom they left at home. Upon finishing their job contracts or seasonal work, some settled in the United States and others returned to Mexico.

A turning point in twentieth century immigration came about when the U.S. Congress passed the Immigration and Nationality Act of 1965. This legislation, combined with late modifications in U.S. immigration policy, including tighter control of the U.S.-Mexican border, and changing political relations between the U.S. and other hemispheric governments, fundamentally transformed the nature of Latin American immigration. Whereas Hispanics had historically tended to immigrate to a limited number of U.S. urban regions, they were now spreading out all over the United States. Moreover, because the 1965 immigration law placed more emphasis on the reunification of families, increased numbers of women, children, and entire families were beginning to enter the United States to work and settle permanently. In a process known as "chain migration," Hispanic communities developed strong social networks linking their new American communities with their home regions in other countries. Latin American began organizing and participating more fully in the civic and political lives of their new communities, and were becoming visible at both the local and national levels.

Many Latin American immigrants have maintained dual citizenship, which allows them to vote in elections in both the United States and their

Latin American immigrants

home countries and to continue to remain connected with the social and cultural facets of life in their home countries. Latin American immigrants have tended to travel frequently to their home countries, and many of them send remittances, primarily monetary, to family members outside the United States.

Large-scale Latin American immigration has had a measurable impact on the demographic structure of the United States. Hispanics are, on average, younger than the general population. Moreover, they are adding significant numbers of young people to labor forces in regions of the United States where native-born populations are aging. By expanding the pool of those who work labor-intensive and, typically, low-wage jobs, they have helped to reinvigorate parts of the United States that had been experiencing net population losses. Because many of them are also settling in rural, as well as urban, areas, their sheer numbers are causing local communities to rethink how they will integrate the newly arrived groups into the civic and cultural lives of their towns and cities. Increased Hispanic participation in political processes has helped to shift emphases to issues important to immigrant communities and to change voting patterns in many regions.

PUSH-PULL FACTORS

The reasons why Latin Americans have immigrated to the United States have changed since the early nineteenth century. In the past, and particularly during the mid-nineteenth century, educated upper- and middle-class Latin Americans tended to migrate to the United States either to work as professionals and then return home or to send their children to U.S. schools. This was especially true among Hispanics in the island countries of the Caribbean. During the late nineteenth and twentieth century, however, members of other socioeconomic classes began arriving in the United States, a trend that has continued up to the twenty-first century. Latin America can be viewed as divided into four distinct zones:

- Mexico
- Caribbean basin, or West Indies
- Central America
- South America

MEXICAN IMMIGRANTS

Historically, most Latin American immigrants have come from Mexico. During the nineteenth and early twentieth centuries, movement across the U.S.-Mexican border was fluid; people from both sides could cross with little obstruction. Consequently, Mexicans could travel north to work and return home easily. During the first decades of the twentieth century, the numbers of people moving north across the border began to increase significantly, and larger numbers of immigrants from Mexico's lower and middle classes began arriving on the U.S. side in search of political stability and economic opportunity.

During the 1940's, the U.S. and Mexican governments negotiated agreements such as the bracero program in order to create more orderly systems of bringing workers into the United States. Under these programs, large numbers of Hispanic migrant workers traveled north to the United States to work in the construction and agricultural sectors of the U.S. economy. After completing their contracts, they generally returned home; however, some remained permanently in the United States. Contract labor programs continued into the 1960's, and through these programs, the U.S. government recognized and formalized an already existing migration pattern.

The border between the United States and Mexico extends approximately 1,920 miles along the southern edges of California, Arizona, New Mexico, and Texas and the northern edges of the Mexican states of Baja California, Sonora, Chihuahua, Coauila, Nuevo León. and Tamaulipas. The border runs through mostly arid terrain ranging from sandy flatlands to rugged mountains.

CARIBBEAN IMMIGRANTS

The West Indies islands of Puerto Rico, Cuba, and Hispaniola—which is shared by the Spanish-speaking Dominican Republic and French-speaking Haiti—constitute the second region of Latin America. Though separated by open expanses of sea, these islands share a geographic proximity to the United States that accounts in part for the movement of many West Indians to the U.S. mainland. During the nineteenth century, upper- and middle-class Hispanic islanders traveled in small numbers from the Caribbean to the United States. By the beginning of the twentieth century, their

numbers had gradually increased but still remained small in actual numbers. The 1920's and 1930's saw an increase in West Indian immigration as job opportunities were becoming scarcer in the Caribbean.

During the mid-twentieth century, West Indian immigration numbers increased substantially. The economic and political circumstances varied among the Hispanic islands, but all these islands were experiencing growing populations and shrinking job bases. People from the Dominican Republic and Puerto Rico—which by then was a U.S. dependency—continued to go to the United States primarily to work, and they formed large communities, primarily in the Northeast. Cuban immigration surged during the 1960's as a result of

the island's communist revolution, and it continued to be strong into the 1980's and 1990's.

CENTRAL AMERICAN IMMIGRANTS

Significant immigration from Central American nations did not begin until the late twentieth century, but immigrants from those nations have dispersed over a wide area of the United States, particularly the South, Midwest, and Far West. Political upheavals during the 1970's and 1980's impelled many people from Guatemala, El Salvador, and Nicaragua to migrate north. A large part of these immigrants were members of the working classes and had less education than other Latin American immigrants. Consequently, they have tended to experience higher levels of poverty after settling in

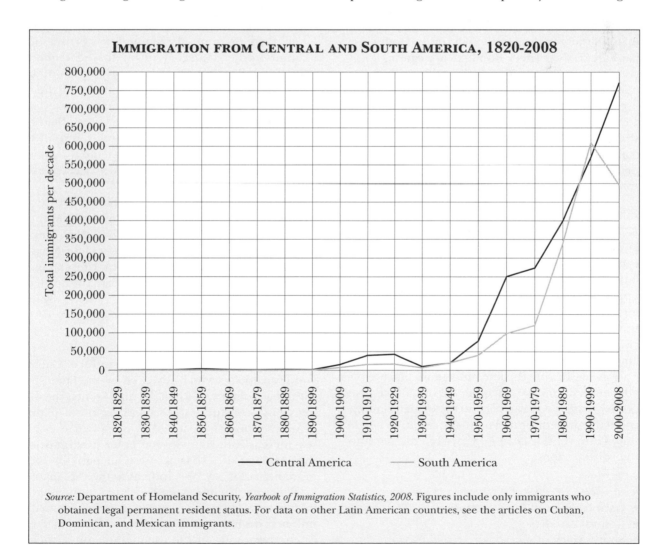

IMMIGRATION FROM CENTRAL AND SOUTH AMERICA, 1820-2008

Source: Department of Homeland Security, *Yearbook of Immigration Statistics, 2008.* Figures include only immigrants who obtained legal permanent resident status. For data on other Latin American countries, see the articles on Cuban, Dominican, and Mexican immigrants.

Protestor waving a Honduran flag at a Miami, Florida, demonstration that was one of many across the United States during a national day of protest against government crackdowns on illegal immigration on May 1, 2006. The predominantly Latin American protestors sought to call attention to the positive economic contributions that undocumented immigrants make to the United States. (AP/Wide World Photos)

the United States. In contrast, immigrants from the more politically stable Costa Rica have tended to be more highly educated and better equipped to find success in the United States. Even after political unrest had largely abated in Central America by the early twenty-first century, immigrants continued to come to the United States in large numbers.

SOUTH AMERICAN IMMIGRANTS

Although South America has the largest population of any of the four Latin American zones, it has historically supplied the fewest immigrants to the United States. However, during the last decade of the twentieth century and the first decade of the twenty-first, the rate of immigration from South American nations more than doubled. The countries sending the most people to the United States have been Brazil, Peru, Ecuador, and Colombia. The numbers of immigrants from Colombia have been particularly high because of political instability

in that country. Meanwhile, increasing numbers of immigrants have come from Argentina, Venezuela, Chile, and Bolivia. Immigrants from South America have settled throughout the United States, but they have tended to concentrate in the Northeast and along the East Coast. Among Latin American nations, the countries of South America are the most distant from the United States. Because of the great distances immigrants from those countries travel to reach the United States, the immigrants have worked especially hard to develop social and support networks to facilitate their journey.

South American immigrants have traditionally brought higher levels of education, and their emigration from their homelands has created serious "brain drains" in their home countries. However, by the early twenty-first century, increasing portions of immigrants were coming from the working classes of their countries. Chilean immigrants have generally had higher levels of education and pro-

fessional skills, while Paraguayan and Bolivian immigrants have tended to be less educated. Paraguay's high rate of population growth has made the immigrants coming from that country younger than those of most other Latin American nations.

CHANGING PATTERNS IN IMMIGRATION

With the large increase of Latin American immigration to the United States after the 1960's, extended family and kinship networks have grown apace. They, in turn, have facilitated the development of chain migration links. Whereas in the past, most Latin Americans coming to the United States were men planning to work and save money before returning home, the late twentieth century saw a large increase in the numbers of women, children, and families following established migration routes to live and work in American communities in which Hispanic family and social contacts were already established.

These social and kinship networks have also led to generally more participation in local civic organizations, clubs, and churches, as well as a renewed use of mutual aid societies to assist and support new immigrants. At the same time, the Spanish-language media and press have become increasingly important disseminators of news, culture, entertainment, and advertising to Spanish-speaking markets.

William A. Teipe, Jr.

FURTHER READING

González, Juan. *Harvest of Empire: A History of Latinos in America.* New York: Viking Press, 2000. Useful general historical overview of the many Hispanic peoples who have immigrated to the United States from all regions of Latin America.

Mahler, Sarah J. *American Dreaming: Immigrant Life on the Margins.* Princeton, N.J.: Princeton University Press, 1995. Close study of Central and South American immigrants in New York's Long Island, who might be viewed as a microcosm of Latin American immigrants in the United States.

Meier, Matt S., and Feliciano Rivera. *Mexican Americans/American Mexicans: From Conquistadors to Chicanos.* 2d ed. Toronto: HarperCollins Canada, 1993. Thorough overview of Mexican immigration into what is now the United States, from the time of early Spanish conquests to the modern American Chicano movement.

Rodriguez, Gregory. *Mongrels, Bastards, Orphans, and Vagabonds: Mexican Immigration and the Future of Race in America.* New York: Pantheon Books, 2007. Broad overview of Mexican immigrants that attempts to assess its implications for future American developments.

Rodríguez, Havidán, Rogelio Sáenz, and Cecilia Menjivar. *Latinas/os in the United States: Changing the Face of America.* New York: Springer, 2008. Broad study of Hispanic communities in the United States, emphasizing their diversity.

Suro, Roberto. *Strangers Among Us: Latino Lives in a Changing America.* New York: Vintage Books, 1999. Balanced view of immigration by Latin Americans.

SEE ALSO: Brazilian immigrants; Chain migration; Colombian immigrants; Cuban immigrants; Dominican immigrants; Ecuadorian immigrants; Guatemalan immigrants; Honduran immigrants; Japanese Peruvians; Latinos and immigrants; Mexican immigrants; Nicaraguan immigrants; Puerto Rican immigrants; Salvadoran immigrants; Spanish-language press; Telemundo.

LATINOS AND IMMIGRANTS

SIGNIFICANCE: American citizens of Latino descent have long had a special relationship with Latin American immigrants, with whom they have shared a common culture and a common language. In addition to these cultural affinities, the geographical proximity of the United States and Latin American nations—particularly Mexico—has helped to foster close ties between Latinos in the United States and the nations from which new immigrants have emigrated. However, while Latinos in the United States have often helped immigrants adjust to life in the United States, others have felt threatened by Latin American immigration.

As Latin American immigrants poured into the United States in increasing numbers during the late twentieth century, many of them were absorbed into established American Latino communities. Many Latinos around the United States have

organized their own social-service agencies to aid immigrants. For example, El Centro de la Raza, in Seattle, has hosted many services for new immigrants of all ethnicities since it was founded in 1972. It began as a Latino-led center but broadened its mission in a multiethnic community. Immigration, especially among Latinos, is a family affair, and El Centro often parses its mission in familial terms.

El Centro and other community centers also have actively maintained Latin American connections, as well as relationships with diplomatic offices in Mexico and other Spanish-speaking countries. Some people at El Centro say that it is a community center with a foreign policy. El Centro, for example, has played a key role in forging Seattle's sister-city relationship with Managua, Nicaragua.

ANTI-IMMIGRATION SENTIMENTS

A minority of Latino immigrants who have become U.S. citizens (or their children) oppose further immigration. An example has been provided by Roberto Suro, the author of *Strangers Among Us: How Latino Immigration is Transforming America* (1998). The son of Puerto Rican and Ecuadorean parents and a reporter for the *Washington Post*, Suro has argued for strengthening U.S. border security, imposing stricter penalties for those immigrants who enter the United States illegally more than once, and restricting aid to countries, such as Mexico, that do not do enough to restrain emigration of their own citizens to the United States.

Suro's views have been criticized for ignoring immigration's motive forces throughout history. Most immigrants, including the parents of Latinos who came into the United States in earlier years, did not leave their original homes until economic necessity or political repression compelled them. Thus, the flow of illegal immigration can be solved only by fundamental political and economic changes in the countries whose people are leaving in large numbers. However, critics have charged that this line of reasoning ignores the safety-valve function of emigration from countries that cannot provide employment for all their citizens.

Suro's book focuses not on Latin American immigrants like himself who have succeeded in the United States, but rather on those whom, he asserts, wallow in the culture of poverty, fail to learn English, and feed on the illegal drug trade and other forms of criminal activity. His perception is selective, critics charge, as he perpetuates stereotypes that fuel much anti-immigrant activity. Suro speaks for a segment of the immigration debate whose advocates believe that the expanding, open economy of earlier years in the United States has stagnated, and that further immigration will only worsen tensions among ethnic groups, causing more problems for already resident Latinos by increasing competition for limited jobs.

Another example of the differing attitudes held by various Latinos vis-à-vis immigration is evident at the U.S-Mexican border, where a large proportion of the federal agents who enforce laws keeping the border secure are themselves Latinos.

Bruce E. Johansen

FURTHER READING

González, Juan. *Harvest of Empire: A History of Latinos in America.* New York: Viking Press, 2000. Good overview of the histories of the many Latino immigrant groups that have come to the United States.

Hopfensperger, Jean. "Hard Times Send Latinos Back Across the Border: Fewer Jobs, Tougher Immigration Rules Force Some Immigrants to Return Home." *Minneapolis Star-Tribune*, May 29, 2009. Extensive examination of Latino immigrants' return to their home countries following economic difficulties in the United States, especially in Minnesota's Twin Cities.

Schrader, Esther. Review of *Strangers Among Us* by Roberto Suro. *Washington Monthly*, October, 1998. Detailed examination of issues raised in Suro's book on Latino immigration, which is reconfiguring North American politics and culture. Suro opposes illegal Latino immigration.

Segura, Gary M., ed. "Latino Immigration and National Identity." *Perspectives on Politics* (June, 2006). Rebuts assumptions that Latino immigrants generally fail to succeed and adapt to social norms in the United States; it finds that public discourse on Latinos and immigration often relies on stereotypes and inaccurate information.

Suro, Roberto. *Strangers Among Us: How Latino Immigration Is Transforming America.* New York: Alfred A. Knopf, 1998. A *Washington Post* reporter, Suro explores immigration issues and con-

cludes that older Latino immigrants sometimes oppose easing of laws for those who come after them.

SEE ALSO: Bilingual education; Bracero program; Chicano movement; Drug trafficking; Employment; Farm and migrant workers; Illegal immigration; Latin American immigrants; Mexican immigrants; Puerto Rican immigrants; West Indian immigrants.

LAU V. NICHOLS

THE CASE: U.S. Supreme Court decision on the education of children with limited English-language skills

DATE: Decided on January 21, 1974

SIGNIFICANCE: Based on the Civil Rights Act of 1964, *Lau v. Nichols* required school districts to provide compensatory training for students with limited proficiency in the use of the English language, but the ruling left it up to educational authorities and school districts to decide which methods of instruction to utilize.

In 1971, San Francisco's school district was racially integrated by court order. At that time, the school district had about 2,800 students of Chinese ancestry who were unable to communicate in the English language. The district provided 1,000 of these students with special instruction in English but provided no such instruction for the remaining 1,800 students. The parents of those not receiving special instruction went to court in a class-action suit, arguing that the district's policy violated Title VI of the Civil Rights Act of 1964, which prohibited educational discrimination based on national origin. In addition, the parents asserted that the district's policy was contrary to the requirements of the equal protection clause of the Fourteenth Amendment.

Although the lower federal courts ruled against the parents, the Supreme Court unanimously held that the district's failure to provide the students with appropriate language instruction denied them equal educational opportunity on the basis of ethnicity. In writing the opinion for the Court, Justice William O. Douglas relied entirely on the Civil Rights Act of 1964 and wrote that there was no need to consider whether the district's actions might also be inconsistent with the Fourteenth Amendment. To buttress his position, Douglas observed that the district received a substantial amount of federal financial assistance and that a 1970 antidiscrimination guideline of the Department of Health, Education, and Welfare required federally funded school districts to rectify the "linguistic deficiencies" of students from non-English-speaking homes. While requiring "affirmative steps" to overcome the language barrier, Douglas did not prescribe any particular means toward that end, whether bilingual instruction, English as a second language (ESL) training, or another approach.

The *Lau* decision significantly expanded the rights of limited-English-proficient (LEP) students throughout the nation. Among other things, it popularized the notion that language is so closely interwoven with a group's national culture that language-based discrimination constitutes a form of national-origin discrimination. The decision helped encourage the Department of Health, Education, and Welfare to issue the "Lau Remedies" of 1975, which required bilingual instruction in elementary schools where enough LEP students of the same language made it practical. Enforced by the Office of Civil Rights, five hundred school districts adopted bilingual programs within the next five years. Experts disagreed, however, about the effectiveness of such programs. The Republican administrations of the 1980's allowed a more flexible, case-by-case approach, and most districts abandoned bilingualism and attempted to help LEP students with ESL classes.

Thomas Tandy Lewis

FURTHER READING

Epstein, Lee, and Thomas Walker. *Constitutional Law for a Changing America: Rights, Liberties, and Justice.* 6th ed. Washington, D.C.: CQ Press, 2006.

O'Brien, David M. *Constitutional Law and Politics.* 7th ed. New York: W. W. Norton, 2008.

SEE ALSO: Bilingual education; Bilingual Education Act of 1968; Citizenship; Constitution, U.S.; Due process protections; Education; English as a second language; History of immigration after 1891; Multiculturalism; Supreme Court, U.S.

Lem Moon Sing v. United States

The Case: U.S. Supreme Court decision on habeas corpus petitions by aliens
Date: Decided on May 27, 1895

Significance: The *Lem Moon Sing* decision upheld a federal law prohibiting district courts from reviewing habeas corpus petitions, thereby empowering immigration authorities to exclude or deport alien immigrants without any concern that judges might find fault with their procedures.

A businessman who had resided many years in California, Lem Moon Sing was born in China to Chinese parents, which made him ineligible for naturalized American citizenship. In 1894, he visited his native land with the intention of returning in a few months to resume living and working in the United States. During his absence, however, the U.S. Congress passed an appropriation act with a provision that immigration officials' decisions were final when excluding aliens from admission into the United States under the Chinese Exclusion Act of 1882. Decisions were subject to review by the secretary of the treasury. When arriving in San Francisco later that year, Sing appeared to meet the qualifications for reentry. He presented two credible witnesses testifying that he had conducted business as a merchant and was not a laborer excluded by the Scott Act of 1888. Immigration officials, nevertheless, denied him permission to enter the country.

Arguing that the exclusion was an unconstitutional denial of due process and that it violated treaties with China, Sing petitioned the U.S. district court for a writ of habeas corpus, which would have allowed a judge to review the decision. Based on the 1894 law, the petition was denied. The Supreme Court, by an 8-1 margin, upheld the judgment of the lower court. Speaking for the majority, Justice John Marshall Harlan reviewed the Court's precedents concerning the power of Congress to make immigration policy. While recognizing the duty of immigration officials to faithfully follow provisions in both laws and treaties, Harlan insisted that the U.S. Constitution empowered Congress to decide that the final judgment would be made by officials within the executive department of the government.

Thomas Tandy Lewis

Further Reading
Hyung-chan, Kim, ed. *Asian Americans and the Supreme Court: A Documentary History.* Westport, Conn.: Greenwood Press, 1992.
McClain, Charles J. *In Search of Equality: The Chinese Struggle Against Discrimination in Nineteenth-Century America.* Berkeley: University of California Press, 1994.

See also: Chinese Exclusion Act of 1882; *Chinese Exclusion Cases*; Chinese immigrants; Congress, U.S.; Due process protections; History of immigration, 1783-1891; *Immigration and Naturalization Service v. St. Cyr*; *Nishimura Ekiu v. United States*; Supreme Court, U.S.; *United States v. Ju Toy*.

Lennon, John

Identification: English musician and political activist
Born: October 9, 1940; Liverpool, England
Died: December 8, 1980; New York, New York

Significance: After winning international fame as one of the lead singers of the British rock band called the Beatles, Lennon moved to the United States in 1971 and joined in a number of radical leftist causes. In 1972, President Richard M. Nixon attempted to have him deported for political reasons.

Upon the breakup of John Lennon's world-famous rock group the Beatles, he and his Japanese-born wife, Yoko Ono, used their celebrity to promote the anti-Vietnam War movement. In 1969, they staged quixotic protests such as "Bed-ins for Peace," and Lennon was denied entry to the United States. Lennon and Ono moved to New York City in 1971, associating with such radicals as Jerry Rubin and Abbie Hoffman. Lennon and Ono also advocated a number of leftist causes in their protest album *Sometime in New York City* (1972).

President Richard M. Nixon, fearing that Lennon's influence on young voters could undermine his reelection and that there could be a Lennon-led

disruption of the 1972 Republican National Convention, ordered Lennon's deportation. In March of that year, Lennon was served a deportation notice by the Immigration and Naturalization Service citing a 1968 misdemeanor drug conviction in England. Lennon appealed the order, which was eventually overturned in 1975. Despite Lennon's radical associations, the Federal Bureau of Investigation's surveillance of him determined the often intoxicated Lennon to be a minimal subversive threat. He gained permanent resident status in 1976 but was killed by a mentally deranged American fan four years later.

Luke A. Powers

FURTHER READING

Norman, Philip. *John Lennon: The Life*. New York: Ecco Press, 2008.

Wenner, Jann. *Lennon Remembers*. 1971. New ed. New York: Verso, 2000.

Wiener, Jon. *Gimme Some Truth: The John Lennon FBI Files*. Berkeley: University of California Press, 1999.

SEE ALSO: Citizenship and Immigration Services, U.S.; Drug trafficking; Due process protections; Films; "Moral turpitude"; Music; New York City.

LIBERIA

IDENTIFICATION: West African nation that originated as a refuge for freed American slaves

SIGNIFICANCE: Since its founding, Liberia has had a unique relationship with the United States. Its history is closely linked with American slavery and the abolitionist movement in the United States, and the West African nation was founded as a colony for former African American slaves and free blacks, who were encouraged to emigrate from the United States during the early nineteenth century. During the early twentieth century, a

John Lennon (left) with his Japanese wife, Yoko Ono, in New York City, in 1972. (AP/Wide World Photos)

black nationalist movement in the United States attempted to send more settlers to Liberia.

Liberia's first American settlers were eighty-eight free-born African Americans who went there in 1820 and settled at Cape Mesurado, at the mouth of the St. Paul River. Most of these people were educated and free, and many owned property in Maryland and Virginia. Although they had not been born into slavery in the United States, they had not enjoyed full citizenship rights as Americans. By the time Liberia declared its independence in 1847, several thousand more free-born African Americans and former slaves had joined them in the new nation. These original immigrants and their descendants were afterward known as Americo-Liberians.

LIBERIA'S EARLY IMMIGRANTS

By 1824, the original Cape Mesurado Colony was home to several hundred settlers and had been renamed the Liberia Colony. Throughout the 1820's, other colonies were established along the

coast. These included New Georgia, which was settled by Africans from other parts of the continent who had been liberated from slave ships by U.S. naval vessels while they were being carried to the Western Hemisphere. After these people were set free in the new colony, they became known as "Congos."

Meanwhile, several additional colonies were established under the sponsorship of colonization societies, including the American Colonization Society, and the state legislatures of Kentucky, Maryland, Mississippi, New York, Pennsylvania, and Virginia. The colonies expanded along Liberia's coast throughout the 1830's and 1840's. The population of the region was made up of three distinct groups of people: the original settlers from America, enslaved Africans who had been liberated from slave ships, and the region's indigenous peoples, primarily from Malinké-speaking societies. Americo-Liberians and Congos would always constitute a small minority of the total population of Liberia, but they dominated the politics and economy of Liberia through the nineteenth century and most of the twentieth century. By the twenty-first century, however, average Liberians no longer made distinctions among descendants of the original settlers of Liberia.

By 1847, when the Republic of Liberia declared its independence, approximately 15,000 Americans had settled in the country, along with a few thousand newly so-called Congos. Several European nations quickly established diplomatic relations with Liberia, but the United States did not recognize the new nation until 1862.

TWENTIETH CENTURY LIBERIA

Liberia was long an anomaly in sub-Saharan Africa, most of which was colonized by European nations during the late nineteenth century. By the twentieth century, Liberia and Ethiopia were the only sub-Saharan countries that had not been colonized by Europe, but Liberia differed from Ethiopia, on the other side of the continent, in being politically dominated by non-African settlers, most of whom came from the United States. The country's Americo-Liberian rulers did not even recognize members of Liberia's indigenous societies as citizens of the new nation until 1904. During the 1920's, Marcus Garvey's Universal Negro Improvement Association tried to start a new resettlement program to send African Americans to Liberia, but only a small number of people emigrated to the country.

Meanwhile, Liberia developed painfully slowly. Even its borders with its colonial neighbors remained poorly defined until well into the twentieth century. In his 1936 book, *Journey Without Maps*, author Graham Greene trekked 350 miles through Liberia's rain forests. The only map available at the time from the U.S. government showed a wide swath of Liberia as being unexplored, with a vast, empty space fancifully labeled "cannibals."

The Americo-Liberians governed Liberia through a single party. Although their governments were often corrupt, the country remained relatively stable until 1980, when an army sergeant named Samuel K. Doe brought down the govern-

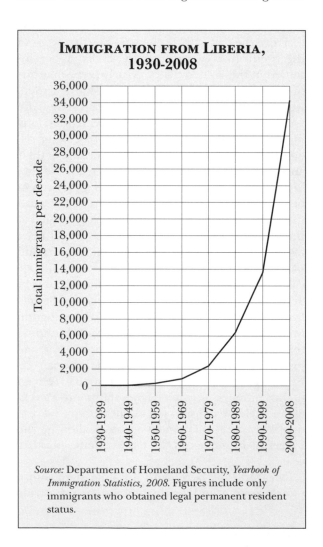

IMMIGRATION FROM LIBERIA, 1930-2008

Total immigrants per decade

Source: Department of Homeland Security, *Yearbook of Immigration Statistics, 2008*. Figures include only immigrants who obtained legal permanent resident status.

ment in a swift coup and had its Americo-Liberian leaders executed. Afterward, ethnic tensions increased until 1989, when Doe's former chief of procurement, Charles Taylor, invaded Liberia from neighboring Côte d'Ivoire and took control of the government. Taylor's regime was marked by a long, bloody civil war, during which 200,000 Liberians died, and about one-third of the nation's population fled to neighboring countries. Thousands of Liberians who had the means to do so fled their war-torn nation and sought refuge in the United States, essentially reversing the trend of Americans returning to the shores of West Africa. Liberia's civil war officially ended in August, 2003, when all the warring parties agreed to a cease-fire. However, by then, much of Liberia lay in ruins, and a massive humanitarian disaster existed.

LIBERIAN IMMIGRATION TO THE UNITED STATES

From the early 1990's through the first years of the twenty-first century, nearly 20,000 Liberians settled in the United States. Nearly three-quarters of them resided in Rhode Island. Many of them were descendants of African American slaves who had long maintained ties with their extended family members in the United States. In seeking refuge, they began returning to the homeland of their ancestors, the United States. To afford these new immigrants legal protection, the U.S. government began granting them temporary protected status (TPS) in 1991. By 2005, TPS had been extended to thousands of Liberians, many of whom had been living in the United States for a decade or more and had either renewed or established new family, social, and economic ties with the United States. In September, 2006, the U.S. Department of Homeland Security announced that the TPS program would stop on October 1, 2007, effectively ending the refugee status Liberian immigrants had enjoyed in the United States. However, Liberians already registered under TPS were allowed to remain in the United States under a new status into March, 2009. As that extension was about to expire, President Barack Obama signed an order allowing the Liberians to remain in the United States another year.

Because Liberia remains a fragile state with a weak economy and nearly nonexistent infrastruc-

ture, many U.S. government leaders believe that forcing the return of nearly 20,000 immigrants to Liberia could easily overwhelm the frail nation. To address the issue, the Liberian Refugee Immigration Fairness Act of 2007 was introduced in the U.S. Senate in February, 2007. A similar bill, the Liberian Refugee Immigration Protection Act of 2007, was introduced in the U.S. House of Representatives in April. 2007. Both forms of legislation were designed to permit eligible Liberians living in the United States to apply for permanent resident status. However, both bills were still awaiting passage in 2009.

Terry A. Anderson

FURTHER READING

Clegg, Claude Andrew. *The Price of Liberty: African Americans and the Making of Liberia.* Chapel Hill: University of North Carolina Press, 2004. Comprehensive history of the origins and early development of Liberia.

Koser, Khalid, ed. *New African Diasporas.* New York: Routledge, 2003. Describes the waves of immigration of the late twentieth century from Africa to the United States and to northern Europe and the United Kingdom.

Murdza, Peter J., Jr. *Immigrants to Liberia, 1865 to 1904: An Alphabetical Listing.* Newark, Del.: Liberian Studies Association of America, 1975. Detailed list of all the African American families who settled in Liberia during the late nineteenth century.

Ndubuike, Darlington. *The Struggles, Challenges, and Triumphs of the African Immigrants in America.* Lewiston, N.Y.: Edwin Mellen Press, 2002. Discusses the struggles of African immigrants in adapting to American society.

Smith, James Wesley. *Sojourners in Search of Freedom: The Settlement of Liberia by Black Americans.* Lanham, Md.: University Press of America, 1987. Another interesting history of the founding of Liberia by African Americans.

SEE ALSO: Abolitionist movement; African Americans and immigrants; African immigrants; American Colonization Society; "Brain drain"; Emigration; Maryland; Remittances of earnings; Slave trade.

LIM, SHIRLEY GEOK-LIN

IDENTIFICATION: Malaysian American author and academic

BORN: December 27, 1944; Malacca, Malaya (now Malaysia)

SIGNIFICANCE: A feminist professor and prolific poet, short-fiction writer, novelist, and literary critic, Shirley Geok-lin Lim researches and writes from the margins as a woman, an English-speaking Malaysian Chinese/Peranakan, and an immigrant Asian American. Her work on language, gender, nation, and ethnicity as engines of cultural production is particularly valuable for an understanding of the identity creation of immigrants.

Shirley Geok-lin Lim was born during World War II at a time when the Japanese army forces had overpowered the British colonial rulers for control of Malaya. Her Chinese father was fluent in Hokkien (a Chinese dialect), Malay, and English. His father had emigrated from Fujian Province, China, to Malaya for work. Lim's Peranakan (Malayan-native Chinese who adopted Malay and Western cultures) mother was fluent in Teochew (another Chinese dialect), Malay, and English. Lim, whose first language was the Malay of her mother, quickly became a predominantly English speaker both at home and at school by the age of six, when she went to a convent school run by Roman Catholic nuns. As a child in Malacca, Lim suffered abuse, poverty, and abandonment—her mother left Lim's father and her five brothers when she was eight years old. She comes from a family of eight brothers (three half brothers) and one half sister.

Lim moved away from her family to Kuala Lumpur to attend the University of Malaya, graduating with a bachelor's degree in 1967 and a master's degree in 1969, both in English literature. In 1969, she moved to the United States to attend Brandeis University on Fulbright and Wien International scholarships. As a new international student from a tropical country, she initially suffered both loneliness and culture shock. Nevertheless, she completed a master's degree (1971) and a doctorate (1973) in English and American literature. In No-

vember, 1972, she married Charles Bazerman, a Jewish New Yorker who also had a doctorate in English and American literature from Brandeis, and they had a son. While pregnant, Lim became a U.S. citizen on February 14, 1980. Her son's American identity solidified her connection to the United States, although she struggled as an immigrant mother to be a part of her local community. Lim has taught at Hostos Community College, City University of New York (1973-1976); Westchester College, State University of New York (1976-1990); and the University of California, Santa Barbara (1990-   ).

Lim's major areas of teaching and research are women's studies, Asian American literature, and Southeast Asian literature. Her poetry and fiction are populated by characters who live in the multilingual, multicultural, multireligious, and multiracial society of her country of origin. Her novels *Joss and Gold* (2001) and *Sister Swing* (2006) deal with characters who have moved from one country to another: Malaysia to Singapore and America to Singapore in the former; Malaysia to America in the latter. Her nonfiction works include *The Forbidden Stitch: An Asian American Women's Anthology* (1989; coeditor), which won an American Book Award/Before Columbus Award in 1990, and her prominent memoir, *Among the White Moon Faces* (1996), which won an American Book Award in 1997.

Lydia Forssander-Song

FURTHER READING

Lim, Shirley Geok-lin. *Among the White Moon Faces: An Asian-American Memoir of Homelands.* New York: Feminist Press at the City University of New York, 1996.

_____. *Sister Swing.* Singapore: Marshall Cavendish, 2006.

Newton, Pauline T. *Transcultural Women of Late Twentieth-Century U.S. American Literature: First Generation Migrants from Islands and Peninsulas.* Burlington, Vt.: Ashgate, 2005.

SEE ALSO: Asian American literature; Lahiri, Jhumpa; Literature; Malaysian immigrants; Mukherjee, Bharati; Sidhwa, Bapsi; Women immigrants.

LINGUISTIC CONTRIBUTIONS

DEFINITION: Contributions to American English made by immigrant speakers of other languages

SIGNIFICANCE: English has long had the largest lexicon, or roster, of vocabulary items, of any language on Earth, in large part because of frequent borrowings from other tongues, especially from Latin, Greek, Old Norse, and French. However, the multicultural nature of the United States, especially from the mid-nineteenth century onward, facilitated the adaptation of borrowed words and phrases into American English at an even greater rate than had been the case in England, the country from which the language derived.

Before the English language was implanted in North America, most of its foreign linguistic influences had been the inadvertent results of military conquests or had come from deliberate attempts at language-engineering by scholars. In the North American colonies and later in the independent United States, changes in the language were more spontaneous and more organic. They were natural outgrowths of the intermingling of peoples from all over the world. The scope of immigrant influences on American English is perhaps best illustrated by examining contributions from the Romance languages of immigrants from countries such as France, Spain, Portugal, Italy, and the many Latin American nations and from the Germanic languages of immigrants from German-, Dutch-, and Scandinavian-speaking countries. Most of the words that have entered American English from the Romance languages pertain to folkways, food, and place names of both natural and artificial locations.

Folklorists employ the term "folkways" to encompass a wide array of professions, social roles, lifestyle issues, customs, dress, recreation, and folk beliefs. Many French terms that have found their way into American English reflect the lifestyles and beliefs of immigrants in regions bordering on Quebec in the northeast and in Louisiana in the south. Examples include

- *voyageur*, trapper or trader who travels long distances
- *traiteur*, folk healer or herbalist
- *lagniappe*, gift or act of kindness extended to guests as a token of cordiality
- *fifolet*, spirit or witch manifesting a nighttime phosphorescence
- *loup garou*, werewolf or similar creature of the night
- *gris-gris*, protective magic devices

Similar terms from Spanish include

- *quincienera*, celebration of a girl's fifteenth birthday
- buckaroo, term for cowboy adapted from the Spanish *vaquero*, literally "cattler"
- *curandero*, folk-healer, the Spanish equivalent of *traiteur*

Words for items of apparel also feature prominently in Spanish loanwords in American English. Examples include poncho, serape, and "ten-gallon hat." The latter originated when English-speakers mistook the Spanish word *galan* for the braid on a hatband for the English word "gallon" for a liquid measurement. Many other words related to the folkways of Spanish-speaking immigrants pertain to items used in ranching, such as "lariat" from Spanish *la reata* for rope or noose. Folk music also has contributed many words, such as "mariachi" for the exuberant form of Mexican music featuring string and wind instruments originally played at marriages—the English word to which the name of the music is directly related. Names of instruments used in mariachi music have also found their way into English. "Guitar" comes from the Spanish *guitaron* for large guitar.

Among the most readily recognized words from Italian are names for crime syndicates, such as "Mafia" and "Cosa Nostra." During the late nineteenth century, American English adopted the Italian *paisano* (sometimes rendered *paisan* in English) for peasant or worker as a jocular term for buddy or compatriot.

ROMANCE FOOD AND FORMATIONS

Words from Romance languages denoting foodstuffs and structures have flooded American English since the founding of the United States, but most especially since the nineteenth century. Ital-

ian words for pasta dishes such as "macaroni" and "spaghetti" entered the English language in England, but after millions of Italians immigrated to the United States during the nineteenth century, Italian restaurants became so commonplace that such Italian terms become more common in American usage than in British English. During the early twentieth century, "pizza" became an American staple, as did a number of coffee drinks of Italian origin such as "espresso," "cappuccino," and "latte."

Spanish gave American English words such as "taco," "tequila," "enchilada," and "burrito." In numerous cases, the dishes were as much American-European hybrids as were the words themselves. For example, enchiladas are a Mexican-American creation, neither fully Spanish nor even wholly Mexican. American pizza has little in common with the Italian dish after which it is named. Many of the Franco-American food terms in American English come from French, French Caribbean, and French Canadian cooking in the American South, especially in Louisiana. Examples include roux, a rich stock for sauces and gravy, and jambalaya, a meat-and-rice dish whose name came into English from Catalan by way of Spanish into Louisiana French. The thick, rich soup known as chowder is a French Canadian innovation in New England cooking terminology.

PLACE NAMES

As numerous as cuisine-related loanwords are in American English, Romance language names for types of places—both geographical and architectural—are equally common. Mexican Spanish has given southwestern American English terms such as

- "hoosegow" (jail), which comes from *juzgado* (place of the judged ones)
- "arroyo," a direct Spanish borrowing for a type of dry riverbed common in the Southwest
- "mesa," a flat, raised area of land from the Spanish word for table

From Cajun French, the dialect of French Canadian immigrants to Louisiana, contributed "bayou" for swamp and "levee" for the earthworks used to protect lowlands from flooding. Another French contribution that has much wider usage in American English is "bureau." The word originally was used for a bedroom desk or dresser; then it was extended to a piece of office furniture, and finally to an office and the agency it housed. In this later sense, both "bureau" and its derivative, "bureaucracy," were borrowed not only by international English but also by a number of other languages.

GERMANIC CONTRIBUTIONS

Borrowings into American English from the Germanic languages followed pathways similar to those from Romance languages. Food-related words have been common. From German have come "strudel," "noodle," "sauerkraut," "pretzel," and the coffee-related equivalent of English "teatime," "kaffeeklatsch." Dutch has given American English "cruller" for a type of pastry and the even more commonly used word "cookie," which was unknown in British English before it was introduced from American English. The equivalent British term has long been "biscuit." The British "biscuit" came from an Old French word for "twice-baked" pastries. In American English, the same word underwent a semantic shift to designate round, scone-like portions of bread. The Dutch *cookie* then filled the niche vacated by "biscuit."

A surprisingly large number of Germanic borrowings have been words denoting types of people; many of these words are derogatory in nature. German examples include "bum" for a lazy or idle person, from the verb *bummeln* (to loaf). Yiddish, the German dialect used primarily by Jews, gave American English a veritable flood of insulting terms. "Yekl," "klutz," "schlemiel," "schlimazel," "schmo," "schmuck," and "schnook" all connote stupidity or ineptitude to some degree. However, perhaps the most enduring and widespread insult from Germanic immigrant languages is the ubiquitous "dumb." For centuries, the homonymic English word "dumb" had meant mute; however, in every other populous Germanic language, spoken collectively by millions of immigrants, a near-identical word meant stupid or foolish. Examples include German's *dumm* and Swedish and Danish's *dum*. The Old English word "dumb" simply borrowed the meaning of its many Germanic cousins.

Not all such Germanic borrowings are negative. "Boss" from Dutch and "ombudsman" from Swedish are both neutral. Yiddish's "mensch" for a good-hearted individual is positive. At the same time, the Romance languages have contributed some insult-

ing terms. American English's "bimbo" for an attractive but unintelligent person is from *bambino*, Italian for baby. "Boob" and "booby" probably derive from Spanish *bobo* for a fool or clown.

OTHER TYPES OF CONTRIBUTIONS

The Romance and Germanic languages are not the only immigrant languages that have made significant contributions to American English. For example, "egg foo young" and "chow mein" are examples of words derived from Chinese for food dishes that were actually devised by Chinese immigrants in the United States. Likewise, "kolache," a pastry popular among Czechs and Slovaks, has evolved in the United States into a sweeter sort of treat reminiscent of American cinnamon rolls while at the same time developing a name that is a singular form in English although derived from a plural form in Czech.

Immigration has left traces on facets of American English that go beyond mere items of vocabulary. For example, among English speakers in areas where dialects of French have long been common, for example, Louisiana, one sometimes hears questions formulated without insertion of the default auxiliary verb "do." Instead of asking "How did your clothes get wet?" a person might say "How your clothes got wet?" The latter sentence structure imitates French syntax. Another example of imitating French phrasing is the rapid-fire repetition of an adjective to suggest intensity, as in "It is hot-hot today."

In regions in which many Americans are bilingual English and Spanish or else in close contact with such speakers, one often hears "leave" used with "to" to indicate a destination, for example, "They are leaving to school" instead of the standard "They are leaving for school," a structure imitative of Spanish, which employs the single-letter preposition *a* (to) in such circumstances.

Another phrase-structure affected by languages of immigrants may be the tag question—making a statement and immediately adding a brief yes/no question seeking confirmation or denial. In formal English, such questions involve complex formulations. For example, the tag on the simple statement, "Roger is drunk" requires copying over the verb ("is"), choosing the appropriate pronoun ("he"), and reversing the polarity of the statement (positive in this case) to negative, thus yielding,

"Roger is drunk, isn't he?" In contrast, most European languages, including members of the Romance and Germanic families, forego such linguistic acrobatics by simply appending to a declarative statement a single word meaning "yes" or "no," for example *si* or *no* in Spanish, *ja* or *nein* in German. During the twentieth century, informal variants of tag questions became increasingly popular in American English, as in "Roger is drunk, right?" Such practices are likely patterned after similar constructions in many immigrant tongues. A peculiarity of grammar in the speech of the American South, the so-called "double modal" constructions such as "might could" or "might should" instead of "might be able" and "perhaps should," may be legacies of Scottish immigrants, as such wording was once common in Scotland.

MORPHOLOGY

American morphology—aspects of English pertaining to roots and stems of words—and pronunciation also bear the imprint of immigration. For example, American English has borrowed the common noun ending -*o* from Romance languages to append to English roots, yielding such hybrids as "weirdo" and "wino." During the late 1990's, the Italian/Spanish noun suffix -*ista* came into similar use, yielding hybrid words such as "fashionista," a term for a person obsessed with clothing trends.

Thomas Du Bose

FURTHER READING

Baron, Dennis. *Grammar and Good Taste*. New Haven, Conn.: Yale University Press, 1982. Definitive discussion of the trends in what is considered appropriate and inappropriate in American English and the forces that have shaped American concepts of linguistic correctness and propriety.

Baugh, Albert, and Thomas Cable. *A History of the English Language*. 5th ed. Upper Saddle River, N.J: Prentice Hall, 2002. Chapter 11 of this book offers a thorough assessment of the forces that have shaped American English and the place of American English in relation to world English.

Bryson, Bill. *Made in America*. New York: Perennial, 1996. Highly enjoyable best-seller about American English with much information about the contributions of various groups of immigrants.

Finegan, Edward, and John Rickford, eds. *Language Variation in North American English*. New

York: Cambridge University Press, 2004. Scholarly but accessible overview of variations within North American English.

Marckwardt, Albert. *American English.* New York: Oxford University Press, 1971. Although originally published during the 1950's, this book remains the standard study of the English language in the United States.

Millward, Celia. *A Biography of the English Language.* 2d ed. Orlando, Fla.: Harcourt, 1996. Exemplary textbook on the history of the English language. Chapter 9 provides a concise review of the special features of American English.

SEE ALSO: Dutch immigrants; Foodways; French immigrants; German immigrants; Italian immigrants; Language issues; Louisiana; Mexican immigrants; Multiculturalism; Scandinavian immigrants.

LITERACY TESTS

DEFINITION: Tests of reading and writing fluency administered to immigrants seeking to attain U.S. citizenship

SIGNIFICANCE: Literacy tests have been a focal point of the controversy between those who would require a minimum standard of educational competence for attaining American citizenship and those who decry what they view as arbitrary restrictiveness. Literacy tests have been a key component of proposed immigration laws and a reason cited for presidential vetoes of legislation that would have instituted them.

Literacy tests as a decision-making barometer have a long heritage dating from their role during the Middle Ages as part of the process to extend "benefit of clergy" status to wayward priests. They afforded preferential treatment in a separate ecclesiastic system of justice to priests who could successfully read the "neck verse" from Psalms. This practice was abolished in the United States in 1827, but the importance of literacy as a gateway

THE AMERICANESE WALL, AS CONGRESSMAN BURNETT WOULD BUILD IT.
UNCLE SAM: You're welcome in — if you can climb it!

Cartoon in a March, 1916, issue of Puck *magazine lampooning the literacy test requirement in the bill that would become the Immigration Act of 1917.* (Library of Congress)

to success in mainstream American life (for both criminal-offender and law-abiding populations) has persisted into the twenty-first century.

The Immigration Act of 1917 was the first major piece of federal legislation to include a literacy test, but earlier attempts to include such tests were vetoed by Presidents Grover Cleveland, William Howard Taft, and Woodrow Wilson in 1897, 1913, and 1915, respectively. The 1897 bill vetoed by Cleveland would have required tests of both reading and writing, while the two later bills included tests for reading only. The wording of the 1917 law, which was eventually passed, precluded admission into the United States for those who were physically able to read but did not have the requisite skills to read English or another language, includ-

ing Hebrew or Yiddish. The proposed test was made up of thirty to forty commonly used words, and examinees were allowed to choose the language or dialect they preferred. Although the law did not set limits on the numbers of immigrants per year or national quotas, it was clearly designed to lower immigration rates, particularly from countries with high levels of illiteracy.

The attitude of President Woodrow Wilson when he vetoed the proposed 1917 legislation restricting immigration is particularly instructive (his veto was ultimately overridden, resulting in passage of the law). Although he had been accused of holding biases against certain minority groups who he felt could not assimilate into a homogenous American middle class, Wilson strongly protested the inclusion of a literacy test. He saw it as a measure of prior educational opportunity, which could result in the rejection of citizenship applications from those with limited educational backgrounds. Their character and motivations would nonetheless render them highly desirable additions to an American middle-class "melting pot" characterized by hard work, dedication to a common set of goals, and ultimate achievement.

Since the early twentieth century, debate about how literacy tests would affect immigration law and policy has continued unabated. Empirical evidence has shown a strong link between fluency in English reading and later vocational success. An attempt initiated in 2001 by the U.S. Citizenship and Immigration Services (USCIS) to revise the naturalization tests was been harshly criticized by a committee under the auspices of the National Research Council. The basis of these criticisms were both methodological and substantive, including the lack of a clearly stated rationale for the literacy tests as well as the process used to develop their content. A new naturalization test was completed for all applicants from October 1, 2009, onward. It includes units on civics and English speaking, reading, and writing.

Eric Yitzchak Metchik

FURTHER READING

Elliott, Stuart, Naomi Chudowsky, Barbara Plake, and Lorraine McDonnell. "Using the *Standards* to Evaluate the Redesign of the U.S. Naturalization Tests: Lessons for the Measurement Community." *Educational Measurement: Issues and Practice* 25, no. 1 (Fall, 2006): 22-26.

McSeveney, Sam. "Immigrants, the Literacy Test, and Quotas: Selected American History College Textbooks' Coverage of the Congressional Restriction of European Immigration, 1917-1929." *The History Teacher* 21, no. 1 (1987): 41-51.

Vaught, Hans. "Division and Reunion: Woodrow Wilson, Immigration, and the Myth of American Unity." *Journal of American Ethnic History* 13, no. 3 (1994): 24-50.

SEE ALSO: Citizenship; Dillingham Commission; Education; English as a second language; Higher education; Immigration Act of 1907; Immigration Act of 1917; Immigration law; Intelligence testing; Language issues; Quota systems; World War I.

LITERATURE

SIGNIFICANCE: Successive waves of immigration to the United States have produced myriad literary works by immigrants. Likewise, native-born writers have also traveled and lived abroad throughout the country's history and have written from the unique perspective of being far from home. In both fiction and nonfiction, the literature of immigration highlights issues that are at the heart of the American experience: the search for self, the conflict between ethnic or national roots and individual identity, and the clash between cultures and generations.

Whatever metaphor is used to describe the ethnic makeup of the country—symphony, salad bowl, or patchwork quilt—the United States has been a nation of immigrants since its founding, and immigration has been a constant subject and theme of its literature. The very first works of American literature—such as John Smith's *The Generall Historie of Virginia, New England, and the Summer Isles* (which was first published in 1624 and included the story of Pocahontas) or William Bradford's *Of Plymouth Plantation* (1630)—were accounts of immigration and settlement in the New World.

Many of the classic works of American literature were in fact written by Europeans first venturing to America: J. Hector St. John de Crevecoeur, whose *Letters from an American Farmer* (1782) so accurately

According to John Smith's account of the settling of Virginia, the Native American chief Powhatan was about to have him executed when Powhatan's daughter Pocahontas intervened to save his life. This story became part of American lore, but some modern scholars believe that Pocahontas may merely have acted out a prearranged role in a tribal ritual that Smith did not understand. (Gay Brothers)

describes the new country and its inhabitants, was born in France. Thomas Paine, who wrote effectively in support of the American Revolution, was born in England. Anne Bradstreet, considered the first American poet, was also born in England and immigrated to Massachusetts with her husband in 1630. *The Interesting Narrative of the Life of Olaudah Equiano: Or, Gustavus Vassa, the African* (1789) was the start of a long line of African American literature, much of it the story of forced immigration during slavery. Even some of the classic works of the nineteenth century are tales of immigration. One of the most popular works by the poet Henry Wadsworth Longfellow was *Evangeline* (1847), which recounts the expulsion of French Canadians from Nova Scotia and their move to Louisiana during the eighteenth century, while the three central characters in Nathaniel Hawthorne's classic novel *The Scarlet Letter* (1850) are all recent English immigrants working out their fates in early Boston.

LITERATURE OF SECOND-WAVE IMMIGRATION

The first great wave of immigration after the founding of the republic occurred between 1830 and 1860 and was northern European in origin, including English, Irish, and German settlers. However, it was during the second major wave—from the 1880's to the 1920's and mainly from southern and eastern Europe—that the literature of immigration became a distinct literary form. The Statue of Liberty was dedicated in New York Harbor in 1886, and the lines from the Jewish American poet Emma Lazarus graced its base:

> Give me your tired, your poor
> Your huddled masses yearning to breathe free.

In 1892, Ellis Island began operating as the port of entry, and millions of immigrants from Greece, Italy, Poland, and other Slavic countries poured into East Coast ghettos.

Clearly, to the more established residents of the United States, these new travelers—darker complexioned and speaking different languages—were the true immigrants, and the literature they produced only confirmed their foreign origins. Books by and about the new immigrants highlighted their struggles. One of the first works of American realism was Rebecca Harding Davis's "Life in the Iron Mills" (1861), a story of Welsh factory workers in Virginia and the first in a line of exposés of the industrial exploitation of immigrants that would lead to Upton Sinclair's *The Jungle* (1906), the story of Lithuanian immigrants scraping out a living in the meatpacking industry in Chicago (and a novel that helped enact the country's first Pure Food and Drug Act).

Works such as Mary Antin's autobiography *The Promised Land* (1912) described how the dream of Americanization could come true for European immigrants. Most accounts of immigration during the late nineteenth century tended to focus on the hardships of the process: The Danish-born journalist Jacob Riis's *How the Other Half Lives* (1890), for example, documented unsafe conditions in crowded New York City tenements. Even when life was not physically hard, as in Kate Chopin's novel *The Awakening* (1899), set in Creole areas around New Orleans, the conflict of different cultural codes could cause tragedy.

In 1916, the critic Randolph Bourne wrote in his essay "Trans-national America" that the idea of the melting pot was misleading. The first settlers did not have to assimilate into any existing culture, Bourne argued; immigrant cultures have always given vitality and variety to the country, and recent immigrants should hold on to their distinctive cultural habits. Many of the literary works of the period confirmed Bourne's assumptions, even while most Americans ignored his plea. The protagonists in Abraham Cahan's *Yekl* (1896) and *The Rise of David Levinsky* (1917) are Russian Jews who end up lost between two worlds, their culture of origin and the country where they dream of success. Anzia Yezierska's stories and novels, such as *Hungry Hearts* (1923), depict similar difficulties of assimilation, especially for eastern European Jews. Willa Cather's *My Ántonia* (1918) fictionalizes the hardships of Bohemian (Czech) immigrants trying to eke out a living on the Western plains, while O. E. Rölvaag's *Giants in the Earth* (1927) is also set on the Western prairie and involves the difficulties for Norwegian immigrants trying to farm that harsh land.

ASSIMILATION AND CELEBRATION

Restrictive federal legislation enacted in 1921 and 1924 limited immigration through more than one-half century. When immigration picked up again after 1965, the main points of debarkation were not European but Asian, Caribbean, and Central American. At the same time, the Civil Rights movement after the 1940's had created a new ethnic awareness, a consciousness of ethnic contributions to so many areas of life in America.

This new pride in turn spawned the rediscovery of older works of immigrant literature, and the creation of a new generation of ethnic writers. Both Mike Gold's *Jews Without Money* (1930) and Henry Roth's *Call It Sleep* (1934), for example, strongly autobiographical accounts of immigrant Jewish family life in New York's lower East Side, were rediscovered during the 1960's, while a decade later Carlos Bulosan's classic autobiography of Filipino immigration, *America Is in the Heart* (1943), was first reprinted (1973). During that same period, Maxine Hong Kingston's powerful fictional memoirs *The Woman Warrior* (1976) and *China Men* (1980) were published, as well as Ernesto Galarza's *Barrio Boy* (1971), an account of his family's migration from Mexico to the United States.

Historians started to question the underlying assumptions and the very terms used to describe immigration and assimilation: Namely, Nathan Glazer and Daniel Patrick Moynihan in *Beyond the Melting Pot: The Negroes, Puerto Ricans, Jews, Italians, and Irish of New York City* (1963) and Michael Novak in *The Rise of the Unmeltable Ethnics: Politics and Culture in the Seventies* (1971). The renewed interest in ethnic and immigrant literature led to new studies—for example, Marcus Klein's *Foreigners: The Making of American Literature* (1981) and Werner Sollors's *Beyond Ethnicity: Consent and Descent in American Culture* (1986)—which in turn led to a number of new ways of viewing American literature. Ethnic literature, Sollors argued, is the pattern for American literature; according to Klein, most twentieth century American writers are "foreigners," immigrants or the heirs of immigrants who reshaped the century's literature.

During the last decades of the twentieth cen-

tury, the American literary canon was transformed, as publishers rushed to include forgotten or rediscovered writers in their anthologies. Ethnic writers stepped forward to claim literary prizes: N. Scott Momaday won the Pulitzer Prize in fiction in 1969 for *House Made of Dawn* (1968), Alice Walker in 1983 for *The Color Purple* (1982), and Toni Morrison five years later for *Beloved* (1987). Writers emerged to tell the stories of every ethnic thread in the historical quilt of the United States. This discovery of ethnicity's centrality in American life, as in the literary canon, meant that Americans increasingly embraced their immigrant backgrounds, often making or maintaining close contact with their countries of origin. Rather than producing stories of being torn between cultures, as in so many earlier twentieth century accounts of immigration, writers by the end of the century increasingly celebrated their ability to live in two cultures, to transcend borders and boundaries. Frank McCourt's popular memoir of his impoverished Irish childhood, *Angela's Ashes* (1996), was both a celebration of the strengths of his Irish mother in the face of grinding poverty and a tribute to his success in the United States. Increasingly, writers could view both their pasts and their futures without fear or tension.

Any survey of American literature of the previous century or so confirms these trends. Such an examination might begin with the English Jewish writer Israel Zangwill's popular 1908 play *The Melting-Pot*, which described the immigration process at the same time that it coined a misnomer to describe it. Finley Peter Dunne, the Chicago newspaper columnist, created the fictional Irish bartender Mr. Dooley, who commented on every social and political event up to World War I, including immigration. A Dutch immigrant to the United States called his autobiography *The Americanization of Edward Bok* (1920), while an immigrant from Slovenia, Louis Adamic, published *Laughing in the Jungle: The Autobiography of an Immigrant in America* in 1932 and *My America* in 1938. Irish immigration was touched on in James T. Farrell's *Studs Lonigan* trilogy (1935); Italian American life in Pietro di Donato's *Christ in Concrete*

(1939) and John Fante's *Wait Until Spring* and *Bandini* (1938). Thomas Bell wrote *Out of This Furnace* (1941), a novel detailing the hardships of immigrant Slovak laborers in western Pennsylvania steel mills, while William Saroyan made comedy out of the difficulties of his Armenian family in Fresno, California, in *The Daring Young Man on the Flying Trapeze* (1934) and *My Name Is Aram* (1940). All of these works explored, in various degrees, the struggles of assimilation, the loss of individual identity in that process, and the pain of being torn between two cultures.

With the rise of a new ethnic consciousness after World War II, immigrant literature underwent an enormous transformation. The change was marked by the publication of *Roots: The Saga of an American Family* (1976), which traced Alex Haley's ancestors back to Africa before slavery, became an enormously popular television series and helped to encourage similar discoveries in other ethnic histories. After Haley, new ethnic literary groups emerged,

Israel Zangwill, author of the 1908 play that introduced the concept of the "melting pot" to the English language. (Library of Congress)

and new attitudes toward immigrant history were born. Older European immigrant groups would continue to be represented in the more diverse American literary range—for example, Polish American Jerzy Kosinski's novel *The Painted Bird* (1965) or Italian American Mario Puzo's *The Godfather* (1969)—but more immigrant literature was coming from other continents.

CARIBBEAN LITERATURE

Caribbean immigration actually rose during the 1920's, when the flow from Europe was slowing. Early writers such as Claude McKay, who migrated from Jamaica in 1912, became a part of the African American literary boom of the Harlem Renaissance of the 1920's. McKay's poetry was collected in *Harlem Shadows* (1922), and his novel *Home to Harlem* was published in 1928. The next generation helped to carve out a more distinctive Caribbean identity. Paula Marshall's *Brown Girl, Brownstones* (1959) is her best-known novel, but she published fiction for the next four decades, novels and short stories in which her characters (often women) work out their identities in a conflict between New York City and the West Indies.

The literary outpouring since the 1960's has been even more prolific, and almost every Caribbean island-state has been represented. Cuban American writers have included Cristina Garcia, whose novel *Dreaming in Cuban* appeared in 1992, and Paula Fox, who has written adult fiction (such as her novel *A Servant's Tale*, in 1984) but who is better known as a children's writer. Her book *The Slave Dancer* (1973) received the Newbery Medal. Oscar Hijuelos has written a series of novels set in both Cuba and the United States, and *The Mambo Kings Play Songs of Love* (1989) won the Pulitzer Prize in fiction. Writers who have immigrated from the Dominican Republic include Julia Alvarez, who wrote the novel *How the García Girls Lost Their Accents* (1991), and Junot Díaz, whose short-story collection *Drown* (1996) was favorably reviewed, and whose first novel, *The Brief Wondrous Life of Oscar Wao* (2007), won the Pulitzer Prize in fiction.

Jamaica Kincaid was born in Antigua in the West Indies in 1949 and came to the United States when she was seventeen. She has written often of the Caribbean immigrant experience: in the novels *Annie John* (1985), *Lucy* (1990), and *The Autobiography of My Mother* (1996), as well as in short stories (*At the Bottom of the River*, 1983) and essays (*A Small Place*, 1988). Haitian Americans have been represented by Edwidge Danticat, the highly respected writer whose novel *Breath, Eyes, Memory* was published in 1994, whose collection of short stories *Krik? Krak!* (1995) was nominated for a National Book Award, and whose memoir of her family's dual citizenship, *Brother, I'm Dying* (2007), was given the National Book Critics Circle Award.

Puerto Rican writers have included Piri Thomas, whose *Down These Mean Streets* (1967) has become a classic coming-of-age urban memoir, and Nicholosa Mohr, whose *El Bronx Remembered* (1975) and *In Nueva York* (1977) fictionalized the coming-of-age struggles of poor Puerto Rican women in New York. Judith Ortiz Cofer published poetry, a novel (*The Line of the Sun*, 1988), and a memoir (*Silent Dancing: A Partial Remembrance of a Puerto Rican Childhood*, 1990) in which two cultures and languages are only part of the mix of ethnic, class, and gender issues.

ASIAN LITERATURE

Even greater diversity and richness have characterized immigrant Asian American literature of the last decades of the twentieth century and into the twenty-first century, as the numerous anthologies and studies of this ethnic literature attest: for example, Jessica Hagedorn's collection *Charlie Chan Is Dead: An Anthology of Asian American Fiction* (1993) and Shirley Geok-lin Lim and Amy Ling's *Reading the Literatures of Asian America* (1992). Although Chinese immigrants have long been a part of American history, their literature was not always available (for example, *Island: Poetry and History of Chinese Immigrants on Angel Island, 1910-1940*, published in 1980). It was not until the appearance of Maxine Hong Kingston and then Amy Tan that Chinese American literature blossomed. Tan's popular novels *The Joy Luck Club* (1989) and *The Kitchen God's Wife* (1991) highlighted the conflicts between assimilation and the desire for ethnic identity, and between generations. A flurry of Chinese American fiction dealing with these immigrant conflicts quickly followed: Gish Jen's *Typical American* (1991), Gus Lee's *China Boy* (1991), David Wong Louie's *Pangs of Love* (stories, 1992), and Fae Myenne Ng's *Bone* (1993).

These themes of dual identity, the conflict be-

tween the desire for both ethnic roots and individual identity, characterize other Asian American literatures as well. The hardships of immigrant life were magnified for the Japanese Americans, who were interned in camps in the West during World War II, and that horrific experience has colored the fiction since then, including Jeanne Wakatsuki Houston and James Houston's *Farewell to Manzanar* (1973), Hisaye Yamamoto's *Seventeen Syllables, and Other Stories* (1988), and Cynthia Kadohata's *The Floating World* (1989).

Korean American literature—such as Ronyoung Kim's *Clay Walls* (1987) and Chang-Rae Lee's *Native Speaker* (1995)—has highlighted the hardships of immigration and the difficulties of dual identity. The same can be said for Indian American fiction—namely Bharati Mukherjee's *Jasmine* (1989), and the works of Jhumpa Lahiri, whose collection of stories, *Interpreter of Maladies* (1999), won the Pulitzer Prize in fiction in 2000, and whose novel *The Namesake* (2003) was made into a popular film.

IMMIGRATION AND THE AMERICAN LITERARY CANON

Literature and art do not recognize national borders as walls or fences but, like ideas, flow easily back and forth from one country or continent to another, and this is particularly true in the literature of immigration and emigration. In addition to immigrants writing about their experiences coming to the United States, writers throughout American history have emigrated to other countries and written from that perspective. For example, Henry James based many of his novels and stories in Europe, often dramatizing the clash between nineteenth century American innocence and European experience. Both Ezra Pound and T. S. Eliot spent most of their careers writing in Europe. James and Eliot eventually became British subjects; Pound died in Italy. African American writers Richard Wright and James Baldwin found France a more congenial environment after World War II than an America they experienced as racially oppressive.

Both immigrant and emigrant fiction and memoir record the lasting tension between ethnic or national roots and the desire for assimilation, the sense of living between two worlds. In the increasingly globalized, shrinking world of the twenty-first century, the literature of immigration can describe the movement of people between countries and cultures and thus make the journey for readers before they attempt their own. For this and other reasons, the literature of immigration will undoubtedly continue as a valuable and vital form in the American literary canon.

David Peck

FURTHER READING

Ferraro, Thomas J., ed. *Ethnic Passages: Literary Immigrants in Twentieth-Century America.* Chicago: University of Chicago Press, 1993. Includes essays on Mario Puzo, Anzia Yezierska, and Maxine Hong Kingston, among other immigrant writers.

Fine, David M. *The City, the Immigrant, and American Fiction, 1880-1920.* Metuchen, N.J.: Scarecrow Press, 1977. Fine studies the literature of the early twentieth century, when European immigrants crowded into urban ghettos—for example, Abraham Cahan's *The Rise of David Levinsky* (1917).

Klein, Marcus. *Foreigners: The Making of American Literature, 1900-1940.* Chicago: University of Chicago Press, 1981. Literary history of the first half of the twentieth century from a radical perspective, which emphasizes its ethnic and proletarian nature. Concludes with detailed analyses of Mike Gold, Nathanael West, and Richard Wright.

Payant, Katherine B., and Toby Rose, eds. *The Immigrant Experience in North American Literature.* Westport, Conn.: Greenwood Press, 1999. Contains a dozen essays, including studies of O. E. Rölvaag and Paule Marshall, Jewish immigrant women's autobiographies and Asian American narratives.

Prchal, Tim, and Tony Trigilio, eds. *Visions and Divisions: American Immigration Literature, 1870-1930.* Piscataway, N.J.: Rutgers University Press, 2008. Anthology of selections from key writers of the Progressive Era, when immigration increased and debates about it likewise rose.

Simone, Roberta, ed. *The Immigrant Experience in American Fiction: An Annotated Bibliography.* Lanham, Md.: Scarecrow Press, 1994. More than six hundred entries describe individual authors, anthologies, and secondary sources for more than forty immigrant groups—from Armenian,

through Irish and Italian and Jewish, to West Indian.

Whitlark, James, and Wendell Aycock, eds. *The Literature of Emigration and Exile.* Lubbock: Texas Tech University Press, 1992. Includes essays on American female immigrants in Canada, Maxine Hong Kingston's *China Men,* and a dozen other topics and writers.

SEE ALSO: Alvarez, Julia; Antin, Mary; Art; Asian American literature; Danticat, Edwidge; *The Jungle*; Lahiri, Jhumpa; Lim, Shirley Geok-lin; Mukherjee, Bharati; *My Ántonia*; Santiago, Esmeralda; Sidhwa, Bapsi; Tocqueville, Alexis de; Yezierska, Anzia.

LITTLE HAVANA

IDENTIFICATION: Cuban enclave within Miami, Florida

SIGNIFICANCE: Little Havana was the focal point for Cuban immigration to the United States following the Cuban Revolution of 1959. The neighborhood still maintains a large Cuban-born population and distinct culture and politics. The residents, in large part, see themselves more as a community in exile than as assimilated Americans.

Miami, Florida's "Little Havana" (*La Pequeña Habana*) has been the cultural and political center not only of Miami's Cuban American immigrant community but also of the Cuban community of the entire United States. The neighborhood has been home to everything from political organizations hatching plots against Fidel Castro's communist regime to Latino music bands, art festivals, and religious parades. Formed after 1960 following the exodus from Cuba of hundreds of thousands of exiles from Castro's revolution of 1959, Little Havana continues to play an important part in the political life of Miami, the state of Florida, U.S. presidential elections, and even the anti-Castro dissident movement in Cuba. Unlike other immigrant communities in the United States, such as New York's Little Italy, it has lost neither its original ethnic composition nor political power over time.

Although officially designated as a "neighborhood" by the U.S. Census of 2000, with the Miami River, Southwest Eleventh Street, Southwest Second Avenue, and Interstate 95 for boundaries, Little Havana is best located and understood by both residents and outsiders by its landmarks and places of historical importance. Calle Ocho (Southwest Eighth Street), which Cuban Americans call *La Saguacera* in the hybrid argot of Spanglish, is the gateway to the neighborhood. A giant mural overlooking the Eighth Street entrance to Little Havana depicts crucial scenes from pre-Castro Cuban history, reinforcing the notion that this is a community in exile, and not, culturally speaking, an integrated part of the United States. Another cultural and political signpost is the Versailles Restaurant, which many residents consider the epicenter of Little Havana. Here, over dishes of chicken, rice, beans, and plantains—Cuban staples—conversations often turn to exile politics. The neighborhood economy rests largely on small shops selling everything from guayaberas—the white linen, short-sleeved shirts traditionally worn by Cuban men—to statues and talismans associated with Santería, the Afro-Cuban syncretic religion of African deities and Roman Catholic saints.

Little Havana has changed little demographically since the first wave of exiles arrived in 1960. More than 90 percent of its population is Latino, with Cubans constituting almost the entire Hispanic bloc. Many residents still occupy the same homes and own the businesses they purchased during the 1960's. The area is more politically conservative than the rest of Cuban Miami, and the population is less willing to engage in any sort of dialogue with the Castro regime.

The graying, and physical demise, of many of the first-generation Cubans and the boom in tourism to the neighborhood, bringing other Latinos and non-Hispanic Americans to spend their money in local enterprises, have the potential to alter the political and cultural features that have made Little Havana distinct. At the beginning of the twenty-first century, the obsession of the locals with anti-Castro politics is slowly giving way to the notion that most residents will never see their homeland again, and tourist dollars have transformed traditional political and religious festivals into street parties rather than evocations of Cuban history. Little Havana seems destined to be incorporated into a new *patria* (homeland), the United States.

Julio César Pino

FURTHER READING
García, Cristina María. *Havana USA: Cuban Exiles and Cuban Americans in South Florida, 1959-1994.* Berkeley: University of California Press, 1996.
Poey, Delia, and Virgil Suárez, eds. *Little Havana Blues: A Cuban-American Anthology.* Houston: Arte Público Press, 1996.
Rieff, David. *The Exile: Cuba in the Heart of Miami.* New York: Simon & Schuster, 1993.

SEE ALSO: Cuban immigrants; Ethnic enclaves; Florida; Freedom Airlift; González case; Haitian immigrants; Latin American immigrants; Latinos and immigrants; Mariel boatlift; Miami; Settlement patterns.

LITTLE ITALIES

DEFINITION: Ethnic enclaves in American cities that have transplanted village communities from Italy

SIGNIFICANCE: Within major urban cities such as New York, Philadelphia, Boston, and Chicago, "Little Italy" communities formed to provide Italian immigrants with a sense of unity and Italian nationalism that they did not have in Italy.

Many of the first Italians who immigrated to the United States landed and then settled in New York City. However, many immigrants also populated Italian enclaves in other cities throughout the United States. Arriving in large numbers between 1880 and 1920, the Italian immigrants tended to rely on *padrones*, or more established immigrants, who helped them adjust to their new environment. However, *padrones* often took advantage of illiterate newcomers by exacting heavy payments for housing and employment services.

CAUSES OF IMMIGRATION
During the 1840's and 1850's, small groups of emigrants from northern Italy sought financial security in the United States. Unlike members of the later migration of southern Italians, members of this earlier group proudly identified themselves as Italians. After Italy itself was finally unified in 1870, these early Italian immigrants gloried in their new-found national identity. Southern Italians, by contrast, left Italy in great numbers after unification. For them, Italy was a nation in name only. Although the Risorgimento strengthened Italy overall, the northern provinces alone experienced its economic and political benefits. To immigrants from the southern regions of Abruzzo, Molise, Campania, Basilicata, Apulia, Calabria, and Sicily, northern Italy was as foreign as America.

For southern Italians who suffered the pangs of starvation, high taxes, and dislocation under Italy's unification government, the possibility of employment and a better place in which to live was worth the journey across the Atlantic. Thanks to cheaper and safer oceanic transatlantic transportation and the promise of riches overseas, more than five million southern Italians immigrated to the United States and countries in South America and North Africa between 1876 and 1930. Plagued with outbreaks of cholera in the Italian countryside that killed more than 55,000 people, many southern Italians left their homeland only to be turned away at the various ports of entry, the most famous being Ellis Island in New York.

THE NORTH
Although Italian immigrants suffered degradation in America from native-born residents who believed that southern Europeans were too ignorant to assimilate, the newcomers compensated for their unfriendly reception by forming their own communities in small enclaves in major American cities. Dubbed "Little Italies" in most cities, these neighborhoods were essentially transplanted Italian villages, or *paesi*.

After arriving in New York Harbor, Italian immigrants moved from the port to Manhattan, and then on to that island's crime-ridden Five Points district. The immigrants soon staked their claims within the enclave. Many earned their livings as organ grinders, street performers, and rag pickers. Despite the fact that the majority of the immigrants had been farmers in their homeland, most accepted work in crowded East Coast American cities to avoid having to travel great distances inland in the unfamiliar land.

Italians who settled in New York City eventually moved beyond Manhattan's Point to other boroughs, such as Queens, the Bronx, and Staten Island. Some went much farther and toiled in the

coal mines in Pennsylvania, Illinois, and West Virginia, while others followed the rails farther west.

Although Italians had settled in Philadelphia even before the American Revolution, they did not immigrate *en masse* to the United States until the 1850's. Within fifty years, 45,000 Italians from Calabria and Sicily were making their homes in Philadelphia. By the first decade of the twentieth century, the southern Italians outnumbered their compatriots from the north. Introducing the pushcart to the local neighborhood, Italians pedaled their merchandise on the streets of the city; they opened restaurants, and made their livings as tailors and construction workers. Nonetheless, they still suffered indignities. Segregated sections were designated for Italians in movie theaters, and the filthy streets of their neighborhoods became breeding grounds of disease.

Following the Great Irish Famine of the late 1840's, Boston, like Philadelphia, became a port of call for immigrants. Italians from Genoa, Campania, and Sicily arriving in Boston settled first in the north end of the city, which they dominated by the time of World War I (1914-1918). Many Sicilians who had been fishermen in their native land took up fishing in Boston. As the city's population increased, the Italian immigrants moved from its North End to the suburbs in Lawrence, Massachusetts. Significantly, New England Italians engaged in fierce rivalry with the Irish, who had already established themselves in Democratic politics. This prompted a number of Italians to gravitate toward the Republican Party, which enticed them with the promise of a full dinner pail and minor recognition—at least until Irish Democrats were willing to share their political opportunities with them.

MIDDLE AMERICA

Following the national Panic of 1873, many southern Italians followed a general migration from

Mulberry Street, the heart of New York City's Little Italy, around 1900. (Library of Congress)

New York City to Chicago to look for work and, as a result, supplanted the Irish and Swedes in Chicago's so-called Little Hell section. Because workers were in such demand, especially during World War I, Italians were a welcome source of cheap labor for employers. Although dreadful conditions in Little Hell predated the Italian migration, native-born Americans began identifying Italians with the area's criminal environment. This caused many Italians to join labor unions and fight for better conditions and wages.

RESULTS

Little Italies provided Italian immigrants with familiar communities within an unfamiliar country. Although some Italians never learned to speak the English language, others acclimated easily to their new surroundings and achieved wealth in America. Because farming land was becoming more scarce, many Italians who immigrated to America had no choice but to settle in the cities. They also migrated to the South and West Coast, earning notoriety and profiting by operating wineries in San Francisco's Little Italy and fisheries in San Diego. Establishing colonies throughout the United States, from Providence, Rhode Island to New Orleans, Louisiana, the Italians made significant contributions to American culture.

Debra A. Mulligan

FURTHER READING

Barkan, Elliott Robert. *From all Points: America's Immigrant West, 1870's-1952.* Bloomington: Indiana University Press, 2007. Excellent source on Little Italies in the West.

Dinnerstein, Leonard, and David M. Reimers. *Ethnic Americans: A History of Immigration.* 4th ed. New York: Columbia University Press, 1999. Textbook that provides an excellent outline on the trends of migration in the United States.

Iorizzo, Luciano J., and Salvatore Mondello. *The Italian Americans.* Boston: Twayne, 1980. Concise narrative of the Italian American experience.

Mangione, Jerre, and Ben Morreale. *La Storia: Five Centuries of the Italian-American Experience.* New York: Harper Perennial, 1992. Informative study of Italian immigration and Italian contributions to American culture and government.

SEE ALSO: Chicago; Criminal immigrants; Ethnic enclaves; *Godfather* trilogy; Italian American press; Italian immigrants; Nativism; New York City; Philadelphia; Rhode Island.

LITTLE TOKYOS

DEFINITION: Japanese ethnic enclaves that developed within existing U.S. cities, especially along the West Coast, during the late nineteenth and early twentieth centuries

SIGNIFICANCE: Urban enclaves provided a source of social and economic stability for Japanese immigrants, despite the fact that the difficulty of finding employment led many toward rural and agricultural pursuits. The cultural conservatism fostered within these enclaves helped deepen the gap between Issei, or first-generation immigrants, and the fast-changing national culture of Japan. It also deepened the gap between Issei and Nisei, the second-generation immigrants.

Little Tokyos, or "Japantowns," arose in cities and towns across the United States for reasons that reflected the natural needs of a new immigrant population. Their greatest concentration occurred along the West Coast. The continued robust existence of these enclaves into the 1930's and early 1940's, however, was partly the result of the sometimes severe racial prejudice and discrimination against Asians, and specifically the Japanese, that prevailed in the United States during the late nineteenth and early to mid-twentieth centuries.

Among the influences leading to the formation of Little Tokyos, the dormitory-style boardinghouses run by early Japanese had particular importance. In Seattle, for example, sixty-five such boardinghouses were in operation by 1905. In addition to providing welcoming living quarters for new arrivals, these houses provided centers of operation for *keiyaku-nin*, the Japanese contractors who acted as agents between immigrant laborers and American railroad, farm, and cannery employers.

Although the enclaves proved important for community reasons, the tendency of many Japanese immigrants to work at agricultural occupa-

Shop in Los Angeles's Little Tokyo that was forced to sell out its entire stock before its proprietor was sent to an internment camp during World War II. (AP/Wide World Photos)

tions encouraged their moving away from urban areas. The Nisei tendency to distance themselves from their Japanese heritage, moreover, worked against the long-term success of the enclaves as active communities. The enclaves' existence remained strong up to the time of World War II, however, due to prejudicial land-ownership policies in California and elsewhere, and also to the difficulty Nisei encountered in obtaining jobs elsewhere, even when possessing college degrees. A large percentage of Nisei ended up working for their parents, temporarily stemming the flow of populace away from the enclaves.

LITTLE TOKYO, LOS ANGELES

The Japanese enclave located a few blocks south of the Los Angeles city hall became the one most strongly associated with the "Little Tokyo" name, although it was also called "J-Town." Founded during the 1890's, it had a resident population of some 30,000 Japanese Americans at its peak.

The equivalent enclave in San Francisco was usually called "Nihonmachi," or "Japantown." In the United States as a whole, forty-three Japantowns came into existence before the United States entered World War II in 1941. That number included small, rural enclaves. The enclaves provided important centers for Japanese-language schools, newspapers, Buddhist temples, Christian churches, and, in a few communities, hospitals.

Enclaves were of importance not only for the mutual economic support but for nurturing a nascent Japanese American culture. The literary magazine *Leaves*, for example, was the work of Los

Angeles Nisei, as was the Sunday literary supplement, in English, of Japanese daily *Kashu Mainichi.* Amateur theater also thrived, with groups including the Little Tokyo Players in Los Angeles.

In contrast to the forward-thinking Nisei, the Issei developed a mode of life within the Japanese enclaves based on their memories of traditional Japanese life that was already becoming outmoded in Japan itself. This conservatism among the Issei led to a growing gap not only between Issei culture and Japanese national culture, but also between Issei and Nisei attitudes toward life in America. By 1930, the Nisei constituted a significant percentage of the Japanese American population, and outnumbered the Issei in California. Given that the Nisei were more inclined to pursue assimilation into American culture, however difficult it was to achieve, this demographic shift further worked against the expansion of Japantowns.

With the forced removal of Japanese Americans from coastal areas in the aftermath of the Japanese attack on Pearl Harbor on December 7, 1941, the continued existence of most U.S. Japantowns was rendered nearly impossible. Promises that personal property of internees would be safeguarded during their internment often proved empty. In Los Angeles, a reported three thousand African Americans moved into housing vacated by Japanese internees in Little Tokyo in July, 1943, tripling their ranks as the war progressed, and leading to the neighborhood's being rechristened "Bronzeville." Although the 1943 Little Tokyo crisis related to ethnic conflict, it involved non-Japanese residents. Peaceful race relations later would mark Japanese and African American interactions, after the incarcerated Japanese began returning.

The wartime propaganda film titled *Little Tokyo, USA,* gave the "Little Tokyo" name nationwide currency, and created an association between the ethnic enclaves and subversive politics. The Hollywood film mixed actual newsreel footage with invented action in portraying Japanese Americans as sources of treachery against the United States, even while using actors of miscellaneous Asian descent to portray Japanese Americans.

Resettlement policies in the wake of World War II led to the intentional geographical dispersal of large numbers of Japanese Americans, upon their release from prison camps. This dispersal accelerated the integration of the Nisei into larger American society and acted as a further element in the diminution of importance of the Japantowns in Japanese American life.

By the early twenty-first century, only three officially designated "Japantowns" still existed. These included Los Angeles's Little Tokyo, which was declared a National Historic Landmark District in 1995; Japantown, San Francisco; and Japantown, San Jose, California.

Mark Rich

FURTHER READING

Daniels, Roger. *Asian America: Chinese and Japanese in the United States Since 1850.* Seattle: University of Washington Press, 1988. Solid overview of the immigration histories of the two Asian immigrant groups.

Hosokawa, Bill. *Nisei: The Quiet Americans.* New York: William Morrow, 1969. Written by an important Japanese American journalist, this book provides a broadly inclusive, fact-filled portrait of an American generation and remains a definitive study.

Lyman, Stanford Morris. *Chinatown and Little Tokyo: Power, Conflict, and Community Among Chinese and Japanese Immigrants in America.* Millwood, N.Y.: Associated Faculty Press, 1986. Illuminating comparison of Chinese and Japanese immigrant populations, documenting their differences of cultural outlook and the impact this had on the assimilation of each group into American society.

Takahashi, Jere. *Nisei/Sansei: Shifting Japanese American Identities and Politics.* Philadelphia: Temple University Press, 1997. Examination of the complicated relationship between first-, second-, and third- (Sansei) generations of Japanese Americans.

Yoo, David K. *Growing Up Nisei: Race, Generation, and Culture Among Japanese Americans of California, 1924-49.* Champaign: University of Illinois Press, 2000. Valuable account that provides a detailed examination of life in Japantowns, with notable focus on the press.

SEE ALSO: Alien land laws; Anti-Japanese movement; Ethnic enclaves; Japanese American press; Japanese immigrants; Los Angeles; Settlement patterns.

LOS ANGELES

IDENTIFICATION: Cosmopolitan Southern California city that is the largest in its state and the second largest in the United States

SIGNIFICANCE: A major world city with a population of 3.8 million people in 2009, Los Angeles has the largest concentration of immigrants of any American city. An estimated 38 percent of its residents were born outside the United States, and they have come from more than 140 different countries, making Los Angeles one of the most ethnically diverse cities in the world.

Founded in 1781 as a Spanish port city, Los Angeles became a Mexican city after Mexico won its independence from Spain in 1821. After the United States defeated Mexico in the Mexican War of 1846-1848, Los Angeles became an American city, but was slow to grow as most of the new state of California's growth was concentrated in the north.

The arrival of the first railroads was the first catalyst to attract significant numbers of people to Los Angeles. During the 1880's, the Santa Fe Railroad made Los Angeles its western terminus, and city officials paid the Southern Pacific Railroad to extend a rail line from San Francisco to Los Angeles. The railroads hired thousands of Chinese immigrants to work on rail lines. By 1880, one-quarter of all workers in California were Chinese men. Passenger fare wars between competing rail companies brought many new residents to the area, including European immigrants from the Midwest.

After a series of federal immigration laws began restricting immigration from Asia, the railroads recruited Mexicans to maintain rail lines in the Southwest and were consequently instrumental in drawing Mexican immigrants to Los Angeles. During the early twentieth century, Los Angeles's Mexican population virtually exploded, growing from 5,000 people in 1900 to more than 150,000 in 1930. However, nearly one-third of these Mexican immigrants were deported from the region during the early years of the Great Depression by U.S. Labor Department officials. Mexicans began returning to the region during the 1940's, after the United States inaugurated a new bracero program to bring Mexican workers into the United States to help during the wartime labor shortage.

As Los Angeles became industrialized during the 1930's, its automobile, airplane, and other industries attracted numerous different immigrant groups. The rapidly expanding factories gave jobs to thousands of non-English-speaking immigrants and were influential in expanding the city's borders.

LATE TWENTIETH CENTURY TRENDS

The city's immigration patterns underwent a major shift after 1960, as the numbers of European immigrants began to decline and non-European immigration began rising rapidly. In 1965, the U.S. Congress passed the Immigration and Nationality Act, which abolished the country-based quota system formerly in place. The new law benefited many nationalities—most notably Asians—who had previously been unable to come to the United States because of the quotas. Before the passage of the 1965 law, Asians accounted for only 7 percent of all immigrants arriving in the United States. By the 1980's, about 44 percent of all immigrants were coming from Asian countries. Many of these new immigrants settled in Los Angeles, which experienced a four-fold growth in Asian population between 1970 and 1990. Immigrants from Vietnam, Cambodia, and Laos arrived in greater numbers after the Vietnam War ended in 1975. They were followed by an influx of Filipinos during the 1980's. By the early twenty-first century, Los Angeles was second only to New York City in the size of its Asian population.

The years following 1970, also saw a large rise in immigration from Mexico and other Latin American countries, and Hispanics became the single largest category of foreign immigrants to Los Angeles. Due in part to the city's nearness to the Mexican border, the Greater Los Angeles region became home to nearly 2 million Mexican immigrants—the single largest concentration of Mexican nationals within the United States.

As Mexicans continued to immigrate in large numbers to Los Angeles and other parts of California, they faced increasing scrutiny from anti-immigration activists. In March, 2006, Los Angeles was the site of the largest immigration rally in the country, as similar rallies took place across the country to protest proposed federal legislation de-

signed to increase penalties for undocumented immigrants.

Bethany E. Pierce

FURTHER READING

Abu-Lughod, Janet L. *New York, Chicago, Los Angeles: America's Global Cities.* Minneapolis: University of Minnesota Press, 1999.

Ochoa, Enrique C., and Gilda L. Ochoa, eds. *Latino Los Angeles: Transformations, Communities, and Activism.* Tucson: University of Arizona Press, 2005.

Rieff, David. *Los Angeles: Capital of the Third World.* New York: Simon & Schuster, 1991.

Sawhney, Deepak Narang, ed. *Unmasking L.A.: Third Worlds and the City.* New York: Palgrave, 2002.

Waldinger, Roger, and Mehdi Bozorgmehr, eds. *Ethnic Los Angeles.* New York: Russell Sage Foundation, 1996.

SEE ALSO: Asian immigrants; *Born in East L.A.*; California; Captive Thai workers; Coalition for Humane Immigrant Rights of Los Angeles; El Rescate; Little Tokyos; Mexican immigrants; Proposition 187.

LOUISIANA

SIGNIFICANCE: One of the most culturally diverse of all American states, Louisiana is well known for its French colonial heritage, which has remained evident in the southern parts of the state, especially in New Orleans. However, immigrants from many other countries have also contributed to the state's rich heritage, and the northern part of the state is noted for its Scotch-Irish heritage.

Located at the mouth of the Mississippi River, which would become a major trade and transportation route into the heartland of the United States, Louisiana originated as a colony of France. In 1699, Pierre le Moyne, Sieur d'Iberville, and his brother, Jean Baptiste, Sieur de Bienville, built Fort Maurepas, near the mouth of the Mississippi River, and brought in Canadian settlers to develop a colony. However, the place proved to be so unhealthy

that it had to be abandoned. In 1717, Bienville began to developed another post at what would eventually become the city of New Orleans.

At first, the French government forced convicts, vagrants, and prostitutes to go to Louisiana, but many of these people were too unhealthy, too unwilling to work, or too unfamiliar with agriculture to make satisfactory colonists. The government then tried offering generous grants, but the French farmers they hoped would go to Louisiana would not emigrate. However, so many German and Swiss peasants were willing to seize this opportunity that an area along the Mississippi River north of New Orleans became known as the German Coast. The name survived, even though the descendants of these immigrants adopted French culture and made French their language.

During the early years of French colonization, Native American tribes often attacked new settlements. Eventually, however, tribal infighting and European diseases reduced their numbers until they were no match for the superior military strength of the invaders. Nevertheless, some communities of the Houma, Koasati (Coushatta), Choctaw, and Apalachee peoples still survived in Louisiana in the early twenty-first century.

After Spain acquired Louisiana in 1762, new land grant policies attracted large numbers of European immigrants to the colony, but few of them were from Spain. Thousands were French-speaking Acadians who had been driven out of Nova Scotia. Some of these people, who became known in Louisiana as Cajuns, have maintained their distinctive language and customs.

U.S. OCCUPATION

The United States purchased the vast Louisiana Territory from France in 1803, and the state of Louisiana entered the union shortly afterward. These developments attracted more Anglo-American settlers. Many immigrants with Scotch-Irish backgrounds became small farmers in the northern part of the state, while those whose ancestries were Scottish and English became merchants and planters in the south. Development of the state's agricultural plantation system began the importation of slaves from Africa and the West Indies. However, since the period of French rule, there had always been free blacks in Louisiana; most of them lived in New Orleans.

During the 1840's and 1850's, many Irish and German immigrants came to Louisiana to work as manual laborers. Later in the nineteenth century, Americans from midwestern states relocated to Cajun Louisiana to raise rice and to work on the railroads; many of them were quickly absorbed into the Cajun way of life. However, the Croatians who established the oyster industry in Plaquemines Parish retained their distinct identity, as did Italians, primarily from Sicily, who would begin immigrating into Louisiana during the early twentieth century.

During the mid-twentieth century, thousands of Honduran immigrants from all levels of society arrived in New Orleans. Some came to acquire convent educations, others to work in casinos and restaurants. During the 1970's, Vietnamese immigrants began settling in the coastal areas, where they worked in the fishing industry, and in New Orleans, where they opened small businesses. Louisiana also became home to immigrants from India, China, and the Philippines. Meanwhile, increasing numbers of Latin Americans were moving into the state. By 2006, almost one-half of all foreign-born residents in Louisiana were Hispanic. About 17 percent of these immigrants had been born in Mexico. One reason for the influx of Mexicans into the state was that after hurricane Katrina, there were good jobs in the construction industry. Since many of these workers were undocumented, it was unclear how many would remain in the state permanently.

Rosemary M. Canfield Reisman

FURTHER READING

Brasseaux, Carl A. *French, Cajun, Creole, Houma: A Primer on Francophone Louisiana.* Baton Rouge: Louisiana State University Press, 2005.

Garvey, Joan B., and Mary Lou Widmer. *Beautiful Crescent: A History of New Orleans.* Rev. ed. New Orleans: Garmer Press, 1997.

Lowe, John, ed. *Louisiana Culture from the Colonial Era to Katrina.* Baton Rouge: Louisiana State University Press, 2008.

PROFILE OF LOUISIANA

Region	Gulf coast
Entered union	1812
Largest cities	New Orleans, Baton Rouge (capital), Shreveport, Metairie, Lafayette
Modern immigrant communities	Mexicans, Hondurans, Vietnamese

Population	Total	Percent of state	Percent of U.S.	U.S. rank
All state residents	4,288,000	100.0	1.43	25
All foreign-born residents	125,000	2.9	0.33	34

Source: U.S. Census Bureau, *Statistical Abstract for 2006.*

Notes: The U.S. population in 2006 was 299,399,000, of whom 37,548,000 (12.5%) were foreign born. Rankings in last column reflect total numbers, not percentages.

Taylor, Joe Gray. *Louisiana: A History.* New York: W. W. Norton, 1984.

SEE ALSO: African Americans and immigrants; Alabama; Disaster recovery work; French immigrants; German immigrants; Honduran immigrants; Irish immigrants; Italian immigrants; Linguistic contributions; Mississippi; Mississippi River; Vietnamese immigrants.

LOYALTY OATHS

DEFINITION: Required expressions of allegiance to a country or government that are often employed to test the loyalty of immigrants

SIGNIFICANCE: Popular during times of war, loyalty oaths and their variants have been imposed upon immigrants as conditions of admission and eventual citizenship, as well as requirements for certain types of public employment.

As formal expressions of allegiance to a given country or government, loyalty oaths have a long history in North America. For example, Puritan settlers required loyalty oaths from community members. After the U.S. Civil War (1861-1865), loyalty oaths were a condition for the reintegration into Ameri-

can political life of former Confederate states during Reconstruction. Modern American political officeholders, such as the president of the United States, take loyalty oaths when they are sworn into office. During the Cold War, many U.S. states tried to suppress communist sympathies by requiring loyalty oaths of public employees, most notably teachers. However, many of these efforts were later deemed unconstitutional by the U.S. Supreme Court. In general, the prevalence of loyalty oaths in the United States has risen during times of war and upheaval, including the Revolutionary War, the Civil War, both world wars, and the Cold War.

Immigrants to the United States have also frequently been targets of loyalty oaths and tests. This is due in part to popular fears of divided country loyalties, combined with the perception, particularly during the early twentieth century, that immigrants were responsible for bringing dangerous political ideologies, such as anarchism and socialism, into the United States. The very first federal Naturalization Act, passed by the U.S. Congress in 1790, included an oath of allegiance as a requirement for citizenship. It was followed eight years later by the Alien and Sedition Acts, which empowered the president of the United States to deport immigrants with unpalatable political views.

It was only after the assassination of President William McKinley by an avowed anarchist in 1901 that Congress added mandatory political screening of arriving immigrants, barring the admission of all those suspected of advocating anarchism or the overthrow of the government of the United States. This requirement was followed nearly two decades later by the World War I-era Espionage and Sedition Acts and the infamous Palmer raids, which included the deportation of thousands of immigrants due to their radical political activities and beliefs.

Loyalty oaths also played an important role during the internment of Japanese Americans during World War II. Military boards required the completion of loyalty examinations by all internees over the age of seventeen. To qualify for release from internment, male intern-

ees had to agree to serve in the U.S. armed forces—women in the Women's Army Corps. All had to renounce all forms of allegiance to the Japanese government and swear to abide by the laws of the United States, even if they had not yet been granted American citizenship.

Since the passage of the Naturalization Act of 1790, loyalty oaths affirming support for the United States and the U.S. Constitution have been a consistent requirement for the granting of citizenship to resident aliens. In 2009, this requirement was still in place, demanding that prospective citizens take a public oath "to support and defend the Constitution and the laws of the United States against all enemies, foreign and domestic," to renounce any foreign allegiances, and to offer military or other service if required.

Sarah Bridger

FURTHER READING

Hyman, Harold. *To Try Men's Souls: Loyalty Tests in American History.* Berkeley: University of California Press, 1958.

Levinson, Sanford. "Constituting Communities Through Words That Bind: Reflections on Loyalty Oaths." *Michigan Law Review* 84, no. 7 (1986): 1440-1470.

Preston, William S. *Aliens and Dissenters: Federal Suppression of Radicals, 1903-1933.* 2d ed. Champaign: University of Illinois Press, 1994.

SEE ALSO: Alien and Sedition Acts of 1798; Citizenship; Deportation; Dual citizenship; Espionage and Sedition Acts of 1917-1918; Immigration Act of

---

U.S. OATH OF CITIZENSHIP

I hereby declare, on oath, that I absolutely and entirely renounce and abjure all allegiance and fidelity to any foreign prince, potentate, state, or sovereignty of whom or which I have heretofore been a subject or citizen; that I will support and defend the Constitution and laws of the United States of America against all enemies, foreign and domestic; that I will bear true faith and allegiance to the same; that I will bear arms on behalf of the United States when required by the law; that I will perform noncombatant service in the Armed Forces of the United States when required by the law; that I will perform work of national importance under civilian direction when required by the law; and that I take this obligation freely without any mental reservation or purpose of evasion; so help me God.

1903; Japanese American internment; Naturalization; Naturalization Act of 1790; Red Scare; Science; World War I; World War II.

LUCE-CELLER BILL OF 1946

DATE: Signed into law on July 3, 1946
THE LAW: Federal law that eased immigration sanctions on Asian Indians and Filipinos
ALSO KNOWN AS: Immigration Act of 1946

> **SIGNIFICANCE:** The Luce-Celler Bill overturned several decades of federal immigration laws that discriminated against specific Asian nationalities by reopening immigration from India and the Philippines and granting the right of naturalization to immigrants from those countries.

Before entering World War II in late 1941, the U.S. government sought to enlist the assistance of a number of countries to join forces against the expansionist German regime that threatened to destroy much of Europe. Filipinos and Asian Indians were enlisted in the cause, but they soon found they were not allowed to immigrate to the United States and become citizens because of legal restrictions imposed on even those who served the United States during the war.

The Luce-Celler Bill permitted Filipinos and Indians who had entered the United States legally to be naturalized as citizens. At the same time, the law imposed a quota of one hundred Indian immigrants per year, effectively activating a provision of a federal law enacted earlier during the twentieth century. When a wave of Indian people began during the late nineteenth century, the United States responded with the Naturalization Act of 1870, which denied Asians the right to gain citizenship. The discrimination that followed the Indian race stemmed from the word "caucasian" and the courts' interpretation of what race was "white enough" to gain citizenship.

The Luce-Celler Bill also permitted the naturalization of Filipinos, who had lost their status as American nationals with the passage of the Tydings-McDuffie Act of 1934, when the Philippines took its first legal step toward independence from the United States. President Harry S. Truman signed the bill into law on July 3, 1946—the day before the Philippines became fully independent.

Karel S. Sovak

FURTHER READING

Daniels, Roger. *Guarding the Golden Door: American Immigration Policy and Immigrants Since 1882.* New York: Hill & Wang, 2004.

Jensen, Joan M. *Passage from India: Asian Indian Immigrants in North America.* New Haven, Conn.: Yale University Press, 1988.

Karnow, Stanley. *In Our Image: America's Empire in the Philippines.* New York: Random House, 1989.

Leonard, Karen Isaksen. *The South Asian Americans.* Westport, Conn.: Greenwood Press, 1997.

Stern, Jennifer. *The Filipino Americans.* New York: Chelsea House, 1989.

SEE ALSO: Asian immigrants; Asian Indian immigrants; Asiatic Barred Zone; Asiatic Exclusion League; Congress, U.S.; Filipino immigrants; Filipino Repatriation Act of 1935; History of immigration after 1891; Immigration Act of 1943; Immigration and Nationality Act of 1965; Immigration law; *United States v. Bhagat Singh Thind.*

M

McCarran Internal Security Act of 1950

The Law: Federal legislation requiring the registration of communist organizations
Also known as: Subversive Activities Control Act
Date: Enacted on September 23, 1950

SIGNIFICANCE: An outgrowth of the anticommunist hysteria during the early Cold War known as McCarthyism, the law prohibited individuals who were or had been members of registered communist organizations from entering the United States. It also allowed for the deportation of communists and other individuals deemed subversive by the federal government.

During the early Cold War period, the United States entered a period of intense fear and persecution of communism. The successful Soviet test of an atomic weapon in 1949, the establishment of a communist government in China that same year, and the outbreak of the Korean War in 1950 contributed to these fears. Wisconsin senator Joseph McCarthy is generally associated as the demagogue most responsible for exacerbating these tensions. Indeed, the anticommunist witch hunt of the early 1950's is known as McCarthyism, but others in the federal government supported a similar agenda.

Pat McCarran, the Democratic senator from Nevada, was one of these supporters, and he sponsored the Internal Security Act of 1950 as a means of combating communism in the United States. The major thrust of the law was to prevent communist sympathizers from obtaining employment in defense industries. In order to accomplish this goal, organizations sympathetic to communist objectives were required to register with the newly created Subversive Activities Control Board (SACB). Past or present members of those organizations were then denied federal employment. The law also denied registered individuals from obtaining passports so that they were unable to leave the country.

McCarran also opposed immigration, and portions of the law directly targeted immigrants. Specifically, it prevented past or present members of communist organizations from entering the United States or from obtaining citizenship. The law had poorly defined standards for what constituted support of communism. As a result, members of foreign labor organizations or citizens of nations with communist governments could be denied entry without actually being practicing communists. Additionally, the law allowed the deportation of communist immigrants already within the United States, and it provided for the creation of detention centers where individuals deemed subversive could be held during times of emergency without trial. In effect, it changed the deportation from a punishment for actual crimes committed into a tool for eliminating political dissent in the immigrant community.

President Harry S. Truman vetoed the security measures as a threat to civil liberties, but the next

Senator Pat McCarran in 1947. (Library of Congress)

day, Congress overrode his veto by a substantial majority. Truman's objections proved prophetic, and cases challenging the act quickly appeared before the U.S. Supreme Court. The first, *Carlson v. Landon* (1952), challenged the right of the government to detain immigrants without bail pending deportation hearings. The court ruled that while the U.S. Constitution protected naturalized citizens, it provided no such protections for resident aliens. The subsequent Immigration and Nationality Act of 1952, which was also sponsored by McCarran, further regulated immigration of communists and individuals deemed subversive by the government. Meanwhile, the Internal Security Act required the registration of communist organizations until the Supreme Court ruled in *Albertson v. Subversive Activities Control Board* (1963) that communists could not be required to register with the government because that violated the Fifth Amendment rights to avoid self-incrimination.

John K. Franklin

FURTHER READING

Oshinsky, David M. *A Conspiracy So Immense: The World of Joe McCarthy.* New York: Oxford University Press, 2005.

Patenaude, Marc. *The McCarran Internal Security Act, 1950-2005.* Saarbrücken, Germany: VDM Verlag, 2008.

SEE ALSO: Deportation; History of immigration after 1891; Immigration and Nationality Act of 1952; Immigration law; Industrial Workers of the World; Korean War; Labor unions; Loyalty oaths.

McCreary Amendment of 1893

THE LAW: Amendment to the Geary Act of 1892 to extend the registration period for Chinese living in the United States by an additional six months

ALSO KNOWN AS: McCreary Act

DATE: Enacted on November 3, 1893

SIGNIFICANCE: The McCreary Amendment made unncessary the wholesale deportation of Chinese persons from the United States and marked a significant change in U.S. immigration policy by requiring for the first time that photographic identification be included on all registration certificates.

The Geary Act passed in 1892 was much harsher than the original Chinese Exclusion Act of 1882. In addition to extending exclusion, the Geary Act required that all Chinese laborers register for certificates of residence that proved their right to remain in the United States. The Chinese community organized extensive opposition to the law. They refused to register and challenged the constitutionality of the Geary Act in the U.S. Supreme Court. To avoid immediate massive Chinese deportation, the Senate passed the McCreary bill, proposed by Representative James B. McCreary, into law on November 3, 1893, extending the required registration time for six more months. The bill stipulated that after that time, a Chinese person could be held without bail pending deportation.

The McCreary Amendment required compliance by Chinese persons who resided in the United States prior to its passage who sought reentry into the United States. It defined laborers to include merchants, laundry owners, miners, and fishers. Although the McCreary Amendment received little historical attention, it significantly changed existing immigration policy by requiring photographs on all identity certificates. This was the first statutory requirement for photographic identification on immigration documentation and remained part of subsequent immigration policy.

Alvin K. Benson

FURTHER READING

Cassel, Susie Lan, ed. *The Chinese in America: A History from Gold Mountain to the New Millennium.* Walnut Creek, Calif.: AltaMira Press, 2002.

Lee, Erika. *At America's Gates: Chinese Immigration During the Exclusion Era, 1882-1943.* Chapel Hill: University of North Carolina Press, 2003.

SEE ALSO: Chinese Exclusion Act of 1882; *Chinese Exclusion Cases*; Chinese immigrants; Geary Act of 1892; Gresham-Yang Treaty of 1894; Taiwanese immigrants.

MACHINE POLITICS

DEFINITION: Nonideological form of local politics dominated by small and typically corrupt elites and based on exchanges of material benefits for political support

SIGNIFICANCE: At its peak during the late nineteenth and early twentieth centuries, machine politics was a response to the needs of the growing urban populations. Operating under a spoils system, many late nineteenth century political machines offered new immigrants jobs and housing in exchange for votes.

The birth of the American political machine can be traced to the waves of immigration to the United States during the late nineteenth century. Following the U.S. Civil War (1861-1865), America saw tremendous expansion in industry and a rapid increase in urbanization. Many immigrants who entered the United States between 1860 and 1890 were poorly educated and unable to speak English. Urban political machines emerged to help alleviate abject poverty, as they could address the needs of the immigrants better than government agencies could. Many immigrants needed jobs and resources faster than traditional means could provide them. Thus, in large cities such as Chicago, New York City, and Kansas City, Missouri, political machines were created to meet these needs.

Machine "bosses," as the leaders of the machines came to be known, provided immigrants help with naturalization, finding jobs, and negotiating rent agreements. Although not often in charge of hiring immigrants directly, bosses persuaded elected officials to give jobs to immigrants or to ensure that government contracts were made with businesses that would employ the faithful immigrants. Machine bosses were seen as beacons of hope for the downtrodden and in many cases took on paternalistic roles. In return for their patronage they expected unwavering loyalty at the voting booth. Although this system has been difficult to enforce during the twenty-first century, it was simple to maintain during the nineteenth century. At that time, privacy in voting booths was limited. Many immigrants arrived at polling places, where they received already marked ballots that they dropped into ballot boxes to be counted—all under the watchful eyes of machine bosses. In many cases, the undemocratic methods of political machines were the only means immigrants had to get jobs. Many immigrants became party leaders within their own neighborhoods and thus helped draw new immigrants into established political machines.

TOM PENDERGAST

A famous example of a machine boos was Tom Pendergast of Kansas City, Missouri. Pendergast's older brother Jim ran a saloon and hotel in Kansas City. As a bartender Jim heard about people's problems and did what he could to help them. Later, when a friend of Jim ran for political office, Jim asked his customers to vote for his friend. The friend won, and shortly thereafter Jim ran for political office himself as an alderman; he also won. Tom Pendergast saw the potential political influence that could be gained from helping needy voters. He found people jobs, gave them food, and persuaded them to vote for his favored candidates. In 1900, the Pendergast machine helped elect Kansas City's mayor, and Pendergast himself was able to oversee the appointments of two hundred workers for a street-paving program. By the early 1920's, Pendergast was spending six hours a day listening to people's needs, and the rest of his time was spent meeting those needs in exchange for votes.

In 1922 and 1926, Pendergast got future U.S. president Harry S. Truman elected to county positions. This relationship with Pendergast would later cause trouble for Truman when he ran for the U.S. Senate and for president. By 1932, Pendergast was able to swing votes for Missouri state and national offices. In return for his assistance in supporting Franklin D. Roosevelt for president, Roosevelt directed five million dollars worth of federal aid to Pendergast through New Deal programs.

The Pendergast machine was practically invincible within Missouri and might have lasted decades longer had not the immigration pattern in Kansas City changed. Most immigrants settling in Kansas City during the 1930's were Italians who resented the Irish leaders and party workers who made up a large percentage of the Pendergast machine. Physical fights ensued, and a once purely political machine began to evolve into a gangster-related mafia. Pendergast himself was later jailed for tax evasion, and his political career came to an abrupt end.

Kathryn A. Cochran

FURTHER READING

Cornwell, Elmer E., Jr. "Bosses, Machines, and Ethnic Groups." *Annals of the American Academy of Political and Social Science* 353, no. 1 (1964): 27-39. Traces the influence of ethnic groups on politics after the decline of the machines during the 1920's.

Gerstle, Gary, and John H. Mollenkopf. *E Pluribus Unum? Contemporary and Historical Perspectives on Immigrant Political Incorporation.* New York: Russell Sage Foundation, 2005. Highlights the struggles of immigrants to assimilate into American political society.

Heidenheimer, Arnold J., and Michael Johnston. *Political Corruption: Concepts and Contexts.* 3d ed. New Brunswick, N.J.: Transaction Publishers, 2002. This compilation explores the historical concept of political corruption via the nineteenth century political machines.

McCullough, David. *Truman.* New York: Simon & Schuster, 1992. Chapters 5 and 6 give a detailed account of how the Pendergast machine selected Harry S. Truman for the U.S. Senate.

Roosevelt, Theodore. "Machine Politics in New York City." *The Century* 33, no 1 (1886): 74-83. Timely look at political machines operating in New York City and a rationalization of why they exist.

Royko, Mike. *Boss: Richard J. Daley of Chicago.* New York: Penguin Books, 1971. Classic work in the field of machine politics, Royko explores the only major political machine to survive in the second half of the twentieth century.

SEE ALSO: Employment; Irish immigrants; New York City; Political parties; Presidential elections; Progressivism; Tammany Hall.

MAIL-ORDER BRIDES

DEFINITION: Women involved in marriages with residents of the United States that are arranged through postal correspondence, Internet connections, and international dating and introduction services

SIGNIFICANCE: Mail-order brides are women who marry their partners after having responded to advertisements for wives or having been selected from their own personals that were posted in newspapers, catalogs, Internet sites, or through marriage broker services. This practice has been used as a legal method of migrating to the United States since the early colonial era.

In the history of the United States, men traditionally immigrated to the new colonies and across the frontiers in far greater numbers than did women. As they settled and began building communities, they wanted marital partners. Single men, who often could not find spouses, needed alternative methods of introduction to women. Finding women who were willing to migrate to remote areas and become spouses to men they hardly knew required effort. Sometimes, men hoped to find a wife through the creation of advertisements or by responding to them. Long-distance location of spouses through advertisements continues to be practiced in America in the early twenty-first century.

EARLY AMERICAN HISTORY

During the American colonial era, in locations where the population of women was low, some colonies brought in women who were eager for a new start in the New World. An early known incidence of this was in 1619, when the Virginia Company of London sent its first ship that carried "mail-order brides" to colonists. Interested men reimbursed the company by paying 120 pounds of tobacco for the women's transportation. During the early eighteenth century, France began shipping women to New Orleans. Later, during the western frontier and California gold rush days, bachelors from the West sought women from the eastern states and other countries to join them. Some men contacted friends and church groups, while others advertised in newspapers.

During the nineteenth century, mail-order catalogs advertising prospective brides as well as marriage brokerage services emerged. Like seeds and clothing, women could be ordered through catalogs; hence, they were dubbed "mail-order brides." While some men who lived in remote areas used these services because of a continued lack of women in the vicinity, others chose mail-order services as a convenient method of selecting particular characteristics in their spouses. At the turn of the twentieth century, for example, Japanese and

other Asian immigrants often resorted to selecting mates from pictures; those chosen "picture brides" then migrated to the United States. These men hoped to marry women from similar cultural backgrounds.

LATE TWENTIETH CENTURY DEVELOPMENTS

By the 1970's, career options were moving more and more American women away from the traditional role of the stay-at-home wife. Many Western men adapted to and supported these changes, while others met traditional wives, but other men chose to seek an alternative option through the use of mail-order bride services. These men were in search of a spouse from a traditional or non-Western background. They purchased advertisement literature that described eligible women, selected their choice from among those depicted, and worked toward obtaining their brides. Most of the bridal candidates who advertised were underprivileged women from developing countries. Poverty and other woes enticed them to seek their fortunes in an entirely new culture.

Throughout the 1980's, the majority of the women who sought fiancé visas, ninety-day entry permits for marriage purposes, were Southeast Asians, particularly women in the Philippines. During the 1990's, deteriorating economic conditions in Russia and Ukraine dramatically increased the interest of Russian and Ukrainian women in becoming mail-order brides. They hoped to enrich their lives, escape socioeconomic depression, and make new starts. By that time, mail-order bride services had replaced most of the print catalogs with similar advertisements that were available via the Internet on the World Wide Web. With this new technology, couples could much more readily exchange pictures and correspondence than in the past.

The mail-order bride practice has a long tradition in the United States. The practice has supporters who believe it is an acceptable custom and opponents who consider the process to be unethical trafficking of women. A high percentage of mail-order brides remain married to their original domestic partners, but some have been trapped in abusive relationships. In an effort to reduce potential problems, President George W. Bush signed the International Marriage Broker Regulation Act in 2006. This law required that candidates for mail-

order brides be at least eighteen years old, be given criminal and marital background check information on the men with whom they wished to correspond, and be provided with legal rights and contact information regarding domestic violence. Mail-order brides make up only a small percentage of the total number of immigrants to the United States, but they remain an important part of the country's history.

Cynthia J. W. Svoboda

FURTHER READING

Belleau, Marie-Claire. "Mail-Order Brides in a Global World." *Albany Law Review* 67, no. 2 (Winter, 2003): 595-608. Discusses the laws in the United States and Canada and makes recommendations for changes.

Constable, Nicole. *Romance on a Global Stage: Pen Pals, Virtual Ethnography, and "Mail Order" Marriages.* Berkeley: University of California Press, 2003. An anthropologist reviews the myths, fairy tales, political economy, and history of mail-order brides.

Enss, Chris. *Hearts West: True Stories of Mail-Order Brides on the Frontier.* Guilford, Conn.: TwoDot, 2005. Relates true accounts of mail-order brides during the nineteenth and early twentieth centuries.

Lindee, Kirsten M. "Love, Honor, or Control: Domestic Violence, Trafficking, and the Question of How to Regulate the Mail-Order Bride Industry." *Columbia Journal of Gender and Law* 16, no. 2 (Summer, 2007): 551-602. Discusses international marriage brokerage rationale for regulation and the International Marriage Broker Regulation Act of 2006.

So, Christine. "Asian Mail-Order Brides, the Threat of Global Capitalism, and the Rescue of the U.S. Nation-State." *Feminist Studies* 32, no. 2 (Summer, 2006): 395-419. Cites several mail-order bride publications and concludes that Asian mail-order brides are perceived as tools for obtaining traditional families.

SEE ALSO: Chinese immigrants; Families; Fiancées Act of 1946; Filipino immigrants; Japanese immigrants; Marriage; "Marriages of convenience"; Picture brides; Russian and Soviet immigrants; War brides; Women immigrants.

MAINE

SIGNIFICANCE: A predominantly white state, most of whose immigrants have come from nearby parts of Canada, Maine has also become the home of small but increasingly significant numbers of African and Asian immigrants, who have become economic and cultural assets.

Most inhabitants of Maine lived on farms at the time Maine became a state during the early nineteenth century. Early immigrants helped produce dairy products and crops such as hay, potatoes, apples, and blueberries. Aroostook County became one of the major potato-producing areas of the United States. Most of the state's early immigrants were French Canadians, many of whom worked in the lumber industry. Newcomers from the Canadian coastal region found opportunities in fishing along the state's extensive Atlantic coast and in another important Maine industry, shipbuilding, especially in Bath. Before 1870, however, these northern immigrants formed a very small part of the total population.

IMMIGRANTS IN THE MILLS

The first large textile mill was built in 1826 in Saco. Lewiston later became the main textile center in the state. Earlier nineteenth century immigrants tended to be Irish but were less numerous than in other New England states, and they tended to leave the mills for other types of work. Between 1870 and 1930, with a peak during the 1880's, French Canadian workers with relatively short routes to travel arrived in railroad stations in southwestern Maine towns such as Biddeford and Lewiston. Many of them planned later to return to Canada, but continuing economic troubles in their former homeland often made them stay in Maine. Some immigrants worked in paper-making, one of the state's largest industries after the early 1880's.

Franco-Americans became steady and reliable workers who expected their children to follow in their footsteps, but they limited the educational opportunities of the next generation. This limitation and linguistic difficulties with English impeded social development of younger immigrants. As late as 1970, 43 percent of Maine's Franco-American residents had only grade-school levels of education or less. During the late twentieth and early twenty-first century, however, cultural centers were established in public colleges at Fort Kent, near the Canadian border, and in Lewiston. Special television programs were also established for Franco-American children.

EARLY TWENTY-FIRST CENTURY DEVELOPMENTS

Fabric mills and the towns that depended on them declined sharply during the late twentieth century. An unusual form of integration has provided new life for Lewiston, a town generally perceived to be dying. Hundreds of African immigrants, particularly from Somalia, began arriving after 2000. Many opened restaurants and small businesses, and some introduced their own versions of textile arts. African immigrants have energized the state's cultural life with their oral poetry, music, and colorful clothing. Some Sudanese and Congolese have followed the Somali initiative. A large increase in the number of people studying English as a second language indicates that they are also accommodating themselves to their new linguistic situation.

PROFILE OF MAINE

Region	New England
Entered union	1820
Largest cities	Portland, Lewiston, Bangor
Modern immigrant communities	Somalis, Cambodians, Chinese

Population	Total	Percent of state	Percent of U.S.	U.S. rank
All state residents	1,322,000	100.0	0.44	40
All foreign-born residents	42,000	3.2	0.11	44

Source: U.S. Census Bureau, *Statistical Abstract for 2006.*
Notes: The U.S. population in 2006 was 299,399,000, of whom 37,548,000 (12.5%) were foreign born. Rankings in last column reflect total numbers, not percentages.

Immigrants from China and Cambodia have injected Asian culture into Maine's largest city, Portland. Although Maine natives have been thought of as distant to outsiders, they seem to have welcomed these African and Asian newcomers.

Robert P. Ellis

FURTHER READING

Brault, Gerard J. *The French-Canadian Heritage in New England.* Hanover, N.H.: University Press of New England, 1986.

Fairfield, Roy P. *Sands, Spindles, and Steeples.* Portland: York Institute, 1956.

Judd, Richard William, et al. *Maine: The Pine Tree State from Prehistory to the Present.* Orono: University of Maine Press, 1995.

Rivard, Paul E. *A New Order of Things: How the Textile Industry Transformed New England.* Hanover, N.H.: University Press of New England, 2002.

SEE ALSO: African immigrants; Asian immigrants; Canadian immigrants; Connecticut; Language issues; Massachusetts; Rhode Island; Vermont.

MALAYSIAN IMMIGRANTS

SIGNIFICANCE: Immigrants from the Southeast Asian nation of Malaysia began entering the United States in significant numbers after Malaysia (called Malaya until 1963) became independent in 1957. Malaysian immigration to the United States has never been large, but Malaysian immigrants have established significant communities in a number of western American cities. Malaysian immigration has tended to rise and fall with economic fluctuations in Southeast Asia.

When the British-ruled Federation of Malaya became independent in 1957, it was beset with political instability because its much larger neighbor Indonesia initially objected to creation as an independent state. Internal strife, combined with the outbreak of armed hostilities between the new government and various groups of Chinese communist guerrillas, prompted many Malayan citizens to emigrate to the United States.

American business interests in Malaysia go back

PROFILE OF MALAYSIAN IMMIGRANTS

Country of origin	Malaysia
Primary languages	Malay, English
Primary regions of U.S. settlement	West Coast states and Hawaii
Earliest significant arrivals	1959
Peak immigration period	1990-2000
Twenty-first century legal residents*	16,757 (2,095 per year)

*Immigrants who obtained legal permanent resident status in the United States.
Source: Department of Homeland Security, *Yearbook of Immigration Statistics, 2008.*

to the era of British rule. Numerous large American corporations have large investments in Malaysia; these include General Electric, Chevron, and Coca-Cola. During the late twentieth century, the United States became Malaysia's primary trading partner, and the two countries have generally had friendly relations.

Since the 1960's, Malaysian immigration to the United States has generally fluctuated with economic ups and downs in Malaysia and Southeast Asia. In fact, economic forces have been the primary factor drawing Malaysians to the United States. Frustrated by limited investment opportunities in Malaysia, many immigrants come to the United States to invest in small businesses. Emigration to the United States became even more appealing after Malaysia's currency was revalued in 2005. Many Malaysians believed they would be better off in the long run by investing their capital in American dollars.

During the last decade of the twentieth century, the number of Malaysians who immigrated to the United States was three times greater than it had been during the previous decade. The global recession of the early twenty-first century prompted even greater levels of immigration as unemployment and inflation rates in Malaysia rose. By 2008, approximately 50,000 Malaysians were living in the United States. Evidence of the growing num-

bers of Malaysians in the United States could be seen in the development of sizable Malaysian enclaves such cities as Los Angeles, San Francisco, and Boston.

Robert D. Mitchell

FURTHER READING

Gould, James W. *The United States and Malaysia.* Cambridge, Mass.: Harvard University Press, 1969.

Lim, Lin Lean. *Impact of Immigration on Labor Markets in Peninsular Malaysia.* Tokyo: Nihon University Population Research Institute, 1986.

Yeoh, Michael, ed. *Twenty-first Century Malaysia: Challenges and Strategies in Attaining Vision, 2020.* London: ASEAN Academic Press, 2002.

SEE ALSO: Asian immigrants; Economic opportunities; Filipino immigrants; History of immigration after 1891; Indonesian immigrants; Lim, Shirley Geok-lin; Thai immigrants; Vietnamese immigrants.

MARIEL BOATLIFT

THE EVENT: Massive influx of Cuban refugees who reached the United States on small boats
DATE: April 1-September 25, 1980
LOCATION: Cuba; Florida; Florida Straits

SIGNIFICANCE: The sudden arrival in South Florida of approximately 125,000 Cuban refugees in the Mariel boatlift may have been the largest single migratory influx in one region in American history. It elicited a reappraisal of U.S. refugee policy and provoked a negative public reaction to Cuban refugees.

During the first decades after Fidel Castro's communist government took power in 1959, emigration from Cuba brought more than 300,000 refugees to the United States. Most of them settled in South Florida. However, while the largest Cuban exodus, between 1965 and 1973, was due mostly to the federal government's Cuban Adjustment Act of 1965, which gave Cuban immigrants special consideration, it was not the most dramatic. The most divisive and disruptive Cuban immigration wave occurred in the Mariel boatlift of 1980.

By the late 1970's, pressures on Cuban opponents to leave their homeland were reaching new levels. In April of 1980, about 10,000 Cubans sought political asylum in the Peruvian embassy in Havana. The Cuban government responded by opening the port of Mariel to allow all who wanted to emigrate to do so. From then until September, approximately 125,000 Cubans sailed for Florida on more than two thousand mostly small boats owned or chartered by Cuban Americans.

The bulk of the people who left Cuba on boats were young male members of the working class. A small number were political prisoners, petty criminals, substance abusers, and people known to have mental disorders. Initially, the refugees were affectionately dubbed "Marielitos." However, the term eventually became a pejorative term associated with depravity, violent behavior, and laziness, and the American media and some politicians characterized the Mariel boatlift refugees as having been made up of "lower-class" deviants and criminals. However, fewer than 2 percent of the refugees were found to have been convicted of felony crimes.

When the Mariel refugees began arriving, South Florida's large Cuban American community rushed to their aid with the full backing of their highly organized private charitable institutions. In Dade County alone, the Cuban Americans raised more than $2 million to assist their compatriots. However, growing concern that this new wave of Cubans would tarnish the image of the established, family-oriented Cuban American community prompted some business and political leaders to withdraw the support.

In June, 1980, President Jimmy Carter ordered all Mariel refugees who had not found relatives or others to sponsor them to be placed in federal detention camps in Wisconsin, Pennsylvania, and Arkansas. In Pennsylvania and Arkansas, the refugees, bored and fearful about their future, rioted. By October, the majority of the Marielitos had been released into various communities, and the detention camps were closed. Meanwhile, the riots created a public backlash against the Mariel refugees. The much-publicized presence of criminals among the refugees also helped generate a feeling of revulsion against the entire group: Marielitos were blamed for the upsurge in violent crime in Miami in 1981. In 1980, a year of economic downturn,

Florida shrimpboat returning from Mariel, Cuba, loaded with Cuban refugees as it lands at the U.S. Navy's Key West naval base in April, 1980. (AP/Wide World Photos)

many people in the United States feared that more Cuban refugees would mean higher unemployment.

In 1985, President Ronald Reagan secured a promise from Castro to take back Marielito criminals. However, after a few hundred had been returned to Cuba, Castro's government became enraged at U.S. sponsorship of the anti-Castro Radio Martí and canceled the agreement. In November, 1987, the United States reached a new agreement with Cuba that provided for deporting to Cuba known Marielito criminals in return for U.S. acceptance of Cuban political prisoners. Some Marielitos held in federal prisons in Louisiana and Georgia rioted and took hostages. The riots ended after the Reagan administration promised that no prisoners would be returned to Cuba without individual reviews of their cases and that those whose offenses were minor would be released into the community. However, hundreds of Marielitos remained in federal prisons several years later.

Despite the difficult reception that many of the Marielitos experienced, many of them went on to achieve economic success in the United States.

Darius V. Echeverría

FURTHER READING

Diaz, Guarione M. *The Cuban American Experience: Issues, Perceptions, and Realities.* St. Louis, Mo.: Reedy Press, 2007.

Engstrom, David W. *Presidential Decision Making Adrift: The Carter Administration and the Mariel Boatlift.* Lanham, Md.: Rowman & Littlefield, 1997.

Larzelere, Alex. *The 1980 Cuban Boatlift: Castro's Ploy, America's Dilemma.* Washington, D.C.: National Defense University Press, 1988.

SEE ALSO: Criminal immigrants; Cuban immigrants; Education; Florida; Freedom Airlift; Haitian boat people; Immigration and Nationality Act of 1965; Miami; Push-pull factors; Stereotyping.

MARRIAGE

DEFINITION: Socially recognized institution whereby two adults are joined in a special kind of social and legal dependence

SIGNIFICANCE: From the earliest years of the United States, marriage has been a central part of American immigration policy and practice. Marrying American citizens or residents has become the easiest and most common way to enter the United States legally—a fact that has attracted additional government scrutiny to so-called marriages of convenience. The rise of same-sex marriage as a social issue has also posed difficult new legal questions about marriage and immigration.

The first major piece of federal legislation on immigration, the Chinese Exclusion Act of 1882, barred most immigration from China to the United States. Chinese born in the United States were still regarded as American citizens. However, Chinese-born workers then already residing in the United States could reenter the United States after leaving the country only with reentry certificates issued by American customs collectors. This early legislation involved marriage because the wives of Chinese-born laborers were prohibited from entering the country, even if the men had valid reentry certificates, and because women were defined by the status of their husbands. This meant that a U.S.-born woman could lose her citizenship by being married to a Chinese man without citizenship.

PREFERENCES FOR SPOUSES BEFORE 1965

Although the Chinese Exclusion Act treated marriage as a basis for exclusion, American immigration policies have historically used marriage as a basis for inclusion. The Emergency Immigration Act of 1921 established a national origins quota by temporarily limiting the annual number of immigrants from any country to 3 percent of the number of persons from that country who had been living in the United States in 1910. The Immigration Act of 1924, also known as the Johnson-Reed Act, made quotas permanent and pushed them back to 2 percent of the number of people from a given country living in the United States in 1890. However, the new immigration law also recognized

preference quota status for spouses of U.S. citizens aged twenty-one and older and for immigrants skilled in agriculture, together with their wives and their dependent children under the age of sixteen, as well as for parents of citizens. Citizens, wives and unmarried children under age eighteen could enter outside the quotas, as could people in several other categories.

The Immigration and Nationality Act of 1952, also known as the McCarran-Walter Act, retained the national origin criterion, but it also strengthened the preference system. The first basis was economic, as immigrants with special skills were given first preference. Other preferences, however, rested on the social norm that family relationships enjoy a special status. Parents of U.S. citizens constituted the second preference, spouses and children of resident aliens the third, and other relatives the fourth.

Spouses, usually wives, were also able to enter the United States through special provisions for the marital partners of members of the U.S. armed forces. An estimated 150,000 to 200,000 European women married U.S. soldiers between 1944 and 1950. During the same period of time, 50,000 to 100,000 Asian women married U.S. servicemen. American immigration laws were very restrictive, and made it especially difficult for Asians to enter the United States, so on December 28, 1945, the U.S. Congress passed the War Brides Act, which waived most of the immigration requirements for women who had married members of the American armed forces serving overseas. Later, marriages with U.S. soldiers brought significant numbers of spouses into the country from Korea, the Philippines, and Vietnam.

PREFERENCES FOR SPOUSES AFTER 1965

Thirteen years after the McCarran-Walter Act, a new amendment to American immigration law pushed preference categories to the forefront and largely removed the national origins restrictions. Under the new system of categories, family reunification became the central principle of American immigration law. Moreover, the unification of spouses became the most important form of family reunification. In addition, spouses of U.S. citizens could be admitted to the United States outside the preference system altogether.

By 1986, the first year for which categories of ad-

mission are available in the U.S. Census Bureau's *Yearbook of Immigration Statistics*, spouses of residents admitted under the preferences and spouses of citizens together accounted for more than 41 percent of all legal immigrants. Even as overall numbers of immigrants grew in the succeeding years, spouses continued to make up more than one-third of all those admitted. Moreover, spouses of U.S. residents made up the largest category of people permitted to enter the country under any preference, and in most years they constituted the majority of family-sponsored immigrants.

American immigration law also has enabled people from other countries to form marriages leading to permanent residence. U.S. citizens may petition U.S. Citizenship and Immigration Services (known as Immigration and Naturalization Services before 2002) for K-1, fiancé visas, so that foreign fiancés can enter the country and apply for a marriage license in one of the states.

Because American immigration law so strongly favors marriage as a reason for inclusion, marriages of convenience—those conducted only in order to obtain permanent legal residence—have become a matter of serious concern. The 1986 Immigration Marriage Fraud Amendments amended the Immigration and Nationality Act of 1952 to impose residency requirements and heightened scrutiny and to provide penalties for marriage fraud.

SAME-SEX MARRIAGE

The rise of same-sex marriage as a social issue at the end of the twentieth century raised questions about whether gay and lesbian U.S. citizens and permanent residents should be eligible for marital immigration benefits for their partners of the same sex. In the case of *Adams v. Howerton* in 1982, an American citizen named Richard Adams argued, in his home state of Colorado, that his partner, Andrew Sullivan, should be classified as his spouse for immigration purposes. However, U.S. law excluded homosexual immigrants until 1990. In denying Adams his bid for marital immigration rights, a federal circuit court cited as evidence that the U.S. Congress did not intend spousal benefits to extend to same-sex couples. With the 1990 end of exclusion on the basis of same-sex involvement, some observers felt that the legal grounds for denying marital immigration benefits to same-sex partners had been removed. Accordingly, advocates

maintained that denying same-sex couples the same immigration opportunities as opposite-sex couples constituted unfair discrimination. Against this, other commentators responded that the opposite-sex couple was the foundation of American social order and that it should receive special recognition and support in national immigration policy.

The recognition of same-sex marriage in some states raised the possibility that debates over marriage and immigration policy could intensify. Historically, what constitutes "marriage" has been defined by individual states, not by the federal government, and states have usually recognized marriages conducted in other states. However, while same-sex marriage has been recognized in a few states, a majority of states passed statutes or constitutional amendments during the 1990's and the early twenty-first century defining marriage as limited to unions between two opposite-sex individuals. Moreover, a federal law known as the Defense of Marriage Act of 1996 specified that no state needed to recognize another state marriage between members of the same sex and that the federal government itself now defined marriage as a union of one man and one woman. This legislation made it unlikely that marital immigration benefits would be extended to same-sex partners, even though U.S. immigration policy no longer blocked entry on the basis of homosexuality.

Carl L. Bankston III

FURTHER READING

Badgett, M. V. Lee. *When Gay People Get Married: What Happens When Societies Legalize Same-Sex Marriage.* New York: New York University Press, 2009. Examination of how same-sex marriage influences societies that includes some consideration of implications for immigration.

Bray, Ilona. *Fiancé and Marriage Visas: A Couple's Guide to U.S. Immigration.* 5th ed. Berkeley, Calif.: Nolo, 2008. Intended as a how-to book, this volume provides a good, easy-to-follow guide to immigration policies on fiancé and marriage visas.

Constable, Nicole. *Romance on a Global Stage: Pen Pals, Virtual Ethnography, and "Mail Order" Marriages.* Berkeley: University of California Press, 2003. Anthropological study of the ways in which American men have searched for wives from other countries, with special attention to the business of mail-order brides.

Cott, Nancy F. *Public Vows: A History of Marriage and the Nation.* Cambridge, Mass.: Harvard University Press, 2002. Comprehensive history of marriage in American law and society.

Shanks, Cheryl. *Immigration and the Politics of American Sovereignty, 1880-1990.* Ann Arbor: University of Michigan Press, 2001. Excellent overview of American immigration policy that includes some discussion of marriage issues.

SEE ALSO: Cable Act of 1922; Families; Gay and lesbian immigrants; *Green Card*; Immigration and Nationality Act of 1965; Intermarriage; Mail-order brides; "Marriages of convenience"; Page Law of 1875; Picture brides; War brides; War Brides Act of 1945; Women immigrants.

"Marriages of convenience"

DEFINITION: Marriages entered into for reasons other than permanent union, such as gaining permanent resident status in the United States

SIGNIFICANCE: Often contracted to evade immigration law, "marriages of convenience" have become an increasingly common method by which immigrants have obtained permanent resident status in the United States. Because marriage is a basic social institution, U.S. immigration policy has been designed to keep married people together. Immigrants traveling to the United States have been encouraged to bring their spouses. Other immigrants, however, have found a route to permanent residence and even citizenship through marriages of convenience.

The concept of "marriages of convenience" has given rise to terms such as "sham marriages," "fraudulent marriages," and "green card marriages." In the context of immigration law, all these terms pertain to essentially the same thing: marriages undertaken for the purpose of circumventing legal requirement for obtaining permanent residency status. It should also be understood that such marriages differ from marriages to so-called mail-order brides. Although women may enter the latter type of marriage for the purpose of immigrating the United States, they do so in the knowledge that their American husbands are seeking permanent marriage partners.

Since the mid-twentieth century, U.S. immigration policy has actively championed marriage and family unification as vital to a stable society. However, marriages are not always undertaken to unite couples who are deeply in love and committed to sharing their lives together. In many societies, families join couples together in arranged marriages, promoting unions between people who may not even know each other in advance, but they do not do this to skirt immigration policies. In contrast, marriages of convenience do exactly that.

One of the easiest ways to become a naturalized American citizen has been to marry a citizen to avoid major immigration difficulties. The immigrant spouses do not need to wait for visa numbers or even need labor certificates. Marriage to an American citizen automatically makes an alien eligible for the legal status of a permanent resident. During the 1980's, the numbers of immigrants who entered the United States after marrying American citizens rose from 87,221 in 1981 to 124,093 in 1985, and 140,000 in 1986. However, the Immigration and Naturalization Service (INS) estimated that 30 percent these immigrants' marriages were fraudulent. In many cases, the American citizens were knowing parties to sham marriages. In others, however, they entered their marriages in good faith only to learn later that they were not the true objects of their immigrant spouses' affection, but instead merely their spouses' means to permanent residency status, one step away from full citizenship.

Arranging sham marriages, which costs an immigrant from two hundred to five thousand dollars, has become a business. In August, 1986, the INS deported the head of a West Coast company that had arranged seventy sham marriages after charging immigrants from three to five thousand dollars for each wedding. Single mothers were particular targets of immigrant seeking "green card marriages."

IMMIGRATION MARRIAGE FRAUD AMENDMENTS OF 1986

Concerned about the increasing numbers of aliens receiving permanent residency status through marriage and convinced that more than one-third

of such marriages were fraudulent, Congress enacted the Immigration Marriage Fraud Amendments (IMFA) on November 10, 1986. This law created a two-year "conditional" permanent residency status for immigrants marrying American citizens. During the ninety days leading up the end of the two-year period, couples were required to submit joint petitions for permanent legal status. So couples could prove their marriages were still valid, INS officials were authorized to make home visits. To verify that couples were living as man and wife, officials interviewed apartment managers, employers, friends, and neighbors. They also interviewed the spouses themselves—separately—asking questions about their weddings, division of household chores, home furnishings and decor, and other matters to see whether the couples were cohabiting. Although instructed not to do, some INS officials have asked intimate questions about the couples' relationships. These interviews have led to a number of law suits about invasion of privacy. When investigators determine that a marriage is fraudulent, they may rescind the immigrant partner's permanent resident status or citizenship, order the immigrant's deportation, or even instigate criminal proceedings against both spouses.

Marriage Fraud in the Media

The magnitude of the sham-marriage problem was so great during the 1980's that television's *Nightline* program broadcast a special on the subject in August, 1985. The program featured an interview with Senator Alan Simpson, the chair of the Senate Subcommittee on Immigration. Sham marriages have also been treated lightly in the media. The 1990 film *Green Card* is a romantic story about an American woman and a French man entering a completely fraudulent marriage for different purposes. The woman needs to be married to lease the apartment of her dreams; the Frenchman needs to marry a citizen so he can gain permanent resident status. The couple's efforts to fool INS officials become the subject of levity. A story line for a 2009 episode of the popular television series *Desperate Housewives* included a scheme for "green card marriage."

Although marriages of convenience may be treated humorously in fiction, the reality has been less than comic. The sham-marriage business has continued to thrive into the twenty-first century, arranging marriages for immigrants for hefty fees and coaching couples on how to respond to official immigration investigations. The news media are filled stories about marriage-fraud rings. Immigrants seeking marriages and the "green cards" come from all over the world. With many aliens willing to pay thousands of dollars for marriages, American citizens in desperate need of money may find sham marriages tempting.

After the terrorist attacks of September 11, 2001, the issue of sham marriages took on another aspect: Fully one-half of thirty-six foreign-born suspected terrorists who were in the United States from the early 1990's to 2004 gained their legal resident status by marrying Americans. Consequently, government agencies began stepping up efforts to uncover sham marriages. In 2008, U.S. Immigration and Customs Enforcement agents rounded up three dozen suspects in Operation Knot So Fast. Government efforts to curtail marriage fraud has continued, but marriage has remained a major route to immigration into the United States.

Marcia B. Dinneen

Further Reading

Chau-Eoan, Howard G. "Tightening the Knot." *Time*, December 15, 1986, 35. Brief discussion of how the Immigration Marriage Fraud Amendments of 1986 were expected to be tougher on marriage fraud.

Farrell, Mary H. J. "For Immigrants Trying to Obtain the Coveted Green Card, Marriage May Be a Treacherous Strategy." *People Weekly*, February 25, 1991, 93-96. Story that includes examples of green card marriages.

Glasser, Jeff. "The Benefits of Marriage." *U.S. News & World Report*, April 2, 2001, 18. Article showing how a new law may actually promote marriage fraud.

Lopez, Elena Maria. "Marriage Fraud." *USA Today*, April 7, 2006, p. 13A. Discusses the ease, through marriage, of getting permanent access to the United States.

Pear, Robert. "In Bureaucracy, Aliens Find Another Unprotected Border." *The New York Times*, October 19, 1986. Statistics show the increase in marriages as a way to enter the United States.

See also: Citizenship; Citizenship and Immigration Services, U.S.; *Green Card*; Green cards; Im-

migration and Naturalization Service, U.S.; Immigration Reform and Control Act of 1986; Intermarriage; Marriage; Permanent resident status.

MARYLAND

SIGNIFICANCE: Between the time of the American Revolution and World War I, more than one million immigrants entered the United States through the port of Baltimore. One reason for this traffic through Baltimore was that the city was the westernmost port on the East Coast, which made it closer to the inland areas where many new immigrants wished to settle. Completion of the National Road to the Ohio River in 1818 and the construction of the Baltimore and Ohio Railroad a decade later also contributed to western movement. However, there were also many opportunities for work in nineteenth century Maryland, particularly in Baltimore.

Small numbers of Germans and Irish migrated to colonial Maryland, and French political refugees came during the 1790's, but the first large-scale immigrant waves that began during the 1830's brought Germans and Irish. By 1860, 32,613 Germans were living in Baltimore, a city whose population was one-quarter foreign born. Germans worked as furniture and piano makers, butchers, brewers, and skilled craftsmen generally. The German Society of Maryland, founded in 1783, provided German newcomers with clothing, fuel, jobs, health care, and even legal assistance. By mid-century the city had German newspapers and German cultural organizations. Jews from southern Germany also found refuge in this community.

The Irish found work building railroads and cities. Baltimore was growing especially fast, with as many as two thousand new buildings being erected every year by mid-century. The Irish also found work as shopkeepers, clerks, and tavern owners. During the 1850's seven Roman Catholic churches had opened in Baltimore; four of them were predominantly Irish. The Irish also opened their own schools. Their devotion to Catholicism led to oppression by the Know-Nothing Party in Maryland, as in many other states in this period.

POST-CIVIL WAR IMMIGRATION

After the Civil War ended in 1865, cooperation between a German shipping line and a Germanic Maryland businessman named Albert Schumacher led to a large increase of Northern European immigrants who entered the United States through Baltimore on their way to western locations. However, many stayed in Baltimore. As the century waned, they were joined by Poles, Czechs, Ukrainians, and Greeks. Many Italian immigrants came to Baltimore from Philadelphia by rail and created a section of the city that became known as Little Italy. Significant numbers of Jews began arriving during the 1880's, fleeing religious persecution in Russia and Poland. Many of them established sweatshops, whose numbers reached two hundred in 1890. The shops also employed Lithuanians and Bohemians.

As in many other eastern states, foreign immigration into Maryland peaked shortly before World War I began in 1914. The war itself and new federal restrictions on immigration enacted during the 1920's severely retarded im-

---

PROFILE OF MARYLAND

Region	Atlantic coast
Entered union	1788
Largest cities	Baltimore, Columbia, Silver Spring
Modern immigrant communities	Mexicans, Chinese

Population	Total	Percent of state	Percent of U.S.	U.S. rank
All state residents	5,616,000	100.0	1.88	19
All foreign-born residents	683,000	12.2	1.82	12

Source: U.S. Census Bureau, *Statistical Abstract for 2006.*
Notes: The U.S. population in 2006 was 299,399,000, of whom 37,548,000 (12.5%) were foreign born. Rankings in last column reflect total numbers, not percentages.

migration into Maryland until after World War II. However, it would not be until the 1980's that foreign immigration again became significant in the state's development.

TWENTY-FIRST CENTURY TRENDS

In the year 2000, 10 percent of Maryland's residents were foreign born. This was the same percentage that the state had had in 1870. However, in 2000, 35 percent of the immigrants were Asians and 34 percent were Latin Americans. The bulk of the latter were Mexicans, who numbered about 40,000. Another change from nineteenth century immigration patterns was that the majority of newcomers settled not in Baltimore but in counties to its south and southwest. Prince George's and Montgomery Counties had the largest portions of foreign-born residents.

During the early years of the twenty-first century, Latin Americans—including Puerto Ricans who were already American citizens—overtook Asians as the largest immigrant group. However, Asians continued to enter the state in large numbers, and they were joined by African immigrants, who accounted for more than one-fifth of all new immigrants.

China has supplied the largest number of Asian immigrants during the twenty-first century, followed by Korea and Vietnam. The Latin American group contains the heaviest concentration of immigrants who do not speak English well. Hispanic immigrants have been especially evident in the construction trades. Asians are most often found in the professional, scientific, and technical areas.

Robert P. Ellis

FURTHER READING

Bode, Carl. *Maryland: A Bicentennial History*. New York: W. W. Norton, 1978.

Miller, Kerby A., et al. *Irish Immigrants in the Land of Canaan: Letters and Memoirs from Colonial and Revolutionary America, 1675-1815*. New York: Oxford University Press, 2003.

Olson, Sherry H. *Baltimore: The Building of an American City*. Baltimore: Johns Hopkins University Press, 1997.

Powell, Barbara M., and Michael A. Powell. *Mid-Maryland History: Conflict, Growth and Change*. Charleston, S.C.: History Press, 2008.

SEE ALSO: Asian immigrants; Chinese immigrants; German immigrants; Irish immigrants; Know-Nothing Party; Maryland; Virginia; Washington, D.C.

MASSACHUSETTS

> **SIGNIFICANCE:** Before New York Harbor's Ellis Island became the major East Coast immigration reception center in 1892, many European immigrants entered the United States through Boston, Massachusetts. Irish immigrants predominated during the middle decades of the nineteenth century, with large numbers of Italians arriving during the decades surrounding the turn of the twentieth century. Later immigration became much more diverse, with large influxes of Jamaicans, Portuguese-speaking peoples, and Chinese entering the state during the late twentieth century.

Populated chiefly by English settlers during its century-and-a-half existence as a British colony, Massachusetts attracted more immigrants from England, British North America, and Ireland during the early decades of the nineteenth century. By the 1840's, famine conditions in Ireland were provoking tens of thousands of Irish people to cross the Atlantic Ocean; most of them entered the United States through New York and Boston. These immigrants were mostly poor and had no means of traveling beyond the American cities in which they first arrived, but most of them had farmed small plots of land and had no experience working in an urban environment. In 1845, nearly one-third of all people living in Boston were either foreign born or children of foreign-born immigrants; many of these were from English backgrounds. By 1850, a large Irish influx had helped raise this figure to 45.7 percent in 1850. By 1855, more than one-half the people in Boston were immigrants and their children. Through most of that period, Irish immigrants outnumbered all other ethnic groups combined.

LATER IMMIGRANTS

Irish Americans gradually moved out of Boston into rural Massachusetts as men found work as

farmhands and day laborers, but others became smiths, hostlers, stablers, carpenters, and waiters. Because these newcomers trusted and understood one another, many of them found work serving their neighbors as butchers, grocers, and tailors. One field of endeavor particularly open to Irish women was domestic help. In contrast to many other immigrants, Irish immigrants arrived in the United States already speaking English, and many young single women were satisfied to work for little more than their board and lodging.

The Irish who remained in poor and overcrowded conditions in Massachusetts cities increased disease and crime. Within the predominantly Protestant state, the immigrants' Roman Catholic religion was viewed with suspicion. In 1834, an Ursuline convent in Charlestown was attacked by a Protestant mob and burned to the ground. During the 1850's, a nativist movement known as the Know-Nothing Party raised fears that the devotion of Catholics to the pope would challenge American democracy. This movement was short-lived, but the fear of Catholics that it engendered persisted until 1960, when John F. Kennedy, of the Irish Catholic descent, ran for the presidency.

Catholic immigrants in Massachusetts generally maintained their religious affiliations, but Protestant immigrants often did not. Swedish immigrants, for example, were mostly Lutherans when they arrived, but when they could not easily find Lutheran congregations, they were inclined to turn to more convenient churches of other Protestant denominations. Other features of immigrants' culture reshaped and became part of the mainstream, but immigrants also shed features of culture that did not fit into the pattern of life in Massachusetts. Immigrants generally adopted mainstream clothing, food, music, and games, even when these differed considerably from those of their homelands.

The growth of large fabric mills throughout the nineteenth century brought many French Canadians into Massachusetts. Their form of Roman Catholicism was less unpopular in Massachusetts than that of the Irish, but their French-speaking children exerted a strain on an educational system with little experience of absorbing non-English-speaking children.

EARLY TWENTIETH CENTURY DEVELOPMENTS

During the years immediately preceding and following 1900, new waves of immigrants began entering Massachusetts: Jews from Russia, and non-English-speaking newcomers from southern and eastern Europe. The largest number came from Italy, and most of these came from southern Italy. Italians tended to live in ethnic enclaves in big cities, such as Boston's North End. They did not readily mix with established communities—either native-born residents or other immigrants. The Italians' darker skins set them apart from the Irish and German immigrants whom Massachusetts natives had already encountered.

Many first-generation Italian immigrant men worked at pick-and-shovel jobs in various locations. The women generally did not work outside their homes but often did piecework and sewing at home to supplement their husbands' incomes. Children were sent out to work as soon as they were old enough to take jobs. Some were taken out of school so they could go to work as early as possible.

Many immigrant workers determined that the Industrial Workers of the World (IWW)

PROFILE OF MASSACHUSETTS

Region	New England
Entered union	1788
Largest cities	Boston, Worcester, Springfield, Lowell, Cambridge
Modern immigrant communities	Mexicans, Brazilians, Portuguese, Chinese

Population	Total	Percent of state	Percent of U.S.	U.S. rank
All state residents	6,437,000	100.0	2.15	13
All foreign-born residents	908,000	14.1	2.41	8

Source: U.S. Census Bureau, *Statistical Abstract for 2006*.
Notes: The U.S. population in 2006 was 299,399,000, of whom 37,548,000 (12.5%) were foreign born. Rankings in last column reflect total numbers, not percentages.

French Canadian immigrants working at a Winchendon, Massachusetts, mill in 1911. (Library of Congress)

served their needs better than the American Federation of Labor. After the mostly unskilled immigrant workers received a pay cut in mills along the Merrimack River in Lawrence, the IWW organized a general strike on their behalf. The strike lasted two months during the winter of 1912 and led to violence and prosecution of workers. Before it ended, hundreds of Russian, Italian, and French Canadian laborers went back to their homelands.

Prospective immigrants, many of whom were family members and relatives of those who had come earlier, found new federal laws blocking them during the 1920's, particularly the Immigration Act of 1924, which reduced the number of admissible immigrants to 2 percent of the population from any country already living in the United States in 1890. This law virtually excluded new immigrants from southern and eastern European countries. The law also included an act specifically

banning Asian populations entirely. Thus immigration for the next few decades consisted mainly of northern and western Europeans.

LATE TWENTIETH CENTURY DEVELOPMENTS

In 1965, the U.S. Congress replaced the 1924 immigration law with one that based immigration standards not on race or nationality but on skills. This allowed many more southern and eastern Europeans to enter the country, as well as educated Asians who would make important contributions to the nation.

After 1965, immigration from the Caribbean increased, particularly from the English-speaking island nation of Jamaica. Many Jamaican professionals and skilled workers settled in Massachusetts. By the year 2000, most of the state's immigrants were coming from the Caribbean, Portugal, and Canada. A Northeastern University study covering

1999-2001 found that 47 percent of Massachusetts's immigrants possessed some post-secondary education, and 25 percent engaged in professional services. Among all skilled and semiskilled blue-collar workers in Massachusetts. 45 percent were foreign born.

A Census Bureau community survey in 2006 established Brazil, China, and Portugal (including Portuguese islands) as the top sources of Massachusetts immigration. Early during the twenty-first century only Florida attracted more Brazilians than Massachusetts. Brazilian immigrants found many jobs in food services, but a large portion of them were in professional services.

Robert P. Ellis

FURTHER READING

Handlin, Oscar. *Boston's Immigrants.* Cambridge, Mass.: Belknap Press, 1969. Study of Boston's immigrants up to the time of the Civil War by one of the leading scholars of American immigration history.

Puleo, Stephen. *The Boston Italians.* Boston: Beacon Press, 2007. Well-researched book on the history of one ethnic group settling in one large city.

Rivard, Paul E. *A New Order of Things: How the Textile Industry Transformed New England.* Hanover: University Press of New England, 2002. Detailed study of immigrant textile workers in Massachusetts by a former official of the American Textile History Museum in Lowell.

Solomon, Barbara Miller. *Ancestors and Immigrants: A Changing New England Tradition.* Cambridge, Mass.: Harvard University Press, 1956. Exploration of the development of restrictions on New England immigration between the 1850's and 1920's.

Ueda, Reed, and Conrad Edick Wright, eds. *Faces of Community: Immigrant Massachusetts, 1860-2000.* Boston: Massachusetts Historical Society, 2003. Collection of essays demonstrating how several immigrant groups adapted to their Massachusetts environment during the later nineteenth century.

Watson, Bruce. *Bread and Roses: Mills, Migrants, and the Struggle for the American Dream.* New York: Viking Press, 2005. Detailed look at the situation that confronted immigrant textile workers in Lowell during the early twentieth century.

SEE ALSO: Anti-Catholicism; Boston; Brazilian immigrants; Connecticut; German immigrants; Industrial Workers of the World; Mexican immigrants; Pilgrim and Puritan immigrants; Religions of immigrants; Women immigrants.

MELTING POT THEORY

DEFINITION: Idea that immigrants to the United States would be fused into one culture

SIGNIFICANCE: An idealistic view of cultural assimilation that was forced upon groups of immigrants during the early twentieth century, the melting pot theory was later discredited as more realistic perspectives concerning immigration prevailed.

The concept of the "melting pot" originated in the English Jewish dramatist Israel Zangwill's play *The Melting-Pot*, which was first performed in Washington, D.C., in 1908. Zangwill's play advanced the idea that a special social and cultural integration of immigrants occurred in America. In its reprocessing of William Shakespeare's sixteenth century play *Romeo and Juliet,* Zangwill's play depicts a pair of lovers from feuding Russian families who emigrate to the United States, where they find themselves and their families in a "crucible," in which all old antagonisms fall away and they become "refined" in their new American identity.

ASSIMILATION PRESSURES

Inspired by the notion that different cultural groups would be combined and blended to form a new composition, like metals being melded at great heat to become stronger alloys, the melting pot theory was enormously popular. Accordingly, the United States had been transformed repeatedly by earlier waves of immigrants, who, as loyal, patriotic Americans, contributed to America's progress. To facilitate this end, immigration laws were passed during the 1920's that restricted the immigration of members of ethnic groups that were more difficult to assimilate—those who would not "melt" together with Americans of western and northern European heritages.

American expectations of immigrants included a commitment to all things American. There was

little tolerance of "hyphenated Americanism," such as "German-Americans." Immigrants were expected to learn to speak English and to divorce themselves completely from the countries of their birth. This "melting" into an American identity was embraced by many European immigrants, who, fleeing from poverty and prejudice, proclaimed intense loyalty to America in World War I and renounced their own ethnic identities.

The federal Immigration Act of 1924 severely restricted the immigration of Asians, southern and eastern Europeans, and Jews, ensuring that future immigration would come mostly from northern and western Europe. Consequently, the American identity resulting from the melting pot through the first half of the twentieth century retained an essentially white face. After World War II, however, federal immigration policy became less restrictive, allowing new ethnic variations.

Attitudes concerning assimilation had also modified, with more people supporting the idea of cultural pluralism that was first advanced by Horace Kallen and Randolph Bourne in 1915-1916. Cultural pluralism, in which smaller ethnic groups band together within a larger nation, allows members of the smaller groups to take pride in their own ethnic identities while remaining loyal to the host nation. Later, other assimilation theories appeared that included the "salad bowl" theory, suggesting the lettuce is the host country and the other ingredients represented various ethnic groups being assimilated into the dominant group.

AFTER 1965

Following the federal Civil Rights Act of 1964, which legally ended discrimination against members of racial minorities in public accommodations and other areas, and the expanded Immigration and Nationality Act of 1965, Americans held more tolerant attitudes toward other ethnicities and also had more negative views of the melting pot idea. Indeed, many prominent Americans began to denounce the "Americanization" of immigrants, and others, such as Nathan Glazer and Daniel P. Moynihan, made a major contribution to the national perspective

with their bestselling book *Beyond the Melting Pot* (1963), which argues that the melting pot had "never really happened." To support this argument, the book cites the ethnic enclaves in New York.

The 1965 immigration reform act that abolished the immigrant quotas and aimed at family reunification, allowed drastic increases in the number of immigrants and an extreme shift in the countries of their origin. During the late 1960's and 1970's, immigrants began coming in huge numbers from Latin America, the Philippines, and Asia—regions whose immigrants in the past had

Poster issued by the federal government during World War II reminding Americans of the positive contributions made to the nation by immigrants, while drawing upon the concept of the "melting pot." (NARA)

been restricted from entering the United States. However, assimilation has continued to occur in some form, although less it is less forced than it was during the early twentieth century, despite the resistance of some immigrants to being absorbed.

Among the factors that influence the rate of assimilation of immigrants are the education levels and resources that the immigrants bring with them. Not all who come to America are impoverished, uneducated, or persecuted. While the formal schooling of many Latin American immigrants is limited to an average of six or seven years, many immigrants from Asia, particularly those from India, have doctoral and medical degrees that permit them to move quickly into scientific and entrepreneurial positions. Korean immigrants have ranked high in ownership of independent businesses.

Multiculturalism, a controversial idea based on the idea that all cultures are of equal worth, has not been totally embraced in the United States. This has been particularly true since the terrorist attacks on the United States of September 11, 2001, that were made by Muslim extremists. Also, the American public has become increasingly concerned about the massive influx of Spanish-speaking Latin American and the impact they are having on American society. In fact, during the early twenty-first century, the issue of immigration was again becoming a contentious one, with several writers denouncing multiculturalism as a barrier to a return to the melting pot idea with its insistence upon the continuity of American beliefs and values.

Mary G. Hurd

FURTHER READING

Jacoby, Tamar, ed. *Reinventing the Melting Pot: The New Immigrants and What It Means to Be an American.* New York: Perseus Books Group, 2004. Collection of essays reflecting diverse attitudes toward assimilation.

Namias, June. *First Generation: In the Words of Twentieth-Century American Immigrants.* Rev. ed. Champaign: University of Illinois Press, 1992. In their own words, American immigrants recount the issues that compelled them to come to America.

Sanabria, Robert. *Stewing in the Melting Pot: The Memoir of a Real American.* Sterling, Va.: Capital Books, 2002. Relates the author's childhood

experience of being forced to assimilate in a Methodist-operated orphanage for Latino children in Los Angeles during the Great Depression.

Sue, Derald Wing, and David Sue. *Counseling the Culturally Diverse: Theory and Practice.* Hoboken, N.J.: John Wiley & Sons, 2002. Controversial study that aims to raise awareness of discriminatory and racist behavior in the United States as the basis of counseling individuals from diverse cultures.

Susser, Ida, and Thomas C. Patterson, eds. *Cultural Diversity in the United States: A Critical Reader.* Hoboken, N.J.: Wiley Blackwell, 2001. Collection of essays that explore cultural diversity through examining complex connections between race, ethnicity, class, and gender.

SEE ALSO: Assimilation theories; Cultural pluralism; Ethnic enclaves; European immigrants; Hansen effect; Identificational assimilation; Immigration and Nationality Act of 1965; Multiculturalism; *A Nation of Immigrants.*

MEXICAN AMERICAN LEGAL DEFENSE AND EDUCATIONAL FUND

IDENTIFICATION: National nonprofit whose mission is to protect the civil rights of Latinos in the United States

DATE: Founded in 1968

SIGNIFICANCE: The Mexican American Legal Defense and Educational Fund advocates for the nearly 45 million Latinos living in the United States, providing legal assistance, educational support, and employment assistance. It is the leading Latino civil rights organization in the United States.

The Mexican American Legal Defense and Educational Fund (MALDEF) was founded in 1968 by Pete Tijerina, a civil rights attorney working with the League of United Latin American Citizens (LULAC). Impressed with the work of the Legal Defense Fund, a project of the National Association for the Advancement of Colored People

(NAACP), he concluded that Mexican Americans needed a similar source of organization and funding to protect their civil rights. With a five-year, $2.2 million grant from the Ford Foundation, Tijerina and a board of directors established MALDEF, with headquarters in San Antonio, Texas, and offices in Arizona, California, Colorado, and New Mexico. The grant was to support the legal defense of Mexican Americans' civil rights, with $250,000 set aside for scholarships to Chicano law students. MALDEF also received a pledge of support and guidance from the more experienced Legal Defense Fund. By 2009, MALDEF had additional offices in Chicago, Atlanta, and Washington, D.C.

According to its mission statement, MALDEF works to ensure "that there are no obstacles preventing [Latinos] from realizing [their] dreams" and "to secure the rights of Latinos, primarily in the areas of employment, education, immigrants' rights, political access, and public resource equity." To accomplish its goals, MALDEF operates several targeted programs. Its Employment and Equal Opportunity Program helps Latino workers obtain fair wages and benefits by educating workers about their rights and by litigating against illegal discrimination. The Parent School Partnership and Community Education and Leadership Development programs help people understand and advocate for their rights. The Public Resource Equity Program works to ensure that Latino communities receive their fair share of public funding and other public resources; to support child-care programs, domestic violence shelters, health clinics, and other programs; and to see that there are enough bilingual staff members at appropriate agencies to assist Latinos in understanding their rights and responsibilities.

MALDEF's legal division has won several important cases, helping to protect the rights of Latinos on issues of language and access to medical care and housing. It successfully fought to overturn California's Proposition 187 (1994), which was designed to bar illegal immigrants from public education, health care, and social services. MALDEF also fought against the expansion of authority of the U.S. Border Patrol and against illegal voter redistricting in Los Angeles that would have weakened Latino political power. It has convened meetings and litigated cases regarding the rights of guest workers and has filed suits to clarify and limit the authority of the Immigration and Naturalization

Service (later U.S. Citizenship and Immigration Services) to conduct searches. In addition to legal work, MALDEF has sponsored radio spots in Spanish to help new immigrants navigate their new environment.

Cynthia A. Bily

FURTHER READING

Acosta, Teresa Palomo, and Ruthe Winegarten. *Las Tejanas: Three Hundred Years of History*. Austin: University of Texas Press, 2003.

Chavez, Linda. *Out of the Barrio: Toward a New Politics of Hispanic Assimilation*. New York: Basic Books, 1991.

Storey, John W., and Mary L. Kelley. *Twentieth-Century Texas: A Social and Cultural History*. Denton: University of North Texas Press, 2008.

SEE ALSO: Border Patrol, U.S.; Chicano movement; Civil Rights movement; Guest-worker programs; Immigrant aid organizations; Immigration and Naturalization Service, U.S.; Latinos and immigrants; Mexican immigrants; Proposition 187; Sociedad Progresista Mexicana.

MEXICAN DEPORTATIONS OF 1931

THE EVENT: Mass deportations of Mexican immigrant workers in order to redistribute jobs to U.S. citizens during the Great Depression

DATE: January-September, 1931

LOCATION: Primarily Los Angeles County, California

SIGNIFICANCE: The deportations highlighted white Americans' anti-immigrant sentiments and encouraged resentment on behalf of both Mexican nationals and Mexican Americans.

After the Great Depression struck in 1929, rapidly rising unemployment provoked white Americans to perceive Mexican nationals and even Mexican Americans as the main source of competition for jobs. Anti-immigrant, and particularly anti-Mexican, sentiment was on the rise, as white Americans

deemed themselves more worthy of relief aid and jobs than "foreigners" in the country.

In order to quell white Americans' anxiety and desperation during the Great Depression, Secretary of Labor William N. Doak, under the administration of President Herbert Hoover, enacted various policies to repatriate at least 100,000 deportable Mexicans of the 400,000 undocumented Mexican immigrants in the United States. The purpose of repatriation was to send idle Mexican workers back to their homeland, save social welfare agencies money, and produce jobs for white Americans. The first nine months of 1931 saw the greatest numbers of Mexicans leaving the United States at once, especially from the Los Angeles area. Authorities such as Charles P. Visel, director of the Los Angeles Citizens' Committee on Coordination of Unemployment Relief, took actions to create a hostile environment for Mexican immigrants to "encourage" their repatriation. Consequently, both ordered and "voluntary" repatriations ensued, as some Mexican nationals sought refuge from increased unemployment and discrimination in the United States, while others were forced to leave.

THE DEPORTATIONS

The mass exodus may have affected as many as two million people of Mexican ancestry, half of whom had been born in the United States. Authorities ignored the fact that some of the repatriated people were naturalized U.S. citizens and that others were citizens by virtue of birth in the United States. Merely having a Spanish surname could subject a person to screening. Deportation raids of public and private spaces occurred all over the country, as Mexicans were not isolated to specific regions, working in both industrial sectors as well as migrant farmworker communities.

The federal government allowed cities, counties, and states to manage repatriation as deemed necessary. Nativism and xenophobia during this period caused inhumane treatment of Mexicans in the United States, as people were repatriated ruthlessly via various modes of transportation, including ships, trains, cars, trucks, and buses. Parents were torn from their children, and husbands and wives were separated. Hospital patients, mentally ill people, and elderly people were also repatriated. Altogether, Mexican families and even those with American citizens as their members were torn apart.

Nonetheless, some American groups were opposed to these repatriations, especially the ranchers and agricultural growers in the Southwest who needed Mexicans as a source of cheap and exploitable labor. Mexicans, these growers claimed, did the work that other Americans were unwilling to do. The repatriation policy threatened the businesses of these growers, as they could lose crops. Merchants too realized that Mexicans were integral to their businesses. During the repatriations, merchants lost profits from their loyal Mexican customers. Moreover, bankers were concerned as Mexicans withdrew their money as they anticipated repatriation. Despite such opposition, repatriates continued to be pushed southward.

Sara A. Ramírez

FURTHER READING

Acuña, Rodolfo F. *Occupied America: A History of Chicanos.* 6th ed. New York: Pearson Longman, 2007.

Balderrama, Francisco, and Raymond Rodríguez. *Decade of Betrayal: Mexican Repatriation in the 1930's.* Rev. ed. Albuquerque: University of New Mexico Press, 2006.

Vargas, Zaragosa. *Labor Rights Are Civil Rights: Mexican American Workers in Twentieth-Century America.* Princeton, N.J.: Princeton University Press, 2005.

SEE ALSO: Border Patrol, U.S.; Bracero program; Chicano movement; Contract labor system; Deportation; El Paso incident; Great Depression; Guestworker programs; Los Angeles; Mexican immigrants; Operation Wetback; Xenophobia.

MEXICAN IMMIGRANTS

SIGNIFICANCE: Mexican immigrants represent the largest minority ethnic group in the United States and differ from other immigrant groups in the nearness of their home country, which makes movement back and forth easier and makes their culture more visible within American society.

Mexico was originally inhabited by Native American peoples who originated in Asia many millennia before the first European explorers and settlers

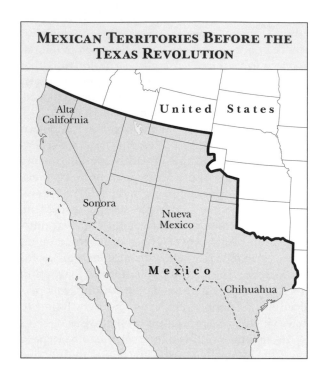

MEXICAN TERRITORIES BEFORE THE TEXAS REVOLUTION

Alta California

United States

Sonora

Nueva Mexico

Mexico

Chihuahua

arrived in the Western Hemisphere. The Native American peoples developed advanced cultures that gave rise to civilizations such as those of the Aztecs and Mayas in what are now Mexico and Central America that were responsible for impressive achievements in technology and mathematics. These civilizations were eventually conquered by Spain during the early sixteenth century. The Spanish introduced their language and the Roman Catholic religion to the original inhabitants of Mexico. Over time, the newcomers mixed with the Native peoples and created the mestizo, or mixed-race, peoples who would become known as modern Mexicans.

Spanish Mexico, or New Spain, extended well into the southwestern parts of what is now the United States, and those regions became part of Mexico when that country won its independence in 1821. However, American settlers wrested Texas from Mexico during the 1830's, and the American victory in the Mexican War of 1846-1848 cost Mexico California, Arizona, New Mexico, and parts of what would become other U.S. states. In one stroke, the Treaty of Guadalupe Hidalgo that settled the war transformed about 85,000 Mexican citizens into the largest minority ethnic group in U.S. territory.

PUSH-PULL FACTORS

Beginning in 1910 with the building of the railroad across the Sonoran Desert, the first wave of Mexican migration was ushered in with the flow of Mexicans "pushed" by the lack of jobs in Mexico under the president-dictator Porfirio Díaz. Moreover, with the large-scale irrigation project of the Colorado Desert in California, agriculture became a lucrative business in the Southwest. Many Mexicans were enticed to the area for jobs in agribusiness, where fruit and vegetable pickers were required in the San Joaquin Valley of California, the Lower Rio Grande Valley of Texas, and the Salt River Valley of Arizona. In addition, similar agribusinesses created jobs for picking sugar beets in Minnesota, Colorado, and Michigan. Besides the sugar beet, Michigan's car industry drew Mexican workers toward the assembly lines of Detroit, where in 1914 Henry Ford paid a daily wage of five dollars.

Another factor pushing Mexicans to go north was the Mexican Revolution that began in 1910 and kept Mexico in a state of virtual civil war into the late 1920's and devastated the country. In the face of violent upheavals, unemployment, and hunger, as many as 2 million Mexicans may have immigrated to the United States by the late 1920's. During the year 1923 alone, an average of 1,000 people crossed the border every day.

WORLD WAR I

In August, 1914, World War I began in Europe, pitting Germany against Great Britain and France and other nations. The United States remained neutral, but in early 1917, an incident involving Mexico occurred that helped to draw the United States into the war. Germany's foreign secretary, Arthur Zimmerman, sent a telegram to Mexico's President Venustiano Carranza in which he offered Germany's pledge to restore to Mexico the U.S. states of Texas, New Mexico, and Arizona in return for Mexico's cooperation with Germany in the event that the United States entered the war. The telegram was intercepted by the British, who passed it along to the U.S. government. The government had the contents of the telegram published in newspapers across the United States. In addition to helping President Woodrow Wilson take the United States into the war, the telegram helped launch a new era of American distrust of Mexicans.

Later that same year, the U.S. Congress passed the Immigration Act of 1917, which imposed an eight-dollar head tax on each immigrant—a hefty impost on Mexican immigrants. The new law also added a literacy test, which made it even more difficult for many Mexicans to enter the United States legally. However, although American suspicions of Mexicans were high, the U.S. entry into World War I created a worker shortage in the United States that forced American employers to look to Mexico for labor. After relaxing the literacy requirement and the head tax, the U.S. Department of Labor set up a system with the agribusiness companies, in which each company could apply for the number of Mexican laborers it required, thereby creating a government-controlled guest-worker program. This arrangement differed from later bracero programs in that it did not guarantee worker protections or wage increases. To ensure that Mexican workers returned to Mexico, the Labor Department held part of their pay until they were back in Mexico.

REPATRIATION

The 1920's saw the first major wave of Mexican immigration, but after the stock market crash of 1929 started the Great Depression, those numbers began reversing. Mexicans became the scapegoats for job losses in the United States, and impover-ished American farmers in the Midwest, which was devastated by dust bowl conditions, began migrating west in search of seasonal agricultural work that had previously been done mostly by immigrants. By 1934, more than half of California's crop pickers were white American migrant workers.

Meanwhile, additional resentment fell on American citizens of Mexican descent who were receiving federal benefits in New Deal programs during the Depression, and Mexican Americans were blamed for using taxpayer money. The federal government came under pressure to send Mexicans back to Mexico. Deportation required time-consuming legal proceedings, so the government engaged in tactics designed to intimidate Mexicans into leaving the country voluntarily. However, in 1931, the government began instituting legal proceedings to deport Mexicans who were found to have violated the conditions of their visas.

In February, 1931, agents of the U.S. Department of Labor began staging public raids across California's Los Angeles County, using local police to help identify Mexicans. Persons who could not produce documentation of their American citizenship or valid passports were bused to the Mexican border. In their haste to round up suspected Mexican nationals, government agents sent some American citizens and persons of Asian ancestry to Mexico.

The mass deportations had the desired effect of creating the fear of expulsion in the minds of Mexican immigrants, many of whom began accepting offers of free passage to Mexico. Eventually, Los Angeles set up county-sponsored trains that provided free transportation to all the Mexicans who wished to leave the country voluntarily. Many of those sent to Mexico were later unable to prove their American citizenship, which they consequently lost.

BRACERO PROGRAM

After the United States entered World War II at the end of 1941, Mexican workers were again persuaded to migrate north to fill jobs left by American workers who had entered the armed forces or gone to work in the expanding defense industry. Since 1917, the Mexican government had tried, with little success, to ensure that Mexicans working in the United States would receive better treatment. By 1942, however, the U.S. government was

---

PROFILE OF MEXICAN IMMIGRANTS

Country of origin	Mexico
Primary language	Spanish
Primary regions of U.S. settlement	California, Texas, southwestern states
Earliest significant arrivals	Pre-1776
Peak immigration periods	1923-1930, 1992-1996
Twenty-first century legal residents*	1,389,201 (173,650 per year)

*Immigrants who obtained legal permanent resident status in the United States.

Source: Department of Homeland Security, Yearbook of Immigration Statistics, 2008.

Mexican immigrants passing through the border station at El Paso, Texas, in 1938. (Library of Congress)

finally ready to pay attention to the Mexican demands. In July, 1942, the U.S. and Mexican governments signed an accord in Mexico City to create the bracero program, in which the U.S. government would take responsibility for overseeing and protecting Mexicans working in the United States under the program. Between 1942 and 1947, more than 200,000 bracero workers were employed across the United States; more than half of them worked in California's agricultural fields.

Criticisms of the bracero program soon emerged. Most of the conditions for workers that Mexico had set were not met. Substandard housing of the workers was a particular problem, but this was remedied in 1943 when new housing units were built by the federal government. Another criticism was the failure of wage rates to increase along with those in areas where braceros were not working, such as Texas. Another criticism of the program was that it encouraged illegal immigration by workers who did not return to Mexico when they completed their contracts. When the program was finally ended by the U.S. government in 1964, Mexico was left with the problem of having large numbers of workers who needed employment.

OPERATION WETBACK

During the early 1950's, the U.S. Immigration and Naturalization Service (INS) was urged by President Dwight D. Eisenhower to begin deporting illegal immigrants. In June, 1953, the INS began a series of surprise raids in the program dubbed "Operation Wetback." The program continued into the following year and was publicized. In contrast to the mass repatriations of the early 1930's, the INS made sure that the people sent back to Mexico were released at points five hundred to one thousand miles south of the border to discourage them

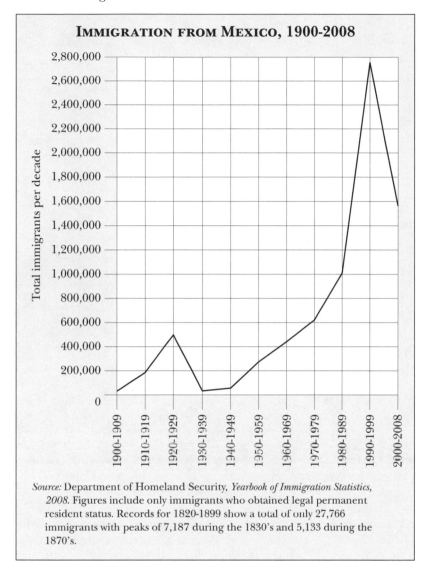

IMMIGRATION FROM MEXICO, 1900-2008

Source: Department of Homeland Security, *Yearbook of Immigration Statistics, 2008.* Figures include only immigrants who obtained legal permanent resident status. Records for 1820-1899 show a total of only 27,766 immigrants with peaks of 7,187 during the 1830's and 5,133 during the 1870's.

groups, Mexicans are often stereotyped as scofflaws and miscreants. At ports of entry along the border, Mexicans were historically forced to undergo humiliating body searches. Moreover, Mexican border posts were the only ports of entry into the United States that forced new arrivals to undergo delousing. During the swine flu outbreak in 2009, fears of Mexicans bringing the disease over the border were common throughout the United States, with many Americans renewing calls for the erection of a border wall.

Shannon Oxley

FURTHER READING

Andreas, Peter. *Border Games: Policing the U.S.-Mexico Divide.* Ithaca, N.Y.: Cornell University Press, 2001. Scholarly study of issues surrounding the policing of the U.S.-Mexican border.

Gutierrez, David G. *Walls and Mirrors: Mexican Americans, Mexican Immigrants, and the Politics of Ethnicity.* Berkeley: University of California Press, 1995. Discusses the issue of race in Mexican and Mexican American identities.

Hoffman, Abraham. *Unwanted Mexican Americans in the Great Depression: Repatriation Pressures, 1929-1939.* Tucson: University of Arizona Press, 1974. Comprehensive study of the massive repatriation of Mexicans during the Great Depression, with detailed data from each state that was involved

Jones, Maldwyn A. *American Immigration.* 2d ed. Chicago: University of Chicago Press, 1992. Objective historical summary of immigration in the United States, providing general information about Mexican immigration.

Meier, Matt S., and Feliciano Ribera. *Mexican Americans/American Mexicans: From Conquistadors to*

from returning to the United States. Once again, many of the people who were deported were American citizens, and again families were torn apart by the deportations. At least 300,000 people were returned to Mexico, and as many as 1 million more were stopped from entering the United States at the border.

ANTI-MEXICAN SENTIMENTS

Stereotypes about "wetbacks"—a derogatory term for illegal Mexican immigrants—stealing American jobs are perpetuated in political circles, and they increase in frequency during economic recessions. Like members of other immigrant

Chicanos. 2d ed. Toronto: HarperCollins Canada, 1993. Thorough summary of Mexican immigration, from the earliest Spanish conquests to the modern Chicano movement. Includes concise accounts of the Depression-era repatriation and the bracero program.

Moquin, Wayne, and Charles Van Doren, eds. *A Documentary History of the Mexican Americans.* New York: Praeger Publishers, 1971. Detailed history of Mexican ties to the United States, with full histories of Mexicans in New Mexico, California, and Texas.

Rodriguez, Gregory. *Mongrels, Bastards, Orphans, and Vagabonds: Mexican Immigration and the Future of Race in America.* New York: Pantheon Books, 2007. Broad overview of immigration law and Mexican identity in United States history.

Telles, Edward, and Vilma Ortiz. *Generations of Exclusion: Mexican Americans, Assimilation and Race.* New York: Russell Sage Foundation, 2008. Good investigation of four decades of the Mexican American experience.

SEE ALSO: Border fence; Bracero program; Chicano movement; Farm and migrant workers; Latin American immigrants; Latinos and immigrants; Mexican American Legal Defense and Educational Fund; Mexican deportations of 1931; Mexican Revolution; Operation Wetback; Sociedad Progresista Mexicana; Spanish-language press.

MEXICAN REVOLUTION

THE EVENT: Political and military struggle that overthrew Mexico's dictator and prompted a mass migration to the United States
DATE: 1910 to 1928
LOCATION: Mexico

SIGNIFICANCE: Aimed against the ruling classes, the violent Mexican Revolution overthrew a dictatorship that had lasted thirty-four years and ushered in more than a decade of political and social disorder that impelled many Mexicans to seek sanctuary in the United States.

Mexico experienced a violent revolution from 1910 to 1928. Initially, rebels sought to overthrow the dictator Porfirio Díaz, who had been in power since 1876. The disparity between rich and poor was significant in the country, with 75 percent of the population living off agriculture but owning only 5 percent of the land. Díaz had essentially placed control of the country in the hands of the landed class, foreign companies, and the Roman Catholic Church, which was allowed to control its extensive landholdings. The revolution erupted in 1910 under the leadership of an idealistic banker named Francisco I. Madero, whose supporters included the famous peasant warriors Emiliano Zapata and Pancho Villa. Those surrounding Díaz were primarily white elitist Mexicans who rejected the contributions of the 80 percent majority of the population who were Indians or mixed-blood mestizos. The goal of the revolution was to implement land reform, expel dominant foreign companies, and limit the power of the Church. Díaz was quickly defeated, but Madero's assassination in 1913 was followed by a violent struggle among the remaining leaders.

During a decade and a half of almost constant civil war—resulting in the death of more than 250,000 Mexicans, the burning of farms and factories, and the destruction of villages and cities—Mexico's economic stability was shattered. Both revolutionaries and those of the former ruling classes were left in disarray. As a result, a wave of immigrants began to cross into the United States. In 1909, fewer than 5,000 Mexicans had immigrated to the United States. However, after the revolution began during the following year, that figure jumped to nearly 90,000 immigrants per year. The revolution caused a state of constant turmoil in Mexico, especially among the landless peasants, but from 1914, when the fiercest period of fighting began, even the upper classes began to immigrate in significant numbers. By 1920, more than 900,000 Mexicans had fled north.

U.S. REACTION

During this same period, the U.S. Congress was concerned with the mass of immigrants coming into the United States from southern and eastern Europe. As a result, Congress passed the Immigration Act of 1917, which required immigrants over the age of sixteen to be literate in English or in their own languages. American agricultural interests successfully lobbied the government to ex-

empt Mexican immigrants from the law's provisions; thus, the flow of Mexicans to serve as agricultural laborers and railroad workers continued unimpeded. Because the Immigration Act of 1921 did not set quotas for immigrants from Latin America, thousands of Mexicans entered the United States on permanent visas annually, with 1924 being the peak year, when 100,000 Mexican immigrants arrived.

In 1917, Mexico's revolutionary government enacted a new constitution that gave to the state control of all land distribution and outlawed foreign ownership of land. It also severely limited the rights of the Roman Catholic Church. It nationalized all Church lands, prohibited the Church from any role in education, and limited the power of the clergy, requiring priests to register with the state. Under revolutionary president Plutarco Elías Calles (1924-1928), the new constitution was harshly implemented, resulting in a revolt of the clergy and their followers in a second stage of the revolution that became known as the Cristero War (1926-1929). This conflict continued the large emigrant flow into the United States, with many immigrants considering themselves to be religious refugees.

The eighteen years of the Mexican Revolution resulted in the first major wave of Mexican immigrants into the United States, totaling nearly two million. These immigrants found life in the United States somewhat natural, as the Southwest, where most of them eventually settled, had for two hundred years been part of Spain or Mexico.

Raymond J. Gonzales

FURTHER READING

Gonzales, Michael J. *The Mexican Revolution, 1910-1940.* Albuquerque: University of New Mexico Press, 2002.

Meyer, Jean A. *The Cristero Rebellion: The Mexican People Between Church and State, 1926-1929.* New York: Cambridge University Press, 1976.

Womack, John. *Zapata and the Mexican Revolution.* New York: Alfred A. Knopf, 1968.

SEE ALSO: Bracero program; Chicago; History of immigration after 1891; Illinois; Immigration Act of 1921; Latin American immigrants; Latinos and immigrants; Mexican immigrants.

MIAMI

IDENTIFICATION: Largest city in South Florida and a major transportation and immigration hub

SIGNIFICANCE: Miami is the major hub of Latin American and Caribbean immigration to the United States, and the immigrant communities have both transformed the city and turned it into a nexus between the United States and its southern neighbors. The city is a hybrid of American and Latino cultures, with many immigrants maintaining close economic and political ties to their native lands.

Miami is the third-largest immigrant city in the United States, after New York and Los Angeles, but differs significantly from those two metropolises in that the immigrant population is still largely concentrated into enclaves, with the Cuban contingent outnumbering the others by a significant margin. Cuban immigration after Fidel Castro's revolution of 1959 transformed the city's economy, society, and politics. Cuban migration to the United States usually involved three generations of parents, children, and at least one elderly relative. The typical Cuban immigrant to Miami was born in a large urban center. Havana alone was home to more than half of those who arrived between 1959 and 1963. One-third of the heads of households who arrived in the United States between 1960 and 1962 had been proprietors or managers back in Cuba, while others came from the ranks of lawyers, doctors, judges, and skilled or semiskilled workers. More than 96 percent were Hispanic whites.

The 1970 U.S. Census estimated that of the one million Cubans who had migrated to the United States since 1959, more than 80 percent had settled in Miami. The exiles of this generation mainly settled in the Riverside neighborhood that came to be known as Little Havana. The biggest consignment came to Miami during the first three years of the Castro regime, and next during the so-called freedom flights of 1965-1973. A huge wave of immigration, estimated at 200,000, occurred in 1980 with the Mariel boatlift. However, after 1980 Cuban immigration once again slowed down to a trickle, until the rafters' crisis of 1994, when Cubans tried to make their way to Miami by using small, makeshift

boats; eventually, some thirty thousand were granted permanent residence in the United States, mostly in the Miami area.

Cuban American immigration to Miami gave an enormous boost to a city that as late as the 1940's was seen as only a vacation spot. Cuban Americans became architects, bankers, doctors, and teachers, as well as blue-collar workers. By 2006, close to 800,000 Cubans were living in Miami-Dade County, constituting three-quarters of the Cuban American population in the United States. Ties of language, religion, and the experience of exile led many to see themselves not as part of a larger Latino or Hispanic community but rather as Cuban residents of Miami. The average Cuban adult in Miami by the end of the twentieth century earned an annual income greater than his Anglo-American neighbors, and Cuban women were more likely to participate in the labor force than any other Hispanic females. Graduation rates for both high school and college also surpassed those of the rest of the city population. As more Cuban immigrants became naturalized citizens, they flexed their political muscle. Their anti-Castro politics persuaded most Cubans to vote Republican in local, state, and national elections. In 1985, Miami elected its first Cuban American mayor, Xavier Suarez, who delivered on his promise to make the city a nexus of trade between the United States and Latin America in everything from luxury cars to shoes.

LATIN AMERICAN AND CARIBBEAN IMMIGRATION AFTER 1980

Political upheaval in Latin America and the Caribbean after 1980 brought new immigrant groups to Miami in large numbers. Nicaraguans fleeing their country's Sandinista revolution of 1979 arrived by the thousands, but many were forced by the U.S. government to return home following the defeat of the Sandinistas in elections in 1990. However, others stayed on, particularly in the downtown neighborhoods around Flagler Street. Colombians seeking refuge from the thirty-year-old civil war at home also migrated to Miami, taking up many of the blue-collar jobs previously held by Cubans. However, it was Haitian immigration during the 1990's, following the installation and then overthrow of President Jean-Bertrand Aristide, that had the greatest impact on the city's ethnic composition. Concentrated in a northeastern

neighborhood of the city that soon came to be dubbed Little Haiti, Haitian immigrants faced ostracism from both the Hispanic and African American communities—the stigma associated with the spread of AIDS in Haiti was particularly harmful—but some were able to climb into the Miami middle class and even attain elected office.

At the start of the new millennium, Miami still resembled the salad bowl rather than melting pot model of immigration and settlement in the United States. Nevertheless, outright physical friction between immigrant groups was rare, and the city's reputation as the economic capital of the Caribbean continued to draw tens of thousands of migrants per year, making Miami one of the largest Latin American cities in the Western Hemisphere.

Julio César Pino

FURTHER READING

Allman, T. D. *Miami: City of the Future.* New York: Atlantic Monthly Press, 1987. History of the city during the twentieth century that stresses the ability of immigrants to assimilate while maintaining a separate cultural identity.

Didion, Joan. *Miami.* New York: Simon & Schuster, 1987. The famed novelist presents a nonfiction account of Miami as a Third World city located in the United States that holds Cuban immigrants responsible for extremist politics.

Grenier, Guillermo J., and Alex Stepick, eds. *Miami Now! Immigration, Ethnicity and Social Change.* Gainesville: University Press of Florida, 1992. This collection of essays stresses how Latin American immigration has turned Miami into a de facto capital city of Latin America, with frequent racial and political upheaval but also cooperation among groups.

Portes, Alejandro, and Alex Stepick. *City on the Edge: The Transformation of Miami.* Berkeley: University of California Press, 1993. Optimistic look at how the post-1980 wave of Cuban immigrants and later arrivals, including Haitians and Nicaraguans, has forged a more tolerant Miami.

Shell-Weiss, Melanie. *Coming to Miami: A Social History.* Gainesville: University Press of Florida, 2009. History of immigration to Miami since 1880 that emphasizes the struggle of Cubans, Haitians, and other Latin American peoples for citizenship and labor rights.

SEE ALSO: Colombian immigrants; Cuban immigrants; Florida; Freedom Airlift; González case; Haitian immigrants; Latin American immigrants; Little Havana; Mariel boatlift; West Indian immigrants.

MICHIGAN

SIGNIFICANCE: Michigan's closeness to Canada has always made Canada its chief source of foreign immigrants. The harshness of the land and weather on the Upper Peninsula made farming impossible, so that immigrants did not come in large numbers until mining and logging became profitable.

French fur traders and missionaries from Montreal began working in what is now the state of Michigan during the seventeenth century. France later built forts at the Straits of Mackinac in 1671 and at the site of Detroit in 1701. After the American Revolution, several hundred French Canadian farmers settled at Detroit. Political difficulties in Ontario and a financial depression in Canada led to the immigration of more Canadians. By 1870, Canadians constituted the largest out-of-state group in Michigan's "thumb" area between Saginaw Bay and Lake Huron; they were also numerically predominant in the northern half of the Lower Peninsula. German immigrants were also numerous, especially after the failed European revolutions of 1848. However, Yankees, who came from New York and New England via the Erie Canal and the lakes via steamship after 1832, often dominated politics and business.

The Upper Peninsula's economy boomed during the last years of the nineteenth century and the first decades of the twentieth. Iron mining in the western part of the peninsula brought Finns, and logging brought Swedes, Irish, Italians, various eastern Europeans, and more Canadians. Most of the latter were French Canadian lumberjacks. During the early twentieth century, newspapers in the Upper Peninsula were published in Italian, Finnish, Swedish, and other languages. However, the forests and mines were exhausted by 1920, and many immigrants moved elsewhere. The region lost population between 1920 and 1930, from around 333,000 to 319,000.

With the growth of the automotive industry, Detroit's position on the Great Lakes, close to transportation from steel mills, led to a new wave of immigration. By 1930, Poles were the largest group of international immigrants, followed by Italians, Russians, Hungarians, Romanians, and Greeks. They were also joined by African Americans eager to leave the segregated South, and by whites from southern Appalachia.

LATE TWENTIETH CENTURY DEVELOPMENTS

In 1960, Michigan counted almost 400,000 residents who still spoke their ancestral languages at home. Half of them lived in Detroit. There, Polish was the most common foreign language, followed by German, Italian, French, and Hungarian. About 26,000 German speakers lived between Detroit and Saginaw Bay, and 26,000 Dutch speakers remained in the Holland colonies. In the Upper Peninsula remained between seven and nine thousand speakers each of Russian, Swedish, Ukrainian, and Finnish. In southern Michigan, the English that was spoken often re-

PROFILE OF MICHIGAN

Region	Upper Midwest
Entered union	1837
Largest cities	Detroit, Grand Rapids, Warren, Flint, Sterling Heights, Lansing (capital), Ann Arbor
Modern immigrant communities	Canadians

Population	Total	Percent of state	Percent of U.S.	U.S. rank
All state residents	10,096,000	100.0	3.37	8
All foreign-born residents	599,000	5.9	1.59	15

Source: U.S. Census Bureau, *Statistical Abstract for 2006.*
Notes: The U.S. population in 2006 was 299,399,000, of whom 37,548,000 (12.5%) were foreign born. Rankings in last column reflect total numbers, not percentages.

flected Yankee influences, but farther north Canadian accents could be heard.

Michigan's location continued to make the state an attractive target for Canadians even after World War II. As late as 1980, Canada was the largest source of foreign-born residents. In 2000, almost 39,000 Michigan residents—most probably from Canada's Quebec province—reported speaking French at home.

Timothy C. Frazer

FURTHER READING

May, George S. *Michigan: A History of the Wolverine State.* Grand Rapids, Mich.: William B. Eerdmans, 1995.

_____. *Michigan: The Great Lakes State.* Sun Valley, Calif.: American Historical Press, 2005.

Michigan: Collected Works of the Federal Writers' Project. Bel Air, Calif.: Reprint Services Corporation, 1991.

SEE ALSO: Arab immigrants; Canadian immigrants; Dutch immigrants; German immigrants; Labor unions; Linguistic contributions; Muslim immigrants; New York State; Polish immigrants.

"MIDDLEMAN" MINORITIES

DEFINITION: Members of an identifiable ethnic, religious, linguistic, or cultural group that occupies an intermediate economic and social prestige position between the domestic minority and the dominant majority

SIGNIFICANCE: "Middleman" minorities form significant economic bridges between generally poorer classes of consumers and generally wealthier classes of producers. Such minorities are often involved in small-scale retail operations or other entrepreneurial activities to provide goods and services to underserved populations.

The term "middleman minority" first became common among American sociologists during the 1960's. It describes the status and function of minority groups, whether recent immigrants or long-standing residents, who serve the retail and small commercial needs of dominant minority groups, whose members themselves have little access to the economic and social status of the majority group. The term "petty retailers" has historically been applied to middleman minorities in the United States who open small retail stores to provide basic commodities in low-income and predominantly minority neighborhoods that larger retailers and service providers tend to avoid.

DISTRIBUTION AND CHARACTERISTICS

Middleman minorities can be found around the globe. Their ethnic and cultural designations vary among the groups that form the dominant minorities within any given society. Middleman minorities throughout the world exhibit several shared characteristics. For example, members of primarily middleman minorities tend to be self-employed or work for members of their own ethnic groups until they begin their own entrepreneurial activities. Their businesses tend to be small and financed initially by ethnic aid groups. Middleman minorities have limited access to the dominant majority to buy resources, but the access they do have tends to be greater than that of the dominant minority. The middleman minorities resell these goods and services to minority populations with whom they have only transactional relationships. Members of middleman minorities rarely attempt to form social ties with members of the larger minority group in a culture.

Members of middleman minorities share a number of personal characteristics as well. For example, they tend to be hard workers and long-term planners and savers. They also tend to have strong beliefs in the value of education for their children, even when they themselves have had little formal education or opportunity to penetrate the social networks of the majority group in a culture. Education is rarely the success factor for first-generation middleman minorities. Likewise, neither is political activism. Hard work and capital accumulation provide the means for success for these people in their quest to provide educational opportunities for their children.

IMAGE OF MIDDLEMAN MINORITIES

Despite providing essential goods and services to neighborhoods that would otherwise lack them, members of middleman minorities are generally viewed with hostility by members of the minority

and majority groups. They have often been the targets of discrimination and physical violence. As members of minority classes with little access to members of wealthier and more powerful majority groups, members of middleman minorities offer convenient targets on whom others may vent their frustration and feelings of anger for having being taken advantage of economically. Middleman minorities do not themselves produce the commodities they sell, but they profit from selling what others have produced. Their prosperity relative to the minority group is resented by their lower-income customers who do not share in that prosperity.

Members of middleman minorities and their children tend to outperform other minority group members in both capital accumulation and educational levels. Rather than imitate the behavior patterns of middleman minorities, other minority group members often view the entire economic and social system as be deliberately stacked against them. Thus, middleman minority businesses are often the first businesses to suffer damage during instances of urban unrest.

With the United States, members of various different ethnic and cultural group have held the status of middleman minorities. During the nineteenth and early twentieth centuries, for example, Jews of a variety of ethnic backgrounds, as well as a variety of European immigrants, constituted the bulk of middleman minorities. Members of these groups were generally able to assimilate into the economic and social mainstream by the second generation. By contrast, immigrants of Asian ethnic background have retained their middleman minority labels for much longer periods of time. Their assimilation has been slower and more difficult than that of European immigrants because of greater language barriers and physical appearances that have served as marks of differentiation from members of the majority group. Middleman minorities of Asian ethnicity have suffered hostility from other members of their own minority groups, as Asian entrepreneurs have progressed economically, and their children have assimilated socially through education leading to higher job status. While education has not been a primary factor in the success of first-generation middleman minority members, it has traditionally had a strongly positive impact on their children. As these entrepreneurs have enjoyed success, they have generally been able to release their children from having to work in their family businesses so they can concentrate on their educational activities.

One of the most obvious hostile situations for members of middleman minorities in the United States has involved Korean owners of convenience stores in predominantly low-income minority neighborhoods. Resident minorities have tended to resent the success of the Korean middlemen, with whom they have few social connections and whom they tend to regard as exploitative outsiders. Moreover, resident minorities also tend to see favoritism in government programs that assist small business owners. The more the Korean middleman prospers seemingly by taking money from resident minorities, the more powerful and potentially lethal the hostility. Such hostility was especially evident in the April, 1992, Los Angeles rioting that followed the acquittal of the police officers who beat Rodney King. Much of the violent anger felt by African Americans was directed against Korean American entrepreneurs operating within predominantly black communities.

Victoria Erhart

FURTHER READING

Butler, John. *Immigrant and Minority Entrepreneurship: The Continuous Rebirth of American Communities.* Westport, Conn.: Praeger, 2004. Examines how different ethnic minorities behave in their attempts to enter the American economic mainstream.

Kaufman, Eric. *Rethinking Ethnicity: Majority Groups and Dominant Minorities.* New York: Routledge, 2004. Studies patterns of ethnic migration caused by the pressures of globalization as various ethnic groups try to improve their status.

Sowell, Thomas. *Black Rednecks and White Liberals.* New York: Encounter Books, 2005. Sociological study of various middleman minorities around the globe and their psychological characteristics. Pays particular attention to Afro-American cultural history.

_____. *Migrations and Cultures: A World View.* New York: Basic Books, 1997. Study of various ethnic groups within different cultures to see which cultures are better at accumulating human capital based through various behaviors.

SEE ALSO: Asian immigrants; Family businesses; Korean immigrants; Stereotyping.

MIGRANT SUPERORDINATION

DEFINITION: Process through which immigrants use force to overwhelm and subdue the original inhabitants of the territories they settle

SIGNIFICANCE: Migrant superordination occurs principally in countries that are colonized by outsiders, and U.S. history provides a classic example of this process.

The superordinate/subordinate relationships that result from migrant superordination processes can take economic, political, and cultural forms. Such relationships are characterized by the institutionalization of dominant-minority relations in which the migrants enjoy disproportionate power, resources, and prestige. Power relationships are then justified by systems of beliefs that rationalize the superiority of the immigrant groups in relation to the indigenous peoples.

Reactions to migrant superordination on the part of the indigenous peoples may range from physical resistance and rebellion to accommodation and assimilation. Historical examples of migrant superordination include the European conquest of Native Americans in the Western Hemisphere and of Africans in South Africa.

M. Bahati Kuumba

FURTHER READING

Cook, Terrence E. *Separation, Assimilation, or Accommodation: Contrasting Ethnic Minority Policies.* Westport, Conn.: Praeger, 2003.

Zølner, Mette. *Re-imagining the Nation: Debates on Immigrants, Identities and Memories.* New York: Peter Lang, 2000.

SEE ALSO: History of immigration, 1620-1783; History of immigration, 1783-1891; Westward expansion; World migration patterns.

MILITARY CONSCRIPTION

DEFINITION: Actions by the U.S. government to direct immigrants to perform military service

SIGNIFICANCE: Efforts by the federal government at various periods in American history to conscript immigrants who had not yet been granted citizenship were met with mixed reaction among ethnic communities; while some groups resisted the draft in principle or protested against its being unfairly administered, many others welcomed the opportunity to serve and took advantage of provisions in the various draft laws that allowed them to become citizens more quickly.

During the Revolutionary War, the War of 1812, and the Mexican War of 1846-1848, the U.S. government filled the ranks of its fighting forces through voluntary enlistments. That practice was seen to be in keeping with the country's professed belief in respecting individual liberties; the general feeling was that no person should be forced to serve the country, even in times of national distress. However, the outbreak of the U.S. Civil War in 1861 changed the dimensions of military conflict in America, as both the Union and the Confederacy instituted conscription to build up the massive armies required to carry on the war. Moreover, both governments decided that both citizens and resident aliens who had declared their intention of becoming citizens should be eligible for conscription.

Authorities reasoned that those who wished to enjoy the benefits of citizenship—even at a future date—were obligated to defend their adopted homeland in times of crisis. This practice was not common among European nations, however, and many European governments protested, claiming that their own citizens should not have to fight for another country until they became full-fledged citizens of that country. The requirement for mandatory military service was also not well received by many recently arrived immigrants, many of whom had come to America to escape similar practices in their native countries.

CIVIL WAR PROTESTS

The Confederacy was the first of the Civil War combatants to establish a draft. Its 1862 law pro-

vided for many exemptions, however, and most aliens were able to avoid conscription even though the South relied heavily on conscripts to fill the ranks of its army. When the Union passed its first draft law one year later, in 1863, protests were mounted throughout the North almost immediately. New immigrants were especially suspicious of plans for conscription; many were certain that the poor would be drafted in greater numbers, and because most new immigrants were poor, that would mean they had a much greater chance of being inducted into the armed forces involuntarily. Their fears were fueled by two provisions in the Union law that favored those with greater financial means: Men who were drafted could either pay three-hundred-dollar bounties to the government to avoid service or hire substitutes to take their places.

Although protests were organized in several cities—the first one in Buffalo, New York, and later riots in Wisconsin—by far the most violent demonstration against the draft occurred in New York City in July, 1863, just days after officials began drawing names for conscription. The majority of the protesters were Irish immigrants, who suddenly discovered that their willingness to get involved in the political process by signing up to vote in local elections—usually as Democrats—was being used against them by Republican lawmakers responsible for draft legislation. Registering to vote was considered a sign of one's intent to remain permanently in America, and those who had registered were automatically considered eligible for the draft.

Thousands of immigrants volunteered to join the Union's Irish Brigade that was formed in New York, but many other Irish feared that if the North won the war, slaves freed from plantations in the South would migrate north and compete for jobs then being done by Irishmen. That concern, coupled with the perception that the Irish and other immigrant groups would be overrepresented among draftees, sparked a violent outburst against city and state officials. Over a five-day period, mobs roamed the streets of New York City, looting business establishments and burning buildings, including the mayor's home and several police stations. Damage to property was later estimated at one million dollars. The protesters' anger quickly focused on African Americans living in the city; shootings and lynchings claimed more than a hundred lives. Lo-

cal police units proved incapable of quelling the violence. In fact, the city's police commissioner himself suffered serious injury in an assault. The governor of New York was forced to call back militia units that had been serving with the Union forces at the Battle of Gettysburg to put down the riots.

A retrospective look at the practice of conscription during the Civil War reveals two great ironies. First, records indicate that the percentage of resident aliens who were drafted during the conflict was no greater than that of citizens. Second, many of the substitutes hired by draftees were immigrants, who evidently found the payments a way to put aside some savings that would help secure their futures, should they make it through the war.

WORLD WAR I

The first federal government draft was allowed to expire at the end of hostilities in 1865 and was not reinstated until 1917, when the United States entered World War I. After the United States entered war in April, 1917, the administration of President Woodrow Wilson determined that conscription would be necessary for the nation to assemble an expeditionary force to assist its European allies. This time, officials were careful to craft a draft law that corrected some of the inequities of the laws passed during the Civil War. Most resident aliens found the Selective Service Act of 1917 much more palatable than earlier mandates for service. The new law offered no provisions for hiring substitutes or paying bounties to avoid service. Additionally, local draft boards were established to examine each potential inductee, determine his fitness for service, and consider granting an exemption. Generally, exemptions were granted on the basis of occupation or health. When resident aliens asked for exemptions by citing their citizenship in other countries, they were told that accepting exemptions would make them ineligible for future U.S. citizenship. In general, most immigrants felt that the process was fair.

Nevertheless, as had occurred during the Civil War, pockets of resistance sprang up in various ethnic communities. Some activists attempted to convince immigrant groups, particularly Italians and Jews, to resist conscription because the war was being waged merely to further international or national business interests at the expense of the work-

ing poor. The Irish were especially skeptical because the United States was entering the conflict on the side of Great Britain, whose government was at that time resisting the movement for Irish independence.

A ploy used to turn European immigrants against conscription was the claim that the draft displayed a dangerous tendency toward "Prussianization"—a reference to the militaristic German regime that many Americans blamed for having started the war. In general, however, immigrants drafted during World War I reported for duty without demur. Moreover, many did not wait to be called but instead chose to enlist. They often did this in units organized locally along ethnic lines, allowing young men to serve alongside others with whom they shared a common heritage. At the same time, however, draftees were typically assigned to units in which men of various ethnic and socioeconomic classes served side by side; this practice actually proved beneficial to many immigrants, because it provided them experiences that allowed them to assimilate more quickly into the general population.

WORLD WAR II

The Selective Service Act of 1940 was virtually identical to that of 1917, but perhaps because America's enemies in World War II were perceived as particularly threatening, virtually no protests were raised to drafting noncitizens. Any hesitancy about the draft that existed among immigrant groups during World War I virtually evaporated by the time the United States reinstituted conscription on the eve of its entrance into the new world war in late 1941. Immigrants of virtually every nationality perceived the Axis powers of Japan, Germany, and Italy as threats to liberty for both their adopted country and their native homelands.

Xenophobic feelings that had caused some German Americans to suffer discrimination during World War I were virtually absent. Although many Japanese Americans were interned throughout the war—ostensibly to prevent espionage—thousands of their young served honorably in the U.S. armed forces, including many who were drafted. As had happened twenty-five years earlier, the experience of serving with a variety of individuals of different backgrounds from other parts of the country allowed immigrants who had been drafted to assimi-

late more rapidly into the mainstream of American society. One immigrant group that benefited notably from this opportunity for assimilation was Mexican Americans.

POST-WORLD WAR CONSCRIPTION

Although the Selective Service Act of 1940 expired in 1947, a new act was passed a year later, and immigrants once again found themselves subject to conscription as the United States built up its armed forces as a defensive measure against the threat of communism. Because the new law continued the provision that resident aliens were eligible to be drafted, immigrants were called up for service in the Korean War between 1950 and 1953 as well.

During the 1950's and 1960's, the newest wave of immigrants from Europe, many from Germany and Eastern European countries, found themselves subject to the draft. Some chose to enlist in the National Guard or military reserves to guarantee they would be able to fulfill the bulk of their six-year military obligation near family members who may have come to America with them. Resident aliens were also subject to conscription during the Vietnam War. Most served willingly, and those who protested their induction usually did so because they had scruples about the war itself, not because they felt they were being discriminated against because they were not yet citizens.

CONSCRIPTION AND CITIZENSHIP

Although federal penalties for resisting the draft have often been harsh, many immigrants found that being conscripted into the military has provided significant benefits as well. Since the American Revolution, aliens who agreed to take up arms for the United States have been allowed to accelerate their journey toward becoming American citizens. Routinely, immigrants applying for citizenship could point to their honorable service as sufficient proof of good moral character, one of the requirements for naturalization.

After World War I, aliens who served in the military, including those drafted during peacetime, were granted waivers of several years on the time required for residence in the United States before being eligible to apply for citizenship. This practice was continued even after the United States did away with the draft during the 1970's. In fact, after

2001, several proposals were put forward in Congress to provide a mechanism for granting citizenship to immigrants—including those who entered the country illegally—who chose to enlist in the armed forces.

Laurence W. Mazzeno

FURTHER READING

Anbinder, Tyler. "Which Poor Man's Fight? Immigrants and the Federal Conscription of 1863." *Civil War History* 52, no. 4 (December, 2006): 344-372. Carefully researched essay demonstrating that, despite concerns that they would be singled out for conscription, immigrants were not selected in disproportionate numbers for military service during the Civil War.

Anderson, Martin, ed. *The Military Draft: Selected Readings on Conscription.* Stanford, Calif.: Hoover Institution Press, 1982. Comprehensive analysis of the history of American drafts. Includes essays on conscription law and on the political theory justifying conscription of resident aliens.

Bergquist, James M. *Daily Life in Immigrant America 1820-1870.* Westport, Conn.: Greenwood Press, 2008. Describes living conditions for immigrants, many of whose lives were disrupted by the Civil War. Comments briefly on the 1863 draft by the Union and the rioting that followed.

Bernstein, Iver. *The New York City Draft Riots: Their Significance for American Society and Politics in the Age of the Civil War.* New York: Oxford University Press, 1990. Describes social and political conditions that prompted segments of the urban poor to mount violent protests against the 1863 draft law.

Flynn, George Q. *The Draft, 1940-1973.* Lawrence: University Press of Kansas, 1993. Examines the impact of the draft on the armed forces and American society from the establishment of a draft prior to World War II through the Vietnam War.

Hay, Jeff, ed. *Military Draft.* Farmington Hills, Mich.: Greenhaven Press, 2008. Collection of essays describing the history of the draft and the government's operations to enforce conscription laws during several periods of armed conflict and in peacetime.

Jacobs, James B., and Leslie Anne Hayes. "Aliens in the U.S. Armed Forces: A Historico-Legal Analysis." *Armed Forces and Society* 7, no. 2 (Winter, 1981): 187-208. Detailed examination of the federal government's recruitment and conscription of noncitizens from the time of the Civil War to the establishment of modern all-volunteer army.

Moore, Albert B. *Conscription and Conflict in the Confederacy.* New York: Hillary House, 1963. Examines the impact of conscription in the Confederate States of America and outlines options open to immigrants who had not yet become citizens.

Sterba, Christopher. *Good Americans: Italian and Jewish Immigrants During the First World War.* New York: Oxford University Press, 2003. Assesses the responses of two ethnic communities to American involvement in the war, including their willingness to serve in the armed forces.

SEE ALSO: Citizenship; Civil War, U.S.; Irish immigrants; Korean War; New York City; Prisoners of war in the United States; Vietnam War; World War I; World War II.

MINNESOTA

SIGNIFICANCE: Growing populations, land shortages, and rigid political and social systems prompted many northern Europeans to immigrate to Minnesota during the nineteenth century. The state was made especially attractive to European immigrants by the availability of cheap land under the federal Homestead Act of 1862. The late twentieth century, however, saw the arrival of immigrants from other parts of the world.

Minnesota is well known for its many residents of Scandinavian ancestry. Scandinavian immigration began during the nineteenth century, when Sweden and Norway were experiencing rapid population growth and began sending emigrants to North America. Both countries had limited arable land, and rich farmland could be purchased cheaply in Minnesota, making the midwestern territory, and later state, an attractive destination for settlement. Persecution by Sweden's state Lutheran church and the country's military draft were additional incentives for emigration.

Minnesota monthly newspaper serving two of the state's immigrant communities with articles in English, Spanish, and Somali. (AP/Wide World Photos)

Norwegians moved to Minnesota for the same economic and demographic reasons as the Swedes. Another factor contributing to Norwegian emigration was the country's rigid class system, which limited voting to members of the upper classes.

Minnesota also attracted many German immigrants who shared the Scandinavians' quest for cheap farmland. German immigration was also fueled by the failed revolutions of 1830 and 1848. Other midwestern states absorbed most of the German immigrants, but many of the immigrants settled in southern Minnesota. Smaller numbers settled in northern parts of the state.

LATE TWENTIETH CENTURY

By 1990 the largest immigrant groups in Minnesota were Latin Americans and Hmong from Southeast Asia, Both groups were part of a surge in immigration that began during the late 1970's. Financial and agricultural crises brought Mexicans

to Minnesota. Between 1990 and 2000. the numbers of Latinos in Minnesota tripled to 143,382. By 2004 the Minnesota State Demographic Center estimated the state's Latino population at about 175,000.

The Hmong are a non-Vietnamese people from Laos and Vietnam who sided with the United States during the Vietnam War and afterward became political refugees. The approximately 60,000 Hmong living in Minnesota in 2004 made Minnesota home to the largest number of Hmong in the United States. The state also had about 25,000 ethnic Vietnamese residents, along with smaller numbers of immigrants from Laos, Burma, and Cambodia.

World events also brought other nationalities to Minnesota. For example, during the 1990's, the collapse of the Soviet Union brought many Russians to Minnesota, and the civil wars following the breakup of Yugoslavia brought Bosnian refugees. In 2002, the collapse of the government in Somalia

brought a surge of Somalis to the state. Minnesota's need for high-tech workers also brought immigrants from India, Pakistan, and China.

The influence of Scandinavian immigrants has remained evident in the varieties of English spoken in Minnesota. The 1996 motion picture *Fargo* satirizes Scandinavian accents in the state. In one scene, a young Minnesota man of apparent Asian ancestry enters a restaurant in Minneapolis. When he speaks, he uses a strong Scandinavian accent exactly like that of the modern descendants of Minnesota's early Swedish and Norwegian immigrants.

Timothy C. Frazer

PROFILE OF MINNESOTA

Region	Upper Midwest
Entered union	1858
Largest cities	Minneapolis, St. Paul (capital), Duluth, Rochester, Bloomington
Modern immigrant communities	Hispanics, Hmong, Somalis, Russians

Population	Total	Percent of state	Percent of U.S.	U.S. rank
All state residents	5,167,000	100.0	1.73	21
All foreign-born residents	339,000	6.6	0.90	21

Source: U.S. Census Bureau, *Statistical Abstract for 2006.*
Notes: The U.S. population in 2006 was 299,399,000, of whom 37,548,000 (12.5%) were foreign born. Rankings in last column reflect total numbers, not percentages.

FURTHER READING

Blegen, Theodore C. *Minnesota: A History of the State.* St. Paul: University of Minnesota Press, 1963.

Lass, William E. *Minnesota: A History.* New York: W. W. Norton, 1998.

Nelson, Helge. *The Swedes and Swedish Settlements in North America.* 1943. Reprint. New York: Arno Press, 1979.

Nordstrom, Byron, ed. *The Swedes in Minnesota.* Minneapolis: T. S. Denison, 1976.

SEE ALSO: German immigrants; Hmong immigrants; Homestead Act of 1862; Language issues; Linguistic contributions; Mexican immigrants.

MISSIONARIES

DEFINITION: Representatives of Christian denominations who work abroad, seeking converts to their faiths

SIGNIFICANCE: The proselyting and educational work of various Christian missionary groups in countries around the world has often had the unintended effect of encouraging foreign converts to immigrate to the United States. Consequently, rates of immigration have been higher from countries with American missionaries than from those not missionized.

American missionaries of all Christian denominations have used a wide assortment of programs to make converts in other countries, particularly those of developing nations and the newly liberated countries of the former Eastern Bloc. Their activities have included work in underdeveloped and undeveloped countries, and countries plagued by natural disaster and ethnic rivalry such as the Sudan. Their approaches have differed from country to country, and the extent of their success is not fully known. However, an unintended consequence of missionary work has been for many new converts to immigrate to the United States.

MISSIONARY TOOLS

Many of the tools employed by Christian missionaries have been used for centuries; others have only recently become available. The various different denominations have employed different tactics in their missionary work, but it is not always easy to generalize about specific denominations. A few broad points can, however, be made confidently. All Christian denominations preach to the oneness of humankind. As part of their teachings, missionaries proclaim Jesus Christ as the Lord and offer

the universalism of the Christian gospel. The concepts of resurrection and the forgiveness of sin are elements used in an effort to convert people.

MOTIVATIONS FOR IMMIGRATION

Because the great passion of many Christian converts is to enjoy the benefits of a stable society that are preached by missionaries, immigrating to the United States is a natural attraction. As part of their proselyting work, missionaries preach the virtues of democracy, which many of their converts cannot enjoy in their native lands. Missionary schools tend to foster high levels of expectations among converts, who are inculcated with American values. To some extent, this results from deliberate missionary planning. For example, the Episcopal Church sends missions to Central America yearly to construct and maintain an infrastructure whose purpose is to "civilize" local peoples. Representatives of the Roman Catholic Church—the

dominant religion in Central America—and of other denominations compete with Episcopal missionaries in the effort to "save souls for Christ." Missionaries of all denominations teach hygiene and Bible studies, promote attitudes of self-confidence among members of religious minorities, and work to create atmospheres conducive to learning.

MEDICAL AND AGRICULTURAL WORK

An important part of missionary work in many developing countries is the introduction of modern Western medicine among the indigenous peoples. The Roman Catholic Church has excelled in this work, and other denominations, such as the Mormons, also send equipment and trained personnel on missions. To increase local acceptance of Western medicine, missionaries typically provide documentation written in the local languages and make sure that medicines they distribute are labeled in the local languages. Within communities

Mormon missionary reading scripture to members of a Tongan family in 2007. Thanks to the strong missionary program of the Church of Jesus Christ of Latter-day Saints, Tonga has one of the highest percentages of Mormons of any nation in the world, and many Mormon Tongans immigrate to the United States. (Getty Images)

lacking modern medical services, health restoration can be viewed as a miracle and contribute to acceptance of the religious messages.

Missionary preaching about the importance of modern health care can also contribute to converts' interest in immigrating to America. However, in areas where missionaries send professional medical personnel and equip and maintain permanent health care facilities, access to health care becomes less of an incentive for immigration. The Denton Program, a nondenominational missionary organization. uses American military aircraft to transport medical personnel and equipment and works with various federal government departments and agencies and the Agency for International Development as well as individual missionary bodies. American churches are careful to send people fluent in the local languages.

The Christian missionary movement has also offered agricultural training in other countries, particularly in unfertile regions. Some groups stress self-help and teach local farmers in the use of modern fertilizers, feeds, shelters, and farm equipment. Agricultural training often leads to encouraging converts to immigrate to regions of the United States that need agrarian workers.

MODERN COMMUNICATION TOOLS

One of the most striking developments in modern missionary work is the availability of powerful tools of communication, many of which are available at little or no cost. Missionary action is supported internationally by a chain of sites on the World Wide Web designed to provide support. In India, for example, missionaries use a Web site that assists in language learning and helps to understand diverse cultures. Christian missionary work in that predominantly Hindu and Muslim country has been sufficiently successful to move the national government to suppress it.

Some companies, such as the on-line SOON ministries, provide evangelical movements with computer hardware at bargain prices, or even for free, for dissemination in developing countries. Missionary ham radio operators also assist novices in other countries to become acquainted with American culture, often helping converts prepare for immigration.

Evangelical missionary bodies have audio and video services that provide free support to many churches. For example, missionaries can download electronic texts of the Bible in 140 different languages. Some missionary bodies also provide information and assistance to foreign converts who wish to immigrate to the United States.

The Episcopal Church and other denominations sponsor retreats for converts considering immigration to the United States. Those aspiring to come to America attend sessions designed to strengthen the converts in their new religious beliefs and to teach them about life in the United States. A special aspect of the training is to inculcate a sense of community.

Arthur K. Steinberg

FURTHER READING

Addison, Steve. *Movements That Change the World.* Smyrna, Del.: Missional Press, 2009. Examination of the dynamics of successful missionary movements by the Australian director of Church Resource Ministries. Written for readers who are already believers, but also useful for insights into missionaries' minds.

Haddad, Yvonne Yazbeck, Jane I. Smith, and John L. Esposito, eds. *Religion and Immigration: Christian, Jewish, and Muslim Experiences in the United States.* Walnut Creek, Calif.: AltaMira Press, 2003. Collection of articles examining the religious backgrounds and religious experiences of modern immigrants to the United States.

Hiebert, Paul. *Anthropological Insights for Missionaries.* Grand Rapids, Mich.: Baker Book House, 1985. Handbook for Christian missionaries by a professional anthropologist who attempts to show missionaries how to understand the people among whom they are working. Provides helpful insights into the cultural challenges faced by missionaries in foreign lands.

Levitt, Peggy. *God Needs No Passport: Immigrants and the Changing American Religious Landscape.* New York: New Press, 2007. Sociological study that emphasizes the ways in which religious identities ensure strong self-identification with native countries.

Reed, James. *The Missionary Mind and American East Asia Policy, 1911-1915.* New York: New York University Press, 1983. Scholarly study of missionary work during a brief but critical phase in U.S.-China relations, when missionary views played an important role in American foreign policy.

Sanneh, Lamin. *Translating the Message: The Missionary Impact on Culture.* 2d ed. Maryknoll, N.Y.: Orbis Books, 2008. A Christian perspective on the history of how missionary messages are understood by converts in other cultures. Emphasis is given to translations of the Scriptures and to post-Reformation missionary work in Africa, the author's area of special expertise.

Walls, Andrew F. *The Missionary Movement in Christian History: Studies in Transmission of Faith.* Maryknoll, N.Y.: Orbis Books, 1996. Broad study of missionaries throughout the full history of Christianity. Many chapters address aspects of missionary interactions with non-Western cultures.

SEE ALSO: Gospel Society; Korean immigrants; Mormon immigrants; Religion as a push-pull factor; Religions of immigrants.

MISSISSIPPI

SIGNIFICANCE: Compared to many other states, Mississippi has experienced relatively little foreign immigration over the course of its modern history. Nevertheless, the state does have several immigrant communities whose members have faced unique conditions and problems. Vietnamese and Mexican immigrants began to increase in numbers during the late twentieth century.

Mississippi has always had much lower levels of immigration than most of the rest of the United States. However, its immigrant population began to growing more rapidly toward the end of the twentieth century and the beginning of the twenty-first century, particularly along the state's Gulf coast. Among the earliest immigrants to the state, who began arriving during the first half of the nineteenth century, Germans and Irish figured most prominently. Members of these groups generally entered the United States through the port of New Orleans, Louisiana, and then moved eastward to enter Mississippi. Many of the early German-speaking immigrants were Jews from the Austro-Hungarian Empire fleeing religious oppression in their native land.

LATE NINETEENTH CENTURY IMMIGRATION

After the U.S. Civil War ended in 1865, Chinese immigrants began entering Mississippi, particularly in the state's Delta region. As newly freed African American slaves in that region began trying to better their lives during the Reconstruction era (1865-1877), many of them not only attempted to assert their political rights but also started moving among plantations in search of higher wages. Plantation owners sought to reduce their dependence on the labor of former slaves by campaigning to bring in Chinese workers, believing that Asian laborers would be easier to control than their former slaves. However, many of the Chinese workers who came to Mississippi proved less tractable than expected by abandoning agricultural work and establishing small stores.

The end of Reconstruction in the late 1870's also saw the reestablishment of white dominance over black Mississippians, reducing the demand of white plantation owners for Chinese manual labor. This development increased opportunities for the Chinese to become members of what sociologists would later call a "middleman minority"—people

---

PROFILE OF MISSISSIPPI

Region	Gulf coast
Entered union	1817
Largest cities	Jackson (capital), Gulfport, Biloxi, Hattiesburg
Modern immigrant communities	Vietnamese, Mexicans

Population	Total	Percent of state	Percent of U.S.	U.S. rank
All state residents	2,910,000	100.0	0.97	31
All foreign-born residents	51,000	1.8	0.14	42

Source: U.S. Census Bureau, *Statistical Abstract for 2006.*
Notes: The U.S. population in 2006 was 299,399,000, of whom 37,548,000 (12.5%) were foreign born. Rankings in last column reflect total numbers, not percentages.

Manuel, a five-year-old shrimp-picker who understands no English, stands amid a mountain of oyster shells at a Biloxi, Mississippi, company in 1911. (Library of Congress/Lewis Wickes Hine)

who purchased wholesale goods from white suppliers and resold them to a customer base that included many African Americans. Often these Mississippi Chinese immigrants became caught in the middle in another sense under the regime of segregation, fitting neither the categories of "black" nor "white" in Mississippi society.

Another group of foreign immigrants who began settling in Mississippi during the half century following the U.S. Civil War was Arab Lebanese immigrants. The Lebanese found work in the state mainly as peddlers, traveling from place to place selling goods. They established communities in some of the larger cities, such as Vicksburg, Jackson, and Clarksdale.

LATE TWENTIETH CENTURY ARRIVALS

Through most of the years between the end of World War I in 1918 and the twenty-first century, foreign immigration to Mississippi remained extremely low. However, the growth of the seafood industry along the Gulf coast did attract some Italian immigrants, who came mainly by way of New Orleans. During the late 1970's and early 1980's, Vietnamese refugees who had resettled in the South began moving to Mississippi's Gulf coast, especially around Biloxi, seeking work in the seafood-processing industry. As these Southeast Asian immigrants settled in the region during the 1980's, they entered the fishing and shrimping industry, which became an ethnic niche business for them. During the following decade, Gulf coast Vietnamese moved into a new ethnic occupational concentration as casino gambling became a major industry that provided them with jobs. However, at the same time this new industry provided them with employment, it also drove up housing prices within the areas in which they had settled.

The 1990's also saw a significant increase in the Mexican population of Mississippi, and Mexicans became the state's fastest-growing immigrant population during the early twenty-first century. Members of this group tended to concentrate in the construction and restaurant industries. Damage wrought by Hurricane Katrina along the Gulf coast, particularly to the Gulfport-Biloxi region in August, 2005, greatly increased the need for workers in the building trades, thereby attracting more Mexican immigrants to the construction industry. The arrival of these new immigrants also brought new problems. An unknown but apparently substantial number of these Mexican immigrant workers were undocumented, and some of the immigrants reported problems in being paid for their work by contractors.

Carl L. Bankston III

FURTHER READING

Bond, Bradley G., ed. *Mississippi: A Documentary History.* Jackson: University Press of Mississippi, 2005.

Do, Hien Duc. *The Vietnamese Americans.* Westport, Conn.: Greenwood Press, 1999.

Durrenberger, E. Paul. *Gulf Coast Soundings: People and Policy in the Mississippi Shrimp Industry.* Lawrence: University Press of Kansas, 1996.

Herrmann, Denise von, ed. *Resorting to Casinos: The Mississippi Gambling Industry.* Jackson: University Press of Mississippi, 2006.

SEE ALSO: African Americans and immigrants; Alabama; Arab immigrants; Arkansas; Chinese immigrants; German immigrants; Louisiana; Mexican immigrants; Mississippi River; Vietnamese immigrants.

MISSISSIPPI RIVER

IDENTIFICATION: Primary waterway of the central United States

SIGNIFICANCE: A mighty river whose watershed forms the continent's heartland, the Mississippi provided inexpensive transit for immigrants bound for the Midwest and the western frontier. Many settled in the riverfront cities or on nearby lands. Their work increased the output of the region's fields and factories, whose products were then shipped out via river transit. Unique cultural features evolved from the mix of immigrant settlers in major riverfront cities such as New Orleans.

The Mississippi River functioned as a magnet for immigrants even before becoming part of the United States. Discovered by the sixteenth century Spanish explorer Hernando de Soto and explored by the seventeenth century French nobleman Sieur de La Salle, both the river and its vast watershed were alternately claimed by France and Spain during the seventeenth and eighteenth centuries. The upper reaches remained the preserve of Native Americans and a few trappers until the American Revolution, but the economic and strategic importance of the river's Delta region was recognized early. New Orleans was founded in 1719. Its eighteenth century population grew to ten thousand, including Spanish soldiers, West African slaves, refugees from Caribbean plantations, Portuguese fishermen, French Creoles, and entrepreneurs from the newly independent United States.

In the surrounding Delta country, French Acadians settled after being expelled from Canada in the wake of its British takeover in the mideighteenth century. Isleños, former Canary Islands inhabitants, migrated to the Delta during the region's Spanish rule, also bringing their culture and fishing-based economy to the bayous. The many coves and islands of the region provided shelter for legendary pirates such as Jean Lafitte.

IMPACT OF THE LOUISIANA PURCHASE

President Thomas Jefferson's purchase of the Louisiana Territory in 1803 not only gave an expanding nation a huge new storehouse of natural resources but also secured a water route that eased transit to all the areas that bordered the river and its major tributaries. Both immigration and shipping benefited from no longer having to make onerous overland trips through the wilderness. After the Battle of New Orleans (1815) cut short a British land-grab attempt in the region, the territory was secured for settlers who wanted to build new lives there. The North American continent now offered unpopulated lands and opportunities, just as many European countries were entering an era of economic and political crises.

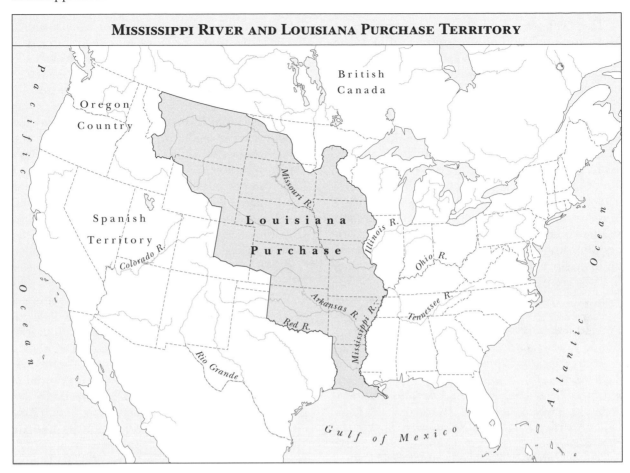

MISSISSIPPI RIVER AND LOUISIANA PURCHASE TERRITORY

One early aspect of the Louisiana Purchase was that it granted automatic U.S. citizenship to those already living in the territory. These people included a fairly large population in the Delta region, and scattered settlements in the more sparsely inhabited areas upriver. In the first decade after the purchase, more than 10,000 new French-speaking immigrants poured into New Orleans, refugees from the Haitian revolution and other slave uprisings on French Caribbean islands.

French immigrants also predominated at this time in the river's upper reaches. St. Louis and some other river cities had been founded by French voyageurs during the eighteenth century, first as an outpost for fur traders, then serving as a supply base and port for the settlers in the countryside. Lead mining began early in the city's hinterland, and by 1723 French entrepreneur Philip Francois Renault was shipping lead down the Mississippi to diverse foreign markets. Other metals,

furs, and timber were gathered or produced by the largely French early immigrants to the mid-Mississippi region.

Early during the nineteenth century, the wilderness was partially cleared and states were established in the former Northwest Territory. Their settlers often came via the Mississippi's eastern tributaries such as the Ohio River. New towns sprang up, peopled by both these internal migrants and European immigrants who arrived via the Mississippi route. Throughout most of the mid-nineteenth century, immigrants tended to come from northern or western European countries: Scandinavia, the British Isles, France, and Germany. Many were rural folk. Some of these joined the burgeoning populations of the states on the river's eastern bank, notably Illinois and Indiana, where town life and farms were already flourishing. Others set out to farm the rich, virgin soil of trans-Mississippi states, including Iowa, Minnesota, Missouri, Kan-

sas, and Nebraska. Still others settled in riverfront cities and became shopkeepers, or carried on the crafts, ranging from tailoring to metalwork, which they had followed in their homelands.

Like the French migrants to the Mississippi Delta, many other immigrants came as refugees from disasters in their homeland. The Irish faced starvation at home from the potato blight of the mid-nineteenth century. France and Germany churned with political turbulence and the uprooting of a centuries-old social order. If the Mississippi Valley was "untamed" in comparison, it still offered the chance to build a new life without being caught up in civic unrest.

POST-CIVIL WAR EXPANSION

With prospective statehood on the horizon during the early 1850's, Kansas and Missouri were caught in the struggle over slave- versus free-state status. During the ensuing Civil War (1861-1865), it was clear that control of the Mississippi was vitally important to both sides. The war endangered ordinary river traffic, and immigration slowed drastically. There was a fair amount of immigrant participation in the war, however, supporting both sides. St. Louis, for example, had large communities of both German and Irish immigrants. Open clashes occurred between the two during the war. Many from the city's Irish Roman Catholic community joined the Confederate forces, along with Father John Bannon, who accompanied them as a chaplain and later served as a Confederate emissary to the Vatican. The Germans, with their strong martial tradition and marching societies, were staunchly antislavery and enlisted in the Union cause.

In the post-Civil War North, industry expanded to become the driving engine of the U.S. economy. The West was transformed from frontier to an integral part of the nation. The Homestead Act of 1862 offered free land to settlers for farming. Once again, immigrants, mostly from Europe, arrived in large numbers to work the farms and factories in the Mississippi Valley. Those with special skills—coopers and blacksmiths, for example—were targeted by pamphleteers, and sometimes businessmen or state governments even paid their passage to the sponsoring area. Arkansas, Iowa, and Minnesota were among the states directly or indirectly offering such aid.

Most of the first wave of post-Civil War immigrants, like their predecessors, came from northern and western Europe and assimilated fairly well into the existing river towns. The raw materials they produced—hardwood lumber, ore, grain, and other agricultural produce from the upper Mississippi basin, and rice, cotton, pine and cypress wood, and cane sugar from its lower reaches—were shipped in great quantities down the river and to far-flung markets. The craftsmen's work, in contrast, tended to stay localized. Every town needed metalworkers and carpenters, for example, and their need to deal with customers and sponsors meant that these immigrants rapidly acquired rudimentary knowledge of the English language and American customs.

By 1890, the midwestern and Great Lakes states were becoming industrial powerhouses, and the composition of the immigrant flow changed. More than 18 million migrants were to enter the United States in the next thirty years, a rate double that of earlier times. These immigrants came largely from eastern and southern Europe: from Italy, Slavic areas and other parts of the Austro-Hungarian Empire, Russia, and the Baltic region. They immigrated to find work in factories and mines, and their mores and culture were different enough from those of established inhabitants to arouse suspicion. For example, a low-lying district called Bohemian Flats sprang up in Minneapolis. While it was inhabited by hardworking families, the fact that most residents were Czechs or Slovaks was nearly as suspect as the shantylike houses and frequent floods that predominated there.

During this period too, some unexpected immigrant enclaves developed. In Mississippi, immigrant Italians set up fishing and canning enterprises; others became wholesalers of seafood and imported food items. Into the same area moved Lebanese, who often started as itinerant peddlers and then worked their way up to the ownership of groceries and specialty restaurants. In Arkansas, Chinese men were imported as laborers in the cotton fields to serve as replacements for the lost slave labor. When this program did not work out, the Chinese stayed and became grocers despite exclusionary laws aimed at them. Further north, Belgian and Greek workers moved into the Quad Cities area of Iowa, drawn by the many unskilled jobs in the John Deere factory and those in similar

assembly-line factories that were part of the new industrial America.

NEW PATTERNS AND PEOPLES

World War I drastically slowed the inflow of migrants. Although a certain number of Europeans still came as refugees from the war and its aftermath, its net effect put a lid on mass migration to the Mississippi Valley as well as the rest of the nation. During the early 1920's, there was a rebound in immigration from the war-torn European countries, but this was cut off by legislation in 1924 that established national quotas and for the first time limited the total number of immigrants allowed to enter the United States. It is notable that the only strong opposition to these measures was in the northeastern states, not the Mississippi Valley, which had also benefited much from immigrants' contributions. In fact, anti-German sentiment that accompanied the war was intense in the Middle West. It probably sped up the assimilation process in this region for the many residents of German or middle European origin. Because it was no longer acceptable to speak the German language, much less express any solidarity with their (or their ancestors') homeland, such residents redoubled their efforts to blend into the "melting pot."

With the Great Depression of the 1930's, World War II, and the quota system all contributing, the region experienced a dearth of new immigrants for several decades. Those who did come were often the beneficiaries of special provisions based on world events: war brides in the wake of U.S. servicemen's wide deployment during World War II and after, or refugees from such events as the Hungarian uprising of 1956 and the Cuban Revolution in 1959. Members of the first two groups might end up in Mississippi Valley towns depending on their own personal situation. Although most Cubans settled in Florida, a significant minority found refuge in New Orleans and the Delta region, relatively close to their Caribbean origins.

Immigration possibilities changed drastically with passage of the Immigration and Nationality Act of 1965. This law repealed the existing quota system and based most immigration decisions, in theory, on family-related or skills-related considerations. Air travel and the automobile had replaced riverboats as a way for immigrants to reach their destination. For the first time, large numbers of migrants came to America's heartland from Asia and Latin America. These new migrants had a wide variety of work and educational backgrounds. Like native-born Americans, they went where the jobs were.

The Vietnam War's aftermath brought thousands of Vietnamese to America. Many found work in the Gulf coast shrimp industry. Others scattered up and down the whole Mississippi Valley, working in various occupations from health care to agricultural processing. During the 1980's and 1990's, Mexican and Central American immigrants, legal and illegal, moved to midwestern towns. They found work not only in agriculture but also in meatpacking and construction. After Hurricane Katrina devastated the Gulf coast in 2005, Mexican workers were the single largest group involved in reconstruction efforts. Within a few months, the Latino population of New Orleans soared from 3.1 percent to an estimated 9.6 percent. Most of these new Delta residents were not newly arrived in the United States, but came from other U.S. locations.

Emily Alward

FURTHER READING

Ambrose, Stephen E., and Douglas G. Brinkley. *The Mississippi and the Making of a Nation*. Washington, D.C.: National Geographic Society, 2002. Lavishly illustrated volume written by two distinguished historians. Shows the river as both a channel for commerce and a natural resource. Biographical sketches of many famous immigrants.

McDermott, John Francis, ed. *Frenchmen and French Ways in the Mississippi Valley*. Champaign: University of Illinois Press, 1969. Studies of the contributions of French explorers and immigrants to the Mississippi region.

_____. *The Spanish in the Mississippi Valley, 1762-1804*. Champaign: University of Illinois Press, 1974. Papers on the era of Spanish ownership and maximum influence.

Massey, Douglas S., ed. *New Faces in New Places: The Changing Geography of American Immigration*. New York: Russell Sage Foundation, 2008. Symposium articles showing how non-Western and Latino immigrants have brought a new diversity to American life since the 1960's. Includes studies of midwestern and southern destinations.

Thornell, John. "Struggle for Identity in the Most

Southern Place on Earth: The Chinese in the Mississippi Delta." *Chinese America: History and Perspectives* (January, 2003): 63. Scholarly but lively article tracing the survival strategies of the Chinese community from 1870 on.

SEE ALSO: Louisiana; Mississippi; Missouri; Mormon immigrants; National Road; Natural disasters as push-pull factors; Transportation of immigrants; Westward expansion.

MISSOURI

SIGNIFICANCE: Located by the Mississippi River on the threshold of the western frontier, Missouri has had a somewhat different immigrant experience from those of neighboring midwestern states. Nevertheless, like many other states, it attracted significant numbers of European immigrants during the nineteenth century, and it has had similar experiences with illegal immigration since the late twentieth century.

Most early settlers in Missouri were Americans of English origin who entered the territory from Kentucky, Tennessee, Ohio, Indiana, and Illinois. These groups spread into the river valleys into the central part of Missouri during the 1820's and into western Missouri during the 1830's. Meanwhile, the Mississippi River port of St. Louis emerged as the gateway to the western frontier. Over the next twenty years, the state's population tripled, from 19,783 to 66,586, while trading posts in both Kansas City and St. Joseph outfitted wagons trains heading west along the Santa Fe and Oregon trails.

Substantial overseas immigration began during the 1830's with the arrival of Germans, who established farms west of St. Louis and south of the Missouri River. On the eve of the U.S. Civil War,

more 15 percent of the state's residents were foreign born—mostly Germans and Irish. By the end of the nineteenth century, the state was beginning to attract Italian, Greek, Polish, and east European Jewish immigrants.

TWENTIETH CENTURY IMMIGRATION

The basis of Missouri's economy gradually shifted from agriculture to industry through the early twentieth century. Between 1900 and 1970, the state's rural population dropped from 70 to less than 30 percent of the state total. However, Missouri differed from other midwestern states whose metropolitan centers grew significantly through that period. In fact, its major cities shrank. St. Louis lost almost half its population between 1950 and 1980. St. Louis and Kansas City responded by undertaking massive urban renewal programs during the 1980's to deal with air pollution, traffic, crime, and dilapidated housing, and Missouri's economy slowly began to improve. By the twenty-first century, more than half of the state's residents were clustered within its two largest metropolitan areas, St. Louis and Kansas City.

By the turn of the twenty-first century, Missouri's immigrant heritage was reflected in large numbers of people of German, Irish, English, and French descent. During the 1990's, they were joined by approximately 40,000 to 60,000 immigrants from wartorn Bosnia. By the year 2004, the state was home to 195,000 foreign-born residents, about 5 percent of

---

PROFILE OF MISSOURI

Region	Midwest
Entered union	1821
Largest cities	Kansas City, St. Louis, Springfield, Independence
Modern immigrant communities	Bosnians

Population	Total	Percent of state	Percent of U.S.	U.S. rank
All state residents	5,843,000	100.0	1.95	18
All foreign-born residents	194,000	3.3	0.52	28

Source: U.S. Census Bureau, *Statistical Abstract for 2006.*
Notes: The U.S. population in 2006 was 299,399,000, of whom 37,548,000 (12.5%) were foreign born. Rankings in last column reflect total numbers, not percentages.

whom spoke languages other than English in their homes.

Missouri was also home to between 35,000 and 65,000 undocumented immigrants, who represented less than 1 percent of the estimated 12 million undocumented immigrants believed to be living in the United States. In 2009, state lawmakers decided to crack down on illegal immigration by requiring all public employers, including state and local agencies, to use a database that searches records from the Social Security Administration and the Department of Homeland Security to determine whether potential employees are in the country legally.

Gayla Koerting

FURTHER READING

Aron, Stephen. *American Confluence: The Missouri Frontier from Borderland to Border State.* Bloomington: Indiana University Press, 2006.

Blouet, Brian W., and Frederick C. Luebke. *The Great Plains: Environment and Culture.* Lincoln: University of Nebraska Press, 1979.

Foley, William E. *A History of Missouri.* Columbia: University of Missouri Press, 2000.

Gjerde, Jon. *The Minds of the West: The Ethnocultural Evolution of the Rural Middle West, 1830-1917.* Chapel Hill: University of North Carolina Press, 1979.

Kamphoefner, Walter D. *The Westfalians: From Germany to Missouri.* Princeton, N.J.: Princeton University Press, 1987.

Thelen, David. *Paths of Resistance: Tradition and Dignity in Industrializing Missouri.* Columbia: University of Missouri Press, 1991.

SEE ALSO: Arkansas; German immigrants; Illinois; Kansas; Machine politics; Mississippi River; Nebraska; Westward expansion.

"MODEL MINORITIES"

DEFINITION: Popular conception of certain minority groups whose members tend to attain educational and economic success and achieve high degrees of assimilation into the mainstream society

SIGNIFICANCE: The term "model minority" has most often been applied to Asian Americans, particularly Japanese, Chinese, and, more recently, Indian Americans. This issue is a significant one because it sets up strata within the category of minorities that imply that those who are most easily "assimilated" are the "best." This hierarchy allows the majority group to apply criteria of acceptance to other groups. It also is significant because the existence of this concept puts great pressure on younger members of groups labeled "model minorities" to reach high levels of achievement.

"Model minority" is a label applied to an ethnic, racial, or otherwise identifiable group, many of whose members achieve higher levels of success—as identified by the majority group—than average members of society. Measures of success may include household incomes, living conditions, or educational levels. Researchers who have studied minority groups have labeled "model minorities." Some of them consider the concept to be a myth and a form of racial and ethnic stereotyping. In the United States, Asian Americans and Asian immigrants are often given this label, as are some immigrants from India.

REACTIONS TO THE LABEL

Members of groups that have been called model minorities have varied in their responses to this label. Some are naturally proud to be considered high achieving. However, as more scholarly study has been applied to the concept, the model minority stereotype has been shown to be detrimental to many members of affected ethnic groups. It has, for example, played a role in disqualifying individuals from receiving aid from assistance programs.

Moreover, as with any stereotype, "model minority" tends to become a label that is applied to all members of a group, only some of whom are actually high achievers. This tendency can create unnecessary pressure on individuals to succeed or attempt to force individuals into molds in which they do not fit. This has been especially been a problem among Asian immigrants, whose many subgroups are very different from one another. The tendency to group all Asians together is a form of stereotyping and works to hide problems that do exist.

The label "model minority" might also lead Asians to think that their battles for equality within

American society have been won. Demographers have pointed out that this is not the case. For example, Asian Americans are highly underrepresented in political officeholding in the United States. They are also underrepresented as chief executive officers, board members, and high-level supervisors in the American corporate world.

STATISTICAL PERSPECTIVES

The concept of "model minority" depends on the computation of an average—a mathematical entity involving the addition of values attributed to everyone and divided by the number of individuals included. This statistic often hides the truth when a distribution is bimodal (that is, when many individuals are at either end of a continuum, not concentrated in the middle). In the case of a "model minority," a group might look very affluent given statistical averages, but this appearance might hide the fact that the group is actually a collection with many individuals clustered at both the high and low ends of the economic continuum.

Most of the stereotypical concepts related to the "model minority" label are most easily applied to Asians who have immigrated from China or Japan. Most of these immigrant populations derive from the middle and upper classes in their home countries. These immigrants tend to arrive in the United States already sharing the values of middle- and upper-class American society. Meanwhile, it is often forgotten that the group considered "Asian" includes such populations as Laotians, Hmong, Cambodians, Vietnamese, and Indonesians who have higher-than-average levels of poverty in the United States.

IMPLICATIONS FOR AFFIRMATIVE ACTION

The myth of the model minority works against any efforts to extend any affirmative action benefits or policies to Asian Americans, and in some cases Indian Americans. As the concept itself is a myth, many people have suggested that affirmative

Students of a Japanese-language school in Sacramento, California, around 1910. A long tradition of strong family support for education has contributed to the image of Asian Americans as "model minorities." (Sacramento Ethnic Survey, Sacramento Archives and Museum Collection Center)

action programs should work to disaggregate the Asian population in the United States and determine which populations' members do need assistance. There have also been calls to examine the areas in which Asian Americans have hit the so-called "glass ceiling" in corporate and political leadership with a view toward removing obstacles to their advancement in those fields.

Mary C. Ware

FURTHER READING

Chou, Rosalind S., and Joe R. Feagin. *The Myth of the Model Minority: Asian Americans Facing Racism.* Boulder, Colo.: Paradigm, 2008. Debunks the

model minority myth by showing the depth of racism that Asian Americans actually encounter.

Fong, Timothy. *The Contemporary Asian American Experience: Beyond the Model Minority.* 3d ed. Upper Saddle River, N.J.: Prentice Hall. 2008. Focuses on how gender, race, and class intersect to affect Asian Americans.

Lee, Stacey. *Unraveling the "Model Minority" Stereotype: Listening to Asian American Youth.* New York: Teachers College Press, 1996. Drawing on interviews with many Chinese American, Japanese American, and Hmong youths, Lee uses the words of the young people themselves to show how mythic the model minority concept is by revealing the differences among Asian Americans that the stereotype works to hide.

Min, Pyong Gap, ed. *Asian Americans: Contemporary Trends and Issues.* Thousand Oaks, Calif.: Pine Forge Press, 2005. This book is distinguished from many others by focusing on issues directly affecting contemporary Asian Americans.

Takaki, Ronald. *Strangers from a Different Shore: A History of Asian Americans.* San Francisco: Back Bay Books, 1998. Popular history of Asian Americans, written by a well-known expert in the field. who illustrates the history with many primary sources.

SEE ALSO: Affirmative action; Amerasian children; Anti-Japanese movement; Asian immigrants; Assimilation theories; Chinese immigrants; Education; Immigrant advantage; Japanese immigrants; Korean immigrants; Stereotyping.

MOLLY MAGUIRES

IDENTIFICATION: Secret society of Irish miners
DATE: 1860's to 1878
LOCATION: Primarily eastern Pennsylvania

> **SIGNIFICANCE:** The Molly Maguires illustrate the frustrations and disappointments that certain groups of immigrants encountered in the United States as they found harsh working conditions and a quality of life little better than that in their homeland.

The Molly Maguires were a secret brotherhood of Irish Roman Catholic miners who were believed to have used threats, bashings, and murder to intimidate mining supervisors in the anthracite coalfields of eastern Pennsylvania in the 1860's and 1870's. The Molly Maguires sought both revenge for unfair treatment and better working conditions. Molly Maguirism in the region came to an end when the leaders were arrested, tried, and executed for murder in a court proceeding that took place entirely under the authority of the coal companies.

Franklin B. Gowen, president of the Philadelphia and Reading Railroad and the Philadelphia and Reading Coal and Iron Company, hired Allan Pinkerton's detective agency to investigate the activities of the miners and paid a private police force to arrest them. The agency sent James McParlan to infiltrate the Molly Maguires and gather evidence regarding their activities. Posing as James McKenna, McParlan succeeded in gaining the trust of the miners and testified at the trials that he had participated in their meetings and activities. McParlan's testimony, corroborated by other witnesses who were employees in the mines, stated that the accused men committed the murders. Gowen served as special prosecutor at the trials. The jury, containing not a single Irish Catholic but made up primarily of non-English-speaking Pennsylvania Dutch, found the men guilty. In 1878, they were sentenced to death by hanging. The execution of the convicted Molly Maguires not only eliminated the violence in the coal mining region but also brought union activity to a halt.

According to McParlan, all the society members were Irish or sons of Irishmen and were Catholics. Members also belonged to the Ancient Order of Hibernians (AOH), a benevolent society whose purpose was to provide financial aid to any of their members who were in need. In addition, they belonged to the Workingmen's Benevolent Association (WBA), the union founded by John Siney in 1868. Both the AOH and the WBA were dedicated to improving the lives of the miners and their families, but neither advocated the use of violence and terrorism. There were accusations that the AOH was simply a front organization for the Molly Maguires. McParlan stated that any Molly Maguire who had a grievance against a mine supervisor or official could ask for retribution in the form of beating or murder. The membership voted and a Molly was assigned to carry out the punishment.

This was usually a Molly from another county in the region.

Historians fail to agree as to the actual existence of the Molly Maguires in the eastern Pennsylvania mining region. The Molly Maguires left no tangible evidence of their existence. Molly Maguires did exist in Ireland as a secret society of Irish Catholic tenant farmers who retaliated against wealthy Protestant landowners, both Irish and English, in the agrarian conflict over land usage. The Molly Maguires dressed in disguise as women, painted their faces with cork, and used intimidation and violence. Many of the Irish miners in Pennsylvania were from the regions of Ireland where the society was active. As mine laborers, they faced much of the same hardships and lack of fair treatment that they had fled. Dangerous working conditions, frequent disasters resulting in deaths, long hours, low wages, payment in scrip, and the policy of firing any miner who dared to complain appear reason enough for these workers to again unite as Molly Maguires.

Shawncey Webb

FURTHER READING

Dubofsky, Melvyn, and Foster Rhea Dulles. *Labor in America: A History.* Wheeling, Ill.: Harlan Davidson, 2004.
Kenny, Kevin. *Making Sense of the Molly Maguires.* New York: Oxford University Press, 1998.

SEE ALSO: Coal industry; Employment; Fenian movement; Great Irish Famine; Immigrant aid organizations; Irish immigrants; Labor unions; Pennsylvania; Pinkerton, Allan; Settlement patterns.

"MONGRELIZATION"

DEFINITION: Nonscientific theory that racial interbreeding causes degeneration of the human species

SIGNIFICANCE: As an expression of a conservative nationalist vision of America as a Protestant northern European country, ideas about "mongrelization" represented an entrenched mind-set that opposed extending open immigration to countries and races that were perceived to sully bloodlines of Nordic purity, which was regarded as the noblest manifestation of the American character.

Although from its inception America had been shaped by virtually unrestricted immigration, late nineteenth century conservatives began expressing their fears that allowing peoples such as Irish Catholics, eastern and southern Europeans, and Asians into the country threatened the American identity. The incendiary rhetoric surrounding controversial legislation curbing—or in some cases eliminating altogether—immigration from specific countries and regions deemed alien was based on the argument hat such immigrants compromised the racial makeup of the nation. Proponents of this view, who regarded themselves as fierce nationalists, defined American identity as based on western and northern European stock—which was white in skin color and primarily Protestant in religious beliefs.

The argument insisted that characteristics intrinsic to that Nordic American identity—intelligence, moral character, self-reliance, faith in democracy, sobriety, virtue, honesty, and a committed work ethic—adhered to some racial and ethnic groups but not to others. According to the argument, groups routinely designated as inferior would inevitably pollute the Nordic American bloodlines, creating "mongrel" generations of hyphenated ethnicity. The designation most often used to describe the immigration flow of these peoples was "hordes." Africans, Asians, and Mexicans were the peoples most commonly referred to as "hordes," but the term was also applied to Italians, Poles, Jews, Slavs, and other peoples from the Mediterranean basin. Advocates of the "mongrelization" theory wanted the immigration of all these peoples to be stopped or restricted.

The 1882 Chinese Exclusion Act and nearly six decades of subsequent legislation aimed at eliminating Asian immigration were manifestations of this argument. Unlike other types of immigrant restrictions—those based on the potential for political subversion or the potential for a health threat—the argument of mongrelization played to the bigotry and racist fears of the white Protestant American majority by designating certain ethnicities as undesirables.

The controversial eugenicist and self-proclaimed anthropologist Madison Grant published *The Pass-*

ing of the Great Race in 1916. In print for more than thirty years, this book made the unapologetic argument that the greatest evil facing the burgeoning American empire came from unrestricted immigration. Drawing on the metaphors—if not the science—of Charles Darwin, proponents of the mongrelization theory argued a kind of scientific racism. In proposing eugenics as a way to maintain American racial integrity, these vocal and impassioned public figures, most notably Senators Benjamin (Pitchfork Ben) Tillman of South Carolina and J. Thomas Helfin of Alabama, saw unrestricted immigration of such unsavory ethnicities as doing irreparable damage to the racial makeup and hence the moral integrity of Nordic America.

Mongrelization was largely discredited first by the groundbreaking work of professionally trained anthropologists during the 1930's who railed against such biological generalizations as the mongrelization theory as forms of fear-mongering. They argued for the influence of environment on shaping character and later cited the rise of Nazism in Adolf Hitler's Germany as an example of the dangers of notions of Nordic racial purity.

Joseph Dewey

FURTHER READING

Bennett, David H. *The Party of Fear: From Nativist Movements to the New Right in American History.* Chapel Hill: University of North Carolina Press, 1988.

Gerstle, Gary. *American Crucible: Race and Nation in the Twentieth Century.* New Brunswick, N.J.: Rutgers University Press, 2001.

Tirman, John, ed. *The Maze of Fear: Security and Migration After 9/11.* New York: New Press, 2004.

SEE ALSO: Anti-Chinese movement; Anti-Japanese movement; Anti-Semitism; Asian immigrants; Eugenics movement; European immigrants; History of immigration after 1891; Quota systems; Stereotyping; Xenophobia.

MONTANA

SIGNIFICANCE: Montana's links to immigration have a great deal to do with the mining industry. As the state's mines developed and became specialized, immigrant labor was frequently brought in to work the mines and to service the mining industry in supporting roles. Immigration into Montana has been limited since the late twentieth century. A rising number of newcomers are entering the state to take advantage of its economic and social benefits.

At the time Montana became a state in 1889, the mining industry had been well established throughout the territory for thirty years. Prospectors began working the hills of southern Montana during the 1850's. In 1862, the discovery of gold in Grasshopper Creek began a small gold rush that brought miners and speculators from California, Wyoming, and Colorado. Another gold strike was made during the following year, near the location of modern Virginia City, increasing the flow of people into Montana. As the mining industry developed, laborers were brought in to perform the demanding and dangerous work of extracting ore from the ground.

LATE NINETEENTH CENTURY IMMIGRATION

During the nineteenth century, much of the difficult and dangerous mining work in Montana was done by Chinese immigrants and African Americans. These workers were generally paid at much lower rates than white workers and were frequently given perilous and demeaning tasks that other workers refused to do. Immigrants from Ireland, England, Germany, and the Scandinavian nations also entered the region to work as miners, merchants, and investors, hoping to strike it rich during Montana's boom years. As the twentieth century approached, different regions of Montana began to specialize in certain ores. For example, Butte became a primary copper supplier for the entire United States, and Philipsburg specialized in silver production. Butte's copper mines employed workers from Greece, Bulgaria, Romania, Serbia, Poland, Czechoslovakia, Finland, and Italy.

TWENTIETH CENTURY DEVELOPMENTS

During the twentieth century, Montana's population began to stabilize as the boom-and-bust mining and land speculation industries became secondary to the state's agricultural and ranching industries. With the revisions to the Homestead Act of 1862 during the early twentieth century, immigrants were attracted to Montana by the availability of 320-acre plots of farmland for low prices. Many of these new arrivals relocated from areas in the American Midwest, particularly from Illinois and Indiana, and moved into southern and western Montana in search of good farmland and sites for home construction. The people moving into Montana were also increasingly foreign. By 1910, more than 25 percent of Montana's population was classified as foreign born. New immigrants not involved in the mining industry typically worked in agriculture, growing Montana's primary crops—wheat, barley, sugar beets, and rye. Some became ranchers, raising cattle and sheep. Throughout the twentieth century, agriculture dominated Montana's economy.

By the early twenty-first century, Montana's population was typical of states in the northern Rocky Mountain region. More than 92 percent of the population were classified as "white," with very small numbers of African Americans, Asians, and Pacific Islanders. Native American accounted for about 4 percent of all Montanans, with a growing Hispanic population making up another 3 percent. The largest Hispanic concentration was located within the urban region of Billings.

Robert D. Mitchell

FURTHER READING

Lee, Rose Hum. *The Growth and Decline of Chinese Communities in the Rocky Mountain Region.* New York: Arno Press, 1978.

Montana Writers' Program. *Copper Camp: Stories of the World's Greatest Mining Town, Butte, Montana.* New York: Hastings House, 1943.

Murphy, Mary. *Mining Cultures: Men, Women and Leisure in Butte, 1914-41.* Champaign: University of Illinois Press, 1997.

PROFILE OF MONTANA

Region	Northwest
Entered union	1889
Largest cities	Billings, Missoula, Great Falls
Modern immigrant communities	Hispanics, Chinese

Population	Total	Percent of state	Percent of U.S.	U.S. rank
All state residents	945,000	100.0	0.32	44
All foreign-born residents	18,000	1.9	0.05	47

Source: U.S. Census Bureau, *Statistical Abstract for 2006.*
Notes: The U.S. population in 2006 was 299,399,000, of whom 37,548,000 (12.5%) were foreign born. Rankings in last column reflect total numbers, not percentages.

SEE ALSO: African Americans and immigrants; Chinese immigrants; Economic opportunities; Employment; History of immigration after 1891; Idaho; Italian immigrants; Labor unions; Railroads.

"MORAL TURPITUDE"

DEFINITION: Loosely defined term that is generally construed to encompass any behavior that gravely shocks or violates the sentiments or accepted standards of a community

SIGNIFICANCE: In American immigration law, the term "moral turpitude" first appeared in the Immigration Act of 1891, in which it was provided as a basis for excluding immigrants suspected of possessing low morals from entering the country or as grounds for deporting previously admitted immigrants.

The concept of "moral turpitude" can be traced to a Middle English expression term with Latin roots that means "shame" and connotes immoral behavior. In modern legal parlance, moral turpitude suggests behavior that is evil in and of itself and not merely because it is prohibited by law. For example, drunk driving is not a crime of moral turpitude, but drunk driving without a license is.

An elusive concept related more to cultural con-

cepts of sin than to statutory law, moral turpitude is sometimes associated with the sins outlined in the Old Testament's Ten Commandments. Ambiguity in the meaning of the term has allowed U.S. immigration officers such a wide latitude that they can rule to exclude or deport persons whom they personally dislike, including those presumed to engage in victimless crimes, such as consensual sexual conduct and substance abuse.

For example, immigrants suspected of being homosexuals were usually rejected before 1973, when the American Psychiatric Association stopped calling homosexuality a mental disorder. However, gay people can still be excluded because the law allows exclusion of "psychopathic personalities" apart from crimes of "moral turpitude." Foreigners who marry Americans in same-sex ceremonies have, for example, been excluded. Border agents have the power to stop persons from entering the country on the basis of a list of about thirty "indicators" of homosexuality while they survey visitors lined up at immigration checkpoints. Those who enter and are subsequently deemed sexual psychopaths may have their passports stamped "sexual deviate" as they leave the country, thereby subjecting them to the possibility of being incarcerated upon arrival in their home countries.

CATEGORIES OF CRIMES

The term "moral turpitude" encompasses a wide variety of actual crimes, which fall under four headings:

- Crimes against property, such as fraud and robbery and even shoplifting
- Crimes against government, most notably bribery, counterfeiting, and perjury
- Crimes against persons, including victimless offenses
- Aiding, abetting, or engaging in conspiracies to commit crimes of moral turpitude

The Immigration and Nationality Technical Corrections Act of 1994 increased the number of "aggravated felonies" that can provide grounds for deportation. In 1996, the law was amended to permit the attorney general of the United States to deport, without a prior hearing, any person convicted of any recent crime of "moral turpitude."

Michael Haas

FURTHER READING

Freilich, Joshua D., and Graeme Newman, eds. *Crime and Immigration.* Burlington, Vt.: Ashgate, 2007.

New York State Defenders Association. *Representing Immigrant Defendants in New York.* 4th ed. New York: Author, 2008.

Weissbrodt, David, and Laura Danielson. *Immigration Law and Procedure in a Nutshell.* 5th ed. St. Paul, Minn.: Thomson/West, 2005.

SEE ALSO: *Boutilier v. Immigration and Naturalization Service;* Congress, U.S.; Deportation; Gay and lesbian immigrants; Immigration Act of 1891; Immigration Reform and Control Act of 1986; Lennon, John.

MORMON IMMIGRANTS

IDENTIFICATION: Converts to the Church of Jesus Christ of Latter-day Saints who immigrated to North America

SIGNIFICANCE: Immigration of Mormon converts from outside the United States was an important part of the building of the Mormon Church into an international organization. The immigration of tens of thousands who saw the United States as a "New Zion" is another example of immigrants seeking religious freedom in the United States.

One of the first major religious movements entirely indigenous to the United States, the Church of Jesus Christ of Latter-day Saints—who are better known as Mormons—was founded in New York State by Joseph Smith in 1830. Almost immediately after the church was organized, Smith began sending missionaries to Europe to recruit new members. At a time when many Europeans were already warming to the idea of emigrating to North America, the missionaries' message of a "New Zion" was warmly received. The missionaries found thousands of converts in northern and western European nations during the 1840's and 1850's, creating a vibrant Mormon movement in Europe. However, because the religion was founded on the belief that the United States represented a New

Zion, Mormon leaders began making plans to transport European converts across the Atlantic.

IMMIGRANT GROUPS

One of the first significant groups of European converts to come to North America were English immigrants who arrived on the British ship *Britannia* in 1840. Its passengers immediately went to the main Mormon settlement in Nauvoo, a booming Illinois town on the Mississippi River. The leader of this group, John Moon, soon sent glowing reports back to England that convinced other Mormon converts to start for the United States. In 1849, by which time church headquarters had relocated to Salt Lake City, Utah, the church's new president, Brigham Young, founded the Perpetual Emigration Fund Company. Financed by church donations, this body paid for the transatlantic passages of impoverished converts. It also provided money for transportation, food, clothing, and wagons to help the immigrants travel overland to settlements in the West.

The peak years of Mormon immigration occurred between the 1850's and 1890's, during which tens of thousands of European converts came to the United States. Among these were more than 50,000 British converts and about 20,000 Scandinavians. The largest group of Scandinavians were Danes, who began emigrating in 1852 during a period of domestic turmoil and military conflict between Denmark and nearby German kingdoms. The Mormon leader in Denmark, Erastus Snow, organized transport for more than 10,000 Danish converts. Europeans always constituted the largest portion of Mormon immigrants, but some came from other parts of the world, most notably Australia.

IMMIGRATION ROUTES

Most European converts reached North America by way of Liverpool, England, from which to they sailed to New Orleans, Louisiana. A Mormon agent in Liverpool helped converts to find ships and provided them with contacts in the United

Mormon immigrants moving west on the Oregon Trail. Some immigrants who were unable to afford draft animals crossed the plains pushing and pulling handcarts. (Library of Congress)

States. Some Mormon-chartered boats were also used for immigrants. New Orleans was the favored port of entry into the United States because it was on the mouth of the Mississippi River, up which immigrants could ride steamboats to Nauvoo during the 1840's. After most Mormons relocated to the West, new immigrants could take steamboats up the Mississippi to the Missouri River, on which they could continue west on steamboats. However, many immigrants faced arduous overland journeys to reach New Zion until the first transcontinental railroad was completed in 1869. Passing through northern Utah, the railroad provided fast, safe, and direct transportation to Mormon territory from points in the East. Consequently, increasingly numbers of European immigrants reached Utah by sailing to New York City.

HAZARDS OF TRAVEL

Sailing across the North Atlantic and Pacific in passenger ships was generally a hazardous undertaking in mid-nineteenth century sailing ships, but most Mormon immigrants enjoyed relatively safe journeys. In 1854, however, the ship *Julia Ann* was en route from Australia to North America with several Mormon immigrants when it struck a coral reef and sank. Although casualties were limited, the sinking was a reminder of the dangers facing all transoceanic immigrants. Moreover, the perils of travel did not end when the immigrants landed in North America. Cross-country overland journeys were full of perils, and freshwater transportation had its own deadly perils. In April, 1852, a large number of Mormon converts from Wales and England were traveling up the Missouri River on the steamboat *Saluda*, when its boilers exploded near Lexington, Missouri. The explosion quickly sank the boat, killed scores of passengers, and left several orphaned children.

MORMON STRUGGLES

The Mormons' success in settling and developing the Utah Territory may have had the ironic effect of harming their immigration efforts. Under Brigham Young's leadership, many church members practiced plural marriage. The growing size of the church and the development of Utah attracted widespread attention to Mormon polygamy in the East. Criticisms of polygamy and other unusual Mormon practices prompted the federal government to pay closer attention to the administration of Utah Territory. The government shut down the church's immigration fund, slowing Mormon immigration by making it more difficult for European immigrants to reach the country. Federal officials also closely questioned many Mormon immigrants and sent some back to their home countries. As government pressures on the Mormon polygamy mounted, some polygamist families emigrated to colonies in Mexico and Canada.

Eventually, however, the church officially abandoned its support for plural marriage, and Utah was admitted to the union as a state in 1896. During the twentieth century, the church continued an aggressive missionary program throughout the world but did not make a practice of encouraging new converts to immigrate to the United States.

More than a century after the great wave of Mormon immigration ended, the church created the Mormon Immigration Index, a list of more than 90,000 converts who came to the United States during the nineteenth century. The compilation of names includes the diaries and other writings of immigrants detailing their journeys to their new Zion.

Douglas Clouatre

FURTHER READING

Abanes, Richard. *One Nation Under Gods: A History of the Mormon Church.* New York: Four Walls Eight Windows, 2002. Well-documented book that covers the Mormon Church's struggles with the U.S. government and its efforts to convert followers.

Arrington, Leonard J. *Brigham Young: American Moses.* New York: Alfred A. Knopf, 1985. Biography of one of the founding leaders of the Mormon Church. Includes details of Brigham Young's efforts to spread the religion around the world.

Mulder, William. *Homeward to Zion: The Mormon Migration from Scandinavia.* Minneapolis: University of Minnesota Press, 2000. Recounts stories of survival and tragedy as Mormons migrated from Scandinavia through the United States and into Utah.

Roberts, David. *Devil's Gate: Brigham Young and the Great Mormon Handcart Tragedy.* New York: Simon & Schuster, 2008. Account of the Mormon

handcart migration from Iowa to Utah, a tragic trek across the inhospitable American West.

Stegner, Wallace. *The Gathering of Zion: The Story of the Mormon Trail.* New York: McGraw-Hill, 1964. Overview of the Mormon Church that includes sections on Mormon migration.

SEE ALSO: British immigrants; Congress, U.S.; Immigrant aid organizations; Missionaries; Nativism; Pacific Islander immigrants; Utah; Westward expansion.

MOTEL INDUSTRY

DEFINITION: Guest-accommodation industry that arose during the twentieth century to serve people traveling on highways

SIGNIFICANCE: Due to changing economic conditions in the United States and changes in immigration laws, immigrants from South Asia—particularly Indians—began to dominate the middle tier of the American motel industry during the last two decades of the twentieth century.

The path of South Asians to the United States has been a convoluted one. During the long era of the British Empire, the British sent many people from their Indian possession to other colonies in regions such as East Africa and the West Indies. In these places the transplanted Indians performed many types of labor, particularly in service industries. After Great Britain lost most of its colonies, most of the transplanted Indians remained in their new homes, continuing to work as tradespeople, civil servants, and clerks. However, during the late twentieth century, political instability in many of the former British colonies made it difficult for Asians to live and work safely. Some of these people relocated to Great Britain, but others came to the United States.

Around the same period that Indians were immigrating to the United States from other countries around the world, the American budget motel industry was becoming economically distressed. Immigrants often found that they could purchase a roadside motel for as little as forty thousand dollars. This was an amount that many Indian immigrants could afford. Moreover, the motel business was particularly well suited to Hindus, who accounted for the vast majority of Indian immigrants. Operating restaurants catering to American tastes would have been problematic, as Hindus are not allowed by their religion to handle meat. Grocery stores required large investments, and many other businesses required licensing or special training. Consequently, the budget motel industry seemed almost ideal for Indian immigrants. Motel managers could live at their places of business, thereby minimizing their personal housing costs. The language barrier was not overly difficult for Indians to surmount. Indeed, most motel managers have reported that the most important criterion for business success was a willingness to work long hours.

The depth of Asian Indian involvement in the American accommodations industry can be seen

---

THE PATEL CLAN

Throughout the United States, travelers taking rooms in public accommodations such as Days Inn, Motel 6. and other economical middle-tier motel chains might wonder why nearly all the motel managers and owners whom they encounter appear to be immigrants from India. They also might wonder why the most common surname among these individuals is "Patel." To a casual observer, it might seem that nearly all motels are owned and managed by someone who appears to be from India and is named Patel. This has not been far from the true.

The Patel clan was one of the largest clans represented among the South Asians who have immigrated to the United States, and its members have been particularly entrepreneurial. Members of the Patel clan were such prominent shopkeepers and businesspeople in their native India and in East Africa that it was jokingly said of them that they carried a "commerce gene." During the 1960's and 1970's, Patels began coming to the United States and Canada in large numbers. At that time, U.S. immigration laws allow anyone willing and able to invest forty thousand dollars in a business enterprise to apply for permanent residence that could lead to citizenship. It was thus natural for many of them to move into the motel industry.

in the size of the Asian American Hotel Owners Association, a professional organization whose members operated more than twenty thousand motels and hotels across the United States in the year 2009. These twenty thousand establishments represented than 50 percent of all middle-tier public lodging in the country, and association members also owned or managed 40 percent of all American hotel properties, including upscale hotels. These numbers represent a remarkable entrepreneurial achievement by members of the Indian American population, who collectively account for fewer than 1 percent of the total U.S. population. Equally remarkable is the fact that Indian Americans reached this level of involvement in fewer than three decades.

Mary C. Ware

FURTHER READING

Asian American Hotel Owners Association Annual Report. Atlanta, Ga.: AAHOA, 2008.

Duttagupta, Ishani. "March of the Indian Entrepreneurs." *The Economic Times* (Mumbai, India), February 6, 2009.

Helweg, Arthur W. *Strangers in a Not-So-Strange Land: Indian American Immigrants in the Global Age.* Florence, Ky.: Wadsworth, 2004.

SEE ALSO: Asian immigrants; Asian Indian immigrants; Association of Indians in America; Congress, U.S.; Economic opportunities; Employment; History of immigration after 1891.

MUIR, JOHN

IDENTIFICATION: Scottish-born American writer, naturalist, and conservationist
BORN: April 21, 1838; Dunbar, Scotland
DIED: December 24, 1914; Los Angeles, California

SIGNIFICANCE: Muir loved the wilderness in North America, which contrasted with the rocky, bare coast of his native Dunbar, Scotland. He helped found the conservation movement in the United States and cofounded the Sierra Club, originally dedicated to the protection of Yosemite National Park and later to the preservation of wilderness in the United States.

John Muir. (Library of Congress)

In *The Story of My Boyhood and Youth* (1913), John Muir wrote that he felt no regret when his father moved the family in 1849 from Scotland to America, as he immediately fell in love with the North American wilderness. Initially headed for Canada, the Muir family settled in southeastern Wisconsin. In 1880, Muir married Louisa Wanda Strentzel, the daughter of a Polish immigrant father and an American-born mother.

Muir explored and lived for a while in the Sierra Nevadas in California. He made several expeditions to Alaska and wrote numerous articles and books about his travels. He had a particular affinity for the Yosemite region in east central California. Indeed, Muir was largely responsible for the establishment of Yosemite as a national park in 1890, and through his efforts other national parks were set up. Considered the "father of the national parks," Muir also cofounded the environmental organization Sierra Club in 1892.

Richard Tuerk

FURTHER READING

Cohen, Michael P. *The Pathless Way: John Muir and American Wilderness.* Madison: University of Wisconsin Press, 1984.

Miller, Sally M., and Daryl Morrison, eds. *John Muir: Family, Friends, and Adventures.* Albuquerque: University of New Mexico Press, 2005.

Turner, Frederick. *Rediscovering America: John Muir in His Time and Ours.* New York: Viking Press, 1985.

SEE ALSO: Assimilation theories; British immigrants; Canada vs. United States as immigrant destinations; Intermarriage; Wisconsin.

MUKHERJEE, BHARATI

IDENTIFICATION: Indian-born American teacher and author

BORN: July 27, 1940; Calcutta (now Kolkata), India

SIGNIFICANCE: A writer, professor, and forceful speaker on immigration, Mukherjee is best known for her fictional works about Indian immigrants in North America. Through 2008, she had published seven novels, several collections of short stories, and a number of nonfictional essays and books, many of which touch on immigration issues.

Born in India in 1940, Bharati Mukherjee was the daughter of a pharmaceutical chemist. At an early age, she demonstrated literary ability. She could read and write by the age of three and decided to be an author by the age of ten. Life in Calcutta meant sharing a home with her father's extended family, with as many as fifty relatives living in one establishment. In 1947, her family emigrated to Great Britain, where she lived for more than three years. After returning to India, she earned bachelor's and master's degrees in English and ancient Indian culture in her home country. She then became an immigrant again, when she went to the United States to earn a master of fine arts degree in creative writing and a doctorate in English and comparative literature at the University of Iowa. In 1963, she married Canadian writer Clark Blaise after a two-week acquaintance.

After completing her doctorate in 1969, Mukherjee immigrated to Canada, where she became a naturalized citizen in 1972. Many of her writings describe her years in Canada as a time of discrimination, as she found Canadian citizens generally antagonistic toward Asian immigrants. This view can particularly be seen in her first collection of short stories, *Darkness* (1985), which echoes the occurrences of ethnic division she observed and underwent while living in Canada.

In 1980, Mukherjee moved to the United States, where she became a permanent resident. She regarded her immigration status in the United States as triumphant and embraced the "melting pot" philosophy that allowed her to become an American citizen in 1987. In becoming a citizen of the United States, she eschewed the idea that she was an "Asian American" or an "Indian American" as racist. Instead, she called herself an American with Bengali Indian origins.

Mukherjee's work has often been criticized for its inclusion of immigration issues, and she has challenged the stereotypes of immigrants that she has often seen reinforced in academic and publishing realms. Although her characters are typically female immigrants who have experienced discrimination in some form, her stories provide a powerful survival theme as their characters overcome the handicaps of their foreign backgrounds, experiences, and sorrows to find new directions.

In an attempt to break the stereotype that all Indian immigrants come from the same cultural background, Mukherjee stresses the individuality of each of her characters, rather than the overall immigrant experience. Moreover, rather than allowing herself to be absorbed into the postcolonial tradition, her objective in writing is not only to show that a person can be influenced by past experiences, culture, and beliefs, but also to demonstrate that the present experiences, culture, and beliefs play an integral part of who one will become in the future. To show the realistic span of ideas about immigration, Mukherjee incorporates characters from a range of immigration experiences, including characters who behave as postcolonials and expatriates—holding onto their pasts with nostalgic fervor—as well as characters who embrace a new life despite their race or ethnicity.

Theresa L. Stowell

FURTHER READING

Alam, Fakrul. *Bharati Mukherjee.* New York: Twayne, 1996.

Kumar, Amitava. *Away: The Indian Writer as an Expatriate.* New York: Routledge, 2004.

Zhou, Xiaojing, and Samina Najmi. *Form and Transformation in Asian American Literature.* Seattle: University of Washington Press, 2005.

SEE ALSO: Asian American literature; Asian Indian immigrants; Association of Indians in America; Lahiri, Jhumpa; Lim, Shirley Geok-lin; Literature; Sidhwa, Bapsi.

MULTICULTURALISM

DEFINITION: View that no single ethnic group should impose its culture onto the rest of the population of a diverse country but instead will benefit from greater familiarity with and respect for contributions of all cultural groups.

SIGNIFICANCE: Since the mid-1960's, multiculturalists have worked to counter tendencies of immigrant groups and minorities to be denigrated. They have succeeded in gaining adoption of on-the-job cultural sensitivity programs and educational curricula presenting positive images of nonmainstream groups. Government agencies have implemented multicultural reforms in response to pressure from minorities to decrease discrimination and prejudice, much of which resulted from ignorance of the contributions and customs of diverse cultural groups in American society.

In July, 1941, as World War II was being waged by ultranationalists in Germany and Japan, an obscure book review in the *New York Herald-Tribune* advocated "multiculturalism" as an antidote to nationalism. The term reappeared in a Canadian government report on bilingualism in 1965 that recommended that "multiculturalism" replace the "bicultural" policies of Canada that had been granting linguistic equality to English and French.

CIVIL RIGHTS MOVEMENT

Meanwhile, in the United States, the federal Civil Rights Act of 1964 outlawed discrimination in employment, government facilities and programs, public accommodations, and voting, thereby outlawing racial segregation in most areas of public life. In an executive order the following year, President Lyndon B. Johnson mandated government contractors to engage in "affirmative action" by hiring qualified members of minority groups previously excluded. Discrimination was also outlawed in the Immigration and Nationality Act of 1965, which resulted in a considerable increase in non-European immigrants.

The movement that produced civil rights legislation also pressured American universities to establish ethnic studies programs, on the premise that the historical status of nonmainstream cultures in the United States had been neglected, consistent with a policy of assimilationist Anglo-conformity, so the research agenda was to uncover the contributions of diverse minority groups to the United States, document patterns of discrimination, and otherwise enrich American scholarship by focusing on the cultural diversity of the United States. Educational institutions then voluntarily adopted programs of affirmative action, even though they were not required by law to do so.

Because not all employers voluntarily complied with affirmative action and nondiscrimination requirements, members of minority groups felt as frustrated as government officials who monitored that lack of progress. Concrete programs were needed to overcome resistance attributable to stereotypes and other factors. Immigrants with cultural practices that did not conform to the mainstream were particularly disadvantaged. For example, members of minority groups traditionally known for being employed in menial labor had difficulty being hired for white-collar jobs. In addition, federally funded mental health programs serviced few minorities, partly because many members of minorities were recent immigrants from countries in which the concept of mental illness was not understood as a treatable medical condition. To overcome favoritism toward members of the majority group, employers and directors of mental health and other government-funded programs were urged to adopt cultural sensitivity training, which relied heavily on the scholarship of ethnic studies researchers.

Cultural sensitivity training was designed for adults, and it appeared it would be needed as long

as children grew up with mistaken and stereotypical ideas about ethnic groups based on ignorance. Accordingly, curriculum reform from kindergarten to college was on the education agenda during the 1970's to ensure that young people would have more respect for minority cultures that would translate into better utilization of government programs and nondiscrimination in employment. In *Lau v. Nichols* (1972), the U.S. Supreme Court ordered schools to assist language minority children, primarily immigrants, through bilingual and English-as-a-second-language programs.

Multiculturalism soon enjoyed many new forms of government support: approval of radio and television stations in minority languages, funding for minority arts and music, financial aid to minority businesses, scholarships for minority students, voting on ballots in minority languages, and acceptance of holidays for minorities. The establishment of African American civil rights leader Martin Luther King, Jr.'s birthday as a federal holiday in 1983 is an example of the latter.

Focus on the special needs of underrepresented groups broadened in scope. Women were the first to benefit, as employment discrimination based on gender was outlawed in the Civil Rights Act of 1964. Other forms of discrimination were banned in subsequent years. The term "multicultural" was soon interpreted to encompass respect for people of different ages, physical and mental capabilities, and sexual orientations.

Commercially, multiculturalism has been profitable. From the sale of traditional furniture and items such as "Black Is Beautiful" sweatshirts, marketing campaigns directed at members of different cultural groups has been successful. At the same time, owners of cinemas have converted single-screen theaters into multiplex operations that can offer films to multiple niche markets simultaneously.

BACKLASH AGAINST MULTICULTURALISM

Perhaps inevitably, some multicultural innovations were badly designed or implemented. How-

In one of the most multicultural naturalization ceremonies in U.S. history, 14,000 immigrants from 111 different countries were sworn in as American citizens in Fort Lauderdale, Florida, in September, 2000. (Getty Images)

ever, the general, incremental progress of multiculturalism gradually rankled many people in the mainstream who resented being labeled as "Americentric," "Eurocentric," "parochial," or "prejudiced," or who otherwise felt that they were being vilified. The main premise of the counterattack was that the United States was basically a product of Western civilization, so any attempt to divert attention from that foundation imperiled national unity and undermined fundamental values. For the critics, multiculturalism had gone too far.

One of the endangered values was said to be respect for competence. Some beneficiaries of affirmative action, notably students at leading universities, were told that they had been admitted to the institution merely because of their ethnicity, not because they were qualified. When private businesses were pressured to fill what they perceived as ethnic quotas in their workforce, white male job applicants cried out against "reverse discrimination." The same was true of many disappointed applicants for entry to prestigious universities.

Whereas cultural pluralists view each culture as making unique and valuable contributions to a collectively shared mainstream, multiculturalists were accused of being more concerned with preserving the distinctions among cultures. Accordingly, the aim of bilingual education morphed from serving as a transition to English-language literacy for immigrants into a permanent track in elementary and secondary education in which the entire educational curriculum might be learned in a language other than English, thereby stunting the ability of immigrants to rise in social mobility. In Hawaii, for example, residents with Native Hawaiian ancestry were provided opportunities to attend schools in which the initial language of instruction was Hawaiian, with English introduced for the first time in the fourth grade.

Another criticism of multiculturalism was that the teaching of basic American history was being eclipsed by too much attention to minority history. Because fundamental principles of American culture and democracy were treated as an orthodoxy that needed to be challenged, the result, according to critics, was cacophony and confusion in the minds of students, including members of minority groups themselves.

Multiculturalism was said to unleash identity politics and political correctness. Identity politics involved the pursuit of public policies by each ethnic group without cooperating with other ethnic groups, sometimes resulting in advocacy of conflicting solutions and lack of progress for all groups. Political correctness meant that one would be accused of being a racist for making factual statements about group characteristics or for posing hypotheses about differences among various ethnic groups. Multiculturalists responded that such statements created a "hostile environment" for students and workers, producing a chilling effect on what could be said in public, according to their critics.

Philosophically, multiculturalists were attacked for advocating a relativism in which everything is both true and not true, depending on one's cultural perspective. Social science was questioned as inherently ideological, so college debates regarding differences of opinion on public policy issues were no longer focused on achieving consensus but instead on mobilizing support among minorities to prevail over the traditional mainstream view or vice versa.

ALTERNATIVES TO MULTICULTURALISM

Both monoculturalism and multiculturalism were eventually challenged by interculturalism. The latter view holds that members of different cultures should learn from one another, rather than have one culture prevail or allow diverse cultures to become separatist. Interculturalists strive to find commonalities and consider differences as subcultures.

Another alternative, polyculturalism, insists that the world's cultures have been in flux in part because they have influenced one another for centuries, are interrelated, and therefore possess common values that should be stressed. Those who have long said that they are "citizens of the world," rather than nationalists, now reside under the banner of polyculturalism.

The election of Barack Obama to the U.S. presidency in 2008 may have opened a new chapter on multiculturalism, as many expect that this first African American president will adopt "postracial" public policies that bring Americans together after decades of "culture wars." Obama spent the first eighteen years in his life in Indonesia and Hawaii, outside the American mainland, and with relatives on four continents as well as in the mid-Pacific. His

values were shaped by multicultural experiences. He also taught American constitutional law with a focus on civil rights. His apparent interculturalist message was that diverse Americans should listen to one another in order to achieve pragmatic solutions to festering problems. Many observers hoped that his message would be translated into action during his presidency.

Michael Haas

FURTHER READING

Bennett, Milton J. *Basic Concepts of Intercultural Communication.* Boston: Intercultural Press, 1998. Develops a methodology for intercultural communication.

Bloom, Allan. *Closing of the American Mind: How Higher Education Has Failed Democracy and Impoverished the Souls of Today's Students.* New York: Simon & Schuster, 1989. By the most prominent early opponent of the multiculturalist ethos, which the author compares to the malaise in pre-Hitler Germany. Bloom was concerned that multiculturalists saw all "truth" as relative, while the best-financed entertainers promoted mindless hedonism and narcissism.

Haas, Michael, ed. *Multicultural Hawai'i: The Fabric of a Multiethnic Society.* New York: Garland Press, 1998. Collection of articles on aspects of multiculturalism in Hawaii, ranging from literature and music to education and politics. Contributions describe a form of multiculturalism that developed not from government intervention but from social necessity. Some of the state's diverse cultural groups were historically bitter rivals and had to learn to live together in close proximity on Hawaii's small islands.

Kivisto, Peter, and Georganne Rundblad, eds. *Multiculturalism in the United States: Current Issues, Contemporary Voices.* Thousand Oaks, Calif.: Pine Forge Press, 2000. Anthology of article presenting nearly fifty diverse views on aspects of multiculturalism.

Kymlicka, Will. *Multicultural Citizenship: A Liberal Theory of Minority Rights.* Oxford, England: Clarendon Press, 1995. Written by a Canadian, a classic statement supporting multiculturalism.

Okin, Susan M. *Is Multiculturalism Bad for Women?* Princeton, N.J.: Princeton University Press, 1999. Focuses on how the preservation of cultural diversity may overshadow or even block the effort to dismantle male dominance in American society by marginalizing women's rights issues, including the right to an abortion and to avoid the humiliating roles assigned to women in traditional non-Western cultures.

Prashad, Vijay. *Everybody Was Kung Fu Fighting: Afro-Asian Connections and the Myth of Cultural Purity.* Boston: Beacon Press, 2001. Classic statement of polyculturalism.

Schlesinger, Arthur M., Jr. *The Disunitinig of America: Reflections on a Multicultural Society.* Rev. ed. New York: W. W. Norton, 1998. While accepting cultural pluralism, in which diverse cultures join together in a democratic culture, Schlesinger attacks the "cult of ethnicity" for endangering national unity by focusing on crimes committed by Western civilization on non-Western cultures while ignoring the positive elements of Western heritage.

SEE ALSO: Affirmative action; Anglo-conformity; Assimilation theories; Civil Rights movement; Cultural pluralism; Education; Immigration and Nationality Act of 1965; Language issues; *Lau v. Nichols*; Stereotyping.

MUSIC

SIGNIFICANCE: As successive waves of immigrants arrived in North America, their musical traditions provided a link with their homelands and served as an aspect of group identity. With time, these traditions changed in response to new contexts and merged with other traditions as new forms of music were created.

During the period of European colonization of America, settlers, missionaries, and traders from Spain, Holland, England, France, and other nations began to interact with some of the many Native American nations and communities that they encountered, initially in the Atlantic, Pacific, and Gulf coastal regions. Often an integral part of ceremonies, Native American musical styles reflect the various belief systems, environments, and narratives of diverse Amerindian cultures. After the voice, which is used in group singing as well as in

solo genres, the most common indigenous instruments are drums and other percussion instruments.

Despite dislocations, genocide, and assimilation, many Native Americans maintained musical practices along with language and rituals, and sometimes adopted instruments and forms from nonnative communities, especially in rural areas. During the latter half of the twentieth century, activists in the pan-Indian movement utilized music, occasionally blending native elements with familiar rock and country styles, to raise political consciousness. The institution of the powwow often includes traditional music and dance performances in large cultural gatherings. Native American music has also been associated with meditation and the environmental movement. Nonnative American music has been influenced by native concepts of individuality in music, in that certain songs come into existence through private experiences associated with personal growth.

SPANISH SETTLERS AND HISPANIC COMMUNITIES

Spanish settlements in Florida, in Texas, and along the California coast during the sixteenth through eighteenth centuries brought Roman Catholic liturgical music to the area as part of the mission system, and eventually settlers brought secular Spanish music as well, including stringed instruments such as the *vihuela*, guitar, and violin. Over time, cultural blending between Spanish and Native Americans resulted in syncretic practices, especially with regard to religious festivals. During the nineteenth century, Mexican song genres such as the *ranchera* and *corrido* were sung and accompanied by traveling groups, who also incorporated musical elements from central European immigrant cultures.

Mexicans waiting to find day jobs in East Los Angeles play mariachi tunes, perhaps the most emblematic form of Mexican music. (Getty Images)

After the northern parts of Mexico became part of the United States in 1848, Hispanic and mestizo (blended) musical culture continued to develop in those regions and was further augmented by continued immigration from Latin America to the United States. In addition to the older communities in the American Southwest, newer immigrants from Puerto Rico and other areas created vibrant enclaves in many American cities, particularly in New York, and contributed to the development of salsa, Latin rock, and other genres.

NORTHERN EUROPEAN SETTLERS AND COMMUNITIES

English and Dutch colonists brought their music with them as they established settlements in Virginia, in Massachusetts, and along the Hudson River during the seventeenth century. Congregational hymn singing was very important, especially in the Plymouth Bay settlement that was originally established as a religious community. Singing schools, taught by traveling musicians known as singing masters, became a way for communities to enjoy social gatherings as people learned part-singing, often with the aid of "shape notes" (solfeggio symbols combined with staff notation). Singing schools spread throughout the United States during the nineteenth century and led to the development of Sacred Harp singing in the South.

Secular music and instruments were also brought from England and other northern European countries. Often, the secular music was associated with social dancing (usually country dancing, square dancing, and quadrilles). During the nineteenth century, band music was cultivated, and the piano became an important instrument for middle- and upper-class families, who often gathered around the piano for recreational singing. As in England, women were encouraged to learn piano for playing within the home but discouraged from public performances. Concerts of classical music were sometimes given by European musicians for American audiences. Less sophisticated Anglo-American audiences enjoyed humorous minstrel shows, which portrayed derogatory stereotypes of African Americans to the accompaniment of lively music. French-speaking settlers who had been removed from eastern Canada during conflicts of the late eighteenth century eventually settled in western Louisiana, which alternated being a French and

Spanish colony. They became known as Cajuns (or Acadians), maintained their language, and developed a unique musical style known as zydeco.

AFRICAN AMERICAN COMMUNITIES

Beginning in the early seventeenth century, West African captives were forcibly brought to the American colonies as part of the Atlantic slave trade, and in reaction to physical and cultural oppression, they developed powerful forms of musical expression. The primary vocal tradition became known as spirituals: religious songs that also carried coded messages for escape and community support. Themes of redemption and justice in spirituals were both transcendent and concrete.

A secondary genre was functional vocal music to accompany manual labor. Both forms utilized West African concepts of "call and response," in which musical phrases would alternate between a solo voice and group singing. Often, repetition would be used, with emotional intensity increasing through embellishment and inflection. Although drums were forbidden (with the notable exception of Spanish- and French-controlled areas), the banjo was reconstructed from African prototypes and eventually entered into the rural American mainstream.

After the U.S. Civil War ended and slavery was finally abolished in 1865, newer immigrants of African descent came voluntarily to the United States from the Caribbean region and, eventually, from Africa itself. Gospel music, an extension of spirituals and hymnody within African American churches, rose to prominence during the twentieth century. Blues, a secular style with melodic similarities to African American sacred music, became well known at about the same time. In the blues, a rhymed couplet, with the first line repeated, is set to a three-phrase musical structure, often with the second phrase harmonized with the subdominant. The blues was also used in instrumental music, forming an essential element of jazz and becoming the foundation for rock and other popular genres.

Near the beginning of the twentieth century, African American musicians in New Orleans and other cities spearheaded the creation of ragtime, followed by what is often regarded as the quintessential American music style: jazz, which incorporates many elements from European as well as West African musical practices. African Americans rose

to fame as popular music stars—at first in jazz, later in rock, and especially in rhythm and blues (R&B), among other styles. Spirituals continued to be an important African American tradition during the twentieth century, inspiring classical settings and arrangements by Harlem Renaissance composers and being referenced in writing by W. E. B. Du Bois and in speeches by the Reverend Martin Luther King, Jr. Spirituals inspired solidarity and courage during the Civil Rights movement of the 1950's and 1960's. During the late twentieth and early twenty-first centuries, new urban styles developed, including rap, which built on African and African American traditions of incorporating rhythmic designs into speech, and hip-hop, which was begun by disc jockeys manipulating recorded music and superimposing their own sounds in live performances.

CELTIC MUSICAL TRADITIONS

During the eighteenth century, immigrants from Ireland, Scotland, Wales, and other regions settled in the Appalachian mountains. Fiercely independent and living in relative isolation, they cultivated narrative song and instrumental dance music traditions that they had brought from their homelands. In some cases, Appalachian ballads remained almost unchanged from their counterparts in Europe. Over time, the instrumental dance music acquired some African American inflectional and rhythmic influences, eventually leading to the development of bluegrass. During the nineteenth century, newer waves of immigrants from Ireland arrived but settled primarily in large communities within major cities such as New York and Boston. Because of these communities, Irish music was well documented and preserved in the United States, and some of the repertoire was eventually brought back to Ireland.

OTHER EUROPEAN IMMIGRANTS

During British North America's colonial period, German settlers, often escaping religious persecution and war, settled in many areas, especially in Pennsylvania, where they became known as the Pennsylvania Dutch. Most of their music was religious, but Germans also added musical dance forms such as the waltz to North American and Latin American music. In smaller ensembles, the accordion became a mainstay, and an inexpensive

and highly portable German instrument, the harmonica, was introduced in the United States in 1868, where it was received with great enthusiasm. The harmonica was adaptable to many musical styles, including blues and country, and its plaintive, lonesome sound became identified with travelers such as cowboys, and fortune seekers who rode the railroads in search of opportunities.

German and other central European communities contributed to the development and popularity of brass band music, and another lively dance form, the polka, echoed in the large German and Polish communities of American cities. Euro-American descendants of earlier generations of immigrants often looked to Europe for guidance in matters of culture, and until the twentieth century they frequently preferred exotic new European immigrants with classical training over their homespun American counterparts for teaching posts, compositions, and concerts. During the early twentieth century, immigration from Ashkenazi Jewish communities in eastern Europe increased, bringing Klezmer music and Yiddish theater to the United States. Many first- and second-generation immigrant musicians from Yiddish-speaking communities in Europe participated in the development of musical theater, music publishing, and the emergence of the popular music industry.

In American urban centers, Italian, Greek, and other immigrant communities created ethnic enclaves during the late nineteenth and early twentieth centuries. Music, along with language, cuisine, religious worship, and other shared experiences, contributed to community identity. Eventually, through assimilation and relocation to the suburbs, some of the enclaves became less distinct, but music and dance forms were cultivated, especially the Italian *tarantella* and Greek *rebetiko* music. Americans from outside these groups are sometimes invited to experience this music and dance in cultural festivals sponsored by city governments.

ASIAN IMMIGRANTS

Most of the first Asian immigrants to the United States were from southern China. During the mid-nineteenth century, they were primarily male gold prospectors and manual laborers coming through San Francisco and other western ports. Cantonese opera and other southern Chinese music genres were occasionally supported as Chinatown en-

claves grew in the cities, and Chinese Christian churches shared hymn repertoire with missionary churches in China. During the twentieth century, immigrants from other Asian nations arrived, especially in Hawaii, where Asian musicians contributed to the island's multicultural heritage. During the late twentieth century, newer immigrants from Asia were often highly educated and supported elite forms of music, often inviting visiting musicians from their home countries.

COMMUNITIES IN EXILE

The twentieth century brought unprecedented upheavals and relocations to the world, from the Armenians fleeing genocide in Turkey in 1915 through World War I, global depression during the 1930's, the Holocaust, World War II, the Cold War, wars in Vietnam and Cambodia, the Iranian revolution, and more. Many of those who were displaced or threatened by these events sought refuge in the United States. In some cases, music traditions that would have otherwise been destroyed were preserved. Although tolerance was not always a factor in America's musical history, the increasing recognition of music as a marker of personal and community identity, and the increasing value placed on musical diversity, bode well for the future.

John E. Myers

FURTHER READING

Bohlman, Philip Vilas, Edith Blumhofer, and Maria Chow, eds. *Music in American Religious Experience.* New York: Oxford University Press, 2006. Collection of detailed chapters (based on presentations for a conference at the University of Chicago) highlighting specific dimensions of the topic and spanning many ethnic groups, religious faiths and/or denominations, and historical periods.

Chase, Gilbert. *America's Music, from the Pilgrims to the Present.* 3d ed. Champaign: University of Illinois Press, 1987. Spans classical, folk, and popular music.

Roberts, John Storm. *The Latin Tinge: The Impact of Latin American Music on the United States.* 2d ed. New York: Oxford University Press, 1999. Encompasses the evolution of Latin American musical forms as well as their influence in the United States.

Rubin, Rachel, and Jeffrey Paul Melnick. *Immigra-
tion and American Popular Culture: An Introduction.* New York: New York University Press, 2007. Includes extensive treatment of music, spanning the 1930's to the early twenty-first century.

Southern, Eileen. *The Music of Black Americans: A History.* 3d ed. New York: W. W. Norton, 1997. Comprehensive study includes all major genres and figures.

SEE ALSO: Art; Berlin, Irving; Cultural pluralism; Lennon, John; Linguistic contributions; Literature; Multiculturalism; Television and radio.

MUSLIM IMMIGRANTS

SIGNIFICANCE: By the early twenty-first century, approximately two million Muslim immigrants were living in the United States. The Muslim immigrant community is diverse, encompassing followers of different Islamic sects and people from virtually all regions of the world. In the face of increasing American hostility, especially since the terrorist attacks on the United States of September 11, 2001, members of this diverse immigrant community have begun to recognize their commonalities and mobilize for their rights.

Common data collection methods make it difficult to provide concise demographic information about the Muslim immigrant community in the United States. While the U.S. Census Bureau reported that approximately 0.6 percent of all people living in United States during the early twenty-first century were Muslims, that figure was derived from a survey of a representative population sample. The Census Bureau does not collect information on individual respondents' religions in the census itself and therefore cannot provide overall population numbers based on religious affiliation.

Estimates of the numbers of Muslims in the United States produced by other organizations usually range between 5 and 8 million individuals, and common consensus places the number at approximately 6 million. Since immigrants are estimated to constitute about one-third of the Muslims in the United States, the number of people who are

both Muslims and immigrants is approximately 2 million. This figure is consistent with the numbers of immigrants who have come to the United States from predominantly Muslim countries, after adjusting for the proportions of non-Muslims in those countries.

EARLIEST MUSLIM IMMIGRANTS

Some of the earliest Muslim immigrants to come to what is now the United States were slaves who traveled with Spanish explorers during the sixteenth century. Some of the African slaves brought to British colonies during the seventeenth century were also slaves. Scholars have estimates that as many as 10 to 20 percent of all slaves imported to the United States practiced some forms of Islam in their homelands. Estimates on the size of this population range in number from as few as 40,000 Muslim slaves in the United States to 3 million Muslim slaves in all the Americas.

One of the most comprehensive records of the experiences of these early Muslim immigrants is the autobiography of Omar ibn Sayyid, who was brought to North Carolina from West Africa as a slave during the late nineteenth century. Omar ibn Sayyid was literate in Arabic; in 1831, he wrote a detailed account of his experiences. Slaveholders valued Muslim slaves for their literacy skills, but their religious practices were usually discouraged. Consequently, Islamic practices were not passed along to later generations of slaves. However, Islamic practices did survive in a few small and isolated communities. During the early twentieth century, oral historians found evidence of Muslim cultural and religious influences in African American communities living on islands off the coast of Georgia.

The first documented Muslim immigrants to come to the United States voluntarily came during the late nineteenth and early twentieth centuries. During the 1880's thousands of Muslims immigrated from the Ottoman Empire, mainly from parts of what are now the independent countries of Syria and Lebanon. Between 1890 and 1910, several hundred South Asian immigrants, who included some Muslims, came to the United States to work on railroads and in lumber mills in the American West. The early midwestern auto industry also had many Arab immigrant employees, many of whom were Muslims. Some of the first social and religious Muslim immigrant institutions in the United States were established by these people.

Changes in U.S. immigration laws that restricted

NATIONS WITH PREDOMINANTLY MUSLIM POPULATIONS

Countries are grouped below by the estimated percentages of Muslims within their total populations. Within each group, the countries are listed alphabetically.

96-99 PERCENT			50-59 PERCENT
Afghanistan	Somalia	Bangladesh	Burkina Faso
Algeria	Tunisia	Guinea	Chad
Azerbaijan	Turkey	Indonesia	Kazakhstan
Comoros	Uzbekistan	Kyrgyzstan	Lebanon
Djibouti	Western Sahara	Oman	Nigeria
Iran	Yemen	Tajikistan	
Iraq			40-42 PERCENT
Jordan	90-95 PERCENT	70-79 PERCENT	Bosnia-Herzegovina
Libya	Egypt	Albania	Guinea-Bissau
Maldives	Gambia	Qatar	
Mauritania	Kuwait	Sierra Leone	30-36 PERCENT
Morocco	Mali	Sudan	Eritrea
Niger	Syria	United Arab Emirates	Ethiopia
Pakistan	Turkmenistan		Ivory Coast
Saudi Arabia		60-69 PERCENT	Macedonia
Senegal	80-89 PERCENT	Brunei	Tanzania
	Bahrain	Malaysia	

Muslim immigrants praying at the Karbalaa Islamic Center in Dearborn, Michigan, in early 2003. The center provides a variety of services to help new immigrants adjust to life in the United States. (AP/Wide World Photos)

the entry of non-Europeans and established a system of national origins quotas slowed down the rate of Muslim immigration to the United States during the early to mid-twentieth century. From the 1920's to the 1950's, most Muslim immigrants arriving in the United States came from eastern European regions. By the time the national origins quota system was abolished by the Immigration and Nationality Act of 1965, only between 100,000 and 150,000 Muslims were living in the United States.

POST-1965 IMMIGRATION

The 1965 immigration law replaced national origin quotas and with new criteria for admitting immigrants based on family relationships, work skills, and refugee status. After this law went into effect, Muslims began immigrating to the United States

from countries all over the world. Research conducted by the Center for Immigration Studies suggests that the largest numbers of Muslim immigrants immediately after 1965 came from South Asian countries, particularly Pakistan, Bangladesh, and India. Immigrants from these former British colonies had the advantage of having learned English in school and were consequently highly competitive applicants for immigration based on their skills needed to fill American jobs. Large numbers of Muslims also came to the United States from the Middle East and Central Asia during this time.

During the late 1980's and 1990's. increasing numbers of Muslims came to the United States as refugees. Some were fleeing ethnic conflicts in Africa; others were escaping from religious persecution in South Asia and the Middle East. Many were refugees who had been displaced by military con-

flicts in Iraq, Israel, Kuwait, Lebanon, Pakistan, Somalia, Sudan, and the successor states to Yugoslavia.

POST-9/11 ISSUES

Negative stereotypes of Muslims and Muslim immigrants have been common in the United States since the colonial era. International events, particularly wars and other conflicts, have clearly contributed to negative American views of Muslims. Since the early 1970's, airplane hijackings and terrorist actions have strengthened negative public perceptions of Muslims, especially when such actions have directly affected Americans, such as the late 1970's Iranian hostage crisis. However, the Muslim extremist attacks on the United States of September 11, 2001 ("9/11") elevated negative American views of Muslims to a new level and inaugurated a new era of discrimination and violence directed against Muslims in the United States. The Federal Bureau of Investigation's annual survey of hate crimes for 2001 recorded a dramatic increase in crimes against Muslims: from 28 reported incidents directed against Muslims in 2000 to 481 in 2001—a seventeen fold increase.

The first decade of the twenty-first century has also seen the involvement of the United States in seemingly intractable wars in the predominantly Muslim countries of Afghanistan and Iraq. According to post-9/11 public opinion polls conducted by both the Pew Research Center and the Council on American-Islamic Relations, a majority of Americans have come to associate Islam with violence. Most Christian Americans also do not recognize commonalities between their own religious beliefs and those held by Muslims. Meanwhile, hate crimes directed against Muslims have continued to rise. According to data collected by the Council on American-Islamic Relations, the number of assaults and incidents of discrimination against Muslims in the United States rose from 1,019 documented cases in 2003 to 1,972 cases in 2005.

Both immigrant and nonimmigrant Muslims have been victims of hate crimes and discrimination since 9/11, but immigrants have been more frequently targeted. Significantly, many persons who have committed hate crimes seem to believe that *all* Muslims in the United States are immigrants, as many of their hate crimes are accompanied by cries of "Go Home."

In addition to the threat of hate crimes faced by Muslim immigrants, there are numerous allegations of post-9/11 legal discrimination against this community. The Patriot Act of 2001 required many immigrants from Muslim-majority countries to register with the federal government, and it enacted new restrictions on travel by individuals from those countries. By 2003, fewer green cards and visas were being issued to people in Muslim-majority countries, particularly people from Pakistan, Morocco, and Iran. Muslim immigrants generally have faced increased problems traveling as they report being profiled for more rigorous security checks than other passengers in airports.

Although there is little demographic data about the impact that these crimes and legal discrimination have had on the number of Muslim immigrants in the United States, anecdotal evidence suggests that many Muslim immigrants have chosen to return to their countries of origin or to move on to other countries, such as Canada, rather than remain in the hostile social and political climate of the United States. At the same time, however, many of the Muslims who have remained in the United States have begun to organize to educate the American public about Islam and Muslim people, and they have also worked to educate members of their own communities about their legal rights in the United States.

U.S. CIVIL SOCIETY AND POLITICAL LIFE

During the first decade of the twenty-first century, more than 1.5 billion Muslims lived in countries around the world, and forty-seven different nations had populations that were more than 50 percent Muslim. Moreover, several large countries in which Muslims accounted for much smaller percentages of total populations nevertheless had large numbers of Muslims, including India, Russia, and China. Indeed, India had the third-largest Muslim population in the world, even though its 160,945,000 Muslims accounted for only 13.4 percent of its total population.

Although Muslim immigrants have come to the United States from a wide variety of countries and cultural backgrounds, Muslims living in the United States have been able to organize around common social and religious interests. The first national Muslim conference was held in Iowa in 1952. This conference was attended by only 400 Muslims from

the United States and Canada, but it marked the inception of the International Muslim Society. At a later conference in 1954, American Muslims, including a sizable number of immigrants, formed the Federation of Islamic Associations of the United States and Canada (FIA). The primary organizational goal of FIA was to address religious and cultural issues in the United States. However, members of this organization also worked as an advocacy group for the U.S. Muslim community. The FIA also provided a forum in which Muslim immigrants could come together to develop a sense of shared identity across cultural boundaries. However, although these organizations fulfilled an important role in the Muslim community, they always had small memberships. Indeed, as late as the 1980's and 1990's, Muslim Americans appear to have had fewer political organizations than other ethnic and religious groups of similar sizes.

After 9/11, Muslim immigrants and other Muslims in the United States began to participate more actively in civil organizations that would represent their concerns and work as advocates for their community. Education and advocacy groups were formed to oppose the backlash against Muslims living in the United States. According to the American Muslim Task Force on Civil Rights and Elections, a number of grassroots organizations worked to register Muslim voters, educate Muslim immigrants about their rights, and lobby against federal policies that were harmful to Muslim immigrants. Islamic centers have expanded their social programs to offer English classes and free legal assistance to Muslim immigrants. Groups such as the Council on American-Islamic Relations have collected data on hate crimes against Muslims, offered advice on promoting community safety, and increased outreach work to address negative stereotypes about Muslims and Muslim immigrants in the United States.

Jacqueline H. Fewkes

FURTHER READING

Curtis, Edward E., IV, ed. *The Columbia Sourcebook of Muslims in the United States.* New York: Columbia University Press, 2008. Comprehensive collection of primary sources and essays about Muslims and Islam in the United States. Covers diverse viewpoints within the Muslim community and includes reflections on Muslim experiences in post-9/11 America.

D'Alisera, JoAnn. *An Imagined Geography: Sierra Leonean Muslims in America.* Philadelphia: University of Pennsylvania Press, 2004. Study of attempts by Sierra Leonean Muslims to retain their religion, customs, and ethnic identity in the United States. Sierra Leone is a small West African country with a 71.3-percent Muslim population.

Ewing, Katherine Pratte, ed. *Being and Belonging: Muslims in the United States Since 9/11.* New York: Russell Sage Foundation, 2008. Eight ethnographic essays exploring how issues of identity and assimilation have been addressed in contemporary Arab Christian and Muslim communities in the United States.

Haddad, Yvonne Yazbeck, ed. *The Muslims of America.* New York: Oxford University Press, 1993. Collection of essays about Muslim communities in both the United States and Canada, written by both non-Muslim and Muslim authors. Most focus on Muslim American institutions, and many discuss the role that American foreign policy has played in the lives of Muslim immigrants.

Lawrence, Bruce B. *New Faiths, Old Fears: Muslims and Other Asian Immigrants in American Religious Life.* New York: Columbia University Press, 2002. Compares religious backgrounds of Asian immigrants to examine what role they play in the integration of Asian immigrants into American religious life, with a particular focus on Muslims from Asia.

Mohammad-Arif, Amminah. *Salaam America: South Asian Muslims in New York.* New York: Anthem Press, 2002. Ethnographic study of South Asian Muslims living in New York. Provides a strong historical background and pays particular attention to the impact of 9/11 on this community.

Rajagopalan, Kavitha. *Muslims of Metropolis: The Stories of Three Immigrant Families in the West.* New Brunswick, N.J.: Rutgers University Press, 2008. Stories of three different Muslim immigrant families, from Palestine, Iraq, and Bangladesh, that immigrated to England, Germany, and the United States.

Shaheen, Jack. *Reel Bad Arabs: How Hollywood Vilifies a People.* New York: Olive Branch Press, 2001. Fascinating source of information on portrayals of Arabs and other Muslims in more than eight hundred alphabetically arranged films, with

special attention given to scenes in which negative stereotyping occurs.

SEE ALSO: Arab immigrants; Asian immigrants; Indonesian immigrants; Iranian immigrants; 9/11 and U.S. immigration policy; Pakistani immigrants; Religion as a push-pull factor; Religions of immigrants; Stereotyping; Turkish immigrants.

MY ÁNTONIA

IDENTIFICATION: Novel by Willa Cather depicting the lives of nineteenth century European immigrants in rural Nebraska

DATE: First published in 1918

SIGNIFICANCE: A novel about pioneers, *My Ántonia* recounts stories of European immigrants who sought prosperity in Nebraska at the end of the nineteenth century, focusing on how these immigrants transformed America and how America changed them.

The title character of Willa Cather's 1918 novel *My Ántonia* is Bohemian immigrant Ántonia Shimerda. Narrator Jim Burden first encounters the Shimerda family as a boy traveling from Virginia to Black Hawk, Nebraska. The family is indicative of many eastern Europeans who began new lives in Nebraska. As the English tutor of the teenage Ántonia, Jim learns about the hardships endured by the Shimerdas and other neighboring families, who are subjected to discrimination from Anglo-Saxon Americans and more established immigrant families from western and northern Europe.

Often, new immigrants are exploited in business, as the Shimerdas are by the fellow countryman who sells them their farm. They are also criticized for what is perceived to be their primitive culture and superstitious religious beliefs. Nevertheless, the European cultures of the immigrant families brighten the tapestry of Great Plains life for Jim. From the Austrian stories told by Otto Fuchs, the Burdens' hired man, to the brazen sensuality of young Norwegians such as Lena Lingard, to the raucous dance hall run by the Italian Vannis family, Jim comes to understand the rich vitality of ethnic life. Jim's view of European immigrants imbues the novel with a message of cultural pluralism rather than assimilation. In Lena, the American ideal of succeeding and blending into society is typified, but in Ántonia, who retains her culture and speaks her language with her American-born children, a multicultural ideal is emphasized.

Hugh Burkhart

FURTHER READING

Prchal, Tim. "The Bohemian Paradox: *My Ántonia* and Popular Images of Czech Immigrants." *MELUS* 29, no. 2 (2004): 4-25.

Smith, Christopher, ed. *Readings on "My Ántonia."* San Diego, Calif.: Greenhaven Press, 2001.

SEE ALSO: Anglo-conformity; Assimilation theories; Czech and Slovakian immigrants; European immigrants; Literature; Multiculturalism; Nebraska.

N

NAME CHANGING

DEFINITION: Voluntary and involuntary changing of family surnames by immigrants

SIGNIFICANCE: Modern Americans researching their family histories have often been stymied by name changes made when their ancestors immigrated to the United States. For many, it can be unsettling to learn that a family name held in much pride is little more than one century old. Some Americans have changed their names back to their ancestors' original surnames, but understanding the reasons for the name changes can help in providing a better understanding of what ancestors experienced when they immigrated.

It is sometimes difficult for twenty-first century Americans to understand why immigrants of the past were willing to change their surnames when they entered the United States, as name changing tended to cut them off from their ancestors and even from their contemporary relatives. However, connections between immigration and name changing are not merely from the past. As late as the early twenty-first century, the very first section of the U.S. government form on which immigrants apply for naturalization still contained a space for name-change requests. Its location near the top of the form highlights the continuing connection between changing one's citizenship and changing one's name. However, while the motivations of modern immigrants for changing their names are seldom as strong as they were for immigrants a century earlier, many immigrants still choose to start their new lives in the United States with new names.

INVOLUNTARY NAME CHANGES

Many modern Americans believe that their family names were changed by lazy or careless immigration officials at immigration reception centers such as Ellis Island in New York Harbor and Angel Island in San Francisco Bay. This idea has become entrenched in American thought by family traditions, popular literature, films, and even some scholarly works. However, a close study of the procedures followed at these immigration centers shows that casual name changes were rare. Government regulations were not always followed by immigration officers, but it is important to note that a federal regulation specifically prohibited officials from altering the names of immigrants. However, this regulation was not drafted to protect the integrity of ancestral histories, but to prevent the entry of undesirable aliens into the country.

One reason behind misconceptions about name changing at immigration reception centers is the false notion that immigration officials asked immigrants what their names were and then simply wrote down something phonetically close to what they heard without bothering to ask the immigrants how to spell their names. In reality, however, immigration officials did not get the names from the immigrants, but from the passenger lists of the ships on which the immigrants arrived. Many photographs of newly arrived immigrants at Ellis Island show them standing in long lines wearing what appear to be name tags. In fact, the tags the immigrants were wearing bore the names of their ships and the numbers of the lines on the ships' manifests on which they were listed. Immigration officer simply copied the names from the passenger lists, including whatever errors may have been on those lists.

Language differences can certainly cause confusion with names, particularly when the languages are written in different alphabets or systems. However, immigration officials at major centers such as Ellis Island usually spoke the languages of the immigrants to whom they were assigned. In fact, around the turn of the twentieth century, one-third of all Ellis Island officials were themselves immigrants. A small army of translators were also on duty, available to assist in getting correct information. Because immigrants later often described their entire immigration processing simply as "Ellis Island" or "Angel Island," it was easy for family traditions to incorporate the idea that their surname had been changed at one of those reception centers.

There is little doubt that many immigrant name changes were involuntary; however, it is much more likely that such changes can be attributed to errors

FATE OF THE PASSENGER LISTS

During the 1940's and 1950's, the National Archives and Records Administration placed all passenger lists of ships used by immigration reception centers on microfilm. Because microfilming was a new technology during those decades, some of the older passenger lists are difficult to decipher. However, because the original lists were later destroyed, the microfilms are the only copies that remain. In 2003, Ancestry.com began a project to digitize the information on the microfilm and to make it available online to their subscribers.

in the ships' passenger lists than to mistakes made by immigration officials. Errors could find their way into those lists several different ways. For example, some surnames had no single spelling that was recognized as standard at the time they were recorded. Moreover, many immigrants were illiterate and could not spell their own names if they were asked when they boarded the ships taking them to America. Those who could spell their names may not have been asked for the preferred spellings by shipping line clerks.

Some involuntary name changes came after the formal immigration process was completed. In one representative case, when a child of Polish immigrants reached school age, a school refused to register the child unless the long Polish family name was simplified. The child took the mother's maiden name as a family name and later passed it on to his own descendants. In another case, a well-meaning teacher persuaded the parents of the only Jewish boy in a small school to call him "Jack" instead of "Israel," his real name. She was concerned that the boy would be teased by the Christian children. The parents complied but made sure the boy understood that "Jack" was short for "Jacob," who took on the name "Israel" in the Bible. During the twenty-first century, such actions by schoolteachers would bring on lawsuits and firings, but until the late twentieth century, immigrants were rarely in a position to argue against changing their names.

VOLUNTARY NAME CHANGES

Immigrants arriving in America actually changed their names voluntarily much more often than they did involuntarily. The vast majority of them had al-

ready left their homes and relatives behind and made an arduous journey across the ocean to build new lives in a country whose main language many of them did not even speak. During the early twentieth century, few employers had qualms about discriminating against prospective employees for any reason they chose. If an immigrant's name was difficult to pronounce or spell, many employers would simply hire someone else with a more "American" name. While changing a family name may seem an extreme step to modern, native-born Americans, it was probably seen as a minor sacrifice by impoverished early immigrants who had already given up so much simply to reach America.

ETHNIC NAMING CONVENTIONS

Confusion caused by differences in naming conventions among different ethnic groups has often been the cause of immigrant name changes. Even during the twenty-first century, such differences cause some immigrants sufficient problems to move them to change their names.

Chinese naming conventions place family names first, followed by given names. Sometimes given names include generation names, which are shared by other members of the same generation. Generation names fall between the family and individual given names. For example, the name "Lee Qin Chun" indicates a person in the Lee family and the Qin generation with the given name "Chun." If Lee Qin Chun were to have two sons, they might be called "Lee Han Li" and "Lee Han Chou." Because Western naming conventions have no equivalent for generation names, opportunities for confusion are obvious.

Another Chinese convention that causes confusion for Westerners is the practice of Chinese women retaining their own family names when they marry. However, they sometimes add their husbands' family names to their own given names. Children take the family names of their fathers. Western women have only recently begun to retain their maiden names after marriage, but this relatively new custom has done little to eliminate Westerners' misunderstandings of Chinese married names. A question faced by married Chinese women when they immigrate to the United States is whether they will retain their maiden names or take their husbands' family names.

Before the nineteenth century, German Jews

did not use surnames. Fathers' first names were used in a form that would translate into English as "Jacob the son of Isaac." In 1808, Napoleon I decreed that all Jews living within his empire must adopt family names. In some places, the government gave them a list of names from which to choose and assigned names to those who failed to make selections. When these European Jews came to America, their attachment to the family names imposed on them was often tenuous, making them more prone to change their names after arriving. In addition, Jewish merchants quickly learned that in America their gentile customers were more likely to patronize stores with Anglo-Saxon-sounding names than those with Jewish names. Discrimination in hiring, housing, and other aspects of everyday life also made name changing acceptable to Jewish immigrants.

By the early twenty-first century, a large portion of immigrants to the United States were Hispanics, making the naming conventions used in Spanish-speaking countries important. Traditional Spanish names combine the surnames of both mothers and fathers. Full names are usually made up of two given names and two surnames. For example, the name "José Rafael Sepulveda Calderon" indicates a person whose mother's surname is Calderon and whose father's surname is Sepulveda. However, confusion arises from the practice of omitting the mother's surname in informal usage. Small differences such as these can cause problems when filling out forms such as employment applications.

SPELLING AND PRONUNCIATION

The Cyrillic alphabet is used by dozens of Central Asian and eastern European languages, most notably Russian. Created during the early nineteenth century, this alphabet has many characters that resemble characters in the Latin alphabet used by English and many other languages. However, some of the characters that appear to be the same actually represent different sounds, and each alphabet has characters not in the other. Because Cyrillic and Latin characters do not match perfectly, names transliterated from Cyrillic forms often have several different possible spellings in the Latin alphabet. Moreover, some transliterated names appear to Westerners to be missing vowels,

such as the name "Aleksandr." Spelling and pronunciations of Slavic names are particularly difficult for Americans and non-Slavic people. Recognizing this fact, many Slavic immigrants chose to simplify the spellings of their own names or to change their names entirely to avoid problems in their newly adopted country.

Chinese languages present even more difficult pronunciation challenges. Cantonese and Mandarin are tonal languages in which the meanings of words depend on their rising or falling tones when spoken. Mandarin, for example, uses four different tones to give meaning to spoken words: mid-level, low falling, high rising, and high creaky-rising. For a Westerner used only to placing stress on some syllables more than others, subtle tonal variations used to convey differences of meaning of a word open the door to considerable confusion. Consequently, some Chinese immigrants avoid such problems by simplifying their names.

Wayne Shirey

FURTHER READING

Belli, Melvin, and Allen P. Wilkinson. *Everybody's Guide to the Law: All the Legal Information You Need in One Comprehensive Volume.* New York: HarperCollins, 2003. Contains a good chapter on the legalities of name changing.

Morgan, George G. *How to Do Everything with Your Genealogy.* New York: McGraw-Hill Osborne, 2004. Excellent guide to genealogical research; contains a good section on name changing.

Szucs, Loretto Dennis, and Luebking Hargreaves. *Guidebook to American Genealogy.* Provo, Utah: Ancestry Publishing, 2005. Informative book on genealogy with sections on immigrant name changing.

Wilton, David, and Ivan Brunetti. *Word Myths: Debunking Linguistic Urban Legends.* New York: Oxford University Press, 2004. Contains an informative section on the myths surrounding involuntary name changing.

SEE ALSO: Angel Island Immigration Station; Anglo-conformity; Anti-Semitism; Atlas, Charles; Chinese immigrants; Ellis Island; Employment; Identificational assimilation; Jewish immigrants; Stereotyping.

A NATION OF IMMIGRANTS

IDENTIFICATION: Posthumously published survey of U.S. immigration policy by John F. Kennedy

DATE: First published in 1958; first expanded and revised edition published in 1964

SIGNIFICANCE: *A Nation of Immigrants*, written while John F. Kennedy was still a senator, espouses reform of exclusionary immigration policies. After Kennedy was elected president of the United States in 1960, he called on Congress to reform immigration law.

In 1958, the Anti-Defamation League asked Senator John F. Kennedy, Pulitzer Prize winner for *Profiles in Courage* (1955), to write an essay advocating reform of U.S. immigration policy. Politically, Kennedy hoped to ensure support from Jewish and other immigrant communities for his 1960 bid for the presidency. He used the occasion to compose a meditation on the United States as "a nation of immigrants."

For Kennedy, the leveling effects of Old World oppression shaped the egalitarian nature of American democracy, built upon successive waves of immigration. In the book, Kennedy skirts the economic issues associated with cheap immigrant labor, but he eloquently documents the abuses of nineteenth and twentieth century nativist movements. He summarizes exclusionary U.S. immigration policy from the Naturalization Act of 1790 to the Immigration Act of 1924. According to Kennedy, America is not a "melting pot" for immigrants. Rather, invoking the language of cultural pluralism, he promotes immigration as the engine of democracy that allows new ideas in the arts, politics, economics, and the sciences to challenge the status quo. The book calls for legislative action to remove the immigration quota system—which was achieved after his assassination in 1963 in the Immigration and Nationality Act of 1965.

Luke A. Powers

FURTHER READING

Giglio, James. *The Presidency of John F. Kennedy.* 2d ed. Lawrence: University Press of Kansas, 2006.

Kennedy, John F. *A Nation of Immigrants.* Expanded ed. Introduction by Edward Kennedy. Foreword by Abraham Foxman. New York: HarperPerennial, 2008.

Melhman, Ira. "John F. Kennedy and Immigration Reform." *The Social Contract* 1, no. 4 (Summer, 1991): 201-206.

SEE ALSO: Anti-Defamation League; Commission on Immigration Reform, U.S.; Cultural pluralism; Immigration Act of 1924; Immigration and Nationality Act of 1965; Jewish immigrants; Melting pot theory; Nativism; Naturalization Act of 1790; Xenophobia.

John F. Kennedy. (John F. Kennedy Library)

NATIONAL ROAD

IDENTIFICATION: First federally funded interstate transportation project

DATE: 1811-1840

LOCATION: Maryland, Pennsylvania, West Virginia (then part of Virginia), Ohio, Indiana, and Illinois

SIGNIFICANCE: This trans-Appalachian highway provided both employment for new im-

migrants in its construction as well as a central artery for their westward migration, traveling across mountains and rivers and through the state capitals of Columbus and Indianapolis. Although originally planned to extend to St. Louis, political wrangling, the advent of the railroad, and the end of congressional support caused the road to terminate in central Illinois.

As early as 1802, U.S. Treasury secretary Albert Gallatin articulated the need for a National Road. In 1806, and with the support of President Thomas Jefferson, Congress passed a bill that provided for such a highway between Cumberland, Maryland, and the Mississippi River with the provision that it run through state capitals along its route. In 1811, the work began on the western edge of Cumberland, Maryland, on a twenty-foot-wide roadway with a sixty-six-foot right-of-way, built initially of stone, earth, and gravel, and later of macadam. There was no provision for eminent domain and no compensation provided to landowners, since the course of the road itself was considered sufficient recompense.

Although local citizens and farmers were employed on the project, there was a significant coterie of recent Irish immigrants who followed the westward course of the road, some of whom worked as well on the building of the Erie (completed 1825) and other canals. Mail delivery was facilitated as sections of the National Road were completed, connecting literate immigrants with family and friends on the East Coast and in Europe. The final federal appropriation was in 1838, and construction concluded in 1840 in Vandalia, Illinois.

Richard Sax

FURTHER READING

Dunaway, Wilma A. *The First American Frontier: Transition to Capitalism in Southern Appalachia, 1700-1860.* Chapel Hill: University of North Carolina Press, 1996.

Raitz, Karl B., ed. *A Guide to the National Road.* Baltimore: Johns Hopkins University Press, 1996.

SEE ALSO: Canals; German immigrants; History of immigration, 1783-1891; Iron and steel industry; Land laws; Mississippi River; Railroads; Transportation of immigrants; Westward expansion.

NATIVE AMERICANS

IDENTIFICATION: Aboriginal inhabitants of North America

SIGNIFICANCE: Although Native Americans had occupied the Western Hemisphere for at least thirteen millennia before the first modern Europeans, Africans, and Asians arrived, they, like the immigrant peoples who would follow them, originally came to the New World as immigrants.

There is substantial agreement among historians, anthropologists, archaeologists, and other scholars that the native peoples of North America originated in Asia. Most researchers believe that the ancestors of modern Indians, as they have come to be known, migrated from Siberia across the Bering Strait to Alaska. These early immigrants must have come to North America during periodic ice ages that caused the sea level to drop far enough to create a landmass approximately nine hundred miles wide that connected the Eurasian and North American continents. These early migrants probably followed the migratory mammals they hunted into North America. They eventually traveled southward and eastward until they populated most parts of the North American continent and continued advancing into Central and South America.

Despite widespread agreement on this basic theory of the origin of Native Americans, there is great disagreement concerning the timing of the migration. Furthermore, some Native American historians and writers have questioned the basic idea of explaining their origins with scientific theories that discredit the creation stories of many tribes. Indeed, such theories call into question the very idea that Native Americans are "native," implying instead that they are merely another immigrant group that happened to arrive very early.

SCIENTIFIC THEORIES

The theory that Native Americans migrated from Asia was first suggested long before scientific evidence was collected to support it. Christopher Columbus and other early European explorers and settlers in the New World assumed that Asia and North America were connected. After the vast distance between Eurasia and North America was

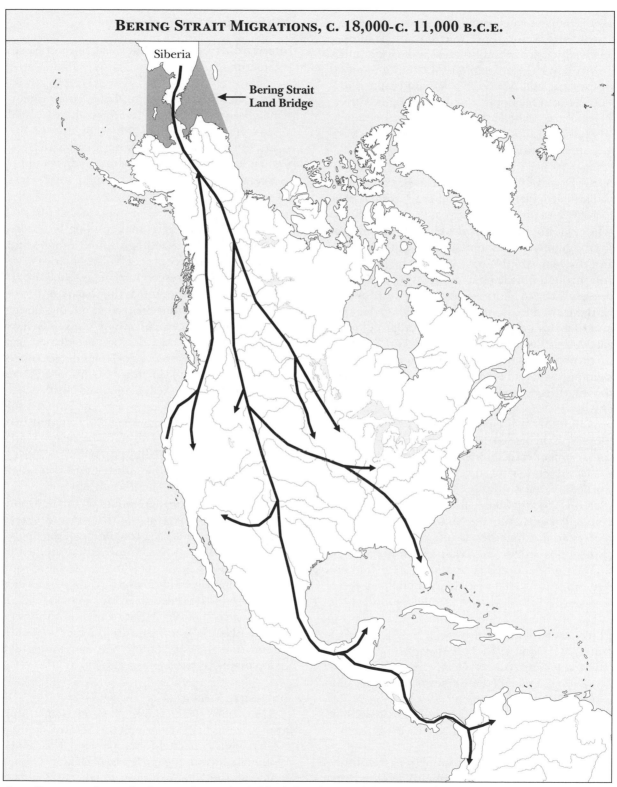

BERING STRAIT MIGRATIONS, C. 18,000–C. 11,000 B.C.E.

Siberia

Bering Strait
Land Bridge

According to one theory, the first people to arrive in North America traveled over a land bridge between modern-day Siberia and Alaska. Once on the continent, they gradually spread southward and eastward.

later understood, scholars recognized that the presence of Native Americans in what they called the New World contradicted the biblical account of Creation, which says that human beings were created in one and only one place. During the late sixteenth century, the Spanish Jesuit missionary José de Acosta proposed a migration theory to explain the existence of Native Americans, thereby vindicating the biblical account of creation. In 1728, when Vitus Bering discovered the strait between Siberia and Alaska that would later be named after him, Acosta's migration theory was discredited because no one believed that primitive peoples could have crossed the strait by boat.

During the twentieth century, scientists finally found evidence to support Acosta's theory despite the existence of the Bering Strait. During several periods within the Pleistocene period, glaciers interrupted the normal flow of water back into the ocean, causing the sea level to drop as much as three hundred feet. During the last period of glaciation, which occurred between 70,000 and 12,000 years ago, a land bridge linked the coast of Siberia with the coast of Alaska. Archaeologists named this land bridge Beringia because it follows the course of the Bering Strait. Furthermore, there is general agreement that the geologic record suggests that Beringia would have provided a practical route for human migration between 70,000 and 45,000 years ago and again between 25,000 and 14,000 years ago. However, disagreement on two points remains: exactly when human migration occurred and whether there was a single period of migration or multiple migrations over a longer period of time.

ASIAN-NATIVE AMERICAN TIES

During the twentieth century, scientists assembled overwhelming evidence proving that a migration from Eurasia to North America did, in fact, occur. In addition to the geological evidence showing that the existence of a land bridge made migration possible, anthropologists have shown that Native Americans share many characteristics with Asians, particularly the inhabitants of northern Siberia. In his 1998 book *The Origins of Native Americans*, anthropologist Michael Crawford points to four types of evidence for Asian-Native American connections: genetic, morphological, craniometric, and cultural.

Modern studies of deoxyribonucleic acid (DNA) have demonstrated that Native Americans have close genetic ties to several modern Asian peoples. Moreover, some genetic markers that appear in Native Americans appear in only one other genetic group: Asians. Crawford traces this connection down to something as mundane as earwax, pointing out that both New World and Asian peoples exhibit a high incidence of dry and brittle ear wax that is unlike the sticky and wet variety that characterizes other populations of the world. One practical result of this similarity is an unusually high level of ear infections among populations in Alaska and Siberia.

Even before the migration theory had real scientific evidence to back it up, it shared with modern science what Crawford calls "morphological" and "craniometric" evidence. Consequently, it had from its start a kind of plausibility. In simple terms, the Native Americans whom José de Acosta saw during the sixteenth century looked to him as if they had come from Asia. Among other facial and bodily characteristics, the Native Americans shared these physical features with Asians:

- straight black hair
- sparse facial and body hair
- high cheek bones
- flat faces
- skin folds (in some cases) covering upper eyelids

Modern science and archeology have added to these similarities dental evidence. Craniometric measurements of Asian and Native American skulls have also supported the migration theory, as skull characteristics tie Native Americans to Asians, not to western Europeans or Africans.

Among the cultural similarities between Native Americans and Asians are beliefs in a natural world that is animated by spirits of animals and plants that must be placated at various times and in holy men and medicine men who have visions and can cure the sick. Even a cursory knowledge of Native American spirituality suggests that it has much more in common with Eastern religions that it does with Western religious beliefs.

NATIVE AMERICAN ORIGIN STORIES

The Native Americans' traditions of their own origins contain no hints of migration from Asia. In fact, they almost entirely dispute the notion of Na-

tive peoples wandering into North America from anywhere else. Instead, traditional stories suggest that Native peoples emerged from the earth. The modern Kiowan writer N. Scott Momaday recounts the Kiowan story of origin in his 1969 book *The Way to Rainy Mountain*:

> You know everything had to begin and this is how it was: the Kiowas came one by one into the world through a hollow log. There were many more than now, but not all of them got out. . . . They looked around and saw the world. It made them glad to see so many things. They called themselves Kwuda, "coming out."

The Choctaw writer Valjean McCarty Hessing tells a similar creation story from the Pacific Northwest region of the United States. In his version, a lonely raven saw a bubbling clamshell come out of the sand. As the raven watched, people emerged from the shell. The raven was delighted that he had company on this lonely earth. In the Zuñi creation story, a lonely Sunfather hears the cries of his children in Mother Earth as he wanders the sky. Seeing two columns of foam at the base of a waterfall, he engenders life in them, ordering that they become gods who will descend into the womb of Mother Earth and bring his children up into the light. Edmund J. Ladd, a member of the Shiwi tribe, has observed that "Most, if not all" traditions of origin "teach that human beings were born out of mother earth."

Scientific research has shown that Native Americans wandered into North America from Asia in search of food and in search of a home. Native American stories suggest that Native Americans were so much a part of this continent that they emerged from beneath it. Rather than seeking a home as so many others who came to America, they were already home—a part of the very soil.

POLITICAL IMPLICATIONS

The Sioux writer Vine Deloria, Jr. has called the Bering Strait theory of Native American origin "a triumph of doctrine over facts." He points out that "there are no well-worn paths which clearly show migratory patterns," and even if there were, there would be no indication of where the footprints were heading. Deloria has also pointed out the irony in the fact that the basic Western story of ori-

gin, the biblical account of Creation, undergirds modern scientific accounts in interesting ways.

Jose de Acosta could not reconcile the existence of Native Americans with the biblical account of Creation, so he theorized that Native Americans came from Asia. In so doing, he found a place for them in the story of Creation that he had brought with him to the New World, confirming that human beings were essentially exiles, wandering from a paradise from which they had been expelled for having sinned. Whether the explanation for the wandering is expulsion from the Garden of Eden or a desperate search for food leading human beings across the Bering Strait, the outcome is the same: All of human life is wandering in search of a lost home, a journey that can only end when the wandering ceases in death. In such a context, the land itself is a prison, a place where one must toil to survive until the better world arrives. In contrast, Native American stories of origin suggest that Paradise is below the feet of Native people, that it is the very earth from which they emerged. They do not have to wander to find it—they have merely to live in its context and understand it.

Much like Deloria, James Wilson in his 1999 history of Native America, *The Earth Shall Weep*, argues that in explaining Native Americans, western science and western religion have worked hand in hand. Modern scientists have even traced the genetic history of man back to a single woman, whom they have named "Eve" after the biblical mother of humankind. They have also theorized that humankind originated in one place, Africa, from which it spread into other parts of the world. Thus, whether the account is tilted toward the biblical or the scientific view of creation, the conclusion is the same: All Americans are wanderers who wound up here in this alien land and must somehow learn to live together as immigrants. Moreover, no one is "native," not even *Native* Americans.

CONCLUSIONS

Just as for many, there is no reconciling of the biblical account of Creation with modern scientific theories of creation, such as evolution or the Big Bang, so Native American stories of creation will likely never be reconciled with the science of the migration theory of Native American origins. More importantly, however, Native American stories of creation carry with them an idea of rootedness and

belonging that contradicts the biblical story of Creation as well as the science of the migration theory or even the science of evolution. In so doing, these stories dramatize for native people why they are a part of the land, "natives" in a land of immigrants.

H. William Rice

FURTHER READING

Ballantine, Betty, and Ian Ballantine. *Native Americans: An Illustrated History.* Atlanta, Ga.: Turner, 1992. Well-illustrated book that includes a Native American account of Native American origins.

Crawford, Michael H. *The Origins of Native Americans: Evidence from Anthropological Genetics.* New York: Cambridge University Press, 1998. Detailed examination of the scientific evidence for Native American origins. Although the book is written for anthropologists, nonspecialists can grasp its basic arguments.

Hoxie, Frederick E. *Encyclopedia of North American Indians.* Boston: Houghton Mifflin, 1996. Encyclopedic reference work containing entries on Native American origins from the perspectives of both modern science and Native American cultures.

Kehoe, Alice B. *North American Indians: A Comprehensive Account.* Englewood Cliffs, N.J.: Prentice-Hall, 1981. Traces the evolution of the first inhabitants of North America, region by region, from prehistory to the present. Contains recommended readings and sources at the end of each chapter.

Momaday, N. Scott. *The Way to Rainy Mountain.* Albuquerque: University of New Mexico Press, 1969. A Kiowan Indian, Momaday reconstructs not only the stories of the origin of his people, but also the stories of their migration from the Great Plains to Oklahoma.

Underhill, Ruth M. *Red Man's America: A History of Indians in the United States.* Rev. ed. Chicago: University of Chicago Press, 1971. Concise volume surveying origins, history, and definitive accounts of social customs, material culture, religion, and mythology. Written from the perspective of the first peoples of North America.

Wilson, James. *The Earth Shall Weep: A History of Native America.* New York: Grove, 1999. Comprehensive and highly readable history of Native Americans whose first part covers origins from

the perspectives of both modern science and Native American traditions.

SEE ALSO: Alaska; Asian immigrants; Nativism; Natural disasters as push-pull factors; Pilgrim and Puritan immigrants.

NATIVE SONS OF THE GOLDEN STATE

IDENTIFICATION: Immigrant support group and benevolent organization
ALSO KNOWN AS: Chinese American Citizens Alliance (1927 on)
DATE: Founded in 1895; rechartered in 1915

SIGNIFICANCE: Organized initially in California to provide its Chinese American immigrants community support and to encourage them in the process of assimilation at a time when they faced entrenched bigotry and government-sanctioned discrimination, the Native Sons of the Golden State (not to be confused with the white nativist organization "Native Sons of the Golden West") became a national model for immigrant organizations interested in promoting good citizenship through respect for and commitment to the ideals of their adopted country.

By the closing decade of the nineteenth century, Chinese American immigrants in California were facing unprecedented discrimination. Initially welcomed as cheap labor during the gold rush era and then later during the massive enterprise of completing the transcontinental railroad, Chinese immigrants quickly became objects of hostility and violence by Californians convinced the Chinese were a particular threat both economically in an era of heated competition for work and culturally as the Chinese shared neither language, religion, nor social customs with the larger community of mostly European descendants.

After the landmark federal Chinese Exclusion Act of 1882 banned Chinese immigration for ten years, the Chinese community already in California struggled to find stability amid an environment of escalating bigotry that saw the steady removal of

their civil rights through a succession of discriminatory state laws. Moreover, with immigration effectively curtailed, the Chinese American community faced the threat of rapid cultural extinction unless some movement was made toward assimilation.

In response to this, in 1895 a small but determined group of second-generation and English-speaking Chinese Americans met in San Francisco to found an organization designed to provide Chinese immigrants the kind of fraternal club routinely denied them because of their ethnicity. However, their specific goal was to help Chinese Americans assimilate by providing avenues through which members might participate in community activities. Members pledged to uphold the ideals of American democracy and adopted as their organization's name "Native Sons of the Golden State" to emphasize the fact they were born in California and were thus Americans by birth.

Against vocal hostility from some Chinese Americans concerned that such a mission would deprive the next generations of any sense of their Chinese heritage, members of the Native Sons nevertheless championed having Chinese Americans take leadership roles in their neighborhoods as a way to direct them into positions of authority and trust. By encouraging community participation and the moral instruction of youth, the organization quickly made national headlines and spread to other cities, first in California but nationwide within a decade. In 1915, the Native Sons of California was rechartered as the Chinese American Citizens Alliance.

Joseph Dewey

FURTHER READING

Lee, Erika. *At America's Gate: Chinese Immigration During the Exclusion Era, 1882-1943*. Chapel Hill: University of North Carolina Press, 2007.
Lien, Pei-te. *The Making of Asian Americans Through Political Participation*. Philadelphia: Temple University Press, 2001.
Pfaelzer, Jean. *The Forgotten War Against Chinese Americans*. Berkeley: University of California Press, 2008.

SEE ALSO: Anti-Chinese movement; Asian immigrants; Assimilation theories; Chinese American Citizens Alliance; Chinese Exclusion Act of 1882; Chinese immigrants; Citizens Committee to Repeal Chinese Exclusion; History of immigration after 1891; Immigration Act of 1943; "Yellow peril" campaign.

NATIVISM

DEFINITION: Negative form of ethnocentrism that is typically expressed by opposition to what is perceived as alien contamination by members of minority and immigrant groups

SIGNIFICANCE: Throughout the history of the United States, nativism has been an ideology that has driven Americans to strong, and frequently harsh, reactions against members of groups, particularly immigrants, who are perceived to be different. During the nineteenth and early twentieth centuries, nativist movements were influential in helping to pass restrictive immigration laws.

Since the founding of the United States, Americans has frequently shown ambivalence toward immigrants. Because the country has been built on immigration, it has generally welcomed new immigrants as necessary additions to the labor force and as sources of new economic growth. On the other hand, immigrants have also been feared and resented because of their alien ways and their competition with native-born Americans for jobs and political power. Nativists, the most outspoken critics of immigration, feared that the American way of life, and even the republic itself, was in danger from the constant stream of newcomers. They developed an ideology of nativism that comprised three identifiable strains:

- anti-Catholic nativism
- racial nativism
- antiradical nativism

These three strains often overlapped in the various nativist organizations that emerged in the nineteenth and twentieth centuries.

ANTI-ROMAN CATHOLIC NATIVISM

Anti-Catholic nativism had its roots in the religious views of the earliest English settlers in the American colonies. As products of the Protestant

Reformation in Europe, the early colonists viewed the pope as a foreign monarch who exercised dangerous influence through the Roman Catholic Church. The large influx of Irish Catholic immigrants during the early nineteenth century fueled an upsurge of anti-Catholic propaganda, which alleged that Irish Catholics were agents of the pope intent on undermining republican institutions. During the 1830's, inventor Samuel F. B. Morse wrote a tract, *Foreign Conspiracy Against the Liberties of the United States* (1834), in which he called for the formation of the Anti-Popery Union to resist the papal plot. His tract became required reading in many Protestant Sunday schools. In 1834, an anti-Catholic mob burned the Ursuline Convent in Charlestown, Massachusetts. Ten years later, riots erupted in Philadelphia when Irish Catholics opposed the use of the Protestant King James version of the Bible in public schools.

The American Protective Association (APA), organized in 1887, was the most visible manifestation of anti-Catholic nativism during the late nineteenth century. Its members swore they would never vote for Catholic candidates, employ Catholic workers over Protestants, or join with Catholic strikers. The APA drew strong support from workers in the midwestern and Rocky Mountain states who feared competition from cheap Irish labor. By the late 1890's, however, as Irish and German Catholics became an important part of the electorate, the more extreme anti-Catholic sentiment dissipated. The APA itself disappeared during the 1890's.

RACIAL NATIVISM

During the late nineteenth century, a racial strain of nativism, cultivated by the self-professed guardians of Anglo-Saxon culture and apparently supported by scientific research, began to be di-

Short-lived nativist newspaper published in Boston in 1852. (Library of Congress)

rected against immigrant groups. Ever since colonial times, white settlers had viewed themselves as culturally and physically different from, and superior to, Native Americans and African Americans. Some intellectuals adapted the research of Charles Darwin on biological evolution to argue that certain races would inevitably triumph over others because of their inherent superiority. English and American intellectuals confidently trumpeted the superiority of the Anglo-Saxon "race" and its institutions, and researchers set out to "prove" their cultural assumptions by measuring the cranial volumes of skulls from members of various ethnic groups and devising crude intelligence tests. As a new wave of immigrants from Asia and southern and eastern Europe began to arrive, these newcomers were quickly labeled racially inferior.

Racial nativism reached its zenith during the early twentieth century. Influenced by the European eugenics movement, with its emphasis on breeding the right racial groups, American nativists expressed alarm over the impact of the new immigrants. Madison Grant's widely read *The Passing of the Great Race* (1916) summarized many of the racial nativist arguments. Grant argued that the superior Nordic "race" was being destroyed by the influx of southern and eastern Europeans, and warned that race mixing would result in an inferior hybrid race and the destruction of Anglo-Saxon civilization. Jewish and Italian immigrants, in particular, were often singled out for criticism in nativist publications because of their alleged racial inferiority.

ANTIRADICAL NATIVISM

Immigrants also came under attack for political reasons during the late nineteenth century. Nativist writers worried that most immigrants came from nondemocratic societies, harbored socialist or anarchist sympathies, and would foment revolution in the United States. The participation of some immigrants in the labor agitation of the period seemed to confirm these fears of alien radicalism. Antiradical nativism intensified following the 1917 Russian Revolution and the onset of an economic crisis in the United States. Although most immigrants were not socialists, immigrants nevertheless constituted a majority of the membership of the American Socialist Party. During the Red Scare of 1919-1920, when many Americans feared that a communist

revolution was imminent, immigrants and radicalism became synonymous in the public mind.

IMPACT ON PUBLIC POLICY

Nativism had its most significant impact on public policy in the area of immigration restrictions designed to discriminate against Asians and southern and eastern Europeans. In 1882, the federal Chinese Exclusion Act cut off further immigration by Chinese laborers. During World War I, Congress overrode a presidential veto to enact literacy tests for all immigrants, which discriminated against southern and eastern Europeans who had less access to basic education. During the 1920's, the United States adopted a system of quotas based on national origins for European immigration, imposing a maximum annual limit of 150,000 and allocating most of the slots to northern and western European countries. The national origins quota system formed the basis of immigration law until it was abolished in 1965.

Richard V. Damms

FURTHER READING
Bennett, David H. *The Party of Fear: From Nativist Movements to the New Right in American History.* Chapel Hill: University of North Carolina Press, 1988. Scholarly study of evolution of nineteenth century nativism into twentieth century political conservatism.

Billington, Ray Allen. *The Protestant Crusade, 1800-1860: A Study of the Origins of American Nativism.* New York: Macmillan, 1938. Classic historical work on early nineteenth century nativism.

Curran, Thomas J. *Xenophobia and Immigration, 1820-1930.* Boston: Twayne, 1975. Overview of the historical background behind restrictive immigration policies throughout U.S. history, focusing on nativism and such groups as the Ku Klux Klan.

Gabaccia, Donna R. *Immigration and American Diversity: A Social and Cultural History.* Malden, Mass.: Blackwell, 2002. Survey of American immigration history, from the mid-eighteenth century to the early twenty-first century, with an emphasis on cultural and social trends, with attention to ethnic conflicts, nativism, and racialist theories.

Higham, John. *Strangers in the Land: Patterns of American Nativism, 1860-1925.* New Brunswick, N.J.: Rutgers University Press, 2002. Classic ac-

count of anti-immigrant hostility in the United States from the Civil War to the final victory for restriction during the 1920's.

Lee, Erika. *At America's Gates: Chinese Immigration During the Exclusion Era, 1882-1943*. Chapel Hill: University of North Carolina Press, 2003. Study of immigration from China to the United States from the time of the Chinese Exclusion Act to the loosening of American immigration laws during the 1960's, with an afterword on U.S. immigration policies after the terrorist attacks of September 11, 2001.

Navarro, Armando. *The Immigration Crisis: Nativism, Armed Vigilantism, and the Rise of a Countervailing Movement*. Walnut Creek, Calif.: AltiMira Press, 2008. Comprehensive history of the politics of immigration to the United States since the early colonial era, focusing on the role played by nativist movements.

SEE ALSO: American Protective Association; Americanization programs; Anti-Catholicism; Anti-Chinese movement; Anti-Filipino violence; Anti-Japanese movement; Anti-Semitism; Eugenics movement; Know-Nothing Party; Ku Klux Klan; Xenophobia.

NATURAL DISASTERS AS PUSH-PULL FACTORS

DEFINITION: Natural occurrences such as hurricanes, earthquakes, volcanic eruptions, pandemics, and other disasters that prompt human migrations

SIGNIFICANCE: Permanent or temporary migration to a safer environment is the traditional survival strategy of populations faced with overwhelming natural or environmental disasters. Often such disasters not only result in destruction of living environments, but also destroy the social and economic fabrics of a society, forcing entire communities to seek new social, economic, and cultural environments in which to thrive.

Natural disasters often function as initiatives to push populations to migrate to new, more favor-

able living conditions. Less frequently, areas struck by natural disasters may serve to pull in small group populations if they believe the post-disaster living conditions can be exploited to their advantage. A broad and extensive record of migrations, both forced and voluntary, exists in the geological, archeological, and written historical records documenting human culture.

DISASTERS AND HISTORICAL MIGRATIONS

Evidence exists suggesting environmental change initiated the first humanoid migrations out of the African continent as early as 60 to 70 millennia in the past, dispersing human ancestry northward in an attempt to find more favorable living conditions. Geological evidence from about 70 millennia ago indicates that a super-volcanic eruption of the Lake Toba Caldera on the Indonesian island of Sumatra resulted in a massive climate-changing event. The dating of this eruption coincides with fossil evidence and DNA indexing suggesting that a massive reduction in the human population of the time from estimates of 60 million to as few as 10,000 survivors globally. The resulting bottlenecking of human evolution precipitated an outward radiation of survivors to new habitats.

In much more recent times, a massive flooding of the Black Sea through the Bosporus Straits around 5600 B.C.E. devastated the near-shore cultures and resulted in a mass migration out of the area populating new regions of Asia Minor. This flood was mythologized in both the Tale of Gilgamesh and the biblical Book of Genesis. More recently still, the super-volcanic eruption of the Santorini Caldera in the southern Aegean Sea around 1600 B.C.E. caused the downfall of the Minoan and other Bronze Age cultures, and the climatic outfall from the eruption severely stressed Egyptian and early Greek cultures. Survivors of the eruption dispersed throughout the Mediterranean basin to repopulate new territories and give rise to new cultures. In North and South America, inclusive evidence has linked droughts caused by climatic changes to the collapse and migration of native cultures, including the ancient Pueblo peoples of the American Southwest, the Maya and Olmec peoples of Mexico and Central America, and the Nazca culture of the South American Andes.

DISASTER-DRIVEN MIGRATIONS TO NORTH AMERICA

During the late tenth century, the Vikings of northern Europe were pushed to explore and settle North America after their colonies had deforested Greenland. However, they had to abandon their North American colonies when the Little Ice Age developed and new Arctic ice floes blocked sailing routes. The Little Ice Age, which lasted from the mid-thirteenth to the early seventh centuries, worked as a major push-pull factor in human migrations. Cooling in the northern hemisphere resulted in severe long-term crop losses, food shortages, and prolonged famines. It also led to the outbreak of numerous diseases, most notably the bubonic plague. The freezing of shipping lanes devastated trade. Sustained droughts ensued, forests were cut down for heating fuel, and warfare became almost constant among communities competing for shrinking resources. All these condi-tions resulted in massive disruptions of social and cultural systems.

Northern European and Asian peoples mi-grated to escape the harsh climatic conditions or to fill living niches left by deaths and emigration. By the late fifteenth century, the need to search out re-sources and flee social upheavals gave rise to an era of exploration. Over the next several hundred years, large numbers of Europeans were pushed and pulled into emigrating to North America.

During the mid-nineteenth century, two large-scale famines proved major push factors in North American immigration: the Great Irish Famine be-tween 1845 and 1852, and the Great Northern China Famine of 1877-1878. Survivors of both fam-ines were pushed out of their homelands by the de-teriorating economic and social conditions, and pulled to the prospects of a better life in North America. In the same manner, during the late twentieth century, severe drought, desertification,

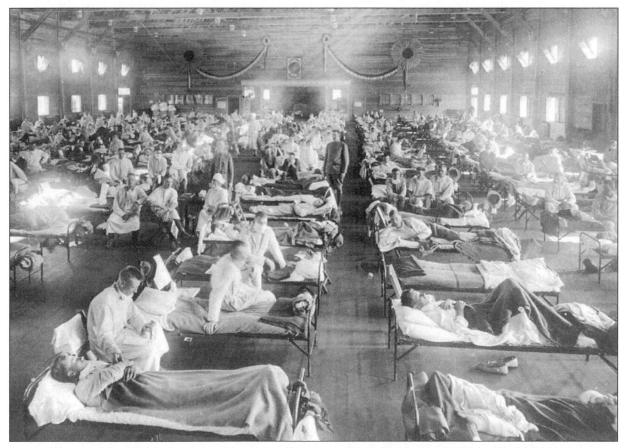

Victims of the 1918 influenza pandemic in a Kansas emergency hospital. (AP/Wide World Photos)

and famine resulted in large migrations of peoples from central and sub-Saharan Africa. As global climate changes have continued to advance during the twenty-first century, rising sea levels, climatic variations, and habitat loss will most likely bring about major new population migrations in the future.

DISASTER-DRIVEN MIGRATIONS WITHIN NORTH AMERICA

An early twentieth century disaster that directly affected North America was the great influenza pandemic of 1918-1919, in which more than 500 million people were infected and 100 million died worldwide, mostly young adults. Between 700,000 and 1 million people are estimated to have died from influenza within the United States. Influenza deaths became a pull factor that drew people to migrate to new regions to fill jobs and properties previously held by influenza victims. Another early twentieth century disaster that prompted a massive internal migration was the Great Mississippi Flood of 1927, in which more than 700,000 persons were displaced from their homes. It helped propel the Great Migration of African Americans from the South to northern cities, particularly Chicago and Detroit.

The disastrous North American hurricane season of 1928, while devastating vast areas of southern Florida, became a pull for migration as rebuilding efforts promoted the region as a vacation destination. The Dust Bowl years of the 1930's, brought on by poor farming practices and drought, pushed people from the Great Plains to northern cities and West Coast states.

In 2005, Hurricane Katrina destroyed large portions of Louisiana, Mississippi, and Alabama, most notably the city of New Orleans. The hurricane resulted in the evacuation of more than 1,000,000 people, the largest migration of Americans since the Dust Bowl years. Of these people, 700,000 became displaced persons from New Orleans, and after two years only 40 percent had returned home; the remaining number relocated to other cities throughout the United States. On a smaller scale, a tornado in Picher, Oklahoma, in 2008 resulted in the town being destroyed to such an extent it was abandoned in 2009, forcing all its residents to migrate to new locations.

Randall L. Milstein

FURTHER READING

Bullard, Robert D., and Beverly Wright, eds. *Race, Place, and Environmental Justice After Hurricane Katrina.* Boulder, Colo.: Westview Press, 2009. Revealing look at the roles of different ethnic communities in the rebuilding of the Gulf coast after Hurricane Katrina struck.

Clark, Jeffrey J. *Tracking Prehistoric Migrations: Pueblo Settlers Among the Tonto Basin Hohokam.* Tucson: University of Arizona Press, 2001. Of the migrations of early Native American groups in the American Southwest.

Diamond, Jared. *Guns, Germs, and Steel.* New York: W. W. Norton, 1997. Extended essay on world history offering many ideas on how physical geography has influenced human events such as population movements.

Fagan, Brian. *The Little Ice Age: How Climate Made History, 1300-1850.* New York: Basic Books, 2000. Interesting study of the relationship between climatic changes, food supply, and population movements during the Little Ice Age.

Gregory, James N. *American Exodus: The Dust Bowl Migration and Okie Culture in California.* New York: Oxford University Press, 1989. History of the migrants from Oklahoma and other southern Great Plains states who fled to California to escape the Dust Bowl conditions of the 1930's.

Gribben, Arthur, ed. *The Great Famine and the Irish Diaspora in America.* Amherst: University of Massachusetts Press, 1999. Collection of twelve essays commemorating the 150th anniversary of the Great Irish Famine that drove more than 1.5 million people to leave Ireland.

Levey, Richard, and Daniel Franck. *Dust Bowl! The 1930's Black Blizzards.* New York: Bearport, 2005. Graphic account of the effects of dust storms in the Midwest.

Rain, David. *Eaters of the Dry Season: Circular Labor Migration in the West African Sahel.* Boulder, Colo.: Westview Press, 1999. Encroaching desertification has made West Africa's Sahel region one of the most precarious human environments in the world. This work explores the dynamics of the population that lives in the Sahel, from the seasonal migrants to the farmers and herders.

Rosario, Kevin. *The Culture of Calamity: Disaster and the Making of Modern America.* Chicago: University of Chicago Press, 2007. Broad survey of the role of natural disasters in U.S. history.

Williams, A. R. "After the Deluge: Central America's Storm of the Century." *National Geographic*, November, 1999, 108-129. Well-illustrated account of Hurricane Mitch, which devastated Central America in 1998 and drove tens of thousands of people to emigrate to the United States.

SEE ALSO: Disaster recovery work; Economic opportunities; Great Depression; Great Irish Famine; Mississippi River; Push-pull factors; Refugees; Return migration; Salvadoran immigrants.

NATURALIZATION

DEFINITION: Process by which aliens become citizens of the new countries in which they reside

> **SIGNIFICANCE:** The naturalization process in the United States has offered citizenship to persons born in other countries but the process itself has historically raised issues about fairness, national security concerns, and public perceptions of certain immigrant groups.

The issue of citizenship is so important that naturalization is mentioned within the foundation law of the United States, the U.S. Constitution. Article I, section 8 of that document authorizes the U.S. Congress to "establish an uniform Rule of Naturalization." In 1790, the year after the Constitution was ratified, Congress enacted its first naturalization law. The Fourteenth Amendment, which was ratified in 1868, expanded the constitutional definition of citizenship. Since that time, additional legislation has continued to refine the legal rules concerning naturalization.

EARLY YEARS OF THE REPUBLIC

When the Framers of the U.S. Constitution considered the issue of naturalization, they decided that Congress should have the power to establish uniform laws and procedures governing the process by which citizens of other countries could become American citizens. Before the Constitution was ratified, naturalization procedures were conducted by the courts of individual states, but the members of the Constitutional Convention of 1787 decided that leaving such an important matter to the states would create confusion. They agreed that decisions concerning naturalization should be ruled upon only by courts with common law jurisdiction. It was also necessary for the procedures to be conducted with prothonotaries (court clerks) and official seals.

Congress's passage of the Naturalization Act of 1790 created guidelines for U.S. citizenship. In limiting citizenship to "free white persons," the law denied the possibility of citizenship to indentured servants, free blacks, Native Americans, and, later, Asians. The law also stated that white immigrants of "good moral character" could petition state courts for citizenship after they had been residents of the United States for two years and were residents of the states to which they made their petitions. Only five years later, that law was superseded by the Naturalization Act of January 29, 1795. The new law increased the period of residence from two to five years. It also mandated that immigrants wanting to become American citizens had formally to declare their intention to become citizens three years before they formally applied. New citizens were also required formally to renounce all allegiance to their former countries.

In 1798, Congress again increased the period of residence necessary to apply for citizenship, from five to fourteen years. Although proponents of this new requirement argued that it was necessary for issues of national security, many historians believe that the change was made for political reasons—to limit the number of new citizens who might support and vote for Thomas Jefferson's Democratic-Republican Party and against the ruling Federalist Party. Indeed, naturalized citizens from Ireland and France did tend to side with the Democratic-Republicans. Considered part of the Alien and Sedition Acts of 1798, this law was repealed in 1802, when Jefferson was president.

NINETEENTH CENTURY LEGISLATION

The Fourteenth Amendment to the U.S. Constitution extended citizenship to all persons born within the territory of the United States, regardless of their parents' citizenship:

> All persons born or naturalized in the United States and subject to the jurisdiction thereof, are citizens of the United States and of the State wherein they reside. No State shall make or en-

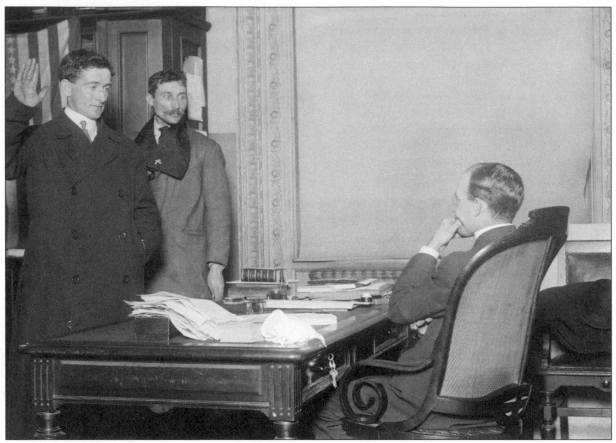

Swearing in of a new citizen before a New York judge in 1910. (Library of Congress/George Grantham Bain Collection)

force any law which shall abridge the privileges or immunities of citizens of the United States . . .

Although the words "All persons born . . . in the United States . . . are citizens" seem unequivocal, there are actually two exceptions to this principle—children of foreign diplomats and children of occupying enemy military personnel.

The Naturalization Act of 1870 made explicit the principle articulated in the Fourteenth Amendment by providing for the naturalization of all African Americans born in the United States, including former slaves.

The 1870 law also established new penalties for fraudulent naturalization applications, and it specified that Asians living in the United States were not eligible for American citizenship. The Chinese Exclusion Act of 1882 further codified these restrictions by forbidding further immigration from China and making even more explicit the ban on naturalization for Chinese residents of the United States. However, a significant challenge to Chinese exclusion came in 1898, when the U.S. Supreme Court ruled in the case of *United States v. Wong Kim Ark* that citizenship had to be granted to children born in the United States to Chinese parents. Meanwhile, the Geary Act of 1892 continued to enact the ban on naturalization by Chinese residents.

In 1862, Congress had passed a law allowing immigrants who had served honorably in the U.S. Army to apply for naturalization after only one year of residence. In 1894, this privilege was extended to honorably discharged veterans of the U.S. Navy and Marine Corps who had served a minimum of five years. These measures allowed a significant number of Irish immigrants who had served in the Mexican War and the U.S. Civil War to become citizens and helped make possible a strong Irish pres-

ence in the politics of such cities as New York, Boston, and Chicago.

The Immigration Act of 1882 sought to exclude "convicts (except those convicted of political offenses), lunatics, idiots and persons likely to become public charges" from entry into the United States. Such persons already in the country were excluded from the naturalization process. The law set up a series of immigration offices at various ports of entry and levied a fifty-cent tax on all immigrants landing at these ports.

TWENTIETH CENTURY LEGISLATION

The Naturalization Act of 1906 tightened the requirements for naturalization. Prospective citizens had to produce verification of their entry into the United States and verification of the identities of their spouses and children. They also had to demonstrate their ability to speak English. The Emergency Quota Act of 1921 set national quotas for entry into the United States based on 3 percent of the number of residents from each country who had been residing in the United States during the year 1890. The quota system effectively limited immigration from eastern and southern European countries but, perhaps oddly, set no quotas on immigration from Latin America. Consequently, the numbers of immigrants from Mexico and other Latin American countries who applied for naturalization dramatically increased over the next two decades. Meanwhile, the Nationality Act of 1940 sought to clarify the status of those born in United States territories and made residence in the United States a key to retaining citizenship for those born in the United States of foreign parents.

The Chinese Exclusion Act was finally repealed by the Immigration Act of 1943, which was also known as the Magnuson Act. Afterward, a steady stream of Cantonese-speaking immigrants began to enter the United States who were likely to learn to speak English and apply for naturalization. Repeal of the Chinese Exclusion Act also paved the way for Chinese nationals already living in the United States to apply for naturalization. The Immigration and Nationality Act of 1952, also known as the McCarran-Walter Act, added some new restrictions to immigration but granted U.S. citizenship by birth to persons born in the U.S. territories of Guam, the Northern Mariana Islands, Puerto Rico, and the U.S. Virgin Islands. Before this law

was passed, persons born in those territories had to apply for naturalization to become U.S. citizens. The Immigration and Nationality Act of 1965 allowed residents of any country of origin presently residing in the United States equal access to the naturalization process.

SPECIAL ISSUES

By the 1980's, illegal immigration had become a concern for many in the United States. The Immigration Reform and Control Act of 1986 addressed the realities of undocumented residents in the United States by providing the opportunity for undocumented immigrants to apply for naturalization provided they could prove that they had been in the United States for at least four years. Although the law was criticized by some for providing "amnesty" to people who had lived in the United States illegally, the legislation included new sanctions against American employers who knowingly hired undocumented workers.

During the 1980's and 1990's, many American couples looked to other countries to adopt children. The Child Citizenship Act of 2000 made the process of naturalization much easier for foreign adoptees. Under this law, children under the age of eighteen who were adopted by American citizens and were under their adoptive parents' custody automatically became naturalized upon their entry into the United States.

MODERN NATURALIZATION PROCESSES

During the early twenty-first century, immigrants who had attained permanent resident status and obtained green cards could apply for naturalization after five years of residence in the United States or only three years if they were married to American citizens. Applicants for naturalization had to demonstrate permanent residence in the states or districts in which they made their applications. They also had to show "good moral character," which was determined through criminal background checks, and "an attachment to the Constitution," which was demonstrated through a basic civics test. Finally, applicants also had to be able to communicate in basic English and swear an oath of allegiance to the United States.

Between the mid-1990's and the early twenty-first century, the number of immigrants who became naturalized citizens increased dramatically.

In 1996, there were approximately 6.5 million naturalized citizens in the United States. In 2005, that figure had risen to more than 11 million. By that time, almost one-half of all foreign-born immigrants who were legally residing within the United States had been naturalized. Reasons for this large increase in naturalization included several negative incentives, such as the trend to restrict certain public benefits to U.S. citizens. Another incentive to naturalize was the government's making the cost of replacing green cards comparable to the cost of applying for naturalization.

Most recently naturalized citizens live in California, New York, Texas, Florida, New Jersey, and Illinois, and most have come from European and Asian nations. However, the fastest-growing segment of the naturalized population comes from Mexico and Central America.

During the late twentieth century, the subject of dual citizenship began receiving national attention. At issue has been how immigrants can reconcile their dual citizenship with the oath they take in which they renounce their previous citizenship. Despite this apparent contradiction, there have been some high-profile cases of naturalized citizens who have retained their previous citizenship. California governor Arnold Schwarzenegger, who has retained his Austrian citizenship, is perhaps the best-known example. The U.S. State Department's policy on dual citizenship has been that the U.S. government does not recommend it but will recognize it. The government recognizes that some newly naturalized citizens may have responsibilities to fulfill to the countries of their birth. For example, naturalized U.S. citizens from Israel may still be liable for Israeli military service that does not affect their U.S. citizenship. However, the Department of Homeland Security has come under criticism for detaining naturalized U.S. citizens traveling with foreign passports.

William Carney

FURTHER READING

Aleinikoff, Thomas A., et al. *Immigration and Citizenship: Process and Policy.* 6th ed. St. Paul, Minn.: West Group, 2008. Popular legal textbook that discusses legislation and court cases relating to all aspects of immigration and naturalization.

Bray, Ilona. *Becoming a U.S. Citizen: A Guide to the Law, Exam, and Interview.* 4th ed. Berkeley, Calif.: Nolo Press, 2008. Practical and clearly written guide explaining the advantages and disadvantages of obtaining American citizenship, as well as current American rules for naturalization.

LeMay, Michael C., and Elliott Robert Barken, eds. *U.S. Immigration and Naturalization Laws and Issues: A Documentary History.* Westport, Conn.: Greenwood Press, 1999. Collection of 150 unabridged historical documents pertaining to immigration and naturalization issues.

Schreuder, Sally A. *How to Become a United States Citizen.* 5th ed. Berkeley, Calif.: Nolo Press, 1996. Concise guidebook that clearly explains the rules and procedures of the naturalization process.

Schuck, Peter. *Citizens, Strangers, and In-Betweens: Essays on Immigration and Citizenship.* Boulder, Colo.: Westview, 1998. Collection of essays on a wide variety of topics relating to citizenship and naturalization by a recognized authority on legal aspects of immigration and naturalization.

Smith, Roger M. *Civic Ideals: Conflicting Visions of Citizenship in U.S. History.* New Haven, Conn.: Yale University Press, 1999. Liberal analysis emphasizing racial and gender discrimination in naturalization laws from the colonial era to the early twentieth century.

Spiro, Peter J. *Beyond Citizenship: American Identity After Globalization.* New York: Oxford University Press, 2008. Investigation into the changing nature of American identity that touches on the changing nature of citizenship and nationality in an increasingly globalized culture.

SEE ALSO: *Boutilier v. Immigration and Naturalization Service*; Citizenship; Citizenship and Immigration Services, U.S.; Dual citizenship; Immigration and Nationality Act of 1965; Naturalization Act of 1790; *Ozawa v. United States*; Permanent resident status; Resident aliens; *United States v. Bhagat Singh Thind*.

NATURALIZATION ACT OF 1790

THE LAW: Federal legislation establishing rules and procedures for naturalization of aliens

DATE: Enacted on March 26, 1790

ALSO KNOWN AS: An Act to Establish an Uniform Rule of Naturalization

SIGNIFICANCE: This act was the first federal law to establish procedures for naturalization under the U.S. Constitution. Although it required only two years' residence prior to naturalization, less time than any succeeding law, it restricted the right of naturalization to white male immigrants.

In accordance with Article I, section 8, clause 4 of the Constitution, which grants Congress the power "to establish an uniform Rule of Naturalization," Congress passed a naturalization act, which was signed into law on March 26, 1790. The act granted foreign-born free white men the ability to naturalize after two years' residence in the United States.

When weighing the provisions and residency requirements, congressional legislators debated the relative merits of a liberal conception of citizenship, and its transferability, while also debating whether the danger of immigrants refusing to shed their antirepublican, old-world traditions outweighed their value as a source of wealth and increased population. Idealists who viewed the United States as a republican asylum allied themselves with moderates whose mercantilist outlook caused them to see new migrants, rich or poor, as an asset to the nation. Future Democratic-Republicans John Page and James Madison of Virginia and future Federalist John Lawrence were particularly active in the debates that shaped the law into its final form.

Congressmen also debated to what degree the law should supersede or defer to existing state naturalization laws. Concerns about conflicts with state laws ultimately led to another change from the original bill, which had stipulated that the rights of citizenship would be granted in steps, withholding the right to hold office until the second year of residence. Rather than entangle the law with conflicting state requirements, the final bill that was passed granted all rights of citizenship at the end of the second year. This conflict would come to the fore in U.S. courts, with federal authority over citizenship being fully confirmed in the 1817 decision *Chirac v. Chirac*. Also left unanswered was the status of foreign-born colonists who had allied themselves with the patriot cause in the American Revolution, which led to controversy over the seating of Swiss-born U.S. senator Albert Gallatin in 1793.

The act built upon earlier existing legislation and legal tradition, modeling the law on existing state naturalization laws. A precedent for citizenship at the national level already existed in article IV of the Articles of Confederation. The law differed from Articles of Confederation provisions chiefly in explicitly restricting naturalization to whites only. The 1790 act also followed trends in the legal concept of naturalization, and the existing common-law tradition of feme covert, attaching the legal identity to the implicitly male head of household, to the exclusion of his wife, dependent children, slaves, and indentured servants. Although citizenship status descended to the acknowledged free white sons, the law excepted the children of fathers who had never resided in the United States.

The act also reflected the trend of the increasing concentration of citizenship at the federal or national level of government. Through the passage of the act, it was possible to be a citizen of the United States and, owing to religious or residency restrictions, not a citizen of one's state of residence; conversely, a person could be a citizen of a state but not of the United States. The Naturalization Act of 1795 would attempt to further federalize citizenship and was aided by court cases confirming the federalization trend in evolving legal precedent.

The Naturalization Act of 1790 had a shorter residency requirement for heads of household than any succeeding federal legislation: The 1795 act lengthened the residency requirement to five years, to which it returned in 1802 after the longer, fourteen-year requirement under the Alien Friends Act of 1798.

John O'Keefe

FURTHER READING

Baseler, Marilyn C. *"Asylum for Mankind": America, 1607-1800.* Ithaca, N.Y.: Cornell University Press, 1998.

Kettner, James H. *The Development of American Citizenship, 1608-1870.* Chapel Hill: University of North Carolina Press for the Omohundro Institute of Early American History and Culture, 1978.

LeMay, Michael C., and Elliott Robert Barkin, eds. *U.S. Immigration and Naturalization Laws and Issues: A Documentary History.* Westport, Conn.: Greenwood Press, 1999.

Somerville, Siobhan B. "Notes Toward a Queer History of Naturalization." *American Quarterly* 57, no. 3 (September, 2005) 659-679, 1002.

SEE ALSO: Alien and Sedition Acts of 1798; Congress, U.S.; Constitution, U.S.; Immigration law; Naturalization.

NEBRASKA

SIGNIFICANCE: Nebraska has always been primarily an agricultural state. During the nineteenth century, its chief attraction to immigrants was its cheap farm land. By the end of the century, fully one-half of the state's farmers were foreign born. Throughout the twentieth century, the state's population growth was relatively slow, but toward the end of the century the state began receiving an influx of Latin American immigrants, primarily from Mexico.

Early European settlement of the Nebraska region was spurred by the Homestead Act of 1862, a federal land law that made public lands in the West almost free to immigrant families. It gave settlers 160-acre plots of land in return for minimal registration fees and the promise to improve the land and live on it for at least five years. The Timber Culture Act of March 3, 1873, introduced by Nebraska's Senator Phineas W. Hitchcock, added to the allure of Nebraska land. Under this law, homesteaders could get additional land by planting trees and caring for them for a period of ten years.

NINETEENTH CENTURY IMMIGRATION AND RAILROADS

Wagon trains carried the first settlers into Nebraska, but by the 1850's, railroads were becoming the primary means of transportation. The railroad companies were aggressive in campaigning and used a variety of promotional campaigns. They placed standing advertisements in East Coast papers and offered trips to editors and their wives on their lines. Pamphlets were often published in vast quantities and distributed in various foreign languages to attract more settlers. Immigration agents were sent to European countries to conduct lectures and public forums about the availability of free land on the western plains. The railroads occasionally even reduced fares for large family groups. In 1864, the federal government granted the railroad companies twenty-mile-wide blocks of land on both sides of their tracks west of the Missouri River that the railroads were entitled to sell to settlers. Settlers naturally preferred to farm as near the tracks as possible, but the railroads generally sold the land to speculators.

To attract new settlers to Nebraska, the state government aggressively promoted Nebraska's agricultural potential. Under the leadership of Governor Robert W. Furnas, the state agricultural board sent native-born plants and crops to exhibitions in the

---

PROFILE OF NEBRASKA

Region	Midwest
Entered union	1867
Largest cities	Omaha, Lincoln (capital), Bellevue, Grand Island
Modern immigrant communities	Hispanics

Population	Total	Percent of state	Percent of U.S.	U.S. rank
All state residents	1,769,000	100.0	0.59	38
All foreign-born residents	100,000	5.6	0.27	38

Source: U.S. Census Bureau, *Statistical Abstract for 2006.*
Notes: The U.S. population in 2006 was 299,399,000, of whom 37,548,000 (12.5%) were foreign born. Rankings in last column reflect total numbers, not percentages.

East to counter the belief that the regions west of the Mississippi River were unsuitable for agriculture.

Because they owned 17 percent of Nebraska's land, the railroad companies had a vested interest in attracting settlers. As the railroads extended their lines and built bridges, they also developed new towns in rural areas. Built on local agricultural economies, these towns tended to follow a common pattern: Grain elevators were erected next to railroad tracks, followed by schools, churches, post offices, and business districts within walking distances of the railroads that developed into the classic American "Main Streets." Grocery stores and post offices frequently became centers where local immigrants gathered and bonded with other members of the communities. The towns' clubs, lodges, and churches helped to cement social ties.

Large numbers of Swedish immigrants settled in Nebraska's Saunders and Polk counties, but Germans constituted the largest immigrant group. They settled primarily in the northeastern section of the state. Eventually, Nebraska became home to more Swedes, Danes, and Czechs than any other state in the region.

TWENTIETH CENTURY DEVELOPMENTS

Nebraska's population growth throughout most of the twentieth century was slow compared to that of the United States as a whole. The 1900 census recorded 1,066,910 residents of Nebraska. By the year 2004, the state had 1,711,000 residents. The Great Depression of the 1930's devastated Nebraska's economy. Many farmers went west to find agricultural work in California, Oregon, and Washington. The latter half of the century saw an influx of Hispanics, many of whom took jobs in the meatpacking and construction industries. By the early twenty-first century, illegal immigration was a major issue, and many native-born Nebraskans were complaining that undocumented workers were taking jobs away from American citizens. In 2009, Nebraska's unicameral legislature took up the subject of implementing a new system to verify the legal status of foreign-born applicants for jobs.

Gayla Koerting

FURTHER READING

Blouet, Brian W., and Frederick C. Luebke. *The Great Plains: Environment and Culture.* Lincoln: University of Nebraska Press, 1979.

Gjerde, Jon. *The Minds of the West: The Ethnocultural Evolution of the Rural Middle West, 1830-1917.* Chapel Hill: University of North Carolina Press, 1979.

Olson, James C., and Ronald Nagle. *The History of Nebraska.* Lincoln: University of Nebraska Press, 1997.

Wishart, David J., ed. *Encyclopedia of the Great Plains.* Lincoln: University of Nebraska Press, 2004.

SEE ALSO: Czech and Slovakian immigrants; Flanagan, Edward J.; German immigrants; Iowa; Kansas; Literature; Missouri; *My Ántonia*; Westward expansion.

NEVADA

SIGNIFICANCE: Long a lightly populated, arid, and undeveloped region, Nevada began its modern development during the mid-nineteenth century, after silver was discovered in its west-central area. Since that time, Nevada has always depended on immigrant labor to help develop its economy. Beginning with railroads and mining and continuing with its modern entertainment and hospitality service industries, immigrant groups have provided a large and effective workforce throughout Nevada.

Nevada became a U.S. territory in 1861 and a state in 1864, but major events in 1859 had a dramatic impact on its future development and began attracting immigrants into the region. Discovery of the famous Comstock silver lode quickly established Gold Hill and Virginia City as major mining centers, and new immigrants began pouring in, hoping to strike it rich in the booming silver mining industry. Along with American investors and miners came large numbers of foreign laborers who worked in the mines and provided essential services to the growing population. Immigrants from Ireland, Greece, Italy, Japan, Mexico, and the Balkan peninsula all came to Nevada seeking employment or fortune. These immigrants joined already established communities of Chinese laborers who had been brought in to help build railroad lines connected to the transcontinental railroad.

PROFILE OF NEVADA

Region	West
Entered union	1864
Largest cities	Las Vegas, Paradise, Reno, Henderson, Sunrise Manor
Modern immigrant communities	Hispanics, Chinese

Population	*Total*	*Percent of state*	*Percent of U.S.*	*U.S. rank*
All state residents	2,496,000	100.0	0.83	35
All foreign-born residents	476,000	19.1	1.27	17

Source: U.S. Census Bureau, *Statistical Abstract for 2006.*

Notes: The U.S. population in 2006 was 299,399,000, of whom 37,548,000 (12.5%) were foreign born. Rankings in last column reflect total numbers, not percentages.

By 1870, the state had almost 3,000 Chinese workers, who trailed only American-born residents and Irish immigrants in numbers. Ten years later, the state had more than 5,000 Chinese, who by then outnumbered the Irish immigrants. U.S. Census figures for 1880 show Nevada with the highest percentage of foreign-born residents in the union.

TWENTIETH CENTURY ARRIVALS

Although most of Nevada's immigrant communities had been brought in to provide cheap and efficient labor, many of the immigrants faced discrimination and violence throughout the nineteenth and early twentieth centuries. In 1908, Reno's city government tried to discourage more Chinese from coming by burning down the city's Chinatown for "sanitary reasons." Such actions were not, however, directed only against Asian immigrants. For example, the town of McGill tried to expel all its Greek residents in 1908. Violence was also routinely directed against Italian and Serbian immigrants as nativist fervor captivated much of Nevada during the early twentieth century.

Mexicans began immigrating into Nevada during the silver boom years but did not arrive in large numbers until the mid-twentieth century, when the state participated in the bracero guest-worker program, which was stated in 1942 to provide low-cost labor for American farmers. Most bracero workers returned to Mexico after completing their labor contracts, but some remained and estab-lished homes in and around the main urban centers of Las Vegas and Reno. By 1950, nearly 10 percent of the residents of Las Vegas's Clark County were counted as Hispanic.

As the cities of Las Vegas and Reno established themselves as major national centers of gaming and tourism, new immigrants were drawn to the expanding employment opportunities that the cities offered. Since the late 1940's, Nevada's casinos have steadily multiplied and grown ever larger, creating an increasing need for service workers. Immigrants from both foreign countries and other parts of the United States have flooded into the state. A high percentage of the foreign immigrants have been Latin Americans, particularly Mexicans. By 1980, Clark County's Hispanic population had increased by 600 percent since 1950.

By the year 2007, Nevada was one of the fastest-growing states in the union, with a total population of approximately 2.5 million people. Nevada was also the most culturally diverse state within the Rocky Mountain region, with African Americans accounting for 7 percent of the total population and Asian Americans 6 percent. The state's Hispanic population was second only to its "white" population in numbers, with approximately 500,000 residents, who accounted for 20 percent of the total population. The state's largest cities have also developed notable ethnic enclaves. Within the major urban areas, Las Vegas, for example, has a dynamic Chinatown along the western edge of Interstate 15 and a large shopping district catering to Asians in its downtown area.

Robert D. Mitchell

FURTHER READING

BeDunnah, Gary P. *A History of the Chinese in Nevada.* San Francisco: R&E Research Associates, 1973.

Elliott, Russell R. *History of Nevada.* 2d ed. Lincoln: University of Nebraska Press, 1987.

Hulse, James W. *The Silver State: Nevada's Heritage Reinterpreted.* 3d ed. Reno: University of Nevada Press, 2004.

James, Ronald M. *Comstock Women: The Making of a Mining Community.* Reno: University of Nevada Press, 1998.

Shepperson, Wilbur S. *Restless Strangers: Nevada's Immigrants and Their Interpreters.* Reno: University of Nevada Press, 1970.

SEE ALSO: Arizona; California; Chinese immigrants; Economic opportunities; Employment; History of immigration after 1891; Irish immigrants; Italian immigrants; Labor unions; Railroads.

NEW HAMPSHIRE

SIGNIFICANCE: Because it borders Canada's Quebec province, New Hampshire has long attracted French Canadian immigrants but relatively few immigrants from other countries. During the late twentieth century, increasing numbers of Asians began coming to New Hampshire.

The earliest New Hampshire immigrants were chiefly French Canadians who had farmed in Quebec. Many of these people took up farming in New Hampshire, but others worked as lumberjacks in the state's timber industry. During the late nineteenth century, many of them worked in the state's expanding textile mills, which often employed entire families. They characteristically tended to retain their language and culture.

The history of Manchester, New Hampshire's, Amoskeag textile mill, at one time the largest fabric plant in the world, provides a window into immigrant life in the state. Its labor force was at first dominated by young descendants of early English settlers. During the 1850's and 1860's these workers were gradually replaced by the incoming Irish immigrants. By 1860, the city of Manchester's population was 27 percent foreign born, more than 70 percent of whom were Irish. Other immigrants included much smaller numbers of Germans and Swedes, many of whom were skilled craftspeople.

During the 1870's, land scarcity in Quebec impelled more French Canadians to go to New Hampshire, where many of them worked in the Amoskeag textile mill. These people were found to make docile, industrious, and stable workers. Moreover, French Canadians generally had large families and were willing to let their children work in the mill, so the company solicited more emigration from Quebec. By the turn of the twentieth century, Greek and Polish immigrants were being absorbed into the mill's workforce, which by then numbered 17,000.

Until 1922, Amoskeag had avoided the labor strikes that had begun to disrupt production in other New England textile mills. However, during that year, the company's simultaneous increase of hours and reduction of wages provoked a strike. After the strike was settled, worker confidence in both their company and their union declined. During the Great Depression of the next decade, the century-old company went out of business. However, despite the hard times they faced, relatively few of the displaced workers left Manchester.

TWENTY-FIRST CENTURY TRENDS

New Hampshire has attracted fewer immigrants than the majority of states. During the early years of the twenty-first century,

---

PROFILE OF NEW HAMPSHIRE

Region	New England
Entered union	1788
Largest cities	Manchester, Nashua, Concord (capital)
Modern immigrant communities	Hispanics, Asian Indians, Chinese, Koreans

Population	Total	Percent of state	Percent of U.S.	U.S. rank
All state residents	1,315,000	100.0	0.44	41
All foreign-born residents	71,000	5.4	0.19	40

Source: U.S. Census Bureau, *Statistical Abstract for 2006.*
Notes: The U.S. population in 2006 was 299,399,000, of whom 37,548,000 (12.5%) were foreign born. Rankings in last column reflect total numbers, not percentages.

only about 5 percent of its citizens were foreign-born immigrants—a percentage less than half of the national average. However, between 2000 and 2005, new immigration saw an increase of 36 percent in the state's Hispanic population and 40 percent in the Asian population. Both groups are quite diverse in New Hampshire. The Hispanics include Puerto Ricans, Mexicans, and immigrants from several Central American countries. The Asians include Indians, Chinese, and Koreans. The majority of the Asian immigrants are already well educated when they arrive and generally find high-paying jobs without difficulty. Many of the immigrants have been attracted by the high quality of life in New Hampshire, as well as its good schools and low crime rates.

New immigration has brought new concerns to New Hampshire. While many residents of the state welcome the immigrants' contributions to the workforce, others are worried about the numbers of undocumented immigrants entering the state. The state legislature has enacted laws providing penalties for employers who hire undocumented immigrants. Related to this issue is concern that illegal immigration is tied to rising crime rates. A 2007 report presented on public radio found that New Hampshire's residents were becoming less welcoming to immigrants than the residents of many other states.

Robert P. Ellis

FURTHER READING

Armstrong, John Borden. *Factory Under the Elms: A History of Harrisville, New Hampshire, 1774-1969.* Cambridge, Mass.: MIT Press, 1969.

Brault, Gerard J. *The French-Canadian Heritage in New England.* Hanover, N.H.: University Press of New England, 1986.

Hareven, Tamara K., and Randolph Langenbach. *Amoskeag: Life and Work in an American Factory-City.* New York: Pantheon Books, 1978.

Heffernan, Nancy Coffey, and Ann Page Stecker. *New Hampshire: Crosscurrents in Its Development.* 3d ed. Hanover, N.H.: University Press of New England, 2004.

SEE ALSO: British immigrants; Canada vs. United States as immigrant destinations; Canadian immigrants; French immigrants; Great Depression; Illegal immigration; Labor unions; Vermont.

NEW HARMONY

IDENTIFICATION: German immigrant utopian community later purchased by a Scottish reformer

DATE: 1814-1827

LOCATION: New Harmony, Indiana

SIGNIFICANCE: New Harmony proved to be a failed millenarian utopia for German Har-

Architect's rendering of Robert Owen's vision for New Harmony. (Library of Congress)

monists and a failed secular utopia for the Scottish-led Owenites, but it helped spread reform and socialist ideals.

In 1803, George Rapp, a German who called himself a prophet and proclaimed that the millennium was near, led hundreds of his followers to Pennsylvania. There they formed the Harmony Society, giving up everything they owned to live communally and pledging themselves to celibacy. In 1814, the society moved to Indiana, where they founded the town of New Harmony. New Harmony prospered as new immigrants increased the population, and the inhabitants were successful at farming. While they awaited the millennium, they kept their German language and customs. Trouble with surrounding towns, however, led Rapp to move his flock back to Pennsylvania, selling the town to Robert Owen.

Owen had made his fortune from textile mills in his native Scotland, but his great concern for his workers led him to favor reform. He purchased New Harmony in 1825 as a utopian experiment to prove the viability of socialism. About eight hundred reformers and educators at New Harmony shared their property communally and favored gender equality. Unlike the Harmonists' commune, Owen's was purely secular on the assumption that rationality could create a more moral society.

Owen's experiment soon failed. The town drained his finances, and the freethinking reformers turned out not to be as manageable as Scottish laborers. The utopia disbanded in 1827, but its ideas later influenced other American reform communities.

Lincoln Austin Mullen

FURTHER READING

Taylor, Anne. *Visions of Harmony: A Study in Nineteenth-Century Millenarianism.* New York: Oxford University Press, 1987.

Thompson, Brian. *Devastating Eden: The Search for Utopia in America.* New York: HarperCollins, 2004.

Wilson, William E. *The Angel and the Serpent: The Story of New Harmony.* Bloomington: Indiana University Press, 1964.

SEE ALSO: British immigrants; German immigrants; History of immigration, 1783-1891; Indiana; Rapp, George; Religion as a push-pull factor; Westward expansion.

NEW JERSEY

SIGNIFICANCE: Because of New Jersey's location next to New York Harbor, the state historically drew many immigrants entering the United States through its main port of entry. This pattern has continued into the twenty-first century, as new immigrants have arrived at Newark, New Jersey's, and nearby New York City's international airports. The state's earliest immigrants were mostly from Europe; by the end of the twentieth century, New Jersey was one of the top-ranking states in percentages of immigrants from Mexico, China, and the Philippines, and it was also welcoming significant numbers of Asian Indians.

One of Great Britain's original North American colonies, New Jersey drew its earliest immigrants from England. Many of them were Quakers and Baptists seeking religious freedom. After the United States achieved its independence, the heaviest influx of European immigrants into New Jersey began arriving during the 1840's. Later, Irish immigrants came as laborers. Possessing the advantage of already speaking English, they quickly became prominent in political life and would eventually come to dominate the governments of such major cities as Jersey City, Trenton, and Paterson. German immigrants were slower to arrive, but by 1890 there were about 120,000 foreign-born Germans settled in New Jersey. They were prominent as craftsmen and established reputations as skilled glassmakers and woodworkers. Many Italian immigrants relocated from New York City to New Jersey. Others came directly from Italy and worked as farmers in the rural southern portion of the state. Over time, however, many of these people gravitated to industrial cities such as Trenton and Newark.

MODERN TRENDS

By the turn of the twenty-first century, New Jersey had one of the richest mixtures of world cultures in the United States, with people from nearly one hundred different nations speaking more than 165 different languages. In 2009, an advisory panel on the state's immigrant policy reported that fully 20 percent of the state's 8.7 million residents

PROFILE OF NEW JERSEY

Region	Atlantic coast
Entered union	1787
Largest cities	Newark, Jersey City, Paterson, Elizabeth, Edison
Modern immigrant communities	Asian Indians, Mexicans, Chinese, Filipinos

Population	Total	Percent of state	Percent of U.S.	U.S. rank
All state residents	8,724,000	100.0	2.91	11
All foreign-born residents	1,754,000	20.1	4.67	6

Source: U.S. Census Bureau, Statistical Abstract for 2006.

Notes: The U.S. population in 2006 was 299,399,000, of whom 37,548,000 (12.5%) were foreign born. Rankings in last column reflect total numbers, not percentages.

were foreign born, and most of these people had entered within the previous twenty years. About 46 percent of the foreign-born residents were Latin Americans, 30 percent were Asians, 18.6 percent were Europeans, and 4.5 percent were Africans. The largest single national group among the foreign-born New Jersey residents were Asian Indians, who constituted almost 10 percent of the immigrant population. They were followed by immigrants from Mexico, China, the Philippines, and Colombia, in that order.

The advisory report also noted that New Jersey has a comparatively high rate of naturalization among its immigrant communities. In 2006, 48 percent of its foreign-born residents were naturalized citizens. Although immigrants as a whole were more likely than native-born Americans to live in poverty, naturalized immigrants were less likely to live in poverty than natives. The advisory report did not deal at length with the subject of illegal immigration but noted the U.S. Department of Homeland Security estimate of approximately 430,000 undocumented immigrants in New Jersey.

Among other findings of the advisory report on immigration was the fact that one-third of all children in New Jersey were members of families with at least one foreign-born parent. Consequently, the state needed more instruction in English as a second language and more resources for preschool children.

Several positive factors were noted in the report. Immigrants were less likely than native-born New Jersey residents to be incarcerated or on public assistance. Immigrants were also more likely to be employed, although they generally received lower wages. More than 40 percent of the state's scientists and engineers with higher degrees were foreign born, as were medical professionals. Without these foreign-born professionals New Jersey would face serious shortages.

Robert P. Ellis

FURTHER READING

Fleming, Thomas J. *New Jersey: A Bicentennial History.* New York: W. W. Norton, 1977.

Green, Howard L., ed. *Words That Make New Jersey History: A Primary Source Reader.* Piscataway, N.J.: Rutgers University Press, 2006.

Mappen, Mark. *Jerseyana: The Underside of New Jersey History.* Piscataway, N.J.: Rutgers University Press, 1992.

Montalto, N. *One of the Many: Integrating Immigrants in New Jersey.* Washington, D.C.: National Integration Forum, 2006.

SEE ALSO: Alien land laws; Brazilian immigrants; Delaware; German immigrants; Irish immigrants; New York State; Political parties; Statue of Liberty; Transportation of immigrants.

NEW MEXICO

SIGNIFICANCE: As one the last American frontier territories to be settled, New Mexico offered opportunities for better lives to a wide variety of immigrants from throughout the world during the nineteenth century. After becoming a state in 1912, New Mexico developed into an area in which immigrants have been able to integrate into the community while still preserving their cultural heritages.

During the nineteenth and twentieth centuries, immigrants from both Asia and Europe joined

large numbers of immigrants from Mexico to New Mexico. New Mexico shares a long border with Mexico, which it had been part of until the United States won the Mexican War in 1848. The most numerous European groups were Germans, including significant numbers of German Jews, through both centuries; Italians came during the nineteenth century and Spaniards during the twentieth.

The first German immigrants in New Mexico were Jewish merchants and traders who had pushed west to sell their wares along the Santa Fe Trail. They opened stores in the towns that developed along the trail and soon arranged for additional family members to follow them to New Mexico. German Lutherans started immigrating during the 1880's; most of them settled in and around Albuquerque, to which they encouraged other Germans to come. The next significant wave of Germans came after World War II, when many German scientists worked at the state's White Sands Missile Range. The German immigrants readily assimilated to the life and culture of New Mexico, particularly during the war years when anti-German sentiment was strong throughout the United States.

Italian immigrants began arriving in Albuquerque at the same time as the railroad. These immigrants found success in all types of business ventures and particularly in construction trades. During the twentieth century, a small number of

Spanish immigrants came to New Mexico. Many of them became affiliated with the Cervantes Institute, which promotes Spanish culture and heritage in the state.

New Mexico's Asian communities are mostly concentrated in Albuquerque. The first Asians to arrive were Chinese and Japanese laborers who came during the late nineteenth century. Many of them worked on the railroads. Not fully accepted into the life of the city, they established their own communities and built businesses that served their own people. After the Vietnam War ended in 1975, Albuquerque's Asian community was augmented by the arrival of about 3,000 Vietnamese immigrants. Like the other Asians who had preceded them, they established their own restaurants and shops.

Around the turn of the twenty-first century, New Mexico's Asian population became even more diversified as Koreans and Filipinos began settling in the state. By this time, Asians were fully integrated into the life of Albuquerque, where they found opportunities in all sectors of business and the professions. Asian professionals include engineers, physicians, university professors, and information technology specialists. The culture of the various Asian communities has also become an important part of New Mexico's lifestyle. Asian restaurants and groceries are found throughout Albuquerque. Culture centers and ethnic festivals not only maintain Asian traditions but also have made them part of the culture of New Mexico.

Despite the important contributions of European and Asian immigrants, the strongest cultural influences in New Mexico are Mexican. The state's large Mexican American community includes families who trace their ancestry back to the time when New Mexico was part of Mexico and even earlier, when the region was ruled by Spain. Other families trace their roots to nineteenth and early twentieth century Mexican immigrants, but a substantial part of the state's early twenty-first century population was made up of both docu-

PROFILE OF NEW MEXICO

Region	Southwest
Entered union	1912
Largest cities	Albuquerque, Las Cruces, Santa Fe (capital), Rio Rancho
Modern immigrant communities	Mexicans, Vietnamese, Koreans, Filipinos

Population	Total	Percent of state	Percent of U.S.	U.S. rank
All state residents	1,954,000	100.0	0.65	36
All foreign-born residents	197,000	10.1	0.52	27

Source: U.S. Census Bureau, *Statistical Abstract for 2006.*
Notes: The U.S. population in 2006 was 299,399,000, of whom 37,548,000 (12.5%) were foreign born. Rankings in last column reflect total numbers, not percentages.

mented and undocumented immigrants who were born in Mexico.

Shawncey Webb

FURTHER READING

Citola, Nicholas P. *Italians in Albuquerque*. Chicago: Arcadia Publishing, 2002.

Gutiérrez, David G. *Walls and Mirrors: Mexican Americans, Mexican Immigrants, and the Politics of Ethnicity*. Berkeley: University of California Press, 1995.

Rodriguez, Havidán, Rogelio Sáenz, and Cecilia Menjivar. *Latinas/os in the United States: Changing the Face of America*. New York: Springer, 2008.

Zolberg, Aristide. *A Nation by Design: Immigration Policy in the Fashioning of America*. Cambridge, Mass.: Harvard University Press, 2006.

SEE ALSO: Arizona; Bracero program; German immigrants; Italian immigrants; Mexican immigrants; Texas; Vietnamese immigrants; Westward expansion.

NEW YORK CITY

IDENTIFICATION: Largest city in the United States and the most important business and financial center in the nation since colonial times

SIGNIFICANCE: The most important metropolis in the United States, New York City was essentially built and populated by immigrants and their children. Its Ellis Island was the leading port of entry for immigrants from 1892 until 1954, and its Statue of Liberty was an important symbol of welcome.

The first European immigrants to New York were Dutch who settled the southern end of Manhattan Island during the early seventeenth century. Before the Dutch arrived, Manhattan was sparsely populated by the Lenape people, from whom Peter Minuit famously purchased the island for the equivalent of twenty-four dollars in 1626. The Dutch named their colony New Amsterdam and built it into a bustling, heterogeneous commercial port that attracted visitors from all over the world. The same traits would continue to characterize New York City through the next four centuries, as the city developed into the leading destination for immigrants in the United States and perhaps in the entire world.

EARLY IMMIGRANTS

After the English seized New Amsterdam from the Dutch in 1664, they renamed the city New York. Under English, and later British, sovereignty, thousands of English, Welsh, and Scots immigrated to Manhattan, and slaves were imported from Africa. The next great wave of immigration occurred during the 1830's and 1840's, with the arrival of hundreds of thousands of German immigrants fleeing the political and economic turmoil of revolutionary Europe, and Irish immigrants escaping the ravage of their homeland's great potato famine.

By 1855, more than one-half of New York City's residents were foreign born. These immigrants represented a new alignment in American history. Most were Roman Catholics and did not speak English as their first language. They settled in New York City's ethnic enclaves and looked to maintain their cultural traditions. Poorer immigrants were packed into tenements such as the notorious Five Points Slum. Anti-immigrant sentiments increased as well, as exemplified by the nativist and Americanist movements and the rise of the Know-Nothing Party. Tensions reached a peak in draft riots during the Civil War over the issue of conscription. By the 1870's, however, immigrants had become a political force within the city, their votes courted by urban political machines such as the infamous Tammany Hall of William Marcy "Boss" Tweed. Ethnic politics would remain a dominant feature of New York City history.

ELLIS ISLAND AND THE STATUE OF LIBERTY

Through the first century of American independence, immigration remained basically open and unregulated. Immigrants arrived at ports, went through state customs houses, and became American residents. In New York City, shipping companies submitted the passenger lists to the local collector of customs. However, on August 1, 1855, the state of New York began operating a processing center for arriving immigrants on the southern tip of Manhattan known as Castle Garden. It was the first such center in the United States. After the federal Immigration Act of 1882 gave jurisdiction over immigration to the U.S. Department of the Trea-

New York City's bustling Hester Street in the city's lower East Side Jewish ghetto in 1914. (Getty Images)

sury, the secretary of the Treasury contracted with New York State to continue its processing of immigrants.

The federal Immigration Act of 1891 made supervision over immigration policy an exclusively federal process, so Castle Garden was closed. On January 1, 1892, the federal government opened its own processing center on Ellis Island, off the southern tip of Manhattan, to examine newly arrived immigrants and determine whether they should be admitted to the United States. Over the next thirty-two years, more than 16 million immigrants passed through Ellis Island, accounting for 71 percent of all immigrants to the United States. Most of those immigrants passed through New York City after being processed. Many stayed in the city—some temporarily before moving on to other

places, but approximately one-third settled permanently in New York City or the surrounding area.

The Statue of Liberty, located on Liberty Island near Ellis Island in New York Harbor, was also owned and administered by the federal government. A gift from France in 1886, the statue had no formal connection to the immigration process, but as one of the first sights that greeted passengers of ships sailing into the harbor, its glowing presence was accepted as a symbol of welcome to the new nation.

A CITY OF IMMIGRANTS

By the late nineteenth century, New York stood as the most populous and commercially significant city in North America. It was also the leading immigration destination in the nation and perhaps the

world. Immigrants took up multifarious forms of employment within the city and established their own ethnic neighborhoods up and down Manhattan.

During the second half of the nineteenth century, the demographics of immigration changed again. The 1880's and 1890's began an era of mass immigration from eastern and southern Europe. Consequently, New York City absorbed hundreds of thousands of Italian and Jewish immigrants, the latter primarily from Russia and Poland. Smaller but still significant numbers of new immigrants came from the Austro-Hungarian Empire, Greece, Poland, Spain, the West Indies, and China. Manhattan was becoming a bustling collection of ethnic neighborhoods: Chinatown and Little Italy in Lower Manhattan, Jewish enclaves in the lower East Side and the Grand Concourse in the Bronx, an Irish neighborhood in Hell's Kitchen, Germans and Czechs in Yorkville. The northern end of the island has an Italian Harlem, a Spanish Harlem, and an African American Harlem, the last of which would witness the famous Harlem Renaissance of the 1920's.

The term "melting pot" was coined to describe the incredible mix of groups that had become New York. The lives of the new immigrants drew both hostility and sympathy. Pressures to restrict immigration persisted. Jacob Riis's book *How the Other Half Lives* (1890) documented the miserable conditions of urban slums. The Triangle Shirtwaist Factory fire in 1911, in which 146 mostly young European-born female garment workers died, demonstrated the miserable working conditions of many immigrants.

In 1898, New York City expanded into greater New York, adding the boroughs of Brooklyn, Queens, and Staten Island to its charter. At that time, Queens and Staten Island were largely rural, but Brooklyn already had the cosmopolitan make-up that immigration had given to Manhattan and the South Bronx, with Scandinavian and Italian neighborhoods in Bay Ridge, Jewish neighborhoods in Williamsburg, Flatbush, and Brownsville, German neighborhoods in Ridgewood, and Syrians in Red Hook. New York was a teeming mixture of ethnic groups, but many Americans across the country were becoming alarmed by the numbers of immigrants flooding into the United States. Federal legislation was enacted during the 1880's and 1890's

to gain control over the immigration process—with more administrative oversight, but also with an eye to shaping the country's ethnic make-up.

TWENTIETH CENTURY IMMIGRATION

During the twentieth century, immigration continued largely unabated, even though immigration to the United States as a whole was becoming more restrictive with the introduction of national origins quotas in 1921 and 1924. However, the quota system tended to affect the ethnic mixture more than the numbers of new immigrants coming into New York. Because immigration from other countries in the Western Hemisphere remained relatively unrestricted through the quota system years, much of the immigration to New York immediately after World War II was from Latin America. Residents of Puerto Rico, regarded as U.S. citizens since 1917, were unaffected by immigration quotas. During the 1950's more than 1 million Puerto Ricans came to New York City. As British subjects, residents of the British West Indies were also privileged in immigration and flocked to the city. The overall rate of immigration into the city slowed somewhat throughout the century until passage of the Immigration and Nationality Act of 1965, which repealed national quotas.

The revival of New York City from an economic slump during the 1980's saw the city's rate of immigration climb again. As native-born New Yorkers moved to suburban communities, they were replaced within the city by immigrants. In 1970, 18.2 percent of the city's population were immigrants; by 2005, that percentage had doubled. Between 1964 and 1990, the leading sources of immigrants to New York City were

- Dominican Republic (202,102 immigrants)
- China and Taiwan (145,362)
- Jamaica (101,580)
- Guyana (70,523)
- Haiti (65,287)
- Colombia (61,383)
- Soviet Union (60,110)
- Korea (55,688)

Between 1990 and 2000, about 1.25 million immigrants settled in New York City, with others settling in nearby suburbs. By 2007, it was estimated that more than 3 million immigrants were living in New York City, out of a total population of approxi-

mately 8 million. Moreover, about 60 percent of New York City's residents were either immigrants themselves or children of immigrants. By the early twenty-first century, one-third of the city's immigrants during the twenty-first century were from Latin America, with the majority from the Dominican Republic, Ecuador, Mexico, and Colombia. One-quarter of the city's immigrants were Asian; Chinese were the largest group, but there were also many Koreans, Asian Indians, and Filipinos. A large number of immigrants from Caribbean countries have transformed the city's traditionally black neighborhoods. During the early years of the twenty-first century, Dominicans, Chinese, Jamaicans, and people from the former Soviet Union made up the largest of arriving groups to New York. About 170 languages are spoken in the city.

QUEENS AS A MICROCOSM OF THE CITY

New York City is a city of neighborhoods that reflect the ethnic origins of different immigrant groups. In no part of the city, however, have the transformations wrought by immigration been more apparent than in the borough of Queens. Once an ethnically homogenous and rural suburb, Queens has become the most ethnically diverse county in the United States. During the early twenty-first century, one-half of its residents were foreign born. Most of New York City's 275,000 Asian Indians and other South Asians live in Queens. A similar pattern is true of the city's approximately 215,000 Filipino residents. Queen's Astoria neighborhood has the largest concentration of Greeks outside Athens, Greece. Flushing has one of the largest Chinatowns in the country. Arabic and Middle Eastern populations are clustered around Steinway Street. Colombians and South Asians are clustered in Jackson Heights; Bangladeshis and Brazilians on the Astoria-Long Island City border.

The history of Queens is a microcosm of New York City immigration history. Like Manhattan, it was first settled by the Dutch and English. Irish, German, and Italian immigrants settled in western Queens during the nineteenth century. The beginning of the twentieth century saw millions of immigrants arriving from southern and western Europe. Around the turn of the twenty-first century, new immigrants poured in from Latin America, the West Indies, and Asia.

Howard Bromberg

FURTHER READING

Almeida, Linda. *Irish Immigrants in New York City, 1945-1995*. Bloomington: Indiana University Press, 2001. Study of late twentieth century Irish immigration into the city. Although most Irish immigrants arrived during the mid-nineteenth century, they remained an important stream of immigrants into the following century.

Baily, Samuel. *Immigration in the Land of Promise: Italians in Buenos Aires and New York City, 1870-1914*. Ithaca, N.Y.: Cornell University Press, 2004. Comparative study of the large turn-of-the-twentieth-century waves of Italian immigration into New York City and Argentina's capital city, Buenos Aires.

Foner, Nancy. *From Ellis Island to JFK: New York's Two Great Waves of Immigration*. New Haven, Conn.: Yale University Press, 2000. Study by a leading immigration historian comparing the mass migrations of Russian Jews and Italians to New York City around 1900 to the wave of immigrants from Asia, Latin America, and the Caribbean a century later.

_____, ed. *Islands in the City: West Indian Migration to New York*. Berkeley: University of California, 2001. Collection of scholarly essays on the impact of immigration to New York from the multicultural West Indies.

_____. *New Immigrants in New York*. New York: Columbia University Press, 2001. Collection of sociological studies of New York City's recent Chinese, Dominican, Jamaican, Korean, Mexican, Soviet Jew, and West African immigrants, examining how members of these groups have interacted with the city.

Glazer, Nathan, and Daniel Moynihan. *Beyond the Melting Pot: The Negroes, Puerto Ricans, Jews, Italians, and Irish of New York City*. 2d ed. Cambridge, Mass.: MIT Press, 1970. First published in 1963, this study of the assimilation of ethnic New York immigrants into American culture is a classic of American sociology.

Kasinitz, Philip. *Caribbean New York: Black Immigrants and the Politics of Race*. Ithaca, N.Y.: Cornell University Press, 1992. Examines migratory patterns of Caribbean New Yorkers, with tables and figures documenting the highly mobile West Indian immigration patterns.

Kasinitz, Philip, John Mollenkopf, and Mary Waters, eds. *Becoming New Yorkers: Ethnographies of the*

New Second Generation. New York: Russell Sage Foundation, 2004. Collection of sociological essays examining the experiences of New Yorkers under the age of eighteen who are children of immigrants.

Kessner, Thomas. *The Golden Door: Italian and Jewish Immigrant Mobility in New York City, 1880-1915.* New York: Oxford University Press, 1977. Quantitative study of the experiences of the greatest immigration wave to the "Immigrant City," with twenty-five tables showing occupational distribution.

Smith, Robert Courtney. *Mexican New York: Transnational Lives of New Immigrants.* Berkeley: University of California, 2005. Ethnographic study of the families of transnational Mexican immigrants living in Mexico and New York. With a methodological appendix.

Waldinger, Roger. *Still the Promised City? African Americans and New Immigrants in Postindustrial New York.* Cambridge, Mass.: Harvard University Press, 1999. Study of employment, demographics, ethnicity, and race in recent immigration to New York. With appendixes on shift-share analysis and field research methods.

SEE ALSO: Ellis Island; Ethnic enclaves; Garment industry; Little Italies; Machine politics; Melting pot theory; New York State; Puerto Rican immigrants; Statue of Liberty; Tammany Hall; Triangle Shirtwaist fire.

NEW YORK STATE

SIGNIFICANCE: The history of immigration into the state of New York has been dominated by immigration into New York City, in which about 90 percent of the state immigrant population lives. The rest of the state has had a somewhat different but nonetheless significant immigration history.

In the first U.S. Census of 1790, New York ranked as the fifth-most populous of the country's eighteen states and territories with a total population of 340,120. About one-half of its residents were of English descent and one-fifth were of Dutch descent. By 1820, New York ranked as the most populous state in the union and remained so until the 1960's, when it was overtaken by California. The state's earliest Jewish immigrants were mostly Spanish and Portuguese, but German Jews began arriving during the 1830's. From then until the end of the nineteenth century, the Irish, Germans, and English furnished the largest numbers of immigrants to the state.

Through New York's history, the majority of new immigrants to the state have settled, at least initially, in New York City, which was both the largest city in the United States and the country's primary port of entry for immigrants. During a single year, 1853, about 300,000 immigrants passed through the port of New York City. Most of these people were Irish fleeing from their homeland's devastating potato famine, and most of them crowded into the tenements of New York City.

Between the 1880's and World War I (1914-1918), the numbers of Italian, Polish, Greek, and Russian immigrants entering New York increased rapidly. Most of these immigrants were laborers, but many of their children became important professional figures, politicians, and entertainers. Fiorello La Guardia, who was mayor of New York City for eleven years; Herbert H. Lehman, who was state governor for nearly ten years; and Jacob K. Javits, who represented New York in the U.S. Senate for twenty-four years, were all children of immigrants.

TWENTIETH CENTURY TRENDS

Studies of immigration into the state of New York typically focus on New York City, through which many millions of immigrants have entered the country. This is natural, as during the early years of the twenty-first century, 90 percent of the state's entire immigrant population resided in the city. However, more than 200,000 other immigrants were living in other parts of the state. Immigration patterns in upstate New York are quite different from those of the city. A study of the foreign-born population of upstate New York completed in 2007 by the Federal Reserve Bank of New York revealed some of those differences, drawing on data from the 2000 U.S. Census.

According to the 2007 report, Latin American immigrants constituted more than one-half of all foreign-born residents of New York City but only 13 percent of the populations of such major upstate

cities as Buffalo, Rochester, Albany, and Syracuse. In contrast, European immigrants accounted for 43 percent of all foreign-born residents in the upstate cities but only 17 percent of New York City's foreign born. Recent immigrants from Germany and Poland were prominent among the foreign born in the upstate cities, along with newcomers from eastern Europe and the former Soviet republics. As might be expected, the percentage of Canadian immigrants is much higher upstate than in New York City, especially in Buffalo, which stands on the Canadian border. However, the proportions of Asian immigrants both upstate and in the city are roughly the same: 25 percent in the city and 30 percent upstate.

Upstate New York and Long Island also differ from New York City in having many immigrant agricultural workers. Their exact numbers are difficult to establish, because many of these immigrants are undocumented. However, of the 47,000 immigrants known to be working on fruit, vegetable, and dairy farms at the turn of the twenty-first century, 80 percent were Mexicans. As many as one-half of these people may have been undocumented. As in other states, many of them are impoverished and without heath care insurance.

The Hispanic immigrant population of upstate New York also includes many Portuguese and Brazilians. A 2006 state government report on Hispanic immigrants and their children, including Puerto Ricans, in upstate areas found that members of the younger generations still faced many of the same problems that their immigrant ancestors faced. Limited education and English language proficiency were particular problems.

Robert P. Ellis

FURTHER READING

Bogen, Elizabeth. *Immigration in New York.* New York: Praeger, 1987.

Klein, Milton M. *The Empire State: A History of New York.* Ithaca, N.Y.: Cornell University Press, 2005.

Pencak, William, et al., eds. *Immigration to New York.* Philadelphia: Balch Institute Press, 1991.

Youssef, Nadia H. *The Demographics of Immigration: A*

PROFILE OF NEW YORK

Region	Atlantic coast
Entered union	1788
Largest cities	New York City, Hempstead, Brookhaven, Islip, Oyster Bay, Buffalo
Modern immigrant communities	Chinese, Mexicans, Asian Indians

Population	Total	Percent of state	Percent of U.S.	U.S. rank
All state residents	19,306,000	100.0	6.45	3
All foreign-born residents	4,179,000	21.6	11.13	2

Source: U.S. Census Bureau, *Statistical Abstract for 2006.*

Notes: The U.S. population in 2006 was 299,399,000, of whom 37,548,000 (12.5%) were foreign born. Rankings in last column reflect total numbers, not percentages.

Socio-Demographic Profile of the Foreign-Born Population in New York State. New York: Center for Migration Studies, 1991.

SEE ALSO: Asian immigrants; Canadian immigrants; Canals; Dutch immigrants; Farm and migrant workers; *Golden Venture* grounding; Jewish immigrants; New Jersey; New York City.

NEW YORK V. MILN

THE CASE: U.S. Supreme Court decision on state regulation of immigrants

DATE: February 16, 1837

SIGNIFICANCE: Ignoring congressional power under the U.S. Constitution's commerce clause, the *Miln* decision gave individual states power over arriving immigrants by allowing them to regulate passengers on ships entering their ports under the doctrine of the state police powers. In later years, however, the Court would reverse this ruling.

In an attempt to gain control over indigent aliens and others likely to become public charges, New York's state legislature enacted a law requiring ships docking in New York Harbor to pay a head tax on each passenger and to provide an accurate rec-

ord of all passengers. Failure to comply with the law was to result in hefty penalties. Because the transportation and ingress of persons was considered a form of commerce, the law raised the explosive issue of the U.S. Constitution's commerce clause, which gave the federal government ultimate authority to regulate all foreign and interstate commerce. When New York City fined the master of the ship *Emily* for not reporting a hundred passengers, the master argued in federal court that the New York law was unconstitutional.

After the case reached the U.S. Supreme Court, the Court upheld the New York law by a 6-1 margin. Writing for the Court, Associate Justice Philip P. Barbour ignored the explosive issue of the commerce clause, while asserting that the state's "police power" was just as applicable to "precautionary measures against the moral pestilence of paupers, vagabonds, and possible convicts, as it is to guard against the physical pestilence, which may arise from unsound and infectious articles imported." The state's right to protect the health and welfare of its citizens, moreover, was "complete, unqualified, and exclusive." Justice Joseph Story issued a strong dissent. The *Miln* decision, insofar as it related to the regulation of commerce with foreign nations, would later be overturned in the *Passenger Cases* (1848) and *Henderson v. New York* (1875).

Thomas Tandy Lewis

FURTHER READING

Legomsky, Stephen. *Immigration and the Judiciary: Law and Politics in Britain and America.* New York: Oxford University Press, 1987.

LeMay, Michael, and Elliott Robert Barkan, eds. *U.S. Immigration and Naturalization Laws and Issues: A Documentary History.* Westport, Conn.: Greenwood Press, 1999.

SEE ALSO: Congress, U.S.; Constitution, U.S.; Due process protections; History of immigration, 1783-1891; Immigration law; *Passenger Cases*; Supreme Court, U.S.

NGUYEN V. IMMIGRATION AND NATURALIZATION SERVICE

THE CASE: U.S. Supreme Court decision concerning citizenship of immigrant children
DATE: Decided on January 9, 2001

SIGNIFICANCE: The *Nguyen* ruling upheld a federal law giving a gender-based preference in rights to citizenship of illegitimate children born abroad when only one parent is a U.S. citizen.

Tuan Anh Nguyen, who was born out of wedlock in Vietnam, was the son of an American father and a Vietnamese mother. At the age of five, the boy was brought to the United States and raised by his father. When he was twenty-two years old, Nguyen was found guilty of sexually abusing a young child. Under U.S. law, a child born to an unmarried American mother was automatically considered a natural-born citizen, whereas a child born to an unmarried father was not a citizen unless the father proved paternity with a blood test and formally claimed paternity before the child's eighteenth birthday. Because the father had not satisfied these requirements, the Immigration and Naturalization Service (INS) ruled that Nguyen was not a citizen and therefore deportable. Nguyen argued in federal court that the gender distinction in the law was discriminatory and therefore unconstitutional.

By a 5-4 margin, the Supreme Court held that Nguyen could be deported and that the gender distinction in the law was "consistent with the constitutional guarantee of equal protection." Writing for the majority, Justice Anthony Kennedy explained that such distinctions are permissible if they serve "important governmental objectives" and employed means that are "substantially related to the achievement of those objectives." While the majority concluded that the law satisfied the two standards because of different relationships between children with their mothers and fathers, Justice Sandra Day O'Connor and three other justices vigorously disagreed.

Thomas Tandy Lewis

FURTHER READING

O'Brien, David M. *Constitutional Law and Politics.* 7th ed. New York: W. W. Norton, 2008.

Phelan, Margaret, and James Gillespie. *Immigration Law Handbook.* 5th ed. New York: Oxford University Press, 2007.

SEE ALSO: Amerasian children; Amerasian Homecoming Act of 1987; Child immigrants; Citizenship; Congress, U.S.; Constitution, U.S.; Deportation; Supreme Court, U.S.; Vietnamese immigrants.

NICARAGUAN IMMIGRANTS

SIGNIFICANCE: Despite deep historical ties between Nicaragua and the United States, significant Nicaraguan immigration did not begin until after the start of the Sandinista revolution of the 1970's. Since then, Nicaraguans have become one of the largest groups of Central American immigrants and have made their presence especially felt in South Florida and Southern California.

Ties between the United States and Nicaragua have historically been marked by U.S. political, economic, and military intervention in the Central American nation. In 1909, for example, the U.S. government supported a revolution that replaced

PROFILE OF NICARAGUAN IMMIGRANTS

Country of origin	Nicaragua
Primary language	Spanish
Primary regions of U.S. settlement	South Florida and Southern California
Earliest significant arrivals	Late nineteenth century
Peak immigration period	1990's-2008
Twenty-first century legal residents*	53,176 (6,647 per year)

*Immigrants who obtained legal permanent resident status in the United States.
Source: Department of Homeland Security, *Yearbook of Immigration Statistics, 2008.*

a liberal military ruler with a conservative regime. Afterward, the United States maintained a military presence in the country until 1933, when it defeated an uprising by rebel leader Augusto César Sandino. With support from the United States, General Anastasio Somoza seized control of Nicaragua in 1936. His sons, Luis and Anastasio Somoza Debayle, assumed control of the country and continued the family rule through more than four decades.

EARLY IMMIGRATION

Early immigration from Nicaragua to the United States was facilitated by the country's political and economic dependency on the United States. Like other Central Americans, some of the earliest Nicaraguans who came to the United States were industrialists and workers associated with the nation's coffee industry who began going to San Francisco, California, during the late nineteenth and early twentieth centuries.

During the 1930's, Nicaragua's repressive Somoza regime drove large numbers of people to flee the country. Many of these people settled in Southern California and the state of New York. During World War II and afterward, many Nicaraguans found employment at U.S.-based shipyards and wartime industries in the U.S.-administered Panama Canal Zone, and many of them later moved to San Francisco. By the 1940's, Nicaraguans were the largest Central American community in the San Francisco Bay area and second only to Mexicans among Latin American immigrants.

According to data from the U.S. Census, some 28,620 Nicaraguans were living in the United States in 1970. Many had immigrated after passage of the federal Immigration and Nationality Act of 1965, which significantly loosened U.S. immigration rules. Interestingly, most Nicaraguan immigrants during the late 1960's were women. Most of them were domestic workers who found employment through well-established immigrant networks in San Francisco and Los Angeles.

IMPACT OF THE SANDINISTA REVOLUTION

By 1979, Nicaragua's Somoza regime had alienated most of its political base and was toppled by a leftist guerrilla organization, the Sandinista National Liberation Front (FSLN). The Sandinistas' unsteady assumption of power over the next de-

cade triggered the largest exodus of Nicaraguans in the country's history.

The Sandinista revolution spurred three waves of Nicaraguan immigration to the United States. The first took place during the time of the revolution, when perhaps 20,000 members of wealthy families closely associated with the Somoza regime fled to Miami, Florida.

The second wave occurred during the early 1980's. It brought many non-Sandinista members of the new government coalition, along with business people and professionals whose companies had been seized by the state or who found it increasingly difficult to maintain their lifestyle within the constraints of the socialist-leaning government.

Meanwhile, because of the Sandinista government's efforts to sever Nicaragua's dependence on the United States and fears of the U.S. government that Nicaragua would boost Soviet communist influence in the region, the United States launched a multifaceted assault against the Sandinista regime. U.S. actions included a trade embargo against Nicaragua and support for a counterrevolutionary army in exile that was known as the "Contras." By 1990, Nicaragua was engulfed in a severe economic crisis and growing violence, and the Sandinistas were voted out of power. The third wave of immigration took place during this period, and brought to the United States thousands of young men of all classes dodging military conscription, along with poor families fleeing the country's harsh economic conditions and the ravages of a festering civil war.

By the time of the 1990 U.S. Census, the three recent waves of Nicaraguan immigration had brought into the United States 202,658 documented immigrants and an unknown but probably substantial number of undocumented immigrants. The bulk of these people settled in South Florida, where the total Nicaraguan population in Miami alone was estimated at 175,000 during the early 1990's. That number made Nicaraguans the second-largest Hispanic community in South Florida after Cubans.

Nicaraguans fleeing the Sandinista regime did not receive automatic refugee status or asylum privileges in the United States. Indeed, of those who applied for asylum, only about one-quarter were successful during the 1980's. In 1997, U.S. deportations of Nicaraguans who were not granted asylum were temporarily halted in 1997. However, during the following year, when the U.S. Congress froze

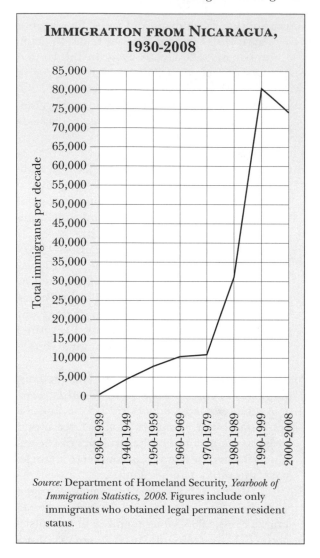

IMMIGRATION FROM NICARAGUA, 1930-2008

Source: Department of Homeland Security, *Yearbook of Immigration Statistics, 2008.* Figures include only immigrants who obtained legal permanent resident status.

military support for the Contras and Nicaraguan immigration began increasing again, the government reversed its position and began treating Nicaraguans as illegal immigrants. The 1997 federal Nicaraguan Adjustment and Central American Relief Act allowed Nicaraguans who had entered the United States before 1995 to obtain permanent residency.

The exodus from Nicaragua continued during the 1990's and into the early twenty-first century because of the country's shattered economy and social conditions. Meanwhile, Nicaraguans have become part of the flood of undocumented immigrants coming to the United States. Most have settled in the well-established Nicaraguan communi-

ties of Southern California and South Florida, but others have settled in large cities in Texas. By 2008, the number of Nicaraguans living in the United States was estimated at 300,000, but that figure must be considered conservative because of the undocumented status of many of the immigrants.

Mauricio Espinoza-Quesada

FURTHER READING

Bucuvalas, Tina. *South Florida Folklife.* Jackson: University of Mississippi Press, 1994. One of the chapters in this book provides an overview of Nicaraguan immigration to Miami and traditions maintained by this community.

Fernández-Kelly, Patricia, and Sara Curran. "Nicaraguans: Voices Lost, Voices Found." In *Ethnicities: Children of Immigrants in America*, edited by Rubén Rumbaut and Alejandro Portes. Berkeley: University of California Press, 2001. Essay detailing the impact of settling in the United States on the children of Nicaraguan immigrants.

Menjívar, Cecilia. "Salvadorans and Nicaraguans: Refugees Become Workers." In *Illegal Immigration in America*, edited by David Haines and Karen Rosenblum. Westport, Conn.: Greenwood Press, 1999. Account of the struggles of Nicaraguans fleeing the Sandinista conflict to attain legal status in the United States.

Solaún, Mauricio. *U.S. Intervention and Regime Change in Nicaragua.* Lincoln: University of Nebraska Press, 2005. Well-organized historical account of U.S intervention in Nicaraguan politics and its impact.

Walker, Thomas. *Nicaragua: Living in the Shadow of the Eagle.* Boulder, Colo.: Westview Press, 2003. History of the Nicaraguan nation and its ties with the United States.

SEE ALSO: Deportation; El Rescate; Florida; Honduran immigrants; Illegal immigration; Immigration waves; Latin American immigrants; Latinos and immigrants; Miami; Refugees; Salvadoran immigrants.

9/11 AND U.S. IMMIGRATION POLICY

THE EVENT: Reexamination of U.S. immigration laws from a security perspective following the terrorist attacks of September 11, 2001 on New York City and Washington, D.C.

SIGNIFICANCE: The fusing of immigration policy to the U.S. war on terrorism—and the resultant tightening of access to the country by foreign students, professionals, and immigrants from areas regarded as most likely to contain potential terrorists—generated a major debate over the goals of immigrant policy, and led to substantial changes in the day-to-day operation of U.S. policies toward the nationals of other countries.

The immigration policy of the United States was already in the process of being revised in 2001, when Middle Eastern operatives of the Muslim extremist organization al-Qaeda hijacked four American jet airliners for use as flying bombs against targets in New York City and Washington, D.C., on September 11 of that year. Prior to that moment, however, the main issue driving the national immigration debate had been primarily economic—the charge that the influx of illegal immigrants was driving down U.S. wages and depriving American citizens of employment. To that argument, the attacks on the World Trade Center and Pentagon building added a major national security issue to immigration reform.

The significance of that change in policy direction was quickly dramatized when the U.S. Immigration and Naturalization Service (INS) was reconstituted as the U.S. Citizenship and Immigration Services (USCIS) and placed under the aegis of the newly created Department of Homeland Security on March 1, 2003. Elsewhere, the government moved aggressively to tighten the rules governing admission to the United States, to secure its borders more tightly to prevent hostile aliens from entering the country illegally, and to identify illegal immigrants who were already inside the country.

RESTRICTING ADMISSION TO THE UNITED STATES

The most widely criticized of the government's post-9/11 actions were proposals—later aban-

doned—to criminalize entering the United States illegally. Nearly as controversial, however, were administrative reforms mandating special registration of certain categories of immigrants. For example, international students were to register their names and addresses with the government and regularly update that information. Even more draconian were requirements for male immigrants from twenty-four predominantly Muslim countries to be photographed, fingerprinted, and annually interviewed by government officials. The new regulations also made it easier to deport aliens for even minor criminal transgressions. Visa application and renewal procedures were expanded, along with the discretionary authority of U.S. officials stationed abroad to deny visas to applicants unable to meet the heightened security requirements for entry to the United States. Critics have argued that the net result of these moves has been to deny entry or reentry to many valued people because their points of origin happened to be in the Muslim world.

SEALING THE BORDERS AND IDENTIFYING ILLEGAL IMMIGRANTS

A collateral consequence of the 9/11 attacks was that they focused new attention on the large numbers of non-European aliens who were in the United States illegally, thereby generating new calls to bolster border security against unsanctioned immigrants. The focus of these calls was the long U.S. border with Mexico. The U.S. Congress responded

---

THE EVENTS OF SEPTEMBER 11, 2001

At 8:45 A.M. on September, 11, 2001, an airliner flying out of Boston crashed into the north tower of New York City's World Trade Center, ripping a hole in several upper floors and starting a fire so intense that people on higher floors could not evacuate the building. At first, the crash was believed to be an accident. However, when a second airliner struck the Trade Center's south tower eighteen minutes later, it was clear that neither crash had been accidental. Fearing that a large-scale terrorist attack was underway, government agencies shut down local airports, bridges, and tunnels. Less than one hour after the first crash, the Federal Aviation Administration ordered—for the first time in history—a stop to all flight operations throughout the United States. Only moments later, a third airliner crashed into the Pentagon Building outside Washington, D.C.

Meanwhile, the intense fires in the Trade Center towers—fed by the airliners' jet fuel—so weakened the buildings that they could no longer support their upper floors. At 10:05 A.M., the entire south tower collapsed; twenty-three minutes later, the north tower collapsed. Between those events, a fourth airliner crashed in a field outside Pittsburgh, Pennsylvania.

As was later determined, all four airliners had been hijacked by operatives of a shadowy Middle Eastern organization known as al-Qaeda that was determined to kill as many Americans and do as much damage to the United States as possible. By any measure, the scheme was a great success. The cost of the physical damage of the attacks could be measured in billions of dollars. Although the extent of human fatalities was not as great as was initially feared, about three thousand people lost their lives—a number greater than all the American fatalities during the Japanese attack on Pearl Harbor on December 7, 1941. In addition, the sense of security from outside threats that Americans had long enjoyed was shattered. The impact of the terrorist attacks on American attitudes toward immigrants would be significant.

Dust clouds enveloping Lower Manhattan after the collapse of the World Trade Center towers on September 11, 2001. (www.bigfoto.com)

in 2006 by authorizing the expansion of a secure fence along the border. Another step taken to advance border security was requiring, on a phased-in basis, U.S. citizens to carry passports when traveling to—and especially when returning from—neighboring Mexico and Canada, which were once free from that requirement.

To prevent future terrorist attacks on the United States, new and often highly controversial policies were implemented to identify and respond to the growing number of illegal immigrants already inside the country. The Patriot Act, passed less than six weeks after 9/11, expanded the Federal Bureau of Investigation's authority to monitor people living inside the United States. The National Security Entry-Exit Regulation System put into effect in 2002 required male noncitizens over the age of sixteen to register with the government. A computerized entry-exit system at ports of entry enhanced the federal government's ability to identify more easily those staying beyond the time permitted by their visas.

Meanwhile, raids were launched on the sites of companies suspected of employing illegal immigrants, especially at locations judged to be near potential terrorist targets, such as construction areas near Dulles International Airport outside Washington, D.C. In this endeavor, federal agents were often assisted by state and local enforcement agencies. In fact, the latter often carried the greater burden. Ironically, federal scrutiny of firms suspected of harboring illegal employees actually declined in the years immediately following 9/11, when the government focused more on identifying likely Arab terrorists.

To heighten national security, Congress passed the Real ID Act in 2005. This law's main purpose was to standardize procedures across the United States involving the acquisition of driving licenses by specifying the requirements that must be met for state licenses and for identity cards used for such "official purposes" as entering federal buildings and security-sensitive private facilities such as nuclear power plants, and for boarding commercial aircraft. The federal act also authorized federal magistrates to require additional proofs of identity and status of aliens already in the country who are seeking asylum.

Joseph R. Rudolph, Jr.

FURTHER READING

Alden, Edward H. *The Closing of the American Border: Terrorism, Immigration, and Security Since 9/11.* New York: Harper, 2008. Thoughtful assessment of post-9/11 immigration policy based on interviews with Bush administration officials and persons adversely affected by those policies.

Farnam, Julie. *U.S. Immigration Laws Under the Threat of Terrorism.* New York: Algora, 2005. Thorough treatment of the subject that examines the post-9/11 restrictions on immigration in the context of the restrictive immigration and asylum laws that resulted from the first World Trade Center bombing in 1993.

Kettl, Donald F. *System Under Stress: Homeland Security and American Politics.* Washington, D.C.: Congressional Quarterly Press, 2004. Excellent introductory reading for those seeking to place post-9/11 changes in immigration policy into the broader context of U.S. counterterrorism policy.

McEntire, David A. *Introduction to Homeland Security: Understanding Terrorism with an Emergency Management Perspective.* Hoboken, N.J.: John Wiley & Sons, 2009. Covers the same ground as Kettl's work but in a more extensive manner.

U.S. Senate. *War on Terrorism: Immigration Enforcement Since September 11, 2001: Hearing Before the Subcommittee on Immigration, Border Security, and Citizenship.* Washington, D.C.: Government Printing Office, 2003. For researchers with access to public documents, an outstanding source for testimonial arguments for and against the tightening of U.S. borders after 9/11.

SEE ALSO: Arab immigrants; Aviation and Transportation Security Act of 2001; Border fence; History of immigration after 1891; Homeland Security, Department of; Loyalty oaths; Muslim immigrants; Patriot Act of 2001; Supreme Court, U.S.

NISHIMURA EKIU V. UNITED STATES

THE CASE: U.S. Supreme Court decision concerning habeas corpus petitions by aliens
DATE: Decided on January 18, 1892

SIGNIFICANCE: The *Nishimura Ekiu* decision recognized the constitutionality of a federal law that authorized immigration officials to refuse to admit aliens into the country, without any opportunity for habeas corpus relief. The ruling also ignored minor procedural mistakes by immigration officials acting in pursuance of the law.

Nishimura Ekiu, a female citizen of Japan, arrived at the port of San Francisco in 1891. When she was interviewed by immigration officials, she claimed that she was going to meet her husband, who was living in the United States, but did not know his address. Having only twenty-two dollars in her possession, she said that she would stay at a hotel until her husband called her. A recent federal law of 1891 required the U.S. Treasury Department to refuse admittance to several categories of persons, including persons without succicient financial resources to avoid becoming public charges. After officials refused to allow Nishimura into the country, she petitioned the district court for a writ of habeas corpus, claiming that denial of such relief would deprive her of liberty without due process of law.

The U.S. Supreme Court voted 8-1 to approve both the constitutionality of the 1891 law and the officials' refusal to allow Nishimura to land. Writing the majority opinion, Justice Horace Gray concentrated on the wording of the relevant statute, which referred to the concurrent jurisdiction of the district and circuit courts. He concluded that Congress had clearly and explicitly authorized immigration officials within the Treasury Department to make the final determination for refusing admittance of the categories of aliens enumerated in the statute.

Thomas Tandy Lewis

FURTHER READING
Galloway, Donald. *Immigration Law.* Concord, Ont.: Irwin Law, 1997.

LeMay, Michael, and Elliott Robert Barkan, eds. *U.S. Immigration and Naturalization Laws and Issues: A Documentary History.* Westport, Conn.: Greenwood Press, 1999.

SEE ALSO: Congress, U.S.; Due process protections; History of immigration, 1783-1891; *Immigration and Naturalization Service v. St. Cyr*; Japanese immigrants; *Lem Moon Sing v. United States*; Supreme Court, U.S.; *United States v. Ju Toy.*

NORTH AMERICAN FREE TRADE AGREEMENT

THE TREATY: International agreement among the United States, Canada, and Mexico creating the largest free trade zone in the world
DATE: Ratified in 1993; went into effect on January 1, 1994
ALSO KNOWN AS: NAFTA

SIGNIFICANCE: This international agreement facilitated the movement of trade goods and persons among the United States, Canada, and Mexico, and had the effect of accelerating the influx of undocumented Mexican migrants into the United States.

The North American Free Trade Agreement (NAFTA) was signed in 1992 and ratified in 1993 by the governments of the United States, Canada, and Mexico and took effect on January 1, 1994. NAFTA established a free trade zone in North America by immediately lifting tariffs on the majority of goods produced by the signatory nations. It also called for the gradual elimination, over a period of fifteen years, of most remaining barriers to cross-border investments and to the movement of goods and services among the three countries.

MOBILITY OF IMMIGRANTS
Chapter 16 of NAFTA specifically concerns cross-border movement of persons within the NAFTA region. It makes four categories of travelers eligible for temporary entry from one NAFTA country into another: business visitors, traders and investors, intracompany transferees, and profes-

*NAFTA initialing ceremony in October, 1992. Standing, from left to right: Mexican president Carlos Salinas de Gortari,
U.S. president George H. W. Bush, and Canadian prime minister Brian Mulroney. Seated: Jaime Serra Puche, Carla
Hills, and Michael Wilson.* (George Bush Presidential Library and Museum)

sionals. There are more than sixty listed qualifying
NAFTA Professional (TN) titles, including computer systems analysts, accountants, hotel managers, management consultants, economists, engineers, scientists, and teachers. NAFTA defines
"temporary entry" as entry without the intent to establish permanent residence. For example, the
United States specifies that visiting aliens must satisfy inspecting immigration officers that their proposed stays are temporary. A temporary period has
a reasonable, finite end that does not equate to
permanent residence. In order to establish that visits will be temporary, alien visitors must demonstrate to the satisfaction of inspecting immigration
officers that their work assignments in the United
States will end at predictable times and that they
will promptly return home upon completion of
their assignments. For each of the above four categories, spouses and dependents can enter NAFTA
member countries as visitors so long as they meet

the member country's existing temporary entry
immigration regulations.

Citizens of Canada and Mexico who wish to enter and work as professionals in the United States
need NAFTA-based nonimmigrant TN visas. To apply for and receive such visas, applicants must provide the U.S. immigration agencies with all necessary documentation, such as passports to prove
their Canadian or Mexican citizenship. They must
also show proof of their professional qualifications,
such as transcripts of grades, licenses, certificates,
degrees, or records of previous employment, and
letters verifying their employment in the United
States. Application fees of fifty U.S. dollars are
charged.

Canadian citizens can apply for TN visas at U.S.
ports of entry; Mexican citizens must do this at U.S.
embassy consular sections and submit to appointed interviews there. The maximum period of
stay for TN visa holders in the United States was

originally one year; this period was extended to three years in October, 2008, and U.S. Citizenship and Immigration Services (USCIS) can grant extensions in increments of one year. There is no limit on the number of years that a TN visa holder may stay in the United States. When the applicants are already in the United States, their employers may file Form I-129 (Petition for Non-immigrant Worker) with the Nebraska Service Center of the USCIS, or the applicants may reapply at a port of entry using the same application and documentation procedures above as required for the initial entry.

According to the Department of Homeland Security's *Yearbook of Immigration Statistics*, during fiscal year 2006 (October, 2005, through September, 2006), 74,098 foreign professionals (64,633 Canadians and 9,247 Mexicans) were admitted into the United States for temporary employment under NAFTA. Additionally, 17,321 of their family members (13,136 Canadians, 2,904 Mexicans, as well as a number of third-country nationals married to Canadians and Mexicans) entered the United States.

INCREASED ILLEGAL IMMIGRATION

Implementation of NAFTA accelerated the movement of undocumented immigrants from Mexico to the United States in several ways. First, the economic integration under NAFTA created increased cross-border traffic, which made illegal migration easier. Second, NAFTA functioned to expand and then contract Mexico's *maquiladora* industry, which assembled a large, mobile workforce just across the Rio Grande, leading to the unemployment of many Mexican workers. Third, the import of inexpensive American agricultural goods caused the bankruptcy of many Mexican farmers and therefore pushed large numbers of Mexican farmworkers out of work. These dislocated Mexican workers increasingly chose to seek a new life in the United States.

Before NAFTA went into effect, undocumented Mexican immigrants came mainly from four or five Mexican states and a limited number of mostly rural municipalities. Since NAFTA has been in effect, immigrants have come from all Mexican states and practically all municipalities. The counterpart of this hollowing out of the Mexican countryside is the growth of the Mexican migrant population in the United States, much of it undocumented.

American states that had only handfuls of Hispanics in 1990 counted sizable Hispanic populations by 2006. In Georgia, for example, the Latin-origin population went from 1.7 percent in 1990 to 5.3 percent in 2000, due to an inflow of 300,000 persons, overwhelmingly from Mexico. Cities such as Charlotte, North Carolina, whose Hispanics in 1990 consisted of a few wealthy Cuban and South American professionals, had more than 80,000 Hispanic residents in 2006, mostly undocumented Mexican laborers. These Mexican migrants were without any significant political voices and proved vulnerable to exploitation.

To prevent or discourage undocumented migrants from entering the United States, U.S. authorities began working to tighten border enforcement in 1993 by building new physical fortifications and virtual surveillance systems. By 2006, more than $20 billion had been spent on this project. Nevertheless, the project proved ineffective, and massive illegal Mexican migration to the United States continued. To evade apprehension by the U.S. Border Patrol and to reduce the risks posed by natural hazards, Mexican migrants have turned increasingly to people smugglers (coyotes), which in turn has enabled smugglers to charge more for their services. With clandestine border crossing an increasingly expensive and risky business, U.S. border enforcement policy has unintentionally encouraged undocumented migrants to remain in the United States for longer periods and settle permanently in the United States in much larger numbers.

Yunqiu Zhang

FURTHER READING

Ashbee, Edward, Helene Balslev Clausen, and Carl Pedersen, eds. *The Politics, Economics, and Culture of Mexican-U.S. Migration: Both Sides of the Border.* New York: Palgrave Macmillan, 2007. Collection of essays examining all aspects of Mexican immigration to the United States from both American and Mexican perspectives.

Belous, Richard S., and Jonathan Lemco, eds. *NAFTA as a Model of Development.* Washington, D.C.: National Planning Association, 1993. Collection of twenty-one conference papers presents a good variety of viewpoints, including several from the perspective of Canada and Mexico.

Cameron, Maxwell A., and Brian W. Tomlin. *The Making of NAFTA: How the Deal Was Done.* Ithaca,

N.Y.: Cornell University Press, 2000. Covers the background of the diplomatic process and offers a full account of the negotiations resulting in the NAFTA agreement.

Cornelius, Wayne A., and Jessa M. Lewis, eds. *Impacts of Border Enforcement on Mexican Migration: The View from Sending Communities.* La Jolla, Calif.: Center for Comparative Immigration Studies, 2007. Essays examining Mexican perspective on immigration to the United States.

Grayson, George W. *The North American Free Trade Agreement: Regional Community and the New World Order.* Lanham, Md.: University Press of America, 1995. Presents a narrative history of the debates and negotiations surrounding NAFTA up to the time the treaty was approved.

Kingsolver, Ann E. *NAFTA Stories: Fears and Hopes in Mexico and the United States.* Boulder, Colo.: Lynne Rienner, 2001. Presents a wide variety of viewpoints about NAFTA as revealed in stories told by people from many different backgrounds.

Weintraub, Sidney, ed. *NAFTA's Impact on North America: The First Decade.* Washington, D.C.: Center for Strategic and International Studies, 2004. Collection of essays examining the political, social, and nontrade impact of NAFTA through its first decade.

SEE ALSO: Border fence; Border Patrol, U.S.; Canada vs. United States as immigrant destinations; Canadian immigrants; Economic opportunities; Homeland Security, Department of; Illegal immigration; Mexican immigrants.

NORTH CAROLINA

SIGNIFICANCE: One of the original thirteen colonies, North Carolina began its existence as an immigrant society. After the United States became independent, it received few foreign immigrants until the 1960's and 1970's, when significant economic growth brought waves of new people looking for work. By the turn of the twenty-first century, the state had one of the nation's fastest growing population of Latinos, a large but unknown number of whom were undocumented laborers.

The non-Native American population of early colonial North Carolina was necessarily a product of immigration, not all of it foreign. Many of North Carolina's earliest settlers came from other colonies, such as Virginia, Maryland, South Carolina and Pennsylvania. Indeed, the first permanent white settlers came to Albemarle Sound from Virginia during the 1650's. Mostly of English extraction, they numbered several hundred farmers and traders. North Carolina's first significant conflict with Native Americans, the Tuscarora War of 1711, was in part sparked by the settlement of Swiss and German colonists at New Bern. Its outcome, the defeat of the Indians, spurred new European immigration to North Carolina's Coastal Plain.

COLONIAL SOCIETY

The colony's growing population was quite diverse. In addition to settlers of English ancestry, Scottish, Irish, Welsh, French, German, and Swiss settlers were well represented. Black slaves, most of whom came from either the West Indies or directly from West Africa, arrived in increasing numbers. They were concentrated mostly in the Lower Cape Fear region, where the plantations of affluent South Carolina and Virginia immigrants produced naval stores, indigo, and rice.

North Carolina had the distinction of attracting more Scottish Highlanders in the eighteenth century than any other future state. From 1732 to 1775, between 15,000 and 30,000 Highlanders came to North Carolina's Cape Fear Valley. Among them were the poet John MacRae and the Jacobite heroine Flora MacDonald. Their communities were highly insular, and Gaelic prevailed as the majority language—even for slaves in the region—into the early nineteenth century.

Westward expansion into North Carolina's Piedmont region was similarly diverse. While the first settlers there were English colonists from the coast, they were soon joined by others—including the stream of Germans and Scotch-Irish who by the mid-eighteenth century had begun moving southward from Pennsylvania along the Great Valley of Virginia. In 1753, Pennsylvania Moravians began work on the planned community of Salem. They would also establish several other settlements in the region. Immigration into the mountain region—which, by 1830, would give western North Carolina a preponderance of the population—

followed a similar ethnic profile. Most migrants were of Scotch-Irish, English, or German ancestry. Many came directly from the Piedmont region.

NINETEENTH CENTURY TRENDS

Because of a slow-down in immigration and a significant degree of out-migration during the nineteenth and early twentieth centuries, several attempts to attract immigrants to North Carolina were concocted. These began during the post-Civil War era under the auspices of the state Department of Agriculture, Immigration, and Statistics and its subordinate organization, the North Carolina Bureau of Immigration. The bureau's successes were mostly modest; they included the settlement of sixty-nine immigrants described as "German Polanders" in Salisbury in 1881. Private citizens also attempted to attract foreign labor and capital to the state through colonization schemes. The most famous of these, Wilmington entrepreneur Hugh Mac-Rae, founded several settlements of Italian, Polish, Dutch, German, and Hungarian immigrants in the southeastern part of the state between 1905 and 1908.

TWENTIETH CENTURY DEVELOPMENTS

North Carolina had little significant immigration until the 1960's and 1970's, when economic growth and the end of racial segregation in public accommodations encouraged people from out of state and overseas to enter the state. Most of the population growth since that period has been centered in the state's major urban regions—the so-called Research Triangle that encompasses the major university towns of Raleigh, Durham and Chapel Hill; the Piedmont Triad of Winston-Salem, Greensboro, and High Point; and Asheville and Wilmington. Many immigrants from around the world have settled in these areas in search of economic opportunities and education, bringing a degree of cultural diversity unprecedented in North Carolina history.

PROFILE OF NORTH CAROLINA

Region	Atlantic coast
Entered union	1789
Largest cities	Charlotte, Raleigh (capital), Greensboro, Durham, Winston-Salem, Fayetteville
Modern immigrant communities	Mexicans, Asian Indians, Chinese, Vietnamese, Koreans

Population	Total	Percent of state	Percent of U.S.	U.S. rank
All state residents	8,856,000	100.0	2.96	10
All foreign-born residents	614,000	6.9	1.64	14

Source: U.S. Census Bureau, *Statistical Abstract for 2006.*
Notes: The U.S. population in 2006 was 299,399,000, of whom 37,548,000 (12.5%) were foreign born. Rankings in last column reflect total numbers, not percentages.

During the 1970's and 1980's many Southeast Asian immigrants entered North Carolina. A large portion of these people were refugees fleeing the aftermath of the Vietnam War, which ended in 1975. Of the 125,000 Vietnamese refugees authorized to enter the United States during President Gerald Ford's administration, about 2,400 were living in North Carolina by 1980. They were joined by another stream of Vietnamese migration during the 1980's. Many Montagnards joined this stream of post-Vietnam War refugees. By the early twenty-first century, North Carolina had the largest population of Montagnards—about 5,000—outside Vietnam. Hmong immigrants fleeing Laos's Vietnam-backed government also came in large numbers to the United States. The estimated 7,100 to 12,000 refugees who settled in North Carolina formed one of the largest Hmong communities in the United States.

The 1960's also saw the immigration of people from other parts of Asia into North Carolina. Many are involved in business, education, research and other middle-class pursuits, and most live in the Raleigh-Durham-Chapel Hill Triangle. By 2000, roughly 26,000 Asian Indians, 19,000 Chinese, 15,000 Vietnamese, 12,000 Koreans, and 9,000 Filipinos resided in the state.

The single largest-growing immigrant group in North Carolina, however, has been Latinos. Mostly

of Mexican origin but also including people from South and Central America, the Latino population of North Carolina saw the highest increase in the nation (394 percent) between 1990 and 2000. This growth has been in large part due to the U.S. demand for cheap, unskilled labor, combined with the potent push factor of poverty and limited jobs in Mexico and other countries. It was sped by an economic boom experienced in the South during the 1990's that was particularly strong in Charlotte and Raleigh-Durham.

Latinos have been especially attracted to the construction industry in North Carolina, in which they made up about 29 percent of the labor force during the early twenty-first century. They have also been heavily employed in North Carolina's agricultural and agricultural processing sectors, in which they have rapidly displaced African American workers. About one-third of the nation's documented guest workers labor on farms in North Carolina. However, a large but unknown number of Latino workers are undocumented.

Jeremiah Taylor

FURTHER READING

Blethen, H. Tyler, and Curtin W. Wood, Jr. *From Ulster to Carolina: The Migration of the Scotch-Irish to Southwestern North Carolina.* Raleigh: North Carolina Department of Cultural Resources, Division of Archives and History, 1998.

Haines, David W., ed. *Refugees as Immigrants: Cambodians, Laotians, and Vietnamese in America.* Totowa, N.J.: Rowman & Littlefield, 1989.

Nazario, Sonia. *Enrique's Journey.* New York: Random House, 2006.

Sherman, Spencer. "The Hmong in America: Laotian Refugees in the Land of the Giants." *National Geographic* (October, 1988).

SEE ALSO: British immigrants; Economic opportunities; Ethnic enclaves; European immigrants; Georgia; German immigrants; Guest-worker programs; Mexican immigrants; South Carolina; Vietnamese immigrants; Westward expansion.

NORTH DAKOTA

SIGNIFICANCE: North Dakota stands apart from most U.S. states in its geographical remoteness, the small size of its population, and the small number of non-European immigrants it has attracted. As younger residents of rural counties have gravitated to the major cities of Bismarck and Fargo or left the state permanently to seek employment elsewhere, the state's traditionally strong agricultural industry has faced a growing labor shortage that has not been alleviated by significant new immigration.

Located in the upper Midwest, North Dakota has experienced its own unique pattern of ethnic group immigration. Most of the states in its region had received most of the immigrants that would come to them before 1890. During the early twentieth century, North Dakota was the only state in the region to continue receiving significant numbers of new immigrants. Most of these late arrivals were northern Europeans who settled in the western part of the state, which had a strong agricultural economy.

NINETEENTH AND TWENTIETH CENTURY TRENDS

Dakota Territory, which was created in 1861, was split in 1889, when the states of North and South Dakota entered the union. During the late nineteenth century, European immigrants settled throughout the Great Plains. The 1900 U.S. Census revealed that 30 percent of North Dakota's residents were Scandinavians, particularly Norwegians. Most of them settled in the eastern and northern areas of the state. Germans formed the second-largest immigrant group. Ethnic Germans from the Russian Empire were particularly prominent in the south-central part of the state. In North Dakota's northern counties, Canadians were the largest immigrant group.

In contrast to most other states, North Dakota did not undergo a surge in population growth or experience an infusion of non-European immigrants during the late twentieth century. In 1970, fully one-third of the state's population still spoke German at home, and one-sixth retained Norwegian and Swedish as their mother tongues. However, since the mid-twentieth century, the state has

undergone a significant demographic shift, as the youngest generations of immigrant families have sought economic opportunities outside North Dakota. Between 1950 and 1970 alone, 382 of the state's towns lost 80 percent of their population. Over the ensuing decades, the use of ethnic languages faded as third-generation family members left the state for good. Nevertheless, the immigrants' core values of family, church, and community remained strong.

North Dakota's aging workforce has created a labor shortage that was approaching crisis proportions during the early twenty-first century. The traditionally strong agricultural economy has been particularly threatened. However, native-born North Dakotans have resisted proposals to invite new manufacturing industries into the state, fearing that they might attract a wave of illegal immigrants who would undermine longstanding traditions within the tight communities of northern European immigrant descendants. Declining rural population has led to farm consolidations, as well as school district consolidations, and mergers of church congregations.

Gayla Koerting

PROFILE OF NORTH DAKOTA

Region	North-central
Entered union	1889
Largest cities	Fargo, Bismarck (capital), Grand Forks
Modern immigrant communities	Germans

Population	Total	Percent of state	Percent of U.S.	U.S. rank
All state residents	635,000	100.0	0.21	48
All foreign-born residents	13,000	2.1	0.03	50

Source: U.S. Census Bureau, *Statistical Abstract for 2006.*

Notes: The U.S. population in 2006 was 299,399,000, of whom 37,548,000 (12.5%) were foreign born. Rankings in last column reflect total numbers, not percentages.

FURTHER READING

Blouet, Brian W., and Frederick C. Luebke. *The Great Plains: Environment and Culture.* Lincoln: University of Nebraska Press, 1979.

Gjerde, Jon. *The Minds of the West: The Ethnocultural Evolution of the Rural Middle West, 1830-1917.* Chapel Hill: University of North Carolina Press, 1979.

Kiely, Kathy. "Can Aging N.D. Resist Change Amid Immigration Debate?" *USA Today,* November 25, 2007.

Wilkins, Robert P., and Wynona Wilkins. *North Dakota: A Bicentennial History.* New York: W. W. Norton, 1977.

Wishart, David J., ed. *Encyclopedia of the Great Plains.* Lincoln: University of Nebraska Press, 2004.

SEE ALSO: German immigrants; Minnesota; Nebraska; Scandinavian immigrants; South Dakota; Westward expansion.

O

OHIO

SIGNIFICANCE: Although Ohio was one of the first territories in the Midwest to become a state, its history of foreign immigration began relatively late, after major conflicts with Native Americans opened the region to settlement.

Ohio's first immigrants were Native Americans of the Miami, Shawnee, Ottawa, Tuscarora, Wyandotte, Seneca, and Delaware tribes. Many of these people were relatively late arrivals who moved to the region to get away from expanding European settlements to the east and from conflicts with the Iroquois and Cherokee peoples. In 1763, during the British colonial era, white settlement in the Ohio region was banned to prevent conflicts with Native Americans. However, after the United States became independent in 1783, restrictions on settlement were lifted. A coalition of Native American forces under the Miami war chief Little Turtle fought a four-year war against U.S. occupation of the region, but the U.S. victory at the Battle of Fallen Timbers in 1794 effectively ended Native American resistance.

IMMIGRATION UNDER STATEHOOD

After the United States became independent, the future of the Ohio Territory was defined by the Northwest Ordinance of 1787. That law's banning of slavery north of the Ohio River profoundly affected the character of all the future midwestern states, especially those which the Ohio River separated from the slave states of Kentucky and Virginia. In 1788, Marietta, a Massachusetts colony on an island in the Ohio River, became Ohio's first permanent American settlement.

Although New England Yankees were making claims on Ohio territory, the first settlers who came in significant numbers were Scotch-Irish. Most of these people were children and grandchildren of immigrants from Ulster in Northern Ireland who had settled in Virginia, Kentucky, and Pennsylvania. These early immigrants spread out along the Ohio River, northward from Marietta. By 1803,

their numbers were large enough to make Ohio eligible for U.S. statehood. The federal government's liberal land sales policy attracted many more settlers to the southern part of the state. By 1810, Ohio had more than 230,000 American and foreign residents.

The first immigrants to enter Ohio directly from Europe in substantial numbers were six hundred French, who were lured to Ohio by a land scheme promoted in France. In 1790, they founded a colony called Gallipolis on the Ohio River and soon assimilated into American culture. More French immigrants came during the nineteenth and twentieth centuries. Many of them were fleeing political and economic crises in Europe. Ohio also received immigrants from French-speaking Quebec. According to the U.S. Census, in the year 2000, almost 45,000 Ohio residents reported speaking French at home—a number exceeded only by German and Spanish speakers.

GERMAN IMMIGRATION

After the War of 1812 ended, the first German-speaking immigrants arrived in eastern Ohio, where they settled along a ridge of high land nicknamed the "Backbone." However, these people did not come directly from Europe; they were mostly Pennsylvania Dutch who were already American citizens—Amish and Mennonites who lived in close-knit communities and maintained their ancestral language. Their communities, their language, and conservative style of dress have survived into the twenty-first century, in both Ohio and other parts of the Midwest. The 2000 U.S. Census recorded more than 16,000 Ohio residents who still spoke the Pennsylvania Dutch dialect of German at home.

Revolutions in 1830 and 1848 helped propel the first German immigrants who came directly to Ohio. By 1850, Germans made up 5.6 percent of the state's total population and were more numerous even than British and Irish immigrants, who collectively constituted 4.4 percent. The densest concentration of Germans was in the Cincinnati area, along the Ohio River. In 1830, Germans made up only 5 percent of that city's population, but by 1850 that figure had risen to 23 percent. Cincinnati

by then was becoming known for its German breweries and opera. Similar increases in German population occurred in Chillicothe, Dayton, and Portsmouth.

The northern part of Ohio was also receiving its share of foreign immigrants. Cuyahoga County, which included Cleveland, was more than one-third foreign born by 1870. Most of its immigrants were Germans. By the turn of the twentieth century, the Germans had been joined by substantial numbers of Bohemians, Canadians, Hungarians, Poles, Austrians, and Italians.

A little-known but important aspect of Ohio's immigrant communities has been German's influence on the English spoken in the state. Many of southern Ohio's first American settlers came from Kentucky and Virginia, but traces of southern accent are mostly confined to rural areas. New England Yankees, who spoke a dialect of English that has been popularly, though mistakenly, called "general American," settled mostly in cities. There they were joined by German immigrants, many of whom learned their English from Yankee teachers. Because the Germans rarely learned English from Southerners in Ohio, they helped make southern accents less evident in the state's cities.

LATE TWENTIETH CENTURY TRENDS

The late twentieth century saw the first waves of Hispanic immigrants entering Ohio. Most of these people were Mexicans, whose immigration grew even heavier after the turn of the twenty-first century. By 2006, the state's Hispanic population reached 265,762—about 2.3 percent of Ohio's total population. Just over 50 percent of these people were Mexicans.

Although Mexicans have constituted a smaller percentage of the total population in Ohio than in some other states, their growing presence has led to a revival of nativism and racism. In October, 2004, an arson fire in Ohio's largest city, Columbus, burned ten Mexican workers to death. Similar hate

crimes have occurred in other cities, and the state has intensified its efforts to reduce illegal immigration.

Timothy C. Frazer

FURTHER READING

Daniels, Roger. *Coming to America: A History of Immigration and Ethnicity in American Life.* New York: HarperCollins, 1990. Thorough but readable treatment of groups of immigrants from the seventeenth century through the 1980's: why they came, where they settled.

Frazer, Timothy C., ed. *"Heartland" English: Variation and Transition in the American Midwest.* Tuscaloosa: University of Alabama Press, 1993. Collection of essays that describe the impact immigrants and settlement had on the spoken English of several midwestern states, including Ohio.

Izant, Grace Goulder. *Ohio Scenes and Citizens.* Cleveland: World Publishing Company, 1964. Sketches and case histories illustrating twentieth century life in Ohio.

Quinones, Sam. *Antonio's Gun and Delphino's Dream: True Tales of Mexican Migration.* Albuquerque: University of New Mexico Press, 2007. Narrates the causes for the economic crisis in Mexico, which led to the large Mexican immigration into the United States that began during the 1970's. Describes the experiences of eight Mexicans who arrived after 1990.

PROFILE OF OHIO

Region	Midwest
Entered union	1803
Largest cities	Columbus (capital), Cleveland, Cincinnati, Tolelo, Akron, Dayton
Modern immigrant communities	Mexicans

Population	Total	Percent of state	Percent of U.S.	U.S. rank
All state residents	11,478,000	100.0	3.83	7
All foreign-born residents	412,000	3.6	1.10	19

Source: U.S. Census Bureau, *Statistical Abstract for 2006.*

Notes: The U.S. population in 2006 was 299,399,000, of whom 37,548,000 (12.5%) were foreign born. Rankings in last column reflect total numbers, not percentages.

SEE ALSO: Connecticut; French immigrants; German immigrants; Irish immigrants; Iron and steel industry; Italian immigrants; Kentucky; Language issues; Pennsylvania.

OKLAHOMA

> **SIGNIFICANCE:** During the nineteenth century, the availability of free public land in Oklahoma played a major role in attracting immigrants to the United States from Europe. The building of railroads and the development of coal mines and oil fields brought additional waves of immigrants.

During the nineteenth century, poverty, harsh living conditions, and religious persecution caused vast numbers of Europeans to immigrate to the United States. Many settled in the major cities of the East and Midwest and in the coal mining regions of Pennsylvania and West Virginia. Others went to the agricultural areas of the Midwest and Great Plains where they successfully established farms. By the late nineteenth century, European immigrants, seeking to improve their lives, were still coming to the United States; however, they found a lack of both jobs and land in the east and the Midwest. The best land in the Great Plains had also been claimed. In April of 1889, Oklahoma, which at that time was administratively an Indian territory of the United States, was opened for white settlement, and the first great "land run" took place that same year. A large majority of the new immigrants sought land and a new life in the territory.

FARMERS AND MERCHANTS

Many of Oklahoma's first foreign immigrants were Germans from Europe's German states and from the Russian Empire. Many of them also shared a common religion, as members of either the Mennonite Church or the Lutheran Church. They set-tled in areas of north central, northwestern, and southwestern Oklahoma. Those who had come from the Russian steppes and the eastern part of Germany were able to tolerate the dry, windy climate of Oklahoma and prospered as farmers. They tended to keep to themselves, establish their own churches, and maintain both their language and their customs. During World War I, they faced severe discrimination and personal danger as the anti-German sentiment intensified in Oklahoma. The teaching of German in school was forbidden, and German newspapers were burned. Even making German sauerkraut was condemned as subversive. In an attempt to prove their allegiance to the United States, members of the German community that had founded the town of Kiel in 1894 renamed it Loyal.

Around the same time the first German immigrants were arriving, many Jewish merchants from Bavaria and Austria were coming into Oklahoma to supply the crews building railroads. After the main railroad lines were completed, many of these merchants stayed and opened shops in the newly formed towns. In 1899, the first Jewish temple was established at Ardmore. More Jewish merchants as well as Syrian peddlers came after oil was discovered and boomtowns began arising after 1900.

During the early years of the twentieth century, peasant farmers from Bohemia arrived. Many of them were from the region known as Czechoslova-

---

PROFILE OF OKLAHOMA

Region	Midwest
Entered union	1907
Largest cities	Oklahoma City (capital), Tulsa, Norman, Lawton
Modern immigrant communities	Mexicans, Vietnamese, Asian Indians

Population	Total	Percent of state	Percent of U.S.	U.S. rank
All state residents	3,579,000	100.0	1.20	28
All foreign-born residents	176,000	4.9	0.47	30

Source: U.S. Census Bureau, *Statistical Abstract for 2006.*
Notes: The U.S. population in 2006 was 299,399,000, of whom 37,548,000 (12.5%) were foreign born. Rankings in last column reflect total numbers, not percentages.

kia after 1918. Most engaged in farming, but others established flour mills or became merchants selling agricultural equipment. The Bohemians generally clustered together in and around Oklahoma City and maintained the traditions of their homeland.

COAL MINING

Land was not the only attraction that drew immigrants to Oklahoma. Coal mining began in the territory in 1872, and the first commercial coal mining was started in 1873. Most of the coal was mined in eastern Oklahoma, in districts belonging to Native American tribes. However, enterprising entrepreneurs, such as James McAlester, married into the tribes or paid special taxes that permitted them to use non-Indian labor to work the coal mines. Consequently, many immigrants who had hoped to find work in the mines of Pennsylvania and West Virginia instead went to Oklahoma. Many of these people had immigrated from Ireland, Scotland, and Wales. Others came from Poland, Lithuania, Hungary, Russia, Germany, England, and Italy. Although mining wages were relatively high in Oklahoma, the work was difficult and dangerous. The miners typically worked in inadequately ventilated shafts so cramped they were unable to stand erect.

Among immigrant coal miners, Italians were most numerous. In 1910, they constituted the largest group of foreign-born residents in the three major coal-producing counties of Pittsburg, Coal, and Latimer. After 1920, the state's coal mining industry steadily declined, reducing its need for labor. Many of the immigrant coal miners from Poland, Lithuania, and Ukraine sought new jobs in the slaughterhouses and on the farms in the Oklahoma City area. Many Italian coal miners bought farms and businesses and stayed in the mining region.

MEXICAN AND ASIAN IMMIGRANTS

Mexican immigration into Oklahoma began around the turn of the twentieth century, but many of these early immigrants came only as seasonal agricultural workers and returned home. The railroad crews of that time were predominantly Mexican, and Mexican immigrants also worked in a wide variety of other jobs, from picking cotton to mining coal to working on oilfields. Eventually, some of these workers brought their families with

them and established homes in Oklahoma. By 1930, approximately 7,500 Mexicans were permanent residents of Oklahoma.

After World War II, the numbers of Mexicans immigrating to Oklahoma increased, but the first truly large wave of Mexican immigration did not occur until the last two decades of the twentieth century. Mexicans spread throughout the state, working primarily as laborers on farms, in factories, in construction, and as restaurant employees. By the early twenty-first century, Mexican culture and the Spanish language played very visible and important roles in Oklahoma.

The first substantial number of Asians to enter Oklahoma were Vietnamese, who began coming in 1975, after the Vietnam War ended. They readily adapted and opened various businesses, particularly restaurants and grocery stores. During the 1980's, considerable numbers of other Asian immigrants moved to Oklahoma. These included Korean, Chinese, Japanese, and Asian Indians. The Asian immigrants, while maintaining their own culture, have been successful in adapting to life in Oklahoma.

Shawncey Webb

FURTHER READING

Bicha, Karel D. *The Czechs in Oklahoma.* Norman: University of Oklahoma Press, 1982. Excellent and thorough coverage, discussing where Czechs have settled, their culture, and their role in the state's agriculture.

Franks, Kenny Arthur, and Paul F. Lambert. *Oklahoma: The Land and Its People.* Morris Plains, N.J.: Unicorn Publishing, 1994. Good discussion of where immigrant groups have settled in Oklahoma and what their lives in the state have been like.

Luebke, Frederick C. *Germans in the New World: Essays in the History of Immigration.* Champaign: University of Illinois Press, 1990. Particularly good for language issues and prejudices faced by Germans in Oklahoma.

Portes, Alejandro, and Rubén G. Rumbaut. *Immigrant America: A Portrait.* 3d ed. Berkeley: University of California Press, 2006. Good presentation of the life of immigrants in different social and economic situations. Also treats assimilation.

Zolberg, Aristide. *A Nation by Design: Immigration Policy in the Fashioning of America.* Cambridge,

Mass.: Harvard University Press, 2006. Excellent for its objective presentation of U.S. immigration policy and its changes. Good for Mexican immigration.

SEE ALSO: Coal industry; Czech and Slovakian immigrants; German immigrants; Homestead Act of 1862; Irish immigrants; Italian immigrants; Jewish immigrants; Railroads.

OPERATION WETBACK

THE EVENT: Massive federal-state effort to remove unauthorized Mexican workers from the United States
DATE: June-September, 1954
LOCATION: U.S.-Mexican border areas

> **SIGNIFICANCE:** Considered an extreme example of overaggressive immigration enforcement, Operation Wetback rounded up and deported nearly 300,000 Mexicans working in the United States and detained more than 1 million more Mexicans who crossed the U.S. border.

Operation Wetback was a response to mounting American sentiment against the large numbers of Mexicans who entered the United States illegally after World War II and the Mexican government's concern that its citizens working in the United States should not be employed without labor contracts. Between 1942 and 1964, almost 5 million Mexicans were admitted into the United States as bracero workers under a series of U.S.-Mexican agreements that became progressively more favorable to American farm employers over the years. Under the program, the U.S. government guaranteed the wages promised to braceros during World War II. Afterward, however, the American farmers who employed the workers were made responsible for paying both the wages of the workers and their transportation costs from the interior of Mexico to their farms.

Meanwhile, the large numbers of Mexicans who continued to enter the United States illegally saved many American employers the cost of their transportation. Known as "wetbacks" even in official documents, these workers were returned to the border when they were detected inside the United States and were then issued work permits and returned to the farms on which they had been previously employed. Between 1947 and 1949, two "wetbacks" were legalized in this way for every Mexican who was legally admitted to the United States under the bracero program.

The Migratory Labor Agreement of 1951 shifted more authority over bracero workers from the Mexican government to American farm employers. The Mexican government wanted American employers to recruit their workers within the interior of Mexico, but under the 1951 agreement, the U.S. Department of Labor opened five reception centers along the international border to which Mexicans seeking American jobs could report. Employers arranged and paid for transportation from the reception centers to their farms.

One day after he signed the Migratory Labor Agreement into law, President Harry S. Truman asked the U.S. Congress to approve legislation making it a federal crime knowingly to hire unauthorized immigrant workers. Congress refused. Two sections of the Immigration and Nationality Act of 1952 included the so-called Texas proviso, which made harboring illegal immigrants subject to a two-thousand-dollar fine and up to five years imprisonment, while exempting employment from the definition of "harboring."

Meanwhile, illegal immigration from Mexico surged, and U.S. attorney general Herbert Brownwell called what he observed "shocking" during his August, 1953, visit to the Mexican border. Brownwell appointed General Joseph Swing to be commissioner of the Immigration and Naturalization Service (INS), instructing him to "clean up" the border. Operation Wetback began June 17, 1954, in Arizona and California, with 750 INS agents assigned to farming areas trying to arrest 1,000 unauthorized Mexican immigrants a day.

State and local police joined the sweeps of Latino barrios as the program spread to other states, and thousands of Mexicans returned home on their own. The setting up of highway checkpoints and railroad checks resulted in the detainment of thousands of Mexicans and Mexican Americans on vagrancy charges until INS agents could verify their status. When the INS ran out of funding in mid-September, 1954, the operation was halted. By

then, some 1.1 million unauthorized foreigners had been apprehended during the federal fiscal year that had ended on June 30, 1954, but only 254,000 had been apprehended during the following fiscal year. Meanwhile, the U.S. Department of Labor had made it easier for farmers to hire braceros by relaxing rules such as minimum six-week contracts and the enforcement of wage and housing regulations. Consequently, the number of braceros admitted to the United States rose from 200,000 in 1953 to 400,000 in 1955.

Operation Wetback had several long-term effects. The first was the public revulsion at the rough rounding up of families who included U.S. citizens with young babies. It seemed unlikely that the U.S. government would again attempt a similar mass repatriation. Second, easing farmers' access to bracero workers encouraged the expansion of labor-intensive agriculture without raising wages, sowing the seeds for subsequent unauthorized migration. Finally, Operation Wetback made future efforts of the United States to negotiate migration agreements with Mexico more difficult.

Philip L. Martin

FURTHER READING

Garcia, Juan Ramon. *Operation Wetback: The Mass Deportation of Mexican Undocumented Workers.* Westport, Conn.: Greenwood Press, 1980.

Garcia y Griego, Manuel. "The Importation of Mexican Contract Laborers to the United States, 1942-64." In *Between Two Worlds: Mexican Immigrants in the United States*, edited by David G. Gutierrez. Wilmington, Del.: Scholarly Resources, 1996.

Kirstein, Peter. *Anglo over Bracero. A History of the Mexican Worker in the United States from Roosevelt to Nixon.* San Francisco: R&E Associates, 1977.

SEE ALSO: Border Patrol, U.S.; Bracero program; Deportation; El Paso incident; Guest-worker programs; Mexican deportations of 1931; Mexican immigrants; Texas.

ORDERLY DEPARTURE PROGRAM

THE EVENT: U.S.-supported United Nations program designed to facilitate immigration of Vietnamese refugees

DATE: 1979-1999

LOCATION: Bangkok, Thailand, and Ho Chi Minh City (Saigon), Vietnam

SIGNIFICANCE: The Orderly Departure Program was instituted by the communist government of Vietnam in cooperation with the United Nations to ease the plight of refugees attempting to leave Southeast Asia on small boats. Through the program, about 500,000 Vietnamese immigrated to North America.

After the communist victory ended the Vietnam War in early 1975, tens of thousands of Vietnamese people wanted to escape from the newly reunited country's communist regime. In 1978, the Socialist Republic of Vietnam turned against the ethnic Chinese minority in Vietnam known as Hoa. Repressive measures drove many of these people to leave the country on small boats. The great perils that these boat people faced on the high seas aroused international attention. In the face of growing international concern, leaders of the Vietnamese government began meeting with representatives of the office of the U.N. High Commissioner of Refugees (UNHCR) and the U.S. government to find a mutually satisfactory settlement.

THE PROGRAM IN OPERATION

After intense negotiations, Vietnam and the UNHCR signed a memorandum of understanding on May 30, 1979. The agreement established the Orderly Departure Program (ODP) for Vietnamese citizens requesting to emigrate from Vietnam to Western countries. The United States agreed to accept a majority of the emigrants.

The program got off to a slow start. In January 1980, the ODP opened its offices in Bangkok, Thailand. From there, ODP missions went to Ho Chi Minh City—as Saigon had been renamed by the Vietnamese government—to interview potential immigrants and process their departures. However, immediately after U.S. president Ronald Rea-

Young Vietnamese refugees, who were relocated to the Philippines after the closure of refugee camps in Thailand, staging a demonstration at the U.S. embassy in Manila in September, 1996, urging the U.S. government to resettle them in the United States, as they believed it had promised to do. (AP/Wide World Photos)

gan took office on January 20, 1981, Vietnam suspended the program. In October, 1981, Vietnam resumed the program after resolving differences with the new U.S. administration. It was not until 1983 that the ODP was running smoothly. By then, the majority of Vietnamese refugees who went to the United States were leaving through the program's provisions rather than risking perilous ocean voyages on their own.

After U.S.-Vietnamese relations improved with the lifting of a U.S. trade embargo against Vietnam in early 1994, the two countries decided to close registration for the ODP on September 14, 1994. In 1999, the ODP office in Bangkok shut its doors and the remaining work was handled by the U.S. Refugee Resettlement Section at the U.S. consulate in Ho Chi Minh City. On November 15, 2005, the United States and Vietnam agreed to allow the last Vietnamese who had been eligible to emigrate to the United States under the program but had missed the 1994 deadline for registration to do so.

In all, about 500,000 Vietnamese immigrated to the United States under the ODP. Most of these people either had worked with Americans during the Vietnam War or were family members of people who had. Others were relatives of Vietnamese already living in the United States. While eventually reducing the numbers of desperate boat people, the ODP contributed substantially to Vietnamese immigration to America.

In American popular culture, the ODP was immortalized in the musical *Miss Saigon* (pr., pb. 1989) and the autobiography of Kien Nguyen, *The Unwanted* (2001), depicting the plight of the Vietnamese affected by its operation.

R. C. Lutz

FURTHER READING

Kumin, Julie. "Orderly Departure from Vietnam: Cold War Anomaly or Humanitarian Innovation?" *Refugee Survey Quarterly* 27, no. 1 (2008): 104-117.

Nguyen, Kien. *The Unwanted.* Boston: Back Bay Books, 2001.

U.S. General Accounting Office. *Refugee Program: The Orderly Departure Program from Vietnam.* Washington, D.C.: Government Printing Office, 1990.

SEE ALSO: Amerasian children; Amerasian Homecoming Act of 1987; Asian immigrants; Child immigrants; Refugees; Vietnam War; Vietnamese immigrants.

OREGON

> **SIGNIFICANCE:** A destination for immigration since before it was a state, Oregon has drawn immigrants from all over the world. However, through much of its history as a state, it actively resisted the immigration of people from regions other than northern and western Europe.

White settlers, both European and Americans of European descent, poured into Oregon during the middle of the nineteenth century, seeking land for homesteading. The settlers clashed violently with Native Americans, many of whom were killed, died of disease, or sent to reservations. At the same time, the state's territorial and state governments enacted laws to reserve Oregon citizenship for white settlers. Black people were barred from Oregon in 1844, and both African Americans and Chinese were barred from voting or owning land by Oregon's state constitution. An 1866 miscegenation law prohibited white people from marrying blacks, Chinese, or Native Americans. Founded as a white, agrarian, frontier state, Oregon retained an ambivalence and even hostility toward immigration into the twentieth century.

NINETEENTH CENTURY PATTERNS

At the time Oregon became a state in 1859, only about 10 percent of its residents were foreign born. Afterward, however, foreign immigration increased, but many of the new immigrants were secondary migrants who had originally settled in the Midwest. Many were attracted to Oregon's mild climate and good farmlands.

Early on, the state of Oregon established a clear preference for German and Scandinavian immigrants, believing that these people would integrate well and achieve social and economic success. Southern and eastern European immigrants, however, were unwelcome and were described as "undesirable" in a 1912 report of the Oregon State Immigration Commission. Oregonians tended to view themselves as thrifty, independent farmers and pioneers and regarded southern and eastern Europeans as having values that were incompatible with their own.

By 1910, Scandinavian immigrants from Sweden, Denmark, Norway, and Finland made up 40 percent of Oregon's population. In addition to farming, these immigrants worked as carpenters, longshoremen, and in lumber mills. Many of the women worked as domestics or ran boardinghouses. Despite the state's bias against eastern Europeans, Jews from Germany and eastern Europe also did well in Oregon during the late nineteenth century. Taking advantage of a relatively open class structure and growing economy with few labor unions, the Jews were generally regarded as shopkeepers and small business owners and were consequently not perceived as competing with native-born laborers.

ASIAN IMMIGRATION

Members of other ethnic groups, however, were not welcome—especially immigrants from China and Japan. Chinese workers who had come to the western states to escape poverty found themselves barred from holding mining claims and land in Oregon soon after statehood. About 5 percent of Oregon's residents were Chinese in 1880, but they were finding life increasingly difficult in the face of violent nativist opposition. After the federal Chinese Exclusion Act of 1882 was passed, mobs of Oregonians drove Chinese residents out of Oregon City, Salem, and Yamhill. Attempts to drive the Chinese out of Portland failed, but the city's Chinese population afterward went down. In 1887, horse thieves murdered forty-three Chinese miners at the Snake River and were subsequently acquitted. As in California, white citizens perceived the Chinese as

strange, pagan, and unwilling to assimilate, and also saw them as undercutting American wages.

Anti-Chinese violence subsided by the 1890's, but the state government continued to explore methods of reducing the Chinese population. In 1903, the state Bureau of Labor collected data on Chinese and Japanese immigrants to determine the extent to which they were in competition with white workers.

During the first four decades of the twentieth century, Japanese workers became targets of violence and negative public feelings in Oregon. Nevertheless, many Japanese immigrants achieved success as farmers, hotel owners, and business operators. They also established the Japanese Association of Oregon, which gave legal and financial aid to new arrivals. However, after Japan launched its sneak attack on the U.S. naval base at Pearl Harbor on December 7, 1941, Japanese immigrants felt the effects of a major backlash. Most of the Japanese nationals and Japanese Americans were interned throughout World War II, giving white Oregonians opportunities to take over Japanese-owned businesses. Some Oregonians hoped to drive the Japanese out of their state permanently. After the war ended in 1945, returning internees were met with suspicion. By the late 1940's, Oregon's state government had partially compensated Japanese American families for their economic losses during their internment and began lifting laws that had restricted Japanese from owning land.

After the Vietnam War ended in 1975, many Vietnamese people immigrated to Oregon. By the early twenty-first century, the Vietnamese were one of the largest immigrant communities in Oregon.

LATIN AMERICAN IMMIGRANTS

Latin American immigration into Oregon began in earnest during the 1930s, when Hispanic workers began arriving to work in the state's agricultural industry. Many Hispanics took jobs that opened up as American citizens found employment in the growing defense industry on the eve of American entry into World War II. Mexican immigration to Oregon increased sharply with the 1942 establishment of the bracero program, which was designed to import seasonal agricultural workers during the war. Braceros working in Oregon were often subjected to substandard working and living conditions, but the program continued until 1964. Meanwhile, as native-born American workers found better-paying jobs in other industries, Oregon's farmers became increasingly dependent on Mexican and other Latin American workers.

Mexican immigrants also worked in Oregon's food, construction, and manufacturing industries and began small businesses. They formed organizations to assist immigrants and advocate for workers' rights and established church- and community-based organizations to provide job training and other services for new arrivals. The long history of Hispanic immigration into Oregon has created multiple-generation households in which some members are naturalized American citizens, while others may be undocumented immigrants. This complicates integration of immigrants into society and makes their utilization of social services difficult.

REFUGEES AND IMMIGRATION REFORM

During the 1960's, efforts to admit refugees from Cuba and other countries and lift discriminatory quotas met with resistance in Oregon, as prejudice against Asian, southern and eastern European, and Latin American immigrant groups continued. How-

PROFILE OF OREGON

Region	Northwest Pacific coast
Entered union	1859
Largest cities	Portland, Eugene, Salem (capital), Gresham
Modern immigrant communities	Mexicans, Vietnamese

Population	Total	Percent of state	Percent of U.S.	U.S. rank
All state residents	3,701,000	100.0	1.24	27
All foreign-born residents	360,000	9.7	0.96	20

Source: U.S. Census Bureau, Statistical Abstract for 2006.
Notes: The U.S. population in 2006 was 299,399,000, of whom 37,548,000 (12.5%) were foreign born. Rankings in last column reflect total numbers, not percentages.

ever, with the passage of the federal Immigration and Nationality Act of 1965, Oregon's immigration rates increased dramatically. During the 1980's, the state became a popular destination for refugees, particularly from the Soviet Union. After the collapse of the Soviet Union in 1991, many refugees from Soviet republics were fundamentalist Christians seeking greater religious freedom—a fact that helped win them sympathy and acceptance in Oregon. By that time, the numbers of refugees from African and Southeast Asian nations were also increasing. Many of these people, like the eastern Europeans, made use of church and state assistance for refugees as well as kinship networks to ease their transition into American society. African and Asian immigrants have encountered some resistance, particularly after the terrorist attacks on the United States of September 11, 2001, but many have established businesses and strong communities.

TWENTY-FIRST CENTURY TRENDS

By the turn of the twenty-first century, Oregon ranked eleventh among all states in numbers of refugees taken in, and the state could be fairly described as a major immigrant gateway. Reasons for this change in demographics have included the decline of employment opportunities in other traditional immigrant gateway states, agricultural opportunities in Oregon that have drawn new immigrants from Mexico and other Latin American countries, and the presence of strong resettlement and social service networks that serve refugees and other immigrants. The state's refugee social service organizations provide refugees with housing, employment, and other services during their first year in Oregon.

Despite Oregon's growing diversity, its history as a primarily European-descended state hostile to immigrants has made it difficult for many immigrants, especially refugees, to integrate into mainstream society. Moreover, a growing percentage of Oregon's jobs are in technology fields that require more specialized training and skills than jobs in traditional immigrant occupations, such as lumbering, farming, and fishing.

By the year 2005, 9.7 percent of the residents of Oregon were foreign born, and 60 percent of these people had arrived in the state since 1990. Most of the state's immigrants were living in the Portland metropolitan area near the state's northern border with Washington.

Melissa A. Barton

FURTHER READING

Do, Hien Duc. *The Vietnamese Americans.* Westport, Conn.: Greenwood Press, 1999. Brief history of Vietnamese Americans, who constituted one of Oregon's largest immigrant communities during the early twenty-first century.

Hoobler, Dorothy, and Thomas Hoobler. *The Scandinavian American Family Album.* New York: Oxford University Press, 1998. Illustrated with historic photographs, this book covers the history of Scandinavian immigration to the United States, including to Oregon.

Nokes, R. Gregory. "'A Most Daring Outrage': Murder at Chinese Massacre Cove, 1887." *Oregon Historical Quarterly* 107, no. 3 (2006): 326-353. Detailed reconstruction of the massacre of Chinese miners at Snake River.

Ross, Alexander. *Adventures of the First Settlers on the Oregon or Columbia River, 1810-1813.* Lincoln: University of Nebraska Press, 1986. Ross, one of the original clerks at Astoria, gives a colorful firsthand account of the venture.

Tolzmann, Don Heinrich. *The German-American Experience.* Amherst, N.Y.: Humanity Books, 2000. Study of German immigrants in America, including western settlement.

SEE ALSO: Anti-Japanese movement; Bracero program; Farm and migrant workers; Japanese American internment; Japanese immigrants; Mexican immigrants; Snake River Massacre; *United States v. Bhagat Singh Thind*; Vietnamese immigrants; Washington State.

OYAMA V. CALIFORNIA

THE CASE: U.S. Supreme Court decision concerning the right of aliens to own land
DATE: Decided on January 19, 1948

SIGNIFICANCE: The influential *Oyama* decision overturned the portions of the California Alien Land Laws that discriminated against U.S. citizens on the basis of race, but the Supreme Court chose not to rule on the

constitutionality of discrimination against noncitizens based on their race or ethnicity.

During the 1930's, Kajiro Oyama, a Japanese immigrant ineligible for American citizenship, purchased eight acres of land in Southern California. Because the state's Alien Land Laws of 1913 and 1920 prohibited noncitizens from owning land, he deeded the property to his minor son, Fred Oyama, who was a U.S. citizen by birth. The father then succeeded in gaining legal guardianship over his son. The local court at the time ignored a provision in the 1920 law requiring proof that land transfers in such circumstances were genuine gifts, not subterfuges to evade the restrictions on alien ownership. During World War II, when the Oyama family was displaced and residing in Utah, the state of California seized the family's eight acres in an escheat trial, based on the accusation that Kajiro Oyama had violated the 1920 law. The state's highest court upheld the action. Fred Oyama, with the support of the American Civil Liberties Union (ACLU), petitioned the Supreme Court for a writ of certiorari.

By a 6-3 vote, the U.S. Supreme Court ruled in Fred Oyama's favor and struck down relevant portions of the Alien Land Laws as inconsistent with the equal protection clause of the Fourteenth Amendment. Writing the opinion for the majority, Chief Justice Fred M. Vinson considered only the issue of discrimination against Fred Oyama and other U.S. citizens who had the difficult burden of proving that their ownership of land was not the result of an intentional effort to evade the 1920 law—a burden not required of other citizens. Vinson's opinion ignored the broader issue of the state's discrimination against Kajiro Oyama and other alien residents illegible for naturalization. In concurring opinions, three liberal members criticized the narrowness of the opinion. Four years later, however, California's Supreme Court would decide the case of *Sei Fujii v. State of California* (1952), which overturned both Alien Land Laws as incompatible with the state's constitution.

Thomas Tandy Lewis

FURTHER READING

Chuman, Frank. *The Bamboo People: The Law and Japanese Americans.* Del Mar, Calif.: Publisher's Inc., 1976.

Itō, Kazuo. *Issei: A History of Japanese Immigrants in North America.* Seattle: Japanese Community Service, 1973.

SEE ALSO: Alien land laws; California; Citizenship; Due process protections; History of immigration after 1891; *Sei Fujii v. State of California*; Supreme Court, U.S.; *Terrace v. Thompson.*

OZAWA V. UNITED STATES

THE CASE: U.S. Supreme Court decision concerning whether Asian immigrants were eligible for naturalization
DATE: Decided on November 13, 1922

SIGNIFICANCE: The *Ozawa* ruling interpreted the word "white" in U.S. naturalization law as referring exclusively to persons of European ancestry (or Caucasians), thereby holding that federal legislation disqualified all persons of Asian ancestry from becoming naturalized citizens.

U.S. naturalization laws enacted between 1790 and 1870 limited the privilege of American citizenship to "free white persons." In 1870, the privilege was extended to persons of African descent but not to immigrants from Asia. Although the Naturalization Act of 1906 was somewhat ambiguous on this point, it implicitly continued the long-standing racial restriction on eligibility for naturalization.

Takao Ozawa, a resident of Hawaii, was a person of Japanese ancestry born in Japan. In 1914, after continuously living in the United States for over twenty years, he applied for U.S. citizenship. Both he and his children had attended American schools. The family used English at home, and they attended an American Christian church. Based on these facts, combined with his relatively light skin color, Ozawa claimed that he could be classified as a "white person." He argued that the purpose of the relevant laws had been to exclude African and Native Americans. The district court, however, rejected the claim and denied his application.

Agreeing to review the case, the Supreme Court upheld the decision of the lower court. Writing for a unanimous Court, Justice George Sutherland considered two issues: first, whether the 1906 stat-

ute allowed the naturalization of a nonwhite person, and second, whether a person of Japanese ancestry might be classified as white. In an exegesis of the relevant portions of the statute, Sutherland found no evidence that the 1906 law eliminated the racial exclusion. If Congress desired to alter "a rule so well and so long established," Sutherland asserted that such a purpose would have been definitely disclosed in unambiguous language.

Discussing the term "white person" in the 1790 law, Sutherland rejected the argument that its purpose was to exclude only Africans and American Indians. A color-test definition of "white," moreover, seemed inadequate, because all racial groups had complex gradations of darkness. Anglo-Saxons were frequently of darker complexions than persons belonging to the "brown and yellow races of Asia." Deciding that the term "white person" was synonymous with the words "a person of the Caucasian race," Sutherland wrote that the applicant was "clearly of a race which is not Caucasian." Because of the dominant ideas in 1790, combined with the U.S. Constitution's explicit authorization of Con-

gress to enact naturalization laws, he saw no need to question whether a racial exclusion might be inconsistent with the due process clause of the Fifth Amendment. The ineligibility of Japanese immigrants for naturalization would continue until passage of the Immigration and Nationality Act of 1952, which was also known as the McCarran-Walter Act of 1952.

Thomas Tandy Lewis

FURTHER READING

Chuman, Frank. *The Bamboo People: The Law and Japanese Americans.* Del Mar, Calif.: Publisher's Inc., 1976.

Hyung-chan, Kim, ed. *Asian Americans and the Supreme Court: A Documentary History.* Westport, Conn.: Greenwood Press, 1992.

SEE ALSO: Citizenship; Congress, U.S.; Constitution, U.S.; Immigration law; Japanese immigrants; Naturalization; Naturalization Act of 1790; Supreme Court, U.S.; "Undesirable aliens"; *United States v. Bhagat Singh Thind.*

P

PACIFIC ISLANDER IMMIGRANTS

SIGNIFICANCE: Although Pacific Islander immigrants have probably received less attention than most other immigrant communities, more Pacific Islanders reside in the United States—including the Pacific Island state Hawaii—than remain in many of their island homelands. Coming from many separate islands with many very different cultures and languages, Islander immigrants are almost impossible to identify in early U.S. censuses, in which they were typically counted under the category of "others" or lumped with Asians.

Pacific Islander immigration to the United States is best understood by recognizing that Pacific Oceanic peoples have a long history of long-distance ocean voyages. Prehistoric inhabitants of South Pacific islands—especially the widespread archipelagoes of Melanesia and Polynesia—constructed sturdy canoes and developed surprisingly advanced navigation systems to find their way around the distantly separated islands. Their island-based regional interactions resulted in marriages, trade contacts, and political relationships, including warfare. During the sixteenth century, the Islanders' regional dynamics were disrupted by the arrival of European explorers, who brought novel technologies, new diseases, and very different cultural concepts to the region.

THE AMERICAN PRESENCE IN THE PACIFIC

Over the ensuing centuries, the Pacific Islands and their inhabitants came increasingly under the domination of Euro-American political rule, economic expansion, and religious beliefs. With increasing contacts came increased population movements, including European settlements on many islands. Many indigenous inhabitants moved away from the islands; some relocated within the Pacific region, others went as far as Europe and the Americas. Most of these population movements were sporadic, small scale, and poorly documented.

By the mid-nineteenth century, American whaling ships were operating regularly in the Pacific Ocean, and Samoans and Hawaiians began to work in the whaling industry. Ultimately, some of these people ended up far from their island homes. Oceanic people were further incorporated into American spheres by the sudden U.S. colonial expansion into the Philippines, Guam, Samoa, and Hawaii between 1898 and 1900, when the United States annexed the Hawaiian islands and occupied Spain's Pacific Island possessions after winning the Spanish-American War.

Extensive military, missionary, and trading links between the United States and its Pacific Island possessions helped prompt large numbers of Islanders to immigrate to the mainland United States. During World War II (1941-1945), the presence of American military bases on many of the region's islands brought the U.S. war with Japan directly into the homelands of Pacific Islanders. The result was tremendous carnage and destruction that would contribute to postwar migration.

PUSH-PULL FACTORS

Pacific Islander immigration can be understood broadly as the product of several push factors that operated across the islands, and also several pull factors that made the United States a compelling migration destination. Push factors have included local political conditions, such as Tonga's monarchy, which many commoners find oppressive. Environmental disasters have also been important, especially hurricanes, which often create havoc on small islands. Other push factors have included economic conditions, especially low wages on many islands; limited higher educational facilities; health services that are inadequate for treating some ailments; and limited opportunities for skilled and professional workers.

The most important pull factors that have drawn Islanders to the United States have been relief from all the Islanders' push factors: nonoppressive government, greater safety from natural disasters, higher wages, and almost unlimited educational and professional opportunities. Moreover, established Pacific Islander communities within the United States provide kin networks that ease

adjustments to immigration by giving newcomers places to stay on their arrival and strong support groups. Local contacts also assist new immigrants with health, educational, and work opportunities.

POPULATION DATA

The hundreds of populated islands spread across the Pacific Ocean, particularly in the South Pacific, are made of independent nations, European dependencies, and American possessions. A sizable number of Pacific Islanders live on territories that were incorporated into the United States during the late nineteenth century. Some sporadic Pacific Islander immigration to the mainland United States probably occurred before that time, but large numbers of Islanders did not begin com-

ing to the United States until the 1950's and 1960's and particularly during the 1970's.

At the time of the 1990 U.S. Census, 365,000 Pacific Islanders lived in the United States. This figure compares with about 30,000 Islanders living in Australia and 531,000 in New Zealand. Only ten years later, the U.S. Pacific Islander population had jumped to 874,000. However, a variety of changes in the methods used in the 2000 U.S. Census mean that the 2000 data are not directly comparable to earlier census information. For example, the 2000 figure for total Islanders includes some people who also reported some non-Pacific Islander ancestry.

Approximately 58 percent of the 2000 U.S. Census group counted as "Native Hawaiian and Other Pacific Islander" were living in Hawaii and California, with sizeable populations also found in Wash-

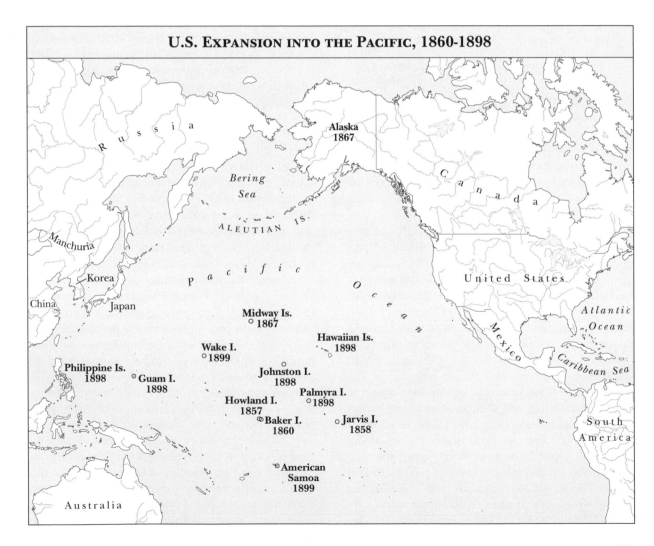

U.S. EXPANSION INTO THE PACIFIC, 1860-1898

PROFILE OF PACIFIC ISLANDER IMMIGRANTS

Countries of origin	American Samoa, Fiji, Guam, French Polynesia, Kiribati, Marshall Islands, Micronesia, Palau, Samoa, Tonga, Solomon Islands
Primary languages	English, Polynesian languages
Primary regions of U.S. settlement	Hawaii, California, Utah, and Washington
Earliest significant arrivals	Late nineteenth century
Peak immigration period	Mid- to late twentieth century
Twenty-first century legal residents*	16,925 (2,116 per year)

*Immigrants who obtained legal permanent resident status in the United States. Figures do not include Hawaiians.
Source: Department of Homeland Security, *Yearbook of Immigration Statistics, 2008.*

ington, Oregon, Texas, Utah, Nevada, Arizona, New York State, and Florida. Pacific Islanders, including Native Hawaiians, made up more than 22 percent of the population of Honolulu.

In the mainland United States, significant proportions of Pacific Islanders lived in urban locations, with major concentrations in California (especially Hayward, Vallejo, Oceanside, Long Beach, Sacramento, and Daly City), Utah (West Valley City, Salt Lake City), and Washington (Tacoma). Much of this population concentration has occurred as the result of chain migration, with important founding families often identifiable in many of these locations.

In Utah, religion plays a special role. Many of the early Hawaiian and Tongan immigrants to the state were members of the Church of Jesus Christ of Latter-day Saints, which is better known as the Mormon Church. The church has long sent missionaries to the islands and has had particular success in Tonga, and Mormon links have been strong throughout Utah, Hawaii, and Tonga, which explains ongoing shifts in population. There are also

strong connections between the Mormon tertiary education facility, Brigham Young University (BYU), which was founded in Provo, Utah, in 1875, and BYU-Hawaii, which was founded in 1955. The Mormon Church assisted many Pacific Islander church members to immigrate to the mainland United States, especially to California and Utah. These connections are ongoing, and continue to facilitate immigration of Pacific Islanders.

The 2000 U.S. Census also reported that the largest Pacific Islander group in the United States was Native Hawaiians (401,162 people), followed by Samoans (133,281), and Guamanians or Chamorros (92,611). Approximately 70 percent of the Pacific Islander population in the United States fit into these three ethnic categories. Additional groups represented in the census included Tongans (36,840), Fijians (13,581), Marshallese (6,650), Palauans (3,469), and Tahitians (3,313).

Census data have also shown that members of these immigrant groups are young, on average. They include large numbers of individuals in their child-bearing years, and children. Because Oceanic peoples favor large families, it seemed that the U.S. Pacific Islander population would continue to grow rapidly through natural increase, along with ongoing immigration from the islands. Another projected trend was a growth in the number of Pacific Islanders who identify with more than one ethnic group. There are already high levels of intermarriage among different island communities, and also with non-Pacific Islander people. Although this generalization holds less with Tongan and Fijian populations, it suggests that Pacific Islander communities in the United States are increasing in their internal diversity. Older Islanders tend to worry that marriage with outsiders will weaken communal cohesion and eventually cause the loss of languages and cultural traditions, but members of the younger generation typically do not share these concerns.

Intermarriage and other intercultural links are also facilitated by participation in church activities. Many Christian congregations offer services in Pacific Islander languages, and some have Pacific Islander ministers in areas with high numbers of Oceanic people. Pacific Islanders living in the United States tend to identify socially through their memberships in specific church congregations, much as people living on the islands identify

themselves as originating from specific villages on specific islands.

PACIFIC ISLANDER AMERICAN CULTURE

Although Pacific Islander groups originate from different island archipelagoes, and their members possess different cultural practices, and speak different languages, certain broad cultural norms prevail across the islands that have been imported to the United States in varying degrees. For example, in contrast to the American cultural emphasis on individualistic traits, Oceanic peoples place greater value on collectivism, which encourages them to subordinate their personal interests to those of the family or wider kinship network. This trait may often be described by members of the Pacific Islander community as the respect owed by young people to their elders, and there are many cultural ideals about how it should be expressed, including lack of questioning of the older generation by youngsters, and the lowering of one's eyes and body height before elders. Differences between American and Islander styles of socialization sometimes result in conflicts between generational groups. Elder immigrants believe in greater levels of communal involvement and decision-making power by family networks, while their American-born children tend to focus more on their individual needs and desires and personal decision-making.

Divisions between the younger and older generations also may be exacerbated by language differences. Older immigrants typically find it more challenging to learn new languages than their children do, which often means that the children have greater skills in English than their parents or grandparents. Pacific Islander children who grow up the United States also tend not to learn the languages of their parents or to learn to speak them only at rudimentary levels. Community elders may consequently feel disappointment when young members of their communities do not speak their home languages well enough to participate in traditional orations at culturally important events, such as weddings and funerals.

At the same time, non-English-speaking family members may find their employment opportunities are limited and also have difficulty communicating with mainstream cultural brokers, such as teachers, community leaders, and government of-ficials. Outsiders often do not realize the extent of these language problems when they interact with Pacific Islanders, whose cultural norms encourage politeness that may be expressed through head nods, or other body language that seems to indicate agreement or understanding to Americans.

Accustomed to a communal way of life, Pacific Islanders often cook and eat together and live in close proximity to one another. This sometimes translates to situations in which members of extended families share American houses designed for small nuclear families. Their non-Islander neighbors and local social workers and health authorities may find it difficult to understand why so many people would wish to live together. Pacific Islanders also tend to view kinship ties in a more expansive manner than non-Islander Americans. For example, they are more likely to include all their extended family members in their conception of "family," not merely members of their nuclear families, as Americans are more likely to think of "family."

These broader conceptions of family may also include adopted siblings. In the Pacific, people often practice formal and informal adoption. For example, if a woman has no biological children, her brother may give her one or two of his own children, whom she will then raise as her own. The adoptions may never be formalized, and this arrangement is considered to be an expression of love from a brother for his sister, and does not devalue the adopted child or children according to local norms. Children may also live for considerable periods of time with relatives in order to attend schools or for other reasons. Many of these informal adoptions are never documented officially. For this reason, often Pacific people may describe households with fluctuating numbers of children and acknowledge as "sisters" and "brothers" individuals who may not even be biologically or legally related to them. These practices can cause problems to families wishing to immigrate to the United States together, or who are in the United States and wish to obtain health care and educational benefits.

Pacific Islanders typically settled in towns in the United States that already have sizeable Pacific Islander populations. This allows them to replicate much of their island lifestyles if they so desire. Older immigrants especially wish to retain impor-

Members of the Brigham Young University football team performing a Polynesian war dance under the leadership of one of the team's many Polynesian American players before a 2006 game. For many young Pacific Islanders, football has provided a ticket to college education in the United States, and some of them have achieved prominence in professional football. (WireImage/Getty Images)

tant aspects of their home cultures. For example, Samoans practice their *Fa'a-Samoa* belief system, the "Samoan way," and Tongans their *Anga Faka-tonga* belief system, or "Tongan way." At times, however, maintaining cultural norms may simply mean eating the same kinds of food that is typically consumed in the islands.

U.S.-PACIFIC ISLAND LINKS

Many Pacific Islanders living in the United States during the early twenty-first century believed that they would one day return to their island homelands. This belief would be more typical of the older first-generation immigrants than younger American-born family members. Reverse migration does occur, but less frequently than immigrants typically imagine when they first arrive in the United States. The initial dream of immigrants is to make a lot of money and then retire to the islands and live out their lives in style. In reality, by the time many elderly members of the Pacific Islander community are ready to retire, they find little in the islands to which to return. Many of their

family members are in the United States, and many of their old friends and networks are spread across the United States, Australia, New Zealand, and other islands. Elderly Islanders may also have health needs that are best treated in the United States. Some people do, however, maintain strong connections to their island homelands that draw them back.

More immigrants return to the islands for temporary visits than ever return permanently. There is much prestige in visiting, and providing gifts for those who remain. Moreover, maintaining links to the homelands and their people are important for community well-being and self-identity.

In addition to taking gifts with them on visits home, people in the United States often send remittances, in the form of money or goods, back to the islands. Island homelands benefit immensely from these cash infusions into their local economies. Some immigrants load large shipping containers with goods to send home. Like other traditions, this one means more to older members of the immigrant communities than to their offspring.

Although many young people oppose the idea of sending remittances and gifts, they sometimes become involved in this exchange network. There is a tradition in both the United States, and other diaspora communities of sending misbehaving youngsters back to their homelands for socialization into appropriate cultural norms. After miscreant children have spent a year in the islands looked after by extended family members, they may be deemed sufficiently well behaved to be returned to their U.S. homes.

An issue for all ethnic community members living in the United States is the prevalence of stereotypes and ongoing discrimination. Pacific Islanders may be easy targets because they are often identifiable based on their appearance, which means that American-born members of the community may be equally vulnerable. Members of Pacific Islander communities often are active in service organizations and educational initiatives to counteract the local effects of these stereotypes. Communities may also harshly sanction Pacific Islanders who act according to the stereotypes, such as those who join gangs, or are violent to their families since this behavior affects the entire group in a negative manner. Communities also celebrate the achievements of Pacific Islanders and strive to make mainstream Americans aware of these success stories and the history of their ethnic group in the United States.

Susan J. Wurtzburg

FURTHER READING

Duranti, Alessandro, Elinor Ochs, and Elia K. Ta'ase. "Change and Tradition in Literacy Instruction in a Samoan American Community." In *Many Pathways to Literacy: Young Children Learning with Siblings, Grandparents, Peers, and Communities*, edited by Eve Gregory, Susi Long, and Dinah Volk. New York: RoutledgeFalmer, 2004. Study of Samoan methods of instruction and how these may be incorporated into American educational institutions.

Halualani, Rona Tamiko. "Connecting Hawaiians: The Politics of Authenticity in the Hawaiian Diaspora." In *Intercultural Alliances: Critical Transformation*, edited by Mary Jane Collier. Thousand Oaks, Calif.: Sage Publications, 2003. Discussion of cultural authenticity, or what it means to be Hawaiian for people living outside Hawaii—a study that has implications for all Pacific Islanders.

Lee, Helen Morton. *Tongans Overseas: Between Two Shores.* Honolulu: University of Hawaii Press, 2003. Anthropological study of the lives of Tongan community members living in Melbourne, Australia that provides insights into the challenges that Pacific Islanders face when they immigrate to the United States.

McGrath, Barbara Burns. "Seattle Fa'a Samoa." *The Contemporary Pacific* 14, no. 2 (2002): 307-340. Discussion of how Samoan immigrants living in Seattle, Washington, have structured their lives to maintain Samoan culture while adapting to the United States.

Small, Cathy A. *Voyages: From Tongan Villages to American Suburbs.* Ithaca, N.Y.: Cornell University Press, 1997. Anthropological study of twenty-five years of migration from Tonga to Northern California viewed from the perspectives of both the immigrants to the United States and people who remained in Tonga.

Spickard, Paul R., Joanne L. Rondilla, and Debbie Hippolite Wright, eds. *Pacific Diaspora: Island Peoples in the United States and Across the Pacific.* Honolulu: University of Hawaii Press, 2002. Broad history of Pacific Islander migrations across the Pacific Ocean with an emphasis on their contemporary incursions into the United States.

Wurtzburg, Susan J. "Households and Families: Micronesia and Polynesia." In *Routledge International Encyclopedia of Women's Studies: Global Women's Issues and Knowledge*, edited by C. Kramarae and D. Spender. Vol. 1. New York: Routledge, 2000. Brief outline of commonalities in family structures and social organization across the Pacific Islands that is applicable to understanding the challenges that Pacific Islander families face in the United States.

SEE ALSO: Asian Pacific American Labor Alliance; Australian and New Zealander immigrants; California; Chain migration; Families; Hawaii; Mormon immigrants; Remittances of earnings; Stereotyping; Utah.

PACIFIC MAIL STEAMSHIP COMPANY

IDENTIFICATION: Shipping company that carried mail and passengers between Asia and the United States

DATE: Established on April 12, 1848

SIGNIFICANCE: Formed to carry mail from Central America to California, the Pacific Mail Steamship Company also carried many immigrants up the Pacific coast. During the early decades of Asian immigration to the United States, the Pacific Mail Steamship Company was the primary shipping line that carried Chinese and Japanese immigrants to the West Coast.

Between the time gold was discovered in California in 1848, and 1869, when the first transcontinental railroad was completed, a large portion of the people going from the East Coast to the West Coast of the United States traveled primarily by ship, usually crossing Central America by overland routes along the way. During this same period, increasing numbers of Asians—particularly Chinese—were coming to California to work in the mines and railroads. For a large number of these travelers, ships of the Pacific Mail Steamship Company provided not only oceanic transportation but also the mail service to communicate with families left behind.

The Pacific Mail Steamship Company was chartered in New York in April, 1848, by William Aspinwall. In October, the company was granted a contract by the U.S. government to carry mail from the Isthmus of Panama to San Francisco, in the recently acquired territory of California. The company went into service with three new paddlewheel steamers. In addition to carrying the U.S. mail, the company's ships carried immigrants, businessmen, and gold seekers on the twelve- to fourteen-day voyage up the Pacific Coast. In 1855, completion of a railroad line across Panama made the overland part of travelers' journeys quicker, safer, and more comfortable. However, completion of the transcontinental railroad across the United States in 1869 would eventually doom the company's Panama to California service. However, between 1848 and 1869, the company's ships carried 19,000 passengers per year to California.

Meanwhile, the company's immediate future was assured in 1865, when it was granted a contract to carry U.S. mail between the West Coast of the United States and East Asia. After collecting mail in San Francisco, company ships sailed to Yokohama, Japan, and Hong Kong, China. By this period, large numbers of Asians, mostly Chinese, were coming to the United States and Canada to work. As Pacific Mail expanded its fleet, it carried tens of thousands of Asians to the United States, typically charging the immigrants forty dollars to make the passage in steerage class. By 1873, Pacific Mail was running forty ships on various routes. A large majority of them worked the Asian routes. The company also had smaller vessels running routes among U.S. and Canadian ports along the West Coast.

Federal restrictions on Asian immigration that began with the Chinese Exclusion Act of 1882 gradually cut into the Pacific Mail's Asian passenger trade, but the shipping company opened new routes to other regions, including Australia. However, over time, the company failed to keep up with competing lines. In 1893, it was purchased by the Southern Pacific Railroad Company, which resold it to another shipping company in 1916. In 1938, its ownership passed to the American President Lines, but by then the company existed only on paper. It was formally dissolved eleven years later.

Robert J. Stewart

FURTHER READING

Barde, Robert Eric. *Immigration at the Golden Gate: Passenger Ships, Exclusion, and Angel Island.* Westport, Conn.: Praeger, 2008.

Chandler, Robert J., and Stephen J. Potash. *Gold, Silk, Pioneers and Mail: The Story of the Pacific Mail Steamship Company.* San Francisco: Friends of the San Francisco Maritime Museum Library, 2007.

Page, Thomas W. "The Transportation of Immigrants and Reception Arrangements in the Nineteenth Century." *Journal of Political Economy* 19, no. 9 (1911): 732-749.

SEE ALSO: California; California gold rush; Chinese immigrants; Hamburg-Amerika Line; Japanese immigrants; Korean immigrants; Railroads; San Francisco; Transportation of immigrants.

PAGE LAW OF 1875

THE LAW: Federal legislation prohibited entry of Chinese contract workers and prostitutes into the United States

DATE: Enacted on March 3, 1875

ALSO KNOWN AS: Act Supplementary to the Acts in Relation to Immigration

SIGNIFICANCE: Originally designed to prohibit Chinese contract workers and prostitutes from entering the United States, this federal law eventually excluded Asian women in general.

On February 10, 1875, California congressman Horace F. Page introduced federal legislation designed to prohibit the immigration of Asian female prostitutes into the United States. Officially titled An Act Supplementary to the Acts in Relation to Immigration, the Page Law evolved into a restriction of vast numbers of Chinese immigrating into the country regardless of whether they were prostitutes. Any person convicted of importing Chinese prostitutes was subject to a maximum prison term of five years and a fine of not more than five thousand dollars.

An amendment to the law prohibited individuals from engaging in the "coolie trade," the importation of illegal Chinese contract laborers. Punishment for this type of violation, however, was less severe and much more difficult to effect, given the large numbers of Asian male immigrants arriving at the time. Consequently, the law was applied in a gender-specific manner, effectively deterring immigration of Asian females into the United States. Within seven years following the implementation of the law, the average number of Chinese female immigrants dropped to one-third of its previous level.

An elaborate bureaucratic network established to carry out the Page Law's gender-specific exclusions was a cata-

lyst for the decline in Chinese immigration rates. American consulate officials supported by American, Chinese, and British commercial, political, and medical services made up the law's implementation structure. Through intelligence gathering, interrogation, and physical examinations of applicants, the consulate hierarchy ferreted out undesirable applicants for immigration and those suspected of engaging in illegal human trafficking.

This investigative procedure was complicated. Any characteristic or activity that could be linked, even in the most remote sense, to prostitution became grounds for denial of the right to immigrate. Most applications to immigrate came from women from the lower economic strata of Chinese society; low economic status was linked to prostitution and therefore became a reason for immigration exclusion. Navigating language barriers through official

Chinese woman with her children and brother-in-law awaiting a streetcar in San Francisco around 1904. The sedate black outfit worn by the woman is typical of the dress worn by married Chinese women who wanted to distinguish themselves from prostitutes. (Library of Congress)

interviews aimed at evaluating personal character often produced an atmosphere of rigid interrogation, bringing subsequent denial of the right to immigrate. In addition, passing stringent physical examinations performed by biased health care officials was often impossible.

Because Hong Kong was the main point of departure for Chinese immigrating to the United States, all required examinations were performed there with a hierarchy of American consulate officials determining immigrant eligibility. The consular general had such authority in implementing the Page Law that there was a wide opportunity for abuse of power. In 1878, Hong Kong consul general John S. Mosby accused his predecessors, David Bailey and H. Sheldon Loring, of having amassed thousands of dollars in extra income by charging additional examination fees regardless of whether an examination was performed and by falsifying test results to deny immigration permission to otherwise legal immigrants. Federal investigations of Bailey and Loring produced no official indictments; instead, they revealed the simple fact of overly aggressive officials who made preventing the immigration of Chinese women to the United States a top priority of their respective tenures, rather than an opportunity for profit.

Regardless of the personalities of the consulate officials in charge of implementing the Page Law, the results were the same: The number of Chinese who immigrated to the United States decreased dramatically between the 1875 enactment of the law and the enactment of its successor, the Chinese Exclusion Act of 1882.

Cynthia Gwynne Yaudes

EXTRACTS FROM THE PAGE LAW

Be it enacted by the Senate and House of Representatives of the United States of America in Congress-assembled, That in determining whether the immigration of any subject of China, Japan, or any Oriental country, to the United States, is free and voluntary, as provided by section two thousand one hundred and sixty two of the Revised Code, title "Immigration," it shall be the duty of the consul-3-general or consul of the United States residing at the port from which it is proposed to convey such subjects, in any vessels enrolled or licensed in the United States, or any port within the same, before delivering to the masters of any such vessels the permit or certificate provided for in such section, to ascertain for a term of service within the United States, for lewd and immoral purposes; and if there be such contract or agreement, the said consul-general or consul shall not deliver the required permit or certificate. . . .

SEC. 3. That the importation into the United States of women for the purposes of prostitution is hereby forbidden; and all contracts and agreements in relation thereto, made in advance or in pursuance of illegal importation and purposes, are hereby declared void; and whoever shall knowingly and willfully hold, or attempt to hold, any woman to such purposes, in pursuance of such illegal importation and contract or agreement, shall be deemed guilty of a felony, and, on conviction thereof, shall be imprisoned not exceeding five years and pay a fine not exceeding five thousand dollars.

SEC. 5. That it shall be unlawful for aliens of the following classes to immigrate into the United States, namely, persons who are undergoing sentence for conviction in their own country of felonious crimes other than political or growing out of or the result of such political offenses, and women "imported for the purposes of prostitution." Every vessel arriving in the United States may be inspected under the direction of the collector of the port at which it arrives . . .

FURTHER READING

Foner, Philip, and Daniel Rosenberg. *Racism, Dissent, and Asian Americans from 1850 to the Present.* Westport, Conn.: Greenwood Press, 1993.

Peffer, George Anthony. "Forbidden Families: Emigration Experiences of Chinese Women Under the Page Law, 1875-1882." *Journal of American Ethnic History* 6 (Fall, 1986): 28-46.

SEE ALSO: Bayard-Zhang Treaty of 1888; Chinese Exclusion Act of 1882; *Chinese Exclusion Cases*; Chinese immigrants; Citizens Committee to Repeal Chinese Exclusion; Coolies; History of immigration, 1783-1891; Marriage; Women immigrants.

PAKISTANI IMMIGRANTS

SIGNIFICANCE: Pakistani immigration only became a distinctive part of South Asian immigration during the 1960's. The United States has never been a primary destination for Pakistani immigrants, but they have formed distinctive subgroups in certain areas of settlement. After the September 11, 2001, terrorist attacks on the United States, their Muslim identity became problematic.

Pakistan did not exist as a distinct nation until 1947, when both it and India were formed from British India. The reason for the split was primarily religious. Though it had a secular government, India became a Hindu-majority state, while Pakistan became a primarily Muslim state.

In terms of U.S. government statistics, no separate statistics of Pakistani immigration were kept until after 1981. Before that year, Pakistanis were grouped under "Other South Asians." Of the South Asians, only Indian immigrants had their own separate category. Statistics are further confused by the emergence of Bangladesh as a separate country in 1971 out of what was previously known as East Pakistan, the eastern wing of the two-part country formed in 1947. Bangladeshis and Pakistanis were grouped together until 1973, though probably very few Bangladeshis did immigrate at that time. In 1973, fewer than two hundred Bangladeshis were counted in the United States.

Before 1947, Pakistani immigration would have been counted as Indian. At the beginning of the twentieth century, there had been a small-scale immigration of farmers and farm laborers to Southern California, mainly to work in the newly developed rice farms of the Sacramento Valley, but no other significant influx.

FIRST GROWTH

After independence, most Pakistani emigrants went to the United Kingdom. British law at that time allowed previous colonials unfettered entry into Great Britain. Other Commonwealth countries, especially Canada and Australia, also had generous provisions for other Commonwealth immigrants. By contrast, U.S. immigration policy allowed little possibility for Pakistani entry.

This policy began to change after 1965, when passage of the Immigration and Nationality Act of 1965 allowed professionals and other people with needed skills entry. A slow trickle of Pakistani professionals began to take advantage of the liberalized immigration policy, aided by tightening restrictions in the United Kingdom and lack of job opportunities in their native country. The tendency of Pakistan to drift into undemocratic military regimes also alienated a number of professionals and skilled workers.

The main professions of these immigrants were in medicine and engineering. In 1971, just over two thousand immigrants joined the five thousand or so Pakistanis already in the United States, mainly in the larger population centers of New York, Chicago, Los Angeles, and San Francisco. Numbers edged up during the 1970's and 1980's but never reached more than six thousand per year. Some also came as students or tourists and then changed their status while in the United States.

At first, the trend was for single men to come, establish themselves, then sponsor spouses to join them, or return to Pakistan, marry, and bring their spouses back with them. Those who failed to qualify as doctors or pharmacists in the United States reinvented themselves as small businessmen, often running convenience stores or gas stations. Taxi driving was a favored occupation among those who came with less education.

SUBSEQUENT DEVELOPMENT

The turning point in numbers came in 1991, when the annual immigration suddenly jumped to 20,355. The lottery system allowed a number of unskilled Pakistanis to immigrate. Meanwhile, provisions for wider family sponsorship allowed a number of brothers, sisters, and parents to enter. Pakistani society is very family-oriented, with the extended family being the norm. During the 1990's, some 124,500 Pakistanis were admitted, making the Pakistani community the ninth-largest of all Asian communities.

Certain stresses began to manifest themselves as a second generation grew up in the United States. The arranged marriage system was still enforced where possible to maintain cultural identity, but spouses from Pakistan found it difficult to adjust to new gender roles within American culture. Divisions between religious groups, especially Sunnis

PROFILE OF PAKISTANI IMMIGRANTS

Country of origin	Pakistan
Primary languages	Urdu, English, others
Primary regions of U.S. settlement	California, New York, and Chicago
Earliest significant arrivals	1950's
Peak immigration period	1990's
Twenty-first century legal residents*	117,143 (14,643 per year)

*Immigrants who obtained legal permanent resident status in the United States.

Source: Department of Homeland Security, *Yearbook of Immigration Statistics, 2008.*

and Shias, kept communities divided. Though Pakistanis mixed easily with other South Asian Muslims, they found it difficult to mix with Muslims from the Middle East or of African origin. The desire for fair-skinned spouses was especially troublesome, fed as it was by the Bollywood movie culture.

The September 11, 2001, terrorist attacks in New York City and Washington, D.C., and the subsequent involvement of Pakistan on the American political stage were especially problematic for both the existing community and new immigrants. Numbers of immigrants actually declined, with 51,600 entering between 2001 and 2004 and 14,900 in 2005. Persian Gulf states absorbed a growing number of Pakistani migrant workers, who were much more at home there in a Muslim culture. Also, immigration to the Commonwealth countries continued at quite high levels. Movement among the worldwide Pakistani diaspora was also a significant feature.

David Barratt

FURTHER READING

Aswad, Barbara C., and Barbara Bilgé, eds. *Family and Gender Among American Muslims: Issues Facing Middle Eastern Immigrants and Their Descendants.* Philadelphia: Temple University Press, 1996. Sociological study with a chapter devoted to the problems of South Asians, especially in terms of family ties, marriage, and education.

Leonard, Karen. *The South Asian Americans: The New Americans.* Westport, Conn.: Greenwood Press, 1997. Studies the impact South Asian immigrants have made on American culture.

McCloud, Aminah Beverly. *Transnational Muslims in American Society.* Gainesville: University Press of Florida, 2006. Places Pakistani immigration in the wider context of Muslim South Asians and distinguishes the various religious subgroups.

Narayan, Anjana, and Bandana Purkayastha. *Living Religions: Hindu and Muslim South Asian-American Women Narrate Their Experiences.* Sterling, Va.: Kumarian Press, 2009. Written in light of the September 11, 2001, terrorist attacks, individual women narrate their experiences as South Asian immigrants and how they challenge borders and stereotypes.

Prashad, Vijay. *The Karma of Brown Folk.* Minneapolis: University of Minnesota Press, 2000. Interviews and analyses of South Asians, piecing together how their image as a successful immigrant group has been constructed.

U.S. Census Bureau. *Statistical Abstract of the United States: 2007.* Washington, D.C.: Author, 2006. Includes separate figures for Pakistani immigrants from 1981.

Waters, Mary C., and Reed Ueda, eds. *The New Americans: A Guide to Immigration Since 1965.* Cambridge, Mass.: Harvard University Press, 2007. The chapter on South Asia, by Nazli Kibria, sufficiently discusses Pakistani immigrants.

Williams, Raymond B. *Religions of Immigrants from India and Pakistan: New Threads in the American Tapestry.* New York: Cambridge University Press, 1988. Studies various religions and how they have adapted to and influenced American culture.

SEE ALSO: Asian immigrants; Asian Indian immigrants; Canada vs. United States as immigrant destinations; History of immigration after 1891; Immigration and Nationality Act of 1965; Muslim immigrants; Religions of immigrants; Sidhwa, Bapsi.